CRIME IN THE UNITED STATES

CRIME IN THE UNITED STATES

2013
SEVENTH EDITION

Edited by Shana Hertz Hattis

 **Bernan** Press

Lanham, MD

Published in the United States of America
by Bernan Press, a wholly owned subsidiary of
The Rowman & Littlefield Publishing Group, Inc.
4501 Forbes Boulevard, Suite 200
Lanham, Maryland 20706

Bernan Press
800-865-3457
www.bernan.com

ISBN: 978-1-59888-622-1
eISBN: 978-1-59888-623-8

∞™ The paper used in this publication meets the minimum requirements of American National Standard for Information Sciences—Permanence of Paper for Printed Library Materials, ANSI/NISO Z39.48-1992. Manufactured in the United States of America.

CONTENTS

SECTION I:
SUMMARY OF THE UNIFORM CRIME REPORTING (UCR) PROGRAM

SUMMARY OF THE UNIFORM CRIME REPORTING (UCR) PROGRAM

Bernan Press is proud to present its seventh edition of *Crime in the United States*. This title was formerly published by the Federal Bureau of Investigation (FBI), but is no longer available in printed form from the government. This edition contains final data from 2011, the latest data that are currently available.

This section describes the history of the UCR program, which collects the data used in *Crime in the United States,* and it examines the best way to use the data in this publication.

About the UCR Program

The UCR program's primary objective is to generate reliable information for use in law enforcement administration, operation, and management; however, over the course of the program, its data has stood as one of the country's leading social indicators.

The UCR program is a nationwide, cooperative statistical effort of more than 18,000 city, university and college, county, state, tribal, and federal law enforcement agencies voluntarily reporting data on crimes brought to their attention. Since 1930, the FBI has administered the UCR program and continued to assess and monitor the nature and type of crime in the nation. Criminologists, sociologists, legislators, municipal planners, the media, and other students of criminal justice use the data for varied research and planning purposes. In 2011, law enforcement agencies active in the UCR program represented more than 304 million United States inhabitants—97.8 percent of the total population. The coverage amounted to 98.8 percent of the population in metropolitan statistical areas, 92.3 percent of the population in cities outside metropolitan areas, and 93.1 percent of the population in nonmetropolitan counties.

Note for Users

It is important for UCR data users to remember that the FBI's primary objective is to generate a reliable set of crime statistics for use in law enforcement administration, operation, and management. The FBI does not provide a ranking of agencies; instead, it provides alphabetical tabulations of states, metropolitan statistical areas, cities with over 10,000 inhabitants, suburban and rural counties, and selected colleges and universities. Law enforcement officials use these data for their designed purposes. Additionally, the public relies on these data for information about the fluctuations in levels of crime from year to year, while criminologists, sociologists, legislators, city planners, media outlets, and other students of criminal justice use them for a variety of research and planning purposes. Since crime is a sociological phenomenon influenced by a variety of factors, the FBI discourages data users from ranking agencies and using the data as a measurement of the effectiveness of law enforcement.

To ensure that data are uniformly reported, the FBI provides contributing law enforcement agencies with a handbook that explains how to classify and score offenses and provides uniform crime offense definitions. Acknowledging that offense definitions may vary from state to state, the

FBI cautions agencies to report offenses according to the guidelines provided in the handbook, rather than by local or state statutes. Most agencies make a good faith effort to comply with established guidelines.

The UCR program publishes the statistics most commonly requested by data users. More information regarding the availability of UCR program data is available by telephone at (304) 625-4995, by fax at (304) 625-5394, or by e-mail at <cjis_comm@leo.gov>. E-mail data requests cannot be processed without the requester's full name, mailing address, and contact telephone number.

Variables Affecting Crime: Caution Against Ranking

Until data users examine all the variables that affect crime in a town, city, county, state, region, or college or university, they can make no meaningful comparisons. In each edition of *Crime in the United States*, many entities—including news media, tourism agencies, and other organizations with an interest in crime in the nation—use reported figures to compile rankings of cities and counties. However, these rankings are merely a quick choice made by that data user; they provide no insight into the many variables that mold the crime in a particular town, city, county, state, or region. Consequently, these rankings may lead to simplistic and/or incomplete analyses, which can create misleading perceptions and thus adversely affect cities and counties, along with their residents.

Considering Other Characteristics of a Jurisdiction

To assess criminality and law enforcement's response from jurisdiction to jurisdiction, data users must consider many variables, some of which (despite having significant impact on crime) are not readily measurable or applicable among all locales. Geographic and demographic factors specific to each jurisdiction must be considered and applied in order to make an accurate and complete assessment of crime in that jurisdiction. Several sources of information are available to help the researcher explore the variables that affect crime in a particular locale. U.S. Census Bureau data, for example, can help the user better understand the makeup of a locale's population. The transience of the population, its racial and ethnic makeup, and its composition by age and gender, educational levels, and prevalent family structures are all key factors in assessing and understanding crime.

Local chambers of commerce, planning offices, and similar entities provide information regarding the economic and cultural makeup of cities and counties. Understanding a jurisdiction's industrial/economic base, its dependence upon neighboring jurisdictions, its transportation system, its economic dependence on nonresidents (such as tourists and convention attendees), and its proximity to military installations, correctional institutions, and other types of facilities all contribute to accurately gauging and interpreting the crime known to and reported by law enforcement.

The strength (including personnel and other resources) and aggressiveness of a jurisdiction's law enforcement agency are also key factors in understanding the nature and extent of crime occurring in that area. Although information pertaining to the number of sworn and civilian employees can be found in this publication, it cannot be used alone as an assessment of the emphasis that a community places on enforcing the law. For example, one city may report more crime than another comparable city because its law enforcement agency identifies more offenses. Attitudes of citizens toward crime and their crime reporting practices—especially for minor offenses—also have an impact on the volume of crimes known to police.

Making Valid Crime Assessments

It is essential for all data users to become as well educated as possible about understanding and quantifying the nature and extent of crime in the United States and in the jurisdictions represented by law enforcement contributors to the UCR program. Valid assessments are possible only with careful study and analysis of the various unique conditions that affect each local law enforcement jurisdiction.

Some factors that are known to affect the volume and type of crime occurring from place to place are:

- Population density and degree of urbanization

- Variations in composition of population, particularly in the concentration of youth

- Stability of the population with respect to residents' mobility, commuting patterns, and transient factors

- Modes of transportation and highway systems

- Economic conditions, including median income, poverty level, and job availability

- Cultural factors and educational, recreational, and religious characteristics

- Family conditions, with respect to divorce and family cohesiveness

- Climate

- Effective strength of law enforcement agencies

- Administrative and investigative emphases of law enforcement

- Policies of other components of the criminal justice system (that is, prosecutorial, judicial, correctional, and probational policies)

- Residents' attitudes toward crime

- Crime reporting practices of residents

Although many of the listed factors equally affect the crime of a particular area, the UCR program makes no attempt to relate them to the data presented. **The data user is therefore cautioned against comparing statistical data of individual reporting units from cities, counties, metropolitan areas, states, or colleges or universities solely on the basis on their population coverage or student enrollment.** Until data users examine all the variables that affect crime in a town, city, county, state, region, or college or university, they can make no meaningful comparisons.

Historical Background

Since 1930, the FBI has administered the UCR program; the agency continues to assess and monitor the nature and type of crime in the nation. Data users look to the UCR program for various research and planning purposes.

Recognizing a need for national crime statistics, the International Association of Chiefs of Police (IACP) formed the Committee on Uniform Crime Records in the 1920s to develop a system of uniform crime statistics. After studying state criminal codes and making an evaluation of the record-keeping practices in use, the committee completed a plan for crime reporting that became the foundation of the UCR program in 1929. The plan included standardized offense definitions for seven main offense classifications known as Part I crimes to gauge fluctuations in the overall volume and rate of crime. Developers also instituted the Hierarchy Rule as the main reporting procedure for what is now known as the Summary Reporting System of the UCR program.

Seven main offense classifications, known as Part I crimes, were chosen to gauge the state of crime in the nation. These seven offense classifications included the violent crimes of murder and nonnegligent manslaughter, forcible rape, robbery, and aggravated assault; also included were the property crimes of burglary, larceny-theft, and motor vehicle theft. By congressional mandate, arson was added as the eighth Part I offense category. Data collection for arson began in 1979.

During the early planning of the program, it was recognized that the differences among criminal codes precluded a mere aggregation of state statistics to arrive at a national total. Also, because of the variances in punishment for the same offenses in different states, no distinction between felony and misdemeanor crimes was possible. To avoid these problems and provide nationwide uniformity in crime reporting, standardized offense definitions were developed. Law enforcement agencies use these to submit data without regard for local statutes. UCR program offense definitions can be found in Appendix II.

In January 1930, 400 cities (representing 20 million inhabitants in 43 states) began participating in the UCR program. Congress enacted Title 28, Section 534, of the *United States Code* that same year, which authorized the attorney general to gather crime information. The attorney general, in turn, designated the FBI to serve as the national clearinghouse for the collected crime data. Since then, data based on uniform classifications and procedures for reporting have been obtained annually from the nation's law enforcement agencies.

Advisory Groups

Providing vital links between local law enforcement and the FBI for the UCR program are the Criminal Justice Information Systems Committees of the IACP and the National Sheriffs' Association (NSA). The IACP represents the thousands of police departments nationwide, as it has since the program began. The NSA encourages sheriffs throughout the country to participate fully in the program. Both committees serve the program in advisory capacities.

In 1988, a Data Providers' Advisory Policy Board was established. This board operated until 1993, when it combined with the National Crime Information Center Advisory Policy Board to form a single Advisory Policy Board (APB) to address all FBI criminal justice information services. The current APB works to ensure continuing emphasis on UCR-related issues. The Association of State Uniform Crime Reporting Programs (ASUCRP) focuses on UCR issues within individual state law enforcement associations and also promotes interest in the UCR program. These organizations foster widespread and responsible use of uniform crime statistics and lend assistance to data contributors.

Redesign of UCR

Although UCR data collection was originally conceived as a tool for law enforcement administration, the data were widely used by other entities involved in various forms of social planning by the 1980s. Recognizing the need for more detailed crime statistics, law enforcement called for a thorough evaluative study to modernize the UCR program. The FBI formulated a comprehensive three-phase redesign effort. The Bureau of Justice Statistics (BJS) agency in the Department of Justice responsible for funding criminal justice information projects, agreed to underwrite the first two phases. These phases were conducted by an independent contractor and structured to determine what, if any, changes should be made to the current program. The third phase would involve implementation of the changes identified.

The final report, the *Blueprint for the Future of the Uniform Crime Reporting Program,* was released in the summer of 1985. It specifically outlined recommendations for an expanded, improved UCR program to meet future informational needs. There were three recommended areas of enhancement to the UCR program:

- Offenses and arrests would be reported using an incident-based system

- Data would be collected on two levels. Agencies in level one would report important details about those offenses comprising the Part I crimes, their victims, and arrestees. Level two would consist of law enforcement agencies covering populations of more than 100,000 and a sampling of smaller agencies that would collect expanded detail on all significant offenses

- A quality assurance program would be introduced

In January 1986, Phase III of the redesign effort began, guided by the general recommendations set forth in the *Blueprint.* The FBI selected an experimental site to implement the redesigned program, while contractors developed new data guidelines and system specifications. Upon selecting the South Carolina Law Enforcement Division (SLED), which enlisted the cooperation of nine local law enforcement agencies, the FBI developed automated data capture specifications to adapt the SLED's state system to the national UCR program's standards, and the BJS funded the revisions. The pilot demonstration ran from March 1 through September 30, 1987, and resulted in further refinement of the guidelines and specifications.

From March 1 through March 3, 1988, the FBI held a national UCR conference to present the new system to law enforcement and to obtain feedback on its acceptability. Attendees of the conference passed three overall recommendations without dissent: first, that there be established a new, incident-based national crime reporting system; second, that the FBI manage this program, and third, that an Advisory Policy Board composed of law enforcement executives be formed to assist in directing and implementing the new program. Furthermore, attendees recommended that the implementation of national incident-based reporting proceed at a pace commensurate with the resources and limitations of contributing law enforcement agencies.

Establishing the NIBRS

From March 1988 through January 1989, the FBI developed and assumed management of the UCR program's National Incident-Based Reporting System (NIBRS), and by April 1989, the first test of NIBRS data was submitted to the national UCR program. Over the next few years, the national lUCR program published information about the redesigned program in five documents:

- *Uniform Crime Reporting Handbook*, NIBRS Edition (1992) provides a nontechnical program overview focusing on definitions, policies, and procedures of the IBRS
- *Data Submission Specifications* (May 1992) is used by local and state systems personnel, who are responsible for preparing magnetic media for submission to the FBI
- Approaches to Implementing an Incident-Based System (July 1992) is a guide for system designers
- *Error Message Manual* (revised December 1999) contains designations of mandatory and optional data elements, data element edits, and error messages
- *Data Collection Guidelines* (revised August 2000) contains a system overview and descriptions of the offense codes, reports, data elements, and data values used in the system

As more agencies inquired about the NIBRS, the FBI, in May 2002, made the *Handbook for Acquiring a Records Management System (RMS) That Is Compatible with the NIBRS* available to agencies considering or developing automated incident-based records management systems. The handbook, developed under the sponsorship of the FBI and the BJS, provides instructions for planning and conducting a system acquisition and offers guidelines on preparing an agency for conversion to the new system and to the NIBRS.

Originally designed with 52 data elements, the redesigned NIBRS captures up to 57 data elements via 6 types of data segments: administrative, offense, victim property, offender, and arrestee. Although, in the late 1980s, the FBI committed to hold all changes to the NIBRS in abeyance until a substantial amount of contributors implemented the system, modifications have been necessary. The system's flexibility has allowed the collection of four additional pieces of information to be captured within an incident: bias-motivated offenses (1990), the presence of gang activity (1997), data for law enforcement officers killed and assaulted (2003), and data on cargo theft (2005).

The FBI began accepting NIBRS data from a handful of agencies in January 1989. As more contributing law enforcement agencies become educated about the rich data available through incident-based reporting and as resources permit, more agencies are implementing the NIBRS. As of June 2012, approximately 43 percent of reporting agencies are certified for NIBRS participation, covering about 25 percent of the population. These agencies include one individual agency each in Alabama, Illinois, Mississippi, and the District of Columbia, as well as the state UCR programs of the following 32 states: Arizona, Arkansas, Colorado, Connecticut, Delaware, Idaho, Iowa, Kansas, Kentucky, Louisiana, Maine, Massachusetts, Michigan, Missouri, Montana, Nebraska, New Hampshire, North Dakota, Ohio, Oklahoma, Oregon, Rhode Island, South Carolina, South Dakota, Tennessee, Texas, Utah, Vermont, Virginia, Washington, West Virginia, and Wisconsin. Eight state UCR programs have tested the NIBRS. Five other programs are planning and developing the NIBRS, including three state agencies and Washington, D.C. A state can be returned to developmental status due to issues such as computer problems.

Suspension of the *Crime Index* and the *Modified Crime Index*

In June 2004, the CJIS APB approved discontinuing the use of the *Crime Index* in the UCR program and its publications and directed the FBI to publish a violent crime total and a property crime total. The Crime Index, first published in *Crime in the United States* in 1960, was the title used for a simple aggregation of the seven main offense classifications (Part I offenses) in the Summary Reporting System. The Modified Crime Index was the number of Crime Index offenses plus arson.

For several years ,the CJIS Division studied the appropriateness and usefulness of these indices and brought the matter before many advisory groups including the UCR Subcommittee of the CJIS APB, the ASUCRP, and a meeting of leading criminologists and sociologists hosted by the BJS. In short, the *Crime Index* and the *Modified Crime Index* were not true indicators of the degrees of criminality because they were always driven upward by the offense with the highest number, typically larceny-theft. The sheer volume of those offenses overshadowed more serious but less frequently committed offenses, creating a bias against a jurisdiction with a high number of larceny-thefts but a low number of other serious crimes such as murder and forcible rape.

Recent Developments in UCR Program

In response to federal legislation outlined in the USA Patriot Improvement and Reauthorization Act of 2005, the UCR program began accepting cargo theft data from local, state, tribal, and federal agencies on January 1, 2010. Congress commissioned the FBI to begin capturing crime data on human trafficking in the William Wilberforce Trafficking Victims Protection Reauthorization Act of 2008. The Matthew Shepard and James Byrd, Jr. Hate Crime Prevention Act of 2009 requires the collection of data on crimes motivated by "gender and gender identity" bias, as well as "crimes committed by, and crimes directed against, juveniles." The national UCR program staff is developing collection strategies to meet both of these most recent mandates.

In addition, to meet a directive of the U.S. Government's Office of Management and Budget, the national UCR program will expand race categories from four (White, Black, American Indian or Alaska Native, and Asian or Other Pacific Islander) to five (White, Black, American Indian or Alaska Native, Asian, and Native Hawaiian or Other Pacific Islander). The ethnicity categories will change from "Hispanic" to "Hispanic or Latino Origin" and from "Non-Hispanic" to "Not of Hispanic or Latino Origin."

UCR Redevelopment Project Update

To streamline the program's database management and quality control activities, the FBI created the UCR Redevelopment Project (UCRRP). The UCRRP's goal is to improve the efficiency, usability, and maintainability of the UCR program while increasing the value to users. The redevelopment project will:

- Decrease the time it takes to analyze data,

- Reduce, to the point of elimination, the exchange of printed materials between agencies and the FBI,

- Provide an enhanced external data query tool so that the public can view and analyze published UCR data from the Internet, and

- Decrease the time needed to release and publish crime data.

To reach this goal, an effort is underway to transition all submissions to an electronic format on or before January 2013. After January 2013, the UCR program will no longer accept paper or the electronic submissions of documents (for example, Portable Document Format files). The UCRRP is working with agencies to collect information and identify ways to assist in the transition, including the adoption of an electronic submission via the NIBRS, electronic Summary Reporting System, or Extensible Markup Language.

Expanded Offense Tables

Expanded offense data are the details of the various offenses that the Uniform Crime Reporting Program collects beyond the count of how many crimes law enforcement agencies report. These details may include the type of weapon used in a crime, the type or value of items stolen, and so forth. Expanded homicide data provide supplemental details about murders such as the age, sex, and race of both the victim and the offender, the weapon used in the homicide, the circumstances surrounding the offense, and the relationship of the victim to the offender. In addition, expanded data includes trends (for example, 2-year comparisons) and rates per 100,000 inhabitants.

Expanded offense data, including expanded homicide data, are information collected beyond the reports of the number of crimes known. As a result, law enforcement agencies can report an offense without providing the supplemental data about that offense. These additional tables can be found at http://www.fbi.gov/about-us/cjis/ucr/crime-in-the-u.s/2011/crime-in-the-u.s.-2011/offenses-known-to-law-enforcement/expanded-offense-data.

About the Editor

Shana Hertz Hattis is a consulting writer-editor with Bernan. She holds a master of science in education degree in from Northwestern University, as well as a bachelor's degree in journalism from the same university. She has previously edited *Housing Statistics of the United States* and several volumes of *The United States Government Internet Directory* for Bernan.

SECTION II:
OFFENSES KNOWN TO POLICE

VIOLENT CRIME OFFENSES

- Murder
- Forcible Rape
- Robbery
- Aggravated Assault

PROPERTY CRIME OFFENSES

- Burglary
- Larceny-Theft
- Motor Vehicle Theft
- Arson

VIOLENT CRIME

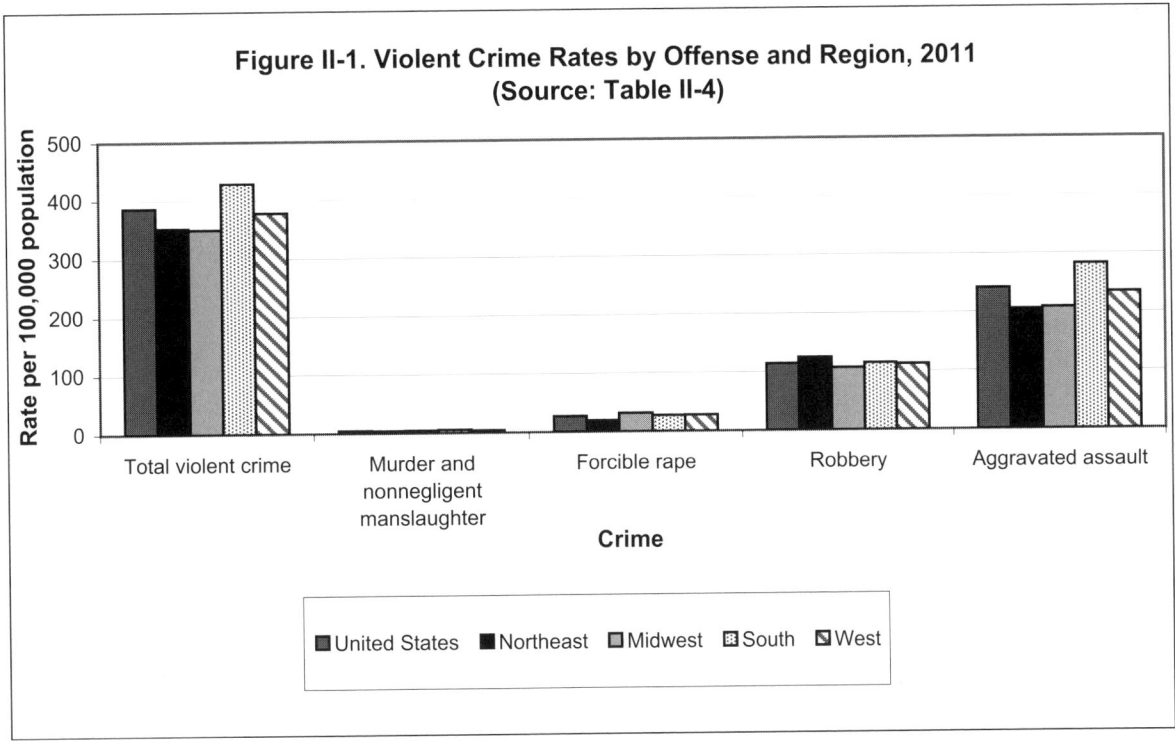

**Figure II-1. Violent Crime Rates by Offense and Region, 2011
(Source: Table II-4)**

Definition

Violent crime consists of four offenses: murder and non-negligent manslaughter, forcible rape, robbery, and aggravated assault. According to the Uniform Crime Reporting (UCR) program, run by the Federal Bureau of Investigation (FBI), violent crimes involve either the use of force or the threat of force.

Data Collection

The data presented in *Crime in the United States* reflect the Hierarchy Rule, which counts only the most serious offense in a multiple-offense criminal incident. In descending order of severity, the violent crimes are murder and nonnegligent manslaughter, forcible rape, robbery, and aggravated assault; these are followed by the property crimes of burglary, larceny-theft, and motor vehicle theft. More information on the expanded violent crime tables (which are available online but not included in this publication) can be found in Section I.

National Volume, Trends, and Rate

In 2011, an estimated 1,203,564 violent crimes occurred in the United States, showing a decrease of 3.8 percent from the 2010 estimate. An estimated 386.3 violent crimes were committed per 100,000 inhabitants in 2011. Aggravated assaults accounted for 62.4 percent of violent crimes, the highest number of violent crimes reported to law enforcement. Robbery made up 29.4 percent of violent crimes,

forcible rape accounted for 6.9 percent, and murder accounted for 1.2 percent (no change from 2009 or 2010) of estimated violent crimes in 2011. (Table II-1)

All violent crimes decreased in 2011 from 2010, a continuation of the trend in the previous year. Murder decreased 0.7 percent, forcible rape fell 2.5 percent, aggravated assault declined 3.9 percent, and robbery dropped 4.0 percent. The 2011 murder rate, 4.7 offenses per 100,000 inhabitants, was also a decrease of 1.5 percent when compared with the rate for 2010. (Tables II-1 and II-1A)

The 2011 estimated violent crime total was 15.4 percent below the 2007 level and 15.5 percent below the 2002 level. The 5-year and 10-year trend data showed that the violent crime rate decreased 18.1 percent between 2007 and 2011 and decreased 21.9 percent between 2002 and 2011. (Tables II-1 and II-1A)

In 2011, offenders used firearms in 67.7 percent of the nation's murders, 41.3 percent of robberies, and 21.2 percent of aggravated assaults. Although the largest percent of murders and robberies were committed with firearms, weapons such as clubs and blunt objects accounted for the majority (32.8 percent) of aggravated assaults. (Weapon data are not collected for forcible rape offenses.) (Expanded Homicide Table 7, Expanded Offense Robbery Table 3, and Expanded Aggravated Assault Table, see http://www.fbi.gov/about-us/cjis/ucr/crime-in-the-u.s/2011/crime-in-the-u.s.-2011/offenses-known-to-law-enforcement/expanded-offense-data for more information)

Regional Offense Trends and Rate

The UCR program divides the United States into four regions: the Northeast, the South, the Midwest, and the West. (More details concerning geographic regions are provided in Appendix III.) The population distribution of the regions can be found in Table II-3, and the estimated volume and rate of violent crime by region are provided in Table II-4.

The Northeast

The Northeast accounted for an estimated 17.8 percent of the nation's population in 2011 and an estimated 16.2 percent of its violent crimes. (Table II-3) The estimated number of violent crimes decreased 1.4 percent from 2010 to 2011. Murder decreased 6.2 percent in the Northeast. Forcible rapes decreased 2.1 percent. Aggravated assaults decreased 2.0 percent from the 2010 rate. In 2011, there were an estimated 352.1 violent crimes per 100,000 inhabitants. (Table II-4)

The Midwest

With an estimated 21.6 percent of the total population of the United States, the Midwest accounted for 19.5 percent of the nation's estimated number of violent crimes in 2011. (Table II-3) The region had a 4.0 percent decrease in violent crime from 2010 to 2011. The estimated number of aggravated assaults declined 5.7 percent and the estimated number of robberies fell 2.1 percent, while the number of murders rose 2.7 percent percent and the number of forcible rapes rose 0.2 percent. The rate of violent crime per 100,000 inhabitants in the Midwest declined 4.3 percent from 2010 to 2011. (Table II-4)

The South

The South, the nation's most populous region, accounted for 37.2 percent of the nation's population in 2011. Almost 42 percent (41.3 percent) of violent crimes in 2011 occurred in the South. (Table II-3) Violent crime in the South decreased by 4.1 percent. The estimated number of forcible rapes fell 2.2 percent in the South. Robberies had the largest decline (5.6 percent) of the four offenses, followed by aggravated assault (3.7 percent), forcible rape (2.2 percent), and murder (0.9 percent). The estimated rate of violent crime in the South was 428.8 incidents per 100,000 inhabitants in 2011. (Table II-4)

The West

With 23.4 percent of the nation's population in 2011, the West accounted for an estimated 22.9 percent of the nation's violent crime. (Table II-3) Violent crime in the West decreased 4.8 percent from 2010 to 2011. All four violent offense categories decreased in number from 2010 to 2011, except for murder, which rose 0.4 percent; aggravated assault decreased 4.2 percent, robbery fell 5.9 percent, and forcible rape dropped 6.0 percent. The region's violent crime rate in 2011 was 378.0 per 100,000 population, a 5.71 percent decrease from the 2010 rate. (Table II-4)

Community Types

The UCR program aggregates crime data into three community types: metropolitan statistical areas (MSAs), cities outside MSAs, and nonmetropolitan counties outside MSAs. Appendix III provides additional information regarding community types. In 2011, 83.5 percent of the nation's population lived in MSAs. Residents of cities outside MSAs continued to account for 6.6 percent of the country's population, and residents living in nonmetropolitan counties continued to account for 9.9 percent of the population. (Table II-2)

Approximately 88.0 percent of the areas actually reporting violent crimes in the United States occurred in MSAs, 6.0 percent occurred in cities outside MSAs, and 4.4 percent occurred in nonmetropolitan counties. By community type, the violent crime rates were estimated at 410.3 incidents per 100,000 inhabitants in MSAs, 382.1 incidents per 100,000 inhabitants in cities outside MSAs, and 186.1 incidents per 100,000 inhabitants in nonmetropolitan counties. (Table II-2)

Population Groups: Trends and Rates

In the UCR program, data are also aggregated into population groups; these groups are described in more detail in Appendix III. The nation's cities had an overall decrease of another 3.5 percent in the estimated number of violent crimes from 2010 to 2011. By city population group, cities with 50,000 to 99,999 inhabitants had the largest percentage decline in the estimated number of violent crimes (4.9 percent). (Table II-12)

The law enforcement agencies in the nation's cities collectively reported a rate of 467.3 violent crimes per 100,000 inhabitants in 2011. Law enforcement agencies in cities subset of 500,000 to 999,999 inhabitants reported the highest violent crime rate, with 819.6 violent crimes per 100,000 inhabitants; the violent crime rate for all cities with 250,000 or more inhabitants was 754.5 per 100,000 inhabitants. Agencies in cities with 10,000 to 24,999 inhabitants reported the lowest violent crime rate (279.4 incidents per 100,000 inhabitants). Law enforcement agencies in the nation's metropolitan counties reported a collective violent crime rate of 256.9 per 100,000 inhabitants, while agencies in nonmetropolitan counties reported a collective rate of 180.8 violent crimes per 100,000 inhabitants. (Table II-16)

MURDER

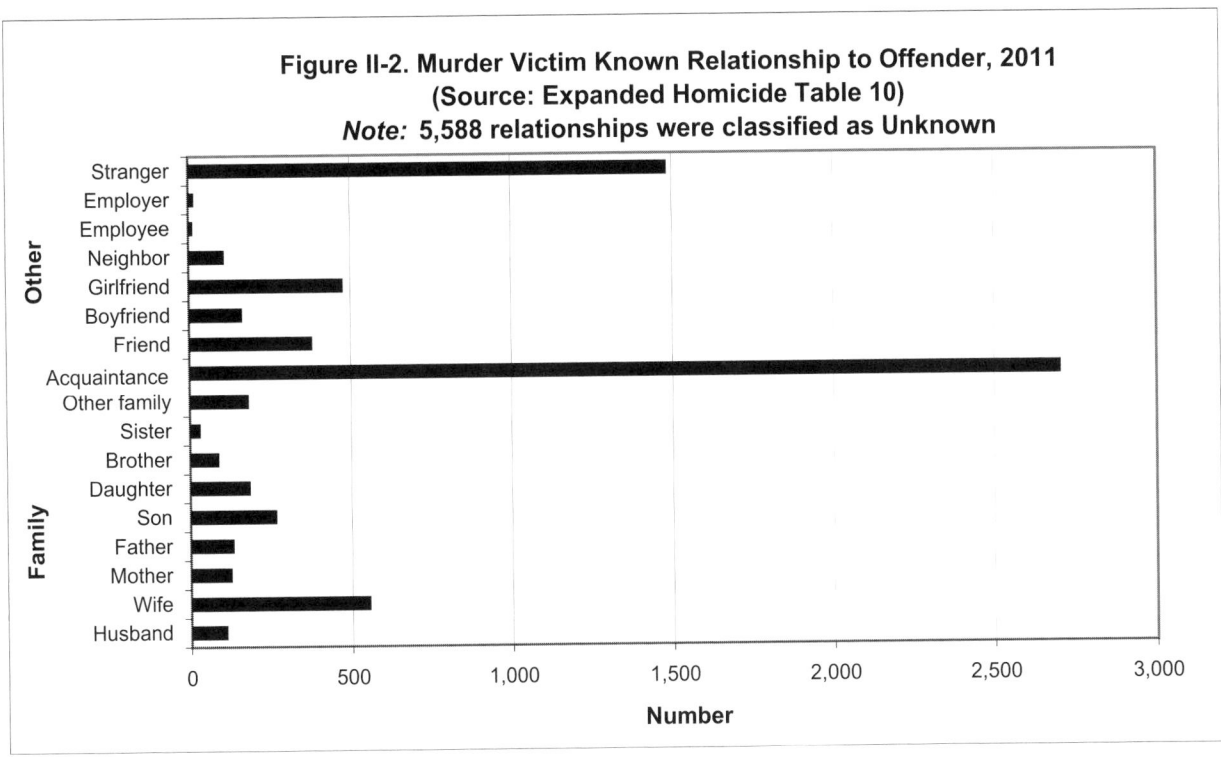

**Figure II-2. Murder Victim Known Relationship to Offender, 2011
(Source: Expanded Homicide Table 10)**
Note: 5,588 relationships were classified as Unknown

Definition

The UCR program defines murder and non-negligent manslaughter as the willful (non-negligent) killing of one human being by another. The classification of this offense is based solely on police investigation, rather than on the determination of a court, medical examiner, coroner, jury, or other judicial body. The UCR program does not include the following situations under this offense classification: deaths caused by negligence, suicide, or accident; justifiable homicides; and attempts to murder or assaults to murder, which are considered aggravated assaults.

Data Collection/Supplementary Homicide Reports (SHR)

The UCR program's *Supplementary Homicide Report* (SHR) provides information about murder victims and offenders by age, sex, and race; the types of weapons used in the murders; the relationships of the victims to the offenders; and the circumstances surrounding the incident. Law enforcement agencies are asked to complete an SHR for each murder reported to the UCR program. Data from SHRs can be viewed in the Expanded Homicide Data section, found on the FBI web site: http://www.fbi.gov/about-us/cjis/ucr/crime-in-the-u.s/2010/crime-in-the-u.s.-2010/offenses-known-to-law-enforcement/expanded/expandhomicidemain. More information on these reports and the expanded homicide tables can be found in Section I. Highlights from these tables have been included below.

National Volume, Trends, and Rates

An estimated 14,612 persons were murdered nationwide in 2011. This number was a 0.7 percent decrease from the 2010 estimate, a 14.7 percent decrease from the 2007 figure, and a 10.0 percent decrease from the 2002 estimate. The 2011 murder rate, 4.7 offenses per 100,000 inhabitants, was a 2.1 percent decrease when compared with the rate for 2010. For a third year, murder accounted for 1.2 percent of the overall estimated number of violent crimes in 2011. (Tables II-1 and II-1A)

Regional Offense Trends and Rates

The UCR program divides the United States into four regions: the Northeast, the South, the Midwest, and the West. (More details concerning geographic regions are provided in Appendix III.) In 2011, nearly 44 percent (43.6 percent) of murders were reported in the South, the most populous region. The West reported 21.0 percent of murders, 20.6 percent were reported in the Midwest, and 14.8 percent were reported in the Northeast.

The Northeast

In 2011, the Northeast accounted for an estimated 17.8 percent of the nation's population and 14.8 percent of its estimated number of murders. With an estimated 2,169 murders, the Northeast saw a 6.2 percent decrease compared with the

2010 figure. The offense rate for the Northeast was 3.9 murders per 100,000 inhabitants, down from 4.2 murders per 100,000 inhabitants in 2010. (Tables II-3 and II-4)

The Midwest

The Midwest accounted for an estimated 21.6 percent of the nation's total population and 20.6 percent of the country's estimated number of murders in 2011. The Midwest reported an estimated 3,003 murders in 2011. The region experienced a rate of 4.5 murders per 100,000 inhabitants in 2011, slightly above the 2010 rate. (Tables II-3 and II-4)

The South

The South accounted for an estimated 37.2 percent of the nation's population in 2011 and 43.6 percent of the nation's murders, the highest proportion among the four regions. The estimated 6,371 murders represented a 0.9 percent decrease in the estimated number of murders from 2010 to 2011. The region's estimated rate of 5.5 murders per 100,000 inhabitants represented a decrease of 1.9 percent from the estimated rate for 2010. (Tables II-3 and II-4)

The West

The West again accounted for an estimated 23.4 percent of the nation's population and 21.0 percent of the estimated number of murders in 2011. The West experienced an estimated 3,069 murders, a 0.4 percent increase from the 2010 estimate. The region's murder rate was 4.2 per 100,000 inhabitants, virtually unchanged from the 2010 rate. (Tables II-3 and II-4)

Community Types

The UCR program aggregates data for three community types: metropolitan statistical areas (MSAs), cities outside MSAs, and nonmetropolitan counties outside MSAs. (See Appendix III for definitions.) In 2011, MSAs accounted for 83.5 percent of the nation's population and 86.9 percent of the estimated total number of murders. With 12,703 estimated homicides, MSAs experienced a rate of 4.9 murders per 100,000 inhabitants in 2011. Cities outside MSAs accounted for 6.6 percent of the U.S. population and (with an estimated 830 murders) accounted for 5.7 percent of the estimated murders in the nation. The murder rate for cities outside MSAs was 4.4 per 100,000 inhabitants. In 2011, 9.9 percent of the nation's population lived in nonmetropolitan counties outside MSAs. An estimated 895 murders took place in these counties, accounting for 6.1 percent of the nation's estimated total. (Table II-2)

Population Groups: Trends and Rates

The UCR program uses the following population group designations in its data presentations: cities (grouped according to population size) and counties (classified as either metropolitan or nonmetropolitan). A breakdown of these classifications is provided in Appendix III.

From 2010 to 2011, the nation's cities experienced a 0.8 percent decrease in homicides. Three city groups experienced increases (3.3 percent in cities with 100,000 to 249,999 inhabitants, 11.5 percent in cities with 10,000 to 24,999 inhabitants, and 20.0 percent in cities with fewer than 10,000 inhabitants). The city group with the largest decrease (12.6 percent) was in cities with 50,000 to 99,999 inhabitants. Metropolitan counties experienced a decrease in homicides of 4.4 percent from 2010 to 2011, while nonmetropolitan counties experienced a decrease of 0.6 percent. (Table II-12)

In 2011, cities collectively had a rate of 5.5 murders per 100,000 inhabitants. Cities with 250,000 to 499,999 inhabitants had the highest murder rate (11.7 murders per 100,000 inhabitants). Cities with 10,000 to 24,999 inhabitants had the lowest murder rates, with 2.8 murders per 100,000 inhabitants. The homicide rate for metropolitan counties was 3.3 murders per 100,000 inhabitants, and for nonmetropolitan counties, it was 3.2 murders per 100,000 inhabitants. Suburban areas had a homicide rate of 2.9 per 100,000 inhabitants. (Table II-16)

Supplementary Homicide Reports Data

Victims/Offenders

Based on 2011 supplemental homicide data (where the ages, sexes, or races of the murder victims were *identified*), 94.7 percent of victims were over 18 years of age, 23.5 percent were under age 22, 5.3 percent were under 18 years of age, and the age of 1.0 percent of the victims was unknown. Of the 12,642 murder victims represented in the 2011 expanded tables whose gender was identified, 77.6 percent were male. Concerning race, 46.6 percent of victims were White, 50.7 percent were Black, and 2.7 percent were from other races. Race was unknown for 175 victims. (Expanded Homicide Tables 1 and 2) For murders where the gender of the offender was identified, 89.3 percent were males. For the offenders for whom race was identified, 52.4 percent were Black, 45.2 percent were White, and 2.4 percent were other races; 4,077 offenders were of unknown race. (Expanded Homicide Data Table 3)

Victim-Offender Relationships

For incidents in which the victim-offender relationship was specified (including the designation of "unknown"), 13.8 percent of victims were slain by family members, 11.7 percent were murdered by strangers, and 30.3 percent were killed by acquaintances (neighbor, friend, boyfriend, employer, etc.). (Expanded Homicide Data Table 10)

Circumstances/Weapons

Concerning the known circumstances surrounding murders, and including murders with unknown circumstances, 28.4 percent of victims were murdered during arguments (including romantic triangles) in 2011. Felony circumstances (rape, robbery, burglary, etc.) accounted for 14.3 percent of murders. Circumstances were unknown for 38.0 percent of reported homicides. (Expanded Homicide Data Table 12) Of the homicides for which the type of weapon was specified (including the designation of "unknown"), 67.8 percent involved the use of firearms. Of the identified firearms used, handguns comprised 72.5 percent. (Expanded Homicide Data Table 8)

Justifiable Homicide

Certain willful killings must be reported as justifiable, or excusable, homicide. In the UCR program, justifiable homicide is defined as, and is limited to, the following:

- The killing of a felon by a peace officer in the line of duty.

- The killing of a felon, during the commission of a felony, by a private citizen.

Because these killings are determined by law enforcement investigation to be justifiable, they are tabulated separately from murder and nonnegligent manslaughter. Law enforcement reported 653 justifiable homicides in 2011. Of those, law enforcement officers justifiably killed 393 individuals, and private citizens justifiably killed 260 individuals. (Expanded Homicide Data Tables 14 and 15)

FORCIBLE RAPE

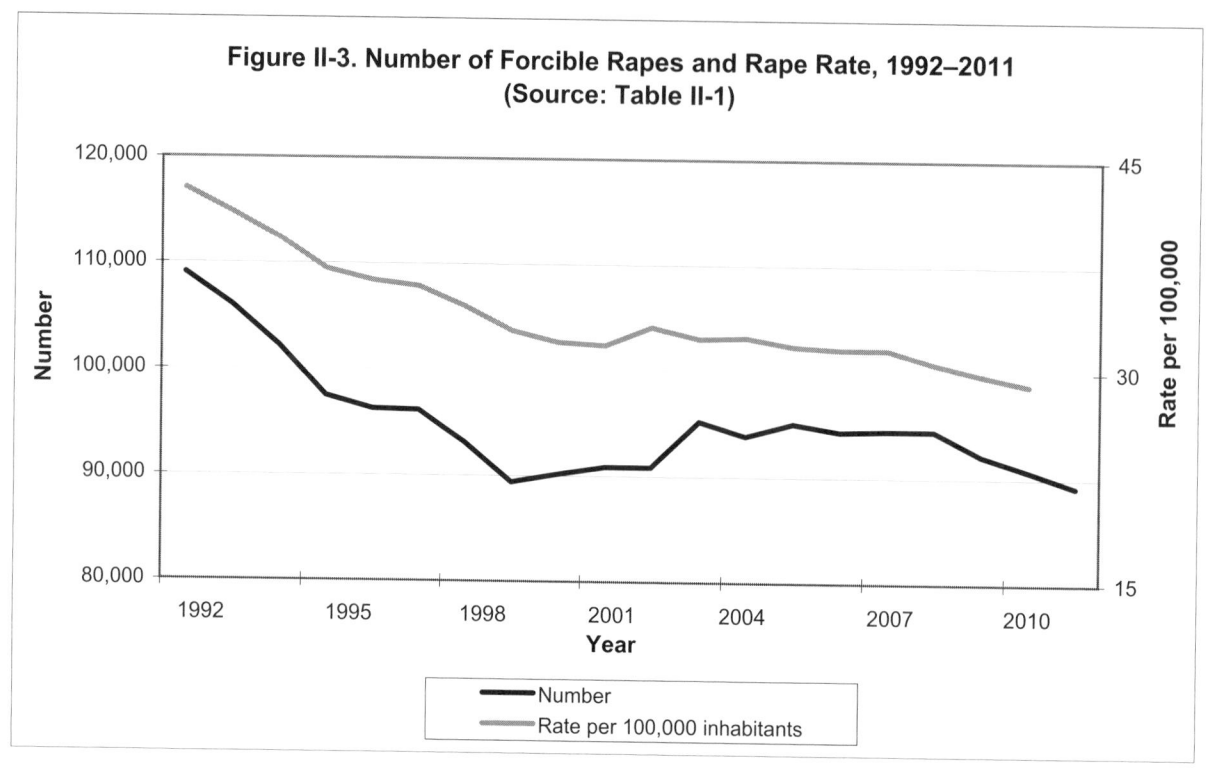

Figure II-3. Number of Forcible Rapes and Rape Rate, 1992–2011
(Source: Table II-1)

Definition

Forcible rape is the carnal knowledge of a female forcibly and against her will. Assaults and attempts to commit rape by force or threat of force are included; however, statutory rape (without force) and other sex offenses are excluded.

Data Collection

The UCR program counts one offense for each female victim of a forcible rape, attempted forcible rape, or assault with intent to rape, regardless of the victim's age. A rape by force involving a female victim and a familial offender is counted as a forcible rape, not as an act of incest. The program collects only arrest statistics concerning all other crimes of a sexual nature. The offense of statutory rape, in which no force is used but the female victim is under the age of consent, is included in the arrest total for the sex offenses category. Sexual attacks on males are counted as aggravated assaults or sex offenses, depending on the circumstances and the extent of any injuries.

National Volume, Trends, and Rates

In 2011, the estimated number of forcible rapes (83,425)—the lowest figure in the last 22 years—decreased 2.5 percent from the 2010 estimate. The estimated volume of rapes in 2011 was 9.5 percent lower than in 2007 and was 12.4 percent below the 2002 level. (Tables II-1 and II-1A)

Of the forcible rapes known to law enforcement agencies in 2011, rapes by force made up 93.0 percent of reported rape offenses, and in 2010 assaults to rape-attempts accounted for 7.0 percent of reported rape offenses. (Tables II-1 and II-19)

Regional Offense Trends and Rates

The UCR program divides the United States into four regions: the Northeast, the South, the Midwest, and the West. (More details concerning geographic regions are provided in Appendix III.) Regional analysis offers estimates of the volume of female rapes, the percent change from the previous year's estimate, and the rate of rape per 100,000 female inhabitants in each region.

The Northeast

The Northeast made up 17.8 percent of the U.S. population in 2011. In 2011, an estimated 10,641 forcible rapes of females—12.8 percent of the national total—occurred in the Northeast. This was a decrease of 2.1 percent from the 2010 estimated figure. (Tables II-3 and II-4)

The Midwest

The Midwest accounted for 21.6 percent of the U.S. population in 2011. Over one-quarter (25.3 percent) of all forcible rapes in the nation occurred in the Midwest in 2011. The 2011 estimate (21,097 forcible rapes) represented an increase of 0.2 percent from the 2010 estimate. (Tables II-3 and II-4)

The South

The South, the nation's most populous region, accounted for an estimated 37.2 percent of the nation's population in 2011; the region also accounted for an estimated 37.8 percent of the nation's estimated number of forcible rapes. An estimated 31,560 female victims reported forcible rape in the South in 2011, down 2.2 percent from 32,225 in 2010. (Tables II-3 and II-4)

The West

The West accounted for 23.4 percent of the nation's population in 2011. The region also accounted for 24.1 percent of the nation's total number of estimated forcible rapes with an estimated 20,127 offenses. The West saw a 6.0 percent decline in forcible rapes from 2010 to 2011. (Tables II-3 and II-4)

Community Types

Using the U.S. Office of Management and Budget's designations, the UCR program aggregates crime data by type of community in which the offenses occur: metropolitan statistical areas (MSAs), cities outside MSAs, and nonmetropolitan counties outside MSAs. (Appendix III provides more detailed information about community types.)

MSAs

In 2011, MSAs accounted for 83.5 percent of the nation's population and 79.8 percent of the nation's estimated number of forcible rapes. An estimated 66,574 females were forcibly raped in metropolitan areas. (Table II-2)

Cities Outside MSAs

Cities outside MSAs are mostly incorporated areas served by city law enforcement agencies. Although accounting for only 6.6 percent of the U.S. population in 2011, cities outside MSAs accounted for 9.0 percent of the nation's estimated forcible rapes (8,259 offenses). (Table II-2)

Nonmetropolitan Counties

In 2011, approximately 9.9 percent of the nation's population lived in nonmetropolitan counties outside MSAs (counties made up of mostly non-incorporated areas served by noncity law enforcement agencies). Collectively, these areas had an estimated 5,781 forcible rapes, representing 6.9 percent of the nation's estimated total. (Table II-2)

Population Groups: Trends and Rates

The UCR program uses the following population group designations in its data presentations: cities (grouped according to population size) and counties (classified as either metropolitan or nonmetropolitan). A breakdown of these classifications is provided in Appendix III.

From 2010 to 2011, the nation's cities experienced a 2.7 percent decrease in forcible rapes. Cities with 100,000 to 249,999 inhabitants and cities with fewer than 10,000 inhabitants experienced the greatest declines (5.5 percent and 4.7 percent, respectively). Metropolitan counties experienced a decrease in forcible rapes of 6.4 percent from 2010 to 2011, while nonmetropolitan counties experienced a decrease of 8.7 percent. (Table II-12)

In 2011, cities collectively had a rate of 29.8 forcible rapes per 100,000 inhabitants. Cities with 250,000 to 499,999 inhabitants had the highest rate of forcible rape (43.1 forcible rapes per 100,000 inhabitants). Cities with 10,000 to 24,999 inhabitants had the lowest rate, with 25.2 forcible rapes per 100,000 inhabitants. The forcible rape rate for metropolitan counties was 20.3 per 100,000 inhabitants, and for nonmetropolitan counties, it was 21.0 per 100,000 inhabitants. Suburban areas had a forcible rape rate of 20.7 per 100,000 inhabitants. (Table II-16)

ROBBERY

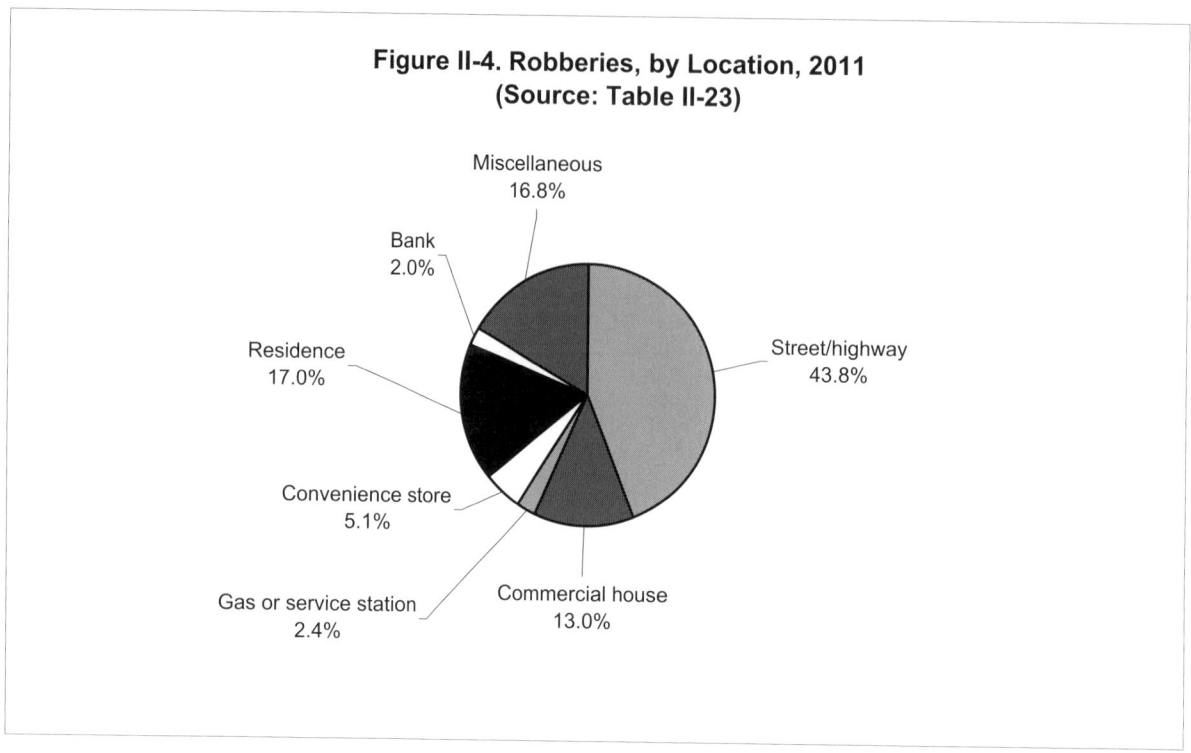

Figure II-4. Robberies, by Location, 2011
(Source: Table II-23)

Miscellaneous
16.8%

Bank
2.0%

Residence
17.0%

Street/highway
43.8%

Convenience store
5.1%

Gas or service station
2.4%

Commercial house
13.0%

Definition

The UCR program defines robbery as the taking or attempting to take anything of value from the care, custody, or control of a person or persons by force or threat of force or violence and/or by putting the victim in fear.

National Volume, Trends, and Rates

In 2011, the estimated robbery total (354,396) decreased 4.0 percent from the 2010 estimate. The 5-year robbery trend (2007 data compared with 2011 data) showed an decrease of 20.8 percent. The 2011 estimated robbery rate (113.7 per 100,000 inhabitants) showed a decrease of 4.7 percent when compared with the 2010 rate. (Tables II-1 and II-1A)

Regional Offense Trends and Rates

The UCR program divides the United States into four regions: the Northeast, the South, the Midwest, and the West. (More details concerning geographic regions are provided in Appendix III.)

The Northeast

The Northeast, with an estimated 17.8 percent of the nation's population in 2011, accounted for 19.4 percent of its estimated number of robberies. (Table II-3) The estimated number of robberies decreased 0.2 percent from 2010. The rate for this region was 124.0 robberies per 100,000 inhabitants, down from 124.6 robberies per 100,000 inhabitants in 2010. (Table II-4)

The Midwest

The Midwest accounted for 21.6 percent of the total population of the United States and 20.1 percent of its estimated number of robberies in 2011. (Table II-3) An estimated 71,345 robberies occurred in the Midwest in 2011, a 2.1 percent decrease from the estimated figure from 2010. The region's robbery rate was 106.2 robberies per 100,000 inhabitants in 2011. (Table II-4)

The South

The South, the nation's most highly populated region, accounted for an estimated 37.2 percent of the nation's population and 37.4 percent of the nation's estimated number of robberies in 2011. (Table II-3) Robberies accounted for an estimated 132,467 violent crimes in this region in 2011, representing a 5.6 percent decrease from the 2010 figure. The 2011 robbery rate in the South was 114.1, down 6.6 percent from 2010. (Table II-4)

The West

The West was home to an estimated 23.4 percent of the nation's population and accounted for 23.1 percent of the nation's estimated number of robberies in 2011. (Table II-3) The estimated number of robberies (86,779) in the region in 2011 represented a 10.0 percent decrease from the 2010 figure. The rate of robberies per 100,000 inhabitants in the West was 120.6, a 10.4 percent decrease from the 2010 rate. (Table II-4)

Community Types

The UCR program aggregates data for three community types: metropolitan statistical areas (MSAs), cities outside MSAs, and nonmetropolitan counties outside MSAs. MSAs include a central city or urbanized area with at least 50,000 inhabitants, as well as the county that contains the principal city and other adjacent counties that have, as defined by the U.S. Office of Management and Budget, a high degree of social and economic integration as measured through commuting. Cities outside MSAs are mostly incorporated areas, and nonmetropolitan counties are made up of mostly unincorporated areas served by noncity law enforcement.

In 2011, MSAs were home to an estimated 83.5 percent of the nation's population, and 95.0 percent of the nation's estimated number of robberies took place in these areas. Robberies in MSAs occurred at a rate of 129.9 per 100,000 inhabitants. Cities outside MSAs accounted for 6.6 percent of the U.S. population and accounted for 3.0 percent of the estimated number of robberies in the nation. The robbery rate for cities outside MSAs was 56.0 per 100,000 inhabitants. Nonmetropolitan counties made up 9.9 percent of the nation's estimated population and 1.2 percent of the nation's estimated robberies, at a rate of 15.5 robberies per 100,000 inhabitants. (Table II-2)

Population Groups: Trends and Rates

The national UCR program aggregates data by various population groups, which include cities, metropolitan counties, and nonmetropolitan counties. A definition of these groups can be found in Appendix III. The number of robberies in cities as a whole decreased 3.5 percent. Among the population groups labeled *city*, those cities with 50,000 to 99,999 inhabitants had the greatest decrease in the number of robberies (4.9 percent). Nonmetropolitan counties had a 5.4 percent decrease in the estimated number of robberies, and metropolitan counties showed a 7.1 percent decrease. The number of robberies in suburban areas fell 5.6 percent. (Table II-12)

Among the population groups, the nation's cities collectively had a rate of 152.7 robberies per 100,000 inhabitants. Of the population groups and subsets designated *city*, those 500,000 to 999,999 inhabitants had the highest rate (296.2 per 100,000 inhabitants), while those with fewer than 10,000

inhabitants had the lowest rate (47.2 per 100,000 inhabitants) of robberies. Of the two county groups, metropolitan counties had a rate of 54.1 robberies per 100,000 inhabitants, while nonmetropolitan counties had a rate of 14.2 robberies per 100,000 inhabitants. Suburban areas had a robbery rate of 57.7 per 100,000 inhabitants. (Table II-16)

Offense Analysis

The UCR program collects supplemental data about robberies to document the use of weapons, the dollar loss associated with the offense, and the location types.

Robbery by Weapon

Firearms were used in 41.4 percent of robberies in 2011. Strong-arm robberies accounted for 42.0 percent of the total. Offenders used knives or cutting instruments in 7.9 percent of these crimes. In the remainder of the robberies, the offenders used other types of weapons. (Table II-19)

Loss by Dollar Value

Based on the supplemental reports from law enforcement agencies, robberies cost victims, collectively, an estimated $409 million in 2011. (Tables II-1 and II-23) The average loss per robbery was $1,153. Average dollar losses were the highest for banks, which suffered an average loss of $4,704 per offense. Gas and service stations lost an average of $890 per offense. Commercial houses, which include supermarkets, department stores, and restaurants, had average losses of $1,783. An average of $1,489 was taken from residences. An average of $667 was lost in each offense against convenience stores. (Table II-23)

Robbery Trends by Location

Among the location types, bank robberies had the greatest percentage decrease from 2010 to 2011, declining 12.6 percent. Robberies that occurred at convenience stores decreased 5.1 percent. The number of robberies that occurred at commercial houses fell 4.6 percent, robberies on streets and highways decreased 3.3 percent, and robberies at residences decreased 4.3 percent. Robberies at gas or service stations increased 0.1 percent. (Table II-23)

By location type, the greatest proportion of robberies in 2011 occurred on streets and highways (43.8 percent). Robbers targeted commercial houses in 13.0 percent of offenses and residences in 17.0 percent of offenses. Convenience stores accounted for 5.1 percent of robberies, followed by gas and service stations (2.4 percent) and banks (2.0 percent). (Table II-23)

AGGRAVATED ASSAULT

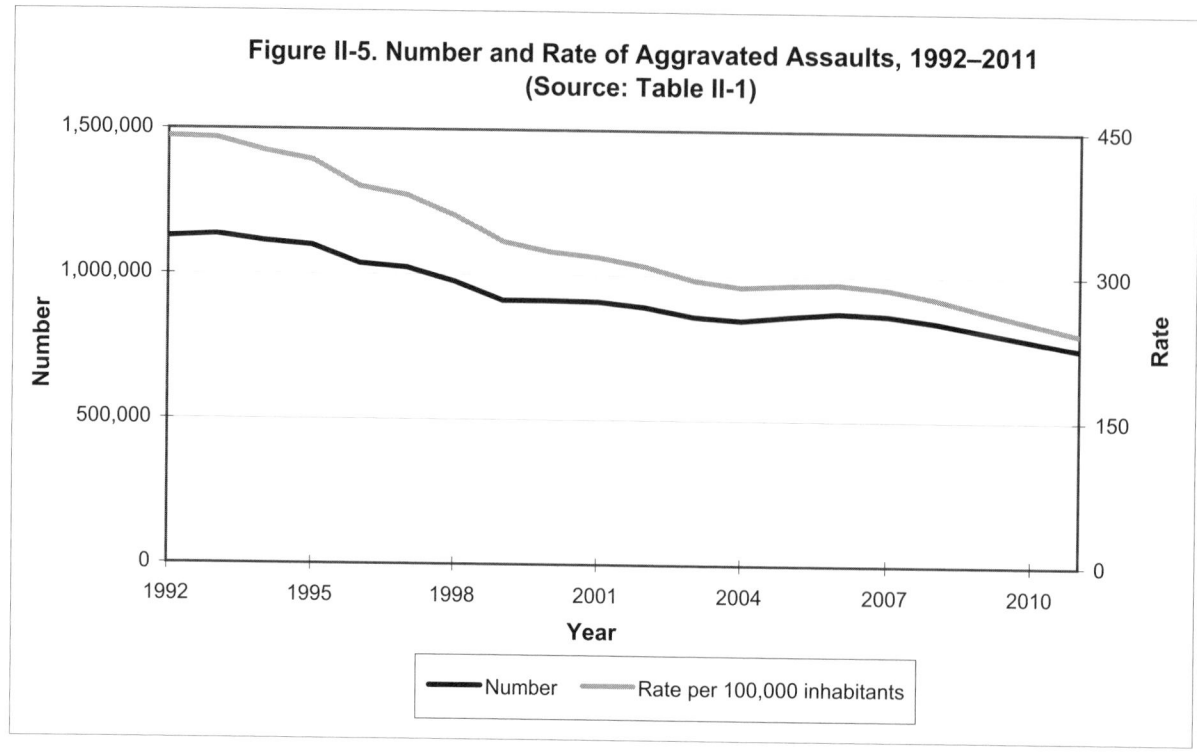

Figure II-5. Number and Rate of Aggravated Assaults, 1992–2011
(Source: Table II-1)

Definition

The UCR program defines aggravated assault as an unlawful attack by one person upon another for the purpose of inflicting severe or aggravated bodily injury. This type of assault is usually accompanied by the use of a weapon or by other means likely to produce death or great bodily harm. Attempted aggravated assaults that involve the display or threat of a gun, knife, or other weapon are included in this crime category because serious personal injury would likely result if these assaults were completed. When aggravated assault and larceny-theft occur together, the offense falls under the category of robbery.

National Volume, Trends, and Rates

In 2011, estimated occurrences of aggravated assaults totaled 751,131, a 3.9 percent decrease from the 2010 figure, and a 15.7 percent decline when compared with the estimates for 2002. The 2011 data also show a decrease for the fifth consecutive year in the rate of aggravated assaults per 100,000 U.S. inhabitants. This rate, estimated at 241.1, represents a 4.6 percent decrease from the 2010 rate. However, it also represents a 16.1 percent decrease from the 2007 (5-year trend) rate and a 22.1 percent decrease from the 2002 (10-year trend) rate. (Tables II-1 and II-1A)

Among the four types of violent crime offenses (murder, forcible rape, robbery, and aggravated assault), aggravated assault typically has the highest rate of occurrence. This trend continued in 2011 with aggravated assault accounting for 62.4 percent of all violent crime. (Table II-1)

Regional Offense Trends and Rates

The UCR program divides the United States into four regions: the Northeast, the South, the Midwest, and the West. (More details concerning geographic regions are provided in Appendix III.)

The Northeast

The region with the smallest proportion of the nation's population (an estimated 17.8 percent in 2011) also accounted for the smallest proportion of the nation's estimated number of aggravated assaults (15.2 percent). (Table II-3) Occurrences of aggravated assault decreased 2.0 percent from 2010 to 2011, dropping by an estimated 2,343 incidents. However, the region continued to have the lowest aggravated assault rate in the nation, at 205.0 incidents per 100,000 inhabitants. (Table II-4)

The Midwest

With 21.6 percent of the nation's total population in 2011, the Midwest accounted for approximately 18.6 percent of the nation's estimated number of aggravated assaults. (Table II-3) Occurrences of this offense decreased 5.7 percent from the estimated total for 2010, declining to an estimated 139,577 incidents. The region's aggravated assault rate, at 207.8 incidents per 100,000 inhabitants, represented a 6.0 percent decrease from the 2010 rate. (Table II-4)

The South

The South, the nation's most highly populated region, accounted for an estimated 37.1 percent of the nation's population in 2011 and the largest amount of the nation's estimated number of aggravated assaults (43.6 percent, the same rate as 2010). (Table II-3) From 2010 to 2011, the estimated number of aggravated assaults decreased 3.7 percent, falling to a total of 327,265 incidents. The rate of aggravated assaults declined to 282.0 per 100,000 inhabitants. (Table II-4)

The West

In 2011, the West was home to an estimated 23.4 percent of the nation's population. The region accounted for 22.7 percent of the nation's estimated number of aggravated assaults. (Table II-3) From 2010 to 2011, the estimated number of offenses decreased 4.2 percent to 170,472 incidents. The rate, estimated at 234.0 offenses per 100,000 inhabitants, fell 5.1 percent from 2010. (Table II-4)

Community Types

The UCR program aggregates data for three community types: metropolitan statistical areas (MSAs), cities outside MSAs, and nonmetropolitan counties outside MSAs. MSAs include a central city or urbanized area with at least 50,000 inhabitants, as well as the county that contains the principal city and other adjacent counties that have a high degree of social and economic integration as measured through commuting. Cities outside MSAs are mostly incorporated areas, and nonmetropolitan counties are made up of mostly unincorporated areas. (For additional information about community types, see Appendix III.)

In 2011, 83.7 percent of the nation's population lived in MSAs, where the rate of aggravated assault was an estimated 249.1 per 100,000 inhabitants. Cities outside MSAs (with 6.6 percent of the U.S. population) had the highest rate of aggravated assault at 281.0 offenses per 100,000 inhabitants. Nonmetropolitan counties accounted for 9.9 percent of the U.S. population and had an offense rate of 146.8 aggravated assaults per 100,000 inhabitants. (Table II-2)

From 2010 to 2011, the number of aggravated assaults fell for all cities. Cities with 50,000 to 99,999 inhabitants experienced the greatest decrease (5.0 percent), followed by cities with 250,000 to 499,999, which fell 4.6 percent. In metropolitan counties, the number of aggravated assaults declined 6.2 percent; in nonmetropolitan counties, this number also decreased 3.7 percent. Aggravated assaults in suburban areas declined 5.0 percent from 2010 to 2011. (Table II-12)

Aggravated assault occurred at an estimated rate of 243.5 offenses per 100,000 inhabitants nationwide. The collective rate for cities was 279.4 aggravated assaults per 100,000 inhabitants. Among city population groups, rates ranged from a high of 471.9 offenses per 100,000 inhabitants (in cities with 500,000 to 999,999 inhabitants) to a low of 197.6 offenses per 100,000 inhabitants (in cities with 25,000 to 49,999 inhabitants). The aggravated assault rate was 179.1 in metropolitan counties and 142.5 in nonmetropolitan counties. It was 170.8 in suburban areas. (Table II-16)

Offense Analysis

Aggravated Assault by Weapon

Of the aggravated assault offenses for which law enforcement agencies provided expanded data in 2010, 33.1 percent were committed with blunt objects or other dangerous weapons; 27.4 percent involved personal weapons such as hands, fists, and feet; 20.6 percent were committed with firearms; and 19.0 percent involved knives or other cutting instruments. (Table II-19)

PROPERTY CRIME

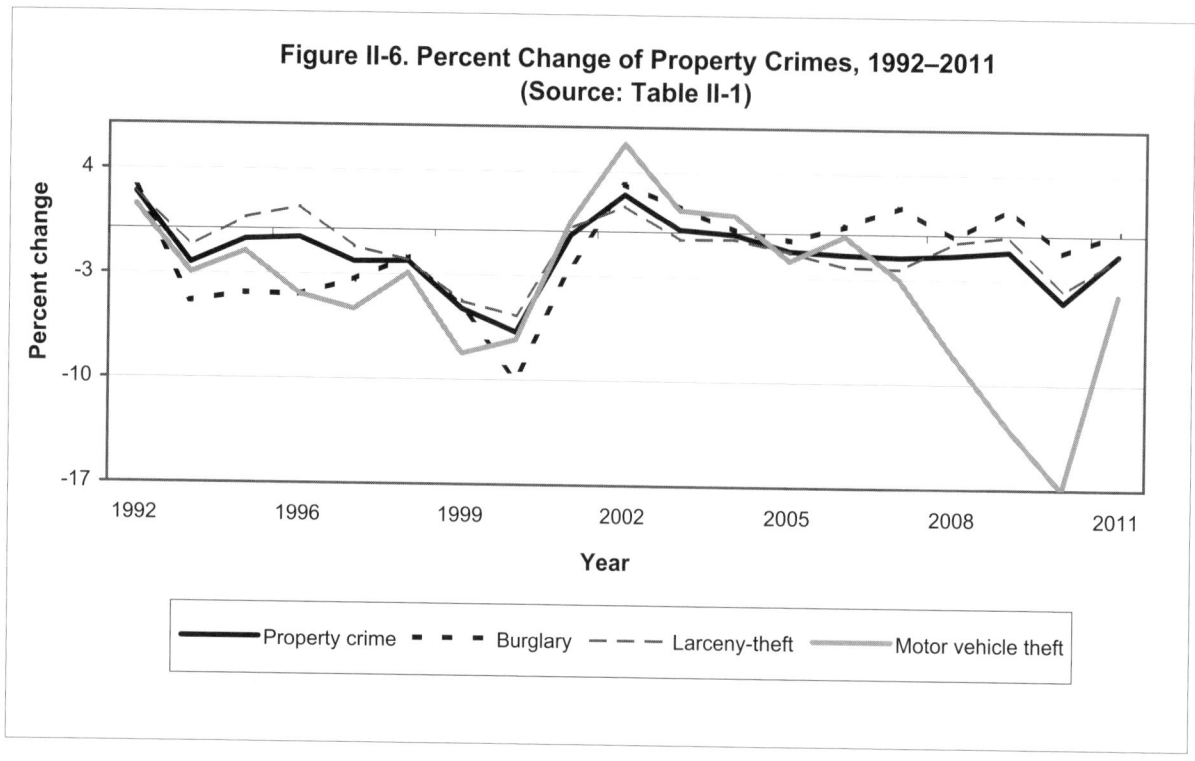

Figure II-6. Percent Change of Property Crimes, 1992–2011
(Source: Table II-1)

Definition

The Uniform Crime Reporting (UCR) program's definition of property crime includes the offenses of burglary, larceny-theft, motor vehicle theft, and arson. The object of theft-type offenses is the taking of money or property without the use of force or threat of force against the victims. Property crime includes arson because the offense involves the destruction of property; however, arson victims may be subjected to force. Because of limited participation and the varying collection procedures conducted by local law enforcement agencies, only limited data are available for arson. Arson statistics are included in the trend, clearance, and arrest tables in *Crime in the United States*, but they are not included in any estimated volume data. More information on the expanded arson tables (which are available online but not included in this publication) can be found in Section I.

Data Collection

The data presented in *Crime in the United States* reflect the Hierarchy Rule, which counts only the most serious offense in a multiple-offense criminal incident. In descending order of severity, the violent crimes are murder and nonnegligent manslaughter, forcible rape, robbery, aggravated assault; these are followed by the property crimes of burglary, larceny-theft, and motor vehicle theft. The Hierarchy Rule does not apply to the offense of arson.

National Volume, Trends, and Rates

An estimated 9,063,173 property crimes were committed in the United States in 2011, representing a 0.5 percent decrease from the 2010 (2-year trend) estimate, a 9.3 percent decrease from the 2007 (5-year trend) estimate, and a 13.3 percent decrease from the 2002 (10-year trend) estimate. (Tables II-1 and II-1A)

From 2010 to 2011, motor vehicle theft fell 3.3 percent. Larceny-theft showed a decrease from its 2010, 2007, and 2002 estimates, while burglary rose 0.9 percent from 2010 and 1.7 percent from 2002, but fell 0.1 percent from 2007. (Tables II-1 and II-1A)

The estimated property crime rate per 100,000 inhabitants in 2011 was 2,908.7, a 1.3 percent decrease from the 2010 rate, an 11.2 percent decrease from the 2007 rate, and a 19.9 percent decrease from the 2002 rate. The rate of burglaries fell 6.0 percent from 2002 to 2011. The motor vehicle theft rates per 100,000 residents fell 47.0 percent from 2002 to 2011. (Tables II-1 and II-1A)

Regional Offense Trends and Rates

The UCR program separates the United States into four regions: the Northeast, the Midwest, the South, and the West. (Geographic breakdowns can be found in Appendix III.)

Property crime data collected by the UCR program and aggregated by region reflected the following results.

The Northeast

The Northeast region accounted for 17.8 percent of the nation's population in 2011. The region also accounted for 13.0 percent of the nation's estimated number of property crimes in 2011. (Table II-3) Law enforcement in the Northeast saw a 0.5 percent decrease in the estimated number of property crimes from 2010 to 2011. The property crime rate for the Northeast, estimated at 2,121.8 incidents per 100,000 inhabitants, was virtually unchanged from the 2010 rate. (Table II-4)

The Midwest

The Midwest, with 21.6 percent of the U.S. population in 2011, accounted for 21.1 percent of the nation's estimated number of property crimes. (Table II-3) Law enforcement in the Midwest saw the number of property crimes remain virtually unchanged from 2010 to 2011. The rate of property crime in the Midwest in 2011, estimated at 2,844.3 incidents per 100,000 inhabitants, represented a 0.3 percent decrease from the 2010 rate. (Table II-4)

The South

The South, the nation's most populous region, accounted for 37.2 percent of the U.S. population in 2011. The region also accounted for an estimated 43.2 percent of the nation's property crimes. (Table II-3) The South experienced a 0.9 percent decrease in its estimated number of property crimes from 2010 to 2011. The 2011 property crime rate, an estimated 3,370.8 incidents per 100,000 inhabitants, was 1.9 percent lower than the 2010 rate. (Table II-4)

The West

In 2011, the West accounted for 23.4 percent of the nation's population. The West also accounted for 22.8 percent of the nation's estimated number of property crimes. (Table II-3) From 2010 to 2011, the estimated number of property crimes in this region decreased 0.8 percent. The estimated property crime rate in the West in 2011, 2,831.5 incidents per 100,000 inhabitants, was 1.8 percent lower than the 2010 rate. (Table II-4)

Community Types

The UCR program aggregates data by three community types: metropolitan statistical areas (MSAs), cities outside metropolitan areas, and nonmetropolitan counties. (Additional in-depth information regarding community types can be found in Appendix III.) In 2011, 83.5 percent of the U.S. population lived in MSAs. The property crime rate for MSAs was 3,004.8 per 100,000 inhabitants. Cities outside metropolitan areas, which accounted for 6.6 percent of the total population in 2011, had a property crime rate of 3,596.6 per 100,000 inhabitants. Nonmetropolitan counties, with 9.9 percent of the nation's population in 2011, had a property crime rate of 1,638.6 per 100,000 inhabitants. (Table II-2)

Population Groups: Trends and Rates

The UCR program organizes the agencies that contribute data into population groups, which include cities, metropolitan counties, and nonmetropolitan counties. (Appendix III provides further details about these groups.) From 2010 to 2011, law enforcement in the nation's cities collectively reported a 0.7 percent decrease in the number of property crimes. Most city groups experienced decreases in the number of property crimes; cities with 1 million or more inhabitants had the largest decline at 2.3 percent. Metropolitan counties experienced a decrease of 1.0 percent from 2010 to 2011, while property crime increased in nonmetropolitan by 2.5 percent. (Table II-12)

The nation's cities collectively had a property crime rate of 3,385.4 incidents per 100,000 inhabitants in 2011. Nonmetropolitan counties had a rate of 1,624.0 incidents per 100,000 inhabitants, and metropolitan counties had a rate of 2,101.4 incidents per 100,000 inhabitants. The rate was 2,364.8 in suburban areas. (Table II-16)

Offense Analysis

The estimated dollar loss attributing to property crimes, not including arson, in 2011 was $15.3 billion. Among the individual property crime categories, the dollar losses were an estimated $4.8 billion for burglary, $6.1 billion for larceny-theft, and $4.4 billion for motor vehicle theft. In 2011, the average dollar value per motor vehicle stolen in the United States was $6,089. The average dollar value of property taken during burglaries was $2,185; during robberies, $1,153; and during larceny-thefts, $988. (Tables II-1 and II-23) Arson had an average dollar loss of $13,196. Arsons of industrial/manufacturing structures resulted in the highest average dollar losses ($68,349), followed by other commercial structures, with average losses of $37,855. (Expanded Arson Table 2)

BURGLARY

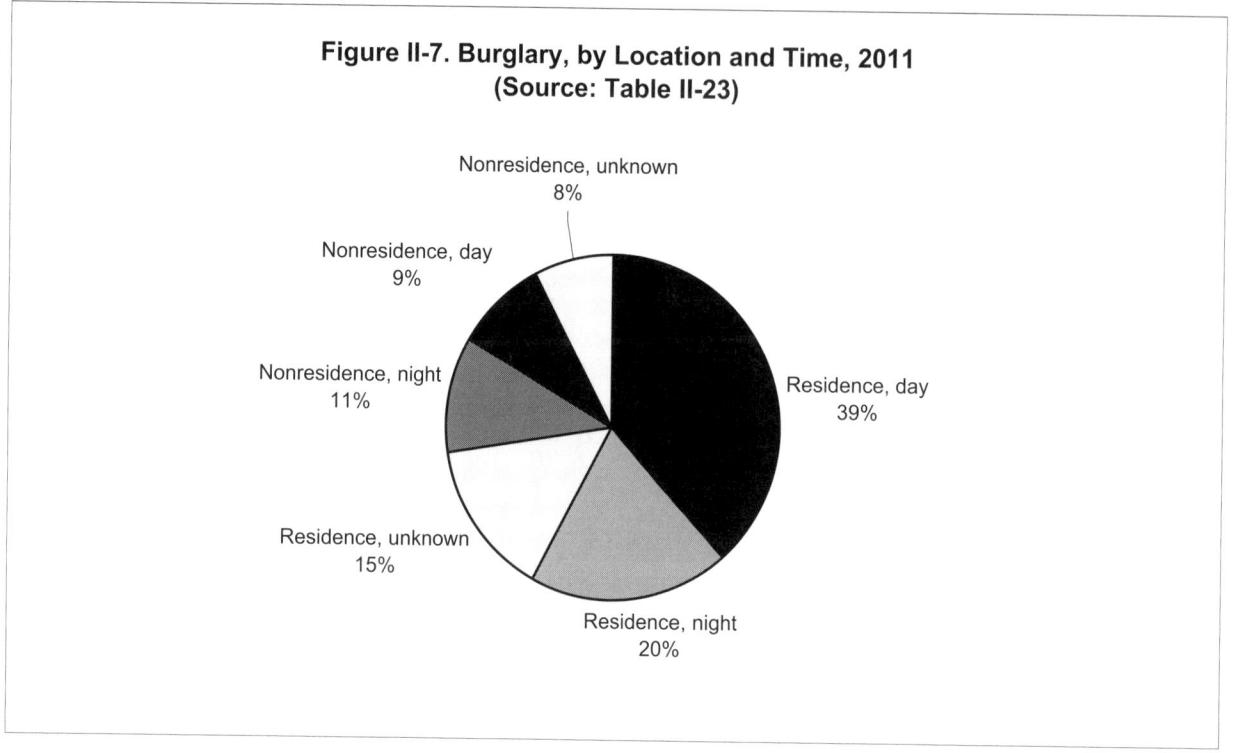

Figure II-7. Burglary, by Location and Time, 2011
(Source: Table II-23)

Nonresidence, unknown 8%
Nonresidence, day 9%
Nonresidence, night 11%
Residence, unknown 15%
Residence, night 20%
Residence, day 39%

Definition

The UCR program defines burglary as the unlawful entry of a structure to commit a felony or theft. To classify an offense as a burglary, the use of force to gain entry need not have occurred. The program has three subclassifications for burglary: forcible entry, unlawful entry where no force is used, and attempted forcible entry. The UCR definition of "structure" includes, but is not limited to, apartments, barns, house trailers or houseboats (when used as permanent dwellings), offices, railroad cars (but not automobiles), stables, and vessels (such as ships).

National Volume, Trends, and Rate

In 2011, there were an estimated 2,188,005 burglaries—an increase of 0.9 percent when compared with 2010 data. There was a decrease of 0.1 percent in the number of burglaries in 2011 when compared with the 2007 estimate, and an increase of 1.7 percent when compared with the 2002 estimate. Burglary accounted for 24.1 percent of the estimated number of property crimes committed in 2011. The burglary rate for the United States in 2011 was 702.2 incidents per 100,000 inhabitants, a 0.2 percent increase from the 2010 rate. (Tables II-1 and II-1A)

Regional Offense Trends and Rates

The UCR program divides the United States into four regions: the Northeast, the Midwest, the South, and the West. (Details regarding these regions can be found in Appendix III.) An analysis of burglary data by region showed the following details.

The Northeast

In 2011, 17.8 percent of the nation's population lived in the Northeast. This region accounted for 11.1 percent of the estimated total number of burglary offenses in the nation in 2011. The region's burglary rate, an estimated 437.5 offenses per 100,000 inhabitants, represented a increase of 3.0 percent from the 2010 rate. (Tables II-3 and II-4)

The Midwest

The Midwest accounted for 21.6 percent of the nation's population in 2011. This region accounted for 21.0 percent of the nation's estimated number of burglaries. The estimated number of burglaries in this region increased 1.4 percent from 2010 to 2011. The Midwest had a burglary rate of 685.0 offenses per 100,000 inhabitants, a 1.4 percent increase from the 2010 rate. (Tables II-3 and II-4)

The South

The South, the nation's most highly populated region, had the most burglaries in 2011 (an estimated 1,017,528), a number less than one-tenth of one percent away from its 2010 level. With 37.2 percent of the nation's population, this region accounted for 46.5 percent of all burglaries in the

United States. The estimated rate of burglary in the South was 876.8 incidents per 100,000 inhabitants, a 1.0 percent decrease from the 2010 rate. (Tables II-3 and II-4)

The West

The West accounted for 23.4 percent of the nation's population in 2011. This region accounted for an estimated 21.4 percent of the nation's burglaries. The region's burglary rate was 641.6, a 0.2 percent decrease from the 2010 rate. The total number of burglaries (467,533) represented a 0.8 percent increase from the 2010 figure. (Tables II-3 and II-4)

Community Types

The UCR program aggregates data by three community types: metropolitan statistical areas (MSAs), cities outside MSAs, and nonmetropolitan counties. (See Appendix III for more information regarding community types.) In 2011, 83.5 percent of the U.S. population lived in MSAs, and an estimated 83.6 percent of all burglaries occurred in this type of community. Inhabitants of cities outside MSAs accounted for 6.6 percent of the total population in 2011 and 7.1 percent of the estimated number of burglaries; nonmetropolitan counties, with 9.9 percent of the U.S. population, accounted for 7.4 percent of all burglaries. The burglary rates per 100,000 inhabitants were 708.6 in MSAs, 821.7 in cities outside MSAs, and 568.4 in nonmetropolitan counties. (Table II-2)

Population Groups: Trends and Rates

In addition to analyzing data by region and community type, the UCR program aggregates crime statistics by population groups. Cities are categorized into six groups based on the number of inhabitants; counties are categorized into two groups, metropolitan and nonmetropolitan. (Appendix III offers further details regarding these population groups.)

An examination of data from law enforcement agencies showed that the nation's cities again experienced a collective 0.4 percent increase in burglaries from 2010 to 2011. Burglaries increased in all but two city groups, with cities of 50,000 to 99,999 posting the greatest increase (1.5 per-

cent). The volume of burglaries increased 0.3 percent in metropolitan counties, 0.6 percent in suburban areas, and 0.9 percent in nonmetropolitan counties. (Table II-12)

The UCR program calculates burglary rates for population groups from the information provided by participating agencies that submitted all 12 months of offense data for the year. In 2011, the nation's cities had 762.9 offenses per 100,000 inhabitants. Cities with 500,000 to 999,999 population had the highest burglary rate at 1,132.4 incidents per 100,000 inhabitants. Cities with 10,000 to 24,999 inhabitants had the lowest burglary rate—613.0 incidents per 100,000 inhabitants. Metropolitan counties had a rate of 584.8 per 100,000 inhabitants, and nonmetropolitan counties had a rate of 563.3 per 100,000 inhabitants. The rate in suburban areas was 560.8 per 100,000 inhabitants. (Table II-16)

Offense Analysis

The UCR program requests that participating law enforcement agencies provide details regarding the nature of burglaries in their jurisdictions, such as type of entry, type of structure, time of day, and dollar loss associated with each offense.

Of all burglaries, 60.5 percent involved forcible entry, 33.2 percent were unlawful entries (without force), and the remainder (6.3 percent) were forcible entry attempts. (Table II-19)

Victims of burglary offenses suffered an estimated $4.8 billion in lost property in 2011; overall, the average dollar loss per burglary offense was $2,185. (Tables II-1 and II-23)

As in the past, burglars targeted residences more often than nonresidential structures. In 2011, burglaries of residential properties accounted for 74.5 percent of all burglary offenses. Law enforcement agencies were unable to determine the time of day for 21.1 percent of all reported burglaries. However, of the burglaries for which time of day could be established, most burglaries of residences (39.3 percent of all reported burglaries) occurred during the day, while most burglaries of nonresidential structures (10.4 percent of all reported burglaries) occurred at night. (Table II-23)

LARCENY-THEFT

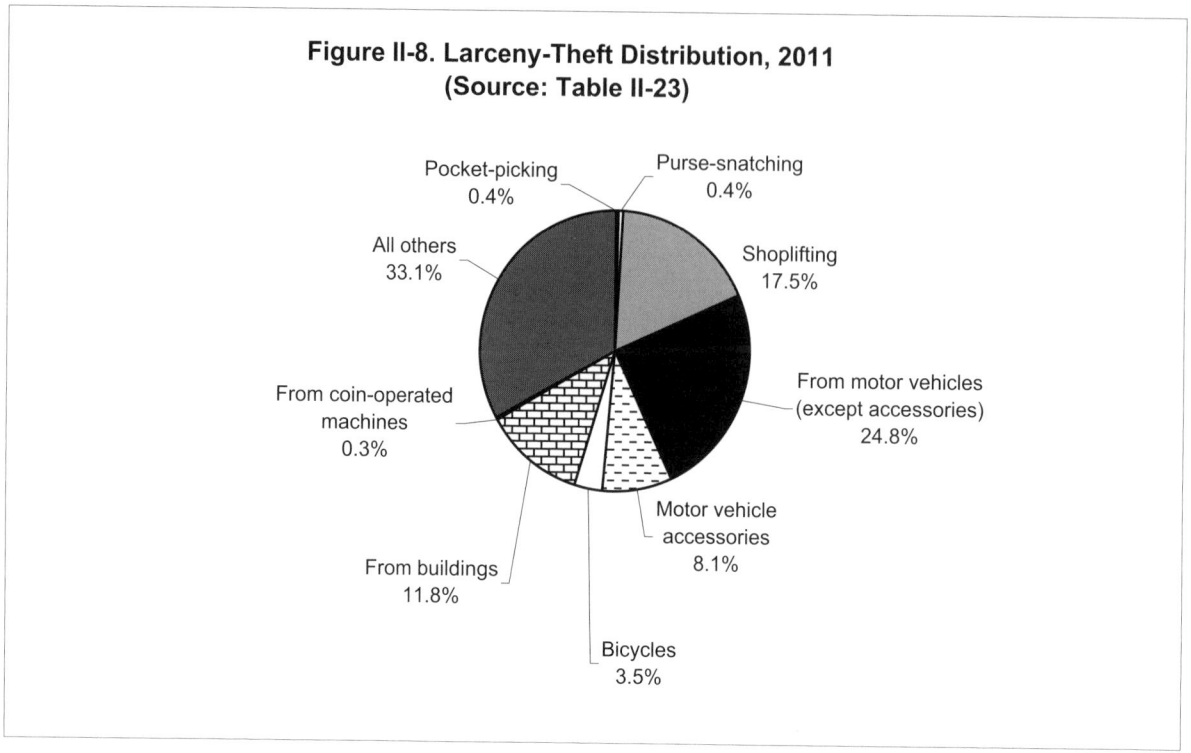

Figure II-8. Larceny-Theft Distribution, 2011
(Source: Table II-23)

Pocket-picking 0.4%

Purse-snatching 0.4%

All others 33.1%

Shoplifting 17.5%

From coin-operated machines 0.3%

From motor vehicles (except accessories) 24.8%

From buildings 11.8%

Motor vehicle accessories 8.1%

Bicycles 3.5%

Definition

The UCR program defines larceny-theft as the unlawful taking, carrying, leading, or riding away of property from the possession or constructive possession of another. Examples are thefts of bicycles, motor vehicle parts and accessories, shoplifting, pocket picking, or the stealing of any property or article not taken by force and violence or by fraud. Attempted larcenies are included. Embezzlement, confidence games, forgery, check fraud, and so on, are excluded from this category.

National Volume, Trends, and Rates

Larceny-thefts accounted for an estimated 68.0 percent of property crimes in 2011—an estimated 6 million (6,159,795) larceny-thefts nationwide. The estimated number of larceny-thefts dropped 0.7 percent from 2010 to 2011. The 2011 figure showed a 12.7 percent decline compared with the 2002 estimate. The trend data also showed decreases in the larceny-theft rates per 100,000 inhabitants during these periods. The rate of larceny-thefts declined 1.4 percent from 2010 to 2011 and 19.3 percent from 2002 to 2011. (Tables II-1 and II-1A)

Regional Offense Trends and Rates

The UCR program defines four regions within the United States: the Northeast, the Midwest, the South, and the West. (See Appendix III for a geographical description of each region.) Larceny-theft decreased in all four regions;

the South and West each declined 0.8 percent, while the Northeast and Midwest each dropped 0.6 percent. (Table II-4) The following paragraphs provide a region overview of larceny-theft.

The Northeast

The Northeast was the region with the smallest proportion (17.8 percent) of the U.S. population in 2011. The region also experienced the fewest larceny-thefts in the country, accounting for only 13.9 percent of all larceny-thefts. (Table II-3) The estimated number of offenses in 2011 (859,259) represented a 0.6 percent decline from 2010, and the estimated rate—1,547.6 incidents per 100,000 inhabitants—represented a 0.8 percent decline. (Table II-4)

The Midwest

With 21.6 percent of the U.S. population in 2011, the Midwest accounted for an estimated 21.3 percent of the nation's larceny-thefts. (Table II-3) The estimated number of offenses (1,311,642) declined 0.6 percent compared with the 2010 data, and the estimated rate of occurrences (1,953.0 incidents per 100,000 inhabitants) declined 0.9 percent. (Table II-4)

The South

With more than one-third of the U.S. population in 2011 (37.2 percent), the South had the nation's highest proportion of larceny-theft offenses: an estimated 42.8 percent.

(Table II-3) Estimated offenses in this region totaled 2,634,765, a 0.8 percent decrease from the 2010 estimate. The South's larceny-theft rate—estimated at 2,270.4 offenses per 100,000 inhabitants—decreased 1.8 percent from the 2010 estimate. (Table II-4)

The West

In 2011, an estimated 23.4 percent of the U.S. population lived in the West. This region was also where 22.0 percent of the nation's estimated number of larceny-thefts took place, the same percentage as 2010. (Table II-3) Occurrences of larceny-theft declined 0.8 percent from 2010 to 2011, dropping to an estimated total of 1,354,129 offenses. The region's larceny-theft rate, estimated at 1,858.4 offenses per 100,000 inhabitants, declined 1.8 percent from the 2010 rate. (Table II-4)

Community Types

The UCR program aggregates data for three community types: metropolitan statistical areas (MSAs), cities outside MSAs, and nonmetropolitan counties outside MSAs. MSAs include a central city or urbanized area with at least 50,000 inhabitants, as well as the county that contains the principal city and other adjacent counties that share a high degree of social and economic integration as measured through commuting. Cities outside MSAs are mostly incorporated areas, and nonmetropolitan counties are composed of unincorporated areas. (See Appendix III for more information regarding community types.)

In 2011, MSAs were home to an estimated 83.5 percent of the nation's population and again experienced 85.5 percent of the nation's larceny-theft incidents. Cities outside MSAs accounted for 6.6 percent of the U.S. population and 8.1 percent of larceny-theft offenses. Nonmetropolitan counties, which were home to 9.9 percent of the nation's population, accounted for 4.5 percent of the estimated number of larceny-theft offenses. (Table II-2)

Population Groups: Trends and Rates

In cities, collectively, occurrences of larceny-theft declined 0.9 percent between 2010 and 2011. Cities with 1,000,000 or more inhabitants experienced the greatest decrease (2.9 percent). In metropolitan and suburban areas, larceny-theft

decreased 1.0 percent and 0.8 percent, respectively. Nonmetropolitan counties experienced an increase of 4.1 percent. (Table II-12)

Based on reports of larceny-theft offenses from U.S. law enforcement agencies that submitted 12 months of complete data for 2011, this offense occurred at a rate of 1,988.6 offenses per 100,000 inhabitants. The collective rate for cities was 2,345.4 offenses per 100,000 inhabitants. Among city population groups, cities with 500,000 to 999,000 inhabitants had the highest larceny-theft rate, 3,009.5 incidents per 100,000 inhabitants. Cities with more than 1,000,000 inhabitants had the lowest rate, at 2,059.8. In metropolitan counties, the rate was 1,354.7 incidents per 100,000 inhabitants; in nonmetropolitan counties, the rate was 964.3 incidents per 100,000 inhabitants. The rate in suburban areas was 1,649.4 per 100,000 inhabitants. (Table II-16)

Offense Analysis

Distribution

Table II-23 provides a further breakdown of larceny-theft offenses, including shoplifting, thefts from buildings, thefts of motor vehicle accessories, thefts of bicycles, thefts from coin-operated machines, purse snatching, and pocket picking. The "all other" category, which includes the less-defined types of larceny-theft, accounted for 33.1 percent of all offenses.

Loss by Dollar Value

Larceny-theft offenses cost victims an estimated $6.1 billion dollars in 2011, similar to the cost in 2010. The average value of property stolen was $988 per offense. Larceny-theft from buildings had the highest average dollar loss per offense at $1,443. Thefts from motor vehicles (except accessories) had an average dollar loss of $818 per offense; thefts of motor vehicle accessories, $540; purse snatching, $412; pocket picking, $539; thefts from coin-operated machines, $368; thefts of bicycles, $367; and shoplifting, $199. (Tables II-1 and II-23)

Offenses in which the stolen property was valued at more than $200 accounted for 46.3 percent of all larceny-thefts, up 2.2 percent from 2010. Table II-23 provides further analysis, including the average dollar value per offense of all offenses in the overall category of property crime. (Table II-23)

MOTOR VEHICLE THEFT

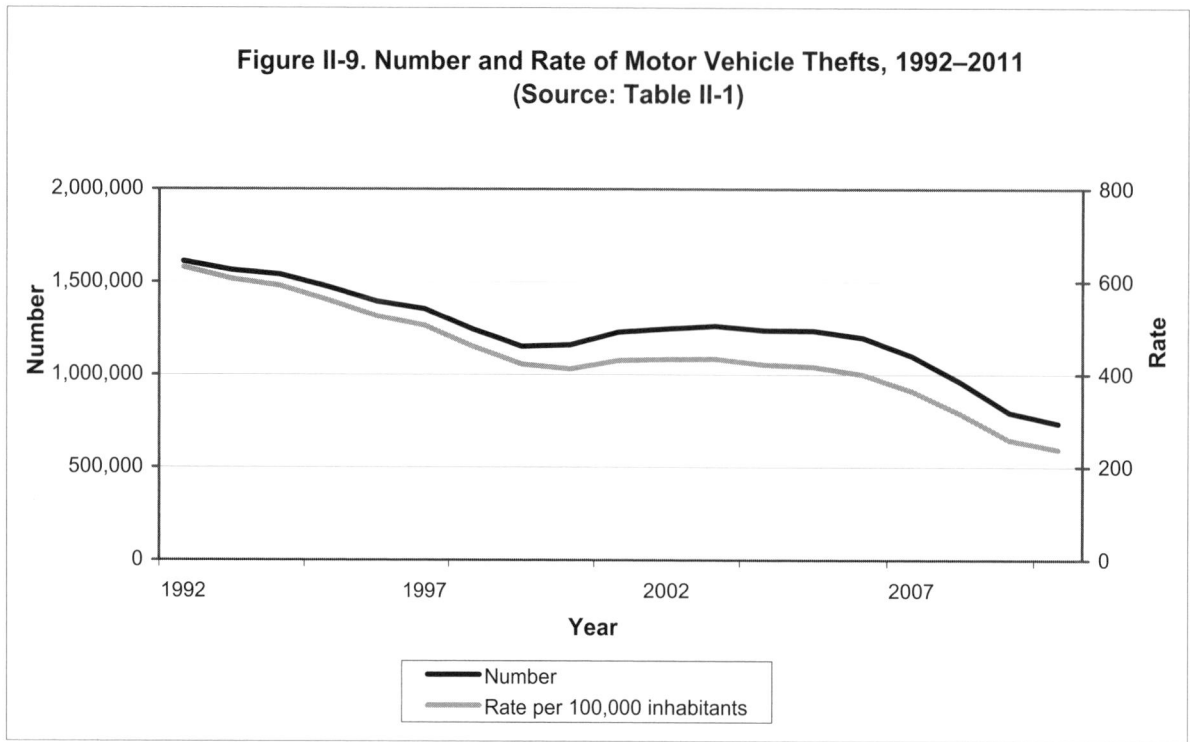

Figure II-9. Number and Rate of Motor Vehicle Thefts, 1992–2011
(Source: Table II-1)

Definition

The UCR program defines motor vehicle theft as the theft or attempted theft of a motor vehicle. The offense includes the stealing of automobiles, trucks, buses, motorcycles, snowmobiles, etc. The taking of a motor vehicle for temporary use by a person or persons with lawful access is excluded.

National Volume, Trends, and Rates

In 2011, an estimated 715,373 motor vehicle thefts took place in the United States. The estimated number of motor vehicle thefts declined 3.3 percent when compared with data from 2010, 35.0 percent when compared with 2007 figures, and 42.6 percent when compared with 2002 figures. (Tables II-1 and II-1A)

The estimated rate of motor vehicle theft in 2011 was 229.6 incidents per 100,000 inhabitants. In the 2-year, 5-year, and 10-year trend data, this rate showed decline: the 2011 rate was 4.0 percent lower than the 2010 rate, 37.1 percent lower than the 2007 rate, and 47.0 percent lower than the 2002 rate. (Tables II-1 and II-1A)

Regional Offense Trends and Rates

In order to analyze crime by geographic area, the UCR program divides the United States into four regions: the Northeast, the Midwest, the South, and the West. (Appen-

dix III provides a map delineating the regions.) This section provides a regional overview of motor vehicle theft.

The Northeast

The Northeast accounted for an estimated 17.8 percent of the nation's population in 2011. The region also accounted for an estimated 10.6 percent of its motor vehicle thefts. (Table II-3) An estimated 75,906 motor vehicle thefts occurred in the Northeast in 2011, virtually unchanged from the 2010 estimate. The estimated rate of 136.7 motor vehicle thefts per 100,000 inhabitants in the Northeast in 2011 represented a 0.3 percent decline from the 2010 rate. (Table II-4)

The Midwest

An estimated 21.6 percent of the country's population resided in the Midwest in 2011. The region accounted for 19.4 percent of the nation's motor vehicle thefts. (Table II-3) The Midwest had an estimated 138,522 motor vehicle thefts in 2011, a 0.3 percent decrease from the previous year's total. The motor vehicle theft rate was estimated at 206.3 motor vehicles stolen per 100,000 inhabitants, a 0.6 percent decrease from the 2010 rate. (Table II-4)

The South

The South, the nation's most populous region, was home to an estimated 37.2 percent of the U.S. population in 2011 and accounted for 36.3 percent of the nation's motor vehicle thefts. (Table II-3) The estimated 259,424 motor vehicle thefts in the South decreased 4.8 percent from the 2010 estimate. Motor vehicles in the South were stolen at an estimated rate of 223.6 per 100,000 inhabitants in 2011, a rate that was 5.8 percent lower than the 2010 rate. (Table II-4)

The West

With approximately 23.4 percent of the U.S. population in 2011, the West accounted for 33.8 percent of all motor vehicle thefts in the nation in 2011. (Table II-3) An estimated 241,521 motor vehicle thefts occurred in this region. This number represented a 4.2 percent decrease from the previous year's estimate. The motor vehicle theft rate for the West was also lower in 2011 than in 2010; the 2011 rate of 331.5 motor vehicles stolen per 100,000 inhabitants was 5.2 percent lower than the 2010 rate. (Table II-4)

Community Types

The UCR program aggregates data by three community types: metropolitan statistical areas (MSAs), cities outside MSAs, and nonmetropolitan counties. MSAs are areas that include a principal city or urbanized area with at least 50,000 inhabitants and the county that contains the principal city and other adjacent counties that have, as defined by the U.S. Office of Management and Budget, a high degree of economic and social integration.

In 2011, the vast majority (83.5 percent) of the U.S. population resided in MSAs, where approximately 91.4 percent of motor vehicle thefts occurred. For 2011, the UCR program estimated an overall rate of 252.7 motor vehicles stolen per 100,000 MSA inhabitants. Cities outside MSAs accounted for 3.7 percent of motor vehicle thefts, and nonmetropolitan counties accounted for 3.9 percent of motor vehicle thefts. The UCR program estimated a 2011 rate of 136.4 motor vehicles stolen for every 100,000 inhabitants in cities outside MSAs, and a rate of 96.9 motor vehicles stolen per 100,000 inhabitants in nonmetropolitan counties. (Table II-2)

Population Groups: Trends and Rates

The UCR program aggregates data by various population groups, which include cities, metropolitan counties, and nonmetropolitan counties. (A definition of these groups can be found in Appendix III.)

In cities, collectively, the number of motor vehicle thefts decreased 2.6 percent from 2010 to 2011. The number of motor vehicle thefts decreased, even by a little, for all city groups. Cities with 100,000 to 249,999 inhabitants experienced the greatest decline—4.1 percent. Suburban areas experienced a decrease of 4.5 percent, metropolitan counties experienced a decrease of 5.8 percent, and nonmetropolitan counties experienced a decrease of 2.6 percent. (Table II-12)

In 2011, cities had a collective motor vehicle theft rate of 277.1 per 100,000 inhabitants. Among the population groups, cities with 500,000 to 999,999 inhabitants experienced the highest rate of motor vehicle thefts with 529.9 motor vehicle thefts per 100,000 inhabitants. Conversely, the nation's smallest cities, those with populations under 10,000, had the lowest rate of motor vehicle theft with 128.5 incidents per 100,000 in population. Within the county groups, metropolitan counties had a rate of 161.9 motor vehicles stolen per 100,000 inhabitants, while nonmetropolitan counties had a rate of 96.5 incidents per 100,000 inhabitants. Suburban areas had a rate of 154.7 per 100,000 inhabitants. (Table II-16)

Offense Analysis

Based on the reports of law enforcement agencies, the UCR program estimated the combined value of motor vehicles stolen nationwide in 2011 at approximately $4.4 billion. In 2011, the average dollar value per motor vehicle stolen in the United States was $6,089. (Tables II-1 and II-23) Automobiles were, by far, the most frequently stolen vehicle, accounting for 73.9 percent of all vehicles stolen. Trucks and buses accounted for 15.7 percent of stolen vehicles, and other vehicles accounted for 10.4 percent of stolen vehicles. (Expanded Motor Vehicle Theft Table)

By type of vehicle, automobiles were stolen at a rate of 180.3 cars per 100,000 inhabitants in 2010. Trucks and buses were stolen at a rate of 40.9 vehicles per 100,000 in population, and other types of vehicles were stolen at a rate of 26.1 vehicles per 100,000 inhabitants. (Table II-19)

ARSON

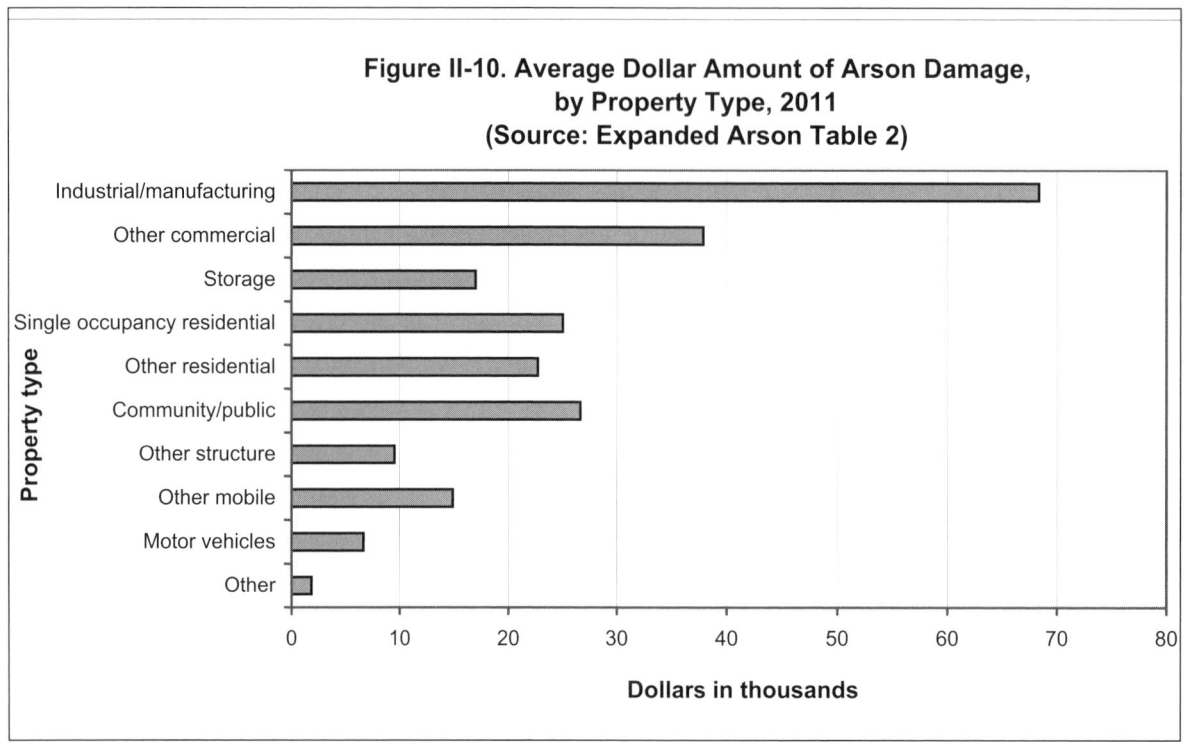

Figure II-10. Average Dollar Amount of Arson Damage, by Property Type, 2011 (Source: Expanded Arson Table 2)

Definition

The UCR program defines arson as any willful or malicious burning or attempt to burn (with or without intent to defraud) a dwelling house, public building, motor vehicle, aircraft, or personal property of another, and so on.

Data Collection

Only fires that investigators determined were willfully set (not fires labeled as "suspicious" or "of unknown origin") are included in this arson data collection. Points to consider regarding arson statistics include:

National offense rates per 100,000 inhabitants (found in Tables II-1, II-2, and II-4) do not include arson data; the FBI presents rates for arson separately. Arson rates are calculated based upon data received from all law enforcement agencies that provide the UCR program with data for 12 complete months.

Arson data collection does not include estimates for arson, because the degree of reporting arson offenses varies from agency to agency. Because of this unevenness of reporting, arson offenses are excluded from Tables II-1 through II-7, all of which contain offense estimations.

The number of arsons reported by individual law enforcement agencies is available in Tables II-8 through II-11. Arson trend data (which indicate year-to-year changes) can be found in Tables II-12 through II-15.

Population Groups: Trends and Rates

The number of arsons reported in 2011 decreased 4.7 percent from the 2010 figure. Law enforcement agencies in the nation's cities collectively reported a 4.0 percent decline in the number of arsons from the 2010 figure. The number of arsons declined for all population groups. Among the population groups labeled *city,* the subset with 1,000,000 or more inhabitants had the largest year-to-year decrease in reported arsons, 7.4 percent. Agencies in the nation's metropolitan counties reported a 5.9 percent decrease in the number of arsons, and those in non-metropolitan counties reported an 9.3 percent decline. Those in suburban areas reported a 6.7 percent decline. (Table II-12)

Arson rates were based on information received from 13,045 agencies that provided 12 months of complete arson data to the UCR program. An examination of data indicated that in 2011, the highest rate among city groups—32.8 arsons per 100,000 inhabitants—was reported in cities with 250,000 or more inhabitants. Among cities with 250,000 or more inhabitants, those with a population of 250,000 to 499,999 had the highest rate at 38.6 per 100,000 inhabitants. Cities with 10,000 to 24,999 inhabitants had the lowest rate of arson at 13.3 per 100,000 inhabitants. Metropolitan counties had 13.2 arsons per 100,000 inhabitants, and non-metropolitan counties had 12.2 arsons per 100,000 inhabitants, the lowest of all the population groups. The rate in suburban areas was 12.8 per 100,000 inhabitants. (Expanded Arson Table 1)

Offense Analysis

The UCR program breaks down arson offenses into three property categories: structural, mobile, and other. In addition, the structural property type is broken down into seven types of structures, and the mobile property type consists of two subgroupings. The program also collects information on the estimated dollar value of the damaged property.

Property Type

The total number of arsons decreased in 2011. Arsons for the structural property type decreased 5.2 percent, mobile property type dropped 15.5 percent, and other arsons fell 4.9 percent from 2010 to 2011. (Table II-15)

Distribution by Property Type

Arsons involving structures (residential, storage, public, etc.) accounted for 45.9 percent of the total number of arson offenses; arsons involving mobile property accounted for 23.9 percent; and other types of property (such as crops, timber, fences, etc.) accounted for 30.2 percent of reported arsons. Of the arsons involving structures, 63.8 percent involved residential properties. Of the residential arsons, 75.8 percent were single-occupancy residences. Approximately 18.6 percent of structures were not in use when the arson occurred. Mobile arsons accounted for 23.9 percent of all arsons. Within this category, 95.0 percent of offenses involved the burning of motor vehicles. (Expanded Arson Table 2)

Dollar Loss

In monetary terms, the average dollar loss in 2011 for arson was $13,196. The average dollar loss for a structural arson was $23,918. Within the structural arson category, the industrial/manufacturing subcategory had the highest average dollar loss at $68,349. Within that same category, single-occupancy dwellings had an average dollar loss of $24,990. Mobile property had an average dollar loss of $7,016. Other property types had an average dollar loss of $1,813. (Expanded Arson Table 2)

Table II-1.   Crime in the United States, by Volume and Rate per 100,000 Inhabitants, 1992–2011

(Number, rate per 100,000 population, percent.)

Year	Population[1]	Violent crime		Murder and nonnegligent manslaughter		Forcible rape		Robbery		Aggravated assault	
		Number	Rate	Number	Rate	Number	Rate	Number	Rate	Number	Rate
1992	255,029,699	1,932,274	757.7	23,760	9.3	109,062	42.8	672,478	263.7	1,126,974	441.9
1993	257,782,608	1,926,017	747.1	24,526	9.5	106,014	41.1	659,870	256.0	1,135,607	440.5
1994	260,327,021	1,857,670	713.6	23,326	9.0	102,216	39.3	618,949	237.8	1,113,179	427.6
1995	262,803,276	1,798,792	684.5	21,606	8.2	97,470	37.1	580,509	220.9	1,099,207	418.3
1996	265,228,572	1,688,540	636.6	19,645	7.4	96,252	36.3	535,594	201.9	1,037,049	391.0
1997	267,783,607	1,636,096	611.0	18,208	6.8	96,153	35.9	498,534	186.2	1,023,201	382.1
1998	270,248,003	1,533,887	567.6	16,974	6.3	93,144	34.5	447,186	165.5	976,583	361.4
1999	272,690,813	1,426,044	523.0	15,522	5.7	89,411	32.8	409,371	150.1	911,740	334.3
2000	281,421,906	1,425,486	506.5	15,586	5.5	90,178	32.0	408,016	145.0	911,706	324.0
2001[2]	285,317,559	1,439,480	504.5	16,037	5.6	90,863	31.8	423,557	148.5	909,023	318.6
2002	287,973,924	1,423,677	494.4	16,229	5.6	95,235	33.1	420,806	146.1	891,407	309.5
2003	290,788,976	1,383,676	475.8	16,528	5.7	93,883	32.3	414,235	142.5	859,030	295.4
2004	293,656,842	1,360,088	463.2	16,148	5.5	95,089	32.4	401,470	136.7	847,381	288.6
2005	296,507,061	1,390,745	469.0	16,740	5.6	94,347	31.8	417,438	140.8	862,220	290.8
2006	299,398,484	1,435,123	479.3	17,309	5.8	94,472	31.6	449,246	150.0	874,096	292.0
2007	301,621,157	1,422,970	471.8	17,128	5.7	92,160	30.6	447,324	148.3	866,358	287.2
2008	304,059,724	1,394,461	458.6	16,465	5.4	90,750	29.8	443,563	145.9	843,683	277.5
2009	307,006,550	1,325,896	431.9	15,399	5.0	89,241	29.1	408,742	133.1	812,514	264.7
2010[3]	309,330,219	1,251,248	404.5	14,722	4.8	85,593	27.7	369,089	119.3	781,844	252.8
2011	311,591,917	1,203,564	386.3	14,612	4.7	83,425	26.8	354,396	113.7	751,131	241.1

Year	Property crime		Burglary		Larceny-theft		Motor vehicle theft	
	Number	Rate	Number	Rate	Number	Rate	Number	Rate
1992	12,505,917	4,903.7	2,979,884	1,168.4	7,915,199	3,103.6	1,610,834	631.6
1993	12,218,777	4,740.0	2,834,808	1,099.7	7,820,909	3,033.9	1,563,060	606.3
1994	12,131,873	4,660.2	2,712,774	1,042.1	7,879,812	3,026.9	1,539,287	591.3
1995	12,063,935	4,590.5	2,593,784	987.0	7,997,710	3,043.2	1,472,441	560.3
1996	11,805,323	4,451.0	2,506,400	945.0	7,904,685	2,980.3	1,394,238	525.7
1997	11,558,475	4,316.3	2,460,526	918.8	7,743,760	2,891.8	1,354,189	505.7
1998	10,951,827	4,052.5	2,332,735	863.2	7,376,311	2,729.5	1,242,781	459.9
1999	10,208,334	3,743.6	2,100,739	770.4	6,955,520	2,550.7	1,152,075	422.5
2000	10,182,584	3,618.3	2,050,992	728.8	6,971,590	2,477.3	1,160,002	412.2
2001[2]	10,437,189	3,658.1	2,116,531	741.8	7,092,267	2,485.7	1,228,391	430.5
2002	10,455,277	3,630.6	2,151,252	747.0	7,057,379	2,450.7	1,246,646	432.9
2003	10,442,862	3,591.2	2,154,834	741.0	7,026,802	2,416.5	1,261,226	433.7
2004	10,319,386	3,514.1	2,144,446	730.3	6,937,089	2,362.3	1,237,851	421.5
2005	10,174,754	3,431.5	2,155,448	726.9	6,783,447	2,287.8	1,235,859	416.8
2006	10,019,601	3,346.6	2,194,993	733.1	6,626,363	2,213.2	1,198,245	400.2
2007	9,882,212	3,276.4	2,190,198	726.1	6,591,542	2,185.4	1,100,472	364.9
2008	9,774,152	3,214.6	2,228,887	733.0	6,586,206	2,166.1	959,059	315.4
2009	9,337,060	3,041.3	2,203,313	717.7	6,338,095	2,064.5	795,652	259.2
2010[3]	9,112,625	2,945.9	2,168,459	701.0	6,204,601	2,005.80	739,565	239.1
2011	9,063,173	2,908.7	2,188,005	702.2	6,159,795	1,976.90	715,373	229.6

Note: Although arson data are included in the trend and clearance tables, sufficient data are not available to estimate totals for this offense. Therefore, no arson data are published in this table.
[1] Populations are U.S. Census Bureau provisional estimates as of July 1 for each year except 2000 and 2010, which are decennial census counts.
[2] The murder and nonnegligent homicides that occurred as a result of the events of September 11, 2001, are not included in this table.
[3] The crime figures have been adjusted.

Table II-1A.   Crime in the United States, Percent Change in Volume and Rate per 100,000 Inhabitants for 2 Years, 5 Years, and 10 Years, 2002–2011

(Percent change.)

Year	Violent crime		Murder and nonnegligent manslaughter		Forcible rape		Robbery		Aggravated assault	
	Number	Rate	Number	Rate	Number	Rate	Number	Rate	Number	Rate
2002–2011	-15.5	-21.9	-10.0	-16.8	-12.4	-19.0	-15.8	-22.2	-15.7	-22.1
2007–2011	-15.4	-18.1	-14.7	-17.4	-9.5	-12.4	-20.8	-23.3	-13.3	-16.1
2010–2011	-3.8	-4.5	-0.7	-1.5	-2.5	-3.2	-4.0	-4.7	-3.9	-4.6

Year	Property crime		Burglary		Larceny-theft		Motor vehicle theft	
	Number	Rate	Number	Rate	Number	Rate	Number	Rate
2002–2011	-13.3	-19.9	+1.7	-6.0	-12.7	-19.3	-42.6	-47.0
2007–2011	-8.3	-11.2	-0.1	-3.3	-6.6	-9.5	-35.0	-37.1
2010–2011	-0.5	-1.3	+0.9	+0.2	-0.7	-1.4	-3.3	-4.0

Table II-2.   Crime in the United States, by Community Type, 2011

(Number, percent, rate per 100,000 population.)

Area	Population[1]	Violent crime	Murder and non-negligent manslaughter	Forcible rape	Robbery	Aggravated assault	Property crime	Burglary	Larceny-theft	Motor vehicle theft
United States..	311,591,917	1,203,564	14,612	83,425	354,396	751,131	9,063,173	2,188,005	6,159,795	715,373
Rate per 100,000 inhabitants		386.3	4.7	26.8	113.7	241.1	2,908.7	702.2	1,976.9	229.6
Metropolitan Statistical Areas....................	260,215,678	1,059,804	12,703	66,574	336,567	643,960	7,747,779	1,828,333	5,265,628	653,818
Area actually reporting (percent)[2]..............	98.8									
Estimated total (percent).............................	100.0	1,067,657	12,760	68,685	338,096	648,116	7,818,836	1,843,917	5,317,464	657,455
Rate per 100,000 inhabitants		410.3	4.9	26.4	129.9	249.1	3,004.8	708.6	2,043.5	252.7
Cities Outside Metropolitan Areas..............	20,555,101	72,724	830	7,521	10,565	53,808	682,496	155,484	500,878	26,134
Area actually reporting (percent)[2]..............	92.3									
Estimated total (percent).............................	100.0	78,536	902	8,361	11,512	57,761	739,288	168,902	542,348	28,038
Rate per 100,000 inhabitants		382.1	4.4	40.7	56.0	281.0	3,596.6	821.7	2,638.5	136.4
Nonmetropolitan Counties	30,821,138	53,500	895	5,781	4,369	42,455	466,571	161,955	276,760	27,856
Area actually reporting (percent)[2]..............	93.1									
Estimated total (percent).............................	100.0	57,371	950	6,379	4,788	45,254	505,049	175,186	299,983	29,880
Rate per 100,000 inhabitants		186.1	3.1	20.7	15.5	146.8	1,638.6	568.4	973.3	96.9

Note: Although arson data are included in the trend and clearance tables, sufficient data are not available to estimate totals for this offense. Therefore, no arson data are published in this table.

[1] Population figures are U.S. Census Bureau provisional estimates as of July 1, 2011.

[2] The percentage reported under "Area actually reporting" is based on the population covered by agencies providing 3 months or more of crime reports to the FBI.

Table II-3.   Crime in the United States, Population and Offense Distribution, by Region, 2011

(Percent distribution.)

Region	Population	Violent crime	Murder and non-negligent manslaughter	Forcible rape	Robbery	Aggravated assault	Property crime	Burglary	Larceny-theft	Motor vehicle theft
United States[1]..	100.0	100.0	100.0	100.0	100.0	100.0	100.0	100.0	100.0	100.0
Northeast..	17.8	16.2	14.8	12.8	19.4	15.2	13.0	11.1	13.9	10.6
Midwest...	21.6	19.5	20.6	25.3	20.1	18.6	21.1	21.0	21.3	19.4
South...	37.2	41.3	43.6	37.8	37.4	43.6	43.2	46.5	42.8	36.3
West..	23.4	22.9	21.0	24.1	23.1	22.7	22.8	21.4	22.0	33.8

Note: Although arson data are included in the trend and clearance tables, sufficient data are not available to estimate totals for this offense.

Therefore, no arson data are published in this table.

[1] Because of rounding, the percentages may not add to 100.0.

Table II-4.   Crime, by Region, Geographic Division, and State, 2010–2011

(Number, rate per 100,000 population, percent.)

Area	Population[1]	Violent crime		Murder and nonnegligent manslaughter		Forcible rape		Robbery		Aggravated assault	
		Number	Rate	Number	Rate	Number	Rate	Number	Rate	Number	Rate
United States[2,3,4,5]											
2010.................................	309,330,219	1,251,248	404.5	14,722	4.8	85,593	27.7	369,089	119.3	781,844	252.8
2011.................................	311,591,917	1,203,564	386.3	14,612	4.7	83,425	26.8	354,396	113.7	751,131	241.1
Percent change		-3.8	-4.5	-0.7	-1.5	-2.5	-3.2	-4.0	-4.7	-3.9	-4.6
Northeast											
2010.................................	55,366,108	198,333	358.2	2,312	4.2	10,868	19.6	68,993	124.6	116,160	209.8
2011.................................	55,521,598	195,482	352.1	2,169	3.9	10,641	19.2	68,855	124.0	113,817	205.0
Percent change		-1.4	-1.7	-6.2	-6.4	-2.1	-2.4	-0.2	-0.5	-2.0	-2.3
New England											
2010.................................	14,453,587	48,174	333.3	420	2.9	3,618	25.0	12,170	84.2	31,966	221.2
2011.................................	14,492,360	45,549	314.3	378	2.6	3,559	24.6	12,119	83.6	29,493	203.5
Percent change		-5.4	-5.7	-10.0	-10.2	-1.6	-1.9	-0.4	-0.7	-7.7	-8.0
Connecticut											
2010............................	3,575,498	10,083	282.0	133	3.7	595	16.6	3,553	99.4	5,802	162.3
2011............................	3,580,709	9,767	272.8	128	3.6	686	19.2	3,677	102.7	5,276	147.3
Percent change..............		-3.1	-3.3	-3.8	-3.9	+15.3	+15.1	+3.5	+3.3	-9.1	-9.2
Maine											
2010............................	1,327,379	1,621	122.1	24	1.8	389	29.3	412	31.0	796	60.0
2011............................	1,328,188	1,636	123.2	26	2.0	393	29.6	369	27.8	848	63.8
Percent change..............		+0.9	+0.9	+8.3	+8.3	+1.0	+1.0	-10.4	-10.5	+6.5	+6.5
Massachusetts											
2010............................	6,555,466	30,737	468.9	214	3.3	1,784	27.2	6,897	105.2	21,842	333.2
2011............................	6,587,536	28,219	428.4	185	2.8	1,628	24.7	6,768	102.7	19,638	298.1
Percent change..............		-8.2	-8.6	-13.6	-14.0	-8.7	-9.2	-1.9	-2.3	-10.1	-10.5
New Hampshire											
2010............................	1,316,807	2,204	167.4	13	1.0	411	31.2	450	34.2	1,330	101.0
2011............................	1,318,194	2,478	188.0	17	1.3	429	32.5	474	36.0	1,558	118.2
Percent change..............		+12.4	+12.3	+30.8	+30.6	+4.4	+4.3	+5.3	+5.2	+17.1	+17.0
Rhode Island											
2010............................	1,052,528	2,709	257.4	29	2.8	298	28.3	782	74.3	1,600	152.0
2011............................	1,051,302	2,602	247.5	14	1.3	304	28.9	746	71.0	1,538	146.3
Percent change..............		-3.9	-3.8	-51.7	-51.7	+2.0	+2.1	-4.6	-4.5	-3.9	-3.8
Vermont											
2010............................	625,909	820	131.0	7	1.1	141	22.5	76	12.1	596	95.2
2011............................	626,431	847	135.2	8	1.3	119	19.0	85	13.6	635	101.4
Percent change..............		+3.3	+3.2	+14.3	+14.2	-15.6	-15.7	+11.8	+11.7	+6.5	+6.5
Middle Atlantic											
2010.................................	40,912,521	150,159	367.0	1,892	4.6	7,250	17.7	56,823	138.9	84,194	205.8
2011.................................	41,029,238	149,933	365.4	1,791	4.4	7,082	17.3	56,736	138.3	84,324	205.5
Percent change		-0.2	-0.4	-5.3	-5.6	-2.3	-2.6	-0.2	-0.4	+0.2	-0.1
New Jersey											
2010............................	8,799,593	27,055	307.5	371	4.2	981	11.1	11,818	134.3	13,885	157.8
2011............................	8,821,155	27,203	308.4	380	4.3	1,006	11.4	12,209	138.4	13,608	154.3
Percent change..............		+0.5	+0.3	+2.4	+2.2	+2.5	+2.3	+3.3	+3.1	-2.0	-2.2
New York											
2010............................	19,395,206	76,492	394.4	868	4.5	2,797	14.4	28,630	147.6	44,197	227.9
2011............................	19,465,197	77,490	398.1	774	4.0	2,752	14.1	28,396	145.9	45,568	234.1
Percent change..............		+1.3	+0.9	-10.8	-11.2	-1.6	-2.0	-0.8	-1.2	+3.1	+2.7
Pennsylvania											
2010............................	12,717,722	46,612	366.5	653	5.1	3,472	27.3	16,375	128.8	26,112	205.3
2011............................	12,742,886	45,240	355.0	637	5.0	3,324	26.1	16,131	126.6	25,148	197.3
Percent change..............		-2.9	-3.1	-2.5	-2.6	-4.3	-4.5	-1.5	-1.7	-3.7	-3.9
Midwest[3]											
2010.................................	66,976,458	244,866	365.6	2,924	4.4	21,056	31.4	72,856	108.8	148,030	221.0
2011.................................	67,158,835	235,022	349.9	3,003	4.5	21,097	31.4	71,345	106.2	139,577	207.8
Percent change		-4.0	-4.3	+2.7	+2.4	+0.2	-0.1	-2.1	-2.3	-5.7	-6.0
East North Central											
2010.................................	46,439,372	177,281	381.7	2,186	4.7	14,480	31.2	59,469	128.1	101,146	217.8
2011.................................	46,519,084	169,872	365.2	2,295	4.9	14,606	31.4	58,151	125.0	94,820	203.8
Percent change		-4.2	-4.3	+5.0	+4.8	+0.9	+0.7	-2.2	-2.4	-6.3	-6.4
Illinois											
2010............................	12,841,980	57,132	444.9	704	5.5	3,066	23.9	20,386	158.7	32,976	256.8
2011............................	12,869,257	55,247	429.3	721	5.6	3,708	28.8	20,254	157.4	30,564	237.5
Percent change..............		-3.3	-3.5	+2.4	+2.2	+20.9	+20.7	-0.6	-0.9	-7.3	-7.5

Note: Although arson data are included in the trend and clearance tables, sufficient data are not available to estimate totals for this offense. Therefore, no arson data are published in this table.

* = Less than one-tenth of one percent.

[1] Populations are U.S. Census Bureau provisional estimates as of December 2011.

[2] The crime figures have been adjusted.

[3] The data collection methodology for the offense of forcible rape used by the Minnesota state Uniform Crime Reporting (UCR) Program (with the exception of Minneapolis and St. Paul, Minnesota) does not comply with national UCR Program guidelines. Consequently, its figures for forcible rape and violent crime (of which forcible rape is a part) are not published in this table.

[4] Includes offenses reported by the Zoological Police and the Metro Transit Police.

[5] Because of changes in the state's reporting practices, figures are not comparable to previous years' data.

Table II-4.   Crime, by Region, Geographic Division, and State, 2010–2011—*Continued*

(Number, rate per 100,000 population, percent.)

Area	Property crime		Burglary		Larceny-theft		Motor vehicle theft	
	Number	Rate	Number	Rate	Number	Rate	Number	Rate
United States[2, 3, 4, 5]								
2010.................................	9,112,625	2,945.9	2,168,459	701.0	6,204,601	2,005.8	739,565	239.1
2011.................................	9,063,173	2,908.7	2,188,005	702.2	6,159,795	1,976.9	715,373	229.6
Percent change	-0.5	-1.3	+0.9	+0.2	-0.7	-1.4	-3.3	-4.0
Northeast								
2010.................................	1,175,122	2,122.5	235,105	424.6	864,104	1,560.7	75,913	137.1
2011.................................	1,178,072	2,121.8	242,907	437.5	859,259	1,547.6	75,906	136.7
Percent change	+0.3	*	+3.3	+3.0	-0.6	-0.8	*	-0.3
New England								
2010.................................	336,004	2,324.7	75,328	521.2	237,678	1,644.4	22,998	159.1
2011.................................	332,919	2,297.2	76,422	527.3	234,161	1,615.8	22,336	154.1
Percent change	-0.9	-1.2	+1.5	+1.2	-1.5	-1.7	-2.9	-3.1
Connecticut.................		187.4						
2010.................................	78,259	2,188.8	15,145	423.6	56,413	1,577.8	6,701	187.4
2011.................................	77,609	2,167.4	15,679	437.9	55,218	1,542.1	6,712	187.4
Percent change	-0.8	-1.0	+3.5	+3.4	-2.1	-2.3	+0.2	*
Maine..........................		81.2						
2010.................................	32,900	2,478.6	7,364	554.8	24,547	1,849.3	989	74.5
2011.................................	33,809	2,545.5	7,854	591.3	24,877	1,873.0	1,078	81.2
Percent change	+2.8	+2.7	+6.7	+6.6	+1.3	+1.3	+9.0	+8.9
Massachusetts								
2010.................................	154,496	2,356.8	37,903	578.2	105,124	1,603.6	11,469	175.0
2011.................................	148,790	2,258.7	36,533	554.6	101,471	1,540.3	10,786	163.7
Percent change	-3.7	-4.2	-3.6	-4.1	-3.5	-3.9	-6.0	-6.4
New Hampshire								
2010.................................	29,230	2,219.8	5,444	413.4	22,789	1,730.6	997	75.7
2011.................................	30,106	2,283.9	5,749	436.1	23,383	1,773.9	974	73.9
Percent change	+3.0	+2.9	+5.6	+5.5	+2.6	+2.5	-2.3	-2.4
Rhode Island								
2010.................................	26,959	2,561.4	6,124	581.8	18,432	1,751.2	2,403	228.3
2011.................................	28,141	2,676.8	6,964	662.4	18,890	1,796.8	2,287	217.5
Percent change	+4.4	+4.5	+13.7	+13.8	+2.5	+2.6	-4.8	-4.7
Vermont								
2010.................................	14,160	2,262.3	3,348	534.9	10,373	1,657.3	439	70.1
2011.................................	14,464	2,309.0	3,643	581.5	10,322	1,647.7	499	79.7
Percent change	+2.1	+2.1	+8.8	+8.7	-0.5	-0.6	+13.7	+13.6
Middle Atlantic								
2010.................................	839,118	2,051.0	159,777	390.5	626,426	1,531.1	52,915	129.3
2011.................................	845,153	2,059.9	166,485	405.8	625,098	1,523.5	53,570	130.6
Percent change	+0.7	+0.4	+4.2	+3.9	-0.2	-0.5	+1.2	+0.9
New Jersey								
2010.................................	183,042	2,080.1	38,732	440.2	128,754	1,463.2	15,556	176.8
2011.................................	189,719	2,150.7	43,238	490.2	129,066	1,463.1	17,415	197.4
Percent change	+3.6	+3.4	+11.6	+11.4	+0.2	*	+12.0	+11.7
New York								
2010.................................	379,710	1,957.8	65,839	339.5	293,232	1,511.9	20,639	106.4
2011.................................	372,255	1,912.4	65,397	336.0	287,547	1,477.2	19,311	99.2
Percent change	-2.0	-2.3	-0.7	-1.0	-1.9	-2.3	-6.4	-6.8
Pennsylvania								
2010.................................	276,366	2,173.1	55,206	434.1	204,440	1,607.5	16,720	131.5
2011.................................	283,179	2,222.3	57,850	454.0	208,485	1,636.1	16,844	132.2
Percent change	+2.5	+2.3	+4.8	+4.6	+2.0	+1.8	+0.7	+0.5
Midwest[3]								
2010.................................	1,910,619	2,852.7	452,331	675.4	1,319,359	1,969.9	138,929	207.4
2011.................................	1,910,201	2,844.3	460,037	685.0	1,311,642	1,953.0	138,522	206.3
Percent change	*	-0.3	+1.7	+1.4	-0.6	-0.9	-0.3	-0.6
East North Central								
2010.................................	1,339,456	2,884.3	334,148	719.5	906,207	1,951.4	99,101	213.4
2011.................................	1,336,305	2,872.6	339,256	729.3	898,668	1,931.8	98,381	211.5
Percent change	-0.2	-0.4	+1.5	+1.4	-0.8	-1.0	-0.7	-0.9
Illinois								
2010.................................	349,064	2,718.1	77,472	603.3	242,681	1,889.7	28,911	225.1
2011.................................	346,025	2,688.8	77,746	604.1	239,510	1,861.1	28,769	223.5
Percent change	-0.9	-1.1	+0.4	+0.1	-1.3	-1.5	-0.5	-0.7

Note: Although arson data are included in the trend and clearance tables, sufficient data are not available to estimate totals for this offense. Therefore, no arson data are published in this table.

* = Less than one-tenth of one percent.

[2] The crime figures have been adjusted.

[3] The data collection methodology for the offense of forcible rape used by the Minnesota state Uniform Crime Reporting (UCR) Program (with the exception of Minneapolis and St. Paul, Minnesota) does not comply with national UCR Program guidelines. Consequently, its figures for forcible rape and violent crime (of which forcible rape is a part) are not published in this table.

[4] Includes offenses reported by the Zoological Police and the Metro Transit Police.

[5] Because of changes in the state's reporting practices, figures are not comparable to previous years' data.

Table II-4.   Crime, by Region, Geographic Division, and State, 2010–2011—*Continued*

(Number, rate per 100,000 population, percent.)

Area	Population[1]	Violent crime		Murder and nonnegligent manslaughter		Forcible rape		Robbery		Aggravated assault	
		Number	Rate	Number	Rate	Number	Rate	Number	Rate	Number	Rate
Indiana											
2010	6,490,622	20,983	323.3	268	4.1	1,760	27.1	6,559	101.1	12,396	191.0
2011	6,516,922	21,626	331.8	312	4.8	1,757	27.0	6,978	107.1	12,579	193.0
Percent change		+3.1	+2.6	+16.4	+15.9	-0.2	-0.6	+6.4	+6.0	+1.5	+1.1
Michigan											
2010	9,877,143	48,693	493.0	580	5.9	4,733	47.9	11,522	116.7	31,858	322.5
2011	9,876,187	43,983	445.3	613	6.2	4,347	44.0	10,393	105.2	28,630	289.9
Percent change		-9.7	-9.7	+5.7	+5.7	-8.2	-8.1	-9.8	-9.8	-10.1	-10.1
Ohio											
2010	11,537,968	36,306	314.7	479	4.2	3,730	32.3	16,486	142.9	15,611	135.3
2011	11,544,951	35,484	307.4	513	4.4	3,631	31.5	16,057	139.1	15,283	132.4
Percent change		-2.3	-2.3	+7.1	+7.0	-2.7	-2.7	-2.6	-2.7	-2.1	-2.2
Wisconsin											
2010	5,691,659	14,167	248.9	155	2.7	1,191	20.9	4,516	79.3	8,305	145.9
2011	5,711,767	13,532	236.9	136	2.4	1,163	20.4	4,469	78.2	7,764	135.9
Percent change		-4.5	-4.8	-12.3	-12.6	-2.4	-2.7	-1.0	-1.4	-6.5	-6.8
West North Central[3]											
2010	20,537,086	67,585	329.1	738	3.6	6,576	32.0	13,387	65.2	46,884	228.3
2011	20,639,751	65,150	315.7	708	3.4	6,491	31.4	13,194	63.9	44,757	216.8
Percent change		-3.6	-4.1	-4.1	-4.5	-1.3	-1.8	-1.4	-1.9	-4.5	-5.0
Iowa											
2010	3,050,202	8,191	268.5	38	1.2	883	28.9	1,012	33.2	6,258	205.2
2011	3,062,309	7,826	255.6	46	1.5	834	27.2	825	26.9	6,121	199.9
Percent change		-4.5	-4.8	+21.1	+20.6	-5.5	-5.9	-18.5	-18.8	-2.2	-2.6
Kansas											
2010	2,859,143	10,602	370.8	97	3.4	1,146	40.1	1,538	53.8	7,821	273.5
2011	2,871,238	10,162	353.9	110	3.8	1,085	37.8	1,459	50.8	7,508	261.5
Percent change		-4.2	-4.6	+13.4	+12.9	-5.3	-5.7	-5.1	-5.5	-4.0	-4.4
Minnesota[3]											
2010	5,310,658	12,515	235.7	96	1.8	1,798	33.9	3,388	63.8	7,233	136.2
2011	5,344,861	11,825	221.2	74	1.4	1,664	31.1	3,386	63.4	6,701	125.4
Percent change		-5.5	-6.1	-22.9	-23.4	-7.5	-8.0	-0.1	-0.7	-7.4	-7.9
Missouri											
2010	5,995,715	27,440	457.7	420	7.0	1,445	24.1	6,185	103.2	19,390	323.4
2011	6,010,688	26,889	447.4	366	6.1	1,458	24.3	6,269	104.3	18,796	312.7
Percent change		-2.0	-2.3	-12.9	-13.1	+0.9	+0.6	+1.4	+1.1	-3.1	-3.3
Nebraska											
2010	1,830,141	5,093	278.3	54	3.0	674	36.8	1,020	55.7	3,345	182.8
2011	1,842,641	4,665	253.2	67	3.6	695	37.7	997	54.1	2,906	157.7
Percent change		-8.4	-9.0	+24.1	+23.2	+3.1	+2.4	-2.3	-2.9	-13.1	-13.7
North Dakota											
2010	674,629	1,548	229.5	10	1.5	245	36.3	90	13.3	1,203	178.3
2011	683,932	1,689	247.0	24	3.5	259	37.9	91	13.3	1,315	192.3
Percent change		+9.1	+7.6	+140.0	+136.7	+5.7	+4.3	+1.1	-0.3	+9.3	+7.8
South Dakota											
2010	816,598	2,196	268.9	23	2.8	385	47.1	154	18.9	1,634	200.1
2011	824,082	2,094	254.1	21	2.5	496	60.2	167	20.3	1,410	171.1
Percent change		-4.6	-5.5	-8.7	-9.5	+28.8	+27.7	+8.4	+7.5	-13.7	-14.5
South[4,5]											
2010	114,857,529	518,808	451.7	6,428	5.6	32,255	28.1	140,371	122.2	339,754	295.8
2011	116,046,736	497,663	428.8	6,371	5.5	31,560	27.2	132,467	114.1	327,265	282.0
Percent change		-4.1	-5.1	-0.9	-1.9	-2.2	-3.2	-5.6	-6.6	-3.7	-4.7
South Atlantic[4]											
2010	59,916,816	271,650	453.4	3,324	5.5	14,716	24.6	76,767	128.1	176,843	295.1
2011	60,513,771	258,452	427.1	3,296	5.4	14,514	24.0	73,947	122.2	166,695	275.5
Percent change		-4.9	-5.8	-0.8	-1.8	-1.4	-2.3	-3.7	-4.6	-5.7	-6.7
Delaware											
2010	899,792	5,608	623.3	51	5.7	326	36.2	1,839	204.4	3,392	377.0
2011	907,135	5,075	559.5	41	4.5	289	31.9	1,538	169.5	3,207	353.5
Percent change		-9.5	-10.2	-19.6	-20.3	-11.3	-12.1	-16.4	-17.0	-5.5	-6.2
District of Columbia[4]											
2010	604,912	8,026	1,326.8	132	21.8	187	30.9	4,325	715.0	3,382	559.1
2011	617,996	7,429	1,202.1	108	17.5	173	28.0	4,093	662.3	3,055	494.3
Percent change		-7.4	-9.4	-18.2	-19.9	-7.5	-9.4	-5.4	-7.4	-9.7	-11.6
Florida											
2010	18,838,613	101,969	541.3	987	5.2	5,373	28.5	26,086	138.5	69,523	369.0
2011	19,057,542	98,199	515.3	984	5.2	5,274	27.7	25,622	134.4	66,319	348.0
Percent change		-3.7	-4.8	-0.3	-1.4	-1.8	-3.0	-1.8	-2.9	-4.6	-5.7

Note: Although arson data are included in the trend and clearance tables, sufficient data are not available to estimate totals for this offense. Therefore, no arson data are published in this table.
* = Less than one-tenth of one percent.
[1] Populations are U.S. Census Bureau provisional estimates as of December 2011.
[3] The data collection methodology for the offense of forcible rape used by the Minnesota state Uniform Crime Reporting (UCR) Program (with the exception of Minneapolis and St. Paul, Minnesota) does not comply with national UCR Program guidelines. Consequently, its figures for forcible rape and violent crime (of which forcible rape is a part) are not published in this table.
[4] Includes offenses reported by the Zoological Police and the Metro Transit Police.
[5] Because of changes in the state's reporting practices, figures are not comparable to previous years' data.

Table II-4.   Crime, by Region, Geographic Division, and State, 2010–2011—*Continued*

(Number, rate per 100,000 population, percent.)

Area	Property crime		Burglary		Larceny-theft		Motor vehicle theft	
	Number	Rate	Number	Rate	Number	Rate	Number	Rate
Indiana								
2010............................	199,274	3,070.2	48,570	748.3	137,204	2,113.9	13,500	208.0
2011............................	206,055	3,161.8	50,551	775.7	140,688	2,158.8	14,816	227.3
Percent change	+3.4	+3.0	+4.1	+3.7	+2.5	+2.1	+9.7	+9.3
Michigan								
2010............................	271,501	2,748.8	74,345	752.7	169,748	1,718.6	27,408	277.5
2011............................	257,979	2,612.1	71,596	724.9	160,887	1,629.0	25,496	258.2
Percent change	-5.0	-5.0	-3.7	-3.7	-5.2	-5.2	-7.0	-7.0
Ohio								
2010............................	376,836	3,266.1	107,125	928.5	248,581	2,154.5	21,130	183.1
2011............................	387,297	3,354.7	112,709	976.3	253,520	2,195.9	21,068	182.5
Percent change	+2.8	+2.7	+5.2	+5.1	+2.0	+1.9	-0.3	-0.4
Wisconsin								
2010............................	142,781	2,508.6	26,636	468.0	107,993	1,897.4	8,152	143.2
2011............................	138,949	2,432.7	26,654	466.7	104,063	1,821.9	8,232	144.1
Percent change	-2.7	-3.0	+0.1	-0.3	-3.6	-4.0	+1.0	+0.6
West North Central[3]								
2010...................................	571,163	2,781.1	118,183	575.5	413,152	2,011.7	39,828	193.9
2011...................................	573,896	2,780.5	120,781	585.2	412,974	2,000.9	40,141	194.5
Percent change	+0.5	*	+2.2	+1.7	*	-0.5	+0.8	+0.3
Iowa								
2010............................	68,740	2,253.6	16,746	549.0	48,194	1,580.0	3,800	124.6
2011............................	71,361	2,330.3	17,400	568.2	50,025	1,633.6	3,936	128.5
Percent change	+3.8	+3.4	+3.9	+3.5	+3.8	+3.4	+3.6	+3.2
Kansas								
2010............................	89,109	3,116.6	19,315	675.6	63,774	2,230.5	6,020	210.6
2011............................	88,438	3,080.1	18,789	654.4	62,972	2,193.2	6,677	232.5
Percent change	-0.8	-1.2	-2.7	-3.1	-1.3	-1.7	+10.9	+10.4
Minnesota[3]								
2010............................	136,431	2,569.0	24,415	459.7	103,429	1,947.6	8,587	161.7
2011............................	136,264	2,549.4	25,724	481.3	102,358	1,915.1	8,182	153.1
Percent change	-0.1	-0.8	+5.4	+4.7	-1.0	-1.7	-4.7	-5.3
Missouri								
2010............................	200,858	3,350.0	44,197	737.1	140,526	2,343.8	16,135	269.1
2011............................	198,882	3,308.8	44,822	745.7	138,743	2,308.3	15,317	254.8
Percent change	-1.0	-1.2	+1.4	+1.2	-1.3	-1.5	-5.1	-5.3
Nebraska								
2010............................	48,827	2,667.9	8,318	454.5	36,896	2,016.0	3,613	197.4
2011............................	50,726	2,752.9	8,714	472.9	37,909	2,057.3	4,103	222.7
Percent change	+3.9	+3.2	+4.8	+4.1	+2.7	+2.0	+13.6	+12.8
North Dakota								
2010............................	12,010	1,780.2	2,000	296.5	9,137	1,354.4	873	129.4
2011............................	13,246	1,936.7	2,433	355.7	9,833	1,437.7	980	143.3
Percent change	+10.3	+8.8	+21.7	+20.0	+7.6	+6.2	+12.3	+10.7
South Dakota								
2010............................	15,188	1,859.9	3,192	390.9	11,196	1,371.1	800	98.0
2011............................	14,979	1,817.7	2,899	351.8	11,134	1,351.1	946	114.8
Percent change	-1.4	-2.3	-9.2	-10.0	-0.6	-1.5	+18.3	+17.2
South[4,5]								
2010...................................	3,946,323	3,435.8	1,017,240	885.7	2,656,545	2,312.9	272,538	237.3
2011...................................	3,911,717	3,370.8	1,017,528	876.8	2,634,765	2,270.4	259,424	223.6
Percent change	-0.9	-1.9	*	-1.0	-0.8	-1.8	-4.8	-5.8
South Atlantic[4]								
2010...................................	1,994,677	3,329.1	505,222	843.2	1,347,995	2,249.8	141,460	236.1
2011...................................	2,002,003	3,308.3	507,847	839.2	1,360,332	2,248.0	133,824	221.1
Percent change	+0.4	-0.6	+0.5	-0.5	+0.9	-0.1	-5.4	-6.3
Delaware								
2010............................	31,078	3,453.9	7,550	839.1	21,593	2,399.8	1,935	215.0
2011............................	30,939	3,410.6	7,531	830.2	21,878	2,411.8	1,530	168.7
Percent change	-0.4	-1.3	-0.3	-1.1	+1.3	+0.5	-20.9	-21.6
District of Columbia[4]								
2010............................	28,802	4,761.4	4,233	699.8	19,514	3,225.9	5,055	835.7
2011............................	29,636	4,795.5	3,850	623.0	21,330	3,451.5	4,456	721.0
Percent change	+2.9	+0.7	-9.0	-11.0	+9.3	+7.0	-11.8	-13.7
Florida								
2010............................	669,035	3,551.4	169,119	897.7	458,454	2,433.6	41,462	220.1
2011............................	671,200	3,522.0	170,171	892.9	461,408	2,421.1	39,621	207.9
Percent change	+0.3	-0.8	+0.6	-0.5	+0.6	-0.5	-4.4	-5.5

Note: Although arson data are included in the trend and clearance tables, sufficient data are not available to estimate totals for this offense. Therefore, no arson data are published in this table.

* = Less than one-tenth of one percent.

[3] The data collection methodology for the offense of forcible rape used by the Minnesota state Uniform Crime Reporting (UCR) Program (with the exception of Minneapolis and St. Paul, Minnesota) does not comply with national UCR Program guidelines. Consequently, its figures for forcible rape and violent crime (of which forcible rape is a part) are not published in this table.

[4] Includes offenses reported by the Zoological Police and the Metro Transit Police.

[5] Because of changes in the state's reporting practices, figures are not comparable to previous years' data.

Table II-4.   Crime, by Region, Geographic Division, and State, 2010–2011—*Continued*

(Number, rate per 100,000 population, percent.)

Area	Population[1]	Violent crime		Murder and nonnegligent manslaughter		Forcible rape		Robbery		Aggravated assault	
		Number	Rate	Number	Rate	Number	Rate	Number	Rate	Number	Rate
Georgia											
2010..........................	9,712,157	39,068	402.3	555	5.7	2,107	21.7	12,372	127.4	24,034	247.5
2011..........................	9,815,210	36,634	373.2	554	5.6	2,053	20.9	12,148	123.8	21,879	222.9
Percent change..............		-6.2	-7.2	-0.2	-1.2	-2.6	-3.6	-1.8	-2.8	-9.0	-9.9
Maryland											
2010..........................	5,785,681	31,607	546.3	426	7.4	1,228	21.2	11,054	191.1	18,899	326.7
2011..........................	5,828,289	28,797	494.1	398	6.8	1,194	20.5	10,343	177.5	16,862	289.3
Percent change..............		-8.9	-9.6	-6.6	-7.3	-2.8	-3.5	-6.4	-7.1	-10.8	-11.4
North Carolina											
2010..........................	9,560,234	34,679	362.7	474	5.0	2,002	20.9	9,620	100.6	22,583	236.2
2011..........................	9,656,401	33,774	349.8	508	5.3	1,995	20.7	9,550	98.9	21,721	224.9
Percent change..............		-2.6	-3.6	+7.2	+6.1	-0.3	-1.3	-0.7	-1.7	-3.8	-4.8
South Carolina											
2010..........................	4,637,106	27,923	602.2	265	5.7	1,551	33.4	5,017	108.2	21,090	454.8
2011..........................	4,679,230	26,760	571.9	320	6.8	1,612	34.5	4,313	92.2	20,515	438.4
Percent change..............		-4.2	-5.0	+20.8	+19.7	+3.9	+3.0	-14.0	-14.8	-2.7	-3.6
Virginia											
2010..........................	8,023,953	17,184	214.2	376	4.7	1,580	19.7	5,678	70.8	9,550	119.0
2011..........................	8,096,604	15,923	196.7	303	3.7	1,536	19.0	5,430	67.1	8,654	106.9
Percent change..............		-7.3	-8.2	-19.4	-20.1	-2.8	-3.7	-4.4	-5.2	-9.4	-10.2
West Virginia											
2010..........................	1,854,368	5,586	301.2	58	3.1	362	19.5	776	41.8	4,390	236.7
2011..........................	1,855,364	5,861	315.9	80	4.3	388	20.9	910	49.0	4,483	241.6
Percent change..............		+4.9	+4.9	+37.9	+37.9	+7.2	+7.1	+17.3	+17.2	+2.1	+2.1
East South Central[5]											
2010..........................	18,460,132	75,875	411.0	1,026	5.6	5,897	31.9	19,750	107.0	49,202	266.5
2011..........................	18,553,961	77,560	418.0	1,066	5.7	5,723	30.8	19,176	103.4	51,595	278.1
Percent change		+2.2	+1.7	+3.9	+3.4	-3.0	-3.4	-2.9	-3.4	+4.9	+4.3
Alabama[5]											
2010..........................	4,785,401	18,363	383.7	275	5.7	1,355	28.3	4,864	101.6	11,869	248.0
2011..........................	4,802,740	20,174	420.1	301	6.3	1,371	28.5	4,910	102.2	13,592	283.0
Percent change..............		+9.9	+9.5	+9.5	+9.1	+1.2	+0.8	+0.9	+0.6	+14.5	+14.1
Kentucky											
2010..........................	4,347,223	10,604	243.9	188	4.3	1,438	33.1	3,748	86.2	5,230	120.3
2011..........................	4,369,356	10,406	238.2	153	3.5	1,463	33.5	3,693	84.5	5,097	116.7
Percent change..............		-1.9	-2.4	-18.6	-19.0	+1.7	+1.2	-1.5	-2.0	-2.5	-3.0
Mississippi											
2010..........................	2,970,072	7,999	269.3	204	6.9	931	31.3	2,777	93.5	4,087	137.6
2011..........................	2,978,512	8,036	269.8	239	8.0	865	29.0	2,492	83.7	4,440	149.1
Percent change..............		+0.5	+0.2	+17.2	+16.8	-7.1	-7.4	-10.3	-10.5	+8.6	+8.3
Tennessee											
2010..........................	6,357,436	38,909	612.0	359	5.6	2,173	34.2	8,361	131.5	28,016	440.7
2011..........................	6,403,353	38,944	608.2	373	5.8	2,024	31.6	8,081	126.2	28,466	444.5
Percent change..............		+0.1	-0.6	+3.9	+3.2	-6.9	-7.5	-3.3	-4.0	+1.6	+0.9
West South Central											
2010..........................	36,480,581	171,283	469.5	2,078	5.7	11,642	31.9	43,854	120.2	113,709	311.7
2011..........................	36,979,004	161,651	437.1	2,009	5.4	11,323	30.6	39,344	106.4	108,975	294.7
Percent change		-5.6	-6.9	-3.3	-4.6	-2.7	-4.1	-10.3	-11.5	-4.2	-5.5
Arkansas											
2010..........................	2,921,588	14,711	503.5	134	4.6	1,321	45.2	2,369	81.1	10,887	372.6
2011..........................	2,937,979	14,129	480.9	162	5.5	1,213	41.3	2,428	82.6	10,326	351.5
Percent change..............		-4.0	-4.5	+20.9	+20.2	-8.2	-8.7	+2.5	+1.9	-5.2	-5.7
Louisiana											
2010..........................	4,545,343	25,241	555.3	500	11.0	1,230	27.1	5,297	116.5	18,214	400.7
2011..........................	4,574,836	25,406	555.3	513	11.2	1,268	27.7	5,239	114.5	18,386	401.9
Percent change..............		+0.7	*	+2.6	+1.9	+3.1	+2.4	-1.1	-1.7	+0.9	+0.3
Oklahoma											
2010..........................	3,760,184	18,100	481.4	195	5.2	1,469	39.1	3,345	89.0	13,091	348.1
2011..........................	3,791,508	17,243	454.8	208	5.5	1,403	37.0	3,282	86.6	12,350	325.7
Percent change..............		-4.7	-5.5	+6.7	+5.8	-4.5	-5.3	-1.9	-2.7	-5.7	-6.4
Texas											
2010..........................	25,253,466	113,231	448.4	1,249	4.9	7,622	30.2	32,843	130.1	71,517	283.2
2011..........................	25,674,681	104,873	408.5	1,126	4.4	7,439	29.0	28,395	110.6	67,913	264.5
Percent change..............		-7.4	-8.9	-9.8	-11.3	-2.4	-4.0	-13.5	-15.0	-5.0	-6.6

Note: Although arson data are included in the trend and clearance tables, sufficient data are not available to estimate totals for this offense. Therefore, no arson data are published in this table.

* = Less than one-tenth of one percent.

[1] Populations are U.S. Census Bureau provisional estimates as of December 2011.

[5] Because of changes in the state's reporting practices, figures are not comparable to previous years' data.

Table II-4.   Crime, by Region, Geographic Division, and State, 2010–2011—*Continued*

(Number, rate per 100,000 population, percent.)

Area	Property crime		Burglary		Larceny-theft		Motor vehicle theft	
	Number	Rate	Number	Rate	Number	Rate	Number	Rate
Georgia								
2010............................	353,449	3,639.2	96,947	998.2	226,161	2,328.6	30,341	312.4
2011............................	355,952	3,626.5	95,657	974.6	230,820	2,351.7	29,475	300.3
Percent change	+0.7	-0.3	-1.3	-2.4	+2.1	+1.0	-2.9	-3.9
Maryland								
2010............................	173,309	2,995.5	36,704	634.4	118,578	2,049.5	18,027	311.6
2011............................	166,699	2,860.2	35,784	614.0	114,847	1,970.5	16,068	275.7
Percent change	-3.8	-4.5	-2.5	-3.2	-3.1	-3.9	-10.9	-11.5
North Carolina								
2010............................	329,202	3,443.5	102,826	1,075.6	208,057	2,176.3	18,319	191.6
2011............................	340,562	3,526.8	106,144	1,099.2	217,386	2,251.2	17,032	176.4
Percent change	+3.5	+2.4	+3.2	+2.2	+4.5	+3.4	-7.0	-8.0
South Carolina								
2010............................	181,098	3,905.4	46,261	997.6	121,544	2,621.1	13,293	286.7
2011............................	182,685	3,904.2	46,921	1,002.8	122,100	2,609.4	13,664	292.0
Percent change	+0.9	*	+1.4	+0.5	+0.5	-0.4	+2.8	+1.9
Virginia								
2010............................	187,403	2,335.5	30,804	383.9	145,990	1,819.4	10,609	132.2
2011............................	182,141	2,249.6	30,597	377.9	141,820	1,751.6	9,724	120.1
Percent change	-2.8	-3.7	-0.7	-1.6	-2.9	-3.7	-8.3	-9.2
West Virginia								
2010............................	41,301	2,227.2	10,778	581.2	28,104	1,515.6	2,419	130.4
2011............................	42,189	2,273.9	11,192	603.2	28,743	1,549.2	2,254	121.5
Percent change	+2.2	+2.1	+3.8	+3.8	+2.3	+2.2	-6.8	-6.9
East South Central[5]								
2010.................................	601,449	3,258.1	167,673	908.3	396,565	2,148.2	37,211	201.6
2011.................................	611,924	3,298.1	177,326	955.7	398,302	2,146.7	36,296	195.6
Percent change	+1.7	+1.2	+5.8	+5.2	+0.4	-0.1	-2.5	-3.0
Alabama[5]								
2010............................	168,828	3,528.0	42,484	887.8	115,564	2,414.9	10,780	225.3
2011............................	173,190	3,606.1	51,117	1,064.3	111,411	2,319.7	10,662	222.0
Percent change	+2.6	+2.2	+20.3	+19.9	-3.6	-3.9	-1.1	-1.5
Kentucky								
2010............................	111,170	2,557.3	30,443	700.3	74,488	1,713.5	6,239	143.5
2011............................	118,358	2,708.8	32,553	745.0	79,132	1,811.1	6,673	152.7
Percent change	+6.5	+5.9	+6.9	+6.4	+6.2	+5.7	+7.0	+6.4
Mississippi								
2010............................	88,596	2,983.0	30,453	1,025.3	52,784	1,777.2	5,359	180.4
2011............................	90,115	3,025.5	30,907	1,037.7	54,283	1,822.5	4,925	165.4
Percent change	+1.7	+1.4	+1.5	+1.2	+2.8	+2.5	-8.1	-8.4
Tennessee								
2010............................	232,855	3,662.7	64,293	1,011.3	153,729	2,418.1	14,833	233.3
2011............................	230,261	3,595.9	62,749	979.9	153,476	2,396.8	14,036	219.2
Percent change	-1.1	-1.8	-2.4	-3.1	-0.2	-0.9	-5.4	-6.1
West South Central								
2010.................................	1,350,197	3,701.1	344,345	943.9	911,985	2,499.9	93,867	257.3
2011.................................	1,297,790	3,509.5	332,355	898.8	876,131	2,369.3	89,304	241.5
Percent change	-3.9	-5.2	-3.5	-4.8	-3.9	-5.2	-4.9	-6.1
Arkansas								
2010............................	103,820	3,553.5	32,463	1,111.1	65,796	2,252.1	5,561	190.3
2011............................	110,295	3,754.1	34,471	1,173.3	70,012	2,383.0	5,812	197.8
Percent change	+6.2	+5.6	+6.2	+5.6	+6.4	+5.8	+4.5	+3.9
Louisiana								
2010............................	165,667	3,644.8	45,437	999.6	110,260	2,425.8	9,970	219.3
2011............................	168,744	3,688.5	46,320	1,012.5	113,301	2,476.6	9,123	199.4
Percent change	+1.9	+1.2	+1.9	+1.3	+2.8	+2.1	-8.5	-9.1
Oklahoma								
2010............................	129,464	3,443.0	37,848	1,006.5	81,303	2,162.2	10,313	274.3
2011............................	127,252	3,356.2	36,341	958.5	79,880	2,106.8	11,031	290.9
Percent change	-1.7	-2.5	-4.0	-4.8	-1.8	-2.6	+7.0	+6.1
Texas								
2010............................	951,246	3,766.8	228,597	905.2	654,626	2,592.2	68,023	269.4
2011............................	891,499	3,472.3	215,223	838.3	612,938	2,387.3	63,338	246.7
Percent change	-6.3	-7.8	-5.9	-7.4	-6.4	-7.9	-6.9	-8.4

Note: Although arson data are included in the trend and clearance tables, sufficient data are not available to estimate totals for this offense. Therefore, no arson data are published in this table.

* = Less than one-tenth of one percent.

[5] Because of changes in the state's reporting practices, figures are not comparable to previous years' data.

Table II-4.   Crime, by Region, Geographic Division, and State, 2010–2011—*Continued*

(Number, rate per 100,000 population, percent.)

Area	Population[1]	Violent crime		Murder and nonnegligent manslaughter		Forcible rape		Robbery		Aggravated assault	
		Number	Rate	Number	Rate	Number	Rate	Number	Rate	Number	Rate
West[5]											
2010	72,130,124	289,241	401.0	3,058	4.2	21,414	29.7	86,869	120.4	177,900	246.6
2011	72,864,748	275,397	378.0	3,069	4.2	20,127	27.6	81,729	112.2	170,472	234.0
Percent change		-4.8	-5.7	+0.4	*	-6.0	-7.0	-5.9	-6.9	-4.2	-5.1
Mountain[5]											
2010	22,133,139	86,182	389.4	943	4.3	8,355	37.7	18,744	84.7	58,140	262.7
2011	22,373,411	82,414	368.4	987	4.4	8,103	36.2	17,959	80.3	55,365	247.5
Percent change		-4.4	-5.4	+4.7	+3.5	-3.0	-4.1	-4.2	-5.2	-4.8	-5.8
Arizona											
2010	6,413,158	26,528	413.6	408	6.4	2,191	34.2	6,953	108.4	16,976	264.7
2011	6,482,505	26,311	405.9	405	6.2	2,264	34.9	7,127	109.9	16,515	254.8
Percent change		-0.8	-1.9	-0.7	-1.8	+3.3	+2.2	+2.5	+1.4	-2.7	-3.8
Colorado											
2010	5,047,692	16,339	323.7	129	2.6	2,230	44.2	3,164	62.7	10,816	214.3
2011	5,116,796	16,383	320.2	149	2.9	2,278	44.5	3,306	64.6	10,650	208.1
Percent change		+0.3	-1.1	+15.5	+13.9	+2.2	+0.8	+4.5	+3.1	-1.5	-2.9
Idaho											
2010	1,571,102	3,464	220.5	22	1.4	533	33.9	213	13.6	2,696	171.6
2011	1,584,985	3,184	200.9	36	2.3	435	27.4	184	11.6	2,529	159.6
Percent change		-8.1	-8.9	+63.6	+62.2	-18.4	-19.1	-13.6	-14.4	-6.2	-7.0
Montana[5]											
2010	990,958	2,733	275.8	25	2.5	332	33.5	154	15.5	2,222	224.2
2011	998,199	2,670	267.5	28	2.8	357	35.8	169	16.9	2,116	212.0
Percent change		-2.3	-3.0	+12.0	+11.2	+7.5	+6.8	+9.7	+8.9	-4.8	-5.5
Nevada											
2010	2,704,283	17,929	663.0	158	5.8	965	35.7	5,298	195.9	11,508	425.5
2011	2,723,322	15,309	562.1	141	5.2	912	33.5	4,299	157.9	9,957	365.6
Percent change		-14.6	-15.2	-10.8	-11.4	-5.5	-6.2	-18.9	-19.4	-13.5	-14.1
New Mexico											
2010	2,065,913	12,147	588.0	140	6.8	959	46.4	1,616	78.2	9,432	456.6
2011	2,082,224	11,817	567.5	156	7.5	857	41.2	1,722	82.7	9,082	436.2
Percent change		-2.7	-3.5	+11.4	+10.6	-10.6	-11.3	+6.6	+5.7	-3.7	-4.5
Utah											
2010	2,775,479	5,925	213.5	53	1.9	983	35.4	1,269	45.7	3,620	130.4
2011	2,817,222	5,494	195.0	54	1.9	854	30.3	1,081	38.4	3,505	124.4
Percent change		-7.3	-8.6	+1.9	+0.4	-13.1	-14.4	-14.8	-16.1	-3.2	-4.6
Wyoming											
2010	564,554	1,117	197.9	8	1.4	162	28.7	77	13.6	870	154.1
2011	568,158	1,246	219.3	18	3.2	146	25.7	71	12.5	1,011	177.9
Percent change		+11.5	+10.8	+125.0	+123.6	-9.9	-10.4	-7.8	-8.4	+16.2	+15.5
Pacific											
2010	49,996,985	203,059	406.1	2,115	4.2	13,059	26.1	68,125	136.3	119,760	239.5
2011	50,491,337	192,983	382.2	2,082	4.1	12,024	23.8	63,770	126.3	115,107	228.0
Percent change		-5.0	-5.9	-1.6	-2.5	-7.9	-8.8	-6.4	-7.3	-3.9	-4.8
Alaska											
2010	714,146	4,537	635.3	31	4.3	533	74.6	594	83.2	3,379	473.2
2011	722,718	4,383	606.5	29	4.0	420	58.1	576	79.7	3,358	464.6
Percent change		-3.4	-4.5	-6.5	-7.6	-21.2	-22.1	-3.0	-4.2	-0.6	-1.8
California											
2010	37,338,198	164,133	439.6	1,809	4.8	8,331	22.3	58,116	155.6	95,877	256.8
2011	37,691,912	154,944	411.1	1,792	4.8	7,663	20.3	54,292	144.0	91,197	242.0
Percent change		-5.6	-6.5	-0.9	-1.9	-8.0	-8.9	-6.6	-7.5	-4.9	-5.8
Hawaii											
2010	1,363,359	3,603	264.3	25	1.8	377	27.7	1,065	78.1	2,136	156.7
2011	1,374,810	3,949	287.2	17	1.2	434	31.6	1,042	75.8	2,456	178.6
Percent change		+9.6	+8.7	-32.0	-32.6	+15.1	+14.2	-2.2	-3.0	+15.0	+14.0
Oregon[2]											
2010	3,838,332	9,648	251.4	96	2.5	1,239	32.3	2,421	63.1	5,892	153.5
2011	3,871,859	9,586	247.6	82	2.1	1,217	31.4	2,222	57.4	6,065	156.6
Percent change		-0.6	-1.5	-14.6	-15.3	-1.8	-2.6	-8.2	-9.0	+2.9	+2.0
Washington											
2010	6,742,950	21,138	313.5	154	2.3	2,579	38.2	5,929	87.9	12,476	185.0
2011	6,830,038	20,121	294.6	162	2.4	2,290	33.5	5,638	82.5	12,031	176.1
Percent change		-4.8	-6.0	+5.2	+3.9	-11.2	-12.3	-4.9	-6.1	-3.6	-4.8
Puerto Rico											
2010	3,721,978	10,246	275.3	977	26.2	39	1.0	6,516	175.1	2,714	72.9
2011	3,706,690	10,540	284.4	1,136	30.6	45	1.2	6,465	174.4	2,894	78.1
Percent change		+2.9	+3.3	+16.3	+16.8	+15.4	+15.9	-0.8	-0.4	+6.6	+7.1

Note: Although arson data are included in the trend and clearance tables, sufficient data are not available to estimate totals for this offense. Therefore, no arson data are published in this table.

* = Less than one-tenth of one percent.

[1] Populations are U.S. Census Bureau provisional estimates as of December 2011.

[2] The crime figures have been adjusted.

[5] Because of changes in the state's reporting practices, figures are not comparable to previous years' data.

Table II-4.   Crime, by Region, Geographic Division, and State, 2010–2011—*Continued*

(Number, rate per 100,000 population, percent.)

Area	Property crime		Burglary		Larceny-theft		Motor vehicle theft	
	Number	Rate	Number	Rate	Number	Rate	Number	Rate
West[5]								
2010.................................	2,080,561	2,884.5	463,783	643.0	1,364,593	1,891.8	252,185	349.6
2011.................................	2,063,183	2,831.5	467,533	641.6	1,354,129	1,858.4	241,521	331.5
Percent change	-0.8	-1.8	+0.8	-0.2	-0.8	-1.8	-4.2	-5.2
Mountain[5]								
2010.................................	666,613	3,011.8	147,888	668.2	460,835	2,082.1	57,890	261.6
2011.................................	659,625	2,948.3	147,629	659.8	456,732	2,041.4	55,264	247.0
Percent change	-1.0	-2.1	-0.2	-1.2	-0.9	-2.0	-4.5	-5.6
Arizona								
2010	226,802	3,536.5	50,932	794.2	154,137	2,403.4	21,733	338.9
2011............................	230,422	3,554.5	54,929	847.3	155,664	2,401.3	19,829	305.9
Percent change	+1.6	+0.5	+7.8	+6.7	+1.0	-0.1	-8.8	-9.7
Colorado								
2010	135,001	2,674.5	26,196	519.0	97,534	1,932.2	11,271	223.3
2011............................	133,361	2,606.3	25,768	503.6	96,546	1,886.8	11,047	215.9
Percent change	-1.2	-2.5	-1.6	-3.0	-1.0	-2.3	-2.0	-3.3
Idaho								
2010	31,436	2,000.9	6,513	414.5	23,594	1,501.7	1,329	84.6
2011............................	32,787	2,068.6	6,920	436.6	24,534	1,547.9	1,333	84.1
Percent change	+4.3	+3.4	+6.2	+5.3	+4.0	+3.1	+0.3	-0.6
Montana[5]								
2010	25,409	2,564.1	3,692	372.6	20,166	2,035.0	1,551	156.5
2011............................	23,155	2,319.7	3,390	339.6	18,307	1,834.0	1,458	146.1
Percent change	-8.9	-9.5	-8.2	-8.8	-9.2	-9.9	-6.0	-6.7
Nevada								
2010	75,004	2,773.5	22,286	824.1	42,533	1,572.8	10,185	376.6
2011............................	69,731	2,560.5	20,214	742.3	40,032	1,470.0	9,485	348.3
Percent change	-7.0	-7.7	-9.3	-9.9	-5.9	-6.5	-6.9	-7.5
New Mexico								
2010	70,776	3,425.9	21,023	1,017.6	44,503	2,154.2	5,250	254.1
2011............................	73,534	3,531.5	21,423	1,028.9	46,703	2,242.9	5,408	259.7
Percent change	+3.9	+3.1	+1.9	+1.1	+4.9	+4.1	+3.0	+2.2
Utah								
2010	88,316	3,182.0	15,095	543.9	67,242	2,422.7	5,979	215.4
2011............................	83,758	2,973.1	13,122	465.8	64,453	2,287.8	6,183	219.5
Percent change	-5.2	-6.6	-13.1	-14.4	-4.1	-5.6	+3.4	+1.9
Wyoming								
2010	13,869	2,456.6	2,151	381.0	11,126	1,970.8	592	104.9
2011............................	12,877	2,266.4	1,863	327.9	10,493	1,846.8	521	91.7
Percent change	-7.2	-7.7	-13.4	-13.9	-5.7	-6.3	-12.0	-12.6
Pacific								
2010.................................	1,413,948	2,828.1	315,895	631.8	903,758	1,807.6	194,295	388.6
2011.................................	1,403,558	2,779.8	319,904	633.6	897,397	1,777.3	186,257	368.9
Percent change	-0.7	-1.7	+1.3	+0.3	-0.7	-1.7	-4.1	-5.1
Alaska								
2010	20,259	2,836.8	3,105	434.8	15,535	2,175.3	1,619	226.7
2011............................	19,028	2,632.8	2,826	391.0	14,859	2,056.0	1,343	185.8
Percent change	-6.1	-7.2	-9.0	-10.1	-4.4	-5.5	-17.0	-18.0
California								
2010	981,939	2,629.9	228,857	612.9	600,558	1,608.4	152,524	408.5
2011............................	973,901	2,583.8	230,090	610.4	596,963	1,583.8	146,848	389.6
Percent change	-0.8	-1.7	+0.5	-0.4	-0.6	-1.5	-3.7	-4.6
Hawaii								
2010	45,667	3,349.6	8,706	638.6	31,681	2,323.7	5,280	387.3
2011............................	45,889	3,337.8	10,008	728.0	31,697	2,305.6	4,184	304.3
Percent change	+0.5	-0.4	+15.0	+14.0	+0.1	-0.8	-20.8	-21.4
Oregon[2]								
2010	116,657	3,039.3	20,035	522.0	87,494	2,279.5	9,128	237.8
2011............................	120,594	3,114.6	20,448	528.1	91,099	2,352.8	9,047	233.7
Percent change	+3.4	+2.5	+2.1	+1.2	+4.1	+3.2	-0.9	-1.7
Washington								
2010	249,426	3,699.1	55,192	818.5	168,490	2,498.8	25,744	381.8
2011............................	244,146	3,574.6	56,532	827.7	162,779	2,383.3	24,835	363.6
Percent change	-2.1	-3.4	+2.4	+1.1	-3.4	-4.6	-3.5	-4.8
Puerto Rico								
2010.................................	51,036	1,371.2	17,494	470.0	26,773	719.3	6,769	181.9
2011.................................	51,717	1,395.2	16,591	447.6	29,273	789.7	5,853	157.9
Percent change	+1.3	+1.8	-5.2	-4.8	+9.3	+9.8	-13.5	-13.2

Note: Although arson data are included in the trend and clearance tables, sufficient data are not available to estimate totals for this offense. Therefore, no arson data are published in this table.
* = Less than one-tenth of one percent.
[2] The crime figures have been adjusted.
[5] Because of changes in the state's reporting practices, figures are not comparable to previous years' data.

Table II-5.   Crime, by State and Area, 2011

(Number, percent, rate per 100,000 population.)

Area	Population	Violent crime	Murder and non-negligent man-slaughter	Forcible rape	Robbery	Aggravated assault	Property crime	Burglary	Larceny-theft	Motor vehicle theft
Alabama[1]										
Metropolitan statistical area	3,431,868	X	X	X	X	X	X	X	X	X
Area actually reporting (percent)	97.8	15,393	252	981	4,345	9,815	131,484	39,276	83,753	8,455
Estimated total (percent)	100.0	15,575	254	998	4,375	9,948	133,029	39,846	84,632	8,551
Cities outside metropolitan areas	625,776	X	X	X	X	X	X	X	X	X
Area actually reporting (percent)	98.4	3,199	31	241	461	2,466	28,863	7,122	20,324	1,417
Estimated total (percent)	100.0	3,228	31	244	464	2,489	29,048	7,188	20,436	1,424
Nonmetropolitan counties	745,096	X	X	X	X	X	X	X	X	X
Area actually reporting (percent)	97.8	1,341	16	126	69	1,130	10,870	3,994	6,204	672
Estimated total (percent)	100.0	1,371	16	129	71	1,155	11,113	4,083	6,343	687
State total	4,802,740	20,174	301	1,371	4,910	13,592	173,190	51,117	111,411	10,662
Rate per 100,000 inhabitants	X	420.1	6.3	28.5	102.2	283.0	3,606.1	1,064.3	2,319.7	222.0
Alaska										
Metropolitan statistical area	345,208	X	X	X	X	X	X	X	X	X
Area actually reporting (percent)	100.0	2,646	15	306	507	1,818	11,664	1,304	9,626	734
Cities outside metropolitan areas	125,661	X	X	X	X	X	X	X	X	X
Area actually reporting (percent)	93.9	678	2	75	41	560	3,639	426	2,976	237
Estimated total (percent)	100.0	722	2	80	44	596	3,876	454	3,170	252
Nonmetropolitan counties	251,849	X	X	X	X	X	X	X	X	X
Area actually reporting (percent)	100.0	1,015	12	34	25	944	3,488	1,068	2,063	357
State total	722,718	4,383	29	420	576	3,358	19,028	2,826	14,859	1,343
Rate per 100,000 inhabitants	X	606.5	4.0	58.1	79.7	464.6	2,632.8	391.0	2,056.0	185.8
Arizona										
Metropolitan statistical area	5,998,271	X	X	X	X	X	X	X	X	X
Area actually reporting (percent)	99.5	22,804	331	1,631	6,980	13,862	215,453	50,478	146,557	18,418
Estimated total (percent)	100.0	22,877	332	1,637	6,996	13,912	216,378	50,678	147,233	18,467
Cities outside metropolitan areas	205,812	X	X	X	X	X	X	X	X	X
Area actually reporting (percent)	88.6	2,392	58	499	96	1,739	9,869	2,732	6,135	1,002
Estimated total (percent)	100.0	2,742	65	606	108	1,963	11,140	3,084	6,925	1,131
Nonmetropolitan counties	278,422	X	X	X	X	X	X	X	X	X
Area actually reporting (percent)	98.1	680	8	21	23	628	2,850	1,145	1,478	227
Estimated total (percent)	100.0	692	8	21	23	640	2,904	1,167	1,506	231
State total	6,482,505	26,311	405	2,264	7,127	16,515	230,422	54,929	155,664	19,829
Rate per 100,000 inhabitants	X	405.9	6.2	34.9	109.9	254.8	3,554.5	847.3	2,401.3	305.9
Arkansas										
Metropolitan statistical area	1,770,662	X	X	X	X	X	X	X	X	X
Area actually reporting (percent)	95.8	10,344	112	851	2,020	7,361	74,609	22,110	48,309	4,190
Estimated total (percent)	100.0	10,597	114	875	2,037	7,571	76,149	22,676	49,174	4,299
Cities outside metropolitan areas	512,170	X	X	X	X	X	X	X	X	X
Area actually reporting (percent)	96.5	2,326	32	205	320	1,769	21,995	7,421	13,877	697
Estimated total (percent)	100.0	2,410	33	212	332	1,833	22,792	7,690	14,380	722
Nonmetropolitan counties	655,147	X	X	X	X	X	X	X	X	X
Area actually reporting (percent)	92.9	1,043	14	117	55	857	10,549	3,814	6,000	735
Estimated total (percent)	100.0	1,122	15	126	59	922	11,354	4,105	6,458	791
State total	2,937,979	14,129	162	1,213	2,428	10,326	110,295	34,471	70,012	5,812
Rate per 100,000 inhabitants	X	480.9	5.5	41.3	82.6	351.5	3,754.1	1,173.3	2,383.0	197.8
California										
Metropolitan statistical area	36,836,745	X	X	X	X	X	X	X	X	X
Area actually reporting (percent)	99.9	151,568	1,757	7,370	53,902	88,539	954,328	224,122	585,150	145,056
Cities outside metropolitan areas	100.0	151,642	1,757	7,374	53,926	88,585	954,893	224,257	585,505	145,131
Area actually reporting (percent)	278,451	X	X	X	X	X	X	X	X	X
Estimated total (percent)	100.0	1,503	6	116	210	1,171	9,841	2,598	6,538	705
Nonmetropolitan counties	576,716	X	X	X	X	X	X	X	X	X
Area actually reporting (percent)	100.0	1,799	29	173	156	1,441	9,167	3,235	4,920	1,012
State total	37,691,912	154,944	1,792	7,663	54,292	91,197	973,901	230,090	596,963	146,848
Rate per 100,000 inhabitants	X	411.1	4.8	20.3	144.0	242.0	2,583.8	610.4	1,583.8	389.6
Colorado										
Metropolitan statistical area	4,417,535	X	X	X	X	X	X	X	X	X
Area actually reporting (percent)	98.8	14,918	132	2,042	3,211	9,533	119,439	23,321	85,624	10,494
Estimated total (percent)	100.0	15,045	132	2,062	3,229	9,622	120,630	23,529	86,519	10,582
Cities outside metropolitan areas	333,267	X	X	X	X	X	X	X	X	X
Area actually reporting (percent)	90.4	835	8	154	59	614	8,868	1,337	7,248	283
Estimated total (percent)	100.0	923	9	170	65	679	9,806	1,478	8,015	313
Nonmetropolitan counties	365,994	X	X	X	X	X	X	X	X	X
Area actually reporting (percent)	84.0	349	7	39	10	293	2,457	639	1,690	128
Estimated total (percent)	100.0	415	8	46	12	349	2,925	761	2,012	152
State total	5,116,796	16,383	149	2,278	3,306	10,650	133,361	25,768	96,546	11,047
Rate per 100,000 inhabitants	X	320.2	2.9	44.5	64.6	208.1	2,606.3	503.6	1,886.8	215.9

Note: Although arson data are included in the trend and clearance tables, sufficient data are not available to estimate totals for this offense. Therefore, no arson data are published in this table.

X = Not applicable.

[1] Because of changes in the state's reporting practices, figures are not comparable to previous years' data.

Table II-5.   Crime, by State and Area, 2011—*Continued*

(Number, percent, rate per 100,000 population.)

Area	Population	Violent crime	Murder and non-negligent man-slaughter	Forcible rape	Robbery	Aggravated assault	Property crime	Burglary	Larceny-theft	Motor vehicle theft
Connecticut										
Metropolitan statistical area..................	2,880,136	X	X	X	X	X	X	X	X	X
Area actually reporting (percent).................	100.0	9,235	123	604	3,581	4,927	70,282	13,775	50,161	6,346
Cities outside metropolitan areas	161,436	X	X	X	X	X	X	X	X	X
Area actually reporting (percent).................	100.0	217	1	34	45	137	2,880	488	2,274	118
Nonmetropolitan counties..................	539,137	X	X	X	X	X	X	X	X	X
Area actually reporting (percent).................	100.0	315	4	48	51	212	4,447	1,416	2,783	248
State total..................	3,580,709	9,767	128	686	3,677	5,276	77,609	15,679	55,218	6,712
Rate per 100,000 inhabitants..................	X	272.8	3.6	19.2	102.7	147.3	2,167.4	437.9	1,542.1	187.4
Delaware										
Metropolitan statistical area..................	707,970	X	X	X	X	X	X	X	X	X
Area actually reporting (percent).................	100.0	4,120	37	215	1,337	2,531	23,654	5,280	17,075	1,299
Cities outside metropolitan areas..................	48,021	X	X	X	X	X	X	X	X	X
Area actually reporting (percent).................	100.0	329	0	28	100	201	2,772	580	2,142	50
Nonmetropolitan counties..................	151,144	X	X	X	X	X	X	X	X	X
Area actually reporting (percent).................	100.0	626	4	46	101	475	4,513	1,671	2,661	181
State total..................	907,135	5,075	41	289	1,538	3,207	30,939	7,531	21,878	1,530
Rate per 100,000 inhabitants..................	X	559.5	4.5	31.9	169.5	353.5	3,410.6	830.2	2,411.8	168.7
District of Columbia[2]										
Metropolitan statistical area..................	617,996	X	X	X	X	X	X	X	X	X
Area actually reporting (percent).................	100.0	7,429	108	173	4,093	3,055	29,636	3,850	21,330	4,456
Cities outside metropolitan areas..................	X	X	X	X	X	X	X	X	X	X
Nonmetropolitan counties..................	X	X	X	X	X	X	X	X	X	X
District total..................	617,996	7,429	108	173	4,093	3,055	29,636	3,850	21,330	4,456
Rate per 100,000 inhabitants..................	X	1,202.1	17.5	28.0	662.3	494.3	4,795.5	623.0	3,451.5	721.0
Florida										
Metropolitan statistical area..................	17,931,051	X	X	X	X	X	X	X	X	X
Area actually reporting (percent).................	99.9	93,488	938	4,976	25,088	62,486	641,973	160,797	442,693	38,483
Estimated total (percent).................	100.0	93,499	938	4,976	25,092	62,493	642,066	160,818	442,760	38,488
Cities outside metropolitan areas..................	191,511	X	X	X	X	X	X	X	X	X
Area actually reporting (percent).................	98.7	1,374	10	82	233	1,049	8,449	2,184	5,978	287
Estimated total (percent).................	100.0	1,391	10	83	236	1,062	8,557	2,212	6,054	291
Nonmetropolitan counties..................	934,980	X	X	X	X	X	X	X	X	X
Area actually reporting (percent).................	100.0	3,309	36	215	294	2,764	20,577	7,141	12,594	842
State total..................	19,057,542	98,199	984	5,274	25,622	66,319	671,200	170,171	461,408	39,621
Rate per 100,000 inhabitants..................	X	515.3	5.2	27.7	134.4	348.0	3,522.0	892.9	2,421.1	207.9
Georgia										
Metropolitan statistical area..................	7,950,984	X	X	X	X	X	X	X	X	X
Area actually reporting (percent).................	99.4	30,696	477	1,713	11,046	17,460	293,471	78,801	187,750	26,920
Estimated total (percent).................	100.0	30,861	479	1,721	11,102	17,559	295,307	79,227	189,019	27,061
Cities outside metropolitan areas..................	687,967	X	X	X	X	X	X	X	X	X
Area actually reporting (percent).................	86.5	3,034	30	175	736	2,093	29,100	7,180	21,089	831
Estimated total (percent).................	100.0	3,506	35	202	850	2,419	33,624	8,298	24,366	960
Nonmetropolitan counties..................	1,176,259	X	X	X	X	X	X	X	X	X
Area actually reporting (percent).................	95.2	2,158	38	124	187	1,809	25,715	7,739	16,592	1,384
Estimated total (percent).................	100.0	2,267	40	130	196	1,901	27,021	8,132	17,435	1,454
State total..................	9,815,210	36,634	554	2,053	12,148	21,879	355,952	95,657	230,820	29,475
Rate per 100,000 inhabitants..................	X	373.2	5.6	20.9	123.8	222.9	3,626.5	974.6	2,351.7	300.3
Hawaii										
Metropolitan statistical area..................	963,465	X	X	X	X	X	X	X	X	X
Area actually reporting (percent).................	100.0	2,469	17	228	890	1,334	29,758	5,215	21,269	3,274
Cities outside metropolitan areas..................	X	X	X	X	X	X	X	X	X	X
Nonmetropolitan counties..................	411,345	X	X	X	X	X	X	X	X	X
Area actually reporting (percent).................	16.5	244	0	34	25	185	2,659	790	1,719	150
Estimated total (percent).................	100.0	1,480	0	206	152	1,122	16,131	4,793	10,428	910
State total..................	1,374,810	3,949	17	434	1,042	2,456	45,889	10,008	31,697	4,184
Rate per 100,000 inhabitants..................	X	287.2	1.2	31.6	75.8	178.6	3,337.8	728.0	2,305.6	304.3
Idaho										
Metropolitan statistical area..................	1,039,576	X	X	X	X	X	X	X	X	X
Area actually reporting (percent).................	99.9	2,231	20	296	151	1,764	23,711	4,765	18,039	907
Estimated total (percent).................	100.0	2,232	20	296	151	1,765	23,722	4,767	18,048	907
Cities outside metropolitan areas..................	244,961	X	X	X	X	X	X	X	X	X
Area actually reporting (percent).................	99.4	591	10	90	27	464	5,872	1,154	4,486	232
Estimated total (percent).................	100.0	595	10	91	27	467	5,907	1,161	4,513	233
Nonmetropolitan counties..................	300,448	X	X	X	X	X	X	X	X	X
Area actually reporting (percent).................	100.0	357	6	48	6	297	3,158	992	1,973	193
State total..................	1,584,985	3,184	36	435	184	2,529	32,787	6,920	24,534	1,333
Rate per 100,000 inhabitants..................	X	200.9	2.3	27.4	11.6	159.6	2,068.6	436.6	1,547.9	84.1

Note: Although arson data are included in the trend and clearance tables, sufficient data are not available to estimate totals for this offense. Therefore, no arson data are published in this table.
X = Not applicable.
[2] Includes offenses reported by the Zoological Police and the Metro Transit Police.

Table II-5.   Crime, by State and Area, 2011—*Continued*

(Number, percent, rate per 100,000 population.)

Area	Population	Violent crime	Murder and non-negligent man-slaughter	Forcible rape	Robbery	Aggravated assault	Property crime	Burglary	Larceny-theft	Motor vehicle theft
Illinois										
Metropolitan statistical area	11,192,664	X	X	X	X	X	X	X	X	X
Area actually reporting (percent)	93.6	49,258	670	2,949	19,439	26,200	294,897	65,767	201,983	27,147
Estimated total (percent)	100.0	50,871	687	3,124	19,887	27,173	310,391	68,799	213,754	27,838
Cities outside metropolitan areas	919,496	X	X	X	X	X	X	X	X	X
Area actually reporting (percent)	70.3	2,489	16	319	237	1,917	19,494	4,398	14,641	455
Estimated total (percent)	100.0	3,543	23	454	337	2,729	27,748	6,260	20,840	648
Nonmetropolitan counties	757,097	X	X	X	X	X	X	X	X	X
Area actually reporting (percent)	91.4	761	10	119	27	605	7,205	2,455	4,491	259
Estimated total (percent)	100.0	833	11	130	30	662	7,886	2,687	4,916	283
State total	12,869,257	55,247	721	3,708	20,254	30,564	346,025	77,746	239,510	28,769
Rate per 100,000 inhabitants	X	429.3	5.6	28.8	157.4	237.5	2,688.8	604.1	1,861.1	223.5
Indiana										
Metropolitan statistical area	5,104,685	X	X	X	X	X	X	X	X	X
Area actually reporting (percent)	89.5	18,664	255	1,361	6,187	10,861	163,652	40,866	110,120	12,666
Estimated total (percent)	100.0	19,389	265	1,440	6,312	11,372	173,726	43,199	117,207	13,320
Cities outside metropolitan areas	510,618	X	X	X	X	X	X	X	X	X
Area actually reporting (percent)	83.9	848	22	117	207	502	16,830	3,093	12,966	771
Estimated total (percent)	100.0	1,011	26	139	247	599	20,067	3,688	15,460	919
Nonmetropolitan counties	901,619	X	X	X	X	X	X	X	X	X
Area actually reporting (percent)	77.5	950	16	138	325	471	9,500	2,839	6,214	447
Estimated total (percent)	100.0	1,226	21	178	419	608	12,262	3,664	8,021	577
State total	6,516,922	21,626	312	1,757	6,978	12,579	206,055	50,551	140,688	14,816
Rate per 100,000 inhabitants	X	331.8	4.8	27.0	107.1	193.0	3,161.8	775.7	2,158.8	227.3
Iowa										
Metropolitan statistical area	1,730,732	X	X	X	X	X	X	X	X	X
Area actually reporting (percent)	99.9	5,317	29	609	696	3,983	49,402	11,370	35,188	2,844
Estimated total (percent)	100.0	5,322	29	610	696	3,987	49,450	11,379	35,225	2,846
Cities outside metropolitan areas	614,048	X	X	X	X	X	X	X	X	X
Area actually reporting (percent)	92.0	1,666	8	155	106	1,397	15,499	3,734	11,067	698
Estimated total (percent)	100.0	1,810	9	168	115	1,518	16,844	4,058	12,027	759
Nonmetropolitan counties	717,529	X	X	X	X	X	X	X	X	X
Area actually reporting (percent)	85.2	592	7	48	12	525	4,316	1,672	2,362	282
Estimated total (percent)	100.0	694	8	56	14	616	5,067	1,963	2,773	331
State total	3,062,309	7,826	46	834	825	6,121	71,361	17,400	50,025	3,936
Rate per 100,000 inhabitants	X	255.6	1.5	27.2	26.9	199.9	2,330.3	568.2	1,633.6	128.5
Kansas										
Metropolitan statistical area	1,961,511	X	X	X	X	X	X	X	X	X
Area actually reporting (percent)	99.2	7,627	91	764	1,296	5,476	64,037	13,043	45,437	5,557
Estimated total (percent)	100.0	7,665	91	769	1,300	5,505	64,390	13,103	45,707	5,580
Cities outside metropolitan areas	584,158	X	X	X	X	X	X	X	X	X
Area actually reporting (percent)	96.7	1,850	13	230	139	1,468	18,900	3,987	14,132	781
Estimated total (percent)	100.0	1,913	13	238	144	1,518	19,550	4,124	14,618	808
Nonmetropolitan counties	325,569	X	X	X	X	X	X	X	X	X
Area actually reporting (percent)	94.7	554	6	74	14	460	4,262	1,480	2,508	274
Estimated total (percent)	100.0	584	6	78	15	485	4,498	1,562	2,647	289
State total	2,871,238	10,162	110	1,085	1,459	7,508	88,438	18,789	62,972	6,677
Rate per 100,000 inhabitants	X	353.9	3.8	37.8	50.8	261.5	3,080.1	654.4	2,193.2	232.5
Kentucky										
Metropolitan statistical area	2,541,214	X	X	X	X	X	X	X	X	X
Area actually reporting (percent)	99.5	7,887	85	778	3,040	3,984	83,613	20,924	58,015	4,674
Estimated total (percent)	100.0	7,924	85	784	3,055	4,000	84,118	21,045	58,375	4,698
Cities outside metropolitan areas	518,140	X	X	X	X	X	X	X	X	X
Area actually reporting (percent)	96.9	999	11	184	382	422	17,022	3,916	12,447	659
Estimated total (percent)	100.0	1,030	11	190	394	435	17,558	4,039	12,839	680
Nonmetropolitan counties	1,310,002	X	X	X	X	X	X	X	X	X
Area actually reporting (percent)	94.9	1,378	54	464	232	628	15,837	7,091	7,517	1,229
Estimated total (percent)	100.0	1,452	57	489	244	662	16,682	7,469	7,918	1,295
State total	4,369,356	10,406	153	1,463	3,693	5,097	118,358	32,553	79,132	6,673
Rate per 100,000 inhabitants	X	238.2	3.5	33.5	84.5	116.7	2,708.8	745.0	1,811.1	152.7

Note: Although arson data are included in the trend and clearance tables, sufficient data are not available to estimate totals for this offense. Therefore, no arson data are published in this table.
X = Not applicable.

Table II-5. Crime, by State and Area, 2011—*Continued*

(Number, percent, rate per 100,000 population.)

Area	Population	Violent crime	Murder and non-negligent man-slaughter	Forcible rape	Robbery	Aggravated assault	Property crime	Burglary	Larceny-theft	Motor vehicle theft
Louisiana										
Metropolitan statistical area	3,411,659	X	X	X	X	X	X	X	X	X
Area actually reporting (percent)	98.5	18,397	437	910	4,488	12,562	127,086	33,626	85,844	7,616
Estimated total (percent)	100.0	18,682	440	925	4,527	12,790	129,355	34,068	87,599	7,688
Cities outside metropolitan areas	394,448	X	X	X	X	X	X	X	X	X
Area actually reporting (percent)	83.8	2,879	31	109	384	2,355	17,602	5,333	11,811	458
Estimated total (percent)	100.0	3,436	37	130	458	2,811	21,009	6,365	14,097	547
Nonmetropolitan counties	768,729	X	X	X	X	X	X	X	X	X
Area actually reporting (percent)	98.1	3,226	35	209	249	2,733	18,040	5,778	11,390	872
Estimated total (percent)	100.0	3,288	36	213	254	2,785	18,380	5,887	11,605	888
State total	4,574,836	25,406	513	1,268	5,239	18,386	168,744	46,320	113,301	9,123
Rate per 100,000 inhabitants	X	555.3	11.2	27.7	114.5	401.9	3,688.5	1,012.5	2,476.6	199.4
Maine										
Metropolitan statistical area	775,621	X	X	X	X	X	X	X	X	X
Area actually reporting (percent)	100.0	961	16	193	293	459	20,759	4,679	15,425	655
Cities outside metropolitan areas	272,487	X	X	X	X	X	X	X	X	X
Area actually reporting (percent)	100.0	433	7	138	65	223	8,483	1,650	6,647	186
Nonmetropolitan counties	280,080	X	X	X	X	X	X	X	X	X
Area actually reporting (percent)	100.0	242	3	62	11	166	4,567	1,525	2,805	237
State total	1,328,188	1,636	26	393	369	848	33,809	7,854	24,877	1,078
Rate per 100,000 inhabitants	X	123.2	2.0	29.6	27.8	63.8	2,545.5	591.3	1,873.0	81.2
Maryland										
Metropolitan statistical area	5,514,983	X	X	X	X	X	X	X	X	X
Area actually reporting (percent)	100.0	27,808	391	1,139	10,174	16,104	157,597	33,417	108,437	15,743
Cities outside metropolitan areas	83,421	X	X	X	X	X	X	X	X	X
Area actually reporting (percent)	100.0	457	0	24	87	346	3,952	784	3,097	71
Nonmetropolitan counties	229,885	X	X	X	X	X	X	X	X	X
Area actually reporting (percent)	100.0	532	7	31	82	412	5,150	1,583	3,313	254
State total	5,828,289	28,797	398	1,194	10,343	16,862	166,699	35,784	114,847	16,068
Rate per 100,000 inhabitants	X	494.1	6.8	20.5	177.5	289.3	2,860.2	614.0	1,970.5	275.7
Massachusetts										
Metropolitan statistical area	6,560,666	X	X	X	X	X	X	X	X	X
Area actually reporting (percent)	97.4	27,632	183	1,590	6,665	19,194	144,601	35,541	98,532	10,528
Estimated total (percent)	100.0	28,158	185	1,627	6,762	19,584	147,980	36,376	100,857	10,747
Cities outside metropolitan areas	26,795	X	X	X	X	X	X	X	X	X
Area actually reporting (percent)	100.0	57	0	1	5	51	810	157	614	39
Nonmetropolitan counties	75	X	X	X	X	X	X	X	X	X
Area actually reporting (percent)	100.0	4	0	0	1	3	0	0	0	0
State total	6,587,536	28,219	185	1,628	6,768	19,638	148,790	36,533	101,471	10,786
Rate per 100,000 inhabitants	X	428.4	2.8	24.7	102.7	298.1	2,258.7	554.6	1,540.3	163.7
Michigan										
Metropolitan statistical area	8,027,009	X	X	X	X	X	X	X	X	X
Area actually reporting (percent)	98.6	39,968	577	3,221	10,134	26,036	219,831	62,405	133,328	24,098
Estimated total (percent)	100.0	40,295	577	3,259	10,207	26,252	222,823	63,065	135,429	24,329
Cities outside metropolitan areas	641,557	X	X	X	X	X	X	X	X	X
Area actually reporting (percent)	82.7	1,217	6	341	104	766	14,185	2,090	11,701	394
Estimated total (percent)	100.0	1,438	7	406	123	902	16,858	2,465	13,921	472
Nonmetropolitan counties	1,207,621	X	X	X	X	X	X	X	X	X
Area actually reporting (percent)	92.4	2,078	27	630	58	1,363	16,901	5,603	10,656	642
Estimated total (percent)	100.0	2,250	29	682	63	1,476	18,298	6,066	11,537	695
State total	9,876,187	43,983	613	4,347	10,393	28,630	257,979	71,596	160,887	25,496
Rate per 100,000 inhabitants	X	445.3	6.2	44.0	105.2	289.9	2,612.1	724.9	1,629.0	258.2
Minnesota[3]										
Metropolitan statistical area	4,002,202	X	X	X	X	X	X	X	X	X
Area actually reporting (percent)	99.7	X	62	X	3,251	5,317	111,479	20,563	84,086	6,830
Estimated total (percent)	100.0	X	62	X	3,256	5,328	111,842	20,613	84,384	6,845
Cities outside metropolitan areas	512,001	X	X	X	X	X	X	X	X	X
Area actually reporting (percent)	97.3	X	4	X	105	891	14,558	2,317	11,594	647
Estimated total (percent)	100.0	X	4	X	108	916	14,969	2,382	11,922	665
Nonmetropolitan counties	830,658	X	X	X	X	X	X	X	X	X
Area actually reporting (percent)	99.2	X	8	X	22	453	9,374	2,706	6,002	666
Estimated total (percent)	100.0	X	8	X	22	457	9,453	2,729	6,052	672
State total	5,344,861	11,825	74	1,664	3,386	6,701	136,264	25,724	102,358	8,182
Rate per 100,000 inhabitants	X	221.2	1.4	31.1	63.4	125.4	2,549.4	481.3	1,915.1	153.1

Note: Although arson data are included in the trend and clearance tables, sufficient data are not available to estimate totals for this offense. Therefore, no arson data are published in this table.

X = Not applicable.

[3] The data collection methodology for the offense of forcible rape used by the Minnesota state Uniform Crime Reporting (UCR) Program (with the exception of Minneapolis and St. Paul, Minnesota) does not comply with national UCR Program guidelines. Consequently, its figures for forcible rape and violent crime (of which forcible rape is a part) are not published in this table.

Table II-5.   Crime, by State and Area, 2011—*Continued*

(Number, percent, rate per 100,000 population.)

Area	Population	Violent crime	Murder and non-negligent man-slaughter	Forcible rape	Robbery	Aggravated assault	Property crime	Burglary	Larceny-theft	Motor vehicle theft
Mississippi										
Metropolitan statistical area	1,336,058	X	X	X	X	X	X	X	X	X
Area actually reporting (percent)	88.1	3,742	104	370	1,418	1,850	41,467	12,629	25,875	2,963
Estimated total (percent)	100.0	4,007	110	399	1,477	2,021	44,845	13,633	28,044	3,168
Cities outside metropolitan areas	593,438	X	X	X	X	X	X	X	X	X
Area actually reporting (percent)	76.4	1,849	63	217	609	960	21,741	7,601	13,351	789
Estimated total (percent)	100.0	2,419	82	284	797	1,256	28,452	9,947	17,472	1,033
Nonmetropolitan counties	1,049,016	X	X	X	X	X	X	X	X	X
Area actually reporting (percent)	55.0	886	26	100	120	640	9,250	4,030	4,822	398
Estimated total (percent)	100.0	1,610	47	182	218	1,163	16,818	7,327	8,767	724
State total	2,978,512	8,036	239	865	2,492	4,440	90,115	30,907	54,283	4,925
Rate per 100,000 inhabitants	X	269.8	8.0	29.0	83.7	149.1	3,025.5	1,037.7	1,822.5	165.4
Missouri										
Metropolitan statistical area	4,481,246	X	X	X	X	X	X	X	X	X
Area actually reporting (percent)	100.0	22,382	311	1,183	5,999	14,889	161,124	36,046	111,574	13,504
Cities outside metropolitan areas	655,159	X	X	X	X	X	X	X	X	X
Area actually reporting (percent)	99.6	2,567	24	156	220	2,167	25,031	4,374	19,765	892
Estimated total (percent)	100.0	2,578	24	157	221	2,176	25,130	4,391	19,843	896
Nonmetropolitan counties	874,283	X	X	X	X	X	X	X	X	X
Area actually reporting (percent)	99.2	1,914	31	117	49	1,717	12,525	4,349	7,266	910
Estimated total (percent)	100.0	1,929	31	118	49	1,731	12,628	4,385	7,326	917
State total	6,010,688	26,889	366	1,458	6,269	18,796	198,882	44,822	138,743	15,317
Rate per 100,000 inhabitants	X	447.4	6.1	24.3	104.3	312.7	3,308.8	745.7	2,308.3	254.8
Montana[1]										
Metropolitan statistical area	351,772	X	X	X	X	X	X	X	X	X
Area actually reporting (percent)	100.0	898	6	96	100	696	11,329	1,584	9,098	647
Cities outside metropolitan areas	201,871	X	X	X	X	X	X	X	X	X
Area actually reporting (percent)	97.5	907	12	142	45	708	6,677	921	5,319	437
Estimated total (percent)	100.0	930	12	146	46	726	6,850	945	5,457	448
Nonmetropolitan counties	444,556	X	X	X	X	X	X	X	X	X
Area actually reporting (percent)	98.8	833	10	114	23	686	4,917	851	3,707	359
Estimated total (percent)	100.0	842	10	115	23	694	4,976	861	3,752	363
State total	998,199	2,670	28	357	169	2,116	23,155	3,390	18,307	1,458
Rate per 100,000 inhabitants	X	267.5	2.8	35.8	16.9	212.0	2,319.7	339.6	1,834.0	146.1
Nebraska										
Metropolitan statistical area	1,080,927	X	X	X	X	X	X	X	X	X
Area actually reporting (percent)	99.1	3,583	52	459	902	2,170	35,119	5,811	25,866	3,442
Estimated total (percent)	100.0	3,588	52	460	902	2,174	35,243	5,836	25,956	3,451
Cities outside metropolitan areas	405,148	X	X	X	X	X	X	X	X	X
Area actually reporting (percent)	92.2	795	10	171	77	537	11,007	1,838	8,758	411
Estimated total (percent)	100.0	861	11	185	83	582	11,935	1,993	9,496	446
Nonmetropolitan counties	356,566	X	X	X	X	X	X	X	X	X
Area actually reporting (percent)	77.8	168	3	39	9	117	2,761	689	1,912	160
Estimated total (percent)	100.0	216	4	50	12	150	3,548	885	2,457	206
State total	1,842,641	4,665	67	695	997	2,906	50,726	8,714	37,909	4,103
Rate per 100,000 inhabitants	X	253.2	3.6	37.7	54.1	157.7	2,752.9	472.9	2,057.3	222.7
Nevada										
Metropolitan statistical area	2,452,465	X	X	X	X	X	X	X	X	X
Area actually reporting (percent)	100.0	14,560	121	857	4,258	9,324	65,403	19,012	37,167	9,224
Cities outside metropolitan areas	46,407	X	X	X	X	X	X	X	X	X
Area actually reporting (percent)	100.0	301	3	28	21	249	1,468	387	981	100
Nonmetropolitan counties	224,450	X	X	X	X	X	X	X	X	X
Area actually reporting (percent)	78.1	350	13	21	16	300	2,235	637	1,472	126
Estimated total (percent)	100.0	448	17	27	20	384	2,860	815	1,884	161
State total	2,723,322	15,309	141	912	4,299	9,957	69,731	20,214	40,032	9,485
Rate per 100,000 inhabitants	X	562.1	5.2	33.5	157.9	365.6	2,560.5	742.3	1,470.0	348.3
New Hampshire										
Metropolitan statistical area	820,159	X	X	X	X	X	X	X	X	X
Area actually reporting (percent)	93.8	1,601	9	230	351	1,011	17,773	3,315	13,847	611
Estimated total (percent)	100.0	1,648	9	239	358	1,042	18,475	3,440	14,400	635
Cities outside metropolitan areas	445,693	X	X	X	X	X	X	X	X	X
Area actually reporting (percent)	90.0	702	7	156	102	437	10,180	1,948	7,939	293
Estimated total (percent)	100.0	780	8	173	113	486	11,316	2,165	8,825	326
Nonmetropolitan counties	52,342	X	X	X	X	X	X	X	X	X
Area actually reporting (percent)	3.1	13	0	5	1	7	88	19	66	3
Estimated total (percent)	100.0	50	0	17	3	30	315	144	158	13
State total	1,318,194	2,478	17	429	474	1,558	30,106	5,749	23,383	974
Rate per 100,000 inhabitants	X	188.0	1.3	32.5	36.0	118.2	2,283.9	436.1	1,773.9	73.9

Note: Although arson data are included in the trend and clearance tables, sufficient data are not available to estimate totals for this offense. Therefore, no arson data are published in this table.

X = Not applicable.

[1] Because of changes in the state's reporting practices, figures are not comparable to previous years' data.

Table II-5. Crime, by State and Area, 2011—*Continued*

(Number, percent, rate per 100,000 population.)

Area	Population	Violent crime	Murder and non-negligent man-slaughter	Forcible rape	Robbery	Aggravated assault	Property crime	Burglary	Larceny-theft	Motor vehicle theft
New Jersey										
Metropolitan statistical area	8,821,155	X	X	X	X	X	X	X	X	X
Area actually reporting (percent)	100.0	27,203	380	1,006	12,209	13,608	189,719	43,238	129,066	17,415
Cities outside metropolitan areas	X	X	X	X	X	X	X	X	X	X
Nonmetropolitan counties	X	X	X	X	X	X	X	X	X	X
State total	8,821,155	27,203	380	1,006	12,209	13,608	189,719	43,238	129,066	17,415
Rate per 100,000 inhabitants	X	308.4	4.3	11.4	138.4	154.3	2,150.7	490.2	1,463.1	197.4
New Mexico										
Metropolitan statistical area	1,385,862	X	X	X	X	X	X	X	X	X
Area actually reporting (percent)	100.0	8,090	61	550	1,414	6,065	51,271	13,834	33,060	4,377
Cities outside metropolitan areas	395,776	X	X	X	X	X	X	X	X	X
Area actually reporting (percent)	97.9	2,757	62	217	253	2,225	17,163	5,160	11,312	691
Estimated total (percent)	100.0	2,816	63	222	258	2,273	17,532	5,271	11,555	706
Nonmetropolitan counties	300,586	X	X	X	X	X	X	X	X	X
Area actually reporting (percent)	94.3	859	30	80	47	702	4,461	2,186	1,969	306
Estimated total (percent)	100.0	911	32	85	50	744	4,731	2,318	2,088	325
State total	2,082,224	11,817	156	857	1,722	9,082	73,534	21,423	46,703	5,408
Rate per 100,000 inhabitants	X	567.5	7.5	41.2	82.7	436.2	3,531.5	1,028.9	2,242.9	259.7
New York	17,894,951	X	X	X	X	X	X	X	X	X
Metropolitan statistical area	99.4	74,802	753	2,389	28,057	43,603	339,446	58,057	263,122	18,267
Area actually reporting (percent)	100.0	74,948	754	2,398	28,105	43,691	341,125	58,348	264,442	18,335
Estimated total (percent)	584,129	X	X	X	X	X	X	X	X	X
Cities outside metropolitan areas	97.7	1,454	7	162	213	1,072	16,437	3,249	12,767	421
Area actually reporting (percent)	100.0	1,488	7	166	218	1,097	16,823	3,325	13,067	431
Estimated total (percent)	986,117	X	X	X	X	X	X	X	X	X
Nonmetropolitan counties	97.3	1,026	13	183	71	759	13,918	3,623	9,765	530
Area actually reporting (percent)	100.0	1,054	13	188	73	780	14,307	3,724	10,038	545
State total	19,465,197	77,490	774	2,752	28,396	45,568	372,255	65,397	287,547	19,311
Rate per 100,000 inhabitants	X	398.1	4.0	14.1	145.9	234.1	1,912.4	336.0	1,477.2	99.2
North Carolina										
Metropolitan statistical area	6,789,371	X	X	X	X	X	X	X	X	X
Area actually reporting (percent)	99.0	24,351	342	1,449	7,419	15,141	238,548	70,217	155,841	12,490
Estimated total (percent)	100.0	24,542	343	1,463	7,468	15,268	241,312	70,839	157,889	12,584
Cities outside metropolitan areas	876,406	X	X	X	X	X	X	X	X	X
Area actually reporting (percent)	92.6	4,688	83	237	1,373	2,995	46,394	12,772	31,991	1,631
Estimated total (percent)	100.0	5,032	90	255	1,472	3,215	49,844	13,729	34,366	1,749
Nonmetropolitan counties	1,990,624	X	X	X	X	X	X	X	X	X
Area actually reporting (percent)	97.0	4,076	73	269	592	3,142	47,940	20,936	24,385	2,619
Estimated total (percent)	100.0	4,200	75	277	610	3,238	49,406	21,576	25,131	2,699
State total	9,656,401	33,774	508	1,995	9,550	21,721	340,562	106,144	217,386	17,032
Rate per 100,000 inhabitants	X	349.8	5.3	20.7	98.9	224.9	3,526.8	1,099.2	2,251.2	176.4
North Dakota										
Metropolitan statistical area	330,907	X	X	X	X	X	X	X	X	X
Area actually reporting (percent)	99.5	847	4	126	75	642	7,866	1350	6077	439
Estimated total (percent)	100.0	850	4	126	75	645	7,911	1,356	6,113	442
Cities outside metropolitan areas	158,858	X	X	X	X	X	X	X	X	X
Area actually reporting (percent)	92.4	640	18	102	12	508	3,624	635	2,637	352
Estimated total (percent)	100.0	692	19	110	13	550	3,921	687	2,853	381
Nonmetropolitan counties	194,167	X	X	X	X	X	X	X	X	X
Area actually reporting (percent)	97.2	143	1	22	3	117	1,375	379	843	153
Estimated total (percent)	100.0	147	1	23	3	120	1,414	390	867	157
State total	683,932	1,689	24	259	91	1,315	13,246	2,433	9,833	980
Rate per 100,000 inhabitants	X	247.0	3.5	37.9	13.3	192.3	1,936.7	355.7	1,437.7	143.3
Ohio										
Metropolitan statistical area	9,306,231	X	X	X	X	X	X	X	X	X
Area actually reporting (percent)	94.7	31,971	460	3,056	15,096	13,359	315,457	94,459	202,074	18,924
Estimated total (percent)	100.0	32,718	467	3,165	15,384	13,702	328,935	97,271	212,255	19,409
Cities outside metropolitan areas	950,318	X	X	X	X	X	X	X	X	X
Area actually reporting (percent)	79.4	1,348	17	253	436	642	29,831	6,436	22,709	686
Estimated total (percent)	100.0	1,697	21	319	549	808	37,563	8,104	28,595	864
Nonmetropolitan counties	1,288,402	X	X	X	X	X	X	X	X	X
Area actually reporting (percent)	91.7	981	23	135	114	709	19,074	6,726	11,619	729
Estimated total (percent)	100.0	1,069	25	147	124	773	20,799	7,334	12,670	795
State total	11,544,951	35,484	513	3,631	16,057	15,283	387,297	112,709	253,520	21,068
Rate per 100,000 inhabitants	X	307.4	4.4	31.5	139.1	132.4	3,354.7	976.3	2,195.9	182.5

Note: Although arson data are included in the trend and clearance tables, sufficient data are not available to estimate totals for this offense. Therefore, no arson data are published in this table.

X = Not applicable.

Table II-5. Crime, by State and Area, 2011—*Continued*

(Number, percent, rate per 100,000 population.)

Area	Population	Violent crime	Murder and non-negligent man-slaughter	Forcible rape	Robbery	Aggravated assault	Property crime	Burglary	Larceny-theft	Motor vehicle theft
Oklahoma										
Metropolitan statistical area	2,433,110	X	X	X	X	X	X	X	X	X
Area actually reporting (percent)	100.0	13,040	153	996	2,929	8,962	94,681	27,394	58,252	9,035
Cities outside metropolitan areas	727,258	X	X	X	X	X	X	X	X	X
Area actually reporting (percent)	99.9	3,103	26	292	319	2,466	24,848	6,197	17,371	1,280
Estimated total (percent)	100.0	3,106	26	292	319	2,469	24,876	6,204	17,391	1,281
Nonmetropolitan counties	631,140	X	X	X	X	X	X	X	X	X
Area actually reporting (percent)	100.0	1,097	29	115	34	919	7,695	2,743	4,237	715
State total	3,791,508	17,243	208	1,403	3,282	12,350	127,252	36,341	79,880	11,031
Rate per 100,000 inhabitants	X	454.8	5.5	37.0	86.6	325.7	3,356.2	958.5	2,106.8	290.9
Oregon										
Metropolitan statistical area	3,010,261	X	X	X	X	X	X	X	X	X
Area actually reporting (percent)	99.1	7,941	64	913	1,990	4,974	96,145	15,353	73,288	7,504
Estimated total (percent)	100.0	7,983	64	919	1,997	5,003	96,676	15,462	73,672	7,542
Cities outside metropolitan areas	410,825	X	X	X	X	X	X	X	X	X
Area actually reporting (percent)	98.5	968	8	187	175	598	16,581	2,843	12,962	776
Estimated total (percent)	100.0	983	8	190	178	607	16,832	2,886	13,158	788
Nonmetropolitan counties	450,773	X	X	X	X	X	X	X	X	X
Area actually reporting (percent)	98.7	612	10	107	46	449	6,997	2,074	4,215	708
Estimated total (percent)	100.0	620	10	108	47	455	7,086	2,100	4,269	717
State total	3,871,859	9,586	82	1,217	2,222	6,065	120,594	20,448	91,099	9,047
Rate per 100,000 inhabitants	X	247.6	2.1	31.4	57.4	156.6	3,114.6	528.1	2,352.8	233.7
Pennsylvania										
Metropolitan statistical area	10,719,812	X	X	X	X	X	X	X	X	X
Area actually reporting (percent)	99.2	41,266	597	2,737	15,525	22,407	246,517	49,104	181,844	15,569
Estimated total (percent)	100.0	41,434	597	2,750	15,571	22,516	248,136	49,369	183,138	15,629
Cities outside metropolitan areas	958,036	X	X	X	X	X	X	X	X	X
Area actually reporting (percent)	94.3	2,166	14	194	354	1,604	18,704	3,542	14,698	464
Estimated total (percent)	100.0	2,297	15	206	375	1,701	19,835	3,756	15,587	492
Nonmetropolitan counties	1,065,038	X	X	X	X	X	X	X	X	X
Area actually reporting (percent)	100.0	1,509	25	368	185	931	15,208	4,725	9,760	723
State total	12,742,886	45,240	637	3,324	16,131	25,148	283,179	57,850	208,485	16,844
Rate per 100,000 inhabitants	X	355.0	5.0	26.1	126.6	197.3	2,222.3	454.0	1,636.1	132.2
Puerto Rico										
Metropolitan statistical area	3,515,571	X	X	X	X	X	X	X	X	X
Area actually reporting (percent)	100.0	10,127	1,100	42	6,305	2,680	48,976	15,461	27,756	5,759
Cities outside metropolitan areas	191,119	X	X	X	X	X	X	X	X	X
Area actually reporting (percent)	100.0	413	36	3	160	214	2,741	1,130	1,517	94
Territory total	3,706,690	10,540	1,136	45	6,465	2,894	51,717	16,591	29,273	5,853
Rate per 100,000 inhabitants	X	284.4	30.6	1.2	174.4	78.1	1,395.2	447.6	789.7	157.9
Rhode Island										
Metropolitan statistical area	1,051,302	X	X	X	X	X	X	X	X	X
Area actually reporting (percent)	100.0	2,596	13	301	746	1,536	28,092	6,962	18,879	2,251
Cities outside metropolitan areas	X	X	X	X	X	X	X	X	X	X
Nonmetropolitan counties	X	X	X	X	X	X	X	X	X	X
Area actually reporting (percent)	100.0	6	1	3	0	2	49	2	11	36
State total	1,051,302	2,602	14	304	746	1,538	28,141	6,964	18,890	2,287
Rate per 100,000 inhabitants	X	247.5	1.3	28.9	71.0	146.3	2,676.8	662.4	1,796.8	217.5
South Carolina										
Metropolitan statistical area	3,577,275	X	X	X	X	X	X	X	X	X
Area actually reporting (percent)	99.9	19,404	232	1,256	3,404	14,512	139,810	34,553	94,178	11,079
Estimated total (percent)	100.0	19,429	232	1,257	3,408	14,532	140,023	34,594	94,339	11,090
Cities outside metropolitan areas	283,043	X	X	X	X	X	X	X	X	X
Area actually reporting (percent)	97.8	2,743	34	101	472	2,136	15,678	3,752	11,322	604
Estimated total (percent)	100.0	2,803	35	103	482	2,183	16,023	3,835	11,571	617
Nonmetropolitan counties	818,912	X	X	X	X	X	X	X	X	X
Area actually reporting (percent)	100.0	4,528	53	252	423	3,800	26,639	8,492	16,190	1,957
State total	4,679,230	26,760	320	1,612	4,313	20,515	182,685	46,921	122,100	13,664
Rate per 100,000 inhabitants	X	571.9	6.8	34.5	92.2	438.4	3,904.2	1,002.8	2,609.4	292.0

Note: Although arson data are included in the trend and clearance tables, sufficient data are not available to estimate totals for this offense. Therefore, no arson data are published in this table.

X = Not applicable.

Table II-5.   Crime, by State and Area, 2011—*Continued*

(Number, percent, rate per 100,000 population.)

Area	Population	Violent crime	Murder and non-negligent man-slaughter	Forcible rape	Robbery	Aggravated assault	Property crime	Burglary	Larceny-theft	Motor vehicle theft
South Dakota										
Metropolitan statistical area	373,529	X	X	X	X	X	X	X	X	X
Area actually reporting (percent)	98.7	1,018	9	254	135	620	9,321	1,821	6,996	504
Estimated total (percent)	100.0	1,022	9	255	135	623	9,386	1,831	7,049	506
Cities outside metropolitan areas	217,574	X	X	X	X	X	X	X	X	X
Area actually reporting (percent)	89.5	819	8	173	26	612	4,080	676	3,106	298
Estimated total (percent)	100.0	914	9	193	29	683	4,557	755	3,469	333
Nonmetropolitan counties	232,979	X	X	X	X	X	X	X	X	X
Area actually reporting (percent)	78.6	124	2	38	2	82	814	246	484	84
Estimated total (percent)	100.0	158	3	48	3	104	1,036	313	616	107
State total	824,082	2,094	21	496	167	1,410	14,979	2,899	11,134	946
Rate per 100,000 inhabitants	X	254.1	2.5	60.2	20.3	171.1	1,817.7	351.8	1,351.1	114.8
Tennessee										
Metropolitan statistical area	4,701,796	X	X	X	X	X	X	X	X	X
Area actually reporting (percent)	100.0	32,191	310	1,622	7,435	22,824	178,899	47,425	120,148	11,326
Cities outside metropolitan areas	605,926	X	X	X	X	X	X	X	X	X
Area actually reporting (percent)	100.0	3,728	28	219	483	2,998	27,974	6,567	20,384	1,023
Nonmetropolitan counties	1,095,631	X	X	X	X	X	X	X	X	X
Area actually reporting (percent)	100.0	3,025	35	183	163	2,644	23,388	8,757	12,944	1,687
State total	6,403,353	38,944	373	2,024	8,081	28,466	230,261	62,749	153,476	14,036
Rate per 100,000 inhabitants	X	608.2	5.8	31.6	126.2	444.5	3,595.9	979.9	2,396.8	219.2
Texas										
Metropolitan statistical area	22,549,888	X	X	X	X	X	X	X	X	X
Area actually reporting (percent)	99.9	95,634	1,018	6,544	27,626	60,446	821,834	194,265	567,433	60,136
Estimated total (percent)	100.0	95,657	1,018	6,545	27,632	60,462	822,133	194,327	567,652	60,154
Cities outside metropolitan areas	1,436,594	X	X	X	X	X	X	X	X	X
Area actually reporting (percent)	99.3	6,026	50	552	617	4,807	44,367	11,492	31,274	1,601
Estimated total (percent)	100.0	6,060	50	556	618	4,836	44,599	11,556	31,437	1,606
Nonmetropolitan counties	1,688,199	X	X	X	X	X	X	X	X	X
Area actually reporting (percent)	98.5	3,108	57	333	143	2,575	24,388	9,197	13,637	1,554
Estimated total (percent)	100.0	3,156	58	338	145	2,615	24,767	9,340	13,849	1,578
State total	25,674,681	104,873	1,126	7,439	28,395	67,913	891,499	215,223	612,938	63,338
Rate per 100,000 inhabitants	X	408.5	4.4	29.0	110.6	264.5	3,472.3	838.3	2,387.3	246.7
Utah										
Metropolitan statistical area	2,496,222	X	X	X	X	X	X	X	X	X
Area actually reporting (percent)	99.9	4,992	39	757	1,059	3,137	77,046	11,637	59,509	5,900
Estimated total (percent)	100.0	4,992	39	757	1,059	3,137	77,058	11,639	59,518	5,901
Cities outside metropolitan areas	160,485	X	X	X	X	X	X	X	X	X
Area actually reporting (percent)	86.8	237	9	62	13	153	3,773	746	2,895	132
Estimated total (percent)	100.0	272	10	71	15	176	4,346	859	3,335	152
Nonmetropolitan counties	160,515	X	X	X	X	X	X	X	X	X
Area actually reporting (percent)	87.2	200	4	23	6	167	2,052	544	1,395	113
Estimated total (percent)	100.0	230	5	26	7	192	2,354	624	1,600	130
State total	2,817,222	5,494	54	854	1,081	3,505	83,758	13,122	64,453	6,183
Rate per 100,000 inhabitants	X	195.0	1.9	30.3	38.4	124.4	2,973.1	465.8	2,287.8	219.5
Vermont	211,494	X	X	X	X	X	X	X	X	X
Metropolitan statistical area	100.0	363	3	48	36	276	5,530	954	4,400	176
Area actually reporting (percent)	204,085	X	X	X	X	X	X	X	X	X
Cities outside metropolitan areas	96.5	282	1	37	39	205	5,206	1,100	3,963	143
Area actually reporting (percent)	100.0	291	1	38	40	212	5,394	1,140	4,106	148
Nonmetropolitan counties	210,852	X	X	X	X	X	X	X	X	X
Area actually reporting (percent)	98.0	189	4	32	9	144	3,472	1,519	1,781	172
Estimated total (percent)	100.0	193	4	33	9	147	3,540	1,549	1,816	175
State total	626,431	847	8	119	85	635	14,464	3,643	10,322	499
Rate per 100,000 inhabitants	X	135.2	1.3	19.0	13.6	101.4	2,309.0	581.5	1,647.7	79.7
Virginia	6,969,785	X	X	X	X	X	X	X	X	X
Metropolitan statistical area	100.0	14,174	250	1,292	5,156	7,476	161,299	26,268	126,341	8,690
Area actually reporting (percent)	281,010	X	X	X	X	X	X	X	X	X
Cities outside metropolitan areas	96.8	663	9	78	154	422	8,425	1,220	6,895	310
Area actually reporting (percent)	100.0	685	9	81	159	436	8,700	1,260	7,120	320
Nonmetropolitan counties	845,809	X	X	X	X	X	X	X	X	X
Area actually reporting (percent)	100.0	1,064	44	163	115	742	12,142	3,069	8,359	714
State total	8,096,604	15,923	303	1,536	5,430	8,654	182,141	30,597	141,820	9,724
Rate per 100,000 inhabitants	X	196.7	3.7	19.0	67.1	106.9	2,249.6	377.9	1,751.6	120.1

Note: Although arson data are included in the trend and clearance tables, sufficient data are not available to estimate totals for this offense. Therefore, no arson data are published in this table.

X = Not applicable.

Table II-5.   Crime, by State and Area, 2011—*Continued*

(Number, percent, rate per 100,000 population.)

Area	Population	Violent crime	Murder and non-negligent man-slaughter	Forcible rape	Robbery	Aggravated assault	Property crime	Burglary	Larceny-theft	Motor vehicle theft
Washington										
Metropolitan statistical area	5,992,954	X	X	X	X	X	X	X	X	X
Area actually reporting (percent)	99.9	18,220	137	1,985	5,411	10,687	218,883	49,668	146,028	23,187
Estimated total (percent)	100.0	18,222	137	1,985	5,412	10,688	218,920	49,675	146,054	23,191
Cities outside metropolitan areas	345,464	X	X	X	X	X	X	X	X	X
Area actually reporting (percent)	98.0	1,215	12	198	178	827	15,169	3,314	10,935	920
Estimated total (percent)	100.0	1,240	12	202	182	844	15,481	3,382	11,160	939
Nonmetropolitan counties	491,620	X	X	X	X	X	X	X	X	X
Area actually reporting (percent)	100.0	659	13	103	44	499	9,745	3,475	5,565	705
State total	6,830,038	20,121	162	2,290	5,638	12,031	244,146	56,532	162,779	24,835
Rate per 100,000 inhabitants	X	294.6	2.4	33.5	82.5	176.1	3,574.6	827.7	2,383.3	363.6
West Virginia										
Metropolitan statistical area	1,034,072	X	X	X	X	X	X	X	X	X
Area actually reporting (percent)	92.7	3,401	33	247	607	2,514	24,817	6,716	16,785	1,316
Estimated total (percent)	100.0	3,610	36	260	636	2,678	26,713	7,113	18,193	1,407
Cities outside metropolitan areas	224,618	X	X	X	X	X	X	X	X	X
Area actually reporting (percent)	73.7	689	2	41	131	515	4,993	982	3,817	194
Estimated total (percent)	100.0	936	3	56	178	699	6,776	1,333	5,180	263
Nonmetropolitan counties	596,674	X	X	X	X	X	X	X	X	X
Area actually reporting (percent)	91.7	1,206	38	66	88	1,014	7,979	2,518	4,925	536
Estimated total (percent)	100.0	1,315	41	72	96	1,106	8,700	2,746	5,370	584
State total	1,855,364	5,861	80	388	910	4,483	42,189	11,192	28,743	2,254
Rate per 100,000 inhabitants	X	315.9	4.3	20.9	49.0	241.6	2,273.9	603.2	1,549.2	121.5
Wisconsin										
Metropolitan statistical area	4,160,131	X	X	X	X	X	X	X	X	X
Area actually reporting (percent)	99.0	11,630	123	896	4,343	6,268	108,970	20,568	81,145	7,257
Estimated total (percent)	100.0	11,685	123	903	4,357	6,302	110,002	20,704	82,011	7,287
Cities outside metropolitan areas	655,218	X	X	X	X	X	X	X	X	X
Area actually reporting (percent)	94.0	1,083	5	156	78	844	17,383	2,314	14,636	433
Estimated total (percent)	100.0	1,152	5	166	83	898	18,498	2,462	15,575	461
Nonmetropolitan counties	896,418	X	X	X	X	X	X	X	X	X
Area actually reporting (percent)	100.0	695	8	94	29	564	10,449	3,488	6,477	484
State total	5,711,767	13,532	136	1,163	4,469	7,764	138,949	26,654	104,063	8,232
Rate per 100,000 inhabitants	X	236.9	2.4	20.4	78.2	135.9	2,432.7	466.7	1,821.9	144.1
Wyoming										
Metropolitan statistical area	168,530	X	X	X	X	X	X	X	X	X
Area actually reporting (percent)	100.0	414	4	55	53	302	4,997	798	4,004	195
Cities outside metropolitan areas	239,560	X	X	X	X	X	X	X	X	X
Area actually reporting (percent)	97.0	621	12	73	16	520	6,279	737	5,307	235
Estimated total (percent)	100.0	639	12	75	16	536	6,472	760	5,470	242
Nonmetropolitan counties	160,068	X	X	X	X	X	X	X	X	X
Area actually reporting (percent)	100.0	193	2	16	2	173	1,408	305	1,019	84
State total	568,158	1,246	18	146	71	1,011	12,877	1,863	10,493	521
Rate per 100,000 inhabitants	X	219.3	3.2	25.7	12.5	177.9	2,266.4	327.9	1,846.8	91.7

Note: Although arson data are included in the trend and clearance tables, sufficient data are not available to estimate totals for this offense. Therefore, no arson data are published in this table.
X = Not applicable.

Table II-6.   Crime, by Selected Metropolitan Statistical Area, 2011

(Number, percent, rate per 100,000 population.)

Area	Population	Violent crime	Murder and non-negligent man-slaughter	Forcible rape	Robbery	Aggravated assault	Property crime	Burglary	Larceny-theft	Motor vehicle theft
Abilene, TX M.S.A.	168,729									
Includes Callahan, Jones, and Taylor Counties										
City of Abilene	119,526	428	5	33	120	270	4,384	1,119	3,093	172
Total area actually reporting	100.0	502	5	36	122	339	5,112	1,338	3,569	205
Rate per 100,000 inhabitants	X	297.5	3.0	21.3	72.3	200.9	3,029.7	793.0	2,115.2	121.5
Aguadilla-Isabela-San Sebastian, PR M.S.A.	304,633									
Includes Aguada, Aguadilla, Anasco, Isabela, Lares, Moca, Rincon, and San Sebastian Municipios										
Total area actually reporting	100.0	336	30	1	158	147	3,150	1,398	1,648	104
Rate per 100,000 inhabitants	X	110.3	9.8	0.3	51.9	48.3	1,034.0	458.9	541.0	34.1
Akron, OH M.S.A.	703,715									
Includes Portage and Summit Counties										
City of Akron	199,256	1,779	27	165	718	869	10,864	4,268	5,790	806
Total area actually reporting	91.6	2,192	32	248	865	1,047	21,531	6,436	13,891	1,204
Estimated total	100.0	2,281	33	261	900	1,087	23,158	6,771	15,125	1,262
Rate per 100,000 inhabitants	X	324.1	4.7	37.1	127.9	154.5	3,290.8	962.2	2,149.3	179.3
Albany, GA M.S.A.	159,379									
Includes Baker, Dougherty, Lee, Terrell, and Worth Counties										
City of Albany	78,454	640	13	37	176	414	4,719	1,332	3,174	213
Total area actually reporting	0.994	838	16	51	201	570	6,918	1,958	4,631	329
Estimated total	99.4	841	16	51	202	572	6,958	1,966	4,660	332
Rate per 100,000 inhabitants	X	527.7	10.0	32.0	126.7	358.9	4,365.7	1,233.5	2,923.8	208.3
Albany-Schenectady-Troy, NY M.S.A.	874,629									
Includes Albany, Rensselaer, Saratoga, Schenectady, and Schoharie Counties										
City of Albany	98,296	939	4	33	320	582	4,611	895	3,514	202
City of Schenectady	66,432	633	4	43	204	382	3,098	904	2,011	183
City of Troy	50,354	371	0	23	112	236	2,318	775	1,442	101
Total area actually reporting	100.0	2,472	13	157	763	1,539	21,818	4,480	16,592	746
Rate per 100,000 inhabitants	X	282.6	1.5	18.0	87.2	176.0	2,494.5	512.2	1,897.0	85.3
Albuquerque, NM M.S.A.	897,005									
Includes Bernalillo, Sandoval, Torrance, and Valencia Counties										
City of Albuquerque	551,961	4,207	35	264	998	2,910	27,976	5,985	19,168	2,823
Total area actually reporting	100.0	5,938	45	355	1,168	4,370	36,335	8,561	24,236	3,538
Rate per 100,000 inhabitants	X	662.0	5.0	39.6	130.2	487.2	4,050.7	954.4	2,701.9	394.4
Alexandria, LA M.S.A.	155,330									
Includes Grant and Rapides Parishes										
City of Alexandria	48,159	651	2	11	159	479	3,560	869	2,517	174
Total area actually reporting	98.1%	1,037	5	52	180	800	6,663	1,726	4,520	417
Estimated total	100.0	1,053	5	53	182	813	6,795	1,752	4,622	421
Rate per 100,000 inhabitants	X	677.9	3.2	34.1	117.2	523.4	4,374.6	1,127.9	2,975.6	271.0
Allentown-Bethlehem-Easton, PA-NJ M.S.A.	823,807									
Includes Warren County, NJ and Carbon, Lehigh, and Northampton Counties, PA										
City of Allentown, PA	118,408	647	10	61	339	237	4,575	1,101	3,041	433
City of Bethlehem, PA	75,221	219	3	17	97	102	1,862	371	1,405	86
Total area actually reporting	99.9%	1,764	23	154	609	978	18,758	3,191	14,601	966
Estimated total	100.0	1,765	23	154	609	979	18,765	3,192	14,607	966
Rate per 100,000 inhabitants	X	214.2	2.8	18.7	73.9	118.8	2,277.8	387.5	1,773.1	117.3
Altoona, PA M.S.A.	127,494									
Includes Blair County										
City of Altoona	46,468	143	0	26	39	78	1,090	301	745	44
Total area actually reporting	100.0	326	2	56	48	220	2,529	527	1,922	80
Rate per 100,000 inhabitants	X	255.7	1.6	43.9	37.6	172.6	1,983.6	413.4	1,507.5	62.7
Amarillo, TX M.S.A.	255,139									
Includes Armstrong, Carson, Potter, and Randall Counties										
City of Amarillo	194,708	1,223	10	104	235	874	9,388	2,016	6,756	616
Total area actually reporting	100.0	1,318	12	112	241	953	10,315	2,296	7,346	673
Rate per 100,000 inhabitants	X	516.6	4.7	43.9	94.5	373.5	4,042.9	899.9	2,879.2	263.8

X = Not applicable.

Table II-6. Crime, by Selected Metropolitan Statistical Area, 2011—*Continued*

(Number, percent, rate per 100,000 population.)

Area	Population	Violent crime	Murder and non-negligent man-slaughter	Forcible rape	Robbery	Aggravated assault	Property crime	Burglary	Larceny-theft	Motor vehicle theft
Ames, IA M.S.A.	90,011									
Includes Story County										
City of Ames	59,274	178	0	18	10	150	1,670	351	1,263	56
Total area actually reporting	100.0	250	0	30	13	207	2,351	497	1,775	79
Rate per 100,000 inhabitants	X	277.7	0.0	33.3	14.4	230.0	2,611.9	552.2	1,972.0	87.8
Anchorage, AK M.S.A.	310,965									
Includes Anchorage Municipality and Matanuska-Susitna Borough										
City of Anchorage	296,955	2,388	12	283	465	1,628	9,455	1,080	7,750	625
Total area actually reporting	100.0	2,454	13	289	471	1,681	10,268	1,161	8,456	651
Rate per 100,000 inhabitants	X	789.2	4.2	92.9	151.5	540.6	3,302.0	373.4	2,719.3	209.3
Anderson, SC M.S.A.	189,305									
Includes Anderson County										
City of Anderson	26,997	209	3	9	50	147	2,028	481	1,405	142
Total area actually reporting	100.0	1,103	15	64	138	886	9,699	2,720	6,078	901
Rate per 100,000 inhabitants	X	582.7	7.9	33.8	72.9	468.0	5,123.5	1,436.8	3,210.7	476.0
Ann Arbor, MI M.S.A.	344,531									
Includes Washtenaw County										
City of Ann Arbor	113,848	261	0	36	59	166	2,549	534	1,918	97
Total area actually reporting	100.0	1,066	8	169	214	675	7,935	1,957	5,538	440
Rate per 100,000 inhabitants	X	309.4	2.3	49.1	62.1	195.9	2,303.1	568.0	1,607.4	127.7
Anniston-Oxford, AL M.S.A.[1]	119,143									
Includes Calhoun County										
City of Anniston[1]	23,217	411	11	21	85	294	2,323	996	1,227	100
City of Oxford[1]	17,280	87	3	5	16	63	1,048	182	808	58
Total area actually reporting	100.0	607	14	43	113	437	5,089	1,727	3,169	193
Rate per 100,000 inhabitants	X	509.5	11.8	36.1	94.8	366.8	4,271.3	1,449.5	2,659.8	162.0
Appleton, WI M.S.A.	226,649									
Includes Calumet and Outagamie Counties										
City of Appleton	72,939	217	0	33	29	155	1,458	220	1,213	25
Total area actually reporting	100.0	321	2	45	33	241	3,839	558	3,174	107
Rate per 100,000 inhabitants	X	141.6	0.9	19.9	14.6	106.3	1,693.8	246.2	1,400.4	47.2
Asheville, NC M.S.A.	430,246									
Includes Buncombe, Haywood, Henderson, and Madison Counties										
City of Asheville	84,450	444	5	22	181	236	3,949	753	2,875	321
Total area actually reporting	99.5	932	12	73	269	578	10,808	3,253	6,793	762
Estimated total	100.0	938	12	73	271	582	10,898	3,273	6,860	765
Rate per 100,000 inhabitants	X	218.0	2.8	17.0	63.0	135.3	2,533.0	760.7	1,594.4	177.8
Athens-Clarke County, GA M.S.A.	195,076									
Includes Clarke, Madison, Oconee, and Oglethorpe Counties										
City of Athens-Clarke County	117,114	417	6	30	132	249	4,873	1,359	3,273	241
Total area actually reporting	99.4	731	6	44	146	535	7,224	1,883	4,985	356
Estimated total	100.0	734	6	44	147	537	7,269	1,892	5,018	359
Rate per 100,000 inhabitants	X	376.3	3.1	22.6	75.4	275.3	3,726.2	969.9	2,572.3	184.0
Atlanta-Sandy Springs-Marietta, GA M.S.A.	5,338,234									
Includes Barrow, Bartow, Butts, Carroll, Cherokee, Clayton, Cobb, Coweta, Dawson, DeKalb, Douglas, Fayette, Forsyth, Fulton, Gwinnett, Haralson, Heard, Henry, Jasper, Lamar, Meriwether, Newton, Paulding, Pickens, Pike, Rockdale, Spalding, and Walton Counties										
City of Atlanta	425,533	6,097	88	148	2,343	3,518	30,144	7,499	17,274	5,371
City of Sandy Springs	95,089	153	1	6	94	52	2,475	587	1,728	160
City of Marietta	57,324	386	5	13	125	243	2,624	584	1,864	176
Total area actually reporting	99.7	21,351	318	1,096	8,130	11,807	189,043	51,865	117,096	20,082
Estimated total	100.0	21,403	319	1,099	8,147	11,838	189,614	51,978	117,515	20,121
Rate per 100,000 inhabitants	X	400.9	6.0	20.6	152.6	221.8	3,552.0	973.7	2,201.4	376.9

X = Not applicable.

[1] Because of changes in the state/local agency's reporting practices, figures are not comparable to previous years' data.

Table II-6.   Crime, by Selected Metropolitan Statistical Area, 2011—*Continued*

(Number, percent, rate per 100,000 population.)

Area	Population	Violent crime	Murder and non-negligent man-slaughter	Forcible rape	Robbery	Aggravated assault	Property crime	Burglary	Larceny-theft	Motor vehicle theft
Atlantic City-Hammonton, NJ M.S.A.	275,463									
Includes Atlantic County										
City of Atlantic City	39,690	741	13	22	384	322	2,938	573	2,261	104
City of Hammonton	14,840	17	2	0	7	8	200	60	132	8
Total area actually reporting	100.0	1,396	22	60	603	711	9,392	2,144	6,916	332
Rate per 100,000 inhabitants	X	506.8	8.0	21.8	218.9	258.1	3,409.5	778.3	2,510.7	120.5
Auburn-Opelika, AL M.S.A.[1]	140,922									
Includes Lee County[1]										
City of Auburn[1]	53,637	152	0	12	48	92	2,143	550	1,520	73
City of Opelika[1]	26,604	115	2	17	41	55	2,036	406	1,597	33
Total area actually reporting	100.0	296	3	32	94	167	4,587	1,054	3,400	133
Rate per 100,000 inhabitants	X	210.0	2.1	22.7	66.7	118.5	3,255.0	747.9	2,412.7	94.4
Augusta-Richmond County, GA-SC M.S.A.	563,924									
Includes Burke, Columbia, McDuffie, and Richmond Counties, GA and Aiken and Edgefield Counties, SC										
Total area actually reporting	98.8	2,011	50	204	735	1,022	24,273	6,597	15,568	2,108
Estimated total	100.0	2,035	50	205	743	1,037	24,543	6,650	15,767	2,126
Rate per 100,000 inhabitants	X	360.9	8.9	36.4	131.8	183.9	4,352.2	1,179.2	2,795.9	377.0
Austin-Round Rock-San Marcos, TX M.S.A.	1,752,404									
Includes Bastrop, Caldwell, Hays, Travis, and Williamson Counties										
City of Austin	807,022	3,471	28	211	1,106	2,126	42,250	7,042	33,069	2,139
City of Round Rock	101,989	115	2	25	39	49	2,446	394	2,001	51
City of San Marcos	45,839	159	1	11	37	110	1,568	273	1,206	89
Total area actually reporting	100.0	5,032	50	399	1,317	3,266	60,429	10,820	46,845	2,764
Rate per 100,000 inhabitants	X	287.1	2.9	22.8	75.2	186.4	3,448.3	617.4	2,673.2	157.7
Bakersfield-Delano, CA M.S.A.	849,502									
Includes Kern County										
City of Bakersfield	351,568	1,866	18	39	548	1,261	14,840	4,321	8,123	2,396
City of Delano	53,665	220	1	7	48	164	1,644	773	513	358
Total area actually reporting	100.0	4,447	46	184	1,029	3,188	30,071	9,460	15,725	4,886
Rate per 100,000 inhabitants	X	523.5	5.4	21.7	121.1	375.3	3,539.8	1,113.6	1,851.1	575.2
Baltimore-Towson, MD M.S.A.	2,736,186									
Includes Anne Arundel, Baltimore, Carroll, Harford, Howard, and Queen Anne's Counties and Baltimore City										
City of Baltimore	626,848	8,885	196	341	3,457	4,891	29,824	8,615	17,010	4,199
Total area actually reporting	100.0	17,681	256	681	5,968	10,776	83,249	17,846	57,896	7,507
Rate per 100,000 inhabitants	X	646.2	9.4	24.9	218.1	393.8	3,042.5	652.2	2,115.9	274.4
Bangor, ME M.S.A.	153,903									
Includes Penobscot County										
City of Bangor	33,035	69	2	9	35	23	1,672	249	1,389	34
Total area actually reporting	100.0	123	7	21	47	48	4,316	921	3,255	140
Rate per 100,000 inhabitants	X	79.9	4.5	13.6	30.5	31.2	2,804.4	598.4	2,115.0	91.0
Barnstable Town, MA M.S.A.	217,204									
Includes Barnstable County										
City of Barnstable	45,468	303	1	28	32	242	1,278	360	855	63
Total area actually reporting	100.0	985	3	99	106	777	6,051	2,295	3,565	191
Rate per 100,000 inhabitants	X	453.5	1.4	45.6	48.8	357.7	2,785.9	1,056.6	1,641.3	87.9
Baton Rouge, LA M.S.A.	809,822									
Includes Ascension, East Baton Rouge, East Feliciana, Iberville, Livingston, Pointe Coupee, St. Helena, West Baton Rouge, and West Feliciana Parishes										
City of Baton Rouge	231,592	2,468	64	51	893	1,460	12,666	4,220	7,946	500
Total area actually reporting	98.7	4,692	95	146	1,282	3,169	32,521	8,679	22,733	1,109
Estimated total	100.0	4,752	96	149	1,290	3,217	32,994	8,771	23,099	1,124
Rate per 100,000 inhabitants	X	586.8	11.9	18.4	159.3	397.2	4,074.2	1,083.1	2,852.4	138.8

X = Not applicable.

[1] Because of changes in the state/local agency's reporting practices, figures are not comparable to previous years' data.

Table II-6.   Crime, by Selected Metropolitan Statistical Area, 2011—*Continued*

(Number, percent, rate per 100,000 population.)

Area	Population	Violent crime	Murder and non-negligent man-slaughter	Forcible rape	Robbery	Aggravated assault	Property crime	Burglary	Larceny-theft	Motor vehicle theft
Battle Creek, MI M.S.A..............................	136,043									
Includes Calhoun County										
City of Battle Creek	61,658	567	5	62	98	402	3,089	1,146	1,846	97
Total area actually reporting	98.8	848	8	82	138	620	5,183	1,704	3,324	155
Estimated total..	100.0	853	8	83	139	623	5,227	1,714	3,355	158
Rate per 100,000 inhabitants	X	627.0	5.9	61.0	102.2	457.9	3,842.2	1,259.9	2,466.1	116.1
Bay City, MI M.S.A...................................	107,690									
Includes Bay County										
City of Bay City	34,906	170	0	36	35	99	797	244	524	29
Total area actually reporting	100.0	295	3	74	45	173	2,113	538	1,504	71
Estimated total..	X	273.9	2.8	68.7	41.8	160.6	1,962.1	499.6	1,396.6	65.9
Rate per 100,000 inhabitants										
Beaumont-Port Arthur, TX M.S.A.............................	396,925									
Includes Hardin, Jefferson, and Orange Counties										
City of Beaumont	120,785	1,069	13	65	356	635	6,656	2,035	4,336	285
City of Port Arthur	54,950	434	8	29	156	241	2,853	950	1,740	163
Total area actually reporting	100.0	2,167	26	137	627	1,377	15,375	4,555	10,000	820
Rate per 100,000 inhabitants.......................	X	545.9	6.6	34.5	158.0	346.9	3,873.5	1,147.6	2,519.4	206.6
Bellingham, WA M.S.A...................................	204,296									
Includes Whatcom County										
City of Bellingham	82,154	199	1	35	55	108	3,738	646	2,961	131
Total area actually reporting	100.0	439	3	94	74	268	6,395	1,448	4,721	226
Rate per 100,000 inhabitants.......................	X	214.9	1.5	46.0	36.2	131.2	3,130.3	708.8	2,310.9	110.6
Bend, OR M.S.A...................................	159,412									
Includes Deschutes County										
City of Bend	77,455	204	1	25	27	151	2,416	365	1,978	73
Total area actually reporting	100.0	528	2	55	45	426	4,914	791	3,950	173
Rate per 100,000 inhabitants.......................	X	331.2	1.3	34.5	28.2	267.2	3,082.6	496.2	2,477.9	108.5
Billings, MT M.S.A.[1]	159,454									
Includes Carbon and Yellowstone Counties										
City of Billings..	105,095	313	2	36	36	239	4,693	669	3,689	335
Total area actually reporting	100.0	418	3	42	41	332	5,521	851	4,264	406
Rate per 100,000 inhabitants.......................	X	262.1	1.9	26.3	25.7	208.2	3,462.4	533.7	2,674.1	254.6
Binghamton, NY M.S.A...................................	252,857									
Includes Broome and Tioga Counties										
City of Binghamton	47,589	268	0	17	76	175	2,284	415	1,796	73
Total area actually reporting	100.0	548	3	59	125	361	6,648	1,215	5,257	176
Rate per 100,000 inhabitants.......................	X	216.7	1.2	23.3	49.4	142.8	2,629.2	480.5	2,079.0	69.6
Birmingham-Hoover, AL M.S.A.[1]	1,133,475									
Includes Bibb, Blount, Chilton, Jefferson, St. Clair, Shelby, and Walker Counties[1]										
City of Birmingham[1].....................................	213,258	3,163	54	182	1,011	1,916	17,841	5,806	10,522	1,513
City of Hoover[1]..	82,012	59	0	7	35	17	2,194	422	1,663	109
Total area actually reporting	94.9%	5,805	99	404	1,683	3,619	45,250	14,220	27,992	3,038
Estimated total..	100.0	5,942	101	417	1,704	3,720	46,401	14,658	28,634	3,109
Rate per 100,000 inhabitants.......................	X	524.2	8.9	36.8	150.3	328.2	4,093.7	1,293.2	2,526.2	274.3
Bismarck, ND M.S.A...................................	110,613									
Includes Burleigh and Morton Counties										
City of Bismarck	62,305	166	1	27	15	123	1,865	258	1,494	113
Total area actually reporting	100.0	245	3	41	16	185	2,700	436	2,098	166
Rate per 100,000 inhabitants.......................	X	221.5	2.7	37.1	14.5	167.2	2,440.9	394.2	1,896.7	150.1
Blacksburg-Christiansburg-Radford, VA M.S.A...................	164,905									
Includes Giles, Montgomery, and Pulaski Counties and Radford City										
City of Blacksburg.......................................	43,129	24	0	9	5	10	591	84	490	17
City of Christiansburg..................................	21,292	29	0	7	5	17	733	98	615	20
City of Radford	16,604	55	1	7	8	39	477	97	364	16
Total area actually reporting	100.0	245	3	55	24	163	4,137	716	3,279	142
Rate per 100,000 inhabitants.......................	X	148.6	1.8	33.4	14.6	98.8	2,508.7	434.2	1,988.4	86.1

X = Not applicable.

[1] Because of changes in the state/local agency's reporting practices, figures are not comparable to previous years' data.

Table II-6. Crime, by Selected Metropolitan Statistical Area, 2011—*Continued*

(Number, percent, rate per 100,000 population.)

Area	Population	Violent crime	Murder and non-negligent man-slaughter	Forcible rape	Robbery	Aggravated assault	Property crime	Burglary	Larceny-theft	Motor vehicle theft
Bloomington, IN M.S.A.................................	193,698									
Includes Greene, Monroe, and Owen Counties										
City of Bloomington..	80,816	244	4	18	58	164	3,072	601	2,300	171
Total area actually reporting	87.7	350	6	39	65	240	4,985	997	3,696	292
Estimated total..	100.0	378	6	43	69	260	5,378	1,096	3,964	318
Rate per 100,000 inhabitants...........................	X	195.1	3.1	22.2	35.6	134.2	2,776.5	565.8	2,046.5	164.2
Bloomington-Normal, IL M.S.A.[2].................	170,082									
Includes McLean County[2]										
City of Bloomington[2]......................................	76,841	361	1	69	58	233	1,740	460	1,231	49
City of Normal[2]..	52,655	106	0	16	19	71	1,299	279	994	26
Total area actually reporting	94.5	525	2	92	81	350	3,493	862	2,543	88
Estimated total..	100.0	546	2	94	87	363	3,697	901	2,699	97
Rate per 100,000 inhabitants...........................	X	321.0	1.2	55.3	51.2	213.4	2,173.7	529.7	1,586.9	57.0
Boise City-Nampa, ID M.S.A.......................	623,381									
Includes Ada, Boise, Canyon, Gem, and Owyhee Counties										
City of Boise	207,945	510	1	66	59	384	5,328	809	4,347	172
City of Nampa	82,459	227	0	37	9	181	2,475	514	1,864	97
Total area actually reporting	99	1,302	8	157	91	1,046	12,670	2,412	9,792	466
Estimated total..		1,303	8	157	91	1,047	12,681	2,414	9,801	466
Rate per 100,000 inhabitants...........................		209.0	1.3	25.2	14.6	168.0	2,034.2	387.2	1,572.2	74.8
Boston-Cambridge-Quincy, MA-NH M.S.A.......	4,578,146									
Includes the Metropolitan Divisions of Boston-Quincy, MA; Cambridge-Newton-Framingham, MA; and Peabody, MA and Rockingham County-Strafford County, NH										
City of Boston, MA	621,359	5,252	63	271	1,904	3,014	19,445	3,482	14,064	1,899
City of Cambridge, MA	105,803	479	5	24	152	298	3,159	539	2,465	155
City of Quincy, MA	92,834	394	1	31	91	271	1,776	551	1,087	138
City of Newton, MA	85,665	80	0	2	19	59	1,181	212	942	27
City of Framingham, MA	68,734	187	0	6	21	160	1,126	212	830	84
City of Waltham, MA	61,002	174	0	15	24	135	868	191	639	38
City of Peabody, MA	51,563	124	2	9	13	100	1,282	212	996	74
Total area actually reporting	96.6%	16,727	127	992	4,505	11,103	93,529	19,318	67,134	7,077
Estimated total..	100.0	17,153	129	1,026	4,583	11,415	96,552	20,033	69,260	7,259
Rate per 100,000 inhabitants...........................	X	374.7	2.8	22.4	100.1	249.3	2,109.0	437.6	1,512.8	158.6
Boston-Quincy, MA M.D.	1,899,298									
Includes Norfolk, Plymouth, and Suffolk Counties										
Total area actually reporting	96.4	9,727	93	517	3,020	6,097	43,273	8,919	30,977	3,377
Estimated total..	100.0	9,937	94	532	3,059	6,252	44,643	9,258	31,919	3,466
Rate per 100,000 inhabitants...........................	X	523.2	4.9	28.0	161.1	329.2	2,350.5	487.4	1,680.6	182.5
Cambridge-Newton-Framingham, MA M.D.	1,512,246									
Includes Middlesex County										
Total area actually reporting	96.1	3,629	13	249	776	2,591	25,882	5,374	19,107	1,401
Estimated total..	100.0	3,813	14	262	810	2,727	27,064	5,666	19,920	1,478
Rate per 100,000 inhabitants...........................	X	252.1	0.9	17.3	53.6	180.3	1,789.7	374.7	1,317.2	97.7
Peabody, MA M.D.	747,688									
Includes Essex County										
Total area actually reporting	100.0	2,776	20	120	618	2,018	15,786	3,561	10,223	2,002
Rate per 100,000 inhabitants...........................	X	365.4	2.9	21.3	71.8	269.4	2,198.6	518.0	1,451.1	229.5
Rockingham County-Strafford County, NH M.D.	420,757									
Includes Rockingham and Strafford Counties										
Total area actually reporting	89.3	560	6	95	103	356	7,713	1,312	6,142	259
Estimated total..	100.0	609	6	104	112	387	8,436	1,439	6,712	285
Rate per 100,000 inhabitants...........................	X	144.7	1.4	24.7	26.6	92.0	2,005.0	342.0	1,595.2	67.7
Boulder, CO M.S.A......................................	299,698									
Includes Boulder County										
City of Boulder	99,081	275	2	35	35	203	2,491	467	1,899	125
Total area actually reporting	91.7	631	4	72	76	479	5,786	1,032	4,473	281
Estimated total..	100.0	697	4	81	87	525	6,465	1,134	5,000	331
Rate per 100,000 inhabitants...........................	X	232.6	1.3	27.0	29.0	175.2	2,157.2	378.4	1,668.3	110.4

X = Not applicable.

[2] The data collection methodology for the offense of forcible rape used by Chicago, Illinois, and the Minnesota state UCR Program (with the exception of Minneapolis and St. Paul, Minnesota) does not comply with national UCR Program guidelines. Consequently, its figures for forcible rape and violent crime (of which forcible rape is a part) are not published in this table.

Table II-6.   Crime, by Selected Metropolitan Statistical Area, 2011—*Continued*

(Number, percent, rate per 100,000 population.)

Area	Population	Violent crime	Murder and non-negligent man-slaughter	Forcible rape	Robbery	Aggravated assault	Property crime	Burglary	Larceny-theft	Motor vehicle theft
Bowling Green, KY M.S.A.	126,823									
Includes Edmonson and Warren Counties										
City of Bowling Green	58,468	167	3	31	60	73	2,716	462	2,127	127
Total area actually reporting	100.0	207	3	38	67	99	3,380	654	2,571	155
Rate per 100,000 inhabitants	X	163.2	2.4	30.0	52.8	78.1	2,665.1	515.7	2,027.2	122.2
Bremerton-Silverdale, WA M.S.A.	255,073									
Includes Kitsap County										
City of Bremerton	38,321	241	1	41	53	146	2,038	397	1,457	184
Total area actually reporting	100.0	810	3	122	117	568	7,477	2,029	4,870	578
Rate per 100,000 inhabitants	X	317.6	1.2	47.8	45.9	222.7	2,931.3	795.5	1,909.3	226.6
Bridgeport-Stamford-Norwalk, CT M.S.A.	901,031									
Includes Fairfield County										
City of Bridgeport	144,496	1,447	20	116	610	701	5,607	1,540	3,025	1,042
City of Stamford	122,870	389	6	32	190	161	1,987	282	1,498	207
City of Norwalk	85,761	326	3	15	90	218	1,914	297	1,443	174
City of Danbury	81,043	164	1	34	76	53	1,588	343	1,183	62
City of Stratford	51,479	146	1	9	59	77	1,541	309	1,104	128
Total area actually reporting	100.0	2,645	32	228	1,094	1,291	17,390	3,602	11,989	1,799
Rate per 100,000 inhabitants	X	293.6	3.6	25.3	121.4	143.3	1,930.0	399.8	1,330.6	199.7
Brownsville-Harlingen, TX M.S.A.	414,768									
Includes Cameron County										
City of Brownsville	178,706	500	1	37	109	353	8,187	1,009	7,015	163
City of Harlingen	66,214	337	4	18	65	250	4,078	880	3,099	99
Total area actually reporting	100.0	1,217	8	92	233	884	17,055	3,189	13,416	450
Rate per 100,000 inhabitants	X	293.4	1.9	22.2	56.2	213.1	4,111.9	768.9	3,234.6	108.5
Brunswick, GA M.S.A.	113,849									
Includes Brantley, Glynn, and McIntosh Counties										
City of Brunswick	15,586	251	2	5	68	176	1,261	366	850	45
Total area actually reporting	98.2	569	7	30	149	383	5,190	1,406	3,620	164
Estimated total	100.0	575	7	30	151	387	5,269	1,422	3,678	169
Rate per 100,000 inhabitants	X	505.1	6.1	26.4	132.6	339.9	4,628.1	1,249.0	3,230.6	148.4
Buffalo-Niagara Falls, NY M.S.A.	1,140,613									
Includes Erie and Niagara Counties										
City of Buffalo	262,484	3,250	36	121	1,459	1,634	14,305	4,473	8,711	1,121
City of Cheektowaga Town	79,194	175	2	10	80	83	2,753	362	2,294	97
City of Tonawanda	15,198	26	0	1	2	23	390	41	338	11
City of Niagara Falls	50,419	581	4	31	174	372	2,941	849	1,904	188
Total area actually reporting	100.0	5,010	45	258	1,946	2,761	33,597	8,075	23,609	1,913
Rate per 100,000 inhabitants	X	439.2	3.9	22.6	170.6	242.1	2,945.5	708.0	2,069.9	167.7
Burlington, NC M.S.A.	153,047									
Includes Alamance County										
City of Burlington	50,597	405	2	14	104	285	3,669	880	2,668	121
Total area actually reporting	100.0	644	3	28	135	478	6,003	1,656	4,122	225
Rate per 100,000 inhabitants	X	420.8	2.0	18.3	88.2	312.3	3,922.3	1,082.0	2,693.3	147.0
Canton-Massillon, OH M.S.A.	404,718									
Includes Carroll and Stark Counties										
City of Canton	73,060	810	12	57	438	303	4,787	1,854	2,683	250
City of Massillon	32,173	87	0	15	37	35	1,209	348	832	29
Total area actually reporting	91.6	1,159	14	119	559	467	11,584	3,589	7,492	503
Estimated total	100.0	1,211	15	127	579	490	12,522	3,782	8,203	537
Rate per 100,000 inhabitants	X	299.2	3.7	31.4	143.1	121.1	3,094.0	934.5	2,026.8	132.7
Cape Coral-Fort Myers, FL M.S.A.	627,187									
Includes Lee County										
City of Cape Coral	156,408	235	3	14	58	160	3,990	1,023	2,855	112
City of Fort Myers	63,147	770	20	32	170	548	3,018	667	2,153	198
Total area actually reporting	100.0	2,213	38	107	602	1,466	17,498	5,326	11,375	797
Rate per 100,000 inhabitants	X	352.8	6.1	17.1	96.0	233.7	2,789.9	849.2	1,813.7	127.1

X = Not applicable.

Table II-6. Crime, by Selected Metropolitan Statistical Area, 2011—*Continued*

(Number, percent, rate per 100,000 population.)

Area	Population	Violent crime	Murder and non-negligent man-slaughter	Forcible rape	Robbery	Aggravated assault	Property crime	Burglary	Larceny-theft	Motor vehicle theft
Cape Girardeau-Jackson, MO-IL M.S.A.	96,620									
Includes Alexander County, IL, and Bollinger and										
Cape Girardeau Counties, MO										
City of Cape Girardeau, MO	38,079	252	1	15	94	142	2,473	394	2,017	62
City of Jackson, MO	13,808	24	0	1	1	22	340	62	266	12
Total area actually reporting	100.0	448	1	35	107	305	3,563	717	2,737	109
Rate per 100,000 inhabitants	X	463.7	1.0	36.2	110.7	315.7	3,687.6	742.1	2,832.7	112.8
Carson City, NV M.S.A.	55,740									
Includes Carson City										
Total area actually reporting	100.0	148	4	0	16	128	1,275	316	890	69
Rate per 100,000 inhabitants	X	265.5	7.2	0.0	28.7	229.6	2,287.4	566.9	1,596.7	123.8
Casper, WY M.S.A.	76,057									
Includes Natrona County										
City of Casper	55,761	103	1	10	22	70	2,057	287	1,693	77
Total area actually reporting	100.0	188	2	16	23	147	2,438	404	1,936	98
Rate per 100,000 inhabitants	X	247.2	2.6	21.0	30.2	193.3	3,205.5	531.2	2,545.5	128.9
Cedar Rapids, IA M.S.A.	259,291									
Includes Benton, Jones, and Linn Counties										
City of Cedar Rapids	126,988	358	2	41	86	229	4,879	1,099	3,566	214
Total area actually reporting	99.0	473	2	62	87	322	6,284	1,508	4,499	277
Estimated total	100.0	478	2	63	87	326	6,332	1,517	4,536	279
Rate per 100,000 inhabitants	X	184.3	0.8	24.3	33.6	125.7	2,442.0	585.1	1,749.4	107.6
Champaign-Urbana, IL M.S.A.	232,588									
Includes Champaign, Ford, and Piatt Counties										
City of Champaign	81,299	732	1	56	105	570	2,281	586	1,599	96
City of Urbana	41,374	197	1	35	74	87	1,464	382	1,055	27
Total area actually reporting	93.1	1,285	6	125	209	945	5,457	1,457	3,832	168
Estimated total	100.0	1,321	6	129	219	967	5,812	1,525	4,103	184
Rate per 100,000 inhabitants	X	568.0	2.6	55.5	94.2	415.8	2,498.8	655.7	1,764.1	79.1
Charleston, WV M.S.A.	304,676									
Includes Boone, Clay, Kanawha, Lincoln, and										
Putnam Counties										
City of Charleston	51,466	510	5	23	120	362	3,009	635	2,234	140
Total area actually reporting	85.3	1,169	17	76	189	887	7,988	1,879	5,592	517
Estimated total	100.0	1,286	19	84	202	981	8,970	2,118	6,281	571
Rate per 100,000 inhabitants	X	422.1	6.2	27.6	66.3	322.0	2,944.1	695.2	2,061.5	187.4
Charlotte-Gastonia-Rock Hill, NC-SC M.S.A.	1,780,095									
Includes Anson, Cabarrus, Gaston, Mecklenburg,										
and Union Counties, NC and York County, SC										
City of Charlotte-Mecklenburg, NC	789,478	4,787	56	218	1,612	2,901	32,008	8,536	21,371	2,101
City of Gastonia, NC	72,651	466	4	37	171	254	4,363	951	3,198	214
City of Rock Hill, SC	66,924	410	4	46	71	289	2,996	537	2,298	161
City of Concord, NC	80,069	93	2	8	37	46	3,111	452	2,528	131
Total area actually reporting	97.7	7,501	85	429	2,180	4,807	59,443	14,953	41,077	3,413
Estimated total	100.0	7,621	86	438	2,211	4,886	61,156	15,339	42,346	3,471
Rate per 100,000 inhabitants	X	428.1	4.8	24.6	124.2	274.5	3,435.5	861.7	2,378.9	195.0
Charlottesville, VA M.S.A.	203,966									
Includes Albemarle, Fluvanna, Greene, and Nelson										
Counties and Charlottesville City										
City of Charlottesville	43,994	183	1	27	59	96	1,467	114	1,252	101
Total area actually reporting	100.0	337	6	55	86	190	4,082	503	3,362	217
Rate per 100,000 inhabitants	X	165.2	2.9	27.0	42.2	93.2	2,001.3	246.6	1,648.3	106.4
Chattanooga, TN-GA M.S.A.	533,526									
Includes Catoosa, Dade, and Walker Counties, GA										
and Hamilton, Marion, and Sequatchie Counties, TN										
City of Chattanooga, TN	169,187	1,460	24	36	385	1,015	10,635	2,503	7,338	794
Total area actually reporting	100.0	2,673	34	93	502	2,044	19,799	4,910	13,471	1,418
Rate per 100,000 inhabitants	X	501.0	6.4	17.4	94.1	383.1	3,711.0	920.3	2,524.9	265.8
Cheyenne, WY M.S.A.	92,473									
Includes Laramie County										
City of Cheyenne	59,944	147	2	26	25	94	2,049	255	1,734	60
Total area actually reporting	100.0	226	2	39	30	155	2,559	394	2,068	97
Rate per 100,000 inhabitants	X	244.4	2.2	42.2	32.4	167.6	2,767.3	426.1	2,236.3	104.9

X = Not applicable.

Table II-6.   Crime, by Selected Metropolitan Statistical Area, 2011—*Continued*

(Number, percent, rate per 100,000 population.)

Area	Population	Violent crime	Murder and non-negligent man-slaughter	Forcible rape	Robbery	Aggravated assault	Property crime	Burglary	Larceny-theft	Motor vehicle theft
Chicago-Joliet-Naperville, IL-IN-WI M.S.A.[2]	9,491,301									
Includes the Metropolitan Divisions of Chicago-Joilet-Naperville, IL, Gary, IN, and Lake County-Kenosha County, IL-WI										
City of Chicago, IL[2]	2,703,713		431		13,975	12,408	118,239	26,420	72,373	19,446
City of Joliet, IL	147,877	517	8	30	87	392	3,861	939	2,751	171
City of Naperville, IL	142,280	112	2	4	24	82	2,110	300	1,768	42
City of Elgin, IL	108,514	287	5	78	82	122	2,068	555	1,425	88
City of Gary, IN	80,704	639	30	47	328	234	5,338	2,618	1,926	794
City of Evanston, IL	74,710	178	3	4	76	95	2,126	403	1,669	54
City of Arlington Heights, IL	75,327	48	2	5	17	24	1,083	170	892	21
City of Schaumburg, IL	74,450	63	0	14	23	26	2,358	238	2,056	64
City of Skokie, IL	64,979	141	2	13	39	87	1,723	325	1,323	75
City of Des Plaines, IL	58,540	70	1	6	14	49	795	137	619	39
City of Hoffman Estates, IL	52,051	68	0	15	16	37	682	119	538	25
Total area actually reporting	95.7		599		17,850	18,932	256,093	54,466	174,893	26,734
Estimated total	100.0		609		18,100	19,478	264,951	56,203	181,610	27,138
Rate per 100,000 inhabitants	X		6.4		190.7	205.2	2,791.5	592.2	1,913.4	285.9
Chicago-Joilet-Naperville, IL M.D.[2]	7,906,889									
Includes Cook, DeKalb, DuPage, Grundy, Kane, Kendall, McHenry, and Will Counties										
Total area actually reporting	96.3		533		16,679	17,118	216,005	45,497	146,677	23,831
Estimated total	100.0		540		16,870	17,524	222,513	46,751	151,642	24,120
Rate per 100,000 inhabitants	X		6.8		213.4	221.6	2,814.2	591.3	1,917.8	305.1
Gary, IN M.D.	711,687									
Includes Jasper, Lake, Newton, and Porter Counties										
Total area actually reporting	95.5	2,204	62	178	816	1,148	24,226	6,062	15,723	2,441
Estimated total	100.0	2,242	63	182	822	1,175	24,767	6,196	16,095	2,476
Rate per 100,000 inhabitants	X	315.0	8.9	25.6	115.5	165.1	3,480.0	870.6	2,261.5	347.9
Lake County-Kenosha County, IL-WI M.D.	872,725									
Includes Lake County, IL, and Kenosha County, WI										
Total area actually reporting	90.6	1,193	4	168	355	666	15,862	2,907	12,493	462
Estimated total	100.0	1,381	6	188	408	779	17,671	3,256	13,873	542
Rate per 100,000 inhabitants	X	158.2	0.7	21.5	46.8	89.3	2,024.8	373.1	1,589.6	62.1
Chico, CA M.S.A.	222,586									
Includes Butte County										
City of Chico	87,200	245	5	37	92	111	2,115	487	1,337	291
Total area actually reporting	100.0	576	8	75	158	335	5,375	1,564	3,196	615
Rate per 100,000 inhabitants	X	258.8	3.6	33.7	71.0	150.5	2,414.8	702.6	1,435.8	276.3
Cincinnati-Middletown, OH-KY-IN M.S.A.	2,134,687									
Includes Dearborn, Franklin, and Ohio Counties, IN; Boone, Bracken, Campbell, Gallatin, Grant, Kenton, and Pendleton Counties, KY; and Brown, Butler, Clermont, Hamilton, and Warren Counties, OH										
City of Cincinnati, OH	297,160	3,067	61	183	1,773	1,050	20,462	6,674	12,512	1,276
City of Middletown, OH	48,730	364	4	39	95	226	4,369	1,309	2,949	111
Total area actually reporting	98.8	6,249	99	653	2,878	2,619	74,065	18,797	52,177	3,091
Estimated total	100.0	6,287	99	659	2,891	2,638	74,691	18,934	52,640	3,117
Rate per 100,000 inhabitants	X	294.5	4.6	30.9	135.4	123.6	3,498.9	887.0	2,465.9	146.0
Clarksville, TN-KY M.S.A.	276,234									
Includes Christian and Trigg Counties, KY and Montgomery and Stewart Counties, TN										
City of Clarksville, TN	134,128	883	8	61	128	686	4,217	1,333	2,666	218
Total area actually reporting	99.4	1,199	11	108	197	883	7,792	2,391	4,994	407
Estimated total	100.0	1,204	11	109	199	885	7,851	2,405	5,036	410
Rate per 100,000 inhabitants	X	435.9	4.0	39.5	72.0	320.4	2,842.2	870.6	1,823.1	148.
Cleveland, TN M.S.A.	116,833									
Includes Bradley and Polk Counties										
City of Cleveland	41,657	437	2	21	50	364	2,260	437	1,735	88
Total area actually reporting	100.0	733	7	33	56	637	3,555	799	2,554	202
Rate per 100,000 inhabitants	X	627.4	6.0	28.2	47.9	545.2	3,042.8	683.9	2,186.0	172.9

X = Not applicable.

[2] The data collection methodology for the offense of forcible rape used by Chicago, Illinois, and the Minnesota state UCR Program (with the exception of Minneapolis and St. Paul, Minnesota) does not comply with national UCR Program guidelines. Consequently, its figures for forcible rape and violent crime (of which forcible rape is a part) are not published in this table.

Table II-6. Crime, by Selected Metropolitan Statistical Area, 2011—*Continued*

(Number, percent, rate per 100,000 population.)

Area	Population	Violent crime	Murder and non-negligent man-slaughter	Forcible rape	Robbery	Aggravated assault	Property crime	Burglary	Larceny-theft	Motor vehicle theft
Cleveland-Elyria-Mentor, OH M.S.A.	2,078,757									
Includes Cuyahoga, Geauga, Lake, Lorain, and Medina Counties										
City of Cleveland	397,106	5,426	74	354	3,156	1,842	25,323	10,706	10,524	4,093
City of Elyria	54,573	192	2	18	86	86	2,252	703	1,478	71
City of Mentor	47,194	43	0	9	24	10	1,127	159	910	58
Total area actually reporting	88.7	8,062	96	626	4,062	3,278	55,304	18,037	31,594	5,673
Estimated total	100.0	8,411	99	677	4,194	3,441	61,589	19,368	36,321	5,900
Rate per 100,000 inhabitants	X	404.6	4.8	32.6	201.8	165.5	2,962.8	931.7	1,747.2	283.8
College Station-Bryan, TX M.S.A.	233,472									
Includes Brazos, Burleson, and Robertson Counties										
City of College Station	95,832	288	1	31	32	224	2,993	651	2,289	53
City of Bryan	77,804	425	2	22	78	323	2,906	681	2,130	95
Total area actually reporting	100.0	838	5	72	122	639	7,463	1,676	5,576	211
Rate per 100,000 inhabitants	X	358.9	2.1	30.8	52.3	273.7	3,196.5	717.9	2,388.3	90.4
Colorado Springs, CO M.S.A.	656,862									
Includes El Paso and Teller Counties										
City of Colorado Springs	423,680	1,865	26	319	449	1,071	15,866	3,323	11,375	1,168
Total area actually reporting	99.9	2,448	31	395	478	1,544	19,137	4,141	13,606	1,390
Estimated total	100.0	2,449	31	395	478	1,545	19,159	4,144	13,623	1,392
Rate per 100,000 inhabitants	X	372.8	4.7	60.1	72.8	235.2	2,916.7	630.9	2,074.0	211.9
Columbia, MO M.S.A.	173,414									
Includes Boone and Howard Counties										
City of Columbia	108,894	582	2	37	166	377	4,263	798	3,323	142
Total area actually reporting	100.0	729	4	45	182	498	5,570	1,045	4,324	201
Rate per 100,000 inhabitants	X	420.4	2.3	25.9	105.0	287.2	3,212.0	602.6	2,493.5	115.9
Columbus, GA-AL M.S.A.[1]	298,305									
Includes Russell County, AL,[1] and Chattahoochee, Harris, Marion, and Muscogee Counties, GA										
City of Columbus, GA	192,385	933	15	40	413	465	12,450	3,342	8,059	1,049
Total area actually reporting	97.2	1,195	24	68	456	647	15,488	4,210	9,992	1,286
Estimated total	100.0	1,220	24	69	465	662	15,752	4,285	10,158	1,309
Rate per 100,000 inhabitants	X	409.0	8.0	23.1	155.9	221.9	5,280.5	1,436.4	3,405.2	438.8
Columbus, IN M.S.A.	77,186									
Includes Bartholomew County										
City of Columbus	44,286	84	1	7	20	56	2,597	303	2,087	207
Total area actually reporting	99.5	125	1	13	24	87	3,200	417	2,514	269
Estimated total	100.0	126	1	13	24	88	3,213	419	2,524	270
Rate per 100,000 inhabitants	X	163.2	1.3	16.8	31.1	114.0	4,162.7	542.8	3,270.0	349.8
Columbus, OH M.S.A.	1,837,882									
Includes Delaware, Fairfield, Franklin, Licking, Madison, Morrow, Pickaway, and Union Counties										
City of Columbus	787,609	5,185	87	565	3,244	1,289	49,043	15,169	30,259	3,615
Total area actually reporting	97.3	6,587	103	811	3,738	1,935	75,410	21,121	49,996	4,293
Estimated total	100.0	6,664	104	822	3,768	1,970	76,800	21,407	51,050	4,343
Rate per 100,000 inhabitants	X	362.6	5.7	44.7	205.0	107.2	4,178.7	1,164.8	2,777.7	236.3
Corpus Christi, TX M.S.A.	437,195									
Includes Aransas, Nueces, and San Patricio Counties										
City of Corpus Christi	311,637	1,987	12	194	370	1,411	14,897	2,668	11,762	467
Total area actually reporting	100.0	2,346	18	261	398	1,669	18,593	3,623	14,374	596
Rate per 100,000 inhabitants	X	536.6	4.1	59.7	91.0	381.8	4,252.8	828.7	3,287.8	136.3
Corvallis, OR M.S.A.	86,490									
Includes Benton County										
City of Corvallis	55,042	71	0	13	15	43	1,753	287	1,421	45
Total area actually reporting	100.0	97	3	18	16	60	2,229	397	1,756	76
Rate per 100,000 inhabitants	X	112.2	3.5	20.8	18.5	69.4	2,577.2	459.0	2,030.3	87.9

X = Not applicable.

[1] Because of changes in the state/local agency's reporting practices, figures are not comparable to previous years' data.

Table II-6.　Crime, by Selected Metropolitan Statistical Area, 2011—*Continued*

(Number, percent, rate per 100,000 population.)

Area	Population	Violent crime	Murder and non-negligent man-slaughter	Forcible rape	Robbery	Aggravated assault	Property crime	Burglary	Larceny-theft	Motor vehicle theft
Crestview-Fort Walton Beach-Destin, FL M.S.A...................	183,286									
Includes Okaloosa County										
City of Crestview	21,264	106	0	13	18	75	826	198	605	23
City of Fort Walton Beach	19,773	92	3	7	22	60	853	121	689	43
Total area actually reporting	100.0	782	4	60	113	605	5,251	997	4,037	217
Rate per 100,000 inhabitants...........	X	426.7	2.2	32.7	61.7	330.1	2,864.9	544.0	2,202.6	118.4
Cumberland, MD-WV M.S.A.[1]..............	104,047									
Includes Allegany County, MD,[1] and Mineral County, WV										
City of Cumberland, MD	21,057	153	0	16	42	95	1,425	319	1,081	25
Total area actually reporting	98.5	333	6	35	69	223	2,976	763	2,157	56
Estimated total........................	100.0	338	6	35	70	227	3,023	771	2,194	58
Rate per 100,000 inhabitants...........	X	324.9	5.8	33.6	67.3	218.2	2,905.4	741.0	2,108.7	55.7
Dallas-Fort Worth-Arlington, TX M.S.A............................	6,505,848									
Includes the Metropolitan Divisions of Dallas-Plano-Irving and Fort Worth-Arlington										
City of Dallas............................	1,223,021	8,330	133	428	4,066	3,703	61,859	18,727	35,148	7,984
City of Fort Worth	756,803	4,569	48	350	1,267	2,904	35,117	10,058	22,617	2,442
City of Arlington	373,128	1,874	22	136	540	1,176	17,208	4,388	11,757	1,063
City of Plano	265,309	429	5	40	142	242	6,764	1,193	5,182	389
City of Irving	220,841	514	8	25	151	330	6,794	1,603	4,590	601
City of Carrollton	121,603	206	3	4	93	106	3,322	896	2,152	274
City of Denton	115,769	311	2	53	55	201	3,315	565	2,632	118
City of McKinney	133,876	241	1	33	44	163	2,826	626	2,085	115
City of Richardson......................	101,311	173	0	9	76	88	2,808	680	1,934	194
Total area actually reporting	99.9	23,309	294	1,753	8,088	13,174	227,515	60,017	148,295	19,203
Estimated total........................	100.0	23,316	294	1,753	8,090	13,179	227,610	60,036	148,365	19,209
Rate per 100,000 inhabitants...........	X	358.4	4.5	26.9	124.3	202.6	3,498.5	922.8	2,280.5	295.3
Dallas-Plano-Irving, TX M.D.	4,324,880									
Includes Collin, Dallas, Delta, Denton, Ellis, Hunt, Kaufman, and Rockwall Counties										
Total area actually reporting	99.9	14,559	200	1,018	5,864	7,477	146,675	38,842	93,768	14,065
Estimated total........................	100.0	14,562	200	1,018	5,865	7,479	146,720	38,851	93,801	14,068
Rate per 100,000 inhabitants...........	X	336.7	4.6	23.5	135.6	172.9	3,392.5	898.3	2,168.9	325.3
Fort Worth-Arlington, TX M.D...........	2,180,968									
Includes Johnson, Parker, Tarrant, and Wise Counties										
Total area actually reporting	99.9	8,750	94	735	2,224	5,697	80,840	21,175	54,527	5,138
Estimated total........................	100.0	8,754	94	735	2,225	5,700	80,890	21,185	54,564	5,141
Rate per 100,000 inhabitants...........	X	401.4	4.3	33.7	102.0	261.4	3,708.9	971.4	2,501.8	235.7
Dalton, GA M.S.A............................	144,100									
Includes Murray and Whitfield Counties										
City of Dalton	33,564	90	0	9	28	53	1,304	254	996	54
Total area actually reporting	98.3	314	2	30	37	245	4,189	955	2,976	258
Estimated total........................	100.0	322	2	30	40	250	4,286	974	3,047	265
Rate per 100,000 inhabitants...........	X	223.5	1.4	20.8	27.8	173.5	2,974.3	675.9	2,114.5	183.9
Danville, IL M.S.A.[2].........................	81,871									
Includes Vermilion County[2]										
City of Danville[2]......................	33,126	335	3	50	74	208	2,206	793	1,366	47
Total area actually reporting	98.4	479	3	78	83	315	3,280	1,147	2,032	101
Estimated total........................	100.0	482	3	78	84	317	3,309	1,153	2,054	102
Rate per 100,000 inhabitants...........	X	588.7	3.7	95.3	102.6	387.2	4,041.7	1,408.3	2,508.8	124.6
Danville, VA M.S.A.........................	107,834									
Includes Pittsylvania County and Danville City										
City of Danville.........................	43,569	166	7	28	64	67	2,080	464	1,546	70
Total area actually reporting	100.0	214	11	38	74	91	2,800	714	1,970	116
Rate per 100,000 inhabitants...........	X	198.5	10.2	35.2	68.6	84.4	2,596.6	662.1	1,826.9	107.6
Davenport-Moline-Rock Island, IA-IL M.S.A.[1]....................	381,200									
Includes Henry, Mercer, and Rock Island Counties, IL, and Scott County, IA										
City of Davenport, IA[1]..............	100,207	652	5	53	113	481	4,908	1,140	3,529	239
City of Moline, IL.......................	43,614	211	0	34	18	159	1,587	277	1,242	68
City of Rock Island, IL.................	39,135	290	2	14	52	222	1,235	256	894	85
Total area actually reporting	95.6	1,548	8	171	199	1,170	10,855	2,279	8,081	495
Estimated total........................	100.0	1,586	8	175	210	1,193	11,228	2,351	8,365	512
Rate per 100,000 inhabitants...........	X	416.1	2.1	45.9	55.1	313.0	2,945.4	616.7	2,194.4	134.3

X = Not applicable.

[1] Because of changes in the state/local agency's reporting practices, figures are not comparable to previous years' data.

[2] The data collection methodology for the offense of forcible rape used by Chicago, Illinois, and the Minnesota state UCR Program (with the exception of Minneapolis and St. Paul, Minnesota) does not comply with national UCR Program guidelines. Consequently, its figures for forcible rape and violent crime (of which forcible rape is a part) are not published in this table.

Table II-6. Crime, by Selected Metropolitan Statistical Area, 2011—*Continued*

(Number, percent, rate per 100,000 population.)

Area	Population	Violent crime	Murder and non-negligent man-slaughter	Forcible rape	Robbery	Aggravated assault	Property crime	Burglary	Larceny-theft	Motor vehicle theft
Dayton, OH M.S.A.	842,118									
Includes Greene, Miami, Montgomery, and Preble Counties										
City of Dayton	141,631	1,355	33	98	638	586	8,323	3,121	4,569	633
Total area actually reporting	98.7	2,426	51	289	1,065	1,021	28,652	7,960	19,200	1,492
Estimated total	100.0	2,443	51	291	1,072	1,029	28,957	8,023	19,431	1,503
Rate per 100,000 inhabitants	X	290.1	6.1	34.6	127.3	122.2	3,438.6	952.7	2,307.4	178.5
Decatur, AL M.S.A.[1]	154,569									
Includes Lawrence and Morgan Counties[1]										
City of Decatur[1]	55,951	197	3	19	56	119	2,109	815	1,131	163
Total area actually reporting	100.0	342	3	37	68	234	3,952	1,464	2,217	271
Rate per 100,000 inhabitants	X	221.3	1.9	23.9	44.0	151.4	2,556.8	947.1	1,434.3	175.3
Decatur, IL M.S.A.	111,101									
Includes Macon County										
City of Decatur	76,351	481	10	14	124	333	2,835	1,140	1,581	114
Total area actually reporting	97.3	560	10	32	131	387	3,308	1,299	1,883	126
Estimated total	100.0	567	10	33	133	391	3,374	1,312	1,933	129
Rate per 100,000 inhabitants	X	510.3	9.0	29.7	119.7	351.9	3,036.9	1,180.9	1,739.9	116.1
Deltona-Daytona Beach-Ormond Beach, FL M.S.A.	501,334									
Includes Volusia County										
City of Daytona Beach	61,836	835	3	37	236	559	4,268	994	2,899	375
City of Ormond Beach	38,657	267	1	7	23	236	1,397	249	1,090	58
Total area actually reporting	99.6	2,503	22	117	507	1,857	18,225	4,676	12,527	1,022
Estimated total	100.0	2,511	22	117	510	1,862	18,295	4,692	12,577	1,026
Rate per 100,000 inhabitants	X	500.9	4.4	23.3	101.7	371.4	3,649.3	935.9	2,508.7	204.7
Denver-Aurora-Broomfield, CO M.S.A.	2,587,784									
Includes Adams, Arapahoe, Broomfield, Clear Creek, Denver, Douglas, Elbert, Gilpin, Jefferson, and Park Counties										
City of Denver	610,612	3,708	34	396	1,143	2,135	22,495	4,868	14,040	3,587
City of Aurora	330,740	1,448	9	183	504	752	9,875	2,144	6,861	870
City of Broomfield	56,862	31	1	6	7	17	1,101	81	974	46
Total area actually reporting	99.1	9,135	71	1,281	2,265	5,518	70,402	13,319	49,591	7,492
Estimated total	100.0	9,181	71	1,290	2,270	5,550	70,741	13,399	49,825	7,517
Rate per 100,000 inhabitants	X	354.8	2.7	49.8	87.7	214.5	2,733.7	517.8	1,925.4	290.5
Des Moines-West Des Moines, IA M.S.A.	572,618									
Includes Dallas, Guthrie, Madison, Polk, and Warren Counties										
City of Des Moines	204,498	1,069	8	103	216	742	10,727	2,493	7,400	834
City of West Des Moines	56,905	115	1	26	13	75	1,824	225	1,564	35
Total area actually reporting	100.0	1,590	9	177	254	1,150	17,711	3,848	12,748	1,115
Rate per 100,000 inhabitants	X	277.7	1.6	30.9	44.4	200.8	3,093.0	672.0	2,226.3	194.7
Detroit-Warren-Livonia, MI M.S.A.[1]	4,293,012									
Includes the Metropolitan Divisions of Detroit-Livonia-Dearborn and Warren-Troy-Farmington Hills										
City of Detroit	713,239	15,245	344	427	4,962	9,512	43,818	15,994	16,456	11,368
City of Warren	133,955	719	6	73	156	484	3,853	1,070	1,975	808
City of Livonia	96,869	168	1	19	40	108	2,108	308	1,589	211
City of Dearborn	98,079	359	3	22	104	230	3,757	612	2,705	440
City of Troy	80,919	72	0	17	14	41	1,780	236	1,402	142
City of Farmington Hills	79,680	101	2	11	28	60	1,266	267	895	104
City of Southfield	71,685	377	4	33	116	224	2,681	710	1,592	379
City of Pontiac	63,083	320	0	26	76	218	2,497	671	1,598	228
City of Taylor	55,182	43	3	5	8	27	964	81	847	36
City of Novi	99.2	24,540	416	1,377	7,008	15,739	122,715	33,779	69,635	19,301
Total area actually reporting	100.0	24,633	416	1,387	7,029	15,801	123,574	33,968	70,238	19,368
Estimated total	X	573.8	9.7	32.3	163.7	368.1	2,878.5	791.2	1,636.1	451.2
Rate per 100,000 inhabitants	1,819,213									
Detroit-Livonia-Dearborn, MI M.D.										
Includes Wayne County	99.5	19,117	370	770	5,915	12,062	74,554	23,000	36,519	15,035
Total area actually reporting	100.0	19,145	370	773	5,921	12,081	74,812	23,057	36,700	15,055
Rate per 100,000 inhabitants	X	1,052.4	20.3	42.5	325.5	664.1	4,112.3	1,267.4	2,017.4	827.6

X = Not applicable.

[1] Because of changes in the state/local agency's reporting practices, figures are not comparable to previous years' data.

Table II-6.   Crime, by Selected Metropolitan Statistical Area, 2011—*Continued*

(Number, percent, rate per 100,000 population.)

Area	Population	Violent crime	Murder and non-negligent man-slaughter	Forcible rape	Robbery	Aggravated assault	Property crime	Burglary	Larceny-theft	Motor vehicle theft
Warren-Troy-Farmington Hills, MI M.D.[1]	2,473,799									
Includes Lapeer, Livingston, Macomb, Oakland[1], and St. Clair Counties										
Total area actually reporting	99.1	5,423	46	607	1,093	3,677	48,161	10,779	33,116	4,266
Estimated total	100.0	5,488	46	614	1,108	3,720	48,762	10,911	33,538	4,313
Rate per 100,000 inhabitants	X	221.8	1.9	24.8	44.8	150.4	1,971.1	441.1	1,355.7	174.3
Dothan, AL M.S.A.	146,340									
Includes Geneva, Henry, and Houston Counties										
City of Dothan	64,920	339	2	22	105	210	2,699	599	1,986	114
Total area actually reporting	98.5	581	5	43	122	411	4,310	1,055	3,019	236
Estimated total	100.0	590	5	44	124	417	4,399	1,078	3,079	242
Rate per 100,000 inhabitants	X	403.2	3.4	30.1	84.7	285.0	3,006.0	736.6	2,104.0	165.4
Dover, DE M.S.A.	163,973									
Includes Kent County										
City of Dover	36,416	313	5	15	73	220	2,243	132	2,030	81
Total area actually reporting	100.0	1,020	7	85	193	735	5,992	1,158	4,641	193
Rate per 100,000 inhabitants	X	622.1	4.3	51.8	117.7	448.2	3,654.3	706.2	2,830.3	117.7
Dubuque, IA M.S.A.	94,143									
Includes Dubuque County										
City of Dubuque	57,939	135	1	20	32	82	1,702	416	1,239	47
Total area actually reporting	100.0	146	1	21	33	91	1,911	499	1,353	59
Rate per 100,000 inhabitants	X	155.1	1.1	22.3	35.1	96.7	2,029.9	530.0	1,437.2	62.7
Duluth, MN-WI M.S.A.[2]	281,781									
Includes Carlton and St. Louis Counties, MN[3] and Douglas County, WI										
City of Duluth, MN[2]	86,931		0		82	164	4,346	756	3,424	166
Total area actually reporting	100.0		3		127	327	9,228	1,842	7,007	379
Rate per 100,000 inhabitants	X		1.1		45.1	116.0	3,274.9	653.7	2,486.7	134.5
Durham-Chapel Hill, NC M.S.A.	510,752									
Includes Chatham, Durham, Orange, and Person Counties										
City of Durham	231,225	1,707	27	64	699	917	11,270	3,874	6,768	628
City of Chapel Hill	57,959	106	1	7	38	60	1,523	484	985	54
Total area actually reporting	100.0	2,253	37	117	824	1,275	19,386	6,576	11,889	921
Rate per 100,000 inhabitants	X	441.1	7.2	22.9	161.3	249.6	3,795.6	1,287.5	2,327.7	180.3
Eau Claire, WI M.S.A.	161,853									
Includes Chippewa and Eau Claire Counties										
City of Eau Claire	66,170	139	0	20	21	98	1,959	378	1,531	50
Total area actually reporting	100.0	244	0	40	31	173	3,410	774	2,546	90
Rate per 100,000 inhabitants	X	150.8	0.0	24.7	19.2	106.9	2,106.9	478.2	1,573.0	55.6
El Centro, CA M.S.A.	176,580									
Includes Imperial County										
City of El Centro	43,099	165	2	11	36	116	2,284	695	1,424	165
Total area actually reporting	95.6	453	3	30	83	337	5,703	1,940	3,035	728
Estimated total	100.0	478	3	31	91	353	5,899	1,987	3,158	754
Rate per 100,000 inhabitants	X	270.7	1.7	17.6	51.5	199.9	3,340.7	1,125.3	1,788.4	427.0
Elizabethtown, KY M.S.A.	120,563									
Includes Hardin and Larue Counties										
City of Elizabethtown	28,728	43	2	17	18	6	1,022	131	853	38
Total area actually reporting	100.0	117	2	37	46	32	1,875	342	1,455	78
Rate per 100,000 inhabitants	X	97.0	1.7	30.7	38.2	26.5	1,555.2	283.7	1,206.8	64.7
Elmira, NY M.S.A.	89,229									
Includes Chemung County										
City of Elmira	29,331	70	1	2	25	42	1,141	255	871	15
Total area actually reporting	100.0	177	1	13	28	135	2,101	407	1,653	41
Rate per 100,000 inhabitants	X	198.4	1.1	14.6	31.4	151.3	2,354.6	456.1	1,852.5	45.9
El Paso, TX M.S.A.	817,494									
Includes El Paso County										
City of El Paso	662,780	2,858	16	217	464	2,161	16,312	1,859	12,997	1,456
Total area actually reporting	100.0	3,325	18	241	502	2,564	19,492	2,505	15,277	1,710
Rate per 100,000 inhabitants	X	406.7	2.2	29.5	61.4	313.6	2,384.4	306.4	1,868.8	209.2

X = Not applicable.

[1] Because of changes in the state/local agency's reporting practices, figures are not comparable to previous years' data.

[2] The data collection methodology for the offense of forcible rape used by Chicago, Illinois, and the Minnesota state UCR Program (with the exception of Minneapolis and St. Paul, Minnesota) does not comply with national UCR Program guidelines. Consequently, its figures for forcible rape and violent crime (of which forcible rape is a part) are not published in this table.

[3] The FBI determined that the agency did not follow national Uniform Crime Reporting (UCR) Program guidelines for reporting an offense. Consequently, this figure is not included in this table.

Table II-6.   Crime, by Selected Metropolitan Statistical Area, 2011—*Continued*

(Number, percent, rate per 100,000 population.)

Area	Population	Violent crime	Murder and non-negligent man-slaughter	Forcible rape	Robbery	Aggravated assault	Property crime	Burglary	Larceny-theft	Motor vehicle theft
Erie, PA M.S.A.	281,461									
Includes Erie County										
City of Erie	102,111	431	6	77	150	198	3,738	1,233	2,404	101
Total area actually reporting	100.0	692	8	129	191	364	7,580	1,997	5,378	205
Rate per 100,000 inhabitants	X	245.9	2.8	45.8	67.9	129.3	2,693.1	709.5	1,910.7	72.8
Eugene-Springfield, OR M.S.A.	355,459									
Includes Lane County										
City of Eugene	157,848	460	0	78	177	205	7,878	1,440	5,862	576
City of Springfield	60,035	149	1	15	46	87	2,437	309	1,979	149
Total area actually reporting	100.0	1,001	3	118	254	626	12,639	2,493	9,217	929
Rate per 100,000 inhabitants	X	281.6	0.8	33.2	71.5	176.1	3,555.7	701.3	2,593.0	261.4
Evansville, IN-KY M.S.A.	360,616									
Includes Gibson, Posey, Vanderburgh, and Warrick Counties, IN and Henderson and Webster Counties, KY										
City of Evansville, IN	118,029	491	3	56	154	278	5,456	1,074	4,151	231
Total area actually reporting	76.5	823	5	83	176	559	8,646	1,776	6,528	342
Estimated total	100.0	912	7	94	189	622	9,933	2,127	7,379	427
Rate per 100,000 inhabitants	X	252.9	1.9	26.1	52.4	172.5	2,754.5	589.8	2,046.2	118.4
Fairbanks, AK M.S.A.	34,243									
Includes Fairbanks North Star Borough										
City of Fairbanks	32,089	177	2	17	33	125	1,232	130	1,026	76
Total area actually reporting	100.0	192	2	17	36	137	1,396	143	1,170	83
Rate per 100,000 inhabitants	X	560.7	5.8	49.6	105.1	400.1	4,076.7	417.6	3,416.8	242.4
Fajardo, PR M.S.A.	70,000									
Includes Ceiba, Fajardo, and Luquillo Municipios										
Total area actually reporting	100.0	205	26	2	85	92	1,073	446	562	65
Rate per 100,000 inhabitants	X	292.9	37.1	2.9	121.4	131.4	1,532.9	637.1	802.9	92.9
Fargo, ND-MN M.S.A.[2]	211,760									
Includes Clay County, MN[2], and Cass County, ND										
City of Fargo, ND	107,329	384	1	42	47	294	2,671	423	2,120	128
Total area actually reporting	100.0	X	1	X	64	372	4,390	697	3,483	210
Rate per 100,000 inhabitants	X	X	0.5	X	30.2	175.7	2,073.1	329.1	1,644.8	99.2
Farmington, NM M.S.A.	131,499									
Includes San Juan County										
City of Farmington	46,390	504	2	73	40	389	1,628	244	1,291	93
Total area actually reporting	100.0	822	5	104	53	660	2,758	543	2,058	157
Rate per 100,000 inhabitants	X	625.1	3.8	79.1	40.3	501.9	2,097.4	412.9	1,565.0	119.4
Fayetteville, NC M.S.A.	371,029									
Includes Cumberland and Hoke Counties										
City of Fayetteville	203,107	1,050	25	56	495	474	12,972	4,204	8,088	680
Total area actually reporting	100.0	1,795	33	78	676	1,008	20,252	7,286	11,923	1,043
Rate per 100,000 inhabitants	X	483.8	8.9	21.0	182.2	271.7	5,458.3	1,963.7	3,213.5	281.1
Flagstaff, AZ M.S.A.	136,324									
Includes Coconino County										
City of Flagstaff	66,802	263	0	45	38	180	3,008	235	2,706	67
Total area actually reporting	100.0	565	5	69	57	434	4,585	528	3,941	116
Rate per 100,000 inhabitants	X	414.5	3.7	50.6	41.8	318.4	3,363.3	387.3	2,890.9	85.1
Flint, MI M.S.A.	425,469									
Includes Genesee County										
City of Flint	102,357	2,392	52	85	607	1,648	6,618	3,628	2,220	770
Total area actually reporting	94.4	3,511	64	226	911	2,310	15,918	6,548	8,045	1,325
Estimated total	100.0	3,579	64	234	926	2,355	16,535	6,684	8,478	1,373
Rate per 100,000 inhabitants	X	841.2	15.0	55.0	217.6	553.5	3,886.3	1,571.0	1,992.6	322.7
Florence, SC M.S.A.[1]	207,960									
Includes Darlington and Florence Counties[1]										
City of Florence[1]	37,488	351	3	16	76	256	3,230	537	2,530	163
Total area actually reporting	100.0	1,369	14	60	219	1,076	10,357	2,658	7,120	579
Rate per 100,000 inhabitants	X	658.3	6.7	28.9	105.3	517.4	4,980.3	1,278.1	3,423.7	278.4

X = Not applicable.

[1] Because of changes in the state/local agency's reporting practices, figures are not comparable to previous years' data.

[2] The data collection methodology for the offense of forcible rape used by Chicago, Illinois, and the Minnesota state UCR Program (with the exception of Minneapolis and St. Paul, Minnesota) does not comply with national UCR Program guidelines. Consequently, its figures for forcible rape and violent crime (of which forcible rape is a part) are not published in this table.

Table II-6.   Crime, by Selected Metropolitan Statistical Area, 2011—*Continued*

(Number, percent, rate per 100,000 population.)

Area	Population	Violent crime	Murder and non-negligent man-slaughter	Forcible rape	Robbery	Aggravated assault	Property crime	Burglary	Larceny-theft	Motor vehicle theft
Florence-Muscle Shoals, AL M.S.A.[1]	147,845									
Includes Colbert and Lauderdale Counties[1]										
City of Florence[1]	39,508	88	1	10	29	48	1,592	394	1,155	43
City of Muscle Shoals[1]	13,209	65	1	2	12	50	576	129	413	34
Total area actually reporting	100.0	337	3	22	65	247	3,681	954	2,564	163
Rate per 100,000 inhabitants	X	227.9	2.0	14.9	44.0	167.1	2,489.8	645.3	1,734.2	110.3
Fond du Lac, WI M.S.A.	102,076									
Includes Fond du Lac County										
City of Fond du Lac	43,208	146	2	37	9	98	1,069	117	923	29
Total area actually reporting	100.0	184	2	44	13	125	1,625	238	1,323	64
Rate per 100,000 inhabitants	X	180.3	2.0	43.1	12.7	122.5	1,592.0	233.2	1,296.1	62.7
Fort Collins-Loveland, CO M.S.A.	304,849									
Includes Larimer County										
City of Fort Collins	146,494	420	3	56	46	315	4,272	560	3,553	159
City of Loveland	68,024	107	1	22	11	73	1,725	209	1,464	52
Total area actually reporting	100.0	653	4	96	62	491	7,666	1,081	6,315	270
Rate per 100,000 inhabitants	X	214.2	1.3	31.5	20.3	161.1	2,514.7	354.6	2,071.5	88.6
Fort Smith, AR-OK M.S.A.	301,142									
Includes Crawford, Franklin, and Sebastian Counties, AR and Le Flore and Sequoyah Counties, OK										
City of Fort Smith, AR	86,861	601	5	63	100	433	4,703	1,110	3,389	204
Total area actually reporting	99.8	1,254	9	139	126	980	8,396	2,313	5,695	388
Estimated total	100.0	1,257	9	139	126	983	8,423	2,322	5,712	389
Rate per 100,000 inhabitants	X	417.4	3.0	46.2	41.8	326.4	2,797.0	771.1	1,896.8	129.2
Fort Wayne, IN M.S.A.	418,383									
Includes Allen, Wells, and Whitley Counties										
City of Fort Wayne	254,987	785	24	94	310	357	9,036	1,888	6,768	380
Total area actually reporting	94.5	912	26	117	338	431	11,281	2,278	8,518	485
Estimated total	100.0	935	26	120	341	448	11,612	2,369	8,736	507
Rate per 100,000 inhabitants	X	223.5	6.2	28.7	81.5	107.1	2,775.4	566.2	2,088.0	121.2
Fresno, CA M.S.A.	941,388									
Includes Fresno County										
City of Fresno	500,480	2,915	35	51	1,020	1,809	25,421	5,713	14,928	4,780
Total area actually reporting	98.4	5,123	52	149	1,363	3,559	40,398	9,850	23,527	7,021
Estimated total	100.0	5,172	52	152	1,379	3,589	40,767	9,938	23,759	7,070
Rate per 100,000 inhabitants	X	549.4	5.5	16.1	146.5	381.2	4,330.5	1,055.7	2,523.8	751.0
Gadsden, AL M.S.A.[1]	104,933									
Includes Etowah County[1]										
City of Gadsden[1]	37,033	299	5	25	76	193	2,973	768	1,967	238
Total area actually reporting	100.0	513	5	42	85	381	4,624	1,266	2,996	362
Rate per 100,000 inhabitants	X	488.9	4.8	40.0	81.0	363.1	4,406.6	1,206.5	2,855.2	345.0
Gainesville, FL M.S.A.	267,877									
Includes Alachua and Gilchrist Counties										
City of Gainesville	126,049	912	6	82	184	640	5,356	1,063	4,003	290
Total area actually reporting	100.0	1,603	13	124	283	1,183	9,204	2,119	6,642	443
Rate per 100,000 inhabitants	X	598.4	4.9	46.3	105.6	441.6	3,435.9	791.0	2,479.5	165.4
Gainesville, GA M.S.A.	182,050									
Includes Hall County										
City of Gainesville	34,249	116	2	12	46	56	1,582	332	1,176	74
Total area actually reporting	100.0	284	5	33	82	164	4,505	1,124	3,087	294
Rate per 100,000 inhabitants	X	156.0	2.7	18.1	45.0	90.1	2,474.6	617.4	1,695.7	161.5
Glens Falls, NY M.S.A.	129,502									
Includes Warren and Washington Counties										
City of Glens Falls	14,766	44	0	2	5	37	410	68	331	11
Total area actually reporting	100.0	207	12	34	18	143	2,135	404	1,672	59
Rate per 100,000 inhabitants	X	159.8	9.3	26.3	13.9	110.4	1,648.6	312.0	1,291.1	45.6
Goldsboro, NC M.S.A.	124,178									
Includes Wayne County										
City of Goldsboro	36,899	343	7	2	91	243	2,655	675	1,840	140
Total area actually reporting	97.7	543	10	5	126	402	5,070	1,625	3,163	282
Estimated total	100.0	551	10	6	128	407	5,186	1,651	3,249	286
Rate per 100,000 inhabitants	X	443.7	8.1	4.8	103.1	327.8	4,176.3	1,329.5	2,616.4	230.3

X = Not applicable.

[1] Because of changes in the state/local agency's reporting practices, figures are not comparable to previous years' data.

Table II-6. Crime, by Selected Metropolitan Statistical Area, 2011—*Continued*

(Number, percent, rate per 100,000 population.)

Area	Population	Violent crime	Murder and non-negligent man-slaughter	Forcible rape	Robbery	Aggravated assault	Property crime	Burglary	Larceny-theft	Motor vehicle theft
Grand Forks, ND-MN M.S.A.[2]	99,832									
Includes Polk County, MN[2], and Grand Forks County, ND										
City of Grand Forks, ND	53,729	133	0	32	8	93	1,533	306	1,130	97
Total area actually reporting	98.2	X	0	X	12	137	2,235	457	1,653	125
Estimated total	100.0	X	0	X	12	140	2,280	463	1,689	128
Rate per 100,000 inhabitants	X	X	0.0	X	12.0	140.2	2,283.8	463.8	1,691.8	128.2
Grand Junction, CO M.S.A.	149,279									
Includes Mesa County										
City of Grand Junction	59,586	257	2	74	37	144	2,588	379	2,070	139
Total area actually reporting	99.5	449	3	92	52	302	4,043	719	3,103	221
Estimated total	100.0	450	3	92	52	303	4,062	722	3,118	222
Rate per 100,000 inhabitants	X	301.4	2.0	61.6	34.8	203.0	2,721.1	483.7	2,088.7	148.7
Grand Rapids-Wyoming, MI M.S.A.	773,576									
Includes Barry, Ionia, Kent, and Newaygo Counties										
City of Grand Rapids	187,898	1,395	10	81	464	840	6,174	1,952	3,897	325
City of Wyoming	72,071	262	2	34	71	155	1,591	487	960	144
Total area actually reporting	98.9	2,646	20	328	662	1,636	17,646	4,837	11,980	829
Estimated total	100.0	2,672	20	331	668	1,653	17,875	4,887	12,141	847
Rate per 100,000 inhabitants	X	345.4	2.6	42.8	86.4	213.7	2,310.7	631.7	1,569.5	109.5
Great Falls, MT M.S.A.[1]	82,049									
Includes Cascade County[1]										
City of Great Falls[1]	59,024	176	2	13	33	128	2,699	303	2,287	109
Total area actually reporting	100.0	204	2	16	33	153	2,947	344	2,488	115
Rate per 100,000 inhabitants	X	248.6	2.4	19.5	40.2	186.5	3,591.8	419.3	3,032.3	140.2
Greeley, CO M.S.A.	257,229									
Includes Weld County										
City of Greeley	94,507	437	1	38	75	323	3,118	593	2,377	148
Total area actually reporting	98.1	741	6	65	99	571	5,269	1,106	3,853	310
Estimated total	100.0	754	6	67	101	580	5,401	1,126	3,955	320
Rate per 100,000 inhabitants	X	293.1	2.3	26.0	39.3	225.5	2,099.7	437.7	1,537.5	124.4
Green Bay, WI M.S.A.	307,576									
Includes Brown, Kewaunee, and Oconto Counties										
City of Green Bay	104,510	373	2	54	48	269	2,420	467	1,852	101
Total area actually reporting	100.0	446	2	74	56	314	5,464	1,031	4,237	196
Rate per 100,000 inhabitants	X	145.0	0.7	24.1	18.2	102.1	1,776.5	335.2	1,377.5	63.7
Greenville-Mauldin-Easley, SC M.S.A.	644,406									
Includes Greenville, Laurens, and Pickens Counties										
City of Greenville	59,089	485	5	22	110	348	3,495	732	2,540	223
City of Mauldin	23,156	78	0	7	16	55	493	88	377	28
City of Easley	20,226	107	1	8	10	88	1,056	164	837	55
Total area actually reporting	100.0	3,478	42	217	533	2,686	23,542	5,832	15,954	1,756
Rate per 100,000 inhabitants	X	539.7	6.5	33.7	82.7	416.8	3,653.3	905.0	2,475.8	272.5
Guayama, PR M.S.A.	84,045									
Includes Arroyo, Guayama, and Patillas Municipios										
Total area actually reporting	100.0	177	18	0	73	86	1,066	406	624	36
Rate per 100,000 inhabitants	X	210.6	21.4	0.0	86.9	102.3	1,268.4	483.1	742.5	42.8
Gulfport-Biloxi, MS M.S.A.	249,760									
Includes Hancock, Harrison, and Stone Counties										
City of Gulfport	68,049	192	12	22	94	64	3,605	944	2,523	138
City of Biloxi	44,221	204	2	34	60	108	2,341	766	1,431	144
Total area actually reporting	83.3	518	20	71	185	242	9,304	2,534	6,305	465
Estimated total	100.0	563	21	78	194	270	10,007	2,768	6,721	518
Rate per 100,000 inhabitants	X	225.4	8.4	31.2	77.7	108.1	4,006.6	1,108.3	2,691.0	207.4
Hagerstown-Martinsburg, MD-WV M.S.A.	270,693									
Includes Washington County, MD and Berkeley and Morgan Counties, WV										
City of Hagerstown, MD	40,038	188	1	2	76	109	1,510	382	1,054	74
City of Martinsburg, WV	17,249	79	0	4	20	55	972	171	772	29
Total area actually reporting	99.6	713	9	34	146	524	5,944	1,597	4,046	301
Estimated total	100.0	717	9	34	147	527	5,978	1,603	4,073	302
Rate per 100,000 inhabitants	X	264.9	3.3	12.6	54.3	194.7	2,208.4	592.2	1,504.7	111.6

X = Not applicable.

[1] Because of changes in the state/local agency's reporting practices, figures are not comparable to previous years' data.

[2] The data collection methodology for the offense of forcible rape used by Chicago, Illinois, and the Minnesota state UCR Program (with the exception of Minneapolis and St. Paul, Minnesota) does not comply with national UCR Program guidelines. Consequently, its figures for forcible rape and violent crime (of which forcible rape is a part) are not published in this table.

Table II-6.   Crime, by Selected Metropolitan Statistical Area, 2011—*Continued*

(Number, percent, rate per 100,000 population.)

Area	Population	Violent crime	Murder and non-negligent man-slaughter	Forcible rape	Robbery	Aggravated assault	Property crime	Burglary	Larceny-theft	Motor vehicle theft
Hanford-Corcoran, CA M.S.A.	154,780									
Includes Kings County										
City of Hanford	54,601	174	2	7	48	117	1,447	286	1,002	159
City of Corcoran	25,105	76	1	1	13	61	355	106	207	42
Total area actually reporting	100.0	542	8	30	97	407	3,436	859	2,188	389
Rate per 100,000 inhabitants	X	350.2	5.2	19.4	62.7	263.0	2,219.9	555.0	1,413.6	251.3
Harrisburg-Carlisle, PA M.S.A.	551,228									
Includes Cumberland, Dauphin, and Perry Counties										
City of Harrisburg	49,686	697	8	62	382	245	2,515	662	1,605	248
City of Carlisle	18,742	58	0	8	26	24	464	53	405	6
Total area actually reporting	99.0	1,680	20	180	578	902	12,009	2,457	9,024	528
Estimated total	100.0	1,691	20	181	581	909	12,111	2,474	9,105	532
Rate per 100,000 inhabitants	X	306.8	3.6	32.8	105.4	164.9	2,197.1	448.8	1,651.8	96.5
Harrisonburg, VA M.S.A.	126,724									
Includes Rockingham County and Harrisonburg City										
City of Harrisonburg	49,498	99	1	13	19	66	1,060	158	866	36
Total area actually reporting	100.0	150	2	34	21	93	1,663	266	1,325	72
Rate per 100,000 inhabitants	X	118.4	1.6	26.8	16.6	73.4	1,312.3	209.9	1,045.6	56.8
Hartford-West Hartford-East Hartford, CT M.S.A.	1,022,173									
Includes Hartford, Middlesex, and Tolland Counties										
City of Hartford	125,006	1,639	27	55	602	955	5,502	1,271	3,372	859
City of West Hartford	63,385	68	1	4	46	17	1,517	231	1,180	106
City of East Hartford	51,347	173	0	22	79	72	1,401	325	938	138
City of Middletown	47,736	77	0	10	30	37	1,023	143	820	60
Total area actually reporting	100.0	2,999	36	201	1,134	1,628	24,976	5,000	17,926	2,050
Rate per 100,000 inhabitants	X	293.4	3.5	19.7	110.9	159.3	2,443.4	489.2	1,753.7	200.6
Hickory-Lenoir-Morganton, NC M.S.A.	370,132									
Includes Alexander, Burke, Caldwell, and Catawba Counties										
City of Hickory	40,517	238	5	11	75	147	2,500	536	1,850	114
City of Lenoir	18,459	48	1	1	15	31	871	236	593	42
City of Morganton	17,133	41	0	5	7	29	628	135	465	28
Total area actually reporting	99.5	818	22	50	188	558	12,864	4,155	8,164	545
Estimated total	100.0	823	22	50	189	562	12,944	4,173	8,223	548
Rate per 100,000 inhabitants	X	222.4	5.9	13.5	51.1	151.8	3,497.1	1,127.4	2,221.6	148.1
Hinesville-Fort Stewart, GA M.S.A.	78,942									
Includes Liberty and Long Counties										
City of Hinesville	33,877	155	2	12	41	100	1,605	506	1,042	57
Total area actually reporting	83.6	231	3	13	47	168	2,162	710	1,355	97
Estimated total	100.0	269	4	16	60	189	2,552	829	1,589	134
Rate per 100,000 inhabitants	X	340.8	5.1	20.3	76.0	239.4	3,232.8	1,050.1	2,012.9	169.7
Holland-Grand Haven, MI M.S.A.	263,602									
Includes Ottawa County										
City of Holland	26,015	93	0	19	8	66	852	174	664	14
City of Grand Haven	10,404	19	0	12	1	6	292	39	252	1
Total area actually reporting	100.0	401	2	127	26	246	4,842	967	3,764	111
Rate per 100,000 inhabitants	X	152.1	0.8	48.2	9.9	93.3	1,836.9	366.8	1,427.9	42.1
Hot Springs, AR M.S.A.	96,750									
Includes Garland County										
City of Hot Springs	35,459	328	2	22	47	257	2,847	589	2,130	128
Total area actually reporting	100.0	496	4	51	67	374	5,309	1,758	3,263	288
Rate per 100,000 inhabitants	X	512.7	4.1	52.7	69.3	386.6	5,487.3	1,817.1	3,372.6	297.7
Houma-Bayou Cane-Thibodaux, LA M.S.A.	210,082									
Includes Lafourche and Terrebonne Parishes										
City of Houma	34,035	212	1	17	76	118	1,550	268	1,234	48
City of Thibodaux	14,699	70	1	8	8	53	588	102	473	13
Total area actually reporting	100.0	661	6	52	147	456	6,968	1,714	4,944	310
Rate per 100,000 inhabitants	X	314.6	2.9	24.8	70.0	217.1	3,316.8	815.9	2,353.4	147.6

X = Not applicable.

Table II-6.   Crime, by Selected Metropolitan Statistical Area, 2011—*Continued*

(Number, percent, rate per 100,000 population.)

Area	Population	Violent crime	Murder and non-negligent man-slaughter	Forcible rape	Robbery	Aggravated assault	Property crime	Burglary	Larceny-theft	Motor vehicle theft
Houston-Sugar Land-Baytown, TX M.S.A.[1]	6,071,933									
Includes Austin, Brazoria, Chambers, Fort Bend, Galveston, Harris, Liberty, Montgomery, San Jacinto, and Waller Counties										
City of Houston	2,143,628	20,892	198	771	8,054	11,869	108,336	27,459	68,596	12,281
City of Sugar Land	80,475	96	1	5	29	61	1,429	220	1,176	33
City of Baytown	73,313	212	1	13	79	119	3,555	700	2,628	227
City of Galveston[1]	48,748	302	4	58	88	152	2,291	453	1,697	141
City of Conroe	57,390	194	2	12	60	120	2,086	439	1,550	97
Total area actually reporting	99.9	33,443	330	1,628	11,530	19,955	217,173	54,691	141,872	20,610
Estimated total	100.0	33,444	330	1,628	11,530	19,956	217,186	54,694	141,881	20,611
Rate per 100,000 inhabitants	X	550.8	5.4	26.8	189.9	328.7	3,576.9	900.8	2,336.7	339.4
Huntsville, AL M.S.A.[1]	419,602									
Includes Limestone and Madison Counties[1]										
City of Huntsville[1]	180,972	1,518	13	51	405	1,049	9,749	2,677	6,306	766
Total area actually reporting	100.0	2,106	19	112	498	1,477	14,721	4,347	9,323	1,051
Rate per 100,000 inhabitants	X	501.9	4.5	26.7	118.7	352.0	3,508.3	1,036.0	2,221.9	250.5
Idaho Falls, ID M.S.A.	131,886									
Includes Bonneville and Jefferson Counties										
City of Idaho Falls	57,512	148	1	27	9	111	1,582	289	1,203	90
Total area actually reporting	100.0	255	6	38	12	199	2,718	571	2,008	139
Rate per 100,000 inhabitants	X	193.3	4.5	28.8	9.1	150.9	2,060.9	432.9	1,522.5	105.4
Indianapolis-Carmel, IN M.S.A.	1,765,211									
Includes Boone, Brown, Hamilton, Hancock, Hendricks, Johnson, Marion, Morgan, Putnam, and Shelby Counties										
City of Indianapolis	833,024	9,170	96	435	3,372	5,267	46,967	15,122	26,588	5,257
City of Carmel	79,596	17	1	8	2	6	831	69	729	33
Total area actually reporting	86.3	9,965	101	530	3,525	5,809	61,286	17,124	38,233	5,929
Estimated total	100.0	10,348	107	569	3,599	6,073	66,511	18,232	42,016	6,263
Rate per 100,000 inhabitants	X	586.2	6.1	32.2	203.9	344.0	3,767.9	1,032.9	2,380.2	354.8
Iowa City, IA M.S.A.	153,385									
Includes Johnson and Washington Counties										
City of Iowa City	68,217	163	0	24	18	121	1,580	326	1,207	47
Total area actually reporting	100.0	368	3	49	27	289	2,810	568	2,145	97
Rate per 100,000 inhabitants	X	239.9	2.0	31.9	17.6	188.4	1,832.0	370.3	1,398.4	63.2
Jackson, MS M.S.A.	541,099									
Includes Copiah, Hinds, Madison, Rankin, and Simpson Counties										
City of Jackson	174,170	1,620	52	126	808	634	12,811	4,722	6,632	1,457
Total area actually reporting	90.3	2,039	63	165	915	896	18,310	6,133	10,371	1,806
Estimated total	100.0	2,149	66	175	940	968	19,594	6,492	11,228	1,874
Rate per 100,000 inhabitants	X	397.2	12.2	32.3	173.7	178.9	3,621.1	1,199.8	2,075.0	346.3
Jackson, TN M.S.A.	116,467									
Includes Chester and Madison Counties										
City of Jackson	65,799	675	6	43	156	470	3,746	1,126	2,397	223
Total area actually reporting	100.0	866	9	61	170	626	4,723	1,455	2,966	302
Rate per 100,000 inhabitants	X	743.6	7.7	52.4	146.0	537.5	4,055.2	1,249.3	2,546.6	259.3
Jacksonville, FL M.S.A.	1,363,935									
Includes Baker, Clay, Duval, Nassau, and St. Johns Counties										
City of Jacksonville	834,429	5,182	71	350	1,578	3,183	36,113	8,518	25,733	1,862
Total area actually reporting	100.0	7,141	87	439	1,870	4,745	50,233	11,429	36,366	2,438
Rate per 100,000 inhabitants	X	523.6	6.4	32.2	137.1	347.9	3,682.9	837.9	2,666.3	178.7
Jacksonville, NC M.S.A.	180,026									
Includes Onslow County										
City of Jacksonville	71,034	171	1	25	24	121	2,034	515	1,428	91
Total area actually reporting	100.0	426	4	66	62	294	5,420	1,524	3,621	275
Rate per 100,000 inhabitants	X	236.6	2.2	36.7	34.4	163.3	3,010.7	846.5	2,011.4	152.8
Janesville, WI M.S.A.	161,030									
Includes Rock County										
City of Janesville	63,852	169	2	20	32	115	2,399	407	1,948	44
Total area actually reporting	100.0	393	4	39	96	254	4,877	1,086	3,656	135
Rate per 100,000 inhabitants	X	244.1	2.5	24.2	59.6	157.7	3,028.6	674.4	2,270.4	83.8

X = Not applicable.

[1] Because of changes in the state/local agency's reporting practices, figures are not comparable to previous years' data.

Table II-6.   Crime, by Selected Metropolitan Statistical Area, 2011—*Continued*

(Number, percent, rate per 100,000 population.)

Area	Population	Violent crime	Murder and non-negligent man-slaughter	Forcible rape	Robbery	Aggravated assault	Property crime	Burglary	Larceny-theft	Motor vehicle theft
Jefferson City, MO M.S.A.	150,351									
Includes Callaway, Cole, Moniteau, and Osage Counties										
City of Jefferson City	43,236	245	1	9	58	177	1,613	282	1,305	26
Total area actually reporting	100.0	473	7	22	70	374	3,720	778	2,807	135
Rate per 100,000 inhabitants	X	314.6	4.7	14.6	46.6	248.8	2,474.2	517.5	1,867.0	89.8
Johnson City, TN M.S.A.	200,508									
Includes Carter, Unicoi, and Washington Counties										
City of Johnson City	63,722	278	3	7	59	209	2,958	682	2,187	89
Total area actually reporting	100.0	650	6	19	87	538	6,065	1,515	4,296	254
Rate per 100,000 inhabitants	X	324.2	3.0	9.5	43.4	268.3	3,024.8	755.6	2,142.6	126.7
Johnstown, PA M.S.A.	144,137									
Includes Cambria County										
City of Johnstown	22,572	151	3	7	60	81	961	358	572	31
Total area actually reporting	96.6	369	4	50	85	230	2,877	752	2,042	83
Estimated total	100.0	379	4	51	88	236	2,971	767	2,117	87
Rate per 100,000 inhabitants	X	262.9	2.8	35.4	61.1	163.7	2,061.2	532.1	1,468.7	60.4
Jonesboro, AR M.S.A.	121,942									
Includes Craighead and Poinsett Counties										
City of Jonesboro	67,772	333	1	44	81	207	3,347	1,276	1,968	103
Total area actually reporting	96.2	450	4	57	93	296	4,664	1,706	2,820	138
Estimated total	100.0	467	4	59	95	309	4,795	1,750	2,902	143
Rate per 100,000 inhabitants	X	383.0	3.3	48.4	77.9	253.4	3,932.2	1,435.1	2,379.8	117.3
Joplin, MO M.S.A.	176,156									
Includes Jasper and Newton Counties										
City of Joplin	50,332	249	2	33	54	160	3,533	692	2,562	279
Total area actually reporting	100.0	552	3	66	74	409	6,483	1,352	4,649	482
Rate per 100,000 inhabitants	X	313.4	1.7	37.5	42.0	232.2	3,680.3	767.5	2,639.1	273.6
Kankakee-Bradley, IL M.S.A.	113,791									
Includes Kankakee County										
City of Kankakee	27,620	253	4	31	110	108	1,303	391	859	53
City of Bradley	15,943	67	0	12	10	45	763	93	661	9
Total area actually reporting	89.2	412	4	56	133	219	3,020	702	2,228	90
Estimated total	100.0	440	4	59	141	236	3,291	754	2,435	102
Rate per 100,000 inhabitants	X	386.7	3.5	51.8	123.9	207.4	2,892.1	662.6	2,139.9	89.6
Kansas City, MO-KS M.S.A.[1]	2,045,034									
Includes Franklin, Johnson, Leavenworth, Linn, Miami, and Wyandotte Counties, KS, and Bates, Caldwell, Cass, Clay, Clinton, Jackson, Lafayette, Platte, and Ray Counties, MO										
City of Kansas City, MO	461,458	5,536	108	265	1,665	3,498	25,545	6,848	15,305	3,392
City of Overland Park, KS	174,473	289	2	60	38	189	4,015	468	3,237	310
City of Kansas City, KS[1]	146,712	947	27	95	291	534	7,883	1,827	4,792	1,264
Total area actually reporting	99.6	9,730	161	727	2,460	6,382	69,498	15,209	46,712	7,577
Estimated total	100.0	9,750	161	730	2,462	6,397	69,682	15,241	46,852	7,589
Rate per 100,000 inhabitants	X	476.8	7.9	35.7	120.4	312.8	3,407.4	745.3	2,291.0	371.1
Kennewick-Pasco-Richland, WA M.S.A.	257,314									
Includes Benton and Franklin Counties										
City of Kennewick	75,077	226	2	27	35	162	2,628	404	2,056	168
City of Pasco	60,719	208	2	25	31	150	1,596	368	1,055	173
City of Richland	48,812	89	1	13	8	67	1,398	260	1,075	63
Total area actually reporting	100.0	656	5	90	87	474	6,798	1,423	4,872	503
Rate per 100,000 inhabitants	X	254.9	1.9	35.0	33.8	184.2	2,641.9	553.0	1,893.4	195.5
Killeen-Temple-Fort Hood, TX M.S.A.	413,828									
Includes Bell, Coryell, and Lampasas Counties										
City of Killeen	130,613	815	15	69	172	559	5,210	2,034	2,989	187
City of Temple	67,493	185	0	21	84	80	2,039	575	1,380	84
Total area actually reporting	99.5	1,376	18	137	300	921	11,591	3,882	7,309	400
Estimated total	100.0	1,382	18	138	301	925	11,663	3,897	7,362	404
Rate per 100,000 inhabitants	X	334.0	4.3	33.3	72.7	223.5	2,818.3	941.7	1,779.0	97.6

X = Not applicable.

[1] Because of changes in the state/local agency's reporting practices, figures are not comparable to previous years' data.

Table II-6.   Crime, by Selected Metropolitan Statistical Area, 2011—*Continued*

(Number, percent, rate per 100,000 population.)

Area	Population	Violent crime	Murder and non-negligent man-slaughter	Forcible rape	Robbery	Aggravated assault	Property crime	Burglary	Larceny-theft	Motor vehicle theft
Kingsport-Bristol-Bristol, TN-VA M.S.A...............................	312,618									
Includes Hawkins and Sullivan Counties, TN and										
Scott and Washington Counties and Bristol City, VA										
City of Kingsport, TN..............................	48,640	428	3	22	62	341	3,240	552	2,556	132
City of Bristol, TN	26,943	115	0	20	11	84	1,187	196	943	48
City of Bristol, VA	18,048	57	1	8	13	35	657	106	530	21
Total area actually reporting	100.0	1,136	9	103	134	890	10,219	2,301	7,473	445
Rate per 100,000 inhabitants......................	X	363.4	2.9	32.9	42.9	284.7	3,268.8	736.0	2,390.5	142.3
Kingston, NY M.S.A.	183,313									
Includes Ulster County										
City of Kingston	24,000	93	0	8	34	51	580	115	450	15
Total area actually reporting	100.0	335	2	43	65	225	3,435	749	2,588	98
Rate per 100,000 inhabitants......................	X	182.7	1.1	23.5	35.5	122.7	1,873.8	408.6	1,411.8	53.5
Knoxville, TN M.S.A.	704,327									
Includes Anderson, Blount, Knox, Loudon, and										
Union Counties										
City of Knoxville....................................	180,488	1,691	17	94	559	1,021	12,879	2,544	9,515	820
Total area actually reporting	100.0	3,240	34	190	818	2,198	26,908	6,321	18,935	1,652
Rate per 100,000 inhabitants......................	X	460.0	4.8	27.0	116.1	312.1	3,820.4	897.5	2,688.4	234.6
Kokomo, IN M.S.A.	99,192									
Includes Howard and Tipton Counties										
City of Kokomo	45,700	184	3	20	73	88	2,558	505	1,954	99
Total area actually reporting	98.9	261	5	23	79	154	3,379	820	2,437	122
Estimated total......................................	100.0	264	5	23	80	156	3,417	826	2,467	124
Rate per 100,000 inhabitants......................	X	266.2	5.0	23.2	80.7	157.3	3,444.8	832.7	2,487.1	125.0
La Crosse, WI-MN M.S.A.[2]	134,312									
Includes Houston County, MN[2], and La Crosse										
County, WI										
City of La Crosse, WI	51,544	165	0	18	25	122	1,823	313	1,435	75
Total area actually reporting	99.0	X	0	X	28	166	3,078	603	2,369	106
Estimated total......................................	100.0	X	0	X	29	167	3,113	608	2,398	107
Rate per 100,000 inhabitants......................	X	X	0.0	X	21.6	124.3	2,317.7	452.7	1,785.4	79.7
Lafayette, IN M.S.A.	202,820									
Includes Benton, Carroll, and Tippecanoe Counties										
City of Lafayette	67,483	408	3	38	48	319	3,000	635	2,190	175
Total area actually reporting	95.6	536	3	60	61	412	5,133	1,107	3,754	272
Estimated total......................................	100.0	550	3	62	64	421	5,309	1,146	3,880	283
Rate per 100,000 inhabitants......................	X	271.2	1.5	30.6	31.6	207.6	2,617.6	565.0	1,913.0	139.5
Lafayette, LA M.S.A.	276,242									
Includes Lafayette and St. Martin Parishes										
City of Lafayette	121,726	843	6	15	232	590	6,511	1,194	5,040	277
Total area actually reporting	94.1	1,469	11	51	304	1,103	10,053	2,053	7,617	383
Estimated total......................................	100.0	1,561	12	56	317	1,176	10,781	2,195	8,180	406
Rate per 100,000 inhabitants......................	X	565.1	4.3	20.3	114.8	425.7	3,902.7	794.6	2,961.2	147.0
Lake Havasu City-Kingman, AZ M.S.A.	203,020									
Includes Mohave County										
City of Lake Havasu City	53,271	98	1	26	3	68	1,268	228	974	66
City of Kingman	28,465	101	2	7	14	78	1,520	303	1,153	64
Total area actually reporting	100.0	409	12	45	57	295	6,463	1,653	4,469	341
Rate per 100,000 inhabitants......................	X	201.5	5.9	22.2	28.1	145.3	3,183.4	814.2	2,201.3	168.0
Lakeland-Winter Haven, FL M.S.A.	610,301									
Includes Polk County										
City of Lakeland	98,750	548	6	36	140	366	5,147	1,333	3,612	202
City of Winter Haven	34,336	302	4	12	78	208	1,857	458	1,294	105
Total area actually reporting	100.0	2,543	25	143	528	1,847	20,106	6,057	13,213	836
Rate per 100,000 inhabitants......................	X	416.7	4.1	23.4	86.5	302.6	3,294.4	992.5	2,165.0	137.0
Lancaster, PA M.S.A.	521,101									
Includes Lancaster County										
City of Lancaster....................................	59,511	504	5	37	217	245	3,014	531	2,378	105
Total area actually reporting	100.0	946	7	115	341	483	10,586	1,881	8,349	356
Rate per 100,000 inhabitants......................	X	181.5	1.3	22.1	65.4	92.7	2,031.5	361.0	1,602.2	68.3

X = Not applicable.

[2] The data collection methodology for the offense of forcible rape used by Chicago, Illinois, and the Minnesota state UCR Program (with the exception of Minneapolis and St. Paul, Minnesota) does not comply with national UCR Program guidelines. Consequently, its figures for forcible rape and violent crime (of which forcible rape is a part) are not published in this table.

Table II-6. Crime, by Selected Metropolitan Statistical Area, 2011—*Continued*

(Number, percent, rate per 100,000 population.)

Area	Population	Violent crime	Murder and non-negligent man-slaughter	Forcible rape	Robbery	Aggravated assault	Property crime	Burglary	Larceny-theft	Motor vehicle theft
Lansing-East Lansing, MI M.S.A.	463,686									
Includes Clinton, Eaton, and Ingham Counties										
City of Lansing	114,211	1,169	8	90	275	796	4,287	1,650	2,397	240
City of East Lansing	48,542	82	1	17	7	57	1,043	292	699	52
Total area actually reporting	98.2	1,695	18	214	338	1,125	10,871	3,231	7,155	485
Estimated total	100.0	1,718	18	217	343	1,140	11,083	3,278	7,304	501
Rate per 100,000 inhabitants	X	370.5	3.9	46.8	74.0	245.9	2,390.2	706.9	1,575.2	108.0
Laredo, TX M.S.A.	255,571									
Includes Webb County										
City of Laredo	241,059	1,120	11	76	215	818	10,419	1,790	8,143	486
Total area actually reporting	100.0	1,236	11	84	222	919	10,851	1,907	8,436	508
Rate per 100,000 inhabitants	X	483.6	4.3	32.9	86.9	359.6	4,245.8	746.2	3,300.8	198.8
Las Cruces, NM M.S.A.	211,575									
Includes Dona Ana County										
City of Las Cruces	98,710	424	3	17	68	336	4,546	1,120	3,164	262
Total area actually reporting	100.0	778	7	61	90	620	6,800	1,863	4,514	423
Rate per 100,000 inhabitants	X	367.7	3.3	28.8	42.5	293.0	3,214.0	880.5	2,133.5	199.9
Las Vegas-Paradise, NV M.S.A.	1,967,721									
Includes Clark County										
City of Las Vegas Metropolitan Police Department	1,458,474	10,813	82	651	3,493	6,587	41,426	12,662	21,977	6,787
Total area actually reporting	100.0	12,732	93	769	3,764	8,106	53,676	15,978	29,435	8,263
Rate per 100,000 inhabitants	X	647.0	4.7	39.1	191.3	411.9	2,727.8	812.0	1,495.9	419.9
Lawrence, KS M.S.A.	111,530									
Includes Douglas County										
City of Lawrence	88,200	335	0	33	37	265	3,793	502	3,098	193
Total area actually reporting	100.0	390	0	39	40	311	4,488	642	3,632	214
Rate per 100,000 inhabitants	X	349.7	0.0	35.0	35.9	278.8	4,024.0	575.6	3,256.5	191.9
Lawton, OK M.S.A.	125,426									
Includes Comanche County										
City of Lawton	97,904	829	8	57	175	589	5,531	1,960	3,365	206
Total area actually reporting	100.0	875	8	63	180	624	5,890	2,086	3,575	229
Rate per 100,000 inhabitants	X	697.6	6.4	50.2	143.5	497.5	4,696.0	1,663.1	2,850.3	182.6
Lebanon, PA M.S.A.	133,994									
Includes Lebanon County										
City of Lebanon	25,558	87	0	11	46	30	643	133	486	24
Total area actually reporting	93.7	223	1	25	72	125	2,258	419	1,771	68
Estimated total	100.0	240	1	26	77	136	2,421	446	1,901	74
Rate per 100,000 inhabitants	X	179.1	0.7	19.4	57.5	101.5	1,806.8	332.9	1,418.7	55.2
Lewiston-Auburn, ME M.S.A.	107,688									
Includes Androscoggin County										
City of Lewiston	36,587	77	3	13	29	32	1,351	387	943	21
City of Auburn	23,052	43	0	7	23	13	1,094	200	876	18
Total area actually reporting	100.0	166	4	37	60	65	3,181	839	2,279	63
Rate per 100,000 inhabitants	X	154.1	3.7	34.4	55.7	60.4	2,953.9	779.1	2,116.3	58.5
Lexington-Fayette, KY M.S.A.[1]	475,361									
Includes Bourbon, Clark, Fayette, Jessamine, Scott, and Woodford Counties										
City of Lexington[1]	297,847	1,358	14	105	496	743	12,431	2,724	9,036	671
Total area actually reporting	99.7	1,803	17	154	621	1,011	19,061	4,303	13,906	852
Estimated total	100.0	1,808	17	155	623	1,013	19,120	4,317	13,948	855
Rate per 100,000 inhabitants	X	380.3	3.6	32.6	131.1	213.1	4,022.2	908.2	2,934.2	179.9
Lima, OH M.S.A.	106,409									
Includes Allen County										
City of Lima	38,799	404	1	48	97	258	2,262	786	1,357	119
Total area actually reporting	97.4	499	2	66	115	316	3,904	1,164	2,566	174
Estimated total	100.0	504	2	67	117	318	3,981	1,180	2,624	177
Rate per 100,000 inhabitants	X	473.6	1.9	63.0	110.0	298.8	3,741.2	1,108.9	2,466.0	166.3
Lincoln, NE M.S.A.	304,853									
Includes Lancaster and Seward Counties										
City of Lincoln	260,685	966	4	166	177	619	10,189	1,401	8,424	364
Total area actually reporting	97.5	984	4	173	177	630	10,839	1,503	8,959	377
Estimated total	100.0	989	4	174	177	634	10,926	1,523	9,019	384
Rate per 100,000 inhabitants	X	324.4	1.3	57.1	58.1	208.0	3,584.0	499.6	2,958.5	126.0

X = Not applicable.

[1] Because of changes in the state/local agency's reporting practices, figures are not comparable to previous years' data.

Table II-6. Crime, by Selected Metropolitan Statistical Area, 2011—_Continued_

(Number, percent, rate per 100,000 population.)

Area	Population	Violent crime	Murder and non-negligent man-slaughter	Forcible rape	Robbery	Aggravated assault	Property crime	Burglary	Larceny-theft	Motor vehicle theft
Little Rock-North Little Rock-Conway, AR M.S.A.	705,050									
Includes Faulkner, Grant, Lonoke, Perry, Pulaski, and Saline Counties										
City of Little Rock	194,988	2,905	37	161	858	1,849	15,504	4,655	9,756	1,093
City of North Little Rock	62,775	611	12	20	216	363	5,519	1,101	4,067	351
City of Conway	59,354	247	4	22	82	139	2,719	406	2,208	105
Total area actually reporting	91.1	5,062	67	309	1,257	3,429	35,451	9,947	23,274	2,230
Estimated total	100.0	5,260	69	327	1,268	3,596	36,551	10,365	23,864	2,322
Rate per 100,000 inhabitants	X	746.0	9.8	46.4	179.8	510.0	5,184.2	1,470.1	3,384.7	329.3
Logan, UT-ID M.S.A.	127,757									
Includes Franklin County, ID and Cache County, UT										
City of Logan, UT	49,104	26	0	2	2	22	376	49	314	13
Total area actually reporting	100.0	61	0	13	5	43	1,356	218	1,093	45
Rate per 100,000 inhabitants	X	47.7	0.0	10.2	3.9	33.7	1,061.4	170.6	855.5	35.2
Longview, TX M.S.A.	218,879									
Includes Gregg, Rusk, and Upshur Counties										
City of Longview	80,239	403	4	20	107	272	3,715	800	2,643	272
Total area actually reporting	99.5	840	11	76	135	618	7,329	1,793	4,971	565
Estimated total	100.0	843	11	76	136	620	7,366	1,801	4,998	567
Rate per 100,000 inhabitants	X	385.1	5.0	34.7	62.1	283.3	3,365.3	822.8	2,283.5	259.0
Longview, WA M.S.A.	104,017									
Includes Cowlitz County										
City of Longview	37,223	162	2	35	38	87	1,997	317	1,483	197
Total area actually reporting	100.0	315	4	85	60	166	3,435	683	2,451	301
Rate per 100,000 inhabitants	X	302.8	3.8	81.7	57.7	159.6	3,302.3	656.6	2,356.3	289.4
Los Angeles-Long Beach-Santa Ana, CA M.S.A.	12,979,653									
Includes the Metropolitan Divisions of Los Angeles-Long Beach-Glendale and Santa Ana-Anaheim-Irvine										
City of Los Angeles	3,837,207	20,045	297	828	10,077	8,843	86,330	17,264	53,469	15,597
City of Long Beach	467,691	2,857	25	112	1,320	1,400	12,816	3,275	7,329	2,212
City of Santa Ana	328,343	1,313	13	62	591	647	6,575	1,067	4,222	1,286
City of Anaheim	340,218	1,281	15	105	446	715	8,493	1,410	5,964	1,119
City of Irvine	214,872	120	2	11	40	67	3,280	513	2,649	118
City of Glendale	193,973	258	0	14	108	136	3,452	623	2,506	323
City of Pomona	150,810	927	11	54	339	523	4,444	890	2,578	976
City of Pasadena	138,734	435	7	26	178	224	3,672	1,011	2,382	279
City of Torrance	147,148	185	2	17	91	75	2,767	509	1,957	301
City of Orange	138,020	157	3	6	82	66	2,652	445	2,001	206
City of Fullerton	136,750	306	2	25	104	175	3,550	643	2,548	359
City of Costa Mesa	111,253	231	4	30	83	114	3,534	524	2,743	267
City of Burbank	104,555	191	1	17	68	105	2,555	395	1,926	234
City of Compton	97,589	1,067	17	45	380	625	2,865	800	1,202	863
City of Carson	92,792	444	5	13	106	320	2,492	573	1,360	559
City of Santa Monica	90,791	369	1	24	129	215	2,971	483	2,300	188
City of Newport Beach	86,187	116	0	16	27	73	2,223	441	1,702	80
City of Tustin	76,428	97	1	7	39	50	1,513	243	1,167	103
City of Montebello	63,235	174	1	6	97	70	1,837	671	766	400
City of Monterey Park	60,978	102	1	1	60	40	1,039	213	635	191
City of Gardena	59,521	281	2	11	139	129	1,453	395	789	269
City of Arcadia	57,027	68	1	5	24	38	1,699	408	1,206	85
City of Paramount	54,734	255	1	6	129	119	1,621	268	884	469
City of Fountain Valley	55,963	79	1	8	14	56	1,279	273	941	65
City of Cerritos	49,618	84	0	4	51	29	1,761	375	1,221	165
Total area actually reporting	100.0	52,624	641	2,314	22,147	27,522	289,794	60,048	183,422	46,324
Rate per 100,000 inhabitants	X	405.4	4.9	17.8	170.6	212.0	2,232.7	462.6	1,413.2	356.9
Los Angeles-Long Beach-Glendale, CA M.D.	9,934,033									
Includes Los Angeles County										
Total area actually reporting	100.0	46,116	568	1,904	19,902	23,742	228,136	49,328	138,325	40,483
Rate per 100,000 inhabitants	X	464.2	5.7	19.2	200.3	239.0	2,296.5	496.6	1,392.4	407.5
Santa Ana-Anaheim-Irvine, CA M.D.	3,045,620									
Includes Orange County										
Total area actually reporting	100.0	6,508	73	410	2,245	3,780	61,658	10,720	45,097	5,841
Rate per 100,000 inhabitants	X	213.7	2.4	13.5	73.7	124.1	2,024.5	352.0	1,480.7	191.8

X = Not applicable.

Table II-6.   Crime, by Selected Metropolitan Statistical Area, 2011—*Continued*

(Number, percent, rate per 100,000 population.)

Area	Population	Violent crime	Murder and non-negligent man-slaughter	Forcible rape	Robbery	Aggravated assault	Property crime	Burglary	Larceny-theft	Motor vehicle theft
Louisville/Jefferson County, KY-IN M.S.A.³	1,291,986									
Includes Clark, Floyd, Harrison³, and Washington Counties, IN, and Bullitt, Henry, Jefferson, Meade, Nelson, Oldham, Shelby, Spencer, and Trimble Counties, KY										
City of Louisville Metro, KY	665,152	4,086	48	227	1,643	2,168	31,949	8,127	21,560	2,262
Total area actually reporting	97.2	5,353	57	342	1,963	2,991	47,954	12,421	32,353	3,180
Estimated total	100.0	5,413	57	349	1,977	3,030	48,790	12,607	32,953	3,230
Rate per 100,000 inhabitants	X	419.0	4.4	27.0	153.0	234.5	3,776.4	975.8	2,550.6	250.0
Lubbock, TX M.S.A.	290,884									
Includes Crosby and Lubbock Counties										
City of Lubbock	234,404	1,800	8	70	313	1,409	12,078	3,410	7,975	693
Total area actually reporting	100.0	1,965	11	94	322	1,538	13,652	3,923	8,959	770
Rate per 100,000 inhabitants	X	675.5	3.8	32.3	110.7	528.7	4,693.3	1,348.6	3,079.9	264.7
Lynchburg, VA M.S.A.	255,651									
Includes Amherst, Appomattox, Bedford, and Campbell Counties and Bedford and Lynchburg Cities										
City of Lynchburg	76,471	278	3	22	72	181	2,469	515	1,855	99
Total area actually reporting	100.0	440	6	51	89	294	5,178	1,085	3,867	226
Rate per 100,000 inhabitants	X	172.1	2.3	19.9	34.8	115.0	2,025.4	424.4	1,512.6	88.4
Macon, GA M.S.A.	235,351									
Includes Bibb, Crawford, Jones, Monroe, and Twiggs Counties										
City of Macon	92,554	566	13	33	246	274	7,807	2,154	5,104	549
Total area actually reporting	99.5	908	18	51	304	535	12,938	3,424	8,595	919
Estimated total	100.0	912	18	51	305	538	12,988	3,434	8,632	922
Rate per 100,000 inhabitants	X	387.5	7.6	21.7	129.6	228.6	5,518.6	1,459.1	3,667.7	391.8
Madera-Chowchilla, CA M.S.A.	152,639									
Includes Madera County										
City of Madera	62,138	406	1	15	115	275	1,442	608	528	306
City of Chowchilla	18,940	82	0	2	4	76	453	184	233	36
Total area actually reporting	100.0	799	5	27	139	628	3,805	1,628	1,603	574
Rate per 100,000 inhabitants	X	523.5	3.3	17.7	91.1	411.4	2,492.8	1,066.6	1,050.2	376.1
Madison, WI M.S.A.	571,071									
Includes Columbia, Dane, and Iowa Counties										
City of Madison	234,225	815	8	74	272	461	7,936	1,440	6,152	344
Total area actually reporting	99.8	1,244	10	143	344	747	14,741	2,466	11,728	547
Estimated total	100.0	1,245	10	143	344	748	14,773	2,470	11,755	548
Rate per 100,000 inhabitants	X	218.0	1.8	25.0	60.2	131.0	2,586.9	432.5	2,058.4	96.0
Manchester-Nashua, NH M.S.A.	401,245									
Includes Hillsborough County										
City of Manchester	109,708	618	2	69	181	366	4,194	902	3,136	156
City of Nashua	86,607	212	3	24	50	135	2,130	360	1,693	77
Total area actually reporting	94.2	1,006	8	124	260	614	9,185	1,851	7,020	314
Estimated total	100.0	1,021	8	127	262	624	9,416	1,892	7,202	322
Rate per 100,000 inhabitants	X	254.5	2.0	31.7	65.3	155.5	2,346.7	471.5	1,794.9	80.3
Manhattan, KS M.S.A.	127,888									
Includes Geary, Pottawatomie, and Riley Counties										
Total area actually reporting	99.5	368	5	49	47	267	2,547	626	1,852	69
Estimated total	100.0	369	5	49	47	268	2,561	628	1,863	70
Rate per 100,000 inhabitants	X	288.5	3.9	38.3	36.8	209.6	2,002.5	491.1	1,456.7	54.7
Mankato-North Mankato, MN M.S.A.²	97,487									
Includes Blue Earth and Nicollet Counties²										
City of Mankato²	39,608		1		21	49	1,859	390	1,419	50
City of North Mankato²	13,497		0		3	0	314	47	259	8
Total area actually reporting	99.9		1		26	72	2,825	604	2,126	95
Estimated total	100.0		1		26	72	2,825	604	2,126	95
Rate per 100,000 inhabitants	X		1.0		26.7	73.9	2,897.8	619.6	2,180.8	97.4
Mansfield, OH M.S.A.	124,566									
Includes Richland County										
City of Mansfield	47,856	171	3	32	86	50	3,063	913	2,044	106
Total area actually reporting	98.5	225	3	48	111	63	5,410	1,481	3,769	160
Estimated total	100.0	227	3	48	112	64	5,462	1,492	3,808	162
Rate per 100,000 inhabitants	X	182.2	2.4	38.5	89.9	51.4	4,384.8	1,197.8	3,057.0	130.1

X = Not applicable.

² The data collection methodology for the offense of forcible rape used by Chicago, Illinois, and the Minnesota state UCR Program (with the exception of Minneapolis and St. Paul, Minnesota) does not comply with national UCR Program guidelines. Consequently, its figures for forcible rape and violent crime (of which forcible rape is a part) are not published in this table.

³ The FBI determined that the agency did not follow national Uniform Crime Reporting (UCR) Program guidelines for reporting an offense. Consequently, this figure is not included in this table.

Table II-6. Crime, by Selected Metropolitan Statistical Area, 2011—*Continued*

(Number, percent, rate per 100,000 population.)

Area	Population	Violent crime	Murder and non-negligent man-slaughter	Forcible rape	Robbery	Aggravated assault	Property crime	Burglary	Larceny-theft	Motor vehicle theft
Mayaguez, PR M.S.A.	105,007									
Includes Hormigueros and Mayaguez Municipios										
Total area actually reporting	100.0	210	27	0	105	78	1,903	632	1,154	117
Rate per 100,000 inhabitants	X	200.0	25.7	0.0	100.0	74.3	1,812.3	601.9	1,099.0	111.4
McAllen-Edinburg-Mission, TX M.S.A.	791,072									
Includes Hidalgo County										
City of McAllen	132,610	246	4	27	72	143	5,875	511	5,184	180
City of Edinburg	78,722	282	1	28	54	199	4,652	758	3,666	228
City of Mission	78,679	100	2	6	37	55	2,751	464	2,094	193
City of Pharr	71,881	256	4	17	51	184	2,452	530	1,765	157
Total area actually reporting	100.0	2,337	35	225	468	1,609	31,295	6,316	23,319	1,660
Rate per 100,000 inhabitants	X	295.4	4.4	28.4	59.2	203.4	3,956.0	798.4	2,947.8	209.8
Medford, OR M.S.A.	205,369									
Includes Jackson County										
City of Medford	75,704	387	6	38	60	283	3,895	370	3,375	150
Total area actually reporting	100.0	596	10	71	73	442	6,891	860	5,783	248
Rate per 100,000 inhabitants	X	290.2	4.9	34.6	35.5	215.2	3,355.4	418.8	2,815.9	120.8
Memphis, TN-MS-AR M.S.A.	1,326,648									
Includes Crittenden County, AR; DeSoto, Marshall, Tate, and Tunica Counties; MS, and Fayette, Shelby, and Tipton Counties, TN										
City of Memphis	652,725	10,336	117	398	3,083	6,738	42,355	13,254	25,667	3,434
Total area actually reporting	96.1	12,910	139	568	3,458	8,745	59,349	18,414	36,585	4,350
Estimated total	100.0	13,007	141	578	3,480	8,808	60,532	18,756	37,358	4,418
Rate per 100,000 inhabitants	X	980.4	10.6	43.6	262.3	663.9	4,562.8	1,413.8	2,816.0	333.0
Merced, CA M.S.A.	258,800									
Includes Merced County										
City of Merced	79,886	503	8	20	149	326	3,159	802	2,044	313
Total area actually reporting	100.0	1,409	14	61	274	1,060	9,132	2,604	5,496	1,032
Rate per 100,000 inhabitants	X	544.4	5.4	23.6	105.9	409.6	3,528.6	1,006.2	2,123.6	398.8
Miami-Fort Lauderdale-Pompano Beach, FL M.S.A.	5,640,473									
Includes the Metropolitan Divisions of Fort Lauderdale-Pompano Beach-Deerfield Beach, Miami-Miami Beach-Kendall, and West Palm Beach-Boca Raton-Boynton Beach										
City of Miami	404,901	4,849	68	96	2,002	2,683	22,921	5,141	15,080	2,700
City of Fort Lauderdale	167,777	1,565	12	91	771	691	10,192	3,102	6,489	601
City of Pompano Beach	101,206	917	5	41	343	528	5,524	1,343	3,852	329
City of West Palm Beach	101,281	769	14	48	235	472	5,383	1,354	3,685	344
City of Miami Beach	88,975	887	4	40	370	473	9,585	1,171	7,838	576
City of Boca Raton	85,542	178	0	23	63	92	2,676	495	2,067	114
City of Deerfield Beach	76,040	366	1	23	134	208	2,415	569	1,651	195
City of Boynton Beach	69,147	389	4	7	123	255	3,343	776	2,426	141
City of Delray Beach	61,347	564	4	27	183	350	3,223	699	2,385	139
City of Homestead	61,337	967	4	18	299	646	3,314	954	2,200	160
Total area actually reporting	100.0	33,654	344	1,451	11,512	20,347	236,524	54,367	163,975	18,182
Rate per 100,000 inhabitants	X	596.7	6.1	25.7	204.1	360.7	4,193.3	963.9	2,907.1	322.3
Fort Lauderdale-Pompano Beach-Deerfield Beach, FL M.D.	1,771,889									
Includes Broward County										
Total area actually reporting	100.0	8,749	59	473	3,474	4,743	70,949	18,814	47,633	4,502
Rate per 100,000 inhabitants	X	493.8	3.3	26.7	196.1	267.7	4,004.1	1,061.8	2,688.3	254.1
Miami-Miami Beach-Kendall, FL M.D.	2,530,459									
Includes Miami-Dade County										
Total area actually reporting	100.0	18,320	218	638	6,157	11,307	119,789	24,227	84,714	10,848
Rate per 100,000 inhabitants	X	724.0	8.6	25.2	243.3	446.8	4,733.9	957.4	3,347.8	428.7
West Palm Beach-Boca Raton-Boynton Beach, FL M.D.	1,294,282									
Includes Palm Beach County										
Total area actually reporting	100.0	6,992	83	345	2,018	4,546	46,173	11,534	31,827	2,812
Rate per 100,000 inhabitants	X	540.2	6.4	26.7	155.9	351.2	3,567.5	891.2	2,459.0	217.3

X = Not applicable.

Table II-6.   Crime, by Selected Metropolitan Statistical Area, 2011—*Continued*

(Number, percent, rate per 100,000 population.)

Area	Population	Violent crime	Murder and non-negligent man-slaughter	Forcible rape	Robbery	Aggravated assault	Property crime	Burglary	Larceny-theft	Motor vehicle theft
Michigan City-La Porte, IN M.S.A......................	112,036									
Includes La Porte County										
City of Michigan City...............................	31,460	96	2	9	41	44	1,840	297	1,421	122
City of La Porte......................................	22,166	43	1	6	10	26	1,121	193	886	42
Total area actually reporting	96.9	179	4	25	60	90	3,919	776	2,917	226
Estimated total..	100.0	188	4	26	62	96	4,044	796	3,014	234
Rate per 100,000 inhabitants	X	167.8	3.6	23.2	55.3	85.7	3,609.6	710.5	2,690.2	208.9
Midland, TX M.S.A.[2]...............................	139,752									
Includes Midland County										
City of Midland[2].....................................	113,486	334	4	21	58	251	3,287	715	2,435	137
Total area actually reporting	100.0	399	6	22	62	309	3,816	848	2,797	171
Rate per 100,000 inhabitants	X	285.5	4.3	15.7	44.4	221.1	2,730.6	606.8	2,001.4	122.4
Milwaukee-Waukesha-West Allis, WI M.S.A.......................	1,562,687									
Includes Milwaukee, Ozaukee, Washington, and										
Waukesha Counties										
City of Milwaukee.....................................	597,426	5,969	85	194	2,963	2,727	30,097	6,669	18,890	4,538
City of Waukesha......................................	71,026	92	0	17	17	58	1,130	178	918	34
City of West Allis......................................	60,674	199	2	10	114	73	3,174	571	2,376	227
Total area actually reporting	97.3	6,949	92	288	3,297	3,272	50,249	9,268	35,745	5,236
Estimated total..	100.0	7,003	92	295	3,311	3,305	51,249	9,400	36,584	5,265
Rate per 100,000 inhabitants	X	448.1	5.9	18.9	211.9	211.5	3,279.5	601.5	2,341.1	336.9
Minneapolis-St. Paul-Bloomington, MN-WI M.S.A.[2]...........	3,304,725									
Includes Anoka, Carver, Chisago, Dakota, Hennepin,										
Isanti, Ramsey, Scott, Sherburne, Washington, and										
Wright Counties, MN[2] and Pierce and St. Croix										
Counties, WI										
City of Minneapolis, MN..............................	385,531	3,722	32	386	1,589	1,715	19,190	5,104	12,311	1,775
City of St. Paul, MN...................................	287,665	1,885	8	169	604	1,104	11,932	3,197	6,890	1,845
City of Bloomington, MN[2]............................	83,533	X	0	X	41	70	3,151	251	2,813	87
City of Plymouth, MN[2]................................	71,121	X	0	X	12	31	1,212	276	908	28
City of Eagan, MN[2]..................................	64,702	X	0	X	11	23	1,512	185	1,278	49
City of Eden Prairie, MN[2]............................	61,266	X	0	X	12	14	960	127	811	22
City of Minnetonka, MN[2].............................	50,118	X	0	X	11	13	910	154	725	31
Total area actually reporting	99.9	X	59	X	2,997	4,634	93,940	17,189	70,600	6,151
Estimated total..	100.0	X	59	X	2,998	4,636	94,005	17,198	70,653	6,154
Rate per 100,000 inhabitants	X	X	1.8	X	90.7	140.3	2,844.6	520.4	2,137.9	186.2
Missoula, MT M.S.A.[1]...............................	110,269									
Includes Missoula County[1]										
City of Missoula[1].....................................	67,381	192	0	26	20	146	2,415	299	2,019	97
Total area actually reporting	100.0	276	1	38	26	211	2,861	389	2,346	126
Rate per 100,000 inhabitants	X	250.3	0.9	34.5	23.6	191.4	2,594.6	352.8	2,127.5	114.3
Mobile, AL M.S.A.[1,4]..............................	414,980									
Includes Mobile County[1]										
City of Mobile[1,4].....................................	251,869	1,619	30	48	637	904	13,650	4,058	8,891	701
Total area actually reporting	100.0	2,524	47	87	894	1,496	19,948	6,149	12,518	1,281
Rate per 100,000 inhabitants	X	608.2	11.3	21.0	215.4	360.5	4,807.0	1,481.8	3,016.5	308.7
Modesto, CA M.S.A.................................	520,501									
Includes Stanislaus County										
City of Modesto.......................................	203,530	1,413	14	67	425	907	8,894	2,121	5,410	1,363
Total area actually reporting	100.0	2,484	34	117	702	1,631	19,187	5,346	10,620	3,221
Rate per 100,000 inhabitants	X	477.2	6.5	22.5	134.9	313.4	3,686.3	1,027.1	2,040.3	618.8
Monroe, LA M.S.A..................................	178,055									
Includes Ouachita and Union Parishes										
City of Monroe...	49,261	834	5	23	113	693	3,910	1,340	2,467	103
Total area actually reporting	97.6	1,116	9	38	147	922	7,873	2,575	5,080	218
Estimated total..	100.0	1,139	9	39	150	941	8,059	2,611	5,224	224
Rate per 100,000 inhabitants	X	639.7	5.1	21.9	84.2	528.5	4,526.1	1,466.4	2,933.9	125.8
Monroe, MI M.S.A..................................	151,906									
Includes Monroe County										
City of Monroe...	20,717	107	0	13	24	70	911	244	622	45
Total area actually reporting	94.4	353	3	65	66	219	3,631	1,075	2,358	198
Estimated total..	100.0	377	3	68	71	235	3,852	1,124	2,513	215
Rate per 100,000 inhabitants	X	248.2	2.0	44.8	46.7	154.7	2,535.8	739.9	1,654.3	141.5

X = Not applicable.

[1] Because of changes in the state/local agency's reporting practices, figures are not comparable to previous years' data.

[2] The data collection methodology for the offense of forcible rape used by Chicago, Illinois, and the Minnesota state UCR Program (with the exception of Minneapolis and St. Paul, Minnesota) does not comply with national UCR Program guidelines. Consequently, its figures for forcible rape and violent crime (of which forcible rape is a part) are not published in this table.

[4] The population for the city of Mobile, Alabama, includes 55,819 inhabitants from the jurisdiction of the Mobile County Sheriff's Department.

Table II-6.   Crime, by Selected Metropolitan Statistical Area, 2011—*Continued*

(Number, percent, rate per 100,000 population.)

Area	Population	Violent crime	Murder and non-negligent man-slaughter	Forcible rape	Robbery	Aggravated assault	Property crime	Burglary	Larceny-theft	Motor vehicle theft
Montgomery, AL M.S.A.[1]	376,339									
Includes Autauga, Elmore, Lowndes, and										
Montgomery Counties[1]										
City of Montgomery[1]	206,754	707	31	38	354	284	10,744	2,885	7,043	816
Total area actually reporting	99.7	1,117	39	76	431	571	15,333	4,238	10,004	1,091
Estimated total	100.0	1,121	39	76	432	574	15,375	4,249	10,032	1,094
Rate per 100,000 inhabitants	X	297.9	10.4	20.2	114.8	152.5	4,085.4	1,129.0	2,665.7	290.7
Morristown, TN M.S.A.	137,840									
Includes Grainger, Hamblen, and Jefferson Counties										
City of Morristown	29,400	195	1	13	35	146	1,964	200	1,667	97
Total area actually reporting	100.0	474	3	27	79	365	4,704	1,035	3,419	250
Rate per 100,000 inhabitants	X	343.9	2.2	19.6	57.3	264.8	3,412.7	750.9	2,480.4	181.4
Mount Vernon-Anacortes, WA M.S.A.	118,735									
Includes Skagit County										
City of Mount Vernon	32,241	100	2	24	34	40	1,804	351	1,377	76
City of Anacortes	16,026	24	0	6	4	14	501	91	387	23
Total area actually reporting	100.0	242	3	47	64	128	5,293	1,228	3,801	264
Rate per 100,000 inhabitants	X	203.8	2.5	39.6	53.9	107.8	4,457.8	1,034.2	3,201.2	222.3
Muncie, IN M.S.A.	118,272									
Includes Delaware County										
City of Muncie	70,443	513	1	42	108	362	2,433	553	1,701	179
Total area actually reporting	100.0	602	2	61	117	422	3,352	775	2,354	223
Rate per 100,000 inhabitants	X	509.0	1.7	51.6	98.9	356.8	2,834.1	655.3	1,990.3	188.5
Muskegon-Norton Shores, MI M.S.A.	172,058									
Includes Muskegon County										
City of Muskegon	38,372	364	5	34	86	239	2,157	585	1,500	72
City of Norton Shores	23,976	39	0	3	13	23	759	103	637	19
Total area actually reporting	100.0	746	7	101	165	473	7,092	1,470	5,394	228
Rate per 100,000 inhabitants	X	433.6	4.1	58.7	95.9	274.9	4,121.9	854.4	3,135.0	132.5
Myrtle Beach-North Myrtle Beach-Conway, SC M.S.A.	272,427									
Includes Horry County										
City of Myrtle Beach	27,425	443	4	36	160	243	4,187	590	3,243	354
City of North Myrtle Beach	13,912	108	3	13	43	49	1,501	376	1,032	93
City of Conway	17,302	158	1	11	35	111	887	220	636	31
Total area actually reporting	99.9	1,821	24	178	410	1,209	15,214	3,401	10,676	1,137
Estimated total	100.0	1,822	24	178	410	1,210	15,229	3,404	10,687	1,138
Rate per 100,000 inhabitants	X	668.8	8.8	65.3	150.5	444.2	5,590.1	1,249.5	3,922.9	417.7
Napa, CA M.S.A.	138,089									
Includes Napa County										
City of Napa	77,819	224	1	24	47	152	1,615	344	1,132	139
Total area actually reporting	100.0	452	3	34	69	346	2,799	631	1,919	249
Rate per 100,000 inhabitants	X	327.3	2.2	24.6	50.0	250.6	2,027.0	457.0	1,389.7	180.3
Naples-Marco Island, FL M.S.A.	325,902									
Includes Collier County										
City of Naples	19,803	55	1	1	6	47	615	73	526	16
City of Marco Island	16,637	10	0	2	1	7	202	39	161	2
Total area actually reporting	100.0	1,028	10	45	215	758	6,077	1,485	4,377	215
Rate per 100,000 inhabitants	X	315.4	3.1	13.8	66.0	232.6	1,864.7	455.7	1,343.0	66.0
Nashville-Davidson–Murfreesboro–Franklin, TN M.S.A.	1,604,276									
Includes Cannon, Cheatham, Davidson, Dickson,										
Hickman, Macon, Robertson, Rutherford, Smith,										
Sumner, Trousdale, Williamson, and Wilson Counties										
City of Nashville	612,789	7,239	50	373	1,889	4,927	29,256	7,541	19,987	1,728
City of Murfreesboro	109,736	654	3	30	131	490	4,851	1,383	3,283	185
City of Franklin	63,051	103	0	11	11	81	1,021	88	898	35
Total area actually reporting	100.0	10,440	78	596	2,316	7,450	53,243	13,474	36,858	2,911
Rate per 100,000 inhabitants	X	650.8	4.9	37.2	144.4	464.4	3,318.8	839.9	2,297.5	181.5
New Haven-Milford, CT M.S.A.	810,372									
Includes New Haven County										
City of New Haven	130,019	1,748	34	55	766	893	6,479	1,413	4,124	942
City of Milford	52,857	35	1	0	23	11	1,753	158	1,515	80
Total area actually reporting	100.0	3,008	50	115	1,246	1,597	24,656	4,526	17,775	2,355
Rate per 100,000 inhabitants	X	371.2	6.2	14.2	153.8	197.1	3,042.6	558.5	2,193.4	290.6

X = Not applicable.

[1] Because of changes in the state/local agency's reporting practices, figures are not comparable to previous years' data.

Table II-6.   Crime, by Selected Metropolitan Statistical Area, 2011—*Continued*

(Number, percent, rate per 100,000 population.)

Area	Population	Violent crime	Murder and non-negligent man-slaughter	Forcible rape	Robbery	Aggravated assault	Property crime	Burglary	Larceny-theft	Motor vehicle theft
New Orleans-Metairie-Kenner, LA M.S.A...........	1,178,445									
Includes Jefferson, Orleans, Plaquemines, St. Bernard, St. Charles, St. John the Baptist, and St. Tammany Parishes										
City of New Orleans....................	346,974	2,748	200	163	1,059	1,326	14,013	3,857	7,616	2,540
City of Kenner.................	67,312	161	9	10	69	73	2,604	414	2,040	150
Total area actually reporting	100.0	5,782	279	310	1,781	3,412	39,982	9,562	26,334	4,086
Rate per 100,000 inhabitants.............	X	490.6	23.7	26.3	151.1	289.5	3,392.8	811.4	2,234.6	346.7
New York-Northern New Jersey-Long Island, NY-NJ-PA M.S.A..........	18,974,419									
Includes the Metropolitan Divisions of Edison-New Brunswick, NJ; Nassau-Suffolk, NY; Newark-Union, NJ-PA; and New York-White Plains-Wayne, NY-NJ										
City of New York, NY.............	8,211,875	51,209	515	1,092	19,773	29,829	140,457	18,159	112,864	9,434
City of Newark, NJ..............	278,064	3,243	94	58	1,977	1,114	10,016	2,396	3,921	3,699
City of Edison Township, NJ	100,300	142	2	9	65	66	1,832	343	1,279	210
City of White Plains, NY	57,109	87	1	3	29	54	1,265	46	1,182	37
City of Wayne Township, NJ	54,899	34	0	3	18	13	1,173	144	964	65
City of Union Township, NJ	56,831	116	1	4	63	48	1,002	155	745	102
City of New Brunswick, NJ..........	55,365	479	3	7	250	219	1,609	404	1,102	103
Total area actually reporting	99.9	77,000	852	1,895	31,618	42,635	330,615	56,466	247,451	26,698
Estimated total...............	100.0	77,029	852	1,896	31,628	42,653	330,926	56,514	247,703	26,709
Rate per 100,000 inhabitants...........	X	406.0	4.5	10.0	166.7	224.8	1,744.1	297.8	1,305.5	140.8
Edison-New Brunswick, NJ M.D.	2,348,037									
Includes Middlesex, Monmouth, Ocean, and Somerset Counties										
Total area actually reporting	100.0	3,554	29	185	1,351	1,989	45,227	9,173	34,239	1,815
Rate per 100,000 inhabitants...........	X	151.4	1.2	7.9	57.5	84.7	1,926.2	390.7	1,458.2	77.3
Nassau-Suffolk, NY M.D.	2,845,615									
Includes Nassau and Suffolk Counties										
Total area actually reporting	99.9	4,367	55	114	1,850	2,348	45,947	7,885	35,697	2,365
Estimated total...............	100.0	4,370	55	114	1,851	2,350	45,975	7,889	35,720	2,366
Rate per 100,000 inhabitants...........	X	153.6	1.9	4.0	65.0	82.6	1,615.6	277.2	1,255.3	83.1
Newark-Union, NJ-PA M.D.	2,154,867									
Includes Essex, Hunterdon, Morris, Sussex, and Union Counties, NJ and Pike County, PA										
Total area actually reporting	100.0	8,356	172	246	4,495	3,443	44,685	10,433	26,146	8,106
Rate per 100,000 inhabitants...........	X	387.8	8.0	11.4	208.6	159.8	2,073.7	484.2	1,213.3	376.2
New York-White Plains-Wayne, NY-NJ M.D.	11,625,900									
Includes Bergen, Hudson, and Passaic Counties, NJ and Bronx, Kings, New York, Putnam, Queens, Richmond, Rockland, and Westchester Counties, NY										
Total area actually reporting	99.9	60,723	596	1,350	23,922	34,855	194,756	28,975	151,369	14,412
Estimated total...............	100.0	60,749	596	1,351	23,931	34,871	195,039	29,019	151,598	14,422
Rate per 100,000 inhabitants...........	X	522.5	5.1	11.6	205.8	299.9	1,677.6	249.6	1,304.0	124.1
North Port-Bradenton-Sarasota, FL M.S.A.	711,852									
Includes Manatee and Sarasota Counties										
City of North Port..............	58,139	160	1	15	23	121	1,373	375	966	31
City of Bradenton.................	50,221	362	1	14	79	268	2,165	584	1,486	99
City of Sarasota..............	52,625	513	8	28	172	305	3,226	698	2,414	134
City of Venice.............	21,031	28	0	3	9	16	556	129	414	14
Total area actually reporting	100.0	3,518	32	194	831	2,461	25,997	6,771	18,320	955
Rate per 100,000 inhabitants...........	X	494.2	4.5	27.3	116.7	345.7	3,652.0	951.2	2,573.6	136.8
Norwich-New London, CT M.S.A.	146,560									
Includes New London County										
City of Norwich..............	40,568	133	2	25	45	61	856	235	570	49
City of New London.................	27,671	319	3	18	41	257	814	227	538	70
Total area actually reporting	100.0	583	5	60	107	411	3,260	647	2,471	148
Rate per 100,000 inhabitants...........	X	397.8	3.4	40.9	73.0	280.4	2,224.3	441.5	1,686.0	104.5
Ocala, FL M.S.A.	335,813									
Includes Marion County										
City of Ocala.............	57,082	358	5	26	112	215	3,154	713	2,376	65
Total area actually reporting	100.0	1,668	14	162	191	1,301	8,381	2,540	5,549	292
Rate per 100,000 inhabitants...........	X	496.7	4.2	48.2	56.9	387.4	2,495.7	756.4	1,652.4	87.0

X = Not applicable.

Table II-6. Crime, by Selected Metropolitan Statistical Area, 2011—*Continued*

(Number, percent, rate per 100,000 population.)

Area	Population	Violent crime	Murder and non-negligent man-slaughter	Forcible rape	Robbery	Aggravated assault	Property crime	Burglary	Larceny-theft	Motor vehicle theft
Ocean City, NJ M.S.A.	97,589									
Includes Cape May County										
City of Ocean City	11,740	22	0	1	1	20	581	111	468	2
Total area actually reporting	100.0	309	1	13	84	211	4,544	1,075	3,395	74
Rate per 100,000 inhabitants	X	316.6	1.0	13.3	86.1	216.2	4,656.3	1,101.6	3,478.9	75.8
Odessa, TX M.S.A.	140,016									
Includes Ector County										
City of Odessa	102,043	748	6	37	73	632	3,134	617	2,336	181
Total area actually reporting	100.0	951	11	38	95	807	4,238	900	3,096	242
Rate per 100,000 inhabitants	X	679.2	7.9	27.1	67.8	576.4	3,026.8	642.8	2,211.2	172.8
Ogden-Clearfield, UT M.S.A.	557,743									
Includes Davis, Morgan, and Weber Counties										
City of Ogden	84,423	392	2	20	96	274	4,429	858	3,279	292
City of Clearfield	30,693	54	0	10	9	35	746	108	613	25
Total area actually reporting	100.0	827	8	150	151	518	14,294	2,378	11,249	667
Rate per 100,000 inhabitants	X	148.3	1.4	26.9	27.1	92.9	2,562.8	426.4	2,016.9	119.6
Oklahoma City, OK M.S.A.	1,266,404									
Includes Canadian, Cleveland, Grady, Lincoln, Logan, McClain, and Oklahoma Counties										
City of Oklahoma City	586,208	5,108	58	277	1,232	3,541	34,113	9,855	20,199	4,059
Total area actually reporting	100.0	6,689	78	511	1,501	4,599	54,100	14,513	34,142	5,445
Rate per 100,000 inhabitants	X	528.2	6.2	40.4	118.5	363.2	4,271.9	1,146.0	2,696.0	430.0
Olympia, WA M.S.A.	256,222									
Includes Thurston County										
City of Olympia	47,207	126	0	17	31	78	1,976	342	1,535	99
Total area actually reporting	100.0	587	4	70	90	423	7,123	1,916	4,861	346
Rate per 100,000 inhabitants	X	229.1	1.6	27.3	35.1	165.1	2,780.0	747.8	1,897.2	135.0
Omaha-Council Bluffs, NE-IA M.S.A.	872,617									
Includes Harrison, Mills, and Pottawattamie Counties, IA and Cass, Douglas, Sarpy, Saunders, and Washington Counties, NE										
City of Omaha, NE	412,608	2,309	43	220	696	1,350	18,764	3,321	12,793	2,650
City of Council Bluffs, IA	62,556	656	4	69	61	522	4,251	980	2,776	495
Total area actually reporting	99.9	3,349	51	366	789	2,143	29,256	5,615	19,979	3,662
Estimated total	100.0	3,349	51	366	789	2,143	29,276	5,618	19,995	3,663
Rate per 100,000 inhabitants	X	383.8	5.8	41.9	90.4	245.6	3,355.0	643.8	2,291.4	419.8
Orlando-Kissimmee-Sanford, FL M.S.A.	2,163,500									
Includes Lake, Orange, Osceola, and Seminole Counties										
City of Orlando	241,548	2,591	29	119	697	1,746	17,145	4,165	11,669	1,311
City of Kissimmee	60,495	593	3	24	118	448	3,364	870	2,332	162
City of Sanford	54,300	329	4	23	159	143	3,234	945	2,143	146
Total area actually reporting	100.0	12,887	122	679	2,968	9,118	79,243	22,072	51,775	5,396
Rate per 100,000 inhabitants	X	595.7	5.6	31.4	137.2	421.4	3,662.7	1,020.2	2,393.1	249.4
Oshkosh-Neenah, WI M.S.A.	167,722									
Includes Winnebago County										
City of Oshkosh	66,371	179	0	11	20	148	1,668	315	1,330	23
City of Neenah	25,612	36	0	4	1	31	407	72	327	8
Total area actually reporting	100.0	321	1	24	26	270	3,195	627	2,508	60
Rate per 100,000 inhabitants	X	191.4	0.6	14.3	15.5	161.0	1,904.9	373.8	1,495.3	35.8
Owensboro, KY M.S.A.	115,545									
Includes Daviess, Hancock, and McLean Counties										
City of Owensboro	57,661	143	1	46	37	59	2,323	513	1,711	99
Total area actually reporting	100.0	164	1	56	42	65	3,050	714	2,212	124
Rate per 100,000 inhabitants	X	141.9	0.9	48.5	36.3	56.3	2,639.7	617.9	1,914.4	107.3
Oxnard-Thousand Oaks-Ventura, CA M.S.A.	832,997									
Includes Ventura County										
City of Oxnard	200,225	619	8	26	274	311	3,499	577	2,563	359
City of Thousand Oaks	128,172	137	1	10	34	92	1,788	319	1,409	60
City of Ventura	107,684	326	1	20	135	170	3,320	657	2,468	195
City of Camarillo	65,968	79	2	10	17	50	882	160	675	47
Total area actually reporting	100.0	1,705	15	101	616	973	14,169	2,654	10,501	1,014
Rate per 100,000 inhabitants	X	204.7	1.8	12.1	73.9	116.8	1,701.0	318.6	1,260.6	121.7

X = Not applicable.

Table II-6.   Crime, by Selected Metropolitan Statistical Area, 2011—*Continued*

(Number, percent, rate per 100,000 population.)

Area	Population	Violent crime	Murder and non-negligent man-slaughter	Forcible rape	Robbery	Aggravated assault	Property crime	Burglary	Larceny-theft	Motor vehicle theft
Palm Bay-Melbourne-Titusville, FL M.S.A...........................	550,781									
Includes Brevard County										
City of Palm Bay	104,596	601	2	22	97	480	2,739	808	1,786	145
City of Melbourne	77,105	750	3	25	158	564	4,010	873	3,021	116
City of Titusville	44,357	270	2	27	66	175	1,634	423	1,076	135
Total area actually reporting	100.0	3,262	15	174	561	2,512	18,155	4,616	12,791	748
Rate per 100,000 inhabitants........................	X	592.2	2.7	31.6	101.9	456.1	3,296.2	838.1	2,322.3	135.8
Palm Coast, FL M.S.A.	97,000									
Includes Flagler County...........................										
Total area actually reporting	100.0	311	1	19	37	254	2,064	505	1,484	75
Rate per 100,000 inhabitants........................	X	320.6	1.0	19.6	38.1	261.9	2,127.8	520.6	1,529.9	77.3
Panama City-Lynn Haven-Panama City Beach,										
FL M.S.A.............................	171,153									
Includes Bay County										
City of Panama City	36,981	316	3	11	78	224	2,281	410	1,753	118
City of Lynn Haven	18,745	66	0	2	6	58	499	91	399	9
City of Panama City Beach	12,182	84	1	10	18	55	1,111	194	911	6
Total area actually reporting	100.0	915	12	62	173	668	7,424	1,628	5,472	324
Rate per 100,000 inhabitants........................	X	534.6	7.0	36.2	101.1	390.3	4,337.6	951.2	3,197.1	189.3
Pascagoula, MS M.S.A.	162,859									
Includes George and Jackson Counties										
City of Pascagoula	22,477	74	1	14	41	18	1,509	349	1,083	77
Total area actually reporting	100.0	548	5	69	120	354	5,358	1,628	3,393	337
Rate per 100,000 inhabitants........................	X	336.5	3.1	42.4	73.7	217.4	3,290.0	999.6	2,083.4	206.9
Pensacola-Ferry Pass-Brent, FL M.S.A.	455,110									
Includes Escambia and Santa Rosa Counties										
City of Pensacola	52,631	383	2	28	102	251	2,974	610	2,226	138
Total area actually reporting	100.0	2,397	18	198	581	1,600	16,320	3,963	11,529	828
Rate per 100,000 inhabitants........................	X	526.7	4.0	43.5	127.7	351.6	3,585.9	870.8	2,533.2	181.9
Peoria, IL M.S.A.	380,327									
Includes Marshall, Peoria, Stark, Tazewell, and										
Woodford Counties										
City of Peoria	115,353	814	16	33	288	477	5,438	1,721	3,460	257
Total area actually reporting	83.1	1,319	20	111	329	859	9,242	2,701	6,155	386
Estimated total..	100.0	1,467	22	127	371	947	10,660	2,974	7,237	449
Rate per 100,000 inhabitants........................	X	385.7	5.8	33.4	97.5	249.0	2,802.9	782.0	1,902.8	118.1
Philadelphia-Camden-Wilmington, PA-NJ-DE-MD										
M.S.A.	5,988,988									
Includes the Metropolitan Divisions of Camden, NJ;										
Philadelphia, PA; and Wilmington, DE-MD-NJ										
City of Philadelphia, PA................................	1,530,873	18,268	324	833	8,246	8,865	59,617	12,057	40,113	7,447
City of Camden, NJ	77,604	2,152	47	66	857	1,182	4,462	1,436	2,226	800
City of Wilmington, DE	71,577	1,111	23	30	427	631	3,772	1,148	2,213	411
Total area actually reporting	99.7	31,844	486	1,625	13,047	16,686	164,188	33,358	117,885	12,945
Estimated total..	100.0	31,880	486	1,628	13,057	16,709	164,536	33,415	118,163	12,958
Rate per 100,000 inhabitants........................	X	532.3	8.1	27.2	218.0	279.0	2,747.3	557.9	1,973.0	216.4
Camden, NJ M.D.	1,254,841									
Includes Burlington, Camden, and Gloucester Counties										
Total area actually reporting	100.0	4,412	65	245	1,686	2,416	33,497	7,892	23,547	2,058
Rate per 100,000 inhabitants........................	X	351.6	5.2	19.5	134.4	192.5	2,669.4	628.9	1,876.5	164.0
Philadelphia, PA M.D.	4,021,780									
Includes Bucks, Chester, Delaware, Montgomery,										
and Philadelphia Counties										
Total area actually reporting	99.6	23,559	386	1,200	9,997	11,976	108,016	19,925	78,541	9,550
Estimated total..	100.0	23,595	386	1,203	10,007	11,999	108,364	19,982	78,819	9,563
Rate per 100,000 inhabitants........................	X	586.7	9.6	29.9	248.8	298.4	2,694.4	496.8	1,959.8	237.8
Wilmington, DE-MD-NJ M.D........................	712,367									
Includes New Castle County, DE; Cecil County, MD;										
and Salem County, NJ										
Total area actually reporting	100.0	3,873	35	180	1,364	2,294	22,675	5,541	15,797	1,337
Rate per 100,000 inhabitants........................	X	543.7	4.9	25.3	191.5	322.0	3,183.1	777.8	2,217.5	187.7

X = Not applicable.

Table II-6.   Crime, by Selected Metropolitan Statistical Area, 2011—*Continued*

(Number, percent, rate per 100,000 population.)

Area	Population	Violent crime	Murder and non-negligent man-slaughter	Forcible rape	Robbery	Aggravated assault	Property crime	Burglary	Larceny-theft	Motor vehicle theft
Phoenix-Mesa-Glendale, AZ M.S.A.	4,252,245									
Includes Maricopa and Pinal Counties										
City of Phoenix	1,466,097	8,089	116	559	3,324	4,090	64,479	18,666	38,258	7,555
City of Mesa	445,256	1,838	18	131	497	1,192	15,117	2,769	11,407	941
City of Glendale	229,931	1,114	22	44	431	617	14,738	2,442	10,838	1,458
City of Scottsdale	220,462	400	4	34	125	237	6,724	1,424	5,054	246
City of Tempe	164,008	787	5	45	237	500	8,933	1,579	6,804	550
Total area actually reporting	99.9	16,144	209	1,155	5,352	9,428	155,389	37,490	104,283	13,616
Estimated total	100.0	16,152	209	1,156	5,354	9,433	155,482	37,510	104,351	13,621
Rate per 100,000 inhabitants	X	379.8	4.9	27.2	125.9	221.8	3,656.5	882.1	2,454.0	320.3
Pine Bluff, AR M.S.A.	101,017									
Includes Cleveland, Jefferson, and Lincoln Counties										
City of Pine Bluff	49,454	683	12	41	152	478	4,008	1,565	2,168	275
Total area actually reporting	98.2	768	15	48	162	543	4,988	1,984	2,604	400
Estimated total	100.0	777	15	49	163	550	5,059	2,008	2,648	403
Rate per 100,000 inhabitants	X	769.2	14.8	48.5	161.4	544.5	5,008.1	1,987.8	2,621.3	398.9
Pittsburgh, PA M.S.A.	2,363,799									
Includes Allegheny, Armstrong, Beaver, Butler, Fayette, Washington, and Westmoreland Counties										
City of Pittsburgh	308,609	2,476	44	67	1,126	1,239	10,063	2,686	6,897	480
Total area actually reporting	99.1	7,043	90	422	2,139	4,392	45,075	10,040	33,199	1,836
Estimated total	100.0	7,084	90	425	2,150	4,419	45,480	10,106	33,523	1,851
Rate per 100,000 inhabitants	X	299.7	3.8	18.0	91.0	186.9	1,924.0	427.5	1,418.2	78.3
Pittsfield, MA M.S.A.	132,019									
Includes Berkshire County										
City of Pittsfield	45,010	269	4	31	40	194	1,266	459	738	69
Total area actually reporting	93.5	515	4	65	53	393	3,013	1,012	1,881	120
Estimated total	100.0	542	4	67	58	413	3,183	1,054	1,998	131
Rate per 100,000 inhabitants	X	410.5	3.0	50.8	43.9	312.8	2,411.0	798.4	1,513.4	99.2
Pocatello, ID M.S.A.	91,658									
Includes Bannock and Power Counties										
City of Pocatello	54,855	132	3	15	5	109	1,794	262	1,457	75
Total area actually reporting	100.0	192	3	20	7	162	2,611	335	2,187	89
Rate per 100,000 inhabitants	X	209.5	3.3	21.8	7.6	176.7	2,848.6	365.5	2,386.0	97.1
Ponce, PR M.S.A.	240,170									
Includes Juana Diaz, Ponce, and Villalba Municipios										
Total area actually reporting	100.0	653	81	8	338	226	2,792	865	1,795	132
Rate per 100,000 inhabitants	X	271.9	33.7	3.3	140.7	94.1	1,162.5	360.2	747.4	55.0
Portland-South Portland-Biddeford, ME M.S.A.	514,030									
Includes Cumberland, Sagadahoc, and York Counties										
City of Portland	66,185	190	2	36	92	60	2,639	441	2,096	102
City of South Portland	24,999	60	0	5	12	43	860	81	760	19
City of Biddeford	21,274	79	0	14	21	44	1,169	244	908	17
Total area actually reporting	100.0	672	5	135	186	346	13,262	2,919	9,891	452
Rate per 100,000 inhabitants	X	130.7	1.0	26.3	36.2	67.3	2,580.0	567.9	1,924.2	87.9
Port St. Lucie, FL M.S.A.	429,887									
Includes Martin and St. Lucie Counties										
City of Port St. Lucie	166,846	371	6	30	61	274	3,861	1,128	2,590	143
Total area actually reporting	100.0	1,481	22	95	398	966	12,063	3,360	8,247	456
Rate per 100,000 inhabitants	X	344.5	5.1	22.1	92.6	224.7	2,806.1	781.6	1,918.4	106.1
Poughkeepsie-Newburgh-Middletown, NY M.S.A.	673,314									
Includes Dutchess and Orange Counties										
City of Poughkeepsie	32,883	326	5	22	107	192	1,029	283	693	53
City of Newburgh	28,996	527	4	11	254	258	1,243	401	782	60
City of Middletown	28,212	163	2	9	57	95	947	167	755	25
Total area actually reporting	98.4	1,604	16	95	535	958	12,915	2,353	10,159	403
Estimated total	100.0	1,623	16	96	542	969	13,115	2,384	10,321	410
Rate per 100,000 inhabitants	X	241.0	2.4	14.3	80.5	143.9	1,947.8	354.1	1,532.9	60.9
Prescott, AZ M.S.A.	214,020									
Includes Yavapai County										
City of Prescott	40,407	171	4	12	13	142	1,258	260	960	38
Total area actually reporting	100.0	766	17	35	32	682	4,627	1,115	3,305	207
Rate per 100,000 inhabitants	X	357.9	7.9	16.4	15.0	318.7	2,161.9	521.0	1,544.2	96.7

X = Not applicable.

Table II-6.   Crime, by Selected Metropolitan Statistical Area, 2011—*Continued*

(Number, percent, rate per 100,000 population.)

Area	Population	Violent crime	Murder and non-negligent man-slaughter	Forcible rape	Robbery	Aggravated assault	Property crime	Burglary	Larceny-theft	Motor vehicle theft
Provo-Orem, UT M.S.A.	536,977									
Includes Juab and Utah Counties										
City of Provo	114,659	149	4	27	26	92	2,888	386	2,400	102
City of Orem	90,033	45	0	20	10	15	2,322	166	2,069	87
Total area actually reporting	100.0	398	5	102	58	233	11,834	1,635	9,754	445
Rate per 100,000 inhabitants	X	74.1	0.9	19.0	10.8	43.4	2,203.8	304.5	1,816.5	82.9
Pueblo, CO M.S.A.[1]	161,834									
Includes Pueblo County										
City of Pueblo[1]	108,452	831	12	40	173	606	5,494	1,590	3,434	470
Total area actually reporting	100.0	861	13	41	179	628	7,136	1,923	4,683	530
Rate per 100,000 inhabitants	X	532.0	8.0	25.3	110.6	388.1	4,409.5	1,188.3	2,893.7	327.5
Punta Gorda, FL M.S.A.	162,158									
Includes Charlotte County										
City of Punta Gorda	16,868	15	0	0	3	12	326	55	258	13
Total area actually reporting	100.0	396	2	31	53	310	4,037	1,144	2,780	113
Rate per 100,000 inhabitants	X	244.2	1.2	19.1	32.7	191.2	2,489.5	705.5	1,714.4	69.7
Racine, WI M.S.A.	196,259									
Includes Racine County										
City of Racine	79,204	324	5	14	186	119	3,605	1,239	2,227	139
Total area actually reporting	100.0	455	7	27	225	196	5,652	1,558	3,890	204
Rate per 100,000 inhabitants	X	231.8	3.6	13.8	114.6	99.9	2,879.9	793.8	1,982.1	103.9
Raleigh-Cary, NC M.S.A.	1,144,826									
Includes Franklin, Johnston, and Wake Counties										
City of Raleigh	409,014	1,724	17	127	680	900	13,242	2,985	9,343	914
City of Cary	136,949	108	1	13	41	53	2,093	370	1,658	65
Total area actually reporting	99.6	2,773	30	222	923	1,598	29,533	7,534	20,316	1,683
Estimated total	100.0	2,785	30	223	926	1,606	29,712	7,574	20,449	1,689
Rate per 100,000 inhabitants	X	243.3	2.6	19.5	80.9	140.3	2,595.3	661.6	1,786.2	147.5
Rapid City, SD M.S.A.	127,919									
Includes Meade and Pennington Counties										
City of Rapid City	68,782	437	3	99	57	278	2,960	560	2,244	156
Total area actually reporting	100.0	519	4	127	58	330	3,713	714	2,806	193
Rate per 100,000 inhabitants	X	405.7	3.1	99.3	45.3	258.0	2,902.6	558.2	2,193.6	150.9
Reading, PA M.S.A.	412,754									
Includes Berks County										
City of Reading	88,363	758	13	22	377	346	3,301	1,380	1,501	420
Total area actually reporting	97.2	1,249	19	59	445	726	8,762	2,266	5,857	639
Estimated total	100.0	1,272	19	61	451	741	8,987	2,303	6,037	647
Rate per 100,000 inhabitants	X	308.2	4.6	14.8	109.3	179.5	2,177.3	558.0	1,462.6	156.8
Redding, CA M.S.A.	179,306									
Includes Shasta County										
City of Redding	90,917	701	3	63	100	535	3,396	823	2,237	336
Total area actually reporting	100.0	1,302	6	98	132	1,066	4,954	1,416	2,996	542
Rate per 100,000 inhabitants	X	726.1	3.3	54.7	73.6	594.5	2,762.9	789.7	1,670.9	302.3
Reno-Sparks, NV M.S.A.	429,004									
Includes Storey and Washoe Counties										
City of Reno	227,120	1,108	14	27	383	684	6,550	1,618	4,311	621
City of Sparks	91,025	285	7	46	75	157	2,447	656	1,600	191
Total area actually reporting	100.0	1,680	24	88	478	1,090	10,452	2,718	6,842	892
Rate per 100,000 inhabitants	X	391.6	5.6	20.5	111.4	254.1	2,436.3	633.6	1,594.9	207.9
Richmond, VA M.S.A.	1,273,282									
Includes Amelia, Caroline, Charles City, Chesterfield, Cumberland, Dinwiddie, Goochland, Hanover, Henrico, King and Queen, King William, Louisa, New Kent, Powhatan, Prince George, and Sussex Counties and Colonial Heights, Hopewell, Petersburg, and Richmond Cities										
City of Richmond	206,654	1,428	36	44	676	672	8,647	1,886	5,833	928
Total area actually reporting	100.0	2,990	71	189	1,208	1,522	31,776	6,433	23,295	2,048
Rate per 100,000 inhabitants	X	234.8	5.6	14.8	94.9	119.5	2,495.6	505.2	1,829.5	160.8

X = Not applicable.

[1] Because of changes in the state/local agency's reporting practices, figures are not comparable to previous years' data.

Table II-6.   Crime, by Selected Metropolitan Statistical Area, 2011—*Continued*

(Number, percent, rate per 100,000 population.)

Area	Population	Violent crime	Murder and non-negligent man-slaughter	Forcible rape	Robbery	Aggravated assault	Property crime	Burglary	Larceny-theft	Motor vehicle theft
Riverside-San Bernardino-Ontario, CA M.S.A.	4,274,518									
Includes Riverside and San Bernardino Counties										
City of Riverside	307,443	1,310	13	57	458	782	9,631	2,080	6,278	1,273
City of San Bernardino	212,392	1,861	30	77	720	1,034	8,461	2,359	4,446	1,656
City of Ontario	165,851	493	6	27	209	251	4,858	939	3,057	862
City of Victorville	117,266	686	6	37	261	382	3,931	1,359	2,086	486
City of Temecula	101,274	95	0	7	54	34	2,406	547	1,700	159
City of Chino	78,900	247	2	9	58	178	2,072	530	1,341	201
City of Hemet	79,582	361	5	15	124	217	3,472	1,173	1,911	388
City of Redlands	69,555	197	3	18	90	86	2,621	531	1,766	324
City of Colton	52,767	189	4	8	90	87	1,558	446	844	268
City of Palm Desert	49,015	76	2	2	40	32	2,147	593	1,439	115
Total area actually reporting	100.0	15,172	185	757	4,931	9,299	120,476	34,714	68,600	17,162
Rate per 100,000 inhabitants	X	354.9	4.3	17.7	115.4	217.5	2,818.5	812.1	1,604.9	401.5
Roanoke, VA M.S.A.	312,395									
Includes Botetourt, Craig, Franklin, and Roanoke Counties and Roanoke and Salem Cities										
City of Roanoke	98,191	589	8	33	175	373	4,635	928	3,424	283
Total area actually reporting	100.0	850	10	73	215	552	7,975	1,524	6,035	416
Rate per 100,000 inhabitants	X	272.1	3.2	23.4	68.8	176.7	2,552.9	487.8	1,931.8	133.2
Rochester, MN M.S.A.[2]	187,446									
Includes Dodge, Olmsted, and Wabasha Counties[2]										
City of Rochester[2]	107,593			1	65	102	2,323	425	1,809	89
Total area actually reporting	98.2			1	67	156	3,293	651	2,498	144
Estimated total	100.0			1	68	159	3,382	663	2,571	148
Rate per 100,000 inhabitants	X		0.5		36.3	84.8	1,804.3	353.7	1,371.6	79.0
Rochester, NY M.S.A.	1,059,061									
Includes Livingston, Monroe, Ontario, Orleans, and Wayne Counties										
City of Rochester	211,511	2,029	31	95	755	1,148	10,934	3,384	6,849	701
Total area actually reporting	100.0	3,064	43	220	1,036	1,765	27,384	6,232	19,901	1,251
Rate per 100,000 inhabitants	X	289.3	4.1	20.8	97.8	166.7	2,585.7	588.4	1,879.1	118.1
Rockford, IL M.S.A.	350,483									
Includes Boone and Winnebago Counties										
City of Rockford	153,331	2,106	21	112	566	1,407	7,122	1,890	4,746	486
Total area actually reporting	80.5	2,341	25	155	599	1,562	9,593	2,501	6,515	577
Estimated total	100.0	2,476	27	171	630	1,648	10,868	2,793	7,439	636
Rate per 100,000 inhabitants	X	706.5	7.7	48.8	179.8	470.2	3,100.9	796.9	2,122.5	181.5
Rocky Mount, NC M.S.A.	154,324									
Includes Edgecombe and Nash Counties										
City of Rocky Mount	58,206	569	12	13	151	393	3,916	1,146	2,625	145
Total area actually reporting	99.9%	766	18	21	198	529	5,961	1,966	3,747	248
Estimated total	100.0	770	18	21	199	532	6,022	1,980	3,792	250
Rate per 100,000 inhabitants	X	499.0	11.7	13.6	128.9	344.7	3,902.2	1,283.0	2,457.2	162.0
Rome, GA M.S.A.	97,585									
Includes Floyd County										
City of Rome	36,781	227	4	18	62	143	2,202	472	1,655	75
Total area actually reporting	100.0	486	5	28	77	376	3,724	869	2,683	172
Rate per 100,000 inhabitants	X	498.0	5.1	28.7	78.9	385.3	3,816.2	890.5	2,749.4	176.3
Sacramento Arden-Arcade Roseville, CA M.S.A.	2,174,392									
Includes El Dorado, Placer, Sacramento, and Yolo Counties										
City of Sacramento	471,972	3,354	36	134	1,162	2,022	18,563	4,141	11,087	3,335
City of Roseville	120,184	248	1	24	43	180	3,541	534	2,786	221
City of Folsom	73,052	84	1	15	33	35	1,510	316	1,116	78
City of Woodland	56,120	178	1	28	42	107	1,188	338	721	129
Total area actually reporting	100.0	9,136	95	542	2,848	5,651	61,437	14,730	37,938	8,769
Rate per 100,000 inhabitants	X	420.2	4.4	24.9	131.0	259.9	2,825.5	677.4	1,744.8	403.3
Saginaw-Saginaw Township North, MI M.S.A.[1]	200,018									
Includes Saginaw County[1]										
City of Saginaw[1]	51,469	1,168	8	37	170	953	1,886	1,125	657	104
Total area actually reporting	97.9	1,560	14	85	221	1,240	4,874	1,969	2,677	228
Estimated total	100.0	1,572	14	86	224	1,248	4,982	1,993	2,753	236
Rate per 100,000 inhabitants	X	785.9	7.0	43.0	112.0	623.9	2,490.8	996.4	1,376.4	118.0

X = Not applicable.

[1] Because of changes in the state/local agency's reporting practices, figures are not comparable to previous years' data.

[2] The data collection methodology for the offense of forcible rape used by Chicago, Illinois, and the Minnesota state UCR Program (with the exception of Minneapolis and St. Paul, Minnesota) does not comply with national UCR Program guidelines. Consequently, its figures for forcible rape and violent crime (of which forcible rape is a part) are not published in this table.

Table II-6.   Crime, by Selected Metropolitan Statistical Area, 2011—*Continued*

(Number, percent, rate per 100,000 population.)

Area	Population	Violent crime	Murder and non-negligent man-slaughter	Forcible rape	Robbery	Aggravated assault	Property crime	Burglary	Larceny-theft	Motor vehicle theft
Salem, OR M.S.A.	394,898									
Includes Marion and Polk Counties										
City of Salem	156,283	519	3	32	119	365	5,960	891	4,641	428
Total area actually reporting	100.0	885	12	87	171	615	11,001	1,967	8,270	764
Rate per 100,000 inhabitants	X	224.1	3.0	22.0	43.3	155.7	2,785.8	498.1	2,094.2	193.5
Salinas, CA M.S.A.	419,936									
Includes Monterey County										
City of Salinas	152,210	1,115	15	34	374	692	4,492	1,140	2,189	1,163
Total area actually reporting	100.0	1,951	34	94	572	1,251	9,893	2,650	5,573	1,670
Rate per 100,000 inhabitants	X	464.6	8.1	22.4	136.2	297.9	2,355.8	631.0	1,327.1	397.7
Salisbury, MD M.S.A.	126,390									
Includes Somerset and Wicomico Counties										
City of Salisbury	30,631	369	1	23	74	271	1,832	402	1,369	61
Total area actually reporting	100.0	664	6	27	125	506	3,966	1,056	2,786	124
Rate per 100,000 inhabitants	X	525.4	4.7	21.4	98.9	400.3	3,137.9	835.5	2,204.3	98.1
Salt Lake City, UT M.S.A.	1,145,892									
Includes Salt Lake, Summit, and Tooele Counties										
City of Salt Lake City	190,038	1,213	6	119	340	748	12,798	1,658	9,654	1,486
Total area actually reporting	99.9	3,481	24	457	819	2,181	47,274	6,879	35,808	4,587
Estimated total	100.0	3,481	24	457	819	2,181	47,286	6,881	35,817	4,588
Rate per 100,000 inhabitants	X	303.8	2.1	39.9	71.5	190.3	4,126.6	600.5	3,125.7	400.4
San Angelo, TX M.S.A.	114,176									
Includes Irion and Tom Green Counties										
City of San Angelo	95,161	250	0	32	42	176	3,624	801	2,685	138
Total area actually reporting	100.0	287	0	48	45	194	3,958	886	2,923	149
Rate per 100,000 inhabitants	X	251.4	0.0	42.0	39.4	169.9	3,466.6	776.0	2,560.1	130.5
San Antonio-New Braunfels, TX M.S.A.	2,187,591									
Includes Atascosa, Bandera, Bexar, Comal, Guadalupe, Kendall, Medina, and Wilson Counties										
City of San Antonio	1,355,339	7,038	89	492	1,785	4,672	80,868	15,334	59,641	5,893
City of New Braunfels	58,955	119	2	7	26	84	1,943	298	1,565	80
Total area actually reporting	99.9	8,706	111	676	2,049	5,870	102,071	20,160	74,909	7,002
Estimated total	100.0	8,709	111	676	2,050	5,872	102,108	20,168	74,936	7,004
Rate per 100,000 inhabitants	X	398.1	5.1	30.9	93.7	268.4	4,667.6	921.9	3,425.5	320.2
San Diego-Carlsbad-San Marcos, CA M.S.A.	3,131,701									
Includes San Diego County										
City of San Diego	1,316,919	5,104	38	293	1,456	3,317	29,709	5,840	17,610	6,259
City of Carlsbad	106,566	210	4	11	35	160	1,970	468	1,375	127
City of San Marcos	84,766	233	0	19	60	154	1,424	358	908	158
City of National City	59,271	372	1	12	137	222	1,814	300	1,046	468
Total area actually reporting	100.0	11,009	82	660	3,050	7,217	65,102	13,326	40,420	11,356
Rate per 100,000 inhabitants	X	351.5	2.6	21.1	97.4	230.4	2,078.8	425.5	1,290.7	362.6
Sandusky, OH M.S.A.	77,135									
Includes Erie County										
City of Sandusky	25,812	120	1	7	40	72	1,366	327	1,020	19
Total area actually reporting	98.7	222	1	12	52	157	2,300	590	1,663	47
Estimated total	100.0	224	1	12	53	158	2,329	596	1,685	48
Rate per 100,000 inhabitants	X	290.4	1.3	15.6	68.7	204.8	3,019.4	772.7	2,184.5	62.2
San Francisco-Oakland-Fremont, CA M.S.A.	4,386,357									
Includes the Metropolitan Divisions of Oakland-Fremont-Hayward and San Francisco-San Mateo-Redwood City										
City of San Francisco	814,701	5,374	50	131	3,088	2,105	32,886	4,408	24,304	4,174
City of Oakland	395,317	6,652	104	202	3,365	2,981	20,904	5,170	9,429	6,305
City of Fremont	216,606	384	2	35	156	191	3,952	1,206	2,303	443
City of Hayward	145,881	579	7	44	360	168	3,782	988	1,693	1,101
City of Berkeley	113,903	482	1	19	340	122	5,064	976	3,460	628
City of San Mateo	98,350	246	1	20	69	156	1,732	306	1,288	138
City of San Leandro	85,949	367	7	19	217	124	3,205	671	1,957	577
City of Redwood City	77,718	177	0	26	63	88	1,487	436	918	133
City of Pleasanton	71,111	59	0	4	24	31	1,215	182	949	84
City of Walnut Creek	64,927	69	1	2	14	52	2,024	422	1,472	130
City of South San Francisco	64,380	138	1	13	47	77	1,327	412	764	151
City of San Rafael	58,391	200	2	20	65	113	1,473	309	1,011	153
Total area actually reporting	100.0	22,294	264	891	10,369	10,770	135,104	28,864	83,296	22,944
Rate per 100,000 inhabitants	X	508.3	6.0	20.3	236.4	245.5	3,080.1	658.0	1,899.0	523.1

X = Not applicable.

Table II-6. Crime, by Selected Metropolitan Statistical Area, 2011—*Continued*

(Number, percent, rate per 100,000 population.)

Area	Population	Violent crime	Murder and non-negligent man-slaughter	Forcible rape	Robbery	Aggravated assault	Property crime	Burglary	Larceny-theft	Motor vehicle theft
Oakland-Fremont-Hayward, CA M.D.	2,589,383									
Includes Alameda and Contra Costa Counties										
Total area actually reporting	100.0	14,712	196	574	6,604	7,338	82,633	20,020	45,716	16,897
Rate per 100,000 inhabitants	X	568.2	7.6	22.2	255.0	283.4	3,191.2	773.2	1,765.5	652.5
San Francisco-San Mateo-Redwood City, CA M.D.	1,796,974									
Includes Marin, San Francisco, and San Mateo Counties										
Total area actually reporting	100.0	7,582	68	317	3,765	3,432	52,471	8,844	37,580	6,047
Rate per 100,000 inhabitants	X	421.9	3.8	17.6	209.5	191.0	2,920.0	492.2	2,091.3	336.5
San German-Cabo Rojo, PR M.S.A.	137,202									
Includes Cabo Rojo, Lajas, Sabana Grande, and San German Municipios										
Total area actually reporting	100.0	92	6	0	56	30	1,011	503	464	44
Rate per 100,000 inhabitants	X	67.1	4.4	0.0	40.8	21.9	736.9	366.6	338.2	32.1
San Jose-Sunnyvale-Santa Clara, CA M.S.A.	1,858,506									
Includes San Benito and Santa Clara Counties										
City of San Jose	957,062	3,206	39	226	1,101	1,840	21,972	4,223	12,628	5,121
City of Sunnyvale	141,728	150	3	21	68	58	1,970	393	1,351	226
City of Santa Clara	117,837	177	2	14	67	94	2,933	409	2,202	322
City of Mountain View	74,937	153	0	7	41	105	1,353	167	1,086	100
City of Milpitas	67,575	102	2	10	59	31	1,824	299	1,315	210
City of Palo Alto	65,160	64	0	3	24	37	1,248	286	923	39
City of Cupertino	58,987	46	1	4	18	23	711	139	555	17
Total area actually reporting	100.0	4,760	61	368	1,614	2,717	39,884	7,574	25,429	6,881
Rate per 100,000 inhabitants	X	256.1	3.3	19.8	86.8	146.2	2,146.0	407.5	1,368.2	370.2
San Juan-Caguas-Guaynabo, Puerto Rico M.S.A.	2,468,598									
Includes Aguas Buenas, Aibonito, Arecibo, Barceloneta, Barranquitas, Bayamon, Caguas, Camuy, Canovanas, Carolina, Catano, Cayey, Ciales, Cidra, Comerio, Corozal, Dorado, Florida, Guaynabo, Gurabo, Hatillo, Humacao, Juncos, Las Piedras, Loiza, Manati, Maunabo, Morovis, Naguabo, Naranjito, Orocovis, Quebradillas, Rio Grande, San Juan, San Lorenzo, Toa Alta, Toa Baja, Trujillo Alto, Vega Alta, Vega Baja, and Yabucoa Municipios										
Total area actually reporting	100.0	8,309	894	28	5,439	1,948	37,157	10,826	21,102	5,229
Rate per 100,000 inhabitants	X	336.6	36.2	1.1	220.3	78.9	1,505.2	438.5	854.8	211.8
San Luis Obispo-Paso Robles, CA M.S.A.	272,807									
Includes San Luis Obispo County										
City of San Luis Obispo	45,649	134	2	24	34	74	1,782	330	1,345	107
City of Paso Robles	30,143	95	2	11	12	70	832	148	632	52
Total area actually reporting	100.0	680	5	91	81	503	6,196	1,411	4,360	425
Rate per 100,000 inhabitants	X	249.3	1.8	33.4	29.7	184.4	2,271.2	517.2	1,598.2	155.8
Santa Barbara-Santa Maria-Goleta, CA M.S.A.	428,878									
Includes Santa Barbara County										
City of Santa Barbara	89,449	319	0	37	80	202	2,756	541	2,124	91
City of Santa Maria	100,723	716	7	18	153	538	2,429	655	1,510	264
City of Goleta	30,239	40	0	4	8	28	383	98	268	17
Total area actually reporting	100.0	1,657	10	130	298	1,219	9,083	2,167	6,367	549
Rate per 100,000 inhabitants	X	386.4	2.3	30.3	69.5	284.2	2,117.9	505.3	1,484.6	128.0
Santa Cruz-Watsonville, CA M.S.A.	265,467									
Includes Santa Cruz County										
City of Santa Cruz	60,651	480	1	23	113	343	3,356	568	2,603	185
City of Watsonville	51,801	281	5	14	92	170	1,605	328	967	310
Total area actually reporting	100.0	1,169	10	75	252	832	8,744	1,958	5,964	822
Rate per 100,000 inhabitants	X	440.4	3.8	28.3	94.9	313.4	3,293.8	737.6	2,246.6	309.6
Santa Fe, NM M.S.A.	145,783									
Includes Santa Fe County										
City of Santa Fe	68,707	305	2	19	77	207	3,749	1,943	1,639	167
Total area actually reporting	100.0	552	4	30	103	415	5,378	2,867	2,252	259
Rate per 100,000 inhabitants	X	378.6	2.7	20.6	70.7	284.7	3,689.0	1,966.6	1,544.8	177.7
Santa Rosa-Petaluma, CA M.S.A.	489,566									
Includes Sonoma County										
City of Santa Rosa	169,788	682	5	58	134	485	3,706	637	2,794	275
City of Petaluma	58,622	140	0	11	23	106	884	131	693	60
Total area actually reporting	100.0	1,702	11	138	234	1,319	8,307	1,664	6,041	602
Rate per 100,000 inhabitants	X	347.7	2.2	28.2	47.8	269.4	1,696.8	339.9	1,234.0	123.0

X = Not applicable.

Table II-6.   Crime, by Selected Metropolitan Statistical Area, 2011—*Continued*

(Number, percent, rate per 100,000 population.)

Area	Population	Violent crime	Murder and non-negligent man-slaughter	Forcible rape	Robbery	Aggravated assault	Property crime	Burglary	Larceny-theft	Motor vehicle theft
Savannah, GA M.S.A.	352,188									
Includes Bryan, Chatham, and Effingham Counties										
City of Savannah-Chatham Metropolitan	226,422	889	26	36	488	339	9,579	2,241	6,608	730
Total area actually reporting	100.0	1,202	30	68	548	556	12,773	3,053	8,838	882
Rate per 100,000 inhabitants	X	341.3	8.5	19.3	155.6	157.9	3,626.8	866.9	2,509.5	250.4
Scranton Wilkes-Barre, PA M.S.A.	565,428									
Includes Lackawanna, Luzerne, and Wyoming Counties										
City of Scranton	76,332	226	3	34	95	94	2,556	620	1,810	126
City of Wilkes-Barre	41,630	213	2	12	129	70	1,483	317	1,080	86
Total area actually reporting	97.5	1,494	15	104	392	983	12,364	2,524	9,190	650
Estimated total	100.0	1,523	15	106	400	1,002	12,639	2,569	9,410	660
Rate per 100,000 inhabitants	X	269.4	2.7	18.7	70.7	177.2	2,235.3	454.3	1,664.2	116.7
Seattle-Tacoma-Bellevue, WA M.S.A.	3,493,774									
Includes the Metropolitan Divisions of Seattle-Bellevue-Everett and Tacoma										
City of Seattle	618,209	3,664	20	100	1,418	2,126	31,792	6,807	21,585	3,400
City of Tacoma	201,510	1,507	11	125	446	925	12,062	2,709	7,228	2,125
City of Bellevue	124,283	140	1	23	58	58	3,539	607	2,775	157
City of Everett	104,635	450	5	49	143	253	7,503	1,163	5,415	925
City of Kent	93,861	577	1	60	210	306	4,989	1,223	2,977	789
City of Renton	92,354	292	1	33	115	143	4,223	917	2,748	558
City of Auburn	71,281	279	2	23	107	147	3,797	762	2,435	600
Total area actually reporting	100.0	11,536	73	1,044	3,808	6,611	132,146	29,558	86,948	15,640
Rate per 100,000 inhabitants	X	330.2	2.1	29.9	109.0	189.2	3,782.3	846.0	2,488.7	447.7
Seattle-Bellevue-Everett, WA M.D.	2,686,073									
Includes King and Snohomish Counties										
Total area actually reporting	100.0	8,160	47	749	2,888	4,476	100,812	21,770	67,561	11,481
Rate per 100,000 inhabitants	X	303.8	1.7	27.9	107.5	166.6	3,753.1	810.5	2,515.2	427.4
Tacoma, WA M.D.	807,701									
Includes Pierce County										
Total area actually reporting	100.0	3,376	26	295	920	2,135	31,334	7,788	19,387	4,159
Rate per 100,000 inhabitants	X	418.0	3.2	36.5	113.9	264.3	3,879.4	964.2	2,400.3	514.9
Sebastian-Vero Beach, FL M.S.A.	139,909									
Includes Indian River County										
City of Sebastian	22,228	41	0	3	5	33	442	128	303	11
City of Vero Beach	15,427	46	2	4	13	27	701	175	513	13
Total area actually reporting	100.0	450	5	32	82	331	3,959	1,107	2,742	110
Rate per 100,000 inhabitants	X	321.6	3.6	22.9	58.6	236.6	2,829.7	791.2	1,959.8	78.6
Sheboygan, WI M.S.A.	116,010									
Includes Sheboygan County										
City of Sheboygan	49,503	131	0	16	26	89	1,446	231	1,165	50
Total area actually reporting	100.0	158	1	17	30	110	2,393	364	1,947	82
Rate per 100,000 inhabitants	X	136.2	0.9	14.7	25.9	94.8	2,062.8	313.8	1,678.3	70.7
Sherman-Denison, TX M.S.A.	123,421									
Includes Grayson County										
City of Sherman	39,332	158	1	1	41	115	1,549	325	1,174	50
City of Denison	23,159	91	2	9	14	66	1,145	288	807	50
Total area actually reporting	100.0	336	5	19	60	252	3,905	1,003	2,750	152
Rate per 100,000 inhabitants	X	272.2	4.1	15.4	48.6	204.2	3,164.0	812.7	2,228.1	123.2
Sioux City, IA-NE-SD M.S.A.	144,528									
Includes Woodbury County, IA; Dakota and Dixon Counties, NE; and Union County, SD										
City of Sioux City, IA	83,111	339	1	36	34	268	3,507	709	2,635	163
Total area actually reporting	96.4	415	2	45	36	332	4,333	878	3,248	207
Estimated total	100.0	419	2	46	36	335	4,410	889	3,311	210
Rate per 100,000 inhabitants	X	289.9	1.4	31.8	24.9	231.8	3,051.3	615.1	2,290.9	145.3
Sioux Falls, SD M.S.A.	231,036									
Includes Lincoln, McCook, Minnehaha, and Turner Counties										
City of Sioux Falls	155,760	440	5	108	75	252	4,707	880	3,554	273
Total area actually reporting	99.8	497	5	127	77	288	5,508	1,094	4,103	311
Estimated total	100.0	497	5	127	77	288	5,513	1,095	4,107	311
Rate per 100,000 inhabitants	X	215.1	2.2	55.0	33.3	124.7	2,386.2	474.0	1,777.6	134.6

X = Not applicable.

Table II-6.   Crime, by Selected Metropolitan Statistical Area, 2011—*Continued*

(Number, percent, rate per 100,000 population.)

Area	Population	Violent crime	Murder and non-negligent man-slaughter	Forcible rape	Robbery	Aggravated assault	Property crime	Burglary	Larceny-theft	Motor vehicle theft
South Bend-Mishawaka, IN-MI M.S.A.	320,549									
Includes St. Joseph County, IN and Cass County, MI										
City of South Bend, IN	101,685	744	9	60	406	269	6,096	2,335	3,437	324
City of Mishawaka, IN	48,498	146	3	12	68	63	2,895	517	2,234	144
Total area actually reporting	95.9	1,087	16	105	501	465	11,521	3,582	7,367	572
Estimated total	100.0	1,123	16	109	509	489	11,866	3,657	7,611	598
Rate per 100,000 inhabitants	X	350.3	5.0	34.0	158.8	152.6	3,701.8	1,140.9	2,374.4	186.6
Spartanburg, SC M.S.A.	287,618									
Includes Spartanburg County										
City of Spartanburg	37,444	657	5	12	127	513	2,856	684	1,952	220
Total area actually reporting	99.8	1,399	12	83	254	1,050	10,179	2,746	6,634	799
Estimated total	100.0	1,401	12	83	254	1,052	10,201	2,750	6,651	800
Rate per 100,000 inhabitants	X	487.1	4.2	28.9	88.3	365.8	3,546.7	956.1	2,312.4	278.1
Spokane, WA M.S.A.	478,614									
Includes Spokane County										
City of Spokane	212,194	1,304	4	84	484	732	15,039	3,030	10,231	1,778
Total area actually reporting	100.0	1,644	7	128	582	927	24,591	5,254	16,771	2,566
Rate per 100,000 inhabitants	X	343.5	1.5	26.7	121.6	193.7	5,138.0	1,097.8	3,504.1	536.1
Springfield, IL M.S.A.	210,802									
Includes Menard and Sangamon Counties										
City of Springfield	116,600	1,278	8	103	258	909	7,176	1,883	5,076	217
Total area actually reporting	86.6	1,435	8	133	278	1,016	8,422	2,237	5,921	264
Estimated total	100.0	1,500	9	140	296	1,055	9,045	2,357	6,396	292
Rate per 100,000 inhabitants	X	711.6	4.3	66.4	140.4	500.5	4,290.8	1,118.1	3,034.1	138.5
Springfield, MA M.S.A.	697,165									
Includes Franklin, Hampden, and Hampshire Counties										
City of Springfield	153,993	1,581	20	31	532	998	7,365	2,499	4,072	794
Total area actually reporting	96.8	3,408	25	211	780	2,392	19,772	5,623	12,691	1,458
Estimated total	100.0	3,477	25	216	793	2,443	20,210	5,731	12,993	1,486
Rate per 100,000 inhabitants	X	498.7	3.6	31.0	113.7	350.4	2,898.9	822.0	1,863.7	213.1
Springfield, MO M.S.A.	438,299									
Includes Christian, Dallas, Greene, Polk, and Webster Counties										
City of Springfield	160,078	1,306	5	110	286	905	14,418	2,053	11,391	974
Total area actually reporting	100.0	1,867	9	133	330	1,395	20,106	3,601	15,223	1,282
Rate per 100,000 inhabitants	X	426.0	2.1	30.3	75.3	318.3	4,587.3	821.6	3,473.2	292.5
Springfield, OH M.S.A.	138,434									
Includes Clark County										
City of Springfield	60,652	390	3	32	209	146	4,630	1,614	2,816	200
Total area actually reporting	98.0	406	3	35	214	154	5,680	1,853	3,592	235
Estimated total	100.0	411	3	36	216	156	5,755	1,868	3,649	238
Rate per 100,000 inhabitants	X	296.9	2.2	26.0	156.0	112.7	4,157.2	1,349.4	2,635.9	171.9
State College, PA M.S.A.	154,481									
Includes Centre County										
City of State College	56,608	57	0	12	11	34	893	130	741	22
Total area actually reporting	100.0	171	0	47	31	93	2,470	460	1,952	58
Rate per 100,000 inhabitants	X	110.7	0.0	30.4	20.1	60.2	1,598.9	297.8	1,263.6	37.5
St. Cloud, MN M.S.A.[2]	190,553									
Includes Benton and Stearns Counties[2]										
City of St. Cloud[2]	66,350	X	0	X	45	129	2,578	431	2,040	107
Total area actually reporting	96.5	X	0	X	50	199	4,437	721	3,538	178
Estimated total	100.0	X	0	X	52	204	4,611	745	3,681	185
Rate per 100,000 inhabitants	X	X	0.0	X	27.3	107.1	2,419.8	391.0	1,931.7	97.1
St. Joseph, MO-KS M.S.A.	127,813									
Includes Doniphan County, KS and Andrew, Buchanan, and De Kalb Counties, MO										
City of St. Joseph, MO	77,059	281	4	21	82	174	4,056	907	2,870	279
Total area actually reporting	100.0	352	4	29	83	236	4,826	1,140	3,379	307
Rate per 100,000 inhabitants	X	275.4	3.1	22.7	64.9	184.6	3,775.8	891.9	2,643.7	240.2

X = Not applicable.

[2] The data collection methodology for the offense of forcible rape used by Chicago, Illinois, and the Minnesota state UCR Program (with the exception of Minneapolis and St. Paul, Minnesota) does not comply with national UCR Program guidelines. Consequently, its figures for forcible rape and violent crime (of which forcible rape is a part) are not published in this table.

Table II-6.   Crime, by Selected Metropolitan Statistical Area, 2011—*Continued*

(Number, percent, rate per 100,000 population.)

Area	Population	Violent crime	Murder and non-negligent man-slaughter	Forcible rape	Robbery	Aggravated assault	Property crime	Burglary	Larceny-theft	Motor vehicle theft
St. Louis, MO-IL M.S.A.[2]	2,824,159									
Includes Bond, Calhoun, Clinton, Jersey, Macoupin, Madison, Monroe, and St. Clair Counties, IL[2] and Franklin, Jefferson, Lincoln, St. Charles, St. Louis, Warren, and Washington Counties and St. Louis City, MO										
City of St. Louis, MO	320,454	5,950	113	188	2,127	3,522	25,669	7,015	15,285	3,369
City of St. Charles, MO	66,033	153	0	9	48	96	2,002	257	1,673	72
Total area actually reporting	95.9	13,725	212	684	3,709	9,120	85,802	20,525	58,510	6,767
Estimated total	100.0	13,992	215	713	3,784	9,280	88,365	21,019	60,465	6,881
Rate per 100,000 inhabitants	X	495.4	7.6	25.2	134.0	328.6	3,128.9	744.3	2,141.0	243.6
Stockton, CA M.S.A.	693,362									
Includes San Joaquin County										
City of Stockton	295,136	4,155	58	90	1,323	2,684	15,463	4,133	9,651	1,679
Total area actually reporting	100.0	5,694	87	140	1,723	3,744	29,142	7,931	18,193	3,018
Rate per 100,000 inhabitants	X	821.2	12.5	20.2	248.5	540.0	4,203.0	1,143.8	2,623.9	435.3
Sumter, SC M.S.A.	108,707									
Includes Sumter County										
City of Sumter	40,996	343	3	11	72	257	2,353	789	1,426	138
Total area actually reporting	100.0	550	17	25	116	392	3,866	1,219	2,387	260
Rate per 100,000 inhabitants	X	505.9	15.6	23.0	106.7	360.6	3,556.3	1,121.4	2,195.8	239.2
Syracuse, NY M.S.A.	665,555									
Includes Madison, Onondaga, and Oswego Counties										
City of Syracuse	145,822	1,302	11	63	388	840	5,275	1,705	3,261	309
Total area actually reporting	98.9	1,894	15	154	491	1,234	15,723	3,522	11,562	639
Estimated total	100.0	1,907	15	155	495	1,242	15,860	3,543	11,673	644
Rate per 100,000 inhabitants	X	286.5	2.3	23.3	74.4	186.6	2,383.0	532.3	1,753.9	96.8
Tallahassee, FL M.S.A.	372,419									
Includes Gadsden, Jefferson, Leon, and Wakulla Counties										
City of Tallahassee	183,848	1,661	10	107	511	1,033	9,363	3,252	5,748	363
Total area actually reporting	99.8	2,459	18	157	623	1,661	13,714	4,639	8,531	544
Estimated total	100.0	2,462	18	157	624	1,663	13,737	4,644	8,548	545
Rate per 100,000 inhabitants	X	661.1	4.8	42.2	167.6	446.5	3,688.6	1,247.0	2,295.3	146.3
Tampa-St. Petersburg-Clearwater, FL M.S.A.	2,821,174									
Includes Hernando, Hillsborough, Pasco, and Pinellas Counties										
City of Tampa	340,284	2,228	28	58	587	1,555	10,393	2,718	7,042	633
City of St. Petersburg	248,105	2,532	21	90	720	1,701	12,803	3,412	8,544	847
City of Clearwater	109,153	801	10	40	182	569	4,129	719	3,252	158
City of Largo	78,706	373	1	32	101	239	3,048	617	2,327	104
Total area actually reporting	100.0	12,277	134	687	2,960	8,496	87,498	21,996	60,961	4,541
Rate per 100,000 inhabitants	X	435.2	4.7	24.4	104.9	301.2	3,101.5	779.7	2,160.8	161.0
Terre Haute, IN M.S.A.	173,306									
Includes Clay, Sullivan, Vermillion, and Vigo Counties										
City of Terre Haute	61,095	152	4	17	91	40	3,942	934	2,725	283
Total area actually reporting	86.5	287	6	38	105	138	6,269	1,531	4,308	430
Estimated total	100.0	317	6	41	110	160	6,697	1,632	4,607	458
Rate per 100,000 inhabitants	X	182.9	3.5	23.7	63.5	92.3	3,864.3	941.7	2,658.3	264.3
Texarkana, TX-Texarkana, AR M.S.A.	138,304									
Includes Miller County, AR and Bowie County, TX										
City of Texarkana, TX	37,177	468	3	25	77	363	2,477	746	1,590	141
City of Texarkana, AR	30,145	245	1	10	35	199	2,270	525	1,623	122
Total area actually reporting	100.0	913	10	67	120	716	6,428	1,828	4,191	409
Rate per 100,000 inhabitants	X	660.1	7.2	48.4	86.8	517.7	4,647.7	1,321.7	3,030.3	295.7
Toledo, OH M.S.A.[3]	651,905									
Includes Fulton, Lucas, Ottawa, and Wood Counties										
City of Toledo[3]	287,418	2,868	30	124	1,152	1,562		8,366		1,465
Total area actually reporting	90.2	3,192	39	161	1,247	1,745		9,936		1,745
Estimated total	100.0	3,289	40	175	1,285	1,789		10,299		1,808
Rate per 100,000 inhabitants	X	504.5	6.1	26.8	197.1	274.4		1,579.8		277.3

X = Not applicable.

[2] The data collection methodology for the offense of forcible rape used by Chicago, Illinois, and the Minnesota state UCR Program (with the exception of Minneapolis and St. Paul, Minnesota) does not comply with national UCR Program guidelines. Consequently, its figures for forcible rape and violent crime (of which forcible rape is a part) are not published in this table.

[3] The FBI determined that the agency did not follow national Uniform Crime Reporting (UCR) Program guidelines for reporting an offense. Consequently, this figure is not included in this table.

Table II-6. Crime, by Selected Metropolitan Statistical Area, 2011—*Continued*

(Number, percent, rate per 100,000 population.)

Area	Population	Violent crime	Murder and non-negligent man-slaughter	Forcible rape	Robbery	Aggravated assault	Property crime	Burglary	Larceny-theft	Motor vehicle theft
Topeka, KS M.S.A.	235,354									
Includes Jackson, Jefferson, Osage, Shawnee, and Wabaunsee Counties										
City of Topeka	128,283	698	15	53	235	395	7,529	1,727	5,213	589
Total area actually reporting	98.2	875	15	65	241	554	9,817	2,409	6,703	705
Estimated total	100.0	885	15	66	242	562	9,911	2,425	6,775	711
Rate per 100,000 inhabitants	X	376.0	6.4	28.0	102.8	238.8	4,211.1	1,030.4	2,878.6	302.1
Trenton-Ewing, NJ M.S.A.	367,733									
Includes Mercer County										
City of Trenton	85,196	1,208	23	25	519	641	2,570	1,138	993	439
City of Ewing Township	35,909	85	2	7	44	32	814	257	511	46
Total area actually reporting	100.0	1,604	25	53	691	835	8,010	2,295	5,035	680
Rate per 100,000 inhabitants	X	436.2	6.8	14.4	187.9	227.1	2,178.2	624.1	1,369.2	184.9
Tucson, AZ M.S.A.[3]	994,140									
Includes Pima County										
City of Tucson[3]	527,479	3,440	51	204	1,163	2,022		4,979		2,746
Total area actually reporting	100.0	4,309	75	284	1,406	2,544		8,408		3,827
Rate per 100,000 inhabitants	X	433.4	7.5	28.6	141.4	255.9		845.8		385.0
Tulsa, OK M.S.A.	947,512									
Includes Creek, Okmulgee, Osage, Pawnee, Rogers, Tulsa, and Wagoner Counties										
City of Tulsa	396,101	3,960	49	266	1,090	2,555	21,923	7,353	12,136	2,434
Total area actually reporting	100.0	5,250	64	399	1,236	3,551	33,176	10,324	19,575	3,277
Rate per 100,000 inhabitants	X	554.1	6.8	42.1	130.4	374.8	3,501.4	1,089.6	2,065.9	345.9
Tuscaloosa, AL M.S.A.[1]	220,518									
Includes Greene, Hale, and Tuscaloosa Counties[1]										
City of Tuscaloosa[1]	90,903	432	3	39	194	196	4,402	1,249	2,963	190
Total area actually reporting	94.4	950	9	61	256	624	7,550	2,102	5,028	420
Estimated total	100.0	979	9	64	261	645	7,791	2,194	5,162	435
Rate per 100,000 inhabitants	X	444.0	4.1	29.0	118.4	292.5	3,533.0	994.9	2,340.9	197.3
Tyler, TX M.S.A.	214,127									
Includes Smith County										
City of Tyler	98,939	503	3	46	79	375	4,441	834	3,423	184
Total area actually reporting	100.0	791	8	100	102	581	6,995	1,603	5,055	337
Rate per 100,000 inhabitants	X	369.4	3.7	46.7	47.6	271.3	3,266.8	748.6	2,360.7	157.4
Utica-Rome, NY M.S.A.	300,743									
Includes Herkimer and Oneida Counties										
City of Utica	62,515	382	4	17	102	259	2,501	615	1,809	77
City of Rome	33,877	26	1	1	9	15	441	109	311	21
Total area actually reporting	98.5	691	8	46	143	494	6,623	1,547	4,895	181
Estimated total	100.0	699	8	46	146	499	6,710	1,561	4,965	184
Rate per 100,000 inhabitants	X	232.4	2.7	15.3	48.5	165.9	2,231.1	519.0	1,650.9	61.2
Valdosta, GA M.S.A.	141,426									
Includes Brooks, Echols, Lanier, and Lowndes Counties										
City of Valdosta	55,236	268	5	27	102	134	2,500	815	1,598	87
Total area actually reporting	99.1	480	8	40	122	310	4,363	1,320	2,851	192
Estimated total	100.0	485	8	40	124	313	4,415	1,330	2,889	196
Rate per 100,000 inhabitants	X	342.9	5.7	28.3	87.7	221.3	3,121.8	940.4	2,042.8	138.6
Vallejo-Fairfield, CA M.S.A.	418,203									
Includes Solano County										
City of Vallejo	117,305	903	18	53	435	397	5,244	2,468	1,716	1,060
City of Fairfield	106,559	425	5	21	148	251	2,974	572	2,055	347
Total area actually reporting	100.0	1,802	30	113	694	965	12,087	3,960	6,298	1,829
Rate per 100,000 inhabitants	X	430.9	7.2	27.0	165.9	230.7	2,890.2	946.9	1,506.0	437.3
Victoria, TX M.S.A.	117,812									
Includes Calhoun, Goliad, and Victoria Counties										
City of Victoria	63,909	392	2	38	70	282	3,249	857	2,299	93
Total area actually reporting	98.8	581	3	65	81	432	4,503	1,225	3,118	160
Estimated total	100.0	584	3	65	82	434	4,548	1,234	3,151	163
Rate per 100,000 inhabitants	X	495.7	2.5	55.2	69.6	368.4	3,860.4	1,047.4	2,674.6	138.4

X = Not applicable.

[1] Because of changes in the state/local agency's reporting practices, figures are not comparable to previous years' data.

[3] The FBI determined that the agency did not follow national Uniform Crime Reporting (UCR) Program guidelines for reporting an offense. Consequently, this figure is not included in this table.

Table II-6.   Crime, by Selected Metropolitan Statistical Area, 2011—*Continued*

(Number, percent, rate per 100,000 population.)

Area	Population	Violent crime	Murder and non-negligent man-slaughter	Forcible rape	Robbery	Aggravated assault	Property crime	Burglary	Larceny-theft	Motor vehicle theft
Virginia Beach-Norfolk-Newport News, VA-NC M.S.A.......	1,691,669									
Includes Currituck County, NC and Gloucester, Isle of Wight, James City, Mathews, Surry, and York Counties and Chesapeake, Hampton, Newport News, Norfolk, Poquoson, Portsmouth, Suffolk, Virginia Beach, and Williamsburg Cities, VA										
City of Virginia Beach, VA	443,226	776	15	60	412	289	12,133	2,038	9,645	450
City of Norfolk, VA	245,704	1,424	29	81	625	689	12,258	2,256	9,217	785
City of Newport News, VA..................................	182,878	845	15	52	388	390	6,041	1,094	4,592	355
City of Hampton, VA..................................	139,078	350	9	19	155	167	5,273	820	4,180	273
City of Portsmouth, VA..................................	96,676	550	12	46	235	257	5,237	1,348	3,623	266
Total area actually reporting	100.0	5,488	111	367	2,227	2,783	56,010	10,284	42,961	2,765
Rate per 100,000 inhabitants..................................	X	324.4	6.6	21.7	131.6	164.5	3,310.9	607.9	2,539.6	163.4
Visalia-Porterville, CA M.S.A...................................	447,377									
Includes Tulare County										
City of Visalia	125,905	486	8	40	95	343	5,121	1,110	3,466	545
City of Porterville	54,802	226	2	5	58	161	1,937	519	1,222	196
Total area actually reporting	100.0	1,942	40	99	325	1,478	15,334	3,986	9,433	1,915
Rate per 100,000 inhabitants..................................	X	434.1	8.9	22.1	72.6	330.4	3,427.5	891.0	2,108.5	428.1
Waco, TX M.S.A.	239,849									
Includes McLennan County										
City of Waco	127,431	766	11	70	245	440	6,422	1,670	4,593	159
Total area actually reporting	100.0	1,126	12	130	271	713	9,548	2,414	6,875	259
Rate per 100,000 inhabitants..................................	X	469.5	5.0	54.2	113.0	297.3	3,980.8	1,006.5	2,866.4	108.0
Warner Robins, GA M.S.A.	141,742									
Includes Houston County										
City of Warner Robins	67,096	347	5	22	122	198	4,078	746	3,156	176
Total area actually reporting	100.0	470	5	31	149	285	5,947	1,143	4,543	261
Rate per 100,000 inhabitants..................................	X	331.6	3.5	21.9	105.1	201.1	4,195.7	806.4	3,205.1	184.1
Washington-Arlington-Alexandria, DC-VA-MD-WV M.S.A.	5,651,690									
Includes the Metropolitan Divisions of Bethesda-Rockville-Frederick, MD and Washington-Arlington-Alexandria, DC-VA-MD-WV										
City of Washington, D.C.	617,996	6,985	108	172	3,756	2,949	28,312	3,849	20,124	4,339
City of Alexandria, VA..................................	141,638	252	1	14	129	108	3,181	303	2,506	372
City of Frederick, MD	65,858	306	2	19	96	189	1,787	235	1,474	78
Total area actually reporting	99.9	18,890	251	908	9,002	8,729	134,666	20,083	99,866	14,717
Estimated total..................................	100.0	18,908	251	909	9,005	8,743	134,852	20,115	100,012	14,725
Rate per 100,000 inhabitants..................................	X	334.6	4.4	16.1	159.3	154.7	2,386.0	355.9	1,769.6	260.5
Bethesda-Rockville-Frederick, MD M.D.............................	1,216,589									
Includes Frederick and Montgomery Counties										
Total area actually reporting	100.0	2,282	18	146	1,005	1,113	22,508	3,903	17,153	1,452
Rate per 100,000 inhabitants..................................	X	187.6	1.5	12.0	82.6	91.5	1,850.1	320.8	1,409.9	119.4
Washington-Arlington-Alexandria, DC-VA-MD-WV M.D.	4,435,101									
Includes District of Columbia; Calvert, Charles, and Prince George's Counties, MD; Arlington, Clarke, Fairfax, Fauquier, Loudoun, Prince William, Spotsylvania, Stafford, and Warren Counties and Alexandria, Fairfax, Falls Church, Fredericksburg, Manassas, and Manassas Park Cities, VA; and Jefferson County, WV										
Total area actually reporting	99.9	16,608	233	762	7,997	7,616	112,158	16,180	82,713	13,265
Estimated total..................................	100.0	16,626	233	763	8,000	7,630	112,344	16,212	82,859	13,273
Rate per 100,000 inhabitants..................................	X	374.9	5.3	17.2	180.4	172.0	2,533.1	365.5	1,868.3	299.3
Waterloo-Cedar Falls, IA M.S.A.	168,698									
Includes Black Hawk, Bremer, and Grundy Counties										
City of Waterloo	68,764	357	3	52	60	242	2,159	673	1,401	85
City of Cedar Falls	39,466	71	1	11	4	55	605	119	453	33
Total area actually reporting	100.0	559	4	82	65	408	3,447	994	2,307	146
Rate per 100,000 inhabitants..................................	X	331.4	2.4	48.6	38.5	241.9	2,043.3	589.2	1,367.5	86.5
Wausau, WI M.S.A.	134,647									
Includes Marathon County										
City of Wausau	39,276	123	0	32	21	70	1,178	253	890	35
Total area actually reporting	100.0	200	0	49	28	123	2,415	494	1,844	77
Rate per 100,000 inhabitants..................................	X	148.5	0.0	36.4	20.8	91.3	1,793.6	366.9	1,369.5	57.2

X = Not applicable.

Table II-6. Crime, by Selected Metropolitan Statistical Area, 2011—*Continued*

(Number, percent, rate per 100,000 population.)

Area	Population	Violent crime	Murder and non-negligent man-slaughter	Forcible rape	Robbery	Aggravated assault	Property crime	Burglary	Larceny-theft	Motor vehicle theft
Wenatchee-East Wenatchee, WA M.S.A.	112,624									
Includes Chelan and Douglas Counties										
City of Wenatchee	32,426	87	2	5	22	58	1,315	197	1,056	62
City of East Wenatchee	13,397	31	0	6	7	18	546	64	468	14
Total area actually reporting	100.0	177	6	26	33	112	2,932	582	2,199	151
Rate per 100,000 inhabitants	X	157.2	5.3	23.1	29.3	99.4	2,603.4	516.8	1,952.5	134.1
Wichita, KS M.S.A.	627,017									
Includes Butler, Harvey, Sedgwick, and Sumner Counties										
City of Wichita	384,796	2,950	25	238	490	2,197	19,456	4,005	13,550	1,901
Total area actually reporting	99.6	3,612	31	311	528	2,742	24,648	5,194	17,271	2,183
Estimated total	100.0	3,619	31	312	529	2,747	24,709	5,204	17,318	2,187
Rate per 100,000 inhabitants	X	577.2	4.9	49.8	84.4	438.1	3,940.7	830.0	2,762.0	348.8
Wichita Falls, TX M.S.A.	154,490									
Includes Archer, Clay, and Wichita Counties										
City of Wichita Falls	106,753	459	1	30	147	281	4,876	1,241	3,398	237
Total area actually reporting	100.0	552	1	46	150	355	5,681	1,476	3,936	269
Rate per 100,000 inhabitants	X	357.3	0.6	29.8	97.1	229.8	3,677.3	955.4	2,547.7	174.1
Williamsport, PA M.S.A.	116,481									
Includes Lycoming County										
City of Williamsport	29,475	100	1	8	56	35	1,254	222	982	50
Total area actually reporting	100.0	207	1	24	70	112	2,565	531	1,943	91
Rate per 100,000 inhabitants	X	177.7	0.9	20.6	60.1	96.2	2,202.1	455.9	1,668.1	78.1
Wilmington, NC M.S.A.	366,909									
Includes Brunswick, New Hanover, and Pender Counties										
City of Wilmington	107,826	662	10	32	254	366	5,708	1,454	3,843	411
Total area actually reporting	98.5	1,220	16	96	356	752	13,248	3,696	8,836	716
Estimated total	100.0	1,236	16	97	360	763	13,480	3,748	9,008	724
Rate per 100,000 inhabitants	X	336.9	4.4	26.4	98.1	208.0	3,673.9	1,021.5	2,455.1	197.3
Winchester, VA-WV M.S.A.	129,751									
Includes Frederick County and Winchester City, VA and Hampshire County, WV										
City of Winchester, VA	26,516	63	0	3	29	31	1,117	130	956	31
Total area actually reporting	100.0	246	3	40	47	156	2,932	573	2,219	140
Rate per 100,000 inhabitants	X	189.6	2.3	30.8	36.2	120.2	2,259.7	441.6	1,710.2	107.9
Winston-Salem, NC M.S.A.	483,775									
Includes Davie, Forsyth, Stokes, and Yadkin Counties										
City of Winston-Salem	232,529	1,565	14	93	444	1,014	13,874	4,680	8,522	672
Total area actually reporting	99.4	2,299	20	143	507	1,629	21,322	7,045	13,315	962
Estimated total	100.0	2,307	20	144	509	1,634	21,438	7,071	13,401	966
Rate per 100,000 inhabitants	X	476.9	4.1	29.8	105.2	337.8	4,431.4	1,461.6	2,770.1	199.7
Worcester, MA M.S.A.	803,419									
Includes Worcester County										
City of Worcester	182,145	1,800	11	36	411	1,342	6,077	2,066	3,481	530
Total area actually reporting	98.6	3,495	16	158	587	2,734	17,297	5,031	11,241	1,025
Estimated total	100.0	3,528	16	160	593	2,759	17,516	5,085	11,392	1,039
Rate per 100,000 inhabitants	X	439.1	2.0	19.9	73.8	343.4	2,180.2	632.9	1,417.9	129.3
Yakima, WA M.S.A.	247,047									
Includes Yakima County										
City of Yakima	92,496	481	6	48	156	271	5,120	1,619	2,841	660
Total area actually reporting	100.0	807	16	106	236	449	10,418	3,351	5,802	1,265
Rate per 100,000 inhabitants	X	326.7	6.5	42.9	95.5	181.7	4,217.0	1,356.4	2,348.5	512.0
Yauco, PR M.S.A.	105,916									
Includes Guanica, Guayanilla, Penuelas, and Yauco Municipios										
Total area actually reporting	100.0	145	18	3	51	73	824	385	407	32
Rate per 100,000 inhabitants	X	136.9	17.0	2.8	48.2	68.9	778.0	363.5	384.3	30.2
York-Hanover, PA M.S.A.	436,359									
Includes York County										
City of York	43,857	721	16	60	333	312	1,731	429	1,147	155
City of Hanover	15,338	26	0	3	10	13	675	64	604	7
Total area actually reporting	100.0	1,324	20	139	466	699	8,717	1,385	6,941	391
Rate per 100,000 inhabitants	X	303.4	4.6	31.9	106.8	160.2	1,997.7	317.4	1,590.7	89.6

X = Not applicable.

Table II-6.   Crime, by Selected Metropolitan Statistical Area, 2011—*Continued*

(Number, percent, rate per 100,000 population.)

Area	Population	Violent crime	Murder and non-negligent man-slaughter	Forcible rape	Robbery	Aggravated assault	Property crime	Burglary	Larceny-theft	Motor vehicle theft
Yuba City, CA M.S.A.	168,854									
Includes Sutter and Yuba Counties										
City of Yuba City	65,688	210	1	20	57	132	1,795	348	1,277	170
Total area actually reporting	100.0	684	8	52	102	522	4,716	1,187	3,010	519
Rate per 100,000 inhabitants	X	405.1	4.7	30.8	60.4	309.1	2,792.9	703.0	1,782.6	307.4
Yuma, AZ M.S.A.	198,522									
Includes Yuma County										
City of Yuma	94,381	490	4	33	66	387	3,227	822	2,196	209
Total area actually reporting	87.0	611	13	43	76	479	4,390	1,284	2,795	311
Estimated total	100.0	676	14	48	90	524	5,222	1,464	3,403	355
Rate per 100,000 inhabitants	X	340.5	7.1	24.2	45.3	264.0	2,630.4	737.4	1,714.2	178.8

X = Not applicable.

Table II-7. Offense Analysis, United States, 2007–2011

(Number.)

Classification	2007[1]	2008[1]	2009[1]	2010[1]	2011
Murder	17,128	16,465	15,399	14,722	14,612
Forcible Rape	92,160	90,750	89,241	85,593	83,425
Robbery[2]	447,324	443,563	408,742	369,089	354,396
By location					
Street/highway	195,734	191,050	174,886	159,307	155,065
Commercial house	62,333	61,207	55,980	48,804	46,111
Gas or service station	11,825	11,468	9,881	8,549	8,531
Convenience store	25,056	24,394	21,983	19,282	18,090
Residence	67,841	72,217	69,280	63,779	60,078
Bank	9,298	8,996	8,829	8,034	7,031
Miscellaneous	75,238	74,231	67,903	61,333	59,490
Burglary[2]	2,190,198	2,228,887	2,203,313	2,168,459	2,188,005
By location					
Residence (dwelling)	1,486,405	1,567,682	1,599,047	1,602,056	1,630,791
Residence, night	423,995	438,323	445,983	445,480	442,970
Residence, day	742,403	807,617	819,725	825,163	860,425
Residence, unknown	320,007	321,742	333,339	331,414	327,396
Nonresidence (store, office, etc.)	703,793	661,205	604,266	566,403	557,214
Nonresidence, night	294,958	276,743	255,147	233,765	227,745
Nonresidence, day	228,244	223,303	200,924	192,985	196,719
Nonresidence, unknown	180,591	161,159	148,195	139,652	132,751
Larceny-Theft (Except Motor Vehicle Theft)[2]	6,591,542	6,586,206	6,338,095	6,204,601	6,159,795
By type					
Pocket-picking	27,504	27,140	26,631	24,231	26,556
Purse-snatching	38,191	33,314	30,493	28,137	27,120
Shoplifting	982,402	1,067,655	1,149,406	1,064,608	1,079,316
From motor vehicles (except accessories)	1,712,949	1,714,745	1,727,583	1,638,670	1,526,106
Motor vehicle accessories	601,158	642,964	573,270	549,905	498,684
Bicycles	225,130	221,846	212,362	206,677	217,294
From buildings	791,882	753,450	704,184	699,599	729,080
From coin-operated machines	31,145	26,899	26,085	20,309	19,564
All others	2,181,182	2,098,192	1,888,080	1,972,464	2,036,076
By value					
Under $50	2,221,108	2,155,372	2,060,325	1,971,705	1,903,998
$50 to $200	1,476,222	1,465,002	1,443,919	1,421,342	1,401,463
Over $200	2,894,212	2,965,832	2,833,851	2,803,066	2,854,334
Motor Vehicle Theft	1,100,472	959,059	795,652	739,565	715,373

[1] The crime figures have been adjusted.

[2] Because of rounding, the number of offenses may not add to the total.

Table II-8.   Offenses Known to Law Enforcement, by Selected State and City, 2011

(Number.)

State/City	Population	Violent crime	Murder and non-negligent man-slaughter	Forcible rape	Robbery	Aggravated assault	Property crime	Burglary	Larceny-theft	Motor vehicle theft	Arson[1]
Alabama[2]											
Abbeville	2,701	13	0	1	2	10	65	12	51	2	1
Adamsville	4,544	37	2	2	7	26	300	61	226	13	2
Addison	762	1	0	0	0	1	28	9	15	4	1
Alabaster	30,498	59	2	1	10	46	656	86	541	29	1
Albertville	21,262	43	0	7	5	31	917	247	616	54	0
Alexander City	14,947	138	0	12	11	115	768	206	527	35	0
Andalusia	9,058	31	1	1	4	25	490	90	379	21	0
Anniston	23,217	411	11	21	85	294	2,323	996	1,227	100	14
Arab	8,089	63	1	3	6	53	676	165	460	51	13
Ardmore	1,200	3	0	0	0	3	30	8	21	1	0
Argo	4,091	8	0	1	0	7	43	18	21	4	0
Arley	359	1	0	0	0	1	19	3	15	1	0
Ashford	2,158	9	0	0	0	9	82	30	50	2	1
Ashland	2,047	13	0	2	0	11	42	8	31	3	0
Ashville	2,223	6	2	0	0	4	35	5	29	1	1
Athens	22,002	38	1	4	18	15	771	144	601	26	0
Atmore	10,243	57	2	3	12	40	386	112	260	14	0
Auburn	53,637	152	0	12	48	92	2,143	550	1,520	73	1
Bay Minette	8,083	34	0	4	13	17	325	55	255	15	2
Bayou La Batre	2,570	30	1	1	3	25	208	75	108	25	1
Bessemer	27,588	464	10	23	126	305	3,274	981	2,011	282	16
Birmingham	213,258	3,163	54	182	1,011	1,916	17,841	5,806	10,522	1,513	123
Blountsville	1,692	14	0	0	1	13	78	26	49	3	0
Boaz	9,597	12	0	2	0	10	453	92	345	16	0
Brent	4,971	22	0	1	2	19	120	33	77	10	1
Brewton	5,434	90	0	5	1	84	276	52	215	9	1
Brighton	2,959	0	0	0	0	0	1	0	0	1	4
Brilliant	904	2	0	0	0	2	17	7	9	1	1
Brookside	1,370	4	0	0	0	4	23	11	12	0	0
Brundidge	2,086	4	0	1	1	2	22	2	19	1	0
Butler	1,903	4	0	0	1	3	45	20	24	1	1
Camp Hill	1,019	0	0	0	0	0	5	0	3	2	0
Carbon Hill	2,031	7	0	0	0	7	76	16	46	14	0
Carrollton	1,024	4	0	0	0	4	28	8	18	2	1
Cedar Bluff	1,829	26	1	0	2	23	254	89	150	15	0
Centre	3,506	17	0	1	3	13	190	40	140	10	3
Centreville	2,791	1	0	0	0	1	32	10	21	1	1
Chatom	1,294	9	0	0	0	9	24	7	17	0	0
Chickasaw	6,135	31	0	2	6	23	340	91	225	24	2
Citronelle	3,924	22	1	1	3	17	192	67	112	13	2
Clanton	8,660	55	0	2	7	46	600	124	454	22	1
Clayhatchee	592	0	0	0	0	0	2	0	2	0	0
Collinsville	1,993	8	0	2	2	4	70	17	46	7	0
Columbiana	4,217	11	0	1	0	10	139	35	95	9	0
Coosada	1,230	1	0	0	0	1	33	8	24	1	0
Cordova	2,105	10	0	0	1	9	142	33	98	11	2
Cottonwood	1,295	2	0	0	0	2	18	6	12	0	0
Creola	1,935	11	1	0	0	10	112	13	93	6	0
Cullman	14,846	28	0	11	8	9	777	117	620	40	1
Dadeville	3,246	33	0	1	2	30	129	39	85	5	1
Daleville	5,320	37	0	4	2	31	170	56	105	9	0
Daphne	21,674	36	1	0	12	23	523	116	389	18	0
Dauphin Island	1,244	3	0	0	0	3	50	9	39	2	0
Decatur	55,951	197	3	19	56	119	2,109	815	1,131	163	13
Demopolis	7,519	51	0	5	8	38	365	68	284	13	0
Dora	2,035	16	0	1	2	13	94	30	59	5	0
Dothan	65,811	343	2	22	106	213	2,737	607	2,014	116	0
Double Springs	1,088	1	0	0	0	1	26	9	16	1	1
Douglas	748	4	0	0	0	4	96	43	49	4	0
East Brewton	2,490	27	0	3	2	22	95	21	67	7	0
Eclectic	1,006	12	0	1	0	11	45	7	35	3	0
Elba	3,959	29	0	1	4	24	134	34	93	7	0
Elberta	1,505	8	0	0	0	8	45	18	26	1	0
Enterprise	26,690	122	1	15	23	83	1,081	293	729	59	3
Eufaula	13,200	31	0	8	1	22	634	79	545	10	0
Eutaw	2,948	51	0	2	3	46	96	29	57	10	2
Evergreen	3,963	42	1	6	4	31	214	49	152	13	2
Excel	726	0	0	0	0	0	15	1	13	1	1
Fairfield	11,171	191	4	9	82	96	1,296	446	752	98	1
Fairhope	15,400	46	1	4	9	32	625	124	492	9	0
Fayette	4,641	19	0	0	1	18	119	28	85	6	0
Flomaton	1,447	14	0	0	0	14	53	11	36	6	0
Florala	1,990	6	0	1	0	5	49	9	33	7	0
Florence	39,508	88	1	10	29	48	1,592	394	1,155	43	2

[1] If a blank is presented in the arson column, it indicates that the FBI did not receive 12 complete months of arson data for that agency.

[2] Because of changes in the state/local agency's reporting practices, figures are not comparable to previous years' data.

Table II-8.   Offenses Known to Law Enforcement, by Selected State and City, 2011—*Continued*

(Number.)

State/City	Population	Violent crime	Murder and non-negligent man-slaughter	Forcible rape	Robbery	Aggravated assault	Property crime	Burglary	Larceny-theft	Motor vehicle theft	Arson[1]
Alabama—*Continued*											
Foley	14,688	66	0	4	11	51	693	82	583	28	2
Fort Deposit	1,350	4	0	0	1	3	14	0	13	1	0
Fort Payne	14,079	27	0	2	6	19	488	102	369	17	3
Fultondale	8,420	14	0	1	5	8	434	76	333	25	2
Fyffe	1,023	0	0	0	0	0	38	8	29	1	0
Gadsden	37,033	299	5	25	76	193	2,973	768	1,967	238	18
Gardendale	13,960	22	0	3	5	14	444	90	338	16	0
Geneva	4,473	15	0	1	1	13	107	17	86	4	0
Georgiana	1,746	15	0	0	2	13	30	10	18	2	0
Geraldine	900	1	0	0	1	0	31	12	16	3	0
Glencoe	5,185	10	0	1	0	9	130	56	67	7	0
Gordo	1,758	7	1	0	0	6	21	11	6	4	0
Grant	900	4	0	0	0	4	24	12	10	2	0
Greensboro	2,509	3	0	0	0	3	2	0	2	0	0
Greenville	8,174	69	0	3	8	58	409	65	319	25	0
Grove Hill	1,578	3	0	1	0	2	17	9	8	0	1
Guin	2,387	6	0	1	0	5	34	7	21	6	0
Gulf Shores	9,788	42	0	7	2	33	547	138	391	18	4
Guntersville	8,236	54	0	6	7	41	809	186	595	28	0
Gurley	805	2	0	0	0	2	3	2	1	0	0
Hackleburg	1,523	3	0	0	0	3	35	8	22	5	1
Haleyville	4,193	17	0	1	3	13	212	36	169	7	0
Hamilton	6,918	20	1	3	1	15	191	35	145	11	4
Hanceville	2,996	24	0	1	4	19	111	49	56	6	0
Harpersville	1,645	3	0	0	0	3	10	2	8	0	0
Hartford	2,637	18	0	4	1	13	92	11	75	6	0
Hartselle	14,324	20	0	3	4	13	458	89	352	17	0
Hayneville	936	9	1	0	0	8	29	18	11	0	21
Headland	4,532	2	0	0	1	1	58	14	42	2	1
Heflin	3,497	11	0	1	1	9	129	35	86	8	0
Helena	16,874	10	0	1	0	9	177	28	138	11	0
Henagar	2,355	2	0	0	0	2	57	15	40	2	0
Hokes Bluff	4,307	5	0	1	0	4	54	18	35	1	0
Hollywood	1,005	0	0	0	0	0	13	5	6	2	0
Homewood	25,288	57	0	5	28	24	989	180	744	65	2
Hoover	82,012	59	0	7	35	17	2,194	422	1,663	109	0
Hueytown	16,183	41	2	3	16	20	658	163	474	21	1
Huntsville	180,972	1,518	13	51	405	1,049	9,749	2,677	6,306	766	23
Irondale	12,408	50	2	0	17	31	595	223	338	34	2
Jackson	5,253	28	1	3	3	21	254	61	187	6	0
Jacksonville	12,608	31	0	2	8	21	467	154	301	12	5
Jasper	14,421	95	1	8	26	60	1,019	206	755	58	7
Jemison	2,597	20	0	0	2	18	168	43	109	16	0
Killen	1,113	2	0	0	0	2	46	20	24	2	0
Kimberly	2,724	1	0	0	0	1	23	9	14	0	0
Kinston	543	3	0	1	0	2	21	7	12	2	0
Lafayette	3,017	35	0	3	1	31	172	33	132	7	0
Lake View	1,952	5	0	1	0	4	26	10	14	2	0
Lanett	6,499	81	1	4	4	72	663	182	449	32	0
Leeds	11,830	54	1	1	18	34	528	107	390	31	1
Leesburg	1,032	9	0	0	1	8	69	17	50	2	0
Leighton	733	0	0	0	0	0	16	7	9	0	0
Level Plains	2,095	6	0	0	1	5	52	19	21	12	1
Lincoln	6,296	27	1	2	4	20	315	91	209	15	0
Linden	2,133	2	0	0	0	2	84	37	45	2	0
Lineville	2,407	20	0	1	0	19	39	9	26	4	0
Lipscomb	2,221	18	0	1	4	13	92	40	44	8	4
Littleville	1,016	2	0	0	0	2	18	5	10	3	0
Livingston	3,502	19	0	1	0	18	96	26	65	5	0
Loxley	1,640	7	0	0	0	7	156	22	107	27	0
Madison	43,145	103	1	19	20	63	902	217	630	55	21
Maplesville	711	1	0	1	0	0	16	4	8	4	0
Margaret	4,449	5	0	0	0	5	32	8	23	1	0
Marion	3,704	0	0	0	0	0	0	0	0	0	1
McIntosh	239	7	0	0	4	3	29	5	20	4	0
Midfield	5,391	30	1	1	18	10	346	178	151	17	0
Midland City	2,355	2	0	0	0	2	18	4	11	3	0
Millbrook	14,710	40	0	9	6	25	654	214	421	19	0
Mobile[3]	251,869	1,619	30	48	637	904	13,650	4,058	8,891	701	70
Monroeville	6,550	96	2	8	7	79	494	84	386	24	2
Montevallo	6,353	27	1	2	11	13	191	36	145	10	1
Montgomery	206,754	707	31	38	354	284	10,744	2,885	7,043	816	31
Moody	11,782	14	0	0	2	12	279	56	203	20	0

[1] If a blank is presented in the arson column, it indicates that the FBI did not receive 12 complete months of arson data for that agency.

[3] The population for the city of Mobile, Alabama, includes 55,819 inhabitants from the jurisdiction of the Mobile County Sheriff's Department.

Table II-8. Offenses Known to Law Enforcement, by Selected State and City, 2011—*Continued*

(Number.)

State/City	Population	Violent crime	Murder and non-negligent man-slaughter	Forcible rape	Robbery	Aggravated assault	Property crime	Burglary	Larceny-theft	Motor vehicle theft	Arson[1]
Alabama—*Continued*											
Morris	1,868	4	0	0	1	3	33	5	24	4	1
Moulton	3,488	8	0	1	0	7	101	35	58	8	1
Moundville	2,439	13	0	1	1	11	72	18	50	4	0
Mountain Brook	20,511	12	0	1	6	5	358	75	276	7	1
Mount Vernon	1,582	28	1	1	3	23	114	29	72	13	1
Muscle Shoals	13,209	65	1	2	12	50	576	129	413	34	0
Napier Field	356	2	0	0	0	2	16	4	10	2	0
New Brockton	1,152	12	0	0	3	9	36	17	16	3	0
New Site	777	2	0	0	1	1	11	2	9	0	0
Newton	1,518	4	0	0	0	4	35	11	19	5	0
Northport	23,442	153	3	8	32	110	886	243	579	64	3
Notasulga	970	10	0	1	1	8	93	55	36	2	0
Odenville	3,602	16	0	1	0	15	81	15	53	13	2
Oneonta	6,599	37	0	0	2	35	174	24	137	13	0
Opelika	26,604	115	2	17	41	55	2,036	406	1,597	33	0
Opp	6,691	7	0	0	2	5	158	27	131	0	0
Orange Beach	5,467	12	0	5	0	7	330	61	255	14	0
Owens Crossroads	1,528	0	0	0	0	0	11	3	8	0	0
Oxford	21,451	108	4	6	20	78	1,301	226	1,003	72	2
Ozark	14,979	110	1	6	24	79	886	161	668	57	2
Parrish	987	2	0	0	0	2	40	1	35	4	0
Pelham	21,455	20	1	1	3	15	405	57	332	16	1
Pell City	12,756	63	0	4	8	51	566	101	435	30	3
Phenix City	32,980	214	7	22	39	146	2,185	590	1,379	216	0
Phil Campbell	1,154	3	0	0	0	3	19	5	12	2	0
Piedmont	4,901	22	0	2	2	18	295	75	212	8	0
Pine Hill	980	19	1	2	2	14	36	9	27	0	0
Pleasant Grove	10,159	18	0	2	3	13	200	66	123	11	1
Powell	960	1	0	0	0	1	19	7	11	1	0
Prattville	34,123	60	1	6	24	29	1,289	207	1,001	81	1
Priceville	2,671	0	0	0	0	0	53	11	32	10	0
Prichard	22,768	484	6	10	182	286	1,850	825	798	227	22
Ragland	1,647	4	0	0	1	3	30	8	21	1	0
Rainbow City	9,648	16	0	1	4	11	325	65	237	23	0
Rainsville	4,972	7	0	1	0	6	117	19	93	5	0
Red Bay	3,173	9	0	2	2	5	76	9	61	6	0
Reform	1,710	10	0	2	0	8	51	17	33	1	0
Riverside	2,219	8	0	2	0	6	53	17	34	2	1
Roanoke	6,103	32	0	3	3	26	220	35	172	13	0
Robertsdale	5,301	24	0	3	5	16	276	62	206	8	1
Rogersville	1,263	9	0	1	1	7	77	23	48	6	1
Russellville	9,877	54	0	3	18	33	363	123	223	17	0
Samson	1,949	19	0	2	2	15	90	19	65	6	2
Saraland	13,470	41	0	3	11	27	687	108	554	25	2
Sardis City	1,712	1	0	0	0	1	60	18	36	6	1
Satsuma	6,198	0	0	0	0	0	0	0	0	0	0
Scottsboro	14,841	42	0	1	5	36	550	125	410	15	0
Selma	20,856	333	3	16	71	243	2,464	779	1,547	138	0
Sheffield	9,083	85	0	4	14	67	550	146	369	35	0
Shorter	476	5	0	0	1	4	24	12	10	2	1
Silverhill	709	3	0	0	0	3	56	11	41	4	2
Slocomb	1,990	12	0	0	1	11	81	19	55	7	0
Snead	839	9	0	2	0	7	48	15	29	4	0
Southside	8,452	15	0	2	0	13	92	20	62	10	1
Springville	4,100	1	0	0	1	0	98	24	71	3	0
Steele	1,048	2	0	0	0	2	21	5	8	8	1
Stevenson	2,056	5	0	0	0	5	11	4	7	0	0
St. Florian	415	2	0	1	0	1	20	6	12	2	0
Sulligent	1,936	1	0	0	0	1	63	16	46	1	1
Sumiton	2,532	13	0	0	4	9	191	28	160	3	3
Summerdale	866	8	0	2	0	6	44	8	33	3	0
Sylacauga	12,810	39	1	6	9	23	721	202	503	16	0
Sylvania	1,846	1	0	0	0	1	14	0	13	1	0
Talladega	15,751	115	4	13	14	84	1,276	371	829	76	1
Tarrant	6,428	52	1	6	31	14	559	236	296	27	0
Taylor	2,386	1	0	0	0	1	17	4	13	0	0
Thomasville	4,229	30	0	0	4	26	169	50	103	16	2
Thorsby	1,990	2	0	0	0	2	15	2	10	3	1
Town Creek	1,105	8	0	0	0	8	34	13	17	4	0
Trinity	2,105	6	0	1	0	5	69	27	32	10	0
Troy	18,120	141	1	7	30	103	945	250	648	47	2
Trussville	20,029	0	0	0	0	0	133	106	2	25	0
Tuscaloosa	90,903	432	3	39	194	196	4,402	1,249	2,963	190	20
Tuscumbia	8,464	38	1	0	7	30	397	107	264	26	0
Tuskegee	9,912	77	2	1	14	60	557	266	254	37	4

[1] If a blank is presented in the arson column, it indicates that the FBI did not receive 12 complete months of arson data for that agency.

Table II-8.   Offenses Known to Law Enforcement, by Selected State and City, 2011—*Continued*

(Number.)

State/City	Population	Violent crime	Murder and non-negligent man-slaughter	Forcible rape	Robbery	Aggravated assault	Property crime	Burglary	Larceny-theft	Motor vehicle theft	Arson[1]
Alabama—*Continued*											
Valley	9,570	69	0	6	5	58	613	159	425	29	2
Vance	1,536	10	0	0	1	9	50	11	33	6	0
Vernon	2,010	2	0	0	2	0	29	8	18	3	0
Vestavia Hills	34,197	25	0	4	7	14	524	117	376	31	2
Warrior	3,191	14	0	1	1	12	86	26	53	7	2
Weaver	3,053	31	0	2	0	29	148	47	89	12	2
Wedowee	827	0	0	0	0	0	28	8	19	1	0
Wetumpka	6,559	33	0	3	8	22	329	71	247	11	0
Winfield	4,740	13	0	0	1	12	142	31	106	5	4
Woodstock	1,435	12	0	1	2	9	105	15	79	11	1
York	2,550	9	0	0	7	2	83	25	49	9	2
Alaska											
Anchorage	296,955	2,388	12	283	465	1,628	9,455	1,080	7,750	625	126
Bethel	6,187	63	1	14	3	45	105	35	39	31	2
Bristol Bay Borough	1,015	2	0	0	0	2	27	1	15	11	0
Cordova	2,278	11	0	0	0	11	37	5	27	5	0
Craig	1,222	4	0	0	1	3	41	10	26	5	0
Dillingham	2,370	41	0	14	2	25	61	8	35	18	0
Fairbanks	32,089	177	2	17	33	125	1,232	130	1,026	76	5
Haines	1,743	14	0	0	0	14	27	2	24	1	1
Homer	5,091	34	0	0	0	34	190	36	151	3	0
Juneau	31,825	159	0	14	25	120	1,225	111	1,075	39	18
Kenai	7,225	21	0	3	0	18	228	18	203	7	0
Ketchikan	8,192	28	0	7	2	19	440	36	386	18	2
Kodiak	6,238	92	0	4	2	86	250	33	192	25	4
Nome	3,661	34	1	4	0	29	48	16	23	9	1
North Pole	2,154	11	0	0	3	8	80	9	69	2	1
North Slope Borough	9,596	94	0	13	1	80	116	31	64	21	0
Palmer	6,041	19	0	1	1	17	197	19	176	2	1
Petersburg	3,000	13	0	0	0	13	131	7	122	2	0
Seward	2,740	2	0	0	0	2	92	12	77	3	0
Sitka	9,037	16	0	1	3	12	199	28	167	4	1
Skagway	936	2	0	0	0	2	20	4	13	3	0
Soldotna	4,236	16	0	1	2	13	196	13	173	10	1
Unalaska	4,453	17	0	0	0	17	89	10	70	9	0
Valdez	4,046	11	0	0	0	11	82	6	70	6	0
Wasilla	7,969	42	1	4	3	34	423	59	341	23	1
Wrangell	2,411	3	0	0	0	3	31	4	22	5	0
Arizona											
Apache Junction	36,347	84	4	5	8	67	1,239	308	848	83	0
Avondale	77,317	246	6	6	103	131	3,919	712	2,975	232	16
Bisbee	5,654	91	0	0	0	91	167	14	143	10	1
Buckeye	51,596	43	0	1	11	31	1,341	397	898	46	5
Bullhead City	40,100	57	3	0	25	29	1,491	351	1,068	72	4
Camp Verde	11,027	20	1	0	1	18	213	57	145	11	1
Casa Grande	49,259	232	4	3	53	172	2,664	625	1,892	147	22
Chandler	239,466	681	2	62	171	446	7,416	1,344	5,741	331	35
Chino Valley	10,970	43	0	1	0	42	220	47	157	16	0
Clarkdale	4,155	13	0	0	0	13	103	60	39	4	1
Clifton	3,358	11	0	0	1	10	23	10	11	2	0
Colorado City	4,889	8	0	1	0	7	40	9	29	2	1
Coolidge	11,992	85	0	8	19	58	612	136	454	22	7
Cottonwood	11,424	54	0	1	3	50	462	58	389	15	14
Douglas[4]	17,624		1	0	5		580	65	465	50	4
Eagar	4,954	7	0	0	1	6	148	55	87	6	0
El Mirage	32,247	95	2	14	23	56	1,041	387	585	69	5
Eloy	16,866	98	3	4	10	81	479	162	284	33	10
Flagstaff	66,802	263	0	45	38	180	3,008	235	2,706	67	24
Florence	25,897	34	0	1	1	32	191	54	126	11	2
Fredonia	1,333	2	0	2	0	0	9	3	6	0	0
Gilbert	211,404	178	2	21	56	99	3,854	823	2,896	135	25
Glendale	229,931	1,114	22	44	431	617	14,738	2,442	10,838	1,458	65
Globe	7,639	51	0	7	5	39	349	107	229	13	2
Goodyear	66,199	108	0	19	21	68	1,860	814	940	106	6
Holbrook	5,125	39	0	5	3	31	246	70	168	8	0
Huachuca City	1,879	4	0	0	1	3	23	5	18	0	1
Jerome	450	2	0	0	1	1	20	4	16	0	0
Kingman	28,465	101	2	7	14	78	1,520	303	1,153	64	4
Lake Havasu City	53,271	98	1	26	3	68	1,268	228	974	66	5
Mammoth	1,446	1	0	0	0	1	13	6	7	0	0
Marana	35,456	47	2	7	12	26	1,373	164	1,126	83	5
Maricopa	44,098	60	0	4	12	44	979	263	648	68	1

[1] If a blank is presented in the arson column, it indicates that the FBI did not receive 12 complete months of arson data for that agency.

[4] The FBI determined that the agency's data were overreported. Consequently, those data are not included in this table.

Table II-8. **Offenses Known to Law Enforcement, by Selected State and City, 2011**—*Continued*

(Number.)

State/City	Population	Violent crime	Murder and non-negligent man-slaughter	Forcible rape	Robbery	Aggravated assault	Property crime	Burglary	Larceny-theft	Motor vehicle theft	Arson[1]
Arizona—*Continued*											
Mesa	445,256	1,838	18	131	497	1,192	15,117	2,769	11,407	941	74
Miami	1,863	18	0	0	2	16	80	29	42	9	4
Nogales	21,132	59	1	1	3	54	611	111	433	67	0
Oro Valley	41,592	24	1	2	6	15	744	142	576	26	3
Page	7,350	105	0	1	10	94	498	41	429	28	7
Paradise Valley	13,001	10	0	3	2	5	302	195	104	3	0
Payson	15,518	49	0	3	5	41	374	92	264	18	0
Peoria	156,246	301	2	35	56	208	4,774	1,088	3,360	326	6
Phoenix	1,466,097	8,089	116	559	3,324	4,090	64,479	18,666	38,258	7,555	273
Pima	2,421	1	0	0	0	1	71	21	47	3	0
Pinetop-Lakeside	4,343	42	0	1	6	35	239	54	182	3	3
Prescott	40,407	171	4	12	13	142	1,258	260	960	38	6
Prescott Valley	39,372	113	3	6	6	98	780	120	635	25	6
Sahuarita	25,617	14	0	2	1	11	449	66	370	13	8
Scottsdale	220,462	400	4	34	125	237	6,724	1,424	5,054	246	25
Sedona	10,173	26	0	2	0	24	175	38	134	3	0
Show Low	10,811	81	2	4	6	69	501	110	383	8	5
Sierra Vista	44,509	145	2	21	14	108	1,326	167	1,114	45	9
Snowflake-Taylor	9,839	48	0	0	1	47	162	44	113	5	2
Somerton	14,489	12	0	0	4	8	186	32	137	17	1
South Tucson	5,732	149	3	4	55	87	926	101	801	24	2
Springerville	1,989	10	0	1	0	9	60	13	45	2	0
Surprise	119,181	131	0	12	51	68	2,598	617	1,873	108	22
Tempe	164,008	787	5	45	237	500	8,933	1,579	6,804	550	28
Thatcher	4,934	4	0	0	0	4	119	60	57	2	0
Tolleson	6,638	56	0	7	8	41	775	210	526	39	4
Tombstone	1,400	17	0	0	1	16	101	19	77	5	0
Tucson[5]	527,479	3,440	51	204	1,163	2,022		4,979		2,746	167
Wellton	2,923	1	0	0	0	1	8	2	5	1	0
Wickenburg	6,453	8	1	3	0	4	140	42	93	5	2
Willcox	3,810	6	0	1	0	5	232	34	182	16	5
Williams	3,066	25	0	3	0	22	122	17	101	4	0
Winslow	9,792	121	2	6	2	111	570	69	488	13	2
Yuma	94,381	490	4	33	66	387	3,227	822	2,196	209	23
Arkansas											
Alma	5,460	20	0	3	1	16	231	77	148	6	0
Arkadelphia	10,795	60	0	3	5	52	387	91	281	15	0
Ashdown	4,759	17	0	4	2	11	206	46	157	3	1
Ash Flat	1,090	0	0	0	0	0	14	2	12	0	0
Atkins	3,039	6	0	1	1	4	76	24	51	1	1
Augusta	2,216	0	0	0	0	0	0	0	0	0	0
Austin	2,053	1	0	0	0	1	26	21	5	0	0
Bald Knob	2,919	2	0	0	0	2	101	45	44	12	0
Barling	4,684	13	0	2	1	10	77	27	48	2	2
Bay	1,815	0	0	0	0	0	32	11	20	1	0
Bearden	973	3	0	0	1	2	20	10	7	3	0
Beebe	7,370	44	0	4	1	39	253	87	157	9	0
Bella Vista	26,661	22	0	8	0	14	182	70	111	1	0
Benton	30,913	122	0	4	11	107	1,469	344	1,040	85	3
Bentonville	35,568	85	0	17	1	67	768	135	612	21	2
Berryville	5,397	14	1	4	0	9	286	73	203	10	3
Blytheville	15,738	203	6	7	74	116	1,491	659	785	47	5
Booneville	4,020	31	0	3	1	27	152	56	92	4	1
Bryant	16,814	10	0	5	5	0	911	207	658	46	1
Bull Shoals	1,965	5	0	0	0	5	39	14	25	0	0
Cabot	23,956	46	0	6	2	38	987	481	474	32	0
Caddo Valley	640	3	0	1	1	1	19	4	14	1	0
Camden	12,275	78	1	2	11	64	605	185	409	11	2
Cammack Village	774	0	0	0	0	0	15	12	3	0	0
Carlisle	2,231	1	0	0	1	0	36	17	19	0	0
Cave City	1,918	2	0	0	0	2	33	6	26	1	1
Cave Springs	1,742	0	0	0	0	0	25	15	10	0	0
Centerton	9,587	15	0	4	0	11	86	32	51	3	0
Charleston	2,513	3	0	0	0	3	19	1	18	0	0
Cherokee Village	4,706	6	0	1	0	5	186	77	108	1	0
Clarendon	1,677	2	0	0	1	1	50	26	24	0	0
Clarksville	9,247	22	0	7	1	14	425	72	344	9	0
Clinton	2,622	3	0	0	0	3	45	6	36	3	0
Conway	59,354	247	4	22	82	139	2,719	406	2,208	105	5

[1] If a blank is presented in the arson column, it indicates that the FBI did not receive 12 complete months of arson data for that agency.

[5] The FBI determined that the agency did not follow national Uniform Crime Reporting (UCR) Program guidelines for reporting an offense. Consequently, this figure is not included in this table.

Table II-8.   Offenses Known to Law Enforcement, by Selected State and City, 2011—*Continued*

(Number.)

State/City	Population	Violent crime	Murder and non-negligent man-slaughter	Forcible rape	Robbery	Aggravated assault	Property crime	Burglary	Larceny-theft	Motor vehicle theft	Arson[1]
Arizona—*Continued*											
Crossett	5,549	14	0	3	0	11	276	114	157	5	6
Danville	2,427	1	0	0	0	1	5	4	1	0	0
Dardanelle	4,781	37	0	4	1	32	264	95	164	5	1
Decatur	1,712	1	0	0	0	1	17	10	7	0	0
De Queen	6,644	11	0	0	3	8	117	57	57	3	1
Des Arc	1,730	5	0	0	1	4	8	1	6	1	0
De Witt	3,317	24	0	0	2	22	119	42	74	3	1
Dumas	4,742	14	1	1	3	9	136	49	83	4	0
Earle	2,432	19	0	0	4	15	170	69	101	0	0
El Dorado	19,027	231	2	1	37	191	1,138	555	545	38	13
Eureka Springs	2,089	6	0	1	0	5	102	22	76	4	1
Fairfield Bay	2,356	8	0	1	0	7	43	18	25	0	0
Farmington	6,019	21	0	6	2	13	110	29	78	3	0
Fayetteville	74,137	299	1	47	38	213	3,068	513	2,424	131	8
Flippin	1,365	10	0	0	0	10	55	9	45	1	0
Fordyce	4,333	20	0	1	1	18	153	60	87	6	5
Fort Smith	86,861	601	5	63	100	433	4,703	1,110	3,389	204	20
Gassville	2,094	2	0	0	0	2	24	4	19	1	0
Glenwood	2,245	12	1	2	0	9	31	15	16	0	1
Gosnell	3,575	22	0	2	0	20	125	84	39	2	0
Gravette	2,343	5	0	0	1	4	46	10	33	3	1
Greenbrier	4,742	1	0	0	0	1	1	0	1	0	0
Green Forest	2,782	14	0	7	0	7	78	31	45	2	0
Greenland	1,269	10	0	1	1	8	18	6	12	0	0
Greenwood	9,020	28	0	0	1	27	113	43	69	1	0
Gurdon	2,229	10	0	0	0	10	63	26	36	1	0
Guy	713	1	0	0	0	1	10	0	9	1	0
Hamburg	2,879	7	0	2	2	3	57	13	44	0	1
Hampton	1,334	6	0	0	0	6	32	11	20	1	1
Harrison	13,041	58	1	6	1	50	619	186	406	27	1
Highfill	587	0	0	0	0	0	11	2	8	1	0
Highland	1,053	1	0	0	0	1	14	4	10	0	0
Hope	10,171	101	0	7	12	82	641	190	417	34	5
Horseshoe Bend	2,201	3	0	1	0	2	25	12	13	0	0
Hot Springs	35,459	328	2	22	47	257	2,847	589	2,130	128	3
Jacksonville	28,579	234	0	24	23	187	1,586	428	1,087	71	2
Jonesboro	67,772	333	1	44	81	207	3,347	1,276	1,968	103	15
Judsonia	2,034	3	0	0	0	3	58	13	36	9	1
Keiser	765	1	0	1	0	0	6	5	1	0	0
Lake City	2,098	1	0	1	0	0	10	4	6	0	0
Lake Village	2,594	47	1	0	1	45	69	21	48	0	0
Lepanto	1,907	10	0	2	1	7	40	17	22	1	1
Lewisville	1,290	2	0	0	0	2	29	11	18	0	0
Lincoln	2,266	3	0	2	0	1	28	12	16	0	0
Little Rock	194,988	2,905	37	161	858	1,849	15,504	4,655	9,756	1,093	99
Lonoke	4,277	24	1	0	2	21	197	46	148	3	1
Lowell	7,382	8	0	2	0	6	186	60	116	10	0
Madison	775	2	0	1	0	1	11	3	7	1	0
Magnolia	11,665	51	0	3	7	41	382	185	184	13	6
Malvern	10,396	28	1	2	2	23	233	79	143	11	2
Marianna	4,146	3	0	2	1	0	134	59	74	1	0
Marion	12,438	70	2	8	7	53	426	150	262	14	1
Marked Tree	2,585	1	0	0	1	0	66	16	50	0	0
Maumelle	17,293	30	2	4	1	23	304	130	162	12	0
Mayflower	2,251	10	0	0	0	10	84	22	55	7	0
McGehee	4,251	52	1	0	1	50	124	40	80	4	0
McRae	687	0	0	0	0	0	15	4	11	0	0
Mena	5,780	23	0	6	1	16	274	93	180	1	1
Mineral Springs	1,217	5	0	0	0	5	11	10	1	0	0
Monette	1,512	6	0	1	0	5	9	2	7	0	1
Monticello	9,539	50	2	5	8	35	457	134	307	16	0
Morrilton	6,818	19	1	2	2	14	477	50	416	11	2
Mountain Home	12,542	8	0	1	0	7	526	26	491	9	0
Mountain View	2,769	8	0	1	0	7	78	28	48	2	0
Mulberry	1,668	5	0	1	0	4	71	29	42	0	0
Murfreesboro	1,653	5	0	0	0	5	13	0	13	0	0
Nashville	4,662	11	0	6	0	5	189	51	138	0	1
North Little Rock	62,775	611	12	20	216	363	5,519	1,101	4,067	351	17
Osceola	7,816	96	3	7	7	79	489	151	322	16	11
Ozark	3,712	27	0	7	1	19	127	40	83	4	1
Paragould	26,311	120	1	14	8	97	1,842	574	1,186	82	9
Paris	3,559	6	0	0	0	6	161	65	87	9	3
Pea Ridge	4,830	8	0	2	0	6	56	14	39	3	0

[1] If a blank is presented in the arson column, it indicates that the FBI did not receive 12 complete months of arson data for that agency.

Table II-8.　Offenses Known to Law Enforcement, by Selected State and City, 2011—*Continued*

(Number.)

State/City	Population	Violent crime	Murder and non-negligent man-slaughter	Forcible rape	Robbery	Aggravated assault	Property crime	Burglary	Larceny-theft	Motor vehicle theft	Arson[1]
Arizona —*Continued*											
Perryville	1,471	4	0	1	0	3	31	17	14	0	0
Piggott	3,878	4	0	0	0	4	105	64	40	1	0
Pine Bluff	49,454	683	12	41	152	478	4,008	1,565	2,168	275	49
Plainview	613	1	0	0	0	1	18	7	11	0	0
Plummerville	832	2	0	0	1	1	10	3	7	0	1
Pocahontas	6,658	8	0	0	0	8	23	4	19	0	0
Pottsville	2,859	8	0	0	1	7	25	10	11	4	0
Prairie Grove	4,413	16	0	2	0	14	122	26	96	0	1
Prescott	3,321	14	1	4	1	8	193	77	105	11	1
Quitman	768	1	0	0	0	1	23	1	19	3	0
Ravenden	474	2	0	0	0	2	2	1	1	0	0
Redfield	1,307	0	0	0	0	0	26	10	13	3	0
Rogers	56,387	220	1	38	12	169	2,291	481	1,755	55	9
Rose Bud	486	0	0	0	0	0	12	5	6	1	0
Russellville	28,131	100	0	12	15	73	1,099	256	774	69	3
Salem	1,647	1	0	1	0	0	25	13	11	1	1
Searcy	23,031	79	1	12	11	55	1,190	440	735	15	3
Sheridan	4,638	21	0	4	0	17	182	81	98	3	0
Sherwood	29,746	149	2	5	16	126	982	201	748	33	3
Siloam Springs	15,153	45	0	9	4	32	356	74	270	12	3
Stamps	1,706	3	0	0	0	3	28	8	20	0	0
Star City	2,291	4	0	2	0	2	19	13	6	0	0
Stuttgart	9,397	24	0	5	4	15	476	172	282	22	2
Texarkana	30,145	245	1	10	35	199	2,270	525	1,623	122	3
Trumann	7,298	49	1	4	6	38	537	160	373	4	2
Tuckerman	1,876	9	1	0	0	8	16	13	3	0	2
Van Buren	22,963	70	0	7	6	57	659	196	441	22	1
Vilonia	3,844	4	0	0	0	4	75	34	40	1	0
Waldron	3,645	11	0	4	1	6	219	97	118	4	4
Ward	4,098	24	0	3	2	19	146	71	68	7	0
Warren	6,048	23	1	2	5	15	185	113	68	4	1
West Memphis	26,444	615	4	37	115	459	2,636	1,361	1,166	109	12
White Hall	5,568	3	0	0	2	1	102	27	60	15	0
Wynne	8,430	16	0	7	5	4	344	119	220	5	1
California											
Adelanto	32,138	164	1	18	34	111	885	410	363	112	15
Agoura Hills	20,569	15	0	1	3	11	255	74	168	13	1
Alameda	74,680	207	1	15	94	97	1,898	315	1,323	260	15
Albany	18,757	37	0	4	26	7	476	85	338	53	2
Alhambra	84,066	152	1	7	57	87	1,891	312	1,362	217	6
Aliso Viejo	48,385	30	0	2	8	20	437	75	349	13	2
Alturas	2,860	18	0	3	2	13	54	15	36	3	4
American Canyon	19,683	44	0	3	19	22	527	126	356	45	1
Anaheim	340,218	1,281	15	105	446	715	8,493	1,410	5,964	1,119	26
Anderson	10,049	75	1	3	10	61	417	81	298	38	4
Antioch	103,575	818	5	21	290	502	3,873	1,335	1,571	967	56
Apple Valley	69,948	157	4	16	53	84	1,952	685	1,052	215	16
Arcadia	57,027	68	1	5	24	38	1,699	408	1,206	85	4
Arcata	17,434	48	0	5	12	31	624	74	499	51	20
Arroyo Grande	17,455	23	0	0	4	19	344	88	238	18	13
Artesia	16,716	66	0	1	31	34	327	97	185	45	0
Arvin	19,531	165	1	0	15	149	529	164	250	115	18
Atascadero	28,643	67	0	11	8	48	702	165	502	35	3
Atherton	6,995	3	0	0	0	3	135	11	121	3	2
Atwater	28,499	129	0	5	37	87	1,230	355	773	102	14
Auburn	13,487	52	1	3	10	38	297	58	202	37	0
Avalon	3,772	18	0	0	2	16	51	13	29	9	0
Avenal	15,687	69	1	3	8	57	184	92	82	10	2
Azusa	46,906	239	0	14	49	176	1,048	277	641	130	4
Bakersfield	351,568	1,866	18	39	548	1,261	14,840	4,321	8,123	2,396	125
Baldwin Park	76,276	242	1	9	90	142	1,601	315	883	403	6
Banning	29,951	159	4	9	30	116	710	351	273	86	0
Barstow	22,905	185	2	12	48	123	822	276	407	139	5
Bear Valley	5,233	5	0	0	0	5	93	13	79	1	0
Beaumont	37,311	89	2	6	14	67	980	216	676	88	6
Bell	35,894	291	0	14	101	176	801	235	394	172	0
Bellflower	77,517	286	4	14	116	152	1,832	481	907	444	9
Bell Gardens	42,567	170	8	5	78	79	794	136	310	348	2
Belmont	26,139	16	0	2	6	8	454	98	308	48	2
Belvedere	2,092	0	0	0	0	0	18	5	13	0	0
Benicia	27,314	40	1	6	11	22	409	144	207	58	11

[1] If a blank is presented in the arson column, it indicates that the FBI did not receive 12 complete months of arson data for that agency.

Table II-8. Offenses Known to Law Enforcement, by Selected State and City, 2011—Continued

(Number.)

State/City	Population	Violent crime	Murder and non-negligent man-slaughter	Forcible rape	Robbery	Aggravated assault	Property crime	Burglary	Larceny-theft	Motor vehicle theft	Arson[1]
California—Continued											
Berkeley	113,903	482	1	19	340	122	5,064	976	3,460	628	25
Beverly Hills	34,510	58	1	2	34	21	974	269	675	30	5
Big Bear Lake	5,078	27	1	2	2	22	265	77	171	17	2
Biggs	1,727	12	0	2	1	9	27	9	13	5	0
Bishop	3,925	16	0	1	1	14	110	29	79	2	0
Blythe	21,062	69	3	1	10	55	695	272	403	20	11
Bradbury	1,060	0	0	0	0	0	12	6	5	1	0
Brawley	25,246	54	0	8	12	34	1,047	399	551	97	3
Brea	39,744	58	0	1	27	30	1,419	202	1,156	61	2
Brentwood	52,086	118	0	12	46	60	1,080	249	771	60	18
Brisbane	4,332	10	0	0	1	9	112	17	86	9	2
Broadmoor	4,225	8	0	2	4	2	60	22	27	11	0
Buellton	4,885	7	0	2	1	4	65	15	45	5	0
Buena Park	81,477	230	3	8	76	143	1,879	310	1,230	339	21
Burbank	104,555	191	1	17	68	105	2,555	395	1,926	234	11
Burlingame	29,145	51	1	4	19	27	639	146	434	59	0
Calabasas	23,329	11	0	0	3	8	291	76	205	10	1
Calexico	39,025	112	1	6	28	77	1,394	527	529	338	4
California City	14,286	71	0	12	10	49	510	255	228	27	0
Calimesa	7,972	10	0	0	3	7	159	52	85	22	2
Calistoga	5,216	5	0	1	1	3	60	14	42	4	0
Camarillo	65,968	79	2	10	17	50	882	160	675	47	19
Campbell	39,812	96	0	11	36	49	1,378	307	920	151	7
Canyon Lake	10,685	21	0	1	1	19	225	34	160	31	0
Capitola	10,035	28	1	2	8	17	598	65	518	15	1
Carlsbad	106,566	210	4	11	35	160	1,970	468	1,375	127	2
Carmel	3,766	3	0	0	1	2	78	19	59	0	0
Carpinteria	13,193	24	0	3	3	18	204	43	149	12	1
Carson	92,792	444	5	13	106	320	2,492	573	1,360	559	9
Cathedral City	51,802	226	4	15	53	154	1,783	790	713	280	7
Ceres	45,951	164	0	6	50	108	1,692	374	1,037	281	13
Cerritos	49,618	84	0	4	51	29	1,761	375	1,221	165	3
Chico	87,200	245	5	37	92	111	2,115	487	1,337	291	29
Chino	78,900	247	2	9	58	178	2,072	530	1,341	201	12
Chino Hills	75,678	68	0	4	16	48	978	264	624	90	3
Chowchilla	18,940	82	0	2	4	76	453	184	233	36	11
Chula Vista	246,783	670	6	34	233	397	5,007	807	3,316	884	36
Citrus Heights	84,280	334	1	15	127	191	3,333	607	2,386	340	12
City of Angels	3,881	16	0	3	0	13	60	28	29	3	0
Claremont	35,337	32	0	1	19	12	850	207	601	42	26
Clayton	11,025	8	0	1	2	5	101	25	73	3	2
Clearlake	15,429	143	2	14	21	106	699	251	367	81	15
Cloverdale	8,719	11	0	3	1	7	159	21	129	9	3
Clovis	96,755	211	4	26	55	126	3,933	914	2,608	411	13
Coachella	41,183	276	1	5	76	194	1,697	467	972	258	6
Coalinga	13,537	114	1	4	5	104	676	223	420	33	15
Colma	1,813	11	0	1	6	4	246	33	202	11	0
Colton	52,767	189	4	8	90	87	1,558	446	844	268	13
Colusa	6,041	4	0	0	2	2	126	36	81	9	0
Commerce	12,974	116	0	5	46	65	949	117	507	325	10
Compton	97,589	1,067	17	45	380	625	2,865	800	1,202	863	39
Concord	123,502	430	7	19	167	237	3,803	898	2,268	637	9
Corcoran	25,105	76	1	1	13	61	355	106	207	42	0
Corning	7,753	57	0	4	9	44	349	65	263	21	3
Corona	154,165	200	2	10	105	83	3,354	705	2,298	351	20
Coronado	24,987	25	0	2	6	17	483	68	376	39	0
Costa Mesa	111,253	231	4	30	83	114	3,534	524	2,743	267	14
Cotati	7,350	35	0	3	5	27	97	32	59	6	0
Covina	48,358	142	1	10	43	88	1,719	372	1,195	152	4
Crescent City	7,733	60	0	2	9	49	286	89	182	15	0
Cudahy	24,085	167	0	7	60	100	371	49	195	127	1
Culver City	39,340	146	2	6	74	64	1,669	199	1,363	107	0
Cupertino	58,987	46	1	4	18	23	711	139	555	17	5
Cypress	48,364	60	1	8	18	33	857	150	647	60	4
Daly City	102,312	184	1	14	59	110	1,880	322	1,308	250	15
Dana Point	33,743	53	0	0	5	48	627	101	489	37	0
Danville	42,533	26	0	0	7	19	493	102	361	30	4
Davis	66,393	114	2	33	38	41	1,489	398	1,000	91	10
Delano	53,665	220	1	7	48	164	1,644	773	513	358	40
Del Mar	4,210	16	0	2	1	13	179	29	135	15	0
Del Rey Oaks	1,643	4	0	0	3	1	56	12	43	1	2
Desert Hot Springs	26,243	334	4	14	55	261	1,463	594	693	176	6
Diamond Bar	56,197	58	2	6	24	26	778	254	473	51	5
Dinuba	21,705	156	0	0	21	135	765	297	366	102	5
Dixon	18,567	44	0	4	7	33	355	75	237	43	2

[1] If a blank is presented in the arson column, it indicates that the FBI did not receive 12 complete months of arson data for that agency.

Table II-8.   Offenses Known to Law Enforcement, by Selected State and City, 2011—*Continued*

(Number.)

State/City	Population	Violent crime	Murder and non-negligent man-slaughter	Forcible rape	Robbery	Aggravated assault	Property crime	Burglary	Larceny-theft	Motor vehicle theft	Arson[1]
California—*Continued*											
Dorris	950	7	0	0	1	6	32	8	23	1	0
Dos Palos	5,008	40	0	0	3	37	177	50	105	22	2
Downey	113,086	390	2	23	204	161	3,876	769	2,054	1,053	4
Duarte	21,572	60	0	5	16	39	427	110	263	54	2
Dublin	46,577	79	0	4	16	59	642	115	478	49	4
Dunsmuir	1,669	3	0	0	2	1	71	16	52	3	0
East Palo Alto	28,486	263	8	19	107	129	824	427	239	158	0
Eastvale	54,299	46	1	3	20	22	963	199	637	127	3
El Cajon	100,647	529	2	28	187	312	2,468	603	1,443	422	14
El Centro	43,099	165	2	11	36	116	2,284	695	1,424	165	15
El Cerrito	23,826	104	0	3	58	43	923	228	587	108	1
Elk Grove	154,814	523	3	18	98	404	3,270	664	2,282	324	14
El Monte	114,809	421	1	33	196	191	2,286	544	1,136	606	6
El Segundo	16,850	38	0	4	15	19	550	161	338	51	1
Emeryville	10,199	208	0	2	73	133	1,257	161	977	119	3
Encinitas	60,218	140	0	10	27	103	1,037	222	722	93	0
Escalon	7,216	19	0	0	0	19	282	89	174	19	0
Escondido	145,603	495	3	28	177	287	3,210	557	2,156	497	19
Etna	746	2	0	0	0	2	11	4	5	2	0
Eureka	27,511	122	1	28	35	58	1,644	447	1,012	185	16
Exeter	10,455	45	1	1	10	33	342	138	180	24	5
Fairfax	7,528	23	0	1	0	22	123	27	94	2	0
Fairfield	106,559	425	5	21	148	251	2,974	572	2,055	347	13
Farmersville	10,712	37	1	0	4	32	247	79	134	34	2
Ferndale	1,387	4	0	0	0	4	8	6	2	0	0
Fillmore	15,178	32	0	2	17	13	230	35	164	31	2
Firebaugh	7,638	12	0	0	4	8	131	52	62	17	0
Folsom	73,052	84	1	15	33	35	1,510	316	1,116	78	15
Fontana	198,374	720	5	39	241	435	4,235	1,041	2,411	783	9
Fort Bragg	7,359	41	0	1	5	35	311	78	223	10	3
Fort Jones	849	4	0	0	1	3	15	4	11	0	0
Fortuna	12,066	56	0	11	6	39	381	76	280	25	4
Foster City	30,926	26	1	1	2	22	395	107	255	33	8
Fountain Valley	55,963	79	1	8	14	56	1,279	273	941	65	1
Fowler	5,635	45	0	1	2	42	178	43	106	29	2
Fremont	216,606	384	2	35	156	191	3,952	1,206	2,303	443	19
Fresno	500,480	2,915	35	51	1,020	1,809	25,421	5,713	14,928	4,780	136
Fullerton	136,750	306	2	25	104	175	3,550	643	2,548	359	11
Galt	23,925	44	0	1	25	18	421	111	266	44	9
Gardena	59,521	281	2	11	139	129	1,453	395	789	269	4
Garden Grove	172,892	449	2	19	171	257	3,387	717	2,242	428	17
Gilroy	49,395	204	1	8	65	130	1,382	207	1,006	169	7
Glendale	193,973	258	0	14	108	136	3,452	623	2,506	323	5
Glendora	50,662	65	0	7	35	23	1,309	185	1,068	56	2
Goleta	30,239	40	0	4	8	28	383	98	268	17	1
Gonzales	8,283	23	0	1	8	14	121	31	61	29	4
Grand Terrace	12,182	17	0	1	4	12	238	77	127	34	0
Grass Valley	13,011	64	0	7	13	44	453	77	339	37	3
Greenfield	16,522	82	5	4	29	44	306	87	168	51	8
Gridley	6,661	62	0	2	3	57	251	68	148	35	1
Grover Beach	13,311	36	0	10	3	23	322	77	211	34	3
Guadalupe	7,163	8	0	1	1	6	58	18	36	4	3
Gustine	5,585	34	1	2	5	26	148	46	81	21	1
Hanford	54,601	174	2	7	48	117	1,447	286	1,002	159	12
Hawaiian Gardens	14,422	67	0	0	30	37	216	41	120	55	3
Hawthorne	85,284	623	5	25	302	291	2,124	598	1,136	390	10
Hayward	145,881	579	7	44	360	168	3,782	988	1,693	1,101	16
Healdsburg	11,386	14	0	4	2	8	242	54	187	1	0
Hemet	79,582	361	5	15	124	217	3,472	1,173	1,911	388	3
Hercules	24,343	33	0	2	10	21	312	94	174	44	1
Hermosa Beach	19,735	62	1	7	16	38	605	130	450	25	1
Hesperia	91,233	313	2	25	95	191	2,249	668	1,181	400	20
Hidden Hills	1,878	0	0	0	0	0	15	4	11	0	0
Highland	53,728	236	4	10	81	141	1,457	556	641	260	14
Hillsborough	10,952	0	0	0	0	0	73	29	41	3	0
Hollister	35,339	158	4	10	28	116	621	251	297	73	12
Holtville	6,009	3	0	1	0	2	106	31	65	10	3
Hughson	6,718	7	1	1	2	3	98	19	64	15	0
Huntington Beach	192,226	406	4	34	108	260	4,589	753	3,584	252	20
Huntington Park	58,797	487	1	10	317	159	2,100	209	1,128	763	8
Huron	6,833	100	0	5	21	74	150	44	73	33	7
Imperial	14,931	8	0	0	0	8	88	22	48	18	0
Imperial Beach	26,633	143	0	6	15	122	433	119	193	121	3
Indian Wells	5,016	0	0	0	0	0	151	47	102	2	0

[1] If a blank is presented in the arson column, it indicates that the FBI did not receive 12 complete months of arson data for that agency.

Table II-8. Offenses Known to Law Enforcement, by Selected State and City, 2011—*Continued*

(Number.)

State/City	Population	Violent crime	Murder and non-negligent man-slaughter	Forcible rape	Robbery	Aggravated assault	Property crime	Burglary	Larceny-theft	Motor vehicle theft	Arson[1]
California—*Continued*											
Indio	76,930	430	3	24	110	293	2,610	788	1,453	369	5
Industry	222	44	0	2	22	20	1,136	114	788	234	5
Inglewood	110,962	808	13	33	343	419	2,582	568	1,459	555	32
Ione	8,011	19	0	1	1	17	109	27	80	2	1
Irvine	214,872	120	2	11	40	67	3,280	513	2,649	118	17
Irwindale	1,439	26	2	2	2	20	194	46	121	27	0
Jackson	4,706	18	0	2	1	15	170	49	114	7	0
Kensington	5,137	3	1	0	1	1	93	28	51	14	0
Kerman	13,703	60	1	6	18	35	548	117	299	132	1
King City	13,025	70	1	9	5	55	264	111	113	40	4
Kingsburg	11,516	64	0	2	4	58	369	105	209	55	2
La Canada Flintridge	20,484	14	0	2	3	9	349	94	243	12	2
Lafayette	24,174	9	0	2	2	5	393	110	251	32	0
Laguna Beach	22,990	62	0	6	6	50	604	115	465	24	1
Laguna Hills	30,701	45	0	2	11	32	597	95	475	27	2
Laguna Niguel	63,719	43	0	3	13	27	666	118	524	24	4
Laguna Woods	16,382	8	0	0	5	3	145	25	116	4	0
La Habra	60,947	201	0	3	47	151	1,370	233	1,026	111	1
La Habra Heights	5,388	7	0	1	1	5	71	29	38	4	1
Lake Elsinore	52,430	122	0	3	43	76	1,611	480	908	223	2
Lake Forest	78,172	89	2	1	22	64	947	140	763	44	8
Lakeport	4,809	19	0	2	3	14	261	54	200	7	0
Lake Shastina	2,437	0	0	0	0	0	0	0	0	0	0
Lakewood	80,989	214	2	9	98	105	1,899	341	1,295	263	4
La Mesa	57,736	227	1	11	93	122	1,533	308	997	228	8
La Mirada	49,097	81	0	3	20	58	807	129	536	142	3
Lancaster	158,474	851	4	42	273	532	3,216	986	1,843	387	35
La Palma	15,751	11	1	2	6	2	255	63	169	23	2
La Puente	40,284	157	3	6	44	104	594	136	294	164	2
La Quinta	37,907	188	1	3	33	151	1,428	477	901	50	1
La Verne	31,428	63	0	1	13	49	647	135	481	31	4
Lawndale	33,154	175	5	7	72	91	447	157	196	94	1
Lemon Grove	25,618	137	1	4	29	103	416	105	208	103	0
Lemoore	24,819	81	2	6	12	61	703	130	496	77	13
Lincoln	43,322	29	1	7	5	16	487	170	267	50	6
Lindsay	11,906	70	1	0	10	59	289	73	180	36	2
Livermore	81,920	267	3	14	39	211	1,776	366	1,283	127	10
Livingston	13,212	75	0	5	10	60	350	180	135	35	2
Lodi	62,864	236	2	7	89	138	2,439	713	1,507	219	12
Loma Linda	23,534	53	0	6	15	32	534	144	306	84	1
Lomita	20,494	87	2	5	24	56	334	90	207	37	4
Lompoc	42,933	275	2	28	21	224	971	232	692	47	26
Long Beach	467,691	2,857	25	112	1,320	1,400	12,816	3,275	7,329	2,212	103
Los Alamitos	11,584	12	0	0	6	6	304	80	195	29	3
Los Altos	29,317	6	0	2	2	2	269	55	203	11	2
Los Altos Hills	8,015	4	0	1	0	3	61	33	26	2	3
Los Angeles	3,837,207	20,045	297	828	10,077	8,843	86,330	17,264	53,469	15,597	1,376
Los Banos	36,395	168	3	7	29	129	1,177	397	676	104	1
Los Gatos	29,759	42	0	4	17	21	627	122	464	41	7
Lynwood	70,592	609	4	8	283	314	1,393	429	496	468	22
Madera	62,138	406	1	15	115	275	1,442	608	528	306	0
Malibu	12,794	15	0	2	2	11	268	76	182	10	0
Mammoth Lakes	8,331	38	0	5	4	29	244	66	156	22	1
Manhattan Beach	35,548	44	0	6	10	28	891	204	654	33	2
Manteca	67,885	206	4	7	53	142	2,367	511	1,590	266	19
Marina	19,950	49	1	6	17	25	482	130	328	24	6
Martinez	36,245	68	0	5	21	42	838	191	499	148	1
Marysville	12,214	101	1	6	11	83	460	154	231	75	7
Maywood	27,717	155	2	0	54	99	358	90	135	133	2
McFarland	12,856	57	0	1	10	46	212	80	90	42	13
Menifee	78,430	53	2	2	23	26	1,611	450	901	260	6
Mendota	11,143	64	2	2	20	40	380	114	208	58	24
Menlo Park	32,402	49	2	2	20	25	617	196	386	35	2
Merced	79,886	503	8	20	149	326	3,159	802	2,044	313	42
Millbrae	21,785	28	0	1	9	18	403	105	264	34	3
Mill Valley	14,066	13	0	2	4	7	182	55	118	9	0
Milpitas	67,575	102	2	10	59	31	1,824	299	1,315	210	12
Mission Viejo	94,402	79	0	3	30	46	1,216	193	983	40	4
Modesto	203,530	1,413	14	67	425	907	8,894	2,121	5,410	1,363	56
Monrovia	37,020	75	0	1	34	40	904	150	675	79	1
Montague	1,460	4	0	0	0	4	16	7	7	2	2
Montclair	37,095	191	1	7	81	102	1,694	221	1,170	303	4
Montebello	63,235	174	1	6	97	70	1,837	671	766	400	42

[1] If a blank is presented in the arson column, it indicates that the FBI did not receive 12 complete months of arson data for that agency.

Table II-8. Offenses Known to Law Enforcement, by Selected State and City, 2011—*Continued*

(Number.)

State/City	Population	Violent crime	Murder and non-negligent man-slaughter	Forcible rape	Robbery	Aggravated assault	Property crime	Burglary	Larceny-theft	Motor vehicle theft	Arson[1]
California—*Continued*											
Monterey	28,137	188	2	6	40	140	1,190	229	920	41	8
Monterey Park	60,978	102	1	1	60	40	1,039	213	635	191	0
Monte Sereno	3,380	0	0	0	0	0	20	7	13	0	1
Moorpark	34,826	27	0	1	10	16	365	83	261	21	7
Moraga	16,204	9	0	5	1	3	172	34	121	17	2
Moreno Valley	195,638	732	7	32	330	363	5,762	2,095	2,767	900	3
Morgan Hill	38,327	42	1	8	16	17	690	138	470	82	13
Morro Bay	10,354	20	0	3	2	15	144	28	113	3	0
Mountain View	74,937	153	0	7	41	105	1,353	167	1,086	100	3
Mount Shasta	3,434	6	0	0	0	6	80	25	48	7	0
Murrieta	104,682	105	2	13	34	56	1,495	348	1,031	116	10
Napa	77,819	224	1	24	47	152	1,615	344	1,132	139	9
National City	59,271	372	1	12	137	222	1,814	300	1,046	468	6
Needles	4,901	13	1	0	3	9	198	85	90	23	1
Nevada City	3,104	18	0	1	1	16	123	31	81	11	0
Newark	43,073	170	1	8	55	106	1,386	385	900	101	3
Newman	10,344	22	0	0	5	17	261	61	164	36	0
Newport Beach	86,187	116	0	16	27	73	2,223	441	1,702	80	11
Norco	27,381	34	0	4	12	18	649	185	390	74	1
Norwalk	106,790	371	5	10	138	218	2,274	476	1,156	642	21
Novato	52,514	108	0	10	24	74	992	215	707	70	10
Oakdale	20,918	44	0	5	13	26	900	286	530	84	0
Oakland	395,317	6,652	104	202	3,365	2,981	20,904	5,170	9,429	6,305	138
Oakley	35,849	79	3	3	13	60	526	126	314	86	4
Oceanside	169,050	620	7	58	181	374	3,849	792	2,704	353	22
Ojai	7,549	25	0	2	6	17	171	32	136	3	0
Ontario	165,851	493	6	27	209	251	4,858	939	3,057	862	22
Orange	138,020	157	3	6	82	66	2,652	445	2,001	206	9
Orinda	17,850	4	0	0	2	2	224	83	130	11	1
Orland	7,377	31	0	1	5	25	208	63	107	38	3
Oroville	15,729	67	1	10	23	33	759	226	465	68	14
Oxnard	200,225	619	8	26	274	311	3,499	577	2,563	359	26
Pacifica	37,672	44	0	4	7	33	484	89	350	45	3
Pacific Grove	15,218	24	0	0	3	21	297	104	184	9	3
Palmdale	154,546	785	9	38	246	492	3,273	959	1,906	408	29
Palm Desert	49,015	76	2	2	40	32	2,147	593	1,439	115	3
Palm Springs	45,076	256	1	16	88	151	2,304	742	1,266	296	16
Palo Alto	65,160	64	0	3	24	37	1,248	286	923	39	12
Palos Verdes Estates	13,596	5	0	1	1	3	118	40	71	7	0
Paradise	26,526	78	0	10	14	54	462	200	220	42	0
Paramount	54,734	255	1	6	129	119	1,621	268	884	469	15
Pasadena	138,734	435	7	26	178	224	3,672	1,011	2,382	279	25
Paso Robles	30,143	95	2	11	12	70	832	148	632	52	2
Patterson	20,653	56	1	2	17	36	619	226	270	123	2
Perris	69,190	167	3	3	93	68	2,124	588	974	562	0
Petaluma	58,622	140	0	11	23	106	884	131	693	60	9
Pico Rivera	63,682	243	7	11	87	138	1,568	223	999	346	7
Piedmont	10,792	8	0	0	7	1	282	88	148	46	1
Pinole	18,606	83	1	1	33	48	556	108	328	120	3
Pismo Beach	7,745	31	0	2	5	24	315	84	205	26	0
Pittsburg	64,008	145	3	7	76	59	1,905	554	915	436	2
Placentia	51,127	82	1	2	25	54	891	203	627	61	5
Placerville	10,511	68	1	4	10	53	218	61	135	22	2
Pleasant Hill	33,542	72	0	3	29	40	1,449	214	1,132	103	10
Pleasanton	71,111	59	0	4	24	31	1,215	182	949	84	5
Pomona	150,810	927	11	54	339	523	4,444	890	2,578	976	17
Porterville	54,802	226	2	5	58	161	1,937	519	1,222	196	3
Port Hueneme	21,978	52	0	4	14	34	369	92	244	33	5
Poway	48,373	94	0	8	17	69	615	163	413	39	1
Rancho Cordova	65,538	324	5	12	109	198	1,904	498	1,111	295	5
Rancho Cucamonga	167,212	293	6	13	103	171	3,915	1,173	2,381	361	11
Rancho Mirage	17,420	19	0	1	6	12	723	243	444	36	0
Rancho Palos Verdes	42,133	36	1	1	11	23	550	182	342	26	2
Rancho Santa Margarita	48,416	32	0	1	9	22	368	66	284	18	3
Red Bluff	14,241	104	1	3	17	83	724	218	481	25	1
Redding	90,917	701	3	63	100	535	3,396	823	2,237	336	4
Redlands	69,555	197	3	18	90	86	2,621	531	1,766	324	25
Redondo Beach	67,533	168	0	3	54	111	1,601	313	1,208	80	3
Redwood City	77,718	177	0	26	63	88	1,487	436	918	133	9
Reedley	24,478	202	1	8	29	164	533	178	275	80	2
Rialto	100,337	480	6	18	204	252	2,978	934	1,524	520	21
Richmond	104,920	1,035	26	39	303	667	4,546	1,651	1,533	1,362	32
Ridgecrest	27,941	116	2	12	14	88	521	192	292	37	15
Rio Dell	3,408	4	0	1	1	2	55	11	41	3	1

[1] If a blank is presented in the arson column, it indicates that the FBI did not receive 12 complete months of arson data for that agency.

Table II-8.   Offenses Known to Law Enforcement, by Selected State and City, 2011—*Continued*

(Number.)

State/City	Population	Violent crime	Murder and non-negligent man-slaughter	Forcible rape	Robbery	Aggravated assault	Property crime	Burglary	Larceny-theft	Motor vehicle theft	Arson[1]
California—*Continued*											
Rio Vista	7,447	45	0	0	2	43	161	58	89	14	4
Ripon	14,465	16	0	2	5	9	309	44	246	19	1
Riverbank	22,945	62	0	2	14	46	610	244	288	78	2
Riverside	307,443	1,310	13	57	458	782	9,631	2,080	6,278	1,273	49
Rocklin	57,644	62	0	7	22	33	1,092	267	763	62	11
Rohnert Park	41,453	193	1	16	15	161	801	154	595	52	10
Rolling Hills	1,882	0	0	0	0	0	14	7	6	1	0
Rolling Hills Estates	8,162	6	0	0	3	3	162	43	115	4	0
Rosemead	54,396	170	0	13	69	88	1,140	266	677	197	2
Roseville	120,184	248	1	24	43	180	3,541	534	2,786	221	11
Ross	2,443	1	0	0	0	1	36	9	26	1	0
Sacramento	471,972	3,354	36	134	1,162	2,022	18,563	4,141	11,087	3,335	146
Salinas	152,210	1,115	15	34	374	692	4,492	1,140	2,189	1,163	22
San Anselmo	12,481	25	0	1	3	21	247	77	163	7	1
San Bernardino	212,392	1,861	30	77	720	1,034	8,461	2,359	4,446	1,656	60
San Bruno	41,597	87	1	8	33	45	917	109	674	134	4
San Clemente	64,269	55	0	5	15	35	879	206	631	42	11
Sand City	338	5	0	1	3	1	87	2	83	2	0
San Diego	1,316,919	5,104	38	293	1,456	3,317	29,709	5,840	17,610	6,259	153
San Dimas	33,763	78	0	4	17	57	562	133	390	39	3
San Fernando	23,923	103	0	3	36	64	430	99	270	61	3
San Francisco	814,701	5,374	50	131	3,088	2,105	32,886	4,408	24,304	4,174	161
San Gabriel	40,185	107	0	2	41	64	553	167	338	48	1
Sanger	24,555	314	2	9	20	283	985	297	523	165	4
San Jacinto	44,719	118	4	4	43	67	1,462	507	766	189	3
San Jose	957,062	3,206	39	226	1,101	1,840	21,972	4,223	12,628	5,121	165
San Juan Capistrano	35,000	56	2	4	16	34	450	71	345	34	5
San Leandro	85,949	367	7	19	217	124	3,205	671	1,957	577	14
San Luis Obispo	45,649	134	2	24	34	74	1,782	330	1,345	107	25
San Marcos	84,766	233	0	19	60	154	1,424	358	908	158	7
San Marino	13,302	11	0	2	3	6	192	61	129	2	0
San Mateo	98,350	246	1	20	69	156	1,732	306	1,288	138	4
San Pablo	29,482	256	3	6	126	121	1,342	347	554	441	6
San Rafael	58,391	200	2	20	65	113	1,473	309	1,011	153	13
San Ramon	72,996	27	0	0	11	16	869	166	640	63	5
Santa Ana	328,343	1,313	13	62	591	647	6,575	1,067	4,222	1,286	101
Santa Barbara	89,449	319	0	37	80	202	2,756	541	2,124	91	16
Santa Clara	117,837	177	2	14	67	94	2,933	409	2,202	322	20
Santa Clarita	178,393	262	5	18	76	163	2,568	567	1,766	235	19
Santa Cruz	60,651	480	1	23	113	343	3,356	568	2,603	185	12
Santa Fe Springs	16,414	107	1	6	45	55	1,133	140	833	160	3
Santa Maria	100,723	716	7	18	153	538	2,429	655	1,510	264	9
Santa Monica	90,791	369	1	24	129	215	2,971	483	2,300	188	7
Santa Paula	29,666	130	1	7	45	77	475	104	319	52	1
Santa Rosa	169,788	682	5	58	134	485	3,706	637	2,794	275	16
Santee	54,041	132	1	8	38	85	977	204	666	107	2
Saratoga	30,278	16	1	1	2	12	214	62	139	13	9
Sausalito	7,144	6	0	1	1	4	196	52	139	5	0
Scotts Valley	11,716	13	0	2	3	8	279	63	200	16	1
Seal Beach	24,452	30	8	1	8	13	530	133	367	30	1
Seaside	33,413	112	0	7	23	82	633	149	431	53	10
Sebastopol	7,466	8	0	0	0	8	162	30	125	7	2
Selma	23,492	209	0	9	36	164	1,260	339	722	199	3
Shafter	17,188	41	2	3	11	25	508	162	263	83	19
Sierra Madre	11,045	10	0	1	1	8	137	38	95	4	0
Signal Hill	11,146	32	0	3	13	16	471	99	312	60	2
Simi Valley	125,698	116	0	9	41	66	1,697	314	1,278	105	14
Solana Beach	13,018	33	0	1	12	20	243	68	158	17	0
Soledad	26,041	74	2	4	22	46	251	125	105	21	0
Solvang	5,307	5	0	1	0	4	68	22	42	4	1
Sonoma	10,773	32	0	1	0	31	221	57	157	7	2
Sonora	4,961	30	0	4	8	18	428	69	342	17	2
South El Monte	20,352	122	0	6	41	75	376	75	184	117	3
South Gate	95,506	580	6	10	269	295	2,893	418	1,294	1,181	14
South Lake Tahoe	21,655	130	1	5	22	102	429	153	260	16	1
South Pasadena	25,920	33	0	6	14	13	480	141	281	58	2
South San Francisco	64,380	138	1	13	47	77	1,327	412	764	151	19
Stallion Springs	2,517	3	0	0	0	3	9	5	3	1	1
Stanton	38,635	141	1	7	53	80	629	139	390	100	7
St. Helena	5,882	4	0	1	0	3	113	12	94	7	1
Stockton	295,136	4,155	58	90	1,323	2,684	15,463	4,133	9,651	1,679	86
Suisun City	28,441	50	0	5	21	24	691	186	438	67	2
Sunnyvale	141,728	150	3	21	68	58	1,970	393	1,351	226	14

[1] If a blank is presented in the arson column, it indicates that the FBI did not receive 12 complete months of arson data for that agency.

Table II-8. Offenses Known to Law Enforcement, by Selected State and City, 2011—*Continued*

(Number.)

State/City	Population	Violent crime	Murder and non-negligent man-slaughter	Forcible rape	Robbery	Aggravated assault	Property crime	Burglary	Larceny-theft	Motor vehicle theft	Arson[1]
California—*Continued*											
Susanville	18,158	81	0	4	8	69	313	108	194	11	2
Sutter Creek	2,530	7	1	0	1	5	63	15	47	1	3
Taft	9,437	51	0	1	8	42	345	75	243	27	0
Tehachapi	14,583	29	0	1	7	21	310	108	182	20	0
Temecula	101,274	95	0	7	54	34	2,406	547	1,700	159	0
Temple City	35,976	50	0	2	20	28	344	111	206	27	2
Thousand Oaks	128,172	137	1	10	34	92	1,788	319	1,409	60	12
Tiburon	9,067	5	0	0	0	5	87	15	69	3	1
Torrance	147,148	185	2	17	91	75	2,767	509	1,957	301	11
Tracy	83,897	138	0	12	68	58	2,178	390	1,585	203	12
Truckee	16,370	20	0	1	2	17	259	110	137	12	3
Tulare	59,975	343	5	19	55	264	2,210	515	1,365	330	10
Tulelake	1,022	3	0	0	0	3	23	9	14	0	0
Turlock	69,355	368	1	16	96	255	2,591	806	1,431	354	20
Tustin	76,428	97	1	7	39	50	1,513	243	1,167	103	6
Twentynine Palms	25,342	79	0	10	10	59	523	229	239	55	4
Twin Cities	21,428	36	0	5	12	19	481	149	302	30	1
Ukiah	16,264	115	0	4	18	93	427	154	250	23	5
Union City	70,333	311	3	9	115	184	1,787	459	1,070	258	7
Upland	74,599	183	2	14	80	87	2,214	514	1,349	351	2
Vacaville	93,515	195	3	20	51	121	1,677	261	1,265	151	21
Vallejo	117,305	903	18	53	435	397	5,244	2,468	1,716	1,060	46
Ventura	107,684	326	1	20	135	170	3,320	657	2,468	195	5
Vernon	113	32	0	0	19	13	308	30	183	95	1
Victorville	117,266	686	6	37	261	382	3,931	1,359	2,086	486	26
Villa Park	5,880	2	0	0	0	2	75	12	59	4	0
Visalia	125,905	486	8	40	95	343	5,121	1,110	3,466	545	8
Vista	94,937	387	0	32	121	234	2,025	469	1,213	343	8
Walnut	29,515	40	1	3	8	28	354	107	211	36	4
Walnut Creek	64,927	69	1	2	14	52	2,024	422	1,472	130	6
Waterford	8,555	21	1	2	2	16	201	61	114	26	0
Watsonville	51,801	281	5	14	92	170	1,605	328	967	310	11
Weed	3,002	14	0	0	1	13	88	30	52	6	0
West Covina	107,345	280	1	20	124	135	3,249	526	2,212	511	1
West Hollywood	34,803	337	0	19	125	193	1,437	277	1,041	119	18
Westlake Village	8,367	4	0	0	2	2	181	54	125	2	1
Westminster	90,756	248	3	11	79	155	2,504	409	1,815	280	4
Westmorland	2,251	1	0	0	1	0	11	4	7	0	0
West Sacramento	49,317	172	2	24	61	85	1,376	256	949	171	13
Wheatland	3,497	8	0	0	0	8	52	18	31	3	0
Whittier	86,334	334	4	7	100	223	2,468	435	1,779	254	7
Wildomar	32,554	46	0	6	16	24	719	187	411	121	0
Williams	5,183	14	0	1	1	12	67	27	34	6	2
Willits	4,945	30	0	1	6	23	100	27	64	9	1
Willows	6,238	22	0	2	2	18	229	48	165	16	0
Windsor	27,116	65	0	5	5	55	333	49	271	13	3
Winters	6,702	11	0	1	2	8	103	25	73	5	2
Woodlake	7,365	24	1	1	3	19	144	33	90	21	1
Woodland	56,120	178	1	28	42	107	1,188	338	721	129	23
Yorba Linda	64,989	49	3	4	9	33	819	152	640	27	3
Yountville	2,967	4	0	1	0	3	43	9	33	1	0
Yreka	7,856	41	0	2	4	35	257	49	201	7	2
Yuba City	65,688	210	1	20	57	132	1,795	348	1,277	170	9
Yucaipa	51,971	118	1	7	24	86	900	265	535	100	17
Yucca Valley	20,943	91	1	6	20	64	569	149	355	65	3
Colorado											
Alamosa	8,933	43	1	11	5	26	579	92	477	10	4
Arvada	108,287	162	1	25	34	102	2,546	304	2,053	189	29
Aspen	6,774	8	0	0	0	8	270	22	245	3	0
Ault	1,545	10	0	0	0	10	26	9	17	0	0
Aurora	330,740	1,448	9	183	504	752	9,875	2,144	6,861	870	87
Avon	6,559	6	0	3	0	3	175	19	152	4	2
Basalt	3,924	2	0	0	0	2	46	8	37	1	0
Bayfield	2,374	1	0	0	0	1	6	1	4	1	1
Berthoud	5,194	2	0	0	0	2	71	7	59	5	3
Black Hawk	120	10	0	0	1	9	150	1	147	2	3
Boulder	99,081	275	2	35	35	203	2,491	467	1,899	125	55
Brighton	33,933	88	0	17	4	67	1,088	149	875	64	13
Broomfield	56,862	31	1	6	7	17	1,101	81	974	46	7
Brush	5,558	4	0	0	0	4	68	15	52	1	1
Buena Vista	2,663	0	0	0	0	0	11	0	11	0	0
Burlington	4,328	5	2	0	0	3	67	13	49	5	0

[1] If a blank is presented in the arson column, it indicates that the FBI did not receive 12 complete months of arson data for that agency.

Table II-8.   Offenses Known to Law Enforcement, by Selected State and City, 2011—*Continued*

(Number.)

State/City	Population	Violent crime	Murder and non-negligent man-slaughter	Forcible rape	Robbery	Aggravated assault	Property crime	Burglary	Larceny-theft	Motor vehicle theft	Arson[1]
Colorado—*Continued*											
Campo	111	0	0	0	0	0	0	0	0	0	0
Castle Rock	49,071	30	2	9	6	13	481	74	397	10	3
Cedaredge	2,292	1	0	0	1	0	38	10	27	1	0
Centennial	102,125	162	0	27	23	112	1,353	325	957	71	20
Center	2,269	8	0	0	2	6	86	45	39	2	2
Cherry Hills Village	6,091	2	0	1	1	0	44	17	26	1	0
Colorado Springs	423,680	1,865	26	319	449	1,071	15,866	3,323	11,375	1,168	107
Columbine Valley	1,278	0	0	0	0	0	12	2	9	1	0
Commerce City	46,713	166	1	39	23	103	1,227	243	870	114	6
Cortez	8,630	23	0	0	2	21	359	20	333	6	0
Craig	9,629	27	0	9	2	16	265	50	208	7	2
Crested Butte	1,513	0	0	0	0	0	24	8	14	2	1
Cripple Creek	1,210	7	0	0	0	7	90	8	80	2	1
Dacono	4,224	3	0	0	0	3	8	3	2	3	0
Del Norte	1,715	0	0	0	0	0	26	1	25	0	0
Delta	9,070	24	0	5	1	18	323	44	269	10	1
Denver	610,612	3,708	34	396	1,143	2,135	22,495	4,868	14,040	3,587	95
Dillon	920	1	0	0	0	1	31	4	26	1	0
Durango	17,181	166	0	41	6	119	756	89	627	40	2
Eagle	6,621	4	0	1	0	3	83	5	77	1	0
Eaton	4,441	7	0	0	0	7	3	1	2	0	0
Edgewater	5,260	22	1	6	9	6	251	25	194	32	4
Elizabeth	1,382	2	0	0	1	1	38	5	33	0	0
Empire	287	1	0	0	0	1	9	2	6	1	0
Erie	18,451	11	0	0	0	11	82	20	58	4	1
Estes Park	5,960	8	0	0	0	8	101	23	78	0	1
Evans	18,860	25	0	0	10	15	421	98	287	36	4
Fairplay	691	3	0	0	0	3	19	1	15	3	0
Federal Heights	11,667	53	0	12	17	24	511	59	394	58	5
Firestone	10,324	6	0	4	1	1	81	11	65	5	0
Florence	3,949	4	0	0	0	4	42	13	29	0	0
Fort Collins	146,494	420	3	56	46	315	4,272	560	3,553	159	15
Fort Morgan	11,512	15	0	1	3	11	282	54	220	8	7
Fountain	26,296	28	2	9	12	5	539	99	408	32	8
Fowler	1,203	3	0	0	1	2	6	1	5	0	0
Fraser/Winter Park	2,261	13	0	0	0	13	53	14	37	2	1
Frederick	8,830	1	0	0	0	1	60	16	42	2	0
Frisco	2,730	5	0	1	2	2	63	16	47	0	0
Glendale	4,257	50	0	4	14	32	419	35	363	21	1
Glenwood Springs	9,781	35	0	2	5	28	483	45	426	12	2
Golden	19,196	47	1	2	10	34	441	59	357	25	4
Granby	1,896	4	0	0	0	4	43	6	36	1	0
Grand Junction	59,586	257	2	74	37	144	2,588	379	2,070	139	24
Greeley	94,507	437	1	38	75	323	3,118	593	2,377	148	52
Green Mountain Falls	651	0	0	0	0	0	14	13	0	1	1
Greenwood Village	14,168	22	0	1	7	14	594	96	467	31	1
Gunnison	5,956	27	0	5	1	21	287	37	240	10	3
Haxtun	962	0	0	0	0	0	5	1	4	0	0
Hayden	1,842	0	0	0	0	0	36	2	33	1	0
Holyoke	2,353	0	0	0	0	0	20	1	18	1	1
Idaho Springs	1,747	3	0	1	1	1	73	7	56	10	3
Johnstown	10,059	5	0	0	0	5	102	16	81	5	2
Kersey	1,479	3	0	0	0	3	29	4	22	3	0
Kiowa	736	3	0	1	0	2	20	7	12	1	0
Kremmling	1,469	11	0	0	0	11	26	3	22	1	0
La Junta	7,200	30	0	3	2	25	106	31	67	8	7
Lakeside	8	0	0	0	0	0	14	2	11	1	0
Lakewood	145,470	615	8	88	131	388	6,194	935	4,771	488	15
Lamar	7,940	14	0	2	3	9	250	47	197	6	0
La Salle	1,989	6	0	0	0	6	44	9	33	2	0
Leadville	2,647	17	0	0	0	17	40	13	27	0	0
Limon	1,913	4	1	0	0	3	5	0	4	1	0
Littleton	42,464	55	2	10	14	29	1,132	233	836	63	7
Lone Tree	10,396	9	0	1	2	6	571	24	538	9	2
Longmont	87,773	238	1	18	33	186	1,958	298	1,559	101	66
Louisville	18,696	16	0	1	2	13	257	49	197	11	2
Loveland	68,024	107	1	22	11	73	1,725	209	1,464	52	12
Manitou Springs	5,079	15	0	1	1	13	165	27	134	4	2
Meeker	2,518	2	0	1	0	1	20	4	15	1	0
Milliken	5,708	11	0	3	1	7	46	8	37	1	0
Minturn	1,045	1	0	0	0	1	10	1	9	0	1
Monte Vista	4,521	7	0	3	1	3	121	21	97	3	0
Montrose	19,465	30	0	2	7	21	672	90	561	21	4

[1] If a blank is presented in the arson column, it indicates that the FBI did not receive 12 complete months of arson data for that agency.

Table II-8.   Offenses Known to Law Enforcement, by Selected State and City, 2011—*Continued*

(Number.)

State/City	Population	Violent crime	Murder and non-negligent man-slaughter	Forcible rape	Robbery	Aggravated assault	Property crime	Burglary	Larceny-theft	Motor vehicle theft	Arson[1]
Colorado—*Continued*											
Monument	5,626	7	0	2	1	4	83	12	70	1	1
Morrison	435	2	0	0	1	1	4	1	3	0	0
Mountain View	516	2	0	1	0	1	6	2	2	2	0
Mount Crested Butte	815	3	0	0	0	3	36	2	26	8	0
Nederland	1,470	12	0	0	0	12	29	4	24	1	1
New Castle	4,597	5	0	0	0	5	37	5	28	4	0
Northglenn	36,412	90	0	13	7	70	998	161	725	112	0
Ouray	1,017	0	0	0	0	0	31	2	29	0	0
Pagosa Springs	1,757	18	0	0	0	18	84	22	61	1	0
Palmer Lake	2,462	8	0	1	0	7	10	6	4	0	0
Parachute	1,104	6	0	1	1	4	24	3	19	2	0
Parker	46,086	43	1	9	4	29	541	122	401	18	7
Platteville	2,528	7	0	0	0	7	43	9	33	1	0
Pueblo[2]	108,452	831	12	40	173	606	5,494	1,590	3,434	470	50
Rangely	2,406	4	0	2	0	2	27	1	21	5	0
Rocky Ford	4,026	6	0	0	0	6	82	25	57	0	0
Salida	5,327	4	0	1	1	2	179	16	156	7	4
Sheridan	5,763	15	0	4	3	8	367	44	275	48	5
Silt	2,981	2	0	0	0	2	47	6	40	1	0
Silverthorne	3,955	3	0	1	1	1	115	5	108	2	0
Snowmass Village	2,875	1	0	0	0	1	42	1	41	0	0
Springfield	1,476	1	0	0	0	1	8	3	4	1	0
Steamboat Springs	12,299	34	0	4	2	28	296	31	238	27	0
Sterling	15,034	16	0	3	0	13	353	90	254	9	3
Stratton	669	1	0	0	0	1	25	9	15	1	0
Telluride	2,365	8	0	2	1	5	162	8	148	6	0
Thornton[2]	120,841	695	0	50	50	595	3,438	513	2,644	281	25
Timnath	636	0	0	0	0	0	28	1	27	0	1
Vail	5,397	16	0	1	0	15	312	32	280	0	1
Walsenburg	3,121	5	0	1	0	4	87	27	60	0	0
Westminster	107,962	245	4	34	48	159	2,803	397	2,077	329	13
Wheat Ridge	30,691	132	2	18	26	86	1,283	227	923	133	11
Windsor	18,969	11	0	1	0	10	237	39	193	5	4
Woodland Park	7,325	8	0	0	0	8	93	8	85	0	0
Wray	2,383	0	0	0	0	0	2	0	2	0	0
Yuma	3,585	6	0	2	0	4	36	8	28	0	1
Connecticut											
Ansonia	19,285	30	3	3	17	7	354	44	271	39	2
Avon	18,131	0	0	0	0	0	179	28	149	2	0
Berlin	19,903	15	0	1	6	8	379	80	279	20	1
Bethel	18,618	1	0	0	1	0	306	47	253	6	0
Bloomfield	20,524	43	1	6	8	28	455	83	345	27	3
Branford	28,078	26	0	0	11	15	749	81	613	55	1
Bridgeport	144,496	1,447	20	116	610	701	5,607	1,540	3,025	1,042	24
Bristol	60,589	118	1	10	52	55	1,496	365	1,017	114	9
Brookfield	16,482	10	0	1	5	4	200	34	160	6	0
Canton	10,311	2	0	1	0	1	106	21	82	3	0
Cheshire	29,315	12	0	0	3	9	284	71	204	9	0
Clinton	13,285	19	0	7	2	10	318	54	262	2	2
Coventry	12,458	15	0	5	4	6	191	67	118	6	1
Cromwell	14,031	6	0	1	4	1	340	28	297	15	0
Danbury	81,043	164	1	34	76	53	1,588	343	1,183	62	5
Darien	20,770	6	0	0	2	4	150	21	120	9	1
Derby	12,926	22	0	1	9	12	373	75	271	27	0
East Hampton	12,983	11	1	2	0	8	245	42	197	6	0
East Hartford	51,347	173	0	22	79	72	1,401	325	938	138	10
East Haven	29,311	24	0	0	12	12	835	117	611	107	4
Easton	7,504	1	0	0	0	1	23	3	19	1	3
East Windsor	11,183	14	0	3	3	8	295	55	220	20	7
Fairfield	59,514	24	0	1	9	14	1,131	194	885	52	6
Farmington	25,387	16	0	0	12	4	623	54	562	7	0
Glastonbury	34,491	21	0	2	5	14	323	73	238	12	1
Granby	11,303	9	0	4	3	2	113	25	85	3	1
Greenwich	61,284	27	0	3	14	10	423	79	326	18	1
Groton	10,408	24	0	4	5	15	140	13	122	5	1
Groton Long Point	519	0	0	0	0	0	12	0	12	0	0
Groton Town	29,262	36	0	7	12	17	553	70	458	25	6
Guilford	22,416	16	0	3	1	12	347	65	272	10	1
Hartford	125,006	1,639	27	55	602	955	5,502	1,271	3,372	859	91
Madison	18,303	5	0	0	1	4	123	26	96	1	0
Manchester	58,349	128	1	9	53	65	1,722	256	1,380	86	6
Meriden	60,981	144	0	9	57	78	1,721	444	1,136	141	5

[1] If a blank is presented in the arson column, it indicates that the FBI did not receive 12 complete months of arson data for that agency.

[2] Because of changes in the state/local agency's reporting practices, figures are not comparable to previous years' data.

Table II-8.   Offenses Known to Law Enforcement, by Selected State and City, 2011—*Continued*

(Number.)

State/City	Population	Violent crime	Murder and non-negligent man-slaughter	Forcible rape	Robbery	Aggravated assault	Property crime	Burglary	Larceny-theft	Motor vehicle theft	Arson[1]
Colorado—*Continued*											
Middlebury	7,589	1	0	0	0	1	84	21	60	3	0
Middletown	47,736	77	0	10	30	37	1,023	143	820	60	2
Milford	52,857	35	1	0	23	11	1,753	158	1,515	80	4
Monroe	19,515	6	0	3	1	2	181	37	138	6	3
Naugatuck	31,921	31	0	11	11	9	606	71	498	37	1
New Britain	73,341	328	3	4	143	178	2,967	881	1,768	318	0
New Canaan	19,775	4	0	1	1	2	107	14	93	0	0
New Haven	130,019	1,748	34	55	766	893	6,479	1,413	4,124	942	18
Newington	30,619	26	0	3	12	11	753	104	603	46	2
New London	27,671	319	3	18	41	257	814	227	538	49	6
New Milford	28,194	18	0	3	5	10	474	8	453	13	2
Newtown	27,611	13	0	6	3	4	189	54	130	5	2
North Branford	14,434	1	0	0	1	0	247	33	190	24	0
North Haven	24,138	11	0	0	6	5	599	88	483	28	0
Norwalk	85,761	326	3	15	90	218	1,914	297	1,443	174	4
Norwich	40,568	133	2	25	45	61	856	235	570	51	16
Old Saybrook	10,261	8	0	2	1	5	169	21	143	5	0
Orange	13,982	4	0	1	3	0	406	61	329	16	0
Plainfield	15,433	7	0	2	1	4	50	18	28	4	1
Plainville	17,749	64	0	2	5	57	541	57	462	22	1
Plymouth	12,266	2	0	0	1	1	166	35	126	5	0
Portland	9,526	5	0	0	0	5	84	18	59	7	1
Putnam	9,602	45	0	3	2	40	165	32	127	6	2
Redding	9,175	3	0	0	1	2	59	7	52	0	0
Ridgefield	24,684	0	0	0	0	0	67	12	55	0	0
Rocky Hill	19,745	6	0	1	3	2	266	28	236	2	0
Seymour	16,571	15	0	2	4	9	229	59	162	8	3
Shelton	39,632	27	0	2	10	15	524	131	349	44	0
Simsbury	23,554	6	0	1	2	3	181	20	156	5	2
Southington	43,149	29	1	9	13	6	770	124	620	26	4
South Windsor	25,757	16	0	7	4	5	426	78	335	13	0
Stamford	122,870	389	6	32	190	161	1,987	282	1,498	207	4
Stonington	18,579	12	0	5	3	4	312	52	255	5	0
Stratford	51,479	146	1	9	59	77	1,541	309	1,104	128	7
Suffield	15,764	2	0	0	0	2	95	33	58	4	2
Thomaston	7,902	4	0	0	0	4	131	31	92	8	2
Torrington	36,450	61	0	17	14	30	751	146	584	21	5
Trumbull	36,085	20	0	0	14	6	690	69	598	23	1
Vernon	29,233	30	0	7	8	15	306	67	206	33	1
Wallingford	45,218	28	2	2	15	9	853	126	691	36	3
Waterbury	110,570	359	7	9	183	160	4,571	818	3,326	427	3
Waterford	19,553	52	0	1	1	50	485	46	434	5	0
Watertown	22,556	37	0	3	7	27	448	88	337	23	0
West Hartford	63,385	68	1	4	46	17	1,517	231	1,180	106	1
West Haven	55,667	245	1	0	44	200	1,265	203	880	182	4
Weston	10,198	1	0	0	0	1	54	9	44	1	1
Westport	26,440	20	1	3	5	11	404	89	301	14	0
Wethersfield	26,717	22	0	9	6	7	366	58	291	17	0
Willimantic	17,770	31	1	1	14	15	391	61	301	29	2
Wilton	18,095	2	0	0	0	2	116	17	98	1	0
Winchester	11,263	11	0	4	1	6	223	65	150	8	4
Windsor	29,098	22	0	9	7	6	466	58	391	17	2
Windsor Locks	12,521	12	0	0	4	8	198	33	158	7	0
Wolcott	16,711	4	0	2	1	1	303	56	230	17	0
Woodbridge	9,007	1	0	0	0	1	125	19	97	9	0
Delaware											
Bethany Beach	1,071	4	0	2	0	2	117	14	103	0	0
Blades	1,254	13	0	0	3	10	40	8	31	1	0
Bridgeville	2,069	7	0	2	3	2	92	14	75	3	0
Camden	3,499	11	0	0	3	8	224	14	205	5	0
Cheswold	1,394	2	0	0	0	2	28	4	23	1	0
Clayton	2,948	7	0	2	0	5	45	18	27	0	0
Dagsboro	813	0	0	0	0	0	22	1	21	0	0
Delaware City	1,712	6	0	0	1	5	27	5	21	1	0
Delmar	1,613	8	0	2	4	2	72	17	54	1	1
Dewey Beach	344	17	0	1	2	14	66	16	46	4	0
Dover	36,416	313	5	15	73	220	2,243	132	2,030	81	10
Ellendale	385	0	0	0	0	0	2	0	2	0	0
Elsmere	6,194	20	0	0	8	12	225	59	150	16	0
Felton	1,311	6	0	0	1	5	19	5	14	0	0
Fenwick Island	383	1	0	0	0	1	13	2	11	0	0
Frankford	856	0	0	0	0	0	12	6	6	0	0

[1] If a blank is presented in the arson column, it indicates that the FBI did not receive 12 complete months of arson data for that agency.

Table II-8.   Offenses Known to Law Enforcement, by Selected State and City, 2011—_Continued_

(Number.)

State/City	Population	Violent crime	Murder and non-negligent man-slaughter	Forcible rape	Robbery	Aggravated assault	Property crime	Burglary	Larceny-theft	Motor vehicle theft	Arson[1]
Delaware—_Continued_											
Georgetown	6,488	57	0	6	20	31	326	62	252	12	0
Greenwood	983	3	0	0	1	2	30	11	19	0	0
Harrington	3,598	29	0	2	5	22	171	47	121	3	0
Laurel	3,746	48	0	3	16	29	236	66	162	8	0
Lewes	2,775	7	0	0	0	7	74	15	59	0	0
Middletown	19,064	80	0	8	28	44	404	77	313	14	2
Milford	9,657	86	0	10	24	52	766	126	628	12	0
Millsboro	3,917	18	0	0	7	11	197	32	164	1	0
Milton	2,602	17	0	1	3	13	106	41	62	3	0
Newark	31,776	131	1	7	43	80	949	179	746	24	5
New Castle	5,339	19	0	1	10	8	307	35	252	20	0
Newport	1,066	4	0	0	2	2	44	17	21	6	0
Ocean View	1,901	2	0	1	0	1	45	25	20	0	0
Rehoboth Beach	1,341	6	0	0	2	4	194	31	162	1	1
Seaford	6,999	57	0	3	21	33	528	99	426	3	0
Selbyville	2,189	11	0	1	3	7	126	40	80	6	2
Smyrna	10,126	62	0	1	12	49	306	60	240	6	0
South Bethany	454	1	0	0	0	1	11	4	7	0	0
Wilmington	71,577	1,111	23	30	427	631	3,772	1,148	2,213	411	4
Wyoming	1,326	3	0	0	1	2	33	16	16	1	0
District of Columbia											
Washington	617,996	6,985	108	172	3,756	2,949	28,312	3,849	20,124	4,339	61
Florida											
Alachua	9,182	30	0	1	6	23	292	59	218	15	0
Altamonte Springs	42,062	173	1	7	42	123	1,295	197	1,025	73	2
Altha	543	1	0	0	0	1	1	0	1	0	0
Apalachicola	2,261	6	0	1	0	5	25	7	17	1	0
Apopka	42,108	207	2	13	65	127	1,494	488	915	91	2
Arcadia	7,741	63	0	3	8	52	206	68	129	9	1
Astatula	1,835	5	0	1	0	4	21	9	12	0	0
Atlantic Beach	12,827	81	1	6	18	56	392	91	286	15	1
Atlantis	2,032	10	0	0	0	10	5	4	1	0	0
Auburndale	13,691	100	0	6	17	77	777	219	538	20	4
Aventura	36,249	68	0	2	30	36	2,110	95	1,972	43	0
Avon Park	8,956	55	0	4	14	37	451	153	291	7	2
Bal Harbour Village	2,547	5	0	0	0	5	64	4	60	0	0
Bartow	17,534	120	1	10	21	88	1,030	270	741	19	1
Bay Harbor Islands	5,705	5	0	0	2	3	75	34	36	5	0
Belleair	3,922	1	0	0	0	1	79	9	66	4	0
Belleair Beach	1,581	2	0	0	1	1	37	4	32	1	0
Belleair Bluffs	2,059	3	0	0	2	1	58	8	49	1	0
Belle Glade	17,705	330	9	10	67	244	809	295	470	44	8
Belle Isle	6,070	13	0	2	3	8	162	64	88	10	0
Belleview	4,553	10	0	0	0	10	243	85	150	8	0
Biscayne Park	3,097	6	0	0	1	5	42	36	6	0	0
Blountstown	2,548	2	0	1	1	0	31	4	26	1	0
Boca Raton	85,542	178	0	23	63	92	2,676	495	2,067	114	2
Bonifay	2,831	6	2	1	0	3	14	8	6	0	1
Bowling Green	2,970	14	2	1	1	10	48	15	32	1	0
Boynton Beach	69,147	389	4	7	123	255	3,343	776	2,426	141	3
Bradenton	50,221	362	1	14	79	268	2,165	584	1,486	95	3
Bradenton Beach	1,187	2	0	0	0	2	53	5	47	1	0
Brooksville	7,824	52	0	5	16	31	448	69	364	15	1
Bunnell	2,712	63	0	4	8	51	218	66	137	15	0
Bushnell	2,451	13	0	0	4	9	120	18	93	9	0
Cape Coral	156,408	235	3	14	58	160	3,990	1,023	2,855	112	13
Carrabelle	2,816	6	0	3	0	3	37	13	18	6	0
Casselberry	26,599	164	1	13	36	114	1,057	195	795	67	1
Cedar Key	712	0	0	0	0	0	21	2	19	0	0
Center Hill	1,001	0	0	0	0	0	15	6	7	2	0
Chattahoochee	3,702	24	0	0	4	20	93	33	54	6	1
Chiefland	2,276	5	0	0	0	5	247	91	151	5	0
Chipley	3,654	16	0	0	3	13	85	11	70	4	0
Clearwater	109,153	801	10	40	182	569	4,129	719	3,252	158	15
Clermont	29,134	62	0	2	17	43	927	212	658	57	0
Clewiston	7,253	28	0	3	4	21	236	68	164	4	2
Cocoa	17,374	371	1	23	60	287	1,246	435	747	64	9
Cocoa Beach	11,384	101	0	4	21	76	891	110	752	29	3
Coconut Creek	53,630	112	1	13	42	56	1,485	294	1,089	102	0
Cooper City	28,936	41	0	1	11	29	650	143	475	32	1
Coral Gables	47,418	92	1	5	30	56	2,297	388	1,822	87	1

[1] If a blank is presented in the arson column, it indicates that the FBI did not receive 12 complete months of arson data for that agency.

Table II-8.   Offenses Known to Law Enforcement, by Selected State and City, 2011—*Continued*

(Number.)

State/City	Population	Violent crime	Murder and non-negligent man-slaughter	Forcible rape	Robbery	Aggravated assault	Property crime	Burglary	Larceny-theft	Motor vehicle theft	Arson[1]
Florida—*Continued*											
Coral Springs	122,746	236	1	4	90	141	3,035	633	2,238	164	0
Crescent City	1,598	16	0	0	3	13	64	29	34	1	0
Crestview	21,264	106	0	13	18	75	826	198	605	23	4
Cross City	1,752	8	0	0	1	7	23	4	19	0	0
Crystal River	3,150	44	0	2	9	33	270	26	239	5	0
Cutler Bay	40,835	193	0	10	49	134	1,921	283	1,542	96	1
Dade City	6,525	54	0	3	8	43	369	113	245	11	3
Dania	30,043	177	1	12	63	101	1,837	478	1,225	134	0
Davenport	2,927	4	0	0	3	1	37	20	15	2	0
Davie	93,246	357	1	17	105	234	3,627	709	2,640	278	15
Daytona Beach	61,836	835	3	37	236	559	4,268	994	2,899	375	12
Daytona Beach Shores	4,305	15	0	2	4	9	168	69	89	10	0
Deerfield Beach	76,040	366	1	23	134	208	2,415	569	1,651	195	4
De Funiak Springs	5,248	41	0	5	2	34	268	52	208	8	0
Deland	27,399	139	1	6	39	93	1,436	311	1,088	37	4
Delray Beach	61,347	564	4	27	183	350	3,223	699	2,385	139	3
Doral	46,327	78	0	7	18	53	2,324	259	1,918	147	2
Dunedin	35,802	113	1	15	30	67	916	182	712	22	1
Dunnellon	1,757	8	0	1	0	7	31	9	22	0	0
Eatonville	2,188	31	3	1	6	21	124	52	62	10	0
Edgewater	21,033	45	4	0	11	30	516	134	359	23	2
Edgewood	2,537	8	0	1	1	6	106	9	95	2	0
El Portal	2,357	8	0	2	3	3	106	45	56	5	0
Eustis	18,811	67	1	0	22	44	639	156	449	34	0
Fellsmere	5,268	10	0	0	2	8	69	25	40	4	0
Fernandina Beach	11,644	44	0	4	4	36	352	85	257	10	0
Flagler Beach	4,545	21	0	2	3	16	96	31	61	4	0
Florida City	11,398	304	2	6	83	213	1,295	313	933	49	2
Fort Lauderdale	167,777	1,565	12	91	771	691	10,192	3,102	6,489	601	44
Fort Myers	63,147	770	20	32	170	548	3,018	667	2,153	198	7
Fort Pierce	42,157	482	11	24	194	253	2,589	798	1,676	115	3
Fort Walton Beach	19,773	92	3	7	22	60	853	121	689	43	1
Fruitland Park	4,134	14	0	2	2	10	128	47	77	4	0
Gainesville	126,049	912	6	82	184	640	5,356	1,063	4,003	290	3
Golden Beach	932	0	0	0	0	0	16	8	8	0	0
Graceville	2,309	4	0	0	1	3	42	13	28	1	0
Greenacres City	38,085	217	0	9	56	152	1,169	315	743	111	1
Green Cove Springs	7,002	62	0	8	4	50	234	46	175	13	0
Gretna	1,480	13	0	0	3	10	25	15	10	0	0
Groveland	8,848	18	0	0	6	12	140	45	89	6	0
Gulf Breeze	5,842	3	0	1	0	2	149	23	125	1	0
Gulfport	12,193	45	0	2	12	31	545	117	392	36	4
Gulf Stream	797	2	0	0	0	2	17	2	15	0	0
Haines City	20,815	123	1	7	56	59	739	226	475	38	0
Hallandale	37,619	318	1	14	93	210	1,924	549	1,256	119	2
Hampton	507	4	0	0	0	4	5	2	3	0	0
Havana	1,778	9	0	0	2	7	68	11	49	8	0
Hialeah	227,731	860	4	31	253	572	7,493	1,069	5,473	951	17
Hialeah Gardens	22,040	41	1	5	13	22	930	120	739	71	0
Highland Beach	3,587	0	0	0	0	0	19	8	9	2	0
High Springs	5,423	21	2	1	4	14	157	53	103	1	0
Hillsboro Beach	1,901	4	0	0	1	3	49	10	34	5	0
Holly Hill	11,818	104	1	5	35	63	803	214	522	67	0
Hollywood	142,686	660	4	47	269	340	7,789	2,054	5,163	572	9
Holmes Beach	3,888	3	0	0	2	1	80	17	63	0	0
Homestead	61,337	967	4	18	299	646	3,314	954	2,200	160	6
Howey-in-the-Hills	1,113	1	0	0	0	1	10	3	7	0	0
Hypoluxo	2,623	6	0	1	0	5	35	9	26	0	0
Indialantic	2,757	3	0	1	1	1	69	14	52	3	0
Indian Creek Village	87	0	0	0	0	0	1	1	0	0	0
Indian Harbour Beach	8,337	6	0	1	1	4	173	35	135	3	0
Indian River Shores	3,954	2	0	0	0	2	17	1	15	1	0
Indian Rocks Beach	4,169	11	2	1	1	7	133	30	94	9	0
Indian Shores	3,589	5	0	2	1	2	70	16	53	1	0
Inglis	1,343	7	0	0	0	7	59	24	34	1	2
Interlachen	1,422	7	0	0	1	6	73	17	56	0	0
Jacksonville	834,429	5,182	71	350	1,578	3,183	36,113	8,518	25,733	1,862	108
Jacksonville Beach	21,653	217	4	12	55	146	1,194	173	974	47	3
Jasper	4,608	9	0	0	4	5	61	32	29	0	0
Jennings	890	3	0	0	1	2	30	8	21	1	0
Juno Beach	3,219	5	0	0	3	2	81	23	54	4	0
Jupiter	55,908	146	2	4	51	89	1,113	201	872	40	6
Jupiter Inlet Colony	405	0	0	0	0	0	3	3	0	0	0

[1] If a blank is presented in the arson column, it indicates that the FBI did not receive 12 complete months of arson data for that agency.

Table II-8. Offenses Known to Law Enforcement, by Selected State and City, 2011—*Continued*

(Number.)

State/City	Population	Violent crime	Murder and non-negligent man-slaughter	Forcible rape	Robbery	Aggravated assault	Property crime	Burglary	Larceny-theft	Motor vehicle theft	Arson[1]
Florida—*Continued*											
Jupiter Island	828	0	0	0	0	0	12	6	6	0	0
Kenneth City	5,048	24	0	1	3	20	232	58	163	11	0
Key Biscayne	12,512	4	0	0	0	4	247	10	226	11	0
Key Colony Beach	808	0	0	0	0	0	14	3	11	0	0
Key West	24,985	190	2	12	54	122	1,364	281	1,011	72	2
Kissimmee	60,495	593	3	24	118	448	3,364	870	2,332	162	9
Lady Lake	14,116	39	0	2	7	30	383	75	290	18	0
Lake Alfred	5,083	10	0	2	2	6	152	47	100	5	0
Lake City	12,210	200	0	6	28	166	944	262	658	24	6
Lake Clarke Shores	3,422	6	0	0	2	4	83	24	52	7	0
Lake Hamilton	1,248	6	0	0	3	3	58	17	36	5	0
Lake Helen	2,660	7	0	0	0	7	60	18	39	3	0
Lakeland	98,750	548	6	36	140	366	5,147	1,333	3,612	202	11
Lake Mary	14,010	34	0	2	8	24	322	54	260	8	0
Lake Park	8,266	80	2	7	30	41	717	108	568	41	3
Lake Placid	2,253	13	0	2	5	6	91	26	65	0	1
Lake Wales	14,419	42	1	0	23	18	836	193	623	20	1
Lake Worth	35,386	398	4	16	186	192	1,852	535	1,114	203	20
Lantana	10,565	66	0	7	17	42	564	121	432	11	1
Largo	78,706	373	1	32	101	239	3,048	617	2,327	104	5
Lauderdale-by-the-Sea	6,139	17	0	1	9	7	150	24	117	9	0
Lauderdale Lakes	33,037	342	2	12	163	165	1,743	581	1,081	81	4
Lauderhill	67,799	640	9	22	274	335	3,072	1,338	1,529	205	9
Leesburg	20,391	153	2	5	27	119	1,103	194	876	33	0
Lighthouse Point	10,485	20	0	4	8	8	321	62	242	17	0
Live Oak	6,943	72	0	2	15	55	328	155	162	11	0
Longboat Key	6,982	2	0	0	0	2	110	13	97	0	0
Longwood	13,843	79	0	2	9	68	519	189	315	15	2
Lynn Haven	18,745	66	0	2	6	58	499	91	399	9	0
Madeira Beach	4,321	37	0	1	4	32	269	43	221	5	0
Madison	2,882	41	1	2	6	32	218	69	144	5	1
Maitland	15,966	31	1	4	5	21	469	157	291	21	0
Manalapan	412	1	0	1	0	0	17	3	14	0	0
Mangonia Park	1,914	48	1	1	18	28	225	45	159	21	0
Marco Island	16,637	10	0	2	1	7	202	39	161	2	0
Margate	54,010	143	1	5	43	94	1,276	364	826	86	5
Marianna	6,185	52	1	6	4	41	281	76	198	7	1
Mascotte	5,171	18	0	4	1	13	103	32	66	5	1
Medley	849	5	0	0	0	5	284	30	218	36	0
Melbourne	77,105	750	3	25	158	564	4,010	873	3,021	116	12
Melbourne Beach	3,143	3	0	0	1	2	39	20	18	1	0
Melbourne Village	671	0	0	0	0	0	16	0	14	2	0
Mexico Beach	1,087	5	0	0	2	3	65	19	44	2	0
Miami	404,901	4,849	68	96	2,002	2,683	22,921	5,141	15,080	2,700	124
Miami Beach	88,975	887	4	40	370	473	9,585	1,171	7,838	576	19
Miami Gardens	108,628	999	24	19	413	543	5,397	1,485	3,270	642	26
Miami Lakes	29,761	70	0	1	19	50	636	93	484	59	0
Miami Shores	10,636	43	0	2	18	23	668	139	494	35	0
Miami Springs	13,997	23	0	3	8	12	465	112	319	34	0
Milton	8,946	20	1	4	3	12	380	96	276	8	1
Minneola	9,531	30	0	1	5	24	184	50	124	10	1
Miramar	123,704	514	4	40	192	278	3,208	981	1,969	258	9
Monticello	2,540	21	0	0	1	20	37	22	14	1	0
Mount Dora	12,539	87	0	5	17	65	444	93	321	30	1
Naples	19,803	55	1	1	6	47	615	73	526	16	0
Neptune Beach	7,133	24	0	0	0	24	231	48	178	5	0
New Port Richey	15,114	146	1	4	39	102	887	348	499	40	1
New Smyrna Beach	22,770	112	0	6	20	86	1,069	267	760	42	4
Niceville	12,923	21	0	2	4	15	172	27	136	9	0
North Bay Village	7,234	17	0	1	2	14	195	22	149	24	0
North Lauderdale	41,582	233	1	11	83	138	1,221	544	600	77	7
North Miami	59,587	605	9	35	240	321	3,060	808	1,931	321	8
North Miami Beach	42,089	317	1	13	132	171	1,994	663	1,145	186	3
North Palm Beach	12,179	19	0	0	9	10	232	56	162	14	0
North Port	58,139	160	1	15	23	121	1,373	375	966	32	6
North Redington Beach	1,436	4	0	0	1	3	34	7	26	1	0
Oakland	2,573	11	0	3	5	3	67	32	29	6	0
Oakland Park	41,927	325	2	12	144	167	2,185	659	1,409	117	4
Ocala	57,082	358	5	26	112	215	3,154	713	2,376	65	7
Ocean Ridge	1,810	2	0	0	0	2	42	9	31	2	0
Ocoee	36,064	159	0	16	47	96	1,517	303	1,128	86	4
Okeechobee	5,698	18	0	0	0	18	356	60	279	17	0

[1] If a blank is presented in the arson column, it indicates that the FBI did not receive 12 complete months of arson data for that agency.

Table II-8.   Offenses Known to Law Enforcement, by Selected State and City, 2011—*Continued*

(Number.)

State/City	Population	Violent crime	Murder and non-negligent man-slaughter	Forcible rape	Robbery	Aggravated assault	Property crime	Burglary	Larceny-theft	Motor vehicle theft	Arson[1]
Florida—*Continued*											
Oldsmar	13,776	54	1	4	13	36	451	66	370	15	0
Opa Locka	15,426	438	9	7	136	286	1,242	340	758	144	5
Orange City	10,743	60	0	0	7	53	818	90	703	25	0
Orange Park	8,527	48	0	5	12	31	252	57	188	7	0
Orlando	241,548	2,591	29	119	697	1,746	17,145	4,165	11,669	1,311	45
Ormond Beach	38,657	267	1	7	23	236	1,397	249	1,090	58	2
Oviedo	33,796	81	0	4	13	64	507	103	387	17	0
Pahokee	5,726	89	2	0	12	75	195	68	120	7	2
Palatka	10,702	145	1	10	29	105	790	141	621	28	2
Palm Bay	104,596	601	2	22	97	480	2,739	808	1,786	145	19
Palm Beach	8,462	7	0	1	1	5	146	23	116	7	0
Palm Beach Gardens	49,112	101	1	5	31	64	1,659	207	1,391	61	1
Palm Beach Shores	1,158	1	0	0	1	0	39	7	32	0	0
Palmetto	12,778	159	2	7	33	117	542	182	331	29	0
Palmetto Bay	23,729	66	0	6	16	44	911	211	683	17	1
Palm Springs	19,186	107	0	6	38	63	857	255	535	67	4
Panama City	36,981	316	3	11	78	224	2,281	410	1,753	118	1
Panama City Beach	12,182	84	1	10	18	55	1,111	194	911	6	1
Parker	4,376	33	1	0	1	31	269	68	192	9	1
Parkland	24,289	17	0	0	3	14	301	77	212	12	1
Pembroke Park	6,185	53	1	1	26	25	489	126	301	62	1
Pembroke Pines	156,859	310	4	28	119	159	4,944	1,059	3,591	294	11
Pensacola	52,631	383	2	28	102	251	2,974	610	2,226	138	2
Perry	7,113	94	0	8	5	81	206	73	126	7	3
Pinellas Park	49,748	313	0	15	85	213	2,816	504	2,213	99	11
Plantation	86,113	292	1	15	129	147	3,913	748	2,929	236	9
Plant City	35,194	182	4	8	55	115	1,371	285	983	103	4
Pompano Beach	101,206	917	5	41	343	528	5,524	1,343	3,852	329	9
Ponce Inlet	3,073	3	0	0	0	3	37	2	34	1	0
Port Orange	56,812	86	2	3	6	75	1,437	302	1,086	49	1
Port Richey	2,707	11	0	2	2	7	74	15	54	5	0
Port St. Joe	3,492	12	0	0	1	11	28	12	16	0	0
Port St. Lucie	166,846	371	6	30	61	274	3,861	1,128	2,590	143	11
Punta Gorda	16,868	15	0	0	3	12	326	55	258	13	1
Quincy	8,081	103	1	5	18	79	344	88	251	5	8
Redington Beaches	1,446	2	0	0	1	1	21	9	12	0	0
Riviera Beach	32,931	522	7	16	100	399	1,926	749	1,031	146	4
Rockledge	25,266	76	1	3	16	56	619	164	439	16	1
Royal Palm Beach	34,605	94	2	8	14	70	999	199	731	69	4
Safety Harbor	17,114	41	0	4	3	34	330	83	237	10	1
Sanford	54,300	329	4	23	159	143	3,234	945	2,143	146	2
Sanibel	6,557	5	0	0	0	5	115	24	88	3	0
Sarasota	52,625	513	8	28	172	305	3,226	698	2,414	114	4
Satellite Beach	10,247	51	0	1	2	48	211	60	148	3	4
Sea Ranch Lakes	679	1	0	0	1	0	15	3	12	0	0
Sebastian	22,228	41	0	3	5	33	442	128	303	11	0
Sebring	10,634	35	0	1	3	31	518	147	358	13	1
Seminole	17,468	60	2	3	12	43	643	106	526	11	1
Sewall's Point	2,023	0	0	0	0	0	22	3	18	1	0
Shalimar	727	4	0	0	0	4	3	2	0	1	0
Sneads	1,874	5	0	0	0	5	59	7	51	1	0
South Bay	4,942	47	1	4	9	33	148	36	103	9	3
South Daytona	12,419	104	0	0	11	93	504	144	325	35	0
South Miami	11,816	91	0	6	33	52	837	125	689	23	1
South Palm Beach	1,187	0	0	0	0	0	15	6	8	1	0
South Pasadena	5,032	17	0	1	6	10	137	19	115	3	0
Southwest Ranches	7,445	19	0	0	4	15	173	28	133	12	0
Springfield	9,024	66	3	1	15	47	446	128	302	16	0
Starke	5,523	41	0	3	5	33	312	12	282	18	0
St. Augustine	13,152	84	2	2	22	58	810	104	677	29	4
St. Augustine Beach	6,260	4	0	0	0	4	118	34	81	3	0
St. Cloud	35,662	134	4	7	18	105	924	206	689	29	3
St. Pete Beach	9,473	35	0	1	4	30	391	98	283	10	1
St. Petersburg	248,105	2,532	21	90	720	1,701	12,803	3,412	8,544	847	65
Stuart	15,806	58	2	5	9	42	721	98	613	10	0
Sunny Isles Beach	21,116	22	0	4	11	7	547	76	443	28	0
Sunrise	85,590	269	3	9	100	157	3,590	919	2,511	160	6
Surfside	5,822	4	0	0	2	2	179	26	149	4	0
Sweetwater	13,683	58	1	0	26	31	1,067	70	916	81	0
Tallahassee	183,848	1,661	10	107	511	1,033	9,363	3,252	5,748	363	20
Tamarac	61,251	159	0	20	60	79	1,512	528	890	94	2
Tampa	340,284	2,228	28	58	587	1,555	10,393	2,718	7,042	633	102

[1] If a blank is presented in the arson column, it indicates that the FBI did not receive 12 complete months of arson data for that agency.

Table II-8.   Offenses Known to Law Enforcement, by Selected State and City, 2011—*Continued*

(Number.)

State/City	Population	Violent crime	Murder and non-negligent man-slaughter	Forcible rape	Robbery	Aggravated assault	Property crime	Burglary	Larceny-theft	Motor vehicle theft	Arson[1]
Florida—*Continued*											
Tarpon Springs	23,804	120	7	2	14	97	699	173	496	30	5
Tavares	14,141	21	0	2	2	17	136	30	90	16	0
Temple Terrace	24,875	71	0	5	18	48	743	228	478	37	1
Tequesta	5,706	12	0	1	2	9	135	29	100	6	0
Titusville	44,357	270	2	27	66	175	1,634	423	1,076	135	14
Treasure Island	6,796	17	0	6	1	10	300	42	248	10	0
Trenton	2,026	4	0	0	1	3	39	12	26	1	0
Umatilla	3,503	8	0	0	2	6	119	4	112	3	0
Valparaiso	5,105	2	0	0	0	2	46	12	33	1	0
Venice	21,031	28	0	3	9	16	556	129	414	13	1
Vero Beach	15,427	46	2	4	13	27	701	175	513	13	0
Village of Pinecrest	18,471	21	0	0	7	14	657	97	542	18	1
Virginia Gardens	2,407	2	0	0	1	1	21	9	10	2	0
Waldo	1,029	11	0	1	2	8	56	22	31	3	0
Wauchula	5,069	22	1	1	4	16	216	85	123	8	1
Webster	796	4	0	0	1	3	34	10	20	4	0
Welaka	711	0	0	0	0	0	6	3	2	1	0
Wellington	57,278	143	0	16	27	100	1,389	268	1,050	71	1
West Melbourne	18,605	38	0	1	6	31	655	212	429	14	2
West Miami	6,046	13	0	0	3	10	171	42	115	14	1
Weston	66,223	74	0	3	14	57	742	119	593	30	7
West Palm Beach	101,281	769	14	48	235	472	5,383	1,354	3,685	344	13
West Park	14,349	115	2	5	46	62	692	290	335	67	3
White Springs	788	8	0	0	3	5	22	11	11	0	0
Wildwood	6,800	40	0	5	2	33	133	56	74	3	0
Williston	2,806	24	0	0	11	13	97	24	71	2	0
Wilton Manors	11,791	70	0	1	42	27	617	166	429	22	1
Windermere	2,496	0	0	0	0	0	18	6	11	1	0
Winter Garden	35,039	178	0	11	23	144	1,187	256	857	74	8
Winter Haven	34,336	302	4	12	78	208	1,857	458	1,294	105	9
Winter Park	28,232	77	0	5	27	45	870	226	615	29	0
Winter Springs	33,736	69	1	5	7	56	407	101	283	23	2
Zephyrhills	13,469	62	1	13	10	38	872	150	681	41	1
Georgia											
Abbeville	2,946	6	0	3	0	3	29	9	16	4	2
Acworth	20,694	16	1	0	5	10	472	57	395	20	1
Adairsville	4,709	15	0	1	1	13	164	32	121	11	0
Adel	5,404	24	0	9	6	9	270	90	176	4	0
Alamo	2,834	3	0	0	0	3	25	3	19	3	0
Alapaha	677	8	0	0	1	7	7	3	3	1	0
Albany	78,454	640	13	37	176	414	4,719	1,332	3,174	213	14
Alma	3,512	27	2	8	6	11	167	45	110	12	0
Alpharetta	58,309	58	1	5	24	28	1,438	164	1,241	33	1
Alto	1,187	3	0	0	0	3	14	2	12	0	0
Americus	17,265	225	2	0	31	192	1,302	559	706	37	1
Ashburn	4,207	41	0	5	10	26	167	74	76	17	
Athens-Clarke County	117,114	417	6	30	132	249	4,873	1,359	3,273	241	23
Atlanta	425,533	6,097	88	148	2,343	3,518	30,144	7,499	17,274	5,371	121
Attapulgus	455	0	0	0	0	0	0	0	0	0	0
Auburn	6,978	9	0	4	1	4	61	29	25	7	0
Austell	6,668	32	0	2	3	27	233	60	155	18	1
Avondale Estates	2,999	6	0	0	2	4	92	9	74	9	0
Bainbridge	12,864	77	1	3	13	60	537	139	377	21	
Baldwin	3,322	3	0	1	0	2	95	14	77	4	2
Ball Ground	1,452	1	0	0	1	0	11	5	6	0	0
Barnesville	6,844	37	1	2	3	31	185	32	147	6	0
Barwick	391	0	0	0	0	0	0	0	0	0	0
Baxley	4,458	16	0	2	4	10	307	74	222	11	1
Berlin	558	0	0	0	0	0	0	0	0	0	0
Blairsville	661	0	0	0	0	0	0	0	0	0	0
Blakely	5,135	36	1	3	7	25	188	74	111	3	
Bloomingdale	2,749	1	0	1	0	0	70	24	38	8	
Blythe	730	0	0	0	0	0	15	2	12	1	0
Boston	1,332	15	0	0	0	15	57	10	47	0	0
Bowdon	2,067	22	0	0	0	22	63	11	50	2	0
Braselton	7,610	16	1	4	2	9	105	25	71	9	0
Bremen	6,309	36	0	0	3	33	269	55	194	20	0
Brooklet	1,413	2	0	0	0	2	20	3	16	1	
Brunswick	15,586	251	2	5	68	176	1,261	366	850	45	3
Buchanan	1,119	7	0	0	0	7	37	4	31	2	0
Buena Vista	2,202	4	1	0	2	1	67	18	48	1	0
Butler	1,998	10	0	0	0	10	15	7	6	2	0

[1] If a blank is presented in the arson column, it indicates that the FBI did not receive 12 complete months of arson data for that agency.

Table II-8.   Offenses Known to Law Enforcement, by Selected State and City, 2011—*Continued*

(Number.)

State/City	Population	Violent crime	Murder and non-negligent man-slaughter	Forcible rape	Robbery	Aggravated assault	Property crime	Burglary	Larceny-theft	Motor vehicle theft	Arson[1]
Georgia—*Continued*											
Byron	4,571	42	0	1	4	37	309	100	191	18	2
Cairo	9,733	34	1	7	16	10	346	103	237	6	0
Calhoun	15,856	34	0	2	12	20	760	122	618	20	1
Camilla	5,431	37	0	4	8	25	214	55	154	5	0
Canton	23,260	24	3	3	8	10	420	64	335	21	1
Carrollton	24,709	109	1	17	25	66	1,147	210	900	37	10
Cartersville	19,991	62	0	12	17	33	1,205	215	908	82	4
Cave Spring	1,216	0	0	0	0	0	26	4	19	3	0
Cedartown	9,878	79	0	3	11	65	655	181	458	16	0
Centerville	7,242	18	0	1	6	11	348	46	292	10	
Chamblee	10,022	55	1	1	36	17	775	102	598	75	0
Chatsworth	4,356	6	0	0	1	5	118	19	93	6	1
Chattahoochee Hills	2,409	3	0	0	0	3	45	4	34	7	0
Chickamauga	3,142	16	0	1	1	14	93	29	63	1	0
Clarkesville	1,756	10	0	0	0	10	47	14	31	2	0
Claxton	2,782	5	0	0	0	5	108	29	76	3	0
Cleveland	3,455	46	1	0	1	44	192	37	154	1	0
Climax	284	0	0	0	0	0	0	0	0	0	0
Cochran	5,218	19	2	1	5	11	247	59	186	2	
College Park	14,126	232	5	11	115	101	1,912	526	1,028	358	4
Colquitt	2,018	11	2	1	5	3	26	8	18	0	
Columbus	192,385	933	15	40	413	465	12,450	3,342	8,059	1,049	39
Commerce	6,630	25	0	0	2	23	164	36	128	0	0
Conyers	15,395	80	2	6	34	38	1,163	276	814	73	1
Coolidge	532	1	0	0	0	1	6	3	3	0	0
Cordele	11,294	105	3	12	42	48	1,007	268	721	18	3
Covington	13,291	48	1	3	21	23	859	180	620	59	0
Cumming	5,501	9	0	2	1	6	345	26	314	5	0
Cuthbert	3,924	3	0	0	3	0	46	10	36	0	
Dallas	11,696	37	0	5	12	20	348	75	256	17	0
Dalton	33,564	90	0	9	28	53	1,304	254	996	54	8
Danielsville	567	1	0	0	0	1	18	3	15	0	0
Decatur	19,590	29	0	1	21	7	584	115	421	48	0
Dillard	343	0	0	0	0	0	0	0	0	0	0
Donalsonville	2,685	7	0	0	2	5	57	10	45	2	0
Doraville	8,440	47	0	1	15	31	310	62	225	23	0
Douglasville	31,369	179	0	9	37	133	1,899	223	1,591	85	4
Dublin	16,414	110	1	6	32	71	1,138	263	846	29	0
Duluth	26,950	56	1	8	16	31	543	88	440	15	
Dunwoody	46,876	94	1	2	52	39	1,672	219	1,362	91	
East Dublin	2,473	25	0	0	3	22	129	39	86	4	0
Eastman	5,027	67	0	2	12	53	456	87	361	8	0
East Point	34,156	394	3	9	236	146	3,537	1,163	1,799	575	1
Eatonton[6]	6,565	59	0	3	3	53		35		3	
Edison	1,551	4	0	0	1	3	21	10	11	0	
Elberton	4,714	44	0	1	8	35	359	124	234	1	2
Ellaville	1,836	3	0	0	0	3	33	9	23	1	0
Ellijay	1,640	0	0	0	0	0	0	0	0	0	0
Emerson	1,489	5	0	0	4	1	72	9	59	4	
Enigma	1,295	0	0	0	0	0	27	7	18	2	0
Ephesus	433	0	0	0	0	0	0	0	0	0	0
Eton	922	0	0	0	0	0	22	5	15	2	0
Euharlee	4,190	14	0	4	0	10	38	23	9	6	
Fairburn	13,121	43	3	4	21	15	594	175	353	66	1
Fairmount	729	0	0	0	0	0	16	2	14	0	1
Fayetteville	16,155	39	0	2	9	28	464	35	406	23	
Flowery Branch	5,754	3	1	0	1	1	77	23	52	2	
Folkston	2,535	6	0	0	0	6	114	28	78	8	0
Forest Park	18,711	104	0	4	43	57	872	195	598	79	11
Forsyth	3,838	17	0	0	6	11	221	33	179	9	
Fort Gaines	1,122	0	0	0	0	0	0	0	0	0	0
Fort Oglethorpe	9,385	41	0	2	6	33	636	62	561	13	0
Fort Valley	9,944	116	0	4	19	93	660	196	456	8	0
Franklin Springs	965	0	0	0	0	0	21	2	19	0	0
Gainesville	34,249	116	2	12	46	56	1,582	332	1,176	74	1
Garden City	8,894	123	0	1	19	103	457	110	303	44	2
Glennville	3,616	11	0	1	3	7	164	29	127	8	1
Glenwood	757	0	0	0	0	0	0	0	0	0	0
Gordon	2,044	0	0	0	0	0	52	6	45	1	0
Grantville	3,081	14	0	1	1	12	83	19	59	5	0
Gray	3,319	2	0	0	2	0	39	4	35	0	0
Greensboro	3,403	29	0	1	4	24	138	50	85	3	1
Greenville	888	6	0	0	1	5	54	17	33	4	0

[1] If a blank is presented in the arson column, it indicates that the FBI did not receive 12 complete months of arson data for that agency.

[6] The FBI determined that the agency's data were underreported. Consequently, those data are not included in this table.

Table II-8.   Offenses Known to Law Enforcement, by Selected State and City, 2011—*Continued*

(Number.)

State/City	Population	Violent crime	Murder and non-negligent man-slaughter	Forcible rape	Robbery	Aggravated assault	Property crime	Burglary	Larceny-theft	Motor vehicle theft	Arson[1]
Georgia—*Continued*											
Griffin	23,954	155	1	5	47	102	1,531	304	1,183	44	9
Grovetown	11,364	17	0	6	5	6	223	46	169	8	0
Guyton	1,706	5	0	1	2	2	32	12	19	1	0
Hagan	1,009	2	0	0	0	2	15	6	9	0	
Hahira	2,773	1	0	0	0	1	49	13	33	3	0
Hampton	7,079	6	0	2	2	2	175	40	126	9	0
Hapeville	6,457	49	1	1	21	26	364	69	241	54	
Harlem	2,701	4	0	2	0	2	53	8	43	2	0
Hartwell	4,528	19	0	0	7	12	307	61	243	3	0
Hazlehurst	4,282	11	0	0	6	5	227	46	180	1	1
Helen	517	8	0	0	0	8	77	4	71	2	0
Hephzibah	4,064	25	0	0	1	24	117	29	75	13	0
Hiawassee	892	5	0	0	0	5	27	5	22	0	0
Hinesville	33,877	155	2	12	41	100	1,605	506	1,042	57	
Hiram	3,593	7	0	2	1	4	286	20	261	5	
Hoboken	535	0	0	0	0	0	4	1	3	0	0
Hogansville	3,100	23	1	1	2	19	106	22	77	7	0
Holly Springs	9,310	10	0	2	0	8	79	23	49	7	0
Homeland	922	0	0	0	0	0	0	0	0	0	0
Homerville	2,488	23	0	1	6	16	131	56	74	1	0
Jackson	5,111	29	0	1	9	19	187	44	134	9	0
Jasper	3,733	9	0	0	3	6	239	19	214	6	0
Jefferson	9,556	13	1	1	2	9	166	39	116	11	0
Jesup	10,348	57	0	5	10	42	740	114	597	29	0
Johns Creek	77,738	35	0	3	13	19	574	131	432	11	1
Jonesboro	4,786	31	1	2	7	21	229	43	164	22	0
Kennesaw	30,175	21	0	0	6	15	571	121	425	25	
Kingsland	16,156	74	0	1	8	65	535	126	399	10	2
Kingston	645	2	0	0	0	2	9	4	3	2	0
Lagrange	29,978	136	4	9	71	52	1,733	451	1,193	89	1
Lake City	2,646	8	0	0	7	1	139	14	103	22	
Lakeland	3,410	16	0	2	3	11	75	30	39	6	0
Lavonia	2,184	17	1	0	2	14	144	29	111	4	0
Lawrenceville	28,922	85	3	9	41	32	1,086	219	799	68	1
Leary	626	0	0	0	0	0	2	1	1	0	
Lilburn	11,749	53	0	0	26	27	740	114	594	32	0
Lincolnton	1,587	10	0	0	1	9	35	3	30	2	0
Lithonia	1,949	8	0	0	0	8	119	44	58	17	1
Locust Grove	5,473	20	0	2	3	15	290	35	247	8	
Loganville	10,596	19	0	1	5	13	325	44	258	23	0
Lookout Mountain	1,623	1	0	0	0	1	16	9	5	2	0
Ludowici	1,725	4	0	0	0	4	46	6	38	2	0
Lumber City	1,345	4	0	0	0	4	32	13	19	0	
Lumpkin	1,160	1	0	0	0	1	2	0	0	2	0
Macon	92,554	566	13	33	246	274	7,807	2,154	5,104	549	62
Madison	4,031	17	0	1	7	9	172	50	121	1	0
Manchester	4,286	14	1	0	2	11	245	52	178	15	1
Marietta	57,324	386	5	13	125	243	2,624	584	1,864	176	1
McCaysville	1,070	0	0	0	0	0	44	9	34	1	0
McDonough	22,375	39	0	2	15	22	790	144	593	53	0
McIntyre	659	1	0	0	0	1	22	4	18	0	0
McRae	5,816	12	0	0	1	11	88	22	64	2	0
Meigs	1,049	21	0	1	1	19	32	4	28	0	0
Midville	273	2	0	0	1	1	0	0	0	0	
Midway	2,149	11	0	0	2	9	82	32	43	7	
Milledgeville	17,948	37	0	2	13	22	871	209	642	20	2
Milton	33,091	14	1	2	5	6	327	83	244	0	1
Monroe	13,408	82	0	2	14	66	772	215	535	22	2
Montezuma	3,506	39	0	0	6	33	188	69	114	5	
Morrow	6,530	28	0	4	17	7	838	64	727	47	0
Moultrie	14,456	90	1	6	40	43	1,215	338	845	32	4
Mount Zion	1,718	0	0	0	0	0	20	7	11	2	0
Nashville	5,004	28	1	3	10	14	280	118	157	5	1
Newington	278	0	0	0	0	0	11	1	10	0	0
Newnan	33,474	161	2	1	27	131	1,118	274	808	36	
Newton	663	2	0	0	1	1	5	5	0	0	0
Nicholls	2,835	4	0	0	1	3	38	5	33	0	
Norcross	9,236	52	0	4	20	28	492	120	345	27	0
Oakwood	4,022	7	0	0	1	6	243	39	195	9	0
Ocilla	3,459	19	0	3	2	14	160	26	126	8	
Oxford	2,162	2	0	0	2	0	50	14	35	1	1
Palmetto	4,547	24	0	1	7	16	105	42	54	9	0
Patterson	740	2	0	0	0	2	7	1	6	0	0
Pavo	635	0	0	0	0	0	2	0	0	2	0

[1] If a blank is presented in the arson column, it indicates that the FBI did not receive 12 complete months of arson data for that agency.

Table II-8.   Offenses Known to Law Enforcement, by Selected State and City, 2011—*Continued*

(Number.)

State/City	Population	Violent crime	Murder and non-negligent man-slaughter	Forcible rape	Robbery	Aggravated assault	Property crime	Burglary	Larceny-theft	Motor vehicle theft	Arson[1]
Georgia—*Continued*											
Peachtree City	34,816	8	0	0	5	3	452	50	320	82	4
Pelham	3,949	18	0	3	3	12	224	33	186	5	0
Perry	14,021	34	0	2	8	24	327	61	243	23	
Pine Mountain	1,321	1	0	0	0	1	49	11	37	1	
Pooler	19,392	29	1	7	8	13	530	78	420	32	0
Porterdale	1,448	18	0	0	0	18	116	25	84	7	
Port Wentworth	5,430	13	1	2	2	8	139	39	88	12	1
Poulan	862	1	0	0	1	0	20	5	14	1	
Powder Springs	14,124	33	1	1	12	19	362	161	178	23	1
Quitman	3,901	78	1	3	5	69	249	74	162	13	0
Ray City	1,104	1	1	0	0	0	0	0	0	0	0
Register	177	0	0	0	0	0	0	0	0	0	0
Remerton	1,138	2	0	1	0	1	69	12	55	2	0
Reynolds	1,100	0	0	0	0	0	0	0	0	0	0
Richland	1,492	0	0	0	0	0	0	0	0	0	
Richmond Hill	9,403	13	1	1	1	10	241	36	193	12	0
Rincon	8,952	7	0	2	5	0	194	31	161	2	
Ringgold	3,627	7	0	0	2	5	188	30	150	8	0
Riverdale	15,333	118	0	3	44	71	1,016	311	614	91	
Roberta	1,020	0	0	0	0	0	20	3	16	1	
Rockmart	4,254	31	1	2	5	23	252	52	183	17	0
Rome	36,781	227	4	18	62	143	2,202	472	1,655	75	18
Rossville	4,159	14	0	0	5	9	218	53	139	26	
Roswell	89,509	72	0	11	32	29	1,727	404	1,262	61	0
Royston	2,616	0	0	0	0	0	72	0	72	0	0
Sandersville	5,990	23	0	0	10	13	310	75	231	4	1
Sandy Springs	95,089	153	1	6	94	52	2,475	587	1,728	160	
Sardis	1,012	18	0	0	0	18	5	5	0	0	
Savannah-Chatham Metropolitan	226,422	889	26	36	488	339	9,579	2,241	6,608	730	37
Screven	776	0	0	0	0	0	5	0	5	0	0
Senoia	3,351	5	0	0	3	2	38	8	29	1	0
Shiloh	451	1	0	0	0	1	8	2	6	0	0
Smyrna	51,946	158	3	7	71	77	1,401	381	915	105	13
Snellville	18,482	45	0	1	13	31	782	100	655	27	0
Social Circle	4,318	16	0	1	2	13	123	41	74	8	
Sparks	2,079	6	0	0	1	5	76	26	50	0	0
Sparta	1,418	13	0	1	2	10	44	17	25	2	
Springfield	2,890	4	0	0	2	2	50	4	45	1	0
Statesboro	28,796	100	1	8	58	33	1,239	304	906	29	5
Statham	2,440	17	0	0	0	17	70	20	43	7	0
St. Marys	17,346	66	0	3	9	54	560	137	406	17	
Summerville	4,594	1	0	0	1	0	50	6	39	5	0
Suwanee	15,557	15	0	2	5	8	350	75	259	16	0
Sycamore	720	0	0	0	0	0	0	0	0	0	0
Sylvania	2,995	9	0	4	1	4	94	26	68	0	
Sylvester	6,269	12	0	0	3	9	338	94	223	21	0
Tallapoosa	3,212	3	0	1	0	2	189	30	143	16	
Temple	4,284	18	0	1	0	17	139	41	94	4	0
Tennille	1,559	12	0	1	1	10	99	25	70	4	0
Thomaston	9,291	22	1	3	6	12	404	93	302	9	0
Thomasville	18,655	55	0	4	25	26	1,089	253	793	43	1
Thunderbolt	2,703	1	1	0	0	0	96	22	72	2	0
Tifton	16,565	109	0	5	37	67	1,303	287	980	36	4
Tignall	553	0	0	0	0	0	23	14	9	0	0
Toccoa	8,603	41	0	2	10	29	490	59	426	5	0
Toomsboro	478	0	0	0	0	0	0	0	0	0	0
Trenton	2,331	4	0	0	1	3	33	8	22	3	
Trion	1,851	5	0	0	0	5	26	18	7	1	0
Tunnel Hill	867	1	0	0	0	1	46	6	39	1	0
Tybee Island	3,029	0	0	0	0	0	113	7	104	2	0
Tyrone	6,970	5	0	2	3	0	106	15	79	12	0
Union City	19,712	141	2	3	46	90	1,490	370	907	213	2
Union Point	1,638	2	0	0	2	0	88	34	54	0	1
Valdosta	55,236	268	5	27	102	134	2,500	815	1,598	87	10
Vidalia	10,611	67	0	2	13	52	707	142	534	31	1
Vienna	4,064	13	0	0	3	10	76	18	58	0	0
Villa Rica	14,140	101	0	2	11	88	501	80	388	33	0
Warm Springs	431	0	0	0	0	0	6	3	2	1	0
Warner Robins	67,465	349	5	22	123	199	4,099	750	3,172	177	17
Washington	4,188	36	0	2	3	31	173	36	128	9	0
Watkinsville	2,869	1	0	0	0	1	65	10	51	4	2

[1] If a blank is presented in the arson column, it indicates that the FBI did not receive 12 complete months of arson data for that agency.

Table II-8.   Offenses Known to Law Enforcement, by Selected State and City, 2011—*Continued*

(Number.)

State/City	Population	Violent crime	Murder and non-negligent man-slaughter	Forcible rape	Robbery	Aggravated assault	Property crime	Burglary	Larceny-theft	Motor vehicle theft	Arson[1]
Georgia—*Continued*											
Waverly Hall	745	0	0	0	0	0	7	1	6	0	0
Waycross	14,842	84	1	3	36	44	1,146	173	942	31	2
Waynesboro	5,842	28	2	0	7	19	280	55	205	20	1
West Point	3,520	27	0	3	8	16	222	40	169	13	0
Whigham	477	1	0	0	0	1	0	0	0	0	0
Willacoochee	1,409	8	0	0	0	8	34	18	15	1	0
Winder	14,285	134	1	5	19	109	618	139	448	31	0
Winterville	1,137	2	0	0	0	2	16	1	14	1	0
Woodbury	974	3	0	0	3	0	39	10	27	2	0
Woodstock	24,211	78	0	3	7	68	600	65	525	10	1
Wrens	2,216	14	0	1	2	11	118	27	88	3	0
Zebulon	1,189	5	0	0	0	5	24	6	16	2	0
Idaho											
Aberdeen	2,016	0	0	0	0	0	3	0	3	0	1
American Falls	4,506	11	0	2	0	9	92	14	77	1	0
Bellevue	2,312	3	0	0	0	3	26	13	13	0	0
Blackfoot	12,031	28	0	9	0	19	478	103	367	8	0
Boise	207,945	510	1	66	59	384	5,328	809	4,347	172	53
Bonners Ferry	2,571	2	0	0	0	2	24	2	17	5	0
Buhl	4,168	7	0	0	0	7	121	24	94	3	1
Caldwell	46,748	149	2	4	11	132	1,373	261	1,063	49	7
Challis	1,093	2	0	0	0	2	9	0	9	0	0
Chubbuck	14,076	41	0	2	2	37	599	33	559	7	1
Cottonwood	910	0	0	0	0	0	14	3	8	3	0
Emmett	6,629	14	0	1	0	13	113	18	91	4	1
Filer	2,536	9	0	2	0	7	12	5	5	2	0
Fruitland	4,736	13	0	3	0	10	163	71	90	2	1
Garden City	11,093	49	1	5	3	40	418	67	337	14	1
Gooding	3,606	6	0	1	0	5	52	11	36	5	0
Grangeville	3,176	4	1	0	0	3	48	16	32	0	0
Hagerman	882	0	0	0	0	0	9	1	8	0	0
Hailey	8,048	20	0	0	0	20	77	30	41	6	0
Heyburn	3,123	1	0	0	0	1	28	11	16	1	1
Homedale	2,662	9	0	0	0	9	73	19	53	1	0
Idaho Falls	57,512	148	1	27	9	111	1,582	289	1,203	90	5
Jerome	11,010	31	0	6	2	23	312	62	242	8	2
Kamiah	1,309	2	0	1	0	1	23	4	19	0	0
Kellogg	2,143	7	0	0	1	6	64	11	50	3	2
Ketchum	2,719	13	0	0	0	13	52	14	36	2	0
Kimberly	3,300	4	0	1	0	3	44	13	31	0	0
McCall	3,024	17	1	7	0	9	138	17	118	3	2
Meridian	75,922	108	2	19	3	84	1,049	156	863	30	9
Montpelier	2,626	7	0	1	0	6	79	4	67	8	0
Moscow	24,063	19	1	3	3	12	716	110	591	15	12
Mountain Home	14,363	41	0	4	0	37	246	39	202	5	5
Nampa	82,459	227	0	37	9	181	2,475	514	1,864	97	14
Orofino	3,177	4	0	1	0	3	74	48	23	3	0
Osburn	1,572	2	0	0	0	2	20	2	17	1	0
Parma	2,005	4	0	0	1	3	14	3	9	2	0
Pinehurst	1,637	0	0	0	0	0	29	10	19	0	0
Pocatello	54,855	132	3	15	5	109	1,794	262	1,457	75	5
Ponderay	1,150	0	0	0	0	0	46	3	43	0	0
Post Falls	27,879	46	0	5	3	38	739	127	588	24	9
Preston	5,262	4	0	1	0	3	77	28	48	1	0
Priest River	1,770	2	0	1	0	1	29	6	22	1	0
Rathdrum	6,901	12	0	1	0	11	146	51	94	1	0
Rexburg	25,766	12	0	2	0	10	205	16	182	7	0
Rigby	3,989	2	0	1	0	1	101	16	81	4	0
Rupert	5,615	11	0	4	0	7	117	23	90	4	0
Salmon	3,146	12	0	1	1	10	46	10	35	1	0
Sandpoint	7,446	9	0	0	1	8	268	62	197	9	0
Shelley	4,458	6	0	3	0	3	39	12	26	1	0
Soda Springs	3,092	4	0	0	1	3	20	2	18	0	0
Spirit Lake	1,967	6	0	0	0	6	19	2	14	3	0
St. Anthony	3,581	3	0	0	0	3	36	10	25	1	0
St. Maries	2,429	7	1	0	0	6	14	5	8	1	0
Sun Valley	1,422	1	0	0	0	1	13	1	12	0	0
Twin Falls	44,613	120	2	20	14	84	1,477	225	1,196	56	3
Weiser	5,568	6	0	3	0	3	33	10	22	1	0
Wendell	2,813	4	0	4	0	0	34	4	26	4	0
Wilder	1,550	3	0	0	1	2	15	5	8	2	0

[1] If a blank is presented in the arson column, it indicates that the FBI did not receive 12 complete months of arson data for that agency.

Table II-8. **Offenses Known to Law Enforcement, by Selected State and City, 2011**—*Continued*

(Number.)

State/City	Population	Violent crime	Murder and non-negligent man-slaughter	Forcible rape	Robbery	Aggravated assault	Property crime	Burglary	Larceny-theft	Motor vehicle theft	Arson[1]
Illinois											
Addison	37,053	53	0	11	16	26	748	150	563	35	13
Algonquin	30,136	49	0	0	12	37	521	57	457	7	4
Altamont	2,326	4	0	0	1	3	33	5	27	1	0
Alton	27,949	151	4	20	36	91	1,389	350	987	52	11
Amboy	2,508	28	0	0	0	28	51	27	23	1	0
Antioch	14,473	11	0	1	3	7	316	33	277	6	0
Arcola	2,925	5	0	0	0	5	15	0	13	2	0
Arlington Heights	75,327	48	2	5	17	24	1,083	170	892	21	5
Ashland	1,337	0	0	0	0	0	11	2	9	0	4
Auburn	4,785	3	0	2	0	1	44	14	28	2	1
Aurora	198,495	636	2	58	158	418	3,821	947	2,740	134	20
Bannockburn	1,588	0	0	0	0	0	31	0	30	1	0
Barrington	10,358	4	0	4	0	0	148	28	114	6	2
Barrington Hills	4,222	0	0	0	0	0	41	9	30	2	0
Bartlett	41,332	16	0	3	2	11	288	26	257	5	5
Bartonville	6,490	32	0	8	2	22	231	56	171	4	1
Beardstown	6,141	6	0	0	0	6	38	22	13	3	0
Beecher	4,372	3	0	0	0	3	63	7	54	2	0
Belgium	405	0	0	0	0	0	0	0	0	0	0
Belvidere	25,662	48	0	17	8	23	429	78	343	8	3
Benton	7,108	8	0	0	0	8	239	48	185	6	0
Berkeley	5,225	13	0	0	5	8	84	13	67	4	0
Berwyn	56,828	134	0	19	44	71	1,380	399	900	81	5
Bethalto	9,550	7	0	3	0	4	12	1	11	0	0
Blandinsville	653	0	0	0	0	0	6	1	5	0	2
Bloomingdale	22,084	15	0	4	5	6	717	52	653	12	1
Bloomington	76,841	361	1	69	58	233	1,740	460	1,231	49	16
Blue Island	23,777	112	0	11	61	40	686	181	405	100	1
Bolingbrook	73,587	161	1	25	49	86	1,221	261	915	45	6
Bradley	15,943	67	0	12	10	45	763	93	661	9	1
Braidwood	6,210	7	0	1	0	6	122	13	109	0	5
Bridgeview	16,496	25	0	2	6	17	488	60	396	32	1
Broadview	7,956	34	0	1	16	17	325	47	246	32	0
Brookfield	19,035	11	0	2	1	8	286	58	223	5	3
Buffalo Grove	41,621	9	0	3	4	2	432	59	361	12	0
Burbank	29,012	52	0	1	21	30	537	75	437	25	1
Burr Ridge	10,591	2	0	0	0	2	158	23	134	1	0
Byron	3,764	0	0	0	0	0	51	7	43	1	0
Cahokia	15,287	50	1	3	18	28	834	220	614	0	8
Cairo	2,840	111	0	11	4	96	202	69	131	2	3
Cambridge	2,167	3	0	0	0	3	26	8	16	2	0
Canton	14,748	33	0	12	3	18	353	70	275	8	2
Carbondale	25,980	272	1	32	38	201	1,116	320	768	28	10
Carlinville	5,935	18	0	0	0	18	208	51	149	8	0
Carlyle	3,291	23	0	1	0	22	40	1	39	0	0
Carol Stream	39,831	48	1	8	7	32	498	76	392	30	9
Carpentersville	37,804	39	1	0	13	25	616	154	459	3	3
Carrollton	2,491	12	0	1	0	11	36	10	26	0	1
Cary	18,326	33	0	7	7	19	321	68	248	5	0
Caseyville	4,258	60	1	4	21	34	97	43	43	11	2
Catlin	2,046	1	0	1	0	0	11	1	9	1	0
Centralia	13,071	134	1	15	22	96	859	196	631	32	4
Champaign	81,299	732	1	56	105	570	2,281	586	1,599	96	12
Channahon	12,598	4	0	0	0	4	88	18	64	6	0
Charleston	21,901	47	1	8	6	32	251	58	183	10	0
Chatham	11,535	12	0	2	1	9	83	15	67	1	0
Chenoa	3,226	1	0	0	0	1	31	6	25	0	1
Chicago[7]	2,703,713		431		13,975	12,408	118,239	26,420	72,373	19,446	
Chicago Ridge	14,348	10	0	1	6	3	668	98	542	28	1
Cicero	84,144	344	1	24	162	157	1,981	668	1,042	271	37
Clarendon Hills	8,452	1	0	0	1	0	54	10	43	1	0
Coal City	5,604	6	0	1	2	3	147	13	130	4	2
Coal Valley	3,754	2	0	0	0	2	36	9	26	1	0
Colchester	1,405	1	0	0	0	1	6	0	6	0	0
Collinsville	25,656	57	0	7	15	35	768	127	620	21	2
Columbia	9,736	13	1	3	1	8	89	21	60	8	0
Cortland	4,283	4	0	0	0	4	30	4	26	0	4
Country Club Hills	16,591	64	1	11	20	32	545	139	377	29	4
Countryside	5,913	14	0	5	1	8	254	20	224	10	0
Crest Hill	20,900	27	0	3	9	15	393	108	268	17	1
Crete	8,284	19	0	1	5	13	195	39	153	3	1
Crystal Lake	40,866	67	1	13	4	49	651	84	562	5	8
Danville	33,126	335	3	50	74	208	2,206	793	1,366	47	11

[1] If a blank is presented in the arson column, it indicates that the FBI did not receive 12 complete months of arson data for that agency.

[7] The data collection methodology for the offense of forcible rape used by Chicago, Illinois, and the Minnesota state UCR Program (with the exception of Minneapolis and St. Paul, Minnesota) does not comply with national UCR Program guidelines. Consequently, its figures for forcible rape and violent crime (of which forcible rape is a part) are not published in this table.

Table II-8. Offenses Known to Law Enforcement, by Selected State and City, 2011—*Continued*

(Number.)

State/City	Population	Violent crime	Murder and non-negligent man-slaughter	Forcible rape	Robbery	Aggravated assault	Property crime	Burglary	Larceny-theft	Motor vehicle theft	Arson[1]
Illinois—*Continued*											
Decatur	76,351	481	10	14	124	333	2,835	1,140	1,581	114	29
Deerfield	18,280	4	0	2	1	1	200	6	192	2	0
De Kalb	43,994	206	2	35	35	134	1,409	206	1,177	26	7
De Pue	1,844	2	0	0	0	2	25	4	21	0	0
De Soto	1,595	3	0	0	0	3	8	1	5	2	0
Des Plaines	58,540	70	1	6	14	49	795	137	619	39	13
Divernon	1,176	4	0	1	0	3	18	0	18	0	0
Dixon	15,780	28	0	23	2	3	508	74	428	6	0
Downers Grove	47,977	25	0	3	7	15	855	116	711	28	9
Du Quoin	6,127	7	0	1	0	6	84	18	63	3	1
East Alton	6,320	25	0	12	3	10	245	60	179	6	2
East Dubuque	1,709	9	0	0	0	9	18	3	13	2	0
East Dundee	2,869	6	0	0	1	5	122	6	113	3	0
East Hazel Crest	1,548	2	0	0	0	2	85	27	54	4	0
East Moline	21,366	91	0	21	3	67	553	114	412	27	3
East Peoria	23,472	130	0	21	5	104	946	256	662	28	6
East St. Louis	27,087	1,627	25	52	272	1,278	2,176	990	766	420	35
Edwardsville	24,366	10	0	0	4	6	440	46	384	10	0
Effingham	12,365	37	2	6	8	21	478	60	413	5	2
Elgin	108,514	287	5	78	82	122	2,068	555	1,425	88	6
Elk Grove Village	33,227	17	0	5	2	10	817	112	626	79	2
Elmhurst	44,254	14	0	0	5	9	625	100	498	27	3
Elmwood Park	24,958	31	0	0	11	20	454	101	298	55	2
Eureka	5,311	6	1	1	0	4	52	9	42	1	1
Evanston	74,710	178	3	4	76	95	2,126	403	1,669	54	18
Evergreen Park	19,912	47	0	3	32	12	743	72	645	26	0
Fairfield	5,170	10	0	0	0	10	164	34	125	5	1
Fairmount	644	0	0	0	0	0	4	0	4	0	0
Fairview Heights	17,129	47	0	5	8	34	924	105	787	32	10
Fithian	486	0	0	0	0	0	1	0	1	0	0
Flora	5,085	4	0	1	0	3	131	3	124	4	0
Flossmoor	9,492	9	0	1	5	3	213	44	163	6	1
Forest Park	14,210	72	0	11	33	28	679	109	537	33	0
Fox Lake	10,611	36	0	4	7	25	283	61	207	15	0
Fox River Grove	4,869	7	0	0	3	4	89	19	69	1	0
Frankfort	17,836	13	0	1	1	11	206	25	166	15	1
Franklin Park	18,388	32	0	7	8	17	376	81	265	30	3
Freeport	25,715	51	0	6	20	25	977	243	724	10	6
Galena	3,439	7	0	0	0	7	54	6	48	0	0
Galesburg	32,292	118	2	16	18	82	1,198	222	947	29	5
Geneseo	6,606	16	0	3	0	13	100	9	87	4	1
Geneva	21,560	11	0	1	2	8	225	43	182	0	2
Genoa	5,209	5	0	2	1	2	52	5	46	1	0
Georgetown	3,484	20	0	3	0	17	65	16	45	4	1
Glendale Heights	34,311	38	0	12	10	16	556	67	475	14	4
Glen Ellyn	27,533	17	1	4	5	7	384	47	329	8	1
Glenview	44,827	44	0	8	6	30	613	101	496	16	0
Glenwood	8,996	13	0	0	3	10	229	66	140	23	0
Godfrey	18,036	17	3	1	2	11	290	64	222	4	0
Grafton	676	1	0	0	0	1	20	0	19	1	0
Granite City	29,939	173	0	31	26	116	864	261	591	12	11
Grant Park	1,335	1	0	0	0	1	9	2	7	0	0
Grayslake	21,020	27	0	4	7	16	399	73	317	9	1
Greenfield	1,074	1	0	0	0	1	16	2	14	0	0
Greenville	7,021	4	1	0	0	3	70	16	53	1	0
Gurnee	31,389	33	1	6	8	18	1,301	83	1,203	15	1
Hanover Park	38,087	38	1	3	6	28	459	89	357	13	2
Harvard	9,475	11	0	0	3	8	134	25	109	0	0
Harvey	25,358	430	15	16	249	150	1,750	722	758	270	7
Harwood Heights	8,638	5	0	0	2	3	67	15	42	10	0
Havana	3,311	26	0	7	0	19	90	26	63	1	1
Hawthorn Woods	7,686	2	0	0	0	2	21	4	16	1	1
Hazel Crest	14,142	64	0	11	41	12	566	209	303	54	0
Henning	252	0	0	0	0	0	0	0	0	0	0
Herrin	12,539	166	1	0	7	158	445	206	228	11	3
Herscher	1,596	1	0	1	0	0	8	3	5	0	0
Hickory Hills	14,091	8	0	0	3	5	239	44	181	14	3
Highland	9,949	19	0	5	3	11	129	18	105	6	0
Highwood	5,421	4	0	0	1	3	46	6	38	2	0
Hillsboro	6,226	11	0	1	0	10	74	19	50	5	1
Hinsdale	16,867	2	0	1	0	1	213	23	183	7	0
Hodgkins	1,903	3	0	0	0	3	271	8	256	7	0
Hoffman Estates	52,051	68	0	15	16	37	682	119	538	25	0
Homer Glen	24,293	15	0	3	1	11	220	44	167	9	0
Homewood	19,381	24	0	4	14	6	718	68	638	12	1

[1] If a blank is presented in the arson column, it indicates that the FBI did not receive 12 complete months of arson data for that agency.

Table II-8.   Offenses Known to Law Enforcement, by Selected State and City, 2011—*Continued*

(Number.)

State/City	Population	Violent crime	Murder and non-negligent man-slaughter	Forcible rape	Robbery	Aggravated assault	Property crime	Burglary	Larceny-theft	Motor vehicle theft	Arson[1]
Illinois—*Continued*											
Hoopeston	5,367	28	0	5	4	19	191	45	141	5	1
Huntley	24,364	3	0	0	0	3	215	35	180	0	1
Hutsonville	556	0	0	0	0	0	1	0	0	1	0
Indian Head Park	3,820	1	1	0	0	0	36	8	27	1	2
Indianola	277	0	0	0	0	0	0	0	0	0	0
Island Lake	8,104	5	0	0	4	1	122	34	83	5	0
Itasca	8,675	1	0	0	0	1	103	13	87	3	0
Jacksonville	19,505	78	0	15	5	58	373	80	285	8	3
Jerseyville	8,490	35	0	8	5	22	289	28	254	7	2
Johnsburg	6,356	2	0	2	0	0	142	16	125	1	0
Joliet	147,877	517	8	30	87	392	3,861	939	2,751	171	51
Justice	12,965	11	1	2	2	6	205	63	116	26	0
Kankakee	27,620	253	4	31	110	108	1,303	391	859	53	16
Kenilworth	2,521	0	0	0	0	0	44	9	35	0	0
Kewanee	12,955	43	0	12	2	29	499	35	461	3	2
Kildeer	3,980	0	0	0	0	0	39	9	27	3	0
Kingston	1,168	0	0	0	0	0	10	1	9	0	0
La Grange	15,597	15	0	5	5	5	197	42	151	4	1
La Grange Park	13,620	2	0	0	0	2	110	3	101	6	0
Lake Bluff	5,739	0	0	0	0	0	77	17	59	1	2
Lake Forest	19,433	22	0	0	1	21	111	11	100	0	1
Lake Villa	8,767	17	0	0	0	17	68	11	54	3	1
Lake Zurich	19,690	17	0	5	2	10	255	25	228	2	3
Lansing	28,416	101	0	23	40	38	1,377	222	1,033	122	7
La Salle	9,638	18	0	3	3	12	202	22	177	3	2
Lemont	16,048	3	0	1	1	1	137	15	118	4	7
Libertyville	20,376	10	0	5	1	4	350	56	287	7	1
Lincolnshire	7,297	1	0	0	1	0	72	10	60	2	0
Lincolnwood	12,628	7	0	0	6	1	567	81	469	17	4
Lindenhurst	14,506	3	0	1	0	2	88	15	71	2	0
Lisle	22,457	8	0	0	3	5	286	48	234	4	1
Litchfield	6,960	17	1	3	1	12	257	40	207	10	2
Lockport	24,914	7	0	0	3	4	343	49	289	5	2
Lombard	43,526	58	0	3	9	46	1,067	79	963	25	1
Lyons	10,761	16	0	1	7	8	216	34	173	9	1
Machesney Park	23,570	74	0	5	9	60	608	113	482	13	1
Macomb	19,346	48	0	8	1	39	482	124	350	8	0
Madison	3,903	49	1	4	19	25	300	91	190	19	4
Mahomet	7,280	8	0	0	0	8	85	19	63	3	0
Manhattan	7,072	6	0	0	0	6	23	3	20	0	1
Mascoutah	7,506	4	0	0	0	4	114	5	109	0	0
Matteson	19,066	38	1	1	22	14	730	104	572	54	4
Mattoon	18,611	65	0	11	6	48	360	91	264	5	13
Maywood	24,163	244	13	15	93	123	940	357	493	90	8
McCook	229	6	0	0	0	6	37	9	25	3	0
McHenry	27,073	41	0	10	5	26	594	50	532	12	2
Melrose Park	25,487	53	1	10	16	26	559	98	384	77	5
Mendota	7,394	7	0	0	0	7	164	48	116	0	0
Metropolis	6,557	39	0	6	4	29	212	37	174	1	1
Midlothian	14,864	38	1	3	16	18	327	95	217	15	2
Milan	5,114	18	0	0	3	15	125	22	94	9	0
Minooka	10,957	5	0	1	2	2	142	8	133	1	0
Mokena	18,796	9	0	3	2	4	217	22	184	11	1
Moline	43,614	211	0	34	18	159	1,587	277	1,242	68	5
Momence	3,320	16	0	0	0	16	62	21	40	1	1
Monmouth	9,472	45	0	9	3	33	557	123	427	7	5
Montgomery	18,494	18	0	2	3	13	328	51	272	5	2
Morris	13,677	30	0	1	3	26	455	59	392	4	3
Morrison	4,201	4	0	1	0	3	54	16	36	2	0
Morton	16,316	15	0	0	1	14	176	36	129	11	0
Morton Grove	23,340	25	0	2	4	19	375	69	293	13	0
Mount Carmel	7,306	24	0	2	0	22	282	39	235	8	3
Mount Prospect	54,330	34	0	2	12	20	676	70	583	23	1
Mount Sterling	2,031	5	0	1	0	4	14	6	7	1	1
Mount Vernon	15,323	191	0	11	18	162	920	311	603	6	10
Mount Zion	5,851	3	0	0	0	3	58	29	28	1	0
Mundelein	31,158	17	0	1	4	12	380	62	311	7	3
Murphysboro	7,994	41	0	1	11	29	459	106	353	0	1
Naperville	142,280	112	2	4	24	82	2,110	300	1,768	42	8
New Lenox	24,467	13	0	1	1	11	295	29	262	4	1
Newton	2,858	24	0	1	0	23	61	20	41	0	0
Niles	29,893	22	0	0	9	13	705	78	597	30	1
Normal	52,655	106	0	16	19	71	1,299	279	994	26	5

[1] If a blank is presented in the arson column, it indicates that the FBI did not receive 12 complete months of arson data for that agency.

Table II-8.   Offenses Known to Law Enforcement, by Selected State and City, 2011—*Continued*

(Number.)

State/City	Population	Violent crime	Murder and non-negligent man-slaughter	Forcible rape	Robbery	Aggravated assault	Property crime	Burglary	Larceny-theft	Motor vehicle theft	Arson[1]
Illinois—*Continued*											
Norridge	14,616	18	0	0	9	9	881	52	817	12	0
North Aurora	16,810	34	0	4	8	22	299	38	256	5	3
Northbrook	33,270	12	0	4	4	4	465	80	381	4	0
Northfield	5,436	1	0	0	0	1	97	19	76	2	0
Northlake	12,360	16	0	0	5	11	400	34	356	10	0
North Riverside	6,692	18	0	0	11	7	626	29	581	16	1
Oak Brook	7,907	4	1	0	3	0	584	17	557	10	0
Oakbrook Terrace	2,140	3	0	0	1	2	149	28	114	7	0
Oak Forest	28,046	27	1	2	9	15	406	83	302	21	3
Oak Lawn	56,861	64	0	8	25	31	1,216	137	1,016	63	3
Oak Park	52,034	141	0	7	102	32	1,692	394	1,226	72	1
Oakwood	1,600	2	0	0	0	2	15	5	10	0	0
Oblong	1,470	6	0	0	0	6	23	9	13	1	0
O'Fallon	28,366	29	0	6	4	19	623	113	486	24	2
Oglesby	3,802	9	0	0	1	8	96	9	86	1	3
Okawville	1,438	4	0	0	0	4	15	1	14	0	0
Olney	9,142	25	1	9	3	12	317	47	253	17	1
Olympia Fields	5,003	3	0	1	2	0	126	12	108	6	2
Orion	1,867	0	0	0	0	0	4	1	3	0	0
Orland Park	56,938	18	0	4	3	11	1,616	45	1,553	18	0
Oswego	30,446	23	1	5	2	15	461	54	404	3	3
Ottawa	18,824	15	1	0	2	12	399	61	338	0	3
Palatine	68,763	41	1	10	11	19	814	38	749	27	0
Palos Heights	12,553	3	0	0	2	1	210	16	191	3	0
Palos Hills	17,537	13	0	0	4	9	107	21	77	9	1
Palos Park	4,862	0	0	0	0	0	49	9	40	0	0
Pana	5,865	8	0	0	0	8	113	19	89	5	1
Paris	8,864	33	1	5	0	27	140	39	91	10	2
Park Forest	22,041	61	0	6	24	31	525	275	234	16	5
Park Ridge	37,593	23	0	2	7	14	480	138	336	6	3
Pawnee	2,747	1	0	0	0	1	48	5	39	4	1
Paxton	4,486	10	0	1	1	8	77	21	53	3	2
Pekin	34,197	136	0	26	15	95	779	152	607	20	1
Peoria	115,353	814	16	33	288	477	5,438	1,721	3,460	257	65
Peoria Heights	6,175	30	0	0	5	25	196	38	155	3	1
Peotone	4,154	3	0	1	0	2	41	7	34	0	0
Peru	10,326	8	0	2	0	6	254	21	231	2	3
Pinckneyville	5,665	5	0	0	2	3	41	17	23	1	0
Pittsfield	4,590	0	0	0	0	0	3	0	3	0	0
Plainfield	39,700	22	0	1	5	16	490	90	389	11	5
Pontiac	11,967	49	0	5	4	40	392	60	328	4	3
Pontoon Beach	5,854	9	1	0	3	5	142	30	97	15	0
Posen	6,005	13	0	0	4	9	191	61	114	16	2
Potomac	752	0	0	0	0	0	14	4	10	0	0
Prospect Heights	16,305	20	1	2	3	14	173	44	118	11	1
Quincy	40,755	193	0	30	15	148	1,274	209	1,041	24	4
Rankin	563	1	0	0	0	1	1	0	1	0	0
Rantoul	12,980	133	0	13	10	110	262	111	144	7	1
Richton Park	13,687	44	0	6	28	10	323	108	197	18	1
Ridge Farm	885	0	0	0	0	0	7	3	4	0	0
Riverdale	13,590	201	3	21	128	49	632	306	272	54	0
River Forest	11,206	20	1	2	9	8	312	61	244	7	0
River Grove	10,258	10	0	2	4	4	226	40	172	14	0
Riverside	8,902	8	0	3	4	1	146	31	110	5	0
Riverwoods	3,671	0	0	0	0	0	37	9	28	0	0
Robbins	5,353	26	0	6	10	10	113	67	32	14	1
Rockdale	1,982	6	0	4	1	1	40	11	28	1	0
Rock Falls	9,294	13	0	1	3	9	120	54	59	7	1
Rockford	153,331	2,106	21	112	566	1,407	7,122	1,890	4,746	486	69
Rock Island	39,135	290	2	14	52	222	1,235	256	894	85	7
Rockton	7,708	5	0	0	0	5	104	15	88	1	2
Rolling Meadows	24,172	24	0	3	7	14	338	44	290	4	2
Romeoville	39,799	22	0	2	7	13	764	119	624	21	0
Roselle	22,832	18	0	7	4	7	257	45	205	7	0
Rosemont	4,215	7	0	0	2	5	229	9	213	7	0
Round Lake	18,344	38	0	3	6	29	207	40	160	7	1
Round Lake Beach	28,260	43	0	9	8	26	700	103	590	7	4
Rushville	3,202	5	0	0	0	5	48	14	32	2	0
Salem	7,508	3	0	1	0	2	354	72	274	8	0
Sandwich	7,443	5	0	1	0	4	66	9	57	0	0
Sauk Village	10,538	118	2	12	17	87	608	391	185	32	2
Schaumburg	74,450	63	0	14	23	26	2,358	238	2,056	64	0
Schiller Park	11,829	15	2	1	7	5	223	32	179	12	1
Seneca	2,378	13	0	0	0	13	46	8	38	0	1

[1] If a blank is presented in the arson column, it indicates that the FBI did not receive 12 complete months of arson data for that agency.

Table II-8.   Offenses Known to Law Enforcement, by Selected State and City, 2011—Continued

(Number.)

State/City	Population	Violent crime	Murder and non-negligent man-slaughter	Forcible rape	Robbery	Aggravated assault	Property crime	Burglary	Larceny-theft	Motor vehicle theft	Arson[1]
Illinois—*Continued*											
Shiloh	12,689	21	0	4	3	14	182	43	131	8	1
Shorewood	15,662	14	0	2	3	9	177	34	140	3	1
Sidell	619	0	0	0	0	0	1	0	1	0	0
Silvis	7,502	24	0	3	1	20	308	47	256	5	0
Skokie	64,979	141	2	13	39	87	1,723	325	1,323	75	6
Sleepy Hollow	3,314	0	0	0	0	0	34	5	28	1	0
South Barrington	4,579	2	0	0	0	2	74	19	55	0	0
South Beloit	7,916	13	0	1	3	9	196	34	159	3	6
South Chicago Heights	4,151	11	0	0	5	6	155	27	113	15	2
South Elgin	22,051	17	0	1	1	15	258	33	218	7	1
South Holland	22,096	52	0	4	37	11	521	152	321	48	3
Sparta	4,315	12	0	8	0	4	94	27	66	1	1
Springfield	116,600	1,278	8	103	258	909	7,176	1,883	5,076	217	69
Spring Grove	5,795	2	0	0	0	2	60	9	51	0	1
Spring Valley	5,575	9	0	0	0	9	105	21	83	1	0
St. Charles	33,073	33	0	3	9	21	583	71	502	10	6
Steger	9,599	17	0	2	8	7	428	87	319	22	0
Stone Park	4,961	24	0	5	2	17	105	48	51	6	0
Streamwood	39,978	39	1	4	17	17	620	96	511	13	1
Streator	13,751	22	0	0	1	21	425	69	355	1	0
Summit	11,087	47	1	2	20	24	317	95	169	53	13
Sycamore	17,572	16	0	0	2	14	370	51	317	2	2
Taylorville	11,280	27	0	2	2	23	243	56	175	12	0
Thornton	2,345	2	0	0	1	1	39	14	23	2	0
Tilton	2,732	8	0	4	0	4	69	25	40	4	2
Tinley Park	56,874	35	0	12	9	14	901	99	771	31	6
Tower Lakes	1,287	0	0	0	0	0	7	0	7	0	0
Urbana	41,374	197	1	35	74	87	1,464	382	1,055	27	9
Vandalia	7,063	13	0	0	0	13	121	21	92	8	0
Vernon Hills	25,189	17	1	4	3	9	588	51	535	2	1
Villa Park	21,970	23	0	4	9	10	486	71	401	14	8
Virden	3,435	9	0	0	0	9	53	12	41	0	3
Virginia	1,616	0	0	0	0	0	17	8	9	0	0
Warrensburg	1,214	3	0	1	1	1	10	2	8	0	0
Warrenville	13,180	13	0	7	3	3	234	38	185	11	0
Washington Park	4,209	140	7	2	52	79	249	83	117	49	1
Waterloo	9,841	0	0	0	0	0	72	2	70	0	0
Watseka	5,271	10	0	5	0	5	176	46	130	0	2
Wauconda	13,644	13	0	1	1	11	180	29	144	7	2
Westchester	16,768	8	0	0	6	2	257	69	178	10	1
West Chicago	27,168	23	0	7	1	15	345	48	272	25	6
West City	663	7	0	0	0	7	59	8	51	0	0
West Dundee	7,353	9	0	1	1	7	233	15	216	2	0
Western Springs	13,014	1	0	0	0	1	60	9	50	1	0
Westmont	24,759	25	1	4	11	9	364	58	286	20	5
Westville	3,212	15	0	2	0	13	68	26	37	5	0
Wheaton	53,053	23	0	2	7	14	775	94	674	7	9
Wheeling	37,761	36	0	3	4	29	566	87	444	35	1
Willowbrook	8,566	9	0	0	5	4	162	12	144	6	0
Willow Springs	5,541	2	0	0	1	1	43	7	35	1	0
Wilmette	27,169	9	0	0	4	5	414	81	329	4	1
Wilmington	5,741	5	0	0	0	5	125	8	117	0	0
Winfield	9,107	6	0	0	1	5	59	12	46	1	0
Winnebago	3,110	0	0	0	0	0	51	3	48	0	0
Winnetka	12,224	5	0	1	0	4	156	30	125	1	0
Winthrop Harbor	6,762	12	0	1	1	10	82	23	54	5	0
Wood Dale	13,811	7	0	1	2	4	217	40	169	8	0
Woodridge	33,070	38	2	9	6	21	506	65	417	24	2
Wood River	10,689	27	0	7	3	17	470	89	365	16	1
Woodstock	24,845	26	0	7	7	12	425	43	378	4	2
Worth	10,821	3	0	0	1	2	122	33	77	12	0
Yorkville	16,972	13	0	4	4	5	251	41	206	4	0
Indiana											
Alexandria	5,171	5	0	2	2	1	179	20	147	12	0
Anderson	56,416	203	1	30	87	85	2,949	665	2,052	232	18
Angola	8,656	2	0	0	1	1	538	33	492	13	0
Auburn	12,796	10	0	4	4	2	434	57	369	8	0
Aurora	3,769	15	0	2	4	9	269	29	239	1	0
Avon	12,510	42	0	2	4	36	612	35	563	14	0
Batesville	6,553	22	0	2	0	20	93	19	71	3	0
Bedford	13,482	17	0	5	4	8	476	46	398	32	4
Beech Grove	14,264	32	0	6	16	10	528	102	379	47	3
Berne	4,019	3	0	1	1	1	69	11	54	4	1
Bloomington	80,816	244	4	18	58	164	3,072	601	2,300	171	15

[1] If a blank is presented in the arson column, it indicates that the FBI did not receive 12 complete months of arson data for that agency.

Table II-8.   Offenses Known to Law Enforcement, by Selected State and City, 2011—*Continued*

(Number.)

State/City	Population	Violent crime	Murder and non-negligent man-slaughter	Forcible rape	Robbery	Aggravated assault	Property crime	Burglary	Larceny-theft	Motor vehicle theft	Arson[1]
Indiana—*Continued*											
Bluffton	9,948	11	0	5	2	4	476	60	407	9	0
Boonville	6,278	69	0	1	0	68	148	16	121	11	2
Brazil	7,952	21	0	6	0	15	324	47	261	16	0
Bremen	4,611	6	0	0	1	5	73	18	54	1	0
Brownsburg	21,394	27	0	0	1	26	323	59	247	17	0
Burns Harbor	1,162	2	1	0	1	0	30	5	23	2	0
Carmel	79,596	17	1	8	2	6	831	69	729	33	0
Cedar Lake	11,619	10	0	3	6	1	379	65	299	15	2
Charlestown	7,624	5	0	0	1	4	460	106	348	6	1
Chesterfield	2,560	2	1	0	0	1	49	4	42	3	0
Chesterton	13,135	13	0	2	1	10	233	53	168	12	1
Clarksville	21,835	117	0	10	35	72	1,717	212	1,417	88	3
Clinton	4,918	10	0	0	0	10	44	12	27	5	0
Columbia City	8,795	10	0	3	0	7	176	27	146	3	0
Columbus	44,286	84	1	7	20	56	2,597	303	2,087	207	3
Corydon	3,138	3	0	1	0	2	41	8	32	1	0
Crawfordsville	15,996	30	0	4	2	24	672	146	492	34	2
Crown Point	27,457	17	1	5	7	4	475	50	407	18	1
Culver	1,360	3	0	0	0	3	41	5	35	1	0
Cumberland	5,195	21	2	1	5	13	189	38	142	9	0
Danville	9,047	10	0	0	0	10	138	21	110	7	0
Decatur	9,453	10	0	0	2	8	50	8	36	6	0
Delphi	2,908	10	0	3	1	6	60	10	46	4	0
Dyer	16,474	13	1	3	2	7	337	32	288	17	0
East Chicago	29,850	255	5	16	134	100	1,941	529	1,145	267	2
Ellettsville	6,411	35	0	0	0	35	96	33	53	10	0
Elwood	8,658	16	0	5	5	6	532	104	393	35	4
Evansville	118,029	491	3	56	154	278	5,456	1,074	4,151	231	88
Fairmount	2,969	16	0	0	0	16	48	19	28	1	1
Fishers	77,186	11	0	0	8	3	700	57	626	17	2
Fort Wayne	254,987	785	24	94	310	357	9,036	1,888	6,768	380	41
Frankfort	16,506	47	1	6	15	25	752	106	612	34	0
Franklin	23,833	59	0	5	12	42	991	99	878	14	0
Gary	80,704	639	30	47	328	234	5,338	2,618	1,926	794	45
Gas City	5,995	0	0	0	0	0	176	27	147	2	0
Goshen	31,881	36	1	7	17	11	1,130	212	876	42	5
Greendale	4,543	6	0	0	2	4	126	15	110	1	0
Greenfield	20,707	10	0	3	1	6	381	68	293	20	3
Greensburg	11,551	46	1	1	2	42	237	58	160	19	1
Greenwood	50,045	177	2	0	24	151	1,777	130	1,570	77	4
Griffith	16,979	38	3	3	14	18	641	112	479	50	0
Hagerstown	1,796	0	0	0	0	0	40	9	30	1	0
Hammond	81,243	547	9	45	184	309	3,819	1,032	2,303	484	21
Hartford City	6,252	10	0	0	3	7	213	49	158	6	0
Hebron	3,743	3	0	0	0	3	14	1	12	1	0
Highland	23,848	20	1	1	15	3	885	96	723	66	2
Hobart	29,207	65	0	8	21	36	1,479	161	1,225	93	3
Huntingburg	6,088	0	0	0	0	0	82	16	65	1	0
Huntington	17,480	12	0	5	2	5	478	66	395	17	8
Indianapolis	833,024	9,170	96	435	3,372	5,267	46,967	15,122	26,588	5,257	463
Jasper	15,115	6	2	1	0	3	147	22	110	15	1
Jeffersonville	45,183	454	3	6	44	401	2,258	500	1,588	170	1
Kendallville	9,912	8	0	4	2	2	314	38	266	10	0
Kokomo	45,700	184	3	20	73	88	2,558	505	1,954	99	3
Lafayette	67,483	408	3	38	48	319	3,000	635	2,190	175	20
Lake Station	12,636	35	0	9	5	21	536	107	392	37	13
La Porte	22,166	43	1	6	10	26	1,121	193	886	42	9
Lawrenceburg	5,068	13	0	1	7	5	196	16	178	2	0
Ligonier	4,428	0	0	0	0	0	41	12	26	3	0
Linton	5,441	1	0	0	0	1	220	0	220	0	0
Logansport	18,490	21	1	6	4	10	824	79	714	31	4
Long Beach	1,185	1	1	0	0	0	21	0	19	2	1
Lowell	9,323	24	0	0	0	24	183	13	169	1	1
Marion	30,101	62	0	9	45	8	1,428	259	1,065	104	10
Martinsville	11,888	17	0	7	1	9	1,046	159	855	32	2
Merrillville	35,426	112	2	3	36	71	1,380	151	1,082	147	2
Michigan City	31,460	96	2	9	41	44	1,840	297	1,421	122	8
Mishawaka	48,498	146	3	12	68	63	2,895	517	2,234	144	17
Monticello	5,405	2	0	0	1	1	131	18	102	11	1
Mooresville	9,374	9	0	4	1	4	298	41	240	17	0
Mount Vernon	6,721	36	1	3	2	30	599	206	381	12	5
Muncie	70,443	513	1	42	108	362	2,433	553	1,701	179	33
Munster	23,724	21	0	1	6	14	447	45	387	15	0
Nappanee	6,682	1	0	0	0	1	271	34	227	10	0

[1] If a blank is presented in the arson column, it indicates that the FBI did not receive 12 complete months of arson data for that agency.

Table II-8.   Offenses Known to Law Enforcement, by Selected State and City, 2011—*Continued*

(Number.)

State/City	Population	Violent crime	Murder and non-negligent man-slaughter	Forcible rape	Robbery	Aggravated assault	Property crime	Burglary	Larceny-theft	Motor vehicle theft	Arson[1]
Indiana—*Continued*											
New Albany	36,558	112	1	21	41	49	2,210	428	1,642	140	3
New Castle	18,207	17	1	8	5	3	1,173	231	917	25	2
New Haven	14,870	25	0	5	11	9	401	60	317	24	1
New Whiteland	5,500	11	0	3	0	8	98	12	79	7	0
Noblesville	52,234	60	0	11	20	29	945	132	764	49	12
North Judson	1,781	14	0	1	1	12	82	15	64	3	0
North Liberty	1,906	11	0	1	0	10	27	7	19	1	0
North Vernon	6,762	8	1	2	3	2	280	56	217	7	0
Oakland City	2,441	4	0	0	1	3	72	18	53	1	0
Peru	11,475	21	1	3	6	11	212	57	143	12	2
Plainfield	27,772	43	0	16	6	21	716	75	589	52	2
Plymouth	10,084	3	0	0	1	2	526	70	433	23	1
Portage	37,016	111	1	3	7	100	1,179	183	939	57	2
Porter	4,883	6	1	2	0	3	99	31	58	10	1
Portland	6,255	0	0	0	0	0	227	18	205	4	1
Princeton	8,688	14	0	1	1	12	336	49	282	5	1
Rensselaer	5,889	24	0	1	1	22	246	40	202	4	0
Richmond	37,000	195	3	36	67	89	1,897	609	1,149	139	38
Rushville	6,373	5	0	1	2	2	358	72	275	11	1
Schererville	29,392	13	1	1	7	4	779	50	696	33	0
Scottsburg	6,781	40	0	0	8	32	313	56	254	3	0
Sellersburg	6,159	35	0	0	2	33	138	32	97	9	0
Seymour	17,592	82	1	3	5	73	1,093	153	881	59	3
Shelbyville	19,289	13	0	1	2	10	801	32	742	27	0
South Bend	101,685	744	9	60	406	269	6,096	2,335	3,437	324	43
South Whitley	1,760	0	0	0	0	0	39	6	31	2	0
Speedway	11,872	32	0	1	23	8	609	90	472	47	0
St. John	14,926	14	0	0	1	13	173	24	140	9	0
Tell City	7,309	7	0	0	2	5	204	43	155	6	2
Terre Haute	61,095	152	4	17	91	40	3,942	934	2,725	283	42
Tipton	5,132	12	0	0	3	9	238	50	184	4	1
Union City	3,602	7	0	1	0	6	113	26	83	4	0
Valparaiso	31,892	32	0	4	5	23	958	144	780	34	3
Vincennes	18,517	30	0	5	7	18	1,146	254	839	53	1
Walkerton	2,155	3	0	1	1	1	38	10	23	5	1
Warsaw	13,628	8	0	5	3	0	654	91	540	23	4
Washington	11,568	13	1	1	3	8	454	110	330	14	4
Waterloo	2,253	14	0	2	1	11	75	14	54	7	0
Westfield	30,222	21	0	8	4	9	496	57	413	26	0
West Lafayette	29,747	53	0	3	6	44	459	58	383	18	0
West Terre Haute	2,247	12	0	1	0	11	144	58	77	9	0
Westville	5,883	4	0	1	0	3	49	10	34	5	1
Whitestown	2,882	4	0	0	2	2	29	5	17	7	0
Whiting	5,023	8	1	0	4	3	243	79	154	10	0
Winchester	4,960	0	0	0	0	0	332	35	294	3	0
Winona Lake	4,933	4	0	0	0	4	11	2	7	2	1
Zionsville	14,232	7	0	0	0	7	126	21	98	7	0
Iowa											
Adel	3,701	5	0	0	0	5	60	21	39	0	0
Albia	3,786	7	0	1	0	6	66	9	55	2	1
Algona	5,589	12	0	0	0	12	40	15	24	1	1
Altoona	14,617	19	0	1	4	14	504	66	424	14	2
Ames	59,274	178	0	18	10	150	1,670	351	1,263	56	2
Anamosa	5,562	5	0	0	0	5	87	29	58	0	0
Ankeny	45,821	48	0	9	2	37	677	108	550	19	0
Atlantic	7,149	10	0	2	0	8	152	21	124	7	1
Audubon	2,187	0	0	0	0	0	29	11	18	0	0
Bettendorf	33,391	58	0	5	3	50	533	86	430	17	2
Bloomfield	2,654	6	0	1	0	5	10	3	7	0	0
Boone	12,727	66	0	14	1	51	378	159	208	11	6
Burlington	25,797	143	0	11	19	113	1,122	263	813	46	13
Carlisle	3,896	2	0	0	1	1	29	12	15	2	2
Carroll	10,156	8	0	3	1	4	150	15	124	11	0
Carter Lake	3,805	21	0	4	0	17	135	27	90	18	1
Cedar Falls	39,466	71	1	11	4	55	605	119	453	33	7
Cedar Rapids	126,988	358	2	41	86	229	4,879	1,099	3,566	214	17
Centerville	5,557	29	0	3	1	25	247	74	164	9	1
Chariton	4,344	14	0	0	0	14	113	25	83	5	0
Charles City	7,692	8	0	0	2	6	96	12	79	5	0
Cherokee	5,281	17	0	1	0	16	88	19	64	5	0
Clarinda	5,601	9	0	2	0	7	153	30	118	5	2
Clarion	2,865	9	0	3	0	6	29	11	17	1	0
Clear Lake	7,818	10	0	2	0	8	237	42	192	3	0

[1] If a blank is presented in the arson column, it indicates that the FBI did not receive 12 complete months of arson data for that agency.

Table II-8.   Offenses Known to Law Enforcement, by Selected State and City, 2011—*Continued*

(Number.)

State/City	Population	Violent crime	Murder and non-negligent man-slaughter	Forcible rape	Robbery	Aggravated assault	Property crime	Burglary	Larceny-theft	Motor vehicle theft	Arson[1]
Iowa—*Continued*											
Clinton	27,026	135	0	10	12	113	1,299	255	997	47	13
Coralville	19,006	31	1	9	5	16	493	50	431	12	7
Council Bluffs	62,556	656	4	69	61	522	4,251	980	2,776	495	35
Cresco	3,888	4	0	1	3	0	81	34	41	6	0
Creston	7,875	19	0	0	0	19	159	30	116	13	2
Davenport[2]	100,207	652	5	53	113	481	4,908	1,140	3,529	239	24
Decorah	8,170	4	0	0	0	4	117	10	102	5	0
Denison	8,341	4	0	0	1	3	58	6	48	4	0
Des Moines	204,498	1,069	8	103	216	742	10,727	2,493	7,400	834	44
De Witt	5,350	12	0	3	0	9	88	32	55	1	0
Dubuque	57,939	135	1	20	32	82	1,702	416	1,239	47	34
Eldora	2,746	7	0	0	0	7	27	8	16	3	0
Eldridge	5,681	12	0	1	0	11	68	5	61	2	0
Emmetsburg	3,924	4	0	1	0	3	23	10	12	1	0
Estherville	6,393	10	0	0	0	10	141	30	96	15	0
Evansdale	4,776	11	0	2	0	9	116	39	75	2	3
Fairfield	9,514	20	0	2	1	17	214	61	143	10	6
Fort Dodge	25,338	138	1	14	17	106	1,135	232	834	69	16
Fort Madison	11,109	61	0	6	1	54	344	106	219	19	2
Glenwood	5,297	19	0	3	1	15	175	77	85	13	1
Grinnell	9,266	13	0	1	0	12	162	41	115	6	1
Hampton	4,484	3	0	0	0	3	18	4	9	5	0
Hawarden	2,559	1	0	0	0	1	21	5	16	0	0
Hiawatha	7,061	0	0	0	0	0	92	25	66	1	0
Humboldt	4,715	1	0	0	0	1	37	9	23	5	0
Indianola	14,859	33	0	13	1	19	283	61	208	14	8
Iowa City	68,217	163	0	24	18	121	1,580	326	1,207	47	8
Iowa Falls	5,265	2	0	0	0	2	141	20	118	3	0
Jefferson	4,368	5	0	1	0	4	31	3	28	0	0
Keokuk	10,836	95	1	3	2	89	591	156	401	34	2
Le Mars	9,877	9	0	2	0	7	224	31	177	16	2
Lisbon	2,163	0	0	0	0	0	41	14	27	0	0
Manchester	5,206	26	0	1	0	25	70	13	49	8	0
Maquoketa	6,173	18	0	3	1	14	269	119	136	14	1
Marengo	2,541	6	0	0	0	6	9	4	4	1	0
Marion	34,950	42	0	7	1	34	443	103	319	21	5
Marshalltown	27,696	146	0	0	9	137	972	250	685	37	4
Mason City	28,226	43	1	10	9	23	1,302	314	939	49	4
Missouri Valley	2,853	6	0	0	0	6	46	5	39	2	0
Monticello	3,816	0	0	0	0	0	44	12	31	1	0
Mount Pleasant	8,713	19	0	1	1	17	229	58	156	15	1
Mount Vernon	4,530	4	0	1	0	3	84	15	68	1	0
Muscatine	23,006	161	0	18	3	140	798	202	554	42	6
Nevada	6,834	45	0	2	1	42	179	34	136	9	6
North Liberty	13,444	30	0	0	1	29	83	19	60	4	2
Norwalk	8,992	14	0	1	0	13	114	15	93	6	0
Oelwein	6,449	25	0	0	0	25	124	25	94	5	1
Ogden	2,055	3	0	0	0	3	41	25	16	0	0
Orange City	6,035	3	0	0	0	3	62	16	46	0	1
Osage	3,638	10	0	0	0	10	24	2	22	0	0
Osceola	4,955	6	0	1	1	4	85	14	66	5	1
Oskaloosa	11,523	25	1	3	3	18	273	59	200	14	4
Ottumwa	25,154	72	2	11	9	50	890	199	651	40	14
Pella	10,406	32	0	4	0	28	172	69	101	2	1
Perry	7,742	27	0	0	0	27	141	21	118	2	2
Pleasant Hill	8,831	11	0	0	1	10	178	78	83	17	0
Polk City	3,436	0	0	0	0	0	27	6	18	3	0
Prairie City	1,689	0	0	0	0	0	35	19	15	1	0
Red Oak	5,772	9	0	3	0	6	241	65	163	13	4
Sergeant Bluff	4,249	11	0	0	0	11	76	8	65	3	2
Sheldon	5,215	5	0	0	0	5	69	25	44	0	0
Shenandoah	5,177	1	0	0	0	1	76	8	63	5	1
Sioux City	83,117	339	1	36	34	268	3,507	709	2,635	163	11
Spencer	11,292	2	2	0	0	0	271	109	147	15	1
Spirit Lake	4,865	3	0	0	2	1	181	44	137	0	0
State Center	1,476	4	0	0	0	4	14	4	9	1	0
Storm Lake	10,656	63	0	4	1	58	219	47	170	2	9
Story City	3,449	3	0	0	1	2	44	11	32	1	1
Tipton	3,238	1	0	1	0	0	35	1	33	1	0
Urbandale	39,670	54	0	8	5	41	634	109	501	24	3
Vinton	5,285	8	0	0	0	8	110	18	88	4	1
Washington	7,304	44	1	6	1	36	107	28	72	7	0
Waterloo	68,764	357	3	52	60	242	2,159	673	1,401	85	40
Waukee	13,862	16	0	0	0	16	181	58	117	6	0

[1] If a blank is presented in the arson column, it indicates that the FBI did not receive 12 complete months of arson data for that agency.

[2] Because of changes in the state/local agency's reporting practices, figures are not comparable to previous years' data.

Table II-8.   Offenses Known to Law Enforcement, by Selected State and City, 2011—*Continued*

(Number.)

State/City	Population	Violent crime	Murder and non-negligent man-slaughter	Forcible rape	Robbery	Aggravated assault	Property crime	Burglary	Larceny-theft	Motor vehicle theft	Arson[1]
Iowa—*Continued*											
Waverly	9,926	60	0	2	1	57	192	80	109	3	2
Webster City	8,112	26	0	3	2	21	144	37	102	5	1
West Burlington	2,984	5	0	2	0	3	167	17	149	1	0
West Des Moines	56,905	115	1	26	13	75	1,824	225	1,564	35	10
West Liberty	3,756	2	0	1	0	1	41	9	31	1	0
West Union	2,499	3	0	0	0	3	38	16	20	2	0
Williamsburg	3,084	0	0	0	0	0	28	3	23	2	0
Wilton	2,817	6	0	2	0	4	32	10	22	0	0
Windsor Heights	4,885	6	0	1	2	3	288	23	257	8	0
Winterset	5,217	6	0	1	0	5	165	37	125	3	0
Kansas											
Abilene	6,887	7	0	1	1	5	234	42	187	5	1
Andale	934	0	0	0	0	0	4	1	3	0	0
Andover	11,866	11	0	5	1	5	248	18	221	9	4
Anthony	2,283	2	0	0	0	2	23	9	14	0	0
Arkansas City	12,494	64	1	2	3	58	496	83	393	20	1
Arma	1,490	4	0	0	0	4	22	5	17	0	0
Atchison	11,091	29	0	5	2	22	442	121	303	18	1
Atwood	1,202	1	0	0	0	1	10	2	8	0	0
Augusta	9,333	20	1	6	4	9	307	49	238	20	0
Baldwin City	4,544	4	0	1	0	3	125	9	112	4	1
Basehor	4,642	3	0	0	0	3	45	7	34	4	0
Baxter Springs	4,265	10	0	3	0	7	109	28	66	15	2
Bel Aire	6,812	3	0	1	0	2	49	18	31	0	3
Beloit	3,859	14	0	1	0	13	59	12	46	1	0
Bonner Springs	7,360	22	0	2	2	18	228	28	189	11	4
Bucklin	799	0	0	0	0	0	0	0	0	0	0
Burlington	2,691	1	0	0	0	1	29	12	14	3	0
Bushton	281	0	0	0	0	0	0	0	0	0	0
Cawker City	472	0	0	0	0	0	0	0	0	0	0
Chanute	9,177	37	0	7	0	30	306	121	169	16	2
Chapman	1,402	0	0	0	0	0	15	2	13	0	0
Chetopa	1,132	1	0	1	0	0	8	2	6	0	1
Clay Center	4,362	10	0	2	0	8	96	24	71	1	0
Clearwater	2,497	1	0	0	1	0	29	6	23	0	0
Coffeyville	10,360	86	0	4	8	74	564	142	407	15	2
Colby	5,421	21	0	4	1	16	102	21	76	5	2
Columbus	3,333	1	0	0	0	1	78	16	61	1	1
Concordia	5,429	14	0	4	0	10	165	34	127	4	1
Council Grove	2,196	5	0	0	0	5	34	6	26	2	1
Derby	22,299	54	0	10	4	40	603	99	484	20	5
Dodge City	27,514	115	0	11	17	87	921	215	654	52	2
Edwardsville	4,368	11	0	0	0	11	115	31	69	15	1
El Dorado	13,104	77	0	5	6	66	422	75	324	23	2
Elkhart	2,219	4	0	0	0	4	13	5	7	1	1
Ellinwood	2,145	4	0	1	1	2	39	13	26	0	0
Ellis	2,075	1	0	0	0	1	10	1	8	1	0
Ellsworth	3,140	7	0	2	0	5	52	20	31	1	0
Elwood	1,232	8	0	1	0	7	66	47	18	1	0
Emporia	25,074	77	0	13	4	60	1,050	173	856	21	2
Eskridge	537	0	0	0	0	0	1	0	1	0	0
Eudora	6,175	24	0	3	2	19	175	37	134	4	0
Fairway	3,907	4	0	0	2	2	59	15	36	8	0
Florence	468	0	0	0	0	0	3	1	2	0	0
Fort Scott	8,138	24	0	2	0	22	438	144	266	28	4
Fredonia	2,498	11	0	2	0	9	50	14	34	2	0
Frontenac	3,459	6	0	1	0	5	44	8	33	3	0
Galena	3,105	19	0	0	0	19	108	28	73	7	1
Garden City	26,827	97	1	15	10	71	852	118	702	32	11
Garden Plain	854	1	0	0	0	1	13	8	5	0	1
Gardner	19,244	51	0	7	1	43	306	38	260	8	8
Garnett	3,437	15	0	3	0	12	111	33	77	1	2
Geneseo	269	0	0	0	0	0	0	0	0	0	0
Girard	2,807	12	0	1	0	11	55	14	39	2	1
Goddard	4,372	5	0	2	0	3	83	31	46	6	0
Grandview Plaza	1,570	4	0	0	0	4	54	19	33	2	1
Great Bend	16,097	74	1	13	5	55	752	144	576	32	2
Halstead	2,098	1	0	0	0	1	21	6	15	0	0
Havensville	134	0	0	0	0	0	0	0	0	0	0
Hays	20,640	70	0	13	4	53	553	72	455	26	7
Haysville	10,895	32	0	5	0	27	273	55	206	12	4
Herington	2,542	6	0	1	0	5	52	9	39	4	0
Hesston	3,733	1	0	0	0	1	65	18	47	0	0

[1] If a blank is presented in the arson column, it indicates that the FBI did not receive 12 complete months of arson data for that agency.

Table II-8.   Offenses Known to Law Enforcement, by Selected State and City, 2011—*Continued*

(Number.)

State/City	Population	Violent crime	Murder and non-negligent man-slaughter	Forcible rape	Robbery	Aggravated assault	Property crime	Burglary	Larceny-theft	Motor vehicle theft	Arson[1]
Kansas—*Continued*											
Hiawatha	3,192	3	0	1	0	2	83	2	79	2	0
Highland	1,018	2	0	0	0	2	22	17	5	0	2
Hill City	1,483	1	0	1	0	0	27	4	22	1	0
Hillsboro	3,012	7	0	0	0	7	48	28	20	0	1
Hoisington	2,723	4	0	0	0	4	51	14	36	1	0
Holcomb	2,107	1	0	0	0	1	37	10	26	1	0
Holton	3,350	8	0	1	1	6	72	13	54	5	1
Holyrood	450	0	0	0	0	0	3	2	1	0	3
Hugoton	3,929	2	0	0	0	2	12	0	12	0	0
Hutchinson	42,347	233	1	21	28	183	2,719	499	2,094	126	22
Independence	9,543	32	0	2	4	26	423	90	317	16	6
Inman	1,386	3	0	1	0	2	17	4	12	1	0
Iola	5,740	29	0	3	1	25	296	46	239	11	4
Junction City	23,501	139	0	15	26	98	583	121	444	18	14
Kanopolis	495	0	0	0	0	0	0	0	0	0	0
Kansas City[2]	146,712	947	27	95	291	534	7,883	1,827	4,792	1,264	
Kechi	1,921	0	0	0	0	0	14	1	13	0	0
Kingman	3,197	8	1	2	0	5	55	16	30	9	1
Kiowa	1,033	0	0	0	0	0	0	0	0	0	0
Lake Quivira	912	0	0	0	0	0	0	0	0	0	0
Lansing	11,337	31	0	1	1	29	108	41	58	9	1
Larned	4,080	15	0	1	0	14	117	26	88	3	1
Lawrence	88,200	335	0	33	37	265	3,793	502	3,098	193	14
Leavenworth	35,475	236	3	11	30	192	1,060	304	709	47	15
Leawood	32,069	18	0	1	3	14	445	44	386	15	1
Lebo	946	0	0	0	0	0	1	0	0	1	0
Lenexa	48,496	68	1	11	12	44	1,080	112	862	106	8
Leon	708	0	0	0	0	0	19	7	11	1	0
Liberal	20,655	59	1	7	5	46	515	135	368	12	1
Lindsborg	3,480	2	0	0	0	2	74	27	45	2	3
Lyndon	1,059	0	0	0	0	0	4	0	3	1	0
Lyons	3,763	7	0	0	0	7	11	4	6	1	0
Maize	3,442	9	0	1	0	8	65	10	55	0	0
Maple Hill	624	0	0	0	0	0	0	0	0	0	0
Marion	1,939	4	0	1	0	3	40	12	25	3	0
Marysville	3,315	10	1	3	0	6	61	14	45	2	2
McLouth	886	0	0	0	0	0	27	5	22	0	0
McPherson	13,239	33	1	2	3	27	348	140	195	13	2
Medicine Lodge	2,022	5	0	0	0	5	60	18	38	4	1
Meriden	818	0	0	0	0	0	2	0	2	0	0
Merriam	11,073	28	0	3	7	18	533	54	400	79	1
Minneapolis	2,045	5	0	3	0	2	37	13	24	0	1
Mission Hills	3,520	0	0	0	0	0	45	5	40	0	0
Moran	562	0	0	0	0	0	0	0	0	0	0
Moundridge	1,748	1	0	0	0	1	11	3	7	1	0
Mulberry	523	0	0	0	0	0	13	5	7	1	0
Mulvane	6,150	2	0	0	0	2	124	34	84	6	1
Neodesha	2,502	8	0	2	0	6	41	7	33	1	0
Newton	19,254	104	0	9	7	88	412	102	290	20	5
North Newton	1,770	1	0	0	0	1	19	7	12	0	0
Norton	2,947	2	0	0	0	2	49	4	35	10	0
Oakley	2,058	2	0	0	0	2	39	14	23	2	6
Olathe	126,671	226	6	48	20	152	2,204	259	1,774	171	19
Osage City	2,962	20	0	2	0	18	71	16	51	4	2
Osawatomie	4,475	16	0	6	0	10	146	20	121	5	0
Oskaloosa	1,120	0	0	0	0	0	0	0	0	0	0
Oswego	1,841	1	0	0	0	1	12	4	7	1	0
Ottawa	12,729	29	0	5	2	22	331	94	229	8	3
Overbrook	1,065	1	0	0	0	1	16	4	11	1	0
Overland Park	174,473	289	2	60	38	189	4,015	468	3,237	310	38
Paola	5,638	10	0	1	0	9	214	42	164	8	1
Park City	7,343	25	0	3	0	22	152	25	116	11	0
Parsons	10,567	91	1	7	3	80	546	98	427	21	9
Peabody	1,218	2	0	0	0	2	25	9	16	0	0
Perry	935	0	0	0	0	0	3	0	3	0	0
Prairie Village	21,583	24	0	5	6	13	271	64	194	13	5
Pratt	6,878	20	0	2	0	18	210	40	161	9	4
Rose Hill	3,956	1	0	1	0	0	85	8	72	5	1
Rossville	1,158	0	0	0	0	0	6	0	5	1	0
Russell	4,535	21	0	0	0	21	58	15	41	2	3
Sabetha	2,587	5	0	1	0	4	18	8	7	3	0
Salina	48,010	164	3	40	26	95	2,271	420	1,776	75	32
Scott City	3,840	6	0	1	0	5	44	6	35	3	2
Sedgwick	1,706	0	0	0	0	0	13	2	9	2	0

[1] If a blank is presented in the arson column, it indicates that the FBI did not receive 12 complete months of arson data for that agency.

[2] Because of changes in the state/local agency's reporting practices, figures are not comparable to previous years' data.

Table II-8. Offenses Known to Law Enforcement, by Selected State and City, 2011—*Continued*

(Number.)

State/City	Population	Violent crime	Murder and non-negligent man-slaughter	Forcible rape	Robbery	Aggravated assault	Property crime	Burglary	Larceny-theft	Motor vehicle theft	Arson[1]
Kansas—*Continued*											
Shawnee	62,604	107	1	16	15	75	1,230	159	942	129	12
South Hutchinson	2,473	6	0	0	0	6	80	5	69	6	0
Spearville	778	0	0	0	0	0	18	5	12	1	0
Spring Hill	5,472	12	0	0	1	11	122	15	105	2	4
Sterling	2,343	3	0	1	0	2	48	15	32	1	0
Tonganoxie	5,028	10	0	0	0	10	77	8	64	5	1
Topeka	128,283	698	15	53	235	395	7,529	1,727	5,213	589	
Ulysses	6,200	11	0	0	0	11	75	26	45	4	1
Valley Center	6,865	9	0	0	1	8	112	24	80	8	1
Wa Keeney	1,874	4	0	1	0	3	9	2	7	0	0
Wathena	1,373	3	0	1	0	2	36	6	29	1	1
Waverly	596	0	0	0	0	0	2	0	2	0	0
Wellington	8,224	35	2	6	2	25	414	100	292	22	2
Wellsville	1,869	9	0	0	0	9	35	5	29	1	1
Westwood	2,056	2	0	0	1	1	47	7	36	4	0
Wichita	384,796	2,950	25	238	490	2,197	19,456	4,005	13,550	1,901	139
Winchester	554	0	0	0	0	0	4	0	4	0	0
Winfield	12,379	45	0	2	1	42	446	89	338	19	2
Yates Center	1,426	6	0	0	0	6	15	8	7	0	1
Kentucky											
Albany	2,047	1	0	0	0	1	10	4	6	0	0
Alexandria	8,536	4	0	1	1	2	212	31	177	4	1
Anchorage	2,364	1	0	0	0	1	56	11	45	0	0
Ashland	21,834	70	0	8	36	26	1,309	344	920	45	6
Auburn	1,349	0	0	0	0	0	8	4	3	1	1
Audubon Park	1,483	2	0	0	1	1	62	17	43	2	0
Augusta	1,198	0	0	0	0	0	15	4	11	0	0
Barbourville	3,187	5	0	0	3	2	43	11	28	4	0
Bardstown	11,781	27	0	10	8	9	363	101	256	6	0
Bardwell	728	0	0	0	0	0	1	1	0	0	0
Beattyville	1,316	0	0	0	0	0	12	1	9	2	0
Beaver Dam	3,433	3	0	1	1	1	40	5	30	5	0
Bellefonte	894	0	0	0	0	0	3	1	2	0	0
Bellevue	5,996	8	0	5	2	1	319	70	238	11	0
Benham	503	2	0	1	0	1	6	4	2	0	0
Benton	4,379	6	0	4	1	1	104	22	79	3	1
Berea	13,655	24	1	4	16	3	599	176	389	34	2
Bowling Green	58,468	167	3	31	60	73	2,716	462	2,127	127	1
Brandenburg	2,661	1	0	0	0	1	40	10	23	7	0
Brownsville	842	0	0	0	0	0	15	5	9	1	0
Burkesville	1,532	0	0	0	0	0	9	6	3	0	0
Burnside	615	1	0	0	1	0	47	9	35	3	0
Cadiz	2,576	3	0	0	3	0	138	43	92	3	0
Calhoun	768	0	0	0	0	0	0	0	0	0	0
Calvert City	2,584	4	0	0	0	4	38	14	22	2	0
Campbellsville	9,171	26	0	6	7	13	381	101	272	8	1
Carlisle	2,024	6	1	0	2	3	44	17	24	3	0
Carrollton	3,965	4	0	1	0	3	83	22	54	7	1
Catlettsburg	1,869	3	0	1	1	1	70	21	47	2	0
Cave City	2,255	6	0	0	1	5	33	10	21	2	0
Central City	6,019	2	0	0	0	2	76	2	72	2	0
Clarkson	881	0	0	0	0	0	2	0	2	0	0
Clay City	1,084	3	0	0	0	3	31	11	18	2	0
Cloverport	1,160	0	0	0	0	0	4	0	4	0	0
Coal Run Village	1,718	1	0	0	1	0	17	8	9	0	0
Cold Spring	5,953	3	0	1	2	0	172	13	151	8	1
Columbia	4,483	3	0	2	0	1	40	13	24	3	1
Corbin	7,354	16	0	2	4	10	322	80	227	15	5
Covington	40,921	306	1	36	147	122	2,398	723	1,472	203	16
Cumberland	2,252	7	0	1	0	6	31	21	9	1	0
Cynthiana	6,446	25	0	1	10	14	287	50	230	7	1
Danville	16,330	50	0	5	24	21	646	117	504	25	4
Dawson Springs	2,783	3	0	0	1	2	42	10	32	0	0
Dayton	5,375	18	0	4	6	8	254	82	165	7	2
Dry Ridge	2,206	1	0	0	1	0	20	6	13	1	0
Earlington	1,423	0	0	0	0	0	2	0	1	1	0
Eddyville	2,572	1	0	0	0	1	29	4	23	2	0
Edgewood	8,634	1	0	0	0	1	123	17	103	3	1
Edmonton	1,606	0	0	0	0	0	8	4	4	0	0
Elizabethtown	28,728	43	2	17	18	6	1,022	131	853	38	13
Elkton	2,076	3	0	0	0	3	27	12	15	0	0
Elsmere	8,509	12	0	1	5	6	211	90	110	11	2
Eminence	2,515	10	0	1	2	7	41	10	30	1	0

[1] If a blank is presented in the arson column, it indicates that the FBI did not receive 12 complete months of arson data for that agency.

Table II-8.　Offenses Known to Law Enforcement, by Selected State and City, 2011—*Continued*

(Number.)

State/City	Population	Violent crime	Murder and non-negligent man-slaughter	Forcible rape	Robbery	Aggravated assault	Property crime	Burglary	Larceny-theft	Motor vehicle theft	Arson[1]
Kentucky—*Continued*											
Erlanger	22,034	40	0	8	22	10	575	124	430	21	1
Evarts	969	0	0	0	0	0	1	0	0	1	0
Falmouth	2,184	2	0	1	0	1	58	14	43	1	0
Ferguson	930	0	0	0	0	0	4	4	0	0	0
Flatwoods	7,474	4	0	1	3	0	124	53	68	3	0
Fleming-Neon	775	0	0	0	0	0	3	2	1	0	0
Flemingsburg	2,676	2	0	0	1	1	35	14	20	1	0
Florence	30,158	68	0	9	36	23	1,635	193	1,387	55	4
Fort Mitchell	8,264	6	0	2	2	2	185	30	152	3	0
Fort Thomas	16,438	7	0	1	4	2	242	50	169	23	0
Fort Wright	5,763	10	0	3	7	0	309	31	268	10	0
Frankfort	25,703	102	0	22	49	31	1,337	383	877	77	3
Franklin	8,466	29	0	7	16	6	384	98	268	18	2
Fulton	2,462	9	0	0	4	5	114	26	81	7	4
Gamaliel	379	0	0	0	0	0	1	0	1	0	0
Georgetown	29,299	121	0	17	9	95	1,103	166	910	27	
Glasgow	14,125	24	0	4	1	19	287	47	224	16	5
Graymoor-Devondale	2,890	0	0	0	0	0	53	17	33	3	0
Grayson	4,246	6	0	1	3	2	102	25	72	5	2
Greensburg	2,178	0	0	0	0	0	29	6	23	0	0
Greenup	1,196	0	0	0	0	0	2	0	2	0	0
Greenville	4,342	1	0	0	0	1	34	8	19	7	0
Guthrie	1,429	1	0	0	1	0	11	6	4	1	0
Hardinsburg	2,359	0	0	0	0	0	10	5	3	2	0
Harlan	1,757	4	0	1	0	3	69	15	52	2	0
Harrodsburg	8,398	17	0	1	7	9	153	59	89	5	1
Hartford	2,690	1	0	0	0	1	10	5	3	2	0
Hawesville	952	0	0	0	0	0	5	2	3	0	0
Hazard	4,487	19	0	4	7	8	371	45	315	11	0
Henderson	28,956	61	1	10	14	36	922	174	702	46	1
Heritage Creek	1,083	0	0	0	0	0	12	1	9	2	0
Highland Heights Southgate	10,800	38	0	1	3	34	156	44	105	7	4
Hillview	8,228	7	0	0	5	2	241	92	134	15	0
Hodgenville	3,228	3	0	2	1	0	33	16	15	2	0
Hopkinsville	31,795	113	1	28	47	37	1,307	383	866	58	11
Horse Cave	2,327	1	0	0	0	1	1	1	0	0	0
Hurstbourne Acres	1,824	2	0	0	1	1	12	3	8	1	0
Independence	24,928	18	0	4	5	9	299	95	189	15	0
Indian Hills	2,888	0	0	0	0	0	64	18	44	2	0
Inez	722	1	0	0	0	1	19	4	13	2	0
Irvine	2,734	4	0	0	1	3	41	11	28	2	0
Irvington	1,189	0	0	0	0	0	2	2	0	0	0
Jackson	2,246	2	0	2	0	0	50	13	35	2	0
Jamestown	1,806	1	0	0	0	1	19	4	12	3	0
Jeffersontown	26,779	45	0	6	30	9	614	157	422	35	0
Jenkins	2,218	1	0	0	0	1	4	2	1	1	0
La Center	1,016	0	0	0	0	0	0	0	0	0	0
La Grange	8,138	11	0	1	5	5	175	40	128	7	0
Lakeside Park-Crestview Hills	5,856	2	0	1	0	1	139	18	115	6	0
Lancaster	3,466	4	0	0	1	3	90	37	49	4	0
Lawrenceburg	10,578	7	0	4	1	2	121	25	90	6	0
Lebanon	5,577	19	0	2	6	11	173	82	85	6	1
Lebanon Junction	1,826	1	0	0	1	0	24	9	13	2	0
Leitchfield	6,745	3	0	2	0	1	153	45	101	7	0
Lewisburg	816	1	0	0	0	1	3	2	1	0	0
Lewisport	1,682	0	0	0	0	0	9	3	6	0	0
Lexington[2]	297,847	1,358	14	105	496	743	12,431	2,724	9,036	671	30
Liberty	2,183	3	0	0	0	3	15	2	10	3	0
London	8,048	18	1	4	8	5	395	71	307	17	1
Louisa	2,484	0	0	0	0	0	43	17	24	2	0
Louisville Metro	665,152	4,086	48	227	1,643	2,168	31,949	8,127	21,560	2,262	237
Loyall	1,471	0	0	0	0	0	11	3	7	1	0
Ludlow	4,437	19	0	6	8	5	256	92	154	10	2
Lynnview	920	0	0	0	0	0	2	2	0	0	0
Madisonville	19,726	24	0	9	5	10	656	138	491	27	5
Manchester	1,264	4	0	0	4	0	79	16	63	0	0
Marion	3,060	1	0	0	0	1	57	14	40	3	0
Mayfield	10,093	26	1	8	8	9	225	75	140	10	0
Maysville	9,073	21	0	5	9	7	456	101	337	18	1
Meadow Vale	741	0	0	0	0	0	8	1	7	0	0
Middlesboro	10,405	32	0	3	16	13	671	93	560	18	2
Millersburg	797	0	0	0	0	0	6	0	6	0	0
Monticello	6,231	12	1	2	5	4	209	67	131	11	1
Morehead	6,892	5	0	2	2	1	193	34	156	3	1

[1] If a blank is presented in the arson column, it indicates that the FBI did not receive 12 complete months of arson data for that agency.

[2] Because of changes in the state/local agency's reporting practices, figures are not comparable to previous years' data.

Table II-8. Offenses Known to Law Enforcement, by Selected State and City, 2011—*Continued*

(Number.)

State/City	Population	Violent crime	Murder and non-negligent man-slaughter	Forcible rape	Robbery	Aggravated assault	Property crime	Burglary	Larceny-theft	Motor vehicle theft	Arson[1]
Kentucky—*Continued*											
Morganfield	3,308	5	0	0	2	3	113	27	83	3	0
Morgantown	2,411	0	0	0	0	0	9	6	3	0	0
Mortons Gap	869	0	0	0	0	0	4	0	4	0	0
Mount Sterling	6,943	35	0	7	18	10	549	135	403	11	1
Mount Vernon	2,494	1	0	0	0	1	42	16	24	2	0
Mount Washington	9,180	17	0	4	9	4	238	90	141	7	0
Muldraugh	954	1	0	0	0	1	22	4	16	2	0
Munfordville	1,626	2	0	1	0	1	25	9	14	2	0
Murray	17,864	20	0	3	9	8	594	145	422	27	1
Newport	15,379	54	2	7	26	19	1,154	263	831	60	4
Nicholasville	28,209	79	0	11	42	26	1,395	358	991	46	8
Nortonville	1,212	0	0	0	0	0	6	1	4	1	0
Oak Grove	7,541	25	0	4	10	11	402	147	244	11	2
Olive Hill	1,610	3	0	0	3	0	19	4	13	2	0
Owensboro	57,661	143	1	46	37	59	2,323	513	1,711	99	6
Owenton	1,336	1	0	0	1	0	18	6	12	0	0
Owingsville	1,541	0	0	0	0	0	30	10	19	1	0
Paducah	25,197	80	4	18	28	30	1,148	139	959	50	6
Paintsville	3,483	5	0	2	1	2	152	24	122	6	0
Paris	8,612	33	0	2	22	9	436	142	283	11	0
Park Hills	2,991	6	0	0	1	5	88	28	51	9	0
Pewee Valley	1,466	0	0	0	0	0	5	4	1	0	0
Pikeville	6,951	7	0	2	2	3	440	58	367	15	3
Pineville	1,744	4	0	0	1	3	67	6	60	1	2
Pioneer Village	2,044	0	0	0	0	0	31	10	20	1	0
Prestonsburg	3,277	10	1	2	1	6	84	15	62	7	1
Princeton	6,373	19	0	5	3	11	180	71	97	12	0
Prospect	4,730	0	0	0	0	0	1	0	0	1	0
Providence	3,215	1	0	1	0	0	18	5	10	3	0
Raceland	2,441	0	0	0	0	0	40	18	21	1	0
Radcliff	21,838	59	0	15	27	17	540	100	422	18	6
Ravenna	609	0	0	0	0	0	3	2	1	0	0
Richmond	31,581	114	0	13	56	45	1,854	439	1,369	46	2
Russell	3,403	3	0	1	2	0	96	23	71	2	1
Russell Springs	2,458	3	0	0	1	2	61	7	50	4	0
Russellville	7,008	17	0	5	6	6	264	74	178	12	2
Salyersville	1,896	0	0	0	0	0	2	0	1	1	0
Science Hill	698	0	0	0	0	0	6	1	5	0	0
Shelbyville	14,142	29	0	3	14	12	322	100	204	18	4
Shepherdsville	11,300	26	0	9	8	9	377	143	215	19	1
Shively	15,369	84	2	11	47	24	720	259	387	74	0
Silver Grove	1,110	0	0	0	0	0	27	13	14	0	0
Simpsonville	2,501	1	0	0	1	0	19	1	18	0	0
Smiths Grove	719	0	0	0	0	0	8	0	7	1	0
Somerset	11,273	26	1	6	12	7	698	114	572	12	1
South Shore	1,130	0	0	0	0	0	1	0	1	0	0
Springfield	2,536	2	0	1	0	1	22	12	10	0	0
Stanford	3,511	1	0	0	1	0	45	10	35	0	0
Stanton	2,752	0	0	0	0	0	60	26	30	4	0
St. Matthews	17,593	32	0	1	16	15	682	128	531	23	0
Strathmoor Village	652	0	0	0	0	0	5	2	3	0	0
Sturgis	1,911	0	0	0	0	0	5	2	3	0	0
Taylor Mill	6,650	4	0	1	2	1	104	27	73	4	1
Taylorsville	768	3	0	2	0	1	41	13	26	2	1
Tompkinsville	2,419	2	0	0	0	2	3	2	1	0	0
Trenton	387	0	0	0	0	0	2	1	1	0	0
Uniontown	1,009	2	0	0	0	2	20	8	12	0	0
Vanceburg	1,528	3	0	0	0	3	17	1	15	1	0
Versailles	8,627	26	1	4	6	15	739	222	494	23	3
Villa Hills	7,541	0	0	0	0	0	28	6	17	5	0
Vine Grove	4,551	2	0	0	0	2	70	18	49	3	0
Warsaw	1,626	1	0	0	0	1	21	8	12	1	0
West Liberty	3,459	4	0	1	2	1	64	16	46	2	0
West Point	803	0	0	0	0	0	31	12	16	3	0
Wheelwright	785	0	0	0	0	0	0	0	0	0	0
Whitesburg	2,154	0	0	0	0	0	7	2	5	0	0
Wilder	3,056	3	0	1	2	0	113	11	95	7	0
Williamsburg	5,281	6	0	1	3	2	132	47	84	1	2
Williamstown	3,952	6	0	0	0	6	81	15	59	7	1
Wilmore	3,711	1	0	0	0	1	117	32	79	6	0
Winchester	18,495	147	2	7	32	106	976	210	756	10	6
Worthington	1,620	3	0	3	0	0	8	5	3	0	0

[1] If a blank is presented in the arson column, it indicates that the FBI did not receive 12 complete months of arson data for that agency.

Table II-8. Offenses Known to Law Enforcement, by Selected State and City, 2011—*Continued*

(Number.)

State/City	Population	Violent crime	Murder and non-negligent man-slaughter	Forcible rape	Robbery	Aggravated assault	Property crime	Burglary	Larceny-theft	Motor vehicle theft	Arson[1]
Louisiana											
Abbeville	12,369	106	2	4	17	83	522	182	324	16	
Addis	3,626	4	0	0	0	4	0	0	0	0	0
Alexandria	48,159	651	2	11	159	479	3,560	869	2,517	174	
Amite	4,179	85	1	4	13	67	502	106	380	16	2
Baker	14,022	26	1	2	11	12	462	105	343	14	0
Basile	1,838	1	0	0	0	1	12	3	9	0	0
Bastrop	11,469	135	1	2	31	101	1,318	436	842	40	8
Baton Rouge	231,592	2,468	64	51	893	1,460	12,666	4,220	7,946	500	179
Bernice	1,704	1	0	0	0	1	3	0	3	0	0
Berwick	4,991	4	0	1	0	3	63	15	46	2	0
Bogalusa	12,344	140	2	7	30	101	901	341	520	40	3
Broussard	8,272	20	0	5	1	14	442	127	315	0	
Brusly	2,613	0	0	0	0	0	20	4	15	1	0
Carencro	7,595	52	0	2	9	41	288	76	199	13	0
Clinton	1,668	13	0	0	0	13	29	10	18	1	0
Coushatta	1,982	20	0	0	2	18	50	6	44	0	0
Covington	8,845	36	0	3	4	29	286	50	227	9	0
Crowley	13,386	106	3	1	11	91	520	170	330	20	0
Denham Springs	10,308	72	0	5	18	49	901	127	748	26	0
De Ridder	10,675	78	1	1	5	71	241	65	176	0	1
Erath	2,133	11	0	1	0	10	43	29	7	7	
Eunice	10,493	138	2	7	18	111	688	201	468	19	0
Ferriday	3,543	28	0	2	3	23	114	114	0	0	0
Folsom	723	2	0	0	0	2	21	6	15	0	0
Franklin	7,730	62	1	1	4	56	471	119	350	2	2
Franklinton	3,892	23	0	2	5	16	197	58	133	6	0
French Settlement	1,126	1	0	0	0	1	30	4	26	0	0
Georgetown	330	0	0	0	0	0	2	1	0	1	0
Glenmora	1,354	12	0	1	1	10	23	5	14	4	
Gonzales	9,870	43	1	6	3	33	713	62	635	16	0
Grambling	4,994	20	0	1	4	15	93	93	0	0	0
Gramercy	3,646	19	0	0	1	18	89	12	75	2	0
Greenwood	3,248	7	0	1	1	5	78	23	47	8	0
Gretna	17,898	109	4	10	29	66	629	148	430	51	2
Hammond	20,202	322	2	15	80	225	2,311	879	1,358	74	0
Harahan	9,362	15	0	1	2	12	182	48	126	8	0
Homer	3,267	23	0	1	1	21	119	54	65	0	0
Houma	34,035	212	1	17	76	118	1,550	268	1,234	48	9
Independence	1,680	21	0	1	5	15	135	40	91	4	1
Jeanerette	5,581	24	0	0	4	20	139	50	83	6	0
Jena	3,429	5	0	0	0	5	1	1	0	0	0
Jennings	10,478	41	2	1	4	34	304	50	249	5	2
Kenner	67,312	161	9	10	69	73	2,604	414	2,040	150	21
Kentwood	2,218	19	0	1	7	11	142	40	101	1	0
Kinder	2,500	8	1	0	1	6	84	4	77	3	0
Lafayette	121,726	843	6	15	232	590	6,511	1,194	5,040	277	50
Lake Arthur	2,763	10	2	2	1	5	58	15	42	1	1
Leesville	6,672	35	0	2	3	30	320	26	288	6	2
Lutcher	3,592	11	0	0	0	11	38	16	21	1	0
Mamou	3,272	4	0	1	0	3	105	10	91	4	0
Mandeville	11,666	31	1	2	5	23	377	52	318	7	0
Marksville	5,754	80	0	0	6	74	408	77	322	9	
Monroe	49,261	834	5	23	113	693	3,910	1,340	2,467	103	0
Montgomery	737	1	0	0	0	1	2	0	2	0	0
Morgan City	12,517	56	0	5	12	39	414	52	352	10	
Napoleonville	666	1	0	0	0	1	1	1	0	0	0
Natchitoches	18,491	163	3	10	19	131	1,192	509	661	22	7
New Orleans	346,974	2,748	200	163	1,059	1,326	14,013	3,857	7,616	2,540	
Norwood	325	0	0	0	0	0	1	1	0	0	0
Oil City	1,017	0	0	0	0	0	17	9	5	3	0
Olla	1,398	1	0	0	0	1	35	11	24	0	0
Opelousas	16,786	309	2	17	48	242	1,379	352	970	57	1
Pearl River	2,529	23	1	3	2	17	78	12	63	3	0
Plaquemine	7,184	74	1	0	7	66	422	62	355	5	0
Pollock	473	2	0	0	0	2	12	2	10	0	0
Ponchatoula	6,619	65	0	4	7	54	516	183	325	8	0
Port Allen	5,227	20	2	0	2	16	203	52	144	7	0
Rayville	3,729	29	0	1	1	27	274	58	208	8	0
Scott	8,693	30	0	2	5	23	234	49	173	12	0
Shreveport	201,134	1,544	17	121	355	1,051	9,584	2,775	6,371	438	86
Slidell	27,316	123	1	13	32	77	1,521	232	1,237	52	0
Sorrento	1,414	2	0	0	0	2	12	1	11	0	0

[1] If a blank is presented in the arson column, it indicates that the FBI did not receive 12 complete months of arson data for that agency.

Table II-8.   Offenses Known to Law Enforcement, by Selected State and City, 2011—*Continued*

(Number.)

State/City	Population	Violent crime	Murder and non-negligent man-slaughter	Forcible rape	Robbery	Aggravated assault	Property crime	Burglary	Larceny-theft	Motor vehicle theft	Arson[1]
Louisiana—*Continued*											
Springfield	491	4	0	0	1	3	6	2	4	0	0
Sterlington	1,609	6	0	2	0	4	9	1	8	0	0
St. Francisville	1,781	18	0	0	1	17	44	5	39	0	0
St. Gabriel	6,738	37	0	1	1	35	117	59	54	4	0
St. Martinville	6,170	48	0	0	1	47	119	28	87	4	0
Sulphur	20,597	184	1	9	8	166	1,062	316	734	12	6
Tallulah	7,402	75	2	0	3	70	284	76	203	5	0
Thibodaux	14,699	70	1	8	8	53	588	102	473	13	0
Tickfaw	700	1	0	0	1	0	15	0	15	0	0
Vinton	3,241	10	0	0	0	10	72	19	50	3	0
Walker	6,194	54	0	4	8	42	340	61	269	10	1
Westwego	8,612	30	0	2	6	22	246	61	177	8	0
Wilson	600	0	0	0	0	0	1	1	0	0	0
Zachary	15,097	88	1	1	4	82	280	12	258	10	0
Maine											
Ashland	1,302	1	0	0	0	1	7	5	2	0	0
Auburn	23,052	43	0	7	23	13	1,094	200	876	18	3
Augusta	19,134	69	1	15	15	38	1,303	252	1,028	23	4
Baileyville	1,521	11	0	2	2	7	49	18	30	1	0
Bangor	33,035	69	2	9	35	23	1,672	249	1,389	34	1
Bar Harbor	5,234	1	0	1	0	0	104	6	95	3	0
Bath	8,513	2	0	0	1	1	341	37	293	11	2
Belfast	6,667	7	0	2	0	5	200	45	149	6	0
Berwick	7,245	3	0	0	1	2	160	41	114	5	6
Biddeford	21,274	79	0	14	21	44	1,169	244	908	17	6
Boothbay Harbor	2,165	2	0	0	0	2	61	15	46	0	0
Brewer	9,481	6	0	0	3	3	234	21	206	7	0
Bridgton	5,209	2	0	2	0	0	96	19	75	2	0
Brownville	1,250	4	0	0	0	4	14	7	7	0	0
Brunswick	20,275	18	0	8	3	7	609	124	456	29	4
Bucksport	4,923	21	0	4	0	17	111	31	78	2	1
Buxton	8,033	4	0	1	3	0	97	37	59	1	0
Calais	3,123	12	0	3	1	8	145	16	126	3	0
Camden	4,849	5	0	0	3	2	104	17	85	2	0
Cape Elizabeth	9,014	1	0	0	1	0	108	16	90	2	0
Caribou	8,188	4	0	0	3	1	164	36	121	7	1
Carrabassett Valley	781	1	0	1	0	0	50	4	46	0	0
Clinton	3,486	3	0	0	0	3	67	24	39	4	0
Cumberland	7,210	6	0	3	0	3	61	11	49	1	0
Damariscotta	2,218	0	0	0	0	0	57	9	48	0	0
Dexter	3,894	7	3	1	0	3	99	19	70	10	0
Dixfield	2,550	1	0	1	0	0	69	17	48	4	0
Dover-Foxcroft	4,212	18	2	2	0	14	125	26	97	2	0
East Millinocket	3,072	0	0	0	0	0	18	1	15	2	0
Eastport	1,331	1	0	0	0	1	9	4	5	0	0
Eliot	6,203	2	0	0	0	2	32	14	18	0	0
Ellsworth	7,740	4	0	0	1	3	277	41	225	11	0
Fairfield	6,734	2	0	1	0	1	261	49	204	8	1
Falmouth	11,184	4	0	2	1	1	187	21	164	2	1
Farmington	7,759	13	1	6	3	3	274	40	232	2	0
Fort Fairfield	3,496	8	0	1	0	7	33	10	22	1	0
Fort Kent	4,096	1	0	0	0	1	10	1	9	0	0
Freeport	7,878	6	0	0	2	4	181	16	162	3	1
Fryeburg	3,449	3	0	3	0	0	36	13	22	1	0
Gardiner	5,799	11	0	5	3	3	169	43	126	0	2
Gorham	16,379	18	0	6	6	6	200	61	126	13	7
Gouldsboro	1,737	0	0	0	0	0	8	3	5	0	0
Greenville	1,646	4	0	1	0	3	38	7	31	0	0
Hallowell	2,381	1	0	0	1	0	82	17	64	1	0
Hampden	7,256	0	0	0	0	0	74	18	54	2	0
Holden	3,076	0	0	0	0	0	49	15	34	0	0
Houlton	6,122	2	0	1	0	1	146	24	119	3	0
Islesboro	566	0	0	0	0	0	5	5	0	0	0
Jay	4,850	11	0	5	0	6	106	37	64	5	2
Kennebunk	10,797	5	0	2	1	2	150	46	104	0	2
Kennebunkport	3,474	0	0	0	0	0	70	9	60	1	0
Kittery	9,489	4	0	1	1	2	195	21	170	4	0
Lewiston	36,587	77	3	13	29	32	1,351	387	943	21	14
Limestone	2,314	4	0	1	0	3	35	16	19	0	0
Lincoln	5,084	1	0	0	1	0	168	43	120	5	0
Lincolnville	2,164	6	0	1	0	5	26	14	12	0	0
Lisbon	9,008	4	0	2	0	2	140	42	93	5	1
Livermore Falls	3,187	8	0	3	3	2	93	28	64	1	4

[1] If a blank is presented in the arson column, it indicates that the FBI did not receive 12 complete months of arson data for that agency.

Table II-8.   Offenses Known to Law Enforcement, by Selected State and City, 2011—*Continued*

(Number.)

State/City	Population	Violent crime	Murder and non-negligent man-slaughter	Forcible rape	Robbery	Aggravated assault	Property crime	Burglary	Larceny-theft	Motor vehicle theft	Arson[1]
Maine—*Continued*											
Machias	2,221	7	0	2	1	4	70	13	57	0	0
Madawaska	4,034	2	0	0	0	2	31	6	25	0	0
Madison	4,854	5	0	2	1	2	150	37	106	7	0
Mechanic Falls	3,031	2	0	0	1	1	60	14	43	3	0
Mexico	2,681	4	0	2	1	1	100	29	70	1	1
Milbridge	1,353	0	0	0	0	0	11	4	7	0	0
Millinocket	4,505	3	0	0	1	2	108	33	74	1	0
Milo	2,340	8	0	1	0	7	65	23	39	3	0
Monmouth	4,103	3	0	2	0	1	65	18	45	2	0
Mount Desert	2,053	1	0	0	0	1	41	5	36	0	0
Newport	3,275	4	0	1	1	2	102	23	77	2	0
North Berwick	4,575	1	0	0	0	1	76	36	36	4	1
Norway	5,013	2	0	1	0	1	199	36	160	3	2
Oakland	6,239	4	0	3	0	1	162	23	135	4	0
Ogunquit	892	0	0	0	0	0	26	8	18	0	0
Old Orchard Beach	8,623	9	0	1	3	5	406	123	270	13	3
Old Town	7,839	2	0	1	0	1	213	48	161	4	0
Orono	10,361	2	0	0	1	1	198	28	168	2	1
Oxford	4,109	4	0	3	0	1	175	18	156	1	0
Paris	5,182	7	0	4	1	2	66	13	52	1	0
Phippsburg	2,216	0	0	0	0	0	11	6	4	1	0
Pittsfield	4,214	2	0	0	1	1	85	17	62	6	0
Portland	66,185	190	2	36	92	60	2,639	441	2,096	102	18
Presque Isle	9,691	17	0	4	4	9	445	65	380	0	1
Rangeley	1,168	1	0	0	0	1	27	8	19	0	0
Richmond	3,411	0	0	0	0	0	64	24	38	2	0
Rockland	7,296	8	0	2	3	3	357	34	317	6	1
Rockport	3,330	1	0	0	1	0	38	6	31	1	0
Rumford	5,840	10	0	7	2	1	205	50	152	3	0
Sabattus	4,875	3	0	1	1	1	76	24	50	2	0
Saco	18,480	61	0	5	6	50	568	150	394	24	7
Sanford	20,795	56	0	22	8	26	800	124	655	21	3
Scarborough	18,917	10	0	3	4	3	509	81	417	11	1
Searsport	2,615	1	0	1	0	0	59	20	38	1	1
Skowhegan	8,588	18	1	10	2	5	418	53	349	16	1
South Berwick	7,219	0	0	0	0	0	67	18	48	1	3
South Portland	24,999	60	0	5	12	43	860	81	760	19	2
Southwest Harbor	1,764	1	0	0	0	1	38	4	34	0	0
Swan's Island	332	0	0	0	0	0	0	0	0	0	0
Thomaston	2,781	2	0	1	0	1	90	14	71	5	0
Topsham	8,783	2	0	0	0	2	175	29	139	7	0
Van Buren	2,171	1	0	1	0	0	6	1	5	0	0
Veazie	1,919	1	0	1	0	0	32	4	27	1	0
Waldoboro	5,074	2	0	2	0	0	79	23	54	2	0
Washburn	1,687	1	0	0	0	1	36	11	25	0	0
Waterville	15,720	47	0	17	11	19	665	85	569	11	6
Wells	9,588	4	0	0	2	2	144	46	96	2	0
Westbrook	17,492	26	1	8	10	7	641	91	524	26	5
Wilton	4,115	15	0	8	1	6	141	55	84	2	0
Windham	16,999	11	0	2	3	6	361	69	286	6	2
Winslow	7,793	11	1	4	2	4	140	24	105	11	2
Winter Harbor	516	1	0	0	0	1	3	0	3	0	0
Winthrop	6,091	6	0	1	2	3	171	47	117	7	0
Wiscasset	3,732	1	0	1	0	0	66	18	48	0	0
Yarmouth	8,348	1	0	0	0	1	75	12	61	2	0
York	12,527	5	0	1	1	3	183	57	125	1	1
Maryland											
Aberdeen	15,101	79	1	4	34	40	590	102	458	30	9
Annapolis	38,758	176	1	8	71	96	1,034	186	779	69	8
Baltimore	626,848	8,885	196	341	3,457	4,891	29,824	8,615	17,010	4,199	307
Baltimore City Sheriff	0	0	0	0	0	0	0	0	0	0	0
Bel Air	10,216	50	0	0	7	43	377	32	339	6	4
Berlin	4,528	4	0	1	1	2	140	29	111	0	0
Berwyn Heights	3,153	4	0	0	1	3	77	13	58	6	0
Bladensburg	9,235	99	2	6	40	51	444	100	234	110	0
Boonsboro	3,368	1	0	0	0	1	21	7	11	3	0
Bowie	55,246	79	0	2	45	32	834	185	589	60	1
Brentwood	3,075	2	0	0	0	2	18	3	14	1	0
Brunswick	5,926	3	0	0	0	3	79	17	59	3	0
Cambridge	12,443	97	0	7	16	74	639	111	506	22	0
Capitol Heights	4,378	17	1	2	4	10	82	30	32	20	3
Centreville	4,326	3	0	0	1	2	65	10	53	2	0
Chestertown	5,302	40	0	4	7	29	148	52	91	5	0

[1] If a blank is presented in the arson column, it indicates that the FBI did not receive 12 complete months of arson data for that agency.

Table II-8.   Offenses Known to Law Enforcement, by Selected State and City, 2011—*Continued*

(Number.)

State/City	Population	Violent crime	Murder and non-negligent man-slaughter	Forcible rape	Robbery	Aggravated assault	Property crime	Burglary	Larceny-theft	Motor vehicle theft	Arson[1]
Maryland—*Continued*											
Cheverly	6,232	26	0	0	8	18	181	44	106	31	0
Chevy Chase Village	1,972	0	0	0	0	0	85	14	66	5	0
Colmar Manor	1,417	12	0	1	6	5	41	5	34	2	0
Cottage City	1,317	6	0	1	1	4	41	10	24	7	0
Crisfield	2,752	13	0	1	2	10	48	10	38	0	0
Cumberland	21,057	153	0	16	42	95	1,425	319	1,081	25	6
Delmar	3,031	9	0	0	3	6	94	23	67	4	1
Denton	4,460	16	0	0	8	8	192	58	132	2	1
District Heights	5,892	19	0	0	7	12	187	37	117	33	0
Easton	16,096	61	0	4	18	39	543	114	417	12	2
Edmonston	1,459	5	1	0	2	2	70	11	47	12	0
Elkton	15,589	267	2	14	76	175	1,241	226	979	36	7
Fairmount Heights	1,508	1	0	0	0	1	16	6	4	6	0
Federalsburg	2,765	42	0	2	6	34	130	28	99	3	3
Forest Heights	2,470	17	2	0	5	10	72	44	25	3	0
Frederick	65,858	306	2	19	96	189	1,787	235	1,474	78	14
Frostburg	9,087	14	1	4	5	4	213	63	147	3	1
Fruitland	4,912	48	0	0	5	43	225	44	177	4	2
Glenarden	6,057	23	0	0	8	15	154	38	95	21	0
Greenbelt	23,287	133	0	7	90	36	965	254	596	115	0
Greensboro	1,949	6	0	0	1	5	65	25	37	3	0
Hagerstown	40,038	188	1	2	76	109	1,510	382	1,054	74	31
Hampstead	6,383	5	0	0	2	3	81	13	66	2	2
Hancock	1,560	18	0	0	0	18	63	8	52	3	1
Havre de Grace	13,075	49	0	4	8	37	338	51	275	12	2
Hurlock	2,112	10	0	2	0	8	103	43	56	4	0
Hyattsville	17,723	112	1	2	81	28	1,296	150	1,058	88	0
Landover Hills	1,703	8	0	0	3	5	35	7	19	9	0
La Plata	8,836	47	0	0	6	41	335	35	285	15	0
Laurel	25,353	177	1	4	50	122	889	145	622	122	2
Lonaconing	1,226	0	0	0	0	0	3	0	2	1	0
Luke	66	0	0	0	0	0	0	0	0	0	0
Manchester	4,854	3	0	0	0	3	46	12	32	2	2
Morningside	2,034	14	0	0	6	8	76	26	43	7	0
Mount Rainier	8,157	66	2	1	37	26	342	52	219	71	0
New Carrollton	12,250	51	1	0	23	27	302	82	175	45	0
North East	3,606	9	0	0	6	3	145	31	109	5	5
Oakland	1,943	1	0	0	0	1	32	1	31	0	0
Ocean City	7,169	93	0	4	20	69	1,336	189	1,135	12	2
Ocean Pines	11,821	5	0	0	2	3	121	25	93	3	0
Oxford	657	0	0	0	0	0	1	0	1	0	0
Perryville	4,402	5	0	0	1	4	123	23	91	9	0
Pocomoke City	4,224	44	0	0	2	42	191	39	148	4	2
Port Deposit	659	2	0	0	1	1	34	8	26	0	2
Preston	726	1	0	0	0	1	2	0	1	1	1
Princess Anne	3,321	27	1	1	11	14	120	34	84	2	1
Ridgely	1,655	16	0	0	3	13	103	23	80	0	3
Rising Sun	2,807	3	0	0	2	1	76	8	67	1	0
Riverdale Park	7,022	54	0	0	31	23	256	60	152	44	0
Rock Hall	1,322	0	0	0	0	0	39	16	23	0	0
Salisbury	30,631	369	1	23	74	271	1,832	402	1,369	61	8
Seat Pleasant	4,585	21	1	0	7	13	190	53	102	35	1
Smithsburg	3,003	2	0	0	1	1	18	4	14	0	0
Snow Hill	2,123	12	0	0	0	12	40	8	32	0	0
St. Michaels	1,039	8	0	0	3	5	45	10	35	0	0
Sykesville	4,478	1	0	0	0	1	49	7	41	1	1
Takoma Park	16,873	61	0	3	32	26	503	109	317	77	4
Taneytown	6,792	2	0	0	0	2	113	15	97	1	3
Thurmont	6,228	10	0	1	1	8	96	35	60	1	1
Trappe	1,087	0	0	0	0	0	22	1	21	0	1
University Park	2,572	1	0	0	1	0	67	6	56	5	0
Upper Marlboro	637	0	0	0	0	0	35	14	16	5	
Westminster	18,766	95	0	0	19	76	711	112	581	18	8
Massachusetts											
Abington	16,082	22	0	1	6	15	351	102	226	23	1
Acton	22,058	33	0	0	2	31	201	23	173	5	0
Acushnet	10,366	16	0	0	3	13	120	43	72	5	0
Adams	8,537	26	0	6	1	19	200	65	124	11	0
Agawam	28,611	41	0	5	3	33	199	55	114	30	5
Amesbury	16,382	28	0	4	2	22	249	43	190	16	0
Amherst	38,050	82	0	19	4	59	384	179	187	18	0
Andover	33,403	14	2	2	5	5	309	52	233	24	3
Arlington	43,105	52	0	2	7	43	626	133	458	35	1

[1] If a blank is presented in the arson column, it indicates that the FBI did not receive 12 complete months of arson data for that agency.

Table II-8.　Offenses Known to Law Enforcement, by Selected State and City, 2011—*Continued*

(Number.)

State/City	Population	Violent crime	Murder and non-negligent man-slaughter	Forcible rape	Robbery	Aggravated assault	Property crime	Burglary	Larceny-theft	Motor vehicle theft	Arson[1]
Massachusetts—*Continued*											
Ashburnham	6,118	10	0	2	0	8	68	18	48	2	0
Ashby	3,093	4	0	0	1	3	24	20	2	2	0
Ashfield	1,748	1	0	0	0	1	17	1	16	0	0
Ashland	16,694	19	0	3	2	14	160	53	98	9	1
Athol	11,655	54	0	6	4	44	296	89	197	10	1
Attleboro	43,859	168	1	7	20	140	927	249	607	71	3
Auburn	16,287	50	0	2	7	41	611	69	517	25	2
Avon	4,383	7	1	0	3	3	196	34	158	4	0
Ayer	7,472	19	0	2	1	16	177	89	86	2	2
Barnstable	45,468	303	1	28	32	242	1,278	360	855	63	4
Barre	5,431	29	0	1	0	28	108	35	71	2	0
Becket	1,790	1	0	0	0	1	57	47	10	0	0
Bedford	13,401	5	0	0	1	4	144	32	111	1	0
Bellingham	16,432	29	0	2	5	22	341	38	288	15	0
Belmont	24,880	23	0	5	3	15	289	94	180	15	0
Berkley	6,450	4	0	0	1	3	109	49	55	5	2
Bernardston	2,142	4	0	0	0	4	12	6	5	1	1
Beverly	39,743	92	1	2	9	80	743	130	584	29	2
Billerica	40,488	58	0	10	7	41	619	124	467	28	4
Blackstone	9,081	15	0	1	0	14	135	19	103	13	0
Boston	621,359	5,252	63	271	1,904	3,014	19,445	3,482	14,064	1,899	
Bourne	19,874	61	0	6	9	46	537	225	295	17	1
Boxborough	5,026	6	0	0	1	5	47	13	32	2	0
Boxford	8,014	1	0	0	1	0	28	13	15	0	0
Boylston	4,382	2	0	0	0	2	50	19	31	0	0
Brewster	9,880	25	0	5	2	18	223	59	159	5	0
Brockton	94,380	1,160	9	61	232	858	3,229	1,037	1,805	387	19
Brookline	59,090	124	0	1	29	94	832	178	634	20	0
Cambridge	105,803	479	5	24	152	298	3,159	539	2,465	155	8
Canton	21,692	26	0	0	4	22	301	75	210	16	2
Carlisle	4,882	0	0	0	0	0	19	12	7	0	0
Carver	11,579	30	0	2	2	26	271	95	166	10	6
Chatham	6,162	11	0	3	0	8	126	20	102	4	0
Chelmsford	34,008	32	0	1	4	27	520	60	441	19	1
Chelsea	35,391	617	2	33	228	354	1,353	394	770	189	4
Cheshire	3,255	3	0	0	0	3	6	2	4	0	
Chicopee	55,635	257	1	25	44	187	1,628	436	1,046	146	6
Chilmark	871	1	0	0	0	1	20	4	16	0	0
Cohasset	7,588	11	0	3	0	8	79	30	45	4	0
Cummington	877	0	0	0	0	0	3	3	0	0	0
Dalton	6,797	17	0	1	0	16	66	20	35	11	1
Danvers	26,654	60	1	1	10	48	852	88	739	25	3
Dartmouth	34,239	68	0	2	17	49	881	159	688	34	4
Dedham	24,880	21	0	0	3	18	670	72	573	25	0
Deerfield	5,156	13	0	0	1	12	100	49	50	1	0
Dennis	14,294	64	0	5	6	53	541	208	324	9	4
Dighton	7,129	4	0	2	0	2	38	15	21	2	0
Douglas	8,523	11	0	0	0	11	63	26	35	2	0
Dover	5,623	2	0	0	0	2	34	8	26	0	0
Dracut	29,637	13	0	1	11	1	274	12	232	30	1
Dudley	11,459	22	0	3	2	17	78	37	40	1	0
Duxbury	15,151	5	0	0	0	5	94	15	79	0	0
East Brookfield	2,196	1	0	0	1	0	41	13	23	5	0
Eastham	4,986	17	0	2	2	13	156	36	117	3	0
East Longmeadow	15,816	14	0	0	2	12	334	65	263	6	0
Easton	23,253	25	0	1	5	19	316	135	165	16	0
Edgartown	4,092	8	0	0	1	7	156	45	104	7	1
Egremont	1,232	3	0	0	0	3	21	4	17	0	0
Erving	1,811	1	0	0	0	1	53	18	33	2	0
Essex	3,525	3	0	1	1	1	40	14	26	0	0
Everett	41,921	195	0	25	58	112	1,056	241	681	134	3
Fairhaven	15,970	65	0	8	11	46	452	114	325	13	5
Fall River	89,399	1,089	2	52	274	761	3,187	863	2,027	297	35
Falmouth	31,723	157	0	12	26	119	1,067	581	447	39	6
Fitchburg	40,564	304	2	15	43	244	1,424	464	908	52	7
Framingham	68,734	187	0	6	21	160	1,126	212	830	84	0
Franklin	31,828	5	0	0	3	2	114	25	89	0	0
Freetown	8,924	15	0	0	1	14	165	62	97	6	2
Gardner	20,351	149	0	12	22	115	581	236	326	19	2
Georgetown	8,233	8	0	0	3	5	60	21	36	3	0
Gill	1,509	0	0	0	0	0	11	3	7	1	1
Gloucester	28,964	22	0	6	1	15	553	82	466	5	0
Grafton	17,873	20	0	2	1	17	135	43	87	5	2
Granby	6,278	7	0	0	1	6	65	12	53	0	2

[1] If a blank is presented in the arson column, it indicates that the FBI did not receive 12 complete months of arson data for that agency.

Table II-8.   Offenses Known to Law Enforcement, by Selected State and City, 2011—*Continued*

(Number.)

State/City	Population	Violent crime	Murder and non-negligent man-slaughter	Forcible rape	Robbery	Aggravated assault	Property crime	Burglary	Larceny-theft	Motor vehicle theft	Arson[1]
Massachusetts—*Continued*											
Granville	1,576	1	0	0	0	1	0	0	0	0	0
Great Barrington	7,147	19	0	4	4	11	168	43	120	5	4
Groton	10,711	0	0	0	0	0	19	6	13	0	0
Groveland	6,498	1	0	0	0	1	25	2	21	2	0
Hadley	5,282	10	0	2	1	7	254	31	221	2	1
Halifax	7,564	9	0	1	0	8	81	28	49	4	0
Hamilton	7,811	2	0	0	0	2	52	17	32	3	0
Hampden	5,170	4	0	0	2	2	65	22	41	2	0
Hanover	13,964	2	0	0	1	1	288	31	253	4	0
Hanson	10,271	44	0	6	2	36	131	29	93	9	1
Hardwick	3,008	8	0	0	0	8	49	12	37	0	2
Harvard	6,560	3	0	0	0	3	48	20	28	0	3
Harwich	12,318	42	0	4	3	35	283	144	132	7	5
Hatfield	3,299	3	0	0	0	3	18	6	12	0	0
Haverhill	61,250	362	0	18	55	289	1,461	462	853	146	14
Hinsdale	2,044	6	0	1	0	5	29	17	12	0	1
Holbrook	10,857	61	0	6	18	37	159	42	109	8	0
Holden	17,452	6	0	1	0	5	117	21	91	5	1
Holliston	13,630	6	0	0	0	6	85	17	64	4	0
Holyoke	40,123	404	4	34	75	291	2,421	420	1,829	172	15
Hopedale	5,947	13	0	3	0	10	64	17	45	2	0
Hopkinton	15,016	0	0	0	0	0	95	2	93	0	0
Hubbardston	4,409	16	0	1	0	15	44	22	21	1	0
Hudson	19,179	10	0	4	2	4	209	24	181	4	0
Ipswich	13,255	6	1	0	1	4	191	65	124	2	1
Kingston	12,706	16	0	3	2	11	246	42	192	12	0
Lakeville	10,667	11	0	1	1	9	162	77	79	6	0
Lancaster	8,104	14	0	3	5	6	90	29	55	6	2
Lawrence	76,843	764	10	12	244	498	2,481	682	773	1,026	
Lee	5,979	10	0	2	0	8	127	34	90	3	0
Leicester	11,037	14	0	2	2	10	181	43	121	17	1
Lenox	5,056	4	0	0	0	4	111	24	86	1	0
Leominster	41,007	248	1	17	26	204	1,260	243	947	70	5
Lexington	31,585	13	0	0	0	13	332	69	263	0	4
Lincoln	6,401	8	0	0	0	8	57	16	41	0	0
Littleton	8,978	10	0	1	0	9	93	27	64	2	0
Longmeadow	15,880	11	0	0	3	8	189	41	146	2	5
Lowell	107,167	795	3	36	168	588	3,101	914	1,941	246	33
Ludlow	21,232	11	0	0	9	2	317	76	219	22	0
Lunenburg	10,147	29	0	0	2	27	272	59	207	6	0
Lynn	90,880	804	3	29	181	591	2,620	718	1,559	343	7
Lynnfield	11,667	11	0	0	2	9	228	63	159	6	0
Malden	59,812	250	2	14	80	154	1,307	317	872	118	2
Mansfield	23,325	47	2	9	3	33	395	149	224	22	1
Marblehead	19,929	31	0	0	1	30	211	34	164	13	1
Marion	4,937	5	0	1	0	4	59	13	44	2	0
Marlborough	38,734	183	0	10	11	162	773	129	609	35	2
Mashpee	14,091	36	1	6	7	22	331	61	254	16	2
Mattapoisett	6,082	7	0	0	0	7	100	22	76	2	0
Maynard	10,168	25	1	1	0	23	93	18	67	8	1
Medfield	12,097	7	0	0	1	6	57	16	41	0	0
Medway	12,830	6	1	0	0	5	99	20	78	1	0
Melrose	27,147	46	0	2	14	30	305	62	221	22	1
Mendon	5,875	7	0	0	1	6	30	8	19	3	0
Methuen	47,543	87	0	1	30	56	990	201	685	104	0
Middleboro	23,257	95	1	6	9	79	445	118	307	20	3
Middleton	9,042	10	0	0	0	10	100	3	96	1	0
Millbury	13,342	26	0	1	2	23	309	51	240	18	3
Millville	3,209	3	0	0	0	3	21	6	13	2	0
Milton	27,168	26	0	1	6	19	356	84	258	14	
Monson	8,612	31	0	1	1	29	110	55	50	5	0
Montague	8,488	60	0	0	4	56	213	75	132	6	3
Nahant	3,431	4	0	0	0	4	35	10	25	0	0
Nantucket	10,234	24	0	1	3	20	320	54	258	8	2
Natick	33,207	45	0	4	5	36	637	52	567	18	1
Needham	29,060	4	0	0	0	4	249	30	211	8	0
New Bedford	95,649	1,093	4	59	294	736	3,329	969	2,018	342	30
Newbury	6,707	11	0	1	0	10	47	19	27	1	0
Newburyport	17,522	28	0	1	3	24	206	21	177	8	1
Newton	85,665	80	0	2	19	59	1,181	212	942	27	3
Norfolk	11,295	1	0	0	0	1	80	29	48	3	0
Northampton	28,723	102	0	13	10	79	783	152	610	21	1
North Andover	28,525	9	0	0	0	9	338	52	273	13	0
Northborough	14,241	15	0	1	0	14	130	31	96	3	0
Northbridge	15,803	26	0	2	2	22	280	67	208	5	1

[1] If a blank is presented in the arson column, it indicates that the FBI did not receive 12 complete months of arson data for that agency.

Table II-8. Offenses Known to Law Enforcement, by Selected State and City, 2011—*Continued*

(Number.)

State/City	Population	Violent crime	Murder and non-negligent man-slaughter	Forcible rape	Robbery	Aggravated assault	Property crime	Burglary	Larceny-theft	Motor vehicle theft	Arson[1]
Massachusetts—*Continued*											
North Brookfield	4,709	21	0	1	2	18	77	30	39	8	0
Northfield	3,050	2	0	0	1	1	32	12	18	2	0
North Reading	14,983	18	0	3	4	11	145	28	111	6	1
Norton	19,147	7	0	1	0	6	126	55	64	7	0
Norwell	10,570	9	0	0	2	7	159	60	92	7	1
Norwood	28,776	20	0	4	7	9	469	84	358	27	0
Oak Bluffs	4,555	13	0	0	0	13	176	30	130	16	0
Orange	7,887	37	0	3	2	32	212	111	95	6	1
Orleans	5,926	14	0	1	0	13	236	93	142	1	0
Oxford	13,793	33	0	4	5	24	194	46	128	20	0
Palmer	12,214	54	0	6	3	45	198	59	123	16	1
Paxton	4,835	6	0	1	0	5	26	12	13	1	1
Peabody	51,563	124	2	9	13	100	1,282	212	996	74	2
Pelham	1,329	0	0	0	0	0	3	1	2	0	0
Pembroke	17,946	38	0	8	4	26	246	56	178	12	0
Pepperell	11,567	25	0	2	1	22	185	35	143	7	1
Pittsfield	45,010	269	4	31	40	194	1,266	459	738	69	9
Plainville	8,314	11	0	1	1	9	170	28	137	5	0
Plymouth	56,812	156	2	9	16	129	746	196	533	17	2
Plympton	2,837	7	0	0	1	6	36	12	22	2	0
Princeton	3,434	2	0	1	0	1	30	13	17	0	1
Provincetown	2,960	23	1	1	0	21	98	14	83	1	0
Quincy	92,834	394	1	31	91	271	1,776	551	1,087	138	3
Randolph	32,308	117	1	6	20	90	593	120	448	25	1
Raynham	13,465	32	0	2	13	17	348	78	253	17	1
Reading	24,898	11	0	1	2	8	270	105	158	7	0
Rehoboth	11,679	11	0	2	0	9	156	46	103	7	0
Revere	52,070	181	3	3	49	126	1,340	261	905	174	4
Rochester	5,264	10	0	1	3	6	59	15	41	3	0
Rockport	6,994	2	0	1	0	1	12	6	5	1	0
Rowley	5,892	5	0	0	2	3	23	7	14	2	0
Rutland	8,022	19	1	3	0	15	99	48	48	3	3
Salem	41,592	119	0	15	22	82	986	173	744	69	
Salisbury	8,333	41	0	9	2	30	169	54	108	7	1
Sandwich	20,801	50	0	9	1	40	282	59	220	3	2
Saugus	26,790	84	0	5	23	56	908	174	666	68	4
Scituate	18,244	38	0	1	5	32	197	51	135	11	1
Seekonk	13,806	26	0	3	2	21	392	46	335	11	3
Sharon	17,719	4	0	0	1	3	144	59	80	5	0
Sherborn	4,144	5	0	0	0	5	30	15	10	5	0
Shirley	7,255	11	0	1	0	10	43	14	28	1	1
Shrewsbury	35,825	5	0	0	3	2	283	69	199	15	0
Somerset	18,276	38	0	3	2	33	296	45	229	22	1
Somerville	76,216	282	0	17	90	175	1,742	415	1,178	149	3
Southampton	5,827	11	0	0	0	11	51	17	32	2	1
Southborough	9,827	2	0	0	1	1	69	28	40	1	0
Southbridge	16,821	61	0	3	6	52	446	199	222	25	10
South Hadley	17,621	45	0	4	9	32	274	65	199	10	3
Spencer	11,759	42	0	3	2	37	225	63	156	6	1
Springfield	153,993	1,581	20	31	532	998	7,365	2,499	4,072	794	55
Sterling	7,856	5	0	1	0	4	84	40	39	5	1
Stockbridge	1,959	6	0	2	0	4	91	49	40	2	0
Stoneham	21,568	30	0	1	8	21	314	137	163	14	0
Stoughton	27,126	116	0	3	23	90	590	129	427	34	6
Stow	6,630	4	0	1	2	1	39	14	24	1	0
Sturbridge	9,324	30	0	4	5	21	172	44	120	8	3
Sudbury	17,767	2	0	0	0	2	128	16	111	1	0
Sutton	9,018	3	0	0	0	3	134	54	70	10	0
Swampscott	13,871	12	0	0	3	9	203	42	155	6	1
Swansea	15,962	36	0	5	2	29	353	63	277	13	1
Taunton	56,215	298	0	13	69	216	1,010	451	529	30	4
Templeton	8,062	18	0	1	2	15	125	40	78	7	1
Tewksbury	29,138	80	0	13	10	57	579	122	436	21	2
Topsfield	6,122	0	0	0	0	0	55	14	39	2	0
Townsend	8,980	5	0	0	0	5	112	58	52	2	0
Truro	2,015	5	0	0	0	5	49	18	31	0	0
Tyngsboro	11,361	18	0	1	2	15	193	46	124	23	0
Upton	7,588	4	0	2	0	2	51	12	35	4	1
Uxbridge	13,539	23	0	3	2	18	178	72	95	11	1
Wakefield	25,084	61	1	5	7	48	304	68	220	16	0
Wales	1,849	1	0	0	1	0	6	3	3	0	0
Walpole	24,217	21	0	3	6	12	353	47	301	5	0
Waltham	61,002	174	0	15	24	135	868	191	639	38	3
Ware	9,932	48	0	1	7	40	130	37	81	12	1

[1] If a blank is presented in the arson column, it indicates that the FBI did not receive 12 complete months of arson data for that agency.

Table II-8.   Offenses Known to Law Enforcement, by Selected State and City, 2011—_Continued_

(Number.)

State/City	Population	Violent crime	Murder and non-negligent man-slaughter	Forcible rape	Robbery	Aggravated assault	Property crime	Burglary	Larceny-theft	Motor vehicle theft	Arson[1]
Massachusetts—_Continued_											
Wareham	21,955	130	2	4	13	111	843	264	550	29	8
Watertown	32,110	51	0	2	7	42	492	80	385	27	2
Wayland	13,073	2	1	0	0	1	28	6	21	1	1
Wellesley	28,153	19	0	2	2	15	184	37	140	7	0
Wellfleet	2,767	9	0	0	0	9	54	17	32	5	1
Wenham	4,905	2	0	0	0	2	31	7	24	0	0
West Boylston	7,716	1	0	1	0	0	138	27	105	6	0
West Bridgewater	6,958	16	0	2	5	9	188	36	141	11	0
Westfield	41,344	93	0	16	10	67	703	144	537	22	5
Westford	22,085	19	0	4	3	12	188	37	144	7	0
Westhampton	1,617	0	0	0	0	0	5	4	1	0	0
Westminster	7,321	7	0	0	1	6	258	18	236	4	0
West Newbury	4,261	10	0	0	0	10	38	7	30	1	0
Weston	11,330	6	0	2	0	4	60	15	45	0	0
Westport	15,627	23	0	2	1	20	214	69	126	19	0
West Springfield	28,564	181	0	20	36	125	1,327	271	973	83	3
West Tisbury	2,757	2	0	0	0	2	28	11	16	1	0
Westwood	14,707	16	0	2	3	11	133	36	89	8	0
Weymouth	54,071	183	4	13	35	131	947	166	738	43	5
Whately	1,505	1	0	0	0	1	22	7	14	1	0
Whitman	14,577	40	0	2	6	32	208	50	148	10	1
Wilbraham	14,306	31	0	3	2	26	193	49	140	4	3
Williamstown	7,801	14	0	3	0	11	202	27	173	2	1
Wilmington	22,461	26	0	4	1	21	299	77	218	4	0
Winchendon	10,363	35	0	0	0	35	285	26	247	12	0
Winchester	21,504	5	0	0	2	3	222	45	170	7	0
Winthrop	17,604	40	1	2	6	31	221	77	133	11	1
Woburn	38,352	82	0	9	14	59	739	140	573	26	1
Worcester	182,145	1,800	11	36	411	1,342	6,077	2,066	3,481	530	10
Wrentham	11,022	4	0	2	1	1	200	9	191	0	0
Yarmouth	23,939	162	0	17	18	127	788	400	370	18	5
Michigan											
Adrian	21,117	103	0	35	10	58	679	168	491	20	6
Albion	8,610	66	3	3	10	50	268	88	179	1	2
Algonac	4,107	4	0	0	0	4	71	13	52	6	1
Allegan	4,994	3	0	0	0	3	61	6	55	0	0
Allen Park	28,189	38	0	6	6	26	575	116	402	57	0
Almont	2,672	10	0	1	1	8	79	31	46	2	0
Alpena	10,475	36	0	7	1	28	439	59	372	8	3
Ann Arbor	113,848	261	0	36	59	166	2,549	534	1,918	97	11
Argentine Township	6,908	13	0	4	0	9	41	11	28	2	0
Armada	1,729	1	0	0	0	1	10	2	8	0	0
Auburn	2,085	0	0	0	0	0	11	2	9	0	0
Auburn Hills	21,396	54	1	9	19	25	856	104	716	36	4
Au Gres-Sims	1,982	1	0	0	0	1	1	0	1	0	0
Bad Axe	3,127	7	0	1	0	6	107	8	98	1	0
Bancroft	545	1	0	0	0	1	2	1	1	0	0
Bangor	1,884	10	0	3	0	7	71	11	58	2	1
Baroda-Lake Township	3,842	3	0	0	0	3	55	11	43	1	0
Barry Township	3,375	0	0	0	0	0	39	8	28	3	0
Battle Creek	61,658	567	5	62	98	402	3,089	1,146	1,846	97	25
Bay City	34,906	170	0	36	35	99	797	244	524	29	13
Belding	5,753	11	0	8	1	2	137	23	111	3	1
Bellaire	1,085	1	0	1	0	0	4	1	3	0	0
Belleville	3,988	15	0	3	2	10	102	21	78	3	0
Bellevue	1,281	0	0	0	0	0	2	0	2	0	0
Berkley	14,959	11	1	2	3	5	174	36	124	14	0
Beverly Hills	10,259	5	0	0	3	2	126	24	99	3	0
Birch Run	1,554	3	0	0	1	2	94	12	78	4	0
Birmingham	20,088	23	0	0	7	16	407	48	344	15	2
Blackman Township	37,830	41	0	5	8	28	862	166	655	41	3
Blissfield	3,337	5	0	2	0	3	39	6	33	0	1
Bloomfield Hills	3,866	0	0	0	0	0	59	8	50	1	0
Bloomfield Township	41,039	20	0	0	9	11	457	91	345	21	3
Boyne City	3,732	3	0	1	1	1	89	11	76	2	0
Breckenridge	1,327	2	0	0	0	2	23	8	15	0	0
Bridgeport Township	10,506	31	0	7	1	23	159	68	83	8	1
Bridgman	2,289	3	0	1	0	2	33	4	29	0	0
Brighton	7,438	7	0	3	2	2	200	19	178	3	1
Bronson	2,347	3	0	1	0	2	64	12	52	0	0
Brown City	1,324	1	0	0	0	1	22	2	20	0	0
Brownstown Township	30,604	38	1	5	8	24	553	153	328	72	1
Buena Vista Township	8,669	93	1	7	10	75	336	176	140	20	6

[1] If a blank is presented in the arson column, it indicates that the FBI did not receive 12 complete months of arson data for that agency.

Table II-8.   Offenses Known to Law Enforcement, by Selected State and City, 2011—*Continued*

(Number.)

State/City	Population	Violent crime	Murder and non-negligent man-slaughter	Forcible rape	Robbery	Aggravated assault	Property crime	Burglary	Larceny-theft	Motor vehicle theft	Arson[1]
Michigan—*Continued*											
Burr Oak	827	1	0	0	0	1	15	4	10	1	1
Cadillac	10,347	57	0	17	6	34	623	91	518	14	1
Calumet	725	0	0	0	0	0	13	5	8	0	0
Cambridge Township	5,729	1	0	0	0	1	28	6	22	0	1
Canton Township	90,105	132	0	21	32	79	1,395	222	1,094	79	10
Capac	1,889	5	0	2	0	3	59	8	49	2	0
Carleton	2,343	2	0	1	0	1	37	9	27	1	0
Caro	4,226	13	0	1	1	11	153	20	132	1	1
Carrollton Township	6,098	18	0	3	5	10	139	49	83	7	0
Caseville	776	2	0	2	0	0	45	15	29	1	0
Cass City	2,426	3	0	1	0	2	42	3	38	1	1
Cassopolis	1,773	2	0	0	0	2	26	9	13	4	0
Cedar Springs	3,506	41	0	5	3	33	90	23	63	4	1
Center Line	8,251	33	0	9	3	21	247	30	152	65	0
Central Lake	951	0	0	0	0	0	18	5	13	0	0
Charlevoix	2,511	4	0	4	0	0	112	3	109	0	0
Charlotte	9,067	24	0	13	1	10	281	36	241	4	1
Cheboygan	4,863	12	0	5	0	7	148	15	129	4	0
Chelsea	4,940	4	0	0	2	2	76	7	67	2	0
Chesaning	2,392	3	0	1	0	2	25	9	16	0	1
Chesterfield Township	43,348	143	0	5	12	126	963	120	793	50	2
Chocolay Township	5,899	1	0	0	1	0	66	1	64	1	0
Clare	3,116	10	0	2	1	7	106	16	89	1	0
Clawson	11,816	7	0	2	1	4	110	33	71	6	1
Clay Township	9,059	2	0	0	0	2	89	32	55	2	0
Clinton	2,334	4	0	2	0	2	25	3	20	2	2
Clinton Township	96,723	303	1	23	71	208	2,317	545	1,576	196	10
Clio	2,644	1	0	0	0	1	82	25	55	2	1
Coldwater	10,937	27	0	9	2	16	374	44	323	7	4
Coloma Township	6,498	18	0	5	0	13	133	31	101	1	0
Colon	1,172	0	0	0	0	0	16	2	14	0	1
Columbia Township	7,414	4	0	1	0	3	103	35	64	4	0
Concord	1,049	0	0	0	0	0	8	3	4	1	0
Corunna	3,494	5	0	2	0	3	48	3	44	1	1
Covert Township	2,886	15	0	4	1	10	80	19	55	6	1
Crystal Falls	1,468	1	0	0	0	1	14	1	13	0	0
Davison	5,169	10	0	2	2	6	84	9	64	11	0
Davison Township	19,560	27	1	10	3	13	371	113	233	25	1
Dearborn	98,079	359	3	22	104	230	3,757	612	2,705	440	12
Dearborn Heights	57,730	210	1	16	56	137	1,684	574	897	213	8
Decatur	1,818	4	0	1	0	3	69	10	56	3	1
Denton Township	5,553	4	0	0	0	4	86	8	74	4	0
Detroit	713,239	15,245	344	427	4,962	9,512	43,818	15,994	16,456	11,368	957
Dewitt	4,504	3	0	1	0	2	29	2	27	0	0
Dryden Township	4,764	4	0	0	0	4	34	11	22	1	0
East Grand Rapids	10,686	2	0	2	0	0	128	24	99	5	0
East Jordan	2,349	2	0	2	0	0	24	4	17	3	0
East Lansing	48,542	82	1	17	7	57	1,043	292	699	52	46
Eastpointe	32,418	233	0	18	54	161	1,050	279	537	234	8
Eaton Rapids	5,210	6	0	1	0	5	119	14	101	4	0
Elk Rapids	1,641	2	0	0	0	2	32	1	30	1	0
Elkton	807	0	0	0	0	0	19	2	17	0	0
Elsie	965	3	0	1	0	2	6	3	2	1	0
Emmett Township	11,761	69	0	4	19	46	718	125	581	12	1
Escanaba	12,606	39	1	6	2	30	717	81	625	11	2
Essexville	3,475	10	0	2	0	8	55	8	46	1	0
Evart	1,902	8	0	1	1	6	69	14	50	5	3
Fair Haven Township	1,106	3	0	1	0	2	9	3	5	1	0
Farmington	10,364	8	0	0	4	4	155	27	121	7	0
Farmington Hills	79,680	101	2	11	28	60	1,266	267	895	104	4
Fenton	11,747	18	0	1	6	11	314	49	247	18	2
Ferndale	19,885	82	0	1	30	51	597	139	381	77	2
Flint	102,357	2,392	52	85	607	1,648	6,618	3,628	2,220	770	287
Flint Township	31,905	315	6	20	114	175	2,119	525	1,447	147	7
Flushing	8,383	10	0	0	1	9	148	27	112	9	0
Flushing Township	10,632	6	0	0	1	5	116	54	57	5	0
Forsyth Township	6,159	11	1	5	1	4	68	11	50	7	0
Fowlerville	2,884	4	0	0	0	4	132	21	108	3	0
Frankenmuth	4,940	5	0	0	0	5	88	15	68	5	0
Frankfort	1,285	2	0	0	0	2	25	4	20	1	0
Franklin	3,148	0	0	0	0	0	60	20	38	2	0
Fraser	14,469	28	0	1	8	19	425	49	347	29	2
Gaines	380	0	0	0	0	0	0	0	0	0	0
Galesburg	2,007	1	0	1	0	0	40	18	21	1	0

[1] If a blank is presented in the arson column, it indicates that the FBI did not receive 12 complete months of arson data for that agency.

Table II-8. Offenses Known to Law Enforcement, by Selected State and City, 2011—*Continued*

(Number.)

State/City	Population	Violent crime	Murder and non-negligent man-slaughter	Forcible rape	Robbery	Aggravated assault	Property crime	Burglary	Larceny-theft	Motor vehicle theft	Arson[1]
Michigan—*Continued*											
Garden City	27,671	75	0	6	25	44	689	172	426	91	7
Gaylord	3,642	8	0	4	0	4	232	36	188	8	0
Genesee Township	21,565	91	0	9	15	67	620	250	316	54	5
Gerrish Township	2,991	2	0	1	0	1	25	1	24	0	1
Gibraltar	4,652	6	1	0	0	5	77	15	59	3	1
Gladstone	4,969	4	0	1	0	3	101	14	83	4	0
Gladwin	2,931	9	0	0	0	9	136	21	113	2	0
Grand Blanc Township	37,480	75	0	15	12	48	817	222	548	47	1
Grand Haven	10,404	19	0	12	1	6	292	39	252	1	1
Grand Ledge	7,780	3	0	0	0	3	193	21	171	1	0
Grand Rapids	187,898	1,395	10	81	464	840	6,174	1,952	3,897	325	71
Grandville	15,366	27	0	5	5	17	788	81	696	11	0
Grayling	1,883	7	0	2	1	4	126	5	119	2	0
Green Oak Township	17,463	16	0	3	3	10	255	43	203	9	0
Grosse Ile Township	10,363	4	0	1	0	3	60	7	50	3	0
Grosse Pointe	5,417	2	0	2	0	0	126	23	89	14	0
Grosse Pointe Farms	9,472	7	0	0	1	6	147	13	122	12	0
Grosse Pointe Park	11,546	11	0	0	6	5	239	16	181	42	1
Grosse Pointe Shores	3,006	0	0	0	0	0	6	1	5	0	0
Grosse Pointe Woods	16,123	12	0	1	3	8	211	33	150	28	0
Hamburg Township	21,149	8	0	2	0	6	141	23	115	3	1
Hampton Township	9,645	19	0	3	2	14	245	34	204	7	0
Hamtramck	22,406	307	2	6	115	184	952	394	355	203	14
Hancock	4,631	2	0	2	0	0	78	14	60	4	2
Harbor Beach	1,702	2	0	2	0	0	43	13	30	0	0
Harbor Springs	1,193	0	0	0	0	0	37	4	33	0	0
Harper Woods	14,225	104	0	2	40	62	1,068	101	765	202	3
Hart	2,124	7	0	5	0	2	142	5	136	1	0
Hartford	2,686	9	0	2	0	7	50	9	36	5	1
Hastings	7,344	19	0	6	0	13	223	32	182	9	0
Hazel Park	16,410	64	1	6	20	37	563	161	283	119	3
Hillsdale	8,299	26	0	3	1	22	296	50	240	6	4
Holland	33,026	118	0	24	10	84	1,082	221	843	18	7
Holly	6,081	25	0	6	1	18	174	31	134	9	2
Howard City	1,807	5	0	1	0	4	77	11	62	4	0
Howell	9,482	18	0	5	1	12	249	23	218	8	0
Huntington Woods	6,233	1	0	0	0	1	58	6	52	0	0
Huron Township	15,867	23	0	4	3	16	346	62	258	26	1
Imlay City	3,594	10	0	3	1	6	103	15	84	4	0
Inkster	25,350	459	9	32	96	322	998	440	453	105	22
Ionia	11,385	21	0	6	1	14	263	39	218	6	1
Iron River	3,027	5	0	0	1	4	84	22	54	8	0
Ironwood	5,383	11	0	2	0	9	138	12	124	2	0
Ishpeming	6,465	14	1	4	3	6	124	8	105	11	1
Ishpeming Township	3,510	0	0	0	0	0	12	2	10	0	0
Jonesville	2,256	6	0	0	0	6	76	21	55	0	0
Kalamazoo Township	21,901	86	0	12	16	58	516	183	305	28	5
Kalkaska	2,018	1	0	0	1	0	67	3	62	2	1
Keego Harbor	2,968	18	0	0	1	17	44	13	28	3	0
Kentwood	48,670	179	0	24	53	102	1,371	289	1,026	56	4
Kinross Township	7,555	1	0	0	0	1	42	8	32	2	0
Lake Angelus	290	0	0	0	0	0	10	3	7	0	0
Lake Odessa	2,016	1	0	0	0	1	40	11	29	0	0
Lake Orion	2,971	5	0	1	1	3	51	6	44	1	0
Lakeview	1,006	6	0	1	1	4	36	0	36	0	0
Lansing	114,211	1,169	8	90	275	796	4,287	1,650	2,397	240	24
Lapeer	8,834	33	0	4	0	29	379	42	329	8	1
Lapeer Township	5,052	0	0	0	0	0	19	2	16	1	0
Lathrup Village	4,072	11	0	1	2	8	60	21	34	5	0
Laurium	1,976	2	0	0	0	2	15	4	10	1	0
Lawton	1,899	2	0	0	0	2	39	6	33	0	0
Leslie	1,850	1	0	1	0	0	19	6	13	0	0
Lincoln Park	38,115	211	3	12	36	160	1,620	354	1,057	209	10
Lincoln Township	14,680	16	0	8	2	6	251	33	217	1	0
Linden	3,988	4	0	1	0	3	47	15	32	0	0
Litchfield	1,368	3	0	1	0	2	17	2	14	1	0
Livonia	96,869	168	1	19	40	108	2,108	308	1,589	211	11
Lowell	3,780	6	0	1	0	5	59	19	37	3	1
Luna Pier	1,435	2	0	0	0	2	28	5	22	1	1
Mackinac Island	492	3	0	2	0	1	222	9	213	0	0
Mackinaw City	805	1	0	0	1	0	45	1	44	0	0
Madison Heights	29,672	90	0	13	26	51	955	166	641	148	5
Madison Township	8,614	2	0	1	0	1	82	2	79	1	0
Mancelona	1,389	1	0	0	0	1	46	7	37	2	0

[1] If a blank is presented in the arson column, it indicates that the FBI did not receive 12 complete months of arson data for that agency.

Table II-8.   Offenses Known to Law Enforcement, by Selected State and City, 2011—*Continued*

(Number.)

State/City	Population	Violent crime	Murder and non-negligent man-slaughter	Forcible rape	Robbery	Aggravated assault	Property crime	Burglary	Larceny-theft	Motor vehicle theft	Arson[1]
Michigan—*Continued*											
Manistique	3,095	9	1	1	0	7	114	19	89	6	1
Manton	1,286	1	0	1	0	0	21	3	18	0	0
Marenisco Township	1,726	0	0	0	0	0	5	0	4	1	0
Marquette	21,339	35	1	19	1	14	414	51	355	8	3
Marshall	7,083	20	0	0	0	20	189	39	148	2	1
Mason	8,246	18	1	2	0	15	147	20	123	4	2
Mayville	949	0	0	0	0	0	21	4	17	0	0
Melvindale	10,707	41	0	3	10	28	354	74	226	54	5
Mendon	869	1	0	1	0	0	2	0	2	0	0
Meridian Township	39,658	66	0	15	12	39	900	188	690	22	6
Metamora Township	4,246	7	0	0	0	7	55	16	37	2	0
Midland	41,831	54	1	16	3	34	489	60	425	4	7
Milan	5,832	10	0	3	0	7	103	15	86	2	0
Milford	15,724	9	0	3	1	5	129	32	92	5	2
Monroe	20,717	107	0	13	24	70	911	244	622	45	5
Montague	2,359	2	0	0	0	2	45	3	41	1	2
Montrose Township	7,875	24	0	2	1	21	115	50	60	5	0
Mount Morris	3,084	15	0	1	4	10	152	40	101	11	0
Mount Morris Township	21,485	198	4	21	53	120	1,082	541	457	84	13
Mount Pleasant	25,996	41	0	11	8	22	445	71	354	20	2
Mundy Township	15,071	21	0	2	10	9	457	119	326	12	2
Munising	2,353	2	0	0	0	2	24	1	23	0	1
Muskegon	38,372	364	5	34	86	239	2,157	585	1,500	72	17
Muskegon Heights	10,848	178	1	17	41	119	875	340	472	63	16
Napoleon Township	6,771	3	0	2	0	1	62	18	42	2	0
Nashville	1,627	5	0	0	0	5	52	7	43	2	0
Negaunee	4,565	9	0	3	0	6	170	33	133	4	1
Newaygo	1,975	19	2	1	0	16	174	38	132	4	0
New Baltimore	12,075	7	0	0	0	7	129	10	114	5	1
New Era	451	0	0	0	0	0	3	0	3	0	0
New Haven	4,638	3	0	0	0	3	25	6	17	2	0
Niles	11,591	33	0	12	4	17	420	92	310	18	6
North Branch	1,032	1	0	0	0	1	9	3	6	0	0
Northfield Township	8,239	18	0	4	1	13	165	33	124	8	0
North Muskegon	3,783	3	0	1	1	1	95	10	85	0	1
Northville	5,965	5	0	2	2	1	103	6	93	4	0
Northville Township	28,476	11	0	4	1	6	407	50	338	19	3
Norton Shores	23,976	39	0	3	13	23	759	103	637	19	5
Novi	55,182	43	3	5	8	27	964	81	847	36	0
Oak Park	29,297	147	1	14	48	84	854	295	447	112	5
Olivet	1,604	2	0	0	0	2	18	0	18	0	0
Orchard Lake	2,373	3	0	0	1	2	49	8	41	0	0
Oscoda Township	6,992	13	0	2	0	11	222	75	136	11	2
Otsego	3,953	4	0	0	0	4	53	8	45	0	0
Ovid	1,602	0	0	0	0	0	20	2	17	1	0
Owendale	241	1	0	0	0	1	3	0	3	0	0
Owosso	15,183	71	0	12	4	55	488	93	384	11	4
Oxford	3,433	10	0	2	3	5	40	3	35	2	0
Paw Paw	3,531	11	0	3	0	8	149	28	119	2	0
Petoskey	5,666	5	0	1	0	4	104	17	86	1	3
Pinckney	2,425	1	0	0	0	1	52	6	43	3	2
Pinconning	1,306	3	0	0	0	3	6	2	4	0	0
Pittsfield Township	34,637	80	1	12	21	46	1,000	136	796	68	4
Plainwell	3,801	12	0	7	0	5	84	4	76	4	2
Pleasant Ridge	2,524	0	0	0	0	0	26	6	18	2	0
Plymouth	9,125	11	0	1	1	9	174	29	133	12	1
Plymouth Township	27,503	21	0	3	4	14	325	48	255	22	2
Portage	46,257	85	0	19	13	53	1,660	223	1,409	28	6
Port Austin	663	0	0	0	0	0	16	3	13	0	0
Port Huron	30,161	207	0	13	40	154	1,170	329	791	50	14
Port Sanilac	623	0	0	0	0	0	7	1	5	1	0
Potterville	2,615	1	0	0	0	1	53	3	50	0	0
Prairieville Township	3,401	1	0	1	0	0	14	5	9	0	0
Raisin Township	7,553	2	0	0	0	2	34	9	25	0	0
Reading	1,077	0	0	0	0	0	9	2	7	0	0
Redford Township	48,326	206	1	7	85	113	1,801	638	858	305	14
Reed City	2,423	10	0	1	0	9	56	10	46	0	0
Richfield Township, Genesee County	8,723	14	1	1	3	9	145	71	62	12	1
Richfield Township, Roscommon County	3,728	7	0	0	0	7	33	10	21	2	0
Richland	750	1	0	0	0	1	9	2	7	0	0
Riverview	12,477	13	0	2	1	10	186	20	145	21	1
Rochester	12,701	11	0	0	3	8	150	16	126	8	2
Rockford	5,715	12	0	1	1	10	85	9	75	1	5
Rockwood	3,287	3	0	1	0	2	43	4	32	7	1
Rogers City	2,825	5	0	2	0	3	77	9	68	0	0

[1] If a blank is presented in the arson column, it indicates that the FBI did not receive 12 complete months of arson data for that agency.

Table II-8. Offenses Known to Law Enforcement, by Selected State and City, 2011—*Continued*

(Number.)

State/City	Population	Violent crime	Murder and non-negligent man-slaughter	Forcible rape	Robbery	Aggravated assault	Property crime	Burglary	Larceny-theft	Motor vehicle theft	Arson[1]
Michigan—*Continued*											
Romeo	3,593	6	0	2	0	4	61	14	43	4	0
Romulus	23,971	122	1	13	23	85	887	262	547	78	4
Roosevelt Park	3,828	7	0	0	4	3	264	19	235	10	0
Roseville	47,263	182	1	25	44	112	2,133	337	1,521	275	10
Royal Oak	57,193	79	2	11	8	58	1,058	201	766	91	1
Saginaw	51,469	1,168	8	37	170	953	1,886	1,125	657	104	46
Saginaw Township	40,809	73	0	5	14	54	973	165	789	19	4
Saline	8,803	12	0	0	2	10	110	15	91	4	1
Sand Lake	500	0	0	0	0	0	18	3	14	1	0
Sebewaing	1,758	2	0	1	0	1	18	3	15	0	0
Shelby Township	73,748	97	0	16	11	70	1,091	203	797	91	4
Shepherd	1,514	4	0	2	0	2	29	4	25	0	1
Somerset Township	4,620	0	0	0	0	0	39	9	29	1	0
Southfield	71,685	377	4	33	116	224	2,681	710	1,592	379	5
Southgate	30,024	71	0	4	16	51	1,115	125	868	122	4
South Haven	4,400	23	0	9	6	8	264	44	208	12	0
South Lyon	11,318	12	0	2	1	9	78	8	68	2	1
South Rockwood	1,674	0	0	0	0	0	11	2	7	2	0
Sparta	4,137	8	0	4	0	4	100	9	89	2	1
Spring Arbor Township	8,261	1	0	0	1	0	50	15	34	1	0
Springfield	5,256	20	0	2	1	17	168	57	109	2	1
Spring Lake-Ferrysburg	5,211	10	0	0	1	9	63	14	49	0	1
Standish	1,508	2	0	0	0	2	1	0	1	0	0
St. Charles	2,052	4	0	0	0	4	48	26	19	3	0
St. Clair	5,481	7	0	1	0	6	120	18	93	9	1
St. Clair Shores	59,670	128	1	15	25	87	1,083	247	743	93	6
Sterling Heights[2]	129,601	203	1	11	31	160	2,671	451	2,047	173	6
St. Johns	7,859	12	0	5	2	5	146	38	105	3	0
St. Joseph	8,359	20	0	5	2	13	301	37	262	2	0
St. Joseph Township	10,020	13	0	3	1	9	166	49	113	4	1
St. Louis	7,476	9	0	3	0	6	85	13	71	1	0
Stockbridge	1,217	2	0	1	1	0	71	22	47	2	0
Sturgis	10,986	35	0	14	3	18	310	52	243	15	2
Sumpter Township	9,542	25	0	2	0	23	178	58	107	13	1
Suttons Bay	618	0	0	0	0	0	14	1	13	0	0
Swartz Creek	5,754	7	0	1	1	5	99	19	75	5	0
Sylvan Lake	1,719	3	0	0	0	3	18	2	15	1	0
Tawas	4,632	8	0	2	0	6	100	16	82	2	1
Taylor	63,083	320	0	26	76	218	2,497	671	1,598	228	24
Tecumseh	8,515	4	0	0	1	3	162	43	102	17	1
Thomas Township	11,976	18	0	0	4	14	160	22	134	4	0
Three Rivers	7,805	47	0	9	7	31	318	50	248	20	2
Tittabawassee Township	9,719	7	0	0	1	6	84	20	61	3	1
Trenton	18,839	14	0	2	2	10	238	50	171	17	0
Troy	80,919	72	0	17	14	41	1,780	236	1,402	142	7
Tuscarora Township	3,036	4	0	1	0	3	125	3	122	0	0
Unadilla Township	3,363	3	0	0	1	2	50	14	33	3	0
Union City	1,598	1	0	1	0	0	65	10	54	1	0
Utica	4,753	11	0	2	1	8	205	35	162	8	0
Van Buren Township	28,799	72	0	13	15	44	783	160	537	86	0
Vassar	2,695	7	0	0	0	7	38	3	35	0	0
Vicksburg	2,904	3	0	1	1	1	78	8	69	1	2
Walker	23,519	34	1	7	10	16	755	99	628	28	4
Walled Lake	6,994	12	0	1	1	10	116	19	93	4	2
Warren	133,955	719	6	73	156	484	3,853	1,070	1,975	808	47
Waterford Township	71,653	193	1	39	45	108	1,578	444	1,029	105	14
Watervliet	1,734	0	0	0	0	0	33	8	23	2	0
Wayne	17,580	128	0	17	32	79	692	202	433	57	7
West Bloomfield Township	64,641	42	1	6	8	27	753	175	556	22	2
West Branch	2,137	5	0	3	1	1	77	14	63	0	0
Westland	84,031	348	1	50	88	209	2,380	610	1,470	300	21
White Cloud	1,407	5	1	1	0	3	83	17	62	4	1
Whitehall	2,704	3	0	1	0	2	82	8	73	1	1
White Lake Township	29,996	21	0	1	5	15	470	66	385	19	4
White Pigeon	1,521	4	0	3	0	1	37	4	30	3	0
Williamston	3,851	2	0	1	1	0	44	10	30	4	0
Wixom	13,488	16	0	3	1	12	344	59	255	30	3
Wolverine Lake	4,309	1	0	0	0	1	50	5	43	2	0
Woodhaven	12,865	16	0	0	2	14	227	10	198	19	0
Woodland Township	2,045	0	0	0	0	0	2	0	2	0	0
Wyandotte	25,863	58	0	6	7	45	714	147	489	78	4
Wyoming	72,071	262	2	34	71	155	1,591	487	960	144	10
Ypsilanti	19,420	162	1	17	39	105	811	266	498	47	8
Zeeland	5,500	5	0	3	0	2	127	31	96	0	2
Zilwaukee	1,657	0	0	0	0	0	15	4	11	0	0

[1] If a blank is presented in the arson column, it indicates that the FBI did not receive 12 complete months of arson data for that agency.
[2] Because of changes in the state/local agency's reporting practices, figures are not comparable to previous years' data.

Table II-8.   Offenses Known to Law Enforcement, by Selected State and City, 2011—*Continued*

(Number.)

State/City	Population	Violent crime	Murder and non-negligent man-slaughter	Forcible rape	Robbery	Aggravated assault	Property crime	Burglary	Larceny-theft	Motor vehicle theft	Arson[1]
Minnesota[7]											
Albany	2,581		0		0	1	16	5	10	1	0
Albert Lea	18,155		0		1	24	454	50	389	15	2
Alexandria	11,155		0		1	12	364	37	313	14	1
Annandale	3,253		0		0	5	96	15	77	4	0
Anoka	17,274		1		17	15	878	112	730	36	1
Appleton	1,423		0		0	2	40	10	26	4	0
Apple Valley	49,463		0		13	19	1,191	139	1,029	23	5
Arden Hills	9,626		0		2	3	148	15	123	10	2
Aurora	1,695		0		0	0	0	0	0	0	0
Austin	24,909		0		10	39	757	142	582	33	3
Avon	1,407		0		0	0	22	7	14	1	1
Babbitt	1,486		0		0	0	0	0	0	0	0
Baxter	7,669		0		1	3	384	4	378	2	0
Bayport	3,498		0		0	0	27	5	20	2	0
Becker	4,573		0		0	6	37	5	30	2	0
Belgrade	746		0		0	0	0	0	0	0	0
Belle Plaine	6,712		0		1	3	129	15	111	3	0
Bemidji	13,535		0		6	39	1,090	105	944	41	0
Benson	3,265		0		0	4	82	21	60	1	0
Big Lake	10,138		0		0	18	100	16	76	8	0
Blackduck	791		0		0	1	39	4	35	0	0
Blaine	57,627		0		14	30	1,960	193	1,716	51	10
Bloomington	83,533		0		41	70	3,151	251	2,813	87	21
Blue Earth	3,379		0		0	2	26	3	22	1	0
Brainerd	13,695		0		5	33	671	118	532	21	1
Breckenridge	3,412		0		0	4	53	5	46	2	0
Brooklyn Center	30,336		0		64	53	1,535	252	1,194	89	11
Brooklyn Park	76,366		5		103	102	2,844	506	2,203	135	10
Brownton	768		0		0	0	2	1	1	0	0
Buffalo	15,572		0		3	10	416	46	363	7	0
Burnsville	60,771		1		24	78	1,679	214	1,419	46	5
Caledonia	2,890		0		0	2	57	6	47	4	0
Cambridge	8,174		0		1	5	324	32	274	18	1
Cannon Falls	4,115		0		0	6	105	11	91	3	1
Centennial Lakes	10,842		1		0	4	191	26	160	5	0
Champlin	23,267		0		6	9	474	58	410	6	2
Chaska	23,953		1		6	12	298	37	253	8	3
Chisholm	5,014		0		2	3	90	4	80	6	0
Cloquet	12,218		0		3	13	507	52	439	16	3
Cold Spring	5,489		0		0	5	41	5	34	2	1
Columbia Heights	19,646		0		20	38	612	128	456	28	4
Coon Rapids	61,950		2		16	57	2,672	254	2,361	57	13
Corcoran	5,421		0		0	3	46	4	39	3	0
Cottage Grove	34,856		0		2	5	578	77	485	16	1
Crookston	7,952		0		1	7	77	26	46	5	2
Crosby	2,404		0		0	2	36	7	27	2	0
Crystal	22,322		0		14	21	642	94	518	30	5
Dawson	1,552		0		0	1	16	5	11	0	0
Dayton	4,707		0		0	3	53	10	33	10	0
Deephaven-Woodland	4,110		0		0	1	29	11	18	0	0
Detroit Lakes	8,635		0		2	8	407	27	371	9	0
Dilworth	4,055		0		0	1	121	6	108	7	0
Duluth	86,931		0		82	164	4,346	756	3,424	166	19
Eagan	64,702		0		11	23	1,512	185	1,278	49	5
Eagle Lake	2,441		0		0	2	28	6	21	1	0
East Grand Forks	8,667		0		2	9	208	36	170	2	1
Eden Prairie	61,266		0		12	14	960	127	811	22	5
Edina	48,311		0		7	3	767	108	645	14	0
Elk River	23,151		0		5	6	618	90	513	15	2
Elmore	668		0		0	1	12	3	7	2	0
Ely	3,487		0		0	1	58	2	54	2	0
Eveleth	3,747		0		0	10	117	22	90	5	0
Fairmont	10,748		0		1	7	311	53	248	10	0
Falcon Heights	5,362		0		3	1	102	17	80	5	0
Faribault	23,532		0		8	45	669	143	496	30	14
Farmington	21,249		0		0	23	191	21	163	7	1
Fergus Falls	13,239		0		4	22	392	58	325	9	1
Floodwood	532		0		0	4	33	1	32	0	0
Forest Lake	18,517		0		7	7	474	65	372	37	3
Fridley	27,418		0		29	39	1,270	181	1,029	60	2
Gilbert	1,813		0		0	0	1	1	0	0	0
Glencoe	5,674		0		1	4	89	13	75	1	1
Glenwood	2,584		0		0	0	3	2	1	0	0

[1] If a blank is presented in the arson column, it indicates that the FBI did not receive 12 complete months of arson data for that agency.

[7] The data collection methodology for the offense of forcible rape used by Chicago, Illinois, and the Minnesota state UCR Program (with the exception of Minneapolis and St. Paul, Minnesota) does not comply with national UCR Program guidelines. Consequently, its figures for forcible rape and violent crime (of which forcible rape is a part) are not published in this table.

Table II-8.   Offenses Known to Law Enforcement, by Selected State and City, 2011—*Continued*

(Number.)

State/City	Population	Violent crime	Murder and non-negligent man-slaughter	Forcible rape	Robbery	Aggravated assault	Property crime	Burglary	Larceny-theft	Motor vehicle theft	Arson[1]
Minnesota—*Continued*											
Golden Valley	20,528		0		5	8	438	85	339	14	1
Goodview	4,067		0		0	10	96	26	64	6	0
Grand Rapids	10,953		0		0	9	435	33	387	15	2
Granite Falls	2,919		0		0	5	54	11	43	0	0
Hallock	989		0		0	0	0	0	0	0	0
Hastings	22,343		0		2	24	563	88	450	25	0
Hermantown	9,487		0		1	10	318	56	245	17	0
Hibbing	16,487		0		1	24	181	9	168	4	1
Hilltop	750		0		3	11	66	11	51	4	0
Hokah	584		0		0	1	28	11	16	1	0
Hopkins	17,727		0		11	17	447	98	333	16	6
Houston	987		0		0	3	14	2	12	0	0
Hoyt Lakes	2,033		0		0	0	0	0	0	0	0
Hutchinson	14,287		0		6	10	341	34	299	8	4
Inver Grove Heights	34,141		0		15	55	624	110	494	20	9
Janesville	2,273		0		0	0	34	7	26	1	0
Jordan	5,512		0		0	1	107	3	101	3	0
Kasson	5,977		0		0	2	43	8	32	3	1
Kimball	768		0		0	3	0	0	0	0	0
La Crescent	4,867		0		0	0	55	8	47	0	2
Lake City	5,102		0		0	1	128	16	107	5	0
Lake Crystal	2,569		0		0	1	34	15	18	1	2
Lakefield	1,707		0		0	2	26	5	20	1	0
Lakes Area	9,481		0		0	8	180	30	142	8	0
Lakeville	56,386		0		3	15	771	108	643	20	4
Lauderdale	2,397		0		0	0	44	16	25	3	0
Lester Prairie	1,743		0		0	2	28	4	24	0	0
Lewiston	1,633		0		0	0	1	1	0	0	0
Lino Lakes	20,372		0		0	14	216	41	168	7	3
Litchfield	6,778		0		0	2	100	21	74	5	0
Little Canada	9,848		0		4	2	238	32	166	40	3
Little Falls	8,407		1		0	9	176	16	153	7	0
Long Prairie	3,485		0		0	2	84	4	79	1	0
Madison	1,563		0		0	0	19	5	14	0	0
Mankato	39,612		1		21	49	1,859	390	1,419	50	11
Maple Grove	62,042		0		11	18	1,202	156	1,026	20	3
Mapleton	1,770		0		0	1	23	3	19	1	0
Maplewood	38,311		0		25	34	2,238	269	1,825	144	2
Marshall	13,786		0		2	10	415	60	339	16	1
Medina	4,930		0		1	2	149	19	129	1	0
Melrose	3,626		0		0	0	30	11	17	2	0
Mendota Heights	11,156		0		2	9	256	31	215	10	0
Milaca	2,969		0		0	1	16	1	15	0	0
Minneapolis	385,531	3,722	32	386	1,589	1,715	19,190	5,104	12,311	1,775	140
Minnetonka	50,118		0		11	13	910	154	725	31	9
Minnetrista	8,734		0		0	2	119	17	99	3	0
Montevideo	5,425		0		0	4	156	8	142	6	0
Montgomery	2,979		0		0	2	42	13	29	0	0
Moorhead	38,359		0		13	17	824	101	683	40	3
Moose Lake	2,772		0		0	4	76	3	72	1	0
Morris	5,327		0		0	5	121	15	99	7	0
Mound	9,122		0		0	2	185	40	139	6	0
Mounds View	12,249		0		6	15	380	47	311	22	5
Mountain Iron	2,891		0		0	0	0	0	0	0	0
Mountain Lake	2,120		0		0	0	0	0	0	0	0
New Brighton	21,622		0		10	17	501	72	383	46	1
New Hope	20,496		1		11	14	493	54	409	30	2
Newport	3,462		0		5	4	121	28	81	12	1
New Prague	7,378		0		0	3	161	22	136	3	3
New Richland	1,212		0		0	2	0	0	0	0	0
New Ulm	13,626		0		0	3	283	97	184	2	0
North Branch	10,203		0		1	6	282	25	249	8	1
Northfield	20,161		1		2	6	315	51	249	15	2
North Mankato	13,497		0		3	0	314	47	259	8	3
North Oaks	4,503		0		1	0	32	5	27	0	1
Oakdale	27,589		2		6	28	1,117	125	934	58	8
Oak Park Heights	4,372		0		0	3	230	15	209	6	0
Olivia	2,503		0		0	7	118	12	94	12	0
Orono	11,501		0		2	0	119	19	99	1	1
Ortonville	1,931		0		0	0	16	3	11	2	0
Osakis	1,753		0		0	1	31	10	19	2	0
Owatonna	25,797		0		12	18	491	119	352	20	1
Park Rapids	3,738		1		0	8	217	31	176	10	0
Paynesville	2,451		0		0	1	80	19	58	3	0

[1] If a blank is presented in the arson column, it indicates that the FBI did not receive 12 complete months of arson data for that agency.

Table II-8.   Offenses Known to Law Enforcement, by Selected State and City, 2011—*Continued*

(Number.)

State/City	Population	Violent crime	Murder and non-negligent man-slaughter	Forcible rape	Robbery	Aggravated assault	Property crime	Burglary	Larceny-theft	Motor vehicle theft	Arson[1]
Minnesota—*Continued*											
Plymouth	71,121		0		12	31	1,212	276	908	28	4
Princeton	4,734		0		0	5	171	16	150	5	0
Prior Lake	22,972		0		7	15	454	64	373	17	0
Proctor	3,081		0		3	3	95	19	71	5	0
Ramsey	23,851		0		4	8	548	55	480	13	1
Red Wing	16,586		0		6	22	639	138	479	22	5
Redwood Falls	5,295		0		1	11	160	23	133	4	0
Richfield	35,500		0		39	30	869	162	659	48	2
Robbinsdale	14,061		0		19	20	475	112	342	21	2
Rochester	107,593		1		65	102	2,323	425	1,809	89	20
Rogers	8,663		0		0	6	68	3	65	0	0
Roseau	2,653		0		0	2	22	0	22	0	1
Rosemount	22,043		0		2	7	326	43	280	3	0
Roseville	33,920		0		25	33	1,507	150	1,257	100	3
Sartell	15,999		0		0	9	252	32	217	3	1
Sauk Centre	4,350		0		0	5	83	17	60	6	0
Sauk Rapids	12,872		0		2	2	109	25	81	3	0
Savage	27,119		0		6	13	631	96	515	20	11
Shakopee	37,362		0		4	49	1,026	124	874	28	4
Shoreview	25,236		0		4	7	291	46	229	16	3
Silver Bay	1,902		0		0	2	15	4	10	1	0
Silver Lake	843		0		0	1	5	1	4	0	0
Slayton	2,170		0		1	0	17	1	14	2	0
South Lake Minnetonka	11,747		0		2	3	142	21	119	2	0
South St. Paul	20,316		0		10	71	575	126	433	16	8
Spring Lake Park	6,461		0		4	13	329	38	274	17	3
St. Anthony	8,289		0		5	2	306	59	240	7	0
Staples	3,004		0		0	1	84	14	69	1	0
St. Charles	3,764		0		0	1	29	3	18	8	0
St. Cloud	66,350		0		45	129	2,578	431	2,040	107	8
St. Francis	7,274		0		0	7	136	19	110	7	4
Stillwater	18,366		0		3	8	474	83	377	14	1
St. James	4,641		0		0	2	74	13	58	3	0
St. Louis Park	45,599		1		23	35	1,405	228	1,110	67	2
St. Paul	287,665	1,885	8	169	604	1,104	11,932	3,197	6,890	1,845	106
St. Paul Park	5,320		0		1	9	154	34	109	11	3
St. Peter	11,282		0		2	7	280	35	233	12	0
Thief River Falls	8,639		0		1	3	260	41	214	5	0
Two Harbors	3,774		0		0	3	40	2	37	1	0
Vadnais Heights	12,397		1		2	6	227	32	166	29	0
Virginia	8,779		1		4	28	506	63	433	10	1
Wabasha	2,540		0		0	0	92	7	84	1	0
Wadena	4,120		0		0	3	109	11	94	4	0
Waite Park	6,767		0		7	15	787	44	727	16	1
Warroad	1,795		0		0	3	18	2	16	0	0
Waseca	9,483		0		0	18	174	33	131	10	1
Wayzata	3,716		0		0	2	114	20	92	2	0
West Hennepin	5,313		0		0	0	46	9	34	3	0
West St. Paul	19,691		0		17	34	651	76	515	60	1
Wheaton	1,435		0		0	2	39	9	30	0	0
White Bear Lake	23,981		0		8	19	767	159	580	28	12
White Bear Township	11,034		0		0	1	4	1	2	1	0
Willmar	19,761		0		1	28	489	51	416	22	4
Windom	4,682		0		0	11	115	22	85	8	0
Winnebago	1,448		0		0	0	11	5	6	0	0
Winona	27,805		0		8	23	456	67	368	21	5
Winsted	2,373		0		0	4	39	9	30	0	0
Woodbury	62,439		0		4	14	1,300	192	1,066	42	2
Worthington	12,863		0		6	21	254	46	194	14	1
Wyoming	7,851		0		1	3	159	7	143	9	0
Zumbrota	3,277		0		0	2	40	6	30	4	0
Mississippi											
Aberdeen	5,633	19	0	0	3	16	219	74	132	13	0
Amory	7,344	16	0	1	8	7	324	96	214	14	1
Bay St. Louis	9,295	19	0	2	2	15	420	122	282	16	3
Belzoni	2,243	24	1	1	3	19	22	5	17	0	0
Biloxi	44,221	204	2	34	60	108	2,341	766	1,431	144	4
Brandon	21,787	13	1	2	7	3	247	95	144	8	0
Brookhaven	12,560	21	0	0	13	8	230	59	165	6	0
Byhalia	1,307	11	0	0	4	7	49	8	40	1	0
Carthage	5,094	8	1	0	4	3	43	22	11	10	0
Charleston	2,201	24	0	0	15	9	71	54	17	0	0
Clarksdale	18,030	150	8	4	40	98	1,189	619	503	67	20

[1] If a blank is presented in the arson column, it indicates that the FBI did not receive 12 complete months of arson data for that agency.

Table II-8.   Offenses Known to Law Enforcement, by Selected State and City, 2011—*Continued*

(Number.)

State/City	Population	Violent crime	Murder and non-negligent man-slaughter	Forcible rape	Robbery	Aggravated assault	Property crime	Burglary	Larceny-theft	Motor vehicle theft	Arson[1]
Mississippi—*Continued*											
Cleveland	12,381	53	2	8	11	32	941	168	752	21	7
Collins	2,596	19	0	2	11	6	170	32	132	6	0
Columbia	6,607	18	0	2	7	9	149	81	67	1	0
Columbus	23,729	81	7	9	26	39	1,156	336	784	36	1
Como	1,284	4	1	0	1	2	35	16	17	2	1
Crystal Springs	5,063	7	0	1	3	3	138	40	90	8	2
D'Iberville	9,522	27	6	3	10	8	609	55	535	19	1
Eupora	2,205	7	0	0	0	7	34	12	20	2	0
Florence	4,157	0	0	0	0	0	53	15	38	0	0
Flowood	7,853	38	0	0	4	34	495	77	408	10	0
Fulton	3,976	0	0	0	0	0	70	11	59	0	0
Gautier	18,642	50	1	12	7	30	699	204	453	42	2
Gloster	964	3	1	0	0	2	6	6	0	0	0
Greenwood	15,262	93	7	12	37	37	859	298	539	22	0
Gulfport	68,049	192	12	22	94	64	3,605	944	2,523	138	13
Heidelberg	721	1	0	0	0	1	22	6	14	2	0
Holly Springs	7,728	98	4	2	17	75	304	116	171	17	0
Horn Lake	26,165	24	1	3	15	5	617	154	433	30	5
Indianola	10,723	88	1	5	28	54	603	154	443	6	
Itta Bena	2,057	7	1	0	1	5	192	126	66	0	1
Iuka	3,039	14	0	3	1	10	115	58	55	2	0
Jackson	174,170	1,620	52	126	808	634	12,811	4,722	6,632	1,457	86
Kosciusko	7,430	16	0	2	5	9	176	89	87	0	0
Laurel	18,610	81	0	14	44	23	1,143	414	687	42	3
Leakesville	901	0	0	0	0	0	0	0	0	0	0
Leland	4,498	16	0	0	10	6	178	79	99	0	0
Louisville	6,656	13	0	1	4	8	117	86	26	5	0
Lucedale	2,934	9	0	0	3	6	62	6	54	2	0
Madison	24,240	20	0	1	7	12	220	18	199	3	0
Magee	4,425	29	0	1	4	24	60	33	25	2	2
McComb	12,838	69	4	1	30	34	695	171	504	20	0
Meridian	41,304	236	2	32	105	97	2,453	1,011	1,244	198	11
Morton	3,475	9	1	1	3	4	49	22	21	6	0
Natchez	15,852	65	4	10	33	18	972	234	715	23	16
New Albany	8,064	11	1	2	4	4	78	21	56	1	0
Newton	3,386	2	0	0	0	2	5	1	4	0	0
Ocean Springs	17,508	29	0	0	13	16	528	132	370	26	0
Olive Branch	33,611	92	2	7	21	62	979	414	517	48	2
Pascagoula	22,477	74	1	14	41	18	1,509	349	1,083	77	10
Pass Christian	4,630	7	0	3	0	4	171	43	122	6	0
Pearl	25,187	57	1	10	11	35	673	240	414	19	0
Petal[6, 4]	10,494	1	0	0	1	0				6	0
Philadelphia	7,505	59	0	11	13	35	422	147	271	4	0
Picayune	10,919	48	2	2	15	29	464	107	339	18	3
Port Gibson	1,573	0	0	0	0	0	16	5	11	0	0
Purvis	2,183	1	0	0	0	1	0	0	0	0	0
Ridgeland	24,138	35	3	0	8	24	594	72	504	18	0
Roxie	499	0	0	0	0	0	0	0	0	0	0
Saltillo	4,770	8	0	1	1	6	111	48	63	0	0
Southaven	49,167	140	0	20	26	94	1,542	216	1,261	65	1
Starkville	23,978	41	0	3	15	23	865	187	662	16	3
Summit	1,711	1	0	0	1	0	29	9	19	1	0
Vicksburg	23,946	146	4	25	21	96	1,744	507	1,180	57	6
West Point	11,350	45	2	7	10	26	365	115	249	1	0
Wiggins	4,407	12	0	0	0	12	181	57	122	2	0
Winona	5,062	8	0	0	2	6	50	12	38	0	0
Yazoo City	11,446	36	1	7	10	18	379	181	179	19	2
Missouri											
Adrian	1,683	9	0	0	1	8	44	12	30	2	3
Advance	1,352	5	0	0	0	5	12	4	8	0	0
Alma	403	0	0	0	0	0	0	0	0	0	0
Alton	874	0	0	0	0	0	3	1	2	0	0
Anderson	1,968	4	0	0	1	3	83	26	56	1	0
Appleton City	1,131	4	0	0	0	4	23	4	19	0	0
Arbyrd	511	0	0	0	0	0	2	0	0	2	0
Archie	1,174	1	0	0	0	1	18	4	13	1	0
Arnold	20,884	39	0	2	4	33	861	81	760	20	1
Ash Grove	1,477	2	0	0	0	2	41	21	18	2	0
Ashland	3,720	17	0	1	0	16	47	1	45	1	0
Aurora	7,535	66	0	2	4	60	407	69	319	19	1
Auxvasse	987	6	0	1	0	5	38	10	25	3	0
Ava	3,004	8	0	0	0	8	89	15	71	3	0
Ballwin	30,514	9	0	0	3	6	351	56	283	12	0

[1] If a blank is presented in the arson column, it indicates that the FBI did not receive 12 complete months of arson data for that agency.

Table II-8. Offenses Known to Law Enforcement, by Selected State and City, 2011—*Continued*

(Number.)

State/City	Population	Violent crime	Murder and non-negligent man-slaughter	Forcible rape	Robbery	Aggravated assault	Property crime	Burglary	Larceny-theft	Motor vehicle theft	Arson[1]
Missouri—*Continued*											
Bates City	220	0	0	0	0	0	9	2	4	3	0
Battlefield	5,610	6	0	2	3	1	91	19	69	3	0
Bella Villa	732	3	0	0	0	3	16	8	8	0	0
Belle	1,551	25	0	1	4	20	19	5	12	2	0
Bellefontaine Neighbors	10,899	60	0	5	19	36	419	203	164	52	1
Bellerive	189	0	0	0	0	0	4	0	4	0	0
Bellflower	394	1	0	0	0	1	11	7	4	0	0
Bel-Nor	1,504	3	0	0	0	3	34	14	18	2	0
Bel-Ridge	2,747	35	1	1	4	29	149	73	64	12	0
Belton	23,200	55	1	6	10	38	513	88	386	39	2
Berkeley	9,011	215	0	13	21	181	520	237	248	35	4
Bernie	1,965	4	0	0	0	4	13	2	10	1	0
Bethany	3,304	5	0	0	0	5	45	13	27	5	1
Beverly Hills	576	10	0	0	1	9	50	25	24	1	0
Billings	1,039	10	0	0	0	10	32	6	26	0	1
Birch Tree	681	1	0	0	0	1	13	2	7	4	0
Birmingham	184	0	0	0	0	0	3	2	0	1	0
Blackburn	250	0	0	0	0	0	0	0	0	0	0
Bloomfield	1,940	4	0	0	0	4	44	7	37	0	0
Blue Springs	52,766	116	1	12	32	71	1,520	246	1,153	121	2
Bolivar	10,363	52	0	2	6	44	297	46	245	6	1
Bonne Terre	6,889	11	0	0	0	11	69	15	39	15	0
Boonville	8,349	7	1	0	1	5	303	27	274	2	2
Bourbon	1,638	11	0	0	0	11	21	3	17	1	1
Bowling Green	5,353	5	0	0	1	4	110	16	92	2	0
Branson[4,6]	10,558	132	0	3	15	114		154			1
Branson West	480	5	0	1	0	4	91	11	80	0	0
Breckenridge Hills	4,763	25	1	3	7	14	196	70	116	10	1
Brentwood	8,084	10	0	0	6	4	322	36	278	8	0
Bridgeton	11,592	78	1	5	21	51	881	108	738	35	1
Brookfield	4,559	7	0	1	2	4	126	39	82	5	0
Brunswick	861	2	0	0	0	2	0	0	0	0	0
Bucklin	469	0	0	0	0	0	5	4	1	0	0
Buckner	3,087	12	0	2	3	7	79	18	54	7	0
Buffalo	3,095	7	0	1	0	6	110	20	89	1	0
Butler	4,234	21	0	0	2	19	173	26	142	5	0
Butterfield Village	472	0	0	0	0	0	7	2	5	0	2
Byrnes Mill	2,791	12	0	1	1	10	51	12	37	2	1
Cabool	2,154	5	2	0	0	3	45	14	31	0	0
California	4,294	4	0	0	1	3	59	3	51	5	0
Calverton Park	1,298	4	0	0	0	4	13	7	6	0	0
Camden Point	476	0	0	0	0	0	1	1	0	0	0
Camdenton	3,732	26	0	2	0	24	169	15	152	2	0
Cameron	9,969	32	0	2	0	30	213	38	168	7	2
Campbell	1,999	17	0	2	1	14	92	19	64	9	1
Canton	2,386	2	0	0	0	2	80	14	65	1	1
Cape Girardeau	38,079	252	1	15	94	142	2,473	394	2,017	62	2
Cardwell	716	2	0	0	0	2	5	4	0	1	0
Carl Junction	7,472	7	0	0	1	6	125	30	87	8	2
Carterville	1,898	4	0	1	0	3	25	7	16	2	0
Carthage	14,430	41	0	5	6	30	342	78	249	15	2
Caruthersville	6,190	73	1	1	9	62	243	96	138	9	3
Cassville	3,278	4	1	1	0	2	222	26	194	2	1
Catron	67	0	0	0	0	0	1	1	0	0	0
Center	510	2	0	0	0	2	11	2	9	0	1
Centralia	4,042	11	0	2	0	9	90	25	63	2	0
Chaffee	2,966	4	0	0	0	4	76	25	51	0	0
Charlack	1,368	3	0	0	2	1	66	16	47	3	0
Charleston	5,969	39	1	1	3	34	157	51	101	5	0
Chesterfield	47,657	33	0	3	9	21	745	76	654	15	1
Chillicothe	9,550	38	1	3	2	32	289	92	186	11	4
Clarkton	1,293	1	0	0	0	1	20	8	9	3	0
Claycomo	1,435	0	0	0	0	0	37	8	27	2	0
Clayton	15,997	17	0	0	6	11	298	88	205	5	0
Cleveland	663	0	0	0	0	0	6	2	4	0	0
Clever	2,147	17	1	0	3	13	6	1	5	0	0
Clinton	9,041	35	1	2	3	29	427	86	318	23	0
Cole Camp	1,125	2	0	0	1	1	8	1	6	1	0
Columbia	108,894	582	2	37	166	377	4,263	798	3,323	142	16
Concordia	2,459	3	0	1	0	2	44	12	28	4	0
Conway	791	1	0	0	0	1	12	0	12	0	0
Cool Valley	1,200	5	0	0	2	3	68	23	40	5	0
Corder	405	1	0	0	0	1	0	0	0	0	0
Cottleville	3,086	7	0	0	1	6	74	7	66	1	1
Country Club Hills	1,279	6	0	1	1	4	44	17	25	2	0

[1] If a blank is presented in the arson column, it indicates that the FBI did not receive 12 complete months of arson data for that agency.

[4] The FBI determined that the agency's data were overreported. Consequently, those data are not included in this table.

[6] The FBI determined that the agency's data were underreported. Consequently, those data are not included in this table.

Table II-8.   Offenses Known to Law Enforcement, by Selected State and City, 2011—*Continued*

(Number.)

State/City	Population	Violent crime	Murder and non-negligent man-slaughter	Forcible rape	Robbery	Aggravated assault	Property crime	Burglary	Larceny-theft	Motor vehicle theft	Arson[1]
Missouri—*Continued*											
Country Club Village	2,458	0	0	0	0	0	14	3	11	0	0
Crane	1,467	3	0	0	0	3	47	20	27	0	0
Creighton	350	0	0	0	0	0	0	0	0	0	0
Crestwood	11,955	8	0	0	2	6	323	24	294	5	0
Creve Coeur	17,898	11	0	3	4	4	267	55	203	9	0
Crocker	1,114	7	0	1	0	6	24	9	14	1	0
Crystal City	4,873	10	0	3	1	6	166	10	151	5	0
Cuba	3,368	8	1	0	1	6	151	22	127	2	2
Dellwood	5,043	34	0	0	17	17	161	90	59	12	1
Delta	440	0	0	0	0	0	0	0	0	0	0
Desloge	5,072	21	0	1	1	19	226	28	191	7	0
De Soto	6,423	42	0	2	3	37	305	50	242	13	4
Des Peres	8,403	7	0	0	1	6	475	34	437	4	0
Dexter	7,893	7	0	1	0	6	282	52	217	13	1
Diamond	905	1	0	0	0	1	5	1	4	0	0
Dixon	1,555	3	1	0	0	2	74	11	62	1	0
Doniphan	2,004	2	0	0	0	2	146	18	125	3	0
Doolittle	632	1	0	0	0	1	7	0	7	0	0
Drexel	969	1	0	1	0	0	23	4	18	1	0
Duenweg	1,125	4	0	0	1	3	22	4	16	2	0
Duquesne	1,769	4	0	1	0	3	46	11	32	3	1
East Lynne	304	0	0	0	0	0	1	1	0	0	0
Edgerton	548	4	0	0	0	4	4	1	2	1	0
Edmundson	837	3	0	0	0	3	39	6	24	9	0
Eldon	4,584	21	0	5	0	16	226	63	159	4	0
Ellington	991	2	0	0	0	2	10	0	10	0	0
Ellisville	9,166	9	0	0	3	6	152	16	114	22	1
Ellsinore	448	0	0	0	0	0	0	0	0	0	0
Emma	234	0	0	0	0	0	0	0	0	0	0
Essex	474	3	0	1	0	2	0	0	0	0	0
Eureka	10,226	16	1	1	4	10	215	13	193	9	0
Everton	320	1	0	0	0	1	7	4	3	0	0
Excelsior Springs	11,124	47	0	5	4	38	368	91	262	15	0
Exeter	775	0	0	0	0	0	0	0	0	0	0
Fair Grove	1,398	2	0	0	0	2	17	5	12	0	0
Fair Play	477	0	0	0	0	0	0	0	0	0	0
Farber	323	0	0	0	0	0	0	0	0	0	0
Farmington	16,299	35	0	5	2	28	659	37	603	19	0
Fayette	2,698	3	0	0	0	3	18	3	14	1	0
Ferguson	21,280	103	5	6	45	47	997	263	649	85	0
Ferrelview	453	5	0	0	0	5	5	3	2	0	0
Festus	11,644	41	0	4	4	33	266	43	212	11	1
Fleming	128	0	0	0	0	0	0	0	0	0	0
Flordell Hills	825	7	1	0	3	3	55	28	22	5	2
Florissant	52,348	100	1	4	42	53	1,117	309	695	113	5
Foley	162	0	0	0	0	0	0	0	0	0	0
Fordland	803	1	0	0	0	1	7	2	5	0	4
Foristell	507	0	0	0	0	0	39	6	32	1	0
Forsyth	2,263	7	0	2	0	5	92	16	74	2	1
Frankford	324	0	0	0	0	0	0	0	0	0	0
Fredericktown	3,999	8	0	2	0	6	102	16	82	4	1
Freeman	484	0	0	0	0	0	0	0	0	0	0
Frontenac	3,774	3	0	0	0	3	44	5	39	0	0
Fulton	12,836	30	0	3	4	23	482	80	385	17	1
Gallatin	1,792	2	0	0	0	2	19	0	17	2	0
Garden City	1,648	4	1	0	0	3	47	21	21	5	0
Gerald	1,350	3	0	1	0	2	36	12	20	4	0
Gideon	1,097	8	0	0	1	7	1	1	0	0	0
Gladstone	25,502	67	0	8	17	42	740	137	537	66	5
Glasgow	1,107	1	0	0	0	1	16	5	9	2	0
Glendale	5,947	1	0	0	0	1	72	20	51	1	0
Glen Echo Park	161	2	0	0	2	0	3	1	2	0	0
Goodman	1,253	2	0	0	0	2	24	10	11	3	0
Gower	1,532	0	0	0	0	0	14	4	10	0	0
Grain Valley	12,901	18	0	6	3	9	258	41	194	23	2
Grandin	244	2	0	1	0	1	2	0	2	0	0
Grandview	24,564	195	0	7	56	132	857	222	527	108	5
Greendale	653	2	0	0	1	1	3	1	2	0	0
Greenfield	1,376	9	0	0	0	9	16	5	9	2	1
Greenville	513	2	0	0	0	2	12	1	7	4	0
Greenwood	5,240	7	0	1	0	6	80	11	67	2	0
Hallsville	1,496	0	0	0	0	0	18	3	15	0	0
Hamilton	1,816	5	0	0	1	4	44	12	30	2	0
Hannibal	17,981	54	0	9	8	37	1,123	178	897	48	4

[1] If a blank is presented in the arson column, it indicates that the FBI did not receive 12 complete months of arson data for that agency.

Table II-8.   Offenses Known to Law Enforcement, by Selected State and City, 2011—*Continued*

(Number.)

State/City	Population	Violent crime	Murder and non-negligent man-slaughter	Forcible rape	Robbery	Aggravated assault	Property crime	Burglary	Larceny-theft	Motor vehicle theft	Arson[1]
Missouri—*Continued*											
Hardin	571	0	0	0	0	0	4	2	2	0	0
Harrisonville	10,055	19	0	3	0	16	482	56	408	18	2
Hartville	615	2	0	0	0	2	12	3	9	0	0
Hawk Point	671	0	0	0	0	0	28	5	23	0	0
Hayti	2,950	17	0	0	2	15	183	41	136	6	3
Hazelwood	25,796	76	0	2	27	47	1,011	235	716	60	1
Henrietta	370	1	0	0	0	1	1	0	1	0	0
Herculaneum	3,481	1	0	0	0	1	67	7	57	3	0
Hermann	2,440	15	0	1	0	14	70	19	49	2	0
Higginsville	4,814	3	0	3	0	0	151	26	122	3	0
High Hill	196	0	0	0	0	0	3	0	3	0	0
Highlandville	914	0	0	0	0	0	2	1	1	0	0
Hillsboro	2,831	13	0	2	1	10	84	14	63	7	1
Hillsdale	1,483	37	1	1	3	32	89	41	33	15	1
Holcomb	637	0	0	0	0	0	0	0	0	0	0
Holden	2,260	4	0	0	2	2	98	15	75	8	0
Hollister	4,442	18	0	3	0	15	162	34	120	8	1
Holt	449	1	0	0	0	1	2	0	2	0	0
Holts Summit	3,259	13	1	1	0	11	55	8	45	2	0
Houston	2,089	5	0	0	0	5	170	27	140	3	1
Howardville	384	0	0	0	0	0	6	3	1	2	0
Humansville	1,052	1	0	0	0	1	7	3	4	0	0
Huntsville	1,570	2	0	1	0	1	8	3	5	0	0
Hurley	179	0	0	0	0	0	0	0	0	0	0
Iberia	739	4	0	0	0	4	3	1	1	1	0
Independence	117,255	499	2	45	110	342	6,691	1,178	4,785	728	26
Indian Point	530	0	0	0	0	0	2	1	1	0	0
Ironton	1,465	1	0	1	0	0	26	5	18	3	0
Jackson	13,808	24	0	1	1	22	340	62	266	12	0
Jasper	934	2	0	0	0	2	14	1	13	0	0
Jefferson City	43,236	245	1	9	58	177	1,613	282	1,305	26	10
Jennings	14,765	191	5	6	63	117	1,030	497	448	85	9
Jonesburg	771	5	0	0	1	4	38	10	25	3	0
Joplin	50,332	249	2	33	54	160	3,533	692	2,562	279	12
Kahoka	2,086	6	0	3	0	3	3	0	3	0	0
Kansas City	461,458	5,536	108	265	1,665	3,498	25,545	6,848	15,305	3,392	302
Kearney	8,411	5	0	1	1	3	160	19	135	6	0
Kennett	10,972	42	1	3	6	32	537	147	357	33	4
Kimberling City	2,409	0	0	0	0	0	36	4	32	0	0
Kimmswick	158	0	0	0	0	0	0	0	0	0	0
King City	1,017	0	0	0	0	0	8	3	0	5	0
Kinloch	299	5	0	0	0	5	7	2	2	3	0
Kirksville	17,569	119	0	1	2	116	577	88	480	9	2
Kirkwood	27,640	34	0	4	6	24	758	70	676	12	4
Knob Noster	2,719	5	0	0	2	3	100	23	75	2	0
Ladue	8,552	11	0	0	2	9	141	22	117	2	0
Lake Lafayette	328	0	0	0	0	0	5	2	2	1	0
Lake Lotawana	1,946	0	0	0	0	0	29	8	19	2	0
Lake Ozark	1,592	3	0	0	0	3	45	10	34	1	0
Lakeshire	1,437	1	0	0	1	0	13	4	9	0	0
Lake St. Louis	14,598	25	0	0	5	20	325	43	279	3	0
Lake Tapawingo	733	0	0	0	0	0	13	1	12	0	0
Lake Waukomis	873	2	0	0	0	2	11	1	10	0	0
Lake Winnebago	1,135	0	0	0	0	0	4	0	4	0	0
Lamar	4,548	14	0	8	1	5	128	23	103	2	0
La Monte	1,144	3	0	1	0	2	14	6	8	0	0
Lanagan	421	2	0	0	0	2	0	0	0	0	0
La Plata	1,371	1	0	0	0	1	1	0	1	0	0
Lathrop	2,094	6	0	0	0	6	24	10	10	4	0
Laurie	948	4	0	1	1	2	39	6	31	2	0
Lawson	2,482	6	0	0	0	6	69	22	44	3	4
Leadington	424	2	0	1	0	1	6	1	4	1	0
Leadwood	1,287	12	0	1	1	10	27	8	18	1	0
Leasburg	339	1	0	0	0	1	0	0	0	0	0
Lebanon	14,527	63	0	6	0	57	728	100	605	23	0
Lee's Summit	91,696	107	0	18	30	59	2,116	325	1,676	115	6
Leeton	568	0	0	0	0	0	8	1	7	0	0
Lexington	4,743	13	0	2	0	11	141	31	103	7	0
Liberty	29,255	56	0	1	13	42	476	95	345	36	5
Licking	3,135	3	1	0	1	1	72	12	59	1	0
Lincoln	1,194	1	0	0	0	1	41	7	31	3	0
Linn	1,464	2	0	0	0	2	17	5	12	0	0
Linn Creek	245	1	0	1	0	0	3	1	2	0	0

[1] If a blank is presented in the arson column, it indicates that the FBI did not receive 12 complete months of arson data for that agency.

Table II-8. Offenses Known to Law Enforcement, by Selected State and City, 2011—*Continued*

(Number.)

State/City	Population	Violent crime	Murder and non-negligent man-slaughter	Forcible rape	Robbery	Aggravated assault	Property crime	Burglary	Larceny-theft	Motor vehicle theft	Arson[1]
Missouri—*Continued*											
Louisiana	3,376	17	0	1	0	16	21	5	16	0	1
Lowry City	642	1	0	1	0	0	0	0	0	0	0
Macon	5,491	13	0	0	1	12	204	44	155	5	2
Malden	4,291	12	0	0	0	12	62	23	36	3	0
Manchester	18,160	1	0	1	0	0	362	23	333	6	0
Mansfield	1,301	1	0	0	0	1	76	12	64	0	0
Maplewood	8,075	37	0	1	16	20	504	47	445	12	1
Marble Hill	1,482	24	0	1	6	17	36	5	26	5	0
Marceline	2,241	1	0	0	0	1	59	27	31	1	2
Marionville	2,233	9	0	0	1	8	116	13	95	8	0
Marshall	13,112	33	0	7	0	26	326	55	260	11	0
Marshfield	6,657	10	0	1	0	9	186	30	139	17	0
Marston	505	1	0	0	0	1	2	0	2	0	0
Marthasville	1,140	2	0	0	0	2	4	1	2	1	0
Martinsburg	305	0	0	0	0	0	0	0	0	0	0
Maryland Heights	27,572	40	0	0	8	32	718	117	569	32	3
Maryville	12,016	31	0	1	0	30	269	32	233	4	1
Matthews	630	2	0	0	0	2	19	8	11	0	0
Maysville	1,118	0	0	0	0	0	5	0	5	0	1
Memphis	1,829	0	0	0	0	0	26	3	21	2	0
Merriam Woods	1,767	0	0	0	0	0	0	0	0	0	0
Mexico	11,585	27	0	3	5	19	270	54	207	9	2
Milan	1,967	3	0	0	0	3	18	5	12	1	0
Miller	702	2	0	1	0	1	3	1	2	0	0
Miner	988	14	0	0	0	14	37	6	30	1	0
Moberly	14,025	31	0	0	6	25	462	60	389	13	3
Moline Acres	2,451	17	1	0	6	10	125	52	71	2	0
Monett	8,905	13	0	1	4	8	387	70	299	18	0
Montgomery City	2,844	5	0	1	0	4	40	8	28	4	3
Morehouse	977	2	0	0	0	2	2	1	1	0	0
Mosby	191	2	0	0	0	2	2	0	2	0	0
Moscow Mills	2,518	8	0	1	0	7	68	12	47	9	0
Mound City	1,163	4	0	0	0	4	19	2	16	1	0
Mountain Grove	4,806	21	0	0	3	18	203	33	161	9	0
Mountain View	2,729	5	0	0	0	5	119	37	77	5	0
Mount Vernon	4,592	18	0	0	4	14	190	24	165	1	1
Napoleon	223	0	0	0	0	0	0	0	0	0	0
Naylor	634	1	0	1	0	0	3	0	3	0	0
Neosho	11,878	14	0	3	2	9	424	73	335	16	2
Nevada	8,416	61	0	3	7	51	618	121	468	29	5
New Bloomfield	671	2	0	0	0	2	3	0	3	0	0
Newburg	472	0	0	0	0	0	0	0	0	0	0
New Florence	772	2	0	0	0	2	18	0	18	0	1
New Franklin	1,093	2	0	0	0	2	0	0	0	0	0
New Haven	2,097	14	0	0	0	14	39	12	24	3	1
New London	978	0	0	0	0	0	27	5	21	1	0
New Madrid	3,127	0	0	0	0	0	34	4	29	1	0
New Melle	477	0	0	0	0	0	9	3	5	1	0
Niangua	406	0	0	0	0	0	0	0	0	0	0
Nixa	19,091	17	0	1	5	11	391	50	323	18	1
Noel	1,839	9	0	0	0	9	19	3	13	3	0
Norborne	711	1	0	0	1	0	2	2	0	0	0
Normandy	5,026	32	0	0	7	25	90	32	42	16	2
North Kansas City	4,223	10	0	0	6	4	426	40	346	40	0
Northmoor	326	0	0	0	0	0	9	1	5	3	0
Northwoods	4,242	40	0	2	15	23	139	63	62	14	0
Norwood	667	0	0	0	0	0	0	0	0	0	0
Oak Grove	7,823	11	0	2	1	8	201	39	143	19	1
Oakland	1,386	0	0	0	0	0	17	1	16	0	1
Oakview Village	376	2	0	0	0	2	5	3	1	1	0
Odessa	5,319	3	0	3	0	0	94	25	68	1	2
O'Fallon	79,617	71	0	3	9	59	1,225	135	1,061	29	1
Old Monroe	266	1	0	0	0	1	1	0	0	1	0
Olivette	7,765	20	0	0	6	14	136	42	91	3	0
Oran	1,299	4	0	0	0	4	22	5	17	0	0
Oregon	860	0	0	0	0	0	0	0	0	0	0
Oronogo	2,947	1	0	1	0	0	22	4	17	1	0
Orrick	840	2	0	0	0	2	9	4	3	2	0
Osage Beach	4,367	14	0	0	1	13	284	32	247	5	2
Osceola	950	0	0	0	0	0	1	0	0	1	0
Overland	16,120	45	1	0	14	30	742	209	503	30	5
Owensville	2,686	0	0	0	0	0	64	5	59	0	0
Ozark	17,885	34	0	1	4	29	560	77	460	23	0
Pacific	7,027	19	0	0	2	17	208	25	174	9	1

[1] If a blank is presented in the arson column, it indicates that the FBI did not receive 12 complete months of arson data for that agency.

Table II-8.   Offenses Known to Law Enforcement, by Selected State and City, 2011—*Continued*

(Number.)

State/City	Population	Violent crime	Murder and non-negligent man-slaughter	Forcible rape	Robbery	Aggravated assault	Property crime	Burglary	Larceny-theft	Motor vehicle theft	Arson[1]
Missouri—*Continued*											
Pagedale	3,316	26	0	2	8	16	133	54	68	11	0
Palmyra	3,608	1	0	0	0	1	82	4	74	4	0
Park Hills	8,791	9	0	0	1	8	192	16	161	15	0
Parkville	5,574	7	0	0	0	7	130	18	106	6	0
Parma	716	8	0	1	2	5	14	7	6	1	1
Pasadena Park	472	0	0	0	0	0	6	0	3	3	0
Peculiar	4,625	8	0	1	0	7	92	16	74	2	8
Perry	696	1	0	0	0	1	4	2	2	0	0
Perryville	8,255	12	1	3	0	8	248	43	196	9	0
Pevely	5,504	6	0	0	1	5	133	13	118	2	0
Piedmont	1,984	2	0	0	0	2	81	14	66	1	2
Pierce City	1,297	0	0	0	0	0	22	3	17	2	0
Pilot Knob	749	0	0	0	0	0	0	0	0	0	0
Pine Lawn	3,287	59	0	1	16	42	167	86	57	24	0
Pineville	794	0	0	0	0	0	0	0	0	0	0
Platte City	4,708	5	1	1	1	2	68	11	53	4	5
Platte Woods	386	0	0	0	0	0	11	0	10	1	0
Plattsburg	2,327	3	1	0	0	2	56	8	44	4	1
Pleasant Hill	8,142	2	0	0	0	2	129	24	101	4	0
Pleasant Hope	616	1	0	0	0	1	4	2	2	0	0
Pleasant Valley	2,972	3	0	0	2	1	57	8	43	6	0
Poplar Bluff	17,085	106	2	3	15	86	1,408	272	1,098	38	5
Portageville	3,240	0	0	0	0	0	18	3	15	0	0
Potosi	2,670	10	0	0	2	8	196	20	170	6	0
Purcell	409	0	0	0	0	0	0	0	0	0	0
Purdy	1,102	3	0	0	0	3	28	3	22	3	1
Queen City	600	0	0	0	0	0	0	0	0	0	0
Qulin	460	0	0	0	0	0	8	2	6	0	1
Randolph	52	1	0	0	1	0	6	1	4	1	0
Raymore	19,276	14	0	1	1	12	363	44	301	18	6
Raytown	29,633	88	0	8	35	45	1,232	290	805	137	18
Reeds Spring	916	3	0	1	0	2	6	2	4	0	0
Republic	14,805	79	0	3	5	71	574	108	451	15	0
Rich Hill	1,401	4	0	0	0	4	21	8	12	1	2
Richland	1,870	7	0	1	0	6	87	13	74	0	0
Richmond	5,818	15	0	5	0	10	256	60	193	3	3
Richmond Heights	8,634	14	1	1	5	7	801	58	728	15	0
Riverside	2,948	9	0	1	3	5	198	19	154	25	0
Riverview	2,866	24	0	0	10	14	179	101	59	19	0
Rockaway Beach	844	5	0	0	0	5	13	5	7	1	0
Rock Hill	4,652	2	0	0	1	1	101	22	72	7	0
Rock Port	1,323	1	0	0	0	1	3	1	2	0	0
Rogersville	3,084	4	0	0	1	3	85	16	68	1	0
Rolla	19,630	76	0	2	17	57	796	114	652	30	5
Rosebud	410	1	0	0	0	1	0	0	0	0	0
Salem	4,968	12	0	1	2	9	200	32	164	4	0
Salisbury	1,624	0	0	0	0	0	23	1	22	0	0
Sarcoxie	1,335	4	0	0	0	4	27	8	18	1	0
Savannah	5,075	6	0	0	0	6	60	15	41	4	0
Scott City	4,582	16	0	0	1	15	137	25	107	5	4
Sedalia	21,465	147	2	4	11	130	1,492	302	1,121	69	6
Seligman	854	1	0	0	0	1	17	2	13	2	0
Senath	1,773	14	1	2	1	10	29	8	19	2	1
Seneca	2,344	1	0	0	0	1	62	12	45	5	0
Seymour	1,928	10	0	0	1	9	59	18	37	4	2
Shelbina	1,710	4	0	0	0	4	18	10	6	2	0
Shrewsbury	6,277	8	0	1	2	5	77	12	60	5	0
Sikeston	16,377	266	2	5	28	231	768	129	609	30	8
Slater	1,863	0	0	0	0	0	34	4	29	1	1
Smithville	8,456	11	0	2	2	7	114	13	93	8	0
Southwest City	974	3	0	1	0	2	21	4	15	2	0
Sparta	1,762	3	0	0	1	2	20	14	4	2	0
Springfield	160,078	1,306	5	110	286	905	14,418	2,053	11,391	974	47
St. Ann	13,067	71	1	4	8	58	357	88	231	38	0
St. Charles	66,033	153	0	9	48	96	2,002	257	1,673	72	18
St. Clair	4,741	36	1	4	1	30	298	38	247	13	0
Steelville	1,648	4	0	0	0	4	70	12	55	3	0
Stewartsville	753	0	0	0	0	0	1	1	0	0	0
St. James	4,231	20	0	3	0	17	126	19	103	4	2
St. John	6,541	40	0	3	8	29	255	74	173	8	1
St. Joseph	77,059	281	4	21	82	174	4,056	907	2,870	279	17
St. Louis	320,454	5,950	113	188	2,127	3,522	25,669	7,015	15,285	3,369	191
St. Marys	361	0	0	0	0	0	6	0	6	0	0
Stover	1,098	7	0	0	1	6	52	9	35	8	0

[1] If a blank is presented in the arson column, it indicates that the FBI did not receive 12 complete months of arson data for that agency.

Table II-8.   Offenses Known to Law Enforcement, by Selected State and City, 2011—*Continued*

(Number.)

State/City	Population	Violent crime	Murder and non-negligent man-slaughter	Forcible rape	Robbery	Aggravated assault	Property crime	Burglary	Larceny-theft	Motor vehicle theft	Arson[1]
Missouri—*Continued*											
St. Peters	52,766	138	0	2	16	120	1,439	134	1,270	35	7
Strafford	2,367	0	0	0	0	0	105	7	96	2	0
Strasburg	142	0	0	0	0	0	0	0	0	0	0
St. Robert	4,356	27	0	1	5	21	368	51	309	8	2
Sturgeon	875	0	0	0	0	0	0	0	0	0	0
Sugar Creek	3,357	13	0	0	3	10	211	44	145	22	1
Sullivan	7,107	2	0	1	0	1	405	83	309	13	1
Summersville	504	0	0	0	0	0	16	6	10	0	0
Sunset Hills	8,527	19	0	0	0	19	175	27	136	12	0
Sweet Springs	1,489	10	0	1	0	9	16	4	11	1	0
Tarkio	1,589	1	0	0	0	1	15	3	9	3	0
Terre du Lac	2,328	8	0	1	0	7	55	11	42	2	1
Thayer	2,251	2	0	0	0	2	30	4	24	2	1
Tipton	3,274	3	0	0	0	3	25	4	20	1	0
Town and Country	10,854	8	0	1	4	3	142	28	112	2	0
Tracy	209	1	0	0	0	1	7	2	5	0	0
Trenton	6,023	16	0	4	0	12	159	42	110	7	1
Trimble	648	0	0	0	0	0	0	0	0	0	0
Troy	10,578	9	0	0	2	7	387	39	335	13	0
Truesdale	735	2	0	0	2	0	16	3	13	0	0
Union	10,241	40	0	1	3	36	446	46	392	8	0
Unionville	1,872	0	0	0	0	0	17	6	9	2	0
University City	35,500	194	0	7	68	119	1,456	366	995	95	11
Uplands Park	447	8	0	0	2	6	21	16	4	1	0
Urbana	419	1	0	0	0	1	4	2	2	0	0
Van Buren	822	0	0	0	0	0	18	0	18	0	1
Vandalia	3,913	5	0	0	0	5	56	10	45	1	2
Velda City	1,425	16	0	0	3	13	37	23	9	5	0
Velda Village Hills	1,059	3	0	0	1	2	49	31	14	4	0
Verona	621	2	0	1	0	1	15	7	8	0	1
Versailles	2,491	7	0	0	0	7	64	9	50	5	0
Viburnum	696	0	0	0	0	0	5	1	4	0	0
Vienna	612	2	0	0	0	2	15	4	11	0	0
Vinita Park	1,887	10	0	0	2	8	55	15	37	3	0
Walnut Grove	667	0	0	0	0	0	11	6	5	0	0
Wardell	429	0	0	0	0	0	0	0	0	0	0
Warrensburg	18,906	29	0	5	7	17	561	100	446	15	1
Warrenton	7,909	22	0	0	8	14	405	46	355	4	3
Warsaw	2,135	17	0	1	2	14	104	27	75	2	0
Warson Woods	1,969	1	0	0	1	0	19	3	16	0	0
Washburn	437	0	0	0	0	0	2	1	0	1	3
Washington	14,033	18	0	1	2	15	434	56	363	15	1
Waverly	852	2	0	0	0	2	9	3	6	0	0
Waynesville	4,848	22	1	2	1	18	109	32	75	2	0
Weatherby Lake	1,729	4	0	0	0	4	13	1	10	2	0
Webb City	11,036	0	0	0	0	0	492	48	424	20	0
Webster Groves	23,079	33	0	3	5	25	348	95	228	25	3
Wellington	815	0	0	0	0	0	0	0	0	0	0
Wellston	2,321	55	2	2	14	37	148	64	55	29	8
Wellsville	1,221	1	0	0	0	1	10	4	6	0	0
Wentzville	29,176	32	0	6	4	22	555	77	464	14	2
Weston	1,647	4	0	1	0	3	18	2	14	2	0
West Plains	12,030	66	2	5	7	52	881	135	721	25	0
Wheaton	699	1	0	0	1	0	4	0	3	1	0
Willard	5,307	12	0	0	0	12	89	13	73	3	0
Willow Springs	2,192	13	0	0	0	13	87	22	60	5	0
Winfield	1,409	2	0	0	0	2	7	4	1	2	0
Winona	1,340	7	0	0	1	6	74	30	42	2	0
Wood Heights	720	0	0	0	0	0	5	2	2	1	0
Woodson Terrace	4,078	17	0	2	5	10	137	36	70	31	1
Wright City	3,130	5	0	1	1	3	87	28	58	1	1
Montana[2]											
Baker	1,756	5	0	1	0	4	23	3	17	3	0
Belgrade	7,455	20	0	6	1	13	217	23	190	4	0
Billings	105,095	313	2	36	36	239	4,693	669	3,689	335	9
Boulder	1,194	3	0	0	0	3	7	1	5	1	0
Bozeman	37,611	88	0	21	3	64	1,146	102	991	53	2
Bridger	714	0	0	0	0	0	1	0	1	0	0
Colstrip	2,234	3	0	0	0	3	29	1	25	3	0
Columbia Falls	4,730	5	0	1	0	4	97	8	82	7	0
Columbus	1,910	2	0	2	0	0	29	6	23	0	0
Conrad	2,593	12	0	1	0	11	40	3	34	3	1

[1] If a blank is presented in the arson column, it indicates that the FBI did not receive 12 complete months of arson data for that agency.

[2] Because of changes in the state/local agency's reporting practices, figures are not comparable to previous years' data.

Table II-8.   Offenses Known to Law Enforcement, by Selected State and City, 2011—*Continued*

(Number.)

State/City	Population	Violent crime	Murder and non-negligent man-slaughter	Forcible rape	Robbery	Aggravated assault	Property crime	Burglary	Larceny-theft	Motor vehicle theft	Arson[1]
Montana—*Continued*											
Cut Bank	2,894	16	0	0	0	16	115	15	97	3	1
Dillon	4,171	7	0	0	0	7	58	11	40	7	1
East Helena	2,002	2	0	0	1	1	15	2	12	1	0
Ennis	845	0	0	0	0	0	3	1	2	0	0
Eureka	1,046	3	0	0	1	2	25	6	19	0	0
Fort Benton	1,477	1	0	0	0	1	17	0	15	2	0
Glasgow	3,279	3	0	0	0	3	47	2	36	9	0
Glendive	4,979	11	0	2	0	9	138	30	102	6	1
Great Falls	59,024	176	2	13	33	128	2,699	303	2,287	109	20
Hamilton	4,387	29	0	2	1	26	228	22	203	3	3
Havre	9,393	55	0	4	5	46	443	41	378	24	8
Helena	28,440	135	2	20	11	102	934	123	758	53	6
Hot Springs	549	2	0	0	0	2	2	0	2	0	0
Kalispell	20,104	58	0	9	5	44	853	101	714	38	3
Laurel	6,778	3	0	1	0	2	134	17	111	6	2
Lewistown	5,953	21	0	2	0	19	87	21	58	8	1
Libby	2,651	7	0	0	0	7	101	14	86	1	0
Livingston	7,107	18	0	4	0	14	120	15	98	7	0
Manhattan	1,533	3	0	2	0	1	13	1	10	2	0
Miles City	8,485	19	0	1	0	18	191	15	169	7	1
Missoula	67,381	192	0	26	20	146	2,415	299	2,019	97	14
Plains	1,057	0	0	0	0	0	16	1	13	2	0
Polson	4,528	16	0	2	0	14	286	29	246	11	3
Red Lodge	2,144	7	1	0	1	5	37	7	30	0	1
Ronan City	1,888	12	0	3	1	8	65	5	54	6	0
Sidney	5,237	16	0	2	0	14	97	12	78	7	1
Stevensville	1,825	5	0	0	0	5	25	5	18	2	0
St. Ignatius	849	3	0	1	0	2	17	3	14	0	0
Thompson Falls	1,325	6	0	1	0	5	31	6	23	2	1
Troy	946	1	0	0	0	1	34	3	30	1	1
West Yellowstone	1,282	2	0	0	0	2	2	0	2	0	0
Whitefish	6,413	8	0	4	0	4	177	11	159	7	2
Wolf Point	2,644	12	0	2	0	10	140	43	91	6	0
Nebraska											
Alliance	8,567	25	1	0	2	22	165	53	106	6	1
Ashland	2,475	1	0	1	0	0	6	0	4	2	1
Auburn	3,491	2	0	0	1	1	24	6	17	1	0
Aurora	4,519	8	0	2	0	6	33	15	16	2	0
Beatrice	12,570	71	0	21	2	48	410	81	324	5	2
Bellevue	50,584	49	1	18	7	23	1,230	175	944	111	8
Bennington	1,471	1	0	0	0	1	17	4	12	1	0
Blair	8,061	3	0	0	1	2	97	8	87	2	2
Bridgeport	1,559	0	0	0	0	0	14	2	12	0	0
Broken Bow	3,591	9	0	5	0	4	42	4	37	1	0
Central City	2,960	1	0	0	0	1	52	5	47	0	0
Chadron	5,903	4	0	1	0	3	135	11	117	7	1
Columbus	22,308	19	1	3	3	12	493	78	394	21	2
Cozad	4,012	1	0	1	0	0	54	28	26	0	0
Crete	7,022	25	0	2	2	21	187	50	136	1	1
David City	2,932	1	0	1	0	0	44	1	37	6	0
Falls City	4,364	2	0	0	0	2	66	14	43	9	0
Fremont	26,633	43	0	13	4	26	721	138	560	23	5
Gering	8,576	4	0	0	1	3	157	35	115	7	0
Gothenburg	3,606	2	1	1	0	0	43	9	34	0	0
Grand Island	48,953	149	1	28	29	91	2,448	399	1,958	91	6
Hastings	25,129	47	1	14	8	24	874	108	740	26	6
Holdrege	5,544	8	0	2	0	6	124	19	102	3	0
Imperial	2,089	2	0	1	0	1	5	0	5	0	0
Kearney	31,062	45	0	9	2	34	861	129	714	18	4
La Vista	15,899	10	0	4	1	5	312	36	250	26	1
Lexington	10,321	15	0	6	1	8	316	95	208	13	2
Lincoln	260,685	966	4	166	177	619	10,189	1,401	8,424	364	25
Lyons	859	0	0	0	0	0	5	4	1	0	0
Madison	2,460	2	0	1	0	1	17	3	12	2	0
McCook	7,767	8	0	3	0	5	221	31	175	15	0
Milford	2,109	3	0	2	0	1	24	3	21	0	0
Minden	2,949	2	0	1	0	1	29	4	24	1	0
Mitchell	1,717	1	0	0	0	1	28	13	15	0	0
Nebraska City	7,354	3	0	0	2	1	162	20	134	8	0
Norfolk	24,426	27	0	12	3	12	675	70	581	24	1
North Platte	24,954	61	3	15	7	36	1,054	122	884	48	11
Ogallala	4,779	3	0	2	0	1	157	15	134	8	0
Omaha	412,608	2,309	43	220	696	1,350	18,764	3,321	12,793	2,650	91
O'Neill	3,738	1	0	1	0	0	8	4	3	1	0

[1] If a blank is presented in offense arson column, it indicates that the FBI did not receive 12 complete months of arson data for that agency.

Table II-8. Offenses Known to Law Enforcement, by Selected State and City, 2011—*Continued*

(Number.)

State/City	Population	Violent crime	Murder and non-negligent man-slaughter	Forcible rape	Robbery	Aggravated assault	Property crime	Burglary	Larceny-theft	Motor vehicle theft	Arson[1]
Nebraska—*Continued*											
Papillion	19,063	11	0	7	2	2	340	36	294	10	4
Plainview	1,257	0	0	0	0	0	7	1	5	1	0
Plattsmouth	6,560	8	0	5	0	3	163	18	143	2	1
Ralston	5,996	2	0	0	2	0	155	27	120	8	0
Scottsbluff	15,173	44	2	11	8	23	797	131	650	16	6
Scribner	865	0	0	0	0	0	8	6	2	0	0
Seward	7,026	2	0	2	0	0	70	5	63	2	0
Sidney	6,817	5	0	1	0	4	78	5	70	3	0
South Sioux City	13,472	23	1	3	1	18	389	65	308	16	0
St. Paul	2,310	1	0	0	0	1	5	0	5	0	0
Superior	1,974	3	0	1	0	2	7	5	2	0	0
Valentine	2,761	3	0	1	0	2	34	4	22	8	1
Valley	1,892	5	0	3	1	1	55	9	42	4	1
Wahoo	4,548	3	0	1	0	2	104	30	71	3	2
West Point	3,394	3	0	1	0	2	2	2	0	0	0
Wymore	1,470	0	0	0	0	0	40	2	37	1	0
York	7,835	4	0	0	2	2	213	35	169	9	0
Nevada											
Boulder City	15,150	14	0	1	2	11	143	71	64	8	2
Carlin	2,388	1	0	0	0	1	27	5	21	1	0
Elko	18,451	125	2	12	12	99	596	156	405	35	0
Fallon	8,679	11	0	1	1	9	353	53	281	19	0
Henderson	259,902	571	2	58	197	314	4,777	1,280	3,069	428	44
Las Vegas Metropolitan Police Department	1,458,474	10,813	82	651	3,493	6,587	41,426	12,662	21,977	6,787	232
Lovelock	1,910	22	0	0	1	21	27	15	11	1	0
Mesquite	15,405	21	1	1	1	18	258	51	194	13	0
Reno	227,120	1,108	14	27	383	684	6,550	1,618	4,311	621	26
Sparks	91,025	285	7	46	75	157	2,447	656	1,600	191	22
West Wendover	4,447	20	0	7	1	12	154	38	107	9	3
Winnemucca	7,458	9	0	0	2	7	96	26	63	7	3
New Hampshire											
Alexandria	1,615	1	0	0	0	1	33	13	20	0	0
Alton	5,257	7	0	1	0	6	146	55	91	0	0
Amherst	11,216	8	0	0	2	6	273	30	242	1	2
Antrim	2,640	7	0	3	1	3	64	10	52	2	0
Ashland	2,079	4	0	2	1	1	79	8	63	8	0
Auburn	4,959	4	0	2	1	1	96	45	42	9	0
Barnstead	4,599	2	0	0	0	2	104	39	64	1	0
Barrington	8,587	4	0	1	0	3	134	43	89	2	0
Bartlett	2,792	1	0	0	0	1	48	20	28	0	1
Belmont	7,366	12	0	1	1	10	254	58	189	7	1
Bennington	1,478	1	0	1	0	0	70	5	63	2	0
Berlin	10,064	11	0	4	2	5	164	50	105	9	5
Bethlehem	2,529	2	0	0	1	1	33	11	21	1	1
Boscawen	3,970	4	0	0	0	4	76	8	66	2	2
Bow	7,529	5	0	0	0	5	85	28	54	3	0
Brentwood	4,492	1	0	1	0	0	50	12	37	1	0
Bristol	3,058	7	0	2	0	5	89	31	56	2	0
Campton	3,337	10	0	5	1	4	61	12	48	1	1
Candia	3,914	4	0	0	0	4	63	19	43	1	0
Carroll	764	1	0	0	0	1	81	9	71	1	0
Center Harbor	1,097	0	0	0	0	0	51	13	38	0	0
Charlestown	5,121	8	0	2	0	6	51	16	33	2	0
Claremont	13,372	39	0	8	6	25	452	48	397	7	2
Colebrook	2,304	2	0	0	1	1	54	12	39	3	0
Concord	42,751	120	1	24	25	70	1,288	194	1,058	36	5
Conway	10,128	28	1	7	5	15	418	67	343	8	2
Dalton	980	0	0	0	0	0	17	4	9	4	0
Danville	4,393	1	0	0	0	1	47	10	36	1	1
Deerfield	4,286	2	1	0	1	0	82	28	50	4	2
Deering	1,915	2	0	0	0	2	35	13	21	1	1
Derry	33,152	81	0	10	9	62	863	203	627	33	26
Dover	30,026	30	0	5	11	14	585	90	480	15	2
Dublin	1,599	6	0	0	0	6	13	7	6	0	0
Dunbarton	2,762	2	0	0	0	2	26	14	11	1	0
Durham	14,657	12	0	3	0	9	132	14	117	1	1
Effingham	1,467	0	0	0	0	0	27	10	16	1	0
Enfield	4,588	6	0	0	0	6	70	6	63	1	0
Epping	6,419	5	0	2	1	2	215	24	185	6	3
Epsom	4,572	6	0	1	0	5	78	33	41	4	0
Exeter	14,325	15	0	4	1	10	148	26	118	4	2
Farmington	6,795	22	0	7	4	11	187	67	111	9	7
Fitzwilliam	2,399	0	0	0	0	0	35	16	16	3	0

[1] If a blank is presented in the arson column, it indicates that the FBI did not receive 12 complete months of arson data for that agency.

Table II-8.   Offenses Known to Law Enforcement, by Selected State and City, 2011—*Continued*

(Number.)

State/City	Population	Violent crime	Murder and non-negligent man-slaughter	Forcible rape	Robbery	Aggravated assault	Property crime	Burglary	Larceny-theft	Motor vehicle theft	Arson[1]
New Hampshire—*Continued*											
Franconia	1,105	0	0	0	0	0	30	5	25	0	0
Fremont	4,289	5	0	2	0	3	39	11	24	4	1
Gilford	7,135	11	0	4	1	6	226	44	176	6	0
Gilmanton	3,782	0	0	0	0	0	56	25	28	3	0
Goffstown	17,674	14	0	1	2	11	309	81	226	2	0
Gorham	2,852	6	0	0	2	4	65	11	53	1	2
Greenland	3,554	3	0	0	1	2	60	11	46	3	0
Hampstead	8,534	7	0	0	3	4	90	23	61	6	0
Hampton	14,996	34	0	5	5	24	349	40	296	13	2
Hampton Falls	2,239	3	0	0	1	2	42	12	28	2	0
Hanover	11,275	5	0	4	0	1	170	16	154	0	1
Haverhill	4,703	4	0	0	0	4	102	33	62	7	0
Henniker	4,842	2	0	0	0	2	112	25	87	0	4
Hillsborough	6,019	8	0	2	0	6	124	14	107	3	1
Hinsdale	4,051	12	0	6	1	5	83	20	60	3	0
Hooksett	13,469	18	0	6	4	8	451	92	347	12	0
Hopkinton	5,596	5	0	0	1	4	57	8	47	2	0
Hudson	24,499	29	0	4	7	18	363	60	288	15	3
Jaffrey	5,464	14	0	2	0	12	57	16	38	3	0
Keene	23,440	53	1	10	15	27	811	127	669	15	2
Kingston	6,033	5	0	0	0	5	38	7	27	4	0
Laconia	15,972	64	0	12	13	39	748	128	607	13	3
Lancaster	3,512	4	0	0	1	3	116	18	95	3	0
Lebanon	13,168	25	0	5	4	16	419	37	379	3	8
Lee	4,336	1	0	0	1	0	35	10	23	2	0
Lincoln	1,664	5	0	2	1	2	97	9	86	2	0
Lisbon	1,597	0	0	0	0	0	14	4	10	0	0
Litchfield	8,282	5	0	1	0	4	97	34	58	5	2
Littleton	5,936	24	0	2	1	21	99	29	69	1	1
Londonderry	24,161	18	0	1	0	17	354	78	261	15	1
Loudon	5,324	6	0	5	1	0	153	30	114	9	1
Madison	2,505	2	0	0	2	0	36	7	27	2	9
Manchester	109,708	618	2	69	181	366	4,194	902	3,136	156	70
Meredith	6,249	4	0	1	0	3	137	28	102	7	1
Merrimack	25,527	2	0	0	2	0	269	53	209	7	0
Middleton	1,785	2	0	0	0	2	32	16	14	2	0
Milford	15,135	37	0	2	7	28	322	46	266	10	3
Milton	4,604	14	0	5	0	9	103	38	60	5	1
Mont Vernon	2,412	1	0	0	0	1	21	12	8	1	0
Moultonborough	4,049	2	0	0	0	2	67	18	47	2	0
Nashua	86,607	212	3	24	50	135	2,130	360	1,693	77	19
New Boston	5,328	2	0	2	0	0	57	20	36	1	0
Newbury	2,075	1	0	0	0	1	17	3	14	0	0
New Durham	2,641	3	0	0	0	3	79	15	64	0	0
New Hampton	2,168	2	0	1	0	1	96	14	80	2	0
Newington	754	1	0	0	1	0	214	5	208	1	0
New London	4,403	2	0	0	0	2	39	6	31	2	0
Newport	6,516	10	0	2	0	8	218	31	176	11	2
Newton	4,609	2	0	1	0	1	42	9	32	1	0
Northfield	4,835	10	0	3	2	5	113	27	84	2	1
North Hampton	4,307	1	0	0	0	1	60	15	40	5	0
Northumberland	2,291	5	0	0	1	4	40	14	25	1	0
Northwood	4,247	10	0	3	0	7	104	19	84	1	3
Nottingham	4,791	2	0	0	0	2	83	14	64	5	0
Orford	1,239	0	0	0	0	0	7	2	5	0	0
Ossipee	4,351	15	0	2	0	13	158	26	126	6	0
Pelham	12,914	15	0	2	3	10	195	50	136	9	1
Pembroke	7,124	14	1	3	0	10	132	26	103	3	2
Peterborough	6,292	3	0	3	0	0	114	22	88	4	0
Pittsfield	4,111	10	0	5	0	5	124	28	90	6	0
Plaistow	7,619	3	0	0	1	2	164	13	146	5	0
Plymouth	6,999	17	1	9	3	4	224	25	192	7	11
Portsmouth	21,261	50	0	5	9	36	609	83	510	16	4
Raymond	10,151	14	0	7	0	7	182	38	136	8	2
Rindge	6,022	6	0	1	2	3	78	19	57	2	0
Rochester	29,791	101	0	9	16	76	998	186	787	25	8
Rollinsford	2,530	6	0	3	1	2	44	11	32	1	0
Rye	5,305	3	0	0	0	3	73	4	69	0	0
Salem	28,814	34	0	5	14	15	877	76	748	53	5
Sandown	5,994	2	0	1	0	1	55	18	35	2	0
Sandwich	1,328	1	0	1	0	0	41	14	27	0	0
Seabrook	8,704	13	0	1	2	10	264	23	232	9	0
Somersworth	11,781	41	0	9	7	25	519	40	466	13	6
South Hampton	815	0	0	0	0	0	7	1	6	0	0
Strafford	3,996	0	0	0	0	0	44	15	28	1	0

[1] If a blank is presented in the arson column, it indicates that the FBI did not receive 12 complete months of arson data for that agency.

Table II-8.   Offenses Known to Law Enforcement, by Selected State and City, 2011—*Continued*

(Number.)

State/City	Population	Violent crime	Murder and non-negligent man-slaughter	Forcible rape	Robbery	Aggravated assault	Property crime	Burglary	Larceny-theft	Motor vehicle theft	Arson[1]
New Hampshire—*Continued*											
Stratham	7,265	4	0	1	0	3	73	11	61	1	0
Sunapee	3,369	1	0	1	0	0	15	4	11	0	0
Thornton	2,493	4	0	0	0	4	25	6	17	2	1
Tilton	3,572	12	0	2	2	8	216	24	186	6	1
Troy	2,148	0	0	0	0	0	21	6	7	8	0
Wakefield	5,798	8	0	0	0	8	125	35	83	7	1
Walpole	3,739	3	0	1	1	1	80	21	57	2	1
Warner	2,837	0	0	0	0	0	4	1	0	3	0
Washington	1,124	0	0	0	0	0	19	6	13	0	0
Waterville Valley	247	0	0	0	0	0	23	2	21	0	0
Weare	8,797	9	1	3	1	4	81	34	45	2	0
Webster	1,874	0	0	0	0	0	27	3	21	3	0
Wilton	3,682	3	0	1	0	2	74	33	40	1	1
Winchester	4,347	14	0	4	0	10	136	38	89	9	2
Windham	13,610	13	0	10	0	3	150	31	115	4	1
Wolfeboro	6,277	6	0	2	1	3	119	17	98	4	0
Woodstock	1,376	8	0	3	0	5	41	7	33	1	0
New Jersey											
Aberdeen Township	18,271	18	1	2	4	11	291	62	225	4	2
Absecon	8,439	20	0	0	11	9	218	54	158	6	1
Allendale	6,527	0	0	0	0	0	58	21	36	1	0
Allenhurst	498	0	0	0	0	0	14	1	12	1	0
Allentown	1,834	1	0	0	0	1	27	3	24	0	0
Alpha	2,377	1	0	0	0	1	29	9	20	0	0
Alpine	1,855	1	0	0	1	0	10	3	6	1	0
Andover Township	6,340	1	0	0	1	0	25	11	14	0	0
Asbury Park	16,170	260	4	11	114	131	1,279	412	808	59	3
Atlantic City	39,690	741	13	22	384	322	2,938	573	2,261	104	5
Atlantic Highlands	4,400	7	0	0	0	7	85	9	75	1	0
Audubon	8,848	11	0	0	6	5	306	30	271	5	0
Audubon Park	1,026	2	0	0	2	0	29	7	22	0	0
Avalon	1,338	5	0	0	1	4	266	42	220	4	0
Avon-by-the-Sea	1,907	1	0	0	0	1	54	5	47	2	0
Barnegat Light	576	0	0	0	0	0	10	3	7	0	0
Barnegat Township	21,006	30	0	5	7	18	214	38	174	2	5
Barrington	7,006	6	0	1	2	3	64	24	38	2	0
Bay Head	971	1	0	1	0	0	87	3	84	0	0
Bayonne	63,234	148	3	6	65	74	807	161	534	112	4
Beach Haven	1,174	4	0	0	0	4	162	12	150	0	0
Beachwood	11,082	6	0	0	1	5	251	37	210	4	0
Bedminster Township	8,192	1	0	0	0	1	51	9	40	2	0
Belleville	36,046	115	2	3	60	50	1,013	164	637	212	3
Bellmawr	11,622	23	0	2	8	13	311	84	206	21	0
Belmar	5,813	20	0	0	4	16	312	123	185	4	0
Belvidere	2,690	3	0	0	0	3	35	4	31	0	0
Bergenfield	26,853	18	0	2	2	14	159	34	120	5	1
Berkeley Heights Township	13,227	2	0	0	0	2	72	5	64	3	0
Berkeley Township	41,392	38	0	1	11	26	618	122	483	13	2
Berlin	7,613	8	0	0	0	8	222	36	181	5	0
Berlin Township	5,375	11	0	0	6	5	219	23	194	2	2
Bernards Township	26,741	4	0	1	2	1	156	16	135	5	1
Bernardsville	7,733	2	1	0	0	1	40	2	37	1	0
Beverly	2,586	9	0	0	1	8	69	22	46	1	0
Blairstown Township	5,987	4	0	0	0	4	59	12	46	1	0
Bloomfield	47,472	126	0	5	81	40	1,040	213	650	177	2
Bloomingdale	7,681	13	1	0	0	12	56	10	44	2	0
Bogota	8,214	12	0	0	9	3	71	26	39	6	2
Boonton	8,375	9	1	0	2	6	77	15	61	1	0
Boonton Township	4,277	2	0	0	0	2	25	5	20	0	0
Bordentown	3,937	0	0	0	0	0	43	10	31	2	0
Bordentown Township	11,405	12	2	0	4	6	139	28	101	10	0
Bound Brook	10,437	21	1	2	9	9	249	45	192	12	3
Bradley Beach	4,312	4	0	0	1	3	181	32	144	5	0
Branchburg Township	14,507	5	0	1	1	3	158	22	131	5	0
Brick Township	75,322	100	0	7	20	73	1,313	331	960	22	4
Bridgeton	25,433	307	3	8	120	176	1,063	412	610	41	7
Bridgewater Township	44,612	17	1	2	5	9	658	80	551	27	0
Brielle	4,790	2	0	0	1	1	51	9	40	2	0
Brigantine	9,481	5	0	1	0	4	239	58	179	2	2
Brooklawn	1,962	21	0	4	13	4	236	28	199	9	0
Buena	4,618	19	0	1	2	16	98	27	68	3	0
Burlington	9,953	43	0	6	19	18	239	45	176	18	2

[1] If a blank is presented in the arson column, it indicates that the FBI did not receive 12 complete months of arson data for that agency.

Table II-8.   Offenses Known to Law Enforcement, by Selected State and City, 2011—*Continued*

(Number.)

State/City	Population	Violent crime	Murder and non-negligent man-slaughter	Forcible rape	Robbery	Aggravated assault	Property crime	Burglary	Larceny-theft	Motor vehicle theft	Arson[1]
New Jersey—*Continued*											
Burlington Township	22,669	37	0	7	9	21	401	85	292	24	1
Butler	7,564	5	0	1	1	3	103	38	61	4	0
Byram Township	8,378	10	0	0	3	7	47	14	33	0	0
Caldwell	7,848	6	0	0	1	5	73	19	50	4	0
Califon	1,080	1	0	0	0	1	0	0	0	0	0
Camden	77,604	2,152	47	66	857	1,182	4,462	1,436	2,226	800	136
Cape May	3,619	3	0	1	0	2	199	28	168	3	0
Cape May Point	292	0	0	0	0	0	13	5	8	0	0
Carlstadt	6,147	5	0	1	0	4	160	10	119	31	0
Carney's Point Township	8,076	14	0	1	4	9	198	57	126	15	7
Carteret	22,920	47	2	5	17	23	461	101	317	43	1
Cedar Grove Township	12,452	5	0	1	0	4	140	36	94	10	1
Chatham	8,992	3	0	1	1	1	54	13	38	3	0
Chatham Township	10,487	0	0	0	0	0	33	6	25	2	0
Cherry Hill Township	71,281	112	1	2	59	50	2,387	290	1,969	128	4
Chesilhurst	1,639	1	0	0	1	0	42	16	24	2	1
Chester	1,654	3	0	0	0	3	23	4	19	0	0
Chesterfield Township	7,725	0	0	0	0	0	11	3	7	1	0
Chester Township	7,864	2	1	0	0	1	62	20	41	1	1
Cinnaminson Township	15,621	16	0	5	5	6	386	87	293	6	4
Clark Township	14,805	4	0	0	1	3	196	16	174	6	1
Clayton	8,206	9	0	0	3	6	164	27	127	10	1
Clementon	5,017	17	0	0	12	5	316	102	205	9	2
Cliffside Park	23,673	30	1	0	7	22	189	58	122	9	0
Clifton	84,416	215	2	10	101	102	1,638	311	1,131	196	12
Clinton	2,728	8	0	2	1	5	15	3	11	1	0
Clinton Township	13,523	7	0	0	0	7	80	26	51	3	0
Closter	8,401	4	0	0	4	0	74	17	57	0	0
Collingswood	13,972	34	0	3	21	10	546	107	417	22	2
Colts Neck Township	10,176	3	0	0	1	2	88	21	58	9	0
Cranbury Township	3,870	2	0	0	0	2	36	4	31	1	1
Cranford Township	22,700	8	1	0	2	5	246	42	192	12	0
Cresskill	8,602	3	0	0	0	3	42	12	26	4	0
Deal	752	3	0	0	0	3	77	24	52	1	0
Delanco Township	4,297	5	0	0	1	4	148	25	119	4	3
Delaware Township	4,578	0	0	0	0	0	35	6	25	4	0
Delran Township	16,952	19	0	3	5	11	303	66	225	12	0
Demarest	4,897	0	0	0	0	0	36	10	25	1	0
Denville Township	16,690	4	0	0	1	3	183	26	150	7	0
Deptford Township	30,663	84	0	5	39	40	1,871	324	1,482	65	0
Dover	18,217	51	1	2	28	20	399	84	302	13	0
Dumont	17,537	10	1	1	2	6	96	14	81	1	0
Dunellen	7,251	11	0	0	2	9	198	45	149	4	0
Eastampton Township	6,089	4	0	0	1	3	112	29	82	1	0
East Brunswick Township	47,670	47	0	1	19	27	813	96	705	12	8
East Greenwich Township	9,587	5	0	1	0	4	133	37	89	7	0
East Hanover Township	11,194	4	0	0	0	4	209	29	170	10	0
East Newark	2,414	4	0	0	2	2	25	8	10	7	1
East Orange	64,484	420	6	16	155	243	1,235	458	454	323	20
East Rutherford	8,943	12	0	0	3	9	219	26	171	22	0
East Windsor Township	27,280	20	0	2	4	14	268	49	201	18	0
Eatontown	12,751	34	0	3	14	17	479	66	403	10	0
Edgewater	11,551	4	0	0	2	2	184	29	149	6	0
Edgewater Park Township	8,911	12	0	0	11	1	207	41	157	9	0
Edison Township	100,300	142	2	9	65	66	1,832	343	1,279	210	12
Egg Harbor City	4,257	18	0	1	5	12	150	43	101	6	0
Egg Harbor Township	43,467	120	2	9	32	77	981	213	733	35	9
Elizabeth	125,386	1,315	17	38	723	537	5,099	1,162	2,641	1,296	17
Elk Township	4,230	9	0	0	2	7	113	35	75	3	2
Elmer	1,400	2	0	0	0	2	4	0	4	0	0
Elmwood Park	19,468	22	0	0	12	10	405	68	314	23	1
Elsinboro Township	1,039	4	0	0	2	2	24	6	18	0	0
Emerson	7,426	1	0	0	0	1	67	9	58	0	1
Englewood	27,237	68	1	0	22	45	329	111	198	20	3
Englewood Cliffs	5,299	2	0	0	0	2	65	11	41	13	0
Englishtown	1,853	3	0	0	0	3	15	3	12	0	0
Essex Fells	2,120	0	0	0	0	0	18	0	16	2	0
Evesham Township	45,690	39	0	11	5	23	737	122	597	18	2
Ewing Township	35,909	85	2	7	44	32	814	257	511	46	1
Fairfield Township, Essex County	7,491	11	0	0	6	5	301	60	221	20	0
Fair Haven	6,141	1	0	1	0	0	51	4	44	3	0
Fair Lawn	32,565	27	0	1	18	8	380	73	294	13	6
Fairview	13,881	34	1	0	17	16	190	62	113	15	0
Fanwood	7,342	3	0	0	2	1	89	22	65	2	0
Far Hills	922	0	0	0	0	0	12	2	9	1	0

[1] If a blank is presented in the arson column, it indicates that the FBI did not receive 12 complete months of arson data for that agency.

Table II-8.   Offenses Known to Law Enforcement, by Selected State and City, 2011—*Continued*

(Number.)

State/City	Population	Violent crime	Murder and non-negligent man-slaughter	Forcible rape	Robbery	Aggravated assault	Property crime	Burglary	Larceny-theft	Motor vehicle theft	Arson[1]
New Jersey—*Continued*											
Fieldsboro	542	0	0	0	0	0	0	0	0	0	0
Flemington	4,596	6	0	0	4	2	97	12	84	1	0
Florence Township	12,149	20	0	0	4	16	113	49	63	1	1
Florham Park	11,735	3	0	2	0	1	87	16	69	2	0
Fort Lee	35,463	19	0	3	5	11	331	58	261	12	0
Franklin	5,062	2	0	2	0	0	158	16	140	2	0
Franklin Lakes	10,625	2	0	0	2	0	87	15	66	6	1
Franklin Township, Gloucester County	16,876	14	0	1	3	10	320	116	194	10	0
Franklin Township, Hunterdon County	3,206	3	0	0	1	2	47	9	38	0	0
Franklin Township, Somerset County	62,507	78	1	3	43	31	984	268	656	60	6
Freehold	12,092	22	0	2	9	11	263	76	180	7	0
Freehold Township	36,304	37	1	5	12	19	1,093	124	953	16	3
Frenchtown	1,378	0	0	0	0	0	31	5	26	0	0
Galloway Township	37,473	85	2	8	22	53	751	242	472	37	11
Garfield	30,588	81	0	1	28	52	511	138	328	45	0
Garwood	4,240	1	0	0	0	1	61	14	45	2	0
Gibbsboro	2,282	2	0	0	0	2	48	15	32	1	0
Glassboro	18,641	38	0	5	11	22	414	118	285	11	3
Glen Ridge	7,552	13	0	0	5	8	189	42	137	10	2
Glen Rock	11,640	0	0	0	0	0	71	14	54	3	1
Gloucester City	11,494	36	1	4	16	15	372	105	251	16	0
Gloucester Township	64,849	188	1	10	39	138	1,595	414	1,108	73	5
Green Brook Township	7,227	2	0	0	0	2	152	31	119	2	0
Greenwich Township, Gloucester County	4,915	2	0	0	1	1	183	62	117	4	0
Greenwich Township, Warren County	5,731	4	0	0	1	3	78	4	74	0	0
Guttenberg	11,213	25	0	0	6	19	109	41	62	6	1
Hackensack	43,157	94	0	2	37	55	890	121	697	72	0
Hackettstown	9,756	17	0	0	7	10	149	21	122	6	0
Haddonfield	11,632	9	0	1	1	7	220	45	173	2	1
Haddon Heights	7,498	5	0	2	0	3	154	31	120	3	0
Haddon Township	14,756	21	0	0	12	9	366	76	275	15	0
Haledon	8,346	16	0	0	8	8	244	73	144	27	0
Hamburg	3,288	3	0	0	0	3	39	3	33	3	0
Hamilton Township, Atlantic County	26,591	59	0	5	22	32	993	212	748	33	2
Hamilton Township, Mercer County	88,760	185	0	10	81	94	1,817	513	1,198	106	9
Hammonton	14,840	17	2	0	7	8	200	60	132	8	2
Hanover Township	13,758	14	0	1	3	10	207	39	155	13	0
Harding Township	3,851	2	0	0	0	2	31	13	17	1	1
Hardyston Township	8,240	6	0	0	3	3	145	32	111	2	1
Harrington Park	4,680	0	0	0	0	0	16	1	14	1	0
Harrison	13,665	54	3	1	20	30	354	103	187	64	0
Harrison Township	12,458	9	0	2	4	3	139	31	105	3	1
Harvey Cedars	338	0	0	0	0	0	25	2	23	0	0
Hasbrouck Heights	11,881	3	0	0	2	1	78	15	62	1	0
Haworth	3,393	0	0	0	0	0	14	9	3	2	0
Hawthorne	18,854	14	0	0	8	6	284	65	208	11	0
Hazlet Township	20,402	8	0	0	3	5	266	38	221	7	2
Helmetta	2,185	1	0	0	0	1	26	7	19	0	0
High Bridge	3,660	3	0	1	0	2	28	3	25	0	1
Highland Park	14,029	12	0	1	6	5	204	42	150	12	0
Highlands	5,022	15	0	3	0	12	71	20	50	1	2
Hightstown	5,512	13	0	3	4	6	87	16	67	4	2
Hillsborough Township	38,430	10	0	0	4	6	307	74	226	7	1
Hillsdale	10,253	3	0	0	0	3	47	4	42	1	0
Hillside Township	21,475	89	1	6	63	19	628	138	350	140	0
Hi-Nella	873	3	0	0	0	3	31	12	15	4	0
Hoboken	50,171	195	0	5	66	124	901	171	629	101	1
Ho-Ho-Kus	4,092	0	0	0	0	0	27	8	18	1	0
Holland Township	5,309	2	0	0	0	2	29	3	26	0	0
Holmdel Township	16,829	8	0	0	2	6	278	33	238	7	1
Hopatcong	15,197	7	0	0	0	7	88	23	60	5	0
Hopewell	1,928	3	0	0	0	3	19	5	14	0	0
Hopewell Township	17,362	11	0	0	1	10	129	21	104	4	0
Howell Township	51,245	53	0	2	14	37	703	168	519	16	2
Independence Township	5,681	3	0	0	1	2	37	13	23	1	1
Interlaken	823	1	0	0	1	0	17	7	8	2	0
Irvington	54,105	728	14	24	359	331	1,878	594	721	563	23
Island Heights	1,679	0	0	0	0	0	11	5	6	0	0
Jackson Township	55,039	64	0	6	19	39	852	234	599	19	9
Jamesburg	5,935	10	0	1	6	3	79	27	49	3	0
Jefferson Township	21,385	13	1	0	5	7	214	59	150	5	0
Jersey City	248,423	1,906	18	49	961	878	5,701	1,402	3,439	860	33
Keansburg	10,139	50	0	2	10	38	278	63	210	5	3
Kearny	40,819	86	0	3	31	52	1,121	183	768	170	6
Kenilworth	7,940	7	0	3	3	1	154	21	127	6	0

[1] If a blank is presented in the arson column, it indicates that the FBI did not receive 12 complete months of arson data for that agency.

Table II-8. Offenses Known to Law Enforcement, by Selected State and City, 2011—*Continued*

(Number.)

State/City	Population	Violent crime	Murder and non-negligent man-slaughter	Forcible rape	Robbery	Aggravated assault	Property crime	Burglary	Larceny-theft	Motor vehicle theft	Arson[1]
New Jersey—*Continued*											
Keyport	7,264	23	0	2	10	11	140	40	92	8	2
Kinnelon	10,282	5	0	0	2	3	66	16	48	2	0
Lacey Township	27,736	27	0	0	9	18	736	107	615	14	2
Lake Como	1,765	3	0	0	1	2	22	3	18	1	0
Lakehurst	2,663	2	0	0	1	1	39	7	30	2	0
Lakewood Township	93,152	92	2	6	31	53	1,073	261	786	26	7
Lambertville	3,919	5	0	0	0	5	62	7	53	2	0
Laurel Springs	1,914	5	0	0	1	4	56	23	31	2	0
Lavallette	1,881	3	0	0	0	3	78	15	63	0	0
Lawnside	2,955	15	1	1	8	5	90	21	64	5	0
Lawrence Township, Mercer County	33,583	40	0	3	23	14	1,033	131	874	28	2
Lebanon Township	6,610	2	0	0	0	2	34	12	22	0	0
Leonia	8,967	2	0	0	0	2	99	43	52	4	0
Lincoln Park	10,556	4	0	0	0	4	104	25	75	4	0
Linden	40,634	112	2	1	59	50	1,319	289	847	183	2
Lindenwold	17,672	140	3	5	61	71	618	239	328	51	3
Linwood	7,116	3	0	0	0	3	87	28	59	0	2
Little Egg Harbor Township	20,132	39	0	9	4	26	562	138	409	15	14
Little Falls Township	14,480	16	0	0	4	12	207	45	141	21	0
Little Ferry	10,661	8	0	1	3	4	121	38	75	8	2
Little Silver	5,970	3	0	0	0	3	46	7	38	1	0
Livingston Township	29,464	14	0	1	6	7	470	44	390	36	0
Loch Arbour	195	0	0	0	0	0	22	9	13	0	0
Lodi	24,216	34	0	0	13	21	370	90	252	28	0
Logan Township	6,062	4	0	0	0	4	161	31	119	11	0
Long Beach Township	3,061	2	0	0	0	2	139	16	123	0	0
Long Branch	30,821	131	0	6	51	74	672	200	442	30	0
Long Hill Township	8,731	1	0	0	0	1	72	6	65	1	0
Longport	898	1	0	1	0	0	12	2	10	0	0
Lopatcong Township	8,041	1	0	0	0	1	103	17	83	3	0
Lower Alloways Creek Township	1,776	0	0	0	0	0	17	9	8	0	0
Lower Township	22,942	37	0	1	9	27	544	128	401	15	3
Lumberton Township	12,601	13	0	1	5	7	322	59	255	8	1
Lyndhurst Township	20,622	15	0	0	10	5	356	57	274	25	0
Madison	15,898	8	0	0	2	6	98	26	69	3	0
Magnolia	4,355	12	0	0	7	5	133	44	85	4	0
Mahwah Township	25,976	3	0	0	0	3	106	10	84	12	0
Manalapan Township	39,001	17	0	1	10	6	401	96	285	20	1
Manasquan	5,917	11	0	1	3	7	209	23	185	1	2
Manchester Township	43,213	15	0	2	0	13	400	134	257	9	9
Mansfield Township, Burlington County	8,572	6	0	0	1	5	98	15	81	2	0
Mansfield Township, Warren County	7,751	17	0	1	1	15	164	30	131	3	0
Mantoloking	297	1	0	0	0	1	52	4	48	0	0
Mantua Township	15,268	12	1	1	7	3	312	49	258	5	1
Manville	10,378	4	0	0	3	1	183	12	159	12	2
Maple Shade Township	19,195	33	0	3	9	21	382	73	260	49	2
Maplewood Township	23,946	57	0	3	33	21	391	64	293	34	3
Margate City	6,375	1	0	0	0	1	184	22	155	7	0
Marlboro Township	40,325	19	0	0	8	11	405	80	303	22	1
Matawan	8,839	11	0	0	5	6	123	47	71	5	0
Maywood	9,587	1	0	0	0	1	85	23	58	4	0
Medford Lakes	4,160	1	0	0	0	1	35	2	33	0	0
Medford Township	23,110	13	0	3	4	6	283	55	225	3	2
Mendham	4,998	3	0	0	0	3	34	4	27	3	0
Mendham Township	5,889	2	0	0	0	2	19	2	17	0	0
Merchantville	3,834	7	0	0	1	6	101	18	78	5	0
Metuchen	13,619	6	0	1	3	2	205	51	147	7	2
Middlesex	13,680	5	0	1	1	3	138	26	105	7	0
Middle Township	18,974	70	0	3	15	52	771	158	592	21	0
Middletown Township	66,743	36	1	1	11	23	811	187	602	22	2
Midland Park	7,152	3	0	0	2	1	52	5	46	1	0
Millburn Township	20,216	22	0	0	10	12	721	60	635	26	1
Milltown	6,916	8	0	0	1	7	120	19	98	3	0
Millville	28,495	224	1	15	65	143	1,705	439	1,222	44	7
Mine Hill Township	3,663	0	0	0	0	0	53	15	37	1	0
Monmouth Beach	3,290	1	0	0	1	0	60	7	53	0	0
Monroe Township, Gloucester County	36,249	31	0	2	12	17	719	206	496	17	6
Monroe Township, Middlesex County	39,262	14	1	1	2	10	286	49	230	7	8
Montclair	37,794	80	1	1	46	32	662	188	409	65	5
Montgomery Township	22,328	2	0	0	1	1	165	28	134	3	2
Montvale	7,870	5	0	1	0	4	36	4	29	3	0
Montville Township	21,600	7	0	1	1	5	172	43	120	9	0
Moonachie	2,717	1	0	0	0	1	51	9	39	3	0
Moorestown Township	20,795	13	0	1	7	5	554	74	470	10	1

[1] If a blank is presented in the arson column, it indicates that the FBI did not receive 12 complete months of arson data for that agency.

Table II-8. Offenses Known to Law Enforcement, by Selected State and City, 2011—*Continued*

(Number.)

State/City	Population	Violent crime	Murder and non-negligent man-slaughter	Forcible rape	Robbery	Aggravated assault	Property crime	Burglary	Larceny-theft	Motor vehicle theft	Arson[1]
New Jersey—*Continued*											
Morris Plains	5,550	2	0	0	1	1	76	9	64	3	0
Morristown	18,472	83	0	1	38	44	487	136	340	11	0
Morris Township	22,380	10	0	2	2	6	172	33	128	11	1
Mountain Lakes	4,174	7	1	0	2	4	46	7	36	3	0
Mountainside	6,707	3	0	0	2	1	30	6	23	1	0
Mount Arlington	5,067	7	1	0	0	6	52	14	38	0	0
Mount Ephraim	4,692	11	0	0	8	3	176	27	135	14	1
Mount Holly Township	9,568	38	0	0	17	21	312	67	232	13	0
Mount Laurel Township	42,003	36	0	9	13	14	686	109	558	19	0
Mount Olive Township	28,211	10	0	3	0	7	260	61	191	8	1
Mullica Township	6,167	11	0	0	3	8	125	47	75	3	0
National Park	3,046	10	0	0	6	4	73	17	52	4	0
Neptune City	4,885	12	0	1	2	9	178	35	139	4	0
Neptune Township	28,028	170	0	8	61	101	1,843	341	1,447	55	8
Netcong	3,243	6	0	0	2	4	44	9	34	1	0
Newark	278,064	3,243	94	58	1,977	1,114	10,016	2,396	3,921	3,699	50
New Brunswick	55,365	479	3	7	250	219	1,609	404	1,102	103	12
Newfield	1,558	2	0	0	1	1	19	3	16	0	2
New Hanover Township	7,410	0	0	0	0	0	7	3	3	1	0
New Milford	16,395	7	0	0	3	4	112	22	87	3	0
New Providence	12,212	7	0	0	1	6	107	11	92	4	0
Newton	8,024	3	0	0	1	2	121	10	109	2	1
North Arlington	15,443	19	0	0	5	14	244	44	163	37	2
North Bergen Township	60,975	103	0	4	44	55	744	152	480	112	2
North Brunswick Township	40,878	55	1	5	24	25	766	171	528	67	3
North Caldwell	6,204	2	0	0	1	1	32	7	21	4	0
Northfield	8,653	0	0	0	0	0	112	19	92	1	0
North Haledon	8,445	1	0	0	1	0	56	10	46	0	1
North Hanover Township	7,704	4	0	1	0	3	76	14	58	4	3
North Plainfield	22,009	68	0	6	42	20	344	91	228	25	3
Northvale	4,655	1	0	0	0	1	41	10	31	0	0
North Wildwood	4,054	6	0	0	2	4	395	101	292	2	0
Norwood	5,730	1	0	0	0	1	28	8	20	0	0
Nutley Township	28,464	23	0	0	9	14	327	68	229	30	2
Oakland	12,796	2	0	0	0	2	90	20	64	6	0
Oaklyn	4,051	3	0	1	0	2	122	31	90	1	2
Ocean City	11,740	22	0	1	1	20	581	111	468	2	0
Ocean Gate	2,018	2	0	0	0	2	89	14	74	1	0
Oceanport	5,851	6	0	0	3	3	70	19	49	2	0
Ocean Township, Monmouth County	27,382	43	0	5	14	24	625	99	507	19	4
Ocean Township, Ocean County	8,360	5	0	0	3	2	156	12	139	5	0
Ogdensburg	2,418	1	0	0	0	1	16	3	11	2	0
Old Bridge Township	65,593	62	1	3	13	45	983	189	714	80	6
Old Tappan	5,769	0	0	0	0	0	30	12	18	0	0
Oradell	8,005	1	0	0	0	1	48	3	43	2	0
Orange	30,234	325	8	11	189	117	1,078	401	347	330	3
Oxford Township	2,522	1	0	0	0	1	11	6	5	0	0
Palisades Park	19,687	22	0	0	7	15	188	78	104	6	0
Palmyra	7,423	17	0	0	11	6	193	35	149	9	0
Paramus	26,430	61	0	3	22	36	1,668	89	1,551	28	3
Park Ridge	8,674	2	0	0	0	2	41	8	33	0	0
Parsippany-Troy Hills Township	53,415	28	0	2	18	8	580	186	384	10	0
Passaic	70,013	590	2	6	241	341	1,574	320	1,046	208	3
Paterson	146,685	1,490	17	39	751	683	4,732	1,790	1,888	1,054	5
Paulsboro	6,117	22	1	0	18	3	285	98	178	9	1
Peapack and Gladstone	2,591	2	0	0	0	2	6	1	4	1	0
Pemberton	1,414	9	0	1	0	8	46	7	38	1	0
Pemberton Township	28,005	67	0	7	19	41	817	268	503	46	9
Pennington	2,594	0	0	0	0	0	16	3	13	0	0
Pennsauken Township	36,004	123	0	7	60	56	1,365	307	938	120	3
Penns Grove	5,164	34	0	2	15	17	209	75	129	5	1
Pennsville Township	13,454	30	0	8	6	16	487	108	365	14	1
Pequannock Township	15,592	10	0	0	3	7	174	42	126	6	1
Perth Amboy	50,983	226	0	6	93	127	1,190	395	695	100	3
Phillipsburg	15,000	30	1	6	9	14	452	82	354	16	3
Pine Beach	2,134	1	0	0	0	1	104	2	102	0	0
Pine Hill	10,267	40	0	2	6	32	288	86	185	17	7
Pine Valley	12	0	0	0	0	0	1	1	0	0	0
Piscataway Township	56,231	65	0	0	24	41	686	175	459	52	5
Pitman	9,041	1	0	0	0	1	188	34	145	9	0
Plainfield	49,974	467	10	16	247	194	1,686	605	934	147	19
Plainsboro Township	23,076	4	0	0	0	4	160	25	128	7	1
Pleasantville	20,316	190	3	7	80	100	712	253	396	63	4
Plumsted Township	8,449	4	0	1	1	2	104	27	63	14	1
Pohatcong Township	3,350	1	0	0	0	1	132	10	119	3	0

[1] If a blank is presented in the arson column, it indicates that the FBI did not receive 12 complete months of arson data for that agency.

Table II-8.   Offenses Known to Law Enforcement, by Selected State and City, 2011—*Continued*

(Number.)

State/City	Population	Violent crime	Murder and non-negligent man-slaughter	Forcible rape	Robbery	Aggravated assault	Property crime	Burglary	Larceny-theft	Motor vehicle theft	Arson[1]
New Jersey—*Continued*											
Point Pleasant	18,453	14	0	1	4	9	356	61	292	3	2
Point Pleasant Beach	4,681	9	0	3	2	4	209	30	176	3	0
Pompton Lakes	11,134	11	0	0	0	11	147	32	114	1	0
Princeton	12,348	10	0	0	2	8	381	44	334	3	0
Princeton Township	16,319	3	0	0	3	0	160	34	124	2	0
Prospect Park	5,885	13	0	0	5	8	159	35	106	18	1
Rahway	27,437	85	2	0	33	50	540	114	362	64	6
Ramsey	14,521	13	0	1	1	11	162	9	147	6	0
Randolph Township	25,820	8	1	1	2	4	210	41	166	3	1
Raritan	6,904	8	0	0	3	5	127	23	98	6	0
Raritan Township	22,259	2	0	1	0	1	199	21	168	10	1
Readington Township	16,180	8	0	0	3	5	117	23	93	1	2
Red Bank	12,247	29	1	5	10	13	286	40	236	10	0
Ridgefield	11,069	2	0	0	1	1	77	16	47	14	0
Ridgefield Park	12,771	19	0	0	7	12	183	34	143	6	0
Ridgewood	25,041	8	0	0	1	7	185	36	144	5	2
Ringwood	12,269	1	0	0	0	1	68	10	55	3	0
Riverdale	3,571	8	1	0	2	5	143	8	132	3	0
River Edge	11,378	2	0	1	0	1	108	36	66	6	1
Riverside Township	8,106	24	0	3	15	6	147	50	90	7	0
Riverton	2,788	1	0	1	0	0	65	12	51	2	1
River Vale Township	9,691	3	0	0	0	3	18	4	14	0	0
Robbinsville Township	13,687	7	0	0	3	4	149	30	114	5	0
Rochelle Park Township	5,548	4	0	0	3	1	89	25	56	8	0
Rockaway	6,459	1	0	1	0	0	66	5	60	1	0
Rockaway Township	24,236	15	0	0	4	11	568	41	513	14	0
Rockleigh	533	0	0	0	0	0	1	1	0	0	0
Roseland	5,838	4	0	0	0	4	62	6	47	9	0
Roselle	21,155	69	1	1	39	28	471	224	208	39	2
Roselle Park	13,341	12	0	0	6	6	142	45	89	8	0
Roxbury Township	23,402	9	1	0	4	4	282	72	201	9	0
Rumson	7,146	3	0	0	0	3	82	17	60	5	0
Runnemede	8,496	24	0	1	12	11	396	60	320	16	0
Rutherford	18,121	14	0	0	5	9	268	54	186	28	4
Saddle Brook Township	13,704	11	0	0	5	6	305	35	252	18	0
Saddle River	3,162	0	0	0	0	0	25	9	14	2	0
Salem	5,163	64	0	3	22	39	208	66	138	4	3
Sayreville	42,846	50	1	2	16	31	609	159	406	44	4
Scotch Plains Township	23,588	17	0	0	8	9	240	50	182	8	0
Sea Bright	1,417	0	0	0	0	0	40	2	36	2	0
Sea Girt	1,834	3	0	0	1	2	64	7	56	1	0
Sea Isle City	2,121	8	0	0	2	6	257	70	187	0	0
Seaside Heights	2,897	55	0	2	5	48	304	37	257	10	0
Seaside Park	1,584	6	1	1	2	2	82	13	67	2	0
Secaucus	16,318	14	0	0	6	8	519	51	427	41	0
Ship Bottom	1,160	0	0	0	0	0	62	7	52	3	0
Shrewsbury	3,822	3	0	0	3	0	141	18	118	5	0
Somerdale	5,168	20	0	1	10	9	272	66	203	3	0
Somers Point	10,831	36	0	1	9	26	394	89	301	4	2
Somerville	12,138	22	0	0	12	10	230	55	157	18	1
South Amboy	8,660	12	0	0	1	11	113	32	77	4	3
South Bound Brook	4,578	2	0	0	0	2	51	28	21	2	0
South Brunswick Township	43,561	28	0	4	6	18	508	86	393	29	3
South Hackensack Township	2,386	11	0	2	3	6	58	9	45	4	0
South Harrison Township	3,173	2	0	0	0	2	37	13	19	5	0
South Orange	16,252	59	0	0	48	11	361	68	237	56	0
South Plainfield	23,463	43	0	0	20	23	368	71	278	19	3
South River	16,061	12	0	0	3	9	212	38	168	6	1
South Toms River	3,696	11	0	0	2	9	98	31	63	4	0
Sparta Township	19,788	3	0	0	1	2	110	18	92	0	0
Spotswood	8,284	4	0	0	4	0	114	13	99	2	0
Springfield	15,870	9	0	0	5	4	254	35	202	17	0
Springfield Township	3,425	0	0	0	0	0	51	22	28	1	0
Spring Lake	3,003	3	0	0	0	3	101	12	88	1	0
Spring Lake Heights	4,729	5	0	0	1	4	19	7	11	1	0
Stafford Township	26,623	11	0	1	5	5	468	43	423	2	1
Stanhope	3,622	0	0	0	0	0	41	6	33	2	0
Stillwater Township	4,113	0	0	0	0	0	0	0	0	0	0
Stone Harbor	869	0	0	0	0	0	125	13	112	0	0
Stratford	7,063	26	0	1	13	12	144	51	91	2	0
Summit	21,528	6	0	1	2	3	263	28	227	8	0
Surf City	1,209	1	0	0	0	1	33	1	31	1	0
Swedesboro	2,593	3	0	0	1	2	30	8	21	1	0
Tavistock	5	0	0	0	0	0	1	0	1	0	0
Teaneck Township	39,908	70	2	1	33	34	534	137	379	18	5

[1] If a blank is presented in the arson column, it indicates that the FBI did not receive 12 complete months of arson data for that agency.

Table II-8.   Offenses Known to Law Enforcement, by Selected State and City, 2011—*Continued*

(Number.)

State/City	Population	Violent crime	Murder and non-negligent man-slaughter	Forcible rape	Robbery	Aggravated assault	Property crime	Burglary	Larceny-theft	Motor vehicle theft	Arson[1]
New Jersey—*Continued*											
Tenafly	14,536	3	0	0	2	1	109	29	76	4	1
Teterboro	67	0	0	0	0	0	9	0	7	2	0
Tewksbury Township	6,013	3	0	0	1	2	14	8	6	0	0
Tinton Falls	17,952	17	0	0	7	10	446	74	366	6	0
Toms River Township	91,543	101	1	3	61	36	3,135	589	2,499	47	10
Totowa	10,840	19	0	1	5	13	382	25	332	25	0
Trenton	85,196	1,208	23	25	519	641	2,570	1,138	993	439	25
Tuckerton	3,358	7	0	0	0	7	59	10	45	4	0
Union Beach	6,266	9	0	0	2	7	77	36	41	0	1
Union City	66,676	270	3	3	120	144	1,299	285	849	165	2
Union Township	56,831	116	1	4	63	48	1,002	155	745	102	5
Upper Saddle River	8,235	6	0	0	1	5	40	8	31	1	1
Ventnor City	10,685	20	0	0	8	12	353	114	235	4	0
Vernon Township	24,023	10	0	1	2	7	386	69	311	6	0
Verona	13,376	9	0	1	2	6	184	61	105	18	0
Voorhees Township	29,228	42	1	6	12	23	683	132	529	22	0
Waldwick	9,657	2	0	0	0	2	80	8	72	0	1
Wallington	11,373	12	0	1	3	8	170	35	123	12	1
Wall Township	26,251	16	1	0	2	13	446	114	315	17	0
Wanaque	11,153	5	0	0	3	2	110	6	98	6	0
Warren Township	15,362	2	0	0	1	1	86	36	47	3	0
Washington	6,483	8	0	0	0	8	97	7	85	5	0
Washington Township, Bergen County	9,132	4	0	0	0	4	46	19	26	1	0
Washington Township, Gloucester County	48,720	77	1	3	30	43	1,100	164	895	41	4
Washington Township, Morris County	18,595	10	0	0	1	9	100	28	66	6	1
Washington Township, Warren County	6,673	2	0	0	0	2	59	7	52	0	1
Watchung	5,820	5	0	0	2	3	389	26	356	7	0
Waterford Township	10,684	19	0	2	1	16	170	39	122	9	0
Wayne Township	54,899	34	0	3	18	13	1,173	144	964	65	0
Weehawken Township	12,596	19	0	0	12	7	266	48	195	23	1
Wenonah	2,286	0	0	0	0	0	21	5	16	0	0
Westampton Township	8,842	9	0	1	4	4	163	38	120	5	1
West Amwell Township	3,853	4	0	0	0	4	42	13	29	0	0
West Caldwell Township	10,795	1	0	0	1	0	87	17	67	3	0
West Cape May	1,027	1	0	0	0	1	27	10	17	0	0
West Deptford Township	21,749	20	0	5	7	8	445	101	318	26	0
Westfield	30,417	10	0	0	3	7	334	46	279	9	1
West Long Branch	8,124	4	0	0	3	1	195	39	153	3	0
West Milford Township	25,936	19	0	1	1	17	304	100	196	8	2
West New York	49,873	185	0	1	92	92	603	215	322	66	5
West Orange	46,361	77	1	2	43	31	797	201	518	78	1
Westville	4,302	20	0	2	8	10	161	48	103	10	0
West Wildwood	605	2	0	0	0	2	29	9	20	0	0
West Windsor Township	27,255	14	0	1	6	7	384	46	321	17	0
Westwood	10,944	13	0	0	0	13	63	10	52	1	0
Wharton	6,544	7	0	1	3	3	153	31	116	6	2
Wildwood	5,343	115	1	6	47	61	741	232	500	9	0
Wildwood Crest	3,281	12	0	0	4	8	182	37	145	0	0
Willingboro Township	31,734	109	2	18	40	49	644	241	382	21	2
Winfield Township	1,476	1	0	0	0	1	6	1	5	0	0
Winslow Township	39,630	147	2	6	32	107	634	188	417	29	7
Woodbridge Township	99,915	127	1	8	52	66	2,538	371	2,030	137	6
Woodbury	10,208	29	0	1	16	12	423	77	332	14	3
Woodbury Heights	3,065	6	0	1	4	1	109	16	90	3	0
Woodcliff Lake	5,749	2	0	1	0	1	46	9	37	0	0
Woodland Park	11,858	7	0	0	2	5	255	58	184	13	0
Woodlynne	2,988	21	1	1	5	14	180	74	87	19	1
Wood-Ridge	7,651	4	1	1	0	2	63	16	37	10	0
Woodstown	3,517	10	0	1	2	7	41	11	29	1	0
Woolwich Township	10,234	7	0	1	1	5	95	32	59	4	0
Wyckoff Township	16,752	4	0	0	1	3	124	47	75	2	0
New Mexico											
Alamogordo	30,743	111	2	2	6	101	980	160	777	43	2
Albuquerque	551,961	4,207	35	264	998	2,910	27,976	5,985	19,168	2,823	133
Angel Fire	1,230	1	0	0	0	1	24	11	12	1	0
Artesia	11,427	130	0	7	3	120	472	172	283	17	2
Aztec	6,839	31	0	1	2	28	168	36	120	12	2
Bayard	2,354	20	0	0	0	20	32	10	21	1	0
Belen	7,350	72	0	2	10	60	647	230	387	30	6
Bernalillo	8,413	139	1	3	12	123	371	134	218	19	2
Bloomfield	8,203	74	1	5	2	66	148	41	107	0	1
Bosque Farms	3,948	1	0	0	0	1	55	15	40	0	0
Carlsbad	26,431	192	1	33	15	143	1,062	294	729	39	3
Carrizozo	1,007	1	0	0	0	1	16	8	7	1	0

[1] If a blank is presented in offenses arson column, it indicates that the FBI did not receive 12 complete months of arson data for that agency.

Table II-8. Offenses Known to Law Enforcement, by Selected State and City, 2011—*Continued*

(Number.)

State/City	Population	Violent crime	Murder and non-negligent man-slaughter	Forcible rape	Robbery	Aggravated assault	Property crime	Burglary	Larceny-theft	Motor vehicle theft	Arson[1]
New Mexico—*Continued*											
Cimarron	1,032	0	0	0	0	0	4	1	3	0	0
Clovis	38,198	209	0	31	25	153	2,163	833	1,247	83	31
Corrales	8,422	14	0	2	0	12	61	20	41	0	0
Cuba	739	11	0	0	0	11	8	0	7	1	0
Deming	15,021	118	2	6	13	97	687	173	494	20	6
Dexter	1,280	0	0	0	0	0	7	2	4	1	0
Espanola	10,338	257	1	5	33	218	915	452	420	43	6
Estancia	1,674	0	0	0	0	0	20	6	14	0	0
Eunice	2,955	5	0	0	0	5	66	31	33	2	3
Farmington	46,390	504	2	73	40	389	1,628	244	1,291	93	10
Gallup	21,921	340	1	27	51	261	1,814	297	1,411	106	1
Grants	9,285	99	3	3	9	84	262	152	95	15	3
Hobbs	34,504	163	6	22	14	121	1,459	415	985	59	6
Jal	2,070	2	0	0	1	1	20	5	14	1	1
Las Cruces	98,710	424	3	17	68	336	4,546	1,120	3,164	262	2
Las Vegas	13,907	149	4	12	17	116	484	152	317	15	9
Logan	1,054	1	0	0	0	1	27	9	18	0	0
Lordsburg	2,828	3	0	0	0	3	2	1	0	1	1
Los Alamos	18,151	39	0	6	1	32	255	40	213	2	0
Los Lunas	15,001	173	0	8	3	162	547	79	391	77	0
Lovington	11,132	33	1	3	4	25	305	166	127	12	0
Magdalena	948	5	0	0	0	5	16	7	8	1	2
Mesilla	2,221	4	0	2	1	1	47	18	24	5	0
Milan	3,281	23	0	0	0	23	64	26	36	2	0
Moriarty	1,931	7	0	1	5	1	121	45	67	9	0
Portales	12,417	38	1	4	0	33	473	178	278	17	0
Questa	1,790	8	0	0	0	8	14	6	5	3	0
Raton	6,962	9	0	2	3	4	184	90	83	11	1
Rio Rancho	88,500	180	0	14	15	151	1,619	304	1,208	107	4
Roswell	48,907	300	5	15	36	244	2,686	619	1,978	89	21
Ruidoso	8,119	19	0	3	3	13	360	151	200	9	0
Ruidoso Downs	2,847	10	0	0	0	10	93	27	63	3	0
Santa Clara	1,705	15	1	0	0	14	25	14	11	0	0
Santa Fe	68,707	305	2	19	77	207	3,749	1,943	1,639	167	9
Santa Rosa	2,880	12	0	0	1	11	51	11	40	0	0
Silver City	10,430	82	1	9	4	68	547	134	388	25	4
Socorro	9,152	65	0	0	0	65	377	108	254	15	0
Sunland Park	14,264	12	0	3	2	7	176	43	116	17	1
Taos	5,780	49	1	5	7	36	472	178	277	17	1
Taos Ski Valley	70	1	0	0	0	1	7	0	7	0	0
Tatum	807	1	0	0	1	0	29	0	28	1	1
Texico	1,143	1	0	0	0	1	3	0	3	0	0
Truth or Consequences	6,547	33	0	3	1	29	167	44	114	9	1
Tucumcari	5,423	35	2	0	2	31	289	159	125	5	0
Tularosa	2,874	24	0	0	1	23	99	28	69	2	0
New York											
Adams Village	1,783	0	0	0	0	0	30	8	22	0	0
Addison Town and Village	2,607	1	0	0	0	1	45	13	31	1	0
Akron Village	2,881	3	0	0	1	2	23	4	19	0	0
Albany	98,296	939	4	33	320	582	4,611	895	3,514	202	12
Albion Village	6,083	31	1	2	6	22	256	50	194	12	0
Alexandria Bay Village	1,083	1	0	0	0	1	29	10	19	0	1
Alfred Village	4,193	4	0	0	2	2	43	7	34	2	0
Allegany Village	1,824	7	0	0	0	7	26	5	21	0	0
Altamont Village	1,728	1	0	0	0	1	9	2	6	1	0
Amherst Town	117,610	124	0	7	41	76	2,004	221	1,736	47	2
Amity Town and Belmont Village	2,318	1	0	0	0	1	2	1	1	0	0
Amityville Village	9,566	8	0	0	6	2	169	19	145	5	0
Amsterdam	18,704	28	0	0	13	15	535	151	374	10	1
Andover Village	1,047	0	0	0	0	0	4	1	3	0	0
Angelica Village	873	0	0	0	0	0	3	1	2	0	0
Arcade Village	2,080	0	0	0	0	0	46	1	45	0	0
Ardsley Village	4,472	1	0	0	0	1	39	6	33	0	0
Asharoken Village	657	0	0	0	0	0	2	0	2	0	0
Attica Village	2,558	1	0	0	0	1	16	3	12	1	0
Auburn	27,811	130	2	21	17	90	917	177	716	24	2
Avon Village	3,409	1	0	0	0	1	29	5	22	2	0
Baldwinsville Village	7,411	5	0	1	1	3	120	23	94	3	1
Ballston Spa Village	5,433	18	0	2	1	15	152	31	116	5	0
Batavia	15,535	49	0	10	7	32	507	95	395	17	1
Bath Village	5,812	25	0	3	2	20	153	29	124	0	3
Beacon	15,611	67	0	0	17	50	314	64	239	11	0
Bedford Town	17,413	11	0	1	1	9	82	10	70	2	1
Bethlehem Town	33,807	26	0	5	6	15	514	92	406	16	4

[1] If a blank is presented in the arson column, it indicates that the FBI did not receive 12 complete months of arson data for that agency.

Table II-8. Offenses Known to Law Enforcement, by Selected State and City, 2011—*Continued*

(Number.)

State/City	Population	Violent crime	Murder and non-negligent man-slaughter	Forcible rape	Robbery	Aggravated assault	Property crime	Burglary	Larceny-theft	Motor vehicle theft	Arson[1]
New York—*Continued*											
Binghamton	47,589	268	0	17	76	175	2,284	415	1,796	73	2
Black River	1,354	0	0	0	0	0	10	5	5	0	0
Blooming Grove Town	12,183	8	0	0	0	8	103	25	73	5	0
Bolivar Village	1,052	4	0	0	0	4	9	4	5	0	0
Bolton Town	2,336	0	0	0	0	0	15	1	14	0	0
Boonville Village	2,081	1	0	0	1	0	15	3	12	0	0
Brant Town	2,074	1	0	0	0	1	13	4	9	0	1
Brewster	2,401	0	0	0	0	0	9	1	8	0	0
Briarcliff Manor Village	7,902	2	0	0	2	0	30	8	22	0	0
Brighton Town	36,774	41	0	8	16	17	947	150	766	31	1
Brockport Village	8,404	18	0	2	3	13	151	26	122	3	4
Bronxville Village	6,351	0	0	0	0	0	61	11	47	3	0
Brownville Village	1,124	0	0	0	0	0	5	0	5	0	0
Buffalo[2]	262,484	3,250	36	121	1,459	1,634	14,305	4,473	8,711	1,121	347
Cambridge Village	1,878	1	0	0	0	1	39	7	32	0	1
Camden Village	2,241	7	0	0	1	6	87	8	79	0	0
Camillus Town and Village	24,276	9	0	0	1	8	314	27	275	12	2
Canandaigua	10,592	32	0	4	3	25	312	51	250	11	0
Canisteo Village	2,280	7	0	0	0	7	39	3	35	1	0
Canton Village	6,342	2	0	2	0	0	62	4	58	0	0
Cape Vincent Village	729	2	0	0	0	2	5	2	3	0	0
Carmel Town	34,459	17	1	0	4	12	240	44	190	6	1
Carroll Town	3,540	1	0	0	0	1	6	3	3	0	0
Carthage Village	3,764	1	0	0	0	1	73	10	61	2	1
Caton	2,189	0	0	0	0	0	2	0	2	0	0
Catskill Village	4,099	16	0	0	2	14	132	14	118	0	0
Cayuga Heights Village	3,746	1	0	0	0	1	36	2	34	0	0
Cazenovia Village	2,848	2	0	0	1	1	40	4	35	1	0
Central Square Village	1,856	0	0	0	0	0	38	5	32	1	0
Centre Island Village	412	0	0	0	0	0	2	1	1	0	0
Chatham Village	1,778	13	0	0	0	13	76	14	61	1	0
Cheektowaga Town	79,194	175	2	10	80	83	2,753	362	2,294	97	3
Chester Town	8,048	1	0	1	0	0	6	0	5	1	0
Chittenango Village	5,104	2	0	0	0	2	77	10	62	5	0
Cicero Town	29,774	5	0	0	3	2	376	56	316	4	1
Clarkstown Town	79,221	100	0	5	31	64	1,517	111	1,370	36	3
Clayton Village	1,987	0	0	0	0	0	10	2	8	0	0
Clifton Springs Village	2,137	0	0	0	0	0	27	2	25	0	0
Clyde Village	2,102	2	0	0	1	1	38	9	29	0	0
Cobleskill Village	4,699	2	0	1	0	1	109	16	92	1	0
Coeymans Town	7,451	20	0	0	1	19	61	11	43	7	2
Cohocton Town	2,573	2	0	0	0	2	10	2	8	0	0
Cohoes	16,241	35	0	1	11	23	295	109	172	14	1
Colchester Town	2,086	0	0	0	0	0	6	3	3	0	0
Colonie Town	77,950	54	2	0	32	20	2,197	224	1,955	18	1
Cooperstown Village	1,860	0	0	0	0	0	27	2	25	0	0
Corning	11,233	38	0	5	8	25	365	65	297	3	0
Cornwall Town	9,671	3	0	0	0	3	104	13	89	2	0
Cortland	19,290	48	0	10	5	33	382	96	277	9	1
Crawford Town	9,358	12	0	0	4	8	122	29	87	6	1
Croton-on-Hudson Village	8,106	1	0	0	0	1	65	3	59	3	0
Cuba Town	3,258	7	0	3	0	4	90	18	72	0	1
Deerpark Town	7,937	16	0	1	3	12	198	69	122	7	1
Delhi Village	3,101	5	0	0	0	5	49	11	36	2	1
Depew Village	15,372	25	0	3	6	16	282	38	237	7	1
Deposit Village	1,670	0	0	0	0	0	10	4	6	0	0
Dewitt Town	22,856	33	0	1	13	19	722	89	613	20	0
Dobbs Ferry Village	10,924	15	0	0	9	6	140	17	116	7	1
Dolgeville Village	2,216	2	0	0	0	2	73	15	56	2	0
Dryden Village	1,898	0	0	0	0	0	44	2	40	2	0
Dunkirk	12,619	37	1	1	16	19	397	120	268	9	2
Durham Town	2,737	0	0	0	0	0	7	4	3	0	1
East Aurora-Aurora Town	13,844	10	0	2	3	5	151	26	121	4	4
Eastchester Town	19,642	4	0	0	2	2	166	15	147	4	0
East Greenbush Town	16,547	27	0	2	7	18	397	45	346	6	0
East Hampton Village	1,088	1	0	0	1	0	82	7	73	2	0
East Rochester Village	6,617	6	0	0	3	3	144	25	117	2	0
Eden Town	7,723	6	0	0	2	4	46	12	32	2	0
Ellenville Village	4,154	21	0	3	5	13	109	20	87	2	0
Ellicott Town	5,205	10	0	0	5	5	226	45	167	14	0
Ellicottville	1,605	0	0	0	0	0	104	13	91	0	0
Elmira	29,331	70	1	2	25	42	1,141	255	871	15	3
Elmira Heights Village	4,115	5	0	3	1	1	110	30	78	2	0
Elmira Town	5,986	0	0	0	0	0	1	0	1	0	0
Elmsford Village	4,685	11	0	2	4	5	59	7	39	13	0

[1] If a blank is presented in the arson column, it indicates that the FBI did not receive 12 complete months of arson data for that agency.

[2] Because of changes in the state/local agency's reporting practices, figures are not comparable to previous years' data.

Table II-8. Offenses Known to Law Enforcement, by Selected State and City, 2011—*Continued*

(Number.)

State/City	Population	Violent crime	Murder and non-negligent man-slaughter	Forcible rape	Robbery	Aggravated assault	Property crime	Burglary	Larceny-theft	Motor vehicle theft	Arson[1]
New York—*Continued*											
Endicott Village	13,452	66	1	9	17	39	612	106	488	18	1
Evans Town	16,430	22	0	1	4	17	353	66	270	17	5
Fairport Village	5,377	7	0	0	5	2	60	11	49	0	0
Fallsburg Town	12,077	19	1	0	1	17	252	86	161	5	1
Fishkill Town	20,025	3	0	0	0	3	232	30	198	4	1
Fishkill Village	2,181	2	0	0	0	2	55	12	42	1	0
Floral Park Village	15,934	12	0	0	5	7	56	10	40	6	0
Florida Village	2,846	0	0	0	0	0	12	2	10	0	0
Fort Edward Village	3,390	4	0	1	0	3	20	3	17	0	0
Fort Plain Village	2,332	5	0	2	2	1	73	8	64	1	1
Frankfort Town	5,038	5	0	1	1	3	52	15	34	3	0
Frankfort Village	2,610	3	0	1	0	2	70	10	59	1	2
Franklinville Village	1,748	0	0	0	0	0	26	0	26	0	0
Fredonia Village	11,280	8	0	1	0	7	283	29	248	6	1
Freeport Village	43,053	174	5	7	89	73	914	185	663	66	7
Friendship Town	2,013	0	0	0	0	0	24	11	12	1	0
Fulton City	11,949	22	0	4	5	13	527	88	437	2	0
Garden City Village	22,472	13	1	0	6	6	337	32	302	3	1
Gates Town	28,528	47	2	5	12	28	1,166	99	1,017	50	2
Geddes Town	10,581	1	0	0	0	1	203	24	172	7	0
Geneseo Village	8,067	4	0	3	0	1	142	11	128	3	2
Geneva	13,321	43	0	2	20	21	369	103	262	4	4
Germantown Town	1,963	0	0	0	0	0	2	0	2	0	0
Glen Cove	27,085	18	0	0	8	10	213	39	170	4	4
Glen Park Village	504	0	0	0	0	0	2	0	2	0	0
Glens Falls	14,766	44	0	2	5	37	410	68	331	11	1
Gloversville	15,735	37	0	7	6	24	648	153	474	21	2
Goshen Town	8,266	2	0	0	0	2	78	21	53	4	0
Goshen Village	5,479	3	0	0	0	3	78	7	70	1	0
Gouverneur Village	3,967	10	0	2	0	8	332	71	257	4	0
Gowanda Village	2,721	6	0	0	1	5	52	17	32	3	0
Granville Village	2,554	3	0	0	2	1	34	9	25	0	0
Great Neck Estates Village	2,773	0	0	0	0	0	3	2	1	0	0
Greece Town	96,527	135	0	6	48	81	2,544	355	2,081	108	5
Greenburgh Town	43,055	57	1	3	11	42	698	80	598	20	0
Greene Village	1,587	0	0	0	0	0	0	0	0	0	0
Green Island Village	2,632	2	0	0	0	2	63	12	45	6	0
Greenport Town	4,184	1	0	0	0	1	120	6	112	2	0
Greenwich Village	1,785	2	0	0	0	2	44	9	34	1	0
Greenwood Lake Village	3,168	3	0	0	1	2	21	12	9	0	0
Groton Village	2,374	2	0	0	0	2	69	15	53	1	0
Guilderland Town	33,734	27	0	1	10	16	844	79	759	6	0
Hamburg Town	45,177	51	0	1	17	33	1,036	151	850	35	
Hamburg Village	9,451	8	0	4	0	4	213	35	175	3	0
Hamilton Village	4,258	1	0	0	0	1	29	4	24	1	0
Hammondsport Village	664	0	0	0	0	0	13	1	12	0	0
Hancock Village	1,036	8	0	0	0	8	8	0	7	1	0
Harriman Village	2,435	4	0	0	0	4	7	2	5	0	0
Hastings-on-Hudson Village	7,884	2	0	0	1	1	107	9	98	0	3
Haverstraw Town	36,799	85	2	4	34	45	427	112	302	13	3
Hempstead Village	54,133	439	8	10	207	214	1,049	295	600	154	8
Herkimer Village	7,778	64	0	3	10	51	363	65	298	0	1
Holley Village	1,819	5	0	0	0	5	49	14	33	2	0
Homer Village	3,306	1	0	0	0	1	38	6	32	0	0
Hornell	8,601	8	0	2	1	5	129	14	113	2	1
Horseheads Village	6,490	4	0	0	0	4	131	12	117	2	0
Hudson Falls Village	7,314	17	0	4	2	11	143	31	110	2	0
Hunter Town	2,744	1	0	0	0	1	0	0	0	0	0
Huntington Bay Village	1,431	0	0	0	0	0	9	3	6	0	0
Hyde Park Town	21,668	19	1	4	3	11	170	49	107	14	1
Ilion Village	8,089	20	0	1	2	17	153	23	127	3	0
Independence Town	1,172	0	0	0	0	0	9	1	8	0	0
Inlet Town	334	0	0	0	0	0	13	4	8	1	0
Irondequoit Town	51,924	114	0	11	51	52	1,506	284	1,163	59	2
Irvington Village	6,449	2	0	0	1	1	24	3	18	3	0
Jamestown	31,286	203	0	22	36	145	1,124	335	753	36	11
Johnson City Village	15,242	50	0	3	7	40	891	125	751	15	1
Johnstown	8,782	8	0	0	1	7	330	50	273	7	0
Jordan Village	1,374	0	0	0	0	0	4	1	2	1	0
Kenmore Village	15,492	17	1	0	6	10	296	57	231	8	0
Kensington Village	1,166	0	0	0	0	0	3	0	3	0	0
Kent Town	13,568	1	0	0	0	1	88	26	60	2	0
Kings Point Village	5,027	2	0	0	1	1	10	2	8	0	0
Kingston	24,000	93	0	8	34	51	580	115	450	15	3
Kirkland Town	8,410	0	0	0	0	0	110	33	73	4	0

[1] If a blank is presented in the arson column, it indicates that the FBI did not receive 12 complete months of arson data for that agency.

Table II-8.   Offenses Known to Law Enforcement, by Selected State and City, 2011—*Continued*

(Number.)

State/City	Population	Violent crime	Murder and non-negligent man-slaughter	Forcible rape	Robbery	Aggravated assault	Property crime	Burglary	Larceny-theft	Motor vehicle theft	Arson[1]
New York—*Continued*											
Lackawanna	18,223	130	0	10	21	99	440	107	309	24	4
Lake Placid Village	2,532	4	0	3	0	1	53	10	43	0	0
Lake Success Village	2,947	2	0	0	1	1	22	2	20	0	0
Lakewood-Busti	7,384	2	0	1	0	1	219	21	195	3	0
Lancaster Town	25,431	15	0	2	4	9	492	67	412	13	1
Larchmont Village	5,890	3	0	0	2	1	127	24	100	3	0
Le Roy Village	4,411	8	0	0	1	7	87	13	71	3	1
Lewisboro Town	12,467	0	0	0	0	0	26	1	25	0	0
Liberty Village	4,412	34	0	4	6	24	244	75	160	9	0
Lloyd Harbor Village	3,676	0	0	0	0	0	22	2	20	0	0
Lloyd Town	10,912	0	0	0	0	0	111	23	82	6	2
Lockport	21,260	67	1	12	14	40	734	133	584	17	3
Long Beach	33,425	40	0	0	11	29	275	25	237	13	0
Lowville Village	3,486	8	0	3	0	5	92	9	79	4	0
Lynbrook Village	19,514	22	1	0	10	11	165	19	132	14	0
Lyons Village	3,635	22	0	3	4	15	125	36	89	0	0
Macedon Town and Village	9,189	2	0	0	0	2	30	3	26	1	0
Malone Village	5,938	8	0	4	2	2	296	46	245	5	0
Malverne Village	8,552	0	0	0	0	0	27	5	22	0	0
Mamaroneck Town	12,031	7	0	0	2	5	127	13	109	5	0
Mamaroneck Village	19,014	27	0	2	8	17	171	28	128	15	0
Manchester Village	1,717	0	0	0	0	0	0	0	0	0	0
Manlius Town	24,657	24	0	1	4	19	400	51	340	9	0
Marlborough Town	8,848	9	0	0	0	9	155	27	122	6	2
Massena Village	10,985	27	0	3	4	20	394	80	307	7	1
Mechanicville	5,219	16	0	2	5	9	59	19	35	5	0
Medina Village	6,092	20	0	3	5	12	230	46	179	5	1
Menands Village	4,008	5	0	1	3	1	140	23	115	2	0
Middleport Village	1,848	0	0	0	0	0	28	5	21	2	0
Middletown	28,212	163	2	9	57	95	947	167	755	25	2
Monroe Village	8,402	8	0	1	0	7	208	22	182	4	0
Montgomery Village	3,831	2	0	0	0	2	32	2	30	0	0
Monticello Village	6,756	76	0	3	14	59	266	105	150	11	1
Moravia Village	1,288	1	0	0	0	1	21	3	18	0	0
Moriah Town	3,621	1	0	0	0	1	5	1	4	0	0
Mount Hope Town	7,050	0	0	0	0	0	29	10	16	3	0
Mount Kisco Village	10,926	33	0	1	12	20	163	14	144	5	0
Mount Morris Village	2,999	4	0	0	0	4	62	6	54	2	0
Mount Pleasant Town	26,294	10	0	0	2	8	305	33	265	7	
Mount Vernon	67,594	658	6	9	249	394	1,459	296	1,012	151	5
Nassau Village	1,138	2	0	0	0	2	19	3	16	0	0
Newark Village	9,186	27	0	6	10	11	349	63	279	7	2
New Berlin Town	1,661	1	0	0	0	1	22	10	11	1	0
Newburgh	28,996	527	4	11	254	258	1,243	401	782	60	10
Newburgh Town	29,935	41	0	0	21	20	1,124	113	975	36	1
New Castle Town	17,648	5	0	0	0	5	109	19	87	3	0
New Hartford Town and Village	20,580	20	0	2	4	14	744	68	668	8	0
New Paltz Town and Village	14,066	33	0	4	4	25	248	29	214	5	1
New Rochelle	77,408	214	2	2	118	92	1,343	166	1,100	77	2
New Windsor Town	25,357	26	0	3	5	18	498	95	391	12	1
New York	8,211,875	51,209	515	1,092	19,773	29,829	140,457	18,159	112,864	9,434	
Niagara Falls	50,419	581	4	31	174	372	2,941	849	1,904	188	18
Niagara Town	8,416	22	0	2	4	16	422	53	355	14	1
Niskayuna Town	21,879	13	0	0	5	8	358	61	281	16	1
Nissequogue Village	1,757	0	0	0	0	0	10	4	6	0	0
Norfolk Town	4,607	1	0	1	0	0	27	9	17	1	0
North Castle Town	11,894	4	0	1	1	2	47	9	37	1	0
North Greenbush Town	12,129	9	1	1	2	5	219	36	178	5	0
Northport Village	7,434	3	0	0	2	1	80	12	66	2	0
North Syracuse Village	6,831	26	0	0	2	24	155	19	131	5	1
North Tonawanda	31,710	47	0	4	19	24	607	137	438	32	0
Northville Village	1,104	0	0	0	0	0	9	0	9	0	0
Norwich	7,222	21	0	5	3	13	332	55	275	2	1
Nunda Town and Village	3,078	1	0	0	0	1	12	5	7	0	0
Ocean Beach Village	79	1	0	0	0	1	27	0	26	1	0
Ogdensburg	11,178	26	0	0	2	24	478	125	350	3	2
Ogden Town	19,945	14	0	1	1	12	255	43	202	10	0
Old Westbury Village	4,692	0	0	0	0	0	39	15	24	0	0
Olean	14,517	65	0	5	7	53	549	65	483	1	3
Olive Town	4,439	0	0	0	0	0	3	2	1	0	0
Oneida	11,444	16	0	3	2	11	496	73	414	9	0
Oneonta City	13,963	69	0	1	8	60	392	106	281	5	2
Orangetown Town	36,998	51	1	1	12	37	360	46	298	16	1
Orchard Park Town	29,185	15	0	2	2	11	381	62	304	15	2
Oriskany Village	1,406	0	0	0	0	0	21	7	14	0	0

[1] If a blank is presented in the arson column, it indicates that the FBI did not receive 12 complete months of arson data for that agency.

Table II-8. Offenses Known to Law Enforcement, by Selected State and City, 2011—*Continued*

(Number.)

State/City	Population	Violent crime	Murder and non-negligent man-slaughter	Forcible rape	Robbery	Aggravated assault	Property crime	Burglary	Larceny-theft	Motor vehicle theft	Arson[1]
New York—*Continued*											
Ossining Village	25,173	44	0	1	25	18	234	42	181	11	0
Oswego City	18,224	72	0	8	11	53	679	114	534	31	2
Owego Village	3,914	8	0	0	2	6	77	22	53	2	0
Oxford Village	1,457	0	0	0	0	0	8	3	5	0	0
Oyster Bay Cove Village	2,207	0	0	0	0	0	5	2	3	0	0
Painted Post Village	1,817	1	0	0	0	1	49	4	43	2	0
Peekskill	23,689	34	0	2	9	23	216	37	169	10	0
Pelham Village	6,941	4	0	0	3	1	135	7	120	8	0
Penn Yan Village	5,182	0	0	0	0	0	113	15	98	0	0
Perry Village	3,690	6	0	1	1	4	99	20	75	4	0
Phelps Village	1,998	0	0	0	0	0	3	0	3	0	0
Piermont Village	2,521	0	0	0	0	0	36	1	35	0	0
Pine Plains Town	2,484	0	0	0	0	0	6	1	5	0	0
Plattekill Town	10,546	7	0	0	2	5	126	54	68	4	0
Plattsburgh City	20,079	26	1	4	3	18	545	79	459	7	
Pleasantville Village	7,051	0	0	0	0	0	0	0	0	0	0
Port Byron Village	1,296	0	0	0	0	0	0	0	0	0	0
Port Chester Village	29,097	77	1	2	45	29	882	85	740	57	0
Port Dickinson Village	1,648	1	0	0	0	1	18	4	12	2	0
Port Jervis	8,868	18	1	1	7	9	296	62	227	7	2
Portville Village	1,019	1	0	0	0	1	3	0	3	0	0
Port Washington	18,991	0	0	0	0	0	126	18	106	2	0
Potsdam Village	9,470	13	1	4	1	7	235	23	206	6	0
Poughkeepsie	32,883	326	5	22	107	192	1,029	283	693	53	9
Poughkeepsie Town	38,511	37	0	0	12	25	1,353	106	1,236	11	1
Pulaski Village	2,376	5	0	1	0	4	81	14	67	0	0
Quogue Village	971	1	0	0	0	1	20	8	11	1	0
Ramapo Town	84,431	110	0	3	24	83	883	119	740	24	3
Red Hook Village	1,970	0	0	0	0	0	53	7	45	1	0
Rensselaer City	9,434	17	0	7	2	8	214	51	154	9	1
Rhinebeck Village	2,669	1	0	0	0	1	30	5	25	0	0
Riverhead Town	33,657	75	0	3	18	54	974	168	784	22	1
Rochester	211,511	2,029	31	95	755	1,148	10,934	3,384	6,849	701	177
Rockville Centre Village	24,131	20	0	0	13	7	319	52	252	15	0
Rome	33,877	26	1	1	9	15	441	109	311	21	1
Rosendale Town	6,102	5	0	0	0	5	56	10	44	2	0
Rotterdam Town	29,225	12	0	0	2	10	823	109	691	23	2
Rouses Point Village	2,219	0	0	0	0	0	15	5	10	0	0
Rushford Town	1,155	0	0	0	0	0	8	3	5	0	0
Rye	15,791	1	0	0	1	0	180	14	163	3	0
Rye Brook Village	9,389	2	0	0	0	2	91	11	78	2	0
Sag Harbor Village	2,179	2	0	1	0	1	58	0	58	0	0
Salamanca	5,841	25	0	1	3	21	264	59	198	7	1
Sands Point Village	2,687	0	0	0	0	0	7	1	6	0	0
Saranac Lake Village	5,430	7	0	0	0	7	108	29	77	2	0
Saratoga Springs	26,705	20	0	1	4	15	608	78	524	6	0
Saugerties Town	19,570	15	0	2	1	12	381	118	252	11	1
Scarsdale Village	17,243	2	0	0	0	2	142	19	121	2	0
Schenectady	66,432	633	4	43	204	382	3,098	904	2,011	183	24
Schodack Town	11,308	3	0	0	0	3	92	30	58	4	0
Schoharie Village	926	0	0	0	0	0	10	1	9	0	0
Scotia Village	7,764	8	0	0	1	7	139	15	121	3	0
Seneca Falls Village	6,711	3	0	0	1	2	77	10	67	0	0
Shandaken Town	3,099	2	0	0	0	2	87	32	54	1	0
Shawangunk Town	14,396	6	0	0	0	6	104	32	67	5	0
Sherburne Village	1,373	0	0	0	0	0	7	1	6	0	0
Sherrill	3,085	1	0	0	1	0	36	6	30	0	0
Shortsville Village	1,445	0	0	0	0	0	1	0	1	0	0
Sidney Village	3,918	15	0	3	2	10	165	33	131	1	0
Silver Creek Village	2,668	6	0	0	0	6	40	1	39	0	1
Skaneateles Village	2,461	0	0	0	0	0	6	0	6	0	0
Sleepy Hollow Village	9,914	6	0	0	4	2	107	19	77	11	2
Sodus Point Village	904	0	0	0	0	0	10	2	8	0	0
Sodus Village	1,827	0	0	0	0	0	28	5	23	0	0
Solvay Village	6,614	12	0	0	3	9	216	52	162	2	0
Southampton Village	3,123	3	0	1	1	1	146	19	123	4	0
South Glens Falls Village	3,534	4	0	0	2	2	84	14	67	3	0
South Nyack Village	3,526	5	0	1	0	4	39	8	30	1	0
Southold Town	19,860	20	0	2	2	16	445	108	329	8	1
Spring Valley Village	31,488	160	0	10	59	91	477	80	375	22	1
Stillwater Town	6,578	0	0	0	0	0	17	5	12	0	0
St. Johnsville Village	1,740	5	0	0	0	5	34	4	28	2	0
Stockport Town	2,828	0	0	0	0	0	14	5	9	0	0
Stony Point Town	15,127	10	0	0	4	6	151	28	122	1	0
Suffern Village	10,771	5	0	2	0	3	64	11	50	3	0

[1] If a blank is presented in offense arson column, it indicates that the FBI did not receive 12 complete months of arson data for that agency.

Table II-8. Offenses Known to Law Enforcement, by Selected State and City, 2011—*Continued*

(Number.)

State/City	Population	Violent crime	Murder and non-negligent man-slaughter	Forcible rape	Robbery	Aggravated assault	Property crime	Burglary	Larceny-theft	Motor vehicle theft	Arson[1]
New York—*Continued*											
Syracuse	145,822	1,302	11	63	388	840	5,275	1,705	3,261	309	60
Tarrytown Village	11,328	8	0	1	3	4	115	20	91	4	1
Ticonderoga Town	5,065	22	0	7	0	15	163	48	108	7	2
Tonawanda	15,198	26	0	1	2	23	390	41	338	11	4
Tonawanda Town	58,406	104	0	9	32	63	1,036	215	781	40	4
Troy	50,354	371	0	23	112	236	2,318	775	1,442	101	5
Trumansburg Village	1,805	0	0	0	0	0	43	9	32	2	0
Tuckahoe Village	6,515	3	0	0	1	2	7	1	6	0	0
Tupper Lake Village	3,683	10	0	1	0	9	104	23	80	1	0
Tuxedo Park Village	626	0	0	0	0	0	0	0	0	0	0
Tuxedo Town	3,014	0	0	0	0	0	0	0	0	0	0
Ulster Town	12,382	22	1	2	7	12	518	42	468	8	0
Utica	62,515	382	4	17	102	259	2,501	615	1,809	77	5
Vernon Village	1,177	1	0	0	0	1	18	5	12	1	0
Vestal Town	28,169	15	0	0	6	9	598	42	549	7	0
Walden Village	7,009	20	0	2	1	17	90	14	72	4	0
Wallkill Town	27,549	23	0	5	8	10	804	83	701	20	2
Walton Village	3,102	5	0	2	1	2	40	17	23	0	0
Wappingers Falls Village	5,547	7	0	0	4	3	131	13	114	4	0
Warsaw Village	3,489	6	0	1	0	5	60	3	57	0	0
Waterford Town and Village	8,461	0	0	0	0	0	56	14	41	1	1
Waterloo Village	5,194	21	0	1	1	19	166	26	138	2	2
Watertown	27,144	89	1	9	15	64	1,119	158	847	114	9
Watervliet	10,300	26	0	0	10	16	230	33	185	12	2
Watkins Glen Village	1,867	2	0	0	0	2	73	6	65	2	1
Waverly Village	4,464	3	0	1	0	2	119	16	97	6	1
Wayland Village	1,873	0	0	0	0	0	27	1	26	0	0
Webster Town and Village	42,833	25	4	2	7	12	456	64	378	14	1
Weedsport Village	1,823	0	0	0	0	0	15	0	15	0	0
Wellsville Village	4,700	19	0	0	1	18	186	18	166	2	0
Westfield Village	3,238	1	0	0	0	1	24	6	15	3	0
Westhampton Beach Village	1,729	2	0	0	0	2	40	3	37	0	0
West Seneca Town	44,912	49	1	3	15	30	900	176	684	40	3
Whitehall Village	2,626	5	0	2	0	3	43	8	35	0	1
White Plains	57,109	87	1	3	29	54	1,265	46	1,182	37	2
Whitesboro Village	3,789	7	0	0	0	7	30	6	24	0	0
Whitestown Town	9,199	1	0	0	0	1	102	22	77	3	0
Windham Town	1,711	0	0	0	0	0	24	3	20	1	0
Wolcott Village	1,709	0	0	0	0	0	2	0	2	0	0
Woodbury Town	10,734	3	1	0	2	0	298	16	270	12	0
Woodstock Town	5,910	3	0	0	2	1	63	16	46	1	0
Yonkers	196,857	992	7	35	463	487	3,068	753	2,017	298	15
Yorktown Town	36,243	22	0	0	4	18	460	52	400	8	2
Youngstown Village	1,944	0	0	0	0	0	10	3	7	0	0
North Carolina											
Aberdeen	6,431	27	0	1	9	17	318	51	257	10	2
Ahoskie	5,103	34	1	4	8	21	296	95	196	5	1
Albemarle	16,105	90	2	2	37	49	792	244	504	44	5
Andrews	1,804	10	0	0	1	9	80	25	52	3	0
Angier	4,405	39	0	1	3	35	137	54	78	5	0
Apex	37,951	24	0	2	8	14	592	72	510	10	3
Archdale	11,560	10	0	1	4	5	353	111	229	13	4
Asheboro	25,329	73	0	8	38	27	1,792	419	1,317	56	3
Asheville	84,450	444	5	22	181	236	3,949	753	2,875	321	11
Atlantic Beach	1,514	21	0	4	4	13	206	68	131	7	2
Aulander	906	1	0	0	0	1	13	11	1	1	0
Ayden	4,995	39	0	0	12	27	210	76	123	11	0
Bailey	576	2	0	0	1	1	12	6	6	0	0
Banner Elk	1,041	6	0	0	1	5	34	11	23	0	0
Beaufort	4,090	21	0	1	3	17	155	42	108	5	0
Belhaven	1,709	1	0	0	0	1	57	27	30	0	0
Belmont	10,204	34	1	5	3	25	454	53	386	15	1
Benson	3,353	25	1	2	9	13	279	107	158	14	0
Beulaville	1,312	1	0	0	0	1	47	12	35	0	0
Biscoe	1,722	4	0	0	0	4	204	19	181	4	0
Black Mountain	7,948	6	0	2	0	4	166	44	113	9	1
Blowing Rock	1,257	0	0	0	0	0	45	14	31	0	0
Boiling Spring Lakes	5,440	9	1	1	0	7	84	22	60	2	0
Boiling Springs	4,706	4	0	2	2	0	57	6	47	4	0
Boone	17,339	33	0	7	4	22	405	66	322	17	3
Brevard	7,705	30	0	4	4	22	221	71	147	3	1
Bryson City	1,442	16	1	0	1	14	82	1	81	0	0
Bunn	348	1	0	0	0	1	38	3	35	0	0
Burgaw	3,921	7	0	0	2	5	101	13	87	1	0

[1] If a blank is presented in the arson column, it indicates that the FBI did not receive 12 complete months of arson data for that agency.

Table II-8. Offenses Known to Law Enforcement, by Selected State and City, 2011—*Continued*

(Number.)

State/City	Population	Violent crime	Murder and non-negligent man-slaughter	Forcible rape	Robbery	Aggravated assault	Property crime	Burglary	Larceny-theft	Motor vehicle theft	Arson[1]
North Carolina—*Continued*											
Burlington	50,597	405	2	14	104	285	3,669	880	2,668	121	4
Burnsville	1,714	9	0	2	1	6	96	21	71	4	0
Butner	7,687	24	0	0	2	22	304	89	205	10	5
Canton	4,281	30	2	3	1	24	215	44	157	14	0
Cape Carteret	1,941	2	0	1	1	0	26	5	18	3	0
Carolina Beach	5,778	18	0	0	8	10	277	60	209	8	0
Carrboro	19,830	52	0	4	8	40	702	201	469	32	4
Carthage	2,233	7	0	0	3	4	82	18	59	5	1
Cary	136,949	108	1	13	41	53	2,093	370	1,658	65	8
Catawba	611	4	0	0	0	4	11	2	7	2	0
Chadbourn	1,880	15	1	0	3	11	157	51	99	7	0
Chapel Hill	57,959	106	1	7	38	60	1,523	484	985	54	6
Charlotte-Mecklenburg	789,478	4,787	56	218	1,612	2,901	32,008	8,536	21,371	2,101	195
Cherryville	5,833	20	0	2	3	15	249	44	199	6	1
China Grove	3,608	16	0	1	3	12	86	14	69	3	0
Claremont	1,369	0	0	0	0	0	63	12	47	4	0
Clayton	16,320	20	0	2	10	8	400	112	274	14	5
Cleveland	882	4	0	0	0	4	26	7	18	1	0
Clinton	8,749	51	0	4	14	33	475	142	318	15	2
Coats	2,139	8	0	0	0	8	88	34	49	5	1
Columbus	1,012	5	0	1	1	3	36	7	26	3	0
Concord	80,069	93	2	8	37	46	3,111	452	2,528	131	9
Conover	8,269	19	0	0	10	9	608	79	516	13	1
Cornelius	25,181	39	0	3	11	25	754	126	603	25	9
Cramerton	4,218	9	0	2	4	3	119	32	84	3	0
Creedmoor	4,176	14	0	2	2	10	109	21	84	4	0
Dallas	4,545	20	0	2	2	16	183	40	135	8	1
Davidson	11,083	8	0	0	4	4	107	19	85	3	0
Dobson	1,606	5	0	0	2	3	45	8	34	3	0
Drexel	1,882	3	0	0	2	1	25	8	15	2	0
Duck	374	44	0	0	44	0	93	33	60	0	0
Durham	231,225	1,707	27	64	699	917	11,270	3,874	6,768	628	23
Eden	15,724	68	1	2	9	56	746	185	513	48	3
Edenton	5,067	15	0	0	4	11	252	64	184	4	1
Elizabeth City	18,920	95	0	3	18	74	750	196	541	13	0
Elizabethtown	3,628	25	0	0	15	10	242	42	193	7	1
Elkin	4,052	11	0	0	4	7	292	42	244	6	1
Elon	9,538	17	0	2	4	11	149	59	89	1	0
Emerald Isle	3,701	6	0	1	1	4	331	170	155	6	1
Enfield	2,564	28	0	0	7	21	139	70	62	7	0
Erwin	4,461	11	0	0	5	6	163	6	157	0	0
Fairmont	2,697	29	1	1	14	13	268	83	178	7	2
Farmville	4,713	39	0	1	7	31	212	59	152	1	3
Fayetteville	203,107	1,050	25	56	495	474	12,972	4,204	8,088	680	51
Fletcher	7,278	3	0	0	2	1	173	50	121	2	0
Forest City	7,571	26	0	2	7	17	636	149	464	23	2
Franklin	3,894	9	0	3	1	5	211	51	152	8	2
Franklinton	2,049	7	0	0	4	3	92	25	61	6	1
Fuquay-Varina	18,164	78	1	0	22	55	662	161	473	28	1
Garner	26,071	57	0	4	23	30	1,183	216	931	36	3
Gastonia	72,651	466	4	37	171	254	4,363	951	3,198	214	18
Gibsonville	6,491	11	0	3	5	3	129	65	60	4	1
Goldsboro	36,899	343	7	2	91	243	2,655	675	1,840	140	2
Graham	14,332	69	0	3	7	59	503	140	338	25	0
Granite Falls	4,782	8	0	1	1	6	362	50	294	18	2
Granite Quarry	2,967	10	0	2	0	8	114	30	80	4	0
Hamlet	6,577	38	1	4	8	25	395	127	251	17	3
Haw River	2,327	10	0	0	2	8	95	50	44	1	0
Henderson	15,563	153	5	4	76	68	1,880	416	1,386	78	18
Hendersonville	13,304	55	1	4	19	31	807	141	626	40	1
Hertford	2,170	9	0	0	3	6	85	28	49	8	0
Hickory	40,517	238	5	11	75	147	2,500	536	1,850	114	9
Highlands	936	5	0	0	2	3	47	13	30	4	0
High Point	105,695	600	3	25	200	372	5,057	1,266	3,550	241	24
Hillsborough	6,164	27	0	1	13	13	463	84	358	21	2
Holden Beach	582	3	0	2	0	1	107	63	44	0	0
Holly Ridge	1,284	6	0	1	0	5	40	20	20	0	2
Holly Springs	24,974	36	0	3	3	30	312	90	220	2	2
Hope Mills	15,368	82	0	2	28	52	957	216	704	37	3
Hudson	3,824	2	0	0	1	1	134	25	103	6	0
Huntersville	47,366	68	2	6	16	44	1,017	229	745	43	9
Indian Beach	113	0	0	0	0	0	12	2	10	0	0
Jacksonville	71,034	171	1	25	24	121	2,034	515	1,428	91	3
Jefferson	1,631	1	0	0	0	1	23	6	15	2	0

[1] If a blank is presented in the arson column, it indicates that the FBI did not receive 12 complete months of arson data for that agency.

Table II-8. Offenses Known to Law Enforcement, by Selected State and City, 2011—*Continued*

(Number.)

State/City	Population	Violent crime	Murder and non-negligent man-slaughter	Forcible rape	Robbery	Aggravated assault	Property crime	Burglary	Larceny-theft	Motor vehicle theft	Arson[1]
North Carolina—*Continued*											
Jonesville	2,314	9	0	0	1	8	139	43	96	0	0
Kenansville	866	5	0	1	3	1	28	4	22	2	0
Kernersville	23,416	95	0	3	15	77	1,068	199	836	33	6
King	6,992	22	0	1	2	19	173	38	130	5	3
Kings Mountain	10,427	26	0	2	9	15	447	175	250	22	1
Kinston	21,952	266	11	6	67	182	1,437	491	914	32	9
Kitty Hawk	3,313	2	1	0	0	1	129	31	98	0	2
Knightdale	11,546	20	2	0	5	13	435	81	344	10	1
Lake Lure	1,207	1	0	0	1	0	55	28	26	1	0
Lake Royale	2,538	3	0	0	0	3	85	55	27	3	0
Landis	3,148	2	0	0	0	2	80	19	55	6	0
Laurel Park	2,208	0	0	0	0	0	12	0	12	0	0
Laurinburg	16,164	131	7	4	51	69	1,114	473	610	31	11
Leland	13,699	17	0	2	2	13	356	75	271	10	0
Lenoir	18,459	48	1	1	15	31	871	236	593	42	5
Lexington	19,171	79	3	7	20	49	743	234	476	33	6
Liberty	2,690	2	0	0	0	2	29	2	25	2	0
Lillington	3,235	6	0	0	2	4	203	57	143	3	0
Lincolnton	10,619	48	1	2	8	37	562	107	442	13	1
Long View	4,933	21	1	2	1	17	340	151	164	25	0
Louisburg	3,402	11	1	1	4	5	150	54	87	9	1
Lumberton	21,815	380	6	6	145	223	2,918	837	1,935	146	7
Madison	2,274	9	0	1	1	7	124	28	96	0	0
Magnolia	951	1	0	0	0	1	20	10	9	1	0
Maiden	3,352	4	0	0	1	3	137	30	102	5	1
Marion	7,937	26	1	0	6	19	517	164	332	21	3
Mars Hill	1,893	5	0	3	1	1	52	16	34	2	0
Marshville	2,432	22	0	2	3	17	111	32	78	1	0
Matthews	27,543	36	0	1	9	26	777	82	654	41	10
Maxton	2,457	17	0	1	5	11	159	69	87	3	3
Mayodan	2,509	10	0	0	1	9	224	19	200	5	0
Maysville	1,032	1	0	0	0	1	16	1	15	0	0
Mebane	11,537	58	0	5	15	38	536	95	421	20	1
Middlesex	832	1	0	0	0	1	18	6	12	0	0
Mint Hill	23,010	48	0	5	16	27	429	162	241	26	9
Mooresville	33,126	84	1	7	22	54	1,477	259	1,139	79	16
Morehead City	8,771	63	1	2	7	53	566	151	400	15	2
Morganton	17,133	41	0	5	7	29	628	135	465	28	0
Morrisville	18,812	16	0	3	5	8	365	73	281	11	2
Mount Airy	10,520	59	1	3	5	50	660	128	508	24	1
Mount Gilead	1,196	2	0	0	1	1	37	4	32	1	0
Mount Holly	13,829	27	0	4	4	19	391	107	270	14	1
Mount Olive	4,647	45	0	2	8	35	324	111	202	11	2
Murfreesboro	2,871	4	0	0	2	2	102	30	71	1	0
Murphy	1,648	22	0	0	3	19	119	21	97	1	1
Nashville	5,420	10	2	0	3	5	160	46	104	10	1
New Bern	29,898	175	1	10	51	113	1,807	714	1,053	40	4
Newland	707	1	0	0	1	0	14	6	8	0	0
Newport	4,203	4	0	0	0	4	98	44	53	1	3
Newton	13,132	23	0	5	10	8	601	172	396	33	4
North Topsail Beach	752	0	0	0	0	0	4	2	1	1	0
North Wilkesboro	4,299	25	0	1	8	16	276	49	222	5	1
Oxford	8,568	112	1	6	33	72	695	285	398	12	3
Pilot Mountain	1,496	1	0	0	0	1	103	21	80	2	0
Pinebluff	1,354	4	0	0	2	2	16	9	7	0	0
Pinehurst	13,290	8	0	0	3	5	103	2	99	2	0
Pine Knoll Shores	1,356	2	0	0	0	2	64	21	43	0	0
Pinetops	1,391	12	0	0	5	7	39	11	28	0	0
Pineville	7,574	43	0	2	23	18	1,224	112	1,086	26	10
Pittsboro	3,790	14	0	1	2	11	66	9	50	7	1
Raeford	4,669	38	0	1	15	22	320	70	234	16	1
Raleigh	409,014	1,724	17	127	680	900	13,242	2,985	9,343	914	84
Ramseur	1,713	2	0	0	1	1	90	32	57	1	0
Randleman	4,165	11	0	3	5	3	288	47	239	2	1
Red Springs	3,471	44	1	4	9	30	283	98	173	12	6
Reidsville	14,704	45	0	5	13	27	895	230	647	18	2
Richlands	1,539	3	0	0	1	2	26	4	17	5	0
River Bend	3,159	2	0	0	0	2	9	7	2	0	0
Roanoke Rapids	15,954	62	2	7	19	34	864	306	539	19	4
Robbins	1,111	6	2	0	1	3	40	5	35	0	1
Robersonville	1,507	18	1	0	5	12	54	20	33	1	0
Rockingham	9,679	49	0	3	26	20	1,070	197	856	17	6
Rockwell	2,135	3	0	0	0	3	51	18	31	2	0
Rocky Mount	58,206	569	12	13	151	393	3,916	1,146	2,625	145	19

[1] If a blank is presented in the arson column, it indicates that the FBI did not receive 12 complete months of arson data for that agency.

Table II-8. Offenses Known to Law Enforcement, by Selected State and City, 2011—*Continued*

(Number.)

State/City	Population	Violent crime	Murder and non-negligent man-slaughter	Forcible rape	Robbery	Aggravated assault	Property crime	Burglary	Larceny-theft	Motor vehicle theft	Arson[1]
North Carolina—*Continued*											
Rolesville	3,834	5	0	0	0	5	80	49	30	1	0
Rowland	1,050	7	0	0	5	2	49	23	22	4	0
Roxboro	8,468	66	2	3	19	42	515	131	371	13	1
Rutherfordton	4,266	5	0	0	3	2	142	43	97	2	0
Salisbury	34,089	223	3	10	86	124	2,264	478	1,697	89	8
Sanford	28,450	82	4	0	33	45	960	239	675	46	2
Scotland Neck	2,085	14	0	1	2	11	111	56	55	0	0
Selma	6,150	51	0	3	14	34	428	193	216	19	1
Shallotte	3,722	20	0	0	7	13	209	74	130	5	0
Shelby	20,581	108	0	9	36	63	847	295	516	36	8
Siler City	7,987	19	0	2	6	11	374	86	277	11	1
Smithfield	11,105	98	1	3	22	72	823	181	617	25	3
Southern Pines	12,490	81	1	0	21	59	478	121	340	17	4
Southern Shores	2,748	4	0	2	0	2	65	25	39	1	0
Southport	2,869	3	0	0	2	1	111	10	97	4	1
Sparta	1,792	3	0	2	1	0	48	10	35	3	0
Spencer	3,308	33	1	1	8	23	204	89	111	4	4
Spring Hope	1,337	3	0	0	1	2	36	11	25	0	0
Spring Lake	12,116	33	0	1	3	29	594	220	352	22	2
Spruce Pine	2,203	3	0	3	0	0	58	3	53	2	0
Stallings	14,006	17	0	1	8	8	235	41	189	5	0
Stanley	3,601	11	0	2	4	5	116	32	82	2	0
Star	887	1	0	0	0	1	27	2	25	0	0
Statesville	24,843	250	3	16	55	176	1,884	548	1,238	98	8
Stoneville	1,069	2	0	0	0	2	51	11	40	0	0
St. Pauls	2,061	7	0	0	2	5	138	51	87	0	1
Sunset Beach	3,617	1	0	0	1	0	76	40	35	1	0
Surf City	1,876	14	0	1	2	11	156	76	76	4	0
Swansboro	2,697	10	0	3	2	5	99	17	78	4	0
Sylva	2,621	22	2	1	2	17	195	44	146	5	2
Tabor City	2,543	18	2	1	6	9	193	34	148	11	3
Tarboro	11,560	68	0	4	10	54	493	125	357	11	0
Taylorsville	2,125	3	0	1	0	2	199	53	143	3	1
Thomasville	27,096	130	3	9	35	83	1,266	311	934	21	5
Trent Woods	4,208	1	0	0	0	1	58	10	42	6	0
Troutman	2,413	10	0	0	1	9	75	22	53	0	0
Troy	3,229	19	0	0	0	19	159	23	130	6	0
Tryon	1,667	3	0	0	0	3	57	30	25	2	1
Valdese	4,547	7	0	0	2	5	65	22	39	4	0
Vass	729	2	0	0	1	1	27	2	25	0	0
Wadesboro	5,887	63	2	7	12	42	479	62	406	11	3
Wake Forest	30,499	45	1	2	10	32	725	94	618	13	1
Wallace	3,929	15	0	5	4	6	182	38	138	6	1
Walnut Cove	1,443	1	0	1	0	0	42	7	34	1	0
Warrenton	873	3	0	0	1	2	29	5	23	1	0
Warsaw	3,093	6	0	0	4	2	187	77	109	1	0
Washington	9,868	76	0	5	23	48	677	156	500	21	5
Waxhaw	9,984	23	0	4	1	18	192	51	137	4	3
Waynesville	9,994	21	0	1	2	18	431	152	248	31	1
Weaverville	3,160	4	0	1	1	2	228	9	218	1	0
Wendell	5,919	12	0	4	1	7	124	38	80	6	2
West Jefferson	1,315	0	0	0	0	0	68	6	58	4	0
Whispering Pines	2,965	0	0	0	0	0	14	4	10	0	0
Whitakers	753	4	1	0	2	1	19	5	14	0	0
White Lake	812	5	0	0	0	5	70	11	54	5	0
Whiteville	5,462	52	1	2	15	34	553	106	428	19	3
Wilkesboro	3,456	10	0	1	1	8	402	35	359	8	1
Williamston	5,581	60	1	5	19	35	484	157	317	10	5
Wilmington	107,826	662	10	32	254	366	5,708	1,454	3,843	411	23
Wilson	49,790	244	6	8	71	159	2,212	675	1,420	117	6
Wilson's Mills	2,306	10	0	2	4	4	79	41	33	5	2
Windsor	3,676	9	0	0	2	7	64	19	42	3	0
Wingate	3,535	15	0	1	1	13	89	28	59	2	1
Winston-Salem	232,529	1,565	14	93	444	1,014	13,874	4,680	8,522	672	60
Winterville	9,387	15	0	2	5	8	187	46	135	6	2
Woodfin	6,201	12	0	1	2	9	119	53	59	7	0
Wrightsville Beach	2,508	10	0	6	1	3	203	47	150	6	0
Yadkinville	2,997	13	0	1	1	11	148	28	116	4	2
Youngsville	1,172	0	0	0	0	0	23	3	19	1	0
Zebulon	4,489	31	0	1	8	22	286	29	248	9	0
North Dakota											
Belfield	813	1	1	0	0	0	22	3	17	2	0
Beulah	3,174	2	0	1	0	1	66	14	51	1	0
Bismarck	62,305	166	1	27	15	123	1,865	258	1,494	113	4

[1] If a blank is presented in the arson column, it indicates that the FBI did not receive 12 complete months of arson data for that agency.

Table II-8.   Offenses Known to Law Enforcement, by Selected State and City, 2011—*Continued*

(Number.)

State/City	Population	Violent crime	Murder and non-negligent man-slaughter	Forcible rape	Robbery	Aggravated assault	Property crime	Burglary	Larceny-theft	Motor vehicle theft	Arson[1]
North Dakota—*Continued*											
Carrington	2,100	1	0	0	1	0	9	6	2	1	0
Devils Lake	7,261	33	0	8	2	23	356	71	264	21	7
Dickinson	18,087	51	0	0	1	50	441	53	363	25	0
Ellendale	1,418	1	0	1	0	0	21	1	20	0	2
Fargo	107,329	384	1	42	47	294	2,671	423	2,120	128	13
Grafton	4,356	12	0	2	0	10	97	16	74	7	1
Grand Forks	53,729	133	0	32	8	93	1,533	306	1,130	97	6
Harvey	1,813	2	0	0	0	2	24	7	15	2	0
Jamestown	15,687	30	0	11	0	19	302	42	243	17	2
Lincoln	2,447	7	1	0	0	6	24	1	19	4	0
Linton	1,115	2	0	0	1	1	1	1	0	0	0
Lisbon	2,190	1	0	0	0	1	42	19	21	2	0
Mandan	18,640	44	0	5	0	39	491	66	391	34	2
Medora	114	2	0	0	0	2	0	0	0	0	0
Minot	41,577	117	6	7	5	99	773	114	593	66	5
Napoleon	805	0	0	0	0	0	11	0	11	0	0
Rolla	1,302	0	0	0	0	0	24	9	13	2	0
Rugby	2,924	0	0	0	0	0	59	15	42	2	1
Sherwood	246	0	0	0	0	0	3	3	0	0	0
Thompson	1,003	0	0	0	0	0	6	2	3	1	0
Valley City	6,696	2	0	2	0	0	64	14	45	5	0
Wahpeton	7,897	9	0	3	0	6	154	20	130	4	5
Watford City	1,773	7	0	1	0	6	56	7	43	6	0
West Fargo	26,266	53	0	4	4	45	429	79	330	20	4
Williston	14,964	55	0	15	2	38	388	28	285	75	0
Wishek	1,019	1	0	0	0	1	0	0	0	0	0
Ohio											
Ada	5,956	1	0	1	0	0	64	16	48	0	0
Akron	199,256	1,779	27	165	718	869	10,864	4,268	5,790	806	95
Alliance	22,338	85	2	24	20	39	979	239	715	25	6
Amberley Village	3,588	1	0	0	0	1	47	7	38	2	0
Amelia	4,805	0	0	0	0	0	67	4	62	1	1
Amherst	12,030	9	0	3	3	3	240	47	187	6	1
Arcanum	2,131	1	0	0	0	1	28	9	17	2	0
Arlington Heights	746	1	0	0	1	0	25	6	18	1	0
Ashland	20,377	17	0	9	2	6	593	99	488	6	0
Ashville	4,100	3	0	1	0	2	81	16	61	4	1
Athens	23,849	30	0	9	8	13	486	81	398	7	2
Aurora	15,559	12	0	0	1	11	142	34	107	1	3
Austintown	29,699	29	0	1	28	0	1,344	297	995	52	0
Barberton	26,569	67	1	8	27	31	1,276	232	990	54	14
Barnesville	4,196	1	0	0	1	0	14	5	9	0	1
Batavia	1,510	2	0	0	2	0	83	10	70	3	0
Bath Township, Summit County	9,709	2	0	0	1	1	129	24	104	1	0
Bazetta Township	5,878	3	0	0	0	3	222	34	185	3	0
Beachwood	11,962	37	0	1	8	28	489	61	422	6	0
Beavercreek	45,226	27	0	13	8	6	1,069	90	961	18	3
Beaver Township	6,716	6	0	0	1	5	145	55	90	0	0
Bedford	13,084	21	0	1	4	16	616	54	510	52	1
Bedford Heights	10,759	28	0	5	10	13	313	74	173	66	3
Bellaire	4,281	4	0	0	1	3	31	4	24	3	1
Bellbrook	6,948	2	0	0	1	1	63	10	53	0	1
Bellefontaine	13,380	38	1	6	13	18	806	130	653	23	0
Bellville	1,919	1	0	1	0	0	51	2	48	1	0
Belpre	6,446	5	0	1	2	2	76	16	57	3	2
Berea	19,107	8	0	2	1	5	276	35	225	16	4
Bethel	2,713	4	0	2	2	0	163	22	140	1	0
Bexley	13,067	10	0	1	6	3	348	70	273	5	0
Blue Ash	12,123	9	0	1	5	3	359	51	298	10	0
Bluffton	4,128	3	0	1	0	2	48	11	34	3	0
Bowling Green	30,050	54	1	16	13	24	777	108	652	17	0
Brecksville	13,666	3	0	0	1	2	71	12	58	1	0
Brewster	2,114	0	0	0	0	0	12	2	9	1	0
Brimfield Township	10,384	12	0	6	3	3	277	50	222	5	0
Broadview Heights	19,414	9	0	0	3	6	58	19	36	3	0
Brookfield Township	8,860	18	0	1	5	12	237	74	145	18	3
Brooklyn	11,177	22	0	2	14	6	519	50	418	51	1
Brook Park	19,226	19	0	0	4	15	151	52	77	22	1
Brookville	5,888	3	0	2	0	1	99	15	76	8	0
Brunswick	34,280	108	0	1	1	106	372	51	305	16	0
Brunswick Hills Township	9,905	0	0	0	0	0	27	6	18	3	0
Bryan	8,551	0	0	0	0	0	50	3	47	0	1
Burton	1,456	0	0	0	0	0	3	3	0	0	0

[1] If a blank is presented in the arson column, it indicates that the FBI did not receive 12 complete months of arson data for that agency.

Table II-8. Offenses Known to Law Enforcement, by Selected State and City, 2011—*Continued*

(Number.)

State/City	Population	Violent crime	Murder and non-negligent man-slaughter	Forcible rape	Robbery	Aggravated assault	Property crime	Burglary	Larceny-theft	Motor vehicle theft	Arson[1]
Ohio—*Continued*											
Butler Township	7,874	26	2	6	5	13	251	26	210	15	0
Cadiz	3,355	1	0	0	1	0	88	31	57	0	0
Cambridge	10,643	46	2	9	10	25	688	171	485	32	0
Campbell	8,241	3	0	0	3	0	95	50	41	4	1
Canal Fulton	5,483	4	0	0	1	3	84	22	58	4	0
Canfield	7,521	0	0	0	0	0	110	9	96	5	0
Canton	73,060	810	12	57	438	303	4,787	1,854	2,683	250	25
Cardington	2,048	3	0	1	0	2	33	6	25	2	0
Carlisle	4,919	3	0	0	1	2	99	18	79	2	0
Carrollton	3,243	17	0	0	0	17	16	7	9	0	0
Celina	10,408	23	0	4	5	14	529	70	442	17	1
Centerville	24,017	8	0	3	0	5	433	68	356	9	4
Chagrin Falls	4,116	0	0	0	0	0	39	6	31	2	0
Champion Township	9,619	9	0	1	2	6	250	60	185	5	0
Chardon	5,152	5	0	0	0	5	107	8	99	0	4
Cheviot	8,381	8	0	0	8	0	235	53	177	5	3
Chillicothe	21,917	118	1	8	37	72	2,141	426	1,668	47	18
Cincinnati	297,160	3,067	61	183	1,773	1,050	20,462	6,674	12,512	1,276	328
Circleville	13,324	37	0	5	28	4	1,183	262	905	16	0
Clayton	13,219	4	0	0	2	2	208	62	129	17	1
Clay Township, Ottawa County	2,724	0	0	0	0	0	22	4	16	2	0
Clearcreek Township	14,084	1	0	0	0	1	136	39	93	4	1
Cleveland	397,106	5,426	74	354	3,156	1,842	25,323	10,706	10,524	4,093	319
Cleveland Heights	46,155	143	1	7	102	33	1,018	318	675	25	0
Cleves	3,236	1	0	0	1	0	69	18	50	1	0
Clyde	6,330	9	0	1	2	6	203	50	151	2	0
Coitsville Township	1,393	1	0	0	0	1	41	14	25	2	0
Coldwater	4,430	0	0	0	0	0	47	12	35	0	0
Columbus	787,609	5,185	87	565	3,244	1,289	49,043	15,169	30,259	3,615	
Conneaut	12,850	35	0	4	2	29	353	106	243	4	0
Cortland	7,109	0	0	0	0	0	74	21	53	0	2
Covington	2,586	0	0	0	0	0	37	7	28	2	0
Crestline	4,633	8	0	2	1	5	46	18	24	4	0
Cuyahoga Falls	49,688	60	0	11	17	32	1,363	282	1,017	64	4
Dayton	141,631	1,355	33	98	638	586	8,323	3,121	4,569	633	149
Defiance	16,506	13	0	4	3	6	689	85	602	2	2
Delaware	34,778	74	1	32	20	21	1,020	229	754	37	7
Delhi Township	29,532	14	0	3	5	6	479	103	365	11	0
Delphos	7,106	2	0	2	0	0	243	85	157	1	0
Delta	3,105	1	0	0	0	1	43	11	32	0	0
Dover	12,835	4	0	2	1	1	65	14	49	2	0
Dublin	41,782	16	0	9	4	3	533	69	444	20	3
Eastlake	18,591	8	1	0	2	5	480	33	437	10	3
East Palestine	4,724	4	0	0	2	2	176	43	125	8	3
Eaton	8,413	7	0	2	0	5	407	95	305	7	0
Edgerton	2,013	1	0	0	0	1	17	1	16	0	0
Elida	1,906	2	0	1	0	1	6	1	5	0	0
Elyria	54,573	192	2	18	86	86	2,252	703	1,478	71	17
Englewood	13,475	14	0	1	8	5	364	40	314	10	0
Evendale	2,769	7	0	0	1	6	231	7	224	0	0
Fairborn	32,376	75	0	15	48	12	1,062	289	732	41	2
Fairfield	42,541	112	0	6	16	90	1,283	223	1,015	45	4
Fairfield Township	21,389	37	1	4	7	25	756	121	615	20	3
Fairport Harbor	3,111	12	0	5	3	4	133	23	107	3	2
Findlay	41,232	80	2	23	22	33	1,993	349	1,607	37	11
Forest	1,462	1	0	0	0	1	36	12	23	1	0
Forest Park	18,734	34	0	3	29	2	482	127	335	20	2
Fort Recovery	1,431	0	0	0	0	0	11	1	10	0	0
Fort Shawnee	3,729	1	0	1	0	0	52	15	37	0	0
Fostoria	13,451	25	0	5	5	15	288	84	201	3	2
Fowler	2,597	0	0	0	0	0	18	6	11	1	0
Fredericktown	2,495	1	0	0	0	1	0	69	15	54	0	0
Fremont	16,746	39	0	3	11	25	955	144	793	18	2
Gahanna	33,272	18	0	3	7	8	830	124	687	19	6
Galion	10,520	22	0	6	9	7	576	152	413	11	0
Gallipolis	3,644	7	0	2	2	3	368	44	321	3	0
Gates Mills	2,272	0	0	0	0	0	19	6	13	0	0
Geneva-on-the-Lake	1,289	0	0	0	0	0	15	5	9	1	0
Genoa	2,338	0	0	0	0	0	33	8	24	1	0
Georgetown	4,334	3	0	1	0	2	198	38	157	3	1
Germantown	5,551	2	0	1	0	1	107	22	84	1	1
German Township, Clark County	7,117	1	0	0	1	0	130	19	109	2	0
German Township, Montgomery County	2,884	0	0	0	0	0	68	20	44	4	0
Gibsonburg	2,583	2	0	0	0	2	64	18	46	0	0
Girard	9,965	30	0	0	6	24	367	120	242	5	11

[1] If a blank is presented in the arson column, it indicates that the FBI did not receive 12 complete months of arson data for that agency.

Table II-8.   Offenses Known to Law Enforcement, by Selected State and City, 2011—*Continued*

(Number.)

State/City	Population	Violent crime	Murder and non-negligent man-slaughter	Forcible rape	Robbery	Aggravated assault	Property crime	Burglary	Larceny-theft	Motor vehicle theft	Arson[1]
Ohio—*Continued*											
Glendale	2,157	0	0	0	0	0	25	8	17	0	1
Glouster	1,792	1	0	1	0	0	75	26	49	0	2
Goshen Township, Clermont County	15,516	11	3	2	2	4	397	107	280	10	1
Goshen Township, Mahoning County	3,245	6	0	1	0	5	107	26	77	4	1
Grandview Heights	6,541	1	0	0	1	0	115	26	87	2	0
Granville	5,650	2	0	0	0	2	61	9	49	3	0
Greenfield	4,642	7	0	1	6	0	281	62	208	11	2
Greenhills	3,618	3	0	0	1	2	37	7	29	1	0
Greenville	13,237	48	0	2	7	39	553	132	390	31	6
Grove City	35,601	35	1	7	23	4	1,225	201	997	27	14
Groveport	5,367	9	0	1	1	7	126	20	99	7	0
Harrison	9,904	5	0	0	2	3	288	24	263	1	0
Hartville	2,946	0	0	0	0	0	55	8	47	0	0
Haskins	1,189	1	0	0	0	1	19	1	18	0	0
Heath	10,318	16	0	3	3	10	592	80	502	10	5
Hebron	2,338	0	0	0	0	0	38	9	29	0	0
Hicksville	3,584	1	0	0	0	1	45	10	35	0	1
Highland Heights	8,351	1	0	0	0	1	115	25	85	5	0
Hilliard	28,456	18	2	0	11	5	753	141	592	20	8
Hillsboro	6,610	6	0	2	1	3	368	42	323	3	0
Hinckley Township	7,652	5	0	0	2	3	60	9	48	3	0
Holland	1,765	9	0	0	7	2	178	21	156	1	0
Howland Township	17,340	13	0	1	4	8	527	142	374	11	0
Hubbard	7,880	7	0	1	0	6	194	35	156	3	0
Hubbard Township	5,658	6	0	1	0	5	148	41	99	8	0
Huber Heights	38,129	82	1	7	45	29	1,379	250	1,088	41	24
Hudson	22,278	2	0	0	1	1	135	31	104	0	0
Huron	7,154	3	0	1	0	2	45	3	40	2	0
Independence	7,138	2	0	0	1	1	126	24	98	4	0
Indian Hill	5,789	0	0	0	0	0	56	10	45	1	0
Jackson	6,402	3	0	0	3	0	352	56	288	8	0
Jackson Center	1,463	1	0	1	0	0	10	4	6	0	0
Jackson Township, Montgomery County	3,697	1	0	1	0	0	32	16	12	4	0
Jackson Township, Stark County	40,403	33	0	4	14	15	1,387	188	1,161	38	6
Jamestown	1,994	0	0	0	0	0	73	22	50	1	1
Johnstown	4,635	1	0	0	1	0	61	5	55	1	0
Kent	28,925	58	2	6	17	33	650	146	472	32	16
Kettering	56,204	64	0	23	26	15	1,266	301	907	58	8
Kirtland	6,871	0	0	0	0	0	38	9	29	0	0
Kirtland Hills	646	0	0	0	0	0	7	1	6	0	0
Lake Township	7,959	0	0	0	0	0	101	30	67	4	0
Lakewood	52,169	74	1	9	35	29	1,134	254	795	85	6
Lawrence Township	8,229	3	0	0	0	3	111	32	73	6	0
Lebanon	20,048	36	1	12	8	15	333	51	277	5	3
Lexington	4,826	3	0	2	1	0	91	11	79	1	0
Liberty Township	12,071	17	0	4	5	8	250	61	182	7	0
Lima	38,799	404	1	48	97	258	2,262	786	1,357	119	20
Lincoln Heights	3,288	11	0	2	5	4	47	13	32	2	1
Liverpool Township	4,050	1	0	1	0	0	51	11	39	1	0
Lockland	3,452	21	0	0	17	4	161	62	92	7	2
Logan	7,157	9	1	3	4	1	446	87	350	9	1
London	9,911	8	0	1	1	6	302	58	232	12	1
Lorain	64,144	318	4	37	138	139	3,190	1,320	1,738	132	24
Lordstown	3,420	0	0	0	0	0	89	19	66	4	0
Loudonville	2,643	0	0	0	0	0	71	10	59	2	0
Louisville	9,183	6	0	2	3	1	235	53	176	6	1
Loveland	12,090	5	0	1	2	2	155	24	124	7	0
Madeira	8,732	1	0	1	0	0	51	4	47	0	0
Madison	3,186	1	0	0	1	0	36	9	26	1	0
Madison Township, Franklin County	18,041	9	0	0	6	3	224	76	143	5	0
Madison Township, Lake County	15,711	35	0	4	2	29	208	35	163	10	2
Mansfield	47,856	171	3	32	86	50	3,063	913	2,044	106	15
Mariemont	3,405	1	1	0	0	0	74	0	74	0	0
Marietta	14,095	13	0	2	3	8	204	32	167	5	3
Marion	36,864	98	3	15	52	28	2,501	865	1,586	50	14
Martins Ferry	6,920	8	0	1	3	4	66	16	50	0	0
Marysville	22,110	12	0	7	4	1	442	64	374	4	1
Mason	30,734	10	0	2	1	7	441	54	377	10	1
Massillon	32,173	87	0	15	37	35	1,209	348	832	29	12
Mayfield Heights	19,169	13	0	0	10	3	369	34	320	15	3
McArthur	1,702	4	0	0	2	2	63	15	43	5	0
McComb	1,649	0	0	0	0	0	10	1	9	0	0
Mechanicsburg	1,645	0	0	0	0	0	16	5	9	2	0
Medina Township	8,543	0	0	0	0	0	99	9	88	2	0
Mentor	47,194	43	0	9	24	10	1,127	159	910	58	6

[1] If a blank is presented in the arson column, it indicates that the FBI did not receive 12 complete months of arson data for that agency.

Table II-8.   Offenses Known to Law Enforcement, by Selected State and City, 2011—*Continued*

(Number.)

State/City	Population	Violent crime	Murder and non-negligent man-slaughter	Forcible rape	Robbery	Aggravated assault	Property crime	Burglary	Larceny-theft	Motor vehicle theft	Arson[1]
Ohio—*Continued*											
Mentor-on-the-Lake	7,448	10	1	0	1	8	86	13	72	1	0
Miamisburg	20,196	34	0	6	19	9	801	256	512	33	5
Miami Township, Clermont County	40,878	22	0	0	9	13	884	101	771	12	6
Miami Township, Montgomery County	29,152	48	1	5	17	25	1,230	178	1,018	34	6
Middlefield	2,696	0	0	0	0	0	32	3	29	0	1
Middleport	2,532	0	0	0	0	0	22	10	11	1	1
Middletown	48,730	364	4	39	95	226	4,369	1,309	2,949	111	9
Mifflin Township	2,464	2	0	0	0	2	33	5	27	1	0
Milford	6,714	12	0	1	7	4	407	26	377	4	1
Millersburg	3,027	5	0	4	0	1	78	4	72	2	1
Millersport	1,045	1	0	0	0	1	16	5	11	0	1
Milton Township	2,581	1	0	1	0	0	53	13	35	5	0
Minerva	3,723	2	0	1	0	1	114	20	87	7	0
Mingo Junction	3,457	16	0	0	2	14	38	19	19	0	0
Monroe	14,771	47	0	7	7	33	694	88	591	15	0
Monroeville	1,401	0	0	0	0	0	23	5	17	1	1
Montgomery	10,259	1	0	0	1	0	176	18	154	4	2
Montpelier	4,075	8	0	5	0	3	204	35	166	3	1
Montville Township	11,193	1	0	1	0	0	86	18	66	2	1
Moraine	6,312	37	0	9	13	15	753	94	630	29	6
Moreland Hills	3,322	0	0	0	0	0	19	9	9	1	0
Mount Gilead	3,663	3	0	0	2	1	203	22	176	5	1
Mount Healthy	6,102	11	1	2	8	0	214	65	137	12	0
Mount Sterling	1,783	2	0	0	0	2	38	8	30	0	0
Munroe Falls	5,016	1	0	0	0	1	37	8	29	0	1
Nelsonville	5,396	11	0	3	8	0	260	66	182	12	0
Newark	47,608	84	0	20	38	26	2,066	467	1,554	45	38
New Boston	2,274	8	0	1	6	1	227	47	175	5	0
Newcomerstown	3,825	9	0	3	1	5	91	27	61	3	1
New Franklin	14,237	4	1	3	0	0	133	47	78	8	3
New Lebanon	3,998	4	0	3	0	1	137	30	83	24	0
New Lexington	4,734	5	0	2	1	2	216	36	170	10	0
New London	2,463	2	0	1	0	1	22	8	13	1	0
New Middletown	1,622	0	0	0	0	0	11	5	6	0	0
New Philadelphia	17,301	12	0	1	6	5	123	5	116	2	0
Newtown	2,674	0	0	0	0	0	30	6	24	0	0
New Washington	968	2	0	0	0	2	7	3	4	0	0
North Canton	17,501	15	0	3	5	7	317	81	229	7	2
North Olmsted	32,742	17	0	1	10	6	562	86	448	28	3
North Ridgeville	29,487	13	0	5	0	8	265	68	191	6	0
Northwood	5,269	7	0	1	2	4	318	69	239	10	2
Norwood	19,221	75	3	3	58	11	1,405	281	1,075	49	3
Oberlin	8,292	20	0	6	9	5	241	43	195	3	2
Olmsted Falls	9,031	8	0	3	0	5	66	15	49	2	0
Olmsted Township	13,523	7	0	2	0	5	68	28	37	3	0
Ontario	6,230	9	0	1	4	4	527	29	492	6	0
Orange Village	3,325	1	0	0	0	1	17	6	7	4	0
Oregon	20,306	40	1	1	10	28	847	156	646	45	3
Orrville	8,386	9	1	5	0	3	170	51	115	4	2
Ottawa Hills	4,520	5	0	2	0	3	54	19	33	2	0
Oxford	21,387	81	0	13	5	63	593	151	425	17	7
Painesville	19,577	55	0	8	22	25	537	142	380	15	2
Parma Heights	20,733	25	0	7	7	11	343	58	267	18	0
Pataskala	14,973	5	0	2	3	0	211	44	156	11	0
Paulding	3,608	0	0	0	0	0	7	0	7	0	0
Payne	1,195	0	0	0	0	0	11	5	6	0	0
Peebles	1,783	3	0	1	0	2	39	11	28	0	1
Pepper Pike	5,983	2	0	0	2	0	38	11	27	0	0
Perrysburg	20,638	5	0	0	2	3	394	60	316	18	0
Perry Township, Allen County	3,534	0	0	0	0	0	35	4	31	0	0
Perry Township, Franklin County	3,640	1	0	1	0	0	47	12	35	0	0
Perry Township, Montgomery County	3,357	0	0	0	0	0	35	12	19	4	0
Pickerington	18,304	17	0	3	6	8	349	46	300	3	1
Pierce Township	11,222	3	0	1	2	0	157	40	113	4	0
Pioneer	1,381	2	0	0	0	2	49	8	38	3	3
Piqua	20,537	28	1	10	14	3	1,245	220	1,007	18	3
Poland Township	12,421	2	0	0	0	2	108	26	76	6	0
Poland Village	2,557	0	0	0	0	0	25	2	22	1	0
Port Clinton	6,060	5	0	3	1	1	222	43	174	5	0
Powell	11,508	4	0	1	1	2	101	21	72	8	1
Reminderville	3,406	3	0	0	1	2	19	5	14	0	0
Reynoldsburg	35,919	78	0	9	52	17	1,049	201	813	35	1
Richfield	3,651	0	0	0	0	0	23	3	18	2	0
Richmond Heights	10,554	15	0	1	11	3	313	43	249	21	1
Rittman	6,496	7	0	1	1	5	191	56	131	4	0

[1] If a blank is presented in offenses arson column, it indicates that the FBI did not receive 12 complete months of arson data for that agency.

Table II-8.   Offenses Known to Law Enforcement, by Selected State and City, 2011—*Continued*

(Number.)

State/City	Population	Violent crime	Murder and non-negligent man-slaughter	Forcible rape	Robbery	Aggravated assault	Property crime	Burglary	Larceny-theft	Motor vehicle theft	Arson[1]
Ohio—*Continued*											
Riverside	25,219	55	1	5	11	38	667	155	479	33	1
Roaming Shores Village	1,509	0	0	0	0	0	23	9	13	1	0
Rossford	6,298	1	0	0	1	0	154	23	130	1	1
Ross Township	8,361	0	0	0	0	0	25	4	21	0	0
Russells Point	1,392	3	0	0	0	3	46	10	34	2	0
Russell Township	5,194	1	0	1	0	0	4	2	1	1	0
Sabina	2,566	2	0	1	1	0	70	19	50	1	1
Salem	12,312	2	0	1	0	1	414	35	370	9	0
Sandusky	25,812	120	1	7	40	72	1,366	327	1,020	19	6
Sebring	4,423	6	0	2	0	4	85	17	68	0	1
Seven Hills	11,813	3	0	1	0	2	27	19	8	0	0
Shaker Heights	28,469	34	0	1	25	8	625	196	360	69	0
Sharonville	13,570	23	0	2	16	5	629	109	501	19	2
Shawnee Township	8,713	3	1	0	0	2	106	34	68	4	0
Sheffield Lake	9,144	1	0	0	1	0	153	31	117	5	1
Shelby	9,324	8	0	2	5	1	391	74	310	7	0
Sidney	21,245	58	1	9	19	29	1,209	262	927	20	13
Silverton	4,792	18	0	7	6	5	122	27	83	12	0
Smith Township	4,473	2	0	1	1	0	66	10	53	3	0
Smithville	1,253	2	0	1	1	0	27	6	21	0	0
Solon	23,365	20	0	3	6	11	217	46	163	8	0
Somerset	1,482	5	0	1	2	2	80	2	78	0	0
South Bloomfield	1,745	0	0	0	0	0	41	7	34	0	0
South Charleston	1,694	2	0	0	0	2	32	8	23	1	0
South Euclid	22,311	28	0	1	22	5	434	116	292	26	1
South Point	3,961	14	0	1	4	9	50	16	31	3	2
South Russell	3,813	0	0	0	0	0	5	1	4	0	0
Spencerville	2,225	3	0	2	1	0	62	19	43	0	0
Springboro	17,422	10	0	0	1	9	161	32	126	3	1
Springdale	11,231	23	2	2	12	7	654	59	575	20	3
Springfield	60,652	390	3	32	209	146	4,630	1,614	2,816	200	33
Springfield Township, Hamilton County	36,346	56	1	3	29	23	734	263	438	33	3
Springfield Township, Mahoning County	6,708	2	0	2	0	0	125	56	67	2	0
Springfield Township, Summit County	17,725	22	0	0	10	12	1,042	140	868	34	1
St. Clair Township	7,963	0	0	0	0	0	60	0	60	0	0
Steubenville	18,673	80	2	6	41	31	1,130	212	893	25	2
Stow	34,863	23	0	6	10	7	732	105	618	9	7
St. Paris	2,091	0	0	0	0	0	37	8	27	2	0
Streetsboro	16,040	7	0	0	5	2	65	3	61	1	0
Strongsville	44,783	26	0	3	12	11	932	121	786	25	1
Struthers	10,721	4	0	1	3	0	224	53	162	9	0
Sugarcreek Township	8,047	5	0	0	2	3	284	27	256	1	1
Swanton	3,693	8	0	1	1	6	79	6	73	0	0
Sycamore	862	0	0	0	0	0	11	7	4	0	0
Sylvania Township	29,544	19	0	0	11	8	766	132	599	35	0
Tallmadge	17,550	15	0	6	6	3	370	74	281	15	2
Tipp City	9,696	5	0	2	2	1	209	26	180	3	2
Toledo[5]	287,418	2,868	30	124	1,152	1,562		8,366		1,465	509
Trotwood	24,449	84	2	13	39	30	1,299	570	617	112	14
Troy	25,076	17	0	4	11	2	880	156	705	19	2
Twinsburg	18,809	11	0	4	4	3	169	30	132	7	0
Uhrichsville	5,417	6	0	4	1	1	152	42	102	8	0
Union	6,424	2	0	0	1	1	104	22	82	0	0
Union Township, Clermont County	46,450	49	0	14	32	3	1,963	319	1,611	33	4
University Heights	13,549	17	0	5	7	5	280	49	225	6	0
Upper Arlington	33,796	12	0	4	7	1	472	150	314	8	5
Upper Sandusky	6,601	1	0	1	0	0	11	0	11	0	0
Utica	2,134	2	0	0	0	2	50	9	41	0	0
Vandalia	15,257	18	0	4	7	7	384	114	250	20	5
Van Wert	10,854	29	1	4	5	19	449	138	305	6	8
Vienna Township	3,983	3	0	1	0	2	76	26	42	8	0
Village of Leesburg	1,315	0	0	0	0	0	27	6	20	1	0
Wadsworth	21,583	16	0	6	4	6	382	70	307	5	1
Waite Hill	471	0	0	0	0	0	4	1	3	0	0
Walbridge	3,021	2	0	2	0	0	45	13	31	1	0
Walton Hills	2,283	0	0	0	0	0	19	2	14	3	0
Wapakoneta	9,874	6	0	2	0	4	126	13	108	5	1
Warren	41,587	258	5	28	84	141	2,139	988	1,039	112	6
Warrensville Heights	13,552	58	3	8	36	11	564	264	199	101	3
Warren Township	5,555	5	0	2	0	3	113	29	79	5	1
Washington Court House	14,202	31	0	5	10	16	659	139	504	16	5
Waterville	5,527	0	0	0	0	0	40	7	33	0	0
Wauseon	7,337	4	0	2	1	1	275	21	253	1	3
Wells Township	2,837	2	0	1	0	1	70	19	50	1	0
West Alexandria	1,341	3	0	1	0	2	27	8	19	0	1

[1] If a blank is presented in the arson column, it indicates that the FBI did not receive 12 complete months of arson data for that agency.

[5] The FBI determined that the agency did not follow national Uniform Crime Reporting (UCR) Program guidelines for reporting an offense. Consequently, this figure is not included in this table.

Table II-8. Offenses Known to Law Enforcement, by Selected State and City, 2011—*Continued*

(Number.)

State/City	Population	Violent crime	Murder and non-negligent man-slaughter	Forcible rape	Robbery	Aggravated assault	Property crime	Burglary	Larceny-theft	Motor vehicle theft	Arson[1]
Ohio—*Continued*											
West Carrollton	13,153	24	0	6	11	7	543	133	382	28	4
West Chester Township	58,638	93	0	30	33	30	1,424	255	1,137	32	13
West Jefferson	4,225	8	0	1	1	6	100	23	76	1	0
West Lafayette	2,323	1	0	0	0	1	31	2	29	0	0
West Liberty	1,806	5	0	0	0	5	12	1	11	0	0
Whitehall	18,075	125	2	12	90	21	1,591	307	1,227	57	7
Wickliffe	12,759	32	0	0	3	29	39	27	1	11	0
Willard	6,241	4	0	1	0	3	195	26	166	3	0
Williamsburg	2,492	5	0	2	2	1	93	16	74	3	1
Willoughby	22,284	23	0	3	16	4	394	81	300	13	2
Willowick	14,181	5	0	2	2	1	177	26	141	10	1
Wilmington	12,529	18	2	4	6	6	645	91	552	2	2
Woodmere Village	885	6	0	0	3	3	54	7	43	4	0
Wooster	26,138	72	1	19	17	35	903	191	686	26	8
Worthington	13,585	6	0	1	2	3	373	48	321	4	5
Wyoming	8,434	5	0	0	5	0	154	32	122	0	0
Xenia	25,738	51	2	6	23	20	1,106	227	845	34	4
Yellow Springs	3,490	3	0	0	0	3	79	11	67	1	2
Youngstown	67,031	619	17	29	205	368	3,959	2,036	1,596	327	237
Zanesville	25,506	110	1	19	45	45	1,875	379	1,446	50	28
Oklahoma											
Achille	497	2	0	0	0	2	17	11	6	0	0
Ada	16,990	166	1	21	12	132	693	194	464	35	2
Allen	942	1	0	0	0	1	4	1	3	0	0
Altus	20,025	48	0	5	6	37	591	225	357	9	3
Alva	4,998	5	0	0	0	5	71	23	42	6	1
Anadarko	6,834	24	0	1	2	21	227	68	149	10	5
Antlers	2,479	15	0	0	1	14	77	32	43	2	0
Apache	1,459	0	0	0	0	0	6	3	3	0	0
Ardmore	24,543	405	3	23	32	347	1,291	309	929	53	8
Arkoma	2,010	2	0	0	0	2	14	5	7	2	0
Atoka	3,140	19	0	0	0	19	121	32	87	2	1
Bartlesville	36,133	107	1	9	19	78	1,071	259	769	43	4
Beaver	1,531	2	0	0	0	2	12	4	7	1	0
Beggs	1,335	1	0	0	0	1	23	5	17	1	1
Bethany	19,255	60	2	10	20	28	572	177	327	68	7
Bixby	21,108	31	0	2	2	27	379	167	187	25	6
Blackwell	7,168	8	0	0	0	8	109	33	71	5	4
Blanchard	7,752	2	0	0	0	2	62	21	37	4	0
Boise City	1,280	2	0	1	0	1	1	1	0	0	0
Boley	1,197	2	0	0	0	2	4	3	1	0	0
Bristow	4,267	17	0	1	4	12	202	64	134	4	5
Broken Arrow	99,908	144	0	22	41	81	2,287	426	1,728	133	3
Broken Bow	4,164	26	0	1	3	22	193	48	135	10	4
Caddo	1,008	0	0	0	0	0	3	0	2	1	0
Calera	2,187	3	0	0	0	3	26	12	12	2	0
Caney	207	0	0	0	0	0	15	2	13	0	0
Carnegie	1,741	3	0	0	0	3	12	5	7	0	3
Catoosa	7,228	50	1	3	3	43	154	49	77	28	0
Chandler	3,133	2	0	1	0	1	106	25	74	7	0
Checotah	3,371	1	0	0	0	1	96	11	71	14	1
Chelsea	1,985	0	0	0	0	0	4	1	3	0	0
Cherokee	1,514	1	0	0	0	1	3	1	2	0	0
Chickasha	16,208	134	0	15	9	110	748	196	518	34	6
Choctaw	11,265	23	0	1	3	19	201	61	126	14	1
Chouteau	2,119	4	0	0	0	4	55	12	38	5	0
Claremore	18,780	45	1	8	6	30	511	82	381	48	1
Clayton	830	1	0	0	0	1	7	3	4	0	0
Cleveland	3,286	6	0	1	0	5	83	20	61	2	0
Clinton	9,130	16	0	4	3	9	139	44	81	14	0
Coalgate	1,988	0	0	0	0	0	13	1	11	1	1
Colbert	1,152	5	0	0	1	4	27	12	13	2	0
Collinsville	5,666	7	0	1	1	5	150	67	76	7	1
Comanche	1,681	0	0	0	0	0	22	7	13	2	0
Cordell	2,946	5	0	0	0	5	15	5	9	1	0
Coweta	10,049	16	1	1	2	12	184	28	148	8	0
Crescent	1,426	6	0	0	0	6	6	3	3	0	0
Cushing	7,910	9	0	1	0	8	175	26	140	9	0
Davenport	823	0	0	0	0	0	1	0	1	0	0
Davis	2,712	12	1	0	0	11	114	39	75	0	3
Del City	21,560	156	0	10	28	118	1,345	339	874	132	15
Dewar	898	0	0	0	0	0	2	1	1	0	0
Dewey	3,469	13	0	1	0	12	93	25	68	0	0
Dibble	887	8	0	1	0	7	11	1	9	1	0
Drumright	2,938	4	0	0	1	3	56	17	34	5	0

[1] If a blank is presented in the arson column, it indicates that the FBI did not receive 12 complete months of arson data for that agency.

Table II-8. Offenses Known to Law Enforcement, by Selected State and City, 2011—*Continued*

(Number.)

State/City	Population	Violent crime	Murder and non-negligent man-slaughter	Forcible rape	Robbery	Aggravated assault	Property crime	Burglary	Larceny-theft	Motor vehicle theft	Arson[1]
Oklahoma—*Continued*											
Durant	16,026	159	0	22	11	126	773	223	503	47	3
Edmond	82,276	58	1	7	20	30	1,646	311	1,280	55	5
Elk City	11,818	26	0	4	6	16	331	73	241	17	1
El Reno	16,928	64	0	9	8	47	567	141	403	23	7
Enid	49,908	222	0	22	31	169	1,843	445	1,325	73	4
Eufaula	2,843	9	0	0	0	9	88	37	47	4	0
Fairfax	1,395	2	0	0	0	2	13	5	8	0	1
Fairview	2,607	10	0	0	1	9	99	31	65	3	1
Fletcher	1,190	0	0	0	0	0	9	2	7	0	0
Forest Park	1,009	1	0	0	0	1	12	4	8	0	0
Fort Gibson	4,198	2	0	0	0	2	79	24	53	2	0
Fort Supply	334	0	0	0	0	0	3	1	1	1	0
Frederick	3,982	25	0	4	0	21	84	31	48	5	1
Glenpool	10,924	68	2	5	1	60	213	55	142	16	2
Goodwell	1,307	0	0	0	0	0	2	0	1	1	0
Grove	6,694	18	0	0	0	18	178	26	147	5	0
Guthrie	10,300	20	1	1	1	17	284	50	226	8	4
Guymon	11,564	24	0	1	3	20	293	71	209	13	3
Haileyville	822	3	0	0	0	3	7	5	2	0	0
Hartshorne	2,148	0	0	0	0	0	47	17	29	1	4
Haskell	2,028	0	0	0	0	0	2	1	0	1	0
Healdton	2,818	3	0	0	0	3	18	6	10	2	2
Heavener	3,451	10	0	0	1	9	56	9	44	3	0
Hennessey	2,154	3	0	0	1	2	34	8	25	1	0
Hinton	3,230	2	0	1	1	0	37	8	27	2	0
Hobart	3,796	9	1	2	2	4	90	36	53	1	0
Holdenville	5,833	8	1	0	1	6	73	32	33	8	2
Hollis	2,082	8	0	0	1	7	70	32	35	3	0
Hominy	3,603	10	0	1	0	9	21	7	11	3	0
Hooker	1,939	1	0	0	0	1	19	2	16	1	0
Howe	811	0	0	0	0	0	0	0	0	0	0
Hulbert	596	1	0	0	0	1	2	2	0	0	0
Hydro	979	1	0	0	0	1	16	6	10	0	1
Idabel	7,085	20	0	3	1	16	252	57	180	15	1
Jay	2,474	2	0	0	0	2	77	13	63	1	1
Jenks	17,105	38	0	3	4	31	351	39	299	13	1
Jones	2,721	4	0	0	1	3	35	10	19	6	0
Kiefer	1,703	2	0	0	0	2	6	3	2	1	0
Kingfisher	4,683	2	0	0	0	2	99	19	75	5	0
Kingston	1,618	2	0	0	0	2	6	2	3	1	0
Krebs	2,075	9	0	1	1	7	95	25	64	6	0
Lahoma	618	1	0	0	1	0	1	1	0	0	1
Lawton	97,904	829	8	57	175	589	5,531	1,960	3,365	206	59
Lexington	2,175	11	0	0	1	10	50	11	36	3	1
Lindsay	2,870	6	0	0	0	6	49	21	22	6	0
Locust Grove	1,438	0	0	0	0	0	21	7	13	1	0
Lone Grove	5,108	5	0	0	1	4	107	23	81	3	1
Luther	1,234	0	0	0	0	0	8	4	4	0	0
Madill	3,810	3	0	1	0	2	34	6	28	0	0
Mangum	3,042	4	0	0	0	4	22	11	8	3	2
Mannford	3,109	4	0	0	0	4	39	14	23	2	0
Marietta	2,654	6	0	1	0	5	36	5	24	7	1
Marlow	4,712	5	0	1	0	4	129	28	99	2	0
Maysville	1,245	0	0	0	0	0	29	12	16	1	0
McAlester	18,580	62	0	10	15	37	873	240	595	38	3
McCurtain	522	1	0	0	0	1	7	1	6	0	0
McLoud	4,087	7	0	0	1	6	54	6	38	10	0
Medicine Park	386	0	0	0	0	0	4	2	2	0	0
Meeker	1,156	3	1	0	0	2	28	7	19	2	1
Miami	13,715	64	0	2	6	56	583	133	425	25	6
Midwest City	54,953	264	7	31	48	178	2,674	708	1,724	242	14
Minco	1,649	1	0	0	0	1	15	8	4	3	0
Moore	55,671	119	0	14	28	77	2,418	509	1,709	200	4
Mooreland	1,203	1	0	0	0	1	13	7	5	1	1
Morris	1,495	1	0	0	0	1	3	0	3	0	0
Mountain View	804	2	0	0	0	2	9	2	7	0	0
Muldrow	3,503	6	0	0	0	6	29	15	14	0	1
Muskogee[2]	39,643	231	2	19	37	173	1,006	342	604	60	6
Mustang	17,581	33	1	3	4	25	455	69	362	24	3
Newcastle	7,767	10	0	0	0	10	193	35	138	20	0
Newkirk	2,342	5	0	2	0	3	50	14	34	2	0
Nichols Hills	3,750	1	0	0	0	1	80	21	56	3	0
Nicoma Park	2,419	5	0	1	1	3	64	12	43	9	2
Ninnekah	1,013	0	0	0	0	0	7	1	4	2	0
Noble	6,550	6	0	3	0	3	145	45	89	11	2

[1] If a blank is presented in the arson column, it indicates that the FBI did not receive 12 complete months of arson data for that agency.

[2] Because of changes in the state/local agency's reporting practices, figures are not comparable to previous years' data.

Table II-8.   Offenses Known to Law Enforcement, by Selected State and City, 2011—*Continued*

(Number.)

State/City	Population	Violent crime	Murder and non-negligent man-slaughter	Forcible rape	Robbery	Aggravated assault	Property crime	Burglary	Larceny-theft	Motor vehicle theft	Arson[1]
Oklahoma—*Continued*											
Norman	112,112	191	2	67	51	71	3,480	677	2,656	147	23
North Enid	869	0	0	0	0	0	7	5	2	0	0
Nowata	3,771	19	0	2	0	17	86	23	59	4	2
Oilton	1,024	2	0	0	0	2	26	7	18	1	0
Okemah	3,258	9	0	1	0	8	125	18	100	7	3
Oklahoma City	586,208	5,108	58	277	1,232	3,541	34,113	9,855	20,199	4,059	91
Okmulgee	12,453	70	0	5	13	52	525	139	349	37	3
Oologah	1,158	3	0	1	0	2	31	13	17	1	0
Pauls Valley	6,253	42	0	5	3	34	256	75	170	11	2
Pawhuska	3,622	33	0	0	3	30	114	49	59	6	3
Pawnee	2,220	4	0	1	1	2	25	19	5	1	0
Perkins	2,861	2	0	0	0	2	26	6	20	0	0
Piedmont	5,781	0	0	0	0	0	55	10	42	3	0
Pocola	4,099	1	0	0	0	1	23	4	14	5	0
Ponca City	25,659	130	1	23	22	84	1,103	211	843	49	18
Porum	735	3	0	0	0	3	13	7	4	2	0
Poteau	8,611	38	0	2	0	36	154	43	90	21	1
Prague	2,412	3	0	0	0	3	48	15	28	5	0
Pryor	9,641	69	0	5	1	63	386	92	264	30	2
Purcell	5,947	13	0	1	0	12	273	54	193	26	2
Ringling	1,048	5	0	0	0	5	14	3	6	5	0
Roland	3,203	4	0	0	0	4	33	10	21	2	0
Rush Springs	1,244	3	0	0	0	3	4	2	2	0	0
Sallisaw	8,975	36	0	9	1	26	361	67	284	10	3
Sand Springs	19,108	25	0	3	11	11	668	125	504	39	3
Sapulpa	20,764	47	1	9	7	30	615	148	416	51	12
Sawyer	324	1	0	0	0	1	17	4	12	1	0
Sayre	4,422	10	0	2	0	8	33	12	17	4	0
Seiling	869	1	0	0	0	1	39	7	28	4	0
Seminole	7,568	25	1	5	2	17	373	74	280	19	1
Shawnee	30,177	259	4	20	21	214	1,853	387	1,338	128	1
Skiatook	7,476	23	0	7	3	13	221	49	161	11	2
Snyder	1,409	1	0	0	0	1	12	3	8	1	0
South Coffeyville	793	5	0	0	0	5	5	1	3	1	0
Sparks	171	0	0	0	0	0	0	0	0	0	0
Spencer	3,954	7	0	1	0	6	56	28	24	4	1
Spiro	2,187	4	0	2	0	2	35	10	22	3	1
Stigler	2,714	8	0	0	0	8	82	10	71	1	0
Stillwater	46,177	101	0	9	14	78	1,380	262	1,067	51	6
Stilwell	3,991	3	1	0	1	1	79	15	61	3	1
Stonewall	475	1	0	0	0	1	8	4	1	3	0
Stratford	1,541	1	0	0	0	1	16	7	9	0	0
Stringtown	414	1	0	0	0	1	2	1	1	0	0
Stroud	2,719	3	0	2	0	1	55	13	38	4	0
Sulphur	4,982	4	0	0	0	4	105	45	60	0	0
Talihina	1,126	7	0	0	2	5	50	15	33	2	2
Tecumseh	6,526	10	1	2	0	7	186	61	109	16	3
Texhoma	936	0	0	0	0	0	0	0	0	0	0
The Village	9,025	15	0	1	3	11	327	92	216	19	1
Tishomingo	3,066	7	0	1	0	6	64	26	32	6	0
Tonkawa	3,250	7	0	0	0	7	88	25	61	2	0
Tryon	496	2	0	0	0	2	10	3	6	1	0
Tulsa	396,101	3,960	49	266	1,090	2,555	21,923	7,353	12,136	2,434	259
Tushka	315	0	0	0	0	0	1	0	1	0	0
Tuttle	6,083	41	0	8	1	32	161	35	105	21	1
Valliant	762	2	0	0	0	2	13	1	11	1	0
Verdigris	4,036	4	0	3	1	0	20	6	13	1	0
Vian	1,482	7	0	0	1	6	38	13	24	1	1
Vinita	5,804	12	0	1	1	10	125	26	88	11	1
Wagoner	8,412	92	0	5	7	80	462	127	318	17	5
Walters	2,578	0	0	0	0	0	24	0	24	0	0
Warner	1,659	1	0	0	0	1	30	12	18	0	0
Warr Acres	10,151	65	0	9	24	32	536	138	343	55	2
Washington	625	5	0	0	0	5	4	3	0	1	0
Watonga	5,166	18	0	0	1	17	37	11	24	2	1
Waukomis	1,300	2	0	0	0	2	4	2	2	0	0
Waurika	2,086	0	0	0	0	0	33	7	25	1	0
Waynoka	937	1	0	0	0	1	10	1	5	4	0
Weatherford	10,949	79	0	1	0	78	269	80	179	10	2
Weleetka	1,009	7	0	0	0	7	36	7	27	2	0
Westville	1,657	10	0	0	0	10	37	5	29	3	0
Wetumka	1,296	3	0	0	0	3	23	8	14	1	0
Wewoka	3,467	16	1	0	0	15	110	48	59	3	1
Wilburton	2,873	5	0	0	1	4	33	16	15	2	0
Wilson	1,742	15	0	0	0	15	38	8	23	7	8

[1] If a blank is presented in the arson column, it indicates that the FBI did not receive 12 complete months of arson data for that agency.

Table II-8.   Offenses Known to Law Enforcement, by Selected State and City, 2011—*Continued*

(Number.)

State/City	Population	Violent crime	Murder and non-negligent man-slaughter	Forcible rape	Robbery	Aggravated assault	Property crime	Burglary	Larceny-theft	Motor vehicle theft	Arson[1]
Oklahoma—*Continued*											
Woodward	12,180	10	0	7	1	2	571	196	343	32	0
Wright City	770	1	0	0	1	0	13	0	12	1	1
Wynnewood	2,236	5	2	0	3	0	25	6	16	3	1
Yale	1,240	2	0	0	0	2	32	5	25	2	0
Yukon	22,952	37	0	5	2	30	493	113	371	9	1
Oregon											
Adair Village	849	0	0	0	0	0	4	0	3	1	0
Albany	50,692	44	1	17	9	17	1,439	262	1,083	94	10
Amity	1,631	2	0	1	0	1	38	9	28	1	2
Ashland	20,292	26	1	7	7	11	692	68	602	22	9
Astoria	9,578	11	0	0	2	9	392	66	309	17	1
Athena	1,138	6	0	0	0	6	25	6	19	0	1
Aumsville	3,622	4	0	0	1	3	46	4	38	4	2
Aurora	928	0	0	0	0	0	10	4	6	0	0
Baker City	9,933	2	0	1	0	1	185	22	155	8	1
Bandon	3,099	0	0	0	0	0	106	16	88	2	0
Banks	1,796	4	0	1	0	3	33	7	25	1	0
Beaverton	90,759	166	0	21	36	109	1,779	227	1,410	142	30
Bend	77,455	204	1	25	27	151	2,416	365	1,978	73	29
Black Butte		0	0	0	0	0	7	1	6	0	0
Boardman	3,254	7	0	1	1	5	61	18	40	3	1
Brookings	6,403	5	0	0	0	5	53	6	44	3	
Burns	2,836	0	0	0	0	0	106	30	71	5	
Canby	15,998	8	0	3	2	3	309	56	246	7	0
Cannon Beach	1,708	2	0	1	0	1	30	2	28	0	1
Carlton	2,028	0	0	0	0	0	13	3	10	0	1
Central Point	17,352	19	1	0	0	18	491	53	428	10	2
Clatskanie	1,755	1	0	0	0	1	29	3	24	2	1
Coburg	1,046	0	0	0	0	0	10	0	8	2	0
Condon	689	1	0	0	0	1	1	0	1	0	0
Coos Bay	16,137	89	0	10	10	69	815	141	650	24	
Coquille	3,907	0	0	0	0	0	69	18	49	2	0
Cornelius	11,995	28	0	1	5	22	341	78	234	29	1
Corvallis	55,042	71	0	13	15	43	1,753	287	1,421	45	13
Cottage Grove	9,789	66	0	0	3	63	356	45	285	26	
Creswell	5,085	33	0	1	3	29	186	50	109	27	1
Dallas	14,738	36	1	7	2	26	403	64	318	21	3
Eagle Point	8,559	4	0	1	1	2	261	31	224	6	0
Enterprise	1,961	1	0	0	0	1	15	6	9	0	0
Estacada	2,724	10	0	0	3	7	98	12	77	9	1
Eugene	157,848	460	0	78	177	205	7,878	1,440	5,862	576	63
Fairview	9,015	10	0	4	1	5	251	58	156	37	1
Florence	8,556	5	0	0	2	3	295	62	221	12	2
Forest Grove	21,307	52	2	15	7	28	573	83	464	26	6
Gaston	644	2	0	0	0	2	18	5	13	0	0
Gearhart	1,478	0	0	0	0	0	12	3	8	1	0
Gervais	2,490	7	1	1	1	4	46	4	39	3	0
Gladstone	11,619	36	1	5	5	25	294	53	209	32	3
Gold Beach	2,277	4	0	0	0	4	41	5	34	2	0
Grants Pass	34,901	109	1	15	44	49	1,989	286	1,620	83	9
Gresham	106,718	416	1	31	172	212	4,311	751	2,943	617	26
Hermiston	16,923	46	1	2	14	29	765	154	548	63	0
Hillsboro	92,586	146	1	23	35	87	2,065	252	1,683	130	9
Hines	1,580	0	0	0	0	0	35	15	19	1	
Hood River	7,243	4	0	1	0	3	63	12	46	5	
Hubbard	3,207	1	0	1	0	0	36	18	18	0	2
Independence	8,681	18	0	4	0	14	218	35	170	13	4
Jacksonville	2,815	2	0	0	0	2	24	6	18	0	1
John Day	1,763	2	0	1	0	1	20	3	15	2	1
Junction City	5,449	1	0	0	0	1	54	8	44	2	2
Keizer	36,866	64	3	9	11	41	769	125	609	35	10
King City	3,144	3	0	2	0	1	58	10	47	1	0
Klamath Falls	21,062	80	0	18	21	41	1,002	225	686	91	12
La Grande	13,221	35	0	13	0	22	936	127	772	37	19
Lake Oswego	37,009	19	0	2	3	14	502	77	409	16	5
Lakeview	2,318	24	0	3	0	21	50	11	36	3	0
Lebanon	15,683	36	0	5	7	24	813	134	655	24	6
Lincoln City	8,014	53	1	10	4	38	391	81	299	11	3
Madras	6,110	11	0	2	3	6	265	59	188	18	3
Malin	814	1	0	0	0	1	0	0	0	0	
Manzanita	604	0	0	0	0	0	23	5	18	0	0
McMinnville	32,530	58	0	11	13	34	1,100	212	855	33	8
Medford	75,704	387	6	38	60	283	3,895	370	3,375	150	43
Milton-Freewater	7,125	20	0	0	3	17	210	35	156	19	3

[1] If a blank is presented in the arson column, it indicates that the FBI did not receive 12 complete months of arson data for that agency.

Table II-8.   Offenses Known to Law Enforcement, by Selected State and City, 2011—*Continued*

(Number.)

State/City	Population	Violent crime	Murder and non-negligent man-slaughter	Forcible rape	Robbery	Aggravated assault	Property crime	Burglary	Larceny-theft	Motor vehicle theft	Arson[1]
Oregon—*Continued*											
Milwaukie	20,507	21	0	4	7	10	562	93	433	36	2
Molalla	8,194	8	0	4	2	2	197	23	167	7	3
Monmouth	9,635	10	0	1	0	9	180	39	140	1	0
Mount Angel	3,321	14	1	0	1	12	50	9	40	1	0
Myrtle Creek	3,476	3	0	2	0	1	13	2	9	2	0
Newberg-Dundee	25,499	23	1	6	2	14	529	116	398	15	8
Newport	10,095	43	0	14	4	25	397	49	325	23	7
North Bend	9,798	10	0	3	5	2	457	93	349	15	0
North Plains	1,968	2	0	0	0	2	26	9	16	1	0
Nyssa	3,302	6	0	2	1	3	123	44	72	7	
Oakridge	3,239	14	0	0	3	11	83	27	53	3	1
Ontario	11,487	52	0	5	6	41	813	110	686	17	2
Oregon City	32,198	34	0	9	8	17	799	117	630	52	3
Pendleton	16,789	39	0	15	7	17	597	71	496	30	2
Philomath	4,633	1	0	0	0	1	86	20	60	6	1
Phoenix	4,586	5	0	2	0	3	137	20	114	3	0
Pilot Rock	1,518	2	0	0	0	2	13	3	8	2	0
Portland	589,991	3,037	20	258	917	1,842	30,022	4,303	22,494	3,225	308
Port Orford	1,145	2	0	0	0	2	56	18	36	2	1
Prineville	9,352	20	0	4	0	16	251	43	204	4	
Rainier	1,915	1	0	0	1	0	58	15	34	9	
Redmond	26,494	81	0	16	12	53	1,453	218	1,182	53	15
Reedsport	4,198	0	0	0	0	0	118	25	90	3	1
Rockaway Beach	1,326	5	0	0	1	4	54	27	23	4	0
Rogue River	2,154	3	0	1	2	0	68	12	52	4	0
Roseburg	21,406	53	0	22	17	14	1,168	152	967	49	5
Salem	156,283	519	3	32	119	365	5,960	891	4,641	428	37
Sandy	9,672	8	0	1	5	2	276	36	215	25	1
Scappoose	6,662	32	0	7	1	24	97	15	79	3	0
Seaside	6,526	16	0	3	5	8	438	53	372	13	5
Sherwood	18,388	7	1	4	1	1	182	14	161	7	4
Silverton	9,320	16	0	4	0	12	136	27	106	3	1
Springfield	60,035	149	1	15	46	87	2,437	309	1,979	149	18
Stayton	7,725	30	0	2	1	27	309	47	253	9	1
St. Helens	13,020	9	0	5	2	2	271	52	207	12	7
Sunriver		3	0	0	0	3	56	4	50	2	0
Sutherlin	7,893	12	0	1	1	10	167	29	123	15	3
Sweet Home	9,020	14	1	0	4	9	482	75	392	15	2
Talent	6,131	9	0	1	1	7	196	19	173	4	2
The Dalles	13,765	9	0	4	3	2	585	85	490	10	1
Tigard	48,546	55	0	8	24	23	1,724	173	1,499	52	5
Tillamook	4,988	2	0	0	1	1	182	16	159	7	2
Toledo	3,502	24	2	7	2	13	148	27	114	7	3
Troutdale	16,132	25	1	10	9	5	523	73	409	41	1
Tualatin	26,331	43	0	8	13	22	701	83	579	39	2
Turner	1,874	12	0	1	1	10	25	5	19	1	0
Umatilla	6,980	9	0	2	1	6	157	47	98	12	0
Veneta	4,610	32	0	4	3	25	194	68	111	15	2
Warrenton	5,042	0	0	0	0	0	125	23	97	5	1
West Linn	25,376	10	0	1	3	6	268	29	223	16	0
Wilsonville	19,717	10	0	3	4	3	205	17	169	19	0
Winston	5,436	3	0	0	0	3	83	24	53	6	0
Woodburn	24,336	54	1	4	15	34	542	103	408	31	11
Yamhill	1,035	0	0	0	0	0	18	2	16	0	0
Pennsylvania											
Abington Township, Lackawanna County	1,749	2	0	0	0	2	20	9	9	2	0
Abington Township, Montgomery County	55,486	84	0	5	28	51	1,184	121	1,025	38	6
Adamstown	1,795	3	0	0	1	2	27	9	18	0	0
Adams Township, Butler County	11,689	7	0	1	0	6	87	14	71	2	0
Akron	3,888	2	0	0	0	2	30	5	23	2	0
Alburtis	2,369	1	0	0	0	1	19	1	18	0	0
Aldan	4,165	10	0	0	1	9	155	25	128	2	0
Aleppo Township	1,922	0	0	0	0	0	23	2	21	0	0
Aliquippa	9,468	41	0	1	8	32	188	67	103	18	1
Allegheny Township, Westmoreland County	8,190	4	0	0	3	1	107	11	92	4	0
Allentown	118,408	647	10	61	339	237	4,575	1,101	3,041	433	19
Altoona	46,468	143	0	26	39	78	1,090	301	745	44	18
Ambler	6,437	13	0	2	2	9	147	19	120	8	0
Ambridge	7,072	123	0	5	20	98	308	74	233	1	3
Amity Township	12,623	1	0	0	0	1	127	30	89	8	0
Annville Township	4,782	1	0	0	0	1	74	10	58	6	1
Archbald	7,006	26	0	1	0	25	28	8	20	0	0
Arnold	5,173	12	0	2	5	5	84	29	39	16	1
Ashland	2,826	6	0	0	2	4	50	17	33	0	0

[1] If a blank is presented in the arson column, it indicates that the FBI did not receive 12 complete months of arson data for that agency.

Table II-8.   Offenses Known to Law Enforcement, by Selected State and City, 2011—*Continued*

(Number.)

State/City	Population	Violent crime	Murder and non-negligent man-slaughter	Forcible rape	Robbery	Aggravated assault	Property crime	Burglary	Larceny-theft	Motor vehicle theft	Arson[1]
Pennsylvania—*Continued*											
Aspinwall	2,810	2	0	0	0	2	40	5	34	1	0
Aston Township	16,645	19	0	4	5	10	315	45	253	17	0
Atglen	1,410	1	0	0	0	1	3	0	3	0	0
Athens	3,378	11	0	5	0	6	83	12	71	0	0
Avalon	4,720	17	0	2	5	10	84	21	56	7	0
Avis	1,489	3	0	0	0	3	8	0	8	0	0
Avondale	1,269	2	0	0	0	2	6	2	4	0	0
Avonmore Boro	1,014	0	0	0	0	0	0	0	0	0	0
Baden	4,148	1	0	0	0	1	44	8	34	2	0
Baldwin Borough	19,830	19	1	4	5	9	157	34	110	13	0
Bally	1,093	2	0	0	1	1	0	0	0	0	0
Bangor	5,290	19	0	0	0	19	127	14	111	2	0
Beaver	4,545	2	0	0	1	1	96	16	78	2	0
Beaver Falls	9,016	54	1	2	11	40	297	57	229	11	0
Bedford	2,850	4	0	0	0	4	24	13	11	0	0
Bedminster Township	6,595	3	0	0	1	2	49	10	39	0	0
Bell Acres	1,392	0	0	0	0	0	1	0	1	0	0
Bellefonte	6,207	11	0	1	1	9	104	16	88	0	0
Bellevue	8,397	18	0	1	6	11	227	37	185	5	0
Bellwood	1,834	0	0	0	0	0	18	2	16	0	0
Ben Avon	1,787	0	0	0	0	0	28	3	25	0	0
Ben Avon Heights	372	0	0	0	0	0	3	0	3	0	0
Bendersville	643	0	0	0	0	0	2	0	2	0	0
Bensalem Township	60,620	93	0	14	60	19	2,288	299	1,871	118	35
Benton Area	1,953	0	0	0	0	0	0	0	0	0	0
Berks-Lehigh Regional	30,614	10	0	1	3	6	328	32	288	8	1
Berlin	2,111	0	0	0	0	0	0	0	0	0	0
Bern Township	6,819	22	0	2	2	18	73	10	57	6	1
Berwick	10,510	36	0	7	2	27	434	129	297	8	0
Bessemer	1,115	0	0	0	0	0	0	0	0	0	0
Bethel Park	32,416	26	0	1	3	22	327	39	280	8	0
Bethel Township, Armstrong County	1,187	0	0	0	0	0	0	0	0	0	0
Bethel Township, Berks County	4,125	3	0	0	0	3	35	10	24	1	0
Bethel Township, Delaware County	8,819	11	0	0	1	10	121	28	86	7	0
Bethlehem	75,221	219	3	17	97	102	1,862	371	1,405	86	4
Bethlehem Township	23,806	12	0	0	1	11	409	43	357	9	0
Biglerville	1,204	0	0	0	0	0	29	0	25	4	0
Birdsboro	5,179	6	0	0	0	6	102	27	71	4	1
Birmingham Township	4,221	0	0	0	0	0	23	8	11	4	0
Blacklick Township	2,019	0	0	0	0	0	0	0	0	0	0
Blairsville	3,423	18	0	1	0	17	92	20	72	0	0
Blakely	6,585	5	0	1	2	2	92	14	77	1	2
Blawnox	1,437	7	0	0	0	7	7	2	5	0	0
Bloomsburg Town	14,902	26	0	2	1	23	281	60	218	3	0
Blythe Township	927	0	0	0	0	0	1	0	1	0	0
Bolivar	466	1	0	0	0	1	0	0	0	0	0
Brackenridge	3,270	3	0	0	0	3	76	10	62	4	0
Braddock Hills	1,886	1	0	0	1	0	3	1	2	0	0
Bradford	8,798	47	1	6	3	37	381	50	329	2	4
Bradford Township	4,820	10	0	4	0	6	26	7	18	1	1
Branch Township	1,846	0	0	0	0	0	16	3	13	0	0
Brecknock Township, Berks County	4,600	0	0	0	0	0	26	5	21	0	0
Brentwood	9,674	13	0	0	4	9	190	35	144	11	0
Bridgeport	4,569	9	0	1	2	6	148	19	112	17	0
Bridgeville	5,164	4	0	1	0	3	90	17	71	2	0
Brighton Township	8,253	4	0	0	1	3	44	10	33	1	0
Bristol	9,757	22	0	2	16	4	369	30	314	25	1
Bristol Township	54,756	126	1	15	74	36	1,805	304	1,336	165	13
Brockway	2,079	2	0	0	0	2	10	6	4	0	0
Brookhaven	8,032	11	0	0	3	8	194	27	160	7	0
Brookville	3,937	8	0	2	0	6	68	12	51	5	0
Brownsville	2,338	7	0	0	3	4	57	18	36	3	0
Buckingham Township	20,139	9	1	3	1	4	124	22	97	5	0
Buffalo Township	7,330	10	0	1	0	9	51	15	35	1	0
Bushkill Township	8,204	13	0	3	0	10	81	16	60	5	0
Butler	13,801	85	0	0	29	56	571	98	464	9	7
Butler Township, Butler County	17,303	27	0	1	7	19	427	51	371	5	0
Butler Township, Luzerne County	9,250	40	0	0	2	38	122	33	82	7	0
Butler Township, Schuylkill County	6,006	3	0	0	2	1	31	17	11	3	0
Caernarvon Township, Berks County	4,019	9	0	1	0	8	99	11	88	0	0
California	6,817	20	0	1	1	18	117	23	94	0	0
Caln Township	13,861	66	0	2	6	58	342	29	296	17	2
Cambria Township	6,118	4	0	1	0	3	90	14	67	9	1
Cambridge Springs	2,603	1	0	0	0	1	2	0	2	0	0
Camp Hill	7,913	2	0	0	2	0	125	14	109	2	1

[1] If a blank is presented in the arson column, it indicates that the FBI did not receive 12 complete months of arson data for that agency.

Table II-8.   Offenses Known to Law Enforcement, by Selected State and City, 2011—*Continued*

(Number.)

State/City	Population	Violent crime	Murder and non-negligent man-slaughter	Forcible rape	Robbery	Aggravated assault	Property crime	Burglary	Larceny-theft	Motor vehicle theft	Arson[1]
Pennsylvania—*Continued*											
Canton	1,982	3	0	1	0	2	34	11	22	1	0
Carbondale	8,919	15	0	2	1	12	155	31	114	10	0
Carlisle	18,742	58	0	8	26	24	464	53	405	6	4
Carmichaels	485	0	0	0	0	0	1	0	1	0	0
Carnegie	7,997	10	0	0	6	4	210	40	162	8	1
Carrolltown	856	0	0	0	0	0	12	1	10	1	0
Carroll Township, Washington County	5,658	21	0	1	0	20	58	9	47	2	0
Carroll Township, York County	5,958	7	0	0	1	6	107	24	81	2	0
Cass Township	1,964	5	0	1	0	4	15	4	11	0	1
Castle Shannon	8,343	13	0	0	3	10	88	16	71	1	0
Catasauqua	6,457	7	0	0	1	6	164	33	120	11	1
Catawissa	1,557	4	0	0	0	4	57	5	51	1	2
Cecil Township	11,307	2	0	0	1	1	8	3	5	0	0
Centerville	3,273	1	0	0	1	0	17	2	14	1	0
Central Berks Regional	9,420	14	0	2	4	8	199	26	156	17	3
Chalfont	4,022	4	0	1	0	3	63	6	57	0	0
Chambersburg	20,333	71	0	5	30	36	685	121	543	21	2
Charleroi	5,291	31	0	4	4	23	234	28	202	4	0
Chartiers Township	7,843	2	0	0	0	2	66	12	53	1	0
Cheltenham Township	36,910	76	2	7	45	22	1,026	188	803	35	4
Cherry Tree	365	0	0	0	0	0	0	0	0	0	0
Chester[4]	34,080		21	23	214		1,322	554	626	142	26
Chester Township	3,953	60	0	3	10	47	155	59	89	7	0
Cheswick	1,752	0	0	0	0	0	8	1	6	1	0
Chippewa Township	8,024	1	0	0	0	1	251	16	233	2	0
Christiana	1,172	4	0	0	0	4	16	2	13	1	0
Churchill	3,021	25	0	0	0	25	28	7	20	1	0
Clarion	5,293	3	0	0	0	3	104	19	81	4	0
Claysville	832	0	0	0	0	0	6	1	5	0	0
Clearfield	6,235	13	0	1	0	12	244	22	219	3	0
Cleona	2,087	0	0	0	0	0	16	1	15	0	1
Coaldale	2,288	3	0	0	1	2	10	10	0	0	0
Coal Township	10,416	25	0	2	0	23	191	18	170	3	5
Coatesville	13,142	149	2	2	61	84	462	114	307	41	0
Cochranton	1,140	0	0	0	0	0	11	10	1	0	0
Colebrookdale District	6,039	5	0	0	3	2	97	4	90	3	0
Collegeville	5,105	2	0	1	1	0	77	11	65	1	0
Collier Township	7,103	9	0	0	2	7	188	32	152	4	1
Collingdale	8,814	106	1	2	23	80	276	65	187	24	2
Colonial Regional	19,495	15	0	4	6	5	586	65	506	15	1
Columbia	10,433	23	0	2	13	8	319	67	233	19	2
Colwyn	2,554	17	0	0	6	11	87	35	43	9	0
Conemaugh Township, Somerset County	7,302	9	0	0	1	8	41	7	34	0	0
Conewago Township, Adams County	7,108	1	0	0	0	1	90	13	75	2	1
Conewango Township	3,605	7	0	0	0	7	177	15	161	1	0
Conneaut Lake Regional	3,597	0	0	0	0	0	56	7	49	0	0
Connellsville	7,661	25	1	2	10	12	344	48	288	8	0
Conoy Township	3,204	4	0	0	0	4	39	15	24	0	0
Conshohocken	7,858	20	0	0	0	20	133	16	115	2	0
Conway	2,183	0	0	0	0	0	18	6	12	0	0
Conyngham	1,920	0	0	0	0	0	12	0	12	0	0
Coopersburg	2,394	4	0	0	0	4	17	1	13	3	0
Coplay	3,202	1	0	0	0	1	44	9	35	0	0
Coraopolis	5,695	46	0	2	6	38	110	25	78	7	0
Cornwall	4,125	1	0	0	0	1	1	0	1	0	0
Corry	6,626	30	1	3	2	24	245	45	189	11	1
Crafton	6,426	27	0	0	2	25	147	22	124	1	0
Cranberry Township	28,188	7	0	0	1	6	342	44	292	6	2
Crescent Township	2,648	10	0	0	0	10	44	18	24	2	1
Cresson	1,716	2	0	0	0	2	24	6	18	0	0
Cresson Township	4,350	8	0	0	0	8	31	2	29	0	1
Croyle Township	2,346	0	0	0	0	0	22	0	22	0	0
Cumberland Township, Adams County	6,182	1	0	0	0	1	55	21	33	1	2
Cumberland Township, Greene County	6,644	10	0	2	0	8	168	43	116	9	0
Cumru Township	15,195	10	0	2	5	3	358	49	296	13	0
Curwensville	2,550	10	0	0	1	9	40	9	28	3	0
Dale	1,238	5	0	0	0	5	11	0	10	1	0
Dallas	2,813	1	0	0	0	1	30	5	24	1	0
Dallas Township	9,023	3	0	1	1	1	66	12	49	5	2
Dalton	1,238	4	0	0	0	4	14	4	9	1	1
Danville	4,714	18	1	0	1	16	124	12	110	2	0
Darby	10,721	406	0	11	78	317	588	234	298	56	1
Darby Township	9,294	59	0	1	13	45	231	42	187	2	0
Decatur Township	4,563	22	0	0	0	22	70	17	53	0	0

[1] If a blank is presented in the arson column, it indicates that the FBI did not receive 12 complete months of arson data for that agency.

[4] The FBI determined that the agency's data were overreported. Consequently, those data are not included in this table.

Table II-8.   Offenses Known to Law Enforcement, by Selected State and City, 2011—*Continued*

(Number.)

State/City	Population	Violent crime	Murder and non-negligent man-slaughter	Forcible rape	Robbery	Aggravated assault	Property crime	Burglary	Larceny-theft	Motor vehicle theft	Arson[1]
Pennsylvania—*Continued*											
Delano Township	446	1	0	0	0	1	1	0	1	0	0
Delaware Water Gap	748	0	0	0	0	0	0	0	0	0	0
Delmont	2,695	9	0	0	0	9	28	6	22	0	1
Denver	3,873	10	0	1	1	8	30	2	27	1	0
Derry	2,697	7	0	0	0	7	5	1	4	0	0
Derry Township, Dauphin County	24,758	39	0	0	7	32	532	47	462	23	2
Donegal Township	2,473	0	0	0	0	0	10	4	4	2	0
Dormont	8,620	33	0	0	2	31	87	15	64	8	0
Douglass Township, Berks County	3,317	8	0	0	0	8	37	10	23	4	0
Douglass Township, Montgomery County	10,228	35	3	6	2	24	144	11	126	7	1
Downingtown	7,916	6	0	0	4	2	274	15	246	13	0
Doylestown	8,407	6	0	0	0	6	177	38	136	3	0
Doylestown Township	17,621	15	0	0	4	11	289	41	242	6	1
Dublin Borough	2,165	7	0	0	0	7	15	2	13	0	1
Du Bois	7,819	24	0	1	0	23	286	58	220	8	1
Dunmore	14,102	21	0	1	5	15	132	23	95	14	0
Dunnstable Township	1,011	1	0	0	0	1	5	0	3	2	0
Duquesne	5,583	87	5	4	29	49	316	139	160	17	7
Duryea	4,933	2	0	0	0	2	114	32	73	9	3
Earl Township	7,046	0	0	0	0	0	31	4	22	5	0
East Bangor	1,176	0	0	0	0	0	7	1	6	0	0
East Bethlehem Township	2,362	3	0	1	0	2	39	10	28	1	0
East Brandywine Township	6,763	4	0	1	0	3	46	3	40	3	0
East Buffalo Township	6,434	3	0	0	2	1	35	0	34	1	0
East Cocalico Township	10,343	8	0	0	3	5	120	17	100	3	0
East Conemaugh	1,548	3	0	0	0	3	7	3	4	0	1
East Coventry Township	6,657	3	0	0	0	3	51	8	41	2	0
East Earl Township	6,528	3	0	1	0	2	79	15	58	6	0
Eastern Adams Regional	10,735	9	0	3	2	4	119	20	93	6	1
Eastern Pike Regional	4,807	9	0	2	2	5	242	12	227	3	0
East Hempfield Township	23,597	19	0	4	3	12	476	63	398	15	2
East Lampeter Township	16,476	24	0	6	15	3	852	74	767	11	1
East Lansdowne	2,677	27	0	0	9	18	67	13	50	4	0
East Marlborough Township	7,048	0	0	0	0	0	15	1	14	0	0
East McKeesport	2,715	19	0	0	0	19	45	11	28	6	1
East Norriton Township	13,633	9	0	1	3	5	302	39	253	10	0
East Norwegian Township	866	0	0	0	0	0	0	0	0	0	0
Easton	26,885	96	1	5	42	48	832	133	662	37	3
East Pennsboro Township	20,293	13	1	1	5	6	347	47	294	6	2
East Penn Township	2,890	0	0	0	0	0	13	1	12	0	0
East Petersburg	4,520	1	0	0	0	1	38	5	32	1	2
East Pikeland Township	7,102	10	0	0	2	8	63	11	52	0	0
East Taylor Township	2,735	4	0	0	0	4	16	1	14	1	0
Easttown Township	10,510	2	0	1	0	1	92	21	66	5	2
East Vincent Township	6,843	1	0	0	0	1	53	11	40	2	0
East Washington	2,241	8	0	0	0	8	44	14	29	1	1
East Whiteland Township	10,684	8	0	0	3	5	131	20	109	2	0
Ebensburg	3,362	2	0	0	0	2	59	15	44	0	0
Economy	8,999	3	0	1	0	2	46	12	33	1	0
Eddystone	2,418	11	0	0	0	11	323	15	304	4	0
Edgeworth	1,685	0	0	0	0	0	0	0	0	0	0
Edinboro	6,459	3	0	0	0	3	111	17	92	2	0
Edwardsville	4,831	31	0	2	2	27	175	28	136	11	2
Elizabethtown	11,582	12	0	4	2	6	233	41	190	2	0
Elizabeth Township	13,313	3	0	0	0	3	96	24	67	5	0
Ellwood City	7,946	30	1	3	5	21	243	44	197	2	2
Emlenton Borough	627	1	0	0	0	1	0	0	0	0	0
Emmaus	11,247	12	0	2	4	6	234	26	196	12	0
Emporium	2,080	0	0	0	0	0	15	5	10	0	0
Emsworth	2,457	1	0	1	0	0	26	3	23	0	0
Ephrata	13,437	24	0	4	5	15	271	53	214	4	0
Ephrata Township	9,430	7	0	2	3	2	162	19	138	5	2
Erie	102,111	431	6	77	150	198	3,738	1,233	2,404	101	32
Etna	3,462	22	0	0	3	19	116	18	94	4	0
Evans City	1,839	0	0	0	0	0	15	6	9	0	0
Everett	1,840	2	0	2	0	0	36	5	28	3	1
Everson	796	0	0	0	0	0	0	0	0	0	0
Exeter	5,670	12	0	0	2	10	138	28	101	9	0
Exeter Township, Berks County	25,631	13	1	0	6	6	388	44	334	10	2
Fairview Township, York County	16,721	27	0	3	2	22	281	38	234	9	1
Falls Township, Bucks County	34,409	48	0	9	17	22	969	153	748	68	2
Fawn Township	2,384	4	0	1	0	3	26	7	17	2	0
Fayette City	598	0	0	0	0	0	6	2	4	0	0
Ferguson Township	17,746	13	0	2	3	8	182	32	143	7	1
Ferndale	1,641	2	0	0	0	2	3	0	3	0	0

[1] If a blank is presented in the arson column, it indicates that the FBI did not receive 12 complete months of arson data for that agency.

Table II-8. Offenses Known to Law Enforcement, by Selected State and City, 2011—*Continued*

(Number.)

State/City	Population	Violent crime	Murder and non-negligent man-slaughter	Forcible rape	Robbery	Aggravated assault	Property crime	Burglary	Larceny-theft	Motor vehicle theft	Arson[1]
Pennsylvania—*Continued*											
Fleetwood	4,098	3	0	0	2	1	80	7	68	5	0
Folcroft	6,627	35	0	2	4	29	152	39	106	7	3
Ford City	3,001	7	0	1	2	4	46	6	37	3	0
Forest City	1,917	3	0	0	0	3	45	12	31	2	0
Forest Hills	6,539	3	0	0	1	2	89	23	63	3	0
Forks Township	14,768	3	0	2	0	1	160	28	131	1	0
Forty Fort	4,227	2	0	0	0	2	153	19	129	5	0
Forward Township	3,387	1	0	0	0	1	29	4	25	0	0
Foster Township	4,330	4	0	0	0	4	53	2	50	1	1
Fountain Hill	4,612	11	0	1	3	7	125	25	96	4	0
Fox Chapel	5,405	0	0	0	0	0	22	4	17	1	0
Frackville	3,817	6	0	0	0	6	6	6	0	0	0
Franconia Township	13,106	7	0	2	0	5	84	11	71	2	0
Franklin	6,566	13	0	3	2	8	169	26	138	5	1
Franklin Park	13,513	8	0	1	0	7	47	8	39	0	0
Franklin Township, Carbon County	4,276	14	0	0	1	13	39	14	24	1	0
Frazer Township	1,161	0	0	0	0	0	63	1	62	0	0
Freedom	1,574	8	0	4	1	3	37	10	22	5	0
Freedom Township	3,469	3	0	1	1	1	69	9	59	1	0
Freemansburg	2,644	1	0	0	1	0	56	10	45	1	0
Freeport	1,819	3	0	0	0	3	3	1	2	0	0
Gaines Township	544	0	0	0	0	0	26	0	18	8	0
Gallitzin	1,919	1	0	0	1	0	21	9	12	0	0
Gallitzin Township	1,328	1	0	0	0	1	3	1	2	0	0
Garrett	457	0	0	0	0	0	0	0	0	0	0
Geistown	2,475	1	0	0	1	0	43	6	33	4	0
Gettysburg	7,644	36	0	3	8	25	192	23	166	3	0
Gilpin Township	2,504	0	0	0	0	0	0	0	0	0	0
Girard	3,114	9	0	0	0	9	30	4	26	0	0
Glassport	4,497	13	0	1	2	10	128	34	91	3	2
Glenolden	7,176	18	0	1	7	10	197	36	155	6	1
Granville Township	5,120	4	0	0	0	4	123	15	108	0	0
Greencastle	4,009	4	0	0	2	2	85	16	66	3	1
Greenfield Township, Blair County	4,186	8	0	0	0	8	123	20	101	2	0
Greensburg	14,939	36	0	4	7	25	385	57	317	11	1
Greenville	5,938	17	0	2	2	13	174	53	118	3	1
Greenwood Township	1,958	0	0	0	0	0	0	0	0	0	0
Grove City	8,349	5	0	4	1	0	92	13	78	1	0
Hamburg	4,303	10	0	0	0	10	72	21	49	2	0
Hamiltonban Township	2,380	1	0	0	0	1	8	2	6	0	0
Hampden Township	28,133	11	2	4	3	2	358	58	296	4	1
Hampton Township	18,422	19	0	2	1	16	122	17	101	4	0
Hanover	15,338	26	0	3	10	13	675	64	604	7	4
Hanover Township, Luzerne County	11,111	10	0	4	5	1	186	36	133	17	0
Harleton	284	0	0	0	0	0	1	0	0	1	0
Harmar Township	2,930	11	0	3	1	7	58	4	47	7	0
Harmony Township	3,207	3	0	0	1	2	88	16	70	2	0
Harrisburg	49,686	697	8	62	382	245	2,515	662	1,605	248	13
Harrisville	900	1	0	0	0	1	2	1	1	0	0
Harveys Lake	2,800	1	0	0	0	1	44	8	35	1	0
Hastings	1,282	9	0	0	1	8	32	13	19	0	0
Hatboro	7,383	15	1	1	3	10	95	23	69	3	0
Hatfield Township	20,604	32	0	4	10	18	357	45	295	17	4
Haverford Township	48,646	33	0	1	5	27	654	96	548	10	3
Hawley	1,215	0	0	0	0	0	8	1	7	0	0
Hazleton	25,421	117	4	11	38	64	451	153	236	62	6
Heidelberg Township, Berks County	1,729	1	0	0	1	0	5	1	4	0	0
Hellam Township	8,744	27	1	4	1	21	100	16	82	2	2
Hemlock Township	2,256	1	0	0	1	0	117	0	116	1	0
Hermitage	16,272	31	0	0	11	20	511	70	427	14	1
Highland Township	1,276	0	0	0	0	0	1	0	1	0	0
Highspire	2,407	14	0	0	1	13	37	7	29	1	4
Hilltown Township	15,077	10	0	3	2	5	282	40	238	4	0
Homer City	1,712	4	0	1	0	3	12	1	11	0	0
Homestead	3,175	39	0	4	19	16	276	95	163	18	0
Honesdale	4,494	4	0	2	1	1	143	25	116	2	2
Honey Brook	1,718	0	0	0	0	0	3	0	1	2	0
Hooversville	647	2	0	1	0	1	11	1	10	0	0
Hop Bottom Borough	338	0	0	0	0	0	0	0	0	0	0
Horsham Township	26,230	20	0	0	5	15	300	49	236	15	0
Houston	1,300	0	0	0	0	0	1	0	1	0	0
Hughesville	2,135	7	0	0	1	6	66	7	59	0	0
Hulmeville	1,006	1	0	0	0	1	7	2	5	0	0
Huntingdon	7,116	2	0	0	0	2	97	0	97	0	0
Independence Township, Beaver County	2,511	0	0	0	0	0	14	2	8	4	0

[1] If a blank is presented in offenses the arson column, it indicates that the FBI did not receive 12 complete months of arson data for that agency.

Table II-8.   Offenses Known to Law Enforcement, by Selected State and City, 2011—*Continued*

(Number.)

State/City	Population	Violent crime	Murder and non-negligent man-slaughter	Forcible rape	Robbery	Aggravated assault	Property crime	Burglary	Larceny-theft	Motor vehicle theft	Arson[1]
Pennsylvania—*Continued*											
Indiana	14,020	188	0	9	7	172	269	41	225	3	2
Indiana Township	7,276	8	0	0	0	8	60	9	50	1	1
Industry	1,841	3	0	0	0	3	23	4	19	0	0
Ingram	3,341	4	0	0	1	3	19	4	15	0	0
Ivyland	1,044	0	0	0	0	0	9	0	9	0	0
Jackson Township, Butler County	3,669	8	0	0	0	8	30	5	25	0	0
Jackson Township, Cambria County	4,406	1	0	0	1	0	24	12	12	0	0
Jackson Township, Luzerne County	4,661	6	0	1	0	5	10	3	5	2	1
Jamestown	619	0	0	0	0	0	7	1	6	0	0
Jeannette	9,685	9	0	0	5	4	68	19	49	0	3
Jefferson Hills Borough	10,653	6	0	2	0	4	85	21	57	7	0
Jefferson Township, Mercer County	1,886	1	0	0	0	1	17	5	12	0	0
Jenkins Township	4,456	9	0	0	0	9	155	23	129	3	0
Jenkintown	4,436	2	0	0	1	1	42	8	34	0	0
Jennerstown	697	2	0	0	1	1	2	1	1	0	0
Jermyn	2,176	23	0	0	1	22	59	21	36	2	0
Jim Thorpe	4,796	15	0	1	1	13	135	11	120	4	0
Johnsonburg	2,491	5	0	0	1	4	54	15	38	1	1
Johnstown	22,572	151	3	7	60	81	961	358	572	31	2
Juniata Valley Regional	2,803	0	0	0	0	0	3	0	3	0	0
Kennett Square	6,091	17	0	0	7	10	108	11	88	9	2
Kidder Township	1,941	12	0	0	1	11	112	23	86	3	0
Kilbuck Township	699	0	0	0	0	0	7	1	5	1	0
Kingston	13,224	30	0	1	19	10	379	77	286	16	0
Kingston Township	7,021	13	0	0	1	12	62	10	48	4	0
Kiskiminetas Township	4,815	1	0	0	0	1	56	13	43	0	0
Kittanning	4,057	5	0	0	0	5	25	5	19	1	1
Kline Township	1,443	1	0	1	0	0	45	10	35	0	0
Knox	1,150	1	0	0	0	1	25	0	25	0	0
Koppel	764	5	0	1	0	4	27	12	12	3	0
Kulpmont	2,933	18	0	0	1	17	21	2	18	1	0
Kutztown	5,028	10	0	0	2	8	138	33	101	4	0
Laflin Borough	1,492	5	0	0	0	5	36	7	29	0	0
Lake City	3,041	5	0	1	1	3	69	17	52	0	0
Lamar Township	2,525	1	0	0	0	1	15	1	11	3	0
Lancaster	59,511	504	5	37	217	245	3,014	531	2,378	105	18
Lancaster Township, Butler County	2,540	6	0	0	1	5	23	2	19	2	0
Lancaster Township, Lancaster County	16,200	17	0	1	13	3	598	98	482	18	2
Langhorne Borough	1,627	2	0	0	2	0	26	5	21	0	1
Langhorne Manor	1,447	1	0	0	0	1	4	0	4	0	0
Lansdale	16,321	22	0	7	8	7	317	52	249	16	4
Lansdowne	10,654	29	2	2	13	12	261	84	164	13	0
Lansford	3,954	7	0	0	1	6	31	6	25	0	2
Larksville	4,494	5	0	1	2	2	89	2	80	7	1
Latimore Township	2,588	1	0	0	0	1	23	0	22	1	0
Latrobe	8,365	32	0	2	0	30	211	31	176	4	3
Laureldale	3,923	4	0	0	1	3	23	4	17	2	0
Lawrence Township, Clearfield County	7,705	81	0	1	6	74	316	42	266	8	0
Lawrence Township, Tioga County	1,723	2	0	0	0	2	1	1	0	0	0
Lebanon	25,558	87	0	11	46	30	643	133	486	24	5
Leetsdale	1,222	5	0	1	0	4	39	3	36	0	0
Leet Township	1,639	0	0	0	0	0	0	0	0	0	0
Lehighton	5,518	13	0	0	5	8	153	23	117	13	1
Lehigh Township, Northampton County	10,560	24	0	1	1	22	101	16	76	9	1
Lehman Township	3,519	0	0	0	0	0	0	0	0	0	0
Lewisburg	5,810	13	0	0	4	9	91	22	69	0	0
Liberty Township, Adams County	1,241	1	0	0	0	1	15	2	12	1	0
Ligonier	1,578	2	1	0	0	1	18	1	17	0	0
Ligonier Township	6,624	17	0	0	0	17	36	9	27	0	1
Limerick Township	18,132	10	0	0	5	5	433	45	378	10	3
Lincoln	1,075	0	0	0	0	0	17	7	9	1	0
Linesville	1,043	2	0	0	0	2	8	0	8	0	1
Lititz	9,399	5	0	2	0	3	97	14	76	7	5
Little Beaver Township	1,415	0	0	0	0	0	0	0	0	0	0
Lock Haven	9,803	24	0	1	3	20	266	32	234	0	1
Loretto	1,306	0	0	0	0	0	0	0	0	0	0
Lower Allen Township	18,037	8	1	0	5	2	293	19	273	1	1
Lower Burrell	11,799	6	1	0	2	3	177	45	128	4	0
Lower Frederick Township	4,855	2	0	0	0	2	21	3	18	0	0
Lower Gwynedd Township	11,441	10	0	0	0	10	197	21	173	3	0
Lower Heidelberg Township	5,531	2	0	0	0	2	30	6	24	0	0
Lower Makefield Township	32,663	26	0	2	4	20	483	80	394	9	4
Lower Merion Township	58,009	52	0	0	28	24	1,026	185	803	38	2
Lower Moreland Township	13,023	4	0	0	1	3	176	28	146	2	1
Lower Paxton Township	47,511	119	1	10	33	75	1,218	205	973	40	8

[1] If a blank is presented in the arson column, it indicates that the FBI did not receive 12 complete months of arson data for that agency.

Table II-8. Offenses Known to Law Enforcement, by Selected State and City, 2011—*Continued*

(Number.)

State/City	Population	Violent crime	Murder and non-negligent man-slaughter	Forcible rape	Robbery	Aggravated assault	Property crime	Burglary	Larceny-theft	Motor vehicle theft	Arson[1]
Pennsylvania—*Continued*											
Lower Pottsgrove Township	12,097	19	0	0	2	17	279	46	227	6	0
Lower Providence Township	25,517	42	0	1	2	39	268	39	229	0	2
Lower Salford Township	15,007	7	0	0	0	7	81	5	73	3	1
Lower Saucon Township	10,806	21	0	1	1	19	96	14	77	5	0
Lower Swatara Township	8,294	17	1	0	1	15	130	20	110	0	1
Lower Windsor Township	7,406	16	0	1	1	14	62	13	44	5	0
Luzerne	2,854	10	0	0	1	9	121	13	104	4	0
Luzerne Township	5,984	3	0	0	0	3	32	7	24	1	0
Lykens	1,785	1	0	0	0	1	19	5	14	0	0
Macungie	3,084	5	0	0	0	5	15	2	13	0	0
Madison Township	1,610	0	0	0	0	0	0	0	0	0	0
Mahanoy Township	3,162	0	0	0	0	0	3	2	1	0	0
Mahoning Township, Lawrence County	3,093	4	0	0	4	0	46	2	37	7	1
Mahoning Township, Montour County	4,184	9	0	1	0	8	22	2	19	1	0
Malvern	3,008	8	0	1	0	7	34	5	28	1	0
Manheim	4,873	6	0	2	2	2	121	16	100	5	0
Manheim Township	38,255	33	0	5	17	11	874	97	754	23	0
Manor	3,249	3	0	0	0	3	13	1	11	1	0
Manor Township, Armstrong County	4,240	0	0	0	0	0	0	0	0	0	0
Manor Township, Lancaster County	19,675	9	0	0	4	5	234	44	175	15	0
Mansfield	3,637	0	0	0	0	0	4	0	4	0	0
Marcus Hook	2,405	36	0	0	1	35	103	14	85	4	2
Marietta	2,596	2	0	0	0	2	55	10	45	0	2
Marion Township, Beaver County	916	0	0	0	0	0	4	1	3	0	0
Marion Township, Berks County	1,693	0	0	0	0	0	10	2	8	0	0
Marlborough Township	3,188	4	0	1	0	3	29	4	24	1	0
Marple Township	23,503	10	0	0	1	9	404	44	355	5	2
Mars	1,704	1	0	0	1	0	13	0	13	0	0
Martinsburg	1,964	0	0	0	0	0	41	12	29	0	0
Marysville	2,542	0	0	0	0	0	33	5	27	1	0
Masontown	3,461	7	1	0	0	6	85	15	61	9	0
Mayfield	1,813	1	0	0	0	1	9	1	8	0	1
McAdoo	2,307	2	0	0	0	2	38	4	34	0	0
McCandless	28,548	5	0	0	2	3	246	62	183	1	0
McDonald Borough	2,156	5	0	2	0	3	51	12	38	1	0
McKeesport	19,794	336	3	4	68	261	763	275	447	41	18
McSherrystown	3,048	4	0	0	0	4	46	5	41	0	0
Meadville	13,431	24	1	0	7	16	310	58	252	0	0
Mechanicsburg	9,010	57	0	0	6	51	233	35	196	2	4
Media	5,344	30	0	0	1	29	86	13	73	0	0
Mercer	2,008	6	0	0	0	6	12	4	7	1	0
Mercersburg	1,566	0	0	0	0	0	53	6	47	0	0
Meshoppen	565	0	0	0	0	0	0	0	0	0	0
Meyersdale	2,191	2	0	0	0	2	26	9	17	0	0
Middleburg	1,313	0	0	0	0	0	89	17	71	1	0
Middlesex Township, Butler County	5,407	1	0	0	0	1	34	7	27	0	0
Middletown	8,929	19	0	4	4	11	143	17	120	6	0
Middletown Township	45,581	38	1	3	12	22	1,426	148	1,221	57	3
Midland	2,643	9	0	1	3	5	393	23	365	5	0
Mifflin	644	1	0	0	0	1	5	5	0	0	0
Mifflinburg	3,551	2	0	0	0	2	81	19	62	0	1
Mifflin County Regional	20,835	17	0	4	0	13	278	38	231	9	4
Milford	1,024	1	0	0	0	1	32	5	27	0	0
Millbourne	1,163	15	0	0	6	9	25	7	18	0	0
Millcreek Township, Erie County	53,686	46	0	11	16	19	1,099	248	827	24	0
Millcreek Township, Lebanon County	3,904	5	0	0	1	4	51	10	39	2	1
Millersburg	2,565	11	0	1	0	10	28	6	22	0	1
Millersville	8,194	17	0	5	3	9	89	20	68	1	0
Millvale	3,756	7	0	0	0	7	48	19	26	3	0
Millville	951	0	0	0	0	0	0	0	0	0	0
Minersville	4,411	5	0	0	0	5	22	6	14	2	0
Monaca	5,755	13	0	2	5	6	130	24	96	10	0
Monessen	7,745	65	0	1	9	55	268	75	189	4	0
Monongahela	4,314	17	0	0	1	16	148	21	120	7	1
Monroeville	28,477	54	0	3	17	34	342	75	245	22	0
Montgomery	1,584	2	0	0	0	2	35	0	35	0	0
Montgomery Township	24,869	6	0	1	2	3	514	16	488	10	0
Montoursville	4,630	0	0	0	0	0	10	0	10	0	0
Moon Township	24,262	16	0	0	5	11	263	39	218	6	0
Moore Township	9,227	4	0	0	0	4	61	9	48	4	0
Moosic	5,737	33	0	1	3	29	266	45	212	9	2
Morton	2,678	4	0	0	0	4	149	27	120	2	0
Moscow	2,032	2	0	0	0	2	21	1	19	1	0
Mount Carmel	5,912	9	0	0	2	7	116	19	92	5	1
Mount Carmel Township	3,149	16	0	0	0	16	14	2	11	1	0

[1] If a blank is presented in the arson column, it indicates that the FBI did not receive 12 complete months of arson data for that agency.

Table II-8.   Offenses Known to Law Enforcement, by Selected State and City, 2011—*Continued*

(Number.)

State/City	Population	Violent crime	Murder and non-negligent man-slaughter	Forcible rape	Robbery	Aggravated assault	Property crime	Burglary	Larceny-theft	Motor vehicle theft	Arson[1]
Pennsylvania—*Continued*											
Mount Gretna Borough	197	0	0	0	0	0	0	0	0	0	0
Mount Holly Springs	2,036	4	0	0	1	3	31	9	22	0	1
Mount Jewett	922	4	0	0	0	4	6	4	2	0	0
Mount Joy	7,434	16	0	1	1	14	136	28	103	5	0
Mount Lebanon	33,243	18	0	0	2	16	210	37	170	3	4
Mount Oliver	3,414	36	1	1	19	15	167	52	97	18	0
Mount Pleasant	4,468	2	0	0	0	2	71	10	60	1	0
Mount Pleasant Township	3,526	4	0	0	1	3	28	5	21	2	1
Mount Union	2,455	0	0	0	0	0	29	10	19	0	0
Mountville	2,811	4	0	0	1	3	47	5	41	1	0
Muhlenberg Township	19,691	28	0	2	11	15	748	95	618	35	3
Muncy	2,485	0	0	0	0	0	0	0	0	0	0
Munhall	11,442	21	0	0	6	15	215	49	149	17	0
Murrysville	20,143	6	0	2	1	3	94	33	58	3	1
Myerstown	3,072	14	0	0	1	13	42	0	40	2	0
Nanticoke	10,498	33	0	3	15	15	364	91	257	16	4
Nanty Glo	2,743	14	0	0	2	12	93	30	61	2	0
Narberth	4,296	6	0	0	1	5	43	6	36	1	0
Nazareth Area	5,764	27	0	2	4	21	82	11	71	0	1
Nescopeck	1,588	0	0	0	0	0	9	9	0	0	0
Nesquehoning	3,360	6	0	2	1	3	97	10	87	0	0
Nether Providence Towship	13,750	25	0	2	3	20	189	32	150	7	0
Neville Township	1,087	0	0	0	0	0	59	4	55	0	0
New Beaver	1,507	1	0	0	0	1	6	1	5	0	0
Newberry Township	15,334	17	0	2	4	11	341	50	271	20	1
New Bethlehem	992	1	0	0	0	1	13	2	11	0	0
New Brighton	9,241	62	0	3	9	50	412	72	337	3	0
New Britain Township	11,105	8	0	0	1	7	83	13	68	2	0
New Cumberland	7,300	11	1	5	4	1	125	32	92	1	1
New Garden Township	12,022	10	2	1	2	5	175	31	137	7	0
New Hanover Township	10,974	4	0	1	3	0	90	23	63	4	0
New Holland	5,395	8	0	0	4	4	74	9	61	4	0
New Hope	2,536	15	0	2	0	13	81	7	74	0	0
New Kensington	13,158	44	1	11	17	15	463	132	319	12	7
Newport	1,579	1	0	0	0	1	1	0	1	0	0
Newport Township	5,391	16	0	0	0	16	9	6	3	0	0
New Sewickley Township	7,383	16	0	1	2	13	104	36	61	7	1
Newton Township	2,855	2	0	0	0	2	4	1	3	0	0
Newtown	2,255	2	0	0	0	2	30	3	26	1	0
Newtown Township, Bucks County	22,366	15	0	2	1	12	263	30	228	5	0
Newville	1,330	1	0	0	0	1	42	0	41	1	1
Norristown	34,433	367	4	12	198	153	997	241	641	115	5
Northampton	9,958	6	0	1	2	3	155	36	118	1	2
Northampton Township	39,853	2	0	0	0	2	280	41	230	9	4
North Belle Vernon	1,977	16	0	1	4	11	109	40	67	2	0
North Catasauqua	2,858	3	0	0	0	3	23	1	20	2	0
North Charleroi	1,317	1	0	0	1	0	6	0	6	0	0
North Cornwall Township	7,577	17	0	2	2	13	207	25	178	4	1
North Coventry Township	7,891	6	0	0	2	4	269	22	245	2	0
North East, Erie County	4,308	7	0	4	0	3	150	13	132	5	0
Northeastern Regional	11,456	25	0	16	3	6	160	21	136	3	3
Northern Berks Regional	12,730	9	0	1	2	6	253	22	223	8	0
Northern Cambria Borough	3,847	4	0	2	0	2	86	12	73	1	1
Northern Regional	30,781	4	0	1	0	3	277	30	242	5	1
Northern York Regional	66,820	113	0	9	24	80	1,105	145	928	32	16
North Franklin Township	4,598	14	0	1	5	8	123	19	100	4	0
North Huntingdon Township	30,707	13	1	0	6	6	336	37	287	12	2
North Lebanon Township	11,465	13	0	1	3	9	282	41	237	4	0
North Londonderry Township	8,094	2	0	0	1	1	104	17	87	0	1
North Middleton Township	11,179	5	0	4	0	1	66	13	51	2	0
North Sewickley Township	5,506	6	0	0	0	6	189	41	143	5	1
North Strabane Township	13,451	9	1	1	2	5	152	20	129	3	1
Northumberland	3,816	1	0	0	0	1	62	8	54	0	0
North Union Township	1,481	0	0	0	0	0	2	1	0	1	0
North Versailles Township	12,459	77	0	6	5	66	280	48	217	15	1
North Wales	3,239	5	0	0	0	5	67	11	54	2	0
Northwest Lancaster County Regional	18,190	8	0	2	3	3	173	1	169	3	0
Norwood	5,909	12	0	0	2	10	114	24	85	5	0
Oakmont	6,323	17	0	0	5	12	101	23	72	6	0
O'Hara Township	8,434	0	0	0	0	0	70	18	49	3	0
Ohio Township	4,772	0	0	0	0	0	58	1	56	1	0
Ohioville	3,544	9	0	2	0	7	38	11	26	1	0
Oil City	10,591	22	0	0	5	17	116	15	98	3	1
Old Forge	8,340	3	0	0	0	3	107	33	73	1	7

[1] If a blank is presented in the arson column, it indicates that the FBI did not receive 12 complete months of arson data for that agency.

Table II-8.   Offenses Known to Law Enforcement, by Selected State and City, 2011—*Continued*

(Number.)

State/City	Population	Violent crime	Murder and non-negligent man-slaughter	Forcible rape	Robbery	Aggravated assault	Property crime	Burglary	Larceny-theft	Motor vehicle theft	Arson[1]
Pennsylvania—*Continued*											
Old Lycoming Township	4,954	2	0	1	1	0	125	9	107	9	0
Olyphant	5,167	3	0	0	0	3	34	12	20	2	0
Orangeville Area	1,771	0	0	0	0	0	1	0	1	0	0
Orwigsburg	3,109	2	0	0	0	2	51	8	43	0	0
Osceola Township	661	0	0	0	0	0	0	0	0	0	0
Otto Eldred Regional	2,389	0	0	0	0	0	1	0	1	0	0
Oxford	5,093	30	0	3	3	24	110	21	85	4	0
Paint Township	3,159	37	0	0	0	37	87	19	65	3	0
Palmerton	5,431	11	0	2	2	7	174	10	161	3	0
Palmer Township	20,757	12	0	1	6	5	401	42	349	10	0
Palmyra	7,343	9	0	0	2	7	135	19	114	2	2
Patterson Township	3,039	5	0	2	1	2	69	17	49	3	0
Patton	1,775	1	0	0	0	1	4	1	3	0	0
Patton Township	15,360	6	0	0	6	0	201	29	166	6	1
Paxtang	1,566	4	0	0	2	2	75	20	52	3	0
Pen Argyl	3,606	0	0	0	0	0	50	10	40	0	0
Penbrook	3,018	9	0	0	3	6	67	14	47	6	1
Penndel	2,335	12	0	0	1	11	33	4	26	3	0
Penn Hills	42,464	141	6	16	55	64	850	282	519	49	4
Pennridge Regional	10,997	10	0	3	0	7	104	19	82	3	0
Penn Township, Butler County	5,087	3	0	0	1	2	41	3	36	2	0
Penn Township, Perry County	3,235	0	0	0	0	0	49	11	38	0	0
Penn Township, Westmoreland County	20,069	14	0	0	1	13	122	26	92	4	0
Penn Township, York County	15,662	24	0	1	1	22	257	33	219	5	3
Perkasie	8,538	14	0	0	1	13	210	39	168	3	0
Perryopolis	1,790	0	0	0	0	0	36	9	26	1	1
Peters Township	21,281	8	0	0	2	6	144	19	124	1	1
Philadelphia	1,530,873	18,268	324	833	8,246	8,865	59,617	12,057	40,113	7,447	
Phoenixville	16,492	37	0	2	6	29	395	33	354	8	2
Pine Creek Township	3,225	4	0	0	0	4	14	1	12	1	0
Pine Grove	2,193	9	0	0	0	9	16	0	16	0	0
Pitcairn	3,305	41	0	0	12	29	164	41	114	9	1
Pittsburgh	308,609	2,476	44	67	1,126	1,239	10,063	2,686	6,897	480	195
Plainfield Township	6,158	1	0	0	0	1	57	7	47	3	0
Plains Township	9,993	17	0	1	8	8	210	33	168	9	0
Pleasant Hills	8,294	0	0	0	0	0	90	7	78	5	0
Plumstead Township	12,482	6	0	2	0	4	116	7	106	3	4
Plymouth	5,970	44	0	4	4	36	206	57	137	12	1
Plymouth Township, Montgomery County	16,578	27	0	4	15	8	562	68	475	19	3
Pocono Mountain Regional	39,202	88	1	19	23	45	907	355	529	23	7
Pocono Township	11,100	25	0	4	8	13	328	54	261	13	1
Point Marion	1,163	5	0	0	0	5	22	3	19	0	0
Point Township	3,697	9	0	0	0	9	46	12	33	1	1
Polk	819	0	0	0	0	0	1	1	0	0	0
Portage	2,646	7	0	1	1	5	83	37	46	0	1
Port Allegany	2,164	2	0	0	0	2	44	7	37	0	0
Port Carbon	1,895	1	0	0	1	0	6	0	6	0	0
Portland	521	0	0	0	0	0	2	0	2	0	0
Port Vue	3,810	7	0	0	0	7	48	12	35	1	0
Pottstown	22,448	190	0	26	71	93	1,066	149	870	47	12
Pottsville	14,370	60	1	8	4	47	196	26	162	8	2
Pringle	982	2	1	0	1	0	61	6	54	1	1
Prospect Park	6,475	33	0	1	7	25	178	25	145	8	0
Pulaski Township, Lawrence County	3,463	4	0	0	1	3	37	5	28	4	0
Punxsutawney	5,981	18	0	1	1	16	103	25	78	0	0
Pymatuning Township	3,291	5	0	0	0	5	145	38	101	6	0
Quakertown	9,008	40	1	5	3	31	308	44	256	8	4
Quarryville	2,584	13	0	4	0	9	60	10	48	2	0
Radnor Township	31,632	15	0	0	4	11	379	62	309	8	0
Reading	88,363	758	13	22	377	346	3,301	1,380	1,501	420	32
Reilly Township	728	0	0	0	0	0	10	1	9	0	0
Resa Regional	2,564	2	0	0	0	2	15	4	11	0	0
Reserve Township	3,344	1	0	0	1	0	34	10	24	0	0
Reynoldsville	2,768	1	0	0	1	0	20	5	15	0	0
Rice Township	3,346	0	0	0	0	0	8	4	4	0	0
Richland Township, Bucks County	13,094	6	1	1	2	2	285	22	260	3	0
Richland Township, Cambria County	12,855	9	0	0	3	6	681	43	632	6	0
Ridgway	4,091	4	0	0	0	4	127	26	98	3	0
Ridley Park	7,024	10	0	0	1	9	79	10	66	3	0
Ridley Township	30,886	53	1	1	24	27	557	71	457	29	4
Ringtown	821	0	0	0	0	0	3	0	3	0	0
Riverside	1,938	1	0	0	0	1	23	1	21	1	0
Roaring Spring	2,593	1	0	1	0	0	65	8	56	1	0
Robeson Township	7,239	4	0	1	0	3	86	26	54	6	0
Robinson Township, Allegheny County	13,397	29	0	1	8	20	387	30	348	9	0

[1] If a blank is presented in the arson column, it indicates that the FBI did not receive 12 complete months of arson data for that agency.

Table II-8.   Offenses Known to Law Enforcement, by Selected State and City, 2011—*Continued*

(Number.)

State/City	Population	Violent crime	Murder and non-negligent man-slaughter	Forcible rape	Robbery	Aggravated assault	Property crime	Burglary	Larceny-theft	Motor vehicle theft	Arson[1]
Pennsylvania—*Continued*											
Robinson Township, Washington County	1,937	4	0	2	0	2	35	17	18	0	0
Rochester	3,669	32	1	3	6	22	305	66	231	8	0
Rochester Township	2,811	1	0	0	0	1	60	12	47	1	0
Rockledge	2,551	12	0	0	1	11	48	20	26	2	0
Roseto	1,572	2	0	0	0	2	28	1	23	4	0
Rosslyn Farms	428	0	0	0	0	0	0	0	0	0	0
Ross Township	31,204	30	0	0	12	18	668	75	583	10	1
Rostraver Township	11,399	13	0	2	6	5	392	42	344	6	3
Royalton	910	0	0	0	0	0	2	0	2	0	0
Royersford	4,767	7	0	1	0	6	89	11	76	2	0
Rural Valley	879	0	0	0	0	0	1	0	1	0	0
Ryan Township	2,467	0	0	0	0	0	3	1	2	0	0
Sadsbury Township, Chester County	3,581	4	0	0	0	4	8	4	4	0	0
Salem Township, Luzerne County	4,268	7	0	0	1	6	52	15	36	1	0
Salisbury Township	13,548	6	0	1	4	1	296	48	236	12	3
Saltsburg	876	0	0	0	0	0	9	1	8	0	0
Sandy Township	10,659	20	0	1	1	18	292	52	237	3	0
Sankertown	677	0	0	0	0	0	2	1	1	0	0
Saxton	738	0	0	0	0	0	0	0	0	0	0
Sayre	5,605	5	0	1	0	4	188	38	149	1	0
Schuylkill Township, Chester County	8,543	14	0	0	0	14	123	12	108	3	0
Scottdale	4,398	18	0	1	1	16	92	13	78	1	1
Scott Township, Allegheny County	17,078	16	0	1	5	10	222	29	187	6	3
Scott Township, Columbia County	5,129	1	0	1	0	0	63	5	57	1	0
Scott Township, Lackawanna County	4,921	4	0	0	0	4	18	5	11	2	0
Scranton	76,332	226	3	34	95	94	2,556	620	1,810	126	12
Selinsgrove	5,672	66	0	6	2	58	249	49	193	7	1
Seward	497	0	0	0	0	0	2	2	0	0	0
Sewickley	4,388	10	0	1	0	9	61	7	49	5	0
Sewickley Heights	813	0	0	0	0	0	3	0	3	0	0
Shaler Township	28,849	13	3	1	2	7	323	71	252	0	1
Shamokin	7,398	3	0	0	1	2	61	11	48	2	1
Sharon	14,083	85	0	9	38	38	576	214	335	27	4
Sharon Hill	5,715	65	0	6	14	45	237	30	197	10	0
Sharpsburg	3,457	17	0	0	4	13	75	22	51	2	0
Sharpsville	4,429	32	0	0	0	32	74	0	73	1	0
Shenandoah	5,087	24	1	2	7	14	151	45	104	2	6
Shenango Township, Lawrence County	7,503	13	0	2	6	5	213	49	154	10	2
Shillington	5,290	2	0	0	2	0	92	14	75	3	0
Shinglehouse	1,131	1	0	1	0	0	3	0	3	0	0
Shippensburg	5,510	0	0	0	0	0	90	15	74	1	1
Shohola Township	2,483	0	0	0	0	0	33	13	18	2	0
Silver Lake Township	1,721	0	0	0	0	0	10	5	5	0	0
Silver Spring Township	13,701	6	0	2	1	3	188	9	173	6	1
Sinking Spring	4,021	1	0	0	1	0	75	15	54	6	1
Slatington	4,245	4	0	0	0	4	83	11	70	2	1
Slippery Rock	3,637	2	0	1	0	1	47	6	39	2	0
Smithfield	878	0	0	0	0	0	0	0	0	0	0
Smithton Borough	400	0	0	0	0	0	2	2	0	0	0
Smith Township	4,490	0	0	0	0	0	0	0	0	0	0
Solebury Township	8,720	4	0	0	1	3	64	14	50	0	0
Somerset	6,297	25	0	2	7	16	179	35	136	8	2
Souderton	6,639	19	1	3	2	13	62	12	49	1	0
South Abington Township	9,102	0	0	0	0	0	92	13	75	4	0
South Centre Township	1,943	2	0	0	0	2	31	6	25	0	0
South Coatesville	1,307	9	0	2	1	6	11	1	7	3	0
South Connellsville Borough	1,976	1	0	1	0	0	10	3	7	0	0
Southern Regional York County	10,623	10	0	5	2	3	192	24	163	5	0
South Fayette Township	14,462	11	0	0	4	7	92	19	73	0	1
South Fork	931	1	0	0	0	1	3	0	3	0	0
South Greensburg	2,124	5	0	1	0	4	41	6	34	1	0
South Heidelberg Township	7,294	9	0	0	0	9	60	8	50	2	0
South Heights	477	0	0	0	0	0	0	0	0	0	0
South Lebanon Township	9,493	2	0	0	0	2	78	19	59	0	2
South Londonderry Township	7,013	4	0	1	2	1	71	19	52	0	0
South Park Township	13,459	3	0	1	0	2	53	23	29	1	0
South Pymatuning Township	2,704	3	0	1	0	2	23	8	14	1	0
South Strabane Township	9,376	19	0	8	10	1	472	25	441	6	0
Southwestern Regional	17,586	12	2	3	0	7	152	40	104	8	0
Southwest Greensburg	2,162	8	0	0	0	8	65	12	52	1	0
Southwest Mercer County Regional	10,569	44	1	2	15	26	216	51	153	12	3
Southwest Regional	8,174	4	1	1	0	2	21	4	17	0	0
South Whitehall Township	19,241	20	1	1	7	11	768	66	694	8	9
South Williamsport	6,399	29	0	2	3	24	121	9	107	5	0

[1] If a blank is presented in the arson column, it indicates that the FBI did not receive 12 complete months of arson data for that agency.

Table II-8. Offenses Known to Law Enforcement, by Selected State and City, 2011—*Continued*

(Number.)

State/City	Population	Violent crime	Murder and non-negligent man-slaughter	Forcible rape	Robbery	Aggravated assault	Property crime	Burglary	Larceny-theft	Motor vehicle theft	Arson[1]
Pennsylvania—*Continued*											
Springdale	3,416	6	0	0	0	6	21	3	17	1	0
Springettsbury Township	26,753	45	0	1	20	24	953	49	881	23	2
Springfield Township, Delaware County	24,288	15	0	2	11	2	779	76	693	10	0
Springfield Township, Montgomery County	19,480	36	0	2	6	28	184	28	154	2	0
Spring Garden Township	12,618	37	0	3	18	16	458	45	388	25	0
Spring Township, Berks County	27,205	6	1	1	1	3	283	38	228	17	2
Spring Township, Centre County	7,494	4	0	1	0	3	29	1	26	2	0
Spring Township, Snyder County	1,621	1	0	0	0	1	6	2	4	0	0
State College	56,608	57	0	12	11	34	893	130	741	22	10
Steelton	6,009	27	1	5	14	7	256	59	186	11	2
Stewartstown	2,096	2	0	0	2	0	46	7	37	2	0
St. Marys City	13,112	15	0	5	3	7	227	31	195	1	1
Stowe Township	6,382	22	0	0	7	15	241	50	186	5	1
Strasburg	2,818	1	0	0	0	1	26	7	19	0	0
Stroud Area Regional	34,730	106	2	15	53	36	1,543	145	1,362	36	7
Sugarcreek	5,311	2	0	0	0	2	50	5	43	2	0
Sugarloaf Township, Luzerne County	4,224	1	0	0	0	1	0	0	0	0	0
Sugar Notch	992	0	0	0	0	0	3	2	1	0	0
Summerhill Township	2,475	2	0	0	2	0	39	9	28	2	0
Summit Hill	3,044	2	0	0	0	2	5	3	2	0	1
Summit Township	2,278	0	0	0	0	0	7	0	7	0	0
Sunbury	9,937	106	0	7	4	95	345	64	261	20	6
Susquehanna Depot	1,648	3	0	0	0	3	16	2	12	2	0
Susquehanna Regional	7,780	5	0	0	0	5	99	15	83	1	3
Susquehanna Township, Dauphin County	24,113	45	0	7	16	22	428	89	324	15	2
Sutersville	607	0	0	0	0	0	0	0	0	0	0
Swatara Township	23,436	160	3	0	24	133	796	110	670	16	6
Swissvale	9,012	77	0	0	14	63	218	53	155	10	2
Swoyersville	5,078	5	0	0	0	5	104	26	72	6	1
Sykesville	1,161	0	0	0	0	0	0	0	0	0	0
Tamaqua	7,130	17	0	7	7	3	219	43	166	10	0
Tarentum	4,544	24	0	1	2	21	129	16	109	4	0
Tatamy	1,207	0	0	0	0	0	6	0	6	0	0
Taylor	6,283	32	1	2	2	27	183	19	153	11	0
Telford	4,888	15	0	3	2	10	68	8	59	1	0
Throop	4,101	10	0	0	0	10	57	18	36	3	1
Tiadaghton Valley Regional	6,692	18	0	2	0	16	122	16	105	1	0
Tidioute	690	1	0	0	0	1	7	2	5	0	0
Tinicum Township, Bucks County	4,008	3	0	0	1	2	29	7	22	0	0
Tinicum Township, Delaware County	4,104	26	0	2	4	20	214	20	184	10	0
Tioga	668	1	0	0	0	1	3	0	3	0	0
Titusville	5,619	6	0	1	4	1	183	30	148	5	0
Towamencin Township	17,634	22	1	0	1	20	173	24	149	0	3
Towanda	2,928	5	0	2	0	3	82	13	66	3	0
Trafford	3,184	13	0	1	0	12	52	19	33	0	0
Tredyffrin Township	29,426	12	0	1	2	9	264	57	192	15	1
Tulpehocken Township	3,284	0	0	0	0	0	16	5	10	1	0
Tunkhannock Township, Wyoming County	4,287	2	0	0	0	2	71	10	58	3	0
Turtle Creek	5,366	24	0	0	1	23	11	2	9	0	0
Tyrone	5,494	25	0	4	3	18	162	21	135	6	2
Union City	3,331	4	0	3	1	0	92	25	67	0	0
Uniontown	10,405	54	0	7	27	20	518	104	391	23	0
Union Township, Lawrence County	5,207	10	0	0	3	7	221	11	210	0	0
Union Township, Schuylkill County	1,277	0	0	0	0	0	0	0	0	0	0
Upland	3,249	101	1	2	9	89	143	41	89	13	0
Upper Allen Township	18,117	3	0	2	1	0	210	28	176	6	1
Upper Burrell Township	2,333	0	0	0	0	0	40	6	34	0	0
Upper Chichester Township	16,791	47	1	5	14	27	519	81	412	26	13
Upper Darby Township	83,059	423	3	20	240	160	2,233	347	1,744	142	4
Upper Dublin Township	25,651	25	0	7	3	15	245	33	205	7	2
Upper Gwynedd Township	15,602	11	0	0	0	11	124	15	105	4	1
Upper Leacock Township	8,736	4	0	0	4	0	103	34	67	2	0
Upper Makefield Township	8,216	4	0	0	0	4	58	22	35	1	0
Upper Merion Township	28,486	24	3	0	13	8	1,421	64	1,328	29	1
Upper Moreland Township	24,092	11	0	2	8	1	493	43	431	19	1
Upper Perkiomen	6,815	6	0	2	0	4	133	22	108	3	0
Upper Pottsgrove Township	5,332	7	0	0	1	6	63	15	48	0	0
Upper Providence Township, Montgomery County	21,287	8	0	2	2	4	298	30	263	5	0
Upper Saucon Township	14,855	7	0	4	0	3	203	28	175	0	1
Upper Southampton Township	15,200	8	0	0	2	6	161	32	123	6	0
Upper St. Clair Township	19,290	4	0	0	1	3	95	5	90	0	0
Upper Uwchlan Township	11,263	2	0	1	0	1	37	8	29	0	1
Upper Yoder Township	5,466	13	0	0	2	11	13	0	13	0	0
Uwchlan Township	18,146	18	1	4	2	11	169	31	135	3	0
Valley Township	6,816	44	0	0	2	42	137	29	103	5	0
Vandergrift	5,222	29	0	3	4	22	15	5	9	1	0

[1] If a blank is presented in the arson column, it indicates that the FBI did not receive 12 complete months of arson data for that agency.

Table II-8.   Offenses Known to Law Enforcement, by Selected State and City, 2011—*Continued*

(Number.)

State/City	Population	Violent crime	Murder and non-negligent man-slaughter	Forcible rape	Robbery	Aggravated assault	Property crime	Burglary	Larceny-theft	Motor vehicle theft	Arson[1]
Pennsylvania—*Continued*											
Vandling	753	0	0	0	0	0	2	0	1	1	0
Vernon Township	5,648	1	0	0	0	1	99	6	93	0	0
Verona	2,482	6	0	1	0	5	95	13	81	1	0
Versailles	1,520	8	0	0	0	8	28	7	21	0	0
Vintondale	415	0	0	0	0	0	0	0	0	0	0
Walnutport	2,077	1	0	0	0	1	19	3	15	1	0
Wampum	719	0	0	0	0	0	8	1	7	0	0
Warminster Township	32,786	30	1	5	16	8	584	70	501	13	3
Warren	9,741	41	0	5	0	36	260	36	220	4	0
Warrington Township	23,493	25	2	3	3	17	223	28	189	6	1
Warwick Township, Bucks County	14,483	12	0	0	1	11	103	14	87	2	2
Washington, Washington County	13,707	91	0	17	30	44	596	155	406	35	5
Washington Township, Fayette County	3,914	10	0	0	0	10	62	12	49	1	1
Washington Township, Franklin County	14,054	12	0	4	3	5	257	46	201	10	0
Washington Township, Northampton County	5,138	2	0	1	1	0	55	9	43	3	1
Washington Township, Westmoreland County	7,446	12	2	0	1	9	45	10	34	1	1
Watsontown	2,358	6	0	1	0	5	66	12	51	3	2
Waymart	1,345	0	0	0	0	0	10	2	8	0	0
Waynesboro	10,602	22	1	1	11	9	177	35	137	5	1
Waynesburg	4,189	12	0	0	0	12	79	22	55	2	1
Weatherly	2,533	19	0	1	0	18	93	32	59	2	0
Wellsboro	3,273	1	0	1	0	0	40	3	36	1	0
West Brandywine Township	7,418	13	0	1	0	12	98	19	72	7	0
West Carroll Township	1,300	1	0	1	0	0	5	0	5	0	0
West Chester	18,520	98	1	12	53	32	495	95	377	23	0
West Cocalico Township	7,303	4	0	0	0	4	67	22	41	4	2
West Cornwall Township	1,982	0	0	0	0	0	3	1	2	0	0
West Deer Township	11,809	5	0	1	0	4	128	33	86	9	0
West Earl Township	7,893	11	0	2	0	9	56	9	40	7	0
Western Berks Regional	4,570	4	0	0	1	3	55	9	46	0	0
West Fallowfield Township	2,574	1	0	0	0	1	37	7	30	0	0
West Goshen Township	21,936	24	0	2	5	17	390	37	344	9	1
West Hazleton	4,609	25	0	1	7	17	195	45	141	9	0
West Hempfield Township	16,205	16	1	1	7	7	276	54	218	4	1
West Hills Regional	10,943	2	0	0	0	2	98	30	66	2	1
West Homestead	1,935	17	1	2	5	9	53	13	40	0	0
West Lampeter Township	15,258	8	0	1	3	4	181	32	142	7	1
West Lebanon Township	783	4	0	0	2	2	86	11	74	1	0
West Mahanoy Township	2,881	0	0	0	0	0	12	2	10	0	0
West Manchester Township	18,954	31	0	0	16	15	620	57	553	10	0
West Manheim Township	7,769	2	0	0	1	1	70	21	48	1	0
West Mayfield Borough	1,243	2	0	2	0	0	15	5	9	1	0
West Mead Township	5,266	0	0	0	0	0	15	5	10	0	0
West Mifflin	20,378	45	0	4	20	21	601	95	488	18	1
West Newton	2,641	6	0	0	0	6	82	22	59	1	0
West Norriton Township	15,713	27	0	1	4	22	274	38	221	15	0
West Nottingham Township	2,731	1	0	0	0	1	9	3	6	0	0
West Pike Run	1,592	0	0	0	0	0	13	0	13	0	0
West Pittston	4,884	8	0	0	2	6	159	19	137	3	0
West Pottsgrove Township	3,886	11	0	2	5	4	148	21	121	6	1
West Reading	4,225	19	0	0	4	15	218	24	185	9	0
West Sadsbury Township	2,452	1	0	0	0	1	81	0	76	5	0
West Salem Township	3,549	1	0	0	0	1	42	12	28	2	0
West Shore Regional	7,648	5	0	2	2	1	82	19	56	7	0
Westtown-East Goshen Regional	31,972	13	0	1	3	9	354	34	307	13	5
West View	6,793	15	0	1	2	12	169	18	143	8	1
West Vincent Township	4,582	1	0	0	0	1	30	14	16	0	2
West Whiteland Township	18,332	10	0	1	5	4	487	34	443	10	2
West York	4,632	14	0	3	2	9	71	6	63	2	0
Whitaker Borough	1,275	2	0	0	0	2	33	7	21	5	0
Whitehall	13,988	13	0	0	2	11	64	11	50	3	0
Whitehall Township	26,823	35	0	3	22	10	1,456	108	1,294	54	2
White Haven Borough	1,100	1	0	1	0	0	6	0	4	2	0
Whitemarsh Township	17,404	11	0	0	6	5	211	34	169	8	0
White Oak	7,887	3	0	0	1	2	76	12	59	5	0
White Township	1,398	3	0	0	1	2	34	10	20	4	0
Whitpain Township	18,935	18	0	1	3	14	261	32	224	5	1
Wiconisco Township	1,214	0	0	0	0	0	3	0	3	0	0
Wilkes-Barre	41,630	213	2	12	129	70	1,483	317	1,080	86	4
Wilkes-Barre Township	2,976	15	0	0	10	5	651	16	622	13	3
Williamsburg	1,258	0	0	0	0	0	14	0	13	1	0
Williamsport	29,475	100	1	8	56	35	1,254	222	982	50	8
Willistown Township	10,530	9	0	0	1	8	89	8	80	1	0
Wind Gap	2,729	5	0	3	0	2	52	0	48	4	0
Womelsdorf	2,819	9	0	1	0	8	32	6	13	13	2

[1] If a blank is presented in the arson column, it indicates that the FBI did not receive 12 complete months of arson data for that agency.

Table II-8. Offenses Known to Law Enforcement, by Selected State and City, 2011—*Continued*

(Number.)

State/City	Population	Violent crime	Murder and non-negligent man-slaughter	Forcible rape	Robbery	Aggravated assault	Property crime	Burglary	Larceny-theft	Motor vehicle theft	Arson[1]
Pennsylvania—*Continued*											
Woodward Township	2,380	0	0	0	0	0	85	4	81	0	0
Wrightsville	2,317	17	0	3	4	10	43	2	39	2	0
Wright Township	5,669	2	0	0	0	2	93	5	86	2	0
Wyoming	3,083	4	0	0	1	3	82	11	68	3	2
Wyomissing	10,494	12	0	1	4	7	537	35	497	5	0
Yeadon	11,479	70	0	3	45	22	390	99	254	37	2
York	43,857	721	16	60	333	312	1,731	429	1,147	155	26
York Area Regional	60,596	82	0	5	14	63	653	115	510	28	3
Zelienople	3,824	9	0	0	0	9	67	6	61	0	0
Zerbe Township	1,878	0	0	0	0	0	4	1	3	0	0
Rhode Island											
Barrington	16,290	8	0	1	0	7	181	41	137	3	2
Bristol	22,927	12	0	2	1	9	311	57	252	2	3
Burrillville	15,936	10	0	2	0	8	178	36	124	18	3
Central Falls	19,353	119	0	16	29	74	617	194	346	77	8
Charlestown	7,818	9	0	1	1	7	92	26	64	2	0
Coventry	34,972	22	0	8	1	13	707	130	553	24	11
Cranston	80,290	104	1	18	30	55	2,043	461	1,423	159	14
Cumberland	33,466	34	0	9	6	19	553	141	387	25	8
East Greenwich	13,130	5	0	0	1	4	131	33	95	3	2
East Providence	46,980	64	1	21	8	34	846	172	607	67	8
Foster	4,600	2	0	0	1	1	39	21	18	0	0
Glocester	9,734	3	0	1	0	2	54	13	36	5	1
Hopkinton	8,178	9	0	1	0	8	85	27	51	7	1
Jamestown	5,399	2	0	0	0	2	125	14	107	4	1
Johnston	28,734	38	0	6	9	23	589	150	389	50	8
Lincoln	21,080	15	0	0	3	12	606	66	495	45	2
Little Compton	3,488	1	0	0	0	1	35	8	26	1	0
Middletown	16,131	9	1	2	1	5	262	52	203	7	2
Narragansett	15,849	12	0	2	2	8	293	60	220	13	2
Newport	24,641	111	0	11	19	81	1,087	217	837	33	13
New Shoreham	1,050	1	0	0	0	1	43	7	36	0	0
North Kingstown	26,454	20	0	5	3	12	440	88	341	11	3
North Providence	32,039	51	0	8	8	35	643	175	422	46	6
North Smithfield	11,953	4	0	0	1	3	161	33	120	8	1
Pawtucket	71,062	275	1	34	100	140	2,311	741	1,302	268	14
Portsmouth	17,368	11	0	2	0	9	293	54	226	13	1
Richmond	7,699	4	0	0	1	3	108	22	83	3	0
Scituate	10,317	3	1	0	0	2	101	35	62	4	1
Smithfield	21,404	19	0	1	3	15	279	43	228	8	5
South Kingstown	30,602	25	0	5	4	16	370	99	262	9	2
Tiverton	15,761	14	0	5	4	5	340	83	235	22	1
Warren	10,598	18	0	3	2	13	250	54	192	4	0
Warwick	82,572	84	0	24	18	42	2,194	366	1,734	94	12
Westerly	22,760	18	0	4	2	12	416	85	320	11	0
West Greenwich	6,128	4	0	0	1	3	81	15	55	11	2
West Warwick	29,156	73	0	14	12	47	641	184	421	36	5
Woonsocket	41,137	174	0	22	53	99	1,330	415	833	82	16
South Carolina											
Abbeville	5,298	71	0	6	1	64	147	31	108	8	1
Aiken	29,868	116	2	12	36	66	1,287	171	1,067	49	4
Allendale	3,523	80	0	1	4	75	115	71	40	4	0
Anderson	26,997	209	3	9	50	147	2,028	481	1,405	142	11
Andrews	2,894	12	0	2	3	7	196	50	137	9	0
Aynor	567	1	0	0	1	0	32	6	25	1	1
Bamberg	3,649	13	0	0	2	11	164	41	113	10	1
Barnwell	4,805	37	0	0	18	19	409	134	270	5	2
Batesburg-Leesville	5,424	61	0	3	11	47	321	78	233	10	2
Beaufort	12,505	177	2	7	45	123	769	132	618	19	2
Belton	4,182	14	0	1	2	11	157	30	118	9	2
Bennettsville	9,175	129	3	4	14	108	592	109	471	12	4
Bishopville	3,511	21	0	1	4	16	180	38	129	13	2
Blacksburg	1,870	23	0	0	0	23	119	28	81	10	1
Blackville	2,434	20	0	0	5	15	116	39	73	4	0
Bluffton	12,676	26	0	0	4	22	390	60	314	16	0
Burnettown	2,704	8	0	1	0	7	45	10	34	1	1
Calhoun Falls	2,027	8	0	0	1	7	34	8	23	3	1
Camden	6,918	73	0	0	15	58	467	152	289	26	1
Cayce	12,674	129	0	2	28	99	716	169	479	68	2
Central	5,219	11	0	0	2	9	288	40	234	14	1
Chapin	1,462	3	0	0	2	1	43	9	33	1	0
Charleston	121,481	398	11	30	162	195	3,754	527	2,957	270	6
Cheraw	5,919	53	0	2	12	39	385	75	301	9	0
Chesnee	878	7	0	1	0	6	81	21	58	2	0

[1] If a blank is presented in the arson column, it indicates that the FBI did not receive 12 complete months of arson data for that agency.

Table II-8.   Offenses Known to Law Enforcement, by Selected State and City, 2011—*Continued*

(Number.)

State/City	Population	Violent crime	Murder and non-negligent man-slaughter	Forcible rape	Robbery	Aggravated assault	Property crime	Burglary	Larceny-theft	Motor vehicle theft	Arson[1]
South Carolina—*Continued*											
Chester	5,672	92	0	1	14	77	272	64	191	17	3
Chesterfield	1,489	9	0	0	1	8	52	7	45	0	0
Clemson	14,067	34	0	1	3	30	391	77	272	42	0
Clinton	8,589	78	0	3	11	64	381	84	282	15	0
Clio	734	2	0	0	0	2	35	8	26	1	0
Clover	5,153	122	1	3	4	114	174	42	121	11	4
Conway	17,302	158	1	11	35	111	887	220	636	31	5
Cottageville	771	6	0	0	1	5	23	6	16	1	1
Coward	761	0	0	0	0	0	9	2	6	1	0
Cowpens	2,187	9	0	0	0	9	95	27	61	7	0
Darlington	6,362	78	0	5	12	61	514	85	405	24	1
Denmark	3,579	29	0	1	2	26	209	62	140	7	0
Dillon	6,867	135	0	2	30	103	636	149	456	31	2
Duncan	3,218	8	0	2	4	2	84	15	59	10	1
Easley	20,226	107	1	8	10	88	1,056	164	837	55	1
Edgefield	4,805	7	0	2	1	4	50	7	38	5	0
Edisto Beach	419	0	0	0	0	0	78	32	43	3	0
Ehrhardt	551	1	0	1	0	0	41	8	31	2	1
Elgin	1,326	5	0	1	3	1	97	8	87	2	0
Estill	2,064	37	0	0	2	35	149	46	99	4	3
Eutawville	319	1	0	0	0	1	21	10	11	0	0
Fairfax	2,049	14	1	0	2	11	106	47	53	6	3
Florence	37,488	351	3	16	76	256	3,230	537	2,530	163	6
Forest Acres	10,482	80	1	1	31	47	687	188	462	37	3
Fort Lawn	905	4	0	0	2	2	56	19	36	1	0
Fort Mill	10,937	55	1	4	5	45	245	43	187	15	5
Fountain Inn	7,890	40	1	1	2	36	182	37	131	14	1
Gaffney	12,559	76	4	10	20	42	444	99	315	30	2
Gaston	1,664	5	0	0	1	4	50	14	35	1	1
Georgetown	9,270	119	0	4	18	97	630	125	476	29	3
Goose Creek	36,357	93	0	7	20	66	857	122	671	64	8
Great Falls	2,002	16	0	2	0	14	104	42	58	4	1
Greeleyville	443	12	0	1	0	11	22	5	17	0	0
Greenville	59,089	485	5	22	110	348	3,495	732	2,540	223	5
Greenwood	23,492	395	3	11	43	338	1,703	364	1,291	48	6
Greer	25,812	99	0	15	12	72	766	118	596	52	4
Hampton	2,841	30	0	1	2	27	161	35	121	5	2
Hanahan	18,207	38	0	0	9	29	502	117	347	38	3
Hardeeville	2,986	33	1	0	16	16	208	45	145	18	0
Harleyville	685	7	0	0	1	6	55	12	40	3	0
Hartsville	7,854	104	2	3	23	76	840	205	610	25	6
Hemingway	464	7	0	0	0	7	66	9	55	2	0
Holly Hill	1,292	12	0	0	3	9	98	15	80	3	1
Honea Path	3,639	76	1	7	1	67	285	99	172	14	0
Inman	2,348	13	0	2	0	11	78	18	59	1	0
Irmo	11,226	48	1	3	6	38	344	69	262	13	0
Isle of Palms	4,181	6	0	1	1	4	181	39	138	4	0
Jackson	1,720	3	0	0	0	3	50	13	34	3	0
Jamestown	73	1	0	0	1	0	0	0	0	0	0
Johnsonville	1,497	8	0	0	1	7	27	12	14	1	0
Johnston	2,390	17	0	1	2	14	59	28	27	4	0
Kingstree	3,367	33	2	3	10	18	234	42	180	12	1
Lake City	6,753	93	0	4	13	76	468	124	320	24	4
Lake View	816	9	1	0	4	4	44	12	30	2	1
Lamar	1,001	5	0	0	2	3	20	5	13	2	1
Lancaster	8,625	137	3	3	14	117	389	98	285	6	1
Landrum	2,404	7	0	2	2	3	45	6	37	2	0
Latta	1,395	26	0	2	3	21	116	21	92	3	3
Laurens	9,245	137	3	8	19	107	613	131	463	19	2
Lexington	18,078	61	0	3	9	49	748	44	670	34	0
Liberty	3,307	11	0	0	1	10	190	17	164	9	0
Loris	2,424	18	0	0	5	13	196	36	148	12	1
Lyman	3,281	6	0	1	0	5	107	15	88	4	0
Manning	4,156	49	0	2	8	39	354	71	270	13	4
Marion	7,020	95	3	3	24	65	674	237	414	23	6
Mauldin	23,156	78	0	7	16	55	493	88	377	28	1
Mayesville	740	6	0	0	3	3	45	27	16	2	0
McBee	877	6	0	0	1	5	36	9	25	2	0
McColl	2,199	23	0	0	4	19	84	32	51	1	0
McCormick	2,815	11	0	0	0	11	87	17	67	3	0
Moncks Corner	7,977	52	3	1	14	34	456	65	350	41	0
Mount Pleasant	68,633	158	2	3	27	126	1,234	175	998	61	0
Mullins	4,717	96	1	1	17	77	465	96	346	23	5
Myrtle Beach	27,425	443	4	36	160	243	4,187	590	3,243	354	2
Newberry	10,397	64	0	1	8	55	487	126	354	7	0

[1] If a blank is presented in the arson column, it indicates that the FBI did not receive 12 complete months of arson data for that agency.

Table II-8.   Offenses Known to Law Enforcement, by Selected State and City, 2011—*Continued*

(Number.)

State/City	Population	Violent crime	Murder and non-negligent man-slaughter	Forcible rape	Robbery	Aggravated assault	Property crime	Burglary	Larceny-theft	Motor vehicle theft	Arson[1]
South Carolina—*Continued*											
New Ellenton	2,076	3	0	0	0	3	57	18	36	3	0
Nichols	372	2	0	0	0	2	19	10	8	1	0
Ninety Six	2,021	8	0	0	1	7	39	6	31	2	0
North Augusta	21,597	41	0	3	18	20	956	148	755	53	3
North Charleston	98,606	653	5	35	184	429	5,579	999	4,092	488	19
North Myrtle Beach	13,912	108	3	13	43	49	1,501	376	1,032	93	2
Orangeburg	14,127	72	0	5	24	43	823	283	486	54	4
Pacolet	2,261	13	0	0	3	10	87	35	49	3	0
Pageland	2,792	34	4	1	2	27	145	27	113	5	0
Pamplico	1,240	2	0	0	0	2	8	1	7	0	0
Pelion	682	5	0	0	0	5	28	2	25	1	0
Pickens	3,162	12	0	4	0	8	147	12	112	23	0
Port Royal	10,802	33	0	2	15	16	240	54	176	10	2
Prosperity	1,194	4	0	0	0	4	28	8	20	0	0
Ridgeland	4,083	8	3	0	1	4	53	6	47	0	1
Rock Hill	66,924	410	4	46	71	289	2,996	537	2,298	161	11
Saluda	3,607	66	3	0	12	51	69	14	52	3	0
Santee	972	9	0	1	3	5	117	27	85	5	0
Scranton	943	4	0	0	0	4	11	2	9	0	0
Seneca	8,196	76	0	4	11	61	377	81	276	20	3
Simpsonville	18,450	54	2	5	15	32	681	120	532	29	3
Society Hill	570	1	0	0	1	0	7	2	5	0	0
South Congaree	2,333	9	2	0	0	7	84	15	62	7	0
Spartanburg	37,444	657	5	12	127	513	2,856	684	1,952	220	24
Springdale	2,667	10	0	1	2	7	84	14	63	7	0
St. George	2,108	12	0	0	4	8	117	22	90	5	1
St. Matthews	2,045	17	0	1	1	15	42	11	31	0	0
St. Stephen	1,717	10	0	0	4	6	139	48	83	8	0
Sullivans Island	1,812	0	0	0	0	0	29	3	26	0	0
Summerton	1,012	15	0	1	4	10	63	19	44	0	0
Sumter	40,996	343	3	11	72	257	2,353	789	1,426	138	14
Surfside Beach	3,882	24	0	3	4	17	380	104	263	13	1
Swansea	837	7	0	1	1	5	29	5	22	2	0
Tega Cay	7,709	3	0	1	1	1	75	13	62	0	1
Timmonsville	2,347	21	0	2	2	17	184	66	109	9	3
Travelers Rest	4,629	10	1	0	4	5	225	32	177	16	0
Turbeville	775	6	0	1	0	5	21	11	6	4	0
Union	8,491	71	2	4	13	52	403	76	312	15	1
Wagener	806	5	0	0	1	4	40	11	24	5	0
Walhalla	4,313	12	0	2	1	9	111	29	73	9	0
Walterboro	5,461	50	0	5	14	31	655	108	523	24	3
Ware Shoals	2,195	26	0	2	3	21	132	34	91	7	1
Wellford	2,406	3	0	0	0	3	42	10	31	1	1
West Columbia	15,163	168	0	10	41	117	975	154	750	71	3
Westminster	2,446	14	0	1	4	9	104	24	73	7	0
West Pelzer	890	5	0	0	1	4	104	8	92	4	0
West Union	294	3	0	0	0	3	36	8	28	0	0
Whitmire	1,458	6	0	0	1	5	49	9	40	0	0
Williamston	3,980	20	0	1	0	19	184	40	134	10	0
Williston	3,176	14	0	0	1	13	173	62	108	3	2
Woodruff	4,138	20	0	0	3	17	110	22	85	3	1
Yemassee	1,039	1	0	0	1	0	44	7	33	4	1
York	7,826	99	1	4	12	82	428	78	327	23	1
South Dakota											
Aberdeen	26,408	70	0	21	4	45	488	76	380	32	3
Armour	708	0	0	0	0	0	2	2	0	0	0
Avon	597	0	0	0	0	0	0	0	0	0	0
Belle Fourche	5,662	15	0	5	0	10	90	16	72	2	0
Box Elder	7,895	17	0	4	0	13	174	11	159	4	0
Brandon	8,892	2	0	0	0	2	30	0	30	0	0
Brookings	22,324	7	1	0	0	6	33	6	27	0	0
Burke	611	0	0	0	0	0	0	0	0	0	0
Canton	3,094	5	0	3	0	2	44	8	36	0	0
Centerville	893	1	0	0	1	0	1	1	0	0	0
Chamberlain	2,416	4	0	0	2	2	13	1	11	1	0
Deadwood	1,285	4	0	0	0	4	41	5	36	0	0
Eagle Butte	1,334	1	0	0	0	1	5	1	4	0	0
Estelline	777	0	0	0	0	0	6	4	2	0	0
Faith	426	0	0	0	0	0	2	0	2	0	0
Flandreau	2,369	14	0	0	0	14	45	3	36	6	0
Freeman	1,322	1	0	1	0	0	3	1	2	0	0
Gettysburg	1,176	1	0	1	0	0	1	0	1	0	0
Hermosa	403	0	0	0	0	0	0	0	0	0	0
Hot Springs	3,756	3	0	1	0	2	58	10	43	5	0
Hoven	411	0	0	0	0	0	0	0	0	0	0

[1] If a blank is presented in the arson column, it indicates that the FBI did not receive 12 complete months of arson data for that agency.

Table II-8.   Offenses Known to Law Enforcement, by Selected State and City, 2011—*Continued*

(Number.)

State/City	Population	Violent crime	Murder and non-negligent man-slaughter	Forcible rape	Robbery	Aggravated assault	Property crime	Burglary	Larceny-theft	Motor vehicle theft	Arson[1]
South Dakota—*Continued*											
Irene	425	0	0	0	0	0	1	1	0	0	0
Jefferson	554	0	0	0	0	0	0	0	0	0	0
Kadoka	662	1	0	0	0	1	8	8	0	0	0
Kimball	712	0	0	0	0	0	0	0	0	0	0
Lead	3,162	0	0	0	0	0	15	0	14	1	0
Lemmon	1,242	2	0	1	0	1	6	3	3	0	0
Lennox	2,137	1	0	0	0	1	12	4	8	0	0
Leola	463	0	0	0	0	0	0	0	0	0	0
Madison	6,553	5	0	0	0	5	100	12	80	8	0
Martin	1,084	6	0	1	0	5	6	1	4	1	0
McIntosh	175	0	0	0	0	0	0	0	0	0	0
Menno	615	0	0	0	0	0	0	0	0	0	0
Miller	1,507	0	0	0	0	0	6	1	5	0	0
Mitchell	15,440	44	0	6	2	36	406	50	334	22	1
Mobridge	3,507	7	1	0	0	6	85	8	72	5	0
North Sioux City	2,561	0	0	0	0	0	46	6	40	0	0
Parkston	1,526	0	0	0	0	0	2	1	1	0	0
Philip	788	0	0	0	0	0	2	1	1	0	0
Pierre	13,812	26	0	7	2	17	498	82	392	24	3
Rapid City	68,782	437	3	99	57	278	2,960	560	2,244	156	9
Rosholt	428	0	0	0	0	0	0	0	0	0	0
Scotland	851	0	0	0	0	0	0	0	0	0	0
Selby	650	0	0	0	0	0	0	0	0	0	0
Sioux Falls	155,760	440	5	108	75	252	4,707	880	3,554	273	60
Sisseton	2,500	12	0	1	0	11	99	13	74	12	0
Spearfish	10,622	18	0	3	0	15	337	36	291	10	0
Springfield	2,013	0	0	0	0	0	0	0	0	0	0
Sturgis	6,708	10	0	1	0	9	121	22	91	8	0
Summerset	1,836	0	0	0	0	0	17	5	11	1	0
Tea	3,852	3	0	0	0	3	92	19	66	7	2
Tripp	655	0	0	0	0	0	0	0	0	0	0
Tyndall	1,080	0	0	0	0	0	0	0	0	0	0
Vermillion	10,700	5	0	1	0	4	52	8	39	5	0
Viborg	792	0	0	0	0	0	4	1	3	0	0
Wagner	1,585	0	0	0	0	0	11	0	9	2	2
Watertown	21,743	67	1	15	3	48	531	82	412	37	2
Whitewood	938	5	0	0	1	4	7	0	7	0	0
Wilmot	498	0	0	0	0	0	0	0	0	0	0
Winner	2,932	6	0	1	0	5	16	5	11	0	0
Worthing	888	0	0	0	0	0	0	0	0	0	0
Yankton	14,630	33	1	12	2	18	363	40	302	21	0
Tennessee											
Adamsville	2,227	5	0	0	0	5	48	10	36	2	1
Alamo	2,483	12	0	0	2	10	44	12	30	2	0
Alcoa	8,525	89	0	5	22	62	521	83	418	20	1
Alexandria	975	6	0	0	0	6	24	9	14	1	0
Algood	3,527	10	0	0	1	9	127	21	105	1	0
Ardmore	1,224	5	0	0	0	5	38	14	21	3	0
Ashland City	4,582	20	1	3	2	14	260	61	186	13	1
Athens	13,579	177	1	6	32	138	1,021	185	796	40	2
Atoka	8,463	9	0	1	0	8	130	24	98	8	0
Baileyton	435	2	0	0	1	1	9	3	5	1	0
Baneberry	486	0	0	0	0	0	0	0	0	0	0
Bartlett	55,106	116	0	6	6	104	808	134	632	42	4
Baxter	1,377	7	0	0	1	6	78	20	55	3	0
Bean Station	2,851	11	0	0	5	6	137	34	102	1	0
Belle Meade	2,938	0	0	0	0	0	52	8	44	0	0
Bells	2,459	17	1	1	3	12	40	11	26	3	0
Benton	1,397	3	0	0	0	3	48	10	36	2	0
Berry Hill	542	2	0	0	0	2	74	9	61	4	0
Bethel Springs	724	0	0	0	0	0	2	1	1	0	0
Big Sandy	562	0	0	0	0	0	3	1	2	0	0
Blaine	1,873	4	0	0	1	3	24	7	15	2	0
Bluff City	1,749	11	0	1	1	9	61	8	50	3	0
Bolivar	5,466	36	1	1	3	31	352	134	207	11	2
Bradford	1,057	5	0	0	0	5	12	4	8	0	0
Brentwood	37,394	18	0	1	2	15	373	51	313	9	1
Brighton	2,760	8	0	0	0	8	42	9	30	3	0
Bristol	26,943	115	0	20	11	84	1,187	196	943	48	5
Brownsville	10,385	155	1	8	15	131	585	234	346	5	2
Bruceton	1,491	18	0	1	0	17	25	9	16	0	1
Burns	1,481	2	1	0	0	1	19	9	8	2	0
Calhoun	494	1	0	0	0	1	7	0	7	0	0
Camden	3,614	9	0	1	1	7	200	53	141	6	2
Carthage	2,327	4	0	0	0	4	55	12	43	0	0

[1] If a blank is presented in the arson column, it indicates that the FBI did not receive 12 complete months of arson data for that agency.

Table II-8. Offenses Known to Law Enforcement, by Selected State and City, 2011—*Continued*

(Number.)

State/City	Population	Violent crime	Murder and non-negligent man-slaughter	Forcible rape	Robbery	Aggravated assault	Property crime	Burglary	Larceny-theft	Motor vehicle theft	Arson[1]
Tennessee—*Continued*											
Caryville	2,318	11	0	0	1	10	93	16	70	7	0
Celina	1,508	7	0	0	1	6	22	8	13	1	1
Centerville	3,677	7	1	0	1	5	61	13	47	1	1
Chapel Hill	1,458	3	0	0	0	3	8	2	6	0	0
Charleston	657	1	0	0	0	1	11	3	8	0	0
Chattanooga	169,187	1,460	24	36	385	1,015	10,635	2,503	7,338	794	11
Church Hill	6,798	20	0	0	4	16	118	27	88	3	2
Clarksburg	397	0	0	0	0	0	6	0	4	2	0
Clarksville	134,128	883	8	61	128	686	4,217	1,333	2,666	218	22
Cleveland	41,657	437	2	21	50	364	2,260	437	1,735	88	9
Clifton	2,718	0	0	0	0	0	14	2	11	1	0
Clinton	9,930	49	1	1	6	41	457	76	355	26	3
Collegedale	8,357	11	0	2	1	8	175	30	141	4	1
Collierville	44,362	46	0	6	4	36	690	100	577	13	0
Collinwood	991	1	0	0	1	0	11	7	2	2	0
Columbia	34,994	304	3	21	31	249	1,408	276	1,079	53	2
Coopertown	4,317	3	0	0	0	3	36	13	20	3	0
Copperhill	357	0	0	0	0	0	5	2	3	0	0
Cornersville	1,205	1	0	0	0	1	3	0	2	1	0
Covington	9,120	59	1	4	17	37	460	120	326	14	0
Cowan	1,753	3	0	0	0	3	22	1	20	1	0
Cross Plains	1,729	9	0	1	1	7	44	6	37	1	0
Crossville	10,892	166	0	7	22	137	1,207	252	908	47	1
Crump	1,441	4	0	1	1	2	30	10	19	1	2
Cumberland City	314	1	0	0	0	1	10	3	6	1	0
Cumberland Gap	498	2	1	0	0	1	2	0	2	0	0
Dandridge	2,837	10	0	2	1	7	105	17	83	5	2
Dayton	7,256	13	0	0	4	9	216	32	178	6	0
Decatur	1,612	3	0	0	0	3	47	12	32	3	0
Decaturville	875	1	0	0	0	1	7	1	5	1	0
Decherd	2,382	6	0	1	0	5	54	13	41	0	0
Dickson	14,669	98	4	8	10	76	800	97	678	25	0
Dover	1,430	2	0	0	0	2	25	3	21	1	0
Dresden	3,032	9	0	0	0	9	97	17	79	1	0
Dunlap	4,858	19	0	2	0	17	202	34	152	16	1
Eagleville	609	0	0	0	0	0	1	0	1	0	0
East Ridge	21,168	170	1	4	45	120	979	264	640	75	5
Elizabethton	14,304	44	1	2	9	32	819	131	667	21	2
Elkton	583	0	0	0	0	0	3	2	1	0	0
Englewood	1,546	7	0	0	1	6	35	9	24	2	0
Erin	1,336	3	0	0	0	3	33	5	27	1	1
Erwin	6,152	14	0	0	2	12	152	27	120	5	0
Estill Springs	2,074	2	0	0	1	1	35	10	22	3	0
Ethridge	469	1	0	0	0	1	23	5	18	0	0
Etowah	3,521	16	0	2	3	11	148	41	97	10	1
Fairview	7,790	11	0	1	0	10	112	21	86	5	2
Fayetteville	6,889	61	0	1	11	49	464	93	362	9	3
Franklin	63,051	103	0	11	11	81	1,021	88	898	35	3
Friendship	674	2	0	0	0	2	5	1	4	0	0
Gadsden	474	2	0	0	0	2	5	2	3	0	0
Gainesboro	971	2	0	0	0	2	44	1	43	0	0
Gallatin	30,551	86	0	7	17	62	625	87	519	19	0
Gallaway	686	7	0	0	1	6	20	5	14	1	0
Gates	653	1	0	0	0	1	14	8	6	0	0
Gatlinburg	3,980	22	2	1	5	14	367	132	230	5	3
Germantown	39,194	28	0	3	3	22	473	123	343	7	2
Gibson	400	2	0	0	0	2	9	4	5	0	0
Gleason	1,458	6	0	0	0	6	10	3	7	0	0
Goodlettsville	16,065	71	0	4	24	43	1,078	158	897	23	2
Gordonsville	1,224	3	0	0	1	2	29	9	20	0	0
Grand Junction	328	2	0	0	0	2	15	2	12	1	0
Graysville	1,516	2	0	0	0	2	21	1	20	0	0
Greenbrier	6,491	18	0	0	3	15	100	28	69	3	0
Greeneville	15,198	82	1	4	19	58	861	166	659	36	1
Greenfield	2,202	3	0	0	1	2	37	12	23	2	0
Halls	2,275	4	0	2	0	2	33	10	23	0	0
Harriman	6,407	37	0	6	3	28	342	83	232	27	0
Henderson	6,366	26	1	0	2	23	179	56	118	5	0
Hendersonville	51,835	121	2	5	15	99	908	141	716	51	6
Hohenwald	3,791	24	0	0	1	23	149	23	123	3	0
Hollow Rock	724	6	0	0	0	6	21	7	10	4	0
Hornbeak	428	0	0	0	0	0	3	1	2	0	0
Humboldt	8,528	86	1	6	4	75	412	103	296	13	3
Huntingdon	4,021	10	0	1	1	8	151	16	130	5	0
Huntland	880	4	0	0	0	4	5	1	3	1	0
Jacksboro	2,038	3	0	0	0	3	158	9	149	0	0

[1] If a blank is presented in the arson column, it indicates that the FBI did not receive 12 complete months of arson data for that agency.

Table II-8.   Offenses Known to Law Enforcement, by Selected State and City, 2011—*Continued*

(Number.)

State/City	Population	Violent crime	Murder and non-negligent man-slaughter	Forcible rape	Robbery	Aggravated assault	Property crime	Burglary	Larceny-theft	Motor vehicle theft	Arson[1]
Tennessee—*Continued*											
Jackson	65,799	675	6	43	156	470	3,746	1,126	2,397	223	20
Jamestown	1,977	4	0	0	0	4	146	18	128	0	1
Jasper	3,309	15	0	0	0	15	76	21	51	4	0
Jefferson City	8,120	12	0	2	5	5	471	97	358	16	0
Jellico	2,376	3	0	0	2	1	94	13	71	10	3
Johnson City	63,722	278	3	7	59	209	2,958	682	2,187	89	6
Jonesborough	5,097	12	0	0	2	10	103	24	71	8	0
Kenton	1,293	3	0	0	0	3	24	9	14	1	0
Kimball	1,408	8	0	0	3	5	92	9	76	7	0
Kingsport	48,640	428	3	22	62	341	3,240	552	2,556	132	12
Kingston	5,988	8	0	0	2	6	105	18	80	7	0
Kingston Springs	2,781	2	0	0	1	1	16	5	10	1	0
Knoxville	180,488	1,691	17	94	559	1,021	12,879	2,544	9,515	820	26
Lafayette	4,514	13	0	1	0	12	67	24	39	4	0
La Follette	7,523	61	1	3	11	46	713	251	444	18	2
Lake City	1,797	13	0	1	2	10	100	25	68	7	2
La Vergne	32,882	132	2	9	12	109	823	299	485	39	4
Lawrenceburg	10,522	93	0	7	7	79	547	132	396	19	2
Lebanon	26,426	183	0	9	35	139	1,091	223	808	60	0
Lenoir City	8,720	49	0	1	10	38	527	131	374	22	2
Lewisburg	11,200	70	2	14	7	47	313	80	223	10	5
Lexington	7,721	77	0	0	5	72	498	97	391	10	0
Livingston	4,095	26	0	0	0	26	107	21	78	8	0
Lookout Mountain	1,849	0	0	0	0	0	14	2	10	2	0
Loretto	1,729	1	0	0	0	1	31	9	22	0	0
Loudon	5,430	7	0	0	0	7	63	4	53	6	0
Madisonville	4,618	20	0	0	3	17	303	74	216	13	3
Manchester	10,193	60	1	2	7	50	642	107	500	35	1
Martin	11,576	45	1	3	1	40	295	62	230	3	2
Maryville	27,713	74	0	8	22	44	852	148	665	39	2
Mason	1,624	20	0	0	3	17	29	10	19	0	0
Maury City	680	3	0	0	0	3	5	1	3	1	0
Maynardville	2,435	5	0	0	0	5	113	26	84	3	0
McEwen	1,766	2	0	0	1	1	14	4	8	2	0
McKenzie	5,358	32	1	1	4	26	172	43	126	3	3
McMinnville	13,728	76	0	6	5	65	627	133	462	32	3
Medina	3,510	5	0	0	0	5	50	11	38	1	1
Memphis	652,725	10,336	117	398	3,083	6,738	42,355	13,254	25,667	3,434	319
Milan	7,922	66	1	3	8	54	313	81	228	4	3
Millersville	6,498	13	0	1	0	12	138	44	84	10	0
Millington	10,268	89	0	1	18	70	554	82	438	34	1
Minor Hill	542	0	0	0	0	0	0	0	0	0	0
Monteagle	1,203	3	0	0	1	2	21	7	11	3	1
Monterey	2,876	10	0	1	1	8	48	20	23	5	0
Morristown	29,400	195	1	13	35	146	1,964	200	1,667	97	4
Moscow	561	2	0	0	1	1	25	3	22	0	0
Mountain City	2,554	5	0	0	0	5	37	5	29	3	0
Mount Carmel	5,478	6	0	1	1	4	80	19	58	3	0
Mount Juliet	23,885	55	0	1	10	44	459	77	367	15	0
Mount Pleasant	4,602	29	0	1	0	28	126	27	94	5	1
Munford	5,980	28	2	1	1	24	129	26	97	6	1
Murfreesboro	109,736	654	3	30	131	490	4,851	1,383	3,283	185	2
Nashville	612,789	7,239	50	373	1,889	4,927	29,256	7,541	19,987	1,728	103
Newbern	3,343	22	1	0	3	18	120	33	86	1	0
New Hope	1,092	0	0	0	0	0	0	0	0	0	0
New Market	1,346	1	0	0	1	0	7	2	5	0	0
Newport	7,008	78	0	6	15	57	698	87	585	26	2
New Tazewell	3,064	6	0	0	2	4	54	20	31	3	0
Niota	725	3	0	0	0	3	12	4	8	0	0
Nolensville	5,914	2	0	0	0	2	42	8	31	3	0
Norris	1,504	2	0	0	0	2	43	8	34	1	0
Oakland	6,683	7	0	1	0	6	64	4	60	0	0
Oak Ridge	29,595	137	2	15	24	96	1,154	258	868	28	3
Obion	1,129	8	0	0	0	8	29	4	24	1	1
Oliver Springs	3,260	10	1	0	4	5	133	25	95	13	0
Oneida	3,786	25	1	0	1	23	218	43	164	11	3
Paris	10,248	44	0	5	6	33	493	147	333	13	0
Parsons	2,394	6	0	0	0	6	41	9	29	3	0
Pigeon Forge	5,928	33	0	4	7	22	670	219	396	55	2
Pikeville	1,623	6	0	0	0	6	33	9	24	0	0
Piperton	1,458	5	0	0	1	4	17	2	15	0	0
Pittman Center	507	0	0	0	0	0	20	12	7	1	0
Plainview	2,144	4	1	0	0	3	49	11	37	1	0
Pleasant View	4,186	1	0	1	0	0	53	15	33	5	0
Portland	11,584	37	0	4	3	30	384	99	264	21	3
Powells Crossroads	1,334	1	0	0	0	1	0	0	0	0	0

[1] If a blank is presented in the arson column, it indicates that the FBI did not receive 12 complete months of arson data for that agency.

Table II-8.   Offenses Known to Law Enforcement, by Selected State and City, 2011—*Continued*

(Number.)

State/City	Population	Violent crime	Murder and non-negligent man-slaughter	Forcible rape	Robbery	Aggravated assault	Property crime	Burglary	Larceny-theft	Motor vehicle theft	Arson[1]
Tennessee—*Continued*											
Pulaski	7,941	42	1	3	10	28	336	79	251	6	0
Puryear	677	4	0	0	0	4	13	2	11	0	0
Red Bank	11,756	70	2	5	9	54	571	160	380	31	3
Red Boiling Springs	1,122	3	0	0	0	3	29	12	17	0	0
Ridgely	1,811	5	0	0	1	4	41	9	30	2	0
Ridgetop	1,891	3	0	1	0	2	23	4	17	2	0
Ripley	8,521	103	1	3	17	82	492	257	217	18	1
Rockwood	5,612	22	0	0	4	18	359	42	298	19	5
Rogersville	4,460	28	0	2	5	21	273	68	201	4	0
Rossville	670	5	0	0	0	5	8	0	8	0	0
Rutledge	1,132	1	0	0	0	1	64	10	52	2	0
Saltillo	306	1	1	0	0	0	2	0	2	0	0
Samburg	219	0	0	0	0	0	0	0	0	0	0
Savannah	7,045	54	0	3	7	44	550	102	420	28	0
Scotts Hill	993	3	0	0	0	3	4	1	3	0	0
Selmer	4,436	33	0	2	3	28	213	60	149	4	1
Sevierville	14,941	94	0	8	27	59	908	133	728	47	4
Sewanee	2,332	3	0	2	0	1	73	35	38	0	1
Sharon	953	0	0	0	0	0	16	2	13	1	0
Shelbyville	20,518	98	0	14	5	79	663	113	528	22	3
Signal Mountain	7,622	3	0	0	0	3	51	17	34	0	0
Smithville	4,571	35	0	8	3	24	253	65	174	14	2
Sneedville	1,400	16	0	0	0	16	101	14	84	3	0
Soddy-Daisy	12,829	49	0	5	2	42	411	107	270	34	0
South Carthage	1,334	7	0	0	0	7	39	7	31	1	0
South Fulton	2,375	11	0	0	2	9	59	28	29	2	0
South Pittsburg	3,019	4	0	0	0	4	37	8	28	1	0
Sparta	4,969	12	0	0	9	3	369	69	289	11	2
Spencer	1,615	2	1	0	1	0	12	4	7	1	0
Spring City	1,999	2	0	0	1	1	42	8	32	2	0
Springfield	16,588	161	4	14	36	107	722	111	561	50	6
Spring Hill	29,298	35	0	6	0	29	357	63	289	5	1
St. Joseph	789	8	0	0	0	8	12	7	3	2	0
Surgoinsville	1,817	2	0	0	0	2	24	6	16	2	0
Sweetwater	5,816	35	0	4	1	30	238	65	157	16	0
Tazewell	2,238	18	0	1	5	12	117	25	86	6	1
Tellico Plains	888	3	0	0	0	3	35	14	19	2	0
Tiptonville	4,504	23	0	0	0	23	71	32	38	1	0
Toone	367	1	0	0	0	1	3	2	1	0	0
Townsend	452	1	0	0	0	1	15	4	11	0	0
Trenton	4,302	53	0	2	3	48	246	35	209	2	0
Trezevant	867	1	0	0	0	1	14	0	12	2	1
Trimble	643	0	0	0	0	0	5	4	1	0	0
Troy	1,383	2	0	0	1	1	45	9	36	0	0
Tullahoma	18,823	117	1	4	21	91	806	181	604	21	4
Tusculum	2,687	2	0	0	1	1	23	3	18	2	0
Union City	10,993	55	0	4	11	40	623	123	483	17	11
Vonore	1,487	9	0	0	1	8	91	18	68	5	0
Wartburg	926	1	0	0	0	1	15	3	10	2	0
Wartrace	657	0	0	0	0	0	9	3	5	1	0
Watauga	462	0	0	0	0	0	4	2	2	0	0
Watertown	1,490	4	0	0	1	3	28	10	17	1	0
Waverly	4,142	5	0	1	0	4	103	34	66	3	1
Waynesboro	2,471	3	0	0	0	3	29	3	25	1	0
Westmoreland	2,226	5	0	0	0	5	47	9	36	2	0
White Bluff	3,235	4	0	1	1	2	72	9	57	6	0
White House	10,348	35	1	5	1	28	217	34	168	15	2
White Pine	2,216	9	0	0	5	4	113	15	92	6	0
Whiteville	4,680	9	0	1	0	8	60	13	43	4	0
Whitwell	1,714	8	0	1	0	7	50	5	42	3	0
Winchester	8,607	76	0	3	7	66	334	83	238	13	0
Winfield	976	2	0	0	0	2	7	3	4	0	0
Woodbury	2,704	10	0	1	1	8	61	10	46	5	0
Texas											
Abernathy	2,864	5	0	0	0	5	44	13	29	2	0
Abilene	119,526	428	5	33	120	270	4,384	1,119	3,093	172	31
Addison	13,331	78	0	10	18	50	898	117	676	105	0
Alamo	18,739	164	3	10	19	132	1,409	190	1,141	78	4
Alamo Heights	7,179	4	0	1	2	1	221	29	190	2	0
Alice	19,506	206	1	12	3	190	1,153	238	851	64	18
Allen	86,019	72	0	12	17	43	1,526	248	1,207	71	1
Alpine	6,029	5	0	0	0	5	91	25	62	4	0
Alton	12,601	14	0	0	6	8	374	78	257	39	11
Alvarado	3,865	9	0	2	1	6	113	23	88	2	0
Alvin	24,746	56	2	10	12	32	758	166	551	41	5

[1] If a blank is presented in the arson column, it indicates that the FBI did not receive 12 complete months of arson data for that agency.

Table II-8. Offenses Known to Law Enforcement, by Selected State and City, 2011—*Continued*

(Number.)

State/City	Population	Violent crime	Murder and non-negligent man-slaughter	Forcible rape	Robbery	Aggravated assault	Property crime	Burglary	Larceny-theft	Motor vehicle theft	Arson[1]
Texas—*Continued*											
Amarillo	194,708	1,223	10	104	235	874	9,388	2,016	6,756	616	75
Andrews	11,321	82	0	12	0	70	232	34	179	19	2
Angleton	19,259	64	1	7	15	41	437	96	327	14	1
Anna	8,423	10	0	4	0	6	129	38	86	5	2
Anson	2,481	7	0	0	0	7	57	18	38	1	0
Anthony	5,116	25	0	0	3	22	177	4	169	4	2
Aransas Pass	8,377	56	2	19	5	30	491	114	361	16	2
Archer City	1,873	6	0	1	0	5	7	2	5	0	0
Arcola	1,677	4	0	0	3	1	34	12	17	5	0
Argyle	3,351	2	0	0	0	2	30	7	23	0	0
Arlington	373,128	1,874	22	136	540	1,176	17,208	4,388	11,757	1,063	37
Arp	990	0	0	0	0	0	0	0	0	0	0
Athens	12,977	67	1	11	20	35	505	131	362	12	1
Atlanta	5,794	30	0	4	4	22	245	63	174	8	0
Aubrey	2,650	4	0	2	0	2	66	13	50	3	0
Austin	807,022	3,471	28	211	1,106	2,126	42,250	7,042	33,069	2,139	127
Azle	11,177	23	0	2	1	20	386	94	280	12	10
Baird	1,527	0	0	0	0	0	5	1	4	0	0
Balch Springs	24,227	191	0	17	48	126	1,524	229	1,171	124	0
Balcones Heights	3,003	27	0	1	9	17	540	44	469	27	0
Ballinger	3,846	17	0	0	0	17	79	8	68	3	0
Bangs	1,637	2	0	0	0	2	12	4	8	0	0
Bastrop	7,370	22	0	1	7	14	399	29	360	10	3
Bay City	17,985	38	4	6	9	19	685	148	531	6	3
Bayou Vista	1,569	1	0	0	0	1	12	2	10	0	0
Baytown	73,313	212	1	13	79	119	3,555	700	2,628	227	29
Beaumont	120,785	1,069	13	65	356	635	6,656	2,035	4,336	285	32
Bedford	47,968	170	0	16	21	133	1,525	417	1,024	84	6
Bee Cave	4,008	5	0	1	1	3	123	8	113	2	0
Beeville	13,134	34	0	4	4	26	314	85	219	10	1
Bellaire	17,210	22	0	0	16	6	336	83	239	14	0
Bellmead	10,109	171	0	9	7	155	982	92	862	28	4
Bellville	4,183	6	0	2	0	4	76	11	63	2	0
Belton	18,599	56	0	0	9	47	678	149	524	5	2
Benbrook	21,681	17	1	2	3	11	533	118	397	18	2
Bertram	1,381	4	0	0	0	4	38	12	23	3	0
Beverly Hills	2,037	10	0	0	5	5	90	20	68	2	0
Big Sandy	1,371	1	0	0	0	1	12	6	5	1	0
Big Spring	27,856	190	0	19	9	162	1,035	231	768	36	1
Bishop	3,200	0	0	0	0	0	68	21	47	0	0
Blanco	1,776	10	0	0	0	10	26	3	22	1	0
Bloomburg	413	0	0	0	0	0	0	0	0	0	0
Blue Mound	2,444	0	0	0	0	0	51	14	36	1	0
Boerne	10,691	17	0	2	5	10	277	30	242	5	0
Bogata	1,177	3	0	0	0	3	31	7	22	2	0
Bonham	10,340	17	0	5	1	11	267	72	189	6	3
Borger	13,530	120	1	6	2	111	512	135	358	19	1
Bovina	1,907	11	0	0	0	11	13	5	8	0	0
Bowie	5,328	7	0	4	2	1	271	49	211	11	0
Brackettville	1,724	0	0	0	0	0	0	0	0	0	0
Brady	5,644	12	0	0	2	10	112	32	77	3	2
Brazoria	3,083	3	0	0	0	3	75	5	69	1	0
Breckenridge	5,902	3	0	0	0	3	55	19	36	0	0
Bremond	949	1	0	0	0	1	3	0	3	0	0
Brenham	16,047	43	1	5	6	31	449	92	338	19	2
Bridge City	8,005	29	0	4	2	23	170	32	127	11	0
Bridgeport	6,102	12	0	0	0	12	81	11	69	1	0
Brookshire	4,801	29	2	2	4	21	109	38	62	9	0
Brookside Village	1,555	5	0	1	0	4	23	15	8	0	0
Brownfield	9,860	28	0	4	4	20	211	72	135	4	2
Brownsville	178,706	500	1	37	109	353	8,187	1,009	7,015	163	20
Brownwood	19,694	89	0	17	6	66	771	118	637	16	4
Bruceville-Eddy	1,506	9	0	3	1	5	32	7	24	1	0
Bryan	77,804	425	2	22	78	323	2,906	681	2,130	95	31
Buda	7,449	5	0	0	3	2	181	18	155	8	0
Bullard	2,515	6	0	1	0	5	59	10	48	1	0
Bulverde	4,727	1	0	0	0	1	65	13	52	0	0
Burkburnett	11,038	23	0	8	2	13	281	68	203	10	2
Burleson	37,462	79	0	11	14	54	1,126	232	841	53	3
Burnet	6,113	23	0	3	0	20	138	41	88	9	1
Cactus	3,246	22	0	2	0	20	4	3	1	0	1
Caddo Mills	1,366	1	0	0	0	1	27	14	11	2	0
Caldwell	4,190	5	0	1	0	4	53	25	24	4	0
Calvert	1,217	5	0	0	0	5	42	20	22	0	1
Cameron	5,669	11	0	1	1	9	244	36	207	1	0
Canton	3,656	2	0	0	0	2	101	16	80	5	0

[1] If a blank is presented in the arson column, it indicates that the FBI did not receive 12 complete months of arson data for that agency.

Table II-8. Offenses Known to Law Enforcement, by Selected State and City, 2011—*Continued*

(Number.)

State/City	Population	Violent crime	Murder and non-negligent man-slaughter	Forcible rape	Robbery	Aggravated assault	Property crime	Burglary	Larceny-theft	Motor vehicle theft	Arson[1]
Texas—*Continued*											
Canyon	13,583	15	0	3	1	11	110	24	83	3	0
Carrollton	121,603	206	3	4	93	106	3,322	896	2,152	274	7
Carthage	6,922	31	0	1	2	28	224	48	168	8	0
Castle Hills	4,203	6	0	0	6	0	304	41	255	8	0
Castroville	2,736	6	0	1	0	5	74	11	62	1	0
Cedar Hill	45,975	108	0	8	33	67	1,612	404	1,122	86	6
Cedar Park	49,967	70	0	7	6	57	692	85	580	27	1
Celina	6,155	2	0	0	0	2	84	26	55	3	0
Center	5,302	42	0	1	7	34	208	31	168	9	0
Childress	6,233	19	0	1	0	18	69	21	45	3	3
Chillicothe	722	5	0	0	0	5	14	4	9	1	0
Cibolo	15,672	21	0	7	2	12	204	32	162	10	0
Cisco	3,981	16	1	2	0	13	76	36	35	5	0
Clarksville	3,354	0	0	0	0	0	70	43	27	0	0
Cleburne	29,954	159	0	37	19	103	1,422	293	1,074	55	1
Cleveland	7,836	61	0	9	16	36	608	126	459	23	3
Clifton	3,514	3	0	0	0	3	18	3	15	0	0
Clint	945	2	0	0	0	2	15	2	12	1	0
Clute	11,447	53	0	2	3	48	280	50	216	14	1
Clyde	3,791	7	0	0	0	7	85	26	55	4	0
Cockrell Hill	4,281	20	0	3	6	11	153	35	101	17	1
Coleman	4,808	9	0	0	0	9	158	71	82	5	0
College Station	95,832	288	1	31	32	224	2,993	651	2,289	53	0
Colleyville	23,287	9	0	0	4	5	191	42	144	5	0
Collinsville	1,658	1	0	0	0	1	25	6	18	1	1
Colorado City	4,233	29	0	0	1	28	140	35	97	8	1
Columbus	3,732	21	1	3	5	12	135	36	93	6	1
Comanche	4,426	16	0	3	0	13	203	29	167	7	2
Combes	2,956	3	0	0	0	3	66	31	32	3	1
Commerce	8,248	20	0	5	5	10	343	107	219	17	3
Conroe	57,390	194	2	12	60	120	2,086	439	1,550	97	4
Converse	18,581	32	0	3	9	20	457	80	356	21	3
Coppell	39,472	33	1	5	3	24	644	134	483	27	7
Copperas Cove	32,706	122	1	9	8	104	910	286	603	21	14
Corinth	20,354	19	0	1	2	16	242	61	169	12	2
Corpus Christi	311,637	1,987	12	194	370	1,411	14,897	2,668	11,762	467	68
Corrigan	1,629	11	0	0	0	11	38	9	27	2	0
Corsicana	24,270	243	0	24	23	196	1,142	347	761	34	0
Cottonwood Shores	1,147	2	0	0	0	2	15	8	6	1	0
Crandall	2,918	1	0	0	0	1	27	8	18	1	0
Crane	3,424	3	0	0	0	3	19	3	16	0	1
Crockett	7,096	15	1	0	0	14	205	58	145	2	0
Crosbyton	1,778	3	0	0	0	3	34	13	21	0	0
Crowell	968	0	0	0	0	0	0	0	0	0	0
Crowley	13,108	20	1	2	1	16	253	76	166	11	0
Crystal City	7,288	8	0	0	0	8	69	21	46	2	1
Cuero	6,985	28	0	0	2	26	103	30	62	11	0
Cumby	793	1	0	0	0	1	31	7	22	2	0
Daingerfield	2,614	21	0	4	3	14	120	47	68	5	4
Dalhart	8,097	26	0	8	1	17	160	45	106	9	3
Dallas	1,223,021	8,330	133	428	4,066	3,703	61,859	18,727	35,148	7,984	596
Dalworthington Gardens	2,307	4	0	0	1	3	24	8	13	3	0
Danbury	1,751	5	0	0	0	5	16	2	14	0	0
Dayton	7,394	11	0	3	4	4	173	46	106	21	0
Decatur	6,169	5	0	2	0	3	175	13	155	7	0
Deer Park	32,684	39	0	14	6	19	836	122	682	32	0
De Kalb	1,735	12	0	0	0	12	63	28	30	5	0
De Leon	2,293	8	2	0	0	6	47	16	30	1	0
Del Rio	36,340	91	1	0	12	78	822	217	587	18	8
Denison	23,159	91	2	9	14	66	1,145	288	807	50	1
Denton	115,769	311	2	53	55	201	3,315	565	2,632	118	28
Denver City	4,573	4	0	2	0	2	49	18	29	2	0
Desoto	50,079	150	5	9	66	70	1,654	565	983	106	9
Devine	4,442	8	0	5	0	3	53	14	38	1	0
Diboll	4,876	14	0	4	0	10	112	35	70	7	1
Dickinson	19,073	48	2	3	12	31	539	106	383	50	0
Dilley	3,976	8	0	0	0	8	89	41	43	5	4
Dimmitt	4,485	4	0	0	1	3	109	29	77	3	0
Donna	16,130	116	0	4	12	100	1,104	264	782	58	5
Double Oak	2,927	0	0	0	0	0	8	2	5	1	0
Driscoll	755	0	0	0	0	0	22	7	15	0	0
Dublin	3,731	11	0	1	0	10	151	47	98	6	2
Dumas	15,000	43	1	13	3	26	336	43	277	16	2
Duncanville	39,335	126	1	9	64	52	1,592	450	993	149	2
Eagle Lake	3,716	3	0	1	0	2	38	9	29	0	0

[1] If a blank is presented in the arson column, it indicates that the FBI did not receive 12 complete months of arson data for that agency.

Table II-8.   Offenses Known to Law Enforcement, by Selected State and City, 2011—*Continued*

(Number.)

State/City	Population	Violent crime	Murder and non-negligent man-slaughter	Forcible rape	Robbery	Aggravated assault	Property crime	Burglary	Larceny-theft	Motor vehicle theft	Arson[1]
Texas—*Continued*											
Eagle Pass	26,800	56	2	0	12	42	873	211	651	11	0
Early	2,820	8	0	0	1	7	54	9	44	1	0
Eastland	4,043	8	0	0	0	8	156	39	108	9	4
East Mountain	814	0	0	0	0	0	8	2	5	1	0
Edcouch	3,228	13	0	0	3	10	82	35	39	8	2
Edgewood	1,471	3	0	0	0	3	76	10	65	1	0
Edinburg	78,722	282	1	28	54	199	4,652	758	3,666	228	19
Edna	5,615	8	0	1	0	7	110	29	80	1	0
El Campo	11,846	49	0	2	4	43	400	82	305	13	2
Electra	2,850	7	0	0	0	7	29	5	18	6	1
Elgin	8,306	12	0	3	6	3	249	68	172	9	2
El Paso	662,780	2,858	16	217	464	2,161	16,312	1,859	12,997	1,456	120
Elsa	5,779	34	0	0	3	31	362	98	247	17	2
Ennis	18,903	76	1	7	20	48	735	157	542	36	1
Euless	52,356	128	0	13	44	71	1,751	473	1,130	148	8
Everman	6,237	37	0	4	11	22	223	79	129	15	1
Fairfield	3,013	7	0	0	2	5	33	16	15	2	0
Fair Oaks Ranch	6,112	3	1	0	0	2	22	9	12	1	0
Falfurrias	5,086	13	1	0	0	12	133	65	68	0	5
Farmers Branch	29,218	37	1	3	19	14	1,027	236	695	96	3
Farmersville	3,370	13	0	1	0	12	110	21	87	2	0
Farwell	1,392	3	0	0	1	2	16	3	12	1	1
Ferris	2,487	11	0	0	3	8	89	22	58	9	0
Flatonia	1,412	2	0	2	0	0	15	8	7	0	0
Florence	1,160	2	0	0	0	2	8	3	5	0	0
Floresville	6,584	1	0	0	0	1	218	40	175	3	1
Flower Mound	66,030	51	0	4	3	44	631	95	495	41	2
Floydada	3,102	17	0	3	1	13	69	32	30	7	0
Forest Hill	12,615	78	0	5	20	53	608	222	331	55	0
Forney	14,970	30	0	5	5	20	285	69	199	17	0
Fort Stockton	8,457	56	2	10	0	44	355	83	264	8	1
Fort Worth	756,803	4,569	48	350	1,267	2,904	35,117	10,058	22,617	2,442	143
Frankston	1,255	2	0	0	1	1	73	23	49	1	0
Fredericksburg	10,752	4	0	0	2	2	227	29	193	5	0
Freeport	12,303	41	0	4	6	31	331	88	229	14	0
Freer	2,877	36	0	0	2	34	85	23	58	4	0
Friendswood	36,558	12	0	6	3	3	331	68	253	10	0
Friona	4,210	7	0	1	0	6	39	21	15	3	0
Frisco	119,451	122	3	6	23	90	2,460	483	1,878	99	4
Gainesville	16,339	63	0	2	11	50	896	210	642	44	13
Galena Park	11,116	17	0	6	7	4	243	82	138	23	0
Galveston[2]	48,748	302	4	58	88	152	2,291	453	1,697	141	3
Ganado	2,045	1	0	0	0	1	0	0	0	0	0
Garden Ridge	3,328	0	0	0	0	0	21	4	17	0	0
Garland	231,650	530	5	55	247	223	8,683	2,244	5,794	645	52
Gatesville	16,082	32	0	9	1	22	204	57	141	6	1
Georgetown	48,397	65	1	16	13	35	780	119	631	30	3
Giddings	4,984	45	0	2	4	39	142	20	115	7	0
Gilmer	5,008	52	0	5	2	45	184	20	148	16	2
Gladewater	6,577	30	0	1	3	26	216	61	144	11	1
Glenn Heights	11,515	45	2	1	5	37	223	93	114	16	4
Godley	1,030	3	0	1	0	2	34	5	29	0	0
Gonzales	7,389	63	0	10	6	47	308	67	226	15	0
Gorman	1,106	2	0	0	0	2	17	9	7	1	0
Graham	9,090	16	2	4	2	8	179	29	141	9	0
Granbury	8,146	21	1	3	4	13	458	57	390	11	0
Grand Prairie	179,087	591	9	69	201	312	6,956	1,808	4,330	818	39
Grand Saline	3,202	4	0	0	0	4	62	21	39	2	0
Granger	1,449	3	0	0	0	3	22	6	15	1	0
Granite Shoals	5,013	8	0	2	0	6	88	41	38	9	0
Grapeland	1,520	7	0	1	1	5	14	9	5	0	0
Grapevine	47,309	91	6	12	18	55	1,489	175	1,208	106	4
Greenville	26,095	181	3	25	40	113	1,064	281	741	42	4
Gregory	1,947	18	0	1	1	16	12	5	6	1	0
Groesbeck	4,419	19	0	1	3	15	54	19	32	3	0
Groves	16,484	59	0	3	14	42	569	153	387	29	1
Gruver	1,219	0	0	0	0	0	23	14	9	0	1
Gun Barrel City	5,791	55	0	3	2	50	306	62	237	7	0
Hale Center	2,299	7	0	0	0	7	17	6	10	1	0
Hallettsville	2,604	7	0	1	1	5	90	11	74	5	0
Hallsville	3,652	0	0	0	0	0	37	16	19	2	0
Haltom City	43,301	119	1	11	30	77	1,718	587	995	136	7
Hamlin	2,169	9	0	0	0	9	43	3	38	2	0
Harker Heights	27,262	71	0	9	19	43	1,003	317	645	41	0
Harlingen	66,214	337	4	18	65	250	4,078	880	3,099	99	34

[1] If a blank is presented in the arson column, it indicates that the FBI did not receive 12 complete months of arson data for that agency.

[2] Because of changes in the state/local agency's reporting practices, figures are not comparable to previous years' data.

Table II-8. Offenses Known to Law Enforcement, by Selected State and City, 2011—*Continued*

(Number.)

State/City	Population	Violent crime	Murder and non-negligent man-slaughter	Forcible rape	Robbery	Aggravated assault	Property crime	Burglary	Larceny-theft	Motor vehicle theft	Arson[1]
Texas—*Continued*											
Haskell	3,392	6	0	0	0	6	62	27	35	0	2
Hawk Cove	493	5	0	0	2	3	11	4	5	2	0
Hawkins	1,305	0	0	0	0	0	40	5	33	2	0
Hawley	647	0	0	0	0	0	11	4	6	1	0
Hearne	4,553	27	0	1	8	18	108	39	66	3	2
Heath	7,067	5	0	1	0	4	72	13	56	3	0
Hedwig Village	2,611	5	0	0	4	1	170	15	135	20	0
Helotes	7,495	4	0	1	0	3	77	10	66	1	0
Hemphill	1,223	0	0	0	0	0	42	15	26	1	0
Hempstead	5,891	20	0	0	5	15	199	75	118	6	2
Henderson	14,001	80	0	2	4	74	570	130	409	31	6
Hereford	15,693	54	0	1	1	52	402	123	254	25	2
Hewitt	13,834	21	0	9	2	10	133	35	90	8	0
Hickory Creek	3,315	13	0	1	5	7	71	7	58	6	0
Hidalgo	11,434	13	0	0	4	9	118	26	81	11	0
Highland Park	8,744	0	0	0	0	0	201	30	162	9	2
Highland Village	15,373	7	0	1	2	4	112	18	91	3	0
Hill Country Village	1,006	0	0	0	0	0	34	8	23	3	0
Hillsboro	8,634	22	0	4	1	17	242	54	181	7	0
Hitchcock	7,107	32	0	3	2	27	225	92	119	14	2
Holliday	1,795	0	0	0	0	0	16	6	10	0	0
Hollywood Park	3,126	1	0	0	0	1	70	6	64	0	0
Hondo	8,988	32	1	6	2	23	242	37	201	4	2
Hooks	2,827	7	0	5	0	2	18	4	12	2	0
Horizon City	17,087	17	0	0	3	14	217	102	91	24	2
Horseshoe Bay	3,490	3	0	1	0	2	69	24	43	2	0
Houston	2,143,628	20,892	198	771	8,054	11,869	108,336	27,459	68,596	12,281	765
Howe	2,655	6	0	0	0	6	36	10	25	1	1
Hubbard	1,453	0	0	0	0	0	14	2	12	0	0
Hudson	4,831	11	1	1	0	9	89	35	49	5	1
Hudson Oaks	1,697	5	0	1	0	4	78	13	63	2	0
Hughes Springs	1,797	7	2	0	1	4	31	7	21	3	0
Humble	15,451	114	2	25	45	42	1,706	161	1,420	125	1
Huntington	2,163	12	0	7	0	5	54	13	37	4	2
Huntsville	39,359	188	1	16	24	147	1,045	269	750	26	1
Hurst	38,123	177	1	8	33	135	1,905	300	1,542	63	0
Hutchins	5,450	23	0	2	4	17	145	29	101	15	0
Hutto	15,007	14	0	0	0	14	123	42	80	1	0
Idalou	2,297	5	0	0	0	5	22	7	12	3	0
Ingleside	9,585	18	0	4	2	12	223	78	138	7	6
Ingram	1,842	8	1	5	0	2	41	9	29	3	1
Iowa Park	6,489	10	0	1	0	9	87	20	63	4	0
Irving	220,841	514	8	25	151	330	6,794	1,603	4,590	601	21
Italy	1,902	16	0	2	0	14	46	8	37	1	0
Itasca	1,679	1	0	0	0	1	9	4	5	0	0
Jacinto City	10,775	18	1	0	8	9	371	102	235	34	2
Jacksboro	4,606	7	0	0	0	7	52	17	35	0	0
Jacksonville	14,850	175	0	16	19	140	827	273	526	28	15
Jamaica Beach	1,004	0	0	0	0	0	0	0	0	0	0
Jarrell	1,005	3	0	0	0	3	21	0	20	1	1
Jasper	7,750	29	0	6	4	19	351	59	284	8	2
Jefferson	2,150	14	0	0	2	12	57	13	41	3	1
Jersey Village	7,780	21	1	0	9	11	256	87	152	17	0
Johnson City	1,691	0	0	0	0	0	21	7	14	0	0
Jones Creek	2,063	0	0	0	0	0	3	1	2	0	0
Jonestown	1,873	2	0	0	0	2	51	17	32	2	0
Joshua	6,034	6	0	0	1	5	18	11	5	2	0
Jourdanton	3,952	7	0	0	1	6	22	8	11	3	1
Junction	2,628	5	0	0	0	5	75	16	58	1	0
Karnes City	3,106	11	0	2	0	9	78	12	64	2	1
Katy	14,399	33	0	0	7	26	578	51	500	27	2
Kaufman	6,844	16	0	0	5	11	141	30	103	8	0
Keene	6,234	2	0	0	1	1	96	23	70	3	0
Keller	40,461	24	2	5	2	15	501	90	398	13	0
Kemah	1,810	11	0	0	4	7	105	22	80	3	0
Kemp	1,178	5	0	0	1	4	24	8	15	1	0
Kenedy	3,365	4	0	0	0	4	143	49	93	1	0
Kennedale	6,905	12	0	4	0	8	251	86	149	16	4
Kerens	1,606	11	0	1	0	10	16	6	10	0	0
Kermit	5,828	11	0	0	1	10	34	15	19	0	0
Kerrville	22,817	45	1	0	10	34	619	73	522	24	6
Kilgore	13,248	41	1	6	6	28	599	84	464	51	1
Killeen	130,613	815	15	69	172	559	5,210	2,034	2,989	187	40
Kingsville	26,765	232	0	18	11	203	1,015	353	635	27	1
Kirby	8,168	35	0	0	7	28	241	44	174	23	1
Kountze	2,168	4	1	0	1	2	29	11	16	2	1

[1] If a blank is presented in the arson column, it indicates that the FBI did not receive 12 complete months of arson data for that agency.

Table II-8.   Offenses Known to Law Enforcement, by Selected State and City, 2011—*Continued*

(Number.)

State/City	Population	Violent crime	Murder and non-negligent man-slaughter	Forcible rape	Robbery	Aggravated assault	Property crime	Burglary	Larceny-theft	Motor vehicle theft	Arson[1]
Texas—*Continued*											
Kress	730	0	0	0	0	0	6	0	2	4	0
Kyle	28,606	81	1	15	5	60	405	69	315	21	3
Lacy-Lakeview	6,626	29	0	5	2	22	264	78	178	8	1
La Feria	7,456	4	0	1	1	2	445	110	334	1	1
Lago Vista	6,168	17	0	2	0	15	101	24	71	6	0
La Grange	4,739	5	0	0	1	4	69	18	46	5	0
La Grulla	1,656	3	0	0	0	3	15	10	3	2	0
Laguna Vista	3,183	5	0	2	0	3	82	21	58	3	0
La Joya	4,069	8	0	0	3	5	44	15	29	0	0
Lake Dallas	7,255	9	0	3	1	5	169	29	131	9	1
Lake Jackson	27,414	40	0	9	11	20	559	126	420	13	0
Lakeside	1,335	0	0	0	0	0	23	10	13	0	0
Lakeview, Harris County	6,382	8	0	0	3	5	75	25	44	6	0
Lakeway	11,631	11	0	3	1	7	154	20	128	6	0
Lake Worth	4,680	13	0	0	8	5	600	129	457	14	0
La Marque	14,814	60	2	4	28	26	678	206	440	32	2
Lamesa	9,620	72	0	12	2	58	213	72	132	9	4
Lampasas	6,822	15	0	4	0	11	205	46	153	6	1
Lancaster	37,126	110	2	12	31	65	1,270	436	724	110	0
La Porte	34,511	46	0	18	10	18	642	152	441	49	5
Laredo	241,059	1,120	11	76	215	818	10,419	1,790	8,143	486	95
La Vernia	1,056	5	0	0	0	5	52	7	43	2	0
La Villa	1,998	9	0	0	3	6	57	20	36	1	0
Lavon	2,266	0	0	0	0	0	18	6	11	1	0
League City	85,318	94	3	21	37	33	1,885	374	1,453	58	6
Leander	27,079	20	0	4	3	13	350	36	309	5	8
Leonard	2,032	11	0	0	0	11	66	28	35	3	0
Leon Valley	10,365	25	0	4	12	9	886	119	714	53	0
Levelland	13,827	70	0	23	4	43	392	125	253	14	7
Lewisville	97,295	183	3	22	53	105	3,095	573	2,223	299	6
Liberty	8,574	77	0	4	8	65	464	98	346	20	1
Lindale	4,919	24	0	0	0	24	199	36	157	6	1
Linden	2,030	8	0	0	1	7	40	19	20	1	0
Little Elm	26,443	14	0	0	3	11	224	43	172	9	0
Littlefield	6,506	35	0	2	3	30	259	97	150	12	8
Live Oak	13,407	29	0	8	6	15	676	73	558	45	3
Livingston	5,447	19	0	6	5	8	282	51	224	7	2
Llano	3,300	2	0	1	0	1	74	20	52	2	0
Lockhart	12,965	53	1	7	3	42	356	57	284	15	1
Lockney	1,881	2	0	0	0	2	40	15	24	1	0
Lometa	874	0	0	0	0	0	14	7	7	0	0
Lone Star	1,614	3	0	1	1	1	75	32	41	2	0
Longview	82,148	412	4	20	110	278	3,802	819	2,705	278	28
Lorena	1,727	5	0	0	0	5	34	6	26	2	0
Lorenzo	1,171	5	0	0	0	5	15	8	4	3	0
Los Fresnos	5,659	28	0	0	0	28	126	21	103	2	1
Lott	775	2	0	0	0	2	13	5	8	0	0
Lubbock	234,404	1,800	8	70	313	1,409	12,078	3,410	7,975	693	56
Lufkin	35,805	193	1	19	43	130	1,882	413	1,391	78	1
Luling	5,525	19	0	2	1	16	150	33	113	4	0
Lumberton	12,194	14	0	4	1	9	267	39	217	11	1
Lyford	2,666	4	0	0	1	3	29	20	9	0	3
Lytle	2,544	1	0	0	0	1	92	2	86	4	1
Madisonville	4,489	16	0	2	6	8	173	59	108	6	0
Magnolia	1,422	6	0	0	1	5	26	3	21	2	2
Malakoff	2,373	6	0	2	0	4	51	5	44	2	1
Manor	5,143	17	0	1	1	15	172	54	115	3	0
Mansfield	57,554	62	1	17	17	27	955	211	691	53	4
Manvel	5,288	13	0	1	3	9	86	33	51	2	0
Marble Falls	6,205	13	0	5	0	8	302	46	242	14	0
Marlin	6,093	14	1	1	1	11	58	17	38	3	1
Marshall	24,018	194	2	14	26	152	1,020	317	643	60	4
Mart	2,255	4	0	0	0	4	16	7	9	0	0
Martindale	1,139	0	0	0	0	0	3	1	1	1	0
Mathis	5,046	23	1	4	2	16	159	43	106	10	5
McAllen	132,610	246	4	27	72	143	5,875	511	5,184	180	6
McGregor	5,092	9	0	0	1	8	83	39	44	0	0
McKinney	133,876	241	1	33	44	163	2,826	626	2,085	115	34
Meadows Place	4,758	11	0	1	7	3	121	21	91	9	0
Melissa	4,794	0	0	0	0	0	49	7	42	0	1
Memorial Villages	11,359	9	0	1	4	4	117	21	94	2	0
Memphis	2,338	4	0	0	0	4	12	7	5	0	0
Mercedes	15,898	101	0	7	17	77	826	175	602	49	7
Meridian	1,524	1	0	0	0	1	8	6	2	0	0
Merkel	2,644	4	0	0	0	4	12	4	7	1	0
Mesquite	142,766	397	2	8	177	210	6,542	1,704	4,197	641	10

[1] If a blank is presented in the arson column, it indicates that the FBI did not receive 12 complete months of arson data for that agency.

Table II-8.   Offenses Known to Law Enforcement, by Selected State and City, 2011—*Continued*

(Number.)

State/City	Population	Violent crime	Murder and non-negligent man-slaughter	Forcible rape	Robbery	Aggravated assault	Property crime	Burglary	Larceny-theft	Motor vehicle theft	Arson[1]
Texas—*Continued*											
Mexia	7,616	61	3	4	6	48	349	82	254	13	3
Midland	113,486	334	4	21	58	251	3,287	715	2,435	137	5
Midlothian	18,417	24	0	2	4	18	400	64	310	26	0
Milford	743	5	0	1	0	4	10	3	7	0	0
Mineola	4,610	13	0	0	0	13	193	36	150	7	0
Mineral Wells	17,141	81	2	25	5	49	860	232	605	23	2
Mission	78,679	100	2	6	37	55	2,751	464	2,094	193	26
Missouri City	68,775	90	0	10	35	45	1,172	294	831	47	11
Monahans	7,099	18	0	3	1	14	122	40	72	10	2
Mont Belvieu	3,916	11	0	5	2	4	155	25	114	16	0
Montgomery	634	4	0	0	1	3	21	1	17	3	0
Morgans Point Resort	4,258	1	0	0	0	1	29	5	22	2	0
Mount Pleasant	15,892	37	0	0	7	30	550	164	366	20	2
Muleshoe	5,267	18	0	1	0	17	96	23	67	6	0
Munday	1,327	3	0	1	0	2	14	4	10	0	3
Murphy	18,081	11	0	0	1	10	119	14	103	2	0
Mustang Ridge	879	0	0	0	0	0	0	0	0	0	0
Nacogdoches	33,690	213	1	6	31	175	1,260	317	894	49	1
Naples	1,407	8	0	1	2	5	44	20	23	1	0
Nash	3,022	3	0	0	0	3	51	16	32	3	0
Nassau Bay	4,086	6	0	1	0	5	115	21	85	9	0
Navasota	7,197	78	0	1	4	73	275	92	170	13	1
Nederland	17,916	65	0	9	8	48	643	157	452	34	0
Needville	2,882	6	0	1	1	4	33	10	21	2	0
New Boston	4,646	21	1	2	1	17	245	56	177	12	3
New Braunfels	58,955	119	2	7	26	84	1,943	298	1,565	80	16
New Deal	811	1	0	0	0	1	8	2	6	0	0
Nixon	2,435	4	0	0	1	3	29	12	15	2	1
Nocona	3,097	9	0	1	0	8	46	21	25	0	2
Nolanville	4,349	27	0	1	1	25	76	14	62	0	0
Northlake	1,760	6	0	0	1	5	31	4	24	3	0
North Richland Hills	64,676	185	0	29	33	123	1,904	374	1,438	92	0
Oak Ridge	144	1	0	0	0	1	3	2	1	0	0
Oak Ridge North	3,113	2	0	1	1	0	87	16	69	2	1
Odessa	102,043	748	6	37	73	632	3,134	617	2,336	181	24
O'Donnell	848	0	0	0	0	0	0	0	0	0	0
Olmos Park	2,284	0	0	0	0	0	61	12	46	3	0
Olney	3,354	1	0	0	1	0	75	30	45	0	0
Olton	2,262	4	0	0	0	4	18	9	7	2	0
Onalaska	1,801	0	0	0	0	0	10	3	7	0	0
Orange	18,986	153	0	4	46	103	884	307	527	50	9
Orange Grove	1,346	2	0	0	0	2	20	12	5	3	0
Overton	2,608	10	1	5	0	4	33	12	19	2	0
Ovilla	3,565	2	0	0	1	1	26	8	18	0	0
Oyster Creek	1,134	10	0	0	0	10	37	12	21	4	0
Paducah	1,211	0	0	0	0	0	2	1	1	0	0
Palacios	4,817	9	0	1	3	5	192	64	124	4	3
Palestine	19,106	101	0	22	24	55	947	206	722	19	0
Palmer	2,042	0	0	0	0	0	33	7	26	0	0
Palmhurst	2,662	17	0	0	6	11	138	11	117	10	0
Palm Valley	1,331	2	0	0	0	2	26	9	17	0	0
Palmview	5,575	4	0	0	2	2	218	24	178	16	0
Pampa	18,373	118	0	0	6	112	788	194	561	33	2
Panhandle	2,504	3	0	0	0	3	17	7	9	1	0
Pantego	2,444	16	0	1	3	12	124	20	99	5	0
Paris	25,701	166	2	5	41	118	1,403	352	1,013	38	0
Parker	3,891	1	0	0	0	1	14	5	9	0	0
Pasadena	152,179	566	5	62	135	364	5,266	1,124	3,728	414	20
Pearland	93,172	125	2	15	29	79	1,726	331	1,289	106	0
Pearsall	9,338	22	0	0	6	16	164	46	111	7	0
Pecos	8,965	18	0	0	3	15	164	26	133	5	2
Penitas	4,496	6	0	0	0	6	100	12	80	8	1
Perryton	8,987	4	0	0	0	4	121	32	79	10	0
Pflugerville	47,924	63	0	5	11	47	875	125	715	35	10
Pharr	71,881	256	4	17	51	184	2,452	530	1,765	157	10
Pilot Point	3,937	2	0	1	0	1	53	24	24	5	0
Pinehurst	2,141	12	0	1	3	8	87	21	60	6	0
Pittsburg	4,592	23	0	1	3	19	158	47	105	6	2
Plainview	22,661	66	0	9	11	46	913	196	691	26	7
Plano	265,309	429	5	40	142	242	6,764	1,193	5,182	389	5
Pleasanton	9,122	32	0	5	2	25	417	83	312	22	1
Point Comfort	753	0	0	0	0	0	12	7	5	0	0
Ponder	1,424	0	0	0	0	0	13	6	6	1	0
Port Aransas	3,553	24	0	1	2	21	315	56	243	16	2
Port Arthur	54,950	434	8	29	156	241	2,853	950	1,740	163	44
Port Isabel	5,111	28	0	4	4	20	318	79	224	15	0

[1] If a blank is presented in the arson column, it indicates that the FBI did not receive 12 complete months of arson data for that agency.

Table II-8.   Offenses Known to Law Enforcement, by Selected State and City, 2011—*Continued*

(Number.)

State/City	Population	Violent crime	Murder and non-negligent man-slaughter	Forcible rape	Robbery	Aggravated assault	Property crime	Burglary	Larceny-theft	Motor vehicle theft	Arson[1]
Texas—*Continued*											
Portland	15,417	21	0	4	4	13	452	63	373	16	0
Port Lavaca	12,506	81	0	12	6	63	482	107	357	18	2
Port Neches	13,314	49	0	2	1	46	326	87	225	14	0
Poteet	3,329	12	0	0	0	12	104	29	73	2	0
Poth	1,948	9	0	0	0	9	30	6	22	2	0
Pottsboro	2,205	4	0	0	1	3	33	10	20	3	0
Premont	2,709	10	0	1	1	8	38	18	18	2	3
Presidio	4,519	2	0	0	0	2	11	3	7	1	0
Primera	4,156	8	0	0	0	8	22	6	15	1	0
Princeton	6,950	15	0	3	1	11	124	19	102	3	1
Progreso	5,623	14	0	2	1	11	48	21	18	9	0
Prosper	9,621	13	0	0	1	12	168	60	101	7	0
Queen City	1,507	6	0	2	2	2	84	34	45	5	0
Quitman	1,847	5	0	0	0	5	37	7	28	2	0
Ralls	1,985	1	0	1	0	0	5	5	0	0	0
Rancho Viejo	2,488	1	0	0	0	1	8	4	4	0	1
Ranger	2,520	13	0	1	0	12	87	35	45	7	1
Ransom Canyon	1,119	0	0	0	0	0	1	0	1	0	0
Raymondville	11,521	148	0	4	2	142	527	162	361	4	7
Red Oak	10,996	20	0	2	7	11	275	79	181	15	2
Refugio	2,951	6	0	2	0	4	56	21	34	1	0
Reno	3,233	5	0	1	0	4	28	7	19	2	0
Richardson	101,311	173	0	9	76	88	2,808	680	1,934	194	3
Richland Hills	7,965	11	0	0	3	8	299	75	191	33	0
Richmond	11,925	53	1	6	10	36	289	84	185	20	2
Richwood	3,584	1	0	1	0	0	36	9	24	3	0
Riesel	1,028	0	0	0	0	0	10	1	9	0	0
Rio Grande City	14,125	41	1	2	9	29	489	147	307	35	6
Rio Hondo	2,406	3	0	0	0	3	64	19	43	2	1
Rising Star	853	0	0	0	0	0	0	0	0	0	0
River Oaks	7,583	8	0	3	4	1	204	49	148	7	2
Roanoke	6,087	8	0	0	4	4	145	26	110	9	0
Robinson	10,730	9	0	0	5	4	174	26	144	4	0
Robstown	11,729	21	0	0	5	16	405	119	274	12	0
Rockdale	5,713	10	1	1	0	8	175	53	113	9	0
Rockport	8,950	17	0	0	1	16	373	76	281	16	1
Rockwall	38,279	47	0	10	8	29	1,022	133	820	69	0
Rollingwood	1,442	0	0	0	0	0	14	3	11	0	0
Roma	9,970	26	2	3	4	17	166	48	95	23	0
Roman Forest	1,570	4	0	1	0	3	55	1	54	0	0
Roscoe	1,350	0	0	0	0	0	5	1	4	0	0
Rosebud	1,442	2	0	0	0	2	36	16	17	3	1
Rose City	513	3	0	0	1	2	28	10	14	4	0
Rosenberg	31,262	68	2	9	17	40	632	145	459	28	1
Round Rock	101,989	115	2	25	39	49	2,446	394	2,001	51	1
Rowlett	57,382	65	0	6	9	50	977	228	714	35	12
Royse City	9,546	24	0	2	4	18	128	21	101	6	0
Runaway Bay	1,313	1	0	0	0	1	6	3	3	0	0
Rusk	5,668	12	0	1	0	11	83	17	62	4	2
Sabinal	1,731	4	0	0	0	4	33	7	26	0	0
Sachse	20,757	14	0	4	2	8	216	54	153	9	2
Saginaw	20,223	42	0	3	10	29	489	94	354	41	2
Salado	2,171	2	0	0	1	1	40	15	25	0	0
San Angelo	95,161	250	0	32	42	176	3,624	801	2,685	138	15
San Antonio	1,355,339	7,038	89	492	1,785	4,672	80,868	15,334	59,641	5,893	209
San Augustine	2,152	11	0	0	1	10	24	9	15	0	0
San Benito	24,760	89	0	11	21	57	1,140	302	793	45	5
San Diego	4,582	21	0	0	2	19	49	22	27	0	0
San Felipe	763	1	0	0	0	1	8	4	2	2	0
Sanger	7,062	14	0	4	1	9	130	34	93	3	0
San Juan	34,568	254	1	45	22	186	1,391	221	1,093	77	3
San Marcos	45,839	159	1	11	37	110	1,568	273	1,206	89	3
San Saba	3,164	2	0	0	0	2	38	7	29	2	0
Sansom Park Village	4,785	14	0	0	2	12	143	57	75	11	0
Santa Anna	1,122	5	0	0	0	5	16	8	8	0	0
Santa Fe	12,479	11	0	3	0	8	215	45	146	24	2
Santa Rosa	2,933	6	0	0	0	6	82	18	64	0	0
Schertz	32,127	84	0	9	4	71	626	70	524	32	0
Schulenburg	2,912	25	0	0	4	21	82	28	48	6	0
Seabrook	12,203	7	0	0	2	5	201	54	142	5	0
Seagoville	15,147	15	1	2	8	4	514	146	313	55	0
Seagraves	2,468	7	0	0	1	6	13	2	9	2	0
Sealy	6,146	24	1	2	1	20	153	36	108	9	0
Seguin	25,705	86	1	6	27	52	1,254	301	915	38	3
Selma	5,657	5	0	0	2	3	270	25	221	24	0
Seminole	6,565	4	0	0	0	4	63	10	52	1	0

[1] If a blank is presented in the arson column, it indicates that the FBI did not receive 12 complete months of arson data for that agency.

Table II-8.   Offenses Known to Law Enforcement, by Selected State and City, 2011—*Continued*

(Number.)

State/City	Population	Violent crime	Murder and non-negligent man-slaughter	Forcible rape	Robbery	Aggravated assault	Property crime	Burglary	Larceny-theft	Motor vehicle theft	Arson[1]
Texas—*Continued*											
Seven Points	1,486	8	0	1	1	6	91	27	57	7	0
Seymour	2,798	12	0	1	2	9	38	10	27	1	1
Shallowater	2,536	2	0	0	1	1	28	19	8	1	0
Shamrock	1,950	6	0	1	1	4	31	7	20	4	0
Shavano Park	3,099	2	1	0	0	1	52	3	48	1	0
Shenandoah	2,179	5	0	0	3	2	195	12	178	5	0
Sherman	39,332	158	1	1	41	115	1,549	325	1,174	50	9
Silsbee	6,750	18	0	0	3	15	184	30	148	6	0
Sinton	5,784	29	1	4	0	24	137	31	105	1	1
Slaton	6,250	25	0	3	2	20	137	50	82	5	1
Smithville	3,897	8	0	2	0	6	55	11	43	1	2
Snyder	11,438	68	0	6	5	57	286	91	189	6	1
Socorro	32,687	57	0	3	6	48	511	85	384	42	7
Somerset	1,665	0	0	0	0	0	30	6	21	3	0
Somerville	1,405	6	0	3	1	2	22	7	15	0	0
Sonora	3,091	3	0	1	0	2	27	2	24	1	1
Sour Lake	1,851	4	0	0	0	4	40	10	28	2	0
South Houston	17,340	118	2	7	58	51	763	212	412	139	0
Southlake	27,134	8	0	0	4	4	462	58	400	4	2
South Padre Island	2,875	39	0	8	8	23	558	60	486	12	0
Southside Place	1,751	1	0	0	0	1	17	10	5	2	0
Spearman	3,439	8	0	0	0	8	50	14	35	1	10
Springtown	2,714	14	0	0	0	14	63	19	40	4	0
Spring Valley	3,793	3	0	0	2	1	115	26	83	6	0
Spur	1,346	4	0	0	0	4	9	6	2	1	0
Stafford	18,065	74	1	2	34	37	769	161	537	71	1
Stagecoach	549	0	0	0	0	0	6	3	2	1	1
Stamford	3,190	13	0	0	1	12	97	37	58	2	0
Stanton	2,544	4	0	1	0	3	19	5	12	2	0
Stephenville	17,483	25	0	9	3	13	565	102	441	22	8
Stratford	2,059	11	0	0	0	11	22	8	13	1	0
Sugar Land	80,475	96	1	5	29	61	1,429	220	1,176	33	9
Sullivan City	4,086	2	0	0	0	2	23	11	11	1	1
Sulphur Springs	15,774	32	2	1	2	27	235	63	155	17	3
Sunray	1,967	3	0	0	0	3	11	3	7	1	0
Sunrise Beach Village	728	0	0	0	0	0	6	0	6	0	0
Sunset Valley	765	4	0	0	3	1	108	4	104	0	0
Surfside Beach	492	3	0	0	0	3	16	6	7	3	0
Sweeny	3,762	3	0	2	0	1	82	25	55	2	0
Sweetwater	11,135	99	1	7	5	86	404	127	254	23	3
Taft	3,112	30	0	8	1	21	112	23	86	3	0
Tahoka	2,729	3	0	1	0	2	27	12	15	0	0
Tatum	1,414	7	0	1	0	6	12	5	7	0	0
Taylor	15,511	18	0	1	5	12	461	89	367	5	4
Teague	3,635	31	0	3	5	23	122	57	60	5	0
Temple	67,493	185	0	21	84	80	2,039	575	1,380	84	1
Terrell	16,149	69	2	12	18	37	815	247	531	37	4
Terrell Hills	4,981	3	0	0	1	2	54	14	40	0	0
Texarkana	37,177	468	3	25	77	363	2,477	746	1,590	141	28
Texas City	46,048	152	4	1	57	90	1,566	340	1,161	65	2
The Colony	37,092	51	0	6	12	33	571	133	369	69	1
Thorndale	1,364	1	0	0	0	1	6	2	4	0	0
Thrall	857	4	0	0	0	4	11	2	8	1	0
Three Rivers	1,887	12	0	0	0	12	44	19	25	0	0
Tioga	820	1	0	0	0	1	6	3	3	0	1
Tolar	695	0	0	0	0	0	5	2	3	0	0
Tomball	10,979	33	1	1	4	27	462	61	384	17	1
Tom Bean	1,067	6	0	0	2	4	9	2	7	0	0
Tool	2,287	1	0	0	0	1	63	20	42	1	0
Trenton	648	2	0	0	0	2	27	5	22	0	0
Trinity	2,754	27	0	0	7	20	94	34	55	5	1
Trophy Club	8,193	6	0	3	0	3	127	21	104	2	0
Troup	1,908	5	0	2	0	3	54	16	38	0	0
Troy	1,680	2	0	0	0	2	33	7	26	0	0
Tulia	5,072	7	1	3	1	2	97	27	67	3	0
Tye	1,268	5	0	0	0	5	20	3	14	3	0
Tyler	98,939	503	3	46	79	375	4,441	834	3,423	184	6
Universal City	18,920	53	0	1	12	40	459	103	325	31	3
University Park	23,553	8	0	0	3	5	332	51	257	24	1
Uvalde	16,082	35	0	0	4	31	498	181	317	0	0
Valley Mills	1,228	8	0	0	1	7	25	7	17	1	0
Valley View	773	1	0	0	0	1	3	3	0	0	0
Van	2,687	3	0	0	1	2	46	15	29	2	0
Van Alstyne	3,110	5	0	0	0	5	58	15	41	2	0
Vernon	11,234	59	0	9	7	43	384	85	285	14	3
Victoria	63,909	392	2	38	70	282	3,249	857	2,299	93	18

[1] If a blank is presented in the arson column, it indicates that the FBI did not receive 12 complete months of arson data for that agency.

Table II-8. Offenses Known to Law Enforcement, by Selected State and City, 2011—*Continued*

(Number.)

State/City	Population	Violent crime	Murder and non-negligent man-slaughter	Forcible rape	Robbery	Aggravated assault	Property crime	Burglary	Larceny-theft	Motor vehicle theft	Arson[1]
Texas—*Continued*											
Vidor	10,802	54	0	3	9	42	558	91	426	41	0
Waco	127,431	766	11	70	245	440	6,422	1,670	4,593	159	35
Waelder	1,087	12	1	3	2	6	17	10	7	0	0
Wake Village	5,608	3	0	0	3	0	142	37	97	8	0
Waller	2,375	12	0	1	4	7	91	22	67	2	0
Wallis	1,278	0	0	0	0	0	19	5	14	0	0
Watauga	23,991	93	0	3	17	73	665	140	481	44	1
Waxahachie	30,244	73	1	1	19	52	1,124	200	881	43	3
Weatherford	25,781	39	0	4	11	24	711	139	552	20	5
Webster	10,619	49	0	14	18	17	715	86	553	76	0
Weimar	2,196	0	0	0	0	0	19	6	11	2	0
Weslaco	36,421	154	0	13	37	104	2,215	342	1,765	108	7
West	2,866	0	0	0	0	0	42	11	26	5	1
West Columbia	3,987	21	0	3	2	16	64	9	52	3	0
West Lake Hills	3,127	2	0	0	1	1	72	6	61	5	0
West Orange	3,515	12	1	0	4	7	262	48	211	3	0
Westover Hills	696	0	0	0	0	0	22	4	17	1	0
West Tawakoni	1,609	13	0	0	0	13	56	21	32	3	0
West University Place	15,098	8	0	0	7	1	158	80	70	8	0
Westworth	2,524	2	0	0	0	2	97	24	72	1	0
Wharton	9,018	75	0	1	14	60	437	117	303	17	3
Whitehouse	7,821	11	0	2	0	9	92	13	73	6	1
White Oak	6,605	6	0	0	0	6	100	16	73	11	0
Whitesboro	3,873	2	0	0	1	1	125	21	103	1	3
White Settlement	16,455	54	0	0	9	45	555	149	367	39	2
Whitewright	1,638	5	0	0	0	5	47	15	28	4	0
Whitney	2,131	3	0	1	0	2	87	25	59	3	0
Wichita Falls	106,753	459	1	30	147	281	4,876	1,241	3,398	237	25
Willis	5,781	32	0	1	14	17	186	52	118	16	0
Willow Park	4,066	1	0	0	1	0	44	8	33	3	0
Wills Point	3,598	4	0	0	2	2	65	26	36	3	0
Wilmer	3,759	9	0	0	3	6	114	54	54	6	0
Windcrest	5,477	17	0	2	7	8	330	37	271	22	1
Wink	960	1	0	0	0	1	13	4	9	0	0
Winnsboro	3,506	8	0	0	1	7	22	8	14	0	0
Winters	2,616	15	0	4	2	9	25	13	8	4	0
Wolfe City	1,442	4	0	1	0	3	27	11	13	3	0
Wolfforth	3,747	3	0	1	0	2	46	10	34	2	0
Woodbranch	1,309	1	0	0	0	1	7	3	3	1	0
Woodville	2,640	0	0	0	0	0	22	4	18	0	0
Woodway	8,630	5	0	1	1	3	122	20	101	1	0
Wortham	1,096	5	0	2	0	3	19	13	5	1	0
Wylie	42,299	36	1	2	8	25	685	141	523	21	1
Yoakum	5,937	2	0	0	0	2	171	70	94	7	0
Yorktown	2,136	2	0	0	0	2	15	6	8	1	0
Utah											
American Fork/Cedar Hills	36,755	23	0	11	4	8	940	175	731	34	2
Big Water	484	0	0	0	0	0	7	4	2	1	0
Blanding	3,440	4	0	1	0	3	59	13	43	3	0
Bluffdale	7,745	3	0	1	0	2	150	50	87	13	0
Bountiful	43,373	41	0	15	4	22	803	107	663	33	3
Brian Head	85	0	0	0	0	0	21	3	17	1	0
Brigham City	18,244	35	3	5	5	22	577	144	418	15	7
Cedar City	29,414	52	0	12	4	36	899	175	693	31	5
Centerfield	1,393	1	0	0	0	1	9	2	6	1	0
Centerville	15,631	10	0	1	1	8	455	41	394	20	2
Clearfield	30,693	54	0	10	9	35	746	108	613	25	5
Clinton	20,820	24	0	9	1	14	349	42	297	10	0
Cottonwood Heights	34,078	45	0	6	12	27	961	179	729	53	9
Draper	43,090	45	0	10	7	28	905	216	636	53	8
Enoch	5,915	5	0	1	0	4	60	16	39	5	0
Fairview	1,271	1	0	0	0	1	10	4	4	2	0
Farmington	18,628	6	0	1	0	5	239	22	206	11	3
Grantsville	9,065	11	0	3	0	8	94	42	45	7	1
Harrisville	5,674	8	0	0	4	4	363	23	335	5	0
Heber	11,581	6	0	4	0	2	69	11	57	1	0
Helper	2,243	1	0	0	0	1	38	9	29	0	2
Hildale	2,779	5	0	0	0	5	11	0	11	0	0
Hurricane	14,013	17	0	2	2	13	301	83	204	14	2
Ivins	6,883	4	0	2	0	2	50	19	30	1	0
Kamas	1,846	0	0	0	0	0	26	4	22	0	0
Kanab	4,395	4	1	0	0	3	61	5	55	1	0
Kaysville	27,827	15	1	5	0	9	356	64	278	14	0
La Verkin	4,138	15	0	3	0	12	51	7	38	6	1
Layton	68,610	83	0	28	11	44	1,962	306	1,597	59	9

[1] If a blank is presented in the arson column, it indicates that the FBI did not receive 12 complete months of arson data for that agency.

Table II-8. Offenses Known to Law Enforcement, by Selected State and City, 2011—*Continued*

(Number.)

State/City	Population	Violent crime	Murder and non-negligent man-slaughter	Forcible rape	Robbery	Aggravated assault	Property crime	Burglary	Larceny-theft	Motor vehicle theft	Arson[1]
Utah—*Continued*											
Lehi	48,322	26	1	9	5	11	821	120	652	49	1
Lindon	10,264	4	0	0	0	4	246	45	192	9	1
Logan	49,104	26	0	2	2	22	376	49	314	13	1
Lone Peak	25,562	2	0	0	0	2	269	88	175	6	1
Mapleton	8,133	2	0	0	0	2	83	14	68	1	0
Moab	5,143	11	1	1	1	8	226	34	186	6	3
Moroni	1,450	2	0	0	0	2	15	5	10	0	1
Murray	47,648	198	1	25	47	125	3,065	377	2,391	297	6
Naples	1,789	2	0	0	0	2	63	24	37	2	0
Nephi	5,493	7	0	3	0	4	172	27	134	11	0
North Ogden	17,692	7	1	4	0	2	220	35	180	5	1
North Park	12,336	8	0	3	1	4	161	26	126	9	1
North Salt Lake	16,637	18	0	4	3	11	375	57	282	36	3
Ogden	84,423	392	2	20	96	274	4,429	858	3,279	292	18
Orem	90,033	45	0	20	10	15	2,322	166	2,069	87	5
Park City	7,704	10	0	0	1	9	407	23	369	15	0
Payson	18,647	13	0	1	3	9	745	103	619	23	0
Perry	4,599	2	0	0	0	2	60	13	46	1	0
Pleasant Grove	34,156	17	0	7	4	6	592	104	464	24	1
Pleasant View	8,133	7	0	2	0	5	92	25	63	4	0
Price	8,883	24	0	3	0	21	344	63	279	2	0
Provo	114,659	149	4	27	26	92	2,888	386	2,400	102	10
Richfield	7,697	10	0	6	0	4	232	33	195	4	0
Riverdale	8,589	19	0	4	2	13	555	58	476	21	0
Roosevelt	6,163	19	1	10	2	6	208	28	166	14	0
Roy	37,596	37	1	16	5	15	760	100	641	19	1
Salem	6,547	0	0	0	0	0	87	18	65	4	0
Salina	2,537	8	1	2	0	5	90	8	77	5	2
Salt Lake City	190,038	1,213	6	119	340	748	12,798	1,658	9,654	1,486	36
Sandy	89,149	121	1	17	26	77	2,617	438	1,986	193	7
Santa Clara	6,119	16	0	0	1	15	61	16	38	7	0
Santaquin/Genola	10,700	5	0	0	0	5	191	33	155	3	1
Saratoga Springs	18,124	14	0	3	1	10	200	28	164	8	0
Smithfield	9,678	1	0	0	0	1	69	26	41	2	0
South Jordan	51,391	27	1	8	5	13	962	189	717	56	1
South Ogden	16,851	17	0	4	5	8	366	85	267	14	1
South Salt Lake	24,073	173	2	35	45	91	1,577	264	1,055	258	1
Spanish Fork	35,360	10	0	3	1	6	569	92	459	18	3
Springdale	539	2	0	1	0	1	24	8	16	0	0
Springville	30,035	40	0	12	4	24	880	119	727	34	1
Stockton	628	0	0	0	0	0	1	1	0	0	1
Sunset	5,221	1	0	1	0	0	110	17	90	3	0
Syracuse	24,801	13	0	3	2	8	283	28	251	4	1
Taylorsville City	59,784	211	2	30	54	125	2,467	322	1,863	282	9
Tooele	32,215	66	1	22	5	38	1,316	275	962	79	5
Tremonton	7,795	12	0	6	0	6	215	40	169	6	0
Vernal	9,264	24	1	7	1	15	349	59	273	17	0
Washington	19,123	32	2	4	4	22	431	77	327	27	2
Wellington	1,708	1	0	0	0	1	36	11	25	0	0
West Bountiful	5,367	4	0	1	0	3	137	16	112	9	0
West Jordan	105,713	210	0	31	25	154	2,939	405	2,314	220	12
West Valley	131,979	588	4	77	126	381	5,368	929	3,711	728	10
Woods Cross	9,949	7	0	4	2	1	250	38	194	18	1
Vermont											
Barre	9,062	22	0	8	4	10	447	72	364	11	4
Barre Town	7,933	4	0	0	0	4	131	30	94	7	0
Bellows Falls	3,151	6	0	0	0	6	82	11	70	1	0
Bennington	15,781	22	0	2	1	19	480	102	365	13	0
Berlin	2,890	4	0	2	0	2	48	0	48	0	0
Brandon	3,970	0	0	0	0	0	82	19	61	2	1
Brattleboro	12,059	49	1	3	9	36	429	95	323	11	4
Chester	3,157	3	0	2	0	1	44	31	11	2	0
Colchester	17,086	28	0	2	6	20	590	93	488	9	0
Dover	1,125	1	0	0	0	1	132	11	118	3	0
Essex	19,609	16	0	3	4	9	488	72	405	11	2
Fair Haven	2,737	2	0	1	0	1	74	14	59	1	0
Hardwick	3,013	2	0	0	1	1	70	20	45	5	0
Hartford	9,963	12	0	2	3	7	196	59	127	10	0
Hinesburg	4,401	1	0	0	0	1	48	7	39	2	0
Manchester	4,396	5	0	1	0	4	97	39	55	3	0
Middlebury	8,505	7	0	2	1	4	188	26	161	1	0
Milton	10,363	17	0	1	0	16	219	63	150	6	2
Montpelier	7,864	12	0	2	0	10	334	33	286	15	2
Morristown	5,233	5	0	0	0	5	97	16	81	0	0
Newport	4,594	13	0	3	0	10	111	30	80	1	1

[1] If a blank is presented in the arson column, it indicates that the FBI did not receive 12 complete months of arson data for that agency.

Table II-8.   Offenses Known to Law Enforcement, by Selected State and City, 2011—*Continued*

(Number.)

State/City	Population	Violent crime	Murder and non-negligent man-slaughter	Forcible rape	Robbery	Aggravated assault	Property crime	Burglary	Larceny-theft	Motor vehicle theft	Arson[1]
Utah—*Continued*											
Northfield	6,214	5	0	1	0	4	92	23	63	6	1
Norwich	3,418	0	0	0	0	0	18	6	10	2	0
Randolph	4,783	2	0	0	0	2	42	10	32	0	0
Richmond	4,086	1	0	0	0	1	47	11	36	0	0
Rutland	16,513	59	0	4	14	41	1,081	245	810	26	2
Shelburne	7,152	4	0	1	1	2	54	9	43	2	0
South Burlington	17,924	22	0	7	0	15	711	63	616	32	0
Springfield	9,383	19	0	1	4	14	225	64	152	9	5
St. Albans	6,926	46	0	4	3	39	342	42	290	10	1
St. Johnsbury	7,611	7	0	0	1	6	110	20	88	2	0
Stowe	4,319	3	0	0	0	3	168	19	147	2	0
Swanton	6,434	3	0	0	1	2	58	13	40	5	0
Vergennes	2,591	3	0	1	0	2	27	5	20	2	0
Waterbury	5,070	2	0	0	0	2	21	1	20	0	0
Williston	8,708	5	0	0	0	5	235	31	196	8	0
Wilmington	1,878	0	0	0	0	0	38	6	29	3	0
Windsor	3,557	4	0	1	1	2	44	13	30	1	0
Winooski	7,275	26	0	3	3	20	256	37	210	9	4
Woodstock	3,051	0	0	0	0	0	3	2	1	0	0
Virginia											
Abingdon	8,289	12	0	2	5	5	285	30	244	11	1
Alexandria	141,638	252	1	14	129	108	3,181	303	2,506	372	6
Altavista	3,491	9	0	1	0	8	116	11	102	3	0
Amherst	2,258	1	0	0	1	0	29	5	21	3	0
Appalachia	1,775	9	0	5	0	4	105	29	74	2	0
Ashland	7,311	19	0	2	0	17	230	28	183	19	0
Bedford	6,296	16	0	5	1	10	228	35	182	11	0
Berryville	4,235	4	0	0	0	4	46	9	36	1	0
Big Stone Gap	5,681	11	0	2	2	7	232	30	193	9	2
Blacksburg	43,129	24	0	9	5	10	591	84	490	17	3
Blackstone	3,664	10	0	1	1	8	93	19	73	1	0
Bluefield	5,509	9	0	0	3	6	184	19	159	6	0
Boykins	571	1	0	0	0	1	7	3	4	0	0
Bridgewater	5,711	1	0	1	0	0	35	5	28	2	0
Bristol	18,048	57	1	8	13	35	657	106	530	21	1
Broadway	3,735	0	0	0	0	0	16	5	11	0	0
Cape Charles	1,021	0	0	0	0	0	16	2	13	1	0
Cedar Bluff	1,151	2	0	1	0	1	31	14	14	3	0
Charlottesville	43,994	183	1	27	59	96	1,467	114	1,252	101	5
Chase City	2,379	13	0	3	2	8	80	10	67	3	0
Chatham	1,284	0	0	0	0	0	14	0	13	1	0
Chesapeake	224,864	892	12	46	246	588	7,163	1,237	5,601	325	21
Chilhowie	1,802	1	0	0	1	0	37	3	33	1	1
Chincoteague	2,976	4	0	1	0	3	73	15	55	3	0
Christiansburg	21,292	29	0	7	5	17	733	98	615	20	4
Clarksville	1,153	3	0	1	0	2	23	1	20	2	0
Clifton Forge	3,930	8	0	0	1	7	100	29	70	1	2
Clintwood	1,431	1	0	0	0	1	22	1	20	1	0
Colonial Beach	3,584	7	0	1	0	6	117	10	81	26	0
Colonial Heights	17,619	32	2	5	7	18	924	58	839	27	3
Covington	6,032	22	1	1	7	13	137	24	110	3	0
Crewe	2,354	6	0	0	0	6	81	17	64	0	0
Culpeper	16,575	59	1	3	14	41	438	37	385	16	3
Damascus	824	2	0	0	0	2	36	0	35	1	0
Danville	43,569	166	7	28	64	67	2,080	464	1,546	70	9
Dayton	1,548	0	0	0	0	0	11	2	8	1	0
Dublin	2,564	2	0	0	0	2	84	17	60	7	0
Dumfries	5,020	2	0	0	0	2	70	12	52	6	0
Elkton	2,759	3	0	2	0	1	40	5	33	2	0
Emporia	5,998	40	1	5	14	20	389	115	253	21	1
Exmore	1,477	4	0	0	1	3	48	7	41	0	0
Fairfax City	22,835	36	0	5	12	19	546	39	492	15	1
Falls Church	12,479	10	0	0	5	5	226	21	191	14	0
Farmville	8,314	18	0	2	7	9	276	37	234	5	2
Franklin	8,685	38	0	10	12	16	470	100	355	15	2
Fredericksburg	24,576	101	1	3	24	73	1,063	100	932	31	5
Front Royal	14,612	17	0	6	6	5	492	55	411	26	0
Galax	7,126	31	0	0	4	27	354	32	310	12	0
Gate City	2,058	3	0	0	0	3	65	16	47	2	0
Glade Spring	1,473	1	0	0	1	0	0	0	0	0	0
Glasgow	1,147	0	0	0	0	0	5	0	5	0	0
Gretna	1,282	3	0	0	2	1	13	5	8	0	0
Grottoes	2,700	1	0	1	0	0	22	6	16	0	0
Halifax	1,325	1	0	0	1	0	26	1	24	1	1

[1] If a blank is presented in the arson column, it indicates that the FBI did not receive 12 complete months of arson data for that agency.

Table II-8. **Offenses Known to Law Enforcement, by Selected State and City, 2011**—*Continued*

(Number.)

State/City	Population	Violent crime	Murder and non-negligent man-slaughter	Forcible rape	Robbery	Aggravated assault	Property crime	Burglary	Larceny-theft	Motor vehicle theft	Arson[1]
Virginia—*Continued*											
Hampton	139,078	350	9	19	155	167	5,273	820	4,180	273	31
Harrisonburg	49,498	99	1	13	19	66	1,060	158	866	36	7
Haymarket	1,803	1	0	0	0	1	12	1	11	0	0
Herndon	23,570	44	0	4	13	27	393	24	358	11	0
Hillsville	2,713	13	0	1	0	12	111	13	88	10	0
Honaker	1,466	1	0	0	0	1	13	4	8	1	0
Hopewell	22,861	140	2	5	39	94	954	306	588	60	13
Independence	958	2	0	0	0	2	6	1	5	0	0
Jonesville	1,046	2	1	0	0	1	26	7	18	1	0
Kenbridge	1,272	5	0	0	0	5	12	3	9	0	0
Kilmarnock	1,505	2	0	0	0	2	57	6	50	1	0
Lawrenceville	1,455	3	0	0	3	0	56	20	35	1	1
Lebanon	3,465	3	0	1	0	2	153	11	142	0	1
Leesburg	43,125	58	0	5	6	47	826	53	753	20	3
Lexington	7,126	4	0	2	1	1	75	16	57	2	2
Louisa	1,574	3	0	0	0	3	39	3	36	0	5
Luray	4,953	2	0	0	0	2	161	30	126	5	0
Lynchburg	76,471	278	3	22	72	181	2,469	515	1,855	99	9
Manassas	38,273	129	4	17	52	56	831	121	653	57	4
Manassas Park	14,444	10	0	2	3	5	172	12	147	13	0
Marion	6,039	33	0	2	0	31	198	24	171	3	1
Martinsville	13,986	45	2	2	14	27	498	68	409	21	1
Middleburg	681	0	0	0	0	0	6	0	6	0	0
Middletown	1,280	2	0	1	0	1	17	2	15	0	0
Mount Jackson	2,018	2	0	1	1	0	33	3	26	4	0
Narrows	2,053	2	0	2	0	0	25	1	23	1	0
New Market	2,172	2	0	1	0	1	22	4	18	0	0
Newport News	182,878	845	15	52	388	390	6,041	1,094	4,592	355	84
Norfolk	245,704	1,424	29	81	625	689	12,258	2,256	9,217	785	38
Norton	4,005	2	0	0	1	1	236	7	225	4	0
Onancock	1,278	1	0	0	1	0	16	4	11	1	0
Orange	4,777	5	0	1	4	0	121	13	105	3	1
Parksley	852	1	0	0	1	0	10	1	9	0	0
Pearisburg	2,819	1	0	0	0	1	66	6	57	3	0
Pennington Gap	1,802	0	0	0	0	0	0	0	0	0	0
Petersburg	32,807	156	6	9	53	88	1,470	434	929	107	3
Poquoson	12,295	8	0	1	2	5	149	40	104	5	1
Portsmouth	96,676	550	12	46	235	257	5,237	1,348	3,623	266	11
Pound	1,049	1	0	0	0	1	18	1	16	1	0
Pulaski	9,195	19	0	2	3	14	408	66	314	28	2
Purcellville	7,819	1	0	0	0	1	60	2	57	1	0
Quantico	486	0	0	0	0	0	7	0	6	1	0
Radford	16,604	55	1	7	8	39	477	97	364	16	4
Remington	605	0	0	0	0	0	2	0	2	0	0
Rich Creek	783	0	0	0	0	0	11	2	9	0	0
Richlands	5,893	10	0	0	2	8	256	61	190	5	7
Richmond	206,654	1,428	36	44	676	672	8,647	1,886	5,833	928	58
Roanoke	98,191	589	8	33	175	373	4,635	928	3,424	283	32
Rocky Mount	4,856	20	0	4	8	8	200	28	170	2	1
Salem	25,098	28	0	6	8	14	642	72	544	26	0
Saltville	2,102	2	0	0	0	2	73	3	70	0	0
Shenandoah	2,401	2	0	0	0	2	58	14	42	2	0
Smithfield	8,186	17	0	1	2	14	172	33	130	9	1
South Boston	8,239	35	1	4	15	15	431	100	320	11	1
South Hill	4,706	15	0	3	3	9	199	12	176	11	2
Stanley	1,709	1	0	1	0	0	47	9	38	0	0
Staunton	24,030	47	1	5	16	25	520	39	452	29	6
Stephens City	1,851	2	0	1	1	0	59	13	43	3	0
St. Paul	982	0	0	0	0	0	12	0	12	0	0
Strasburg	6,474	5	0	2	0	3	93	7	84	2	0
Suffolk	85,595	259	3	19	76	161	2,381	518	1,757	106	32
Tappahannock	2,403	11	0	1	1	9	127	10	116	1	1
Tazewell	4,682	4	0	2	0	2	100	15	82	3	0
Timberville	2,552	0	0	0	0	0	19	4	14	1	0
Victoria	1,746	1	0	0	0	1	13	4	8	1	0
Vienna	15,874	17	0	1	8	8	193	9	179	5	1
Vinton	8,195	41	0	3	4	34	239	21	216	2	1
Virginia Beach	443,226	776	15	60	412	289	12,133	2,038	9,645	450	133
Warrenton	9,726	19	0	5	7	7	239	21	213	5	0
Warsaw	1,530	0	0	0	0	0	13	3	10	0	0
Waverly	2,175	6	0	0	3	3	31	5	24	2	0
Waynesboro	21,257	73	0	10	16	47	770	103	628	39	1

[1] If a blank is presented in the arson column, it indicates that the FBI did not receive 12 complete months of arson data for that agency.

Table II-8.   Offenses Known to Law Enforcement, by Selected State and City, 2011—*Continued*

(Number.)

State/City	Population	Violent crime	Murder and non-negligent man-slaughter	Forcible rape	Robbery	Aggravated assault	Property crime	Burglary	Larceny-theft	Motor vehicle theft	Arson[1]
Virginia—*Continued*											
Weber City	1,343	1	0	1	0	0	43	6	36	1	0
West Point	3,345	4	1	1	2	0	58	14	43	1	0
White Stone	356	0	0	0	0	0	3	0	3	0	0
Williamsburg	14,236	27	1	1	14	11	233	21	203	9	0
Winchester	26,516	63	0	3	29	31	1,117	130	956	31	1
Windsor	2,657	3	0	0	1	2	71	46	25	0	0
Wise	3,325	1	0	0	0	1	94	5	87	2	0
Woodstock	5,158	4	0	0	0	4	100	3	93	4	0
Wytheville	8,309	16	0	1	3	12	225	14	205	6	3
Washington											
Aberdeen	17,161	62	1	11	16	34	951	188	694	69	1
Airway Heights	6,210	5	0	0	4	1	183	34	134	15	0
Algona	3,061	4	0	0	0	4	50	8	33	9	0
Anacortes	16,026	24	0	6	4	14	501	91	387	23	4
Arlington	18,207	31	0	5	10	16	782	161	554	67	0
Asotin	1,271	4	0	0	0	4	30	10	18	2	0
Auburn	71,281	279	2	23	107	147	3,797	762	2,435	600	29
Bainbridge Island	23,386	14	0	3	2	9	322	104	217	1	3
Battle Ground	17,847	32	0	9	2	21	406	60	330	16	0
Bellevue	124,283	140	1	23	58	58	3,539	607	2,775	157	25
Bellingham	82,154	199	1	35	55	108	3,738	646	2,961	131	7
Bingen	723	0	0	0	0	0	28	4	22	2	1
Black Diamond	4,216	1	0	0	0	1	60	13	46	1	0
Blaine	4,757	13	0	3	0	10	159	19	138	2	2
Bonney Lake	17,647	31	1	2	4	24	496	93	378	25	2
Bothell	34,031	27	0	7	10	10	899	149	687	63	7
Bremerton	38,321	241	1	41	53	146	2,038	397	1,457	184	14
Brewster	2,407	5	0	1	1	3	43	9	34	0	0
Brier	6,182	2	0	0	0	2	78	14	64	0	2
Buckley	4,906	5	0	0	1	4	134	22	106	6	3
Burien	33,836	223	0	46	68	109	2,353	659	1,207	487	10
Burlington	8,520	15	0	1	11	3	1,026	139	834	53	3
Camas	19,659	9	0	4	2	3	301	45	243	13	2
Carnation	1,814	0	0	0	0	0	34	10	24	0	0
Castle Rock	2,013	2	0	1	0	1	39	11	25	3	0
Centralia	16,592	85	1	16	16	52	789	165	565	59	1
Chehalis	7,373	19	0	3	4	12	388	48	322	18	2
Cheney	10,756	23	0	4	5	14	296	50	230	16	1
Chewelah	2,648	4	0	0	0	4	83	21	56	6	0
Clarkston	7,342	14	0	0	2	12	412	55	355	2	2
Cle Elum	1,901	5	0	1	0	4	122	25	90	7	1
Clyde Hill	3,031	0	0	0	0	0	37	7	29	1	0
Colfax	2,849	2	0	1	1	0	24	3	19	2	0
College Place	8,903	13	0	3	1	9	188	28	154	6	1
Colton	425	0	0	0	0	0	0	0	0	0	0
Colville	4,746	5	0	1	3	1	146	12	131	3	0
Connell	4,275	7	0	2	0	5	36	7	28	1	0
Cosmopolis	1,675	2	0	2	0	0	12	4	8	0	1
Coulee Dam	1,115	5	0	0	0	5	30	7	22	1	0
Coupeville	1,860	1	0	1	0	0	66	31	34	1	0
Covington	17,851	44	0	11	18	15	577	134	393	50	0
Des Moines	30,139	90	1	7	37	45	1,048	230	627	191	8
Dupont	8,328	5	0	0	0	5	37	10	20	7	1
Duvall	6,800	0	0	0	0	0	43	9	33	1	0
East Wenatchee	13,397	31	0	6	7	18	546	64	468	14	3
Eatonville	2,801	2	0	1	0	1	44	12	31	1	1
Edgewood	9,534	14	1	0	4	9	248	98	133	17	1
Edmonds	40,332	71	0	8	22	41	942	255	630	57	11
Ellensburg	18,459	29	1	8	6	14	771	153	580	38	4
Elma	3,156	8	0	2	2	4	164	35	113	16	1
Enumclaw	10,836	15	1	5	2	7	279	55	204	20	2
Ephrata	7,784	16	0	1	6	9	310	74	227	9	3
Everett	104,635	450	5	49	143	253	7,503	1,163	5,415	925	27
Everson	2,520	4	0	1	0	3	43	6	37	0	0
Fife	9,317	62	0	5	13	44	495	104	328	63	0

[1] If a blank is presented in the arson column, it indicates that the FBI did not receive 12 complete months of arson data for that agency.

Table II-8.   Offenses Known to Law Enforcement, by Selected State and City, 2011—Continued

(Number.)

State/City	Population	Violent crime	Murder and non-negligent man-slaughter	Forcible rape	Robbery	Aggravated assault	Property crime	Burglary	Larceny-theft	Motor vehicle theft	Arson[1]
Washington—Continued											
Fircrest	6,599	17	0	2	1	14	133	32	94	7	0
Forks	3,587	14	0	1	2	11	80	16	61	3	0
Gig Harbor	7,238	18	0	1	7	10	489	93	358	38	1
Goldendale	3,460	7	0	0	0	7	95	22	63	10	1
Grand Coulee	1,004	8	0	0	0	8	71	30	38	3	0
Grandview	11,032	20	1	6	6	7	294	83	192	19	16
Granger	3,297	12	0	4	2	6	127	54	66	7	4
Granite Falls	3,417	19	0	3	1	15	130	30	89	11	2
Hoquiam	8,863	34	0	7	5	22	491	97	382	12	2
Ilwaco	951	1	0	0	0	1	21	6	14	1	0
Issaquah	30,911	26	0	4	9	13	735	120	579	36	4
Kelso	12,112	49	1	9	13	26	683	131	506	46	3
Kenmore	20,781	23	0	4	5	14	338	94	233	11	3
Kennewick	75,077	226	2	27	35	162	2,628	404	2,056	168	35
Kent	93,861	577	1	60	210	306	4,989	1,223	2,977	789	18
Kettle Falls	1,620	2	0	1	0	1	57	3	53	1	0
Kirkland	49,552	74	1	20	15	38	1,472	253	1,122	97	5
Kittitas	1,403	0	0	0	0	0	11	5	6	0	0
La Center	2,844	1	0	0	1	0	44	4	37	3	0
Lacey	43,058	95	0	8	19	68	1,381	267	1,056	58	1
Lake Forest Park	12,796	14	0	3	5	6	270	85	168	17	1
Lake Stevens	28,509	35	0	9	10	16	523	108	345	70	19
Lakewood	59,075	506	2	43	117	344	2,729	603	1,839	287	18
Langley	1,051	0	0	0	0	0	26	7	19	0	0
Liberty Lake	7,710	1	0	0	0	1	88	18	68	2	0
Long Beach	1,414	3	0	0	0	3	58	22	35	1	0
Longview	37,223	162	2	35	38	87	1,997	317	1,483	197	57
Lynden	12,138	22	1	2	1	18	189	36	148	5	1
Lynnwood	36,398	101	1	10	41	49	2,124	247	1,751	126	4
Mabton	2,322	3	0	0	0	3	62	13	43	6	1
Maple Valley	23,040	25	0	7	7	11	361	125	213	23	4
Marysville	60,962	94	0	17	20	57	1,844	376	1,227	241	10
McCleary	1,679	0	0	0	0	0	20	5	14	1	0
Medina	3,016	0	0	0	0	0	43	11	31	1	0
Mercer Island	23,055	11	0	0	3	8	407	59	334	14	8
Mill Creek	18,530	16	0	1	3	12	399	89	281	29	4
Milton	7,077	8	0	0	4	4	266	49	194	23	1
Monroe	17,575	33	1	6	5	21	514	79	379	56	2
Montesano	4,038	0	0	0	0	0	73	17	48	8	0
Morton	1,144	2	0	0	0	2	41	15	26	0	1
Moses Lake	20,686	69	1	9	17	42	1,466	277	1,116	73	2
Mountlake Terrace	20,221	33	1	7	11	14	602	137	410	55	9
Mount Vernon	32,241	100	2	24	34	40	1,804	351	1,377	76	9
Moxee	3,360	0	0	0	0	0	33	5	23	5	0
Mukilteo	20,572	17	0	2	5	10	504	123	350	31	3
Napavine	1,794	1	0	0	0	1	47	9	36	2	0
Newcastle	10,543	11	0	6	3	2	211	71	129	11	2
Normandy Park	6,434	3	0	0	1	2	211	49	150	12	0
North Bend	5,821	25	0	7	1	17	224	37	178	9	7
Oak Harbor	22,421	54	0	12	3	39	567	167	390	10	9
Oakville	695	1	0	0	1	0	21	9	9	3	0
Ocean Shores	5,656	6	0	2	1	3	152	48	99	5	0
Odessa	924	1	0	1	0	0	18	8	10	0	0
Olympia	47,207	126	0	17	31	78	1,976	342	1,535	99	6
Omak	4,921	19	0	1	3	15	166	32	118	16	0
Oroville	1,712	1	0	0	0	1	86	30	56	0	0
Orting	6,852	9	0	2	4	3	227	41	177	9	3
Othello	7,480	29	0	1	4	24	462	82	345	35	2
Pacific	6,710	13	0	3	2	8	162	45	92	25	0
Pasco	60,719	208	2	25	31	150	1,596	368	1,055	173	13
Port Angeles	19,337	102	2	17	14	69	963	196	722	45	2
Port Orchard	11,319	60	0	9	4	47	643	123	444	76	2
Port Townsend	9,256	24	0	2	4	18	268	55	203	10	2
Poulsbo	9,344	23	0	3	4	16	315	48	261	6	2

[1] If a blank is presented in the arson column, it indicates that the FBI did not receive 12 complete months of arson data for that agency.

Table II-8. Offenses Known to Law Enforcement, by Selected State and City, 2011—*Continued*

(Number.)

State/City	Population	Violent crime	Murder and non-negligent man-slaughter	Forcible rape	Robbery	Aggravated assault	Property crime	Burglary	Larceny-theft	Motor vehicle theft	Arson[1]
Washington—*Continued*											
Prosser	5,804	19	0	5	3	11	161	48	98	15	2
Pullman	30,267	27	0	1	2	24	481	97	370	14	8
Puyallup	37,603	106	0	12	42	52	2,642	345	2,036	261	9
Quincy	6,856	39	2	3	2	32	363	100	239	24	1
Rainier	1,822	5	0	0	0	5	47	19	26	2	0
Raymond	2,927	4	0	1	0	3	91	24	66	1	0
Reardan	580	0	0	0	0	0	3	1	2	0	0
Redmond	54,993	47	0	18	10	19	1,391	160	1,176	55	4
Renton	92,354	292	1	33	115	143	4,223	917	2,748	558	8
Republic	1,090	3	0	0	0	3	12	3	9	0	0
Richland	48,812	89	1	13	8	67	1,398	260	1,075	63	14
Ridgefield	4,838	2	0	0	0	2	68	10	53	5	1
Ritzville	1,699	1	0	0	0	1	61	20	40	1	1
Roy	805	2	0	0	1	1	26	7	18	1	0
Royal City	2,174	5	0	1	0	4	30	6	24	0	0
Ruston	761	4	0	0	1	3	32	9	20	3	1
Sammamish	46,498	16	0	8	1	7	356	107	235	14	1
SeaTac	27,331	125	0	16	50	59	1,476	311	731	434	0
Seattle	618,209	3,664	20	100	1,418	2,126	31,792	6,807	21,585	3,400	84
Sedro Woolley	10,705	14	0	5	6	3	583	124	411	48	3
Selah	7,259	3	0	0	1	2	198	41	142	15	2
Sequim	6,710	12	0	3	3	6	311	40	263	8	3
Shelton	9,988	74	0	14	8	52	768	167	519	82	1
Shoreline	53,839	84	0	16	34	34	1,692	351	1,210	131	11
Snohomish	9,241	23	0	5	2	16	431	85	321	25	3
Snoqualmie	10,837	5	0	1	0	4	144	19	112	13	1
Soap Lake	1,538	2	0	0	0	2	27	12	14	1	0
South Bend	1,663	3	0	1	0	2	12	6	6	0	0
Spokane	212,194	1,304	4	84	484	732	15,039	3,030	10,231	1,778	72
Spokane Valley	91,163	175	0	22	58	95	5,001	917	3,613	471	17
Stanwood	6,329	12	0	2	4	6	188	46	140	2	0
Steilacoom	6,079	16	0	0	1	15	51	18	30	3	0
Sumas	1,328	1	0	0	0	1	27	5	22	0	0
Sumner	9,599	30	0	4	11	15	532	113	371	48	3
Sunnyside	16,107	45	0	4	5	36	676	153	430	93	1
Tacoma	201,510	1,507	11	125	446	925	12,062	2,709	7,228	2,125	80
Tenino	1,722	2	0	0	0	2	40	10	27	3	1
Tieton	1,210	1	0	0	0	1	14	9	4	1	0
Tonasket	1,048	3	0	0	0	3	48	14	30	4	1
Toppenish	9,089	29	1	5	13	10	540	127	358	55	5
Tukwila	19,407	190	0	16	95	79	2,884	315	2,140	429	6
Tumwater	17,644	44	1	6	7	30	552	119	403	30	3
Twisp	933	2	0	0	0	2	27	7	15	5	0
Union Gap	6,142	36	0	3	12	21	662	88	523	51	1
University Place	31,633	86	1	8	34	43	733	222	449	62	5
Vancouver	164,329	633	9	102	185	337	6,447	950	4,629	868	33
Walla Walla	32,229	130	3	22	20	85	1,383	244	1,104	35	11
Wapato	5,075	37	1	7	12	17	323	143	130	50	3
Warden	2,734	1	0	0	0	1	27	7	12	8	0
Washougal	14,316	36	2	8	3	23	276	39	225	12	10
Wenatchee	32,426	87	2	5	22	58	1,315	197	1,056	62	2
Westport	2,132	0	0	0	0	0	72	17	53	2	0
West Richland	11,996	19	0	4	0	15	166	52	108	6	1
White Salmon	2,259	0	0	0	0	0	55	5	48	2	0
Wilbur	898	2	0	0	0	2	13	4	9	0	0
Winlock	1,360	5	0	0	1	4	35	11	23	1	0
Winthrop	400	1	0	1	0	0	11	2	9	0	0
Woodinville	11,110	11	0	2	2	7	368	87	255	26	0
Woodland	5,595	20	0	2	3	15	159	19	125	15	3
Woodway	1,328	1	0	0	1	0	18	7	11	0	0
Yakima	92,496	481	6	48	156	271	5,120	1,619	2,841	660	17
Yarrow Point	1,017	0	0	0	0	0	11	2	9	0	0
Yelm	6,955	17	0	4	8	5	283	52	217	14	0
Zillah	3,011	7	0	2	4	1	79	17	55	7	0
West Virginia											
Barboursville	3,969	5	0	0	3	2	321	23	295	3	0
Beckley	17,637	134	0	11	36	87	1,050	212	786	52	4
Belington	1,923	11	0	0	0	11	17	4	13	0	0

[1] If a blank is presented in the arson column, it indicates that the FBI did not receive 12 complete months of arson data for that agency.

Table II-8. **Offenses Known to Law Enforcement, by Selected State and City, 2011**—*Continued*

(Number.)

State/City	Population	Violent crime	Murder and non-negligent man-slaughter	Forcible rape	Robbery	Aggravated assault	Property crime	Burglary	Larceny-theft	Motor vehicle theft	Arson[1]
West Virginia—*Continued*											
Benwood	1,422	1	0	0	0	1	4	1	3	0	0
Bethlehem	2,502	1	0	0	0	1	9	3	6	0	0
Buckhannon	5,646	3	0	0	1	2	167	31	127	9	3
Chapmanville	1,258	4	0	0	0	4	43	2	35	6	0
Charleston	51,466	510	5	23	120	362	3,009	635	2,234	140	31
Dunbar	7,917	37	1	3	9	24	173	45	119	9	5
Elkins	7,103	39	0	4	3	32	141	35	101	5	1
Follansbee	2,990	2	0	0	0	2	26	13	12	1	0
Glen Dale	1,528	1	0	0	0	1	22	7	15	0	0
Glenville	1,539	2	0	0	0	2	10	2	8	0	0
Hurricane	6,292	15	0	2	3	10	203	11	186	6	1
Kenova	3,220	3	0	0	0	3	118	21	89	8	0
Kingwood	2,943	1	0	0	0	1	7	6	1	0	0
Lewisburg	3,835	3	0	1	0	2	80	9	69	2	1
Logan	1,781	10	0	2	0	8	136	9	120	7	1
Martinsburg	17,249	79	0	4	20	55	972	171	772	29	9
Mason	969	1	0	0	0	1	7	2	5	0	0
Moorefield	2,547	31	0	0	1	30	55	3	47	5	0
Moundsville	9,330	44	1	2	5	36	477	114	347	16	3
Mount Hope	1,416	0	0	0	0	0	26	13	11	2	0
New Cumberland	1,104	0	0	0	0	0	9	3	6	0	0
New Martinsville	5,373	2	0	0	1	1	57	12	44	1	0
Nitro	7,187	13	0	3	3	7	236	37	184	15	3
Nutter Fort	1,595	2	0	0	0	2	30	6	24	0	0
Oceana	1,396	44	0	0	3	41	127	18	108	1	0
Paden City	2,636	0	0	0	0	0	1	0	1	0	0
Pennsboro	1,172	1	0	0	0	1	1	0	1	0	0
Philippi	2,970	34	0	2	0	32	20	8	12	0	0
Point Pleasant	4,356	13	0	0	4	9	115	23	90	2	0
Ravenswood	3,881	6	0	0	0	6	76	13	62	1	1
Ripley	3,256	0	0	0	0	0	35	3	29	3	0
Romney	1,850	16	0	0	0	16	7	3	4	0	0
Rowlesburg	585	0	0	0	0	0	1	1	0	0	0
Shinnston	2,204	9	0	0	1	8	46	14	30	2	0
Sophia	1,346	2	0	0	0	2	33	6	25	2	1
South Charleston	13,467	66	2	2	7	55	524	72	423	29	1
St. Albans	11,058	26	3	3	11	9	355	72	262	21	1
Summersville	3,577	29	0	0	2	27	122	12	105	5	0
Terra Alta	1,479	1	0	0	0	1	6	4	1	1	0
Triadelphia	812	2	0	0	0	2	3	1	2	0	0
Wardensville	271	0	0	0	0	0	0	0	0	0	0
Wayne	1,415	0	0	0	0	0	15	0	15	0	0
Welch	2,409	15	0	0	0	15	14	1	12	1	0
Wellsburg	2,809	0	0	0	0	0	30	12	14	4	0
Weston	4,115	1	0	0	0	1	0	11	3	6	2	0
West Union	826	0	0	0	0	0	2	0	2	0	0
White Sulphur Springs	2,447	2	0	0	0	2	1	1	0	0	0
Williamson	3,195	8	0	0	4	4	49	19	30	0	0
Wisconsin											
Adams	1,976	3	0	0	1	2	88	21	62	5	0
Albany	1,022	5	0	0	0	5	22	3	18	1	0
Algoma	3,181	5	0	3	0	2	103	5	96	2	0
Altoona	6,735	18	0	4	2	12	122	28	85	9	0
Amery	2,915	4	0	0	0	4	112	16	91	5	0
Antigo	8,270	30	0	0	0	30	488	72	402	14	0
Appleton	72,939	217	0	33	29	155	1,458	220	1,213	25	10
Arcadia	2,938	1	0	0	0	1	16	1	15	0	0
Ashland	8,252	27	1	2	3	21	505	89	403	13	5
Ashwaubenon	17,037	17	0	3	3	11	639	37	587	15	0
Athens	1,110	2	0	1	0	1	8	2	6	0	0
Baraboo	12,100	53	1	8	4	40	447	50	388	9	2
Bayfield	489	2	0	0	0	2	30	6	24	0	0
Beaver Dam	16,285	5	0	1	2	2	472	57	413	2	0
Belleville	2,395	1	0	1	0	0	21	0	21	0	0
Beloit	37,127	156	1	14	54	87	1,333	354	916	63	17
Beloit Town	7,695	24	0	0	3	21	118	31	84	3	2
Berlin	5,548	2	0	1	0	1	131	18	108	5	0
Big Bend	1,296	0	0	0	0	0	45	5	39	1	1
Black River Falls	3,638	4	0	0	0	4	135	3	127	5	0
Blair	1,372	1	0	1	0	0	14	4	10	0	0

[1] If a blank is presented in the arson column, it indicates that the FBI did not receive 12 complete months of arson data for that agency.

Table II-8.   Offenses Known to Law Enforcement, by Selected State and City, 2011—*Continued*

(Number.)

State/City	Population	Violent crime	Murder and non-negligent man-slaughter	Forcible rape	Robbery	Aggravated assault	Property crime	Burglary	Larceny-theft	Motor vehicle theft	Arson[1]
Wisconsin—*Continued*											
Blanchardville	829	0	0	0	0	0	13	1	11	1	0
Bloomer	3,554	2	0	0	0	2	45	9	35	1	1
Bloomfield	6,305	11	0	3	1	7	105	13	86	6	0
Blue Mounds	859	0	0	0	0	0	6	2	3	1	0
Boscobel	3,245	46	0	0	0	46	78	15	63	0	0
Brandon-Fairwater	1,256	0	0	0	0	0	13	0	7	6	0
Brillion	3,162	3	0	1	0	2	22	4	18	0	0
Brodhead	3,307	0	0	0	0	0	93	18	73	2	0
Brookfield	38,085	25	0	0	9	16	1,021	106	895	20	0
Brookfield Township	6,143	12	0	0	0	12	143	12	125	6	0
Brown Deer	12,051	3	0	0	3	0	106	20	82	4	5
Burlington	10,510	16	0	5	2	9	264	43	216	5	1
Butler	1,849	3	0	0	0	3	41	5	32	4	0
Caledonia	24,813	69	0	2	23	44	393	62	317	14	1
Campbellsport	2,025	0	0	0	0	0	16	1	14	1	0
Campbell Township	4,333	0	0	0	0	0	59	10	48	1	0
Cashton	1,107	3	0	0	3	0	5	3	2	0	0
Cedarburg	11,462	7	0	1	0	6	136	8	128	0	0
Chenequa	593	1	0	0	0	1	4	1	3	0	0
Chetek	2,231	3	0	2	0	1	41	17	23	1	0
Chilton	3,950	1	0	0	0	1	78	15	60	3	0
Chippewa Falls	13,721	20	0	2	3	15	218	43	165	10	0
Cleveland	1,491	3	0	2	0	1	8	0	8	0	0
Clinton	2,163	1	0	0	0	1	25	4	21	0	0
Clintonville	4,579	8	0	1	0	7	240	22	218	0	0
Colby-Abbotsford	4,180	2	0	0	0	2	54	13	40	1	0
Columbus	5,013	5	0	0	0	5	91	14	77	0	0
Cornell	1,473	1	0	0	1	0	38	5	33	0	0
Cottage Grove	6,219	1	0	0	0	1	158	15	139	4	0
Crandon	1,928	0	0	0	0	0	40	7	31	2	0
Cross Plains	3,553	0	0	0	0	0	32	3	28	1	0
Cuba City	2,095	0	0	0	0	0	41	5	36	0	0
Cudahy	18,347	62	0	7	21	34	620	134	462	24	1
Cumberland	2,179	3	0	0	0	3	50	7	41	2	0
Dane	999	0	0	0	0	0	0	0	0	0	0
Darien	1,587	0	0	0	0	0	30	1	29	0	0
Darlington	2,462	4	0	0	0	4	26	1	25	0	0
Deforest	8,975	2	0	2	0	0	120	12	104	4	0
Delafield	7,116	5	0	0	3	2	196	13	181	2	0
Delavan	8,500	8	0	0	2	6	297	26	266	5	0
Delavan Town	5,308	1	0	1	0	0	82	15	63	4	1
Denmark	2,132	1	0	0	0	1	12	4	8	0	0
De Pere	23,904	10	0	2	1	7	367	64	298	5	4
Dodgeville	4,713	10	0	1	0	9	71	10	61	0	1
Durand	1,939	0	0	0	0	0	9	1	6	2	0
Eagle River	1,404	1	0	0	0	1	111	9	98	4	0
East Troy	4,300	7	0	4	0	3	95	14	79	2	4
Eau Claire	66,170	139	0	20	21	98	1,959	378	1,531	50	10
Edgar	1,485	0	0	0	0	0	3	0	3	0	0
Edgerton	5,485	0	0	0	0	0	120	14	105	1	0
Eleva	673	0	0	0	0	0	15	2	13	0	0
Elkhart Lake	971	0	0	0	0	0	18	0	18	0	0
Elkhorn	10,128	8	0	4	0	4	226	20	202	4	1
Elk Mound	882	0	0	0	0	0	10	3	7	0	
Ellsworth	3,298	3	0	0	0	3	111	26	80	5	0
Elm Grove	5,960	0	0	0	0	0	74	12	60	2	0
Evansville	5,034	8	0	0	0	8	111	16	92	3	0
Everest	17,111	41	0	10	4	27	375	69	285	21	1
Fall Creek	1,321	1	0	0	0	1	13	4	9	0	0
Fall River	1,719	0	0	0	0	0	12	2	9	1	2
Fennimore	2,508	0	0	0	0	0	75	10	65	0	0
Fitchburg	25,370	59	0	8	14	37	693	66	609	18	0
Fond du Lac	43,208	146	2	37	9	98	1,069	117	923	29	3
Fontana	1,679	0	0	0	0	0	19	1	18	0	0
Fort Atkinson	12,422	15	0	1	2	12	233	32	197	4	0
Fountain City	863	3	0	0	0	3	8	0	8	0	0
Fox Lake	1,526	0	0	0	0	0	8	1	6	1	0
Fox Valley Metro	16,991	13	0	0	0	13	263	33	219	11	1
Franklin	35,605	15	0	2	3	10	627	65	550	12	1

[1] If a blank is presented in the arson column, it indicates that the FBI did not receive 12 complete months of arson data for that agency.

Table II-8.   Offenses Known to Law Enforcement, by Selected State and City, 2011—*Continued*

(Number.)

State/City	Population	Violent crime	Murder and non-negligent man-slaughter	Forcible rape	Robbery	Aggravated assault	Property crime	Burglary	Larceny-theft	Motor vehicle theft	Arson[1]
Wisconsin—*Continued*											
Frederic	1,142	5	0	0	0	5	22	4	18	0	0
Freedom	5,867	0	0	0	0	0	28	5	22	1	0
Geneva Town	5,015	6	0	0	0	6	97	21	76	0	0
Genoa City	3,055	0	0	0	0	0	34	3	30	1	0
Germantown	19,835	9	0	4	3	2	427	48	366	13	0
Gillett	1,392	0	0	0	0	0	34	6	26	2	0
Glendale	12,928	18	0	0	14	4	769	20	720	29	0
Grafton	11,509	3	0	0	1	2	147	9	135	3	0
Grand Chute	21,010	24	0	4	3	17	964	76	858	30	0
Grand Rapids	7,679	1	0	0	0	1	40	11	27	2	0
Green Bay	104,510	373	2	54	48	269	2,420	467	1,852	101	7
Greendale	14,107	10	0	4	3	3	539	28	503	8	0
Greenfield	36,880	51	1	2	24	24	1,175	132	1,016	27	0
Green Lake	964	0	0	0	0	0	30	5	25	0	0
Hales Corners	7,726	7	0	1	0	6	158	8	146	4	2
Hartford	14,285	8	0	0	2	6	338	51	281	6	0
Hartland	9,150	10	0	3	0	7	102	9	88	5	0
Hayward	2,328	8	0	1	0	7	115	12	97	6	1
Hazel Green	1,261	0	0	0	0	0	57	15	42	0	0
Highland	846	0	0	0	0	0	5	2	3	0	0
Hobart-Lawrence	10,512	1	0	0	1	0	58	22	34	2	0
Holmen	9,044	4	0	1	0	3	184	48	129	7	0
Horicon	3,671	1	0	0	0	1	40	1	36	3	0
Hortonville	2,723	2	0	0	0	2	92	6	84	2	0
Hudson	12,774	12	0	1	2	9	501	36	447	18	1
Hurley	1,554	23	0	1	0	22	51	1	42	8	0
Iron River	1,128	2	0	0	0	2	8	3	5	0	0
Jackson	6,782	4	0	0	0	4	35	12	20	3	0
Janesville	63,852	169	2	20	32	115	2,399	407	1,948	44	10
Jefferson	8,008	9	0	4	2	3	225	26	194	5	2
Juneau	2,826	0	0	0	0	0	52	2	49	1	0
Kaukauna	15,529	17	0	1	1	15	172	15	149	8	0
Kenosha	99,650	279	0	50	99	130	3,031	566	2,329	136	9
Kewaskum	4,021	1	0	0	1	0	29	5	24	0	0
Kewaunee	2,965	1	0	0	0	1	38	4	34	0	0
Kiel	3,754	4	0	0	1	3	53	5	46	2	0
Kohler	2,129	0	0	0	0	0	54	0	54	0	0
Kronenwetter	7,241	5	0	1	0	4	53	20	31	2	0
La Crosse	51,544	165	0	18	25	122	1,823	313	1,435	75	3
Lake Delton	2,927	15	0	3	3	9	537	46	483	8	0
Lake Geneva	7,684	39	0	4	3	32	259	22	233	4	0
Lake Hallie	6,476	8	0	1	1	6	217	51	163	3	1
Lake Mills	5,733	12	0	4	0	8	76	8	67	1	0
Lodi	3,063	3	0	1	0	2	84	10	73	1	5
Lomira	2,441	2	0	1	0	1	55	4	49	2	0
Luxemburg	2,526	2	0	1	0	1	19	2	16	1	0
Madison	234,225	815	8	74	272	461	7,936	1,440	6,152	344	50
Manawa	1,377	1	0	1	0	0	14	1	13	0	0
Manitowoc	33,883	53	0	6	7	40	795	109	667	19	4
Marathon City	1,531	6	0	0	0	6	26	6	19	1	0
Marinette	11,016	16	0	2	8	6	352	43	299	10	2
Markesan	1,482	0	0	0	0	0	29	5	24	0	0
Marshall Village	3,879	1	0	1	0	0	76	10	62	4	0
Marshfield	19,201	9	0	1	0	8	515	74	433	8	1
Mauston	4,442	13	0	2	0	11	121	27	90	4	0
Mayville	5,176	1	0	0	0	1	105	17	88	0	0
McFarland	7,842	3	0	0	0	3	175	14	159	2	0
Medford	4,345	1	0	1	0	0	156	8	142	6	0
Menasha	17,429	44	0	3	3	38	424	52	364	8	0
Menomonee Falls	35,781	9	0	1	5	3	460	50	402	8	2
Menomonie	16,335	17	0	2	1	14	388	51	323	14	4
Mequon	23,233	10	2	0	4	4	202	38	162	2	0
Merrill	9,703	22	0	3	0	19	368	50	312	6	2
Middleton	17,518	16	0	1	6	9	461	73	377	11	1
Milton	5,570	11	0	0	4	7	162	10	148	4	2
Milwaukee	597,426	5,969	85	194	2,963	2,727	30,097	6,669	18,890	4,538	262
Mineral Point	2,498	1	0	1	0	0	51	2	43	6	0
Minocqua	4,404	4	0	3	0	1	153	10	138	5	0
Mishicot	1,448	0	0	0	0	0	1	0	1	0	0
Monona	7,566	9	0	0	4	5	462	24	431	7	0

[1] If a blank is presented in the arson column, it indicates that the FBI did not receive 12 complete months of arson data for that agency.

Table II-8.   Offenses Known to Law Enforcement, by Selected State and City, 2011—*Continued*

(Number.)

State/City	Population	Violent crime	Murder and non-negligent man-slaughter	Forcible rape	Robbery	Aggravated assault	Property crime	Burglary	Larceny-theft	Motor vehicle theft	Arson[1]
Wisconsin—*Continued*											
Monroe	10,874	28	0	2	2	24	346	42	299	5	2
Montello	1,502	2	0	0	0	2	30	6	23	1	0
Mosinee	4,005	2	0	1	0	1	108	22	82	4	0
Mount Horeb	7,040	12	0	1	1	10	118	19	98	1	2
Mount Pleasant	26,311	23	0	3	11	9	690	100	571	19	6
Mukwonago	7,387	5	0	1	0	4	175	18	155	2	0
Muskego	24,240	7	0	3	1	3	234	41	188	5	1
Neenah	25,612	36	0	4	1	31	407	72	327	8	1
Neillsville	2,474	0	0	0	0	0	82	15	66	1	0
New Glarus	2,181	2	0	1	1	0	47	3	44	0	0
New Holstein	3,250	3	0	0	0	3	82	6	75	1	0
New Lisbon	2,565	5	0	0	0	5	35	11	18	6	0
New London	7,327	10	1	1	1	7	146	17	124	5	0
New Richmond	8,411	9	0	2	0	7	195	13	172	10	4
Niagara	1,631	0	0	0	0	0	16	3	12	1	0
North Fond du Lac	5,036	9	0	2	1	6	69	7	57	5	1
North Hudson	3,784	0	0	0	0	0	22	2	18	2	0
North Prairie	2,150	1	0	0	0	1	15	0	14	1	0
Oak Creek	34,601	30	0	5	5	20	1,143	82	1,032	29	2
Oconomowoc	15,828	3	0	1	1	1	253	17	235	1	0
Oconomowoc Town	8,445	1	0	0	0	1	38	10	25	3	0
Oconto	4,533	6	0	1	1	4	127	24	97	6	0
Oconto Falls	2,904	0	0	0	0	0	70	14	53	3	0
Omro	3,532	7	0	0	0	7	34	15	19	0	0
Onalaska	17,813	13	0	1	2	10	477	73	400	4	0
Oregon	9,271	8	0	2	0	6	178	33	139	6	0
Osceola	2,579	11	0	0	0	11	49	6	41	2	0
Oshkosh	66,371	179	0	11	20	148	1,668	315	1,330	23	7
Osseo	1,708	0	0	0	0	0	44	1	43	0	0
Oxford	610	0	0	0	0	0	18	5	13	0	0
Park Falls	2,473	0	0	0	0	0	31	0	29	2	0
Pepin	841	0	0	0	0	0	30	2	28	0	0
Peshtigo	3,517	0	0	0	0	0	47	4	38	5	0
Pewaukee Village	8,202	12	0	0	0	12	156	14	137	5	0
Phillips	1,484	6	0	0	0	6	48	7	41	0	0
Plainfield	866	1	0	0	0	1	8	4	4	0	0
Platteville	11,273	10	0	5	0	5	443	38	401	4	0
Pleasant Prairie	19,805	10	0	1	2	7	290	23	262	5	0
Plover	12,176	15	0	2	0	13	188	19	166	3	0
Plymouth	8,482	8	1	1	1	5	237	20	213	4	0
Portage	10,369	35	0	1	3	31	92	27	62	3	0
Port Washington	11,299	7	0	3	0	4	156	10	144	2	1
Poynette	2,539	0	0	0	0	0	22	3	19	0	0
Prescott	4,277	12	0	3	0	9	115	20	93	2	0
Pulaski	3,554	2	0	0	0	2	21	1	19	1	0
Racine	79,204	324	5	14	186	119	3,605	1,239	2,227	139	17
Reedsburg	9,240	9	1	3	1	4	144	7	135	2	1
Rice Lake	8,475	22	0	10	1	11	308	32	265	11	0
Richland Center	5,207	6	0	0	0	6	57	6	50	1	0
Ripon	7,767	9	0	1	1	7	99	9	90	0	1
River Falls	15,065	30	1	4	1	24	396	34	344	18	3
River Hills	1,604	0	0	0	0	0	12	3	9	0	0
Rome Town	2,732	1	0	1	0	0	45	22	22	1	1
Rosendale	1,068	0	0	0	0	0	0	0	0	0	0
Rothschild	5,292	1	0	0	0	1	124	4	119	1	0
Sauk Prairie	4,574	0	0	0	0	0	213	23	189	1	0
Saukville	4,470	5	0	0	0	5	88	7	77	4	0
Seymour	3,466	7	0	1	0	6	28	3	24	1	0
Shawano	9,346	30	0	2	1	27	308	35	269	4	0
Sheboygan	49,503	131	0	16	26	89	1,446	231	1,165	50	5
Sheboygan Falls	7,809	8	0	0	1	7	100	5	91	4	0
Shiocton	925	0	0	0	0	0	13	0	13	0	0
Shorewood	13,219	8	0	0	3	5	332	20	305	7	0
Shorewood Hills	1,572	1	0	0	0	1	56	1	54	1	1
Silver Lake	2,422	2	0	0	0	2	15	5	9	1	0
Siren	810	1	0	0	0	1	31	0	31	0	0
Slinger	5,090	3	0	0	2	1	72	6	66	0	0
South Milwaukee	21,248	16	0	5	7	4	511	76	410	25	1

[1] If a blank is presented in the arson column, it indicates that the FBI did not receive 12 complete months of arson data for that agency.

Table II-8.   Offenses Known to Law Enforcement, by Selected State and City, 2011—*Continued*

(Number.)

State/City	Population	Violent crime	Murder and non-negligent man-slaughter	Forcible rape	Robbery	Aggravated assault	Property crime	Burglary	Larceny-theft	Motor vehicle theft	Arson[1]
Wisconsin—*Continued*											
Sparta	9,563	8	0	0	1	7	278	57	209	12	0
Spencer	1,933	0	0	0	0	0	21	4	17	0	0
Spooner	2,694	3	0	3	0	0	72	7	65	0	0
Stanley	3,624	6	0	1	0	5	67	15	52	0	0
St. Croix Falls	2,142	1	0	0	1	0	89	5	82	2	0
Stevens Point	26,833	47	0	7	4	36	663	83	567	13	1
St. Francis	9,406	16	0	2	6	8	303	34	262	7	0
Stoughton	12,666	9	0	1	4	4	359	65	287	7	0
Strum	1,119	0	0	0	0	0	12	1	11	0	0
Sturgeon Bay	9,184	11	0	1	0	10	153	21	130	2	0
Sturtevant	7,000	6	0	0	1	5	86	15	68	3	0
Summit	4,694	0	0	0	0	0	15	8	7	0	0
Sun Prairie	29,492	43	0	6	7	30	647	69	569	9	1
Superior	27,363	54	0	7	27	20	1,419	274	1,095	50	17
Theresa	1,267	1	0	0	0	1	33	7	23	3	0
Thiensville	3,249	5	0	0	0	5	19	4	13	2	0
Tomah	9,133	24	0	4	1	19	342	46	289	7	0
Tomahawk	3,412	4	0	0	0	4	59	16	35	8	0
Town of East Troy	4,039	0	0	0	0	0	46	12	34	0	0
Town of Madison	6,306	31	0	8	14	9	237	42	165	30	1
Town of Menasha	18,579	23	0	4	1	18	253	70	177	6	1
Trempealeau	1,536	0	0	0	0	0	5	1	4	0	0
Twin Lakes	6,015	5	0	4	0	1	99	15	83	1	1
Two Rivers	11,763	25	0	6	0	19	181	25	145	11	2
Valders	966	0	0	0	0	0	8	0	8	0	1
Verona	10,665	19	1	6	2	10	238	18	220	0	0
Viroqua	4,381	6	0	1	0	5	77	9	68	0	0
Walworth	2,828	4	0	0	0	4	20	1	19	0	0
Washburn	2,126	8	0	1	0	7	19	1	18	0	0
Waterloo	3,348	1	0	0	0	1	28	1	27	0	0
Watertown	23,965	88	0	14	5	69	473	77	386	10	5
Waukesha	71,026	92	0	17	17	58	1,130	178	918	34	7
Waunakee	12,150	12	0	0	3	9	115	22	92	1	0
Waupaca	6,095	23	0	1	3	19	231	9	214	8	0
Waupun	11,389	6	0	1	0	5	144	25	113	6	0
Wausau	39,276	123	0	32	21	70	1,178	253	890	35	6
Wautoma	2,228	6	0	0	0	6	71	5	63	3	0
Wauwatosa	46,598	100	0	2	49	49	1,802	244	1,506	52	0
West Allis	60,674	199	2	10	114	73	3,174	571	2,376	227	26
West Bend	31,213	29	1	2	5	21	745	46	687	12	2
Westby	2,210	3	0	0	0	3	53	20	31	2	0
Westfield	1,259	0	0	0	0	0	20	2	18	0	0
West Milwaukee	4,224	32	0	1	16	15	348	43	280	25	0
West Salem	4,820	3	0	1	0	2	85	27	54	4	1
Whitefish Bay	14,171	2	0	0	2	0	192	7	181	4	0
Whitewater	14,453	19	0	4	3	12	319	58	255	6	0
Williams Bay	2,575	0	0	0	0	0	35	5	30	0	0
Winneconne	2,360	0	0	0	0	0	15	4	11	0	0
Wisconsin Rapids	18,447	8	0	3	3	2	824	103	704	17	1
Wyoming											
Afton	1,926	9	0	0	0	9	13	4	9	0	1
Alpine	835	6	0	1	0	5	20	12	8	0	0
Basin	1,295	2	0	0	0	2	15	7	8	0	0
Buffalo	4,622	18	0	0	0	18	101	12	85	4	1
Casper	55,761	103	1	10	22	70	2,057	287	1,693	77	17
Cheyenne	59,944	147	2	26	25	94	2,049	255	1,734	60	1
Cody	9,597	24	0	4	0	20	266	43	219	4	3
Diamondville	743	1	0	0	0	1	9	2	7	0	0
Douglas	6,169	11	1	0	0	10	251	14	233	4	0
Evanston	12,458	12	0	5	0	7	277	25	241	11	1

[1] If a blank is presented in the arson column, it indicates that the FBI did not receive 12 complete months of arson data for that agency.

Table II-8.   Offenses Known to Law Enforcement, by Selected State and City, 2011—*Continued*

(Number.)

State/City	Population	Violent crime	Murder and non-negligent man-slaughter	Forcible rape	Robbery	Aggravated assault	Property crime	Burglary	Larceny-theft	Motor vehicle theft	Arson[1]
Wyoming—*Continued*											
Evansville	2,564	19	0	0	0	19	31	5	23	3	0
Gillette	29,321	37	0	4	1	32	884	121	734	29	5
Glenrock	2,597	2	0	0	0	2	29	5	23	1	1
Green River	12,616	77	0	3	0	74	249	41	194	14	1
Greybull	1,862	10	0	1	0	9	12	3	8	1	0
Hanna	848	4	0	0	0	4	1	0	1	0	0
Hulett	386	1	0	0	0	1	4	0	4	0	0
Jackson	9,654	41	0	11	0	30	254	28	213	13	0
Kemmerer	2,677	1	0	0	0	1	52	2	49	1	0
Lander	7,547	9	0	1	0	8	243	32	204	7	0
Laramie	31,064	39	0	5	5	29	728	89	614	25	3
Lusk	1,580	1	0	0	0	1	6	2	3	1	0
Mills	3,489	23	1	0	0	22	127	61	64	2	0
Moorcroft	1,017	2	0	1	0	1	25	3	22	0	1
Newcastle	3,560	5	1	2	0	2	86	14	72	0	0
Pine Bluffs	1,138	10	0	0	0	10	39	7	27	5	0
Powell	6,365	16	0	3	2	11	199	17	182	0	3
Rawlins	9,333	44	0	1	0	43	278	40	224	14	0
Riverton	10,700	39	2	4	1	32	503	30	440	33	2
Rock Springs	23,221	76	0	15	4	57	651	69	556	26	2
Saratoga	1,704	0	0	0	0	0	26	5	21	0	0
Sheridan	17,584	31	0	3	1	27	473	58	400	15	3
Sundance	1,192	0	0	0	0	0	13	6	4	3	0
Thermopolis	3,033	0	0	0	0	0	45	3	42	0	0
Torrington	6,553	10	0	2	1	7	153	20	132	1	0
Wheatland	3,656	10	5	1	0	4	146	12	128	6	0
Worland	5,531	1	0	0	0	1	31	1	30	0	0

[1] If a blank is presented in the arson column, it indicates that the FBI did not receive 12 complete months of arson data for that agency.

Table II-9. Offenses Known to Law Enforcement, by Selected State and University and College, 2011

(Number.)

State and University/College	Campus	Student enrollment[1]	Violent crime	Murder and non-negligent manslaughter	Forcible rape	Robbery	Aggravated assault	Property crime	Burglary	Larceny-theft	Motor vehicle theft	Arson[2]
Alabama[3]												
Alabama A&M University		5,814	16	0	1	2	13	183	86	86	11	0
Calhoun Community College		12,134	0	0	0	0	0	29	0	29	0	0
Jacksonville State University		9,504	4	0	0	1	3	102	14	88	0	0
Troy University		28,322	2	0	0	0	2	81	9	72	0	0
University of Alabama, Huntsville		7,614	3	0	2	0	1	104	30	72	2	0
University of Montevallo		3,045	2	0	2	0	0	35	4	29	2	0
University of North Alabama		7,209	3	0	2	1	0	73	13	60	0	0
University of South Alabama		14,776	14	1	2	6	5	228	30	189	9	1
University of West Alabama		5,094	2	0	0	1	1	61	28	33	0	0
Alaska												
University of Alaska												
Anchorage		18,154	3	0	1	1	1	96	3	93	0	0
Fairbanks		9,855	2	0	0	0	2	71	4	64	3	0
Arizona												
Arizona State University		70,440	42	0	3	10	29	1,151	107	1,027	17	9
Central Arizona College		7,117	2	0	0	0	2	65	29	35	1	0
Northern Arizona University		25,197	21	0	7	2	12	367	40	326	1	1
Pima Community College		36,823	4	0	0	3	1	141	5	123	13	1
University of Arizona		39,086	9	1	0	2	6	787	69	707	11	4
Yavapai College		8,410	1	0	0	0	1	35	3	31	1	0
Arkansas												
Arkansas State University, Jonesboro		13,415	8	0	0	1	7	171	42	127	2	0
Arkansas Tech University		9,815	0	0	0	0	0	84	15	66	3	0
Henderson State University		3,708	4	0	2	1	1	58	15	42	1	0
Southern Arkansas University		3,379	3	0	2	0	1	73	20	52	1	0
Southern Arkansas University Tech		1,851	0	0	0	0	0	17	5	12	0	0
University of Arkansas												
Fayetteville		21,405	15	0	1	1	13	236	50	172	14	0
Little Rock		13,176	7	0	2	3	2	197	71	117	9	0
Medical Sciences		2,836	16	0	0	0	16	206	2	201	3	0
Monticello		3,638	1	0	0	1	0	43	14	28	1	0
Pine Bluff		3,428	1	0	0	0	1	78	7	71	0	0
University of Central Arkansas		11,444	6	0	3	1	2	143	48	93	2	1
California												
Allan Hancock College		12,108	0	0	0	0	0	57	16	41	0	1
California State Polytechnic University												
Pomona		20,747	5	0	2	3	0	183	22	146	15	0
San Luis Obispo		18,360	2	0	1	0	1	194	7	177	10	2
California State University												
Bakersfield		7,906	1	0	0	0	1	69	11	56	2	0
Channel Islands		3,828	4	0	0	0	4	56	6	48	2	0
Chico		15,989	4	0	1	2	1	216	11	204	1	1
Dominguez Hills		13,854	15	0	2	6	7	139	72	61	6	0
East Bay		12,889	0	0	0	0	0	131	23	106	2	0
Fresno		20,932	17	0	3	3	11	501	63	416	22	2
Fullerton		35,590	9	0	0	2	7	223	39	169	15	0
Long Beach		33,416	6	0	1	3	2	204	23	176	5	0
Los Angeles		20,142	5	0	0	3	2	187	5	158	24	0
Monterey Bay		4,790	5	0	3	0	2	55	4	50	1	0
Northridge		35,272	12	0	0	5	7	404	33	356	15	0
Sacramento		27,033	6	0	1	3	2	273	14	254	5	4
San Bernardino		16,400	5	0	1	1	3	106	7	87	12	0
San Jose[4]		NA	23	2	1	5	15	401	32	353	16	2
San Marcos		9,722	4	0	0	1	3	41	6	34	1	0
Stanislaus		8,305	1	0	1	0	0	71	12	51	8	3
College of the Sequoias		13,470	1	0	0	0	1	101	13	82	6	0
Contra Costa Community College		7,975	11	0	0	8	3	250	19	210	21	0
Cuesta College		11,335	0	0	0	0	0	20	2	18	0	0
El Camino College		24,756	2	0	0	2	0	177	11	153	13	2
Foothill-De Anza College		41,104	1	0	0	1	0	63	11	50	2	0
Humboldt State University		7,903	2	0	1	0	1	109	3	100	6	0
Marin Community College		7,353	2	0	0	0	2	25	3	22	0	0
Pasadena Community College		27,023	2	0	0	2	0	144	3	132	9	0
Riverside Community College		20,585	5	0	0	2	3	134	14	115	5	0
San Bernardino Community College		13,822	7	0	0	3	4	134	30	96	8	0

NA = Not available.

Note: Caution should be exercised in making any intercampus comparisons or ranking schools because university/college crime statistics are affected by a variety of factors. These include demographic characteristics of the surrounding community, ratio of male to female students, number of on-campus residents, accessibility of the campus to outside visitors, size of enrollment, etc.

[1] The student enrollment figures provided by the United States Department of Education are for the 2010 school year, the most recent available. The enrollment figures include full-time and part-time students.

[2] If a blank is presented in the arson column, it indicates that the FBI did not receive 12 complete months of arson data for that agency.

[3] Because of changes in the state/local agency's reporting practices, figures are not comparable to previous years' data.

[4] Student enrollment figures were not available.

Table II-9.   Offenses Known to Law Enforcement, by Selected State and University and College, 2011—*Continued*

(Number.)

State and University/College	Campus	Student enroll-ment[1]	Violent crime	Murder and non-negligent man-slaughter	Forcible rape	Robbery	Aggra-vated assault	Property crime	Burglary	Larceny-theft	Motor vehicle theft	Arson[2]
San Diego State University	29,187	13	0	5	3	5	574	45	489	40	0	
San Francisco State University	29,718	6	0	3	3	0	298	38	246	14	0	
San Jose/Evergreen Community College	21,671	1	0	0	0	1	86	9	74	3	0	
Santa Rosa Junior College	24,879	7	0	0	1	6	65	2	63	0	2	
Solano Community College	11,801	2	0	0	1	1	70	0	68	2	0	
Sonoma State University	8,395	3	0	1	0	2	103	5	98	0	0	
State Center Community College District	38,821	4	0	0	1	3	328	26	287	15	7	
University of California:												
Berkeley	35,833	32	0	7	11	14	1,011	37	954	20	5	
Davis	31,392	10	0	3	4	3	686	74	603	9	1	
Hastings College of Law	1,304	10	0	0	9	1	25	4	21	0	0	
Irvine	26,994	7	0	3	2	2	489	63	421	5	1	
Los Angeles	38,157	40	0	12	11	17	838	195	625	18	3	
Medical Center, Sacramento[4]		4	0	0	1	3	162	12	142	8	0	
Merced	4,381	1	0	0	0	1	39	2	37	0	0	
Riverside	20,692	7	0	1	4	2	369	26	320	23	1	
San Diego	29,176	6	0	4	0	2	549	39	491	19	5	
San Francisco	3,024	7	0	0	5	2	314	16	286	12	2	
Santa Barbara	22,218	6	0	2	1	3	422	40	378	4	3	
Santa Cruz	17,187	5	0	0	0	5	200	21	177	2	4	
Ventura County Community College District	13,711	0	0	0	0	0	100	0	98	2	3	
West Valley-Mission College	22,783	1	0	0	0	1	86	12	67	7	0	
Colorado												
Adams State College	3,237	2	0	1	0	1	59	23	36	0	3	
Auraria Higher Education Center[4]	NA	0	0	0	0	0	288	29	253	6	0	
Colorado School of Mines	5,287	4	0	0	0	4	39	2	35	2	0	
Colorado State University:												
Fort Collins	30,155	7	0	0	2	5	434	18	415	1	4	
Pueblo	7,379	2	0	1	0	1	87	2	82	3	0	
Fort Lewis College	3,853	3	0	2	0	1	47	8	39	0	2	
Pikes Peak Community College	15,299	1	0	0	0	1	18	0	17	1	1	
Red Rocks Community College	9,826	0	0	0	0	0	16	0	16	0	0	
University of Colorado:												
Boulder	32,697	20	0	7	5	8	459	41	407	11	8	
Colorado Springs	9,745	0	0	0	0	0	82	6	75	1	0	
Denver	24,108	0	0	0	0	0	49	2	43	4	2	
Health Sciences Center[4]		0	0	0	0	0	4	1	3	0	0	
University of Northern Colorado	13,030	3	0	0	0	3	136	3	133	0	1	
Connecticut												
Central Connecticut State University	12,477	0	0	0	0	0	71	9	59	3	0	
Eastern Connecticut State University	5,606	1	0	1	0	0	81	4	76	1	1	
Southern Connecticut State University	11,964	0	0	0	0	0	69	4	65	0	0	
University of Connecticut:												
Health Center[4]	NA	0	0	0	0	0	2	0	2	0	0	
Storrs, Avery Point, and Hartford[4]	NA	12	0	5	2	5	291	50	241	0	7	
Western Connecticut State University	6,582	3	0	2	1	0	53	14	39	0	1	
Yale University	11,701	5	0	0	4	1	315	38	273	4	3	
Delaware												
Delaware State University	3,757	11	0	2	5	4	59	9	50	0	3	
University of Delaware	21,177	17	0	1	4	12	302	24	275	3	1	
Florida												
Edison State College	16,951	2	0	0	1	1	48	0	48	0	0	
Florida A&M University	13,284	13	0	1	5	7	243	11	220	12	1	
Florida Atlantic University	28,270	3	0	1	2	0	273	23	237	13	3	
Florida Gulf Coast University	12,015	2	0	2	0	0	85	7	77	1	0	
Florida International University	42,197	16	0	3	4	9	552	49	486	17	0	
Florida State University:												
Panama City[4]	NA	0	0	0	0	0	14	2	12	0	0	
Tallahassee	40,416	31	0	3	10	18	568	99	461	8	1	
New College of Florida	801	0	0	0	0	0	48	10	37	1	0	
Pensacola Junior College	11,676	5	0	0	0	5	51	13	38	0	0	
Santa Fe College	15,745	0	0	0	0	0	78	3	74	1	0	
Tallahassee Community College	14,739	1	0	0	1	0	57	0	56	1	0	
University of Central Florida	56,106	23	0	3	8	12	490	39	429	22	0	
University of Florida	49,827	10	0	3	1	6	504	27	463	14	0	
University of North Florida	16,153	3	0	0	2	1	159	13	145	1	2	

NA = Not available.

Note: Caution should be exercised in making any intercampus comparisons or ranking schools because university/college crime statistics are affected by a variety of factors. These include demographic characteristics of the surrounding community, ratio of male to female students, number of on-campus residents, accessibility of the campus to outside visitors, size of enrollment, etc.

[1] The student enrollment figures provided by the United States Department of Education are for the 2010 school year, the most recent available. The enrollment figures include full-time and part-time students.

[2] If a blank is presented in the arson column, it indicates that the FBI did not receive 12 complete months of arson data for that agency.

[4] Student enrollment figures were not available.

Table II-9. Offenses Known to Law Enforcement, by Selected State and University and College, 2011—*Continued*

(Number.)

State and University/College	Campus	Student enroll-ment[1]	Violent crime	Murder and non-negligent man-slaughter	Forcible rape	Robbery	Aggra-vated assault	Property crime	Burglary	Larceny-theft	Motor vehicle theft	Arson[2]
University of South Florida:												
St. Petersburg	3,944	6	0	2	2	2	54	8	46	0	0	
Tampa	40,431	10	0	1	1	8	356	48	299	9	0	
University of West Florida	11,599	1	0	1	0	0	121	18	100	3	0	
Georgia												
Abraham Baldwin Agricultural College	3,284	0	0	0	0	0	45	16	29	0	0	
Agnes Scott College	917	1	0	0	1	0	10	0	9	1	0	
Albany State University	4,653	3	0	0	0	3	69	2	66	1	0	
Armstrong Atlantic State University	7,682	2	0	0	1	1	89	8	80	1	0	
Augusta State University	6,919	0	0	0	0	0	57	2	55	0	0	
Berry College	2,087	2	0	1	1	0	34	3	30	1	0	
Clark Atlanta University	3,941	24	0	1	11	12	138	56	78	4	1	
College of Coastal Georgia	3,438	0	0	0	0	0	24	2	22	0		
Columbus State University	8,298	1	0	1	0	0	91	17	74	0	0	
Dalton State College	5,988	0	0	0	0	0	20	3	17	0	0	
Darton College	5,879	0	0	0	0	0	44	4	38	2	0	
Emory University	13,381	11	0	7	3	1	526	13	499	14	2	
Fort Valley State University	3,728	3	0	0	2	1	291	1	289	1	1	
Gainesville State College	8,883	0	0	0	0	0	22	1	21	0	0	
Georgia College and State University	6,737	1	0	1	0	0	65	7	58	0	0	
Georgia Gwinnett College	5,380	1	0	0	0	1	123	1	122	0	1	
Georgia Institute of Technology	20,720	20	0	4	11	5	504	25	458	21		
Georgia Military College	1,549	0	0	0	0	0	7	0	7	0	0	
Georgia Perimeter College	25,113	1	0	0	1	0	102	0	99	3	0	
Georgia Southern University	19,691	5	0	3	2	0	239	10	227	2	0	
Georgia Southwestern State University	3,037	3	0	0	0	3	38	1	35	2	0	
Georgia State University	31,533	31	0	3	26	2	321	9	305	7	0	
Gordon College	5,009	3	0	2	0	1	65	15	49	1	0	
Kennesaw State University	23,452	1	0	1	0	0	155	37	117	1	0	
Macon State College	6,232	1	0	1	0	0	31	0	29	2	0	
Medical College of Georgia[4]	NA	0	0	0	0	0	99	0	90	9	0	
Mercer University	8,236	2	0	1	1	0	51	5	44	2	0	
Middle Georgia College	3,496	7	0	0	0	7	57	4	53	0	0	
Morehouse College	2,586	5	0	0	2	3	142	28	111	3	0	
Morehouse School of Medicine	329	1	0	0	0	1	2	0	2	0	0	
Morris Brown College[4]		0	0	0	0	0	0	0	0	0	0	
North Georgia College and State University	5,912	0	0	0	0	0	39	0	39	0	0	
Piedmont College	2,676	0	0	0	0	0	0	0	0	0	0	
Savannah State University	4,080	9	0	1	5	3	158	10	147	1	0	
Southern Crescent Technical College	6,227	0	0	0	0	0	17	0	17	0	0	
Southern Polytechnic State University	5,514	2	0	0	0	2	84	6	74	4	0	
South Georgia College	2,214	1	0	0	0	1	11	4	7	0	0	
Spelman College	2,177	8	0	1	5	2	31	13	18	0	0	
University of Georgia	34,677	8	0	5	1	2	374	49	320	5	3	
University of West Georgia	11,283	5	0	2	1	2	185	38	147	0	0	
Valdosta State University	12,898	2	0	1	1	0	265	66	197	2	0	
Wesleyan College	690	1	0	0	0	1	9	0	9	0	0	
West Georgia Technical College	8,092	0	0	0	0	0	6	0	6	0	0	
Young Harris College	820	2	0	1	1	0	23	5	18	0	0	
Illinois												
Benedictine University	6,892	0	0	0	0	0	19	1	18	0	0	
Black Hawk College	6,677	0	0	0	0	0	25	0	25	0	0	
Chicago State University	7,354	2	0	0	2	0	47	1	46	0	0	
College of Lake County	18,091	1	0	0	0	1	63	2	61	0	0	
Elgin Community College	12,214	0	0	0	0	0	39	0	39	0	0	
Governors State University	5,660	0	0	0	0	0	13	0	12	1	0	
Harper College	16,060	0	0	0	0	0	59	4	55	0	0	
Illinois State University	21,134	17	0	0	1	16	163	21	140	2	0	
Joliet Junior College	15,676	1	0	0	0	1	58	1	57	0	0	
Morton College	5,459	1	0	0	0	1	28	0	28	0	0	
Northern Illinois University	23,850	8	0	5	0	3	221	22	199	0	0	
Oakton Community College	11,837	8	0	0	0	8	35	0	35	0	0	
Rock Valley College	8,849	2	0	0	0	2	44	1	43	0	1	
Southern Illinois University:												
Carbondale	20,037	14	0	3	4	7	319	70	248	1	3	
Edwardsville	14,133	7	0	2	1	4	157	12	141	4	0	
South Suburban College	7,161	1	0	0	0	1	36	3	33	0	0	
Southwestern Illinois College	13,221	2	0	0	0	2	40	0	40	0	0	

NA = Not available.

Note: Caution should be exercised in making any intercampus comparisons or ranking schools because university/college crime statistics are affected by a variety of factors. These include demographic characteristics of the surrounding community, ratio of male to female students, number of on-campus residents, accessibility of the campus to outside visitors, size of enrollment, etc.

[1] The student enrollment figures provided by the United States Department of Education are for the 2010 school year, the most recent available. The enrollment figures include full-time and part-time students.

[2] If a blank is presented in the arson column, it indicates that the FBI did not receive 12 complete months of arson data for that agency.

[4] Student enrollment figures were not available.

Table II-9.   Offenses Known to Law Enforcement, by Selected State and University and College, 2011—*Continued*

(Number.)

State and University/College	Campus	Student enroll-ment[1]	Violent crime	Murder and non-negligent man-slaughter	Forcible rape	Robbery	Aggra-vated assault	Property crime	Burglary	Larceny-theft	Motor vehicle theft	Arson[2]
Triton College	15,253	1	0	1	0	0	39	1	37	1	0	
University of Illinois:												
Chicago	27,850	11	1	0	10	0	489	6	480	3	0	
Springfield	5,174	0	0	0	0	0	24	2	22	0	0	
Urbana	43,862	15	0	1	4	10	409	36	368	5	2	
Western Illinois University	12,585	12	0	8	2	2	160	49	109	2	1	
Indiana												
Ball State University	22,083	26	0	7	3	16	376	72	302	2	0	
Indiana State University	11,494	9	0	0	3	6	244	6	236	2	0	
Indiana University:												
Bloomington	42,464	17	0	7	0	10	595	78	501	16	4	
Gary	5,969	2	0	1	0	1	29	0	26	3	0	
Indianapolis	30,566	9	0	1	4	4	296	57	227	12	0	
New Albany	7,178	0	0	0	0	0	29	1	28	0	0	
Marian University	2,357	0	0	0	0	0	41	14	27	0	0	
Purdue University	41,063	6	0	2	1	3	450	50	396	4	0	
Iowa												
Iowa State University	28,682	15	0	7	1	7	315	47	266	2	3	
University of Iowa	29,518	10	0	1	1	8	197	20	174	3	0	
University of Northern Iowa	13,201	6	0	6	0	0	89	8	80	1	2	
Kansas												
Emporia State University	6,262	2	0	1	0	1	38	3	34	1	0	
Fort Hays State University	11,883	1	0	1	0	0	61	12	49	0	0	
Kansas State University	23,588	3	0	0	0	3	123	16	106	1	1	
Univeristy of Kansas, main campus	28,697	2	0	0	1	1	216	30	184	2	0	
Washburn University	7,230	0	0	0	0	0	42	13	27	2	0	
Wichita State University	14,577	1	0	0	1	0	89	2	84	3	0	
Kentucky												
Eastern Kentucky University	16,567	6	0	2	2	2	220	46	173	1	1	
Kentucky State University	2,851	6	0	1	2	3	96	20	76	0	1	
Morehead State University	8,541	2	0	2	0	0	68	10	58	0	1	
Murray State University	10,412	1	0	1	0	0	145	25	119	1	1	
Northern Kentucky University	15,716	0	0	0	0	0	146	10	136	0	0	
University of Kentucky	27,108	8	0	2	3	3	554	14	529	11	0	
University of Louisville	21,234	7	0	0	6	1	268	33	224	11	0	
Western Kentucky University	20,897	9	0	5	3	1	178	32	144	2	0	
Louisiana												
Delgado Community College	18,767	0	0	0	0	0	28	9	16	3	0	
Louisiana State University:												
Baton Rouge	29,451	27	0	1	22	4	464	64	392	8	1	
Eunice	3,431	0	0	0	0	0	0	0	0	0	0	
Health Sciences Center, New Orleans	2,699	0	0	0	0	0	0	0	0	0	0	
Health Sciences Center, Shreveport	839	0	0	0	0	0	46	2	44	0	0	
McNeese State University	8,935	0	0	0	0	0	46	4	41	1	0	
Nicholls State University	7,082	0	0	0	0	0	48	7	40	1	0	
Northwestern State University	9,244	1	0	0	0	1	78	50	28	0	0	
Southeastern Louisiana University	15,338	2	0	0	1	1	47	4	43	0	0	
Southern University and A&M College:												
Baton Rouge	6,897	15	0	0	11	4	168	15	151	2	0	
New Orleans	3,165	0	0	0	0	0	2	0	2	0	0	
Tulane University	12,144	1	0	0	0	1	150	15	132	3	1	
University of Louisiana, Lafayette	16,763	15	0	1	5	9	172	22	145	5	0	
University of New Orleans	11,276	2	0	0	2	0	65	18	41	6	0	
Maine												
University of Maine:												
Farmington	2,430	2	0	2	0	0	34	0	34	0	0	
Orono	11,501	2	0	1	0	1	198	5	193	0	8	
University of Southern Maine	9,654	4	0	4	0	0	64	1	62	1	15	
Maryland												
Bowie State University	5,578	11	1	3	1	6	95	35	59	1	0	
Coppin State University	3,800	8	0	0	4	4	68	4	62	2	0	
Frostburg State University	5,470	2	0	2	0	0	60	11	48	1	0	

Note: Caution should be exercised in making any intercampus comparisons or ranking schools because university/college crime statistics are affected by a variety of factors. These include demo-graphic characteristics of the surrounding community, ratio of male to female students, number of on-campus residents, accessibility of the campus to outside visitors, size of enrollment, etc.

[1] The student enrollment figures provided by the United States Department of Education are for the 2010 school year, the most recent available. The enrollment figures include full-time and part-time students.

[2] If a blank is presented in the arson column, it indicates that the FBI did not receive 12 complete months of arson data for that agency.

Table II-9. Offenses Known to Law Enforcement, by Selected State and University and College, 2011—*Continued*

(Number.)

State and University/College	Campus	Student enroll-ment[1]	Violent crime	Murder and non-negligent man-slaughter	Forcible rape	Robbery	Aggra-vated assault	Property crime	Burglary	Larceny-theft	Motor vehicle theft	Arson[2]
Hagerstown Community College		4,715	0	0	0	0	0	7	2	3	2	0
Morgan State University		7,805	23	0	0	19	4	134	27	106	1	0
Salisbury University		8,397	2	0	0	2	0	120	11	108	1	0
St. Mary's College		2,017	1	0	0	0	1	60	12	48	0	0
Towson University		21,840	8	0	3	2	3	129	11	118	0	0
University of Baltimore		6,501	0	0	0	0	0	49	1	48	0	0
University of Maryland												
Baltimore City		6,349	11	0	0	5	6	142	2	139	1	0
Baltimore County		12,888	7	0	2	4	1	125	8	117	0	1
College Park		37,641	12	0	0	3	9	448	59	349	40	0
Eastern Shore		4,540	6	0	1	4	1	126	25	100	1	0
Massachusetts												
Assumption College		2,764	4	0	1	0	3	56	4	51	1	4
Bentley College		5,684	8	0	4	0	4	61	10	51	0	
Boston College		14,868	9	0	4	0	5	159	8	148	3	
Boston University		5,642	2	0	1	1	0	69	3	65	1	0
Brandeis University		11,201	7	0	2	0	5	76	6	69	1	0
Bridgewater State College												
Bristol Community College		12,271	2	0	0	0	2	79	0	77	2	0
Bunker Hill Community College		3,451	5	0	1	1	3	49	8	41	0	0
Clark University		1,266	3	0	1	1	1	30	6	24	0	
Dean College		4,566	3	0	2	0	1	61	3	58	0	
Emerson College												
Fitchburg State College		5,953	2	0	0	0	2	18	12	6	0	0
Framingham State College		1,529	0	0	0	0	0	44	4	40	0	0
Harvard University		27,594	8	0	0	1	7	507	28	476	3	
Holyoke Community College		7,404	2	0	0	0	2	42	0	42	0	
Lasell College		1,798	1	0	1	0	0	39	1	38	0	0
Massachusetts College of Art		2,446	3	0	3	0	0	47	0	47	0	0
Massachusetts College of Liberal Arts		1,974	1	0	0	0	1	23	10	13	0	0
Massachusetts Institute of Technology		10,566	8	0	3	3	2	382	30	351	1	0
Merrimack College		2,168	3	0	1	0	2	28	4	24	0	0
Mount Holyoke College		2,344	1	0	1	0	0	103	4	98	1	0
Northeastern University		29,519	14	0	1	8	5	440	17	422	1	0
North Shore Community College		7,985	0	0	0	0	0	15	0	13	2	0
Salem State College		9,993	7	0	2	1	4	97	26	71	0	0
Smith College		3,113	0	0	0	0	0	74	4	69	1	0
Springfield College		5,364	3	0	0	2	1	92	13	78	1	0
University of Massachusetts												
Amherst		27,569	8	0	3	1	4	294	29	264	1	0
Dartmouth		9,432	17	0	0	2	15	239	33	204	2	17
Harbor Campus, Boston		15,454	1	0	0	0	1	56	1	55	0	0
Wellesley College		2,546	0	0	0	0	0	40	3	37	0	0
Western New England College		3,734	0	0	0	0	0	34	1	33	0	0
Westfield State University		5,885	2	0	2	0	0	50	3	46	1	2
Worcester Polytechnic Institute		5,360	2	0	0	0	2	47	4	43	0	0
Michigan												
Central Michigan University		28,292	4	0	2	1	1	155	12	142	1	1
Delta College		11,572	0	0	0	0	0	39	1	38	0	0
Eastern Michigan University		23,565	5	0	2	2	1	187	12	173	2	7
Grand Rapids Community College		17,870	1	0	0	0	1	157	0	157	0	0
Grand Valley State University		24,541	3	0	1	0	2	136	5	131	0	1
Lansing Community College		21,969	3	0	0	1	2	91	1	88	2	0
Macomb Community College		24,468	0	0	0	0	0	92	0	87	5	0
Michigan State University		46,985	14	0	6	1	7	656	73	573	10	0
Michigan Technological University		6,971	0	0	0	0	0	114	2	112	0	0
Northern Michigan University		9,417	9	0	6	0	3	114	17	96	1	0
Oakland Community College		28,925	1	0	0	0	1	78	3	71	4	0
Oakland University		19,053	9	0	0	2	7	98	10	85	3	0
Saginaw Valley State University		10,656	4	0	1	1	2	99	9	89	1	0
University of Michigan												
Ann Arbor		41,924	23	0	1	9	13	588	27	550	11	3
Dearborn		8,599	0	0	0	0	0	36	0	36	0	0
Flint		8,138	2	0	1	1	0	84	7	68	9	0
Western Michigan University		25,045	1	0	0	0	1	204	4	199	1	3

NA = Not available.

Note: Caution should be exercised in making any intercampus comparisons or ranking schools because university/college crime statistics are affected by a variety of factors. These include demographic characteristics of the surrounding community, ratio of male to female students, number of on-campus residents, accessibility of the campus to outside visitors, size of enrollment, etc.

[1] The student enrollment figures provided by the United States Department of Education are for the 2010 school year, the most recent available. The enrollment figures include full-time and part-time students.

[2] If a blank is presented in the arson column, it indicates that the FBI did not receive 12 complete months of arson data for that agency.

Table II-9.   Offenses Known to Law Enforcement, by Selected State and University and College, 2011—*Continued*

(Number.)

State and University/College	Campus	Student enroll-ment[1]	Violent crime	Murder and non-negligent man-slaughter	Forcible rape	Robbery	Aggra-vated assault	Property crime	Burglary	Larceny-theft	Motor vehicle theft	Arson[2]
Minnesota[5]												
University of Minnesota												
Duluth...................................	11,729	NA	0	NA	0	0	45	2	43	0	0	
Morris.....................................	1,811	NA	0	NA	0	0	20	0	20	0	0	
Twin Cities..............................	51,721	NA	0	NA	6	2	626	51	565	10	0	
Mississippi												
Coahoma Community College	2,741	4	0	0	0	4	10	8	2	0	0	
Mississippi State University	19,644	3	0	0	1	2	215	16	198	1	1	
Northeast Mississippi Community College	3,627	2	0	0	1	1	42	3	39	0	0	
University of Mississippi												
Medical Center	2,452	2	0	0	1	1	126	2	121	3	0	
Oxford.....................................	17,085	9	0	7	1	1	270	46	224	0	0	
Missouri												
Lincoln University.....................................	3,349	12	0	0	2	10	56	23	31	2	0	
Mineral Area College	3,958	1	0	0	0	1	13	5	8	0	0	
Missouri Southern State University	5,802	3	0	1	0	2	53	11	41	1	0	
Missouri University of Science and Technology ...	7,205	1	0	0	0	1	94	9	84	1	1	
Missouri Western State University.....................	6,095	0	0	0	0	0	73	5	68	0	0	
Northwest Missouri State University....................	7,142	2	0	1	0	1	43	4	39	0	0	
Southeast Missouri State University....................	11,033	2	0	1	0	1	47	4	40	3	1	
St. Charles Community College............................	8,202	0	0	0	0	0	31	0	31	0	0	
St. Louis Community College												
Florissant Valley	7,436	0	0	0	0	0	74	1	69	4	0	
Meramec	11,430	2	0	0	0	2	49	1	48	0	0	
Three Rivers Community College........................	3,730	1	0	1	0	0	30	12	18	0	0	
Truman State University........................	6,035	1	0	1	0	0	59	3	56	0	0	
University of Central Missouri	11,351	12	0	1	0	11	173	25	143	5	0	
University of Missouri												
Columbia	32,341	13	0	2	3	8	343	12	328	3	1	
Kansas City	15,259	1	0	1	0	0	167	57	107	3	0	
St. Louis	16,791	5	0	0	0	5	102	19	79	4	0	
Washington University	13,820	0	0	0	0	0	98	9	89	0	0	
Montana[3]												
Montana State University	13,081	3	0	2	0	1	140	12	127	1	1	
Nebraska												
Metropolitan Community College												
Douglas County........................	18,523	0	0	0	0	0	51	1	49	1	0	
Sarpy County[4].........................	NA	0	0	0	0	0	0	0	0	0	0	
University of Nebraska												
Kearney	6,753	1	0	1	0	0	63	13	50	0	NA	
Lincoln	24,610	3	0	2	0	1	257	16	235	6	2	
Nevada												
Truckee Meadows Community College.................	12,587	0	0	0	0	0	31	1	29	1	0	
University of Nevada												
Las Vegas	28,203	8	0	0	6	2	321	46	239	36	1	
Reno	17,680	3	0	1	1	1	193	46	141	6	0	
New Hampshire												
University of New Hampshire	15,095	9	0	2	1	6	186	9	173	4	2	
New Jersey												
Brookdale Community College............................	15,783	0	0	0	0	0	34	2	32	0	0	
Essex County College	13,424	1	0	0	1	0	77	0	77	0	0	
Kean University	15,939	0	0	0	0	0	106	33	73	0	5	
Middlesex County College	12,887	0	0	0	0	0	67	2	64	1	0	
Monmouth University	6,506	1	0	1	0	0	60	16	42	2	2	
Montclair State University	18,402	9	0	1	0	8	205	7	192	6	0	
New Jersey Institute of Technology	8,934	14	0	0	8	6	200	2	188	10	0	
Richard Stockton College of New Jersey	7,879	2	0	0	0	2	52	0	52	0	0	
Rowan University...	11,300	4	0	0	1	3	98	12	86	0	0	
Rutgers University												
Camden												
Newark	6,158	4	0	1	2	1	101	11	89	1	0	
New Brunswick.......................	11,798	16	1	1	7	7	212	11	196	5	0	

NA = Not available.

Note: Caution should be exercised in making any intercampus comparisons or ranking schools because university/college crime statistics are affected by a variety of factors. These include demo-graphic characteristics of the surrounding community, ratio of male to female students, number of on-campus residents, accessibility of the campus to outside visitors, size of enrollment, etc.

[1] The student enrollment figures provided by the United States Department of Education are for the 2010 school year, the most recent available. The enrollment figures include full-time and part-time students.

[2] If a blank is presented in the arson column, it indicates that the FBI did not receive 12 complete months of arson data for that agency.

[3] Because of changes in the state/local agency's reporting practices, figures are not comparable to previous years' data.

[4] Student enrollment figures were not available.

[5] The data collection methodology for the offense of forcible rape used by the Minnesota state Uniform Crime Reporting (UCR) Program does not comply with national UCR Program guidelines. Consequently, its figures for forcible rape and violent crime (of which forcible rape is a part) are not published in this table.

Table II-9.   Offenses Known to Law Enforcement, by Selected State and University and College, 2011—*Continued*

(Number.)

State and University/College	Campus	Student enroll-ment[1]	Violent crime	Murder and non-negligent man-slaughter	Forcible rape	Robbery	Aggra-vated assault	Property crime	Burglary	Larceny-theft	Motor vehicle theft	Arson[2]
Stevens Institute of Technology												
The College of New Jersey	5,629	1	0	0	0	1	31	0	29	2	0	
University of Medicine and Dentistry	7,115	1	0	0	0	1	95	6	83	6	0	
Camden[4]	NA	0	0	0	0	0	5	0	5	0	0	
Newark	6,813	20	0	0	5	15	158	0	148	10	0	
New Brunswick[4]	NA	1	0	0	1	0	25	0	23	2	0	
William Paterson University	11,339	2	0	1	0	1	91	0	91	0	0	
New Mexico												
Eastern New Mexico University	5,075	0	0	0	0	0	NA	NA	NA	2	0	
New Mexico State University	18,600	24	0	0	1	23	461	69	385	7	1	
University of New Mexico	28,688	36	0	2	4	30	650	19	566	65	0	
New York												
Cornell University	20,939	3	0	0	1	2	206	13	191	2	0	
Ithaca College	6,949	1	0	1	0	0	141	11	130	0	2	
Rensselaer Polytechnic Institute	6,704	0	0	0	0	0	68	2	66	0	0	
State University of New York:												
Binghamton	14,895	9	0	4	0	5	184	17	167	0	1	
Buffalo	29,117	9	0	2	3	4	382	67	309	6	0	
Maritime College	1,880	0	0	0	0	0	20	13	7	0	0	
Upstate Medical Center[4]	NA	1	0	0	0	1	101	0	100	1	0	
State University of New York Agricultural and Technical College												
Alfred	3,709	4	0	1	1	2	93	13	79	1	0	
Canton	3,655	1	0	0	1	0	82	2	80	0	0	
Cobleskill	2,566	3	0	0	0	3	54	16	37	1	0	
Farmingdale	6,858	0	0	0	0	0	41	0	40	1	0	
Morrisville	3,454	7	0	1	0	6	75	14	59	2	0	
State University of New York College												
Buffalo	12,419	8	0	1	3	4	147	18	129	0	3	
Cortland	7,358	2	0	1	0	1	76	13	63	0	0	
Environmental Science and Forestry	2,682	0	0	0	0	0	0	0	0	0	0	
Fredonia	5,772	0	0	0	0	0	65	17	47	1	0	
Geneseo	5,665	1	0	1	0	0	103	15	87	1	0	
New Paltz[4]		3	0	2	0	1	79	7	71	1	0	
Old Westbury	4,355	3	0	1	0	2	78	6	70	2	0	
Oneonta	5,989	1	0	0	0	1	75	5	70	0	0	
Optometry	303	0	0	0	0	0	6	1	5	0	0	
Oswego	8,297	2	0	2	0	0	185	31	152	2	3	
Plattsburgh	6,441	4	0	1	1	2	98	17	81	0	0	
Potsdam	4,413	0	0	0	0	0	88	13	75	0	0	
Technology[4]	NA	2	0	0	1	1	59	6	53	0	0	
Utica-Rome[4]	NA	1	0	0	1	0	16	1	15	0	0	
United States Merchant Marine Academy	1,000	1	0	0	0	1	15	8	7	0	0	
North Carolina												
Appalachian State University	17,222	1	0	0	1	0	122	14	105	3	0	
Duke University	15,016	9	0	2	2	5	650	25	615	10	1	
East Carolina University	27,783	8	0	1	4	3	230	20	209	1	0	
Elizabeth City State University	3,307	1	0	0	1	0	31	3	28	0	0	
Elon University	5,709	1	0	1	0	0	56	17	38	1	0	
Fayetteville State University	5,781	11	0	0	7	4	137	61	71	5	1	
North Carolina Agricultural and Technical State University	10,795	9	0	0	3	6	211	35	173	3	0	
North Carolina Central University	8,645	9	0	2	1	6	186	39	144	3	0	
North Carolina School of the Arts	872	0	0	0	0	0	9	0	9	0	0	
North Carolina State University, Raleigh	34,376	15	0	1	6	8	429	39	379	11	0	
University of North Carolina												
Asheville	3,967	0	0	0	0	0	30	2	28	0	0	
Chapel Hill	29,390	4	0	2	2	0	348	24	322	2	1	
Greensboro	18,771	10	0	0	5	5	172	1	168	3	0	
Pembroke	6,944	2	0	0	2	0	90	14	76	0	0	
Wilmington	13,071	2	0	2	0	0	248	17	229	2	0	
Wake Forest University	7,162	4	0	4	0	0	226	81	139	6	1	
Western Carolina University	9,407	3	0	2	0	1	98	6	92	0	0	
Winston-Salem State University	6,333	2	0	0	1	1	72	2	70	0	0	

NA = Not available.

Note: Caution should be exercised in making any intercampus comparisons or ranking schools because university/college crime statistics are affected by a variety of factors. These include demographic characteristics of the surrounding community, ratio of male to female students, number of on-campus residents, accessibility of the campus to outside visitors, size of enrollment, etc.

[1] The student enrollment figures provided by the United States Department of Education are for the 2010 school year, the most recent available. The enrollment figures include full-time and part-time students.

[2] If a blank is presented in the arson column, it indicates that the FBI did not receive 12 complete months of arson data for that agency.

[4] Student enrollment figures were not available.

Table II-9.   Offenses Known to Law Enforcement, by Selected State and University and College, 2011—*Continued*

(Number.)

State and University/College	Campus	Student enroll-ment[1]	Violent crime	Murder and non-negligent man-slaughter	Forcible rape	Robbery	Aggra-vated assault	Property crime	Burglary	Larceny-theft	Motor vehicle theft	Arson[2]
North Dakota												
North Dakota State College of Science..............	2,833	0	0	0	0	0	34	1	33	0	0	
North Dakota State University............................	14,407	0	0	0	0	0	106	8	96	2	2	
University of North Dakota.................................	14,194	4	0	2	0	2	156	4	144	8	1	
Ohio												
Capital University	3,629	1	0	1	0	0	39	12	27	0	0	
Central State University....................................	2,288	1	0	1	0	0	62	19	43	0	0	
Cleveland State University.................................	17,386	3	0	0	3	0	132	4	120	8	0	
College of Mount St. Joseph	2,475	0	0	0	0	0	20	3	17	0	0	
Columbus State Community College....................	30,513	0	0	0	0	0	110	1	106	3	0	
Cuyahoga Community College.............................	31,250	4	0	1	3	0	137	2	129	6	0	
Kent State University..	26,589	2	0	1	1	0	178	17	160	1	0	
Lakeland Community College..............................	9,831	0	0	0	0	0	31	0	31	0	0	
Miami University...	17,472	2	0	1	0	1	191	26	165	0	0	
Notre Dame College	2,091	1	0	0	0	1	22	5	17	0	0	
Ohio State University, Columbus	56,064	15	0	6	6	3	923	22	892	9	3	
Ohio University...	25,108	4	0	3	1	0	205	21	182	2	5	
Sinclair Community College	21,994	0	0	0	0	0	54	0	54	0	0	
University of Akron	27,076	10	0	4	5	1	395	7	374	14	0	
University of Cincinnati	32,283	19	0	2	6	11	438	25	405	8	1	
University of Toledo..	23,085	18	0	0	1	17	606	93	507	6	1	
Wright State University......................................	18,447	4	0	4	0	0	140	23	116	1	0	
Youngstown State University	15,084	2	0	0	1	1	124	5	119	0	0	
Oklahoma												
Cameron University...	6,330	3	0	0	1	2	33	4	28	1	1	
East Central University	4,906	0	0	0	0	0	25	8	17	0	0	
Northeastern Oklahoma A&M College	2,353	2	0	0	0	2	43	13	28	2	0	
Northeastern State University												
Broken Arrow[4]		0	0	0	0	0	7	0	7	0	0	
Tahlequah..	9,558	2	0	1	0	1	41	9	32	0	0	
Oklahoma City University	3,750	0	0	0	0	0	21	1	19	1	0	
Oklahoma State University												
Main Campus..	23,667	7	0	5	0	2	235	45	188	2	0	
Okmulgee..	3,888	1	0	0	0	1	29	6	23	0	0	
Tulsa[4]...	NA	0	0	0	0	0	11	3	8	0	0	
Rogers State University......................................	4,486	2	0	1	0	1	14	6	8	0	0	
Seminole State College.......................................	2,337	0	0	0	0	0	10	0	9	1	0	
Southeastern Oklahoma State University............	4,172	0	0	0	0	0	9	3	5	1	0	
Southwestern Oklahoma State University...........	5,259	0	0	0	0	0	22	6	16	0	0	
Tulsa Community College	20,577	0	0	0	0	0	65	3	62	0	0	
University of Central Oklahoma.........................	17,101	2	0	1	0	1	135	14	120	1	0	
University of Oklahoma												
Health Sciences Center................................	3,847	1	0	0	0	1	215	11	201	3	1	
Norman..	26,476	7	0	3	0	4	313	29	274	10	0	
Oregon												
Portland State University	28,035	4	0	1	2	1	321	40	280	1	1	
Pennsylvania												
Bloomsburg University..	10,091	4	0	2	0	2	74	6	67	1	0	
California University	9,400	0	0	0	0	0	52	2	50	0	0	
Cheyney University...	1,586	11	0	4	1	6	81	34	47	0	0	
Clarion University	7,315	1	0	0	0	1	47	6	40	1	0	
Dickinson College	2,414	2	0	0	0	2	85	7	78	0	0	
East Stroudsburg University...............................	7,387	1	0	0	0	1	44	1	43	0	1	
Edinboro University...	8,642	2	0	1	0	1	63	4	59	0	0	
Elizabethtown College..	2,417	3	0	1	1	1	39	0	39	0	0	
Indiana University...	15,126	2	0	0	0	2	60	4	56	0	0	
Kutztown University..	10,707	7	0	3	0	4	93	4	88	1	0	
Lehigh University..	7,051	1	0	1	0	0	72	9	63	0	0	
Lock Haven University.......................................	5,451	2	0	2	0	0	39	13	25	1	0	
Mansfield University..	3,411	0	0	0	0	0	15	2	13	0	0	
Millersville University	8,729	6	0	2	0	4	55	4	51	0	0	
Moravian College	2,032	6	0	0	0	6	50	3	47	0	2	
Pennsylvania State University												
Altoona...	4,147	0	0	0	0	0	34	3	31	0	1	
Beaver...	906	0	0	0	0	0	9	0	9	0	0	

NA = Not available.

Note: Caution should be exercised in making any intercampus comparisons or ranking schools because university/college crime statistics are affected by a variety of factors. These include demographic characteristics of the surrounding community, ratio of male to female students, number of on-campus residents, accessibility of the campus to outside visitors, size of enrollment, etc.

[1] The student enrollment figures provided by the United States Department of Education are for the 2010 school year, the most recent available. The enrollment figures include full-time and part-time students.

[2] If a blank is presented in the arson column, it indicates that the FBI did not receive 12 complete months of arson data for that agency.

[4] Student enrollment figures were not available.

Table II-9.   Offenses Known to Law Enforcement, by Selected State and University and College, 2011—*Continued*

(Number.)

State and University/College	Campus	Student enroll-ment[1]	Violent crime	Murder and non-negligent man-slaughter	Forcible rape	Robbery	Aggra-vated assault	Property crime	Burglary	Larceny-theft	Motor vehicle theft	Arson[2]
Behrend		4,359	1	0	1	0	0	26	7	19	0	0
Berks		2,771	1	0	0	0	1	29	1	28	0	0
Harrisburg		4,224	0	0	0	0	0	33	0	33	0	0
Hazelton		1,303	0	0	0	0	0	7	1	6	0	0
McKeesport[4]		NA	1	0	0	0	1	7	1	6	0	0
Mont Alto		1,252	0	0	0	0	0	7	0	7	0	0
Schuykill		1,034	2	0	0	0	2	33	8	24	1	0
University Park		45,233	12	0	2	2	8	615	118	493	4	11
Shippensburg University		8,326	3	0	1	1	1	28	4	24	0	0
Slippery Rock University		8,852	2	0	0	0	2	33	1	32	0	0
University of Pittsburgh												
Bradford		1,629	0	0	0	0	0	23	9	14	0	1
Greensburg		1,803	1	0	0	0	1	17	4	13	0	0
Johnstown		2,965	6	0	2	0	4	26	1	25	0	0
Pittsburgh		28,823	11	0	1	6	4	245	16	228	1	0
Titusville		514	0	0	0	0	0	16	1	15	0	0
West Chester University		14,490	5	0	2	1	2	150	17	133	0	0
Rhode Island												
Brown University		8,705	0	0	0	0	0	139	38	101	0	0
University of Rhode Island		16,294	5	0	2	0	3	165	17	146	2	1
South Carolina												
Benedict College		3,137	10	0	3	7	0	333	148	177	8	1
Bob Jones University		3,794	0	0	0	0	0	42	20	22	0	0
Clemson University		19,453	8	0	1	1	6	191	27	153	11	0
Coastal Carolina University		8,706	8	0	4	1	3	345	72	271	2	1
College of Charleston		11,532	3	0	2	1	0	91	7	84	0	0
Columbia College		1,367	0	0	0	0	0	9	1	8	0	0
Denmark Technical College		1,033	1	0	0	1	0	20	3	17	0	0
Francis Marion University		4,032	1	0	0	0	1	61	4	56	1	0
Greenville Technical College		14,879	3	0	0	1	2	75	19	55	1	0
Lander University		3,060	4	0	0	0	4	40	6	34	0	0
Medical University of South Carolina		2,556	2	0	0	1	1	154	2	152	0	0
South Carolina State University		4,362	11	1	0	7	3	130	39	87	4	0
Trident Technical College		15,790	0	0	0	0	0	50	0	48	2	1
University of South Carolina												
Aiken		3,254	0	0	0	0	0	26	3	19	4	0
Columbia		29,599	13	0	1	3	9	419	113	283	23	0
Upstate		5,492	1	0	1	0	0	32	3	29	0	0
Winthrop University		5,998	4	0	2	0	2	60	3	54	3	0
South Dakota												
South Dakota State University		12,816	0	0	0	0	0	71	0	71	0	0
Tennessee												
Austin Peay State University		10,723	4	0	0	3	1	78	6	72	0	1
Christian Brothers University		1,828	2	0	0	1	1	19	2	17	0	0
East Tennessee State University		14,952	2	0	0	0	2	137	20	114	3	1
Middle Tennessee State University		26,430	8	0	1	2	5	301	32	264	5	2
Northeast State Community College		6,775	0	0	0	0	0	10	0	10	0	0
Southwest Tennessee Community College		13,362	5	0	2	0	3	45	2	43	0	0
Tennessee State University		8,930	9	0	0	4	5	139	5	129	5	0
Tennessee Technological University		11,538	4	0	1	0	3	110	28	81	1	1
University of Memphis		22,420	7	0	1	1	5	213	39	171	3	0
University of Tennessee												
Chattanooga		10,781	5	0	1	1	3	151	16	134	1	0
Health Science Center[4]		NA	0	0	0	0	0	50	4	46	0	0
Knoxville		30,300	5	0	3	2	0	469	29	429	11	0
Martin		8,467	2	0	1	1	0	46	16	30	0	0
Vanderbilt University		12,714	12	0	3	5	4	556	16	535	5	1
Walters State Community College		6,959	0	0	0	0	0	15	2	13	0	0
Texas												
Abilene Christian University		4,728	4	0	0	0	4	101	5	95	1	0
Alamo Community College District		60,983	10	0	1	4	5	385	1	356	28	4
Alvin Community College		5,794	0	0	0	0	0	11	1	8	2	0
Amarillo College		11,878	0	0	0	0	0	52	5	46	1	0
Angelo State University		6,856	1	0	0	0	1	75	5	69	1	0
Austin College		1,314	0	0	0	0	0	44	3	41	0	1

NA = Not available.

Note: Caution should be exercised in making any intercampus comparisons or ranking schools because university/college crime statistics are affected by a variety of factors. These include demographic characteristics of the surrounding community, ratio of male to female students, number of on-campus residents, accessibility of the campus to outside visitors, size of enrollment, etc.

[1] The student enrollment figures provided by the United States Department of Education are for the 2010 school year, the most recent available. The enrollment figures include full-time and part-time students.

[2] If a blank is presented in the arson column, it indicates that the FBI did not receive 12 complete months of arson data for that agency.

[4] Student enrollment figures were not available.

Table II-9.   Offenses Known to Law Enforcement, by Selected State and University and College, 2011—*Continued*

(Number.)

State and University/College	Campus	Student enroll-ment[1]	Violent crime	Murder and non-negligent man-slaughter	Forcible rape	Robbery	Aggra-vated assault	Property crime	Burglary	Larceny-theft	Motor vehicle theft	Arson[2]
Baylor Health Care System[4]		3	0	1	1	1	456	11	441	4	0	
Baylor University, Waco	14,900	0	0	0	0	0	212	15	195	2	0	
Blinn College	17,755	6	0	2	2	2	115	21	93	1	0	
Brookhaven College	12,784	0	0	0	0	0	29	0	29	0	0	
Central Texas College	26,055	1	0	1	0	0	30	1	29	0	0	
College of the Mainland	4,352	0	0	0	0	0	35	2	33	0	0	
Eastfield College	12,919	1	0	0	0	1	56	0	55	1	0	
El Paso Community College	29,909	1	0	0	0	1	143	4	120	19	0	
Grayson County College	5,284	1	0	0	0	1	26	11	15	0	0	
Hardin-Simmons University	2,313	0	0	0	0	0	19	5	14	0	0	
Houston Baptist University	2,597	0	0	0	0	0	41	17	24	0	0	
Houston Community College	60,303	6	0	0	1	5	351	53	285	13	0	
Lamar University, Beaumont	14,385	6	0	1	1	4	94	10	81	3	0	
Laredo Community College	10,029	0	0	0	0	0	26	1	25	0	0	
McLennan Community College	9,913	0	0	0	0	0	16	0	16	0	0	
Midwestern State University	6,426	4	0	3	0	1	99	23	76	0	0	
Mountain View College	8,460	4	0	0	3	1	59	21	29	9	0	
North Lake College	12,018	1	0	0	0	1	28	0	28	0	0	
Paris Junior College	6,197	2	0	0	0	2	26	5	21	0	0	
Prairie View A&M University	8,781	11	0	2	4	5	120	31	82	7	0	
Rice University	5,879	4	0	1	2	1	177	10	166	1	0	
Richland College	19,201	3	0	0	0	3	80	1	77	2	0	
Southern Methodist University	10,938	1	0	1	0	0	211	10	195	6	0	
South Plains College	9,900	0	0	0	0	0	14	6	8	0	1	
Southwestern University	1,373	0	0	0	0	0	14	3	11	0	0	
Stephen F. Austin State University	12,954	3	0	1	1	1	176	13	161	2	0	
St. Mary's University	4,105	0	0	0	0	0	68	0	65	3	0	
Sul Ross State University	3,129	1	0	0	0	1	60	16	42	2	1	
Tarleton State University	11,121	1	0	0	0	1	54	13	41	0	0	
Texas A&M International University	6,853	0	0	0	0	0	43	3	40	0	0	
Texas A&M University												
College Station	49,129	3	0	1	1	1	669	28	636	5	0	
Commerce	10,787	5	0	3	0	2	69	13	55	1	2	
Corpus Christi	10,033	0	0	0	0	0	67	2	65	0	0	
Galveston	1,867	3	0	2	0	1	21	2	19	0	0	
Kingsville	9,673	5	0	1	1	3	100	15	85	0	0	
San Antonio[4]	NA	0	0	0	0	0	18	1	17	0	0	
Texas Christian University	9,142	4	0	3	0	1	166	9	152	5	0	
Texas Southern University	9,557	14	0	0	10	4	255	59	192	4	0	
Texas State Technical College												
Harlingen	5,779	2	0	1	0	1	38	5	33	0	0	
Marshall	949	0	0	0	0	0	10	7	3	0	0	
Waco	4,975	2	0	1	0	1	90	34	55	1	0	
Texas State University, San Marcos	32,572	7	0	1	0	6	288	43	244	1	1	
Texas Tech University, Lubbock	31,637	5	0	1	1	3	431	26	398	7	1	
Texas Woman's University	14,180	2	0	1	0	1	35	1	34	0	0	
Trinity University	2,498	0	0	0	0	0	75	20	52	3	0	
Tyler Junior College	11,738	1	0	1	0	0	68	4	63	1	0	
University of Houston												
Central Campus	38,752	6	0	3	2	1	584	75	485	24	0	
Clearlake	8,099	0	0	0	0	0	26	0	26	0	0	
Downtown Campus	12,900	0	0	0	0	0	64	0	64	0	0	
University of Mary Hardin-Baylor	2,956	0	0	0	0	0	32	3	29	0	0	
University of North Texas												
Denton	36,305	6	0	1	1	4	180	28	145	7	0	
Health Science Center	1,579	0	0	0	0	0	14	0	14	0	0	
University of Texas												
Arlington	32,975	9	0	2	1	6	259	27	227	5	0	
Austin	51,195	7	0	1	0	6	555	41	512	2	3	
Brownsville	15,230	3	0	1	1	1	70	0	67	3	0	
Dallas	17,128	3	0	0	0	3	113	3	105	5	0	
El Paso	22,106	6	0	2	1	3	227	28	178	21	0	
Health Science Center, San Antonio	3,310	0	0	0	0	0	74	2	70	2	0	
Health Science Center, Tyler[4]	NA	1	0	0	0	1	15	6	9	0	0	
Houston[4]	NA	5	0	2	1	2	351	17	331	3	0	
Medical Branch	2,660	0	0	0	0	0	103	1	101	1	0	
Pan American	18,744	0	0	0	0	0	149	5	143	1	0	

NA = Not available.

Note: Caution should be exercised in making any intercampus comparisons or ranking schools because university/college crime statistics are affected by a variety of factors. These include demographic characteristics of the surrounding community, ratio of male to female students, number of on-campus residents, accessibility of the campus to outside visitors, size of enrollment, etc.

[1] The student enrollment figures provided by the United States Department of Education are for the 2010 school year, the most recent available. The enrollment figures include full-time and part-time students.

[2] If a blank is presented in the arson column, it indicates that the FBI did not receive 12 complete months of arson data for that agency.

[4] Student enrollment figures were not available.

Table II-9. Offenses Known to Law Enforcement, by Selected State and University and College, 2011—*Continued*

(Number.)

State and University/College	Campus	Student enroll-ment[1]	Violent crime	Murder and non-negligent man-slaughter	Forcible rape	Robbery	Aggra-vated assault	Property crime	Burglary	Larceny-theft	Motor vehicle theft	Arson[2]
Permian Basin	4,063	1	0	0	1	0	21	9	12	0	0	
San Antonio	30,258	6	0	0	3	3	176	11	159	6	0	
Southwestern Medical School	2,499	0	0	0	0	0	175	6	158	11	0	
Tyler	6,476	2	0	1	0	1	25	4	21	0	0	
West Texas A&M University	7,839	1	0	0	0	1	61	14	46	1	0	
Utah												
College of Eastern Utah	2,172	2	0	2	0	0	3	0	2	1	0	
Southern Utah University	8,024	1	0	1	0	0	36	3	32	1	0	
University of Utah	30,819	8	0	3	1	4	532	36	478	18	0	
Utah State University	16,472	1	0	1	0	0	156	12	144	0	0	
Utah Valley University	32,670	0	0	0	0	0	165	7	153	5	0	
Weber State University	24,048	1	0	1	0	0	59	10	49	0	0	
Vermont												
University of Vermont	13,554	2	0	1	1	0	223	16	207	0	0	
Virginia												
Christopher Newport University	4,916	2	0	0	1	1	109	2	107	0	1	
College of William and Mary	8,000	2	0	1	1	0	177	29	142	6	0	
Emory and Henry College	980	0	0	0	0	0	2	0	2	0	0	
George Mason University	32,562	2	0	2	0	0	261	23	237	1	0	
Hampton University	5,254	5	0	0	3	2	83	31	52	0	0	
James Madison University	19,434	1	0	0	1	0	152	8	143	1	0	
J. Sargeant Reynolds Community College	12,629	0	0	0	0	0	37	0	37	0	1	
Longwood University	4,831	2	0	2	0	0	50	8	41	1	0	
Norfolk State University	6,964	7	0	1	4	2	150	24	123	3	3	
Northern Virginia Community College	48,996	2	0	0	1	1	120	3	117	0	0	
Old Dominion University	24,466	5	0	0	4	1	228	12	210	6	0	
Radford University	9,007	7	0	3	0	4	71	8	63	0	2	
University of Mary Washington	5,203	6	0	0	3	3	66	1	65	0	3	
University of Richmond	4,405	9	0	9	0	0	160	26	131	3	3	
University of Virginia	24,391	3	0	2	1	0	283	54	213	16	0	
University of Virginia's College at Wise	1,990	0	0	0	0	0	0	0	0	0	0	
Virginia Commonwealth University	32,027	18	0	1	9	8	511	12	497	2	1	
Virginia Military Institute	1,569	1	0	0	0	1	28	6	22	0	1	
Virginia Polytechnic Institute and State University	31,006	9	0	7	0	2	188	28	158	2	0	
Virginia State University	5,634	6	0	0	1	5	91	4	81	6	0	
Washington												
Central Washington University	11,614	7	0	2	2	3	219	19	198	2	1	
Eastern Washington University	11,534	4	0	2	1	1	72	16	56	0	0	
Evergreen State College	4,833	3	0	2	1	0	85	13	72	0	2	
University of Washington	42,451	8	0	1	4	3	623	87	534	2	2	
Washington State University												
Pullman	26,308	12	0	8	0	4	166	25	136	5	0	
Vancouver[4]	NA	0	0	0	0	0	7	2	4	1	0	
Western Washington University	14,979	4	0	1	0	3	130	5	120	5	0	
West Virginia												
Concord University	2,822	3	0	0	0	3	7	2	5	0	0	
Fairmont State University	4,709	1	0	1	0	0	29	6	23	0	0	
Glenville State College	1,827	0	0	0	0	0	7	2	5	0	0	
Marshall University	14,192	1	0	0	1	0	100	3	97	0	0	
Potomac State College	1,836	2	0	0	0	2	11	4	7	0	2	
Shepherd University	4,234	0	0	0	0	0	18	2	16	0	0	
West Liberty State College	2,738	2	0	0	0	2	10	0	10	0	0	
West Virginia State University	3,190	2	0	1	1	0	22	5	17	0	0	
West Virginia Tech	1,211	2	0	1	0	1	16	0	16	0	0	
West Virginia University	29,306	32	0	0	1	31	160	7	150	3	2	

NA = Not available.

Note: Caution should be exercised in making any intercampus comparisons or ranking schools because university/college crime statistics are affected by a variety of factors. These include demographic characteristics of the surrounding community, ratio of male to female students, number of on-campus residents, accessibility of the campus to outside visitors, size of enrollment, etc.

[1] The student enrollment figures provided by the United States Department of Education are for the 2010 school year, the most recent available. The enrollment figures include full-time and part-time students.

[2] If a blank is presented in the arson column, it indicates that the FBI did not receive 12 complete months of arson data for that agency.

[4] Student enrollment figures were not available.

Table II-9. **Offenses Known to Law Enforcement, by Selected State and University and College, 2011**—*Continued*

(Number.)

State and University/College	Campus	Student enroll-ment[1]	Violent crime	Murder and non-negligent man-slaughter	Forcible rape	Robbery	Aggra-vated assault	Property crime	Burglary	Larceny-theft	Motor vehicle theft	Arson[2]
Wisconsin												
University of Wisconsin												
Eau Claire	11,413	0	0	0	0	0	92	0	92	0	0	
Green Bay	6,636	1	0	1	0	0	35	2	32	1	0	
La Crosse	10,135	0	0	0	0	0	0	0	0	0	0	
Madison	42,180	12	0	4	3	5	370	32	336	2	1	
Milwaukee	30,470	2	0	1	1	0	331	49	282	0	0	
Oshkosh	13,629	4	0	1	0	3	76	3	73	0	3	
Parkside	5,160	0	0	0	0	0	89	3	86	0	0	
Platteville	7,928	4	0	2	0	2	121	19	99	3	3	
River Falls	6,902	2	0	0	0	2	56	1	55	0	1	
Stevens Point	9,500	0	0	0	0	0	79	0	78	1	0	
Stout	9,339	4	0	1	0	3	97	6	91	0	0	
Superior	2,856	0	0	0	0	0	24	0	24	0	0	
Whitewater	11,557	1	0	1	0	0	103	12	91	0	0	
Wyoming												
Sheridan College	3,888	0	0	0	0	0	1	1	0	0	0	
University of Wyoming	12,911	0	0	0	0	0	165	2	162	1	0	

NA = Not available.

Note: Caution should be exercised in making any intercampus comparisons or ranking schools because university/college crime statistics are affected by a variety of factors. These include demographic characteristics of the surrounding community, ratio of male to female students, number of on-campus residents, accessibility of the campus to outside visitors, size of enrollment, etc.

[1] The student enrollment figures provided by the United States Department of Education are for the 2010 school year, the most recent available. The enrollment figures include full-time and part-time students.

[2] If a blank is presented in the arson column, it indicates that the FBI did not receive 12 complete months of arson data for that agency.

Table II-10. Offenses Known to Law Enforcement, by Selected State Metropolitan and Nonmetropolitan Counties, 2011

(Number.)

State/County	Violent crime	Murder and non-negligent man-slaughter	Forcible rape	Robbery	Aggravated assault	Property crime	Burglary	Larceny-theft	Motor vehicle theft	Arson[1]
Alabama—Metropolitan Counties[2]										
Autauga	77	1	7	13	56	469	161	271	37	6
Blount	71	3	9	3	56	964	333	551	80	3
Calhoun	21	0	11	1	9	675	237	437	1	0
Chilton	88	1	16	3	68	772	302	414	56	0
Colbert	31	0	1	1	29	125	33	89	3	0
Elmore	56	2	10	9	35	768	269	454	45	0
Etowah	156	0	12	3	141	669	277	327	65	6
Geneva	30	0	3	1	26	249	82	144	23	1
Greene	50	1	2	2	45	144	62	68	14	1
Henry	33	2	1	1	29	126	44	73	9	1
Houston	83	1	9	7	66	606	193	355	58	1
Jefferson	569	9	55	153	352	4,125	2,348	1,678	99	20
Lauderdale	10	0	1	0	9	143	50	85	8	5
Lawrence	61	0	4	5	52	490	161	293	36	9
Lee	0	0	0	0	0	124	19	105	0	7
Limestone	26	0	1	2	23	200	56	123	21	0
Lowndes	37	0	1	6	30	277	143	115	19	79
Mobile	241	6	19	43	173	2,517	844	1,437	236	4
Montgomery	80	3	1	10	66	613	248	307	58	4
Morgan	38	0	9	3	26	524	269	236	19	0
Russell	29	0	3	2	24	531	185	319	27	0
Shelby	118	1	24	13	80	1,309	409	810	90	3
St. Clair	42	1	16	1	24	669	245	409	15	0
Tuscaloosa	228	2	8	21	197	1,525	427	970	128	5
Alabama—Nonmetropolitan Counties[2]										
Baldwin	91	0	10	13	68	982	374	556	52	7
Barbour	3	0	0	0	3	54	24	26	4	3
Bullock	12	0	2	2	8	70	66	3	1	8
Butler	43	1	5	2	35	277	90	177	10	4
Chambers	0	0	0	0	0	0	0	0	0	0
Cherokee	48	1	2	1	44	535	216	296	23	8
Choctaw	7	1	0	0	6	29	14	11	4	0
Clay	12	0	0	0	12	52	13	34	5	0
Coffee	29	0	1	3	25	239	101	121	17	5
Conecuh	43	0	3	5	35	190	60	117	13	1
Coosa	33	0	1	2	30	245	110	128	7	4
Crenshaw	57	2	0	2	53	198	92	94	12	1
Cullman	113	1	16	3	93	1,235	383	800	52	0
Dale	65	0	9	3	53	205	51	146	8	3
Dallas	73	0	6	11	56	614	207	381	26	3
De Kalb	179	4	21	2	152	908	320	515	73	0
Escambia	42	0	3	4	35	396	126	228	42	0
Fayette	6	0	0	0	6	90	34	50	6	2
Franklin	34	2	4	1	27	319	102	195	22	0
Jackson	78	1	4	1	72	621	232	329	60	4
Lamar	2	0	2	0	0	4	1	3	0	0
Macon	0	0	0	0	0	1	1	0	0	0
Marengo	23	0	4	1	18	180	68	103	9	3
Marion	28	0	1	1	26	247	91	133	23	1
Marshall	55	0	9	1	45	817	312	461	44	3
Monroe	33	0	1	1	31	100	53	44	3	1
Pickens	4	0	1	0	3	17	6	10	1	0
Pike	4	0	0	0	4	33	11	22	0	0
Randolph	44	0	4	2	38	319	124	176	19	1
Sumter	12	0	1	2	9	22	12	7	3	0
Talladega	56	1	4	4	47	957	335	545	77	5
Tallapoosa	17	1	2	1	13	233	109	112	12	0
Washington	26	1	0	0	25	177	44	114	19	2
Winston	13	0	0	0	13	185	76	100	9	0
Arizona—Metropolitan Counties										
Coconino	141	5	10	7	119	531	181	335	15	28
Maricopa	884	6	45	72	761	4,955	1,371	3,143	441	102
Mohave	145	6	11	15	113	2,144	762	1,245	137	11
Pima	607	16	62	163	366	11,711	2,857	8,007	847	96
Pinal	227	5	47	22	153	3,789	710	2,654	425	17
Yavapai	312	9	13	5	285	1,320	465	764	91	12

NA = Not available.

Note: The data shown in this table do not reflect county totals but are the number of offenses reported by the sheriff's office or county police department.

[1] If a blank is presented in the arson column, it indicates that the FBI did not receive 12 complete months of arson data for that agency.

[2] Because of changes in the state/local agency's reporting practices, figures are not comparable to previous years' data.

Table II-10. Offenses Known to Law Enforcement, by Selected State Metropolitan and Nonmetropolitan Counties, 2011—*Continued*

(Number.)

State/County	Violent crime	Murder and non-negligent man-slaughter	Forcible rape	Robbery	Aggravated assault	Property crime	Burglary	Larceny-theft	Motor vehicle theft	Arson[1]
Arizona—Nonmetropolitan Counties										
Apache	45	1	0	1	43	176	95	74	7	20
Cochise	367	3	15	12	337	797	334	400	63	16
Gila	34	1	1	3	29	347	55	261	31	3
Graham[3]		0	0	1		227	62	152	13	10
La Paz	41	0	2	0	39	390	113	253	24	0
Navajo	59	2	1	2	54	610	383	181	46	7
Santa Cruz	7	1	2	2	2	276	103	131	42	9
Arkansas—Metropolitan Counties										
Benton	158	1	21	1	135	459	227	216	16	2
Cleveland	5	0	0	0	5	113	68	37	8	0
Craighead	12	1	0	3	8	296	120	163	13	2
Crawford	139	1	18	1	119	334	67	237	30	1
Crittenden	181	1	7	15	158	454	130	286	38	7
Faulkner	46	0	8	0	38	921	291	554	76	6
Franklin	39	0	4	0	35	191	69	109	13	4
Jefferson	69	2	5	7	55	531	238	200	93	5
Lincoln	3	1	0	1	1	99	52	43	4	3
Lonoke	116	3	9	3	101	787	308	403	76	7
Madison	21	0	5	0	16	122	49	56	17	0
Miller	14	0	4	1	9	279	84	158	37	3
Poinsett	21	0	5	0	16	35	14	16	5	3
Pulaski	409	6	25	31	347	2,244	896	1,144	204	13
Sebastian	83	0	11	3	69	356	183	151	22	3
Washington	148	2	12	4	130	547	199	305	43	7
Arkansas—Nonmetropolitan Counties										
Arkansas	5	0	0	0	5	98	32	57	9	0
Ashley	22	1	1	3	17	218	88	116	14	2
Baxter	30	2	3	0	25	653	114	502	37	0
Boone	21	1	8	0	12	366	114	205	47	5
Carroll	29	0	0	0	29	208	53	145	10	4
Chicot	0	0	0	0	0	39	14	25	0	0
Clark	12	0	1	1	10	142	44	88	10	1
Clay	8	0	2	0	6	76	26	48	2	0
Cleburne	41	1	6	0	34	495	253	195	47	5
Columbia	41	0	0	2	39	212	55	139	18	0
Conway	25	1	1	3	20	322	74	229	19	5
Cross	27	0	4	0	23	28	19	6	3	2
Dallas	1	0	0	0	1	26	7	19	0	1
Drew	30	0	6	1	23	122	38	69	15	2
Fulton	16	0	0	0	16	153	67	79	7	6
Greene	21	0	2	0	19	266	96	154	16	0
Hempstead	42	0	4	0	38	195	47	126	22	6
Howard	14	0	4	0	10	85	36	46	3	0
Independence	136	0	10	12	114	1,546	691	758	97	14
Izard	2	0	1	0	1	186	69	117	0	1
Jackson	23	0	0	2	21	164	49	102	13	2
Johnson	21	0	1	0	20	225	189	36	0	8
Lafayette	4	0	0	0	4	71	17	54	0	0
Lawrence	8	0	1	0	7	129	38	91	0	3
Lee	7	2	0	0	5	66	18	44	4	0
Little River	6	0	0	0	6	72	22	47	3	4
Logan	20	0	9	2	9	311	120	164	27	1
Marion	35	0	2	1	32	219	85	132	2	6
Mississippi	35	0	6	2	27	343	81	226	36	2
Monroe	1	0	0	0	1	51	7	44	0	0
Montgomery	4	0	0	0	4	19	7	12	0	0
Nevada	6	0	0	0	6	45	19	24	2	1
Newton	10	0	2	0	8	79	25	51	3	1
Ouachita	2	0	0	0	2	22	13	9	0	1
Pike	7	1	3	0	3	30	13	13	4	1
Polk	39	0	3	0	36	204	87	103	14	14
Pope	60	0	10	2	48	460	165	256	39	2
Prairie	0	0	0	0	0	50	10	38	2	0
Scott	8	0	4	0	4	66	20	43	3	2
Searcy	10	0	0	0	10	28	16	10	2	0
Sevier	19	1	0	2	16	168	45	101	22	2
St. Francis	23	1	3	5	14	379	105	274	0	2
Stone	18	0	4	0	14	119	56	61	2	3
Union	34	0	0	11	23	436	127	268	41	0

NA = Not available.

Note: The data shown in this table do not reflect county totals but are the number of offenses reported by the sheriff's office or county police department.

[1] If a blank is presented in the arson column, it indicates that the FBI did not receive 12 complete months of arson data for that agency.

[3] The FBI determined that the agency's data were overreported. Consequently, affected data are not included in this table.

Table II-10.   Offenses Known to Law Enforcement, by Selected State Metropolitan and Nonmetropolitan Counties, 2011—*Continued*

(Number.)

State/County	Violent crime	Murder and non-negligent man-slaughter	Forcible rape	Robbery	Aggravated assault	Property crime	Burglary	Larceny-theft	Motor vehicle theft	Arson[1]
Van Buren	46	0	2	0	44	219	51	140	28	5
White	56	3	10	4	39	907	373	438	96	3
Yell	18	0	4	2	12	164	70	82	12	2
California—Metropolitan Counties										
Alameda	725	3	26	218	478	2,192	650	991	551	19
Butte	106	2	13	23	68	1,310	560	744	6	3
Contra Costa	456	13	30	109	304	2,475	1,033	1,423	19	18
El Dorado	192	2	21	21	148	2,273	1,020	1,241	12	10
Fresno	740	6	23	125	586	4,781	1,618	2,331	832	
Imperial	110	0	4	6	100	676	255	399	22	7
Kern	1,822	22	108	358	1,334	10,198	3,301	5,378	1,519	282
Kings	137	2	13	15	107	683	242	386	55	7
Los Angeles	5,595	88	165	1,484	3,858	16,010	4,624	7,730	3,656	222
Madera	311	4	10	20	277	1,634	836	778	20	11
Marin	122	0	8	22	92	739	263	473	3	5
Merced	459	2	22	41	394	2,319	767	1,538	14	6
Monterey	197	8	19	44	126	1,290	504	781	5	18
Napa	52	2	2	1	47	371	125	243	3	4
Orange	251	1	11	42	197	1,301	277	935	89	3
Placer	301	4	25	28	244	1,946	622	1,293	31	3
Riverside	903	13	47	188	655	8,872	2,673	4,884	1,315	18
Sacramento	2,719	33	144	959	1,583	11,797	4,150	7,539	108	77
San Benito	38	1	6	0	31	268	93	161	14	1
San Bernardino	1,081	18	57	178	828	6,207	2,202	2,879	1,126	94
San Diego	1,397	18	84	218	1,077	5,851	1,725	3,202	924	27
San Joaquin	820	23	20	164	613	4,767	1,802	2,831	134	22
San Luis Obispo	208	1	26	13	168	1,356	481	872	3	3
San Mateo	219	0	18	32	169	1,976	312	1,464	200	9
Santa Barbara	255	1	34	30	190	1,539	487	1,045	7	12
Santa Clara	186	4	30	39	113	1,487	316	1,025	146	2
Santa Cruz	362	3	34	36	289	2,301	913	1,382	6	10
Shasta	524	2	32	22	468	970	512	430	28	1
Solano	95	3	4	18	70	423	195	207	21	8
Sonoma	511	5	36	48	422	1,306	490	802	14	13
Stanislaus	323	16	15	77	215	2,404	1,135	1,222	47	61
Sutter	132	3	8	4	117	847	210	589	48	6
Tulare[4]	517	20	31	68	398		1,200	2,191		31
Ventura	155	2	10	23	120	1,124	273	795	56	17
Yolo	82	0	9	4	69	408	125	273	10	7
Yuba	230	3	18	29	180	1,323	457	858	8	5
California—Nonmetropolitan Counties										
Alpine	7	0	0	0	7	105	20	84	1	0
Amador	54	1	5	4	44	598	187	401	10	4
Calaveras	102	1	14	8	79	974	314	655	5	0
Colusa	28	1	2	1	24	281	91	186	4	2
Del Norte	99	2	18	7	72	427	242	180	5	6
Glenn	11	2	0	2	7	169	61	105	3	2
Humboldt	203	2	21	46	134	1,109	436	646	27	14
Inyo	52	1	7	3	41	141	54	85	2	5
Lake	169	1	18	20	130	704	315	383	6	10
Lassen	39	1	5	2	31	143	56	86	1	3
Mariposa	55	0	5	1	49	342	128	214	0	1
Mendocino	295	7	13	23	252	544	247	297	0	10
Modoc	24	0	7	1	16	93	36	53	4	3
Mono	11	0	1	0	10	67	21	46	0	0
Nevada	166	2	10	6	148	533	226	301	6	1
Plumas	104	1	14	3	86	356	124	231	1	7
Sierra	5	0	0	0	5	55	17	38	0	2
Siskiyou	71	2	10	4	55	228	102	124	2	1
Tehama	184	1	5	8	170	316	134	182	0	6
Trinity	34	3	5	1	25	100	63	37	0	0
Tuolumne	75	1	13	13	48	731	354	371	6	18
Colorado—Metropolitan Counties										
Adams	385	2	57	59	267	2,413	622	1,431	360	20
Arapahoe	236	0	29	45	162	1,313	350	856	107	19
Boulder	65	1	11	1	52	554	164	360	30	16
Clear Creek	17	0	4	0	13	68	30	33	5	1

NA = Not available.

Note: The data shown in this table do not reflect county totals but are the number of offenses reported by the sheriff's office or county police department.

[1] If a blank is presented in the arson column, it indicates that the FBI did not receive 12 complete months of arson data for that agency.

[4] The Tulare County Highway Patrol collects the motor vehicle thefts for this county. These data can be found in Table II-11.

Table II-10.   Offenses Known to Law Enforcement, by Selected State Metropolitan and Nonmetropolitan Counties, 2011—*Continued*

(Number.)

State/County	Violent crime	Murder and non-negligent man-slaughter	Forcible rape	Robbery	Aggravated assault	Property crime	Burglary	Larceny-theft	Motor vehicle theft	Arson[1]
Douglas	312	2	197	15	98	1,812	406	1,317	89	21
El Paso	486	2	62	15	407	2,097	604	1,314	179	27
Gilpin	2	0	1	0	1	25	5	19	1	0
Jefferson	127	0	20	18	89	2,323	437	1,779	107	15
Larimer	107	0	18	3	86	973	252	669	52	21
Mesa	181	1	15	12	153	1,201	292	842	67	6
Park	7	0	0	0	7	110	37	61	12	1
Pueblo	28	1	0	6	21	1,545	331	1,157	57	0
Teller	23	1	1	0	21	78	34	43	1	1
Weld	185	5	17	8	155	772	252	435	85	9
Colorado—Nonmetropolitan Counties										
Alamosa	1	0	0	0	1	37	10	27	0	0
Archuleta	15	3	2	0	10	10	4	5	1	0
Bent	2	0	0	1	1	26	7	19	0	1
Chaffee	8	0	2	0	6	89	16	68	5	1
Cheyenne	0	0	0	0	0	3	0	3	0	0
Crowley	4	0	0	0	4	0	0	0	0	0
Custer	7	0	0	0	7	33	8	23	2	0
Delta	19	0	7	0	12	120	25	86	9	2
Dolores	3	0	1	0	2	22	13	7	2	0
Eagle	25	0	4	0	21	386	90	296	0	4
Fremont	36	0	0	1	35	237	96	131	10	2
Grand	10	0	0	0	10	89	10	79	0	0
Gunnison	8	0	0	0	8	32	7	23	2	0
Hinsdale	1	0	0	0	1	12	4	8	0	0
Huerfano	3	0	0	0	3	8	4	4	0	0
Kit Carson	2	0	0	0	2	16	2	11	3	0
Las Animas	0	0	0	0	0	0	0	0	0	0
Lincoln	4	2	0	0	2	0	0	0	0	0
Logan	10	0	2	1	7	110	45	57	8	0
Moffat	4	0	1	0	3	20	8	7	5	1
Montezuma	31	0	2	0	29	163	60	93	10	1
Montrose	36	2	5	0	29	155	36	102	17	0
Morgan	2	0	0	1	1	40	8	30	2	0
Otero	5	0	0	1	4	62	26	36	0	2
Ouray	3	0	0	0	3	12	3	8	1	0
Phillips	0	0	0	0	0	3	1	2	0	0
Pitkin	14	0	0	0	14	50	5	44	1	0
Prowers	8	0	1	0	7	20	8	12	0	0
Rio Grande	4	0	1	1	2	53	11	38	4	2
Routt	12	0	0	0	12	77	21	54	2	1
San Juan	2	0	0	0	2	25	1	19	5	1
San Miguel	0	0	0	0	0	20	7	12	1	1
Sedgwick	7	0	0	0	7	19	5	13	1	0
Washington	14	0	3	0	11	82	21	57	4	0
Delaware—Metropolitan Counties										
New Castle County Police Department	1,122	5	55	341	721	6,117	1,983	3,711	423	5
Florida—Metropolitan Counties										
Alachua	581	4	35	84	458	2,495	794	1,592	109	12
Baker	46	0	4	6	36	312	43	258	11	1
Bay	344	4	38	53	249	2,728	716	1,848	164	5
Brevard	991	6	66	132	787	5,845	1,458	4,170	217	19
Broward	291	2	15	73	201	1,043	260	731	52	8
Charlotte	381	2	31	50	298	3,710	1,089	2,521	100	14
Clay	665	5	32	94	534	4,269	883	3,245	141	28
Collier	956	9	42	208	697	5,250	1,373	3,683	194	14
Escambia	1,782	14	140	463	1,165	10,728	2,600	7,543	585	29
Flagler	227	1	13	26	187	1,751	408	1,287	56	6
Gadsden	88	1	6	12	69	340	150	184	6	0
Gilchrist	31	1	1	1	28	221	84	131	6	0
Hernando	495	8	33	69	385	4,724	1,321	3,241	162	17
Hillsborough	2,130	28	133	530	1,439	19,487	5,104	13,190	1,193	41
Indian River	351	3	25	62	261	2,728	778	1,869	81	5
Jefferson	79	0	5	1	73	171	91	65	15	3
Lake	562	6	27	48	481	3,488	1,159	2,090	239	10
Lee	1,198	15	59	373	751	10,134	3,593	6,064	477	48
Leon	323	4	18	48	253	1,629	699	837	93	16
Manatee	1,518	12	88	348	1,070	9,911	2,532	7,029	350	2

NA = Not available.

Note: The data shown in this table do not reflect county totals but are the number of offenses reported by the sheriff's office or county police department.

[1] If a blank is presented in the arson column, it indicates that the FBI did not receive 12 complete months of arson data for that agency.

Table II-10. Offenses Known to Law Enforcement, by Selected State Metropolitan and Nonmetropolitan Counties, 2011—*Continued*

(Number.)

State/County	Violent crime	Murder and non-negligent man-slaughter	Forcible rape	Robbery	Aggravated assault	Property crime	Burglary	Larceny-theft	Motor vehicle theft	Arson[1]
Marion	1,292	9	135	79	1,069	4,952	1,733	3,000	219	7
Martin	300	1	16	84	199	2,922	690	2,140	92	8
Miami-Dade	6,913	90	311	1,848	4,664	44,395	9,324	30,843	4,228	12
Nassau	85	0	0	8	77	1,153	325	764	64	2
Okaloosa	557	1	38	69	449	3,346	637	2,569	140	2
Orange	5,325	56	284	1,345	3,640	27,348	8,705	16,344	2,299	2
Osceola	866	2	36	91	737	5,408	1,691	3,469	248	1
Palm Beach	2,122	14	120	590	1,398	15,418	4,269	10,031	1,118	84
Pasco	1,190	11	79	261	839	12,380	3,436	8,373	571	80
Pinellas	1,018	8	121	164	725	7,019	1,817	4,887	315	27
Polk	1,288	12	70	185	1,021	9,473	3,274	5,779	420	7
Santa Rosa	199	1	24	13	161	1,913	602	1,219	92	4
Sarasota	769	8	39	165	557	7,912	2,224	5,420	268	10
Seminole	621	6	43	79	493	3,369	907	2,276	186	0
St. Johns	517	4	10	56	447	3,789	841	2,768	180	3
St. Lucie	268	2	20	50	196	1,920	637	1,191	92	3
Volusia	714	10	51	104	549	5,528	1,878	3,362	288	22
Wakulla	90	2	12	7	69	748	167	567	14	7
Florida—Nonmetropolitan Counties										
Bradford	77	0	1	1	75	329	138	172	19	1
Calhoun	9	1	0	0	8	76	33	38	5	0
Citrus	398	5	17	60	316	2,868	806	1,934	128	30
Columbia	233	3	5	11	214	1,406	532	840	34	0
DeSoto	107	1	5	18	83	623	284	318	21	1
Dixie	62	0	14	4	44	415	163	227	25	5
Franklin	92	0	9	1	82	185	55	122	8	2
Glades	41	1	1	6	33	270	77	172	21	0
Gulf	48	1	0	0	47	169	62	103	4	1
Hamilton	34	0	1	1	32	223	94	108	21	0
Hardee	44	1	10	8	25	532	197	312	23	0
Hendry	223	7	9	24	183	1,080	471	562	47	9
Highlands	191	2	10	24	155	1,828	630	1,128	70	0
Holmes	58	1	4	1	52	240	55	168	17	0
Jackson	124	0	17	4	103	715	170	525	20	0
Lafayette	12	0	0	0	12	64	15	47	2	0
Levy	126	1	11	10	104	918	326	545	47	6
Liberty	7	0	0	0	7	38	17	21	0	0
Madison	92	0	2	8	82	250	91	149	10	1
Monroe	164	1	12	14	137	1,847	327	1,468	52	0
Okeechobee	183	0	27	17	139	1,042	433	578	31	1
Putnam	433	1	33	57	342	2,453	1,120	1,258	75	8
Sumter	120	1	14	12	93	656	208	419	29	4
Suwannee	110	1	4	2	103	528	174	325	29	0
Taylor	62	3	1	2	56	170	125	39	6	0
Union	35	0	2	5	28	170	80	85	5	0
Walton	153	3	6	1	143	1,198	376	759	63	3
Washington	52	2	0	3	47	239	77	149	13	0
Georgia—Metropolitan Counties										
Augusta-Richmond	990	26	104	550	310	13,336	3,817	8,108	1,411	74
Barrow	173	0	8	7	158	943	267	614	62	
Bartow	241	2	7	37	195	2,841	805	1,845	191	0
Bibb	218	3	11	35	169	2,762	672	1,855	235	9
Brantley	45	0	7	2	36	293	201	92	0	3
Brooks	28	0	0	1	27	227	68	132	27	
Bryan	32	0	1	2	29	424	120	298	6	1
Burke	148	2	0	0	146	494	147	344	3	0
Butts	42	3	6	18	15	511	147	313	51	1
Carroll	107	2	8	10	87	1,583	503	938	142	10
Catoosa	76	0	9	8	59	1,040	265	666	109	1
Chatham	0	0	0	0	0	0	0	0	0	0
Chattahoochee	18	2	2	3	11	55	24	27	4	2
Cherokee	107	0	13	19	75	2,114	665	1,348	101	4
Clarke	2	0	0	0	2	0	0	0	0	0
Clayton	4	0	0	1	3	8	0	7	1	0
Clayton County Police Department	1,060	28	74	491	467	10,164	3,770	4,989	1,405	32
Cobb	0	0	0	0	0	0	0	0	0	0
Cobb County Police Department	934	18	92	388	436	11,112	3,376	6,836	900	32
Columbia	94	4	19	20	51	2,438	452	1,900	86	10
Coweta	102	2	15	18	67	1,651	453	1,086	112	5
Crawford	28	0	3	1	24	523	158	335	30	1
Dade	62	1	3	0	58	272	90	153	29	1

NA = Not available.

Note: The data shown in this table do not reflect county totals but are the number of offenses reported by the sheriff's office or county police department.

[1] If a blank is presented in the arson column, it indicates that the FBI did not receive 12 complete months of arson data for that agency.

Table II-10. Offenses Known to Law Enforcement, by Selected State Metropolitan and Nonmetropolitan Counties, 2011—*Continued*

(Number.)

State/County	Violent crime	Murder and non-negligent man-slaughter	Forcible rape	Robbery	Aggravated assault	Property crime	Burglary	Larceny-theft	Motor vehicle theft	Arson[1]
Dawson	15	0	0	0	15	551	112	411	28	0
DeKalb County Police Department	3,159	65	139	1,735	1,220	30,194	10,338	15,599	4,257	139
Dougherty	6	0	0	2	4	193	9	179	5	0
Dougherty County Police Department	32	0	7	7	18	431	157	250	24	2
Douglas	176	2	13	68	93	2,191	608	1,394	189	4
Echols	2	0	0	0	2	37	11	23	3	0
Effingham	56	0	14	8	34	348	265	58	25	3
Fayette	33	1	3	7	22	626	201	383	42	6
Floyd	51	0	1	2	48	14	7	7	0	0
Floyd County Police Department	206	1	8	12	185	1,448	383	972	93	15
Forsyth	363	1	22	14	326	1,837	438	1,333	66	2
Fulton	1	0	0	0	1	9	1	8	0	0
Fulton County Police Department	748	13	25	362	348	5,842	1,712	3,242	888	10
Glynn	0	0	0	0	0	0	0	0	0	0
Glynn County Police Department	243	3	17	73	150	3,108	697	2,318	93	2
Gwinnett County Police Department	1,495	24	145	630	696	15,736	5,095	9,451	1,190	75
Hall	154	2	20	33	99	2,553	722	1,624	207	15
Haralson	134	2	2	6	124	532	271	201	60	5
Harris	15	0	2	0	13	271	86	173	12	
Heard	18	0	0	1	17	152	45	79	28	0
Henry	9	0	0	0	9	125	0	124	1	
Henry County Police Department	272	5	30	106	131	4,490	1,360	2,777	353	19
Houston	71	0	6	13	52	1,195	290	853	52	
Jasper	15	0	2	1	12	345	132	203	10	0
Jones	14	1	1	1	11	541	149	344	48	4
Lamar	40	0	0	1	39	269	72	182	15	0
Lanier	9	0	0	0	9	145	51	89	5	0
Lee	79	0	0	1	78	613	161	422	30	1
Liberty	61	1	1	4	55	429	166	232	31	
Lowndes	74	2	6	10	56	746	180	523	43	
Madison	194	0	4	5	185	743	204	488	51	
McDuffie	31	1	1	7	22	303	103	171	29	0
McIntosh	22	2	1	2	17	400	118	256	26	6
Meriwether	24	1	2	0	21	438	159	248	31	0
Monroe	24	0	1	9	14	482	156	295	31	1
Murray	51	1	5	1	44	856	176	611	69	
Muscogee	0	0	0	0	0	0	0	0	0	0
Newton	330	1	18	45	266	2,201	813	1,193	195	
Oconee	44	0	1	2	41	485	105	339	41	1
Oglethorpe	62	0	4	6	52	650	152	485	13	0
Paulding	141	0	18	14	109	2,571	664	1,723	184	13
Pickens	26	2	0	0	24	427	95	317	15	
Pike	2	0	1	0	1	93	30	59	4	
Rockdale	272	1	15	42	214	2,413	677	1,568	168	
Spalding	127	4	15	18	90	1,668	507	1,032	129	0
Terrell	16	2	1	0	13	105	38	60	7	
Twiggs	8	1	0	0	7	175	75	89	11	0
Walton	113	2	4	13	94	1,215	287	813	115	0
Whitfield	166	1	16	7	142	1,823	492	1,205	126	7
Worth	4	0	0	3	1	181	46	120	15	1
Georgia—Nonmetropolitan Counties										
Appling	23	1	2	0	20	455	74	359	22	
Atkinson	4	0	0	0	4	64	32	29	3	
Baldwin	72	1	6	9	56	868	263	582	23	1
Banks	16	0	2	0	14	670	134	500	36	0
Ben Hill	14	1	4	2	7	216	74	131	11	0
Berrien	12	1	1	0	10	257	57	191	9	0
Bleckley	14	0	2	1	11	150	51	90	9	2
Bulloch	27	1	1	7	18	728	259	414	55	
Calhoun	2	0	0	0	2	31	9	21	1	0
Camden	50	2	2	0	46	471	112	339	20	
Charlton	9	0	1	3	5	157	63	89	5	1
Clay	10	2	0	0	8	6	6	0	0	
Clinch	6	0	0	1	5	69	26	35	8	1
Coffee	59	1	6	4	48	856	233	577	46	2
Cook	17	0	0	1	16	133	60	66	7	
Crisp	18	0	0	0	18	429	97	318	14	0
Decatur	33	2	1	5	25	238	74	158	6	1
Dodge	25	1	2	1	21	418	143	265	10	0

NA = Not available.

Note: The data shown in this table do not reflect county totals but are the number of offenses reported by the sheriff's office or county police department.

[1] If a blank is presented in the arson column, it indicates that the FBI did not receive 12 complete months of arson data for that agency.

Table II-10. Offenses Known to Law Enforcement, by Selected State Metropolitan and Nonmetropolitan Counties, 2011—*Continued*

(Number.)

State/County	Violent crime	Murder and non-negligent man-slaughter	Forcible rape	Robbery	Aggravated assault	Property crime	Burglary	Larceny-theft	Motor vehicle theft	Arson[1]
Dooly	19	0	0	3	16	106	17	84	5	
Early	22	0	0	0	22	138	47	85	6	0
Elbert	25	0	1	2	22	582	174	374	34	0
Emanuel	19	0	1	6	12	366	177	165	24	
Evans	13	0	1	1	11	86	46	35	5	
Fannin	95	0	1	2	92	440	150	275	15	0
Franklin	10	1	2	5	2	396	124	255	17	
Gilmer	25	1	3	0	21	427	169	236	22	0
Gordon	148	2	3	2	141	795	233	512	50	0
Grady	28	0	0	1	27	142	70	62	10	
Greene	9	0	0	2	7	247	62	175	10	0
Habersham	38	0	8	1	29	468	168	286	14	0
Hancock	1	0	1	0	0	84	38	44	2	0
Hart	64	0	1	3	60	604	172	403	29	
Irwin	6	0	0	1	5	158	51	99	8	0
Jackson	25	0	1	5	19	1,087	296	737	54	8
Jeff Davis	52	1	0	2	49	306	68	206	32	1
Jefferson	16	0	0	4	12	178	94	67	17	
Laurens	27	0	5	5	17	869	239	536	94	1
Lumpkin	102	0	8	1	93	528	132	373	23	2
Miller	2	0	0	0	2	31	5	26	0	
Mitchell	33	0	4	1	28	250	72	156	22	
Morgan	7	0	1	0	6	209	47	142	20	5
Peach	19	0	0	7	12	377	139	210	28	0
Pierce[5]	7	0	0	1	6		4		5	
Polk	0	0	0	0	0	0	0	0	0	0
Polk County Police Department	63	0	6	3	54	775	280	433	62	7
Pulaski	34	1	0	2	31	263	80	179	4	0
Putnam	66	1	1	1	63	384	127	249	8	0
Rabun	3	0	0	0	3	209	45	157	7	0
Randolph	8	0	1	1	6	92	33	56	3	
Schley	5	0	0	0	5	34	7	27	0	
Screven	12	0	0	3	9	223	80	123	20	1
Seminole	10	3	0	3	4	87	32	51	4	1
Stephens	25	1	9	4	11	492	136	327	29	0
Stewart	2	0	0	0	2	24	12	10	2	0
Taliaferro	8	0	2	1	5	68	27	36	5	0
Taylor	3	1	1	1	0	83	20	49	14	
Telfair	6	0	0	1	5	66	30	34	2	0
Thomas	40	1	2	3	34	580	198	339	43	8
Tift	136	3	8	31	94	860	220	592	48	1
Toombs	18	1	5	3	9	284	91	167	26	0
Towns	3	0	0	1	2	135	65	65	5	0
Treutlen	4	0	0	0	4	84	35	47	2	0
Turner	8	0	0	1	7	104	26	70	8	1
Union	15	1	0	1	13	138	56	70	12	0
Upson	21	1	0	3	17	463	116	314	33	
Ware	57	2	5	4	46	757	199	538	20	0
Warren	21	0	0	0	21	61	29	22	10	0
Washington	21	0	2	3	16	231	52	175	4	0
Wayne	160	1	3	16	140	1,003	233	766	4	0
Webster	1	0	0	1	0	31	20	8	3	1
White	11	0	0	0	11	375	137	202	36	0
Wilcox	8	1	1	0	6	79	25	49	5	0
Wilkes	6	0	0	0	6	36	7	27	2	0
Wilkinson	11	1	0	1	9	124	36	76	12	3
Idaho—Metropolitan Counties										
Ada	122	2	14	3	103	801	165	597	39	20
Bannock	6	0	1	0	5	76	13	59	4	0
Boise	11	0	1	0	10	121	33	87	1	0
Bonneville	81	5	10	3	63	904	213	656	35	5
Canyon	74	0	8	1	65	727	316	364	47	4
Franklin	0	0	0	0	0	57	6	49	2	0
Gem	13	0	1	0	12	41	22	16	3	0
Jefferson	24	0	0	0	24	131	53	68	10	1
Kootenai	121	1	26	7	87	1,328	478	794	56	13
Nez Perce	3	0	0	1	2	123	29	87	7	0
Owyhee	9	0	1	0	8	122	24	93	5	0
Power	2	0	0	0	2	50	13	35	2	0

NA = Not available.

Note: The data shown in this table do not reflect county totals but are the number of offenses reported by the sheriff's office or county police department.

[1] If a blank is presented in the arson column, it indicates that the FBI did not receive 12 complete months of arson data for that agency.

[5] The FBI determined that the agency's data were underreported. Consequently, those data are not included in this table.

Table II-10. Offenses Known to Law Enforcement, by Selected State Metropolitan and Nonmetropolitan Counties, 2011—*Continued*

(Number.)

State/County	Violent crime	Murder and non-negligent man-slaughter	Forcible rape	Robbery	Aggravated assault	Property crime	Burglary	Larceny-theft	Motor vehicle theft	Arson[1]
Idaho—Nonmetropolitan Counties										
Bear Lake	0	0	0	0	0	26	11	15	0	0
Benewah	15	3	0	0	12	26	9	14	3	1
Bingham	10	0	3	0	7	309	80	206	23	1
Blaine	5	0	0	0	5	39	14	20	5	4
Bonner	33	0	5	1	27	454	156	268	30	0
Boundary	9	1	0	0	8	94	47	42	5	0
Butte	3	0	0	0	3	4	0	2	2	0
Camas	1	0	0	1	0	13	7	6	0	0
Caribou	3	0	1	0	2	24	7	17	0	0
Cassia	32	0	4	1	27	317	38	261	18	0
Clark	0	0	0	0	0	12	3	9	0	0
Clearwater	10	0	0	0	10	101	20	75	6	0
Custer	1	0	0	0	1	18	3	12	3	0
Elmore	15	0	1	0	14	65	18	46	1	1
Fremont	4	0	0	0	4	68	9	55	4	2
Gooding	13	1	2	0	10	68	26	36	6	1
Idaho	12	0	0	0	12	111	30	78	3	1
Jerome	11	0	1	0	10	128	41	77	10	0
Latah	20	0	5	0	15	195	87	102	6	0
Lemhi	5	0	0	0	5	37	11	23	3	0
Lewis	5	0	0	0	5	26	7	17	2	0
Lincoln	2	0	2	0	0	9	2	7	0	0
Madison	12	0	4	0	8	80	28	49	3	0
Minidoka	15	0	3	1	11	168	32	126	10	1
Oneida	0	0	0	0	0	29	7	21	1	0
Payette	20	0	1	1	18	119	45	63	11	0
Shoshone	25	0	7	1	17	125	31	84	10	2
Teton	7	0	0	0	7	45	10	35	0	0
Twin Falls	34	1	4	0	29	280	150	110	20	0
Valley	12	0	4	0	8	69	27	40	2	1
Washington	9	0	0	0	9	29	21	8	0	0
Illinois—Metropolitan Counties										
Alexander	8	0	3	0	5	84	23	52	9	1
Bond	2	0	0	0	2	139	42	93	4	0
Champaign	126	3	11	15	97	618	216	382	20	5
Clinton	10	0	1	2	7	110	11	97	2	0
Cook	313	2	36	33	242	1,279	395	776	108	16
De Kalb	28	0	6	2	20	310	69	228	13	2
Ford	25	0	3	0	22	129	42	84	3	0
Grundy	13	0	2	2	9	232	78	141	13	3
Henry	5	0	1	0	4	120	40	77	3	0
Jersey	42	0	8	2	32	149	49	95	5	1
Kane	75	1	12	2	60	692	241	420	31	7
Kankakee	56	0	10	8	38	522	154	348	20	9
Kendall	44	0	9	3	32	311	88	216	7	5
Lake	61	1	9	16	35	1,795	569	1,154	72	5
Macon	69	0	17	3	49	376	118	247	11	4
Macoupin	7	0	0	0	7	233	73	154	6	1
Madison	79	3	5	4	67	882	313	548	21	2
Marshall	2	0	0	0	2	80	41	31	8	1
McHenry	83	4	12	3	64	616	165	425	26	2
McLean	40	1	7	3	29	260	96	153	11	0
Menard	1	0	1	0	0	41	14	23	4	0
Monroe	4	0	1	0	3	65	28	33	4	1
Peoria	142	3	20	12	107	825	225	566	34	3
Piatt	19	1	5	0	13	108	44	60	4	0
Rock Island	57	0	14	2	41	390	117	254	19	1
Sangamon	119	0	24	19	76	823	292	499	32	4
Stark	2	0	0	0	2	102	28	68	6	0
Tazewell	3	0	0	1	2	221	69	146	6	0
Vermilion	69	0	13	5	51	627	229	363	35	0
Will	134	6	13	14	101	1,362	527	730	105	16
Winnebago	93	4	20	13	56	1,039	367	606	66	6
Woodford	7	0	2	0	5	181	68	105	8	1
Illinois—Nonmetropolitan Counties										
Adams	25	0	7	0	18	275	63	200	12	2
Bureau	14	0	2	2	10	159	40	116	3	1
Carroll	0	0	0	0	0	69	12	57	0	0

NA = Not available.

Note: The data shown in this table do not reflect county totals but are the number of offenses reported by the sheriff's office or county police department.

[1] If a blank is presented in the arson column, it indicates that the FBI did not receive 12 complete months of arson data for that agency.

Table II-10. Offenses Known to Law Enforcement, by Selected State Metropolitan and Nonmetropolitan Counties, 2011—*Continued*

(Number.)

State/County	Violent crime	Murder and non-negligent man-slaughter	Forcible rape	Robbery	Aggravated assault	Property crime	Burglary	Larceny-theft	Motor vehicle theft	Arson[1]
Cass	6	0	1	0	5	49	9	40	0	0
Clay	6	1	1	0	4	59	20	35	4	2
Coles	13	0	2	1	10	91	29	58	4	0
Crawford	2	0	1	0	1	58	18	37	3	0
Cumberland	7	1	0	0	6	52	20	31	1	0
De Witt	20	0	6	3	11	84	23	59	2	0
Douglas	5	0	2	0	3	45	13	29	3	0
Edgar	21	0	2	0	19	74	40	31	3	2
Effingham	15	0	0	0	15	122	25	93	4	0
Fayette	4	0	0	1	3	107	24	77	6	0
Franklin	5	0	0	0	5	345	148	180	17	2
Fulton	10	0	0	0	10	170	43	121	6	0
Greene	1	0	0	0	1	46	19	25	2	1
Hamilton	3	0	0	0	3	83	31	50	2	0
Iroquois	10	0	4	0	6	223	92	126	5	0
Jackson	36	0	5	7	24	319	146	161	12	1
Jefferson	40	0	6	2	32	255	109	139	7	4
Jo Daviess	3	0	3	0	0	131	21	107	3	0
Johnson	28	0	0	0	28	112	30	76	6	1
Knox	13	0	4	0	9	212	58	143	11	0
La Salle	31	0	16	1	14	472	163	292	17	4
Lee	6	0	1	1	4	187	80	105	2	2
Livingston	16	4	3	0	9	164	30	130	4	68
Logan	20	0	5	1	14	195	89	101	5	1
Marion	17	1	6	2	8	266	82	165	19	1
Mason	23	2	5	0	16	118	29	86	3	1
Massac	13	0	4	0	9	111	36	73	2	0
McDonough	4	0	1	0	3	71	20	50	1	1
Montgomery	86	0	1	2	83	137	59	78	0	3
Morgan	13	0	6	0	7	92	47	44	1	3
Moultrie	4	0	0	0	4	42	17	25	0	0
Ogle	15	0	3	0	12	222	64	149	9	1
Perry	8	0	3	0	5	74	27	47	0	1
Pike	5	0	1	0	4	9	1	7	1	0
Pulaski	44	0	4	1	39	74	31	38	5	0
Putnam	2	0	0	0	2	45	15	29	1	0
Schuyler	3	0	0	0	3	3	0	3	0	0
Scott	2	0	1	0	1	29	13	15	1	0
Shelby	16	0	0	0	16	104	44	60	0	1
Stephenson	11	0	2	0	9	181	46	130	5	1
Union	7	0	1	0	6	96	15	74	7	0
Wabash	3	0	1	0	2	65	35	25	5	2
Warren	7	0	1	0	6	95	39	51	5	1
Washington	25	0	0	0	25	33	10	23	0	1
Wayne	25	0	0	0	25	141	57	78	6	0
White	14	0	1	0	13	187	55	125	7	0
Whiteside	15	0	0	2	13	234	78	152	4	0
Williamson	28	1	7	1	19	366	145	202	19	2
Indiana—Metropolitan Counties										
Allen	71	2	9	15	45	938	169	711	58	1
Bartholomew	40	0	6	4	30	587	114	414	59	0
Boone	0	0	0	0	0	171	39	132	0	2
Brown	2	0	0	0	2	128	43	73	12	1
Carroll	10	0	0	0	10	221	86	114	21	1
Clark	57	1	5	1	50	651	270	355	26	1
Dearborn	0	0	0	0	0	19	17	2	0	0
Delaware	53	1	8	6	38	525	149	336	40	2
Elkhart	37	1	16	13	7	1,479	532	828	119	9
Floyd	0	0	0	0	0	726	183	500	43	0
Franklin	6	0	0	0	6	189	110	79	0	2
Gibson	12	0	1	0	11	184	28	152	4	2
Greene	2	1	0	0	1	155	25	114	16	1
Hancock	9	0	3	1	5	324	112	201	11	3
Harrison[6]	9	0	0	4	5		157		33	1
Howard	43	0	1	3	39	492	233	246	13	0
Johnson	57	0	3	6	48	871	183	672	16	0
Lake	51	1	8	21	21	1,002	178	713	111	1
La Porte	23	0	6	7	10	811	271	493	47	1
Monroe	37	0	6	7	24	805	248	484	73	0
Newton	29	0	2	1	26	216	72	132	12	0
Porter	44	2	5	3	34	965	176	721	68	0

NA = Not available.

Note: The data shown in this table do not reflect county totals but are the number of offenses reported by the sheriff's office or county police department.

[1] If a blank is presented in the arson column, it indicates that the FBI did not receive 12 complete months of arson data for that agency.

[6] The FBI determined that the agency did not follow national Uniform Crime Reporting (UCR) Program guidelines for reporting an offense. Consequently, this figure is not included in this table.

Table II-10. Offenses Known to Law Enforcement, by Selected State Metropolitan and Nonmetropolitan Counties, 2011—*Continued*

(Number.)

State/County	Violent crime	Murder and non-negligent man-slaughter	Forcible rape	Robbery	Aggravated assault	Property crime	Burglary	Larceny-theft	Motor vehicle theft	Arson[1]
Putnam	16	0	0	3	13	201	89	90	22	0
Shelby	25	0	2	4	19	379	149	199	31	1
St. Joseph	131	3	10	22	96	1,823	529	1,230	64	3
Sullivan	10	0	1	3	6	194	70	114	10	5
Tippecanoe	38	0	9	5	24	907	266	593	48	8
Tipton	17	1	0	0	16	65	27	33	5	0
Vermillion	28	0	4	1	23	65	14	42	9	0
Vigo	34	2	6	7	19	1,279	385	801	93	5
Warrick	120	0	4	1	115	679	121	541	17	1
Wells	4	0	1	0	3	187	67	116	4	0
Indiana—Nonmetropolitan Counties										
Blackford	11	0	0	2	9	42	12	25	5	1
Cass	5	1	1	1	2	296	64	231	1	1
Clark	57	1	5	1	50	651	270	355	26	1
Clinton	21	0	2	8	11	428	118	286	24	0
Crawford	6	0	0	0	6	128	106	19	3	0
Daviess	2	1	0	0	1	133	33	76	24	3
Fulton	11	1	2	0	8	146	56	80	10	1
Grant	6	0	2	1	3	322	105	194	23	2
Henry	5	0	3	2	0	602	223	355	24	0
Huntington	4	0	0	0	4	144	38	96	10	0
Jackson	18	0	3	2	13	491	98	373	20	1
Jay	6	0	0	0	6	115	27	78	10	0
Jennings	42	0	4	0	38	477	235	234	8	0
Knox	0	0	0	0	0	0	0	0	0	0
Kosciusko	33	0	6	2	25	702	138	536	28	6
LaGrange	9	0	4	0	5	251	66	174	11	0
Lawrence	60	0	1	1	58	350	136	195	19	3
Marshall	21	1	3	0	17	377	117	237	23	1
Martin	2	0	0	1	1	72	20	43	9	0
Montgomery	36	0	6	0	30	450	153	266	31	0
Noble	14	0	1	0	13	233	94	122	17	1
Parke	15	1	2	4	8	85	33	50	2	5
Pike	32	0	2	2	28	293	90	194	9	1
Pulaski	18	0	2	0	16	231	57	148	26	3
Randolph	0	0	0	0	0	281	94	179	8	3
Ripley	2	0	0	0	2	298	83	201	14	0
Rush	2	0	1	1	0	247	77	162	8	3
Scott	14	0	1	0	13	346	50	289	7	0
Starke	22	0	3	1	18	206	61	132	13	1
Steuben	16	0	3	2	11	484	136	334	14	0
Wayne	1	1	0	0	0	87	33	53	1	1
White	6	0	1	1	4	62	16	41	5	0
Iowa—Metropolitan Counties										
Black Hawk	37	0	7	0	30	143	48	80	15	1
Bremer	6	0	2	0	4	42	10	30	2	3
Dallas	13	0	0	0	13	133	39	86	8	1
Dubuque	11	0	1	1	9	189	73	104	12	5
Guthrie	3	0	0	0	3	47	19	24	4	1
Harrison	5	0	3	0	2	105	24	70	11	1
Johnson	65	0	5	1	59	220	56	144	20	6
Jones	0	0	0	0	0	79	18	54	7	0
Linn	40	0	13	0	27	285	108	155	22	7
Madison	3	0	0	1	2	58	27	25	6	0
Mills	22	0	2	2	18	215	81	115	19	2
Polk	87	0	7	4	76	779	234	483	62	4
Pottawattamie	50	0	4	1	45	570	215	287	68	3
Scott	40	0	4	1	35	153	45	99	9	2
Story	9	0	3	0	6	143	54	78	11	3
Warren	22	0	3	0	19	275	109	144	22	4
Washington	25	1	4	0	20	130	69	57	4	0
Woodbury	34	0	4	1	29	129	46	71	12	2
Iowa—Nonmetropolitan Counties										
Adair	5	0	0	0	5	54	14	37	3	0
Appanoose	12	0	1	0	11	102	48	48	6	2
Boone	7	0	1	0	6	48	11	24	13	0
Buena Vista	6	0	1	0	5	89	25	55	9	0
Butler	1	1	0	0	0	25	9	8	8	0

NA = Not available.

Note: The data shown in this table do not reflect county totals but are the number of offenses reported by the sheriff's office or county police department.

[1] If a blank is presented in the arson column, it indicates that the FBI did not receive 12 complete months of arson data for that agency.

Table II-10.   Offenses Known to Law Enforcement, by Selected State Metropolitan and Nonmetropolitan Counties, 2011—*Continued*

(Number.)

State/County	Violent crime	Murder and non-negligent man-slaughter	Forcible rape	Robbery	Aggravated assault	Property crime	Burglary	Larceny-theft	Motor vehicle theft	Arson[1]
Calhoun	12	0	0	0	12	87	37	46	4	0
Cass	4	0	0	0	4	76	25	45	6	0
Cedar	10	0	2	1	7	85	1	82	2	1
Cerro Gordo	3	0	0	0	3	131	39	81	11	1
Clarke	3	0	0	0	3	49	16	29	4	0
Clay	6	0	1	0	5	53	37	12	4	0
Clinton	14	1	0	0	13	132	54	74	4	5
Crawford	4	0	0	0	4	8	0	7	1	0
Davis	7	0	0	0	7	19	15	3	1	0
Delaware	8	0	0	0	8	36	13	23	0	0
Des Moines	37	0	0	0	37	153	42	95	16	1
Dickinson	7	0	0	0	7	50	27	22	1	1
Emmet	17	0	0	0	17	32	9	23	0	0
Fayette	10	0	2	0	8	31	7	19	5	0
Floyd	1	0	1	0	0	22	10	12	0	0
Hancock	9	0	0	1	8	41	19	19	3	0
Hardin	7	1	0	0	6	116	47	62	7	1
Henry	12	0	0	0	12	122	54	61	7	0
Howard	5	0	1	3	1	55	14	38	3	1
Humboldt	1	0	0	0	1	37	13	20	4	0
Ida	2	0	1	0	1	37	13	22	2	0
Iowa	15	0	0	0	15	75	25	44	6	0
Jefferson	1	0	0	0	1	59	13	40	6	0
Kossuth	7	0	0	0	7	73	48	22	3	2
Lee	20	1	0	0	19	217	120	89	8	0
Louisa	10	0	1	0	9	68	27	35	6	2
Lucas	5	0	0	0	5	74	29	43	2	3
Lyon	17	0	6	0	11	66	24	39	3	2
Marion	24	1	7	1	15	119	59	50	10	3
Marshall	9	0	0	1	8	92	42	44	6	2
Mitchell	0	0	0	0	0	23	4	18	1	0
Monona	1	0	0	0	1	18	6	9	3	1
Monroe	4	1	1	0	2	27	2	19	6	0
Muscatine	24	0	6	0	18	116	57	48	11	4
O'Brien	10	0	0	0	10	46	19	21	6	0
Osceola	1	0	0	0	1	8	2	5	1	2
Page	5	1	0	0	4	36	9	24	3	0
Palo Alto	14	0	0	0	14	71	26	42	3	0
Plymouth	12	0	0	1	11	77	29	47	1	0
Pocahontas	8	0	2	0	6	76	24	50	2	0
Sioux	10	0	1	0	9	44	20	22	2	1
Story	9	0	3	0	6	143	54	78	11	3
Tama	22	0	1	0	21	83	44	35	4	1
Van Buren	14	0	1	0	13	58	27	26	5	0
Wapello	13	0	0	0	13	96	44	45	7	1
Wayne	4	0	0	0	4	26	10	16	0	0
Webster	16	0	1	0	15	211	71	128	12	3
Winnebago	2	0	0	0	2	14	5	8	1	0
Winneshiek	0	0	0	0	0	16	4	11	1	0
Worth	3	0	0	0	3	96	29	63	4	0
Wright	1	0	0	0	1	46	23	21	2	0
Kansas—Metropolitan Counties										
Butler	40	1	3	0	36	440	123	298	19	6
Doniphan	2	0	1	0	1	37	7	26	4	0
Douglas	25	0	2	0	23	179	64	104	11	1
Franklin	25	0	1	0	24	196	63	120	13	2
Geary	6	0	1	0	5	34	13	19	2	1
Harvey	18	1	0	0	17	86	39	45	2	1
Jackson	18	0	2	0	16	110	33	65	12	5
Jefferson	29	0	3	0	26	330	122	188	20	2
Johnson	38	0	7	0	31	278	73	187	18	7
Leavenworth	48	0	3	1	44	233	85	121	27	15
Linn	15	0	0	0	15	107	51	45	11	3
Miami	18	0	3	0	15	189	70	110	9	6
Osage	13	0	0	1	12	111	45	56	10	2
Pottawatomie	38	0	5	1	32	224	72	140	12	6
Riley County Police Department	173	5	28	20	120	1,467	372	1,062	33	9
Shawnee	65	0	1	4	60	1,281	359	871	51	13
Sumner	17	0	2	2	13	161	71	72	18	2
Wabaunsee	10	0	2	0	8	95	37	53	5	4
Wyandotte	12	0	1	0	11	37	4	27	6	1

NA = Not available.

Note: The data shown in this table do not reflect county totals but are the number of offenses reported by the sheriff's office or county police department.

[1] If a blank is presented in the arson column, it indicates that the FBI did not receive 12 complete months of arson data for that agency.

Table II-10.   Offenses Known to Law Enforcement, by Selected State Metropolitan and Nonmetropolitan Counties, 2011—*Continued*

(Number.)

State/County	Violent crime	Murder and non-negligent man-slaughter	Forcible rape	Robbery	Aggravated assault	Property crime	Burglary	Larceny-theft	Motor vehicle theft	Arson[1]
Kansas—Nonmetropolitan Counties										
Allen	10	0	1	0	9	85	27	55	3	5
Anderson	7	0	0	1	6	60	27	30	3	1
Atchison	15	1	3	1	10	12	8	4	0	1
Barber	3	0	1	0	2	30	6	21	3	0
Barton	9	1	1	0	7	157	61	92	4	3
Bourbon	20	2	1	0	17	129	50	62	17	8
Brown	14	0	4	0	10	44	14	25	5	0
Chase	1	0	0	0	1	14	8	4	2	0
Chautauqua	0	0	0	0	0	19	4	11	4	1
Cherokee	25	0	2	2	21	253	96	146	11	24
Cheyenne	4	0	1	0	3	33	15	16	2	0
Clark	3	0	0	0	3	16	2	14	0	0
Clay	1	0	1	0	0	42	11	24	7	0
Cloud	22	0	7	0	15	62	25	33	4	0
Coffey	4	0	1	0	3	37	10	24	3	0
Cowley	19	0	2	1	16	142	51	84	7	1
Crawford	26	0	3	0	23	229	74	138	17	6
Dickinson	13	0	1	0	12	123	43	71	9	2
Edwards	5	0	1	0	4	24	11	12	1	2
Elk	3	0	0	0	3	23	10	11	2	0
Ellis	8	0	2	0	6	59	23	34	2	0
Ellsworth	7	0	1	1	5	38	17	20	1	2
Finney	25	0	5	2	18	170	47	114	9	4
Ford	7	0	0	0	7	113	33	75	5	0
Graham	0	0	0	0	0	26	3	20	3	1
Grant	6	0	0	0	6	9	2	5	2	0
Gray	4	0	1	0	3	41	9	29	3	0
Greenwood	12	0	2	1	9	94	45	44	5	1
Harper	3	0	1	0	2	16	10	5	1	1
Hodgeman	7	0	0	0	7	44	14	21	9	0
Kingman	2	0	0	0	2	77	24	51	2	2
Kiowa	1	0	0	1	0	43	15	24	4	0
Labette	8	0	2	0	6	109	42	60	7	5
Lane	2	0	1	0	1	14	7	6	1	0
Lincoln	1	0	0	0	1	56	18	34	4	0
Logan	2	0	0	0	2	18	2	16	0	0
Lyon	9	0	0	0	9	102	18	84	0	2
Marion	9	0	0	0	9	5	1	3	1	1
Marshall	3	0	0	0	3	56	14	41	1	0
McPherson	11	0	3	2	6	106	59	39	8	0
Montgomery	30	0	4	1	25	175	65	102	8	6
Morris	9	0	0	0	9	58	23	32	3	0
Morton	4	0	0	0	4	21	4	16	1	1
Nemaha	2	0	0	0	2	30	7	20	3	1
Neosho	3	0	2	0	1	159	69	74	16	7
Ness	4	0	0	0	4	19	2	14	3	0
Pawnee	1	0	0	0	1	31	11	18	2	0
Phillips	2	0	0	0	2	19	11	8	0	0
Pratt	4	0	0	0	4	66	12	47	7	1
Republic	0	0	0	0	0	19	9	9	1	0
Rice	3	0	2	0	1	43	18	19	6	0
Rush	3	0	2	0	1	28	10	17	1	0
Russell	5	0	1	0	4	46	14	30	2	0
Saline	27	1	2	0	24	149	68	77	4	4
Seward	16	0	2	0	14	42	9	31	2	1
Sherman	1	0	0	0	1	17	6	9	2	0
Stafford	1	0	0	0	1	29	6	21	2	0
Washington	11	0	1	0	10	23	11	9	3	3
Wichita	3	0	0	0	3	36	9	24	3	0
Wilson	8	0	0	0	8	68	24	43	1	0
Woodson	8	0	1	0	7	79	32	44	3	0
Kentucky—Metropolitan Counties										
Boone	71	4	21	17	29	1,483	359	1,067	57	3
Bourbon	0	0	0	0	0	88	23	63	2	0
Boyd	25	0	1	10	14	179	43	122	14	0
Bracken	8	0	1	2	5	145	65	79	1	0
Bullitt	18	0	7	6	5	737	383	314	40	1
Campbell County Police Department	11	1	3	2	5	263	78	167	18	1
Christian	17	1	4	2	10	438	173	239	26	3

NA = Not available.

Note: The data shown in this table do not reflect county totals but are the number of offenses reported by the sheriff's office or county police department.

[1] If a blank is presented in the arson column, it indicates that the FBI did not receive 12 complete months of arson data for that agency.

Table II-10. Offenses Known to Law Enforcement, by Selected State Metropolitan and Nonmetropolitan Counties, 2011—*Continued*

(Number.)

State/County	Violent crime	Murder and non-negligent man-slaughter	Forcible rape	Robbery	Aggravated assault	Property crime	Burglary	Larceny-theft	Motor vehicle theft	Arson[1]
Clark	4	0	2	1	1	270	108	151	11	1
Daviess	21	0	10	5	6	628	159	451	18	3
Edmonson	5	0	0	0	5	55	25	24	6	3
Gallatin	2	0	0	0	2	100	45	48	7	0
Grant	3	0	0	2	1	159	49	98	12	1
Greenup	9	1	4	1	3	58	30	19	9	0
Hancock	0	0	0	0	0	19	9	8	2	1
Hardin	4	0	1	0	3	107	34	66	7	3
Henderson	10	0	4	2	4	172	72	90	10	2
Henry	1	0	0	1	0	25	14	11	0	0
Jessamine	16	0	1	7	8	378	179	185	14	0
Kenton	0	0	0	0	0	7	1	6	0	0
Kenton County Police Department	18	0	6	1	11	199	79	111	9	2
Larue	6	0	2	0	4	72	31	34	7	0
McLean	0	0	0	0	0	66	28	33	5	0
Meade	7	0	1	2	4	112	69	38	5	0
Nelson	14	0	4	2	8	303	154	139	10	0
Oldham	0	0	0	0	0	10	3	7	0	0
Oldham County Police Department	19	0	6	8	5	485	184	290	11	2
Pendleton	3	0	1	1	1	109	33	74	2	1
Scott	9	0	3	3	3	262	106	140	16	0
Shelby	17	0	4	4	9	465	131	311	23	0
Spencer	0	0	0	0	0	159	96	52	11	1
Trigg	7	0	1	0	6	149	56	85	8	0
Trimble	0	0	0	0	0	9	3	4	2	0
Warren	26	0	2	4	20	408	130	260	18	1
Webster	0	0	0	0	0	11	6	4	1	0
Woodford	0	0	0	0	0	20	5	13	2	0
Kentucky—Nonmetropolitan Counties										
Adair	2	0	0	0	2	23	7	12	4	0
Allen	3	0	2	0	1	107	53	41	13	1
Anderson	2	0	0	2	0	87	41	39	7	0
Ballard	4	0	0	0	4	149	47	96	6	2
Barren	3	0	0	1	2	111	57	43	11	0
Bell	15	0	2	3	10	165	55	99	11	2
Boyle	4	0	0	0	4	78	37	39	2	1
Breckinridge	3	1	0	0	2	13	9	4	0	0
Butler	6	0	1	0	5	43	22	18	3	0
Caldwell	4	0	1	0	3	61	37	23	1	0
Calloway	12	0	1	1	10	368	159	198	11	2
Carlisle	4	0	1	0	3	43	13	28	2	0
Carroll	1	0	0	0	1	59	18	34	7	2
Carter	5	0	1	0	4	41	20	19	2	0
Casey	1	0	0	0	1	41	22	13	6	1
Clay	5	0	1	2	2	126	42	74	10	2
Crittenden	0	0	0	0	0	41	12	24	5	1
Cumberland	2	0	0	0	2	14	10	4	0	0
Estill	7	0	0	2	5	114	69	44	1	0
Fleming	1	0	0	0	1	8	4	3	1	0
Floyd	3	0	0	0	3	92	18	62	12	1
Franklin	15	0	5	3	7	411	140	254	17	0
Fulton	2	0	0	0	2	32	13	17	2	0
Garrard	2	0	0	1	1	52	16	30	6	0
Graves	16	0	3	3	10	219	94	107	18	4
Grayson	4	0	1	0	3	102	45	48	9	0
Green	4	0	1	0	3	8	3	5	0	0
Harlan	7	0	0	0	7	87	36	43	8	0
Harrison	5	0	0	0	5	209	88	114	7	0
Hart	3	0	2	0	1	18	6	9	3	0
Hickman	0	0	0	0	0	8	5	0	3	0
Hopkins	17	1	5	3	8	332	128	167	37	1
Jackson	0	0	0	0	0	93	39	50	4	1
Johnson	7	0	1	1	5	135	45	76	14	3
Knott	0	0	0	0	0	2	0	2	0	0
Knox	14	0	2	5	7	321	196	103	22	0
Laurel	18	1	0	11	6	538	207	271	60	0
Lawrence	4	0	1	1	2	58	21	25	12	0
Letcher	2	0	0	1	1	49	22	19	8	0
Lewis	8	1	1	2	4	32	16	12	4	0
Lincoln	7	0	0	4	3	89	36	37	16	0
Livingston	5	0	2	0	3	75	30	37	8	0

NA = Not available.

Note: The data shown in this table do not reflect county totals but are the number of offenses reported by the sheriff's office or county police department.

[1] If a blank is presented in the arson column, it indicates that the FBI did not receive 12 complete months of arson data for that agency.

Table II-10. Offenses Known to Law Enforcement, by Selected State Metropolitan and Nonmetropolitan Counties, 2011—*Continued*

(Number.)

State/County	Violent crime	Murder and non-negligent man-slaughter	Forcible rape	Robbery	Aggravated assault	Property crime	Burglary	Larceny-theft	Motor vehicle theft	Arson[1]
Logan	3	0	1	0	2	195	82	102	11	1
Lyon	0	0	0	0	0	94	45	48	1	0
Madison	8	1	3	0	4	483	174	294	15	0
Magoffin	1	0	0	0	1	24	10	12	2	0
Marion	2	0	1	0	1	90	37	45	8	0
Marshall	20	1	4	5	10	300	136	147	17	0
Martin	6	0	1	1	4	70	28	32	10	0
Mason	4	0	0	2	2	193	90	100	3	0
McCracken	46	0	8	15	23	578	178	356	44	1
McCreary	6	0	0	4	2	142	76	60	6	1
Menifee	0	0	0	0	0	50	28	20	2	2
Mercer	5	1	1	0	3	89	48	35	6	0
Metcalfe	1	0	0	0	1	58	20	36	2	0
Montgomery	22	2	2	10	8	574	268	287	19	1
Muhlenberg	7	0	1	3	3	63	30	20	13	0
Ohio	17	0	1	0	16	172	62	81	29	3
Owen	1	0	0	1	0	57	33	19	5	0
Perry	6	0	0	1	5	12	7	2	3	0
Pike	0	0	0	0	0	24	13	9	2	0
Powell	2	0	1	1	0	93	46	45	2	0
Pulaski	12	0	2	5	5	797	447	331	19	4
Rockcastle	3	1	0	1	1	90	57	18	15	0
Rowan	4	0	1	1	2	44	13	28	3	0
Russell	2	0	0	0	2	43	25	13	5	0
Simpson	4	0	1	0	3	142	50	78	14	0
Taylor	15	1	6	0	8	236	127	102	7	2
Todd	3	0	0	1	2	101	43	52	6	0
Union	4	0	1	1	2	48	15	26	7	0
Washington	1	0	0	0	1	38	18	19	1	0
Wayne	0	0	0	0	0	30	14	14	2	3
Whitley	8	0	0	1	7	200	118	64	18	0
Wolfe	0	0	0	0	0	26	10	14	2	0
Louisiana—Metropolitan Counties										
Ascension	373	8	33	41	291	2,837	800	1,887	150	0
Bossier	66	0	0	6	60	487	71	386	30	1
Caddo	113	0	4	8	101	841	211	578	52	3
Calcasieu	375	5	66	41	263	3,893	1,314	2,392	187	24
Cameron	15	0	0	0	15	152	28	117	7	2
East Baton Rouge	536	14	6	193	323	8,008	1,710	6,157	141	25
East Feliciana	1	0	1	0	0	67	25	38	4	0
Grant	10	0	1	0	9	288	77	196	15	0
Iberville	276	0	5	20	251	580	151	408	21	
Jefferson	1,809	49	67	464	1,229	13,028	2,950	9,193	885	94
Lafayette	336	4	19	41	272	1,504	418	1,021	65	21
Lafourche	77	1	0	18	58	1,975	755	1,140	80	2
Livingston	270	2	22	24	222	2,677	796	1,784	97	1
Ouachita	134	2	8	23	101	2,727	950	1,689	88	4
Plaquemines	41	0	1	1	39	387	100	278	9	8
Pointe Coupee	122	1	3	8	110	432	106	305	21	0
Rapides	300	3	32	14	251	2,007	613	1,205	189	9
St. Bernard	75	0	10	14	51	977	220	703	54	
St. Charles	193	3	4	30	156	1,595	449	1,062	84	21
St. Helena	58	0	1	3	54	285	119	136	30	0
St. John the Baptist	113	6	3	42	62	1,266	329	867	70	
St. Martin	125	1	7	10	107	783	139	637	7	
St. Tammany	270	5	18	20	227	2,527	592	1,791	144	9
Terrebonne	295	3	27	45	220	2,783	575	2,043	165	15
West Baton Rouge	50	0	2	8	40	536	65	441	30	0
West Feliciana	26	0	2	0	24	162	32	120	10	1
Louisiana—Nonmetropolitan Counties										
Acadia	102	0	5	4	93	683	182	438	63	0
Allen	22	0	4	1	17	214	60	151	3	4
Assumption	86	0	0	6	80	419	114	286	19	0
Avoyelles	84	3	20	5	56	463	136	307	20	2
Bienville	42	0	2	3	37	207	53	146	8	1
Caldwell	22	0	0	1	21	263	78	174	11	NA
Concordia	66	1	4	2	59	215	61	144	10	NA
East Carroll	25	0	2	1	22	57	19	35	3	0
Evangeline	50	0	3	6	41	517	103	402	12	0
Iberia	390	2	18	89	281	2,126	928	1,131	67	14
La Salle	34	0	0	0	34	138	37	96	5	0

NA = Not available.

Note: The data shown in this table do not reflect county totals but are the number of offenses reported by the sheriff's office or county police department.

[1] If a blank is presented in the arson column, it indicates that the FBI did not receive 12 complete months of arson data for that agency.

Table II-10. Offenses Known to Law Enforcement, by Selected State Metropolitan and Nonmetropolitan Counties, 2011—*Continued*

(Number.)

State/County	Violent crime	Murder and non-negligent man-slaughter	Forcible rape	Robbery	Aggravated assault	Property crime	Burglary	Larceny-theft	Motor vehicle theft	Arson[1]
Madison	25	0	0	1	24	129	20	99	10	0
Morehouse	29	0	0	6	23	253	42	210	1	0
Natchitoches	118	1	3	4	110	596	185	376	35	0
St. James	110	0	4	1	105	444	91	323	30	1
St. Mary	165	2	15	14	134	963	226	697	40	NA
Tangipahoa	797	13	48	46	690	4,222	1,635	2,387	200	0
Tensas	8	1	0	1	6	34	17	16	1	2
Vermilion	77	0	10	8	59	722	216	479	27	0
Vernon	116	3	10	2	101	715	27	640	48	
Washington	139	2	13	15	109	954	330	587	37	0
West Carroll	109	0	0	2	107	381	71	279	31	1
Winn	24	1	1	1	21	177	34	139	4	0
Maine—Metropolitan Counties										
Androscoggin	20	0	9	3	8	240	97	139	4	1
Cumberland	28	0	4	3	21	906	392	468	46	5
Penobscot	8	0	2	5	1	743	265	432	46	0
Sagadahoc	2	0	0	0	2	207	81	110	16	0
York	38	0	5	0	33	471	190	246	35	1
Maine—Nonmetropolitan Counties										
Aroostook	0	0	0	0	0	81	18	60	3	0
Franklin	2	0	0	0	2	96	36	54	6	0
Hancock	1	0	0	0	1	189	30	157	2	0
Kennebec	10	0	4	2	4	460	174	256	30	2
Knox	9	0	1	3	5	194	54	124	16	0
Lincoln	26	0	21	0	5	291	100	178	13	1
Oxford	23	0	8	0	15	313	90	196	27	1
Piscataquis	6	0	3	0	3	149	78	71	0	0
Somerset	11	0	5	1	5	419	159	238	22	2
Waldo	6	0	0	1	5	247	94	144	9	0
Washington	25	0	3	0	22	187	62	116	9	0
Maryland—Metropolitan Counties										
Allegany[2]	27	0	2	4	21	200	48	151	1	0
Anne Arundel	1	0	0	0	1	0	0	0	0	0
Anne Arundel County Police Department	2,485	13	83	526	1,863	13,399	2,073	10,569	757	59
Baltimore County	0	0	0	0	0	0	0	0	0	0
Baltimore County Police Department	4,250	30	142	1,451	2,627	23,800	4,269	17,840	1,691	235
Calvert	121	0	8	30	83	1,746	445	1,246	55	0
Carroll	73	0	26	7	40	619	160	439	20	0
Cecil	137	2	8	38	89	981	348	574	59	0
Charles	539	3	26	170	340	3,428	732	2,431	265	0
Frederick	218	1	9	18	190	1,573	318	1,181	74	20
Harford	399	4	29	86	280	2,271	556	1,577	138	3
Howard	0	0	0	0	0	1	1	0	0	0
Howard County Police Department	597	4	31	211	351	6,556	1,108	5,082	366	57
Montgomery	0	0	0	0	0	0	0	0	0	0
Montgomery County Police Department	1,618	15	112	840	651	17,752	3,061	13,505	1,186	200
Prince George's	54	0	0	0	54	0	0	0	0	0
Prince George's County Police Department	4,075	80	152	2,048	1,795	25,456	5,499	14,977	4,980	214
Somerset	4	0	0	0	4	52	15	37	0	0
Washington	182	1	7	18	156	1,406	415	930	61	0
Wicomico	97	0	1	13	83	863	300	536	27	9
Maryland—Nonmetropolitan Counties										
Caroline	17	1	0	6	10	453	183	255	15	0
Dorchester	29	1	1	3	24	319	85	221	13	1
Garrett	43	2	2	0	39	314	104	200	10	0
Kent	15	0	0	1	14	153	73	71	9	1
St. Mary's	228	0	17	55	156	2,403	649	1,636	118	3
Talbot	12	0	2	1	9	208	68	131	9	0
Worcester	64	1	2	3	58	256	68	185	3	1
Michigan—Metropolitan Counties										
Barry	40	1	13	1	25	397	128	249	20	6
Bay	46	0	13	5	28	680	165	496	19	0
Berrien	116	0	19	13	84	668	192	449	27	6
Calhoun	73	0	3	7	63	567	195	344	28	6
Cass	27	1	11	1	14	503	153	337	13	4
Clinton	17	3	3	4	7	208	90	104	14	0

NA = Not available.

Note: The data shown in this table do not reflect county totals but are the number of offenses reported by the sheriff's office or county police department.

[1] If a blank is presented in the arson column, it indicates that the FBI did not receive 12 complete months of arson data for that agency.

[2] Because of changes in the state/local agency's reporting practices, figures are not comparable to previous years' data.

Table II-10.   Offenses Known to Law Enforcement, by Selected State Metropolitan and Nonmetropolitan Counties, 2011—*Continued*

(Number.)

State/County	Violent crime	Murder and non-negligent man-slaughter	Forcible rape	Robbery	Aggravated assault	Property crime	Burglary	Larceny-theft	Motor vehicle theft	Arson[1]
Eaton	84	3	21	19	41	1,310	305	945	60	4
Genesee	30	0	12	6	12	562	152	399	11	0
Ingham	94	1	14	11	68	713	229	451	33	4
Ionia	31	1	11	1	18	325	122	187	16	3
Jackson	134	2	9	4	119	625	190	403	32	4
Kalamazoo	128	1	26	13	88	1,589	401	1,120	68	11
Lapeer	46	1	6	0	39	466	140	310	16	0
Livingston	43	0	9	7	27	703	156	520	27	3
Macomb	305	1	33	48	223	2,325	522	1,672	131	16
Monroe	188	2	40	30	116	2,303	706	1,470	127	31
Muskegon	34	0	7	2	25	768	122	628	18	3
Oakland[2]	673	10	64	127	472	4,622	1,382	3,005	235	81
Ottawa	263	2	86	16	159	3,332	697	2,542	93	24
Saginaw	78	1	9	9	59	563	182	349	32	4
St. Clair	137	1	17	16	103	1,647	497	1,056	94	22
Van Buren	106	2	30	5	69	603	209	361	33	6
Washtenaw	430	5	83	73	269	2,147	812	1,154	181	18
Wayne	10	0	0	0	10	16	1	14	1	0
Michigan—Nonmetropolitan Counties										
Alcona	9	0	1	0	8	176	55	119	2	1
Allegany	108	1	28	3	76	850	239	560	51	9
Alpena	4	0	2	0	2	71	10	61	0	0
Antrim	18	0	4	3	11	301	91	205	5	0
Arenac	19	0	5	1	13	104	55	42	7	2
Baraga	0	0	0	0	0	25	7	17	1	0
Branch	6	0	1	1	4	174	23	147	4	1
Charlevoix	25	1	12	0	12	147	38	108	1	1
Cheboygan	8	1	2	0	5	100	33	65	2	2
Chippewa	5	0	1	0	4	120	45	68	7	0
Clare	33	1	9	3	20	367	202	162	3	1
Crawford	27	1	4	0	22	200	84	109	7	1
Delta	3	0	0	0	3	63	12	45	6	0
Emmet	10	0	2	1	7	230	42	184	4	0
Gladwin	18	0	2	0	16	135	53	79	3	3
Grand Traverse	92	0	26	3	63	739	128	594	17	4
Gratiot	9	0	3	1	5	182	46	127	9	0
Hillsdale	25	0	2	1	22	196	60	130	6	1
Houghton	5	0	1	1	3	101	24	75	2	0
Huron	13	1	3	0	9	141	54	85	2	0
Iosco	1	0	0	0	1	13	9	3	1	0
Iron	4	1	2	0	1	42	16	25	1	1
Isabella	31	2	11	2	16	398	129	251	18	0
Kalkaska	9	0	5	1	3	261	75	169	17	1
Lake	23	1	5	2	15	269	147	114	8	0
Lenawee	52	0	22	1	29	369	120	230	19	2
Luce	6	0	3	0	3	90	34	54	2	0
Mackinac	3	0	0	0	3	61	16	43	2	0
Marquette	5	0	2	0	3	184	16	165	3	1
Mecosta	192	0	15	2	175	481	114	351	16	1
Montcalm	57	0	12	1	44	530	171	322	37	2
Montmorency	2	0	1	0	1	54	37	14	3	0
Oceana	21	0	7	1	13	287	94	181	12	0
Ogemaw	19	0	1	2	16	288	131	151	6	0
Ontonagon	3	0	1	0	2	23	11	11	1	0
Osceola	25	0	3	0	22	267	83	177	7	2
Oscoda	21	0	2	2	17	256	96	153	7	1
Otsego	3	0	1	0	2	33	10	22	1	0
Presque Isle	7	0	2	0	5	41	18	22	1	0
Roscommon	14	0	6	2	6	155	40	104	11	2
Sanilac	29	0	4	0	25	175	84	83	8	2
Shiawassee	46	0	17	4	25	500	197	289	14	0
St. Joseph	25	0	5	0	20	306	105	188	13	2
Tuscola	39	1	6	0	32	332	121	200	11	3
Wexford	26	0	9	1	16	396	78	310	8	2
Minnesota—Metropolitan Counties[7]										
Anoka	NA	1	NA	2	47	1,675	302	1,297	76	5
Benton	NA	0	NA	0	12	265	51	194	20	3
Blue Earth	NA	0	NA	0	7	177	59	102	16	1
Carlton	NA	2	NA	1	5	323	111	196	16	2

NA = Not available.

Note: The data shown in this table do not reflect county totals but are the number of offenses reported by the sheriff's office or county police department.

[1] If a blank is presented in the arson column, it indicates that the FBI did not receive 12 complete months of arson data for that agency.

[2] Because of changes in the state/local agency's reporting practices, figures are not comparable to previous years' data.

[7] The data collection methodology for the offense of forcible rape used by the Minnesota state UCR Program does not comply with national UCR Program guidelines. Consequently, its figures for forcible rape and violent crime (of which forcible rape is a part) are not published in this table.

Table II-10. Offenses Known to Law Enforcement, by Selected State Metropolitan and Nonmetropolitan Counties, 2011—*Continued*

(Number.)

State/County	Violent crime	Murder and non-negligent man-slaughter	Forcible rape	Robbery	Aggravated assault	Property crime	Burglary	Larceny-theft	Motor vehicle theft	Arson[1]
Carver	NA	0	NA	3	25	736	130	592	14	5
Chisago	NA	0	NA	2	10	442	76	345	21	1
Clay	NA	0	NA	0	3	72	18	51	3	4
Dakota	NA	0	NA	1	38	146	45	95	6	3
Dodge	NA	0	NA	0	33	252	43	202	7	0
Hennepin	NA	0	NA	2	14	141	23	114	4	1
Houston	NA	0	NA	0	4	64	23	38	3	0
Isanti	NA	0	NA	0	10	400	116	249	35	7
Nicollet	NA	0	NA	0	5	110	49	55	6	2
Olmsted	NA	0	NA	2	17	448	151	261	36	1
Polk	NA	0	NA	1	15	157	53	99	5	3
Ramsey	NA	0	NA	1	8	146	19	119	8	1
Scott	NA	0	NA	0	4	119	40	76	3	0
Sherburne	NA	0	NA	1	11	516	125	361	30	1
Stearns	NA	0	NA	1	30	439	118	296	25	0
St. Louis	NA	0	NA	2	33	708	273	382	53	5
Wabasha	NA	0	NA	0	1	26	3	19	4	0
Washington	NA	0	NA	3	18	957	179	734	44	2
Wright	NA	0	NA	9	48	1,716	167	1,490	59	12
Minnesota—Nonmetropolitan Counties[7]										
Aitkin	NA	0	NA	0	16	409	141	237	31	4
Becker	NA	0	NA	1	10	117	38	65	14	3
Beltrami	NA	0	NA	1	36	430	138	271	21	3
Big Stone	NA	0	NA	0	5	44	19	25	0	0
Brown	NA	0	NA	0	2	0	0	0	0	0
Cass	NA	2	NA	0	18	849	232	556	61	0
Chippewa	NA	0	NA	0	8	42	5	36	1	0
Clearwater	NA	0	NA	1	10	192	62	123	7	1
Cook	NA	0	NA	0	5	162	25	135	2	0
Cottonwood	NA	0	NA	0	1	40	11	26	3	1
Crow Wing	NA	1	NA	1	14	448	119	305	24	1
Douglas	NA	0	NA	1	20	216	71	131	14	0
Faribault	NA	0	NA	0	3	53	22	26	5	1
Freeborn	NA	0	NA	0	4	123	32	77	14	0
Goodhue	NA	0	NA	0	7	203	58	119	26	0
Grant	NA	0	NA	0	0	94	23	71	0	1
Hubbard	NA	0	NA	0	6	249	93	146	10	0
Itasca	NA	0	NA	1	26	457	100	340	17	1
Jackson	NA	0	NA	2	3	53	2	47	4	0
Kanabec	NA	0	NA	1	30	441	149	262	30	0
Kandiyohi	NA	1	NA	0	12	207	32	153	22	1
Kittson	NA	0	NA	0	0	38	8	28	2	0
Lac Qui Parle	NA	0	NA	0	2	41	7	33	1	0
Lake	NA	0	NA	0	3	28	10	16	2	0
Lake of the Woods	NA	0	NA	0	3	5	0	5	0	0
Le Sueur	NA	0	NA	0	1	116	39	69	8	1
Lincoln	NA	0	NA	0	10	10	4	6	0	0
Lyon	NA	0	NA	0	4	20	7	12	1	0
Mahnomen	NA	0	NA	0	19	122	31	88	3	0
Marshall	NA	0	NA	0	2	109	9	95	5	1
Martin	NA	1	NA	0	1	25	9	15	1	0
McLeod	NA	0	NA	0	3	94	36	51	7	1
Meeker	NA	0	NA	0	6	243	74	157	12	2
Mille Lacs	NA	0	NA	0	17	454	108	301	45	0
Mower	NA	0	NA	1	9	169	54	93	22	0
Murray	NA	0	NA	0	0	47	18	27	2	0
Nobles	NA	0	NA	1	5	48	18	26	4	0
Otter Tail	NA	2	NA	4	17	401	147	240	14	0
Pennington	NA	0	NA	0	3	53	12	37	4	1
Pine	NA	0	NA	2	28	617	157	406	54	7
Pipestone	NA	0	NA	2	4	65	13	48	4	1
Pope	NA	0	NA	0	3	57	10	37	10	0
Red Lake	NA	0	NA	0	3	22	11	11	0	0
Redwood	NA	0	NA	1	4	60	14	42	4	0
Renville	NA	0	NA	0	1	67	15	35	17	0
Rice	NA	0	NA	0	7	153	43	84	26	0
Rock[3]	NA	0	NA	1		43	7	36	0	0
Roseau	NA	0	NA	0	1	29	6	22	1	0
Sibley	NA	0	NA	0	0	5	5	0	0	0
Steele	NA	0	NA	1	3	115	36	71	8	8

NA = Not available.

Note: The data shown in this table do not reflect county totals but are the number of offenses reported by the sheriff's office or county police department.

[1] If a blank is presented in the arson column, it indicates that the FBI did not receive 12 complete months of arson data for that agency.

[3] The FBI determined that the agency's data were overreported. Consequently, affected data are not included in this table.

[7] The data collection methodology for the offense of forcible rape used by the Minnesota state UCR Program does not comply with national UCR Program guidelines. Consequently, its figures for forcible rape and violent crime (of which forcible rape is a part) are not published in this table.

Table II-10.   Offenses Known to Law Enforcement, by Selected State Metropolitan and Nonmetropolitan Counties, 2011—*Continued*

(Number.)

State/County	Violent crime	Murder and non-negligent man-slaughter	Forcible rape	Robbery	Aggravated assault	Property crime	Burglary	Larceny-theft	Motor vehicle theft	Arson[1]
Stevens	NA	0	NA	0	0	25	9	14	2	0
Swift	NA	0	NA	0	1	36	13	23	0	0
Todd	NA	1	NA	0	8	263	107	148	8	4
Traverse	NA	0	NA	0	3	28	4	20	4	0
Wadena	NA	0	NA	0	3	95	42	45	8	3
Waseca	NA	0	NA	0	1	91	40	49	2	0
Watonwan	NA	0	NA	0	3	38	14	21	3	0
Wilkin	NA	0	NA	0	1	46	11	35	0	0
Winona	NA	0	NA	0	3	104	26	67	11	0
Yellow Medicine	NA	0	NA	0	6	38	9	28	1	0
Mississippi—Metropolitan Counties										
Forrest	24	1	3	3	17	477	173	296	8	1
Harrison	34	0	6	12	16	1,164	371	686	107	2
Hinds	30	2	6	4	18	448	165	206	77	0
Jackson	140	3	30	15	92	1,693	551	1,019	123	28
Lamar	30	4	8	14	4	671	382	277	12	1
Madison	31	1	3	5	22	527	134	344	49	0
Rankin	40	3	4	6	27	618	148	420	50	1
Simpson	39	0	5	3	31	351	121	194	36	3
Tunica	30	0	2	15	13	541	86	409	46	0
Mississippi—Nonmetropolitan Counties										
Adams	67	2	6	8	51	621	297	318	6	1
Chickasaw	16	1	1	4	10	41	18	20	3	0
Choctaw	11	0	0	0	11	90	31	52	7	0
Claiborne	33	1	0	3	29	84	47	36	1	0
Franklin	11	1	1	4	5	54	30	18	6	0
Grenada	18	0	0	7	11	100	49	46	5	0
Itawamba	26	2	4	0	20	271	85	170	16	4
Jefferson	18	1	3	0	14	43	11	26	6	1
Jones	79	2	25	4	48	1,000	373	627	0	0
Kemper	2	0	0	0	2	49	27	18	4	5
Lauderdale	35	0	8	4	23	650	342	271	37	2
Lee	47	0	5	5	37	800	297	462	41	12
Leflore	70	1	6	7	56	430	174	236	20	2
Lincoln	32	0	2	0	30	325	105	199	21	9
Lowndes	53	3	5	12	33	608	309	277	22	0
Marion	32	0	9	9	14	561	242	291	28	5
Oktibbeha	42	0	2	5	35	227	105	113	9	6
Panola	70	2	1	9	58	560	282	262	16	1
Pike	36	1	1	5	29	368	236	131	1	
Pontotoc	22	0	1	12	9	72	26	44	2	3
Scott	47	2	2	3	40	376	126	219	31	6
Tippah	5	0	1	0	4	10	4	6	0	0
Union	4	0	0	0	4	234	84	136	14	3
Warren	16	4	5	1	6	408	129	261	18	0
Washington	41	2	2	8	29	556	123	367	66	0
Winston	1	0	0	0	1	20	4	15	1	0
Missouri—Metropolitan Counties										
Andrew	2	0	0	0	2	74	28	45	1	0
Bates	31	2	2	0	27	201	83	110	8	3
Bollinger	14	0	2	0	12	105	44	52	9	2
Boone	90	1	2	13	74	736	179	508	49	9
Buchanan	22	0	3	1	18	209	62	139	8	1
Caldwell	17	0	1	1	15	54	32	22	0	0
Callaway	60	3	6	1	50	784	205	538	41	6
Cape Girardeau	13	0	1	2	10	276	116	153	7	0
Cass	48	0	2	4	42	465	125	313	27	0
Christian	66	0	0	2	64	401	174	181	46	6
Clay	25	3	2	2	18	210	93	92	25	3
Clinton	49	0	0	2	47	88	18	62	8	1
Cole	48	1	2	3	42	422	105	289	28	1
Dallas	30	0	3	0	27	209	63	140	6	0
De Kalb	8	0	1	0	7	63	21	37	5	0
Franklin	89	1	4	1	83	468	122	294	52	2
Greene	96	3	9	10	74	1,716	573	1,037	106	49
Howard	10	1	1	0	8	39	19	19	1	0
Jackson	42	0	5	6	31	556	190	315	51	1
Jasper	152	0	7	2	143	491	154	282	55	9

NA = Not available.

Note: The data shown in this table do not reflect county totals but are the number of offenses reported by the sheriff's office or county police department.

[1] If a blank is presented in the arson column, it indicates that the FBI did not receive 12 complete months of arson data for that agency.

Table II-10. Offenses Known to Law Enforcement, by Selected State Metropolitan and Nonmetropolitan Counties, 2011—*Continued*

(Number.)

State/County	Violent crime	Murder and non-negligent man-slaughter	Forcible rape	Robbery	Aggravated assault	Property crime	Burglary	Larceny-theft	Motor vehicle theft	Arson[1]
Jefferson	384	2	30	19	333	2,492	404	1,898	190	18
Lafayette	10	0	0	0	10	144	49	85	10	0
Lincoln	89	2	0	0	87	252	82	149	21	0
McDonald	93	2	1	6	84	314	87	206	21	3
Moniteau	5	1	0	0	4	42	9	31	2	0
Newton	40	1	12	3	24	771	202	495	74	4
Osage	39	0	0	0	39	93	42	44	7	0
Platte	53	1	1	2	49	328	95	224	9	7
Polk	88	0	0	2	86	336	127	192	17	0
Ray	19	0	2	0	17	185	73	98	14	0
St. Charles	141	0	8	10	123	1,031	272	720	39	13
St. Louis County Police Department	1,043	17	63	284	679	9,329	2,318	6,387	624	56
Warren	67	1	5	2	59	240	82	145	13	3
Washington	35	0	6	2	27	360	105	217	38	2
Webster	12	0	0	1	11	315	144	135	36	3
Missouri—Nonmetropolitan Counties										
Adair	17	0	2	0	15	159	47	107	5	0
Atchison	0	0	0	0	0	11	3	7	1	0
Audrain	5	0	0	1	4	151	60	81	10	0
Barry	79	0	12	3	64	434	169	239	26	6
Benton	28	0	0	0	28	241	111	109	21	1
Butler	77	0	5	6	66	660	232	395	33	2
Camden	39	0	0	0	39	452	145	284	23	0
Carroll	4	0	0	1	3	41	11	28	2	0
Carter	5	0	0	0	5	62	29	28	5	0
Cedar	12	0	3	0	9	143	48	88	7	0
Chariton	21	0	0	0	21	53	23	28	2	0
Clark	6	0	0	0	6	28	18	5	5	0
Cooper	5	0	2	0	3	132	31	90	11	0
Crawford	32	0	3	0	29	185	73	102	10	0
Dade	4	0	0	0	4	47	37	0	10	0
Daviess	5	0	1	0	4	67	25	33	9	2
Dent	17	4	2	1	10	83	41	32	10	1
Douglas	30	1	1	0	28	94	39	47	8	2
Dunklin	24	0	0	3	21	232	58	159	15	5
Gasconade	19	0	0	1	18	126	48	70	8	2
Gentry	0	0	0	0	0	23	8	15	0	0
Grundy	5	0	1	0	4	57	26	27	4	0
Harrison	8	1	0	2	5	55	9	40	6	3
Henry	43	1	2	0	40	354	115	220	19	7
Hickory	2	0	0	1	1	123	46	59	18	0
Holt	5	0	0	0	5	74	35	32	7	0
Howell	28	1	0	1	26	370	141	203	26	2
Iron	31	0	3	2	26	60	24	29	7	1
Johnson	26	1	1	1	23	416	155	224	37	0
Knox	2	0	0	0	2	46	18	26	2	0
Laclede	138	0	0	0	138	329	81	216	32	2
Lawrence	56	0	4	3	49	415	176	212	27	5
Lewis	0	0	0	0	0	69	24	41	4	0
Linn	16	0	1	0	15	54	29	24	1	2
Livingston	3	0	0	0	3	32	10	17	5	1
Macon	19	0	0	0	19	112	44	64	4	0
Madison	11	0	0	0	11	57	23	29	5	0
Maries	31	0	3	0	28	56	16	36	4	1
Marion	10	0	2	0	8	118	19	96	3	0
Mercer	9	3	0	0	6	14	4	10	0	0
Miller	66	0	8	0	58	229	87	131	11	0
Mississippi	16	0	0	0	16	59	20	37	2	0
Monroe	5	0	0	0	5	51	18	26	7	1
Montgomery	3	1	0	0	2	78	26	48	4	0
Morgan	45	0	3	0	42	274	111	136	27	0
New Madrid	20	0	0	0	20	60	16	38	6	2
Nodaway	36	0	2	1	33	116	35	71	10	0
Oregon	9	0	0	0	9	56	27	25	4	0
Ozark	12	0	0	0	12	141	54	81	6	4
Pemiscot	29	1	3	2	23	120	42	69	9	0
Perry	6	0	0	0	6	63	14	39	10	0
Pettis	9	0	2	0	7	388	130	234	24	0
Phelps	41	1	4	1	35	387	120	234	33	2
Pike	23	0	2	0	21	74	33	35	6	1
Pulaski	91	4	5	4	78	368	186	154	28	3

NA = Not available.

Note: The data shown in this table do not reflect county totals but are the number of offenses reported by the sheriff's office or county police department.

[1] If a blank is presented in the arson column, it indicates that the FBI did not receive 12 complete months of arson data for that agency.

Table II-10.   Offenses Known to Law Enforcement, by Selected State Metropolitan and Nonmetropolitan Counties, 2011—Continued

(Number.)

State/County	Violent crime	Murder and non-negligent man-slaughter	Forcible rape	Robbery	Aggravated assault	Property crime	Burglary	Larceny-theft	Motor vehicle theft	Arson[1]
Putnam	0	0	0	0	0	15	11	1	3	0
Ralls	5	0	0	0	5	152	32	117	3	1
Randolph	6	0	2	0	4	142	37	105	0	1
Reynolds	28	1	0	1	26	78	27	46	5	2
Ripley	29	0	0	0	29	298	94	194	10	0
Saline	23	0	2	2	19	91	44	45	2	0
Schuyler	1	0	0	0	1	42	13	22	7	1
Scott	24	0	0	1	23	96	32	55	9	0
Shannon	3	0	0	0	3	54	15	32	7	1
Shelby	2	0	1	0	1	40	5	33	2	0
St. Clair	6	1	1	1	3	168	48	120	0	0
Ste. Genevieve	59	0	2	0	57	114	23	76	15	5
St. Francois	81	0	6	2	73	460	130	276	54	2
Stoddard	25	0	2	1	22	236	66	158	12	2
Stone	80	2	5	0	73	483	149	310	24	2
Sullivan	10	0	0	0	10	61	31	27	3	0
Taney	117	0	9	4	104	559	164	351	44	0
Texas	6	0	2	0	4	204	87	102	15	4
Vernon	33	1	2	0	30	220	69	132	19	1
Wayne	10	0	1	0	9	84	32	48	4	1
Worth	2	0	0	0	2	37	15	19	3	0
Wright	16	0	5	0	11	85	40	40	5	0
Montana—Metropolitan Counties[2]										
Carbon	15	0	0	0	15	43	11	30	2	0
Cascade	28	0	3	0	25	248	41	201	6	4
Missoula	84	1	12	6	65	404	87	288	29	3
Yellowstone	78	0	4	4	70	610	146	402	62	3
Montana—Nonmetropolitan Counties[2]										
Beaverhead	7	0	0	0	7	63	15	44	4	1
Big Horn	22	3	2	0	17	134	8	118	8	0
Blaine	13	0	0	0	13	15	1	12	2	0
Broadwater	17	0	2	0	15	56	8	42	6	0
Carter	0	0	0	0	0	1	0	1	0	0
Chouteau	6	0	0	0	6	20	3	16	1	0
Custer	1	0	0	0	1	39	6	30	3	0
Daniels	3	0	0	0	3	0	0	0	0	0
Dawson	9	0	2	0	7	66	9	54	3	1
Deer Lodge	25	0	4	1	20	152	15	130	7	2
Fallon	0	0	0	0	0	12	2	9	1	0
Fergus	8	0	5	0	3	52	9	41	2	0
Gallatin	44	0	17	2	25	335	39	273	23	1
Garfield	0	0	0	0	0	0	0	0	0	0
Glacier	20	1	0	0	19	35	6	25	4	0
Golden Valley	1	0	0	0	1	0	0	0	0	0
Granite	1	0	0	0	1	54	4	50	0	0
Hill	19	0	2	0	17	131	19	102	10	1
Jefferson	13	0	1	0	12	36	6	28	2	1
Judith Basin	0	0	0	0	0	1	0	1	0	0
Lake	46	0	10	1	35	294	74	176	44	3
Lewis and Clark	80	2	18	1	59	342	77	239	26	5
Lincoln	25	1	2	1	21	129	24	98	7	0
Madison	6	0	0	0	6	38	6	29	3	0
McCone	1	0	0	0	1	18	3	14	1	0
Meagher	6	0	0	0	6	23	5	17	1	0
Mineral	0	0	0	0	0	1	0	1	0	0
Musselshell	18	0	1	0	17	77	14	61	2	0
Park	20	1	2	1	16	54	18	32	4	3
Phillips	7	0	1	0	6	60	10	44	6	0
Pondera	0	0	0	0	0	7	1	5	1	0
Powell	13	0	0	0	13	87	16	65	6	0
Prairie	1	0	1	0	0	6	1	4	1	0
Ravalli	46	0	4	0	42	310	34	270	6	2
Richland	0	0	0	0	0	32	5	27	0	0
Roosevelt	23	0	2	0	21	52	5	36	11	2
Rosebud	10	0	1	0	9	44	13	29	2	1
Sanders	8	0	5	0	3	67	10	50	7	0
Sheridan	7	0	1	0	6	69	7	50	12	0
Silver Bow	97	2	10	11	74	1,020	149	812	59	12
Stillwater	13	0	3	0	10	61	19	38	4	0
Sweet Grass	5	0	0	0	5	36	4	30	2	0

NA = Not available.

Note: The data shown in this table do not reflect county totals but are the number of offenses reported by the sheriff's office or county police department.

[1] If a blank is presented in the arson column, it indicates that the FBI did not receive 12 complete months of arson data for that agency.

[2] Because of changes in the state/local agency's reporting practices, figures are not comparable to previous years' data.

Table II-10. Offenses Known to Law Enforcement, by Selected State Metropolitan and Nonmetropolitan Counties, 2011—*Continued*

(Number.)

State/County	Violent crime	Murder and non-negligent man-slaughter	Forcible rape	Robbery	Aggravated assault	Property crime	Burglary	Larceny-theft	Motor vehicle theft	Arson[1]
Teton	7	0	0	0	7	53	7	43	3	0
Toole	25	0	2	0	23	128	15	105	8	2
Valley	8	0	2	0	6	23	5	18	0	0
Wheatland	3	0	0	0	3	2	1	1	0	0
Wibaux	0	0	0	0	0	3	0	3	0	0
Nebraska—Metropolitan Counties										
Cass	11	1	4	1	5	313	63	208	42	2
Dakota	3	0	0	0	3	61	13	39	9	0
Dixon	3	0	2	0	1	71	24	43	4	4
Douglas	123	0	8	7	108	1,175	298	786	91	0
Lancaster	9	0	1	0	8	297	78	214	5	2
Sarpy	25	0	10	6	9	730	115	555	60	0
Saunders	6	2	0	0	4	119	31	75	13	0
Nebraska—Nonmetropolitan Counties										
Adams	4	0	2	0	2	170	49	110	11	0
Antelope	1	0	0	0	1	20	4	15	1	0
Arthur	0	0	0	0	0	0	0	0	0	0
Box Butte	0	0	0	0	0	1	0	1	0	0
Boyd	0	0	0	0	0	9	7	2	0	0
Brown	3	1	0	0	2	25	6	18	1	0
Buffalo	9	0	4	2	3	140	39	97	4	0
Burt	3	0	0	0	3	46	17	25	4	0
Butler	2	0	0	0	2	49	12	35	2	0
Cedar	3	0	0	0	3	12	0	12	0	0
Chase	1	0	0	0	1	23	8	14	1	0
Cherry	2	0	0	0	2	9	0	9	0	0
Cuming	4	0	3	0	1	29	6	17	6	0
Custer	2	0	1	1	0	51	19	31	1	0
Dawes	0	0	0	0	0	21	7	13	1	0
Dawson	10	0	6	1	3	74	17	50	7	0
Deuel	2	0	0	0	2	16	3	12	1	0
Dodge	8	0	1	2	5	155	38	112	5	0
Franklin	1	0	0	0	1	7	2	5	0	0
Gage	3	0	0	0	3	136	23	101	12	1
Hall	4	0	1	0	3	228	59	159	10	0
Hamilton	5	0	3	0	2	67	18	46	3	2
Hitchcock	5	0	2	1	2	22	12	7	3	0
Hooker	0	0	0	0	0	0	0	0	0	
Jefferson	3	0	0	0	3	74	17	52	5	0
Kearney	3	0	2	0	1	49	8	40	1	0
Keith	1	0	0	0	1	44	10	28	6	0
Keya Paha	0	0	0	0	0	1	0	1	0	0
Lincoln	10	0	5	0	5	107	30	70	7	1
Madison	4	0	3	0	1	83	10	68	5	0
Morrill	1	0	0	0	1	23	7	14	2	0
Nance	1	0	0	0	1	27	8	19	0	0
Nemaha	0	0	0	0	0	23	5	18	0	0
Nuckolls	1	0	1	0	0	6	2	2	2	0
Pawnee	0	0	0	0	0	41	14	27	0	0
Phelps	1	0	0	0	1	44	9	33	2	0
Pierce	1	0	0	0	1	36	3	32	1	0
Platte	8	0	1	2	5	132	29	96	7	1
Polk	0	0	0	0	0	60	12	45	3	0
Red Willow	1	0	0	0	1	33	14	17	2	0
Rock	0	0	0	0	0	12	5	7	0	0
Saline	1	0	0	0	1	61	27	26	8	0
Scotts Bluff	9	0	2	0	7	99	33	59	7	1
Sheridan	5	0	0	0	5	55	9	42	4	2
Sherman	0	0	0	0	0	20	1	18	1	0
Stanton	7	0	0	0	7	58	8	48	2	0
Thayer	3	0	0	0	3	75	20	49	6	0
Wayne	0	0	0	0	0	21	7	13	1	0
Webster	2	0	0	0	2	39	9	29	1	0
York	1	1	0	0	0	52	14	35	3	0
Nevada—Metropolitan Counties										
Carson City	148	4	0	16	128	1,275	316	890	69	7
Storey	19	0	0	1	18	58	22	36	0	0
Washoe	189	3	7	10	169	934	333	537	64	9

NA = Not available.

Note: The data shown in this table do not reflect county totals but are the number of offenses reported by the sheriff's office or county police department.

[1] If a blank is presented in the arson column, it indicates that the FBI did not receive 12 complete months of arson data for that agency.

Table II-10.   Offenses Known to Law Enforcement, by Selected State Metropolitan and Nonmetropolitan Counties, 2011—*Continued*

(Number.)

State/County	Violent crime	Murder and non-negligent man-slaughter	Forcible rape	Robbery	Aggravated assault	Property crime	Burglary	Larceny-theft	Motor vehicle theft	Arson[1]
Nevada—Nonmetropolitan Counties										
Churchill	18	0	0	1	17	255	90	152	13	1
Douglas	59	1	3	5	50	742	130	588	24	7
Elko	36	7	4	3	22	40	17	16	7	1
Eureka	13	0	3	0	10	31	10	19	2	0
Humboldt	38	0	0	0	38	52	17	29	6	1
Lincoln	9	1	0	0	8	66	8	55	3	2
Lyon	84	3	3	7	71	753	245	458	50	7
White Pine	32	1	3	0	28	143	50	82	11	1
New Hampshire—Metropolitan Counties										
Rockingham	9	0	1	0	8	2	0	2	0	1
New Hampshire—Nonmetropolitan Counties										
Carroll	5	0	1	0	4	56	19	35	2	0
Cheshire	2	0	1	0	1	7	0	6	1	0
Merrimack	5	0	3	0	2	16	0	16	0	0
New Jersey—Metropolitan Counties										
Atlantic	0	0	0	0	0	0	0	0	0	0
Bergen	0	0	0	0	0	0	0	0	0	0
Bergen County Police Department	0	0	0	0	0	0	0	0	0	0
Burlington	0	0	0	0	0	0	0	0	0	0
Camden	0	0	0	0	0	0	0	0	0	0
Cape May	0	0	0	0	0	0	0	0	0	0
Cumberland	0	0	0	0	0	0	0	0	0	0
Essex	0	0	0	0	0	0	0	0	0	0
Gloucester	0	0	0	0	0	0	0	0	0	0
Hudson	0	0	0	0	0	0	0	0	0	0
Hunterdon	0	0	0	0	0	0	0	0	0	0
Mercer	0	0	0	0	0	0	0	0	0	0
Middlesex	0	0	0	0	0	0	0	0	0	0
Monmouth	0	0	0	0	0	0	0	0	0	0
Morris	0	0	0	0	0	0	0	0	0	0
Ocean	0	0	0	0	0	0	0	0	0	0
Passaic	0	0	0	0	0	0	0	0	0	0
Salem	0	0	0	0	0	0	0	0	0	0
Somerset	0	0	0	0	0	0	0	0	0	0
Sussex	0	0	0	0	0	0	0	0	0	0
Union	0	0	0	0	0	0	0	0	0	0
Warren	0	0	0	0	0	0	0	0	0	0
New Mexico—Metropolitan Counties										
Bernalillo	784	4	32	101	647	2,426	882	1,317	227	68
Dona Ana	312	4	39	18	251	1,548	608	808	132	6
Sandoval	23	0	0	2	21	92	49	43	0	0
San Juan	213	2	25	9	177	814	222	540	52	14
Santa Fe	147	2	6	12	127	1,120	693	368	59	7
Torrance	15	0	9	2	4	153	76	55	22	2
Valencia	153	4	18	15	116	1,453	692	618	143	7
New Mexico—Nonmetropolitan Counties										
Catron	1	0	0	0	1	22	9	11	2	0
Chaves	64	1	11	3	49	309	109	169	31	2
Cibola	101	0	5	1	95	108	53	46	9	9
Colfax	2	0	0	0	2	2	0	2	0	0
Curry	15	4	4	1	6	193	95	91	7	1
Eddy	74	1	13	5	55	489	151	317	21	7
Guadalupe	11	0	0	1	10	11	5	6	0	0
Hidalgo	4	1	0	0	3	11	4	5	2	0
Lea	52	4	6	1	41	450	139	288	23	2
Lincoln	15	3	1	0	11	116	50	58	8	0
Luna	58	1	1	2	54	208	92	95	21	0
McKinley	71	1	8	6	56	300	108	148	44	7
Otero	65	0	7	0	58	339	147	167	25	0
Quay	2	0	0	0	2	22	6	15	1	1
Rio Arriba	19	2	2	0	15	76	62	13	1	1
Roosevelt	13	0	4	0	9	101	38	58	5	0
Sierra	12	0	0	0	12	46	9	32	5	2
Taos	106	1	1	2	102	172	127	35	10	0
Union	0	0	0	0	0	20	10	9	1	0

NA = Not available.

Note: The data shown in this table do not reflect county totals but are the number of offenses reported by the sheriff's office or county police department.

[1] If a blank is presented in the arson column, it indicates that the FBI did not receive 12 complete months of arson data for that agency.

Table II-10. Offenses Known to Law Enforcement, by Selected State Metropolitan and Nonmetropolitan Counties, 2011—*Continued*

(Number.)

State/County	Violent crime	Murder and non-negligent man-slaughter	Forcible rape	Robbery	Aggravated assault	Property crime	Burglary	Larceny-theft	Motor vehicle theft	Arson[1]
New York—Metropolitan Counties										
Albany	16	0	6	1	9	178	42	130	6	1
Broome	63	1	10	11	41	911	229	660	22	1
Chemung	36	0	3	0	33	458	85	357	16	2
Dutchess	35	0	4	2	29	691	181	486	24	1
Erie	126	0	9	13	104	1,054	201	819	34	2
Herkimer	0	0	0	0	0	2	0	2	0	0
Livingston	21	0	3	0	18	449	85	350	14	1
Madison	7	0	2	0	5	250	74	165	11	0
Monroe	204	3	16	60	125	3,638	574	2,955	109	6
Nassau	1,420	7	37	696	680	13,160	2,054	10,293	813	119
Niagara	65	0	9	12	44	1,244	354	800	90	5
Oneida	20	1	3	4	12	476	143	314	19	6
Onondaga	199	2	37	42	118	2,308	433	1,793	82	9
Ontario	68	0	15	12	41	969	212	738	19	2
Orange	6	0	0	0	6	35	0	32	3	0
Orleans	19	1	2	2	14	328	108	205	15	0
Oswego	44	2	6	2	34	583	140	405	38	2
Putnam	25	0	1	3	21	336	81	249	6	1
Rensselaer	29	0	2	3	24	212	55	149	8	2
Rockland	19	0	1	0	18	27	1	26	0	0
Saratoga	21	1	1	4	15	1,307	258	1,030	19	2
Schenectady	2	0	0	2	0	13	0	12	1	0
Schoharie	0	0	0	0	0	89	36	51	2	0
Suffolk	85	0	0	0	85	13	1	5	7	0
Suffolk County Police Department	1,862	32	42	748	1,040	24,935	4,342	19,424	1,169	169
Tioga	12	0	1	1	10	223	70	147	6	2
Ulster	40	0	4	5	31	347	94	244	9	0
Warren	49	3	14	5	27	750	134	593	23	1
Washington	30	3	4	1	22	245	65	174	6	0
Wayne	41	0	8	4	29	417	116	284	17	1
Westchester Public Safety	25	0	0	2	23	141	10	129	2	
New York—Nonmetropolitan Counties										
Allegany	0	0	0	0	0	2	0	2	0	0
Cattaraugus	40	0	5	5	30	517	159	335	23	0
Cayuga	21	1	2	0	18	321	77	232	12	1
Chautauqua	20	0	6	7	7	771	239	480	52	2
Chenango	24	0	4	0	20	450	92	352	6	1
Clinton	1	0	0	0	1	15	0	15	0	0
Columbia	23	1	1	2	19	375	100	271	4	0
Cortland	19	0	7	3	9	395	74	301	20	2
Delaware	14	0	7	0	7	127	43	78	6	3
Franklin	0	0	0	0	0	0	0	0	0	0
Fulton	5	0	2	1	2	397	89	298	10	0
Genesee	46	0	8	4	34	655	143	481	31	4
Greene	10	0	2	3	5	69	33	30	6	2
Hamilton	0	0	0	0	0	9	5	4	0	0
Jefferson	27	0	1	2	24	250	23	216	11	0
Lewis	22	1	0	3	18	232	88	116	28	2
Montgomery	14	0	0	2	12	272	22	243	7	0
Otsego	25	1	3	0	21	161	66	87	8	0
Schuyler	7	0	0	0	7	55	17	34	4	1
Seneca	9	1	0	1	7	210	38	165	7	0
Steuben	10	0	4	1	5	212	62	142	8	1
St. Lawrence	27	1	2	0	24	75	15	56	4	0
Sullivan	25	0	2	3	20	529	111	408	10	5
Wyoming	12	0	1	0	11	220	54	161	5	1
Yates	7	0	0	0	7	266	91	173	2	1
North Carolina—Metropolitan Counties										
Alamance	94	1	3	4	86	1,064	409	596	59	1
Alexander	59	3	6	7	43	845	302	507	36	10
Anson	34	0	2	4	28	644	311	312	21	3
Brunswick	140	0	18	31	91	2,079	871	1,100	108	6
Buncombe	155	3	15	33	104	2,059	891	998	170	10
Burke	97	0	4	18	75	1,746	784	893	69	0
Cabarrus	29	0	2	8	19	1,043	383	608	52	4
Caldwell	65	4	5	13	43	1,627	636	930	61	15
Catawba	176	8	9	25	134	2,100	921	1,099	80	9
Chatham	70	3	10	4	53	932	472	437	23	2
Cumberland	538	8	16	112	402	4,265	1,814	2,216	235	43
Currituck	53	2	6	2	43	751	202	522	27	6

NA = Not available.

Note: The data shown in this table do not reflect county totals but are the number of offenses reported by the sheriff's office or county police department.

[1] If a blank is presented in the arson column, it indicates that the FBI did not receive 12 complete months of arson data for that agency.

Table II-10. Offenses Known to Law Enforcement, by Selected State Metropolitan and Nonmetropolitan Counties, 2011—*Continued*

(Number.)

State/County	Violent crime	Murder and non-negligent man-slaughter	Forcible rape	Robbery	Aggravated assault	Property crime	Burglary	Larceny-theft	Motor vehicle theft	Arson[1]
Davie	72	1	7	4	60	714	278	404	32	3
Durham	55	3	5	12	35	765	350	368	47	2
Edgecombe	37	1	0	11	25	654	315	306	33	11
Forsyth	275	3	18	24	230	2,748	905	1,740	103	11
Franklin	78	0	9	7	62	1,148	546	531	71	6
Gaston	4	0	0	0	4	0	0	0	0	0
Gaston County Police Department	201	5	6	30	160	1,300	494	671	135	20
Greene	48	3	14	9	22	613	297	303	13	1
Guilford	159	5	13	22	119	1,807	747	971	89	22
Haywood	102	0	8	5	89	867	393	433	41	4
Henderson	90	1	12	21	56	1,351	556	697	98	1
Hoke	43	0	2	16	25	962	698	216	48	13
Johnston	108	3	19	12	74	2,425	899	1,356	170	5
Madison	0	0	0	0	0	238	116	106	16	1
Nash	60	2	4	14	40	614	295	270	49	5
New Hanover	160	3	19	37	101	2,577	603	1,881	93	9
Onslow	234	3	37	35	159	3,192	954	2,065	173	29
Orange	31	0	5	8	18	704	417	249	38	4
Pender	126	2	12	9	103	682	157	481	44	5
Pitt	198	4	10	16	168	1,433	552	820	61	7
Randolph	107	3	12	22	70	2,531	866	1,579	86	5
Rockingham	72	0	0	15	57	1,421	497	848	76	1
Stokes	151	2	8	5	136	1,059	411	592	56	1
Union	189	2	12	21	154	2,344	850	1,391	103	26
Wake	184	2	21	27	134	2,893	1,019	1,650	224	7
Wayne	155	3	1	27	124	2,091	837	1,123	131	2
Yadkin	85	0	7	7	71	779	334	398	47	2
North Carolina—Nonmetropolitan Counties										
Ashe	30	0	3	5	22	431	220	198	13	0
Avery	24	0	2	0	22	176	55	113	8	2
Beaufort	73	0	1	15	57	744	301	420	23	25
Bertie	29	2	4	8	15	326	142	166	18	6
Bladen	80	1	1	17	61	1,083	481	559	43	11
Camden	7	0	0	0	7	124	48	75	1	0
Caswell	52	0	3	4	45	486	173	294	19	5
Cherokee	31	1	6	0	24	519	202	300	17	4
Chowan	11	0	0	0	11	180	102	74	4	1
Clay	16	1	1	0	14	286	103	167	16	2
Cleveland	39	0	10	25	4	1,440	578	798	64	3
Columbus	106	5	7	26	68	1,630	809	705	116	17
Craven	136	2	12	11	111	1,583	818	668	97	5
Dare	36	0	5	3	28	775	222	547	6	2
Davidson	124	1	8	23	92	2,258	1,000	1,116	142	12
Duplin	175	7	6	10	152	1,156	616	477	63	5
Granville	88	1	6	7	74	968	386	535	47	6
Halifax	125	10	8	20	87	944	475	430	39	12
Harnett	267	6	15	28	218	2,485	982	1,342	161	18
Hertford	23	0	2	4	17	287	131	141	15	3
Iredell	165	1	11	20	133	1,854	752	967	135	11
Jackson	118	0	18	3	97	785	377	378	30	6
Lee	37	0	3	8	26	667	150	444	73	2
Lenoir	113	0	11	11	91	1,015	379	597	39	10
Lincoln	87	0	2	14	71	1,420	537	832	51	9
Macon	20	0	4	1	15	574	218	325	31	2
Martin	36	0	3	1	32	348	151	176	21	2
McDowell	30	1	2	6	21	736	308	389	39	4
Montgomery	34	2	7	3	22	538	283	240	15	4
Moore	60	2	3	10	45	918	406	452	60	7
Northampton	28	0	1	5	22	487	261	203	23	3
Pamlico	27	0	2	6	19	254	96	148	10	0
Pasquotank	68	4	3	7	54	385	142	223	20	2
Perquimans	6	0	2	2	2	138	67	62	9	0
Polk	10	1	2	0	7	236	52	165	19	3
Richmond	164	3	8	34	119	1,383	591	701	91	37
Robeson	527	2	14	125	386	4,110	2,180	1,678	252	48
Rowan	123	3	10	19	91	1,603	534	990	79	4
Scotland	37	0	1	7	29	646	307	286	53	17
Stanly	26	0	6	5	15	547	225	309	13	1
Surry	93	0	5	4	84	1,304	579	648	77	10
Swain	37	0	6	0	31	292	137	153	2	1

NA = Not available.

Note: The data shown in this table do not reflect county totals but are the number of offenses reported by the sheriff's office or county police department.

[1] If a blank is presented in the arson column, it indicates that the FBI did not receive 12 complete months of arson data for that agency.

Table II-10. Offenses Known to Law Enforcement, by Selected State Metropolitan and Nonmetropolitan Counties, 2011—*Continued*

(Number.)

State/County	Violent crime	Murder and non-negligent man-slaughter	Forcible rape	Robbery	Aggravated assault	Property crime	Burglary	Larceny-theft	Motor vehicle theft	Arson[1]
Transylvania	27	1	4	0	22	361	163	180	18	7
Tyrrell	7	2	0	0	5	64	8	50	6	0
Vance	119	3	2	22	92	1,607	811	721	75	7
Watauga	23	0	0	0	23	377	66	286	25	0
Wilkes	151	2	2	16	131	1,553	616	844	93	4
Wilson	62	1	1	1	59	820	253	519	48	3
Yancey	9	0	1	2	6	151	73	76	2	1
North Dakota—Metropolitan Counties										
Burleigh	14	0	5	0	9	198	61	127	10	0
Cass	17	0	5	0	12	167	62	95	10	0
Grand Forks	11	0	0	0	11	87	25	55	7	0
Morton	14	1	4	1	8	122	50	67	5	0
North Dakota—Nonmetropolitan Counties										
Adams	1	0	0	1	0	19	11	7	1	0
Barnes	1	0	0	0	1	44	9	30	5	0
Benson	0	0	0	0	0	15	8	4	3	0
Billings	0	0	0	0	0	4	2	2	0	0
Bottineau	0	0	0	0	0	22	5	16	1	1
Burke	3	0	0	0	3	17	3	13	1	0
Cavalier	2	0	0	0	2	58	11	41	6	1
Dickey	0	0	0	0	0	8	1	6	1	1
Eddy	3	0	0	0	3	16	10	5	1	1
Emmons	0	0	0	0	0	17	9	7	1	0
Golden Valley	4	0	0	0	4	8	1	6	1	0
Grant	0	0	0	0	0	6	3	2	1	0
Griggs	0	0	0	0	0	6	3	1	2	0
Hettinger	2	0	0	0	2	12	6	5	1	1
Kidder	1	0	1	0	0	4	0	3	1	0
Lamoure	0	0	0	0	0	3	0	2	1	0
Logan	0	0	0	0	0	2	0	1	1	0
McHenry	5	0	0	0	5	32	7	20	5	0
McIntosh	3	0	0	1	2	2	0	2	0	0
McKenzie	8	0	2	0	6	58	1	49	8	0
McLean	4	0	0	0	4	80	21	53	6	0
Mercer	5	0	0	0	5	21	11	6	4	0
Mountrail	6	0	0	0	6	105	28	57	20	0
Nelson	2	0	1	0	1	23	11	11	1	0
Oliver	0	0	0	0	0	3	1	2	0	0
Pembina	3	0	0	0	3	46	17	20	9	0
Ramsey	1	0	0	1	0	16	1	13	2	0
Ransom	2	0	1	0	1	6	5	1	0	0
Renville	0	0	0	0	0	25	9	16	0	1
Richland	11	0	4	0	7	92	38	45	9	0
Rolette	3	0	0	0	3	28	13	12	3	0
Sargent	3	0	0	0	3	24	5	18	1	0
Sheridan	1	0	0	0	1	16	4	12	0	0
Stark	4	0	0	0	4	35	5	28	2	0
Steele	0	0	0	0	0	5	2	2	1	1
Stutsman	9	1	5	0	3	27	9	16	2	1
Towner	0	0	0	0	0	10	3	7	0	0
Traill	2	0	1	0	1	43	8	33	2	0
Walsh	5	0	1	0	4	72	26	40	6	1
Ward	30	0	5	0	25	165	49	100	16	2
Wells	0	0	0	0	0	19	8	10	1	0
Williams	19	0	1	0	18	154	15	112	27	2
Ohio—Metropolitan Counties										
Allen	79	0	12	14	53	1,055	235	775	45	5
Belmont	15	2	0	6	7	604	243	323	38	3
Brown	3	0	2	1	0	424	129	256	39	1
Butler	176	1	6	4	165	1,005	314	689	2	4
Carroll	5	0	1	1	3	128	53	71	4	4
Clermont	82	0	16	3	63	2,161	775	1,330	56	19
Delaware	27	1	5	4	17	1,025	373	639	13	4
Erie	61	0	1	1	59	478	162	309	7	1
Fairfield	26	0	6	17	3	1,138	334	765	39	5
Franklin	100	3	12	42	43	1,499	347	1,084	68	10
Fulton	14	0	2	1	11	310	100	200	10	1
Geauga	10	0	1	0	9	196	55	122	19	1
Greene	23	1	5	7	10	582	160	384	38	1

NA = Not available.

Note: The data shown in this table do not reflect county totals but are the number of offenses reported by the sheriff's office or county police department.

[1] If a blank is presented in the arson column, it indicates that the FBI did not receive 12 complete months of arson data for that agency.

Table II-10.   Offenses Known to Law Enforcement, by Selected State Metropolitan and Nonmetropolitan Counties, 2011—*Continued*

(Number.)

State/County	Violent crime	Murder and non-negligent man-slaughter	Forcible rape	Robbery	Aggravated assault	Property crime	Burglary	Larceny-theft	Motor vehicle theft	Arson[1]
Hamilton	318	2	64	121	131	7,427	1,350	5,815	262	22
Jefferson	15	0	0	2	13	200	57	132	11	2
Lake	223	0	20	4	199	595	139	448	8	7
Lawrence	72	0	1	11	60	1,065	381	636	48	3
Licking	363	2	44	10	307	1,095	408	666	21	6
Lorain	45	2	14	18	11	995	488	480	27	12
Lucas	101	2	4	33	62	1,511	404	1,025	82	2
Madison	14	1	2	1	10	465	206	230	29	3
Mahoning	6	0	2	1	3	172	68	101	3	1
Medina	1	0	0	0	1	52	46	6	0	1
Miami	16	0	5	0	11	667	227	408	32	3
Montgomery	272	6	22	105	139	1,636	636	865	135	7
Morrow	5	0	3	0	2	359	105	243	11	0
Ottawa	10	5	1	1	3	351	73	257	21	0
Pickaway	36	1	4	9	22	1,217	565	627	25	5
Portage	34	0	14	15	5	1,673	554	1,044	75	10
Preble	17	1	4	2	10	448	193	233	22	1
Richland	33	0	10	15	8	1,279	452	788	39	3
Stark	87	0	12	39	36	2,023	645	1,252	126	14
Summit	49	1	10	18	20	1,130	303	771	56	10
Trumbull	18	1	2	6	9	653	246	369	38	2
Warren	58	1	16	9	32	1,115	309	790	16	3
Washington	19	0	3	2	14	422	140	263	19	3
Wood	12	0	2	4	6	471	127	330	14	3
Ohio—Nonmetropolitan Counties										
Adams	1	0	1	0	0	36	10	18	8	0
Ashland	17	0	3	2	12	352	188	155	9	1
Athens	10	2	2	2	4	571	147	413	11	2
Auglaize	2	0	1	1	0	119	71	48	0	0
Champaign	17	0	5	0	12	449	151	280	18	4
Clinton	8	0	1	0	7	139	48	80	11	0
Columbiana	9	1	1	0	7	64	44	14	6	0
Coshocton	19	0	1	9	9	851	280	549	22	5
Crawford	12	0	2	2	8	278	115	150	13	0
Defiance	7	1	4	0	2	190	56	128	6	0
Fayette	16	0	2	4	10	720	252	452	16	3
Gallia	18	1	2	6	9	677	248	419	10	3
Guernsey	12	2	4	4	2	416	212	184	20	6
Hancock	11	0	1	1	9	343	136	195	12	0
Hardin	4	0	4	0	0	360	149	199	12	0
Harrison	8	0	0	2	6	95	41	46	8	1
Henry	4	0	0	1	3	279	92	186	1	2
Highland	58	0	0	3	55	668	263	379	26	6
Hocking	4	0	0	0	4	348	135	202	11	3
Holmes	20	1	6	3	10	261	84	170	7	3
Huron	9	0	3	1	5	286	52	214	20	0
Logan	13	2	4	0	7	747	348	380	19	2
Marion	21	0	5	6	10	1,489	327	1,152	10	4
Meigs	16	1	2	2	11	300	131	156	13	2
Mercer	8	0	3	0	5	308	106	192	10	1
Monroe	7	0	3	1	3	100	31	64	5	0
Morgan	4	0	2	0	2	160	81	74	5	4
Muskingum	48	1	24	12	11	1,228	347	800	81	7
Paulding	11	0	1	0	10	203	67	136	0	1
Putnam	4	0	2	2	0	75	24	48	3	0
Ross	25	0	6	13	6	1,914	578	1,239	97	6
Sandusky	116	1	2	10	103	297	195	99	3	0
Scioto	17	0	4	4	9	1,124	456	628	40	20
Seneca	1	0	1	0	0	429	178	248	3	1
Shelby	3	0	0	1	2	232	85	143	4	0
Tuscarawas	10	0	5	1	4	347	149	175	23	2
Van Wert	4	0	1	2	1	254	131	113	10	1
Vinton	17	1	1	4	11	312	110	194	8	0
Wayne	28	2	9	4	13	692	288	375	29	1
Williams	7	0	4	0	3	264	77	169	18	4
Oklahoma—Metropolitan Counties										
Canadian	21	0	3	0	18	185	59	103	23	3
Cleveland	47	0	10	6	31	318	115	163	40	5
Comanche	43	0	6	4	33	313	118	173	22	2
Grady	31	0	3	0	28	266	106	136	24	2
Le Flore	32	2	0	3	27	309	146	144	19	3

NA = Not available.

Note: The data shown in this table do not reflect county totals but are the number of offenses reported by the sheriff's office or county police department.

[1] If a blank is presented in the arson column, it indicates that the FBI did not receive 12 complete months of arson data for that agency.

Table II-10. Offenses Known to Law Enforcement, by Selected State Metropolitan and Nonmetropolitan Counties, 2011—*Continued*

(Number.)

State/County	Violent crime	Murder and non-negligent man-slaughter	Forcible rape	Robbery	Aggravated assault	Property crime	Burglary	Larceny-theft	Motor vehicle theft	Arson[1]
Lincoln	20	3	3	1	13	298	85	193	20	3
Logan	21	2	2	1	16	323	101	202	20	5
McClain	18	0	5	4	9	274	88	154	32	7
Oklahoma	26	0	2	3	21	240	74	130	36	0
Pawnee	19	0	2	0	17	145	59	77	9	1
Rogers	61	0	16	3	42	473	141	237	95	7
Sequoyah	79	1	10	4	64	413	134	263	16	14
Tulsa	211	3	6	14	188	708	301	336	71	3
Wagoner	43	3	5	1	34	509	158	292	59	11
Oklahoma—Nonmetropolitan Counties										
Adair	64	1	3	0	60	259	120	122	17	4
Alfalfa	2	0	1	0	1	24	5	17	2	1
Atoka	0	0	0	0	0	69	32	28	9	1
Beaver	2	0	1	0	1	45	13	27	5	0
Beckham	8	0	1	0	7	71	25	39	7	3
Blaine	2	0	0	0	2	44	11	33	0	1
Bryan	23	2	6	0	15	293	114	140	39	3
Caddo	85	0	3	3	79	182	53	116	13	1
Carter	128	0	12	1	115	213	87	107	19	3
Cherokee	27	0	2	0	25	114	56	43	15	1
Choctaw	20	1	1	0	18	143	53	76	14	5
Cimarron	0	0	0	0	0	4	0	4	0	0
Coal	4	0	1	0	3	58	8	48	2	1
Cotton	8	0	0	0	8	24	11	12	1	1
Craig	16	1	0	1	14	110	38	65	7	4
Custer	7	0	0	2	5	84	39	41	4	4
Delaware	54	3	8	2	41	312	119	163	30	4
Dewey	2	0	1	0	1	19	6	9	4	0
Ellis	9	1	0	0	8	39	15	16	8	1
Garfield	6	0	0	1	5	69	26	42	1	2
Garvin	30	4	7	1	18	214	56	134	24	4
Grant	0	0	0	0	0	51	9	41	1	3
Greer	2	0	0	0	2	15	4	11	0	0
Harmon	0	0	0	0	0	17	3	14	0	0
Harper	0	0	0	0	0	32	15	14	3	0
Haskell	48	2	2	0	44	79	25	40	14	1
Hughes	12	0	2	0	10	155	62	74	19	1
Jackson	6	0	3	0	3	45	13	25	7	0
Jefferson	1	0	0	0	1	17	3	13	1	0
Johnston	14	0	0	0	14	3	2	0	1	0
Kay	23	0	0	1	22	93	38	54	1	0
Kingfisher	0	0	0	0	0	59	5	44	10	0
Kiowa	3	1	0	0	2	37	18	18	1	1
Latimer	7	0	1	0	6	28	11	12	5	0
Love	1	0	0	0	1	58	18	35	5	1
Major	3	0	1	0	2	41	9	32	0	0
Marshall	25	0	1	0	24	48	18	23	7	1
Mayes	24	0	0	1	23	263	77	160	26	0
McCurtain	53	0	8	2	43	535	171	331	33	12
McIntosh	24	0	5	2	17	198	82	103	13	10
Murray	7	0	1	0	6	34	13	15	6	1
Muskogee	72	1	6	2	63	402	153	197	52	19
Noble	2	0	0	0	2	45	13	27	5	0
Nowata	10	0	3	0	7	113	49	48	16	5
Okfuskee	9	0	0	0	9	100	38	52	10	6
Ottawa	8	1	1	0	6	107	54	38	15	0
Pittsburg	22	1	6	2	13	404	142	243	19	12
Pontotoc	31	2	6	1	22	147	59	75	13	2
Pottawatomie	43	2	3	3	35	629	178	354	97	5
Pushmataha	15	2	0	1	12	117	48	52	17	0
Roger Mills	6	0	1	0	5	53	18	33	2	0
Stephens	41	1	6	2	32	233	56	148	29	5
Texas	5	0	1	2	2	55	14	38	3	0
Tillman	5	0	1	1	3	85	38	43	4	2
Washita	4	0	0	0	4	50	22	27	1	1
Woods	2	0	1	0	1	10	3	6	1	0
Woodward	15	1	3	0	11	68	32	28	8	0
Oregon—Metropolitan Counties										
Benton	20	3	3	0	14	200	56	132	12	2
Clackamas	202	3	35	96	68	5,492	891	4,228	373	22
Deschutes	240	1	14	6	219	982	203	734	45	8

NA = Not available.

Note: The data shown in this table do not reflect county totals but are the number of offenses reported by the sheriff's office or county police department.

[1] If a blank is presented in the arson column, it indicates that the FBI did not receive 12 complete months of arson data for that agency.

Table II-10.   Offenses Known to Law Enforcement, by Selected State Metropolitan and Nonmetropolitan Counties, 2011—*Continued*

(Number.)

State/County	Violent crime	Murder and non-negligent man-slaughter	Forcible rape	Robbery	Aggravated assault	Property crime	Burglary	Larceny-theft	Motor vehicle theft	Arson[1]
Jackson	141	2	21	2	116	1,127	281	797	49	5
Lane	241	2	20	17	202	1,146	484	545	117	8
Marion	70	1	19	19	31	1,893	486	1,216	191	3
Multnomah	45	0	6	4	35	841	111	657	73	3
Polk	30	1	2	0	27	378	106	249	23	3
Washington	266	1	66	44	155	2,663	566	1,909	188	22
Yamhill	31	2	8	4	17	582	168	385	29	5
Oregon—Nonmetropolitan Counties										
Baker	2	0	2	0	0	30	15	14	1	0
Clatsop	7	0	0	0	7	134	26	98	10	2
Coos	57	2	1	3	51	589	187	364	38	2
Crook	22	0	2	2	18	125	47	77	1	3
Curry	8	0	0	1	7	231	69	145	17	0
Douglas	35	1	19	2	13	558	160	345	53	15
Gilliam	0	0	0	0	0	16	4	12	0	0
Grant	0	0	0	0	0	40	3	36	1	0
Harney	7	0	0	0	7	27	12	14	1	0
Hood River	10	1	3	2	4	153	28	115	10	1
Jefferson	8	0	1	2	5	184	61	108	15	2
Josephine	64	2	11	10	41	726	237	419	70	3
Klamath	54	0	9	9	36	451	259	140	52	5
Lincoln	52	0	10	0	42	344	133	200	11	3
Linn	19	0	7	4	8	935	246	582	107	4
Malheur	2	0	0	0	2	203	63	129	11	
Morrow	15	0	6	1	8	226	39	170	17	3
Sherman	0	0	0	0	0	34	6	24	4	1
Tillamook	15	0	1	2	12	289	114	161	14	2
Umatilla	59	2	8	5	44	564	184	293	87	3
Union	15	0	0	1	14	310	64	227	19	0
Wallowa	1	0	0	0	1	37	13	21	3	0
Wasco	5	1	0	0	4	112	40	67	5	NA
Pennsylvania—Metropolitan Counties										
Allegheny	5	0	0	1	4	0	0	0	0	0
Beaver	0	0	0	0	0	0	0	0	0	0
Blair	2	0	0	0	2	0	0	0	0	0
Butler	0	0	0	0	0	0	0	0	0	0
Centre	0	0	0	0	0	0	0	0	0	0
Cumberland	0	0	0	0	0	0	0	0	0	0
Lancaster	0	0	0	0	0	0	0	0	0	0
Mercer	0	0	0	0	0	0	0	0	0	0
Montgomery	0	0	0	0	0	0	0	0	0	0
Northampton	1	0	0	0	1	0	0	0	0	0
Pike	0	0	0	0	0	1	0	1	0	0
Washington	4	0	0	0	4	0	0	0	0	0
Westmoreland	0	0	0	0	0	0	0	0	0	0
York	3	0	0	0	3	0	0	0	0	0
Pennsylvania—Nonmetropolitan Counties										
Bedford	0	0	0	0	0	0	0	0	0	0
Clarion	0	0	0	0	0	1	0	1	0	0
Elk	0	0	0	0	0	0	0	0	0	0
Franklin	0	0	0	0	0	0	0	0	0	0
Indiana	0	0	0	0	0	0	0	0	0	0
Lawrence	0	0	0	0	0	0	0	0	0	0
Schuylkill	0	0	0	0	0	0	0	0	0	0
Snyder	0	0	0	0	0	0	0	0	0	0
Tioga	0	0	0	0	0	0	0	0	0	0
Union	0	0	0	0	0	0	0	0	0	0
Warren	0	0	0	0	0	0	0	0	0	0
Wayne	0	0	0	0	0	0	0	0	0	0
South Carolina—Metropolitan Counties										
Aiken	424	11	48	82	283	3,771	1,329	2,075	367	4
Anderson	776	11	46	84	635	6,900	2,061	4,123	716	37
Berkeley	503	5	38	73	387	3,357	951	2,076	330	24
Calhoun	57	1	2	6	48	471	164	251	56	7
Charleston	573	7	24	96	446	2,304	730	1,294	280	14
Darlington	425	3	16	41	365	2,325	876	1,305	144	12
Dorchester	372	2	18	63	289	2,413	771	1,413	229	9
Edgefield	18	2	4	3	9	455	188	240	27	2
Fairfield	120	2	7	9	102	720	233	439	48	5

NA = Not available.

Note: The data shown in this table do not reflect county totals but are the number of offenses reported by the sheriff's office or county police department.

[1] If a blank is presented in the arson column, it indicates that the FBI did not receive 12 complete months of arson data for that agency.

Table II-10. Offenses Known to Law Enforcement, by Selected State Metropolitan and Nonmetropolitan Counties, 2011—*Continued*

(Number.)

State/County	Violent crime	Murder and non-negligent man-slaughter	Forcible rape	Robbery	Aggravated assault	Property crime	Burglary	Larceny-theft	Motor vehicle theft	Arson[1]
Florence	276	6	14	48	208	2,653	737	1,731	185	4
Greenville	1,819	21	118	289	1,391	10,942	3,014	7,042	886	32
Horry	0	0	0	0	0	31	0	31	0	0
Horry County Police Department	1,060	16	111	161	772	7,643	1,997	5,015	631	47
Kershaw	214	6	21	18	169	1,371	396	890	85	21
Laurens	295	1	17	22	255	1,437	499	801	137	12
Lexington	578	10	60	108	400	4,508	1,147	2,953	408	9
Pickens	222	7	11	18	186	2,155	633	1,326	196	4
Richland	2,366	13	93	406	1,854	9,954	2,860	5,947	1,147	26
Saluda	36	0	1	2	33	349	148	178	23	3
Spartanburg	626	7	58	112	449	6,338	1,854	3,953	531	21
York	413	2	28	39	344	2,559	657	1,743	159	25
South Carolina—Nonmetropolitan Counties										
Allendale	9	0	0	0	9	130	47	69	14	1
Bamberg	41	3	1	4	33	266	76	163	27	7
Barnwell	104	1	4	5	94	394	124	249	21	2
Beaufort	606	3	20	86	497	3,849	1,106	2,557	186	16
Chester	129	1	8	16	104	848	238	552	58	2
Chesterfield	117	2	4	4	107	914	286	581	47	6
Clarendon	170	4	11	18	137	927	309	553	65	3
Colleton	172	4	17	13	138	1,297	426	731	140	6
Dillon	240	4	9	20	207	1,014	386	563	65	9
Georgetown	254	0	24	22	208	1,672	504	1,054	114	19
Greenwood[3]		3	5	14		1,583	393	1,106	84	3
Hampton	77	0	3	3	71	426	146	253	27	2
Lancaster	230	3	21	36	170	1,992	591	1,298	103	10
Lee	73	0	7	4	62	429	161	222	46	8
Marion	86	2	10	9	65	878	364	449	65	7
Marlboro	161	2	8	14	137	845	263	517	65	5
McCormick	24	0	2	0	22	61	19	31	11	0
Newberry	54	2	6	5	41	501	114	337	50	0
Oconee	305	4	42	13	246	1,560	511	958	91	5
Union	64	2	12	8	42	602	167	408	27	4
Williamsburg	174	3	9	27	135	780	235	462	83	15
South Dakota—Metropolitan Counties										
Lincoln	10	0	6	0	4	175	56	111	8	0
McCook	2	0	0	0	2	46	12	31	3	0
Meade	11	0	1	1	9	56	8	40	8	0
Minnehaha	30	0	10	1	19	364	101	244	19	8
Pennington	44	1	22	0	21	383	108	259	16	2
Turner	3	0	0	0	3	32	11	20	1	3
Union	2	0	0	0	2	54	7	47	0	0
South Dakota—Nonmetropolitan Counties										
Aurora	0	0	0	0	0	4	1	2	1	0
Beadle	0	0	0	0	0	23	8	15	0	1
Bennett	5	0	0	0	5	8	3	2	3	0
Bon Homme	0	0	0	0	0	0	0	0	0	0
Brookings	1	0	1	0	0	64	6	52	6	1
Brown	3	0	0	0	3	13	5	6	2	0
Butte	1	0	0	0	1	31	11	15	5	0
Campbell	0	0	0	0	0	5	0	4	1	0
Charles Mix	8	0	2	0	6	50	25	21	4	2
Clark	1	0	0	0	1	9	5	4	0	0
Clay	2	0	1	0	1	33	4	27	2	0
Codington	8	0	5	0	3	56	7	45	4	0
Corson	0	0	0	0	0	18	1	16	1	0
Custer	4	0	1	0	3	31	6	20	5	0
Davison	8	0	0	0	8	8	1	6	1	0
Deuel	1	0	0	0	1	21	5	13	3	0
Dewey	1	0	0	0	1	5	1	3	1	0
Douglas	0	0	0	0	0	3	1	2	0	0
Edmunds	0	0	0	0	0	0	0	0	0	0
Faulk	0	0	0	0	0	12	2	9	1	0
Hamlin	7	0	2	0	5	28	8	17	3	1
Hand	0	0	0	0	0	8	4	3	1	0
Hanson	0	0	0	0	0	12	4	8	0	0
Harding	0	0	0	0	0	1	1	0	0	0
Hughes	4	0	0	0	4	26	13	11	2	0
Hutchinson	1	0	0	0	1	4	2	2	0	0

NA = Not available.

Note: The data shown in this table do not reflect county totals but are the number of offenses reported by the sheriff's office or county police department.

[1] If a blank is presented in the arson column, it indicates that the FBI did not receive 12 complete months of arson data for that agency.

Table II-10.   Offenses Known to Law Enforcement, by Selected State Metropolitan and Nonmetropolitan Counties, 2011—*Continued*

(Number.)

State/County	Violent crime	Murder and non-negligent man-slaughter	Forcible rape	Robbery	Aggravated assault	Property crime	Burglary	Larceny-theft	Motor vehicle theft	Arson[1]
Jerauld	0	0	0	0	0	7	2	5	0	0
Lawrence	1	0	0	0	1	24	4	18	2	0
Marshall	6	0	4	1	1	34	19	10	5	0
McPherson	2	0	2	0	0	1	1	0	0	0
Mellette	7	0	2	0	5	11	4	4	3	0
Miner	0	0	0	0	0	19	13	6	0	0
Moody	3	0	0	0	3	23	5	15	3	1
Perkins	0	0	0	0	0	8	2	6	0	0
Potter	1	0	1	0	0	1	0	1	0	0
Roberts	5	0	0	0	5	34	13	10	11	0
Spink	11	0	4	0	7	48	18	28	2	6
Stanley	5	0	4	0	1	31	11	19	1	0
Sully	2	0	0	0	2	7	2	5	0	0
Tripp	0	0	0	0	0	9	1	8	0	0
Walworth	0	0	0	0	0	2	0	0	2	0
Yankton	8	0	1	0	7	77	23	45	9	1
Ziebach	0	0	0	0	0	1	1	0	0	0
Tennessee—Metropolitan Counties										
Anderson	120	0	8	14	98	1,015	443	515	57	4
Blount	271	2	24	21	224	1,840	658	1,054	128	6
Cannon	19	0	2	0	17	132	47	63	22	3
Carter	81	0	0	4	77	704	280	357	67	12
Cheatham	109	1	5	6	97	739	227	427	85	4
Chester	28	1	4	0	23	106	30	66	10	0
Dickson	102	0	14	4	84	591	232	327	32	4
Fayette	81	1	2	6	72	468	139	276	53	1
Hamblen	144	0	4	15	125	697	257	408	32	4
Hamilton	266	4	13	14	235	1,771	642	1,011	118	11
Hartsville/Trousdale	42	0	8	5	29	255	71	175	9	1
Hawkins	52	0	1	6	45	1,077	420	603	54	4
Hickman	47	0	7	0	40	279	120	131	28	1
Jefferson	80	1	6	10	63	960	343	541	76	3
Knox	625	8	23	118	476	5,778	1,458	3,932	388	35
Loudon	56	1	2	11	42	542	214	292	36	3
Macon	71	0	3	0	68	186	38	129	19	2
Madison	136	1	14	12	109	688	242	382	64	1
Marion	62	1	1	0	60	333	97	198	38	1
Montgomery	104	1	8	3	92	882	190	629	63	2
Polk	37	0	1	2	34	350	106	205	39	2
Robertson	59	0	4	3	52	495	160	302	33	2
Rutherford	234	1	15	22	196	1,456	490	872	94	3
Sequatchie	36	1	3	0	32	219	78	114	27	4
Shelby	500	4	35	55	406	3,327	1,123	1,979	225	8
Smith	63	1	5	4	53	267	89	147	31	6
Sullivan	340	3	28	19	290	1,586	499	981	106	18
Sumner	101	3	5	8	85	828	238	551	39	4
Tipton	189	0	14	2	173	671	203	377	91	2
Unicoi	20	0	0	0	20	197	25	170	2	0
Union	48	1	6	6	35	494	208	235	51	2
Washington	200	2	10	11	177	1,009	328	621	60	10
Williamson	41	0	4	3	34	452	166	266	20	5
Wilson	186	0	12	8	166	1,104	422	613	69	1
Tennessee—Nonmetropolitan Counties										
Bedford	42	0	1	0	41	354	132	209	13	1
Benton	27	0	2	1	24	230	55	152	23	0
Bledsoe	11	1	0	2	8	94	22	50	22	0
Campbell	61	1	13	6	41	872	469	355	48	12
Carroll	28	1	1	1	25	329	144	144	41	0
Claiborne	87	1	6	10	70	723	333	350	40	7
Clay	0	0	0	0	0	83	35	42	6	1
Cocke	199	4	8	15	172	1,097	518	505	74	30
Coffee	69	0	1	0	68	390	128	229	33	0
Crockett	13	1	1	0	11	118	50	57	11	2
Cumberland	102	1	3	5	93	985	391	519	75	15
Decatur	8	0	0	0	8	194	71	115	8	1
DeKalb	24	2	2	2	18	287	91	175	21	1
Dyer	44	0	0	2	42	327	112	180	35	2
Fentress	37	1	3	1	32	444	43	388	13	5
Franklin	42	0	5	0	37	336	52	264	20	5
Gibson	63	0	5	3	55	323	139	154	30	1
Giles	37	0	3	3	31	280	96	167	17	1

NA = Not available.

Note: The data shown in this table do not reflect county totals but are the number of offenses reported by the sheriff's office or county police department.

[1] If a blank is presented in the arson column, it indicates that the FBI did not receive 12 complete months of arson data for that agency.

Table II-10. Offenses Known to Law Enforcement, by Selected State Metropolitan and Nonmetropolitan Counties, 2011—*Continued*

(Number.)

State/County	Violent crime	Murder and non-negligent man-slaughter	Forcible rape	Robbery	Aggravated assault	Property crime	Burglary	Larceny-theft	Motor vehicle theft	Arson[1]
Greene	177	1	13	16	147	1,324	548	678	98	10
Grundy	60	0	2	2	56	260	63	156	41	4
Hancock	26	0	1	0	25	159	34	118	7	0
Hardeman	67	0	7	4	56	404	195	159	50	5
Hardin	52	0	6	2	44	444	161	234	49	1
Haywood	47	0	3	4	40	233	100	118	15	0
Henderson	62	1	4	3	54	399	135	234	30	4
Henry	40	0	0	0	40	472	155	297	20	0
Houston	22	0	0	1	21	149	62	77	10	12
Humphreys	20	1	0	1	18	162	56	97	9	0
Jackson	18	1	2	3	12	207	78	112	17	0
Johnson	93	0	2	3	88	251	120	110	21	4
Lake	5	2	0	0	3	21	5	14	2	0
Lauderdale	56	2	3	0	51	428	215	184	29	4
Lawrence	123	0	5	3	115	676	253	395	28	9
Lewis	24	0	0	1	23	179	53	108	18	0
Lincoln	81	0	0	4	77	524	193	302	29	4
Marshall	18	0	1	0	17	173	55	109	9	1
Maury	144	1	15	8	120	709	188	461	60	8
McMinn	75	1	7	8	59	630	266	281	83	5
McNairy	80	0	4	0	76	335	113	191	31	4
Meigs	45	0	4	0	41	289	104	141	44	2
Monroe	100	2	0	3	95	710	218	441	51	3
Moore	2	0	2	0	0	106	23	78	5	1
Morgan	39	1	3	1	34	563	238	295	30	1
Obion	27	0	1	0	26	245	57	161	27	2
Overton	40	0	0	1	39	235	106	119	10	1
Perry	20	0	3	1	16	120	50	66	4	2
Pickett	3	0	0	1	2	61	7	54	0	0
Putnam	90	0	1	4	85	1,028	314	664	50	5
Rhea	74	0	2	3	69	373	103	234	36	0
Roane	36	0	1	3	32	424	155	239	30	0
Scott	27	1	3	1	22	497	221	256	20	0
Sevier	162	3	21	22	116	1,884	830	964	90	2
Van Buren	10	0	1	0	9	53	14	35	4	3
Warren	43	1	5	4	33	443	161	237	45	2
Wayne	21	2	0	0	19	80	38	36	6	3
Weakley	43	1	2	3	37	214	98	101	15	0
White	59	1	5	2	51	458	91	333	34	3
Texas—Metropolitan Counties										
Aransas	21	0	3	1	17	331	119	201	11	0
Archer	3	0	0	0	3	39	10	27	2	0
Armstrong	0	0	0	0	0	15	12	2	1	0
Atascosa	18	0	0	3	15	421	179	230	12	0
Austin	27	1	2	3	21	203	101	98	4	0
Bandera	20	0	1	3	16	180	79	99	2	0
Bastrop	155	2	49	13	91	862	337	467	58	7
Bell	29	2	11	3	13	761	262	463	36	15
Bexar	496	12	61	90	333	6,668	2,013	4,182	473	94
Bowie	140	5	21	3	111	883	332	472	79	12
Brazoria	98	1	13	23	61	1,744	620	1,028	96	1
Brazos	53	2	4	0	47	357	115	222	20	1
Burleson	20	0	7	2	11	123	51	57	15	1
Caldwell	23	1	3	1	18	195	73	105	17	0
Calhoun	11	0	0	0	11	170	55	101	14	0
Callahan	3	0	0	0	3	40	12	25	3	0
Cameron	159	3	9	24	123	1,745	615	1,029	101	10
Carson	13	2	2	0	9	46	15	29	2	0
Chambers	54	1	2	7	44	536	134	364	38	4
Clay	4	0	2	0	2	140	68	66	6	0
Collin	89	2	9	7	71	725	300	355	70	0
Comal	182	0	20	12	150	909	326	553	30	4
Coryell	12	0	0	2	10	140	67	65	8	1
Crosby	3	0	0	0	3	17	9	6	2	0
Dallas	28	0	3	3	22	256	89	148	19	20
Delta	4	0	0	0	4	145	62	73	10	1
Denton	137	1	23	13	100	1,010	342	632	36	1
Ector	182	5	1	22	154	1,009	275	670	64	2
Ellis	51	1	4	5	41	672	228	375	69	2
El Paso	237	2	18	21	196	1,333	357	843	133	19
Fort Bend	902	8	56	117	721	4,155	1,509	2,399	247	10
Galveston	81	2	14	16	49	847	288	478	81	16
Goliad	14	0	0	2	12	69	27	36	6	0

NA = Not available.

Note: The data shown in this table do not reflect county totals but are the number of offenses reported by the sheriff's office or county police department.

[1] If a blank is presented in the arson column, it indicates that the FBI did not receive 12 complete months of arson data for that agency.

Table II-10.   Offenses Known to Law Enforcement, by Selected State Metropolitan and Nonmetropolitan Counties, 2011—*Continued*

(Number.)

State/County	Violent crime	Murder and non-negligent man-slaughter	Forcible rape	Robbery	Aggravated assault	Property crime	Burglary	Larceny-theft	Motor vehicle theft	Arson[1]
Grayson	56	2	9	1	44	802	294	468	40	17
Gregg	81	3	14	7	57	595	160	361	74	8
Guadalupe	78	0	14	4	60	659	277	348	34	12
Hardin	50	3	4	4	39	408	104	259	45	5
Hays	77	2	2	8	65	774	288	468	18	0
Hidalgo	525	20	66	116	323	6,688	2,498	3,779	411	188
Hunt	76	3	0	11	62	1,222	524	604	94	1
Irion	0	0	0	0	0	22	3	19	0	0
Jefferson	25	0	2	1	22	500	176	276	48	3
Johnson	128	3	4	2	119	1,095	340	708	47	17
Jones	1	0	0	0	1	87	23	63	1	0
Kaufman	140	0	18	9	113	1,254	526	605	123	1
Kendall	16	2	8	0	6	232	74	148	10	0
Lampasas	1	0	0	0	1	106	31	72	3	3
Liberty	165	1	0	8	156	1,226	440	655	131	14
Lubbock	111	3	18	5	85	820	361	405	54	1
McLennan	86	1	32	2	51	826	353	435	38	6
Medina	33	1	4	0	28	203	106	89	8	0
Midland	52	2	0	3	47	442	121	290	31	2
Montgomery	648	7	49	119	473	6,328	1,837	4,088	403	12
Nueces	48	1	5	2	40	256	113	138	5	4
Orange	107	0	6	16	85	817	284	470	63	2
Parker	121	1	7	5	108	1,061	408	601	52	0
Potter	26	0	2	3	21	251	75	159	17	5
Randall	36	0	1	2	33	373	127	215	31	8
Robertson	5	0	2	0	3	187	59	112	16	2
Rockwall	30	0	3	1	26	215	69	137	9	0
Rusk	73	0	10	2	61	665	249	356	60	1
San Jacinto	117	0	3	15	99	738	315	349	74	4
San Patricio	32	1	13	2	16	272	85	172	15	0
Smith	238	5	47	23	163	2,043	680	1,224	139	18
Tarrant	124	3	16	12	93	1,256	413	774	69	5
Taylor	21	0	3	1	17	152	78	60	14	1
Tom Green	36	0	16	3	17	237	77	150	10	6
Travis	367	6	11	23	327	3,461	1,039	2,279	143	48
Upshur	57	2	12	4	39	624	250	339	35	5
Victoria	83	1	15	3	64	521	172	320	29	0
Waller	20	0	1	1	18	292	119	154	19	0
Wichita	36	0	1	1	34	107	33	70	4	5
Williamson	106	5	14	14	73	1,288	315	933	40	12
Wilson	33	1	3	0	29	255	81	153	21	0
Wise	30	2	0	3	25	291	96	170	25	15
Texas—Nonmetropolitan Counties										
Anderson	66	2	3	4	57	495	206	232	57	6
Andrews	8	0	1	1	6	71	13	48	10	1
Angelina	86	0	8	9	69	665	255	381	29	0
Bailey	7	0	0	0	7	51	28	21	2	2
Baylor	1	0	0	0	1	11	3	6	2	0
Bee	32	2	4	0	26	148	57	79	12	0
Blanco	5	0	0	0	5	85	35	44	6	2
Borden	0	0	0	0	0	7	1	6	0	0
Bosque	15	0	2	1	12	172	82	84	6	4
Brewster	4	0	0	0	4	28	20	6	2	0
Briscoe	0	0	0	0	0	0	0	0	0	0
Brooks	11	0	1	0	10	15	6	6	3	0
Brown	18	0	0	0	18	176	68	99	9	2
Burnet	27	0	6	2	19	236	93	129	14	1
Camp	7	1	1	1	4	196	92	99	5	0
Cass	30	0	2	0	28	399	160	211	28	0
Castro	3	0	0	0	3	87	32	49	6	2
Cherokee	79	0	11	6	62	641	194	369	78	6
Childress	3	0	0	0	3	21	11	8	2	0
Cochran	2	0	1	0	1	85	18	61	6	1
Coke	1	0	0	0	1	8	2	6	0	0
Coleman	1	0	0	0	1	84	34	46	4	1
Collingsworth	1	1	0	0	0	0	0	0	0	0
Colorado	10	1	1	2	6	218	72	134	12	0
Comanche	7	0	0	0	7	100	30	68	2	0
Concho	2	0	0	0	2	9	6	3	0	0
Cottle	0	0	0	0	0	1	1	0	0	0
Crane	0	0	0	0	0	25	10	15	0	0

NA = Not available.

Note: The data shown in this table do not reflect county totals but are the number of offenses reported by the sheriff's office or county police department.

[1] If a blank is presented in the arson column, it indicates that the FBI did not receive 12 complete months of arson data for that agency.

Table II-10. Offenses Known to Law Enforcement, by Selected State Metropolitan and Nonmetropolitan Counties, 2011—*Continued*

(Number.)

State/County	Violent crime	Murder and non-negligent man-slaughter	Forcible rape	Robbery	Aggravated assault	Property crime	Burglary	Larceny-theft	Motor vehicle theft	Arson[1]
Culberson	3	0	1	0	2	7	1	6	0	0
Dallam	1	0	0	0	1	25	9	14	2	0
Dawson	2	0	0	1	1	46	10	34	2	1
Deaf Smith	17	0	2	0	15	105	31	65	9	1
DeWitt	8	0	0	0	8	107	45	55	7	0
Dickens	0	0	0	0	0	0	0	0	0	0
Dimmit	45	0	1	5	39	218	71	126	21	0
Donley	3	0	0	0	3	27	13	14	0	1
Duval	47	0	4	1	42	142	54	63	25	4
Eastland	5	0	1	0	4	41	25	13	3	0
Edwards	6	0	0	0	6	38	10	25	3	0
Erath	9	2	1	1	5	111	31	73	7	0
Falls	2	0	0	0	2	73	36	27	10	3
Fannin	27	1	1	2	23	206	79	106	21	0
Fayette	12	0	4	0	8	190	75	105	10	1
Fisher	4	0	0	0	4	49	20	28	1	0
Floyd	3	0	0	0	3	12	4	7	1	0
Foard	0	0	0	0	0	5	0	5	0	0
Franklin	20	0	10	1	9	109	38	64	7	2
Freestone	16	1	1	0	14	183	85	87	11	2
Frio	7	0	0	1	6	60	20	37	3	0
Gaines	3	0	0	1	2	59	17	38	4	0
Garza	2	0	0	0	2	38	10	25	3	0
Gillespie	15	0	8	0	7	112	29	80	3	0
Glasscock	2	0	0	1	1	4	1	2	1	0
Gonzales	19	1	0	0	18	135	52	62	21	1
Gray	3	0	0	0	3	113	31	76	6	0
Grimes	13	0	0	0	13	308	102	186	20	2
Hale	7	0	0	0	7	121	39	74	8	0
Hall	0	0	0	0	0	5	4	1	0	0
Hamilton	16	0	2	0	14	135	69	60	6	1
Hansford	0	0	0	0	0	15	1	13	1	0
Hardeman	0	0	0	0	0	81	36	42	3	0
Harrison	97	1	1	4	91	624	266	337	21	0
Hartley	1	0	0	0	1	29	13	12	4	0
Haskell	1	0	0	0	1	7	1	6	0	0
Hemphill	17	0	3	0	14	71	22	48	1	0
Henderson	192	2	39	8	143	1,228	496	613	119	8
Hill	13	3	1	5	4	323	110	193	20	2
Hockley	27	0	6	2	19	103	26	74	3	1
Hood	68	1	9	0	58	559	165	363	31	1
Hopkins	38	1	11	2	24	135	62	70	3	0
Houston	16	3	0	0	13	189	65	111	13	1
Howard	15	0	1	0	14	117	25	82	10	0
Hudspeth	1	0	0	0	1	22	5	16	1	0
Hutchinson	7	1	2	0	4	121	34	80	7	0
Jack	3	0	0	0	3	53	12	35	6	0
Jackson	16	0	0	1	15	76	32	44	0	0
Jasper	61	2	4	3	52	248	112	122	14	0
Jeff Davis	3	0	0	0	3	14	5	7	2	0
Jim Hogg	12	0	1	0	11	21	10	11	0	0
Jim Wells	55	0	10	0	45	392	177	194	21	3
Karnes	11	0	2	1	8	96	29	57	10	0
Kenedy	5	0	1	0	4	4	1	2	1	0
Kent	6	0	0	0	6	27	14	11	2	0
Kerr	33	1	7	2	23	317	93	213	11	6
Kimble	7	0	0	1	6	17	11	6	0	0
King	0	0	0	0	0	1	0	1	0	0
Kinney	0	0	0	0	0	2	0	1	1	0
Kleberg	14	1	6	0	7	239	37	197	5	3
Knox	3	0	0	0	3	20	12	8	0	0
Lamar	32	1	2	3	26	372	143	218	11	0
Lamb	6	0	0	0	6	120	34	81	5	1
La Salle	13	1	0	2	10	28	10	18	0	1
Lavaca	6	0	1	0	5	89	51	31	7	0
Lee	5	0	0	0	5	115	29	78	8	0
Leon	23	0	1	3	19	178	53	110	15	0
Limestone	73	3	8	3	59	355	125	205	25	7
Lipscomb	0	0	0	0	0	18	1	13	4	3
Live Oak	7	0	0	1	6	99	45	43	11	0

NA = Not available.

Note: The data shown in this table do not reflect county totals but are the number of offenses reported by the sheriff's office or county police department.

[1] If a blank is presented in the arson column, it indicates that the FBI did not receive 12 complete months of arson data for that agency.

Table II-10.   Offenses Known to Law Enforcement, by Selected State Metropolitan and Nonmetropolitan Counties, 2011—*Continued*

(Number.)

State/County	Violent crime	Murder and non-negligent man-slaughter	Forcible rape	Robbery	Aggravated assault	Property crime	Burglary	Larceny-theft	Motor vehicle theft	Arson[1]
Llano	8	0	0	1	7	290	97	190	3	1
Loving	0	0	0	0	0	0	0	0	0	0
Lynn	6	1	1	0	4	64	14	45	5	1
Madison	6	0	1	0	5	85	33	38	14	1
Marion	33	1	7	0	25	214	96	108	10	2
Martin	6	1	0	0	5	51	15	35	1	0
Mason	3	0	1	0	2	30	6	23	1	0
Matagorda	53	1	1	0	51	261	87	161	13	0
Maverick	130	1	11	7	111	587	229	332	26	3
McCulloch	5	0	1	0	4	23	7	15	1	0
McMullen	1	0	0	0	1	9	2	4	3	0
Menard	6	0	0	0	6	2	1	1	0	0
Milam	20	1	2	0	17	189	66	117	6	1
Mills	14	0	2	1	11	65	28	32	5	1
Mitchell	2	0	0	0	2	31	10	20	1	0
Montague	17	0	0	0	17	184	50	124	10	0
Moore	3	1	2	0	0	83	27	52	4	0
Morris	13	0	2	0	11	142	68	68	6	0
Motley	1	0	0	0	1	14	4	9	1	0
Nacogdoches	85	0	3	4	78	465	184	247	34	4
Navarro	48	1	11	1	35	595	242	339	14	1
Newton	8	0	0	3	5	91	28	60	3	2
Nolan	7	0	0	0	7	52	27	24	1	0
Ochiltree	4	0	0	0	4	35	6	23	6	0
Oldham	1	0	0	0	1	26	4	20	2	0
Palo Pinto	22	2	1	0	19	148	71	67	10	1
Panola	23	0	3	0	20	329	89	199	41	1
Parmer	1	0	1	0	0	60	25	33	2	0
Pecos	3	0	1	0	2	70	21	46	3	0
Polk	65	2	14	6	43	618	227	347	44	4
Presidio	3	0	0	0	3	13	9	4	0	0
Rains	17	0	7	0	10	187	44	138	5	0
Reagan	1	0	0	0	1	4	4	0	0	1
Real	0	0	0	0	0	13	2	11	0	0
Red River	19	1	2	2	14	170	75	79	16	5
Reeves	18	0	0	0	18	76	16	59	1	0
Refugio	10	0	2	0	8	44	15	28	1	0
Roberts	0	0	0	0	0	18	5	11	2	0
Runnels	0	0	0	0	0	20	1	19	0	0
Sabine	19	0	0	3	16	93	43	48	2	0
San Augustine	22	0	1	0	21	86	39	46	1	3
San Saba	4	0	1	0	3	27	6	17	4	0
Schleicher	0	0	0	0	0	13	6	7	0	0
Scurry	8	0	2	1	5	75	22	50	3	1
Shackelford	1	0	1	0	0	49	5	38	6	0
Shelby	38	2	7	0	29	263	93	152	18	1
Sherman	0	0	0	0	0	1	1	0	0	0
Somervell	5	0	0	0	5	88	39	48	1	0
Starr	71	2	7	2	60	336	151	152	33	3
Stephens	5	0	0	0	5	41	8	29	4	0
Sterling	1	0	0	0	1	4	0	1	3	3
Stonewall	0	0	0	0	0	26	16	10	0	0
Sutton	0	0	0	0	0	1	0	1	0	1
Swisher	4	0	0	0	4	36	9	22	5	0
Terrell	4	0	0	0	4	9	6	3	0	0
Terry	1	0	0	0	1	38	15	20	3	0
Throckmorton	1	0	0	0	1	0	0	0	0	0
Titus	24	0	2	1	21	293	159	124	10	1
Trinity	30	0	7	2	21	196	82	100	14	5
Tyler	77	1	5	4	67	388	187	176	25	4
Upton	1	0	0	0	1	25	2	21	2	0
Uvalde	22	1	0	1	20	129	44	75	10	0
Val Verde	10	0	0	0	10	146	70	67	9	0
Van Zandt	78	0	0	3	75	813	352	397	64	1
Walker	92	3	9	5	75	418	173	204	41	0
Ward	4	0	1	1	2	77	28	45	4	0
Washington	24	0	4	0	20	184	75	97	12	2
Wharton	71	0	0	5	66	479	199	266	14	7
Wheeler	6	0	1	0	5	45	12	31	2	0
Wilbarger	3	0	1	1	1	39	7	27	5	1
Willacy	64	0	9	1	54	195	64	123	8	8
Winkler	3	0	0	1	2	32	7	24	1	0
Wood	46	2	2	1	41	539	204	304	31	1

NA = Not available.

Note: The data shown in this table do not reflect county totals but are the number of offenses reported by the sheriff's office or county police department.

[1] If a blank is presented in the arson column, it indicates that the FBI did not receive 12 complete months of arson data for that agency.

Table II-10.   Offenses Known to Law Enforcement, by Selected State Metropolitan and Nonmetropolitan Counties, 2011—*Continued*

(Number.)

State/County	Violent crime	Murder and non-negligent man-slaughter	Forcible rape	Robbery	Aggravated assault	Property crime	Burglary	Larceny-theft	Motor vehicle theft	Arson[1]
Yoakum	8	0	1	1	6	25	5	20	0	0
Young	15	0	1	0	14	89	29	58	2	3
Zapata	21	0	1	1	19	264	143	106	15	0
Zavala	27	0	1	2	24	85	39	45	1	3
Utah—Metropolitan Counties										
Cache	21	0	6	2	13	460	71	371	18	0
Davis	17	0	5	1	11	203	42	148	13	1
Juab	3	0	1	0	2	70	12	52	6	0
Morgan	5	2	1	0	2	62	21	41	0	0
Salt Lake County Unified Police Department	495	6	65	116	308	7,922	1,338	5,853	731	37
Summit	25	0	2	4	19	480	57	393	30	1
Tooele	19	0	3	1	15	162	51	93	18	1
Utah	36	0	5	0	31	312	80	219	13	1
Washington	17	0	3	0	14	159	48	97	14	3
Weber	40	1	11	4	24	1,115	275	788	52	0
Utah—Nonmetropolitan Counties										
Beaver	4	0	1	0	3	36	11	18	7	0
Box Elder	4	0	0	1	3	227	48	167	12	0
Carbon	8	1	0	1	6	162	34	125	3	1
Daggett	0	0	0	0	0	18	9	9	0	0
Duchesne	36	1	5	0	30	181	40	133	8	1
Emery	1	0	0	1	0	115	39	71	5	0
Grand	5	0	2	0	3	97	44	46	7	0
Iron	38	0	4	1	33	233	84	117	32	0
Millard	18	0	3	0	15	233	42	184	7	1
Rich	3	0	0	0	3	40	7	31	2	0
Sevier	12	1	4	0	7	177	30	141	6	0
Uintah	43	1	1	1	40	265	90	162	13	1
Wasatch	12	0	1	0	11	165	39	119	7	0
Wayne	0	0	0	0	0	33	4	29	0	0
Vermont—Metropolitan Counties										
Franklin	6	0	1	0	5	127	29	89	9	0
Grand Isle	4	0	0	0	4	48	20	25	3	0
Vermont—Nonmetropolitan Counties										
Addison	0	0	0	0	0	0	0	0	0	0
Bennington	0	0	0	0	0	17	10	6	1	0
Caledonia	0	0	0	0	0	0	0	0	0	0
Lamoille	9	0	2	0	7	136	29	102	5	0
Orange	4	0	3	0	1	47	20	24	3	0
Orleans	0	0	0	0	0	57	24	32	1	0
Rutland	3	0	0	0	3	140	17	122	1	0
Washington	0	0	0	0	0	0	0	0	0	0
Virginia—Metropolitan Counties										
Albemarle County Police Department	106	1	21	22	62	1,653	227	1,375	51	12
Amelia	17	0	1	1	15	133	35	81	17	2
Amherst	28	0	7	2	19	525	63	441	21	2
Appomattox	13	1	2	1	9	127	27	94	6	1
Arlington County Police Department	325	0	23	135	167	3,739	251	3,310	178	7
Bedford	43	1	8	4	30	834	278	520	36	2
Botetourt	23	0	2	3	18	286	60	213	13	4
Campbell	49	1	6	7	35	797	147	607	43	2
Caroline	37	0	8	10	19	497	75	403	19	4
Charles City	5	0	1	0	4	17	9	6	2	0
Chesterfield County Police Department	385	8	36	145	196	6,697	1,535	4,925	237	59
Clarke	9	0	4	2	3	141	34	100	7	1
Craig	5	0	0	0	5	10	0	8	2	0
Cumberland	9	0	1	0	8	34	12	19	3	0
Dinwiddie	43	1	7	6	29	431	131	268	32	1
Fairfax County Police Department	909	11	94	421	383	14,775	1,007	12,898	870	73
Fauquier	38	1	11	7	19	684	114	535	35	4
Fluvanna	13	0	2	2	9	214	38	156	20	2
Franklin	39	2	4	5	28	632	118	466	48	1
Frederick	76	2	33	13	28	1,513	337	1,088	88	5
Giles	24	1	1	0	22	176	42	126	8	1
Gloucester	35	8	3	7	17	522	76	421	25	4
Goochland	32	0	0	3	29	206	46	147	13	0

NA = Not available.

Note: The data shown in this table do not reflect county totals but are the number of offenses reported by the sheriff's office or county police department.

[1] If a blank is presented in the arson column, it indicates that the FBI did not receive 12 complete months of arson data for that agency.

Table II-10. Offenses Known to Law Enforcement, by Selected State Metropolitan and Nonmetropolitan Counties, 2011—*Continued*

(Number.)

State/County	Violent crime	Murder and non-negligent man-slaughter	Forcible rape	Robbery	Aggravated assault	Property crime	Burglary	Larceny-theft	Motor vehicle theft	Arson[1]
Greene	26	3	2	2	19	252	24	216	12	2
Hanover	53	2	2	6	43	1,112	124	925	63	2
Henrico County Police Department	428	10	31	232	155	7,634	1,276	5,986	372	94
Isle of Wight	30	0	4	6	20	382	97	264	21	2
James City County Police Department	80	2	19	16	43	971	161	786	24	17
King and Queen	10	0	0	0	10	65	27	33	5	0
King William	7	0	2	3	2	102	48	52	2	0
Loudoun	237	1	45	36	155	2,800	269	2,377	154	27
Louisa	28	0	10	0	18	324	63	261	0	0
Mathews	6	0	2	0	4	117	27	80	10	0
Montgomery	32	0	11	1	20	508	144	349	15	6
Nelson	6	1	1	0	4	191	45	133	13	0
New Kent	30	0	5	1	24	253	54	185	14	0
Pittsylvania	44	4	10	8	22	663	242	390	31	4
Powhatan	13	3	3	1	6	240	79	147	14	2
Prince George County Police Department	37	0	6	4	27	450	93	336	21	0
Prince William County Police Department	537	3	45	181	308	6,965	967	5,603	395	27
Pulaski	33	0	5	2	26	733	117	593	23	2
Roanoke County Police Department	98	0	20	12	66	1,252	297	918	37	4
Rockingham	42	1	17	1	23	276	73	196	7	4
Scott	22	1	6	3	12	444	125	297	22	1
Spotsylvania	270	3	42	64	161	2,580	268	2,216	96	10
Stafford	171	2	34	29	106	1,950	205	1,639	106	12
Surry	14	0	1	0	13	53	22	26	5	0
Sussex	9	0	0	3	6	168	40	114	14	1
Warren	19	0	8	2	9	311	37	256	18	2
Washington	32	1	11	3	17	995	217	749	29	7
York	75	3	4	24	44	1,223	149	1,042	32	16
Virginia—Nonmetropolitan Counties										
Accomack	58	6	11	16	25	563	145	391	27	1
Alleghany	15	1	4	1	9	158	47	103	8	3
Augusta	86	2	13	7	64	817	124	653	40	1
Bland	5	0	1	1	3	49	15	32	2	2
Brunswick	12	1	0	3	8	145	60	65	20	1
Buchanan	27	3	6	1	17	488	131	325	32	0
Buckingham	23	0	5	5	13	238	57	158	23	12
Carroll	28	0	4	2	22	552	165	349	38	6
Charlotte	21	1	1	3	16	121	28	89	4	1
Culpeper	35	2	6	3	24	295	65	199	31	1
Dickenson	16	2	3	2	9	193	37	150	6	8
Essex	13	1	2	1	9	77	34	36	7	1
Floyd	10	0	2	0	8	185	38	139	8	0
Grayson	18	0	5	0	13	171	35	128	8	2
Greensville	16	1	5	3	7	167	53	107	7	0
Halifax	32	1	7	4	20	430	127	272	31	4
Henry	168	7	9	21	131	1,538	423	1,039	76	7
King George	22	0	8	4	10	335	65	247	23	2
Lancaster	11	1	5	0	5	120	33	84	3	1
Lee	32	1	4	1	26	198	37	156	5	0
Lunenburg	9	0	3	1	5	118	40	66	12	1
Madison	15	3	1	2	9	119	19	93	7	1
Mecklenburg	25	0	4	3	18	367	101	250	16	7
Middlesex	12	1	1	4	6	161	36	116	9	0
Northampton	15	0	1	3	11	187	59	121	7	0
Northumberland	9	0	2	2	5	146	39	99	8	2
Nottoway	7	0	0	1	6	88	20	63	5	3
Orange	15	0	3	2	10	232	39	183	10	1
Page	12	0	5	1	6	199	58	138	3	7
Patrick	22	0	2	0	20	361	84	247	30	2
Prince Edward	12	0	2	2	8	62	18	37	7	1
Rappahannock	4	0	0	0	4	76	18	52	6	2
Richmond	10	0	2	0	8	35	10	20	5	0
Rockbridge	23	0	2	3	18	268	49	209	10	2
Russell	21	3	1	2	15	352	136	205	11	7
Shenandoah	28	0	4	3	21	418	106	308	4	0
Smyth	40	3	5	0	32	352	62	271	19	5
Southampton	19	0	2	1	16	282	81	176	25	4
Tazewell	26	0	6	1	19	575	177	359	39	5
Westmoreland	10	0	1	1	8	74	14	53	7	0
Wise	37	0	8	2	27	446	121	293	32	3
Wythe	19	0	4	2	13	174	30	134	10	2

NA = Not available.

Note: The data shown in this table do not reflect county totals but are the number of offenses reported by the sheriff's office or county police department.

[1] If a blank is presented in the arson column, it indicates that the FBI did not receive 12 complete months of arson data for that agency.

Table II-10.   Offenses Known to Law Enforcement, by Selected State Metropolitan and Nonmetropolitan Counties, 2011—*Continued*

(Number.)

State/County	Violent crime	Murder and non-negligent man-slaughter	Forcible rape	Robbery	Aggravated assault	Property crime	Burglary	Larceny-theft	Motor vehicle theft	Arson[1]
Washington—Metropolitan Counties										
Asotin	18	0	0	0	18	215	45	160	10	0
Benton	64	0	10	8	46	645	231	350	64	6
Chelan	36	3	8	3	22	667	189	432	46	2
Clark	248	2	48	65	133	3,853	924	2,525	404	27
Cowlitz	78	1	36	4	37	501	189	275	37	11
Douglas	22	1	7	1	13	399	131	239	29	0
Franklin	24	0	4	2	18	168	53	102	13	3
King	430	5	85	127	213	5,573	2,200	2,749	624	82
Kitsap	441	2	64	52	323	4,000	1,312	2,387	301	13
Pierce	919	10	88	218	603	9,585	3,132	5,341	1,112	48
Skamania	10	0	2	0	8	214	52	151	11	0
Spokane	132	3	16	30	83	3,912	1,189	2,439	284	16
Thurston	294	3	32	24	235	2,726	1,086	1,502	138	18
Whatcom	132	0	38	7	87	1,339	485	789	65	12
Yakima	133	7	27	25	74	2,290	999	995	296	31
Washington—Nonmetropolitan Counties										
Clallam	59	0	8	3	48	850	255	534	61	7
Columbia	7	0	1	0	6	179	42	132	5	0
Ferry	2	0	0	0	2	25	12	12	1	0
Garfield	4	0	1	0	3	62	13	47	2	1
Grant	111	3	7	10	91	1,472	484	868	120	6
Grays Harbor	24	2	3	2	17	434	158	240	36	2
Island	43	1	13	3	26	773	331	426	16	5
Jefferson	22	0	12	1	9	360	109	236	15	1
Kittitas	20	1	5	2	12	448	158	266	24	1
Lewis	58	0	7	1	50	631	237	351	43	2
Lincoln	8	0	1	1	6	135	43	85	7	2
Mason	101	0	17	5	79	1,734	665	900	169	4
Okanogan	55	2	4	4	45	308	103	181	24	0
Pacific	13	1	6	1	5	333	163	154	16	1
Pend Oreille	17	0	1	0	16	411	133	252	26	0
San Juan	19	1	1	0	17	177	51	112	14	4
Stevens	26	2	5	2	17	575	226	294	55	0
Wahkiakum	6	0	0	0	6	12	3	9	0	1
Walla Walla	25	0	8	2	15	365	90	251	24	3
Whitman	8	0	0	0	8	58	28	28	2	0
West Virginia—Metropolitan Counties										
Berkeley	68	4	13	13	38	877	283	554	40	7
Boone	21	0	1	1	19	47	18	20	9	0
Brooke	18	0	4	2	12	83	36	41	6	3
Hampshire	73	1	0	0	72	74	43	27	4	2
Mineral	49	1	1	2	45	38	14	23	1	0
Morgan	10	2	1	2	5	119	51	60	8	1
Preston	54	0	3	1	50	247	127	110	10	1
Putnam	49	1	5	2	41	210	57	143	10	0
West Virginia—Nonmetropolitan Counties										
Barbour	3	0	0	0	3	10	5	5	0	0
Braxton	13	0	0	1	12	54	12	38	4	1
Grant	4	0	0	0	4	16	7	9	0	2
Hardy	7	0	0	0	7	35	15	15	5	0
Harrison	35	3	0	3	29	347	140	190	17	2
Jackson	5	0	0	0	5	36	3	27	6	0
Lewis	5	0	0	0	5	3	2	1	0	0
Logan	54	0	1	0	53	23	10	10	3	1
Mason	4	0	1	0	3	164	0	144	20	0
McDowell	24	1	2	2	19	113	43	63	7	4
Mingo	7	0	0	0	7	7	2	4	1	0
Monroe	7	0	0	1	6	68	16	49	3	0
Nicholas	167	0	3	2	162	209	46	153	10	5
Randolph	44	1	0	0	43	43	15	28	0	1
Ritchie	5	3	0	0	2	65	30	31	4	2
Roane	8	0	0	0	8	49	1	41	7	0
Tyler	16	0	0	0	16	53	21	30	2	1
Upshur	2	1	0	0	1	50	16	34	0	3
Wetzel	2	0	0	0	2	15	8	7	0	0

NA = Not available.

Note: The data shown in this table do not reflect county totals but are the number of offenses reported by the sheriff's office or county police department.

[1] If a blank is presented in the arson column, it indicates that the FBI did not receive 12 complete months of arson data for that agency.

Table II-10. Offenses Known to Law Enforcement, by Selected State Metropolitan and Nonmetropolitan Counties, 2011—*Continued*

(Number.)

State/County	Violent crime	Murder and non-negligent man-slaughter	Forcible rape	Robbery	Aggravated assault	Property crime	Burglary	Larceny-theft	Motor vehicle theft	Arson[1]
Wisconsin—Metropolitan Counties										
Calumet	12	1	1	0	10	156	46	100	10	0
Chippewa	27	0	5	2	20	382	154	219	9	0
Columbia	41	1	7	0	33	426	138	269	19	1
Dane	64	0	6	10	48	1,031	222	760	49	5
Douglas	12	0	6	1	5	381	194	159	28	1
Eau Claire	22	0	7	1	14	257	87	162	8	1
Fond du Lac	18	0	4	2	12	314	96	197	21	2
Kenosha	23	0	7	2	14	805	205	569	31	2
Kewaunee	1	0	0	0	1	65	11	47	7	0
La Crosse	19	0	0	1	18	222	79	136	7	0
Marathon	19	0	4	3	12	481	107	361	13	1
Oconto	3	0	1	2	0	453	154	269	30	0
Outagamie	20	1	5	1	13	422	122	286	14	2
Pierce	38	0	0	0	38	212	62	138	12	0
Racine	14	2	3	2	7	569	86	459	24	0
Rock	24	1	5	3	15	609	250	342	17	6
Sheboygan	11	0	0	2	9	538	108	406	24	3
St. Croix	19	1	0	2	16	474	72	360	42	0
Washington	88	0	7	5	76	507	123	367	17	3
Waukesha	30	1	6	1	22	732	134	557	41	2
Winnebago	28	1	0	0	27	343	99	229	15	4
Wisconsin—Nonmetropolitan Counties										
Adams	15	0	5	1	9	470	207	259	4	0
Ashland	8	0	0	0	8	80	25	51	4	0
Barron	1	0	0	0	1	199	83	110	6	0
Bayfield	11	0	1	3	7	185	61	120	4	0
Buffalo	0	0	0	0	0	22	10	12	0	0
Burnett	25	0	5	0	20	243	116	113	14	2
Clark	77	0	0	2	75	201	72	111	18	3
Crawford	6	0	2	0	4	200	46	145	9	0
Dodge	14	0	1	0	13	223	67	148	8	2
Door	2	0	0	0	2	113	23	89	1	0
Dunn	25	0	2	1	22	171	51	115	5	0
Florence	7	0	1	0	6	88	34	51	3	1
Forest	7	1	1	1	4	217	74	127	16	0
Grant	24	0	0	0	24	331	103	214	14	6
Green	7	0	0	0	7	169	46	120	3	0
Green Lake	1	0	1	0	0	98	40	53	5	0
Iron	3	0	0	0	3	70	20	47	3	0
Jackson	8	0	5	0	3	201	67	104	30	2
Jefferson	36	2	7	7	20	415	109	298	8	8
Juneau	23	0	1	0	22	332	101	214	17	1
Lafayette	1	0	1	0	0	177	31	140	6	0
Langlade	3	0	0	0	3	230	86	137	7	0
Lincoln	11	0	1	0	10	157	51	100	6	0
Manitowoc	21	0	5	0	16	193	47	133	13	0
Marinette	13	0	8	1	4	479	297	172	10	1
Marquette	4	0	3	0	1	164	34	122	8	0
Menominee	1	0	0	0	1	41	21	19	1	0
Monroe	9	0	0	1	8	220	80	127	13	1
Oneida	20	0	3	1	16	225	99	121	5	1
Pepin	4	0	0	0	4	20	11	7	2	0
Polk	85	0	5	4	76	366	128	207	31	1
Portage	14	1	1	0	12	305	77	202	26	1
Price	11	0	0	0	11	105	32	65	8	0
Richland	2	0	0	0	2	61	29	23	9	0
Rusk	23	0	0	1	22	112	31	75	6	2
Sauk	21	0	3	1	17	507	70	423	14	0
Sawyer	39	1	3	0	35	410	154	227	29	1
Shawano	16	0	3	1	12	423	187	219	17	0
Taylor	7	0	3	0	4	142	41	94	7	4
Trempealeau	2	0	1	0	1	155	51	97	7	0
Vernon	6	2	1	0	3	182	71	103	8	1
Vilas	13	0	3	0	10	199	65	123	11	0
Walworth	12	0	3	4	5	314	102	202	10	1
Washburn	9	1	0	0	8	215	68	140	7	1
Waupaca	21	0	8	0	13	547	137	380	30	0
Waushara	23	0	6	0	17	290	78	200	12	1
Wood	4	0	1	0	3	182	55	118	9	2

NA = Not available.

Note: The data shown in this table do not reflect county totals but are the number of offenses reported by the sheriff's office or county police department.

[1] If a blank is presented in the arson column, it indicates that the FBI did not receive 12 complete months of arson data for that agency.

Table II-10. Offenses Known to Law Enforcement, by Selected State Metropolitan and Nonmetropolitan Counties, 2011—*Continued*

(Number.)

State/County	Violent crime	Murder and non-negligent man-slaughter	Forcible rape	Robbery	Aggravated assault	Property crime	Burglary	Larceny-theft	Motor vehicle theft	Arson[1]
Wyoming—Metropolitan Counties										
Laramie	69	0	13	5	51	471	132	307	32	2
Natrona	43	0	6	1	36	223	51	156	16	3
Wyoming—Nonmetropolitan Counties										
Albany	4	0	0	0	4	43	12	30	1	0
Big Horn	4	0	2	0	2	15	12	3	0	0
Campbell	28	0	2	0	26	179	47	119	13	0
Carbon	8	0	0	0	8	76	7	64	5	0
Converse	12	0	1	0	11	46	9	30	7	0
Crook	1	0	0	0	1	28	3	24	1	0
Fremont	17	2	2	0	13	151	42	94	15	1
Goshen	8	0	1	1	6	59	16	41	2	1
Hot Springs	1	0	0	0	1	28	3	24	1	0
Johnson	3	0	0	0	3	30	8	22	0	0
Lincoln	13	0	3	0	10	84	15	66	3	0
Niobrara	1	0	0	0	1	7	0	7	0	0
Park	29	0	2	0	27	68	20	45	3	0
Platte	2	0	0	0	2	32	13	19	0	0
Sheridan	1	0	0	0	1	61	10	47	4	3
Sublette	10	0	1	0	9	151	29	116	6	0
Sweetwater	14	0	0	1	13	166	33	118	15	0
Uinta	0	0	0	0	0	88	6	78	4	0
Washakie	2	0	0	0	2	3	0	3	0	0
Weston	2	0	0	0	2	6	2	4	0	0

NA = Not available.

Note: The data shown in this table do not reflect county totals but are the number of offenses reported by the sheriff's office or county police department.

[1] If a blank is presented in the arson column, it indicates that the FBI did not receive 12 complete months of arson data for that agency.

Table II-11.   Offenses Known to Law Enforcement, by Selected State, Tribal, and Other Agencies, 2011

(Number.)

State/Agency Type	Unit/Office	Violent crime	Murder and non-negligent man-slaughter	Forcible rape	Robbery	Aggra-vated assault	Property crime	Burglary	Larceny-theft	Motor vehicle theft	Arson[1]
Alabama, Tribal Agencies											
Poarch Creek Tribal		25	0	0	3	22	285	46	228	11	0
22nd Judicial Circuit Drug Task Force		0	0	0	0	0	2	0	2	0	0
Alabama, Other Agencies[2]											
24th Judicial Circuit Drug and Violent Crime Task Force		0	0	0	0	0	6	2	3	1	0
Alaska, State Agencies											
Alcohol Beverage Control Board		0	0	0	0	0	0	0	0	0	0
Alaska, Tribal Agencies											
Metlakatla Tribal		1	0	0	0	1	0	0	0	0	0
Alaska, Other Agencies											
Anchorage International Airport		2	0	0	1	1	97	0	96	1	0
Fairbanks International Airport		2	0	0	0	2	13	0	11	2	1
Arizona, State Agencies											
Arizona Department of Public Safety		94	0	0	2	92	27	0	26	1	0
Arizona, Tribal Agencies											
Ak-Chin Tribal		6	0	1	0	5	2	1	1	0	0
Cocopah Tribal		21	0	4	0	17	42	9	29	4	0
Colorado River Agency		30	3	7	0	20	3	2	0	1	0
Colorado River Tribal		11	0	0	0	11	71	38	4	29	19
Fort Apache Agency		89	14	40	2	33	1	0	1	0	8
Fort McDowell Tribal		33	0	0	1	32	44	3	31	10	6
Fort Mojave Tribal		35	0	2	0	33	139	37	94	8	1
Gila River Indian Community		216	4	32	6	174	568	94	332	142	22
Hopi Tribal		128	0	2	0	126	99	3	93	3	0
Hualapai Tribal		142	0	2	1	139	87	42	27	18	5
Kaibab Paiute Tribal		0	0	0	0	0	0	0	0	0	0
Navajo Nation[3]			15		24	388	2,350	870	961	519	339
Pascua Yaqui Tribal		15	1	3	1	10	206	20	139	47	2
Quechan Tribal		10	0	0	0	10	29	8	19	2	1
Salt River Tribal		51	3	6	22	20	559	64	433	62	9
San Carlos Agency		22	10	0	0	12	3	0	2	1	8
San Carlos Apache		103	2	11	0	90	363	82	271	10	114
Tohono O'odham Nation		75	6	19	12	38	238	95	38	105	1
Tonto Apache Tribal		2	0	0	0	2	4	0	2	2	0
Truxton Canon Agency		27	0	1	0	26	26	16	10	0	0
White Mountain Apache Tribal		92	0	27	1	64	409	390	0	19	8
Yavapai-Apache Nation		13	0	0	0	13	31	7	23	1	5
Yavapai-Prescott Tribal		6	0	1	3	2	60	7	50	3	0
Arizona, Other Agencies											
Tucson Airport Authority		0	0	0	0	0	76	5	54	17	0
Arkansas, State Agencies											
State Capitol Police		1	0	1	0	0	13	2	11	0	0
California, State Agencies											
Atascadero State Hospital		60	0	2	0	58	11	0	11	0	0
California State Fair		1	0	0	0	1	41	0	37	4	0
Coalinga State Hospital		45	0	0	0	45	17	1	16	0	0
Department of Parks and Recreation	Angeles	0	0	0	0	0	0	0	0	0	0
	Bay Area	0	0	0	0	0	22	1	21	0	0
	Calaveras County	0	0	0	0	0	2	2	0	0	0
	Capital	0	0	0	0	0	12	3	9	0	0
	Channel Coast	0	0	0	0	0	34	2	31	1	0
	Colorado	0	0	0	0	0	0	0	0	0	0
	Four Rivers District	0	0	0	0	0	8	2	6	0	0
	Gold Fields District	7	0	2	0	5	39	0	37	2	1
	Hollister Hills	0	0	0	0	0	1	1	0	0	0
	Hungry Valley	2	0	0	0	2	2	0	2	0	0
	Inland Empire	1	0	0	0	1	6	1	5	0	0
	Marin County	0	0	0	0	0	0	0	0	0	0
	Mendocino Headquarters	1	0	0	0	1	20	0	20	0	0
	Monterey County	0	0	0	0	0	22	2	20	0	0
	North Coast Redwoods	1	0	0	0	1	19	0	17	2	0
	Northern Buttes	0	0	0	0	0	17	0	17	0	1
	Oceano Dunes	3	0	1	0	2	29	0	26	3	1
	Ocotillo Wells	1	0	0	0	1	1	0	1	0	0
	Orange Coast	0	0	0	0	0	75	17	57	1	0
	Russian River	0	0	0	0	0	11	0	11	0	0
	San Diego Coast	0	0	0	0	0	59	11	46	2	0
	San Joaquin	0	0	0	0	0	5	0	5	0	0

NA = Not available.

[1] If a blank is presented in the arson column, it indicates that the FBI did not receive 12 complete months of arson data for that agency.

[2] Because of changes in the state/local agency's reporting practices, figures are not comparable to previous years' data.

[3] The FBI determined that the agency's data were overreported. Consequently, those data are not included in this table.

Table II-11. **Offenses Known to Law Enforcement, by Selected State, Tribal, and Other Agencies, 2011**—*Continued*

(Number.)

State/Agency Type	Unit/Office	Violent crime	Murder and non-negligent man-slaughter	Forcible rape	Robbery	Aggra-vated assault	Property crime	Burglary	Larceny-theft	Motor vehicle theft	Arson[1]
	San Luis Obispo Coast	1	0	0	0	1	8	1	7	0	0
	Santa Cruz Mountains	0	0	0	0	0	49	0	46	3	0
	Sierra	0	0	0	0	0	17	1	16	0	1
	Silverado	0	0	0	0	0	0	0	0	0	0
	Tehachapi District	1	0	0	0	1	4	1	2	1	0
	Twin Cities	0	0	0	0	0	0	0	0	0	1
Fairview Developmental Center		10	0	0	0	10	8	3	5	0	0
Highway Patrol	Alameda County	1	0	0	0	1	139	1	10	128	0
	Alpine County	0	0	0	0	0	0	0	0	0	0
	Amador County	0	0	0	0	0	32	0	0	32	0
	Butte County	2	0	0	0	2	203	0	36	167	0
	Calaveras County	2	0	0	0	2	120	0	22	98	0
	Colusa County	0	0	0	0	0	21	1	1	19	0
	Contra Costa County	0	0	0	0	0	879	0	25	854	0
	Del Norte County	1	0	0	1	0	48	0	5	43	0
	El Dorado County	0	0	0	0	0	173	0	42	131	0
	Fresno County	3	0	0	0	3	194	2	32	160	0
	Glenn County	1	0	0	0	1	36	0	0	36	0
	Humboldt County	0	0	0	0	0	262	0	47	215	0
	Imperial County	0	0	0	0	0	89	1	10	78	0
	Inyo County	0	0	0	0	0	16	1	5	10	0
	Kern County	0	0	0	0	0	270	0	12	258	0
	Kings County	0	0	0	0	0	46	0	0	46	0
	Lake County	0	0	0	0	0	71	0	12	59	0
	Lassen County	0	0	0	0	0	16	1	8	7	0
	Los Angeles County	28	0	1	4	23	477	12	49	416	0
	Madera County	0	0	0	0	0	271	0	59	212	0
	Marin County	0	0	0	0	0	78	0	12	66	0
	Mariposa County	0	0	0	0	0	23	0	3	20	0
	Mendocino County	1	0	0	0	1	113	0	9	104	0
	Merced County	0	0	0	0	0	511	3	87	421	0
	Modoc County	0	0	0	0	0	2	0	0	2	0
	Mono County	0	0	0	0	0	0	0	0	0	0
	Monterey County	0	0	0	0	0	254	0	26	228	0
	Napa County	0	0	0	0	0	60	0	10	50	0
	Nevada County	0	0	0	0	0	70	0	14	56	0
	Orange County	1	0	0	0	1	19	1	2	16	0
	Placer County	0	0	0	0	0	205	0	56	149	0
	Plumas County	0	0	0	0	0	24	0	6	18	0
	Riverside County	9	0	0	1	8	100	29	4	67	0
	Sacramento County	14	0	1	2	11	3,848	10	801	3,037	1
	San Benito County	0	0	0	0	0	25	0	1	24	0
	San Bernardino County	3	0	0	0	3	40	2	3	35	0
	San Diego County	10	0	0	0	10	150	3	50	97	0
	San Francisco County	0	0	0	0	0	9	0	2	7	0
	San Joaquin County	2	0	0	0	2	739	0	263	476	0
	San Luis Obispo County	0	0	0	0	0	134	0	0	134	0
	San Mateo County	3	0	0	0	3	20	0	11	9	0
	Santa Barbara County	2	0	0	0	2	129	0	35	94	0
	Santa Clara County	1	0	0	0	1	88	0	13	75	0
	Santa Cruz County	0	0	0	0	0	356	0	71	285	0
	Shasta County	2	0	0	0	2	169	0	29	140	0
	Sierra County	0	0	0	0	0	1	0	0	1	0
	Siskiyou County	0	0	0	0	0	41	0	7	34	0
	Solano County	0	0	0	0	0	71	0	5	66	0
	Sonoma County	1	0	0	0	1	211	1	52	158	0
	Stanislaus County	3	0	0	1	2	842	1	35	806	0
	Sutter County	1	0	0	1	0	58	0	5	53	0
	Tehama County	3	0	0	2	1	63	0	7	56	0
	Trinity County	0	0	0	0	0	38	2	2	34	0
	Tulare County	0	0	0	0	0	700	0	91	609	0
	Tuolumne County	1	0	0	0	1	99	0	16	83	0
	Ventura County	1	0	0	0	1	55	0	8	47	0
	Yolo County	0	0	0	0	0	30	0	2	28	0
	Yuba County	0	0	0	0	0	173	0	11	162	0
Lanterman State Hospital		1	0	0	0	1	2	0	2	0	0
Napa State Hospital		119	0	2	1	116	10	1	9	0	0
Patton State Hospital		249	0	3	2	244	16	2	14	0	1
Porterville Developmental Center		5	0	0	1	4	17	3	14	0	0
Sonoma Developmental Center		0	0	0	0	0	6	1	5	0	0

NA = Not available.

[1] If a blank is presented in the arson column, it indicates that the FBI did not receive 12 complete months of arson data for that agency.

Table II-11. Offenses Known to Law Enforcement, by Selected State, Tribal, and Other Agencies, 2011—*Continued*

(Number.)

State/Agency Type	Unit/Office	Violent crime	Murder and non-negligent man-slaughter	Forcible rape	Robbery	Aggra-vated assault	Property crime	Burglary	Larceny-theft	Motor vehicle theft	Arson[1]
California, Tribal Agencies											
Hoopa Valley Tribal................................		163	0	1	5	157	171	61	92	18	38
Tule River Tribal.....................................		37	1	2	1	33	86	9	65	12	7
Yurok Tribal..		36	1	1	1	33	83	34	48	1	1
California, Other Agencies											
East Bay Municipal Utility.......................		0	0	0	0	0	14	0	12	2	0
East Bay Regional Parks..........................	Alameda County	4	1	0	1	2	84	3	79	2	3
	Contra Costa County	12	0	0	10	2	152	2	145	5	1
Fontana Unified School District................		54	0	3	15	36	127	33	89	5	2
Los Angeles County Metropolitan Transportation Authority..........................		8	0	0	0	8	43	0	43	0	0
Los Angeles Transportation Services Bureau...............		502	1	3	261	237	712	13	576	123	5
Monterey Peninsula Airport.....................		0	0	0	0	0	12	1	9	2	0
Port of San Diego Harbor........................		11	0	0	3	8	485	17	468	0	1
San Bernardino Unified School District		90	0	1	81	8	459	217	225	17	12
San Francisco Bay Area Rapid Transit	Alameda County	195	0	1	127	67	1,349	14	1,147	188	4
	Contra Costa County	44	0	0	21	23	692	2	548	142	0
	San Francisco County	68	0	0	37	31	247	3	241	3	0
	San Mateo County	10	0	0	7	3	131	1	112	18	6
Santa Clara Transit District.....................		42	0	1	25	16	101	2	82	17	0
Shasta County Marshal............................		0	0	0	0	0	1	0	1	0	0
Stockton Unified School District		94	0	2	21	71	450	120	327	3	7
Twin Rivers Unified School District		54	0	3	17	34	222	92	122	8	0
Union Pacific Railroad.............................	Alameda County	18	0	0	0	18	113	103	10	0	0
	Amador County	0	0	0	0	0	0	0	0	0	0
	Butte County	0	0	0	0	0	15	3	12	0	0
	Calaveras County	0	0	0	0	0	0	0	0	0	0
	Colusa County	0	0	0	0	0	0	0	0	0	0
	Contra Costa County	8	0	0	0	8	4	1	3	0	0
	El Dorado County	0	0	0	0	0	0	0	0	0	0
	Fresno County	4	0	0	0	4	8	1	7	0	0
	Glenn County	0	0	0	0	0	0	0	0	0	0
	Humboldt County	0	0	0	0	0	0	0	0	0	0
	Imperial County	0	0	0	0	0	8	6	2	0	0
	Inyo County	0	0	0	0	0	0	0	0	0	0
	Kern County	0	0	0	0	0	13	0	13	0	0
	Kings County	0	0	0	0	0	1	0	1	0	0
	Lassen County	0	0	0	0	0	6	0	6	0	0
	Los Angeles County	0	0	0	0	0	195	161	34	0	0
	Madera County	0	0	0	0	0	5	0	5	0	0
	Marin County	0	0	0	0	0	0	0	0	0	0
	Mendocino County	0	0	0	0	0	0	0	0	0	0
	Merced County	0	0	0	0	0	14	0	14	0	0
	Modoc County	0	0	0	0	0	0	0	0	0	0
	Monterey County	0	0	0	0	0	3	0	3	0	0
	Napa County	0	0	0	0	0	0	0	0	0	0
	Nevada County	0	0	0	0	0	0	0	0	0	0
	Orange County	0	0	0	0	0	0	0	0	0	0
	Placer County	2	0	0	0	2	38	9	29	0	0
	Plumas County	0	0	0	0	0	6	0	6	0	0
	Riverside County	4	0	0	0	4	13	6	7	0	0
	Sacramento County	3	0	0	0	3	19	1	18	0	0
	San Benito County	0	0	0	0	0	0	0	0	0	0
	San Bernardino County	0	0	0	0	0	34	13	21	0	0
	San Francisco County	0	0	0	0	0	0	0	0	0	0
	San Joaquin County	8	0	0	0	8	148	129	19	0	0
	San Luis Obispo County	0	0	0	0	0	3	0	3	0	0
	San Mateo County	0	0	0	0	0	2	2	0	0	0
	Santa Barbara County	0	0	0	0	0	2	0	2	0	0
	Santa Clara County	1	0	0	0	1	5	0	5	0	0
	Santa Cruz County	0	0	0	0	0	0	0	0	0	0
	Shasta County	0	0	0	0	0	1	0	1	0	0
	Sierra County	0	0	0	0	0	0	0	0	0	0
	Siskiyou County	0	0	0	0	0	1	0	1	0	0
	Solano County	3	0	0	0	3	12	1	11	0	0
	Sonoma County	0	0	0	0	0	0	0	0	0	0
	Stanislaus County	0	0	0	0	0	4	0	4	0	0
	Sutter County	0	0	0	0	0	3	0	3	0	0
	Tehama County	0	0	0	0	0	1	0	1	0	0
	Trinity County	0	0	0	0	0	0	0	0	0	0
	Tulare County	0	0	0	0	0	1	0	1	0	0
	Ventura County	0	0	0	0	0	2	0	2	0	0
	Yolo County	2	0	0	0	2	8	0	8	0	0
	Yuba County	2	0	0	0	2	5	0	5	0	0

NA = Not available.

[1] If a blank is presented in the arson column, it indicates that the FBI did not receive 12 complete months of arson data for that agency.

Table II-11. Offenses Known to Law Enforcement, by Selected State, Tribal, and Other Agencies, 2011—*Continued*

(Number.)

State/Agency Type	Unit/Office	Violent crime	Murder and non-negligent man-slaughter	Forcible rape	Robbery	Aggra-vated assault	Property crime	Burglary	Larceny-theft	Motor vehicle theft	Arson[1]
Colorado, State Agencies											
Colorado Mental Health Institute..................................		0	0	0	0	0	10	0	10	0	0
Colorado State Patrol		19	0	0	0	19	21	0	6	15	0
Colorado, Tribal Agencies											
Southern Ute Tribal		28	0	5	2	21	16	8	3	5	0
Ute Mountain Tribal		15	0	4	1	10	1	1	0	0	1
Colorado, Other Agencies											
22nd Judicial District Drug Task Force.........................		0	0	0	0	0	0	0	0	0	0
Delta Montrose Drug Task Force..................................		0	0	0	0	0	0	0	0	0	0
Southwest Drug Task Force		0	0	0	0	0	0	0	0	0	0
Connecticut, State Agencies											
Connecticut State Police...		315	4	48	51	212	4,447	1,416	2,783	248	64
State Capitol Police		0	0	0	0	0	5	0	5	0	0
Connecticut, Tribal Agencies											
Mashantucket Pequot Tribal		3	0	0	0	3	10	2	7	1	0
Mohegan Tribal..		4	0	0	0	4	78	2	75	1	0
Connecticut, Other Agencies											
Metropolitan Transportation Authority.........................		5	0	0	2	3	76	0	76	0	0
Delaware, State Agencies											
Attorney General...	Kent County	0	0	0	0	0	0	0	0	0	0
	New Castle County	0	0	0	0	0	0	0	0	0	0
	Sussex County	0	0	0	0	0	0	0	0	0	0
Division of Alcohol and Tobacco Enforcement............		0	0	0	0	0	0	0	0	0	0
Environmental Control		0	0	0	0	0	4	0	4	0	0
Fish and Wildlife		4	0	0	0	4	19	2	17	0	0
Park Rangers		5	0	0	0	5	69	10	59	0	1
River and Bay Authority		1	0	0	0	1	9	2	5	2	0
State Capitol Police		1	0	0	0	1	21	0	19	2	0
State Fire Marshal		18	0	0	0	18	31	29	2	0	233
State Police...	Kent County	514	2	59	84	369	2,418	762	1,567	89	1
	New Castle County	586	1	28	280	277	5,500	590	4,724	186	3
	Sussex County	626	4	46	101	475	4,513	1,671	2,661	181	4
Delaware, Other Agencies											
Amtrak Police..		0	0	0	0	0	3	1	2	0	0
Drug Enforcement Administration...............................	Wilmington Resident Office	0	0	0	0	0	0	0	0	0	0
Wilmington Fire Department		3	0	0	0	3	2	2	0	0	14
District of Columbia, Other Agencies											
Metro Transit Police..		444	0	1	337	106	1,324	1	1,206	117	0
Florida, State Agencies											
Capitol Police..		0	0	0	0	0	7	1	6	0	0
Department of Corrections, Office of the Inspector General..	Baker County	0	0	0	0	0	0	0	0	0	0
	Bradford County	0	0	0	0	0	0	0	0	0	0
	Calhoun County	0	0	0	0	0	0	0	0	0	0
	Franklin County	0	0	0	0	0	0	0	0	0	0
	Hamilton County	0	0	0	0	0	0	0	0	0	0
	Jefferson County	0	0	0	0	0	0	0	0	0	0
	Lake County	0	0	0	0	0	0	0	0	0	0
	Madison County	0	0	0	0	0	0	0	0	0	0
	Marion County	0	0	0	0	0	0	0	0	0	0
	Okeechobee County	0	0	0	0	0	0	0	0	0	0
	Polk County	0	0	0	0	0	0	0	0	0	0
	Santa Rosa County	0	0	0	0	0	0	0	0	0	0
	Sumter County	0	0	0	0	0	0	0	0	0	0
	Taylor County	0	0	0	0	0	0	0	0	0	0
	Walulla County	0	0	0	0	0	0	0	0	0	0
	Washington County	0	0	0	0	0	0	0	0	0	0
Department of Environmental Protection, Division of Law Enforcement.......................................	Alachua County	0	0	0	0	0	2	2	0	0	0
	Bay County	1	0	0	0	1	8	0	8	0	0
	Brevard County	1	0	0	0	1	7	4	3	0	1
	Broward County	0	0	0	0	0	23	2	21	0	0
	Charlotte County	0	0	0	0	0	1	0	1	0	0
	Citrus County	0	0	0	0	0	0	0	0	0	0
	Collier County	0	0	0	0	0	0	0	0	0	0
	Columbia County	0	0	0	0	0	3	1	1	1	0
	DeSoto County	0	0	0	0	0	0	0	0	0	0
	Duval County	0	0	0	0	0	1	0	1	0	0
	Escambia County	0	0	0	0	0	1	0	1	0	0

NA = Not available.

[1] If a blank is presented in the arson column, it indicates that the FBI did not receive 12 complete months of arson data for that agency.

Table II-11.   Offenses Known to Law Enforcement, by Selected State, Tribal, and Other Agencies, 2011—*Continued*

(Number.)

State/Agency Type	Unit/Office	Violent crime	Murder and non-negligent man-slaughter	Forcible rape	Robbery	Aggra-vated assault	Property crime	Burglary	Larceny-theft	Motor vehicle theft	Arson[1]
	Franklin County	0	0	0	0	0	0	0	0	0	0
	Hamilton County	0	0	0	0	0	0	0	0	0	0
	Hendry County	0	0	0	0	0	0	0	0	0	0
	Hernando County	0	0	0	0	0	0	0	0	0	0
	Hillsborough County	0	0	0	0	0	3	0	1	2	0
	Holmes County	0	0	0	0	0	0	0	0	0	0
	Indian River County	0	0	0	0	0	1	0	1	0	0
	Jackson County	0	0	0	0	0	0	0	0	0	0
	Lake County	0	0	0	0	0	1	1	0	0	1
	Lee County	0	0	0	0	0	0	0	0	0	0
	Leon County	0	0	0	0	0	0	0	0	0	0
	Levy County	0	0	0	0	0	10	1	9	0	1
	Liberty County	0	0	0	0	0	0	0	0	0	0
	Manatee County	0	0	0	0	0	4	1	3	0	0
	Marion County	0	0	0	0	0	1	0	1	0	1
	Martin County	0	0	0	0	0	7	0	7	0	0
	Miami-Dade County	0	0	0	0	0	25	2	23	0	0
	Monroe County	0	0	0	0	0	1	0	1	0	0
	Nassau County	0	0	0	0	0	0	0	0	0	1
	Okaloosa County	0	0	0	0	0	5	0	5	0	0
	Okeechobee County	0	0	0	0	0	0	0	0	0	0
	Orange County	0	0	0	0	0	4	2	2	0	1
	Palm Beach County	0	0	0	0	0	4	1	3	0	0
	Pasco County	0	0	0	0	0	0	0	0	0	0
	Pinellas County	0	0	0	0	0	6	4	2	0	0
	Polk County	0	0	0	0	0	0	0	0	0	0
	Putnam County	0	0	0	0	0	1	0	1	0	1
	Santa Rosa County	0	0	0	0	0	2	1	1	0	0
	Sarasota County	0	0	0	0	0	4	1	3	0	0
	Seminole County	0	0	0	0	0	4	0	4	0	1
	St. Johns County	0	0	0	0	0	0	0	0	0	1
	St. Lucie County	0	0	0	0	0	4	0	4	0	0
	Sumter County	0	0	0	0	0	0	0	0	0	0
	Suwannee County	0	0	0	0	0	0	0	0	0	1
	Taylor County	0	0	0	0	0	3	1	2	0	0
	Volusia County	0	0	0	0	0	11	4	7	0	1
	Wakulla County	0	0	0	0	0	2	0	2	0	0
	Walton County	0	0	0	0	0	1	1	0	0	0
	Washington County	0	0	0	0	0	0	0	0	0	0
Department of Insurance	Broward County	0	0	0	0	0	0	0	0	0	0
	Duval County	0	0	0	0	0	0	0	0	0	0
	Escambia County	0	0	0	0	0	0	0	0	0	0
	Hillsborough County	0	0	0	0	0	0	0	0	0	0
	Lee County	0	0	0	0	0	0	0	0	0	0
	Miami-Dade County	0	0	0	0	0	0	0	0	0	0
	Orange County	0	0	0	0	0	0	0	0	0	0
	Palm Beach County	0	0	0	0	0	0	0	0	0	0
	Pinellas County	0	0	0	0	0	0	0	0	0	0
Department of Law Enforcement	Duval County, Jacksonville	0	0	0	0	0	0	0	0	0	0
	Escambia County, Pensacola	0	0	0	0	0	0	0	0	0	0
	Hillsborough County, Tampa	0	0	0	0	0	0	0	0	0	0
	Lee County, Fort Myers	0	0	0	0	0	0	0	0	0	0
	Leon County, Tallahassee	0	0	0	0	0	0	0	0	0	0
	Miami-Dade County, Miami	0	0	0	0	0	0	0	0	0	0
	Orange County, Orlando	2	0	0	0	2	0	0	0	0	0
Division of Alcoholic Beverages and Tobacco..............	Alachua County	0	0	0	0	0	0	0	0	0	0
	Baker County	0	0	0	0	0	0	0	0	0	0
	Bay County	0	0	0	0	0	0	0	0	0	0
	Bradford County	0	0	0	0	0	0	0	0	0	0
	Brevard County	0	0	0	0	0	0	0	0	0	0
	Broward County	0	0	0	0	0	0	0	0	0	0
	Calhoun County	0	0	0	0	0	0	0	0	0	0
	Charlotte County	0	0	0	0	0	0	0	0	0	0
	Citrus County	0	0	0	0	0	0	0	0	0	0
	Clay County	0	0	0	0	0	0	0	0	0	0
	Collier County	0	0	0	0	0	0	0	0	0	0
	Columbia County	0	0	0	0	0	0	0	0	0	0
	DeSoto County	0	0	0	0	0	0	0	0	0	0

NA = Not available.

[1] If a blank is presented in the arson column, it indicates that the FBI did not receive 12 complete months of arson data for that agency.

Table II-11.   Offenses Known to Law Enforcement, by Selected State, Tribal, and Other Agencies, 2011—*Continued*

(Number.)

State/Agency Type	Unit/Office	Violent crime	Murder and non-negligent man-slaughter	Forcible rape	Robbery	Aggra-vated assault	Property crime	Burglary	Larceny-theft	Motor vehicle theft	Arson[1]
	Dixie County	0	0	0	0	0	0	0	0	0	0
	Duval County	0	0	0	0	0	0	0	0	0	0
	Escambia County	0	0	0	0	0	0	0	0	0	0
	Franklin County	0	0	0	0	0	0	0	0	0	0
	Gadsden County	0	0	0	0	0	0	0	0	0	0
	Gilchrist County	0	0	0	0	0	0	0	0	0	0
	Gulf County	0	0	0	0	0	0	0	0	0	0
	Hamilton County	0	0	0	0	0	0	0	0	0	0
	Hardee County	0	0	0	0	0	0	0	0	0	0
	Hendry County	0	0	0	0	0	0	0	0	0	0
	Hernando County	0	0	0	0	0	0	0	0	0	0
	Highlands County	0	0	0	0	0	0	0	0	0	0
	Hillsborough County	0	0	0	0	0	0	0	0	0	0
	Holmes County	0	0	0	0	0	0	0	0	0	0
	Indian River County	0	0	0	0	0	0	0	0	0	0
	Jackson County	0	0	0	0	0	0	0	0	0	0
	Jefferson County	0	0	0	0	0	0	0	0	0	0
	Lafayette County	0	0	0	0	0	0	0	0	0	0
	Lake County	0	0	0	0	0	0	0	0	0	0
	Lee County	0	0	0	0	0	0	0	0	0	0
	Leon County	0	0	0	0	0	0	0	0	0	0
	Levy County	0	0	0	0	0	0	0	0	0	0
	Liberty County	0	0	0	0	0	0	0	0	0	0
	Madison County	0	0	0	0	0	0	0	0	0	0
	Manatee County	0	0	0	0	0	0	0	0	0	0
	Marion County	0	0	0	0	0	0	0	0	0	0
	Martin County	0	0	0	0	0	0	0	0	0	0
	Miami-Dade County	0	0	0	0	0	0	0	0	0	0
	Monroe County	0	0	0	0	0	0	0	0	0	0
	Nassau County	0	0	0	0	0	0	0	0	0	0
	Okaloosa County	0	0	0	0	0	0	0	0	0	0
	Orange County	0	0	0	0	0	0	0	0	0	0
	Osceola County	0	0	0	0	0	0	0	0	0	0
	Palm Beach County	0	0	0	0	0	0	0	0	0	0
	Pasco County	0	0	0	0	0	0	0	0	0	0
	Pinellas County	0	0	0	0	0	0	0	0	0	0
	Polk County	0	0	0	0	0	0	0	0	0	0
	Putnam County	0	0	0	0	0	0	0	0	0	0
	Santa Rosa County	0	0	0	0	0	0	0	0	0	0
	Sarasota County	0	0	0	0	0	0	0	0	0	0
	Seminole County	0	0	0	0	0	0	0	0	0	0
	St. Johns County	0	0	0	0	0	0	0	0	0	0
	St. Lucie County	0	0	0	0	0	0	0	0	0	0
	Sumter County	0	0	0	0	0	0	0	0	0	0
	Suwannee County	0	0	0	0	0	0	0	0	0	0
	Taylor County	0	0	0	0	0	0	0	0	0	0
	Volusia County	0	0	0	0	0	0	0	0	0	0
	Wakulla County	0	0	0	0	0	0	0	0	0	0
	Walton County	0	0	0	0	0	0	0	0	0	0
	Washington County	0	0	0	0	0	0	0	0	0	0
Florida Game Commission	Alachua County	0	0	0	0	0	0	0	0	0	0
	Baker County	0	0	0	0	0	0	0	0	0	0
	Bay County	0	0	0	0	0	0	0	0	0	0
	Bradford County	0	0	0	0	0	0	0	0	0	0
	Brevard County	0	0	0	0	0	0	0	0	0	0
	Broward County	0	0	0	0	0	0	0	0	0	0
	Calhoun County	0	0	0	0	0	0	0	0	0	0
	Charlotte County	0	0	0	0	0	0	0	0	0	0
	Citrus County	0	0	0	0	0	0	0	0	0	0
	Clay County	0	0	0	0	0	0	0	0	0	0
	Collier County	0	0	0	0	0	0	0	0	0	0
	Columbia County	0	0	0	0	0	0	0	0	0	0
	DeSoto County	0	0	0	0	0	0	0	0	0	0
	Dixie County	0	0	0	0	0	0	0	0	0	0
	Duval County	0	0	0	0	0	0	0	0	0	0
	Escambia County	0	0	0	0	0	0	0	0	0	0
	Flagler County	0	0	0	0	0	0	0	0	0	0
	Franklin County	0	0	0	0	0	0	0	0	0	0
	Gadsden County	0	0	0	0	0	0	0	0	0	0
	Gilchrist County	0	0	0	0	0	0	0	0	0	0
	Glades County	0	0	0	0	0	0	0	0	0	0
	Gulf County	0	0	0	0	0	0	0	0	0	0
	Hamilton County	0	0	0	0	0	0	0	0	0	0
	Hardee County	0	0	0	0	0	0	0	0	0	0

NA = Not available.

[1] If a blank is presented in the arson column, it indicates that the FBI did not receive 12 complete months of arson data for that agency.

Table II-11.   Offenses Known to Law Enforcement, by Selected State, Tribal, and Other Agencies, 2011—*Continued*

(Number.)

State/Agency Type	Unit/Office	Violent crime	Murder and non-negligent man-slaughter	Forcible rape	Robbery	Aggra-vated assault	Property crime	Burglary	Larceny-theft	Motor vehicle theft	Arson[1]
	Hendry County	0	0	0	0	0	0	0	0	0	0
	Hernando County	0	0	0	0	0	0	0	0	0	0
	Highlands County	0	0	0	0	0	0	0	0	0	0
	Hillsborough County	0	0	0	0	0	0	0	0	0	0
	Holmes County	0	0	0	0	0	0	0	0	0	0
	Indian River County	0	0	0	0	0	0	0	0	0	0
	Jackson County	0	0	0	0	0	0	0	0	0	0
	Jefferson County	0	0	0	0	0	0	0	0	0	0
	Lafayette County	0	0	0	0	0	0	0	0	0	0
	Lake County	0	0	0	0	0	0	0	0	0	0
	Lee County	0	0	0	0	0	0	0	0	0	0
	Leon County	0	0	0	0	0	0	0	0	0	0
	Levy County	0	0	0	0	0	0	0	0	0	0
	Liberty County	0	0	0	0	0	0	0	0	0	0
	Madison County	0	0	0	0	0	0	0	0	0	0
	Manatee County	0	0	0	0	0	0	0	0	0	0
	Marion County	0	0	0	0	0	0	0	0	0	0
	Martin County	0	0	0	0	0	0	0	0	0	0
	Miami-Dade County	0	0	0	0	0	0	0	0	0	0
	Monroe County	0	0	0	0	0	0	0	0	0	0
	Nassau County	0	0	0	0	0	0	0	0	0	0
	Okaloosa County	0	0	0	0	0	0	0	0	0	0
	Okeechobee County	0	0	0	0	0	0	0	0	0	0
	Orange County	0	0	0	0	0	0	0	0	0	0
	Osceola County	0	0	0	0	0	0	0	0	0	0
	Palm Beach County	0	0	0	0	0	0	0	0	0	0
	Pasco County	0	0	0	0	0	0	0	0	0	0
	Pinellas County	0	0	0	0	0	0	0	0	0	0
	Polk County	0	0	0	0	0	0	0	0	0	0
	Putnam County	0	0	0	0	0	0	0	0	0	0
	Santa Rosa County	0	0	0	0	0	0	0	0	0	0
	Sarasota County	0	0	0	0	0	0	0	0	0	0
	Seminole County	0	0	0	0	0	0	0	0	0	0
	St. Johns County	0	0	0	0	0	0	0	0	0	0
	St. Lucie County	0	0	0	0	0	0	0	0	0	0
	Sumter County	0	0	0	0	0	0	0	0	0	0
	Suwannee County	0	0	0	0	0	0	0	0	0	0
	Taylor County	0	0	0	0	0	0	0	0	0	0
	Union County	0	0	0	0	0	0	0	0	0	0
	Volusia County	0	0	0	0	0	0	0	0	0	0
	Wakulla County	0	0	0	0	0	0	0	0	0	0
	Walton County	0	0	0	0	0	0	0	0	0	0
	Washington County	0	0	0	0	0	0	0	0	0	0
Highway Patrol	Alachua County	3	0	0	0	3	3	0	1	2	0
	Baker County	0	0	0	0	0	1	0	1	0	0
	Bay County	0	0	0	0	0	0	0	0	0	0
	Bradford County	0	0	0	0	0	0	0	0	0	0
	Brevard County	0	0	0	0	0	0	0	0	0	0
	Broward County	11	0	0	2	9	9	0	9	0	0
	Calhoun County	1	0	0	0	1	2	0	0	2	0
	Charlotte County	0	0	0	0	0	0	0	0	0	0
	Citrus County	0	0	0	0	0	0	0	0	0	0
	Clay County	0	0	0	0	0	6	0	0	6	0
	Collier County	7	0	0	0	7	10	0	7	3	0
	Columbia County	5	0	0	0	5	5	1	2	2	0
	DeSoto County	0	0	0	0	0	0	0	0	0	0
	Dixie County	0	0	0	0	0	0	0	0	0	0
	Duval County	2	0	0	0	2	0	0	0	0	0
	Escambia County	2	0	0	0	2	0	0	0	0	0
	Flagler County	0	0	0	0	0	0	0	0	0	0
	Franklin County	0	0	0	0	0	0	0	0	0	0
	Gadsden County	0	0	0	0	0	1	0	0	1	0
	Gilchrist County	0	0	0	0	0	1	0	0	1	0
	Glades County	0	0	0	0	0	0	0	0	0	0
	Gulf County	0	0	0	0	0	0	0	0	0	0
	Hamilton County	1	0	0	0	1	2	0	0	2	0
	Hardee County	0	0	0	0	0	0	0	0	0	0
	Hendry County	0	0	0	0	0	1	0	1	0	0
	Hernando County	1	0	0	0	1	0	0	0	0	0
	Highlands County	0	0	0	0	0	1	0	0	1	0
	Hillsborough County	4	0	0	0	4	3	0	2	1	0
	Holmes County	1	0	0	0	1	5	0	3	2	0
	Indian River County	0	0	0	0	0	1	0	1	0	0
	Jackson County	1	0	0	0	1	2	0	0	2	0

NA = Not available.

[1] If a blank is presented in the arson column, it indicates that the FBI did not receive 12 complete months of arson data for that agency.

Table II-11. Offenses Known to Law Enforcement, by Selected State, Tribal, and Other Agencies, 2011—*Continued*

(Number.)

State/Agency Type	Unit/Office	Violent crime	Murder and non-negligent man-slaughter	Forcible rape	Robbery	Aggra-vated assault	Property crime	Burglary	Larceny-theft	Motor vehicle theft	Arson[1]
	Jefferson County	0	0	0	0	0	0	0	0	0	0
	Lafayette County	0	0	0	0	0	0	0	0	0	0
	Lake County	1	0	0	0	1	2	0	0	2	0
	Lee County	1	0	0	0	1	0	0	0	0	0
	Leon County	2	0	0	0	2	18	0	7	11	0
	Levy County	0	0	0	0	0	0	0	0	0	0
	Liberty County	0	0	0	0	0	0	0	0	0	0
	Madison County	1	0	0	0	1	1	0	1	0	0
	Manatee County	0	0	0	0	0	0	0	0	0	0
	Marion County	0	0	0	0	0	0	0	0	0	0
	Martin County	0	0	0	0	0	0	0	0	0	0
	Miami-Dade County	4	0	0	0	4	6	0	3	3	0
	Monroe County	0	0	0	0	0	0	0	0	0	0
	Nassau County	1	0	0	0	1	0	0	0	0	0
	Okaloosa County	0	0	0	0	0	0	0	0	0	0
	Okeechobee County	0	0	0	0	0	0	0	0	0	0
	Orange County	1	0	0	0	1	0	0	0	0	0
	Osceola County	0	0	0	0	0	0	0	0	0	0
	Palm Beach County	7	0	0	0	7	17	0	5	12	0
	Pasco County	0	0	0	0	0	0	0	0	0	0
	Pinellas County	4	0	0	0	4	0	0	0	0	0
	Polk County	0	0	0	0	0	0	0	0	0	0
	Putnam County	0	0	0	0	0	0	0	0	0	0
	Santa Rosa County	2	0	0	0	2	1	0	0	1	0
	Sarasota County	2	0	0	0	2	7	0	4	3	0
	Seminole County	1	0	0	0	1	4	0	1	3	0
	St. Johns County	0	0	0	0	0	0	0	0	0	0
	St. Lucie County	2	0	0	0	2	5	0	2	3	0
	Sumter County	0	0	0	0	0	1	0	1	0	0
	Suwannee County	1	0	0	0	1	1	0	0	1	0
	Taylor County	1	0	0	0	1	1	0	0	1	0
	Union County	1	0	0	0	1	0	0	0	0	0
	Volusia County	0	0	0	0	0	0	0	0	0	0
	Wakulla County	1	0	0	0	1	0	0	0	0	0
	Walton County	5	0	0	0	5	0	0	0	0	0
	Washington County	1	0	0	0	1	4	0	1	3	0
State Treasurer's Office	Division of Insurance Fraud	0	0	0	0	0	0	0	0	0	0
Florida, Tribal Agencies											
Miccosukee Tribal		3	0	0	0	3	106	10	85	11	0
Seminole Tribal..		69	0	4	15	50	848	49	734	65	1
Florida, Other Agencies											
Duval County Schools.....................................		76	0	6	11	59	758	168	585	5	6
Florida School for the Deaf and Blind		0	0	0	0	0	0	0	0	0	0
Fort Lauderdale Airport...................................		10	0	1	2	7	284	0	269	15	0
Jacksonville Aviation Authority...........................		0	0	0	0	0	89	0	50	39	0
Lee County Port Authority		0	0	0	0	0	108	12	90	6	0
Melbourne International Airport..........................		0	0	0	0	0	1	0	1	0	0
Miami-Dade County Public Schools......................		223	0	5	85	133	1,633	563	1,050	20	7
Northwest Florida Beaches International Airport.......		0	0	0	0	0	3	0	3	0	0
Palm Beach County School District......................		94	0	1	11	82	958	101	850	7	3
Port Everglades..		2	0	1	0	1	51	3	48	0	0
Sarasota-Manatee Airport Authority......................		0	0	0	0	0	6	0	6	0	0
St. Petersburg-Clearwater International Airport		0	0	0	0	0	5	1	4	0	0
Tampa International Airport		3	0	0	1	2	163	9	139	15	0
Volusia County Beach Management........................		12	0	0	11	1	172	0	163	9	0
Georgia, State Agencies											
Atlanta State Farmers Market............................		0	0	0	0	0	44	0	34	10	0
Georgia Department of Public Safety		1	0	0	0	1	80	0	80	0	0
Georgia Department of Transportation	Office of Investigations	0	0	0	0	0	7	0	7	0	0
Georgia Forestry Commission............................		0	0	0	0	0	0	0	0	0	100
Georgia World Congress		9	0	1	5	3	200	1	194	5	0
Ports Authority	Savannah	0	0	0	0	0	16	0	16	0	0
Georgia, Other Agencies											
Augusta Board of Education		3	0	0	1	2	0	0	0	0	5
Bibb County Board of Education		27	0	0	3	24	277	15	261	1	1
Chatham County Board of Education....................		8	0	1	3	4	145	22	122	1	0
Cherokee County Board of Education...................		12	0	0	0	12	121	8	113	0	0
Cobb County Board of Education		35	0	2	6	27	447	33	412	2	2
Decatur County Schools...................................		5	0	0	0	5	0	0	0	0	0
DeKalb County School System		84	0	3	16	65	575	114	441	20	0
Dougherty County Board of Education..................		4	0	0	2	2	41	7	33	1	0

NA = Not available.

[1] If a blank is presented in the arson column, it indicates that the FBI did not receive 12 complete months of arson data for that agency.

Table II-11.   Offenses Known to Law Enforcement, by Selected State, Tribal, and Other Agencies, 2011—*Continued*

(Number.)

State/Agency Type	Unit/Office	Violent crime	Murder and non-negligent man-slaughter	Forcible rape	Robbery	Aggravated assault	Property crime	Burglary	Larceny-theft	Motor vehicle theft	Arson[1]
Fayette County Marshal		0	0	0	0	0	0	0	0	0	0
Forsyth County Fire Investigation Unit		0	0	0	0	0	0	0	0	0	2
Fulton County Marshal		0	0	0	0	0	9	5	4	0	0
Fulton County School System		29	0	13	6	10	109	9	94	6	
Glynn County School System		6	0	0	3	3	72	9	63	0	0
Gwinnett County Public Schools		12	0	0	2	10	247	17	229	1	2
Hartsfield-Jackson Atlanta International Airport		8	0	0	0	8	301	2	255	44	0
Metropolitan Atlanta Rapid Transit Authority		186	3	2	64	117	296	3	237	56	1
Muscogee City Marshal		0	0	0	0	0	0	0	0	0	0
Stone Mountain Park		0	0	0	0	0	19	0	19	0	0
Idaho, State Agencies											
Idaho State Police		12	0	1	0	11	14	3	5	6	1
Fort Hall Tribal		23	1	3	2	17	195	19	149	27	4
Idaho, Other Agencies											
Nez Perce Tribal		9	0	4	0	5	92	20	63	9	0
Illinois, State Agencies											
Illinois Commerce Commission		0	0	0	0	0	0	0	0	0	0
Illinois Department of Natural Resources		3	0	0	0	3	33	7	23	3	1
Secretary of State Police		2	0	0	0	2	33	4	28	1	0
Illinois, Other Agencies											
Chicago Fire Department	Arson Investigations	0	0	0	0	0	0	0	0	0	565
Cook County Forest Preserve		8	0	1	4	3	150	18	128	4	0
Decatur Park District		4	0	0	3	1	29	10	19	0	4
Du Page County Forest Preserve		1	0	1	0	0	27	0	27	0	0
Fon du Lac Park District		0	0	0	0	0	15	2	13	0	0
Indiana Harbor Belt Railroad		0	0	0	0	0	12	0	12	0	0
Kane County Forest Preserve		1	0	0	0	1	30	0	30	0	1
Lake County Forest Preserve		2	0	0	0	2	49	5	44	0	0
McHenry County Conservation District		1	0	0	1	0	3	1	2	0	0
Oak Forest Hospital		0	0	0	0	0	8	0	7	1	0
Indiana, State Agencies											
Indiana State Excise Police		1	0	0	0	1	22	0	22	0	0
Northern Indiana Commuter Transportation District		3	0	1	0	2	45	1	42	2	1
State Police	Adams County	1	0	0	0	1	4	0	3	1	0
	Allen County	2	0	0	0	2	19	0	16	3	0
	Bartholomew County	1	0	0	0	1	16	0	13	3	0
	Benton County	0	0	0	0	0	0	0	0	0	0
	Blackford County	0	0	0	0	0	0	0	0	0	0
	Boone County	0	0	0	0	0	2	0	2	0	0
	Brown County	0	0	0	0	0	1	1	0	0	0
	Carroll County	0	0	0	0	0	0	0	0	0	0
	Cass County	5	2	1	0	2	12	3	7	2	0
	Clark County	18	0	0	3	15	137	11	106	20	0
	Clay County	1	0	1	0	0	4	1	2	1	0
	Clinton County	1	0	0	0	1	10	2	8	0	0
	Crawford County	3	1	0	0	2	9	2	7	0	0
	Daviess County	0	0	0	0	0	5	1	4	0	0
	Dearborn County	2	0	0	0	2	19	1	17	1	0
	Decatur County	5	0	2	1	2	13	2	10	1	0
	De Kalb County	2	0	0	0	2	3	2	1	0	0
	Delaware County	10	0	4	0	6	18	1	15	2	0
	Dubois County	0	0	0	0	0	8	4	4	0	1
	Elkhart County	1	0	0	0	1	20	2	18	0	0
	Fayette County	4	0	0	0	4	5	0	5	0	0
	Floyd County	20	0	0	4	16	58	4	47	7	0
	Fountain County	6	0	2	1	3	5	1	4	0	0
	Franklin County	6	5	0	0	1	27	5	21	1	0
	Fulton County	2	1	0	0	1	7	2	5	0	0
	Gibson County	0	0	0	0	0	12	1	11	0	0
	Grant County	2	0	0	0	2	15	0	14	1	0
	Greene County	2	0	2	0	0	14	6	7	1	0
	Hamilton County	3	0	0	1	2	10	1	9	0	0
	Hancock County	1	0	0	0	1	3	0	3	0	0
	Harrison County	24	2	1	0	21	53	8	38	7	0
	Hendricks County	2	0	0	0	2	18	1	15	2	0
	Henry County	4	0	0	1	3	11	1	8	2	0
	Howard County	3	1	0	0	2	17	4	12	1	0
	Huntington County	4	0	0	2	2	8	2	6	0	0
	Jackson County	6	0	0	2	4	62	19	39	4	0
	Jasper County	11	0	1	0	10	16	2	11	3	0

NA = Not available.

[1] If a blank is presented in the arson column, it indicates that the FBI did not receive 12 complete months of arson data for that agency.

Table II-11. Offenses Known to Law Enforcement, by Selected State, Tribal, and Other Agencies, 2011—*Continued*

(Number.)

State/Agency Type	Unit/Office	Violent crime	Murder and non-negligent man-slaughter	Forcible rape	Robbery	Aggra-vated assault	Property crime	Burglary	Larceny-theft	Motor vehicle theft	Arson[1]
	Jay County	2	0	0	0	2	5	1	4	0	0
	Jefferson County	4	0	1	0	3	29	8	21	0	0
	Jennings County	5	0	3	1	1	10	3	7	0	0
	Johnson County	1	0	0	0	1	8	1	6	1	0
	Knox County	6	0	2	0	4	14	4	9	1	0
	Kosciusko County	1	0	1	0	0	20	3	17	0	0
	LaGrange County	2	0	1	0	1	11	1	8	2	0
	Lake County	31	2	4	5	20	170	12	95	63	0
	La Porte County	9	0	2	2	5	32	4	22	6	0
	Lawrence County	1	0	0	0	1	7	0	7	0	0
	Madison County	30	2	0	3	25	26	2	18	6	0
	Marion County	31	0	4	1	26	116	2	81	33	0
	Marshall County	0	0	0	0	0	31	1	30	0	0
	Martin County	5	0	4	0	1	13	4	9	0	0
	Miami County	14	1	2	2	9	38	5	29	4	0
	Monroe County	6	1	3	0	2	11	1	5	5	0
	Montgomery County	7	0	4	0	3	8	2	6	0	0
	Morgan County	1	0	0	0	1	27	4	23	0	0
	Newton County	0	0	0	0	0	2	0	2	0	0
	Noble County	1	0	0	0	1	8	0	8	0	0
	Ohio County	0	0	0	0	0	1	0	1	0	0
	Orange County	9	0	0	0	9	1	0	1	0	0
	Owen County	6	0	3	0	3	17	5	12	0	1
	Parke County	2	0	1	0	1	4	0	4	0	0
	Perry County	2	0	0	0	2	3	0	3	0	0
	Pike County	5	1	2	0	2	11	4	7	0	0
	Porter County	14	0	0	1	13	32	1	26	5	0
	Posey County	1	0	0	0	1	13	3	9	1	0
	Pulaski County	3	0	0	0	3	15	4	7	4	0
	Putnam County	4	0	3	0	1	8	2	6	0	0
	Randolph County	0	0	0	0	0	4	0	4	0	0
	Ripley County	14	0	2	1	11	97	27	68	2	0
	Rush County	4	0	2	0	2	8	1	7	0	0
	Scott County	14	3	2	0	9	64	17	45	2	0
	Shelby County	8	0	3	0	5	16	1	15	0	0
	Spencer County	0	0	0	0	0	2	0	2	0	0
	Starke County	6	0	2	0	4	10	1	8	1	0
	Steuben County	2	0	2	0	0	14	0	14	0	1
	St. Joseph County	3	0	1	1	1	30	1	27	2	0
	Sullivan County	4	0	1	0	3	6	1	5	0	0
	Switzerland County	1	0	0	0	1	8	2	5	1	0
	Tippecanoe County	11	0	5	0	6	30	2	26	2	0
	Tipton County	2	0	2	0	0	9	1	8	0	0
	Union County	1	0	1	0	0	5	0	4	1	0
	Vanderburgh County	3	0	2	1	0	8	2	6	0	0
	Vermillion County	0	0	0	0	0	10	2	8	0	0
	Vigo County	6	0	1	0	5	13	1	10	2	0
	Wabash County	3	0	0	0	3	2	1	1	0	0
	Warren County	3	0	0	0	3	7	1	4	2	0
	Warrick County	1	0	0	0	1	16	1	15	0	0
	Washington County	12	0	1	2	9	36	5	25	6	0
	Wayne County	8	0	0	3	5	17	3	11	3	0
	Wells County	3	0	0	0	3	3	0	2	1	0
	White County	14	1	1	3	9	24	2	20	2	0
	Whitley County	1	0	0	0	1	6	1	4	1	0
Indiana, Other Agencies											
Indianapolis International Airport.................................		3	0	0	1	2	65	1	58	6	0
St. Joseph County Airport Authority		0	0	0	0	0	10	0	4	6	0
Kansas, State Agencies											
Kansas Alcoholic Beverage Control		0	0	0	0	0	0	0	0	0	0
Kansas Bureau of Investigation....................................		2	0	0	0	2	0	0	0	0	0
Kansas Department of Wildlife and Parks..................		4	0	1	0	3	33	6	26	1	0
Kansas Highway Patrol..		25	0	0	1	24	60	2	42	16	0
Kansas Racing Commission	Security Division	0	0	0	0	0	0	0	0	0	0
State Fire Marshal...		0	0	0	0	0	0	0	0	0	0
Kansas, Tribal Agencies											
Potawatomi Tribal		4	0	0	0	4	45	6	39	0	1
Sac and Fox Tribal		0	0	0	0	0	12	0	9	3	0
Kansas, Other Agencies											
Johnson County Park...		8	0	0	0	8	43	24	18	1	0
Shawnee Mission Public Schools................................		0	0	0	0	0	4	1	3	0	0
Topeka Fire Department..	Arson Investigation	0	0	0	0	0	6	4	2	0	39

NA = Not available.

[1] If a blank is presented in the arson column, it indicates that the FBI did not receive 12 complete months of arson data for that agency.

Table II-11. Offenses Known to Law Enforcement, by Selected State, Tribal, and Other Agencies, 2011—*Continued*

(Number.)

State/Agency Type	Unit/Office	Violent crime	Murder and non-negligent man-slaughter	Forcible rape	Robbery	Aggra-vated assault	Property crime	Burglary	Larceny-theft	Motor vehicle theft	Arson[1]
Unified School District	Goddard	1	0	0	0	1	15	1	14	0	0
	Maize	0	0	0	0	0	7	0	7	0	0
	Seaman	0	0	0	0	0	0	0	0	0	0
	Shawnee Heights	1	0	0	0	1	0	0	0	0	0
Kentucky, State Agencies											
Alcohol Beverage Control		0	0	0	0	0	0	0	0	0	0
Kentucky Fairgrounds Security		0	0	0	0	0	2	0	2	0	0
Kentucky Horse Park		0	0	0	0	0	44	4	38	2	0
Motor Vehicle Enforcement		1	0	0	0	1	5	0	4	1	0
Park Security		1	0	0	0	1	21	5	16	0	0
State Police	Ashland	32	0	17	3	12	376	152	185	39	6
	Bowling Green	53	6	27	4	16	213	116	83	14	8
	Campbellsburg	49	0	28	4	17	322	169	135	18	8
	Cannabis Suppression Section	0	0	0	0	0	0	0	0	0	0
	Columbia	58	6	31	2	19	191	96	77	18	13
	Drug Enforcement Area 2	0	0	0	0	0	7	1	6	0	0
	Dry Ridge	47	3	21	5	18	424	175	214	35	10
	Electronic Crimes	0	0	0	0	0	0	0	0	0	0
	Elizabethtown	60	2	31	2	25	284	130	116	38	7
	Frankfort	33	1	17	4	11	216	83	122	11	9
	Harlan	47	4	15	15	13	499	222	242	35	4
	Hazard	88	3	28	23	34	432	193	186	53	10
	Henderson	28	0	8	1	19	130	55	64	11	4
	London	71	1	38	5	27	477	217	209	51	21
	Madisonville	39	3	22	1	13	197	93	88	16	11
	Mayfield	53	2	22	5	24	258	103	134	21	2
	Morehead	66	4	24	11	27	496	268	194	34	4
	Pikeville	150	4	35	42	69	824	398	325	101	8
	Richmond	61	4	29	6	22	599	316	238	45	22
	Special Investigations	0	0	0	0	0	0	0	0	0	0
	West Drug Enforcement Branch	0	0	0	0	0	3	0	3	0	0
Unlawful Narcotics Investigation	Treatment and Education	0	0	0	0	0	1	0	1	0	0
Kentucky, Other Agencies											
Barren County Drug Task Force		0	0	0	0	0	0	0	0	0	0
Buffalo Trace-Gateway Narcotics Task Force		0	0	0	0	0	0	0	0	0	0
Central Kentucky Area Drug Task Force		0	0	0	0	0	0	0	0	0	0
Cincinnati-Northern Kentucky International Airport		0	0	0	0	0	84	1	82	1	0
Clark County School System		0	0	0	0	0	0	0	0	0	0
Fayette County Schools		1	0	0	0	1	236	10	226	0	0
FIVCO Area Drug Task Force		0	0	0	0	0	4	0	4	0	0
Graves County Schools		0	0	0	0	0	0	0	0	0	0
Greater Hardin County Narcotics Task Force		0	0	0	0	0	0	0	0	0	0
Jefferson County Board of Education		17	0	0	5	12	113	56	56	1	3
Lake Cumberland Area Drug Enforcement Task Force		0	0	0	0	0	0	0	0	0	0
Lexington Bluegrass Airport		0	0	0	0	0	6	0	6	0	0
Louisville Regional Airport Authority		1	0	0	1	0	40	0	22	18	0
McCracken County Public Schools		0	0	0	0	0	4	1	3	0	0
Montgomery County School District		2	0	2	0	0	4	1	3	0	0
Northern Kentucky Narcotics Enforcement Unit		1	0	0	0	1	0	0	0	0	0
Ohio County School System		0	0	0	0	0	1	0	1	0	0
Pennyrile Narcotics Task Force		1	0	0	0	1	0	0	0	0	0
South Central Kentucky Drug Task Force		0	0	0	0	0	1	0	1	0	0
Louisiana, Tribal Agencies											
Chitimacha Tribal		1	0	0	0	1	59	4	55	0	0
Coushatta Tribal		1	0	0	1	0	182	3	174	5	3
Tunica-Biloxi Tribal		14	0	0	0	14	123	7	115	1	0
Maine, State Agencies											
Drug Enforcement Agency	Androscoggin County	0	0	0	0	0	0	0	0	0	0
	Aroostook County	0	0	0	0	0	0	0	0	0	0
	Cumberland County	0	0	0	0	0	0	0	0	0	0
	Franklin County	0	0	0	0	0	0	0	0	0	0
	Hancock County	0	0	0	0	0	0	0	0	0	0
	Kennebec County	0	0	0	0	0	0	0	0	0	0
	Knox County	0	0	0	0	0	0	0	0	0	0

NA = Not available.

[1] If a blank is presented in the arson column, it indicates that the FBI did not receive 12 complete months of arson data for that agency.

Table II-11. Offenses Known to Law Enforcement, by Selected State, Tribal, and Other Agencies, 2011—*Continued*

(Number.)

State/Agency Type	Unit/Office	Violent crime	Murder and non-negligent man-slaughter	Forcible rape	Robbery	Aggra-vated assault	Property crime	Burglary	Larceny-theft	Motor vehicle theft	Arson[1]
	Lincoln County	0	0	0	0	0	0	0	0	0	0
	Oxford County	0	0	0	0	0	0	0	0	0	0
	Penobscot County	0	0	0	0	0	1	0	1	0	0
	Piscataquis County	0	0	0	0	0	0	0	0	0	0
	Sagadahoc County	0	0	0	0	0	0	0	0	0	0
	Somerset County	0	0	0	0	0	0	0	0	0	0
	Waldo County	0	0	0	0	0	0	0	0	0	0
	Washington County	0	0	0	0	0	0	0	0	0	0
	York County	0	0	0	0	0	0	0	0	0	0
State Police................	Androscoggin County	9	1	2	0	6	127	47	71	9	3
	Aroostook County	18	0	5	0	13	252	57	180	15	1
	Cumberland County	3	2	0	0	1	96	35	54	7	15
	Franklin County	11	0	1	0	10	91	36	49	6	3
	Hancock County	7	0	0	0	7	214	75	128	11	4
	Kennebec County	34	1	5	1	27	549	186	343	20	8
	Knox County	7	1	1	0	5	73	15	58	0	4
	Lincoln County	2	0	0	0	2	4	1	3	0	3
	Oxford County	10	0	0	2	8	247	100	133	14	3
	Penobscot County	18	2	5	0	11	407	149	234	24	13
	Piscataquis County	2	0	0	0	2	16	6	7	3	4
	Sagadahoc County	0	0	0	0	0	5	4	1	0	1
	Somerset County	13	1	2	0	10	195	67	117	11	1
	Waldo County	9	0	2	0	7	150	44	97	9	5
	Washington County	10	0	1	1	8	150	43	96	11	16
	York County	7	0	0	1	6	252	103	135	14	18
Maine, Tribal Agencies											
Passamaquoddy Indian Township		0	0	0	0	0	56	19	34	3	1
Passamaquoddy Pleasant Point Tribal		4	0	2	0	2	15	11	3	1	3
Penobscot Nation		4	1	0	0	3	29	8	21	0	0
Maryland, State Agencies											
Comptroller of the Treasury................	Field Enforcement Division	0	0	0	0	0	0	0	0	0	0
Department of Public Safety and Correctional Services................	Internal Investigations Unit	102	0	0	0	102	0	0	0	0	
General Services................	Annapolis, Anne Arundel County	1	0	0	0	1	19	0	16	3	0
	Baltimore City	0	0	0	0	0	34	0	30	4	0
Maryland State Police Statewide		0	0	0	0	0	0	0	0	0	0
Natural Resources Police		14	0	0	0	14	239	16	217	6	31
Springfield Hospital		0	0	0	0	0	20	0	20	0	0
State Fire Marshal		0	0	0	0	0	0	0	0	0	
State Police................	Allegany County	38	3	4	7	24	485	125	353	7	3
	Anne Arundel County	11	0	0	0	11	33	0	30	3	0
	Baltimore City	0	0	0	0	0	1	0	1	0	2
	Baltimore County	23	0	0	0	23	52	7	26	19	0
	Calvert County	18	0	1	1	16	235	47	178	10	5
	Caroline County	13	1	0	0	12	160	65	85	10	1
	Carroll County	77	1	0	12	64	828	198	580	50	4
	Cecil County	149	0	6	38	105	773	236	474	63	15
	Charles County	2	0	0	0	2	15	0	15	0	30
	Dorchester County	6	0	0	2	4	83	32	42	9	1
	Frederick County	56	0	2	12	42	446	95	333	18	18
	Garrett County	26	0	3	3	20	202	82	108	12	1
	Harford County	67	1	2	13	51	375	38	316	21	32
	Howard County	10	2	2	4	2	21	1	12	8	0
	Kent County	12	1	0	1	10	50	24	24	2	4
	Montgomery County	2	0	0	0	2	12	1	5	6	0
	Prince George's County	8	0	0	0	8	84	0	25	59	0
	Queen Anne's County	54	0	0	6	48	178	44	121	13	9
	Somerset County	32	1	0	2	29	235	79	146	10	3
	St. Mary's County	40	0	5	6	29	223	51	157	15	18
	Talbot County	4	0	0	1	3	103	34	59	10	3
	Washington County	60	0	0	2	58	203	44	149	10	15
	Wicomico County	58	3	1	9	45	251	113	124	14	11
	Worcester County	24	0	0	0	24	223	65	139	19	3
Transit Administration................		0	0	0	0	0	0	0	0	0	0
Transportation Authority................		17	0	0	4	13	213	9	170	34	0
Maryland, Other Agencies											
Maryland-National Capital Park Police	Montgomery County	8	0	0	6	2	175	18	153	4	3
	Prince George's County	62	2	2	37	21	189	17	166	6	0

NA = Not available.

[1] If a blank is presented in the arson column, it indicates that the FBI did not receive 12 complete months of arson data for that agency.

Table II-11.   Offenses Known to Law Enforcement, by Selected State, Tribal, and Other Agencies, 2011—*Continued*

(Number.)

State/Agency Type	Unit/Office	Violent crime	Murder and non-negligent man-slaughter	Forcible rape	Robbery	Aggra-vated assault	Property crime	Burglary	Larceny-theft	Motor vehicle theft	Arson[1]
Massachusetts, State Agencies											
Massachusetts Bay Transportation Authority	Bristol County	0	0	0	0	0	5	0	3	2	0
	Essex County	3	0	0	3	0	43	1	42	0	0
	Middlesex County	29	0	0	15	14	160	1	153	6	0
	Norfolk County	12	0	0	8	4	129	1	122	6	0
	Plymouth County	2	0	0	1	1	68	0	67	1	0
	Suffolk County	295	1	0	195	99	341	19	317	5	0
	Worcester County	0	0	0	0	0	7	0	7	0	0
State Police	Barnstable County	6	0	0	0	6	2	0	2	0	0
	Berkshire County	8	0	1	0	7	93	56	35	2	1
	Bristol County	16	0	0	3	13	8	1	5	2	0
	Dukes County	4	0	0	1	3	0	0	0	0	0
	Essex County	1	0	0	0	1	0	0	0	0	0
	Franklin County	19	0	1	0	18	0	0	0	0	0
	Hampden County	16	0	0	0	16	19	0	11	8	0
	Hampshire County	2	0	0	0	2	2	1	1	0	
	Middlesex County	13	0	0	0	13	3	0	3	0	0
	Norfolk County	1	0	0	0	1	3	1	1	1	0
	Plymouth County	9	0	0	1	8	2	0	2	0	0
	Worcester County	22	0	0	0	22	2	0	2	0	0
Michigan, State Agencies											
State Police	Alger County	12	0	1	0	11	63	21	41	1	0
	Allegan County	44	0	13	2	29	378	131	234	13	2
	Alpena County	14	1	3	3	7	198	66	126	6	0
	Antrim County	13	0	12	0	1	20	5	14	1	0
	Arenac County	2	0	2	0	0	20	11	8	1	0
	Baraga County	15	0	2	0	13	35	11	24	0	1
	Barry County	28	1	11	0	16	231	87	132	12	0
	Bay County	47	3	20	3	21	278	82	181	15	0
	Benzie County	6	0	3	0	3	28	7	21	0	0
	Berrien County	36	1	17	1	17	305	89	199	17	1
	Branch County	28	1	13	0	14	133	46	79	8	2
	Calhoun County	33	0	8	3	22	149	54	82	13	2
	Cass County	20	0	9	2	9	73	21	43	9	1
	Charlevoix County	3	0	2	0	1	17	8	8	1	0
	Cheboygan County	15	0	6	0	9	56	20	33	3	0
	Chippewa County	24	2	7	0	15	152	85	59	8	0
	Clare County	4	0	3	0	1	54	30	22	2	0
	Clinton County	1	0	1	0	0	14	3	9	2	0
	Crawford County	5	0	4	0	1	22	9	13	0	0
	Delta County	8	0	4	0	4	79	18	55	6	1
	Dickinson County	8	0	2	0	6	55	29	25	1	1
	Eaton County	8	0	3	0	5	64	27	35	2	2
	Emmet County	18	0	8	0	10	145	28	113	4	0
	Genesee County	54	0	14	10	30	208	110	80	18	2
	Gladwin County	33	0	17	1	15	56	23	30	3	0
	Gogebic County	11	0	5	0	6	20	10	10	0	0
	Grand Traverse County	21	0	12	0	9	126	29	93	4	0
	Gratiot County	31	0	4	0	27	144	62	75	7	2
	Hillsdale County	30	1	13	0	16	172	77	87	8	2
	Houghton County	21	1	11	0	9	137	60	72	5	1
	Huron County	7	1	1	0	5	36	13	22	1	0
	Ingham County	29	1	12	0	16	142	85	45	12	0
	Ionia County	40	0	11	1	28	293	110	167	16	0
	Iosco County	24	0	14	0	10	164	74	80	10	0
	Iron County	1	0	1	0	0	38	14	24	0	0
	Isabella County	20	1	14	0	5	187	48	136	3	0
	Jackson County	51	2	26	1	22	284	82	188	14	2
	Kalamazoo County	7	0	5	1	1	24	2	15	7	0
	Kalkaska County	19	1	9	2	7	76	33	41	2	1
	Kent County	15	0	8	0	7	24	0	22	2	0
	Lake County	9	0	6	0	3	49	22	25	2	1
	Lapeer County	38	1	18	0	19	84	40	41	3	2
	Leelanau County	2	0	1	0	1	5	1	4	0	0
	Lenawee County	58	1	9	0	48	155	62	86	7	1
	Livingston County	69	2	14	3	50	437	103	311	23	3
	Luce County	12	0	5	1	6	50	10	37	3	0
	Mackinac County	10	0	3	0	7	70	22	43	5	0
	Macomb County	12	1	2	0	9	49	15	32	2	1
	Manistee County	15	0	4	2	9	166	68	87	11	0

NA = Not available.

[1] If a blank is presented in the arson column, it indicates that the FBI did not receive 12 complete months of arson data for that agency.

Table II-11. Offenses Known to Law Enforcement, by Selected State, Tribal, and Other Agencies, 2011—*Continued*

(Number.)

State/Agency Type	Unit/Office	Violent crime	Murder and non-negligent man-slaughter	Forcible rape	Robbery	Aggra-vated assault	Property crime	Burglary	Larceny-theft	Motor vehicle theft	Arson[1]
	Marquette County	53	0	12	0	41	319	101	201	17	3
	Mason County	7	0	3	0	4	64	17	47	0	0
	Mecosta County	17	1	9	0	7	91	33	52	6	1
	Menominee County	5	0	1	0	4	66	28	35	3	1
	Midland County	7	0	7	0	0	34	8	26	0	0
	Missaukee County	2	0	0	0	2	16	6	10	0	1
	Monroe County	51	1	10	12	28	305	104	180	21	3
	Montcalm County	28	1	13	0	14	314	115	187	12	2
	Montmorency County	6	1	1	0	4	43	29	13	1	1
	Muskegon County	48	1	21	3	23	303	85	206	12	0
	Newaygo County	53	0	29	0	24	383	135	232	16	4
	Oakland County	33	2	9	6	16	288	137	126	25	1
	Oceana County	14	0	7	0	7	122	41	77	4	0
	Ogemaw County	15	0	6	1	8	210	81	118	11	2
	Ontonagon County	7	0	1	0	6	29	14	15	0	0
	Osceola County	18	0	8	1	9	130	64	64	2	0
	Oscoda County	4	0	3	0	1	20	13	7	0	0
	Otsego County	28	0	10	1	17	172	61	100	11	2
	Ottawa County	8	0	6	0	2	40	7	30	3	0
	Presque Isle County	3	0	1	0	2	12	5	6	1	0
	Roscommon County	18	0	11	0	7	148	35	104	9	3
	Saginaw County	55	4	15	5	31	196	85	93	18	3
	Sanilac County	18	0	9	0	9	141	62	71	8	0
	Schoolcraft County	9	1	1	0	7	72	32	39	1	1
	Shiawassee County	14	0	6	0	8	157	50	95	12	1
	St. Clair County	34	0	8	0	26	314	133	170	11	0
	St. Joseph County	37	1	10	0	26	186	68	106	12	3
	Tuscola County	25	0	13	0	12	147	73	70	4	2
	Van Buren County	66	0	23	1	42	322	116	172	34	3
	Washtenaw County	52	1	11	4	36	169	87	68	14	0
	Wayne County	34	0	13	1	20	116	7	63	46	2
	Wexford County	21	0	9	1	11	187	39	143	5	0
Michigan, Tribal Agencies											
Bay Mills Tribal		0	0	0	0	0	19	3	15	1	0
Hannahville Tribal		26	0	14	0	12	136	25	110	1	0
Kewennaw Bay Tribal		1	0	0	0	1	84	22	61	1	0
Lac Vieux Desert Tribal		6	0	0	0	6	41	11	25	5	0
Little River Band of Ottawa Indians		1	0	0	0	1	23	1	21	1	0
Little Traverse Bay Bands of Odawa Indians		8	0	0	1	7	33	0	33	0	0
Pokagon Tribal		2	0	0	0	2	146	2	142	2	0
Michigan, Other Agencies											
Capitol Region Airport Authority		0	0	0	0	0	7	0	4	3	0
Gerald R. Ford International Airport		0	0	0	0	0	20	0	16	4	0
Wayne County Airport		3	0	0	0	3	218	0	144	74	1
Minnesota, State Agencies[4]											
Capitol Security	St. Paul		0		0	0	23	0	23	0	0
Minnesota State Patrol			0		0	0	0	0	0	0	0
State Patrol	Brainerd		0		0	0	0	0	0	0	0
	Detroit Lakes		0		0	0	0	0	0	0	0
	Duluth		0		0	0	0	0	0	0	0
	Golden Valley		0		0	0	0	0	0	0	0
	Mankato		0		0	0	0	0	0	0	0
	Marshall		0		0	0	0	0	0	0	0
	Oakdale		0		0	0	0	0	0	0	0
	Rochester		0		0	0	0	0	0	0	0
	St. Cloud		0		0	0	0	0	0	0	0
	Thief River Falls		0		0	0	0	0	0	0	0
	Virginia		0		0	0	0	0	0	0	0
Minnesota, Tribal Agencies[4]											
Leech Lake Band of Ojibwe		67	1	5	4	57	136	57	39	40	4
Nett Lake Tribal		2	0	0	0	2	5	5	0	0	0
White Earth Tribal		41	0	3	7	31	364	94	242	28	4
Minnesota, Other Agencies[4]											
Minneapolis-St. Paul International Airport			0		0	0	0	0	0	0	0
Three Rivers Park District			0		0	1	119	4	114	1	0
Mississippi, State Agences											
State Capitol Police		2	0	0	0	2	23	10	12	1	0
Mississippi, Tribal Agencies											
Choctaw Tribal		113	4	16	2	91	269	129	86	54	6

NA = Not available.

[1] If a blank is presented in the arson column, it indicates that the FBI did not receive 12 complete months of arson data for that agency.

[4] The data collection methodology for the offense of forcible rape used by the Minnesota state Uniform Crime Reporting (UCR) Program does not comply with national UCR Program guidelines. Consequently, its figures for forcible rape and violent crime (of which forcible rape is a part) are not published in this table.

Table II-11.   Offenses Known to Law Enforcement, by Selected State, Tribal, and Other Agencies, 2011—*Continued*

(Number.)

State/Agency Type	Unit/Office	Violent crime	Murder and non-negligent man-slaughter	Forcible rape	Robbery	Aggra-vated assault	Property crime	Burglary	Larceny-theft	Motor vehicle theft	Arson[1]
Missouri, State Agencies											
Capitol Police...		0	0	0	0	0	28	1	26	1	0
Department of Conservation		0	0	0	0	0	1	0	0	1	0
Department of Social Services....................................	State Technical										
	Assistance Team	0	0	0	0	0	0	0	0	0	0
Division of Alcohol and Tobacco Control....................		0	0	0	0	0	0	0	0	0	0
Gaming Commission..	Enforcement Division	11	0	0	2	9	182	0	179	3	0
State Fire Marshal		0	0	0	0	0	0	0	0	0	245
State Highway Patrol	Jefferson City	9	2	0	0	7	8	1	4	3	0
	Kirkwood	13	1	0	0	12	2	1	0	1	0
	Lee's Summit	11	0	0	2	9	18	0	8	10	0
	Macon	1	1	0	0	0	13	1	7	5	0
	Poplar Bluff	6	0	0	1	5	10	1	6	3	0
	Rolla	4	3	0	0	1	5	0	0	5	0
	Springfield	3	0	0	0	3	5	0	0	5	0
	St. Joseph	13	0	0	0	13	22	3	9	10	0
	Willow Springs	3	0	0	0	3	4	1	1	2	0
State Park Rangers..		2	0	2	0	0	70	4	65	1	3
State Water Patrol		4	0	0	0	4	123	0	123	0	0
Missouri, Other Agencies											
Bootheel Drug Task Force		0	0	0	0	0	0	0	0	0	0
Clay County Drug Task Force......................................		0	0	0	0	0	0	0	0	0	0
Clay County Park Authority		1	0	0	0	1	17	0	17	0	0
Jackson County Drug Task Force		0	0	0	0	0	0	0	0	0	0
Jackson County Park Rangers		0	0	0	0	0	0	0	0	0	0
Lambert-St. Louis International Airport......................		4	0	0	0	4	153	0	153	0	0
Platte County Multi-Jurisdictional											
Enforcement Group..		0	0	0	0	0	0	0	0	0	0
Springfield-Branson Airport..		0	0	0	0	0	13	0	13	0	0
St. Charles County Park Rangers		0	0	0	0	0	0	0	0	0	0
St. Peters Ranger Division		2	0	0	1	1	33	1	32	0	0
Western Missouri Cyber Crimes Task Force		0	0	0	0	0	0	0	0	0	0
Montana, Tribal Agencies											
Crow Agency...		13	5	0	0	8	77	20	45	12	1
Flathead Tribal...		41	0	3	3	35	85	48	15	22	5
Fort Belknap Tribal		29	0	8	1	20	39	3	32	4	0
Fort Peck Assiniboine and Sioux Tribes		49	1	9	0	39	172	47	110	15	7
Northern Cheyenne Agency		33	2	7	0	24	51	36	1	14	2
Rocky Boys Tribal..		62	0	10	0	52	59	15	31	13	0
Nebraska, State Agencies											
Nebraska State Patrol		20	0	0	0	20	11	0	11	0	0
State Patrol..	Adams County	0	0	0	0	0	2	0	2	0	0
	Antelope County	1	0	0	0	1	1	1	0	0	0
	Arthur County	0	0	0	0	0	0	0	0	0	0
	Banner County	0	0	0	0	0	0	0	0	0	0
	Blaine County	0	0	0	0	0	0	0	0	0	0
	Boone County	0	0	0	0	0	0	0	0	0	0
	Box Butte County	0	0	0	0	0	1	1	0	0	0
	Boyd County	0	0	0	0	0	0	0	0	0	0
	Brown County	0	0	0	0	0	1	0	1	0	0
	Buffalo County	0	0	0	0	0	1	0	1	0	0
	Burt County	0	0	0	0	0	0	0	0	0	0
	Butler County	0	0	0	0	0	0	0	0	0	0
	Cass County	0	0	0	0	0	0	0	0	0	0
	Cedar County	0	0	0	0	0	0	0	0	0	0
	Chase County	0	0	0	0	0	0	0	0	0	0
	Cherry County	0	0	0	0	0	0	0	0	0	0
	Cheyenne County	0	0	0	0	0	0	0	0	0	0
	Clay County	0	0	0	0	0	2	1	1	0	0
	Colfax County	0	0	0	0	0	0	0	0	0	0
	Cuming County	0	0	0	0	0	0	0	0	0	0
	Custer County	0	0	0	0	0	4	2	2	0	0
	Dakota County	0	0	0	0	0	0	0	0	0	0
	Dawes County	0	0	0	0	0	2	0	1	1	0
	Dawson County	0	0	0	0	0	0	0	0	0	0
	Deuel County	0	0	0	0	0	0	0	0	0	0
	Dixon County	0	0	0	0	0	0	0	0	0	0
	Dodge County	0	0	0	0	0	0	0	0	0	0
	Douglas County	1	0	0	0	1	3	0	3	0	0
	Dundy County	0	0	0	0	0	0	0	0	0	0
	Fillmore County	0	0	0	0	0	0	0	0	0	0

NA = Not available.

[1] If a blank is presented in the arson column, it indicates that the FBI did not receive 12 complete months of arson data for that agency.

Table II-11. Offenses Known to Law Enforcement, by Selected State, Tribal, and Other Agencies, 2011—*Continued*

(Number.)

State/Agency Type	Unit/Office	Violent crime	Murder and non-negligent man-slaughter	Forcible rape	Robbery	Aggra-vated assault	Property crime	Burglary	Larceny-theft	Motor vehicle theft	Arson[1]
	Franklin County	0	0	0	0	0	1	0	1	0	0
	Frontier County	0	0	0	0	0	0	0	0	0	0
	Furnas County	0	0	0	0	0	0	0	0	0	0
	Gage County	0	0	0	0	0	1	0	1	0	0
	Garden County	0	0	0	0	0	1	0	1	0	0
	Garfield County	0	0	0	0	0	0	0	0	0	0
	Gosper County	0	0	0	0	0	0	0	0	0	0
	Grant County	0	0	0	0	0	0	0	0	0	0
	Greeley County	0	0	0	0	0	0	0	0	0	0
	Hall County	0	0	0	0	0	4	0	4	0	0
	Hamilton County	0	0	0	0	0	0	0	0	0	0
	Harlan County	0	0	0	0	0	0	0	0	0	0
	Hayes County	0	0	0	0	0	0	0	0	0	0
	Hitchcock County	0	0	0	0	0	1	0	1	0	0
	Holt County	0	0	0	0	0	0	0	0	0	0
	Hooker County	0	0	0	0	0	0	0	0	0	0
	Howard County	1	0	0	0	1	1	1	0	0	0
	Jefferson County	1	1	0	0	0	0	0	0	0	0
	Johnson County	0	0	0	0	0	0	0	0	0	0
	Kearney County	0	0	0	0	0	0	0	0	0	0
	Keith County	1	0	1	0	0	0	0	0	0	0
	Keya Paha County	0	0	0	0	0	0	0	0	0	0
	Kimball County	1	0	0	0	1	0	0	0	0	0
	Knox County	1	0	1	0	0	0	0	0	0	0
	Lancaster County	1	0	0	0	1	1	0	1	0	0
	Lincoln County	0	0	0	0	0	1	0	1	0	0
	Logan County	0	0	0	0	0	0	0	0	0	0
	Loup County	0	0	0	0	0	0	0	0	0	0
	Madison County	0	0	0	0	0	6	0	3	3	0
	McPherson County	0	0	0	0	0	0	0	0	0	0
	Merrick County	0	0	0	0	0	0	0	0	0	0
	Morrill County	0	0	0	0	0	1	0	1	0	0
	Nance County	0	0	0	0	0	0	0	0	0	0
	Nemaha County	0	0	0	0	0	0	0	0	0	0
	Nuckolls County	0	0	0	0	0	0	0	0	0	0
	Otoe County	0	0	0	0	0	2	0	2	0	0
	Pawnee County	0	0	0	0	0	0	0	0	0	0
	Perkins County	0	0	0	0	0	0	0	0	0	0
	Phelps County	1	0	0	0	1	1	0	1	0	0
	Pierce County	0	0	0	0	0	0	0	0	0	0
	Platte County	1	0	0	0	1	1	0	1	0	0
	Polk County	0	0	0	0	0	0	0	0	0	0
	Red Willow County	0	0	0	0	0	0	0	0	0	0
	Richardson County	0	0	0	0	0	0	0	0	0	0
	Rock County	0	0	0	0	0	0	0	0	0	0
	Saline County	1	0	0	0	1	0	0	0	0	0
	Sarpy County	0	0	0	0	0	0	0	0	0	0
	Saunders County	0	0	0	0	0	0	0	0	0	0
	Scotts Bluff County	0	0	0	0	0	4	0	3	1	0
	Seward County	0	0	0	0	0	1	0	1	0	0
	Sheridan County	0	0	0	0	0	0	0	0	0	0
	Sherman County	0	0	0	0	0	0	0	0	0	0
	Sioux County	0	0	0	0	0	0	0	0	0	0
	Stanton County	0	0	0	0	0	0	0	0	0	0
	Thayer County	0	0	0	0	0	0	0	0	0	0
	Thomas County	0	0	0	0	0	1	0	1	0	0
	Thurston County	0	0	0	0	0	0	0	0	0	0
	Valley County	0	0	0	0	0	0	0	0	0	0
	Washington County	0	0	0	0	0	0	0	0	0	0
	Wayne County	0	0	0	0	0	0	0	0	0	0
	Webster County	0	0	0	0	0	0	0	0	0	0
	Wheeler County	0	0	0	0	0	0	0	0	0	0
	York County	0	0	0	0	0	1	0	0	1	0
Nebraska, Tribal Agencies											
Santee Tribal		38	0	0	0	38	22	15	1	6	4
Winnebago Tribal		44	0	0	0	44	6	4	0	2	2
Nevada, Tribal Agencies											
Duckwater Tribal		1	0	0	0	1	4	4	0	0	0
Eastern Nevada Agency		2	0	0	0	2	5	5	0	0	0
Ely Shoshone Tribal		2	0	0	0	2	17	6	11	0	0
Fallon Tribal		2	0	0	1	1	24	11	10	3	0
Las Vegas Paiute Tribal		3	0	0	0	3	75	2	73	0	0
Moapa Tribal		4	0	0	0	4	9	1	7	1	0

NA = Not available.

[1] If a blank is presented in the arson column, it indicates that the FBI did not receive 12 complete months of arson data for that agency.

Table II-11.   Offenses Known to Law Enforcement, by Selected State, Tribal, and Other Agencies, 2011—*Continued*

(Number.)

State/Agency Type	Unit/Office	Violent crime	Murder and non-negligent man-slaughter	Forcible rape	Robbery	Aggra-vated assault	Property crime	Burglary	Larceny-theft	Motor vehicle theft	Arson[1]
Pyramid Lake Tribal		17	0	0	1	16	13	5	3	5	2
Reno-Sparks Indian Colony		29	0	1	3	25	36	13	19	4	0
South Fork Band Tribal		0	0	0	0	0	0	0	0	0	0
Walker River Tribal		12	0	4	0	8	24	16	2	6	1
Washoe Tribal		36	0	1	2	33	43	17	23	3	6
Western Nevada Agency		16	0	3	0	13	36	4	22	10	13
Western Shoshone Tribal		4	1	0	0	3	8	4	2	2	2
Yerington Paiute Tribal		9	0	0	1	8	8	1	4	3	0
Yomba Shoshone Tribal		0	0	0	0	0	7	1	6	0	0
Nevada, Other Agencies											
Clark County School District		65	0	6	26	33	873	143	710	20	41
New Hampshire, State Agencies											
Liquor Commission		1	0	0	1	0	9	0	9	0	0
New Jersey, State Agencies											
New Jersey Transit Police		80	0	0	64	16	396	8	374	14	2
Palisades Interstate Parkway		2	0	0	0	2	0	0	0	0	0
Port Authority of New York and New Jersey		46	0	0	7	39	507	15	451	41	0
State Police	Atlantic County	48	0	4	18	26	793	88	689	16	1
	Bergen County	14	0	0	1	13	100	9	79	12	0
	Burlington County	40	0	4	7	29	587	166	389	32	7
	Camden County	15	0	0	0	15	20	2	18	0	0
	Cape May County	28	0	1	3	24	414	131	265	18	3
	Cumberland County	82	2	8	11	61	974	383	546	45	9
	Essex County	18	0	0	7	11	29	0	22	7	0
	Hunterdon County	22	0	1	3	18	215	64	142	9	2
	Mercer County	4	0	2	1	1	88	2	84	2	0
	Middlesex County	3	0	0	0	3	53	2	45	6	0
	Monmouth County	13	0	1	4	8	257	73	177	7	0
	Morris County	13	0	1	1	11	27	8	16	3	1
	Ocean County	9	0	1	0	8	90	11	77	2	0
	Salem County	33	1	7	4	21	397	189	191	17	3
	Sussex County	27	0	2	5	20	517	139	355	23	3
	Union County	5	0	0	3	2	19	1	16	2	0
	Warren County	15	0	2	1	12	259	95	152	12	2
New Jersey, Other Agencies											
Park Police	Camden County	1	0	0	0	1	10	3	6	1	0
	Morris County	0	0	0	0	0	0	0	0	0	0
	Union County	0	0	0	0	0	0	0	0	0	0
Prosecutor	Atlantic County	0	0	0	0	0	0	0	0	0	0
	Bergen County	0	0	0	0	0	0	0	0	0	0
	Burlington County	0	0	0	0	0	0	0	0	0	0
	Camden County	0	0	0	0	0	0	0	0	0	0
	Cape May County	0	0	0	0	0	0	0	0	0	0
	Cumberland County	0	0	0	0	0	0	0	0	0	0
	Essex County	0	0	0	0	0	0	0	0	0	0
	Gloucester County	0	0	0	0	0	0	0	0	0	0
	Hudson County	0	0	0	0	0	0	0	0	0	0
	Hunterdon County	0	0	0	0	0	0	0	0	0	0
	Mercer County	0	0	0	0	0	0	0	0	0	0
	Middlesex County	0	0	0	0	0	0	0	0	0	0
	Monmouth County	0	0	0	0	0	0	0	0	0	0
	Morris County	0	0	0	0	0	0	0	0	0	0
	Ocean County	0	0	0	0	0	0	0	0	0	0
	Passaic County	0	0	0	0	0	0	0	0	0	0
	Salem County	0	0	0	0	0	0	0	0	0	0
	Somerset County	0	0	0	0	0	0	0	0	0	0
	Sussex County	0	0	0	0	0	0	0	0	0	0
	Union County	0	0	0	0	0	0	0	0	0	0
	Warren County	0	0	0	0	0	0	0	0	0	0
New Mexico, State Agencies											
Motor Transportation Police		1	0	0	0	1	22	4	17	1	0
New Mexico State Police		108	11	5	21	71	1,109	792	235	82	8
New Mexico, Tribal Agencies											
Acoma Tribal		16	0	1	0	15	8	4	4	0	0
Isleta Tribal		85	0	0	0	85	121	19	88	14	0
Jemez Pueblo		37	1	0	0	36	5	2	2	1	0
Laguna Tribal		21	0	5	2	14	98	13	70	15	1
Mescalero Tribal		37	0	2	0	35	57	17	31	9	2
Northern Pueblos Agency		51	7	4	4	36	68	32	33	3	0
Ohkay Owingeh Tribal		6	0	1	3	2	57	17	38	2	1

NA = Not available.

[1] If a blank is presented in the arson column, it indicates that the FBI did not receive 12 complete months of arson data for that agency.

Table II-11.   Offenses Known to Law Enforcement, by Selected State, Tribal, and Other Agencies, 2011—*Continued*

(Number.)

State/Agency Type	Unit/Office	Violent crime	Murder and non-negligent man-slaughter	Forcible rape	Robbery	Aggra-vated assault	Property crime	Burglary	Larceny-theft	Motor vehicle theft	Arson[1]
Pojoaque Tribal		11	0	3	3	5	120	47	60	13	0
Ramah Navajo Tribal		12	1	1	0	10	19	10	9	0	0
Santa Ana Tribal		1	0	0	1	0	10	4	6	0	3
Santa Clara Pueblo		4	0	0	2	2	29	13	15	1	1
Southern Pueblos Agency		35	22	0	2	11	13	8	4	1	2
Taos Pueblo		32	0	3	0	29	6	4	2	0	2
Tesuque Pueblo		1	0	0	0	1	2	0	2	0	0
Zuni Tribal		18	0	2	0	16	17	6	11	0	1
New York, State Agencies											
State Park	Allegany Region	1	0	0	0	1	14	3	10	1	0
	Central Region	0	0	0	0	0	32	3	29	0	0
	Genesee Region	1	0	1	0	0	22	1	21	0	0
	New York City Region	4	0	0	3	1	106	1	104	1	0
	Niagara Region	2	0	0	2	0	59	5	52	2	0
	Palisades Region	1	0	0	1	0	22	2	20	0	1
	Saratoga/Capital Region	1	0	0	0	1	26	2	23	1	0
	Taconic Region	0	0	0	0	0	16	1	15	0	0
	Thousand Island Region	0	0	0	0	0	24	1	22	1	0
State Police	Albany County	7	0	1	0	6	171	17	148	6	1
	Allegany County	25	0	9	0	16	358	112	232	14	NA
	Broome County	43	1	12	5	25	587	126	442	19	2
	Cattaraugus County	24	1	5	2	16	246	58	181	7	1
	Cayuga County	30	0	8	0	22	250	48	194	8	0
	Chautauqua County	12	0	3	0	9	199	42	145	12	1
	Chemung County	62	0	5	2	55	260	25	229	6	3
	Chenango County	20	0	8	0	12	179	64	106	9	0
	Clinton County	43	0	11	2	30	941	204	718	19	5
	Columbia County	16	0	1	4	11	269	85	176	8	0
	Cortland County	4	0	1	0	3	138	25	111	2	NA
	Delaware County	28	1	4	4	19	282	95	175	12	0
	Dutchess County	104	1	12	4	87	737	188	525	24	2
	Erie County	21	0	6	1	14	451	56	384	11	0
	Essex County	19	0	6	0	13	346	125	209	12	2
	Franklin County	35	1	5	0	29	401	121	259	21	4
	Fulton County	11	0	3	1	7	160	34	124	2	0
	Genesee County	9	0	0	0	9	76	9	62	5	0
	Greene County	71	0	6	1	64	461	146	293	22	4
	Hamilton County	1	0	1	0	0	30	15	13	2	0
	Herkimer County	27	1	3	2	21	352	162	182	8	NA
	Jefferson County	57	1	6	6	44	731	148	561	22	2
	Lewis County	3	0	1	0	2	58	26	31	1	0
	Livingston County	10	1	3	0	6	77	15	59	3	0
	Madison County	15	0	6	1	8	211	55	154	2	1
	Monroe County	9	0	3	1	5	69	6	55	8	0
	Montgomery County	6	0	2	1	3	109	18	88	3	0
	Nassau County	4	1	0	0	3	12	0	10	2	0
	New York County	1	0	0	0	1	68	1	67	0	0
	Niagara County	11	0	5	1	5	217	31	172	14	1
	Oneida County	74	1	13	1	59	665	192	456	17	9
	Onondaga County	30	0	9	5	16	663	113	517	33	2
	Ontario County	7	0	3	2	2	271	42	223	6	1
	Orange County	60	1	18	13	28	1,108	145	936	27	1
	Orleans County	6	0	0	0	6	53	8	43	2	0
	Oswego County	34	0	7	3	24	917	249	635	33	0
	Otsego County	24	0	2	4	18	365	74	281	10	1
	Putnam County	23	0	2	1	20	106	26	78	2	0
	Rensselaer County	22	0	5	2	15	591	136	438	17	NA
	Rockland County	5	0	2	0	3	10	0	9	1	1
	Saratoga County	51	1	11	5	34	640	83	540	17	0
	Schenectady County	0	0	0	0	0	104	24	77	3	0
	Schoharie County	10	0	2	1	7	156	53	94	9	2
	Schuyler County	7	0	5	0	2	18	4	13	1	0
	Seneca County	30	0	6	1	23	157	36	112	9	NA
	Steuben County	46	2	13	5	26	496	119	355	22	NA
	St. Lawrence County	35	0	7	1	27	569	189	359	21	NA
	Suffolk County	12	0	2	2	8	63	9	48	6	0
	Sullivan County	44	1	11	1	31	428	167	244	17	3
	Tioga County	10	0	2	0	8	137	41	90	6	0
	Tompkins County	20	0	2	4	14	266	44	217	5	NA
	Ulster County	76	1	18	5	52	462	128	312	22	5
	Warren County	13	0	3	2	8	198	22	168	8	0

NA = Not available.

[1] If a blank is presented in the arson column, it indicates that the FBI did not receive 12 complete months of arson data for that agency.

Table II-11.   Offenses Known to Law Enforcement, by Selected State, Tribal, and Other Agencies, 2011—*Continued*

(Number.)

State/Agency Type	Unit/Office	Violent crime	Murder and non-negligent man-slaughter	Forcible rape	Robbery	Aggra-vated assault	Property crime	Burglary	Larceny-theft	Motor vehicle theft	Arson[1]
	Washington County	39	6	4	1	28	194	47	139	8	2
	Wayne County	45	0	13	5	27	543	173	345	25	0
	Westchester County	42	3	3	5	31	556	132	410	14	2
	Wyoming County	12	0	2	1	9	49	15	30	4	0
	Yates County	6	0	0	0	6	17	3	13	1	0
New York, Tribal Agencies											
Oneida Indian Nation		9	0	0	2	7	349	15	333	1	0
St. Regis Tribal		3	0	0	3	0	130	29	89	12	9
New York, Other Agencies											
Board of Water	Delaware County	0	0	0	0	0	0	0	0	0	0
	Sullivan County	0	0	0	0	0	0	0	0	0	0
	Ulster County	0	0	0	0	0	6	0	6	0	0
	Westchester County	0	0	0	0	0	6	0	6	0	0
Broome County Special Investigations Task Force......		0	0	0	0	0	2	0	2	0	0
New York City Metropolitan Transportation Authority..............		108	0	1	66	41	622	7	603	12	0
Onondaga County Parks		0	0	0	0	0	43	7	36	0	0
Suffolk County Parks...		2	0	0	0	2	40	1	39	0	0
Ulster Regional Gang Enforcement Narcotics Team ..		0	0	0	0	0	0	0	0	0	0
North Carolina, State Agencies											
Department of Human Resources		0	0	0	0	0	5	0	5	0	0
Division of Alcohol Law Enforcement........................		0	0	0	0	0	0	0	0	0	0
North Carolina Highway Patrol		0	0	0	0	0	0	0	0	0	0
State Capitol Police...		0	0	0	0	0	41	2	39	0	0
State Park Rangers..	Eno River	0	0	0	0	0	8	0	8	0	0
	Fort Macon	0	0	0	0	0	1	0	1	0	0
	Hanging Rock	0	0	0	0	0	6	0	6	0	0
	Kerr Lake	0	0	0	0	0	5	0	5	0	0
	Lake Norman	0	0	0	0	0	2	1	1	0	0
	Morrow Mountain	0	0	0	0	0	2	0	1	1	0
	New River-Mount Jefferson	0	0	0	0	0	0	0	0	0	0
North Carolina, Tribal Agencies											
Cherokee Tribal...		94	1	10	12	71	684	168	480	36	6
North Carolina, Other Agencies											
Beaufort County Alcohol Beverage Control Enforcement		0	0	0	0	0	9	0	9	0	0
Pitt County Memorial Hospital		9	0	1	1	7	63	2	59	2	0
Raleigh-Durham International Airport.........................		0	0	0	0	0	65	1	55	9	0
Triad Alcohol Beverage Control Law Enforcement		0	0	0	0	0	9	0	9	0	0
WakeMed Campus Police..		5	0	0	0	5	68	1	67	0	0
North Dakota, Tribal Agencies											
Fort Berthold Agency		44	0	1	0	43	22	3	0	19	1
Fort Totten Agency..		70	3	6	0	61	89	15	60	14	3
Standing Rock Agency		85	0	8	0	77	39	17	16	6	2
Turtle Mountain Agency..		105	8	35	0	62	460	128	260	72	4
Ohio, State Agencies											
Ohio Department of Natural Resources		11	0	1	0	10	68	6	62	0	1
Ohio State Highway Patrol		344	7	8	9	320	415	19	318	78	6
Ohio, Other Agencies											
Cleveland Metropolitan Park District		7	0	1	3	3	102	6	94	2	0
Hamilton County Park District		2	0	0	2	0	31	1	30	0	0
Lake Metroparks...		1	0	0	0	1	7	1	6	0	1
Robinson Memorial Hospital		3	0	0	0	3	9	1	8	0	0
Oklahoma, State Agencies											
Capitol Park Police...		0	0	0	0	0	19	2	17	0	0
Grand River Dam Authority....................................	Lake Patrol	1	0	1	0	0	23	6	17	0	0
Oklahoma, Tribal Agencies											
Absentee Shawnee Tribal.......................................		17	0	3	3	11	53	31	16	6	4
Anadarko Agency...		6	0	0	0	6	39	3	29	7	6
Cherokee Nation..		8	0	1	3	4	40	15	17	8	3
Chickasaw Nation..		56	1	1	8	46	543	37	449	57	4
Choctaw Nation..		4	0	1	0	3	327	34	283	10	0
Citizen Potawatomi Nation		10	0	4	1	5	84	11	55	18	0
Comanche Nation...		5	0	0	0	5	51	9	38	4	1
Concho Agency...		8	0	1	0	7	17	7	5	5	1
Eastern Shawnee Tribal..		2	0	0	1	1	27	3	22	2	0

NA = Not available.

[1] If a blank is presented in the arson column, it indicates that the FBI did not receive 12 complete months of arson data for that agency.

Table II-11.   Offenses Known to Law Enforcement, by Selected State, Tribal, and Other Agencies, 2011—*Continued*

(Number.)

State/Agency Type	Unit/Office	Violent crime	Murder and non-negligent man-slaughter	Forcible rape	Robbery	Aggra-vated assault	Property crime	Burglary	Larceny-theft	Motor vehicle theft	Arson[1]
Iowa Tribal		0	0	0	0	0	2	0	1	1	0
Kaw Tribal		0	0	0	0	0	1	0	1	0	0
Kickapoo Tribal		2	0	0	0	2	26	5	15	6	1
Miami Agency		3	0	1	1	1	56	5	47	4	3
Miami Tribal		0	0	0	0	0	2	1	1	0	0
Muscogee Nation Tribal		5	2	1	0	2	87	20	56	11	3
Osage Nation		10	0	0	6	4	65	31	30	4	2
Otoe-Missouria Tribal		4	0	0	0	4	26	3	20	3	0
Pawnee Agency		6	0	0	1	5	8	4	2	2	1
Pawnee Tribal		1	0	0	0	1	9	3	5	1	0
Ponca Tribal		4	0	0	1	3	49	16	28	5	3
Sac and Fox Tribal		3	0	1	0	2	21	2	18	1	0
Seminole Nation Lighthorse		1	0	0	0	1	23	8	13	2	2
Tonkawa Tribal		2	0	0	0	2	8	3	5	0	0
Wyandotte Nation		20	0	0	2	18	175	7	161	7	0
Oklahoma, Other Agencies											
Guymon Public Schools		0	0	0	0	0	0	0	0	0	0
Jenks Public Schools		4	0	0	1	3	20	1	19	0	0
Madill Public Schools		1	0	0	0	1	0	0	0	0	0
McAlester Public Schools		0	0	0	0	0	5	0	5	0	1
Norman Public Schools		0	0	0	0	0	26	5	20	1	0
Putnam City Campus		1	0	0	1	0	36	1	33	2	0
Oregon, State Agencies											
State Police		152	1	27	2	122	676	62	453	161	43
Oregon, Tribal Agencies											
Coquille Tribal		1	0	0	0	1	15	6	6	3	4
Siletz Tribal		0	0	0	0	0	67	11	54	2	0
Warm Springs Tribal		15	1	2	0	12	170	56	108	6	15
Oregon, Other Agencies											
Blue Mountain Enforcement Narcotics Team	Morrow County	0	0	0	0	0	0	0	0	0	0
	Umatilla County	0	0	0	0	0	1	0	1	0	0
Port of Portland		0	0	0	0	0	302	3	291	8	0
Pennsylvania, State Agencies											
Bureau of Forestry	Adams County	0	0	0	0	0	0	0	0	0	0
	Allegheny County	0	0	0	0	0	0	0	0	0	0
	Armstrong County	0	0	0	0	0	0	0	0	0	1
	Beaver County	0	0	0	0	0	0	0	0	0	0
	Bedford County	0	0	0	0	0	0	0	0	0	1
	Berks County	0	0	0	0	0	0	0	0	0	3
	Blair County	0	0	0	0	0	0	0	0	0	1
	Bradford County	0	0	0	0	0	0	0	0	0	0
	Bucks County	0	0	0	0	0	0	0	0	0	0
	Butler County	0	0	0	0	0	0	0	0	0	0
	Cambria County	0	0	0	0	0	0	0	0	0	1
	Cameron County	0	0	0	0	0	0	0	0	0	0
	Carbon County	0	0	0	0	0	0	0	0	0	3
	Centre County	0	0	0	0	0	0	0	0	0	4
	Chester County	0	0	0	0	0	0	0	0	0	0
	Clarion County	0	0	0	0	0	0	0	0	0	0
	Clearfield County	0	0	0	0	0	0	0	0	0	0
	Clinton County	0	0	0	0	0	0	0	0	0	0
	Columbia County	0	0	0	0	0	0	0	0	0	0
	Crawford County	0	0	0	0	0	0	0	0	0	0
	Cumberland County	0	0	0	0	0	0	0	0	0	0
	Dauphin County	0	0	0	0	0	0	0	0	0	1
	Delaware County	0	0	0	0	0	0	0	0	0	0
	Elk County	0	0	0	0	0	0	0	0	0	0
	Erie County	0	0	0	0	0	0	0	0	0	0
	Fayette County	0	0	0	0	0	0	0	0	0	2
	Forest County	0	0	0	0	0	0	0	0	0	0
	Franklin County	0	0	0	0	0	0	0	0	0	2
	Fulton County	0	0	0	0	0	0	0	0	0	1
	Greene County	0	0	0	0	0	0	0	0	0	0
	Huntingdon County	0	0	0	0	0	0	0	0	0	3
	Indiana County	0	0	0	0	0	0	0	0	0	0
	Jefferson County	0	0	0	0	0	0	0	0	0	0
	Juniata County	0	0	0	0	0	0	0	0	0	0
	Lackawanna County	0	0	0	0	0	0	0	0	0	3
	Lancaster County	0	0	0	0	0	0	0	0	0	0
	Lawrence County	0	0	0	0	0	0	0	0	0	0
	Lebanon County	0	0	0	0	0	0	0	0	0	3
	Lehigh County	0	0	0	0	0	0	0	0	0	6

NA = Not available.

[1] If a blank is presented in the arson column, it indicates that the FBI did not receive 12 complete months of arson data for that agency.

Table II-11.   Offenses Known to Law Enforcement, by Selected State, Tribal, and Other Agencies, 2011—*Continued*

(Number.)

State/Agency Type	Unit/Office	Violent crime	Murder and non-negligent man-slaughter	Forcible rape	Robbery	Aggra-vated assault	Property crime	Burglary	Larceny-theft	Motor vehicle theft	Arson[1]
	Luzerne County	0	0	0	0	0	0	0	0	0	15
	Lycoming County	0	0	0	0	0	0	0	0	0	0
	McKean County	0	0	0	0	0	0	0	0	0	1
	Mercer County	0	0	0	0	0	0	0	0	0	0
	Mifflin County	0	0	0	0	0	0	0	0	0	0
	Monroe County	0	0	0	0	0	0	0	0	0	0
	Montgomery County	0	0	0	0	0	0	0	0	0	0
	Montour County	0	0	0	0	0	0	0	0	0	0
	Northampton County	0	0	0	0	0	0	0	0	0	0
	Northumberland County	0	0	0	0	0	0	0	0	0	5
	Perry County	0	0	0	0	0	0	0	0	0	1
	Philadelphia County	0	0	0	0	0	0	0	0	0	0
	Pike County	0	0	0	0	0	0	0	0	0	0
	Potter County	0	0	0	0	0	0	0	0	0	1
	Schuylkill County	0	0	0	0	0	0	0	0	0	13
	Snyder County	0	0	0	0	0	0	0	0	0	0
	Somerset County	0	0	0	0	0	0	0	0	0	0
	Sullivan County	0	0	0	0	0	0	0	0	0	1
	Susquehanna County	0	0	0	0	0	0	0	0	0	0
	Tioga County	0	0	0	0	0	0	0	0	0	0
	Union County	0	0	0	0	0	0	0	0	0	0
	Venango County	0	0	0	0	0	0	0	0	0	2
	Warren County	0	0	0	0	0	0	0	0	0	0
	Washington County	0	0	0	0	0	0	0	0	0	0
	Wayne County	0	0	0	0	0	0	0	0	0	0
	Westmoreland County	0	0	0	0	0	0	0	0	0	0
	Wyoming County	0	0	0	0	0	0	0	0	0	0
	York County	0	0	0	0	0	0	0	0	0	0
Bureau of Narcotics	Adams County	0	0	0	0	0	0	0	0	0	0
	Allegheny County	0	0	0	0	0	0	0	0	0	0
	Armstrong County	0	0	0	0	0	0	0	0	0	0
	Beaver County	0	0	0	0	0	0	0	0	0	0
	Bedford County	0	0	0	0	0	0	0	0	0	0
	Berks County	0	0	0	0	0	0	0	0	0	0
	Blair County	0	0	0	0	0	0	0	0	0	0
	Bradford County	0	0	0	0	0	0	0	0	0	0
	Bucks County	0	0	0	0	0	0	0	0	0	0
	Butler County	0	0	0	0	0	0	0	0	0	0
	Cambria County	0	0	0	0	0	0	0	0	0	0
	Cameron County	0	0	0	0	0	0	0	0	0	0
	Carbon County	0	0	0	0	0	0	0	0	0	0
	Centre County	0	0	0	0	0	0	0	0	0	0
	Clarion County	0	0	0	0	0	0	0	0	0	0
	Clearfield County	0	0	0	0	0	0	0	0	0	0
	Clinton County	0	0	0	0	0	0	0	0	0	0
	Columbia County	0	0	0	0	0	0	0	0	0	0
	Crawford County	0	0	0	0	0	0	0	0	0	0
	Cumberland County	0	0	0	0	0	0	0	0	0	0
	Dauphin County	0	0	0	0	0	0	0	0	0	0
	Delaware County	0	0	0	0	0	0	0	0	0	0
	Elk County	0	0	0	0	0	0	0	0	0	0
	Erie County	0	0	0	0	0	0	0	0	0	0
	Fayette County	0	0	0	0	0	0	0	0	0	0
	Forest County	0	0	0	0	0	0	0	0	0	0
	Franklin County	0	0	0	0	0	0	0	0	0	0
	Fulton County	0	0	0	0	0	0	0	0	0	0
	Greene County	0	0	0	0	0	0	0	0	0	0
	Huntingdon County	0	0	0	0	0	0	0	0	0	0
	Indiana County	0	0	0	0	0	0	0	0	0	0
	Jefferson County	0	0	0	0	0	0	0	0	0	0
	Juniata County	0	0	0	0	0	0	0	0	0	0
	Lackawanna County	0	0	0	0	0	0	0	0	0	0
	Lancaster County	0	0	0	0	0	0	0	0	0	0
	Lawrence County	0	0	0	0	0	0	0	0	0	0
	Lebanon County	0	0	0	0	0	0	0	0	0	0
	Lehigh County	0	0	0	0	0	0	0	0	0	0
	Luzerne County	0	0	0	0	0	0	0	0	0	0
	Lycoming County	0	0	0	0	0	0	0	0	0	0
	McKean County	0	0	0	0	0	0	0	0	0	0
	Mercer County	0	0	0	0	0	0	0	0	0	0
	Mifflin County	0	0	0	0	0	0	0	0	0	0
	Montgomery County	0	0	0	0	0	0	0	0	0	0
	Montour County	0	0	0	0	0	0	0	0	0	0

NA = Not available.

[1] If a blank is presented in the arson column, it indicates that the FBI did not receive 12 complete months of arson data for that agency.

Table II-11.   Offenses Known to Law Enforcement, by Selected State, Tribal, and Other Agencies, 2011—*Continued*

(Number.)

State/Agency Type	Unit/Office	Violent crime	Murder and non-negligent man-slaughter	Forcible rape	Robbery	Aggra-vated assault	Property crime	Burglary	Larceny-theft	Motor vehicle theft	Arson[1]
	Northampton County	0	0	0	0	0	0	0	0	0	0
	Northumberland County	0	0	0	0	0	0	0	0	0	0
	Perry County	0	0	0	0	0	0	0	0	0	0
	Philadelphia County	0	0	0	0	0	0	0	0	0	0
	Pike County	0	0	0	0	0	0	0	0	0	0
	Potter County	0	0	0	0	0	0	0	0	0	0
	Schuylkill County	0	0	0	0	0	0	0	0	0	0
	Snyder County	0	0	0	0	0	0	0	0	0	0
	Somerset County	0	0	0	0	0	0	0	0	0	0
	Susquehanna County	0	0	0	0	0	0	0	0	0	0
	Tioga County	0	0	0	0	0	0	0	0	0	0
	Union County	0	0	0	0	0	0	0	0	0	0
	Venango County	0	0	0	0	0	0	0	0	0	0
	Warren County	0	0	0	0	0	0	0	0	0	0
	Washington County	0	0	0	0	0	0	0	0	0	0
	Wayne County	0	0	0	0	0	0	0	0	0	0
	Westmoreland County	0	0	0	0	0	0	0	0	0	0
	Wyoming County	0	0	0	0	0	0	0	0	0	0
	York County	0	0	0	0	0	0	0	0	0	0
Moshannon State Forest...		0	0	0	0	0	0	0	0	0	0
Pennsylvania Fish and Boat Commission.....................		0	0	0	0	0	0	0	0	0	0
State Capitol Police...		6	0	0	0	6	68	7	59	2	0
State Park Police..	Pine Grove Furnace	0	0	0	0	0	0	0	0	0	0
	Prince Gallitzin	0	0	0	0	0	0	0	0	0	0
State Police, Bureau of Criminal Investigation	Adams County	0	0	0	0	0	0	0	0	0	0
	Allegheny County	1	0	0	1	0	8	0	6	2	0
	Armstrong County	0	0	0	0	0	0	0	0	0	0
	Beaver County	0	0	0	0	0	0	0	0	0	0
	Bedford County	0	0	0	0	0	0	0	0	0	0
	Berks County	0	0	0	0	0	0	0	0	0	0
	Blair County	0	0	0	0	0	1	0	1	0	0
	Bradford County	0	0	0	0	0	0	0	0	0	0
	Bucks County	0	0	0	0	0	0	0	0	0	0
	Butler County	1	0	1	0	0	3	0	3	0	0
	Cambria County	0	0	0	0	0	0	0	0	0	0
	Cameron County	0	0	0	0	0	0	0	0	0	0
	Carbon County	0	0	0	0	0	0	0	0	0	0
	Centre County	0	0	0	0	0	0	0	0	0	0
	Chester County	0	0	0	0	0	2	0	1	1	0
	Clarion County	0	0	0	0	0	0	0	0	0	0
	Clearfield County	0	0	0	0	0	0	0	0	0	0
	Clinton County	0	0	0	0	0	0	0	0	0	0
	Columbia County	0	0	0	0	0	0	0	0	0	0
	Crawford County	0	0	0	0	0	0	0	0	0	0
	Cumberland County	0	0	0	0	0	0	0	0	0	0
	Dauphin County	0	0	0	0	0	0	0	0	0	0
	Delaware County	0	0	0	0	0	0	0	0	0	0
	Elk County	0	0	0	0	0	0	0	0	0	0
	Erie County	0	0	0	0	0	0	0	0	0	0
	Fayette County	0	0	0	0	0	2	0	1	1	0
	Forest County	0	0	0	0	0	0	0	0	0	0
	Franklin County	0	0	0	0	0	0	0	0	0	0
	Fulton County	0	0	0	0	0	0	0	0	0	0
	Greene County	0	0	0	0	0	0	0	0	0	0
	Huntingdon County	0	0	0	0	0	0	0	0	0	0
	Indiana County	0	0	0	0	0	0	0	0	0	0
	Jefferson County	0	0	0	0	0	0	0	0	0	0
	Juniata County	0	0	0	0	0	0	0	0	0	0
	Lackawanna County	0	0	0	0	0	0	0	0	0	0
	Lancaster County	0	0	0	0	0	0	0	0	0	0
	Lawrence County	0	0	0	0	0	3	0	1	2	0
	Lebanon County	0	0	0	0	0	0	0	0	0	0
	Lehigh County	0	0	0	0	0	0	0	0	0	0
	Luzerne County	0	0	0	0	0	0	0	0	0	0
	Lycoming County	0	0	0	0	0	0	0	0	0	0
	McKean County	0	0	0	0	0	0	0	0	0	0
	Mercer County	0	0	0	0	0	0	0	0	0	0
	Mifflin County	0	0	0	0	0	0	0	0	0	0
	Monroe County	0	0	0	0	0	0	0	0	0	0
	Montgomery County	0	0	0	0	0	1	0	1	0	0
	Montour County	0	0	0	0	0	0	0	0	0	0
	Northampton County	0	0	0	0	0	0	0	0	0	0
	Northumberland County	0	0	0	0	0	0	0	0	0	0

NA = Not available.

[1] If a blank is presented in the arson column, it indicates that the FBI did not receive 12 complete months of arson data for that agency.

Table II-11. Offenses Known to Law Enforcement, by Selected State, Tribal, and Other Agencies, 2011—*Continued*

(Number.)

State/Agency Type	Unit/Office	Violent crime	Murder and non-negligent man-slaughter	Forcible rape	Robbery	Aggra-vated assault	Property crime	Burglary	Larceny-theft	Motor vehicle theft	Arson[1]
	Perry County	0	0	0	0	0	0	0	0	0	0
	Philadelphia County	1	0	0	0	1	2	0	2	0	0
	Pike County	0	0	0	0	0	0	0	0	0	0
	Potter County	0	0	0	0	0	0	0	0	0	0
	Schuylkill County	0	0	0	0	0	1	0	1	0	0
	Snyder County	0	0	0	0	0	0	0	0	0	0
	Somerset County	0	0	0	0	0	0	0	0	0	0
	Sullivan County	0	0	0	0	0	0	0	0	0	0
	Susquehanna County	0	0	0	0	0	0	0	0	0	0
	Tioga County	0	0	0	0	0	0	0	0	0	0
	Union County	0	0	0	0	0	0	0	0	0	0
	Venango County	0	0	0	0	0	0	0	0	0	0
	Warren County	0	0	0	0	0	0	0	0	0	0
	Washington County	0	0	0	0	0	6	0	5	1	0
	Wayne County	0	0	0	0	0	0	0	0	0	0
	Westmoreland County	0	0	0	0	0	0	0	0	0	0
	Wyoming County	0	0	0	0	0	0	0	0	0	0
	York County	0	0	0	0	0	2	0	2	0	0
State Police..	Adams County	73	0	13	8	52	507	140	341	26	4
	Allegheny County	40	0	4	0	36	577	2	572	3	0
	Armstrong County	45	0	16	7	22	435	151	258	26	5
	Beaver County	18	0	2	1	15	166	66	93	7	4
	Bedford County	47	3	18	8	18	443	156	274	13	5
	Berks County	152	4	19	10	119	750	260	464	26	6
	Blair County	28	1	13	1	13	268	85	167	16	4
	Bradford County	50	0	18	2	30	595	220	344	31	11
	Bucks County	46	0	2	2	42	448	85	346	17	7
	Butler County	56	2	16	8	30	566	190	344	32	7
	Cambria County	99	1	36	9	53	271	114	136	21	3
	Cameron County	7	0	1	1	5	81	48	33	0	0
	Carbon County	64	0	9	2	53	347	114	220	13	7
	Centre County	68	0	29	8	31	446	134	295	17	6
	Chester County	121	2	25	23	71	1,235	449	738	48	8
	Clarion County	28	0	6	2	20	419	141	261	17	3
	Clearfield County	47	0	14	4	29	612	187	388	37	4
	Clinton County	49	1	3	1	44	420	81	332	7	1
	Columbia County	23	1	13	1	8	158	48	98	12	1
	Crawford County	30	3	10	6	11	624	256	345	23	0
	Cumberland County	58	1	18	10	29	756	236	497	23	7
	Delaware County	56	0	1	16	39	1,091	137	919	35	0
	Elizabethville	140	0	14	8	118	1,065	263	755	47	16
	Elk County	13	0	11	1	1	281	114	159	8	5
	Erie County	92	1	23	19	49	1,719	359	1,303	57	7
	Fayette County	161	3	30	41	87	2,231	710	1,355	166	76
	Franklin County	72	0	17	12	43	1,193	349	799	45	8
	Fulton County	30	1	8	2	19	211	48	158	5	4
	Greene County	35	3	9	7	16	442	137	284	21	6
	Huntingdon County	55	0	13	2	40	485	150	321	14	3
	Indiana County	72	2	26	16	28	988	257	677	54	4
	Jefferson County	23	0	8	0	15	348	89	235	24	11
	Juniata County	16	1	5	9	1	254	78	168	8	0
	Lackawanna County	25	0	5	2	18	210	78	108	24	25
	Lancaster County	63	1	20	15	27	1,046	370	629	47	13
	Lawrence County	44	0	6	9	29	388	146	215	27	2
	Lebanon County	63	1	10	11	41	457	112	322	23	5
	Lehigh County	90	6	9	6	69	865	138	708	19	10
	Luzerne County	271	4	9	20	238	1,046	232	754	60	13
	Lycoming County	49	0	11	9	29	832	268	538	26	2
	McKean County	5	0	2	0	3	153	61	82	10	0
	Mercer County	26	0	6	1	19	398	176	216	6	2
	Mifflin County	7	0	3	0	4	91	23	62	6	0
	Monroe County	191	0	23	38	130	1,440	435	938	67	6
	Montour County	30	0	7	0	23	75	26	44	5	1
	Northampton County	14	1	2	3	8	544	77	452	15	4
	Northumberland County	83	0	10	1	72	266	64	183	19	0
	Perry County	83	0	27	11	45	689	280	381	28	6
	Philadelphia County	8	0	0	3	5	9	0	6	3	0
	Potter County	19	1	6	1	11	171	68	93	10	2
	Schuylkill County	134	1	18	14	101	725	182	493	50	7
	Skippack	62	1	6	3	52	475	133	326	16	1
	Snyder County	20	1	7	3	9	382	82	290	10	0
	Somerset County	44	4	8	4	28	617	162	423	32	8
	Sullivan County	4	0	0	0	4	117	56	59	2	1

NA = Not available.

[1] If a blank is presented in the arson column, it indicates that the FBI did not receive 12 complete months of arson data for that agency.

Table II-11.　Offenses Known to Law Enforcement, by Selected State, Tribal, and Other Agencies, 2011—*Continued*

(Number.)

State/Agency Type	Unit/Office	Violent crime	Murder and non-negligent man-slaughter	Forcible rape	Robbery	Aggra-vated assault	Property crime	Burglary	Larceny-theft	Motor vehicle theft	Arson[1]
	Susquehanna County	48	0	17	14	17	550	242	270	38	15
	Tioga County	26	2	6	0	18	452	125	293	34	4
	Tionesta	28	0	4	1	23	100	41	56	3	0
	Union County	26	0	10	5	11	278	71	200	7	0
	Venango County	49	0	20	7	22	379	112	249	18	5
	Warren County	22	0	8	1	13	419	145	263	11	3
	Washington County	109	4	26	15	64	949	300	607	42	38
	Wayne County	59	1	20	5	33	533	185	321	27	13
	Westmoreland County	149	2	36	25	86	1,550	367	1,104	79	27
	Wyoming County	7	0	3	2	2	201	44	143	14	0
	York County	66	1	17	7	41	638	186	407	45	9
Pennsylvania, Other Agencies											
Allegheny County District Attorney	Criminal Investigation Division	0	0	0	0	0	41	0	41	0	0
Allegheny County Housing Authority.........................		8	0	1	1	6	21	11	10	0	0
Allegheny County Port Authority		118	0	1	39	78	97	3	91	3	0
County Detective	Berks County	98	0	1	2	95	6	1	4	1	0
	Bucks County	2	0	1	0	1	7	1	6	0	0
	Butler County	0	0	0	0	0	0	0	0	0	0
	Clarion County	0	0	0	0	0	0	0	0	0	0
	Dauphin County	23	0	2	0	21	9	1	8	0	1
	Lackawanna County	10	0	1	0	9	0	0	0	0	0
	Lebanon County	1	0	0	1	0	3	1	2	0	0
	Lehigh County	3	0	1	2	0	90	5	2	83	0
	Pike County	0	0	0	0	0	1	0	1	0	0
	Westmoreland County	2	0	0	0	2	100	0	100	0	0
Delaware County District Attorney	Criminal Investigation Division	20	0	1	0	19	4	0	2	2	0
Delaware County Park		9	0	0	0	9	102	0	101	1	1
Fort Cherry School District.................................		0	0	0	0	0	0	0	0	0	0
Fort Indiantown Gap		0	0	0	0	0	5	0	5	0	0
Westmoreland County Park		1	0	0	0	1	25	2	23	0	0
Rhode Island, State Agencies											
Department of Environmental Management		3	0	0	0	3	32	2	30	0	2
Rhode Island State Airport..................................		0	0	0	0	0	35	0	27	8	0
Rhode Island State Police Headquarters		6	1	3	0	2	49	2	11	36	1
State Police...	Chepachet	4	0	3	0	1	39	3	28	8	0
	Hope Valley	10	1	1	2	6	49	14	33	2	1
	Lincoln	22	1	2	0	19	91	2	54	35	0
	Portsmouth	1	0	0	0	1	5	0	4	1	0
	Wickford	4	0	1	0	3	50	12	36	2	1
Rhode Island, Tribal Agencies											
Narragansett Tribal		1	0	0	0	1	2	2	0	0	0
South Carolina, State Agencies											
Department of Mental Health................................		1	0	0	0	1	10	1	9	0	0
Highway Patrol..	Aiken County	0	0	0	0	0	0	0	0	0	0
	Allendale County	0	0	0	0	0	0	0	0	0	0
	Anderson County	1	0	0	0	1	2	0	0	2	0
	Bamberg County	0	0	0	0	0	0	0	0	0	0
	Barnwell County	0	0	0	0	0	0	0	0	0	0
	Beaufort County	0	0	0	0	0	0	0	0	0	0
	Berkeley County	0	0	0	0	0	0	0	0	0	0
	Cherokee County	0	0	0	0	0	0	0	0	0	0
	Chester County	0	0	0	0	0	0	0	0	0	0
	Clarendon County	0	0	0	0	0	0	0	0	0	0
	Dorchester County	0	0	0	0	0	0	0	0	0	0
	Edgefield County	0	0	0	0	0	0	0	0	0	0
	Fairfield County	0	0	0	0	0	0	0	0	0	0
	Georgetown County	0	0	0	0	0	0	0	0	0	0
	Greenville County	1	0	0	0	1	0	0	0	0	0
	Greenwood County	0	0	0	0	0	1	0	0	1	0
	Horry County	1	0	0	0	1	0	0	0	0	0
	Kershaw County	0	0	0	0	0	0	0	0	0	0
	Lancaster County	0	0	0	0	0	0	0	0	0	0
	Laurens County	0	0	0	0	0	0	0	0	0	0
	Lee County	0	0	0	0	0	0	0	0	0	0
	Lexington County	0	0	0	0	0	0	0	0	0	0
	Orangeburg County	0	0	0	0	0	0	0	0	0	0
	Pickens County	0	0	0	0	0	0	0	0	0	0
	Richland County	1	0	0	0	1	0	0	0	0	0
	Saluda County	0	0	0	0	0	0	0	0	0	0

NA = Not available.

[1] If a blank is presented in the arson column, it indicates that the FBI did not receive 12 complete months of arson data for that agency.

Table II-11.   Offenses Known to Law Enforcement, by Selected State, Tribal, and Other Agencies, 2011—*Continued*

(Number.)

State/Agency Type	Unit/Office	Violent crime	Murder and non-negligent man-slaughter	Forcible rape	Robbery	Aggra-vated assault	Property crime	Burglary	Larceny-theft	Motor vehicle theft	Arson[1]
	Spartanburg County	1	0	0	0	1	0	0	0	0	0
	Sumter County	0	0	0	0	0	0	0	0	0	0
	Williamsburg County	0	0	0	0	0	0	0	0	0	0
	York County	0	0	0	0	0	0	0	0	0	0
South Carolina School for the Deaf and Blind.............		0	0	0	0	0	0	0	0	0	0
State Ports Authority..		0	0	0	0	0	19	1	18	0	0
United States Department of Energy	Savannah River Plant	1	0	1	0	0	32	0	32	0	0
South Carolina, Other Agencies											
Charleston County Aviation Authority		0	0	0	0	0	29	3	23	3	0
Columbia Metropolitan Airport....................................		0	0	0	0	0	7	0	6	1	0
Greenville-Spartanburg International Airport............		0	0	0	0	0	9	0	8	1	0
Lexington County Medical Center................................		2	0	0	0	2	43	1	36	6	0
Whitten Center		0	0	0	0	0	0	0	0	0	0
South Dakota, State Agencies											
Division of Criminal Investigation...............................		18	2	8	1	7	4	3	1	0	0
South Dakota, Tribal Agencies											
Crow Creek Tribal...		8	0	4	0	4	19	5	0	14	1
Flandreau Tribal..		10	0	3	0	7	10	2	6	2	2
Lower Brule Tribal..		23	0	7	0	16	21	17	1	3	1
Oglala Sioux Tribal...		57	1	25	6	25	304	45	211	48	8
Pine Ridge Sioux Tribal		63	2	8	2	51	34	18	11	5	6
Rosebud Tribal..		240	1	44	1	194	68	26	37	5	2
Sisseton-Wahpeton Tribal..		13	0	1	0	12	176	53	100	23	11
Yankton Tribal...		11	0	0	0	11	17	17	0	0	0
Tennessee, State Agencies											
Alcoholic Beverage Commission		0	0	0	0	0	0	0	0	0	0
Department of Correction	Internal Affairs	31	0	0	0	31	0	0	0	0	0
Department of Safety		13	0	0	0	13	31	1	14	16	0
State Fire Marshal...		0	0	0	0	0	0	0	0	0	37
State Park Rangers..	Bicentennial Capitol Mall	0	0	0	0	0	1	0	1	0	0
	Big Hill Pond	0	0	0	0	0	0	0	0	0	0
	Big Ridge	0	0	0	0	0	0	0	0	0	0
	Bledsoe Creek	0	0	0	0	0	0	0	0	0	0
	Booker T. Washington	0	0	0	0	0	0	0	0	0	0
	Burgess Falls Natural Area	0	0	0	0	0	1	0	1	0	0
	Cedars of Lebanon	0	0	0	0	0	0	0	0	0	0
	Chickasaw	0	0	0	0	0	0	0	0	0	0
	Cove Lake	0	0	0	0	0	0	0	0	0	0
	Cumberland Mountain	0	0	0	0	0	0	0	0	0	0
	Cumberland Trail	0	0	0	0	0	0	0	0	0	0
	David Crockett	0	0	0	0	0	0	0	0	0	0
	Davy Crockett Birthplace	0	0	0	0	0	0	0	0	0	0
	Dunbar Cave Natural Area	0	0	0	0	0	2	0	2	0	0
	Edgar Evins	0	0	0	0	0	3	0	3	0	0
	Fall Creek Falls	0	0	0	0	0	4	0	4	0	0
	Fort Loudon State Historic Park	0	0	0	0	0	0	0	0	0	0
	Fort Pillow State Historic Park	0	0	0	0	0	0	0	0	0	0
	Frozen Head Natural Area	0	0	0	0	0	1	0	1	0	0
	Harpeth Scenic Rivers	0	0	0	0	0	0	0	0	0	0
	Harrison Bay	0	0	0	0	0	6	0	6	0	0
	Henry Horton	0	0	0	0	0	0	0	0	0	0
	Hiwassee/Ocoee State Scenic Rivers	0	0	0	0	0	0	0	0	0	0
	Indian Mountain	0	0	0	0	0	0	0	0	0	0
	Johnsonville State Historic Park	0	0	0	0	0	0	0	0	0	0
	Long Hunter	0	0	0	0	0	0	0	0	0	0
	Meeman-Shelby Forest	1	0	0	0	1	3	1	2	0	0
	Montgomery Bell	0	0	0	0	0	1	0	1	0	0
	Mousetail Landing	0	0	0	0	0	0	0	0	0	0
	Natchez Trace	0	0	0	0	0	0	0	0	0	0
	Nathan Bedford Forrest	0	0	0	0	0	0	0	0	0	0
	Norris Dam	0	0	0	0	0	5	1	3	1	0
	Old Stone Fort State Archaeological Park	0	0	0	0	0	0	0	0	0	0

NA = Not available.

[1] If a blank is presented in the arson column, it indicates that the FBI did not receive 12 complete months of arson data for that agency.

Table II-11. Offenses Known to Law Enforcement, by Selected State, Tribal, and Other Agencies, 2011—*Continued*

(Number.)

State/Agency Type	Unit/Office	Violent crime	Murder and non-negligent man-slaughter	Forcible rape	Robbery	Aggra-vated assault	Property crime	Burglary	Larceny-theft	Motor vehicle theft	Arson[1]
	Panther Creek	0	0	0	0	0	2	0	2	0	0
	Paris Landing	0	0	0	0	0	0	0	0	0	0
	Pickett	0	0	0	0	0	3	1	2	0	0
	Pickwick Landing	0	0	0	0	0	5	1	4	0	0
	Pinson Mounds State Archaeological Park	0	0	0	0	0	0	0	0	0	0
	Radnor Lake Natural Area	0	0	0	0	0	3	0	3	0	0
	Red Clay State Historic Park	0	0	0	0	0	0	0	0	0	0
	Reelfoot Lake	0	0	0	0	0	0	0	0	0	0
	Roan Mountain	0	0	0	0	0	0	0	0	0	0
	Rock Island	1	0	0	0	1	5	0	5	0	0
	Sgt. Alvin C. York	0	0	0	0	0	0	0	0	0	0
	South Cumberland Recreation Area	0	0	0	0	0	3	0	3	0	0
	Standing Stone	0	0	0	0	0	0	0	0	0	0
	Sycamore Shoals State Historic Park	0	0	0	0	0	0	0	0	0	0
	Tim's Ford	0	0	0	0	0	0	0	0	0	0
	T.O. Fuller	0	0	0	0	0	0	0	0	0	0
	Warrior's Path	0	0	0	0	0	4	1	3	0	0
TennCare Office of Inspector General		0	0	0	0	0	0	0	0	0	0
Tennessee Bureau of Investigation		18	3	2	1	12	10	1	9	0	0
Tennessee Department of Revenue	Special Investigations Unit	0	0	0	0	0	0	0	0	0	0
Wildlife Resources Agency	Region 1	0	0	0	0	0	0	0	0	0	0
	Region 2	0	0	0	0	0	0	0	0	0	0
	Region 3	0	0	0	0	0	0	0	0	0	0
	Region 4	0	0	0	0	0	0	0	0	0	0
Tennessee, Other Agencies											
Chattanooga Housing Authority		1	0	0	0	1	2	2	0	0	0
Chattanooga Metropolitan Airport		0	0	0	0	0	4	0	4	0	0
Dickson Parks and Recreation		1	0	0	0	1	2	1	1	0	0
Drug Task Force	1st Judicial District	0	0	0	0	0	0	0	0	0	0
	2nd Judicial District	0	0	0	0	0	0	0	0	0	0
	3rd Judicial District	0	0	0	0	0	0	0	0	0	0
	4th Judicial District	0	0	0	0	0	0	0	0	0	0
	5th Judicial District	0	0	0	0	0	0	0	0	0	0
	8th Judicial District	1	0	0	0	1	0	0	0	0	0
	9th Judicial District	0	0	0	0	0	0	0	0	0	0
	10th Judicial District	0	0	0	0	0	1	0	1	0	0
	12th Judicial District	0	0	0	0	0	0	0	0	0	0
	13th Judicial District	0	0	0	0	0	0	0	0	0	0
	14th Judicial District	0	0	0	0	0	0	0	0	0	0
	15th Judicial District	0	0	0	0	0	0	0	0	0	0
	17th Judicial District	0	0	0	0	0	0	0	0	0	0
	18th Judicial District	0	0	0	0	0	2	0	2	0	0
	19th Judicial District	1	0	0	1	0	2	0	2	0	1
	21st Judicial District	0	0	0	0	0	0	0	0	0	0
	22nd Judicial District	0	0	0	0	0	2	0	2	0	0
	23rd Judicial District	0	0	0	0	0	1	0	1	0	0
	24th Judicial District	1	0	0	0	1	3	0	3	0	0
	25th Judicial District	0	0	0	0	0	0	0	0	0	0
	27th Judicial District	0	0	0	0	0	0	0	0	0	0
	31st Judicial District	0	0	0	0	0	0	0	0	0	0
Knoxville Metropolitan Airport		0	0	0	0	0	20	1	18	1	0
Memphis International Airport		2	0	0	0	2	165	0	161	4	0
Metropolitan Nashville Park Police		20	0	1	3	16	116	2	113	1	4
Nashville International Airport		1	0	0	0	1	34	0	21	13	0
Smyrna/Rutherford County Airport Authority		0	0	0	0	0	0	0	0	0	0
Tri-Cities Regional Airport		0	0	0	0	0	2	0	2	0	0
West Tennessee Violent Crime Task Force		0	0	0	0	0	1	0	1	0	0
Texas, Tribal Agencies											
Ysleta Del Sur Pueblo Tribal		91	0	0	0	91	73	10	56	7	0
Texas, Other Agencies											
Amarillo International Airport		1	0	0	0	1	2	1	1	0	0
Dallas-Fort Worth International Airport		4	0	0	0	4	538	11	500	27	0
Hospital District	Dallas County	3	0	0	0	3	377	12	361	4	1
	Tarrant County	2	0	0	1	1	143	4	137	2	0

NA = Not available.

[1] If a blank is presented in the arson column, it indicates that the FBI did not receive 12 complete months of arson data for that agency.

Table II-11.   Offenses Known to Law Enforcement, by Selected State, Tribal, and Other Agencies, 2011—*Continued*

(Number.)

State/Agency Type	Unit/Office	Violent crime	Murder and non-negligent man-slaughter	Forcible rape	Robbery	Aggra-vated assault	Property crime	Burglary	Larceny-theft	Motor vehicle theft	Arson[1]
Houston Metropolitan Transit Authority		1	0	0	1	0	35	0	29	6	0
Independent School District...	Aldine	16	0	0	6	10	96	21	72	3	0
	Alvin	6	0	2	0	4	106	6	100	0	0
	Angleton	0	0	0	0	0	27	2	25	0	0
	Austin	21	0	1	6	14	724	42	676	6	21
	Barbers Hill	0	0	0	0	0	16	1	14	1	0
	Bay City	0	0	0	0	0	33	9	24	0	2
	Cedar Hill	9	0	0	1	8	19	2	15	2	0
	Conroe	11	0	0	3	8	320	5	311	4	3
	East Central	0	0	0	0	0	1	1	0	0	0
	Ector County	33	0	1	0	32	127	9	118	0	0
	Edinburg	5	0	0	0	5	219	7	212	0	3
	El Paso	30	0	1	4	25	388	51	334	3	1
	Floresville	0	0	0	0	0	30	1	29	0	0
	Fort Bend	2	0	1	0	1	398	18	380	0	0
	Hallsville	1	0	0	0	1	9	0	8	1	2
	Humble	3	0	1	0	2	157	2	151	4	0
	Judson	1	0	0	0	1	8	0	8	0	0
	Katy	10	0	3	3	4	341	4	329	8	2
	Killeen	5	0	3	0	2	81	6	74	1	0
	Klein	2	0	0	1	1	35	0	35	0	1
	Lyford	0	0	0	0	0	8	0	8	0	0
	Midland	0	0	0	0	0	34	2	32	0	0
	North East	88	0	3	3	82	363	6	357	0	0
	Pasadena	3	0	1	1	1	275	14	252	9	0
	Pflugerville	4	0	0	0	4	68	1	66	1	4
	Raymondville	0	0	0	0	0	4	2	2	0	0
	Rio Grande City	10	0	0	0	10	62	0	59	3	2
	Socorro	1	0	0	0	1	96	3	93	0	0
	Spring	42	0	0	6	36	97	8	85	4	3
	Spring Branch	3	0	0	2	1	145	12	131	2	0
	Taft	1	0	1	0	0	1	0	1	0	0
	United	0	0	0	0	0	73	1	72	0	1
Port of Houston Authority		0	0	0	0	0	29	4	22	3	0
Utah, State Agencies											
Parks and Recreation..		0	0	0	0	0	3	2	1	0	0
Wildlife Resources		8	0	0	1	7	7	1	6	0	0
Utah, Tribal Agencies											
Goshute Tribal		0	0	0	0	0	0	0	0	0	0
Uintah and Ouray Tribal		8	1	1	0	6	26	18	0	8	0
Utah, Other Agencies											
Cache-Rich Drug Task Force		0	0	0	0	0	4	3	1	0	0
Davis Metropolitan Narcotics Strike Force		1	0	0	1	0	5	0	5	0	0
Granite School District..		5	0	0	0	5	192	34	158	0	12
Utah County Attorney	Investigations Division	0	0	0	0	0	0	0	0	0	0
Utah County Major Crime Task Force		0	0	0	0	0	4	1	1	2	0
Utah Transit Authority..		9	0	0	4	5	2,370	0	2,318	52	0
Vermont, State Agencies											
Fish and Wildlife Department..	Law Enforcement Division	0	0	0	0	0	2	0	2	0	0
State Police..	Bradford	14	0	0	1	13	210	95	94	21	1
	Brattleboro	15	1	4	0	10	136	71	62	3	0
	Derby	18	0	2	1	15	366	158	182	26	1
	Middlesex	3	0	1	1	1	243	89	154	0	2
	New Haven	19	0	6	0	13	353	137	202	14	1
	Rockingham	10	0	1	1	8	272	159	101	12	0
	Royalton	21	3	6	1	11	270	116	133	21	0
	Rutland	21	0	2	2	17	678	327	318	33	2
	Shaftsbury	21	0	2	0	19	211	101	98	12	0
	St. Albans	31	0	7	1	23	419	135	251	33	2
	St. Johnsbury	30	0	3	2	25	315	157	139	19	3
Vermont State Police		0	0	0	0	0	0	0	0	0	0
Vermont State Police Headquarters	Bureau of Criminal Investigations	0	0	0	0	0	12	7	5	0	0
Virginia, State Agencies											
Alcoholic Beverage Control Commission......................		0	0	0	0	0	27	0	27	0	0
Department of Game and Inland Fisheries	Enforcement Division	6	0	0	0	6	9	1	7	1	1
Department of Motor Vehicles.......................................		0	0	0	0	0	70	0	21	49	0
Southside Virginia Training Center..............................		2	0	0	0	2	14	0	14	0	0
State Police..	Accomack County	0	0	0	0	0	14	3	8	3	3
	Albemarle County	0	0	0	0	0	1	0	0	1	0
	Alleghany County	0	0	0	0	0	4	0	3	1	0

NA = Not available.

[1] If a blank is presented in the arson column, it indicates that the FBI did not receive 12 complete months of arson data for that agency.

Table II-11.   Offenses Known to Law Enforcement, by Selected State, Tribal, and Other Agencies, 2011—*Continued*

(Number.)

State/Agency Type	Unit/Office	Violent crime	Murder and non-negligent man-slaughter	Forcible rape	Robbery	Aggra-vated assault	Property crime	Burglary	Larceny-theft	Motor vehicle theft	Arson[1]
	Amherst County	0	0	0	0	0	2	0	2	0	0
	Appomattox County	0	0	0	0	0	0	0	0	0	0
	Augusta County	0	0	0	0	0	0	0	0	0	1
	Bedford County	2	0	0	0	2	17	0	15	2	2
	Bland County	0	0	0	0	0	3	0	3	0	0
	Botetourt County	1	0	0	0	1	1	0	1	0	0
	Buchanan County	4	2	0	0	2	28	4	20	4	2
	Campbell County	0	0	0	0	0	8	2	5	1	0
	Caroline County	0	0	0	0	0	12	1	8	3	1
	Carroll County	0	0	0	0	0	3	0	1	2	0
	Chesapeake	2	0	0	0	2	14	0	5	9	0
	Chesterfield County	1	0	0	0	1	15	0	11	4	0
	Culpeper County	1	0	0	0	1	4	0	2	2	3
	Dickenson County	1	0	0	0	1	11	2	3	6	1
	Dinwiddie County	0	0	0	0	0	1	0	1	0	0
	Fairfax County	8	0	0	0	8	26	0	21	5	0
	Fauquier County	0	0	0	0	0	5	1	0	4	0
	Franklin County	1	0	0	0	1	3	0	0	3	0
	Frederick County	0	0	0	0	0	12	0	8	4	1
	Fredericksburg	0	0	0	0	0	0	0	0	0	0
	Gloucester County	1	0	0	0	1	3	0	3	0	0
	Goochland County	0	0	0	0	0	8	0	7	1	0
	Grayson County	0	0	0	0	0	1	0	1	0	0
	Greensville County	0	0	0	0	0	3	0	2	1	0
	Hampton	11	0	0	0	11	2	0	1	1	0
	Hanover County	1	0	0	0	1	3	0	2	1	0
	Harrisonburg	1	0	0	0	1	6	0	3	3	0
	Henrico County	1	0	0	1	0	8	0	7	1	0
	Henry County	0	0	0	0	0	3	0	2	1	0
	King George County	1	0	0	0	1	3	0	3	0	0
	Lee County	0	0	0	0	0	2	0	0	2	1
	Loudoun County	0	0	0	0	0	2	0	1	1	0
	Mecklenburg County	0	0	0	0	0	6	1	4	1	0
	Montgomery County	4	1	0	0	3	2	0	2	0	0
	Newport News	1	0	0	0	1	2	0	1	1	0
	Norfolk	3	0	0	0	3	7	0	1	6	0
	Northampton County	0	0	0	0	0	0	0	0	0	0
	Page County	0	0	0	0	0	0	0	0	0	0
	Pittsylvania County	1	0	0	0	1	18	1	3	14	0
	Portsmouth	0	0	0	0	0	6	0	3	3	0
	Prince George County	2	0	0	0	2	0	0	0	0	0
	Prince William County	0	0	0	0	0	11	0	6	5	0
	Pulaski County	1	0	1	0	0	11	0	11	0	0
	Richmond	0	0	0	0	0	9	0	5	4	1
	Roanoke	0	0	0	0	0	3	0	3	0	0
	Roanoke County	0	0	0	0	0	3	0	3	0	0
	Rockbridge County	0	0	0	0	0	4	0	4	0	1
	Rockingham County	2	0	0	0	2	26	0	7	19	0
	Russell County	0	0	0	0	0	0	0	0	0	1
	Shenandoah County	1	0	0	0	1	1	0	1	0	0
	Smyth County	0	0	0	0	0	7	2	2	3	0
	Southampton County	0	0	0	0	0	3	0	2	1	0
	Spotsylvania County	0	0	0	0	0	0	0	0	0	0
	Stafford County	0	0	0	0	0	0	0	0	0	0
	Tazewell County	0	0	0	0	0	5	0	5	0	1
	Virginia Beach	1	0	0	0	1	8	0	6	2	0
	Warren County	2	0	0	0	2	1	0	1	0	0
	Washington County	2	0	0	0	2	1	0	0	1	0
	Williamsburg	0	0	0	0	0	1	0	1	0	0
	Winchester	0	0	0	0	0	1	0	1	0	1
	Wise County	1	1	0	0	0	3	0	3	0	0
	Wythe County	1	0	0	0	1	22	1	18	3	0
	York County	0	0	0	0	0	2	0	2	0	0
Virginia State Capitol		1	0	0	1	0	25	0	25	0	0
Virginia, Other Agencies											
Norfolk Airport Authority		0	0	0	0	0	43	0	43	0	0
Port Authority...	Norfolk	0	0	0	0	0	1	0	1	0	0
Reagan National Airport................................		0	0	0	0	0	352	0	306	46	0
Richmond International Airport.....................		0	0	0	0	0	9	0	9	0	0
Washington, State Agencies											
State Insurance Commissioner	Special Investigations Unit	0	0	0	0	0	0	0	0	0	0

NA = Not available.

[1] If a blank is presented in the arson column, it indicates that the FBI did not receive 12 complete months of arson data for that agency.

Table II-11.   Offenses Known to Law Enforcement, by Selected State, Tribal, and Other Agencies, 2011—*Continued*

(Number.)

State/Agency Type	Unit/Office	Violent crime	Murder and non-negligent man-slaughter	Forcible rape	Robbery	Aggra-vated assault	Property crime	Burglary	Larceny-theft	Motor vehicle theft	Arson[1]
Washington, Tribal Agencies											
Chehalis Tribal		6	0	2	2	2	81	13	63	5	0
Colville Tribal		78	0	13	2	63	221	42	150	29	28
Hoh Tribal		0	0	0	0	0	5	2	3	0	0
Jamestown S'Klallam Tribal		0	0	0	0	0	11	1	8	2	0
Kalispel Tribal		18	1	0	3	14	73	16	43	14	0
La Push Tribal		22	0	2	1	19	48	3	36	9	0
Lower Elwha Tribal		3	0	0	1	2	33	13	14	6	2
Lummi Tribal		33	1	7	8	17	319	128	190	1	0
Makah Tribal		15	0	3	0	12	16	7	7	2	1
Nisqually Tribal		1	0	1	0	0	33	8	23	2	0
Nooksack Tribal		7	0	0	0	7	31	8	20	3	0
Puyallup Tribal		38	0	5	19	14	413	61	246	106	1
Quinault Indian Nation		1	0	1	0	0	32	26	0	6	0
Shoalwater Bay Tribal		1	0	0	0	1	7	3	4	0	0
Skokomish Tribal		1	0	0	0	1	23	8	10	5	0
Spokane Agency		44	0	0	2	42	32	30	0	2	0
Stillaguamish Tribal		0	0	0	0	0	39	10	22	7	0
Suquamish Tribal		28	0	1	1	26	111	32	73	6	1
Swinomish Tribal		5	0	0	2	3	155	36	116	3	1
Upper Skagit Tribal		0	0	0	0	0	11	9	0	2	0
Yakama Nation		16	0	10	0	6	534	279	193	62	6
Washington, Other Agencies											
Port of Seattle		35	0	1	0	34	833	25	768	40	0
West Virginia, State Agencies											
Division of Natural Resources	Barbour County	0	0	0	0	0	0	0	0	0	0
	Berkeley County	0	0	0	0	0	0	0	0	0	0
	Boone County	0	0	0	0	0	0	0	0	0	0
	Braxton County	0	0	0	0	0	0	0	0	0	0
	Brooke County	0	0	0	0	0	0	0	0	0	0
	Cabell County	0	0	0	0	0	0	0	0	0	0
	Calhoun County	0	0	0	0	0	0	0	0	0	0
	Clay County	0	0	0	0	0	0	0	0	0	0
	Doddridge County	0	0	0	0	0	0	0	0	0	0
	Fayette County	0	0	0	0	0	0	0	0	0	0
	Gilmer County	0	0	0	0	0	0	0	0	0	0
	Grant County	0	0	0	0	0	0	0	0	0	0
	Greenbrier County	0	0	0	0	0	0	0	0	0	0
	Hampshire County	0	0	0	0	0	0	0	0	0	0
	Hancock County	0	0	0	0	0	0	0	0	0	0
	Hardy County	0	0	0	0	0	0	0	0	0	0
	Harrison County	0	0	0	0	0	0	0	0	0	0
	Jackson County	0	0	0	0	0	0	0	0	0	0
	Jefferson County	0	0	0	0	0	0	0	0	0	0
	Kanawha County	0	0	0	0	0	0	0	0	0	0
	Lewis County	0	0	0	0	0	0	0	0	0	0
	Lincoln County	0	0	0	0	0	0	0	0	0	0
	Logan County	0	0	0	0	0	0	0	0	0	0
	Marion County	0	0	0	0	0	0	0	0	0	0
	Marshall County	0	0	0	0	0	0	0	0	0	0
	Mason County	0	0	0	0	0	0	0	0	0	0
	McDowell County	0	0	0	0	0	0	0	0	0	0
	Mercer County	0	0	0	0	0	0	0	0	0	0
	Mineral County	0	0	0	0	0	0	0	0	0	0
	Mingo County	0	0	0	0	0	0	0	0	0	0
	Monongalia County	0	0	0	0	0	0	0	0	0	0
	Monroe County	0	0	0	0	0	0	0	0	0	0
	Morgan County	0	0	0	0	0	0	0	0	0	0
	Nicholas County	0	0	0	0	0	0	0	0	0	0
	Ohio County	0	0	0	0	0	0	0	0	0	0
	Pendleton County	0	0	0	0	0	0	0	0	0	0
	Pleasants County	0	0	0	0	0	0	0	0	0	0
	Pocahontas County	0	0	0	0	0	0	0	0	0	0
	Preston County	0	0	0	0	0	0	0	0	0	0
	Putnam County	0	0	0	0	0	0	0	0	0	0
	Raleigh County	0	0	0	0	0	0	0	0	0	0
	Randolph County	0	0	0	0	0	0	0	0	0	0
	Ritchie County	0	0	0	0	0	0	0	0	0	0
	Roane County	0	0	0	0	0	0	0	0	0	0
	Summers County	0	0	0	0	0	0	0	0	0	0
	Taylor County	0	0	0	0	0	0	0	0	0	0
	Tucker County	0	0	0	0	0	0	0	0	0	0
	Tyler County	0	0	0	0	0	0	0	0	0	0

NA = Not available.

[1] If a blank is presented in the arson column, it indicates that the FBI did not receive 12 complete months of arson data for that agency.

Table II-11.   Offenses Known to Law Enforcement, by Selected State, Tribal, and Other Agencies, 2011—*Continued*

(Number.)

State/Agency Type	Unit/Office	Violent crime	Murder and non-negligent man-slaughter	Forcible rape	Robbery	Aggra-vated assault	Property crime	Burglary	Larceny-theft	Motor vehicle theft	Arson[1]
	Upshur County	0	0	0	0	0	0	0	0	0	0
	Wayne County	0	0	0	0	0	0	0	0	0	0
	Webster County	0	0	0	0	0	0	0	0	0	0
	Wetzel County	0	0	0	0	0	0	0	0	0	0
	Wirt County	0	0	0	0	0	0	0	0	0	0
	Wood County	0	0	0	0	0	0	0	0	0	0
	Wyoming County	0	0	0	0	0	0	0	0	0	0
State Police....................................	Beckley	31	0	1	3	27	475	110	324	41	1
	Berkeley Springs	6	0	0	0	6	115	47	58	10	1
	Bridgeport	17	1	1	3	12	295	99	172	24	0
	Buckhannon	7	0	1	0	6	107	24	79	4	0
	Clay	12	1	0	1	10	48	15	27	6	0
	Elizabeth	16	0	2	0	14	41	18	23	0	1
	Elkins	15	0	1	1	13	196	58	134	4	5
	Fairmont	9	0	2	1	6	129	43	81	5	0
	Franklin	7	1	2	0	4	32	11	20	1	0
	Gauley Bridge	5	1	0	0	4	60	17	37	6	0
	Gilbert	8	0	3	0	5	71	25	41	5	0
	Glenville	9	1	0	0	8	28	6	22	0	2
	Grafton	2	0	0	0	2	11	3	5	3	0
	Grantsville	18	2	0	0	16	53	8	41	4	1
	Hamlin	49	0	4	1	44	375	130	207	38	5
	Harrisville	7	0	2	0	5	74	10	50	14	0
	Hinton	4	1	0	0	3	78	34	41	3	0
	Hundred	3	0	0	0	3	29	9	19	1	1
	Huntington	13	1	4	0	8	421	40	360	21	1
	Internet Crimes Against Children Unit	0	0	0	0	0	0	0	0	0	0
	Jesse	7	0	1	1	5	38	8	26	4	0
	Kearneysville	30	0	0	1	29	285	79	193	13	2
	Keyser	25	0	3	0	22	254	101	148	5	1
	Kingwood	20	0	5	1	14	155	74	63	18	1
	Lewisburg	8	0	0	0	8	95	23	67	5	0
	Logan	89	2	14	5	68	475	125	301	49	2
	Madison	25	1	1	0	23	226	52	152	22	1
	Marlinton	5	0	0	0	5	72	22	48	2	1
	Martinsburg	99	1	7	14	77	632	183	388	61	4
	Moorefield	16	1	1	1	13	87	43	40	4	0
	Morgantown	62	0	6	5	51	627	193	396	38	2
	Moundsville	2	0	1	0	1	23	8	14	1	0
	New Cumberland	3	0	2	0	1	13	2	11	0	0
	Oak Hill	12	1	3	1	7	157	33	114	10	1
	Paden City	4	0	2	0	2	36	8	25	3	0
	Parkersburg	5	0	0	0	5	117	22	76	19	0
	Parsons	2	0	0	0	2	16	5	11	0	2
	Petersburg	13	0	3	1	9	56	22	32	2	0
	Philippi	5	0	0	0	5	47	20	25	2	0
	Point Pleasant	19	3	3	6	7	124	47	66	11	0
	Princeton	34	0	5	6	23	412	87	298	27	0
	Quincy	13	1	1	0	11	158	30	117	11	2
	Rainelle	2	0	0	0	2	62	21	35	6	0
	Richwood	1	0	0	0	1	15	4	10	1	1
	Ripley	3	0	0	0	3	104	33	66	5	0
	Romney	12	0	2	2	8	114	42	62	10	1
	South Charleston	40	0	9	4	27	502	60	408	34	1
	Spencer	11	1	0	0	10	41	13	24	4	1
	St. Marys	3	0	2	0	1	17	3	10	4	0
	Summersville	3	0	0	0	3	61	12	42	7	0
	Sutton	12	0	1	1	10	76	16	56	4	0
	Union	5	2	0	0	3	45	14	26	5	0
	Upperglade	12	0	0	0	12	53	18	32	3	0
	Wayne	31	0	3	5	23	422	122	264	36	0
	Welch	13	1	0	0	12	110	41	61	8	2
	Wellsburg	0	0	0	0	0	18	5	9	4	0
	Weston	12	1	0	0	11	84	21	54	9	1
	West Union	4	0	0	0	4	24	9	13	2	0
	Wheeling	5	0	5	0	0	54	13	39	2	0
	Whitesville	6	0	0	0	6	82	10	69	3	0
	Williamson	50	2	1	1	46	129	25	92	12	2
	Winfield	11	0	2	0	9	146	26	106	14	0

NA = Not available.

[1] If a blank is presented in the arson column, it indicates that the FBI did not receive 12 complete months of arson data for that agency.

Table II-11.   Offenses Known to Law Enforcement, by Selected State, Tribal, and Other Agencies, 2011—*Continued*

(Number.)

State/Agency Type	Unit/Office	Violent crime	Murder and non-negligent man-slaughter	Forcible rape	Robbery	Aggra-vated assault	Property crime	Burglary	Larceny-theft	Motor vehicle theft	Arson[1]
State Police, Bureau of Criminal Investigation.............	Beckley	0	0	0	0	0	2	1	1	0	0
	Bluefield	0	0	0	0	0	0	0	0	0	0
	Buckhannon	0	0	0	0	0	0	0	0	0	0
	Charleston	0	0	0	0	0	0	0	0	0	0
	Fairmont	0	0	0	0	0	0	0	0	0	0
State Police, Parkway Authority	Fayette County	0	0	0	0	0	0	0	0	0	0
	Kanawha County	0	0	0	0	0	8	0	7	1	0
	Mercer County	0	0	0	0	0	0	0	0	0	0
	Raleigh County	0	0	0	0	0	7	1	6	0	0
West Virginia, Other Agencies											
Central West Virginia Drug Task Force		0	0	0	0	0	0	0	0	0	0
Eastern Panhandle Drug and Violent Crime Task Force		0	0	0	0	0	1	0	1	0	0
Hancock/Brooke/Weirton Drug Task Force		0	0	0	0	0	0	0	0	0	0
Harrison County Drug and Violent Crime Task Force		0	0	0	0	0	0	0	0	0	0
Huntington Drug and Violent Crime Task Force		0	0	0	0	0	0	0	0	0	0
Logan County Drug and Violent Crime Task Force		0	0	0	0	0	0	0	0	0	0
Metropolitan Drug Enforcement Network Team		1	0	0	0	1	0	0	0	0	0
Ohio Valley Drug and Violent Crime Task Force.........		0	0	0	0	0	0	0	0	0	0
Parkersburg Narcotics and Violent Crime Task Force		0	0	0	0	0	0	0	0	0	0
Potomac Highlands Drug and Violent Crime Task Force		0	0	0	0	0	0	0	0	0	0
Three Rivers Drug and Violent Crime Task Force.......		0	0	0	0	0	0	0	0	0	0
Wisconsin, State Agencies											
Capitol Police..		0	0	0	0	0	70	8	61	1	0
Department of Natural Resources...............................		0	0	0	0	0	0	0	0	0	0
Wisconsin State Patrol...		0	0	0	0	0	0	0	0	0	0
Wisconsin, Tribal Agencies											
Lac du Flambeau Tribal...		26	0	3	3	20	361	65	280	16	6
Menominee Tribal..		36	0	3	1	32	111	20	77	14	2
Oneida Tribal...		22	1	1	1	19	102	26	69	7	0
Red Cliff Tribal...		4	0	0	0	4	103	18	77	8	0
St. Croix Tribal..		0	0	0	0	0	44	9	30	5	0
Stockbridge Munsee Tribal		5	0	2	0	3	90	40	49	1	0
Wyoming, Tribal Agencies											
Wind River Agency...		82	3	6	1	72	70	14	35	21	3
Puerto Rico		10,540	1,136	45	6,465	2,894	51,717	16,591	29,273	5,853	NA
Puerto Rico											
Virgin Islands											
St. Croix..		593	27	20	114	432	1,280	545	633	102	32
St. Thomas		735	14	35	167	519	1,674	823	739	112	18
Federal Agencies											
National Institutes of Health		0	0	0	0	0	79	1	77	1	0
Department of the Interior	Bureau of Indian Affairs[5]	5,983	141	1,264	280	4,298	20,597	5,263	12,692	2,642	918
	Bureau of Land Management	11	3	0	1	7	374	8	341	25	61
	Bureau of Reclamation	1	0	0	1	0	5	0	5	0	0
	Fish and Wildlife Service	32	6	5	4	17	444	80	327	37	69
	National Park Service	323	7	34	58	224	2,549	292	2,161	96	73

[1] If a blank is presented in the arson column, it indicates that the FBI did not receive 12 complete months of arson data for that agency.
[5] Tribal figures represented throughout Table 11 are included in the aggregated totals listed under the Bureau of Indian Affairs data.

Table II-12. Crime Trends, by Population Group, 2010–2011

(Number, percent change.)

Population group	Violent crime	Murder and non-negligent man-slaughter	Forcible rape	Robbery	Aggra-vated assault	Property crime	Burglary	Larceny-theft	Motor vehicle theft	Arson	Number of agencies	2011 estimated population
Total, All Agencies												
2010	1,181,882	14,103	78,324	355,154	734,301	8,511,419	2,025,882	5,782,929	702,608	51,620		
2011	1,134,527	13,913	75,341	341,298	703,975	8,458,639	2,034,562	5,743,662	680,415	49,191	14,717	292,506,506
Percent change	-4.0	-1.3	-3.8	-3.9	-4.1	-0.6	+0.4	-0.7	-3.2	-4.7		
Total, Cities												
2010	946,384	10,905	58,220	311,034	566,225	6,652,581	1,485,743	4,608,166	558,672	38,667		
2011	912,979	10,823	56,652	300,223	545,281	6,603,857	1,491,850	4,568,015	543,992	37,124	10,570	197,757,214
Percent change	-3.5	-0.8	-2.7	-3.5	-3.7	-0.7	+0.4	-0.9	-2.6	-4.0		
Group I (250,000 and over)												
2010	431,139	5,755	18,699	168,528	238,157	2,156,411	510,859	1,384,193	261,359	13,426		
2011	416,888	5,606	18,524	163,172	229,586	2,132,880	512,076	1,365,045	255,759	13,083	74	55,434,683
Percent change	-3.3	-2.6	-0.9	-3.2	-3.6	-1.1	+0.2	-1.4	-2.1	-2.6		
1,000,000 and over (Group I subset)												
2010	183,261	2,315	6,062	78,293	96,591	810,340	172,991	535,650	101,699	3,890		
2011	176,602	2,223	5,947	74,249	94,183	791,320	172,588	520,049	98,683	3,604	10	25,247,146
Percent change	-3.6	-4.0	-1.9	-5.2	-2.5	-2.3	-0.2	-2.9	-3.0	-7.4		
500,000 to 999,999 (Group I subset)												
2010	138,154	1,792	6,646	49,258	80,458	753,582	184,393	480,058	89,131	4,807		
2011	133,879	1,756	6,656	48,380	77,087	747,268	184,976	475,738	86,554	4,742	24	16,335,382
Percent change	-3.1	-2.0	+0.2	-1.8	-4.2	-0.8	+0.3	-0.9	-2.9	-1.4		
250,000 to 499,999 (Group I subset)												
2010	109,724	1,648	5,991	40,977	61,108	592,489	153,475	368,485	70,529	4,729		
2011	106,407	1,627	5,921	40,543	58,316	594,292	154,512	369,258	70,522	4,737	40	13,852,155
Percent change	-3.0	-1.3	-1.2	-1.1	-4.6	+0.3	+0.7	+0.2	*	+0.2		
Group II (100,000 to 249,999)												
2010	157,917	1,774	10,072	51,826	94,245	1,164,126	274,124	785,903	104,099	6,775		
2011	152,076	1,833	9,523	50,034	90,686	1,143,385	274,428	769,164	99,793	6,348	207	31,014,905
Percent change	-3.7	+3.3	-5.5	-3.5	-3.8	-1.8	+0.1	-2.1	-4.1	-6.3		
Group III (50,000 to 99,999)												
2010	120,757	1,253	8,418	37,086	74,000	982,605	216,978	689,347	76,280	5,584		
2011	114,889	1,095	8,205	35,279	70,310	981,855	220,298	687,716	73,841	5,272	454	31,501,619
Percent change	-4.9	-12.6	-2.5	-4.9	-5.0	-0.1	+1.5	-0.2	-3.2	-5.6		
Group IV (25,000 to 49,999)												
2010	89,956	910	7,870	24,822	56,354	860,701	180,615	630,543	49,543	4,568		
2011	88,052	891	7,708	24,169	55,284	855,245	181,006	625,519	48,720	4,264	832	28,896,584
Percent change	-2.1	-2.1	-2.1	-2.6	-1.9	-0.6	+0.2	-0.8	-1.7	-6.7		
Group V (10,000 to 24,999)												
2010	79,692	684	6,948	18,112	53,948	799,108	166,599	593,466	39,043	3,832		
2011	76,659	763	6,774	17,288	51,834	799,276	167,963	593,223	38,090	3,679	1,788	28,423,298
Percent change	-3.8	+11.5	-2.5	-4.5	-3.9	*	+0.8	*	-2.4	-4.0		
Group VI (under 10,000)												
2010	66,923	529	6,213	10,660	49,521	689,630	136,568	524,714	28,348	4,482		
2011	64,415	635	5,918	10,281	47,581	691,216	136,079	527,348	27,789	4,478	7,215	22,486,125
Percent change	-3.7	+20.0	-4.7	-3.6	-3.9	+0.2	-0.4	+0.5	-2.0	-0.1		
Metropolitan Counties												
2010	184,513	2,346	14,202	40,054	127,911	1,434,808	390,792	926,675	117,341	9,338		
2011	172,794	2,243	13,298	37,229	120,024	1,419,972	392,065	917,393	110,514	8,790	1,735	67,858,398
Percent change	-6.4	-4.4	-6.4	-7.1	-6.2	-1.0	+0.3	-1.0	-5.8	-5.9		
Nonmetropolitan Counties[1]												
2010	50,985	852	5,902	4,066	40,165	424,030	149,347	248,088	26,595	3,615		
2011	48,754	847	5,391	3,846	38,670	434,810	150,647	258,254	25,909	3,277	2,412	26,890,894
Percent change	-4.4	-0.6	-8.7	-5.4	-3.7	+2.5	+0.9	+4.1	-2.6	-9.3		
Suburban Areas[2]												
2010	325,617	3,593	26,054	76,138	219,832	2,939,418	682,943	2,055,994	200,481	16,831		
2011	308,991	3,499	24,767	71,889	208,836	2,918,518	687,185	2,039,842	191,491	15,704	7,847	124,855,631
Percent change	-5.1	-2.6	-4.9	-5.6	-5.0	-0.7	+0.6	-0.8	-4.5	-6.7		

* = Less than one-tenth of 1 percent.

[1] Includes state police agencies that report aggregately for the entire state.

[2] Suburban areas include law enforcement agencies in cities with less than 50,000 inhabitants and county law enforcement agencies that are within a Metropolitan Statistical Area. Suburban areas exclude all metropolitan agencies associated with a principal city. The agencies associated with suburban areas also appear in other groups within this table.

Table II-13. Crime Trends, by Suburban and Nonsuburban Cities[1], by Population Group, 2010–2011

(Number, percent change.)

Population group	Violent crime	Murder and non-negligent man-slaughter	Forcible rape	Robbery	Aggra-vated assault	Property crime	Burglary	Larceny-theft	Motor vehicle theft	Arson	Number of agencies	2011 estimated population
Suburban Cities												
2010	140,045	1,232	11,741	35,836	91,236	1,494,604	289,681	1,122,173	82,750	7,443		
2011	135,051	1,232	11,347	34,396	88,076	1,487,199	292,054	1,114,706	80,439	6,878	6,104	56,825,644
Percent change	-3.6	0.0	-3.4	-4.0	-3.5	-0.5	+0.8	-0.7	-2.8	-7.6		
Group IV (25,000 to 49,999)												
2010	53,813	559	4,413	15,636	33,205	547,409	109,054	402,355	36,000	2,799		
2011	51,975	512	4,304	15,147	32,012	541,155	110,185	396,276	34,694	2,485	627	21,573,271
Percent change	-3.4	-8.4	-2.5	-3.1	-3.6	-1.1	+1.0	-1.5	-3.6	-11.2		
Group V (10,000 to 24,999)												
2010	50,362	428	4,161	12,928	32,845	522,301	104,271	389,078	28,952	2,514		
2011	47,721	441	3,988	12,237	31,055	521,217	105,692	387,206	28,319	2,333	1,335	21,440,907
Percent change	-5.2	+3.0	-4.2	-5.3	-5.4	-0.2	+1.4	-0.5	-2.2	-7.2		
Group VI (under 10,000)												
2010	35,870	245	3,167	7,272	25,186	424,894	76,356	330,740	17,798	2,130		
2011	35,355	279	3,055	7,012	25,009	424,827	76,177	331,224	17,426	2,060	4,142	13,811,466
Percent change	-1.4	+13.9	-3.5	-3.6	-0.7	*	-0.2	+0.1	-2.1	-3.3		
Nonsuburban Cities												
2010	96,526	891	9,290	17,758	68,587	854,835	194,101	626,550	34,184	5,439		
2011	94,075	1,057	9,053	17,342	66,623	858,538	192,994	631,384	34,160	5,543	3,731	22,980,363
Percent change	-2.5	+18.6	-2.6	-2.3	-2.9	+0.4	-0.6	+0.8	-0.1	+1.9		
Group IV (25,000 to 49,999)												
2010	36,143	351	3,457	9,186	23,149	313,292	71,561	228,188	13,543	1,769		
2011	36,077	379	3,404	9,022	23,272	314,090	70,821	229,243	14,026	1,779	205	7,323,313
Percent change	-0.2	+8.0	-1.5	-1.8	+0.5	+0.3	-1.0	+0.5	+3.6	+0.6		
Group V (10,000 to 24,999)												
2010	29,330	256	2,787	5,184	21,103	276,807	62,328	204,388	10,091	1,318		
2011	28,938	322	2,786	5,051	20,779	278,059	62,271	206,017	9,771	1,346	453	6,982,391
Percent change	-1.3	+25.8	*	-2.6	-1.5	+0.5	-0.1	+0.8	-3.2	+2.1		
Group VI (under 10,000)												
2010	31,053	284	3,046	3,388	24,335	264,736	60,212	193,974	10,550	2,352		
2011	29,060	356	2,863	3,269	22,572	266,389	59,902	196,124	10,363	2,418	3,073	8,674,659
Percent change	-6.4	+25.4	-6.0	-3.5	-7.2	+0.6	-0.5	+1.1	-1.8	+2.8		

* = Less than one-tenth of 1 percent.
[1] Suburban cities include law enforcement agencies in cities with less than 50,000 inhabitants that are within a Metropolitan Statistical Area. Suburban cities exclude all metropolitan agencies associated with a principal city. Nonsuburban cities include law enforcement agencies in cities with less than 50,000 inhabitants that are not associated with a Metropolitan Statistical Area.

Table II-14. Crime Trends, by Metropolitan and Nonmetropolitan Counties[1], by Population Group, 2010–2011

(Number, percent change.)

Population group and range	Violent crime	Murder and non-negligent man-slaughter	Forcible rape	Robbery	Aggra-vated assault	Property crime	Burglary	Larceny-theft	Motor vehicle theft	Arson	Number of agencies	2011 estimated population
Metropolitan Counties												
100,000 and over												
2010	126,789	1,587	8,150	33,334	83,718	936,419	243,633	615,601	77,185	5,630		
2011	117,739	1,472	7,636	30,507	78,124	913,307	240,309	601,479	71,519	5,249	154	41,109,258
Percent change	-7.1	-7.2	-6.3	-8.5	-6.7	-2.5	-1.4	-2.3	-7.3	-6.8		
25,000 to 99,999												
2010	41,633	566	4,444	4,605	32,018	376,332	117,212	235,645	23,475	2,284		
2011	40,248	589	4,083	4,852	30,724	383,124	120,875	239,714	22,535	2,239	428	22,123,925
Percent change	-3.3	+4.1	-8.1	+5.4	-4.0	+1.8	+3.1	+1.7	-4.0	-2.0		
Under 25,000												
2010	15,855	193	1,539	2,104	12,019	119,132	29,076	73,457	16,599	1,415		
2011	14,714	181	1,509	1,851	11,173	120,456	29,904	74,217	16,335	1,288	1,140	4,390,631
Percent change	-7.2	-6.2	-1.9	-12.0	-7.0	+1.1	+2.8	+1.0	-1.6	-9.0		
Nonmetropolitan Counties												
25,000 and over												
2010	22,239	353	2,358	2,193	17,335	193,048	69,619	112,026	11,403	1,255		
2011	21,161	321	2,149	2,063	16,628	199,628	71,535	117,031	11,062	1,203	296	11,691,442
Percent change	-4.8	-9.1	-8.9	-5.9	-4.1	+3.4	+2.8	+4.5	-3.0	-4.1		
10,000 to 24,999												
2010	14,853	216	1,576	954	12,107	127,594	45,075	74,896	7,623	1,045		
2011	14,448	260	1,434	869	11,885	131,754	44,553	79,662	7,539	979	577	9,354,356
Percent change	-2.7	+20.4	-9.0	-8.9	-1.8	+3.3	-1.2	+6.4	-1.1	-6.3		
Under 10,000												
2010	8,761	151	1,218	329	7,063	63,266	20,417	38,095	4,754	855		
2011	8,032	155	1,129	299	6,449	63,345	19,955	38,723	4,667	716	1,362	4,124,315
Percent change	-8.3	+2.6	-7.3	-9.1	-8.7	+0.1	-2.3	+1.6	-1.8	-16.3		

[1] Metropolitan counties include sheriffs and county law enforcement agencies associated with a Metropolitan Statistical Area. Nonmetropolitan counties include sheriffs and county law enforcement agencies that are not associated with a Metropolitan Statistical Area. The offenses from state police agencies are not included in this table.

Table II-15. Crime Trends, Additional Information About Selected Offenses, by Population Group, 2010–2011

(Number, percent change.)

Population group	Forcible rape		Robbery				Aggravated assault			
	Rape by force	Assault to rape-attempts	Firearm	Knife or cutting instrument	Other weapon	Strong-arm	Firearm	Knife or cutting instrument	Other weapon	Hands, fists, feet, etc.
Total, All Agencies										
2010	72,041	5,423	147,510	26,707	30,317	142,628	146,461	131,251	235,043	189,907
2011	68,934	5,293	128,793	24,388	27,170	130,839	138,403	127,857	222,892	185,029
Percent change	-4.3	-2.4	-12.7	-8.7	-10.4	-8.3	-5.5	-2.6	-5.2	-2.6
Total, Cities										
2010	52,545	4,268	125,099	22,966	25,718	124,606	114,283	102,879	175,421	132,504
2011	50,714	4,219	109,059	21,130	23,105	114,092	108,048	100,557	167,723	130,313
Percent change	-3.5	-1.1	-12.8	-8.0	-10.2	-8.4	-5.5	-2.3	-4.4	-1.7
Group I (250,000 and over)										
2010	16,176	1,686	67,462	10,551	11,111	56,640	57,058	38,543	69,050	30,700
2011	15,611	1,702	58,034	9,530	9,704	52,477	53,771	37,530	66,687	31,095
Percent change	-3.5	0.9	-14.0	-9.7	-12.7	-7.3	-5.8	-2.6	-3.4	1.3
1,000,000 and over (Group I subset)										
2010	4,610	663	23,022	4,216	3,867	19,857	15,865	12,223	20,897	7,931
2011	4,345	681	19,193	3,746	3,469	18,064	14,729	11,927	20,680	8,189
Percent change	-5.7	2.7	-16.6	-11.1	-10.3	-9.0	-7.2	-2.4	-1.0	3.3
500,000 to 999,999 (Group I subset)										
2010	5,817	526	25,387	3,510	4,027	18,817	22,823	15,067	27,957	10,741
2011	5,870	523	21,296	3,286	3,581	17,930	21,258	15,133	27,325	11,240
Percent change	0.9	-0.6	-16.1	-6.4	-11.1	-4.7	-6.9	0.4	-2.3	4.6
250,000 to 499,999 (Group I subset)										
2010	5,749	497	19,053	2,825	3,217	17,966	18,370	11,253	20,196	12,028
2011	5,396	498	17,545	2,498	2,654	16,483	17,784	10,470	18,682	11,666
Percent change	-6.1	0.2	-7.9	-11.6	-17.5	-8.3	-3.2	-7.0	-7.5	-3.0
Group II (100,000 to 249,999)										
2010	9,145	607	21,761	4,349	5,137	22,641	20,484	20,442	32,900	18,671
2011	8,672	597	19,954	4,096	4,732	20,224	19,671	19,394	31,783	19,003
Percent change	-5.2	-1.6	-8.3	-5.8	-7.9	-10.7	-4.0	-5.1	-3.4	1.8
Group III (50,000 to 99,999)										
2010	8,111	598	14,554	3,408	3,894	19,253	13,910	15,669	25,935	22,108
2011	7,895	530	12,661	3,307	3,531	17,463	12,748	15,390	24,766	21,021
Percent change	-2.7	-11.4	-13.0	-3.0	-9.3	-9.3	-8.4	-1.8	-4.5	-4.9
Group IV (25,000 to 49,999)										
2010	6,764	415	9,864	2,162	2,628	11,927	9,018	10,579	18,167	17,564
2011	6,675	407	8,509	1,869	2,412	10,969	8,689	10,832	17,037	16,737
Percent change	-1.3	-1.9	-13.7	-13.6	-8.2	-8.0	-3.6	2.4	-6.2	-4.7
Group V (10,000 to 24,999)										
2010	6,425	440	7,361	1,572	1,897	8,810	7,772	9,685	16,132	19,318
2011	6,044	406	6,355	1,465	1,750	8,061	7,288	9,410	15,403	18,958
Percent change	-5.9	-7.7	-13.7	-6.8	-7.7	-8.5	-6.2	-2.8	-4.5	-1.9
Group VI (under 10,000)										
2010	5,924	522	4,097	924	1,051	5,335	6,041	7,961	13,237	24,143
2011	5,817	577	3,546	863	976	4,898	5,881	8,001	12,047	23,499
Percent change	-1.8	10.5	-13.4	-6.6	-7.1	-8.2	-2.6	0.5	-9.0	-2.7
Metropolitan Counties										
2010	13,610	819	20,510	3,351	4,013	16,373	24,544	22,360	47,607	40,751
2011	12,757	737	17,997	2,886	3,544	15,165	23,226	21,354	43,855	39,097
Percent change	-6.3	-10.0	-12.3	-13.9	-11.7	-7.4	-5.4	-4.5	-7.9	-4.1
Nonmetropolitan Counties										
2010	5,886	336	1,901	390	586	1,649	7,634	6,012	12,015	16,652
2011	5,463	337	1,737	372	521	1,582	7,129	5,946	11,314	15,619
Percent change	-7.2	0.3	-8.6	-4.6	-11.1	-4.1	-6.6	-1.1	-5.8	-6.2
Suburban Areas[1]										
2010	23,921	1,503	34,771	6,309	7,674	33,933	37,040	37,981	76,097	75,764
2011	22,938	1,440	30,311	5,607	6,849	31,288	35,043	36,991	70,222	73,603
Percent change	-4.1	-4.2	-12.8	-11.1	-10.8	-7.8	-5.4	-2.6	-7.7	-2.9

[1] Suburban areas include law enforcement agencies in cities with less than 50,000 inhabitants and county law enforcement agencies that are within a Metropolitan Statistical Area. Suburban areas exclude all metropolitan agencies associated with a principal city. The agencies associated with suburban areas also appear in other groups within this table.

Table II-15.   Crime Trends, Additional Information About Selected Offenses, by Population Group, 2010–2011—*Continued*

(Number, percent change.)

Population group	Burglary			Motor vehicle theft			Arson			Number of agencies	2011 estimated population
	Forcible entry	Unlawful entry	Attempted forcible entry	Autos	Trucks and buses	Other vehicles	Structure	Mobile	Other		
Total, All Agencies											
2010	1,194,238	640,096	126,393	518,407	123,101	77,793	23,713	15,009	14,647		
2011	1,166,754	636,558	122,434	481,236	109,266	70,074	22,470	12,680	13,931	14,439	272,150,917
Percent change	-2.3	-0.6	-3.1	-7.2	-11.2	-9.9	-5.2	-15.5	-4.9		
Total, Cities											
2010	864,431	460,892	96,826	420,677	94,940	49,219	17,796	10,507	10,934		
2011	843,526	459,032	93,263	388,351	84,541	45,184	16,911	8,994	10,601	10,386	180,156,135
Percent change	-2.4	-0.4	-3.7	-7.7	-11.0	-8.2	-5.0	-14.4	-3.0		
Group I (250,000 and over)											
2010	319,484	115,224	29,674	178,417	51,657	16,871	6,359	4,976	3,113		
2011	310,714	115,308	27,645	165,380	46,788	15,838	6,029	4,103	3,207	71	45,289,754
Percent change	-2.7	0.1	-6.8	-7.3	-9.4	-6.1	-5.2	-17.5	3.0		
1,000,000 and over (Group I subset)											
2010	94,331	31,731	6,699	51,675	23,518	7,146	1,737	1,848	1,002		
2011	90,745	31,873	6,244	45,235	20,837	6,177	1,512	1,394	984	8	14,654,178
Percent change	-3.8	0.4	-6.8	-12.5	-11.4	-13.6	-13.0	-24.6	-1.8		
500,000 to 999,999 (Group I subset)											
2010	129,354	41,897	13,131	68,942	17,348	5,821	2,176	1,517	1,121		
2011	123,501	42,035	12,171	64,963	16,040	5,766	2,353	1,368	1,019	24	16,775,442
Percent change	-4.5	0.3	-7.3	-5.8	-7.5	-0.9	8.1	-9.8	-9.1		
250,000 to 499,999 (Group I subset)											
2010	95,799	41,596	9,844	57,800	10,791	3,904	2,446	1,611	990		
2011	96,468	41,400	9,230	55,182	9,911	3,895	2,164	1,341	1,204	39	13,860,134
Percent change	0.7	-0.5	-6.2	-4.5	-8.2	-0.2	-11.5	-16.8	21.6		
Group II (100,000 to 249,999)											
2010	157,457	86,173	18,769	82,606	18,314	9,234	2,838	1,680	1,759		
2011	154,456	86,225	18,134	75,680	15,885	8,265	2,838	1,475	1,658	194	28,854,065
Percent change	-1.9	0.1	-3.4	-8.4	-13.3	-10.5	0.0	-12.2	-5.7		
Group III (50,000 to 99,999)											
2010	126,335	79,137	15,763	63,946	10,548	7,538	2,537	1,566	1,854		
2011	123,843	77,490	15,391	59,436	9,293	7,028	2,495	1,248	1,818	444	30,436,777
Percent change	-2.0	-2.1	-2.4	-7.1	-11.9	-6.8	-1.7	-20.3	-1.9		
Group IV (25,000 to 49,999)											
2010	94,994	62,658	11,811	40,192	5,663	5,824	1,908	943	1,609		
2011	94,879	63,251	11,769	37,244	5,018	5,157	1,660	840	1,504	770	26,639,832
Percent change	-0.1	+0.9	-0.4	-7.3	-11.4	-11.5	-13.0	-10.9	-6.5		
Group V (10,000 to 24,999)											
2010	91,642	61,899	11,417	32,122	5,228	5,098	1,884	718	1,148		
2011	87,879	61,582	11,012	29,392	4,374	4,688	1,732	705	1,098	1,684	26,749,154
Percent change	-4.1	-0.5	-3.5	-8.5	-16.3	-8.0	-8.1	-1.8	-4.4		
Group VI (under 10,000)											
2010	74,519	55,801	9,392	23,394	3,530	4,654	2,270	624	1,451		
2011	71,755	55,176	9,312	21,219	3,183	4,208	2,157	623	1,316	7,223	22,186,553
Percent change	-3.7	-1.1	-0.9	-9.3	-9.8	-9.6	-5.0	-0.2	-9.3		
Metropolitan Counties											
2010	239,492	129,516	23,274	81,003	23,771	21,334	4,063	3,651	2,866		
2011	234,110	125,713	22,691	76,357	20,491	18,494	3,771	2,946	2,557	1,687	65,686,356
Percent change	-2.2	-2.9	-2.5	-5.7	-13.8	-13.3	-7.2	-19.3	-10.8		
Nonmetropolitan Counties											
2010	90,315	49,688	6,293	16,727	4,390	7,240	1,854	851	847		
2011	89,118	51,813	6,480	16,528	4,234	6,396	1,788	740	773	2,366	26,308,426
Percent change	-1.3	4.3	3.0	-1.2	-3.6	-11.7	-3.6	-13.0	-8.7		
Suburban Areas[1]											
2010	395,668	238,887	44,589	149,486	34,555	31,670	7,525	5,056	5,510		
2011	386,691	235,012	43,636	138,980	29,724	27,625	6,801	4,210	5,001	7,591	119,228,798
Percent change	-2.3	-1.6	-2.1	-7.0	-14.0	-12.8	-9.6	-16.7	-9.2		

[1] Suburban areas include law enforcement agencies in cities with less than 50,000 inhabitants and county law enforcement agencies that are within a Metropolitan Statistical Area. Suburban areas exclude all metropolitan agencies associated with a principal city. The agencies associated with suburban areas also appear in other groups within this table.

Table II-16.   Rate: Number of Crimes Per 100,000 Population, by Population Group, 2011

(Number, rate.)

Population group	Violent crime		Murder and nonnegligent manslaughter		Forcible rape		Robbery		Aggravated assault	
	Number of offenses known	Rate	Number of offenses known	Rate	Number of offenses known	Rate	Number of offenses known	Rate	Number of offenses known	Rate
Total, All Agencies	1,146,588	392.2	14,022	4.8	78,287	26.8	342,282	117.1	711,997	243.5
Total, Cities	923,695	467.3	10,900	5.5	58,866	29.8	301,739	152.7	552,190	279.4
Group I (250,000 and over)	416,174	754.5	5,572	10.1	19,165	34.7	162,613	294.8	228,824	414.8
1,000,000 and over (Group I subset)	177,315	702.3	2,223	8.8	6,660	26.4	74,249	294.1	94,183	373.0
500,000 to 999,999 (Group I subset)	133,879	819.6	1,756	10.7	6,656	40.7	48,380	296.2	77,087	471.9
250,000 to 499,999 (Group I subset)	104,980	773.1	1,593	11.7	5,849	43.1	39,984	294.5	57,554	423.8
Group II (100,000 to 249,999)	153,518	498.5	1,852	6.0	9,621	31.2	50,394	163.6	91,651	297.6
Group III (50,000 to 99,999)	116,703	367.7	1,108	3.5	8,510	26.8	35,584	112.1	71,501	225.3
Group IV (25,000 to 49,999)	91,372	312.9	901	3.1	8,094	27.7	24,674	84.5	57,703	197.6
Group V (10,000 to 24,999)	79,663	279.4	812	2.8	7,176	25.2	17,980	63.1	53,695	188.3
Group VI (under 10,000)	66,265	297.9	655	2.9	6,300	28.3	10,494	47.2	48,816	219.4
Metropolitan Counties	174,345	256.9	2,262	3.3	13,792	20.3	36,739	54.1	121,552	179.1
Nonmetropolitan Counties[1]	48,548	180.8	860	3.2	5,629	21.0	3,804	14.2	38,255	142.5
Suburban Areas[2]	314,259	252.1	3,564	2.9	25,768	20.7	71,957	57.7	212,970	170.8

Population group	Property crime		Burglary		Larceny-theft		Motor vehicle theft		Number of agencies	2011 estimated population
	Number of offenses known	Rate	Number of offenses known	Rate	Number of offenses known	Rate	Number of offenses known	Rate		
Total, All Agencies	8,553,515	2,925.6	2,055,979	703.2	5,814,034	1,988.6	683,502	233.8	14,550	292,364,075
Total, Cities	6,691,432	3,385.4	1,507,896	762.9	4,635,813	2,345.4	547,723	277.1	10,447	197,654,841
Group I (250,000 and over)	2,144,148	3,887.0	508,459	921.8	1,380,672	2,503.0	255,017	462.3	73	55,161,597
1,000,000 and over (Group I subset)	791,320	3,134.3	172,588	683.6	520,049	2,059.8	98,683	390.9	10	25,247,146
500,000 to 999,999 (Group I subset)	763,142	4,671.7	184,976	1,132.4	491,612	3,009.5	86,554	529.9	24	16,335,382
250,000 to 499,999 (Group I subset)	589,686	4,342.6	150,895	1,111.2	369,011	2,717.5	69,780	513.9	39	13,579,069
Group II (100,000 to 249,999)	1,149,734	3,733.4	276,611	898.2	773,102	2,510.4	100,021	324.8	206	30,796,115
Group III (50,000 to 99,999)	993,725	3,130.9	222,324	700.5	696,782	2,195.4	74,619	235.1	458	31,738,910
Group IV (25,000 to 49,999)	874,257	2,993.9	185,735	636.0	638,500	2,186.5	50,022	171.3	842	29,201,621
Group V (10,000 to 24,999)	822,789	2,885.9	174,764	613.0	608,561	2,134.5	39,464	138.4	1,794	28,510,806
Group VI (under 10,000)	706,779	3,177.1	140,003	629.3	538,196	2,419.3	28,580	128.5	7,074	22,245,792
Metropolitan Counties	1,426,053	2,101.4	396,849	584.8	919,323	1,354.7	109,881	161.9	1,742	67,860,770
Nonmetropolitan Counties[1]	436,030	1,624.0	151,234	563.3	258,898	964.3	25,898	96.5	2,361	26,848,464
Suburban Areas[2]	2,948,086	2,364.8	699,055	560.8	2,056,170	1,649.4	192,861	154.7	7,770	124,664,048

[1] Includes state police agencies that report aggregately for the entire state.

[2] Suburban areas include law enforcement agencies in cities with less than 50,000 inhabitants and county law enforcement agencies that are within a Metropolitan Statistical Area. Suburban areas exclude all metropolitan agencies associated with a principal city. The agencies associated with suburban areas also appear in other groups within this table.

Table II-17.   Rate: Number of Crimes Per 100,000 Inhabitants, by Suburban and Nonsuburban Cities,[1] by Population Group, 2011

(Number, rate.)

Population group	Violent crime		Murder and nonnegligent manslaughter		Forcible rape		Robbery		Aggravated assault	
	Number of offenses known	Rate	Number of offenses known	Rate	Number of offenses known	Rate	Number of offenses known	Rate	Number of offenses known	Rate
Total, Suburban Cities...................	139,919	246.3	1,302	2.3	11,981	21.1	35,218	62.0	91,418	160.9
Group IV (25,000 to 49,999)...................	54,072	248.3	524	2.4	4,544	20.9	15,388	70.7	33,616	154.4
Group V (10,000 to 24,999)...................	49,717	232.0	481	2.2	4,220	19.7	12,765	59.6	32,251	150.5
Group VI (under 10,000)...................	36,130	265.7	297	2.2	3,217	23.7	7,065	51.9	25,551	187.9
Total, Nonsuburban Cities...................	97,381	420.6	1,066	4.6	9,589	41.4	17,930	77.4	68,796	297.1
Group IV (25,000 to 49,999)...................	37,300	502.4	377	5.1	3,550	47.8	9,286	125.1	24,087	324.4
Group V (10,000 to 24,999)...................	29,946	422.7	331	4.7	2,956	41.7	5,215	73.6	21,444	302.7
Group VI (under 10,000)...................	30,135	348.5	358	4.1	3,083	35.7	3,429	39.7	23,265	269.1

Population group	Property crime		Burglary		Larceny-theft		Motor vehicle theft		Number of agencies	2011 estimated population
	Number of offenses known	Rate	Number of offenses known	Rate	Number of offenses known	Rate	Number of offenses known	Rate		
Total, Suburban Cities...................	1,522,033	2,679.5	302,206	532.0	1,136,847	2,001.4	82,980	146.1	6,028	56,803,278
Group IV (25,000 to 49,999)...................	556,570	2,555.7	113,943	523.2	406,955	1,868.7	35,672	163.8	634	21,777,580
Group V (10,000 to 24,999)...................	534,302	2,493.7	109,974	513.3	395,097	1,844.0	29,231	136.4	1,335	21,425,872
Group VI (under 10,000)...................	431,161	3,170.3	78,289	575.7	334,795	2,461.8	18,077	132.9	4,059	13,599,826
Total, Nonsuburban Cities...................	881,792	3,808.2	198,296	856.4	648,410	2,800.3	35,086	151.5	3,682	23,154,941
Group IV (25,000 to 49,999)...................	317,687	4,279.2	71,792	967.0	231,545	3,118.9	14,350	193.3	208	7,424,041
Group V (10,000 to 24,999)...................	288,487	4,071.8	64,790	914.5	213,464	3,012.9	10,233	144.4	459	7,084,934
Group VI (under 10,000)...................	275,618	3,187.8	61,714	713.8	203,401	2,352.6	10,503	121.5	3,015	8,645,966

[1] Suburban cities include law enforcement agencies in cities with less than 50,000 inhabitants that are within a Metropolitan Statistical Area. Suburban cities exclude all metropolitan agencies associated with a principal city. Nonsuburban cities include law enforcement agencies in cities with less than 50,000 inhabitants that are not associated with a Metropolitan Statistical Area.

Table II-18.   Rate: Number of Crimes Per 100,000 Inhabitants, by Metropolitan and Nonmetropolitan Counties[1], by Population Group, 2011

(Number, rate.)

Population group	Violent crime		Murder and nonnegligent manslaughter		Forcible rape		Robbery		Aggravated assault	
	Number of offenses known	Rate	Number of offenses known	Rate	Number of offenses known	Rate	Number of offenses known	Rate	Number of offenses known	Rate
Metropolitan Counties										
100,000 and over	116,437	290.4	1,468	3.7	7,812	19.5	29,790	74.3	77,367	193.0
25,000 to 99,999	42,558	184.1	604	2.6	4,350	18.8	5,021	21.7	32,583	141.0
Under 25,000	15,350	329.4	190	4.1	1,630	35.0	1,928	41.4	11,602	249.0
Nonmetropolitan Counties										
25,000 and over	20,315	173.6	322	2.8	2,190	18.7	1,975	16.9	15,828	135.2
10,000 to 24,999	14,754	156.4	271	2.9	1,548	16.4	894	9.5	12,041	127.6
Under 10,000	8,084	202.6	155	3.9	1,185	29.7	318	8.0	6,426	161.0

Population group	Property crime		Burglary		Larceny-theft		Motor vehicle theft		Number of agencies	2011 estimated population
	Number of offenses known	Rate	Number of offenses known	Rate	Number of offenses known	Rate	Number of offenses known	Rate		
Metropolitan Counties										
100,000 and over	900,761	2,246.9	238,450	594.8	592,668	1,478.4	69,643	173.7	157	40,089,018
25,000 to 99,999	398,940	1,726.1	126,385	546.8	248,958	1,077.2	23,597	102.1	447	23,111,929
Under 25,000	126,352	2,711.5	32,014	687.0	77,697	1,667.4	16,641	357.1	1,138	4,659,823
Nonmetropolitan Counties										
25,000 and over	195,013	1,666.4	70,083	598.9	114,296	976.7	10,634	90.9	297	11,702,846
10,000 to 24,999	136,463	1,446.5	46,279	490.5	82,424	873.7	7,760	82.3	584	9,434,147
Under 10,000	63,793	1,598.5	20,206	506.3	38,885	974.4	4,702	117.8	1,302	3,990,690

[1]Metropolitan counties include sheriffs and county law enforcement agencies associated with a Metropolitan Statistical Area. Nonmetropolitan counties include sheriffs and county law enforcement agencies that are not associated with a Metropolitan Statistical Area. The offenses from state police agencies are not included in this table.

Table II-19. **Rate: Number of Crimes Per 100,000 Inhabitants, Additional Information About Selected Offenses, by Population Group, 2010**

(Number, rate.)

Population group	Forcible rape		Robbery				Aggravated assault			
	Rape by force	Assault to rape-attempts	Firearm	Knife or cutting instrument	Other weapon	Strong-arm	Firearm	Knife or cutting instrument	Other weapon	Hands, fists, feet, etc.
Total, All Agencies										
Number of offenses known	69,896	5,298	127,521	24,204	26,978	129,606	137,857	127,509	221,620	183,457
Rate	26.3	2.0	47.9	9.1	10.1	48.7	51.8	47.9	83.3	69.0
Total, Cities										
Number of offenses known	51,223	4,229	107,747	20,983	22,964	113,085	107,397	100,257	166,228	128,948
Rate	29.0	2.4	60.9	11.9	13.0	63.9	60.7	56.7	94.0	72.9
Group I (250,000 and over)										
Number of offenses known	15,410	1,675	57,349	9,430	9,628	51,807	53,307	37,102	65,515	30,442
Rate	34.7	3.8	129.0	21.2	21.7	116.5	119.9	83.4	147.3	68.5
1,000,000 and over (Group I subset)										
Number of offenses known	4,345	681	19,193	3,746	3,469	18,064	14,729	11,927	20,680	8,189
Rate	29.7	4.6	131.0	25.6	23.7	123.3	100.5	81.4	141.1	55.9
500,000 to 999,999 (Group I subset)										
Number of offenses known	5,669	496	20,611	3,186	3,505	17,260	20,794	14,705	26,153	10,587
Rate	35.5	3.1	129.2	20.0	22.0	108.2	130.4	92.2	164.0	66.4
250,000 to 499,999 (Group I subset)										
Number of offenses known	5,396	498	17,545	2,498	2,654	16,483	17,784	10,470	18,682	11,666
Rate	38.9	3.6	126.6	18.0	19.1	118.9	128.3	75.5	134.8	84.2
Group II (100,000 to 249,999)										
Number of offenses known	8,749	603	19,708	4,088	4,671	20,058	19,528	19,377	31,197	18,558
Rate	30.6	2.1	68.9	14.3	16.3	70.2	68.3	67.8	109.1	64.9
Group III (50,000 to 99,999)										
Number of offenses known	8,101	533	12,485	3,281	3,487	17,324	12,630	15,366	24,668	21,023
Rate	27.0	1.8	41.6	10.9	11.6	57.7	42.0	51.1	82.1	70.0
Group IV (25,000 to 49,999)										
Number of offenses known	6,820	422	8,388	1,863	2,393	10,934	8,662	10,857	16,986	16,722
Rate	26.1	1.6	32.0	7.1	9.1	41.8	33.1	41.5	64.9	63.9
Group V (10,000 to 24,999)										
Number of offenses known	6,306	411	6,341	1,474	1,825	8,123	7,424	9,621	15,926	18,990
Rate	23.8	1.5	23.9	5.6	6.9	30.6	28.0	36.2	60.0	71.5
Group VI (under 10,000)										
Number of offenses known	5,837	585	3,476	847	960	4,839	5,846	7,934	11,936	23,213
Rate	27.8	2.8	16.5	4.0	4.6	23.0	27.8	37.7	56.8	110.4
Metropolitan Counties										
Number of offenses known	13,059	733	18,068	2,858	3,514	14,983	23,368	21,331	44,111	39,091
Rate	20.4	1.1	28.3	4.5	5.5	23.4	36.5	33.4	69.0	61.1
Nonmetropolitan Counties										
Number of offenses known	5,614	336	1,706	363	500	1,538	7,092	5,921	11,281	15,418
Rate	22.2	1.3	6.8	1.4	2.0	6.1	28.1	23.5	44.7	61.1
Suburban Areas[1]										
Number of offenses known	23,518	1,457	30,254	5,573	6,816	31,093	35,231	37,050	70,686	73,526
Rate	20.2	1.3	26.0	4.8	5.9	26.7	30.3	31.8	60.7	63.2

Note: This table has not been updated by the FBI from the 2010 UCR.

[1] Suburban areas include law enforcement agencies in cities with less than 50,000 inhabitants and county law enforcement agencies that are within a Metropolitan Statistical Area. Suburban areas exclude all metropolitan agencies associated with a principal city. The agencies associated with suburban areas also appear in other groups within this table.

Table II-19. Rate: Number of Crimes Per 100,000 Inhabitants, Additional Information About Selected Offenses, by Population Group, 2010—*Continued*

(Number, rate.)

Population group	Burglary			Motor vehicle theft			Number of agencies	2010 estimated population
	Forcible entry	Unlawful entry	Attempted forcible entry	Autos	Trucks and buses	Other vehicles		
Total, All Agencies								
Number of offenses known	1,157,212	634,943	121,163	479,677	108,709	69,432	13,893	266,040,636
Rate	435.0	238.7	45.5	180.3	40.9	26.1		
Total, Cities								
Number of offenses known	833,823	456,908	92,134	386,578	83,968	44,791	9,877	176,845,269
Rate	471.5	258.4	52.1	218.6	47.5	25.3		
Group I (250,000 and over)								
Number of offenses known	306,179	114,112	27,059	163,818	46,441	15,662	70	44,464,682
Rate	688.6	256.6	60.9	368.4	104.4	35.2		
1,000,000 and over (Group I subset)								
Number of offenses known	90,745	31,873	6,244	45,235	20,837	6,177	8	14,654,178
Rate	619.2	217.5	42.6	308.7	142.2	42.2		
500,000 to 999,999 (Group I subset)								
Number of offenses known	118,966	40,839	11,585	63,401	15,693	5,590	23	15,950,370
Rate	745.9	256.0	72.6	397.5	98.4	35.0		
250,000 to 499,999 (Group I subset)								
Number of offenses known	96,468	41,400	9,230	55,182	9,911	3,895	39	13,860,134
Rate	696.0	298.7	66.6	398.1	71.5	28.1		
Group II (100,000 to 249,999)								
Number of offenses known	152,344	85,738	18,024	75,282	15,678	8,172	193	28,585,285
Rate	532.9	299.9	63.1	263.4	54.8	28.6		
Group III (50,000 to 99,999)								
Number of offenses known	122,060	77,413	15,341	60,294	9,340	6,969	439	30,046,974
Rate	406.2	257.6	51.1	200.7	31.1	23.2		
Group IV (25,000 to 49,999)								
Number of offenses known	94,299	62,835	11,658	36,785	5,014	5,101	757	26,176,528
Rate	360.2	240.0	44.5	140.5	19.2	19.5		
Group V (10,000 to 24,999)								
Number of offenses known	88,104	62,519	10,906	29,426	4,360	4,756	1,670	26,541,488
Rate	331.9	235.6	41.1	110.9	16.4	17.9		
Group VI (under 10,000)								
Number of offenses known	70,837	54,291	9,146	20,973	3,135	4,131	6,748	21,030,312
Rate	336.8	258.2	43.5	99.7	14.9	19.6		
Metropolitan Counties								
Number of offenses known	235,173	126,586	22,647	76,922	20,556	18,422	1,713	63,953,300
Rate	367.7	197.9	35.4	120.3	32.1	28.8		
Nonmetropolitan Counties								
Number of offenses known	88,216	51,449	6,382	16,177	4,185	6,219	2,303	25,242,067
Rate	349.5	203.8	25.3	64.1	16.6	24.6		
Suburban Areas[1]								
Number of offenses known	386,615	235,492	43,320	139,080	29,736	27,480	7,379	116,412,187
Rate	332.1	202.3	37.2	119.5	25.5	23.6		

Note: This table has not been updated by the FBI from the 2010 UCR.

[1] Suburban areas include law enforcement agencies in cities with less than 50,000 inhabitants and county law enforcement agencies that are within a Metropolitan Statistical Area. Suburban areas exclude all metropolitan agencies associated with a principal city. The agencies associated with suburban areas also appear in other groups within this table.

Table II-20.   Murder, by Selected State, Territory, and Type of Weapon, 2011

(Number.)

State	Total murders[1]	Total firearms	Handguns	Rifles	Shotguns	Firearms (type unknown)	Knives or cutting instruments	Other weapons	Hands, fists, feet, etc.[2]
Alaska	29	16	5	0	3	8	6	5	2
Arizona	339	222	165	14	9	34	49	59	9
Arkansas	153	110	52	4	6	48	22	17	4
California	1,790	1,220	866	45	50	259	261	208	101
Colorado	147	73	39	3	5	26	22	31	21
Connecticut	128	94	54	1	1	38	18	10	6
Delaware	41	28	18	0	3	7	8	2	3
District of Columbia	108	77	37	0	1	39	21	9	1
Georgia	522	370	326	16	16	12	61	83	8
Hawaii	7	1	0	1	0	0	2	1	3
Idaho	32	17	15	1	0	1	4	8	3
Illinois[3]	452	377	364	1	5	7	29	29	17
Indiana	284	183	115	9	12	47	36	43	22
Iowa	44	19	7	0	2	10	10	10	5
Kansas	110	73	31	3	5	34	11	16	10
Kentucky	150	100	77	6	5	12	13	24	13
Louisiana	485	402	372	10	8	12	28	29	26
Maine	25	12	3	1	1	7	4	7	2
Maryland	398	272	262	2	5	3	75	34	17
Massachusetts	183	122	52	0	1	69	30	22	9
Michigan	613	450	267	29	15	139	43	89	31
Minnesota	70	43	36	3	3	1	12	12	3
Mississippi	187	138	121	6	4	7	26	14	9
Missouri	364	276	158	13	9	96	28	42	18
Montana	18	7	2	3	1	1	4	5	2
Nebraska	65	42	35	2	1	4	7	9	7
Nevada	129	75	46	2	1	26	20	25	9
New Hampshire	16	6	1	2	1	2	4	6	0
New Jersey	379	269	238	1	5	25	51	41	18
New Mexico	121	60	45	2	2	11	21	32	8
New York	774	445	394	5	16	30	160	143	26
North Carolina	489	335	235	26	19	55	60	57	37
North Dakota	12	6	3	0	0	3	4	0	2
Ohio	488	344	187	8	13	136	44	80	20
Oklahoma	204	131	99	8	9	15	26	21	26
Oregon	77	40	13	1	2	24	22	10	5
Pennsylvania	636	470	379	8	19	64	73	66	27
Rhode Island	14	5	1	0	0	4	5	4	0
South Carolina	319	223	126	10	12	75	38	40	18
South Dakota	15	5	3	1	0	1	4	3	3
Tennessee	373	244	172	7	13	52	51	62	16
Texas	1,089	699	497	37	48	117	175	134	81
Utah	51	26	15	4	1	6	5	9	11
Vermont	8	4	2	0	0	2	2	2	0
Virginia	303	208	110	10	15	73	33	41	21
Washington	161	79	58	1	3	17	29	36	17
West Virginia	74	43	23	10	3	7	11	13	7
Wisconsin	135	80	60	7	3	10	21	13	21
Wyoming	15	11	7	0	0	4	0	1	3
Virgin Islands	38	31	27	0	0	4	5	2	0

[1] Total number of murders for which supplemental homicide data were received.

[2] Pushed is included in hands, fists, feet, etc.

[3] Limited supplemental homicide data were received.

Table II-21. Robbery, by State and Type of Weapon, 2011

(Number.)

State	Total robberies[1]	Firearms	Knives or cutting instruments	Other weapons	Strong-arm	Agency count	Population
Alabama	3,106	1,781	161	317	847	300	3,967,912
Alaska	573	130	45	43	355	33	714,559
Arizona	7,057	3,156	671	657	2,573	106	6,281,875
Arkansas	2,210	1,138	108	195	769	212	2,504,030
California	54,227	16,146	4,787	4,865	28,429	733	37,571,959
Colorado	3,229	1,248	299	400	1,282	194	4,848,878
Connecticut	3,588	1,211	361	290	1,726	102	3,474,899
Delaware	1,538	632	120	140	646	55	907,135
District of Columbia	4,093	1,499	235	183	2,176	2	617,996
Florida	25,615	10,769	1,575	2,282	10,989	678	19,052,717
Georgia	11,897	6,819	478	1,137	3,463	483	9,408,130
Idaho	152	51	24	17	60	104	1,493,662
Illinois[2]	566	291	48	44	183	1	153,331
Indiana	6,372	2,953	390	560	2,469	298	5,557,234
Iowa	802	196	87	105	414	184	2,682,969
Kansas	1,421	652	133	128	508	256	2,622,476
Kentucky	3,653	1,688	311	383	1,271	362	4,244,419
Louisiana	4,841	2,512	207	362	1,760	151	3,957,239
Maine	369	77	72	44	176	168	1,328,188
Maryland	10,324	4,611	965	586	4,162	155	5,784,364
Massachusetts	6,564	1,680	1,329	786	2,769	315	6,034,456
Michigan	9,867	4,972	459	750	3,686	516	8,886,852
Minnesota	3,363	1,051	238	480	1,594	311	5,226,982
Mississippi	1,892	1,111	89	190	502	108	1,849,412
Missouri	6,243	3,122	319	441	2,361	602	5,950,416
Montana	151	35	17	20	79	101	926,672
Nebraska	988	427	86	65	410	215	1,678,460
Nevada	4,252	1,703	379	322	1,848	42	2,440,815
New Hampshire	450	111	57	64	218	140	1,129,726
New Jersey	12,118	4,368	937	769	6,044	573	8,759,125
New Mexico	1,707	703	225	151	628	101	2,011,134
New York	8,496	2,516	826	939	4,215	532	10,807,465
North Carolina	8,443	4,221	591	760	2,871	369	8,664,157
North Dakota	90	31	10	9	40	82	646,511
Ohio	14,937	6,358	748	1,324	6,507	464	9,714,166
Oklahoma	3,253	1,540	264	249	1,200	331	3,597,339
Oregon	2,206	557	245	205	1,199	161	3,823,231
Pennsylvania	15,473	6,483	1,117	947	6,926	1,196	11,853,574
Rhode Island	326	111	49	33	133	48	873,472
South Carolina	4,031	2,182	258	371	1,220	249	4,122,555
South Dakota	162	36	20	24	82	122	732,933
Tennessee	7,975	4,532	477	637	2,329	448	6,218,332
Texas	26,247	12,058	2,306	2,356	9,527	1,024	24,016,516
Utah	1,059	295	135	107	522	122	2,687,404
Vermont	68	23	6	9	30	65	531,937
Virginia	5,417	2,856	371	521	1,669	323	8,066,841
Washington	5,409	1,310	507	491	3,101	248	6,322,393
West Virginia	685	241	81	68	295	247	1,498,772
Wisconsin	4,443	2,393	212	387	1,451	366	5,456,018
Wyoming	71	20	8	7	36	62	548,033

[1] The number of robberies from agencies that submitted 12 months of data in 2011 for which breakdowns by type of weapon were included.

[2] Limited data were received.

Table II-22. Aggravated Assault, by State and Type of Weapon, 2011

(Number.)

State	Total aggravated assaults[1]	Firearms	Knives or cutting instruments	Other weapons	Personal weapons	Agency count	Population
Alabama	10,046	1,607	1,545	4,606	2,288	300	3,967,912
Alaska	3,322	575	600	867	1,280	33	714,559
Arizona	15,247	3,603	2,619	4,553	4,472	106	6,281,875
Arkansas	9,398	2,518	1,498	1,967	3,415	212	2,504,030
California	91,035	17,055	14,818	30,474	28,688	733	37,571,959
Colorado	10,277	2,217	2,254	3,165	2,641	194	4,848,878
Connecticut	5,106	697	1,091	1,891	1,427	102	3,474,899
Delaware	3,207	738	752	1,347	370	55	907,135
District of Columbia	3,055	542	967	1,008	538	2	617,996
Florida	66,299	13,153	11,635	24,590	16,921	678	19,052,717
Georgia	20,935	5,517	3,797	6,046	5,575	483	9,408,130
Hawaii	2,204	350	402	770	682	104	1,493,662
Idaho	1,407	677	206	271	253	1	153,331
Illinois[2]	11,666	1,662	1,503	3,267	5,234	298	5,557,234
Indiana	5,702	589	990	1,286	2,837	184	2,682,969
Iowa	7,039	2,016	1,570	2,075	1,378	256	2,622,476
Kansas	5,031	1,067	876	1,905	1,183	362	4,244,419
Kentucky	15,386	3,938	2,553	4,696	4,199	151	3,957,239
Louisiana	848	60	177	281	330	168	1,328,188
Maine	16,780	2,382	4,424	6,392	3,582	155	5,784,364
Maryland	18,587	2,003	4,494	9,104	2,986	315	6,034,456
Massachusetts	26,541	7,679	5,477	9,380	4,005	516	8,886,852
Michigan	6,375	1,177	1,158	1,656	2,384	311	5,226,982
Minnesota	3,048	956	415	738	939	108	1,849,412
Mississippi	18,526	5,290	2,492	4,896	5,848	602	5,950,416
Missouri	1,915	269	258	596	792	101	926,672
Montana	2,814	568	485	892	869	215	1,678,460
Nebraska	8,634	1,301	1,671	4,020	1,642	42	2,440,815
Nevada	1,435	171	409	330	525	140	1,129,726
New Hampshire	13,442	2,360	2,983	4,035	4,064	573	8,759,125
New Jersey	8,813	1,755	1,632	2,582	2,844	101	2,011,134
New Mexico	15,345	2,168	4,908	4,226	4,043	532	10,807,465
New York	19,578	5,843	3,956	5,244	4,535	369	8,664,157
North Carolina	1,261	31	132	247	851	82	646,511
North Dakota	13,679	3,688	2,464	4,702	2,825	464	9,714,166
Ohio	12,086	2,089	1,941	4,270	3,786	331	3,597,339
Oklahoma	5,842	671	1,120	1,926	2,125	161	3,823,231
Oregon	23,575	4,675	3,696	5,690	9,514	1,196	11,853,574
Pennsylvania	869	156	263	327	123	48	873,472
Rhode Island	17,260	5,272	3,214	4,837	3,937	249	4,122,555
South Carolina	1,282	151	467	306	358	122	732,933
South Dakota	27,818	8,555	5,696	10,600	2,967	448	6,218,332
Tennessee	63,330	13,998	14,296	21,559	13,477	1,024	24,016,516
Texas	3,367	573	876	1,145	773	122	2,687,404
Utah	502	67	100	92	243	65	531,937
Vermont	8,605	1,722	2,015	2,865	2,003	323	8,066,841
Virginia	11,496	1,798	2,043	3,553	4,102	248	6,322,393
Washington	3,577	780	500	1,001	1,296	247	1,498,772
West Virginia	7,613	1,495	751	1,523	3,844	366	5,456,018
Wisconsin	964	112	191	261	400	62	548,033
Wyoming	847	79	156	263	349	65	559,126

[1] The number of aggravated assaults from agencies that submitted 12 months of data in 2011 for which breakdowns by type of weapon were included.

[2] Limited data were received.

Table II-23.   Offense Analysis, Number and Percent Change, 2010–2011

(Number, percent, dollars; 14,153 agencies; 2011 estimated population 274,791,753)

Classification	Number of offenses, 2011	Percent change from 2010	Percent distribution[1]	Average value
Murder	12,134	-6.9	NG	
Forcible Rape	70,333	-3.4	NG	
Robbery	291,176	-4.0	100.0	1,153
By location				
Street/highway..	127,403	-3.3	43.8	785
Commercial house	37,885	-4.6	13.0	1,783
Gas or service station	7,009	+0.1	2.4	890
Convenience store	14,863	-5.1	5.1	667
Residence...	49,361	-4.3	17.0	1,489
Bank	5,777	-12.6	2.0	4,704
Miscellaneous..	48,878	-3.9	16.8	1,050
Burglary	1,919,600	+1.0		2,185
By location				
Residence (dwelling)..	1,430,740	+1.9	74.5	2,188
Residence, night..	388,630	-0.9	20.2	1,714
Residence, day...	754,876	+4.2	39.3	2,330
Residence, unknown..	287,234	+0.3	15.0	2,454
Nonresidence (store, office, etc.).........................	488,860	-1.8	25.5	2,179
Nonresidence, night	199,807	-3.0	10.4	1,923
Nonresidence, day	172,587	+1.1	9.0	2,070
Nonresidence, unknown	116,466	-4.0	6.1	2,778
Larceny-Theft (Except Motor Vehicle Theft)	5,391,580	-2.6	100.0	988
By type				
Pocket-picking	23,150	+3.5	0.4	539
Purse-snatching	23,642	-4.2	0.4	412
Shoplifting...	940,903	+1.6	17.5	199
From motor vehicles (except accessories)	1,330,396	-6.7	24.8	818
Motor vehicle accessories	434,732	-8.0	8.1	540
Bicycles..	189,428	+4.2	3.5	367
From buildings...	635,582	+3.6	11.8	1,443
From coin-operated machines	17,055	-3.0	0.3	368
All others...	1,774,967	+3.7	33.1	1,564
By value				
Over $200..	2,488,290	+2.2	46.3	2,067
$50 to $200..	1,221,738	-0.6	22.8	109
Under $50...	1,659,827	-4.1	30.9	16
Motor Vehicle Theft...	623,033	-2.9	NG	6,089

NG = Not given.

Note: For this table, the number of agencies is 14,183. The 2011 population of the United States was 274,791,753.

[1] Because of rounding, the percentages may not add to 100.0.

Table II-24.   Property Stolen and Recovered, by Type and Value, 2011

(Dollars, percent; 13,573 agencies; 2011 estimated population 265,970,598)

Type of property	Value of property		Percent recovered
	Stolen	Recovered	
Total	$13,245,771,907	$2,557,448,141	19.3
Currency, notes, etc.	1,208,118,537	27,690,073	2.3
Jewelry and precious metals.................................	1,783,980,324	81,269,728	4.6
Clothing and furs	272,598,291	35,438,837	13.0
Locally stolen motor vehicles	3,793,147,961	1,984,945,521	52.3
Office equipment..	664,500,881	31,740,789	4.8
Televisions, radios, stereos, etc.	838,553,637	38,165,942	4.6
Firearms...	131,938,134	12,750,035	9.7
Household goods...	377,465,765	12,109,471	3.2
Consumable goods	126,700,845	13,871,866	10.9
Livestock	16,165,288	1,949,450	12.1
Miscellaneous...	4,032,602,244	317,516,429	7.9

Note: For this table, data from 13,605 agencies was used. The estimated 2011 population of the United States is 265,970,598.

SECTION III:
OFFENSES CLEARED

OFFENSES CLEARED

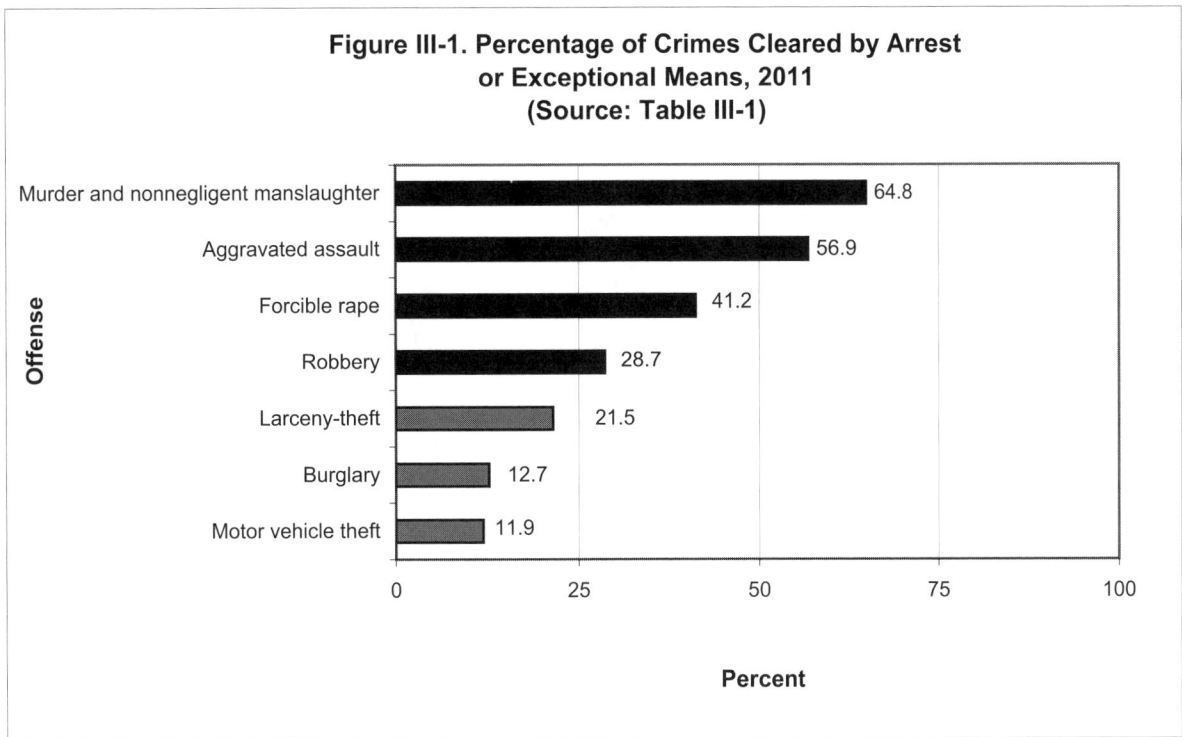

**Figure III-1. Percentage of Crimes Cleared by Arrest
or Exceptional Means, 2011
(Source: Table III-1)**

Law enforcement agencies that report crime to the Federal Bureau of Investigation (FBI) can clear, or "close," offenses in one of two ways: by arrest or by exceptional means. However, the administrative closing of a case by a local law enforcement agency does not necessarily mean that the agency can clear an offense for UCR purposes. To clear an offense within the program's guidelines, the reporting agency must adhere to certain criteria, which are outlined in this section. (*Note:* The UCR program does not distinguish between offenses cleared by arrest and those cleared by exceptional means in its data presentations. The distinction is made solely for the purpose of a definition and not for data collection and publication.) See Appendix I for information on the UCR program's statistical methodology.

Cleared by Arrest

In the UCR program, a law enforcement agency reports that an offense is cleared by arrest, or solved for crime reporting purposes, when at least one person is arrested, charged with the commission of the offense, and turned over to the court for prosecution (whether following arrest, court summons, or police notice). To qualify as a clearance, *all* of these conditions must be met.

In its calculations, the UCR program counts the number of offenses that are cleared, not the number of arrestees. Therefore, the arrest of one person may clear several crimes, and the arrest of many persons may clear only one offense. In addition, some clearances recorded by an agency

during a particular calendar year, such as 2011, may pertain to offenses that occurred in previous years.

Cleared by Exceptional Means

In certain situations, elements beyond law enforcement's control prevent the agency from arresting and formally charging the offender. When this occurs, the agency can clear the offense *exceptionally*. There are four UCR program requirements that law enforcement must meet in order to clear an offense by exceptional means. The agency must have:

- Identified the offender
- Gathered enough evidence to support an arrest, make a charge, and turn over the offender to the court for prosecution
- Identified the offender's exact location so that the suspect could be taken into custody immediately
- Encountered a circumstance outside the control of law enforcement that prohibits the agency from arresting, charging, and prosecuting the offender

Examples of exceptional clearances include, but are not limited to, the death of the offender (e.g., suicide or justifiably killed by a law enforcement officer or a citizen), the victim's refusal to cooperate with the prosecution after the offender has been identified, or the denial of extradition because the offender committed a crime in another jurisdiction and is being prosecuted for that offense. In the UCR program, the recovery of property does not clear an offense.

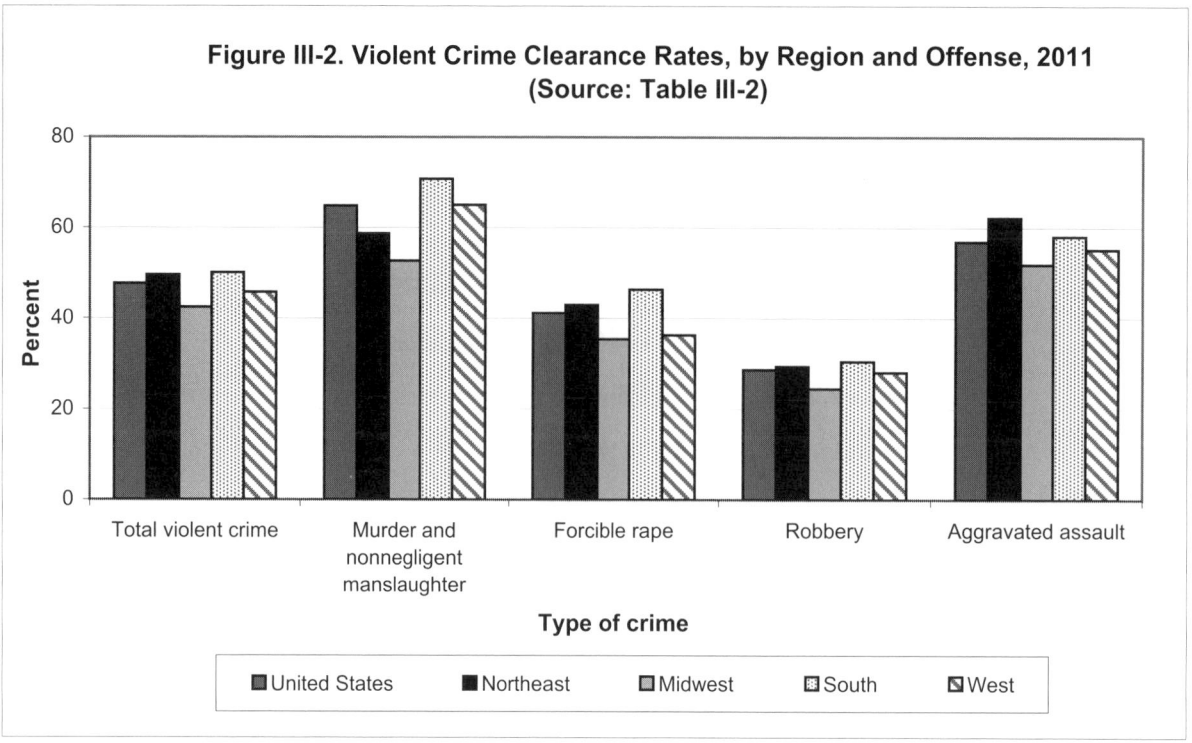

Figure III-2. Violent Crime Clearance Rates, by Region and Offense, 2011 (Source: Table III-2)

National Clearances

A review of the data for 2011 revealed law enforcement agencies in the United States cleared 47.7 percent of violent crimes (murder, forcible rape, robbery, and aggravated assault) and 18.6 percent of property crimes (burglary, larceny-theft, and motor vehicle theft) brought to their attention. In addition, law enforcement cleared 18.8 percent of arson offenses, which are reported in a slightly different manner than the other property crimes. (Table III-1) More details concerning this offense are furnished in the arson text in this section.

As in most years, law enforcement agencies cleared a higher percentage of violent crimes than property crimes in 2011, although clearance rates for both types of crimes were increased from 2010. As a rule, this long-term trend is attributed to the more vigorous investigative efforts put forth for violent crimes. In addition, violent crimes more often involve victims and/or witnesses who are able to identify the perpetrators. Clearance rates for arson crimes, however, dropped slightly from 2010.

A breakdown of the clearances for violent crimes for 2011 revealed that the nation's law enforcement agencies cleared 64.8 percent of murder offenses (unchanged from 2010), 56.9 percent of aggravated assault offenses, 41.2 percent of forcible rape offenses (up nearly a percentage point from 2010), and 28.7 percent of robbery offenses. (Table III-1)

For property crime offenses, law enforcement agencies throughout the nation collectively cleared 18.6 percent of all offenses in 2011, including 12.7 percent of burglary offenses, 21.5 percent of larceny-theft offenses, 11.9 percent of motor vehicle theft offenses, and 18.8 percent of arson offenses. (Table III-1)

Regional Clearances

The UCR program divides the nation into four regions: the Northeast, the Midwest, the South, and the West. (See Appendix III for further details.) A review of clearance data for 2011 by region showed that agencies in the Northeast cleared the greatest proportion of their violent crime offenses (49.6 percent, down nearly a percentage point from 2010). Law enforcement agencies in the South cleared 50.1 percent of their violent crimes (an increase from 2010), while agencies in the West and Midwest cleared 42.5 percent and 45.8 percent, respectively. This represents a respective decrease and increase of nearly three percentage points. (Table III-2)

For murder and nonnegligent manslaughter, the South cleared 70.7 percent of offenses, followed by the West (65.0 percent), the Northeast (58.7 percent), and the Midwest (52.7 percent). Forcible rape offenses were cleared 46.4 percent of the time in the South, 43.0 percent of the time in the Northeast, 36.3 percent in the West, and 35.4 percent in the Midwest. For robbery, the South had the highest clearance rate, at 30.5 percent. The Northeast had the highest proportion of clearances for aggravated assault (62.2 percent). (Table III-2)

Clearance data for 2011 showed that, among the regions, law enforcement agencies in the Northeast cleared the highest percentage of their property crimes (21.1 percent). Agencies in the South and Midwest cleared 19.3 percent and 18.3 percent, respectively. Agencies in the West cleared 16.0 percent of their property crimes. (Table III-2)

Agencies in the Northeast cleared the highest percentage of burglary offenses at 14.5 percent, followed by the South at 13.4 percent, the West at 11.7 percent, and the Midwest at 11.0 percent. For larceny-theft, the Northeast (23.7 percent) was followed by the South at 22.0 percent and the Midwest at 21.6 percent, and then the West (19.0 percent). The South cleared the highest proportion of motor vehicle thefts at 15.0 percent, followed by the Northeast at 13.5 percent. The Northeast cleared the greatest percentage of arson offenses (23.2 percent), followed by the South (19.4 percent). (Table III-2)

Clearances by Population Groups

The UCR program uses the following population group designations in its data presentations: cities (grouped according to population size) and counties (classified as either metropolitan or nonmetropolitan counties). A breakdown of these classifications is furnished in Appendix III.

Cities

In 2011, the clearance data collected showed that law enforcement agencies in the nation's cities cleared 45.6 percent of their violent crime offenses. Among the city population groups, agencies in the smallest cities, those with fewer than 10,000 inhabitants, cleared the greatest proportion of their violent crime offenses (57.3 percent, a gain of nearly four percentage points since 2010), and law enforcement in cities with 500,000 to 999,999 inhabitants cleared the smallest proportion of their violent crime offenses (39.2 percent). (Table III-1)

The clearance data for murder showed that among the city population groups, cities with populations of 10,000 to 24,999 inhabitants cleared the greatest percentage of their murders (76.0 percent). Law enforcement agencies in cities with 500,000 to 999,999 inhabitants cleared the lowest percentage of their murders (53.2 percent). For forcible rape, cities with 1,000,000 or more inhabitants cleared the largest percentage of offenses at 46.6 percent, while cities with 25,000 to 49,999 inhabitants cleared the lowest percentage of offenses at 35.3 percent. Cities with under 10,000 inhabitants cleared the greatest percentage of their robbery offenses at 38.1 percent, and cities with 500,000 to 999,999 inhabitants cleared the lowest proportion of their robbery offenses at 24.1 percent. For aggravated assault, cities with fewer than 10,000 inhabitants cleared the highest proportion of offenses (63.8 percent); cities with 500,000 to 999,999 inhabitants cleared the lowest percentage of offenses (48.3 percent). (Table III-1)

In 2011, agencies in the nation's cities collectively cleared 18.6 percent of their property crime offenses. Law enforcement in cities with 10,000 to 24,999 inhabitants cleared the highest proportion of the property crimes (23.5 percent) brought to their attention; cities with 1,000,000 or more inhabitants cleared the smallest proportion of their property crimes (12.6 percent). (Table III-1)

Law enforcement agencies in cities cleared 12.7 percent of burglaries, 21.5 percent of larceny-thefts, 11.9 percent of motor vehicle thefts, and 18.8 percent of arsons in 2011. (Table III-1) For burglaries, cities with fewer than 10,000 inhabitants cleared the largest percentage of their offenses, at 17.8 percent, while cities with 1,000,000 or more inhabitants cleared the smallest percentage of their offenses, at 7.9 percent. Cities with 10,000 to 24,999 inhabitants cleared the greatest percentage of their larceny-theft offenses (26.4 percent), and cities with 500,000 to 999,999 inhabitants cleared the lowest proportion of larceny-theft offenses (15.1 percent). For motor vehicle theft, cities with fewer than 10,000 inhabitants cleared the highest percentages of their offenses, at 23.4 percent. (Table III-1) Cities with 10,000 to 24,999 inhabitants cleared the greatest percentage of their arson offenses, at 25.7 percent. (Table III-1)

Metropolitan and Nonmetropolitan Counties

In 2011, law enforcement agencies in metropolitan counties cleared 54.0 percent of their violent crime offenses. Of the violent crimes made known to law enforcement agencies in metropolitan counties, murder offenses had the highest proportion of clearance (65.7 percent), followed by aggravated assaults (61.6 percent), forcible rapes (45.2 percent), and robberies (31.7 percent). Law enforcement agencies in metropolitan counties cleared 18.3 percent of their total property crimes, 13.7 percent of burglaries, 20.7 percent of larceny-thefts, 15.0 percent of motor vehicle thefts, and 19.5 percent of their arsons. (Table III-1)

Like their counterparts in metropolitan counties, nonmetropolitan counties collectively cleared a greater proportion of their violent crimes than did the nation as a whole in 2011. Nonmetropolitan counties cleared 60.4 percent of their violent crime offenses and 19.0 percent of property crimes. Of the violent crimes known to them, law enforcement in nonmetropolitan counties had the highest number of clearances for murder (74.8 percent), with 47.7 percent of forcible rapes, 40.7 percent of robberies, and 63.8 percent of aggravated assaults being cleared. Agencies in nonmetropolitan counties reported clearing 16.2 percent of their burglaries, 20.1 percent of their larceny-thefts, 24.5 percent of their motor vehicle thefts, and 24.9 percent of their arsons. (Table III-1)

Clearances by Classification Group and Type

For forcible rape, by classification group and type, law enforcement agencies cleared 43.0 percent of assault to rape attempts and 40.1 percent of rapes by force in 2011. Cleared robbery offenses included 32.2 percent of offenses involving strong-arm tactics, 32.0 percent of offenses involving knives or other cutting instruments, 31.5 percent of offenses involving other weapons, and 23.1 percent of offenses involving firearms. For aggravated assaults, agencies cleared 64.3 percent of offenses involving knives or other cutting instruments; 61.1 percent of offenses involving hands, feet, fists, and so on; 57.0 percent of offenses involving other weapons; and 42.8 percent of offenses involving firearms. (Table III-3)

For property crime clearances grouped by classification and type, data showed that the highest percentage of burglary

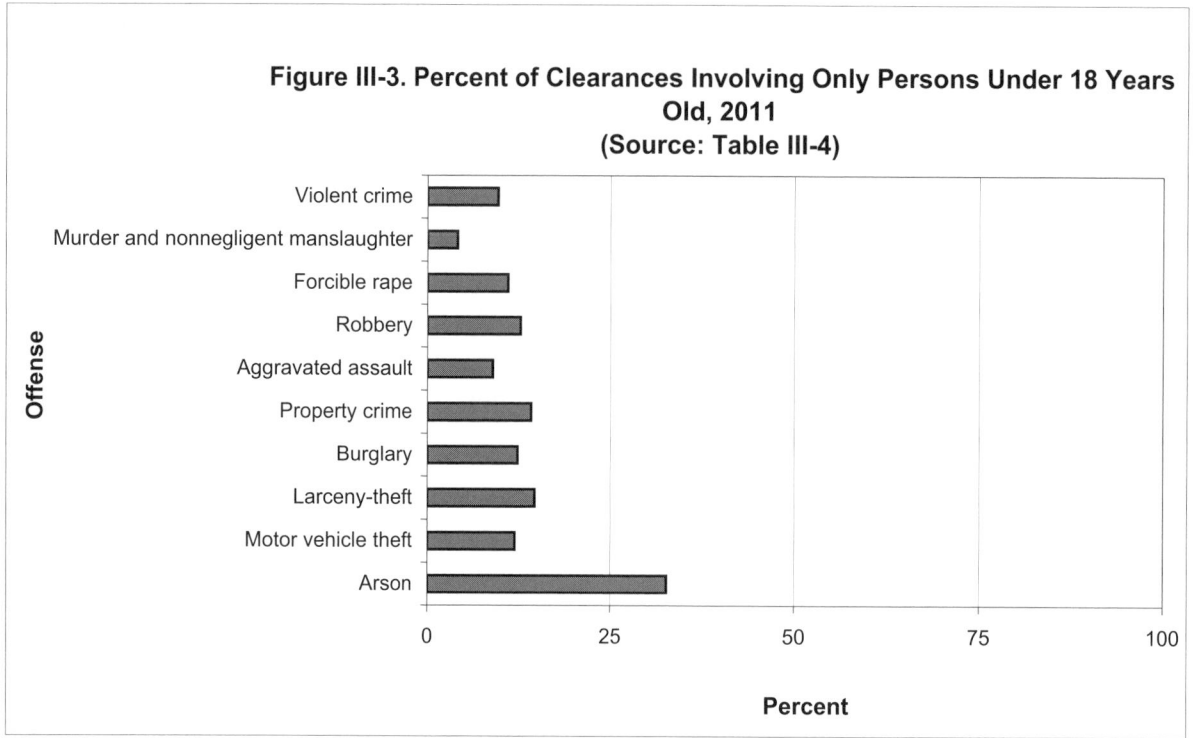

Figure III-3. Percent of Clearances Involving Only Persons Under 18 Years Old, 2011
(Source: Table III-4)

clearances in the nation in 2011 (13.9 percent) were of offenses that involved unlawful entry of structures. Law enforcement agencies cleared 11.7 percent of burglaries involving forcible entry and 10.9 percent of attempted forcible entry offenses. For motor vehicle theft, agencies cleared 12.1 percent of motor vehicle theft offenses involving automobiles and 9.4 percent of motor vehicle theft offenses involving trucks and buses. (Table III-3)

In 2011, 22.8 percent of structural arson offenses were cleared by arrest or exceptional means, while 9.5 percent of mobile arson offenses and 21.0 percent of other arson crimes were cleared. (Table III-3)

Clearances and Juveniles

When an offender under 18 years of age is cited to appear in juvenile court or before other juvenile authorities, the UCR program considers the incident for which the juvenile is being held responsible to be cleared by arrest, although a physical arrest may not have occurred. In addition, according to program definitions, clearances that include both adult and juvenile offenders are classified as clearances for crimes committed by adults. Therefore, the juvenile clearance data are limited to those clearances involving juveniles only, and the figures in this publication should not be used to present a definitive picture of juvenile involvement in crime.

Of the clearances for violent crimes that were reported in the nation in 2011, 9.5 percent involved only juveniles, down from 10.2 percent in 2010. In the nation's cities, collectively, 9.6 percent of violent crime clearances involved

only juveniles, with juveniles in cities exclusively involved in 4.2 percent of murder clearances, 10.2 percent of forcible rape clearances, 12.7 percent of robbery clearances, and 8.8 percent of aggravated assault clearances. These rates represented decreases from 2010. Of the nation's city population groups, cities with fewer than 10,000 inhabitants had the highest percentage of overall clearances for violent crime only involving juveniles (10.6 percent); cities with 1,000,000 or more inhabitants had the lowest percentage (7.6 percent). (Table III-4)

Law enforcement agencies in metropolitan counties reported that 10.3 percent of their violent crime clearances—including 3.5 percent of their murder clearances, 12.8 percent of their forcible rape clearances, 13.2 percent of their robbery clearances, and 9.8 percent of their aggravated assault clearances—involved only juveniles. Agencies in nonmetropolitan counties reported that 7.2 percent of their clearances for violent crime involved only juveniles, including 3.8 percent of their murder clearances, 13.3 percent of their forcible rape clearances, 5.4 percent of their robbery clearances, and 6.7 percent of their aggravated assault clearances. The last number represents a decrease of four percentage points since 2010. (Table III-4)

In 2011, 14.2 percent of clearances for property crime involved only juveniles. In cities collectively, 14.8 percent of the clearances for property crime, 13.0 percent of clearances for burglary, 15.2 percent of clearances for larceny-theft, 12.2 percent of clearances for motor vehicle theft, and 35.5 percent of clearances for arson involved juveniles only. Among the population groups labeled *city*, the percentages of clearances involving only juveniles for overall property crime ranged from a low of 11.9 percent in cities with more than 1,000,000 inhabitants to a high of 16.8 percent in cities with populations of 100,000 to 249,999. (Table III-4)

Metropolitan counties reported 12.9 percent of property crime clearances, 11.6 percent of burglary clearances, 13.4 percent of larceny-theft clearances, 11.4 percent of motor vehicle theft clearances, and 29.5 percent of arson clearances involved persons under 18 years of age. In non-metropolitan counties, 9.0 percent of property crime clearances, 8.7 percent of burglary clearances, 9.0 percent of larceny-theft clearances, 10.0 percent of motor vehicle theft clearances, and 16.9 percent of arson clearances involved juveniles exclusively. In suburban areas, 33.9 percent of arson clearances involved only juveniles. (Table III-4) Arson offenses had the highest percentage of clearances involving only juveniles—32.7 percent—nationally in 2011. (Table III-4)

Table III-1. Number and Percent of Offenses Cleared by Arrest or Exceptional Means, by Population Group, 2011

(Number, percent.)

Population group	Violent crime	Murder and non-negligent man-slaughter	Forcible rape	Robbery	Aggra-vated assault	Property crime	Burglary	Larceny-theft	Motor vehicle theft	Arson[1]	Number of agencies	2011 estimated population
Total, All Agencies												
Offenses known	1,046,123	12,706	72,666	304,089	656,662	8,107,267	1,976,408	5,485,117	645,742	48,348	14,442	276,800,696
Percent cleared by arrest	47.7	64.8	41.2	28.7	56.9	18.6	12.7	21.5	11.9	18.8		
Total Cities												
Offenses known	821,378	9,606	53,842	262,724	495,206	6,244,313	1,428,258	4,307,219	508,836	35,938	10,492	181,952,742
Percent cleared by arrest	45.6	63.8	39.5	28.1	55.2	18.6	12.1	21.7	10.6	18.1		
Group I (250,000 and over)												
Offenses known	336,980	4,652	17,263	128,820	186,245	1,862,252	464,300	1,172,918	225,034	13,324	71	44,231,430
Percent cleared by arrest	40.0	59.3	42.5	24.9	49.7	13.7	9.3	16.6	7.4	14.1		
1,000,000 and over (Group I subset)												
Offenses known	98,579	1,277	4,855	40,501	51,946	532,624	128,009	334,812	69,803	3,604	8	14,331,558
Percent cleared by arrest	40.6	65.2	46.6	26.4	50.5	12.6	7.9	15.8	5.8	11.8		
500,000 to 999,999 (Group I subset)												
Offenses known	133,879	1,756	6,656	48,380	77,087	747,268	184,976	475,738	86,554	4,742	24	16,335,382
Percent cleared by arrest	39.2	53.2	40.1	24.1	48.3	12.8	9.1	15.1	8.1	14.9		
250,000 to 499,999 (Group I subset)												
Offenses known	104,522	1,619	5,752	39,939	57,212	582,360	151,315	362,368	68,677	4,978	39	13,564,490
Percent cleared by arrest	40.5	61.2	41.8	24.5	51.0	15.8	10.8	19.3	8.2	14.9		
Group II (100,000 to 249,999)												
Offenses known	148,578	1,762	9,193	49,049	88,574	1,115,907	266,887	750,082	98,938	6,091	201	30,152,852
Percent cleared by arrest	44.5	63.5	39.4	28.3	53.6	17.5	11.3	20.7	9.9	15.7		
Group III (50,000 to 99,999)												
Offenses known	112,281	1,043	8,002	34,129	69,107	961,962	215,193	674,348	72,421	5,136	439	30,567,766
Percent cleared by arrest	48.4	66.1	37.5	30.3	58.4	20.1	12.5	23.5	11.2	19.9		
Group IV (25,000 to 49,999)												
Offenses known	85,683	849	7,337	23,418	54,079	836,805	178,732	610,353	47,720	4,137	795	27,680,193
Percent cleared by arrest	49.8	71.5	35.3	32.6	58.9	21.7	12.6	25.1	13.4	20.3		
Group V (10,000 to 24,999)												
Offenses known	76,444	776	6,497	17,126	52,045	782,279	167,552	576,771	37,956	3,562	1,699	26,893,603
Percent cleared by arrest	54.2	76.0	38.8	35.3	62.0	23.5	15.0	26.4	17.7	24.2		
Group VI (under 10,000)												
Offenses known	61,412	524	5,550	10,182	45,156	685,108	135,594	522,747	26,767	3,688	7,287	22,426,898
Percent cleared by arrest	57.3	69.5	39.5	38.1	63.8	22.3	17.8	23.4	23.4	25.7		
Metropolitan Counties												
Offenses known	176,184	2,275	13,470	37,500	122,939	1,428,627	396,689	921,069	110,869	9,168	1,696	68,427,437
Percent cleared by arrest	54.0	65.7	45.2	31.7	61.6	18.3	13.7	20.7	15.0	19.5		
Nonmetropolitan Counties												
Offenses known	48,561	825	5,354	3,865	38,517	434,327	151,461	256,829	26,037	3,242	2,254	26,420,517
Percent cleared by arrest	60.4	74.8	47.7	40.7	63.8	19.0	16.2	20.1	24.5	24.9		
Suburban Areas[2]												
Offenses known	309,126	3,472	24,338	71,107	210,209	2,882,202	687,279	2,004,919	190,004	15,842	7,725	122,581,768
Percent cleared by arrest	53.9	67.7	42.2	32.8	62.2	20.1	14.0	22.7	15.0	21.2		

[1] Not all agencies submit data reports for arson to the FBI. Therefore, the agency counts and estimated population presented in this table do not represent participation for the reporting of arson.

[2] Suburban areas include law enforcement agencies in cities with less than 50,000 inhabitants and county law enforcement agencies that are within a Metropolitan Statistical Area. Suburban areas exclude all metropolitan agencies associated with a principal city. The agencies associated with suburban areas also appear in other groups within this table.

Table III-2. Number and Percent of Offenses Cleared by Arrest or Exceptional Means, by Region and Geographic Division, 2011

(Number, percent.)

Geographic region/division	Violent crime	Murder and non-negligent man-slaughter	Forcible rape	Robbery	Aggra-vated assault	Property crime	Burglary	Larceny-theft	Motor vehicle theft	Arson[1]	Number of agencies	2011 estimated population
Total, All Agencies												
Offenses known	1,046,123	12,706	72,666	304,089	656,662	8,107,267	1,976,408	5,485,117	645,742	48,348	14,442	276,800,696
Percent cleared by arrest	47.7	64.8	41.2	28.7	56.9	18.6	12.7	21.5	11.9	18.8		
Northeast												
Offenses known	138,942	1,604	9,211	47,636	80,491	991,231	215,503	712,088	63,640	5,662	3,311	45,474,641
Percent cleared by arrest	49.6	58.7	43.0	29.4	62.2	21.1	14.5	23.7	13.5	23.2		
New England												
Offenses known	43,340	360	3,423	11,552	28,005	318,458	72,761	225,136	20,561	1,699	893	14,083,589
Percent cleared by arrest	50.4	60.0	34.4	27.3	61.8	16.7	12.1	18.7	11.2	23.2		
Middle Atlantic												
Offenses known	95,602	1,244	5,788	36,084	52,486	672,773	142,742	486,952	43,079	3,963	2,418	31,391,052
Percent cleared by arrest	49.2	58.4	48.1	30.0	62.4	23.1	15.7	26.1	14.6	23.1		
Midwest												
Offenses known	168,670	2,153	14,971	48,717	102,829	1,436,443	354,238	980,279	101,926	10,877	3,625	49,878,507
Percent cleared by arrest	42.5	52.7	35.4	24.5	51.9	18.3	11.0	21.6	12.2	16.3		
East North Central												
Offenses known	109,484	1,491	10,094	36,444	61,455	895,311	241,306	588,768	65,237	7,150	1,729	30,200,542
Percent cleared by arrest	36.9	44.3	32.2	22.6	46.0	16.5	9.6	20.0	10.6	14.7		
West North Central												
Offenses known	59,186	662	4,877	12,273	41,374	541,132	112,932	391,511	36,689	3,727	1,896	19,677,965
Percent cleared by arrest	52.9	71.6	42.0	30.0	60.7	21.4	14.1	24.1	15.0	19.5		
South												
Offenses known	473,955	6,046	29,986	127,553	310,370	3,721,340	961,673	2,511,465	248,202	18,532	5,535	111,005,570
Percent cleared by arrest	50.1	70.7	46.4	30.5	58.1	19.3	13.4	22.0	15.0	19.4		
South Atlantic												
Offenses known	248,943	3,170	13,902	72,325	159,546	1,921,400	486,732	1,305,085	129,583	8,575	2,499	57,776,297
Percent cleared by arrest	52.2	72.8	50.9	31.5	61.3	21.0	15.5	23.5	15.9	19.9		
East South Central												
Offenses known	71,630	947	5,219	17,582	47,882	562,944	160,587	368,971	33,386	2,912	1,297	17,254,684
Percent cleared by arrest	48.1	66.1	43.6	29.2	55.2	19.9	13.1	22.8	19.4	22.6		
West South Central												
Offenses known	153,382	1,929	10,865	37,646	102,942	1,236,996	314,354	837,409	85,233	7,045	1,739	35,974,589
Percent cleared by arrest	47.6	69.5	42.0	29.3	54.5	16.5	10.2	19.4	11.8	17.6		
West												
Offenses known	264,556	2,903	18,498	80,183	162,972	1,958,253	444,994	1,281,285	231,974	13,277	1,971	70,441,978
Percent cleared by arrest	45.8	65.0	36.3	28.1	55.2	16.0	11.7	19.0	8.1	18.1		
Mountain												
Offenses known	77,517	848	7,221	17,881	51,567	621,381	140,985	427,674	52,722	3,876	816	21,949,115
Percent cleared by arrest	48.0	70.9	33.3	27.7	56.7	18.9	10.7	22.7	10.2	22.9		
Pacific												
Offenses known	187,039	2,055	11,277	62,302	111,405	1,336,872	304,009	853,611	179,252	9,401	1,155	48,492,863
Percent cleared by arrest	44.9	62.6	38.3	28.1	54.6	14.7	12.1	17.1	7.4	16.2		

[1] Not all agencies submit data reports for arson to the FBI. Therefore, the agency counts and estimated population presented in this table do not represent participation for the reporting of arson.

Table III-3. Number and Percent of Offenses Cleared by Arrest or Exceptional Means, Additional Information About Selected Offenses, by Population Group, 2011

(Number, percent.)

Population group	Forcible rape		Robbery				Aggravated assault			
	Rape by force	Assault to rape-attempts	Firearm	Knife or cutting instrument	Other weapon	Strongarm	Firearm	Knife or cutting instrument	Other weapon	Hands, fists, feet, etc.
Total, All Agencies										
Offenses known	62,700	4,642	114,638	21,942	24,115	117,126	125,844	113,025	191,114	159,414
Percent cleared by arrest	40.1	43.0	23.1	32.0	31.5	32.2	42.8	64.3	57.0	61.1
Total Cities										
Offenses known	47,233	3,732	99,992	19,465	20,840	104,456	100,972	91,486	148,068	117,254
Percent cleared by arrest	38.8	42.9	22.8	31.6	31.3	31.7	38.9	63.5	55.9	61.0
Group I (250,000 and over)										
Offenses known	15,130	1,581	55,082	9,067	9,140	50,727	51,672	36,057	61,076	29,115
Percent cleared by arrest	41.8	44.8	20.2	29.2	28.5	28.3	34.7	62.3	52.0	53.7
1,000,000 and over (Group I subset)										
Offenses known	4,249	606	16,910	3,400	3,166	17,025	13,823	11,603	18,298	8,222
Percent cleared by arrest	46.9	44.9	21.4	29.2	31.1	29.9	37.2	62.7	51.8	52.5
500,000 to 999,999 (Group I subset)										
Offenses known	5,779	527	21,126	3,473	3,572	18,631	20,418	15,271	26,267	11,948
Percent cleared by arrest	39.9	41.7	19.3	28.6	28.1	27.5	34.8	59.3	49.4	52.6
250,000 to 499,999 (Group I subset)										
Offenses known	5,102	448	17,046	2,194	2,402	15,071	17,431	9,183	16,511	8,945
Percent cleared by arrest	39.7	48.4	20.2	30.3	25.5	27.4	32.8	66.8	56.5	56.4
Group II (100,000 to 249,999)										
Offenses known	7,817	522	18,139	3,535	3,985	18,184	17,880	17,026	26,157	17,177
Percent cleared by arrest	38.4	44.1	24.1	30.1	32.1	32.1	35.8	62.1	55.0	60.7
Group III (50,000 to 99,999)										
Offenses known	6,974	408	10,332	2,862	2,945	14,157	10,882	12,839	19,625	17,966
Percent cleared by arrest	37.1	39.7	24.4	31.4	32.7	33.9	42.2	63.6	60.0	63.5
Group IV (25,000 to 49,999)										
Offenses known	6,553	419	7,335	1,846	2,245	9,811	7,968	9,822	15,784	15,761
Percent cleared by arrest	33.9	42.0	28.2	36.0	33.1	35.0	45.9	63.2	58.2	62.2
Group V (10,000 to 24,999)										
Offenses known	5,829	360	5,807	1,370	1,658	6,841	7,242	8,676	14,398	17,431
Percent cleared by arrest	38.6	40.6	28.3	39.6	36.7	40.3	50.0	67.0	61.5	65.4
Group VI (under 10,000)										
Offenses known	4,930	442	3,297	785	867	4,736	5,328	7,066	11,028	19,804
Percent cleared by arrest	39.0	40.3	32.2	41.0	38.2	41.2	56.5	68.7	61.7	64.7
Metropolitan Counties										
Offenses known	10,596	642	13,143	2,176	2,827	11,351	18,207	16,292	32,277	29,088
Percent cleared by arrest	42.8	43.5	23.4	34.2	31.2	36.2	58.3	66.9	60.5	61.0
Nonmetropolitan Counties										
Offenses known	4,871	268	1,503	301	448	1,319	6,665	5,247	10,769	13,072
Percent cleared by arrest	47.4	44.0	37.1	43.5	40.8	42.1	60.0	70.5	61.7	62.7
Suburban Areas[1]										
Offenses known	20,138	1,301	23,762	4,720	5,771	25,302	28,800	29,928	56,262	59,481
Percent cleared by arrest	40.3	42.4	25.3	35.6	33.9	37.1	55.4	67.1	61.3	63.4

[1] Suburban areas include law enforcement agencies in cities with less than 50,000 inhabitants and county law enforcement agencies that are within a Metropolitan Statistical Area. Suburban areas exclude all metropolitan agencies associated with a principal city. The agencies associated with suburban areas also appear in other groups within this table.

Table III-3.   Number and Percent of Offenses Cleared by Arrest or Exceptional Means, Additional Information About Selected Offenses, by Population Group, 2011—*Continued*

(Number, percent.)

Population group	Burglary			Motor vehicle theft			Arson[2]			Number of agencies	2011 estimated population
	Forcible entry	Unlawful entry	Attempted forcible entry	Autos	Trucks and buses	Other vehicles	Structure	Mobile	Other		
Total, All Agencies											
Offenses known	1,095,525	594,376	112,192	451,664	92,696	61,045	20,853	10,852	13,778	13,772	257,496,110
Percent cleared by arrest	11.7	13.9	10.9	12.1	9.4	10.5	22.8	9.5	21.0		
Total Cities											
Offenses known	807,891	434,906	87,486	369,516	73,971	41,046	15,717	7,913	10,305	10,164	172,526,482
Percent cleared by arrest	11.1	13.5	10.7	11.0	8.1	9.5	21.3	8.8	21.0		
Group I (250,000 and over)											
Offenses known	301,734	114,183	27,948	162,138	42,594	14,406	5,806	3,532	3,307	67	42,399,947
Percent cleared by arrest	8.5	10.6	9.3	7.7	5.5	7.6	17.1	5.9	18.4		
1,000,000 and over (Group I subset)											
Offenses known	87,994	33,100	6,915	44,702	19,204	5,897	1,289	1,131	1,146	8	14,331,558
Percent cleared by arrest	7.5	8.5	10.6	6.6	3.9	5.7	19.1	6.2	9.6		
500,000 to 999,999 (Group I subset)											
Offenses known	121,532	42,278	12,648	66,742	13,034	4,916	2,202	1,296	932	23	15,500,953
Percent cleared by arrest	8.4	10.7	8.4	8.0	5.9	10.4	15.9	7.3	24.9		
250,000 to 499,999 (Group I subset)											
Offenses known	92,208	38,805	8,385	50,694	10,356	3,593	2,315	1,105	1,229	36	12,567,436
Percent cleared by arrest	9.6	12.3	9.8	8.3	8.1	6.8	17.0	4.0	21.7		
Group II (100,000 to 249,999)											
Offenses known	145,268	76,977	15,938	71,586	12,500	7,317	2,576	1,389	1,677	184	27,563,681
Percent cleared by arrest	10.3	12.9	10.0	9.7	9.5	8.5	19.5	7.8	19.3		
Group III (50,000 to 99,999)											
Offenses known	111,498	70,193	12,961	53,382	7,967	6,328	2,097	1,111	1,650	409	28,562,894
Percent cleared by arrest	11.3	13.9	13.0	11.5	9.8	8.3	22.2	10.1	22.8		
Group IV (25,000 to 49,999)											
Offenses known	93,285	61,196	11,440	35,265	4,195	5,138	1,674	698	1,510	758	26,321,922
Percent cleared by arrest	11.8	13.7	10.0	14.0	11.2	8.9	24.0	12.9	19.5		
Group V (10,000 to 24,999)											
Offenses known	87,655	59,201	10,156	28,042	3,851	4,065	1,568	680	1,119	1,630	25,790,476
Percent cleared by arrest	14.5	15.8	12.0	18.5	15.7	13.8	28.1	15.0	24.5		
Group VI (under 10,000)											
Offenses known	68,451	53,156	9,043	19,103	2,864	3,792	1,996	503	1,042	7,116	21,887,562
Percent cleared by arrest	18.7	17.2	12.7	25.0	21.0	17.3	27.3	14.3	27.8		
Metropolitan Counties											
Offenses known	199,667	109,443	18,380	66,300	14,853	14,524	3,448	2,332	2,677	1,481	59,484,091
Percent cleared by arrest	12.3	14.4	10.7	15.2	12.3	11.3	26.6	10.3	20.5		
Nonmetropolitan Counties											
Offenses known	87,967	50,027	6,326	15,848	3,872	5,475	1,688	607	796	2,127	25,485,537
Percent cleared by arrest	15.8	16.2	13.6	26.9	22.6	16.1	29.0	16.0	21.9		
Suburban Areas[1]											
Offenses known	345,050	212,461	37,231	124,367	22,383	22,789	6,294	3,438	4,990	7,291	111,165,089
Percent cleared by arrest	12.9	15.0	11.0	15.4	12.3	11.3	27.5	11.0	21.5		

[1] Suburban areas include law enforcement agencies in cities with less than 50,000 inhabitants and county law enforcement agencies that are within a Metropolitan Statistical Area. Suburban areas exclude all metropolitan agencies associated with a principal city. The agencies associated with suburban areas also appear in other groups within this table.

[2] Not all agencies submit data reports for arson to the FBI. Therefore, the agency counts and estimated population presented in this table do not represent participation for the reporting of arson. Agencies must report arson clearances by detailed property classification as specified on the *Monthly Return of Arson Offenses Known to Law Enforcement* to be included in this table; therefore, clearances in this table may differ from other clearance tables.

Table III-4.   Number of Offenses Cleared by Arrest or Exceptional Means and Percent Involving Persons Under 18 Years of Age, by Population Group, 2011

(Number, percent.)

Population group	Violent crime	Murder and non-negligent man-slaughter	Forcible rape	Robbery	Aggra-vated assault	Property crime	Burglary	Larceny-theft	Motor vehicle theft	Arson[1]	Number of agencies	2011 estimated population
Total, All Agencies												
Offenses known	441,316	7,396	26,875	77,866	329,179	1,354,156	220,306	1,064,637	69,213	8,835	13,576	255,070,020
Percent under 18 years	9.5	4.1	10.9	12.7	8.8	14.2	12.3	14.7	11.9	32.7		
Total Cities												
Offenses known	341,606	5,592	19,686	67,666	248,662	1,073,296	156,403	866,900	49,993	6,321	10,108	171,178,410
Percent under 18 years	9.6	4.2	10.2	12.7	8.8	14.8	13.0	15.2	12.2	35.5		
Group I (250,000 and over)												
Offenses known	125,567	2,510	6,883	30,014	86,160	238,566	40,020	182,685	15,861	1,839	66	41,781,951
Percent under 18 years	8.6	4.6	7.7	12.7	7.4	14.1	13.6	14.4	11.5	36.4		
1,000,000 and over (Group I subset)												
Offenses known	39,993	832	2,263	10,684	26,214	66,944	10,162	52,764	4,018	426	8	14,331,558
Percent under 18 years	7.6	3.0	6.8	10.4	6.6	11.9	11.6	12.1	9.0	37.6		
500,000 to 999,999 (Group I subset)												
Offenses known	47,355	773	2,375	10,472	33,735	87,728	15,369	65,800	6,559	698	22	14,882,957
Percent under 18 years	9.5	6.2	6.9	14.9	8.1	15.4	15.8	15.5	12.9	35.0		
250,000 to 499,999 (Group I subset)												
Offenses known	38,219	905	2,245	8,858	26,211	83,894	14,489	64,121	5,284	715	36	12,567,436
Percent under 18 years	8.5	4.6	9.5	12.9	7.1	14.4	12.7	15.0	11.8	37.2		
Group II (100,000 to 249,999)												
Offenses known	58,168	1,018	3,223	12,480	41,447	174,410	26,307	139,410	8,693	948	183	27,441,955
Percent under 18 years	9.9	4.5	9.8	13.5	8.9	16.8	15.0	17.4	13.1	30.8		
Group III (50,000 to 99,999)												
Offenses known	48,313	632	2,743	9,148	35,790	175,769	24,001	144,347	7,421	976	407	28,440,217
Percent under 18 years	10.2	2.5	11.2	13.7	9.4	16.6	12.7	17.4	12.2	37.0		
Group IV (25,000 to 49,999)												
Offenses known	38,557	553	2,384	6,886	28,734	168,613	20,463	142,333	5,817	803	754	26,198,419
Percent under 18 years	10.0	4.7	11.8	12.3	9.4	15.3	12.9	15.8	12.6	39.0		
Group V (10,000 to 24,999)												
Offenses known	37,781	538	2,362	5,507	29,374	170,646	22,994	141,407	6,245	831	1,615	25,563,289
Percent under 18 years	10.0	3.0	12.3	11.0	9.8	13.4	11.5	13.8	12.6	33.8		
Group VI (under 10,000)												
Offenses known	33,220	341	2,091	3,631	27,157	145,292	22,618	116,718	5,956	924	7,083	21,752,579
Percent under 18 years	10.6	5.0	13.0	11.5	10.4	12.2	11.4	12.4	12.0	35.6		
Metropolitan Counties												
Offenses known	73,330	1,228	4,787	8,793	58,522	206,107	41,832	150,881	13,394	1,734	1,417	58,986,177
Percent under 18 years	10.3	3.5	12.8	13.2	9.8	12.9	11.6	13.4	11.4	29.5		
Nonmetropolitan Counties												
Offenses known	26,380	576	2,402	1,407	21,995	74,753	22,071	46,856	5,826	780	2,051	24,905,433
Percent under 18 years	7.2	3.8	13.3	5.4	6.7	9.0	8.7	9.0	10.0	16.9		
Suburban Areas[2]												
Offenses known	137,131	1,986	8,607	18,966	107,572	498,155	79,467	394,489	24,199	3,243	7,197	110,378,170
Percent under 18 years	10.6	3.6	12.3	12.8	10.2	13.6	11.9	14.0	11.5	33.9		

[1] Not all agencies submit data reports for arson to the FBI. Therefore, the agency counts and estimated population presented in this table do not represent participation for the reporting of arson.
[2] Suburban areas include law enforcement agencies in cities with less than 50,000 inhabitants and county law enforcement agencies that are within a Metropolitan Statistical Area. Suburban areas exclude all metropolitan agencies associated with a principal city. The agencies associated with suburban areas also appear in other groups within this table.

SECTION IV:
PERSONS ARRESTED

PERSONS ARRESTED

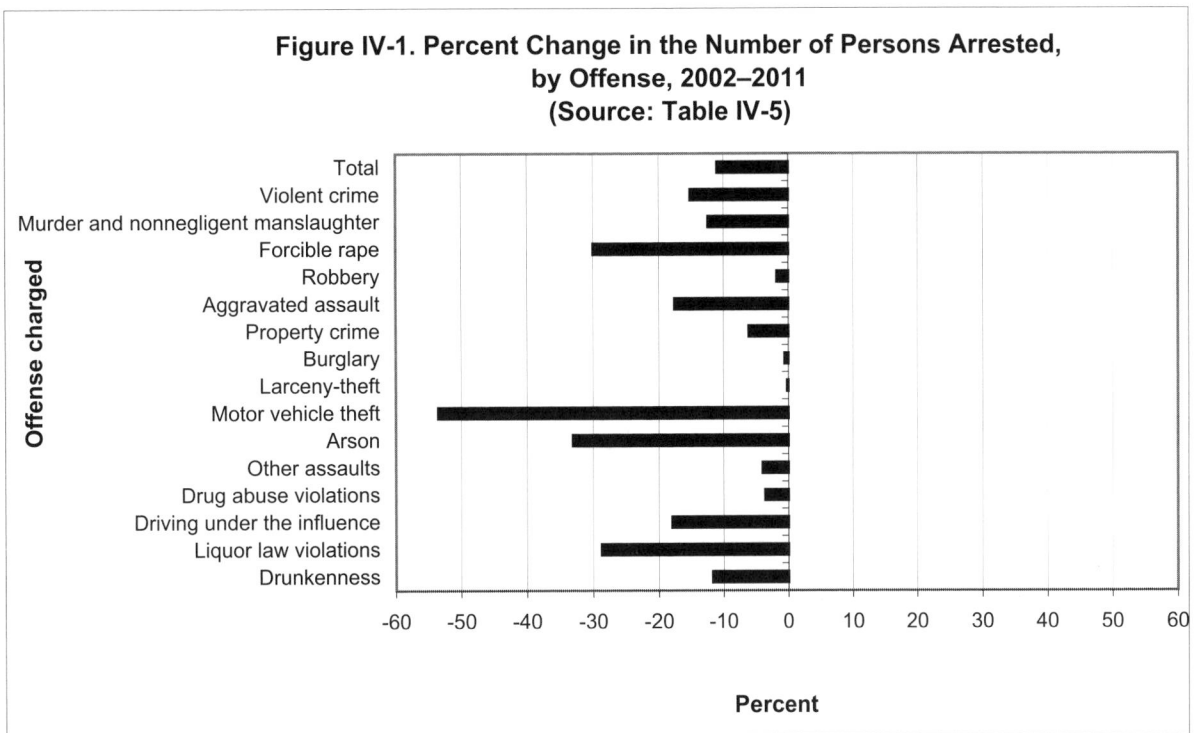

Figure IV-1. Percent Change in the Number of Persons Arrested,
by Offense, 2002–2011
(Source: Table IV-5)

In the Uniform Crime Reporting (UCR) program, one arrest is counted for each separate instance in which an individual is arrested, cited, or summoned for criminal acts in Part I and Part II crimes. (See Appendix II for additional information concerning Part I and Part II crimes.) One person may be arrested multiple times during the year; as a result, the arrest figures in this section should not be taken as the total number of individuals arrested. Instead, it provides the number of arrest occurrences reported by law enforcement. Information regarding the UCR program's statistical methodology and table construction can be found in Appendix I.

National Volume, Trends, and Rates

Volume

The FBI estimated that 12,408,899 arrests occurred in 2011 for all offenses (except traffic violations). Of these arrests, 534,704 were for violent crimes and 1,693,883 were for property crimes. Of the total violent crimes in 2011, aggravated assaults accounted for 74.4 percent of the total, or 408,488 incidents. Robbery had the next highest proportion with just under 20.0 percent, or 106,674 incidents; followed by forcible rape, at 3.6 percent (or 19,491 incidents); and murder and non-negligent manslaughter, at 2.0 percent (or 10,832 incidents). Of the estimated arrests for property crimes in 2011, 1,264,986 (74.7 percent) were for larceny-theft, 296,707 (17.5 percent) were for burglary, 66,414 (3.9

percent) were for motor vehicle theft, and 11,776 (0.2 percent) were for arson. (Table IV-1) The most frequent identifiable arrests made in 2011 were for drug abuse violations (estimated at 1,531,251 arrests). These arrests compose percent of the total number of all arrests.

A comparison of arrest figures from 2010 to 2011 revealed a 4.6 percent decrease. Arrests for violent crimes decreased 4.9 percent and arrests for property crimes decreased 0.1 percent during the 2-year period. (Table IV-8) An examination of the 5-year and 10-year arrest trends showed that the total number of arrests in 2011 fell 12.2 percent from the 2007 total. Arrests for violent crimes showed an 11.5 percent decrease from 2007 to 2011, while property crimes showed a 2.8 percent increase. (Table IV-6) In the 10-year trend data (2002 to 2011), the number of arrests decreased 7.1 percent. For violent crimes, the number of arrests fell 13.2 percent, while arrests for property crimes increased 4.0 percent. (Table IV-4)

The number of adults arrested for violent crime (arrestees age 18 years and over) decreased 4.0 percent from 2010 to 2011, decreased 7.7 percent from 2007 to 2011, and decreased 10.5 percent from 2002 to 2011. The number of juveniles arrested for violent crime (arrestees under 18 years of age) decreased 11.2 percent from 2010 to 2011, decreased 30.9 percent from 2007 to 2011, and decreased 28.5 percent from 2002 to 2011. (Tables IV-4, IV-6, and IV-8)

Trends

The trend data for murder showed that the number of arrests for this offense decreased 4.4 percent from 2010 to 2011, decreased 13.5 percent from 2007 to 2011, and decreased 11.5 percent from 2002 to 2011. The number of adults arrested for murder declined 2.9 percent from 2010 to 2011, decreased 11.2 percent from 2007 to 2011, and fell 10.1 percent from 2002 to 2011. The number of juveniles arrested for murder fell 19.9 percent from 2010 to 2011, decreased 34.6 percent from 2007 to 2011, and fell 26.4 percent from 2002 to 2011. (Tables IV-4, IV-6, and IV-8)

For forcible rape, the 2-year trend data showed that arrests decreased 5.4 percent from 2010 to 2011, with adult arrests decreasing 5.4 percent and juvenile arrests dropping 5.9 percent. The 5-year trend data showed that arrests decreased 14.6 percent from 2007 to 2011; adult arrests decreased 13.3 percent and juvenile arrests declined 21.5 percent during this period. The 10-year trend data showed that forcible rape arrests dropped 30.2 percent from 2002 to 2011, with adult arrests falling 28.6 percent and juvenile arrests falling 38.3 percent. (Tables IV-4, IV-6, and IV-8)

For robbery, the 2-year trend data showed that arrests decreased 5.7 percent from 2010 to 2011, with adult arrests decreasing 3.8 percent and juvenile arrests falling 12.1 percent. The 5-year trend data showed that total robbery arrests fell 14.5 percent from 2007 to 2011; adult arrests decreased 9.0 percent and juvenile arrests dropped 29.4 percent during this period. The 10-year trend data showed that arrests rose 0.4 percent from 2002 to 2011, with adult arrests increasing 2.4 percent and juvenile arrests falling by 6.4 percent. (Tables IV-4, IV-6, and IV-8)

The aggravated assault trend data showed that the number of arrests for this offense fell 4.7 percent from 2010 to 2011, dropped 10.4 percent from 2007 to 2011, and fell 15.2 percent from 2002 to 2011. The number of adults arrested for aggravated assault percent decreased 4.0 percent from 2010 to 2011, declined 7.0 percent from 2007 to 2011, and declined 12.0 percent from 2002 to 2011. The number of juveniles arrested for aggravated assault dropped 10.8 percent from 2010 to 2011, fell 32.3 percent from 2007 to 2011, and dropped 36.4 percent from 2002 to 2011. (Tables IV-4, IV-6, and IV-8)

The 2-year, 5-year, and 10-year trend data showed that the number of arrests for property crime decreased 0.1 percent from 2010 to 2011, increased 2.8 percent from 2007 to 2011, and increased 4.0 percent from 2002 to 2011. The number of adults arrested for property crime offenses (arrestees age 18 years and over) increased 2.6 percent from 2010 to 2011, increased 11.1 percent from 2007 to 2011, and increased 18.5 percent from 2002 to 2011. The number of juveniles arrested for property crime (arrestees under 18 years of age) decreased 9.6 percent from 2010 to 2011, decreased 20.2 percent from 2007 to 2011, and decreased 29.4 percent from 2002 to 2011. (Tables IV-4, IV-6, and IV-8)

The trend data for burglary showed that the number of arrests for this offense decreased 0.3 percent from 2010 to 2011, decreased 3.0 percent from 2007 to 2011, and increased 2.5 percent from 2002 to 2011. The number of adults arrested for burglary rose 1.9 percent from 2010 to 2011, rose 5.3 percent from 2007 to 2011, and rose 16.2 percent from 2002 to 2011. The number of juveniles arrested for burglary decreased 8.2 percent from 2010 to 2011, decreased 25.5 percent from 2007 to 2011, and fell 29.4 percent from 2002 to 2011. (Tables IV-4, IV-6, and IV-8)

For larceny-theft, the 2-year trend data showed that arrests rose 0.1 percent from 2010 to 2011, with adult arrests increasing 3.0 percent and juvenile arrests decreasing 10.0 percent. The 5-year trend data showed that total larceny-theft arrests increased 8.7 percent from 2007 to 2011; adult arrests increased 17.3 percent, while juvenile arrests dropped by 15.7 percent during this period. The 10-year trend data showed that larceny-theft arrests rose 11.3 percent from 2002 to 2011, with adult arrests increasing 26.7 percent and juvenile arrests falling 24.5 percent. (Tables IV-4, IV-6, and IV-8)

For motor vehicle theft, the 2-year trend data showed that arrests declined 4.7 percent from 2010 to 2011, with adult arrests decreasing 2.6 percent and juvenile arrests decreasing 12.0 percent. The 5-year trend data showed that total motor vehicle theft arrests dropped 41.0 percent from 2007 to 2011; juvenile arrests fell by more than half (50.9 percent) and adult arrests dropped 37.6 percent during this period. The 10-year trend data showed that arrests dropped 52.5 percent from 2002 to 2011, with adult arrests falling 45.5 percent and juvenile arrests dropping 68.5 percent. (Tables IV-4, IV-6, and IV-8)

The arson trend data showed that the number of arrests for this offense increased 0.2 percent from 2010 to 2011, fell 22.8 percent from 2007 to 2011, and fell 31.6 percent from 2002 to 2011. The number of adults arrested for arson decreased 1.9 percent from 2010 to 2011, fell 13.4 percent from 2007 to 2011, and fell 19.3 percent from 2002 to 2011. The number of juveniles arrested for arson rose 3.1 percent from 2010 to 2011, dropped 32.7 percent from 2007 to 2011, and dropped 42.8 percent from 2002 to 2011. (Tables IV-4, IV-6, and IV-8)

Rates

The rate of arrests was estimated at 3,991.1 arrests per 100,000 inhabitants in 2011. The arrest rate for violent crime was 172.3 per 100,000 inhabitants, and the arrest rate for property crime was 531.3 per 100,000 inhabitants. Law enforcement agencies throughout the nation reported 3.5 murder arrests, 6.3 forcible rape arrests, 34.5 robbery arrests, and 128.0 aggravated assault arrests per 100,000 inhabitants in 2010. Rates for all violent crimes were down from the 2010 rates. Law enforcement agencies throughout the nation reported 531.3 property crime arrests, 95.6 burglary arrests, 410.6 larceny-theft arrests, 21.4 motor vehicle

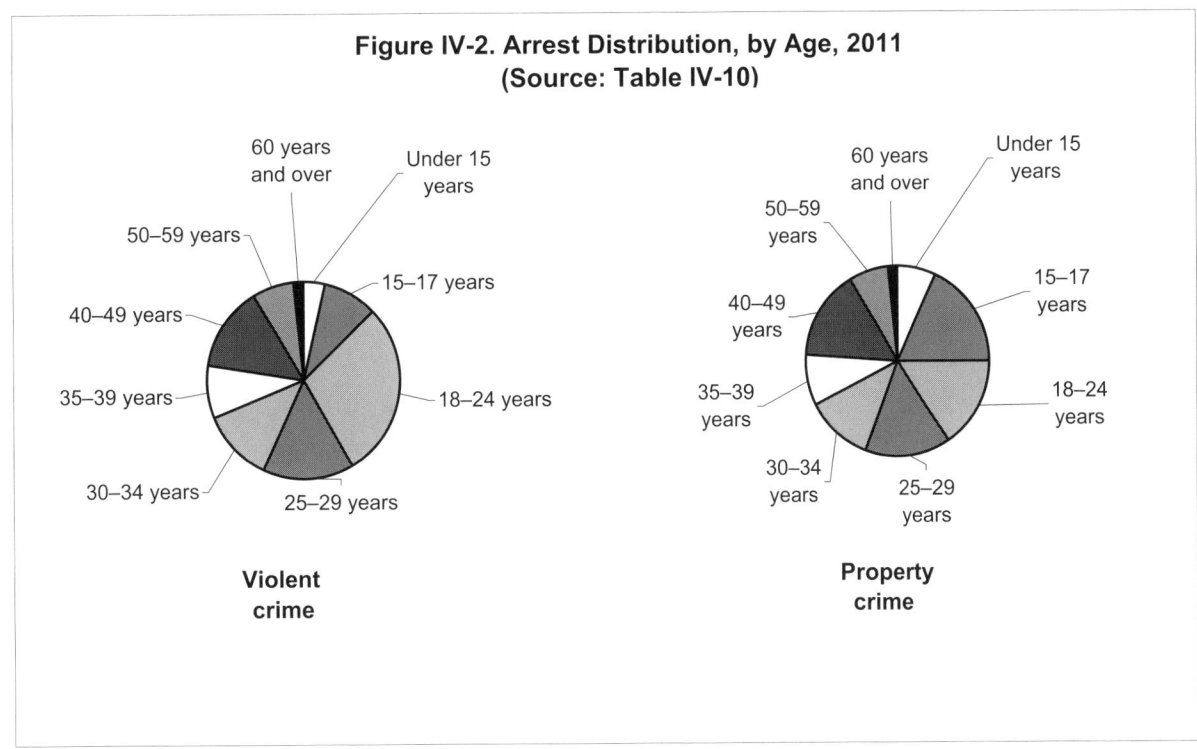

Figure IV-2. Arrest Distribution, by Age, 2011
(Source: Table IV-10)

Violent crime

Property crime

theft arrests, and 3.8 arson arrests per 100,000 inhabitants in 2010. Rates for property crimes were also down from the 2010 rates, except for burglary and arson. (Table IV-2)

By Age, Sex, and Race

Law enforcement agencies that contributed arrest data to the UCR program reported information on the age, sex, and race of the persons they arrested. According to the data for 2011, adults accounted for 88.2 percent of arrestees nationally. (Table IV-10)

A review of arrest data by age from 2010 to 2011 showed that arrests of adults decreased 3.6 percent during this period. Arrests of adults for property crimes, however, increased 2.6 percent, while arrests of adults for violent crimes decreased 4.0 percent over the same time span. The arrest total for juveniles (those under 18 years of age) decreased 11.1 percent from 2010 to 2011. Over the 2-year period, arrests of juveniles for violent crimes fell 11.2 percent; juvenile arrests for property crimes decreased 9.6 percent. (Table IV-8)

By sex, males accounted for 74.1 percent of all persons arrested. Males represented 80.4 percent of arrestees for violent crime, 88.2 percent of arrestees for murder, 98.8 percent of arrestees for forcible rape, 87.8 percent for robbery, and 77.3 percent for aggravated assault. Females accounted for 19.6 percent of violent crime arrestees, 11.8 percent of murder arrestees, 1.2 percent of forcible rape arrestees, 12.2 percent of robbery arrestees, and 22.7 percent of aggravated assault arrestees. (Table IV-14)

In 2011, most arrestees for property crime (79.6 percent) were over 18 years of age. By sex, males accounted for 62.9 percent of arrestees for property crime, 84.4 percent of arrestees for burglary, 56.7 percent of arrestees for larceny-theft, 82.2 percent of arrestees for motor vehicle theft, and 82.1 percent of arrestees for arson. Females accounted for 37.1 percent of property crime arrestees. Of the four property crimes, larceny-theft had the highest proportion of female arrestees at 43.3 percent. (Tables IV-10 and IV-14)

In 2011, 69.2 percent of all persons arrested were White, 28.4 percent were Black, and the remaining 2.4 percent were of other races (American Indian or Alaskan Native and Asian or Pacific Islander). Of all arrestees for violent crimes, 59.4 percent were White, 38.3 percent were Black, and 2.2 percent were of other races. For murder, 48.0 percent of arrestees were White, 49.7 percent were Black, and 2.3 percent were of other races. For forcible rape, 65.0 percent of arrestees were White, 32.9 percent were Black, and 2.1 percent of arrestees were of other races. For robbery, 43.0 percent of arrestees were White, 55.6 percent of arrestees were Black, and 1.5 percent of arrestees were of other races. For aggravated assault, 63.9 percent of arrestees were White, 33.6 percent of arrestees were Black, and 2.5 percent were of other races. (Table IV-15)

Of all arrestees for property crimes, 68.1 percent were White, 29.5 percent were Black, and 2.4 percent were of other races. For burglary, 66.7 percent of arrestees were White, 31.7 percent were Black, and 1.6 percent were of other races. For larceny-theft, 68.6 percent of arrestees were

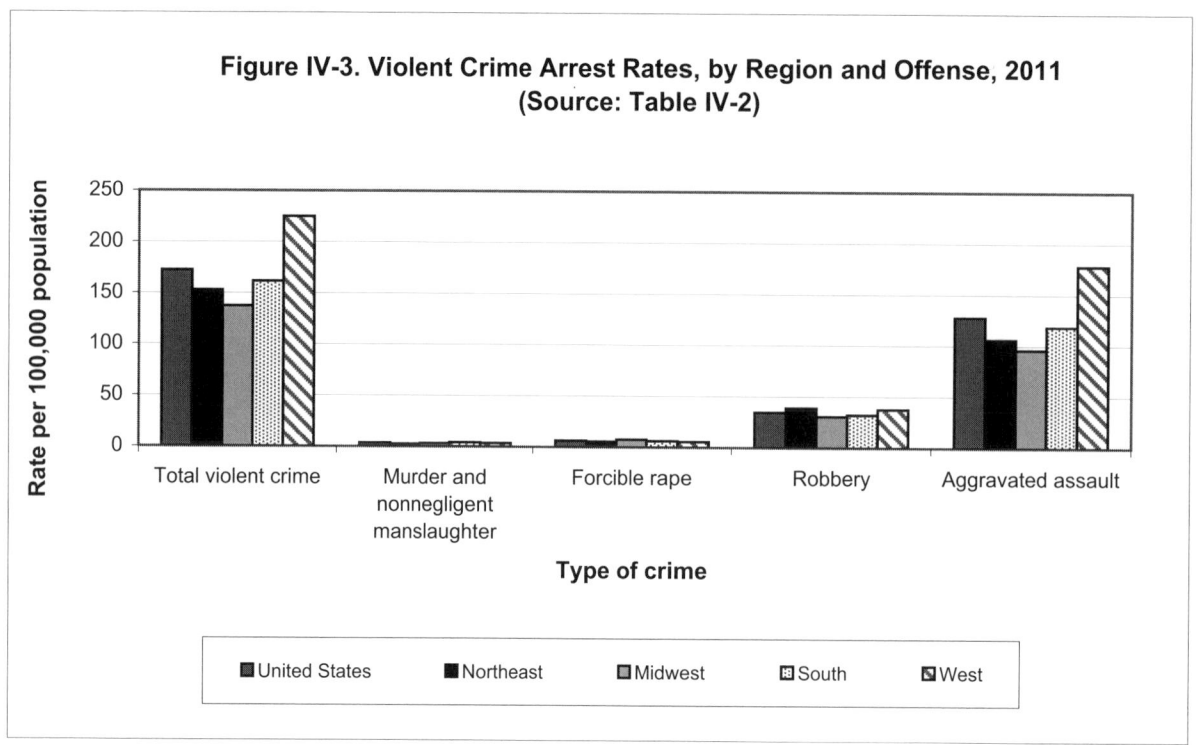

Figure IV-3. Violent Crime Arrest Rates, by Region and Offense, 2011
(Source: Table IV-2)

White, 28.8 percent were Black, and 2.6 percent were of other races. For motor vehicle theft, 64.0 percent of arrestees were White, 33.9 percent of arrestees were Black, and 2.1 percent were of other races. For arson, 72.3 percent of arrestees were White, 25.7 percent of arrestees were Black, and 3.1 percent were of other races. (Table IV-15)

Whites were most commonly arrested for driving under the influence (788,175 arrests) and drug abuse violations (783,564 arrests). Black adults were most frequently arrested for drug abuse violations (371,248 arrests) and other assaults (304,083 arrests). (Table IV-15)

Regional Arrest Rates

The UCR program divides the United States into four regions: the Northeast, the Midwest, the South, and the West. (Appendix III provides more information about the regions.) Law enforcement agencies in the Northeast had an overall arrest rate of 3,373.4 arrests per 100,000 inhabitants, below the national rate (3,991.1 arrests per 100,000 inhabitants). In this region, the arrest rate for violent crimes was 152.9 arrests per 100,000 inhabitants, and for property crime, the arrest rate was 464.1 arrests per 100,000 inhabitants. In the Midwest, law enforcement agencies reported an arrest rate of 3,962.8 arrests per 100,000 inhabitants. The arrest rate for violent crimes was 137.4 and the arrest rate for property crime was 543.0. Law enforcement agencies in the South, the nation's most populous region, reported an arrest rate of 4,570.1 per 100,000 inhabitants. Arrests for violent crime occurred at a rate of 161.6 arrests per 100,000 residents, and for property crime, the arrest rate was 598.2 arrests per 100,000 inhabitants. In the West, law enforce-

ment agencies reported an overall arrest rate of 3,690.6 arrests per 100,000 inhabitants. The region's violent crime arrest rate was 224.9, the highest of the regions, while its property crime arrest rate was 482.6. (Table IV-2)

The regional murder arrest rates were 2.5 in the Northeast, 3.1 in the Midwest, 4.2 in the South, and 3.5 in the West. For forcible rape, the regional arrest rates were 5.6 in the Northeast, 7.6 in the Midwest, 6.3 in the South, and 5.6 in the West. Regional arrest rates for robbery were 38.8 in the Northeast, 30.6 in the Midwest, 32.2 in the South, and 37.6 in the West. For aggravated assault, the regional arrest rates were 106.0 in the Northeast, 96.1 in the Midwest, 118.8 in the South, and 178.1 in the West. (Table IV-2)

The regional burglary arrest rates were 77.3 in the Northeast, 76.1 in the Midwest, 104.2 in the South, and 111.5 in the West. For larceny-theft, the regional arrest rates were 367.6 in the Northeast, 439.4 in the Midwest, 470.9 in the South, and 341.3 in the West. Regional arrest rates for motor vehicle theft were 15.8 in the Northeast, 24.2 in the Midwest, 19.2 in the South, and 25.5 in the West. For arson, the regional arrest rates were 3.4 in the Northeast, 3.3 in the Midwest, 3.9 in the South, and 4.2 in the West. (Table IV-2)

By population group, law enforcement agencies in the nation's cities collectively reported 194.9 violent crime arrests per 100,000 inhabitants in 2011. In the city population groups, cities with 250,000 or more inhabitants reported the highest violent crime arrest rate (274.4) and cities with under 10,000 inhabitants reported the lowest violent crime arrest rate (140.0). Cities reported an overall murder arrest rate of 3.7 per 100,000 inhabitants; cities with

250,000 or more inhabitants had the highest murder arrest rate (6.3) and cities with under 10,000 inhabitants had the lowest murder arrest rate (1.7). The collective city forcible rape arrest rate was 6.7 per 100,000 inhabitants, with the highest rate in cities with 250,000 or more inhabitants (9.2) and the lowest rate in cities with 50,000 to 99,999 inhabitants (5.5). The overall robbery arrest rate for cities was 43.3 per 100,000 inhabitants; cities with 250,000 or more inhabitants had the highest robbery arrest rate (72.6) and cities with fewer than 10,000 inhabitants had the lowest robbery arrest rate (20.1). For aggravated assault, the collective city arrest rate was 141.2 per 100,000 inhabitants, with the greatest arrest rate in cities with 250,000 or more inhabitants (186.3) and the lowest arrest rate in cities with 10,000 to 24,999 inhabitants (109.5). (Table IV-3)

Agencies in metropolitan counties reported a violent crime arrest rate of 132.6 per 100,000 inhabitants, with arrest rates of 3.0 for murder, 4.8 for forcible rape, 18.8 for robbery, and 106.0 for aggravated assault. Agencies in nonmetropolitan counties reported arrest rates of 102.8 for violent crime, 3.0 for murder, 6.2 for forcible rape, 8.4 for robbery, and 85.1 for aggravated assault. (Table IV-3)

By population group, law enforcement agencies in the nation's cities collectively reported 626.7 property crime arrests per 100,000 inhabitants in 2011. In the city population groups, cities with 10,000 to 24,999 inhabitants reported the highest property crime arrest rate (667.3) and cities with 250,000 or more inhabitants reported the lowest property crime arrest rate (597.0). Cities reported an overall burglary arrest rate of 101.5 per 100,000 inhabitants; cities with 100,000 to 249,999 inhabitants had the highest burglary arrest rate (119.0) and cities with 25,000 to 49,999 inhabitants had the lowest burglary arrest rate (88.0). The collective city larceny-theft arrest rate was 497.9 per 100,000 inhabitants, with the highest rate in cities with 10,000 to 24,999 inhabitants (555.0) and the lowest rate in cities with 250,000 or more inhabitants (451.6). The overall motor vehicle theft arrest rate for cities was 23.4 per 100,000 inhabitants; cities with 250,000 or more inhabitants had the highest motor vehicle theft arrest rate (35.0), and cities with 25,000 to 49,999 inhabitants had the lowest motor vehicle theft arrest rate (15.7). For arson, the collective city arrest rate was 3.9 per 100,000 inhabitants, with the greatest arrest rate in cities with fewer than 10,000 inhabitants (6.6) and the lowest arrest rate in cities with 100,000 to 249,999 inhabitants (3.4). (Table IV-3)

Agencies in metropolitan counties reported a property crime arrest rate of 340.8 per 100,000 inhabitants, with arrest rates of 79.5 for burglary, 240.8 for larceny-theft, 17.0 for motor vehicle theft, and 3.4 for arson. Agencies in nonmetropolitan counties reported arrest rates of 285.5 for property crime, 89.7 for burglary, 175.6 for larceny-theft, 16.8 for motor vehicle theft, and 3.3 for arson. (Table IV-3)

In suburban areas, the rates for violent crime and property crime were 133.3 and 468.5, respectively. The rate for murder was 2.5; for forcible rape, 4.9; for robbery, 22.5; and for aggravated assault, 103.5. Specific property crime rates included 81.6 for burglary, 366.9 for larceny-theft, 16.2 for motor vehicle theft, and 3.8 for arson. (Table IV-3)

Community Types

In 2011, law enforcement agencies in the nation's cities reported that 87.0 percent of arrests in their jurisdictions were of adults and 13.0 percent of arrests were of juveniles. Adults accounted for 86.5 percent of arrestees for violent crimes, while juveniles accounted for 13.5 percent. Adults made up 78.6 percent of the arrestees for property crimes, and juveniles accounted for 21.4 percent. (Table IV-18) Of all arrests in the nation's cities in 2011, 42.9 percent were of individuals under 25 years of age. (Table IV-19) In metropolitan counties, 37.2 percent of arrests were of individuals under 25 years of age. (Table IV-25) In nonmetropolitan counties, 32.9 percent of persons arrested were of individuals under 25 years of age. (Table IV-31)

Males accounted for 73.7 percent and females accounted for 26.3 percent of arrestees in the nation's cities in 2011. (Table IV-20) In metropolitan counties, males composed 75.0 percent of arrestees, and in nonmetropolitan counties, males represented 75.4 percent of all arrestees. (Tables IV-26 and IV-32)

By race, 67.0 percent of arrestees in the nation's cities in 2011 were White, 30.6 percent were Black, and 2.4 percent were of other races (American Indian or Alaska Native and Asian or Pacific Islander). (Table IV-21) Whites accounted for 72.9 percent of arrestees in metropolitan counties in 2011, Blacks made up 25.7 percent of arrestees, and persons of other races made up 1.4 percent of the total. (Table IV-27) In nonmetropolitan counties, Whites made up 82.6 percent of arrestees, Blacks accounted for 13.9 percent of arrestees, and other races made up 3.5 percent of the total. (Table IV-33)

Population Groups: Trends and Rates

The national UCR program aggregates data by various population groups, which include cities, metropolitan counties, and nonmetropolitan counties. Definitions of these groups can be found in Appendix III. The total number of arrests in U.S. cities fell 4.9 percent from 2010 to 2011. The number of arrests for violent crimes declined 4.6 percent and arrests for property crimes decreased 1.0 percent during the 2-year time frame. (Table IV-16)

In 2011, law enforcement agencies in cities collectively recorded an arrest rate of 4,359.0 arrests per 100,000 inhabitants. The nation's smallest cities, those with fewer than 10,000 inhabitants, had the highest arrest rate among the city population groups with 5,534.0 arrests per 100,000 inhabitants. Law enforcement agencies in cities with 25,000 to 49,999 inhabitants recorded the lowest rate, 3,969.0. In the nation's metropolitan counties, law enforcement agencies reported an arrest rate of 3,127.9 per 100,000 inhabitants. Agencies in nonmetropolitan counties reported an arrest rate of 3,325.7. (Table IV-3)

Table IV-1. Estimated Number of Arrests, 2011

(Number.)

Offense	Arrests
Total[1]	12,408,899
Violent crime[2]	534,704
Property crime[2]	1,639,883
Murder and nonnegligent manslaughter	10,832
Forcible rape	19,491
Robbery	106,674
Aggravated assault	397,707
Burglary	296,707
Larceny-theft	1,264,986
Motor vehicle theft	66,414
Arson	11,776
Other assaults	1,241,722
Forgery and counterfeiting	70,211
Fraud	168,217
Embezzlement	16,190
Stolen property; buying, receiving, possessing	93,234
Vandalism	237,638
Weapons; carrying, possessing, etc.	153,519
Prostitution and commercialized vice	57,345
Sex offenses (except forcible rape and prostitution)	69,225
Drug abuse violations	1,531,251
Gambling	8,596
Offenses against the family and children	116,723
Driving under the influence	1,215,077
Liquor laws	500,648
Drunkenness	534,218
Disorderly conduct	582,158
Vagrancy	29,203
All other offenses	3,532,195
Suspicion	1,424
Curfew and loitering law violations	76,942

[1] Does not include suspicion.

[2] Violent crimes are offenses of murder and nonnegligent manslaughter, forcible rape, robbery, and aggravated assault. Property crimes are offenses of burglary, larceny-theft, motor vehicle theft, and arson.

Table IV-2. Number and Rate of Arrests, by Geographic Region, 2011

(Number, rate per 100,000.)

Offense charged	United States total (12,023 agencies; population 238,952,977)		Northeast (3,021 agencies; population 42,838,148)		Midwest (2,999 agencies; population 49,075,854)		South (4,317 agencies; population 81,895,840)		West (1,686 agencies; population 65,143,135)	
	Total	Rate	Total	Rate	Total	Rate	Total	Rate	Total	Rate
Total[1]	9,536,787	3,991.1	1,445,100	3,373.4	1,944,775	3,962.8	3,742,708	4,570.1	2,404,204	3,690.6
Murder and nonnegligent manslaughter	8,359	3.5	1,077	2.5	1,526	3.1	3,456	4.2	2,300	3.5
Forcible rape	14,943	6.3	2,398	5.6	3,736	7.6	5,147	6.3	3,662	5.6
Robbery	82,557	34.5	16,600	38.8	15,038	30.6	26,405	32.2	24,514	37.6
Aggravated assault	305,939	128.0	45,420	106.0	47,146	96.1	97,333	118.8	116,040	178.1
Burglary	228,401	95.6	33,097	77.3	37,356	76.1	85,298	104.2	72,650	111.5
Larceny-theft	981,116	410.6	157,453	367.6	215,645	439.4	385,660	470.9	222,358	341.3
Motor vehicle theft	51,027	21.4	6,779	15.8	11,880	24.2	15,739	19.2	16,629	25.5
Arson	8,994	3.8	1,471	3.4	1,598	3.3	3,199	3.9	2,726	4.2
Violent crime[2]	411,798	172.3	65,495	152.9	67,446	137.4	132,341	161.6	146,516	224.9
Property crime[2]	1,269,538	531.3	198,800	464.1	266,479	543.0	489,896	598.2	314,363	482.6
Other assaults	955,620	399.9	165,154	385.5	200,515	408.6	389,609	475.7	200,342	307.5
Forgery and counterfeiting	53,983	22.6	9,112	21.3	8,523	17.4	24,293	29.7	12,055	18.5
Fraud	128,200	53.7	20,448	47.7	21,758	44.3	69,390	84.7	16,604	25.5
Embezzlement	12,496	5.2	1,260	2.9	1,786	3.6	7,108	8.7	2,342	3.6
Stolen property; buying, receiving, possessing	71,890	30.1	13,943	32.5	13,446	27.4	20,584	25.1	23,917	36.7
Vandalism	183,203	76.7	39,018	91.1	39,110	79.7	49,425	60.4	55,650	85.4
Weapons; carrying, possessing, etc.	118,072	49.4	14,867	34.7	24,064	49.0	40,356	49.3	38,785	59.5
Prostitution and commercialized vice	44,174	18.5	5,167	12.1	7,264	14.8	14,999	18.3	16,744	25.7
Sex offenses (except forcible rape and prostitution)	53,048	22.2	8,527	19.9	10,554	21.5	15,766	19.3	18,201	27.9
Drug abuse violations	1,175,083	491.8	193,294	451.2	232,588	473.9	439,664	536.9	309,537	475.2
Gambling	6,517	2.7	479	1.1	2,938	6.0	2,392	2.9	708	1.1
Offenses against the family and children	87,963	36.8	20,406	47.6	19,107	38.9	36,342	44.4	12,108	18.6
Driving under the influence	929,903	389.2	142,830	333.4	217,890	444.0	326,681	398.9	242,502	372.3
Liquor laws	383,903	160.7	44,501	103.9	126,719	258.2	113,872	139.0	98,811	151.7
Drunkenness	414,861	173.6	34,248	79.9	33,383	68.0	241,204	294.5	106,026	162.8
Disorderly conduct	449,694	188.2	103,951	242.7	134,855	274.8	142,860	174.4	68,028	104.4
Vagrancy	22,576	9.4	2,183	5.1	4,350	8.9	7,375	9.0	8,668	13.3
All other offenses (except traffic)	2,704,866	1,132.0	345,820	807.3	499,675	1,018.2	1,164,264	1,421.6	695,107	1,067.0
Suspicion	1,150	0.5	23	0.1	186	0.4	889	1.1	52	0.1
Curfew and loitering law violations	59,399	24.9	15,597	36.4	12,325	25.1	14,287	17.4	17,190	26.4

[1] Does not include suspicion.

[2] Violent crimes are offenses of murder and nonnegligent manslaughter, forcible rape, robbery, and aggravated assault. Property crimes are offenses of burglary, larceny-theft, motor vehicle theft, and arson.

Table IV-3.   Number and Rate of Arrests, by Population Group, 2011

(Number, rate per 100,000 population)

Offense charged	Cities									
	Total (12,023 agencies; population 238,952,977)		Total cities (8,791 cities; population 163,760,401)		Group I (63 cities, 250,000 and over; population 42,961,084)		Group II (169 cities, 100,000 to 249,999; population 25,126,615)		Group III (395 cities, 50,000 to 99,999; population 27,503,319)	
	Total	Rate	Total	Rate	Total	Rate	Total	Rate	Total	Rate
Total[1]	9,536,787	3,991.1	7,138,397	4,359.0	1,926,245	4,483.7	1,025,432	4,081.1	1,098,965	3,995.8
Murder and nonnegligent manslaughter	8,359	3.5	6,085	3.7	2,724	6.3	1,087	4.3	721	2.6
Forcible rape	14,943	6.3	11,014	6.7	3,932	9.2	1,614	6.4	1,505	5.5
Robbery	82,557	34.5	70,832	43.3	31,170	72.6	12,214	48.6	10,082	36.7
Aggravated assault	305,939	128.0	231,162	141.2	80,051	186.3	39,850	158.6	35,804	130.2
Burglary	228,401	95.6	166,221	101.5	45,864	106.8	29,901	119.0	28,237	102.7
Larceny-theft	981,116	410.6	815,356	497.9	194,001	451.6	117,760	468.7	141,194	513.4
Motor vehicle theft	51,027	21.4	38,262	23.4	15,045	35.0	6,161	24.5	5,293	19.2
Arson	8,994	3.8	6,457	3.9	1,573	3.7	844	3.4	1,017	3.7
Violent crime[2]	411,798	172.3	319,093	194.9	117,877	274.4	54,765	218.0	48,112	174.9
Property crime[2]	1,269,538	531.3	1,026,296	626.7	256,483	597.0	154,666	615.5	175,741	639.0
Other assaults	955,620	399.9	716,626	437.6	197,875	460.6	113,426	451.4	113,337	412.1
Forgery and counterfeiting	53,983	22.6	40,470	24.7	9,800	22.8	5,591	22.3	6,263	22.8
Fraud	128,200	53.7	81,037	49.5	16,097	37.5	10,750	42.8	11,980	43.6
Embezzlement	12,496	5.2	9,380	5.7	2,022	4.7	1,425	5.7	1,669	6.1
Stolen property; buying, receiving, possessing	71,890	30.1	52,962	32.3	12,507	29.1	7,991	31.8	10,274	37.4
Vandalism	183,203	76.7	142,860	87.2	36,832	85.7	20,627	82.1	23,220	84.4
Weapons; carrying, possessing, etc.	118,072	49.4	92,728	56.6	36,691	85.4	14,353	57.1	13,530	49.2
Prostitution and commercialized vice	44,174	18.5	41,635	25.4	30,648	71.3	5,078	20.2	2,648	9.6
Sex offenses (except forcible rape and prostitution)............	53,048	22.2	37,653	23.0	12,819	29.8	5,244	20.9	5,885	21.4
Drug abuse violations	1,175,083	491.8	871,342	532.1	276,711	644.1	124,964	497.3	135,012	490.9
Gambling	6,517	2.7	5,668	3.5	3,930	9.1	378	1.5	182	0.7
Offenses against the family and children	87,963	36.8	40,846	24.9	6,109	14.2	7,421	29.5	5,802	21.1
Driving under the influence	929,903	389.2	606,953	370.6	132,522	308.5	80,212	319.2	91,403	332.3
Liquor laws	383,903	160.7	314,311	191.9	52,373	121.9	35,506	141.3	40,978	149.0
Drunkenness	414,861	173.6	357,796	218.5	81,858	190.5	57,906	230.5	61,509	223.6
Disorderly conduct	449,694	188.2	381,490	233.0	85,312	198.6	46,587	185.4	59,378	215.9
Vagrancy	22,576	9.4	20,074	12.3	10,832	25.2	2,433	9.7	3,337	12.1
All other offenses (except traffic)	2,704,866	1,132.0	1,923,852	1,174.8	518,232	1,206.3	270,898	1,078.1	282,307	1,026.4
Suspicion	1,150	0.5	884	0.5	6	0.0	0	0.0	230	0.8
Curfew and loitering law violations	59,399	24.9	55,325	33.8	28,715	66.8	5,211	20.7	6,398	23.3

[1] Does not include suspicion.

[2] Violent crimes are offenses of murder and nonnegligent manslaughter, forcible rape, robbery, and aggravated assault. Property crimes are offenses of burglary, larceny-theft, motor vehicle theft, and arson.

Table IV-3.   Number and Rate of Arrests, by Population Group, 2011—*Continued*

(Number, rate per 100,000 population.)

Offense charged	Cities						Counties				Suburban area[3] (6,522 agencies; population 104,263,328)	
	Group IV (707 cities, 25,000 to 49,999; population 24,481,191)		Group V (1,525 cities, 10,000 to 24,999; population 24,108,467)		Group VI (5,932 cities, under 10,000; population 19,579,725)		Metropolitan counties (1,280 agencies; population 51,699,773)		Nonmetropolitan counties (1,958 agencies; population 22,251,821)			
	Total	Rate	Total	Rate	Total	Rate	Total	Rate	Total	Rate	Total	Rate
Total[1]	971,653	3,969.0	1,032,555	4,283.0	1,083,547	5,534.0	1,617,093	3,127.9	781,297	3,325.7	3,796,517	3,641.3
Murder and nonnegligent manslaughter	660	2.7	554	2.3	339	1.7	1,566	3.0	708	3.0	2,605	2.5
Forcible rape	1,366	5.6	1,354	5.6	1,243	6.3	2,462	4.8	1,467	6.2	5,120	4.9
Robbery	7,353	30.0	6,070	25.2	3,943	20.1	9,744	18.8	1,981	8.4	23,424	22.5
Aggravated assault	27,173	111.0	26,391	109.5	21,893	111.8	54,787	106.0	19,990	85.1	107,868	103.5
Burglary	21,537	88.0	22,008	91.3	18,674	95.4	41,103	79.5	21,077	89.7	85,052	81.6
Larceny-theft	134,143	547.9	133,790	555.0	94,468	482.5	124,496	240.8	41,264	175.6	382,524	366.9
Motor vehicle theft	3,840	15.7	4,190	17.4	3,733	19.1	8,811	17.0	3,954	16.8	16,896	16.2
Arson	852	3.5	877	3.6	1,294	6.6	1,764	3.4	773	3.3	3,951	3.8
Violent crime[2]	36,552	149.3	34,369	142.6	27,418	140.0	68,559	132.6	24,146	102.8	139,017	133.3
Property crime[2]	160,372	655.1	160,865	667.3	118,169	603.5	176,174	340.8	67,068	285.5	488,423	468.5
Other assaults	98,776	403.5	100,255	415.8	92,957	474.8	163,111	315.5	75,883	323.0	362,555	347.7
Forgery and counterfeiting	5,822	23.8	7,023	29.1	5,971	30.5	9,844	19.0	3,669	15.6	22,970	22.0
Fraud	12,971	53.0	12,919	53.6	16,320	83.4	29,665	57.4	17,498	74.5	58,503	56.1
Embezzlement	1,656	6.8	1,529	6.3	1,079	5.5	2,343	4.5	773	3.3	5,104	4.9
Stolen property; buying, receiving, possessing	8,259	33.7	7,978	33.1	5,953	30.4	13,759	26.6	5,169	22.0	31,234	30.0
Vandalism	20,848	85.2	20,669	85.7	20,664	105.5	28,225	54.6	12,118	51.6	70,969	68.1
Weapons; carrying, possessing, etc.	9,527	38.9	8,820	36.6	9,807	50.1	18,406	35.6	6,938	29.5	39,242	37.6
Prostitution and commercialized vice	1,944	7.9	889	3.7	428	2.2	2,387	4.6	152	0.6	5,246	5.0
Sex offenses (except forcible rape and prostitution)	4,541	18.5	4,707	19.5	4,457	22.8	10,705	20.7	4,690	20.0	20,424	19.6
Drug abuse violations	106,588	435.4	107,848	447.3	120,219	614.0	213,452	412.9	90,289	384.3	460,338	441.5
Gambling	282	1.2	270	1.1	626	3.2	600	1.2	249	1.1	1,432	1.4
Offenses against the family and children	6,811	27.8	7,564	31.4	7,139	36.5	33,272	64.4	13,845	58.9	46,626	44.7
Driving under the influence	86,599	353.7	102,221	424.0	113,996	582.2	171,732	332.2	151,218	643.7	389,342	373.4
Liquor laws	41,294	168.7	48,854	202.6	95,306	486.8	43,985	85.1	25,607	109.0	174,027	166.9
Drunkenness	49,762	203.3	52,365	217.2	54,396	277.8	38,633	74.7	18,432	78.5	144,459	138.6
Disorderly conduct	52,106	212.8	62,196	258.0	75,911	387.7	46,743	90.4	21,461	91.4	177,018	169.8
Vagrancy	1,252	5.1	859	3.6	1,361	7.0	2,248	4.3	254	1.1	5,044	4.8
All other offenses (except traffic)	260,794	1,065.3	285,205	1,183.0	306,416	1,565.0	539,545	1,043.6	241,469	1,027.8	1,140,091	1,093.5
Suspicion	348	1.4	71	0.3	229	1.2	77	0.1	189	0.8	571	0.5
Curfew and loitering law violations	4,897	20.0	5,150	21.4	4,954	25.3	3,705	7.2	369	1.6	14,453	13.9

[1] Does not include suspicion.

[2] Violent crimes are offenses of murder and nonnegligent manslaughter, forcible rape, robbery, and aggravated assault. Property crimes are offenses of burglary, larceny-theft, motor vehicle theft, and arson.

[3] Suburban areas include law enforcement agencies in cities with less than 50,000 inhabitants and county law enforcement agencies that are within a Metropolitan Statistical Area. Suburban areas exclude all metropolitan agencies associated with a principal city. The agencies associated with suburban areas also appear in other groups within this table.

Table IV-4. Ten-Year Arrest Trends, 2002 and 2011

(Number, percent change; 9,207 agencies; 2011 estimated population 203,216,356; 2002 estimated population 188,270,573)

Offense charged	Number of persons arrested								
	Total all ages			Under 18 years of age			18 years of age and over		
	2002	2011	Percent change	2002	2011	Percent change	2002	2011	Percent change
Total[1]	8,608,479	7,994,216	-7.1	1,382,486	962,542	-30.4	7,225,993	7,031,674	-2.7
Murder and nonnegligent manslaughter	7,630	6,752	-11.5	679	500	-26.4	6,951	6,252	-10.1
Forcible rape	17,293	12,069	-30.2	2,814	1,735	-38.3	14,479	10,334	-28.6
Robbery	67,523	67,791	+0.4	15,339	14,360	-6.4	52,184	53,431	+2.4
Aggravated assault	305,232	258,765	-15.2	39,849	25,345	-36.4	265,383	233,420	-12.0
Burglary	189,315	193,993	+2.5	56,995	40,253	-29.4	132,320	153,740	+16.2
Larceny-theft	755,039	840,187	+11.3	227,824	172,003	-24.5	527,215	668,184	+26.7
Motor vehicle theft	86,046	40,876	-52.5	26,324	8,301	-68.5	59,722	32,575	-45.5
Arson	10,790	7,385	-31.6	5,616	3,210	-42.8	5,174	4,175	-19.3
Violent crime[2]	397,678	345,377	-13.2	58,681	41,940	-28.5	338,997	303,437	-10.5
Property crime[2]	1,041,190	1,082,441	+4.0	316,759	223,767	-29.4	724,431	858,674	+18.5
Other assaults	802,791	808,239	+0.7	148,787	123,198	-17.2	654,004	685,041	+4.7
Forgery and counterfeiting	76,770	45,543	-40.7	3,454	1,017	-70.6	73,316	44,526	-39.3
Fraud	217,608	112,059	-48.5	5,953	3,531	-40.7	211,655	108,528	-48.7
Embezzlement	13,289	11,075	-16.7	996	296	-70.3	12,293	10,779	-12.3
Stolen property; buying, receiving, possessing	81,686	61,880	-24.2	17,234	8,907	-48.3	64,452	52,973	-17.8
Vandalism	178,566	158,679	-11.1	70,119	45,901	-34.5	108,447	112,778	+4.0
Weapons; carrying, possessing, etc.	100,878	95,423	-5.4	22,175	17,727	-20.1	78,703	77,696	-1.3
Prostitution and commercialized vice	44,376	34,936	-21.3	906	677	-25.3	43,470	34,259	-21.2
Sex offenses (except forcible rape and prostitution)	60,154	46,198	-23.2	12,587	8,400	-33.3	47,567	37,798	-20.5
Drug abuse violations	968,518	954,164	-1.5	117,610	94,134	-20.0	850,908	860,030	+1.1
Gambling	4,214	2,691	-36.1	316	133	-57.9	3,898	2,558	-34.4
Offenses against the family and children	86,762	67,591	-22.1	6,025	2,287	-62.0	80,737	65,304	-19.1
Driving under the influence	857,295	765,635	-10.7	13,543	6,612	-51.2	843,752	759,023	-10.0
Liquor laws	430,374	327,482	-23.9	99,260	61,610	-37.9	331,114	265,872	-19.7
Drunkenness	398,859	370,093	-7.2	12,648	7,959	-37.1	386,211	362,134	-6.2
Disorderly conduct	418,153	367,175	-12.2	121,555	88,744	-27.0	296,598	278,431	-6.1
Vagrancy	16,059	17,700	+10.2	1,427	1,190	-16.6	14,632	16,510	+12.8
All other offenses (except traffic)	2,319,481	2,268,214	-2.2	258,673	172,891	-33.2	2,060,808	2,095,323	+1.7
Suspicion	2,873	932	-67.6	1,092	90	-91.8	1,781	842	-52.7
Curfew and loitering law violations	93,778	51,621	-45.0	93,778	51,621	-45.0	NA	NA	NA

NA = Not available.

[1] Does not include suspicion.

[2] Violent crimes are offenses of murder and nonnegligent manslaughter, forcible rape, robbery, and aggravated assault. Property crimes are offenses of burglary, larceny-theft, motor vehicle theft, and arson.

Table IV-5.   Ten-Year Arrest Trends, by Age and Sex, 2002 and 2011

(Number, percent change; 9,207 agencies; 2011 estimated population 203,216,356; 2002 estimated population 188,270,573)

Offense charged	Male						Female					
	Total			Under 18			Total			Under 18		
	2002	2011	Percent change	2002	2011	Percent change	2002	2011	Percent change	2002	2011	Percent change
Total[1]	6,638,390	5,910,637	-11.0	1,004,071	677,299	-32.5	1,970,089	2,083,579	+5.8	378,415	285,243	-24.6
Murder and nonnegligent manslaughter	6,793	5,951	-12.4	607	456	-24.9	837	801	-4.3	72	44	-38.9
Forcible rape	17,051	11,934	-30.0	2,718	1,694	-37.7	242	135	-44.2	96	41	-57.3
Robbery	60,499	59,410	-1.8	13,984	13,022	-6.9	7,024	8,381	+19.3	1,355	1,338	-1.3
Aggravated assault	243,651	200,755	-17.6	30,422	19,214	-36.8	61,581	58,010	-5.8	9,427	6,131	-35.0
Burglary	163,441	162,496	-0.6	50,386	35,181	-30.2	25,874	31,497	+21.7	6,609	5,072	-23.3
Larceny-theft	473,680	472,669	-0.2	137,966	96,253	-30.2	281,359	367,518	+30.6	89,858	75,750	-15.7
Motor vehicle theft	71,960	33,426	-53.5	21,686	6,951	-67.9	14,086	7,450	-47.1	4,638	1,350	-70.9
Arson	9,155	6,125	-33.1	4,987	2,770	-44.5	1,635	1,260	-22.9	629	440	-30.0
Violent crime[2]	327,994	278,050	-15.2	47,731	34,386	-28.0	69,684	67,327	-3.4	10,950	7,554	-31.0
Property crime[2]	718,236	674,716	-6.1	215,025	141,155	-34.4	322,954	407,725	+26.2	101,734	82,612	-18.8
Other assaults	608,845	584,784	-4.0	101,266	79,252	-21.7	193,946	223,455	+15.2	47,521	43,946	-7.5
Forgery and counterfeiting	46,065	28,542	-38.0	2,209	711	-67.8	30,705	17,001	-44.6	1,245	306	-75.4
Fraud	118,457	66,262	-44.1	3,940	2,302	-41.6	99,151	45,797	-53.8	2,013	1,229	-38.9
Embezzlement	6,638	5,510	-17.0	593	178	-70.0	6,651	5,565	-16.3	403	118	-70.7
Stolen property; buying, receiving, possessing	66,798	49,509	-25.9	14,399	7,397	-48.6	14,888	12,371	-16.9	2,835	1,510	-46.7
Vandalism	149,398	128,600	-13.9	60,623	39,077	-35.5	29,168	30,079	+3.1	9,496	6,824	-28.1
Weapons; carrying, possessing, etc.	92,755	87,682	-5.5	19,846	15,888	-19.9	8,123	7,741	-4.7	2,329	1,839	-21.0
Prostitution and commercialized vice	15,659	10,439	-33.3	279	146	-47.7	28,717	24,497	-14.7	627	531	-15.3
Sex offenses (except forcible rape and prostitution)	55,233	42,872	-22.4	11,461	7,513	-34.4	4,921	3,326	-32.4	1,126	887	-21.2
Drug abuse violations	789,543	761,050	-3.6	97,672	77,744	-20.4	178,975	193,114	+7.9	19,938	16,390	-17.8
Gambling	3,595	2,238	-37.7	301	116	-61.5	619	453	-26.9	15	17	+13.3
Offenses against the family and children	65,459	49,408	-24.5	3,660	1,396	-61.9	21,303	18,183	-14.6	2,365	891	-62.3
Driving under the influence	706,226	579,176	-18.0	10,896	4,958	-54.5	151,069	186,459	+23.4	2,647	1,654	-37.5
Liquor laws	322,989	230,304	-28.7	65,459	37,001	-43.5	107,385	97,178	-9.5	33,801	24,609	-27.2
Drunkenness	343,257	303,138	-11.7	9,906	5,863	-40.8	55,602	66,955	+20.4	2,742	2,096	-23.6
Disorderly conduct	313,550	263,529	-16.0	85,057	57,725	-32.1	104,603	103,646	-0.9	36,498	31,019	-15.0
Vagrancy	12,889	14,406	+11.8	1,092	924	-15.4	3,170	3,294	+3.9	335	266	-20.6
All other offenses (except traffic)	1,809,977	1,714,102	-5.3	187,829	127,247	-32.3	509,504	554,112	+8.8	70,844	45,644	-35.6
Suspicion	2,186	713	-67.4	750	65	-91.3	687	219	-68.1	342	25	-92.7
Curfew and loitering law violations	64,827	36,320	-44.0	64,827	36,320	-44.0	28,951	15,301	-47.1	28,951	15,301	-47.1

[1] Does not include suspicion.

[2] Violent crimes are offenses of murder and nonnegligent manslaughter, forcible rape, robbery, and aggravated assault. Property crimes are offenses of burglary, larceny-theft, motor vehicle theft, and arson.

Table IV-6.　Five-Year Arrest Trends, by Sex, 2007 and 2011

(Number, percent change; 9,207 agencies; 2011 estimated population 203,216,356; 2002 estimated population 188,270,573)

Offense charged	Number of persons arrested								
	Total all ages			Under 18 years of age			18 years of age and over		
	2007	2011	Percent change	2007	2011	Percent change	2007	2011	Percent change
Total[1]	9,688,628	8,502,434	-12.2	1,457,221	1,033,221	-29.1	8,231,407	7,469,213	-9.3
Murder and nonnegligent manslaughter	8,431	7,290	-13.5	855	559	-34.6	7,576	6,731	-11.2
Forcible rape	15,674	13,387	-14.6	2,501	1,963	-21.5	13,173	11,424	-13.3
Robbery	84,420	72,186	-14.5	22,815	16,099	-29.4	61,605	56,087	-9.0
Aggravated assault	295,122	264,383	-10.4	39,792	26,935	-32.3	255,330	237,448	-7.0
Burglary	211,345	204,928	-3.0	57,463	42,816	-25.5	153,882	162,112	+5.3
Larceny-theft	826,390	898,035	+8.7	216,415	182,421	-15.7	609,975	715,614	+17.3
Motor vehicle theft	77,497	45,734	-41.0	19,898	9,764	-50.9	57,599	35,970	-37.6
Arson	10,752	8,305	-22.8	5,198	3,496	-32.7	5,554	4,809	-13.4
Violent crime[2]	403,647	357,246	-11.5	65,963	45,556	-30.9	337,684	311,690	-7.7
Property crime[2]	1,125,984	1,157,002	+2.8	298,974	238,497	-20.2	827,010	918,505	+11.1
Other assaults	911,516	873,167	-4.2	168,909	132,528	-21.5	742,607	740,639	-0.3
Forgery and counterfeiting	71,191	48,151	-32.4	2,195	1,090	-50.3	68,996	47,061	-31.8
Fraud	181,219	116,304	-35.8	5,472	3,728	-31.9	175,747	112,576	-35.9
Embezzlement	16,126	11,021	-31.7	1,245	299	-76.0	14,881	10,722	-27.9
Stolen property; buying, receiving, possessing	84,209	64,882	-23.0	15,914	9,372	-41.1	68,295	55,510	-18.7
Vandalism	207,192	169,934	-18.0	80,176	48,685	-39.3	127,016	121,249	-4.5
Weapons; carrying, possessing, etc.	125,965	103,113	-18.1	29,437	19,296	-34.4	96,528	83,817	-13.2
Prostitution and commercialized vice	50,089	34,091	-31.9	870	593	-31.8	49,219	33,498	-31.9
Sex offenses (except forcible rape and prostitution)	56,809	48,188	-15.2	10,723	8,718	-18.7	46,086	39,470	-14.4
Drug abuse violations	1,242,732	1,055,466	-15.1	136,617	104,528	-23.5	1,106,115	950,938	-14.0
Gambling	8,254	5,106	-38.1	1,518	648	-57.3	6,736	4,458	-33.8
Offenses against the family and children	85,697	76,036	-11.3	3,973	2,305	-42.0	81,724	73,731	-9.8
Driving under the influence	882,720	797,413	-9.7	12,044	7,013	-41.8	870,676	790,400	-9.2
Liquor laws	456,604	346,084	-24.2	103,659	65,713	-36.6	352,945	280,371	-20.6
Drunkenness	422,485	374,040	-11.5	12,233	8,108	-33.7	410,252	365,932	-10.8
Disorderly conduct	504,782	411,633	-18.5	140,293	97,731	-30.3	364,489	313,902	-13.9
Vagrancy	24,465	21,657	-11.5	2,858	1,298	-54.6	21,607	20,359	-5.8
All other offenses (except traffic)	2,732,227	2,378,599	-12.9	269,433	184,214	-31.6	2,462,794	2,194,385	-10.9
Suspicion	1,525	934	-38.8	276	80	-71.0	1,249	854	-31.6
Curfew and loitering law violations	94,715	53,301	-43.7	94,715	53,301	-43.7	NA	NA	NA

NA = Not available.

[1] Does not include suspicion.

[2] Violent crimes are offenses of murder and nonnegligent manslaughter, forcible rape, robbery, and aggravated assault. Property crimes are offenses of burglary, larceny-theft, motor vehicle theft, and arson.

Table IV-7. Five-Year Arrest Trends, by Age and Sex, 2007 and 2011

(Number, percent change; 9,207 agencies; 2011 estimated population 203,216,356; 2002 estimated population 188,270,573)

Offense charged	Male						Female					
	Total			Under 18			Total			Under 18		
	2007	2011	Percent change	2007	2011	Percent change	2007	2011	Percent change	2007	2011	Percent change
Total[1]	7,349,789	6,299,269	-14.3	1,048,359	730,589	-30.3	2,338,839	2,203,165	-5.8	408,862	302,632	-26.0
Murder and nonnegligent manslaughter	7,577	6,440	-15.0	794	517	-34.9	854	850	-0.5	61	42	-31.1
Forcible rape	15,516	13,235	-14.7	2,458	1,917	-22.0	158	152	-3.8	43	46	+7.0
Robbery	74,725	63,369	-15.2	20,700	14,649	-29.2	9,695	8,817	-9.1	2,115	1,450	-31.4
Aggravated assault	232,618	205,156	-11.8	30,602	20,460	-33.1	62,504	59,227	-5.2	9,190	6,475	-29.5
Burglary	180,114	172,632	-4.2	50,681	37,656	-25.7	31,231	32,296	+3.4	6,782	5,160	-23.9
Larceny-theft	496,613	509,826	+2.7	123,243	103,123	-16.3	329,777	388,209	+17.7	93,172	79,298	-14.9
Motor vehicle theft	63,736	37,608	-41.0	16,564	8,230	-50.3	13,761	8,126	-40.9	3,334	1,534	-54.0
Arson	9,122	6,862	-24.8	4,596	3,001	-34.7	1,630	1,443	-11.5	602	495	-17.8
Violent crime[2]	330,436	288,200	-12.8	54,554	37,543	-31.2	73,211	69,046	-5.7	11,409	8,013	-29.8
Property crime[2]	749,585	726,928	-3.0	195,084	152,010	-22.1	376,399	430,074	+14.3	103,890	86,487	-16.8
Other assaults	680,667	633,798	-6.9	112,203	85,344	-23.9	230,849	239,369	+3.7	56,706	47,184	-16.8
Forgery and counterfeiting	43,660	29,978	-31.3	1,483	763	-48.6	27,531	18,173	-34.0	712	327	-54.1
Fraud	99,619	68,102	-31.6	3,510	2,425	-30.9	81,600	48,202	-40.9	1,962	1,303	-33.6
Embezzlement	7,810	5,511	-29.4	731	187	-74.4	8,316	5,510	-33.7	514	112	-78.2
Stolen property; buying, receiving, possessing	66,889	51,847	-22.5	12,990	7,795	-40.0	17,320	13,035	-24.7	2,924	1,577	-46.1
Vandalism	171,824	137,573	-19.9	69,289	41,433	-40.2	35,368	32,361	-8.5	10,887	7,252	-33.4
Weapons; carrying, possessing, etc.	115,979	94,541	-18.5	26,568	17,295	-34.9	9,986	8,572	-14.2	2,869	2,001	-30.3
Prostitution and commercialized vice	15,712	10,524	-33.0	210	163	-22.4	34,377	23,567	-31.4	660	430	-34.8
Sex offenses (except forcible rape and prostitution)	52,507	44,636	-15.0	9,742	7,803	-19.9	4,302	3,552	-17.4	981	915	-6.7
Drug abuse violations	1,006,208	846,679	-15.9	115,007	87,038	-24.3	236,524	208,787	-11.7	21,610	17,490	-19.1
Gambling	7,528	4,598	-38.9	1,495	629	-57.9	726	508	-30.0	23	19	-17.4
Offenses against the family and children	64,032	56,817	-11.3	2,423	1,421	-41.4	21,665	19,219	-11.3	1,550	884	-43.0
Driving under the influence	697,525	601,549	-13.8	9,130	5,246	-42.5	185,195	195,864	+5.8	2,914	1,767	-39.4
Liquor laws	328,192	243,089	-25.9	64,754	39,436	-39.1	128,412	102,995	-19.8	38,905	26,277	-32.5
Drunkenness	354,272	305,668	-13.7	9,097	5,941	-34.7	68,213	68,372	+0.2	3,136	2,167	-30.9
Disorderly conduct	372,970	297,115	-20.3	94,304	63,921	-32.2	131,812	114,518	-13.1	45,989	33,810	-26.5
Vagrancy	19,024	17,468	-8.2	2,012	1,012	-49.7	5,441	4,189	-23.0	846	286	-66.2
All other offenses (except traffic)	2,099,644	1,797,244	-14.4	198,067	135,780	-31.4	632,583	581,355	-8.1	71,366	48,434	-32.1
Suspicion	1,203	723	-39.9	206	64	-68.9	322	211	-34.5	70	16	-77.1
Curfew and loitering law violations	65,706	37,404	-43.1	65,706	37,404	-43.1	29,009	15,897	-45.2	29,009	15,897	-45.2

[1] Does not include suspicion.

[2] Violent crimes are offenses of murder and nonnegligent manslaughter, forcible rape, robbery, and aggravated assault. Property crimes are offenses of burglary, larceny-theft, motor vehicle theft, and arson.

Table IV-8.   Current Year Over Previous Year Arrest Trends, 2010–2011

(Number, percent change; 11,190 agencies; 2011 estimated population 222,444,907; 2010 estimated population 220,412,929)

Offense charged	Number of persons arrested											
	Total all ages			Under 15 years of age			Under 18 years of age			18 years of age and over		
	2010	2011	Percent change	2010	2011	Percent change	2010	2011	Percent change	2010	2011	Percent change
Total[1]	9,252,632	8,831,366	-4.6	320,999	287,474	-10.4	1,171,758	1,041,492	-11.1	8,080,874	7,789,874	-3.6
Murder and nonnegligent manslaughter	7,521	7,188	-4.4	63	60	-4.8	684	548	-19.9	6,837	6,640	-2.9
Forcible rape	14,126	13,357	-5.4	698	681	-2.4	2,040	1,920	-5.9	12,086	11,437	-5.4
Robbery	75,200	70,948	-5.7	3,119	2,731	-12.4	17,087	15,021	-12.1	58,113	55,927	-3.8
Aggravated assault	289,678	276,044	-4.7	9,690	8,928	-7.9	30,831	27,506	-10.8	258,847	248,538	-4.0
Burglary	208,436	207,718	-0.3	12,645	11,683	-7.6	46,635	42,796	-8.2	161,801	164,922	+1.9
Larceny-theft	919,888	921,035	+0.1	58,776	52,880	-10.0	206,343	185,788	-10.0	713,545	735,247	+3.0
Motor vehicle theft	45,572	43,452	-4.7	2,010	1,773	-11.8	9,920	8,730	-12.0	35,652	34,722	-2.6
Arson	8,233	8,246	+0.2	1,999	2,006	+0.4	3,405	3,509	+3.1	4,828	4,737	-1.9
Violent crime[2]	386,525	367,537	-4.9	13,570	12,400	-8.6	50,642	44,995	-11.2	335,883	322,542	-4.0
Property crime[2]	1,182,129	1,180,451	-0.1	75,430	68,342	-9.4	266,303	240,823	-9.6	915,826	939,628	+2.6
Other assaults	914,786	884,705	-3.3	55,357	50,949	-8.0	145,751	131,950	-9.5	769,035	752,755	-2.1
Forgery and counterfeiting	55,427	50,572	-8.8	147	148	+0.7	1,223	1,133	-7.4	54,204	49,439	-8.8
Fraud	136,618	121,580	-11.0	717	589	-17.9	4,301	3,824	-11.1	132,317	117,756	-11.0
Embezzlement	12,435	11,908	-4.2	17	32	+88.2	323	317	-1.9	12,112	11,591	-4.3
Stolen property; buying, receiving, possessing	67,783	66,946	-1.2	2,426	2,060	-15.1	10,743	9,595	-10.7	57,040	57,351	+0.5
Vandalism	179,532	169,905	-5.4	21,620	18,859	-12.8	55,453	48,488	-12.6	124,079	121,417	-2.1
Weapons; carrying, possessing, etc.	106,821	102,426	-4.1	7,209	6,435	-10.7	21,178	18,890	-10.8	85,643	83,536	-2.5
Prostitution and commercialized vice	38,649	34,510	-10.7	74	57	-23.0	656	641	-2.3	37,993	33,869	-10.9
Sex offenses (except forcible rape and prostitution)	51,412	48,626	-5.4	4,563	4,296	-5.9	9,380	8,846	-5.7	42,032	39,780	-5.4
Drug abuse violations	1,120,326	1,039,383	-7.2	21,045	17,970	-14.6	118,367	102,087	-13.8	1,001,959	937,296	-6.5
Gambling	3,480	2,685	-22.8	36	44	+22.2	262	249	-5.0	3,218	2,436	-24.3
Offenses against the family and children	81,585	83,941	+2.9	887	790	-10.9	2,788	2,576	-7.6	78,797	81,365	+3.3
Driving under the influence	925,352	885,339	-4.3	157	128	-18.5	8,478	7,506	-11.5	916,874	877,833	-4.3
Liquor laws	384,843	352,996	-8.3	7,298	6,539	-10.4	73,726	67,399	-8.6	311,117	285,597	-8.2
Drunkenness	432,565	406,131	-6.1	1,161	1,019	-12.2	9,702	8,653	-10.8	422,863	397,478	-6.0
Disorderly conduct	445,628	411,366	-7.7	41,981	38,115	-9.2	112,188	99,099	-11.7	333,440	312,267	-6.3
Vagrancy	23,435	21,135	-9.8	461	391	-15.2	1,576	1,324	-16.0	21,859	19,811	-9.4
All other offenses (except traffic)	2,635,890	2,534,730	-3.8	49,941	44,218	-11.5	211,307	188,603	-10.7	2,424,583	2,346,127	-3.2
Suspicion	747	858	+14.9	19	27	+42.1	91	91	0.0	656	767	+16.9
Curfew and loitering law violations	67,411	54,494	-19.2	16,902	14,093	-16.6	67,411	54,494	-19.2	NA	NA	NA

NA = Not available.

[1] Does not include suspicion.

[2] Violent crimes are offenses of murder and nonnegligent manslaughter, forcible rape, robbery, and aggravated assault. Property crimes are offenses of burglary, larceny-theft, motor vehicle theft, and arson.

Table IV-9.   Current Year Over Previous Year Arrest Trends, by Age and Sex, 2010–2011

(Number, percent change; 11,190 agencies; 2011 estimated population 222,444,907; 2010 estimated population 220,412,929)

Offense charged	Male						Female					
	Total			Under 18			Total			Under 18		
	2010	2011	Percent change	2010	2011	Percent change	2010	2011	Percent change	2010	2011	Percent change
Total[1]	6,865,802	6,514,268	-5.1	822,945	731,656	-11.1	2,386,830	2,317,098	-2.9	348,813	309,836	-11.2
Murder and nonnegligent manslaughter	6,683	6,337	-5.2	609	505	-17.1	838	851	+1.6	75	43	-42.7
Forcible rape	13,976	13,201	-5.5	1,994	1,875	-6.0	150	156	+4.0	46	45	-2.2
Robbery	65,739	62,061	-5.6	15,326	13,647	-11.0	9,461	8,887	-6.1	1,761	1,374	-22.0
Aggravated assault	223,978	213,097	-4.9	23,065	20,611	-10.6	65,700	62,947	-4.2	7,766	6,895	-11.2
Burglary	175,638	174,494	-0.7	40,997	37,558	-8.4	32,798	33,224	+1.3	5,638	5,238	-7.1
Larceny-theft	515,257	520,327	+1.0	112,133	104,407	-6.9	404,631	400,708	-1.0	94,210	81,381	-13.6
Motor vehicle theft	37,526	35,589	-5.2	8,247	7,301	-11.5	8,046	7,863	-2.3	1,673	1,429	-14.6
Arson	6,816	6,830	+0.2	2,958	3,021	+2.1	1,417	1,416	-0.1	447	488	+9.2
Violent crime[2]	310,376	294,696	-5.1	40,994	36,638	-10.6	76,149	72,841	-4.3	9,648	8,357	-13.4
Property crime[2]	735,237	737,240	+0.3	164,335	152,287	-7.3	446,892	443,211	-0.8	101,968	88,536	-13.2
Other assaults	667,516	641,376	-3.9	94,621	85,066	-10.1	247,270	243,329	-1.6	51,130	46,884	-8.3
Forgery and counterfeiting	34,423	31,448	-8.6	878	788	-10.3	21,004	19,124	-9.0	345	345	+0.0
Fraud	79,565	71,749	-9.8	2,827	2,493	-11.8	57,053	49,831	-12.7	1,474	1,331	-9.7
Embezzlement	6,169	6,019	-2.4	194	198	+2.1	6,266	5,889	-6.0	129	119	-7.8
Stolen property; buying, receiving, possessing	54,243	53,313	-1.7	8,923	7,972	-10.7	13,540	13,633	+0.7	1,820	1,623	-10.8
Vandalism	145,464	137,301	-5.6	47,233	41,180	-12.8	34,068	32,604	-4.3	8,220	7,308	-11.1
Weapons; carrying, possessing, etc.	97,847	93,963	-4.0	18,912	16,913	-10.6	8,974	8,463	-5.7	2,266	1,977	-12.8
Prostitution and commercialized vice	11,675	10,622	-9.0	116	159	+37.1	26,974	23,888	-11.4	540	482	-10.7
Sex offenses (except forcible rape and prostitution)	47,485	45,027	-5.2	8,394	7,900	-5.9	3,927	3,599	-8.4	986	946	-4.1
Drug abuse violations	898,176	826,925	-7.9	97,987	84,204	-14.1	222,150	212,458	-4.4	20,380	17,883	-12.3
Gambling	2,932	2,147	-26.8	236	209	-11.4	548	538	-1.8	26	40	+53.8
Offenses against the family and children	60,973	62,980	+3.3	1,833	1,574	-14.1	20,612	20,961	+1.7	955	1,002	+4.9
Driving under the influence	703,577	665,911	-5.4	6,321	5,587	-11.6	221,775	219,428	-1.1	2,157	1,919	-11.0
Liquor laws	274,334	248,047	-9.6	45,152	40,426	-10.5	110,509	104,949	-5.0	28,574	26,973	-5.6
Drunkenness	357,375	331,947	-7.1	7,100	6,367	-10.3	75,190	74,184	-1.3	2,602	2,286	-12.1
Disorderly conduct	319,845	294,988	-7.8	73,225	64,301	-12.2	125,783	116,378	-7.5	38,963	34,798	-10.7
Vagrancy	18,734	17,052	-9.0	1,213	1,019	-16.0	4,701	4,083	-13.1	363	305	-16.0
All other offenses (except traffic)	1,992,595	1,903,296	-4.5	155,190	138,154	-11.0	643,295	631,434	-1.8	56,117	50,449	-10.1
Suspicion	572	670	+17.1	70	64	-8.6	175	188	+7.4	21	27	+28.6
Curfew and loitering law violations	47,261	38,221	-19.1	47,261	38,221	-19.1	20,150	16,273	-19.2	20,150	16,273	-19.2

[1] Does not include suspicion.

[2] Violent crimes are offenses of murder and nonnegligent manslaughter, forcible rape, robbery, and aggravated assault. Property crimes are offenses of burglary, larceny-theft, motor vehicle theft, and arson.

Table IV-10. Arrests, Distribution by Age, 2011

(Number, percent; 12,023 agencies; 2011 estimated population 238,952,977)

Offense charged	Total all ages	Ages under 15	Ages under 18	Ages 18 and over	Under 10	10–12	13–14	15	16	17	18	19	20
Total	9,537,673	307,864	1,129,456	8,408,217	7,240	67,193	233,431	213,055	275,579	332,958	419,517	453,490	444,182
Total percent distribution[1]	100.0	3.2	11.8	88.2	0.1	0.7	2.4	2.2	2.9	3.5	4.4	4.8	4.7
Murder and nonnegligent manslaughter	8,359	72	651	7,708	1	11	60	106	169	304	496	511	513
Forcible rape	14,679	736	2,071	12,608	5	209	522	376	421	538	651	662	621
Robbery	82,557	3,417	18,377	64,180	35	435	2,947	3,717	5,164	6,079	6,999	6,369	5,327
Aggravated assault	305,939	10,036	31,265	274,674	297	2,595	7,144	5,694	7,179	8,356	9,674	10,885	11,568
Burglary	228,401	12,962	47,654	180,747	410	2,743	9,809	9,224	11,713	13,755	16,287	14,612	12,404
Larceny-theft	981,116	55,599	197,159	783,957	950	12,416	42,233	37,960	48,477	55,123	59,812	53,404	45,497
Motor vehicle theft	51,027	2,150	10,786	40,241	15	228	1,907	2,449	3,004	3,183	3,158	2,773	2,371
Arson	8,994	2,117	3,714	5,280	199	694	1,224	614	550	433	367	340	342
Violent crime[2]	411,534	14,261	52,364	359,170	338	3,250	10,673	9,893	12,933	15,277	17,820	18,427	18,029
Violent crime percent distribution[1]	100.0	3.5	12.7	87.3	0.1	0.8	2.6	2.4	3.1	3.7	4.3	4.5	4.4
Property crime[2]	1,269,538	72,828	259,313	1,010,225	1,574	16,081	55,173	50,247	63,744	72,494	79,624	71,129	60,614
Property crime percent distribution[1]	100.0	5.7	20.4	79.6	0.1	1.3	4.3	4.0	5.0	5.7	6.3	5.6	4.8
Other assaults	955,620	55,684	145,424	810,196	1,628	14,618	39,438	27,642	30,953	31,145	29,002	30,500	32,671
Forgery and counterfeiting	53,983	157	1,201	52,782	4	32	121	180	244	620	1,495	2,190	2,449
Fraud	128,200	590	3,912	124,288	13	107	470	665	999	1,658	2,900	4,029	4,527
Embezzlement	12,496	32	325	12,171	0	8	24	19	74	200	544	800	778
Stolen property; buying, receiving, possessing	71,890	2,217	10,269	61,621	26	330	1,861	2,039	2,582	3,431	4,479	4,386	3,720
Vandalism	183,203	20,124	52,229	130,974	903	5,725	13,496	9,984	10,849	11,272	10,805	9,720	8,724
Weapons; carrying, possessing, etc.	118,072	7,202	21,730	96,342	441	2,062	4,699	3,829	4,785	5,914	6,891	6,616	6,095
Prostitution and commercialized vice	44,174	70	763	43,411	0	7	63	113	202	378	1,323	1,796	1,937
Sex offenses (except forcible rape and prostitution)	53,048	4,642	9,584	43,464	182	1,325	3,135	1,658	1,646	1,638	2,003	1,950	1,873
Drug abuse violations	1,175,083	19,201	112,892	1,062,191	117	2,428	16,656	19,338	29,861	44,492	67,940	71,857	68,124
Gambling	6,517	83	766	5,751	1	4	78	131	219	333	438	410	433
Offenses against the family and children	87,963	859	2,748	85,215	56	180	623	504	640	745	1,283	1,562	1,839
Driving under the influence	929,903	130	7,720	922,183	7	24	99	298	1,706	5,586	15,892	23,861	28,821
Liquor laws	383,903	6,620	69,818	314,085	59	559	6,002	10,117	19,741	33,340	63,137	70,985	60,906
Drunkenness	414,861	1,038	8,745	406,116	15	90	933	1,416	2,076	4,215	10,352	12,203	12,631
Disorderly conduct	449,694	39,948	106,303	343,391	595	9,509	29,844	21,730	22,816	21,809	18,960	17,615	17,065
Vagrancy	22,576	400	1,410	21,166	6	59	335	344	389	277	1,035	954	883
All other offenses (except traffic)	2,704,866	46,710	202,424	2,502,442	1,105	8,448	37,157	39,780	52,401	63,533	83,515	102,431	111,992
Suspicion	1,150	35	117	1,033	2	9	24	12	41	29	79	69	71
Curfew and loitering law violations	59,399	15,033	59,399	NA	168	2,338	12,527	13,116	16,678	14,572	NA	NA	NA

NA = Not available.

[1] Because of rounding, the percentages may not add to 100.0.

[2] Violent crimes are offenses of murder and nonnegligent manslaughter, forcible rape, robbery, and aggravated assault. Property crimes are offenses of burglary, larceny-theft, motor vehicle theft, and arson.

Table IV-10. Arrests, Distribution by Age, 2011—*Continued*

(Number, percent; 12,023 agencies; 2011 estimated population 238,952,977)

Offense charged	21	22	23	24	25–29	30–34	35–39	40–44	45–49	50–54	55–59	60–64	65 and over
Total	411,623	380,004	351,553	331,226	1,422,206	1,090,886	800,132	737,859	660,346	474,607	244,854	111,119	74,613
Total percent distribution[1]	4.3	4.0	3.7	3.5	14.9	11.4	8.4	7.7	6.9	5.0	2.6	1.2	0.8
Murder and nonnegligent manslaughter	494	388	421	362	1,422	959	567	490	423	307	177	96	82
Forcible rape	640	529	442	437	2,053	1,620	1,399	1,181	975	678	355	169	196
Robbery	4,577	3,755	3,218	2,956	10,714	6,906	4,259	3,688	2,743	1,645	687	227	110
Aggravated assault	12,367	11,902	11,347	10,954	48,783	39,354	28,646	25,684	22,480	16,001	8,133	3,821	3,075
Burglary	10,743	9,376	8,229	7,287	29,861	21,819	14,723	13,477	11,064	6,524	2,906	930	505
Larceny-theft	39,962	35,255	31,494	29,311	123,819	94,268	69,188	65,944	58,136	40,700	20,711	9,445	7,011
Motor vehicle theft	2,116	1,878	1,800	1,659	7,163	5,644	3,909	3,338	2,370	1,281	500	195	86
Arson	238	215	186	168	818	590	479	439	433	319	189	81	76
Violent crime[2]	18,078	16,574	15,428	14,709	62,972	48,839	34,871	31,043	26,621	18,631	9,352	4,313	3,463
Violent crime percent distribution[1]	4.4	4.0	3.7	3.6	15.3	11.9	8.5	7.5	6.5	4.5	2.3	1.0	0.8
Property crime[2]	53,059	46,724	41,709	38,425	161,661	122,321	88,299	83,198	72,003	48,824	24,306	10,651	7,678
Property crime percent distribution[1]	4.2	3.7	3.3	3.0	12.7	9.6	7.0	6.6	5.7	3.8	1.9	0.8	0.6
Other assaults	36,168	34,971	33,295	32,151	143,818	116,098	87,805	79,783	68,034	45,485	22,166	10,221	8,028
Forgery and counterfeiting	2,184	2,223	2,186	2,174	10,368	8,459	5,964	5,064	3,750	2,411	1,117	477	271
Fraud	4,281	4,440	4,210	4,250	21,105	19,365	15,986	14,001	11,088	7,200	3,812	1,780	1,314
Embezzlement	724	629	567	494	2,004	1,482	1,290	1,046	792	536	280	145	60
Stolen property; buying, receiving, possessing	3,340	3,025	2,775	2,447	10,924	8,328	5,752	4,938	3,668	2,234	1,000	381	224
Vandalism	8,481	7,267	6,335	5,628	22,849	15,289	10,173	8,936	7,512	4,912	2,368	1,124	851
Weapons; carrying, possessing, etc.	5,823	5,296	4,767	4,438	17,756	12,073	7,569	5,955	5,076	3,872	2,075	1,134	906
Prostitution and commercialized vice	1,962	1,967	1,810	1,671	7,201	5,936	4,831	4,901	3,889	2,343	1,020	435	389
Sex offenses (except forcible rape and prostitution)	1,745	1,484	1,383	1,237	5,706	5,014	4,388	4,272	4,172	3,262	2,173	1,339	1,463
Drug abuse violations	61,570	55,338	50,000	46,805	191,308	137,643	89,906	78,079	66,611	44,926	20,748	8,105	3,231
Gambling	312	255	247	210	788	555	446	417	328	330	232	174	176
Offenses against the family and children	2,252	2,455	2,617	2,556	15,470	15,685	12,902	10,789	7,930	4,558	2,000	823	494
Driving under the influence	43,185	42,921	41,353	39,566	167,590	123,557	92,861	87,264	82,148	63,435	36,831	19,582	13,316
Liquor laws	10,201	6,753	5,330	4,343	17,024	13,016	10,832	12,559	14,456	12,431	7,105	3,149	1,858
Drunkenness	19,495	17,377	15,511	14,586	61,150	47,590	38,349	41,716	45,732	37,671	19,767	8,002	3,984
Disorderly conduct	20,717	17,935	15,760	14,156	56,168	40,094	29,517	28,190	27,318	20,781	10,832	4,818	3,465
Vagrancy	679	618	586	498	2,271	1,979	1,758	2,249	2,636	2,629	1,483	605	303
All other offenses (except traffic)	117,302	111,698	105,629	100,846	443,910	347,443	256,537	233,387	206,516	148,093	76,164	33,848	23,131
Suspicion	65	54	55	36	163	120	96	72	66	43	23	13	8
Curfew and loitering law violations	NA	NA	NA	NA	NA	NA	NA	NA	NA	NA	NA	NA	NA

NA = Not available.

[1] Because of rounding, the percentages may not add to 100.0.

[2] Violent crimes are offenses of murder and nonnegligent manslaughter, forcible rape, robbery, and aggravated assault. Property crimes are offenses of burglary, larceny-theft, motor vehicle theft, and arson.

Table IV-11. Male Arrests, Distribution by Age, 2011

(Number, percent; 12,023 agencies; 2011 estimated population 238,952,977)

Offense charged	Total all ages	Ages under 15	Ages under 18	Ages 18 and over	Under 10	10–12	13–14	15	16	17	18	19	20
Total	7,066,303	212,517	799,082	6,267,221	5,924	48,482	158,111	147,305	195,619	243,641	312,052	336,300	328,073
Total percent distribution[1]	100.0	3.0	11.3	88.7	0.1	0.7	2.2	2.1	2.8	3.4	4.4	4.8	4.6
Murder and nonnegligent manslaughter	7,374	64	594	6,780	1	10	53	89	156	285	464	468	471
Forcible rape	14,509	713	2,025	12,484	5	201	507	368	412	532	648	658	617
Robbery	72,498	3,032	16,726	55,772	32	377	2,623	3,406	4,736	5,552	6,353	5,723	4,737
Aggravated assault	236,482	7,410	23,477	213,005	259	1,994	5,157	4,158	5,401	6,508	7,631	8,570	8,896
Burglary	192,659	11,337	42,032	150,627	352	2,402	8,583	8,065	10,324	12,306	14,473	12,816	10,699
Larceny-theft	556,522	32,169	110,923	445,599	695	7,440	24,034	21,323	26,742	30,689	34,249	29,916	25,437
Motor vehicle theft	41,935	1,742	9,086	32,849	11	186	1,545	2,046	2,556	2,742	2,713	2,347	1,961
Arson	7,380	1,823	3,179	4,201	186	603	1,034	513	464	379	327	292	300
Violent crime[2]	330,863	11,219	42,822	288,041	297	2,582	8,340	8,021	10,705	12,877	15,096	15,419	14,721
Violent crime percent distribution[1]	100.0	3.4	12.9	87.1	0.1	0.8	2.5	2.4	3.2	3.9	4.6	4.7	4.4
Property crime[2]	798,496	47,071	165,220	633,276	1,244	10,631	35,196	31,947	40,086	46,116	51,762	45,371	38,397
Property crime percent distribution[1]	100.0	5.9	20.7	79.3	0.2	1.3	4.4	4.0	5.0	5.8	6.5	5.7	4.8
Other assaults	693,887	36,242	93,600	600,287	1,358	10,351	24,533	17,114	19,620	20,624	19,711	21,243	22,521
Forgery and counterfeiting	33,740	130	850	32,890	3	27	100	143	161	416	941	1,398	1,550
Fraud	75,732	396	2,537	73,195	9	70	317	411	620	1,110	1,913	2,628	2,791
Embezzlement	6,304	19	200	6,104	0	5	14	12	46	123	297	429	373
Stolen property; buying, receiving, possessing	57,393	1,753	8,550	48,843	21	268	1,464	1,732	2,160	2,905	3,807	3,634	2,974
Vandalism	148,215	17,007	44,512	103,703	802	4,880	11,325	8,574	9,330	9,601	9,128	8,086	7,023
Weapons; carrying, possessing, etc.	108,468	6,312	19,483	88,985	395	1,776	4,141	3,398	4,326	5,447	6,501	6,245	5,704
Prostitution and commercialized vice	13,767	23	183	13,584	0	1	22	27	52	81	162	259	336
Sex offenses (except forcible rape and prostitution)	49,065	4,162	8,559	40,506	155	1,206	2,801	1,418	1,476	1,503	1,857	1,771	1,745
Drug abuse violations	942,325	15,093	94,072	848,253	98	1,934	13,061	15,972	25,165	37,842	57,497	59,989	56,376
Gambling	5,726	70	718	5,008	1	3	66	123	209	316	423	382	388
Offenses against the family and children	65,978	510	1,690	64,288	37	121	352	318	397	465	913	1,043	1,254
Driving under the influence	701,029	88	5,756	695,273	5	17	66	229	1,259	4,180	11,914	17,829	21,564
Liquor laws	270,022	3,166	42,071	227,951	39	235	2,892	5,484	11,899	21,522	41,678	48,144	42,236
Drunkenness	339,516	630	6,471	333,045	11	57	562	982	1,535	3,324	8,109	9,650	10,109
Disorderly conduct	323,928	25,502	69,325	254,603	499	6,519	18,484	13,613	15,113	15,097	13,824	12,832	12,357
Vagrancy	18,198	301	1,090	17,108	6	41	254	262	296	231	770	692	626
All other offenses (except traffic)	2,040,870	32,710	149,401	1,891,469	826	6,134	25,750	28,383	39,118	49,190	65,684	79,198	84,969
Suspicion	894	24	85	809	1	6	17	8	33	20	65	58	59
Curfew and loitering law violations	41,887	10,089	41,887	NA	117	1,618	8,354	9,134	12,013	10,651	NA	NA	NA

NA = Not available.

[1] Because of rounding, the percentages may not add to 100.0.

[2] Violent crimes are offenses of murder and nonnegligent manslaughter, forcible rape, robbery, and aggravated assault. Property crimes are offenses of burglary, larceny-theft, motor vehicle theft, and arson.

Table IV-11. Male Arrests, Distribution by Age, 2011—*Continued*

(Number, percent; 12,023 agencies; 2011 estimated population 238,952,977)

Offense charged	21	22	23	24	25–29	30–34	35–39	40–44	45–49	50–54	55–59	60–64	65 and over
Total	307,358	282,029	260,249	245,114	1,048,392	803,967	584,577	543,090	496,805	370,750	197,610	90,518	60,337
Total percent distribution[1]	4.3	4.0	3.7	3.5	14.8	11.4	8.3	7.7	7.0	5.2	2.8	1.3	0.9
Murder and nonnegligent manslaughter	450	348	375	326	1,239	834	479	393	351	266	161	84	71
Forcible rape	634	524	436	430	2,028	1,596	1,381	1,175	966	675	353	168	195
Robbery	4,008	3,308	2,772	2,544	9,097	5,850	3,556	3,131	2,351	1,440	599	209	94
Aggravated assault	9,583	9,136	8,647	8,404	37,572	30,401	21,810	19,761	17,309	12,719	6,635	3,299	2,632
Burglary	9,217	7,848	6,833	6,058	24,322	17,664	11,661	10,914	9,075	5,445	2,445	762	395
Larceny-theft	22,349	19,638	17,178	16,065	67,592	52,046	38,695	39,305	35,629	25,311	12,785	5,435	3,969
Motor vehicle theft	1,729	1,535	1,444	1,335	5,700	4,491	3,126	2,741	1,968	1,077	433	170	79
Arson	201	169	154	125	643	454	339	338	324	254	152	65	64
Violent crime[2]	14,675	13,316	12,230	11,704	49,936	38,681	27,226	24,460	20,977	15,100	7,748	3,760	2,992
Violent crime percent distribution[1]	4.4	4.0	3.7	3.5	15.1	11.7	8.2	7.4	6.3	4.6	2.3	1.1	0.9
Property crime[2]	33,496	29,190	25,609	23,583	98,257	74,655	53,821	53,298	46,996	32,087	15,815	6,432	4,507
Property crime percent distribution[1]	4.2	3.7	3.2	3.0	12.3	9.3	6.7	6.7	5.9	4.0	2.0	0.8	0.6
Other assaults	25,357	24,703	24,092	23,454	106,351	87,415	65,678	60,146	51,580	35,616	17,676	8,209	6,535
Forgery and counterfeiting	1,368	1,373	1,324	1,327	6,264	5,003	3,603	3,156	2,466	1,739	818	363	197
Fraud	2,699	2,748	2,589	2,450	12,285	10,595	8,623	8,136	6,775	4,526	2,475	1,156	806
Embezzlement	390	328	281	257	997	744	601	496	407	267	126	76	35
Stolen property; buying, receiving, possessing	2,693	2,385	2,181	1,860	8,296	6,485	4,445	3,872	2,998	1,840	840	335	198
Vandalism	6,869	5,783	4,972	4,392	17,824	11,840	7,797	6,805	5,764	3,881	1,913	929	697
Weapons; carrying, possessing, etc.	5,438	4,919	4,417	4,102	16,376	11,074	6,857	5,363	4,605	3,532	1,940	1,059	853
Prostitution and commercialized vice	396	438	412	450	2,164	2,047	1,631	1,554	1,307	1,074	634	353	367
Sex offenses (except forcible rape and prostitution)	1,599	1,354	1,257	1,141	5,228	4,603	4,067	3,963	3,911	3,134	2,107	1,318	1,451
Drug abuse violations	50,168	44,753	40,123	37,515	151,925	108,479	69,414	58,977	50,496	35,374	17,327	7,004	2,836
Gambling	291	238	235	198	708	489	366	312	274	245	176	140	143
Offenses against the family and children	1,513	1,631	1,779	1,781	10,807	11,673	9,966	8,703	6,566	3,837	1,708	702	412
Driving under the influence	31,584	31,556	30,712	29,618	126,742	94,492	70,195	63,906	60,247	48,415	29,305	16,018	11,176
Liquor laws	7,897	5,246	4,174	3,384	13,449	10,177	8,512	9,992	11,845	10,595	6,225	2,777	1,620
Drunkenness	15,748	14,182	12,801	11,869	49,919	38,772	30,882	33,154	37,436	31,984	17,551	7,232	3,647
Disorderly conduct	15,423	13,336	11,649	10,536	41,297	29,070	21,312	20,499	20,490	16,264	8,867	4,001	2,846
Vagrancy	552	501	484	406	1,767	1,559	1,377	1,796	2,168	2,268	1,317	555	270
All other offenses (except traffic)	89,150	84,013	78,886	75,060	327,681	256,025	188,135	174,442	159,443	118,931	63,024	28,087	18,741
Suspicion	52	36	42	27	119	89	69	60	54	41	18	12	8
Curfew and loitering law violations	NA	NA	NA	NA	NA	NA	NA	NA	NA	NA	NA	NA	NA

NA = Not available.

[1] Because of rounding, the percentages may not add to 100.0.

[2] Violent crimes are offenses of murder and nonnegligent manslaughter, forcible rape, robbery, and aggravated assault. Property crimes are offenses of burglary, larceny-theft, motor vehicle theft, and arson.

Table IV-12. Female Arrests, Distribution by Age, 2011

(Number, percent; 12,023 agencies; 2011 estimated population 238,952,977)

Offense charged	Total all ages	Ages under 15	Ages under 18	Ages 18 and over	Under 10	10–12	13–14	15	16	17	18	19	20
Total	2,471,370	95,347	330,374	2,140,996	1,316	18,711	75,320	65,750	79,960	89,317	107,465	117,190	116,109
Total percent distribution[1]	100.0	3.9	13.4	86.6	0.1	0.8	3.0	2.7	3.2	3.6	4.3	4.7	4.7
Murder and nonnegligent manslaughter	985	8	57	928	0	1	7	17	13	19	32	43	42
Forcible rape	170	23	46	124	0	8	15	8	9	6	3	4	4
Robbery	10,059	385	1,651	8,408	3	58	324	311	428	527	646	646	590
Aggravated assault	69,457	2,626	7,788	61,669	38	601	1,987	1,536	1,778	1,848	2,043	2,315	2,672
Burglary	35,742	1,625	5,622	30,120	58	341	1,226	1,159	1,389	1,449	1,814	1,796	1,705
Larceny-theft	424,594	23,430	86,236	338,358	255	4,976	18,199	16,637	21,735	24,434	25,563	23,488	20,060
Motor vehicle theft	9,092	408	1,700	7,392	4	42	362	403	448	441	445	426	410
Arson	1,614	294	535	1,079	13	91	190	101	86	54	40	48	42
Violent crime[2]	80,671	3,042	9,542	71,129	41	668	2,333	1,872	2,228	2,400	2,724	3,008	3,308
Violent crime percent distribution[1]	100.0	3.8	11.8	88.2	0.1	0.8	2.9	2.3	2.8	3.0	3.4	3.7	4.1
Property crime[2]	471,042	25,757	94,093	376,949	330	5,450	19,977	18,300	23,658	26,378	27,862	25,758	22,217
Property crime percent distribution[1]	100.0	5.5	20.0	80.0	0.1	1.2	4.2	3.9	5.0	5.6	5.9	5.5	4.7
Other assaults	261,733	19,442	51,824	209,909	270	4,267	14,905	10,528	11,333	10,521	9,291	9,257	10,150
Forgery and counterfeiting	20,243	27	351	19,892	1	5	21	37	83	204	554	792	899
Fraud	52,468	194	1,375	51,093	4	37	153	254	379	548	987	1,401	1,736
Embezzlement	6,192	13	125	6,067	0	3	10	7	28	77	247	371	405
Stolen property; buying, receiving, possessing	14,497	464	1,719	12,778	5	62	397	307	422	526	672	752	746
Vandalism	34,988	3,117	7,717	27,271	101	845	2,171	1,410	1,519	1,671	1,677	1,634	1,701
Weapons; carrying, possessing, etc.	9,604	890	2,247	7,357	46	286	558	431	459	467	390	371	391
Prostitution and commercialized vice	30,407	47	580	29,827	0	6	41	86	150	297	1,161	1,537	1,601
Sex offenses (except forcible rape and prostitution)	3,983	480	1,025	2,958	27	119	334	240	170	135	146	179	128
Drug abuse violations	232,758	4,108	18,820	213,938	19	494	3,595	3,366	4,696	6,650	10,443	11,868	11,748
Gambling	791	13	48	743	0	1	12	8	10	17	15	28	45
Offenses against the family and children	21,985	349	1,058	20,927	19	59	271	186	243	280	370	519	585
Driving under the influence	228,874	42	1,964	226,910	2	7	33	69	447	1,406	3,978	6,032	7,257
Liquor laws	113,881	3,454	27,747	86,134	20	324	3,110	4,633	7,842	11,818	21,459	22,841	18,670
Drunkenness	75,345	408	2,274	73,071	4	33	371	434	541	891	2,243	2,553	2,522
Disorderly conduct	125,766	14,446	36,978	88,788	96	2,990	11,360	8,117	7,703	6,712	5,136	4,783	4,708
Vagrancy	4,378	99	320	4,058	0	18	81	82	93	46	265	262	257
All other offenses (except traffic)	663,996	14,000	53,023	610,973	279	2,314	11,407	11,397	13,283	14,343	17,831	23,233	27,023
Suspicion	256	11	32	224	1	3	7	4	8	9	14	11	12
Curfew and loitering law violations	17,512	4,944	17,512	NA	51	720	4,173	3,982	4,665	3,921	NA	NA	NA

NA = Not available.

[1] Because of rounding, the percentages may not add to 100.0.

[2] Violent crimes are offenses of murder and nonnegligent manslaughter, forcible rape, robbery, and aggravated assault. Property crimes are offenses of burglary, larceny-theft, motor vehicle theft, and arson.

Table IV-12. Female Arrests, Distribution by Age, 2011—*Continued*

(Number, percent; 12,023 agencies; 2011 estimated population 238,952,977)

Offense charged	21	22	23	24	25–29	30–34	35–39	40–44	45–49	50–54	55–59	60–64	65 and over
Total	104,265	97,975	91,304	86,112	373,814	286,919	215,555	194,769	163,541	103,857	47,244	20,601	14,276
Total percent distribution[1]	4.2	4.0	3.7	3.5	15.1	11.6	8.7	7.9	6.6	4.2	1.9	0.8	0.6
Murder and nonnegligent manslaughter	44	40	46	36	183	125	88	97	72	41	16	12	11
Forcible rape	6	5	6	7	25	24	18	6	9	3	2	1	1
Robbery	569	447	446	412	1,617	1,056	703	557	392	205	88	18	16
Aggravated assault	2,784	2,766	2,700	2,550	11,211	8,953	6,836	5,923	5,171	3,282	1,498	522	443
Burglary	1,526	1,528	1,396	1,229	5,539	4,155	3,062	2,563	1,989	1,079	461	168	110
Larceny-theft	17,613	15,617	14,316	13,246	56,227	42,222	30,493	26,639	22,507	15,389	7,926	4,010	3,042
Motor vehicle theft	387	343	356	324	1,463	1,153	783	597	402	204	67	25	7
Arson	37	46	32	43	175	136	140	101	109	65	37	16	12
Violent crime[2]	3,403	3,258	3,198	3,005	13,036	10,158	7,645	6,583	5,644	3,531	1,604	553	471
Violent crime percent distribution[1]	4.2	4.0	4.0	3.7	16.2	12.6	9.5	8.2	7.0	4.4	2.0	0.7	0.6
Property crime[2]	19,563	17,534	16,100	14,842	63,404	47,666	34,478	29,900	25,007	16,737	8,491	4,219	3,171
Property crime percent distribution[1]	4.2	3.7	3.4	3.2	13.5	10.1	7.3	6.3	5.3	3.6	1.8	0.9	0.7
Other assaults	10,811	10,268	9,203	8,697	37,467	28,683	22,127	19,637	16,454	9,869	4,490	2,012	1,493
Forgery and counterfeiting	816	850	862	847	4,104	3,456	2,361	1,908	1,284	672	299	114	74
Fraud	1,582	1,692	1,621	1,800	8,820	8,770	7,363	5,865	4,313	2,674	1,337	624	508
Embezzlement	334	301	286	237	1,007	738	689	550	385	269	154	69	25
Stolen property; buying, receiving, possessing	647	640	594	587	2,628	1,843	1,307	1,066	670	394	160	46	26
Vandalism	1,612	1,484	1,363	1,236	5,025	3,449	2,376	2,131	1,748	1,031	455	195	154
Weapons; carrying, possessing, etc.	385	377	350	336	1,380	999	712	592	471	340	135	75	53
Prostitution and commercialized vice	1,566	1,529	1,398	1,221	5,037	3,889	3,200	3,347	2,582	1,269	386	82	22
Sex offenses (except forcible rape and prostitution)	146	130	126	96	478	411	321	309	261	128	66	21	12
Drug abuse violations	11,402	10,585	9,877	9,290	39,383	29,164	20,492	19,102	16,115	9,552	3,421	1,101	395
Gambling	21	17	12	12	80	66	80	105	54	85	56	34	33
Offenses against the family and children	739	824	838	775	4,663	4,012	2,936	2,086	1,364	721	292	121	82
Driving under the influence	11,601	11,365	10,641	9,948	40,848	29,065	22,666	23,358	21,901	15,020	7,526	3,564	2,140
Liquor laws	2,304	1,507	1,156	959	3,575	2,839	2,320	2,567	2,611	1,836	880	372	238
Drunkenness	3,747	3,195	2,710	2,717	11,231	8,818	7,467	8,562	8,296	5,687	2,216	770	337
Disorderly conduct	5,294	4,599	4,111	3,620	14,871	11,024	8,205	7,691	6,828	4,517	1,965	817	619
Vagrancy	127	117	102	92	504	420	381	453	468	361	166	50	33
All other offenses (except traffic)	28,152	27,685	26,743	25,786	116,229	91,418	68,402	58,945	47,073	29,162	13,140	5,761	4,390
Suspicion	13	18	13	9	44	31	27	12	12	2	5	1	0
Curfew and loitering law violations	NA	NA	NA	NA	NA	NA	NA	NA	NA	NA	NA	NA	NA

NA = Not available.

[1] Because of rounding, the percentages may not add to 100.0.

[2] Violent crimes are offenses of murder and nonnegligent manslaughter, forcible rape, robbery, and aggravated assault. Property crimes are offenses of burglary, larceny-theft, motor vehicle theft, and arson.

Table IV-13. Arrests of Persons Under 15, 18, 21, and 25 Years of Age, 2011

(Number, percent; 12,023 agencies; 2011 estimated population 238,952,977)

Offense charged	Total all ages	Number of persons arrested				Percent of total all ages			
		Under 15	Under 18	Under 21	Under 25	Under 15	Under 18	Under 21	Under 25
Total	9,537,673	307,864	1,129,456	2,446,645	3,921,051	3.2	11.8	25.7	41.1
Murder and nonnegligent manslaughter	8,359	72	651	2,171	3,836	0.9	7.8	26.0	45.9
Forcible rape	14,679	736	2,071	4,005	6,053	5.0	14.1	27.3	41.2
Robbery	82,557	3,417	18,377	37,072	51,578	4.1	22.3	44.9	62.5
Aggravated assault	305,939	10,036	31,265	63,392	109,962	3.3	10.2	20.7	35.9
Burglary	228,401	12,962	47,654	90,957	126,592	5.7	20.9	39.8	55.4
Larceny-theft	981,116	55,599	197,159	355,872	491,894	5.7	20.1	36.3	50.1
Motor vehicle theft	51,027	2,150	10,786	19,088	26,541	4.2	21.1	37.4	52.0
Arson...	8,994	2,117	3,714	4,763	5,570	23.5	41.3	53.0	61.9
Violent crime[1]	411,534	14,261	52,364	106,640	171,429	3.5	12.7	25.9	41.7
Property crime[1]	1,269,538	72,828	259,313	470,680	650,597	5.7	20.4	37.1	51.2
Other assaults..	955,620	55,684	145,424	237,597	374,182	5.8	15.2	24.9	39.2
Forgery and counterfeiting	53,983	157	1,201	7,335	16,102	0.3	2.2	13.6	29.8
Fraud	128,200	590	3,912	15,368	32,549	0.5	3.1	12.0	25.4
Embezzlement..	12,496	32	325	2,447	4,861	0.3	2.6	19.6	38.9
Stolen property; buying, receiving, possessing...........	71,890	2,217	10,269	22,854	34,441	3.1	14.3	31.8	47.9
Vandalism	183,203	20,124	52,229	81,478	109,189	11.0	28.5	44.5	59.6
Weapons; carrying, possessing, etc.	118,072	7,202	21,730	41,332	61,656	6.1	18.4	35.0	52.2
Prostitution and commercialized vice	44,174	70	763	5,819	13,229	0.2	1.7	13.2	29.9
Sex offenses (except forcible rape and prostitution)............	53,048	4,642	9,584	15,410	21,259	8.8	18.1	29.0	40.1
Drug abuse violations	1,175,083	19,201	112,892	320,813	534,526	1.6	9.6	27.3	45.5
Gambling	6,517	83	766	2,047	3,071	1.3	11.8	31.4	47.1
Offenses against the family and children...............	87,963	859	2,748	7,432	17,312	1.0	3.1	8.4	19.7
Driving under the influence	929,903	130	7,720	76,294	243,319	*	0.8	8.2	26.2
Liquor laws..	383,903	6,620	69,818	264,846	291,473	1.7	18.2	69.0	75.9
Drunkenness...	414,861	1,038	8,745	43,931	110,900	0.3	2.1	10.6	26.7
Disorderly conduct..	449,694	39,948	106,303	159,943	228,511	8.9	23.6	35.6	50.8
Vagrancy	22,576	400	1,410	4,282	6,663	1.8	6.2	19.0	29.5
All other offenses (except traffic)	2,704,866	46,710	202,424	500,362	935,837	1.7	7.5	18.5	34.6
Suspicion...	1,150	35	117	336	546	3.0	10.2	29.2	47.5
Curfew and loitering law violations........................	59,399	15,033	59,399	59,399	59,399	25.3	100.0	100.0	100.0

* = Less than one tenth of one percent.

[1] Violent crimes are offenses of murder and nonnegligent manslaughter, forcible rape, robbery, and aggravated assault. Property crimes are offenses of burglary, larceny-theft, motor vehicle theft, and arson.

Table IV-14. Arrests, Distribution by Sex, 2011

(Number, percent; 12,023 agencies; 2011 estimated population 238,952,977)

Offense charged	Number of persons arrested			Percent male	Percent female	Percent distribution[1]		
	Total	Male	Female			Total	Male	Female
Total	9,537,673	7,066,303	2,471,370	74.1	25.9	100.0	100.0	100.0
Murder and nonnegligent manslaughter	8,359	7,374	985	88.2	11.8	0.1	0.1	*
Forcible rape	14,679	14,509	170	98.8	1.2	0.2	0.2	*
Robbery	82,557	72,498	10.059	87.8	12.2	0.9	1.0	0.4
Aggravated assault	305,939	236,482	69,457	77.3	22.7	3.2	3.3	2.8
Burglary	228,401	192,659	35,742	84.4	15.6	2.4	2.7	1.4
Larceny-theft	981,116	556,522	424,594	56.7	43.3	10.3	7.9	17.2
Motor vehicle theft	51,027	41,935	9,092	82.2	17.8	0.5	0.6	0.4
Arson	8,994	7,380	1,614	82.1	17.9	0.1	0.1	0.1
Violent crime[2]	411,534	330,863	80,671	80.4	19.6	4.3	4.7	3.3
Property crime[2]	1,269,538	798,496	471,042	62.9	37.1	13.3	11.3	19.1
Other assaults	955,620	693,887	261,733	72.6	27.4	10.0	9.8	10.6
Forgery and counterfeiting	53,983	33,740	20,243	62.5	37.5	0.6	0.5	0.8
Fraud	128,200	75,732	52,468	59.1	40.9	1.3	1.1	2.1
Embezzlement	12,496	6,304	6,192	50.4	49.6	0.1	0.1	0.3
Stolen property; buying, receiving, possessing	71,890	57,393	14,497	79.8	20.2	0.8	0.8	0.6
Vandalism	183,203	148,215	34,988	80.9	19.1	1.9	2.1	1.4
Weapons; carrying, possessing, etc.	118,072	108,468	9,604	91.9	8.1	1.2	1.5	0.4
Prostitution and commercialized vice	44,174	13,767	30,407	31.2	68.8	0.5	0.2	1.2
Sex offenses (except forcible rape and prostitution)	53,048	49,065	3,983	92.5	7.5	0.6	0.7	0.2
Drug abuse violations	1,175,083	942,325	232,758	80.2	19.8	12.3	13.3	9.4
Gambling	6,517	5,726	791	87.9	12.1	0.1	0.1	*
Offenses against the family and children	87,963	65,978	21,985	75.0	25.0	0.9	0.9	0.9
Driving under the influence	929,903	701,029	228,874	75.4	24.6	9.7	9.9	9.3
Liquor laws	383,903	270,022	113,881	70.3	29.7	4.0	3.8	4.6
Drunkenness	414,861	339,516	75,345	81.8	18.2	4.3	4.8	3.0
Disorderly conduct	449,694	323,928	125,766	72.0	28.0	4.7	4.6	5.1
Vagrancy	22,576	18,198	4,378	80.6	19.4	0.2	0.3	0.2
All other offenses (except traffic)	2,704,866	2,040,870	663,996	75.5	24.5	28.4	28.9	26.9
Suspicion	1,150	894	256	77.7	22.3	*	*	*
Curfew and loitering law violations	59,399	41,887	17,512	70.5	29.5	0.6	0.6	0.7

* = Less than one-tenth of 1 percent.

[1] Because of rounding, the percentages may not add to 100.0.

[2] Violent crimes are offenses of murder and nonnegligent manslaughter, forcible rape, robbery, and aggravated assault. Property crimes are offenses of burglary, larceny-theft, motor vehicle theft, and arson.

Table IV-15.　Arrests, Distribution by Race, 2011

(Number, percent; 12,023 agencies; 2011 estimated population 238,952,977)

Offense charged	Total arrests					Percent distribution[1]					Arrests under 18				
	Total	White	Black	American Indian or Alaskan Native	Asian or Pacific Islander	Total	White	Black	American Indian or Alaskan Native	Asian or Pacific Islander	Total	White	Black	American Indian or Alaskan Native	Asian or Pacific Islander
Total	9,499,725	6,578,133	2,697,539	142,422	81,631	100.0	69.2	28.4	1.5	0.9	1,123,992	738,427	359,765	15,023	10,777
Murder and nonnegligent manslaughter	8,341	4,000	4,149	105	87	100.0	48.0	49.7	1.3	1.0	650	293	351	5	1
Forcible rape	14,611	9,504	4,811	170	126	100.0	65.0	32.9	1.2	0.9	2,061	1,284	753	12	12
Robbery	82,436	35,443	45,827	619	547	100.0	43.0	55.6	0.8	0.7	18,353	5,580	12,574	81	118
Aggravated assault	305,220	194,981	102,597	4,540	3,102	100.0	63.9	33.6	1.5	1.0	31,173	17,372	13,176	376	249
Burglary	227,899	151,934	72,244	2,095	1,626	100.0	66.7	31.7	0.9	0.7	47,524	28,388	18,347	392	397
Larceny-theft	977,743	670,768	281,197	15,122	10,656	100.0	68.6	28.8	1.5	1.1	196,228	124,185	66,504	2,822	2,717
Motor vehicle theft	50,902	32,575	17,250	658	419	100.0	64.0	33.9	1.3	0.8	10,754	5,959	4,586	123	86
Arson	8,965	6,479	2,302	107	77	100.0	72.3	25.7	1.2	0.9	3,705	2,700	944	25	36
Violent crime[2]	410,608	243,928	157,384	5,434	3,862	100.0	59.4	38.3	1.3	0.9	52,237	24,529	26,854	474	380
Property crime[2]	1,265,509	861,756	372,993	17,982	12,778	100.0	68.1	29.5	1.4	1.0	258,211	161,232	90,381	3,362	3,236
Other assaults	952,421	625,330	304,083	14,875	8,133	100.0	65.7	31.9	1.6	0.9	144,865	85,813	56,467	1,638	947
Forgery and counterfeiting	53,791	35,239	17,695	295	562	100.0	65.5	32.9	0.5	1.0	1,198	790	388	5	15
Fraud	127,664	84,919	40,621	1,140	984	100.0	66.5	31.8	0.9	0.8	3,884	2,332	1,478	39	35
Embezzlement	12,454	8,155	4,032	65	202	100.0	65.5	32.4	0.5	1.6	322	213	102	1	6
Stolen property; buying, receiving, possessing	71,727	47,434	23,191	542	560	100.0	66.1	32.3	0.8	0.8	10,253	5,798	4,270	81	104
Vandalism	182,482	132,850	45,055	3,029	1,548	100.0	72.8	24.7	1.7	0.8	51,963	39,498	11,338	691	436
Weapons; carrying, possessing, etc.	117,820	68,453	47,515	859	993	100.0	58.1	40.3	0.7	0.8	21,663	13,153	8,100	160	250
Prostitution and commercialized vice	44,090	23,555	19,227	255	1,053	100.0	53.4	43.6	0.6	2.4	760	268	483	1	8
Sex offenses (except forcible rape and prostitution)	52,891	38,422	13,189	729	551	100.0	72.6	24.9	1.4	1.0	9,536	6,651	2,739	77	69
Drug abuse violations	1,171,866	783,564	371,248	8,275	8,779	100.0	66.9	31.7	0.7	0.7	112,427	83,508	26,531	1,277	1,111
Gambling	6,507	1,937	4,351	40	179	100.0	29.8	66.9	0.6	2.8	766	93	664	2	7
Offenses against the family and children	87,586	56,973	28,183	1,848	582	100.0	65.0	32.2	2.1	0.7	2,702	1,882	738	66	16
Driving under the influence	924,210	788,175	111,480	13,618	10,937	100.0	85.3	12.1	1.5	1.2	7,667	7,026	417	150	74
Liquor laws	380,663	312,106	51,446	12,896	4,215	100.0	82.0	13.5	3.4	1.1	69,299	61,403	4,754	2,337	805
Drunkenness	413,723	339,019	64,268	7,619	2,817	100.0	81.9	15.5	1.8	0.7	8,706	7,578	852	206	70
Disorderly conduct	447,201	281,531	153,840	8,771	3,059	100.0	63.0	34.4	2.0	0.7	105,764	60,148	43,749	1,221	646
Vagrancy	22,375	12,989	8,794	447	145	100.0	58.1	39.3	2.0	0.6	1,406	1,026	369	6	5
All other offenses (except traffic)	2,693,823	1,794,893	837,095	42,869	18,966	100.0	66.6	31.1	1.6	0.7	201,082	139,156	57,691	2,400	1,835
Suspicion	1,150	634	506	5	5	100.0	55.1	44.0	0.4	0.4	117	59	57	0	1
Curfew and loitering law violations	59,164	36,271	21,343	829	721	100.0	61.3	36.1	1.4	1.2	59,164	36,271	21,343	829	721

NA = Not available.

[1] Because of rounding, the percentages may not add to 100.0.

[2] Violent crimes are offenses of murder and nonnegligent manslaughter, forcible rape, robbery, and aggravated assault. Property crimes are offenses of burglary, larceny-theft, motor vehicle theft, and arson.

Table IV-15. Arrests, Distribution by Race, 2011—*Continued*

(Number, percent; 12,023 agencies; 2011 estimated population 238,952,977)

Offense charged	Percent distribution[1]					Arrests 18 and over					Percent distribution[1]				
	Total	White	Black	American Indian or Alaskan Native	Asian or Pacific Islander	Total	White	Black	American Indian or Alaskan Native	Asian or Pacific Islander	Total	White	Black	American Indian or Alaskan Native	Asian or Pacific Islander
Total	100.0	65.7	32.0	1.3	1.0	8,375,733	5,839,706	2,337,774	127,399	70,854	100.0	69.7	27.9	1.5	0.8
Murder and nonnegligent manslaughter....................	100.0	45.1	54.0	0.8	0.2	7,691	3,707	3,798	100	86	100.0	48.2	49.4	1.3	1.1
Forcible rape	100.0	62.3	36.5	0.6	0.6	12,550	8,220	4,058	158	114	100.0	65.5	32.3	1.3	0.9
Robbery......................................	100.0	30.4	68.5	0.4	0.6	64,083	29,863	33,253	538	429	100.0	46.6	51.9	0.8	0.7
Aggravated assault.........................	100.0	55.7	42.3	1.2	0.8	274,047	177,609	89,421	4,164	2,853	100.0	64.8	32.6	1.5	1.0
Burglary..	100.0	59.7	38.6	0.8	0.8	180,375	123,546	53,897	1,703	1,229	100.0	68.5	29.9	0.9	0.7
Larceny-theft	100.0	63.3	33.9	1.4	1.4	781,515	546,583	214,693	12,300	7,939	100.0	69.9	27.5	1.6	1.0
Motor vehicle theft.........................	100.0	55.4	42.6	1.1	0.8	40,148	26,616	12,664	535	333	100.0	66.3	31.5	1.3	0.8
Arson	100.0	72.9	25.5	0.7	1.0	5,260	3,779	1,358	82	41	100.0	71.8	25.8	1.6	0.8
Violent crime[2]...............................	100.0	47.0	51.4	0.9	0.7	358,371	219,399	130,530	4,960	3,482	100.0	61.2	36.4	1.4	1.0
Property crime[2]...............................	100.0	62.4	35.0	1.3	1.3	1,007,298	700,524	282,612	14,620	9,542	100.0	69.5	28.1	1.5	0.9
Other assaults	100.0	59.2	39.0	1.1	0.7	807,556	539,517	247,616	13,237	7,186	100.0	66.8	30.7	1.6	0.9
Forgery and counterfeiting..............	100.0	65.9	32.4	0.4	1.3	52,593	34,449	17,307	290	547	100.0	65.5	32.9	0.6	1.0
Fraud	100.0	60.0	38.1	1.0	0.9	123,780	82,587	39,143	1,101	949	100.0	66.7	31.6	0.9	0.8
Embezzlement	100.0	66.1	31.7	0.3	1.9	12,132	7,942	3,930	64	196	100.0	65.5	32.4	0.5	1.6
Stolen property; buying, receiving, possessing........................	100.0	56.5	41.6	0.8	1.0	61,474	41,636	18,921	461	456	100.0	67.7	30.8	0.7	0.7
Vandalism.....................................	100.0	76.0	21.8	1.3	0.8	130,519	93,352	33,717	2,338	1,112	100.0	71.5	25.8	1.8	0.9
Weapons; carrying, possessing, etc..	100.0	60.7	37.4	0.7	1.2	96,157	55,300	39,415	699	743	100.0	57.5	41.0	0.7	0.8
Prostitution and commercialized vice	100.0	35.3	63.6	0.1	1.1	43,330	23,287	18,744	254	1,045	100.0	53.7	43.3	0.6	2.4
Sex offenses (except forcible rape and prostitution)......................	100.0	69.7	28.7	0.8	0.7	43,355	31,771	10,450	652	482	100.0	73.3	24.1	1.5	1.1
Drug abuse violations	100.0	74.3	23.6	1.1	1.0	1,059,439	700,056	344,717	6,998	7,668	100.0	66.1	32.5	0.7	0.7
Gambling...	100.0	12.1	86.7	0.3	0.9	5,741	1,844	3,687	38	172	100.0	32.1	64.2	0.7	3.0
Offenses against the family and children......................................	100.0	69.7	27.3	2.4	0.6	84,884	55,091	27,445	1,782	566	100.0	64.9	32.3	2.1	0.7
Driving under the influence	100.0	91.6	5.4	2.0	1.0	916,543	781,149	111,063	13,468	10,863	100.0	85.2	12.1	1.5	1.2
Liquor laws.....................................	100.0	88.6	6.9	3.4	1.2	311,364	250,703	46,692	10,559	3,410	100.0	80.5	15.0	3.4	1.1
Drunkenness...................................	100.0	87.0	9.8	2.4	0.8	405,017	331,441	63,416	7,413	2,747	100.0	81.8	15.7	1.8	0.7
Disorderly conduct........................	100.0	56.9	41.4	1.2	0.6	341,437	221,383	110,091	7,550	2,413	100.0	64.8	32.2	2.2	0.7
Vagrancy.......................................	100.0	73.0	26.2	0.4	0.4	20,969	11,963	8,425	441	140	100.0	57.1	40.2	2.1	0.7
All other offenses (except traffic)..	100.0	69.2	28.7	1.2	0.9	2,492,741	1,655,737	779,404	40,469	17,131	100.0	66.4	31.3	1.6	0.7
Suspicion	100.0	50.4	48.7	0.0	0.9	1,033	575	449	5	4	100.0	55.7	43.5	0.5	0.4
Curfew and loitering law violations	100.0	61.3	36.1	1.4	1.2	NA	NA	NA	NA	NA	NA	NA	NA	NA	NA

NA = Not available.

[1] Because of rounding, the percentages may not add to 100.0.

[2] Violent crimes are offenses of murder and nonnegligent manslaughter, forcible rape, robbery, and aggravated assault. Property crimes are offenses of burglary, larceny-theft, motor vehicle theft, and arson.

Table IV-16. Arrest Trends, Cities, 2010–2011

(Number, percent change; 8,161 agencies; 2011 estimated population 153,161,714; 2010 estimated population 151,714,983)

Offense charged	Number of persons arrested								
	Total all ages			Under 18 years of age			18 years of age and over		
	2010	2011	Percent change	2010	2011	Percent change	2010	2011	Percent change
Total[1]	6,960,722	6,622,137	-4.9	973,068	860,700	-11.5	5,987,654	5,761,437	-3.8
Murder and nonnegligent manslaughter	5,537	5,190	-6.3	547	427	-21.9	4,990	4,763	-4.5
Forcible rape	10,347	9,790	-5.4	1,482	1,427	-3.7	8,865	8,363	-5.7
Robbery	64,923	61,521	-5.2	15,364	13,499	-12.1	49,559	48,022	-3.1
Aggravated assault	218,472	208,913	-4.4	24,348	21,628	-11.2	194,124	187,285	-3.5
Burglary	153,028	151,634	-0.9	37,030	33,730	-8.9	115,998	117,904	+1.6
Larceny-theft	778,581	772,477	-0.8	182,291	163,091	-10.5	596,290	609,386	+2.2
Motor vehicle theft	34,188	32,168	-5.9	7,779	6,848	-12.0	26,409	25,320	-4.1
Arson	6,103	6,052	-0.8	2,802	2,850	+1.7	3,301	3,202	-3.0
Violent crime[2]	299,279	285,414	-4.6	41,741	36,981	-11.4	257,538	248,433	-3.5
Property crime[2]	971,900	962,331	-1.0	229,902	206,519	-10.2	741,998	755,812	+1.9
Other assaults	685,787	662,839	-3.3	111,600	100,910	-9.6	574,187	561,929	-2.1
Forgery and counterfeiting	41,424	38,303	-7.5	1,000	912	-8.8	40,424	37,391	-7.5
Fraud	86,539	78,076	-9.8	3,400	3,018	-11.2	83,139	75,058	-9.7
Embezzlement	9,256	9,071	-2.0	257	264	+2.7	8,999	8,807	-2.1
Stolen property; buying, receiving, possessing	51,388	50,225	-2.3	9,035	8,065	-10.7	42,353	42,160	-0.5
Vandalism	141,968	133,355	-6.1	45,632	39,266	-14.0	96,336	94,089	-2.3
Weapons; carrying, possessing, etc.	84,876	80,650	-5.0	17,530	15,607	-11.0	67,346	65,043	-3.4
Prostitution and commercialized vice	36,092	32,427	-10.2	589	587	-0.3	35,503	31,840	-10.3
Sex offenses (except forcible rape and prostitution)	36,539	34,601	-5.3	6,570	6,278	-4.4	29,969	28,323	-5.5
Drug abuse violations	836,536	768,898	-8.1	95,707	81,751	-14.6	740,829	687,147	-7.2
Gambling	2,220	1,921	-13.5	230	192	-16.5	1,990	1,729	-13.1
Offenses against the family and children	39,263	38,926	-0.9	2,113	2,037	-3.6	37,150	36,889	-0.7
Driving under the influence	606,974	578,487	-4.7	5,877	5,162	-12.2	601,097	573,325	-4.6
Liquor laws	310,641	284,743	-8.3	56,897	51,979	-8.6	253,744	232,764	-8.3
Drunkenness	370,691	349,359	-5.8	8,498	7,593	-10.6	362,193	341,766	-5.6
Disorderly conduct	380,599	350,418	-7.9	96,976	86,143	-11.2	283,623	264,275	-6.8
Vagrancy	21,442	19,263	-10.2	1,424	1,265	-11.2	20,018	17,998	-10.1
All other offenses (except traffic)	1,883,409	1,811,573	-3.8	174,191	154,914	-11.1	1,709,218	1,656,659	-3.1
Suspicion	630	652	+3.5	84	46	-45.2	546	606	+11.0
Curfew and loitering law violations	63,899	51,257	-19.8	63,899	51,257	-19.8	NA	NA	NA

NA = Not available.

[1] Does not include suspicion.

[2] Violent crimes are offenses of murder and nonnegligent manslaughter, forcible rape, robbery, and aggravated assault. Property crimes are offenses of burglary, larceny-theft, motor vehicle theft, and arson.

Table IV-17. Arrest Trends, Cities, by Age and Sex, 2010–2011

(Number, percent change; 8,436 agencies; 2011 estimated population 153,161,714; 2010 estimated population 151,714,983)

Offense charged	Male						Female					
	Total			Under 18			Total			Under 18		
	2010	2011	Percent change	2010	2011	Percent change	2010	2011	Percent change	2010	2011	Percent change
Total[1]	5,139,765	4,857,973	-5.5	678,845	600,979	-11.5	1,820,957	1,764,164	-3.1	294,223	259,721	-11.7
Murder and nonnegligent manslaughter	4,951	4,614	-6.8	493	404	-18.1	586	576	-1.7	54	23	-57.4
Forcible rape	10,252	9,678	-5.6	1,450	1,389	-4.2	95	112	+17.9	32	38	+18.8
Robbery	56,747	53,784	-5.2	13,756	12,260	-10.9	8,176	7,737	-5.4	1,608	1,239	-22.9
Aggravated assault	167,500	160,048	-4.4	18,134	16,168	-10.8	50,972	48,865	-4.1	6,214	5,460	-12.1
Burglary	128,361	126,815	-1.2	32,331	29,381	-9.1	24,667	24,819	+0.6	4,699	4,349	-7.4
Larceny-theft	426,173	426,305	*	96,798	89,708	-7.3	352,408	346,172	-1.8	85,493	73,383	-14.2
Motor vehicle theft	28,161	26,297	-6.6	6,515	5,743	-11.8	6,027	5,871	-2.6	1,264	1,105	-12.6
Arson	5,048	4,993	-1.1	2,443	2,448	+0.2	1,055	1,059	+0.4	359	402	+12.0
Violent crime[2]	239,450	228,124	-4.7	33,833	30,221	-10.7	59,829	57,290	-4.2	7,908	6,760	-14.5
Property crime[2]	587,743	584,410	-0.6	138,087	127,280	-7.8	384,157	377,921	-1.6	91,815	79,239	-13.7
Other assaults	499,656	480,146	-3.9	71,931	64,799	-9.9	186,131	182,693	-1.8	39,669	36,111	-9.0
Forgery and counterfeiting	25,666	23,926	-6.8	705	629	-10.8	15,758	14,377	-8.8	295	283	-4.1
Fraud	52,372	47,615	-9.1	2,231	1,971	-11.7	34,167	30,461	-10.8	1,169	1,047	-10.4
Embezzlement	4,622	4,532	-1.9	147	167	+13.6	4,634	4,539	-2.1	110	97	-11.8
Stolen property; buying, receiving, possessing	40,934	39,824	-2.7	7,486	6,703	-10.5	10,454	10,401	-0.5	1,549	1,362	-12.1
Vandalism	115,047	107,559	-6.5	39,004	33,416	-14.3	26,921	25,796	-4.2	6,628	5,850	-11.7
Weapons; carrying, possessing, etc.	77,914	74,105	-4.9	15,722	14,042	-10.7	6,962	6,545	-6.0	1,808	1,565	-13.4
Prostitution and commercialized vice	10,625	9,754	-8.2	101	145	+43.6	25,467	22,673	-11.0	488	442	-9.4
Sex offenses (except forcible rape and prostitution)	33,603	31,889	-5.1	5,872	5,580	-5.0	2,936	2,712	-7.6	698	698	0.0
Drug abuse violations	676,417	616,643	-8.8	79,558	67,710	-14.9	160,119	152,255	-4.9	16,149	14,041	-13.1
Gambling	1,874	1,591	-15.1	218	178	-18.3	346	330	-4.6	12	14	+16.7
Offenses against the family and children	26,014	25,552	-1.8	1,364	1,214	-11.0	13,249	13,374	+0.9	749	823	+9.9
Driving under the influence	458,693	432,537	-5.7	4,358	3,880	-11.0	148,281	145,950	-1.6	1,519	1,282	-15.6
Liquor laws	222,398	200,821	-9.7	35,018	31,283	-10.7	88,243	83,922	-4.9	21,879	20,696	-5.4
Drunkenness	307,414	286,295	-6.9	6,215	5,562	-10.5	63,277	63,064	-0.3	2,283	2,031	-11.0
Disorderly conduct	272,983	251,094	-8.0	63,057	55,549	-11.9	107,616	99,324	-7.7	33,919	30,594	-9.8
Vagrancy	17,270	15,673	-9.2	1,105	965	-12.7	4,172	3,590	-14.0	319	300	-6.0
All other offenses (except traffic)	1,424,104	1,359,811	-4.5	127,867	113,613	-11.1	459,305	451,762	-1.6	46,324	41,301	-10.8
Suspicion	478	506	+5.9	64	37	-42.2	152	146	-3.9	20	9	-55.0
Curfew and loitering law violations	44,966	36,072	-19.8	44,966	36,072	-19.8	18,933	15,185	-19.8	18,933	15,185	-19.8

* = Less than one-tenth of one percent.

[1] Does not include suspicion.

[2] Violent crimes are offenses of murder and nonnegligent manslaughter, forcible rape, robbery, and aggravated assault. Property crimes are offenses of burglary, larceny-theft, motor vehicle theft, and arson.

Table IV-18. Arrests, Cities, Distribution by Age, 2011

(Number, percent; 8,791 agencies; 2011 estimated population 163,760,401)

Offense charged	Total all ages	Ages under 15	Ages under 18	Ages 18 and over	Under 10	10–12	13–14	15	16	17	18	19	20
Total	7,139,104	256,392	928,321	6,210,783	5,559	55,370	195,463	178,080	226,306	267,543	329,628	353,115	341,666
Total percent distribution[1]	100.0	3.6	13.0	87.0	0.1	0.8	2.7	2.5	3.2	3.7	4.6	4.9	4.8
Murder and nonnegligent manslaughter	6,085	52	506	5,579	1	9	42	79	125	250	377	393	395
Forcible rape	10,837	545	1,553	9,284	5	155	385	273	324	411	462	483	441
Robbery	70,832	3,107	16,329	54,503	29	389	2,689	3,326	4,602	5,294	6,062	5,410	4,562
Aggravated assault	231,162	7,922	24,608	206,554	234	2,034	5,654	4,516	5,710	6,460	7,481	8,483	8,962
Burglary	166,221	10,307	37,188	129,033	285	2,146	7,876	7,332	9,110	10,439	11,759	10,335	8,746
Larceny-theft	815,356	48,915	171,212	644,144	814	10,933	37,168	33,217	41,923	47,157	50,330	44,585	37,760
Motor vehicle theft	38,262	1,750	8,605	29,657	13	180	1,557	1,977	2,366	2,512	2,415	2,146	1,790
Arson	6,457	1,742	2,980	3,477	175	570	997	502	416	320	248	214	220
Violent crime[2]	318,916	11,626	42,996	275,920	269	2,587	8,770	8,194	10,761	12,415	14,382	14,769	14,360
Violent crime percent distribution[1]	100.0	3.6	13.5	86.5	0.1	0.8	2.7	2.6	3.4	3.9	4.5	4.6	4.5
Property crime[2]	1,026,296	62,714	219,985	806,311	1,287	13,829	47,598	43,028	53,815	60,428	64,752	57,280	48,516
Property crime percent distribution[1]	100.0	6.1	21.4	78.6	0.1	1.3	4.6	4.2	5.2	5.9	6.3	5.6	4.7
Other assaults	716,626	42,785	111,019	605,607	1,128	11,121	30,536	21,273	23,503	23,458	22,220	23,628	25,539
Forgery and counterfeiting	40,470	124	963	39,507	2	25	97	148	197	494	1,175	1,707	1,896
Fraud	81,037	455	3,064	77,973	9	79	367	550	755	1,304	2,165	3,014	3,324
Embezzlement	9,380	20	265	9,115	0	5	15	14	65	166	420	628	641
Stolen property; buying, receiving, possessing	52,962	1,882	8,503	44,459	19	282	1,581	1,717	2,116	2,788	3,478	3,358	2,839
Vandalism	142,860	16,579	41,921	100,939	701	4,712	11,166	8,161	8,538	8,643	8,244	7,457	6,854
Weapons; carrying, possessing, etc.	92,728	5,606	17,702	75,026	280	1,566	3,760	3,177	3,999	4,920	5,731	5,556	5,091
Prostitution and commercialized vice	41,635	64	697	40,938	0	5	59	103	183	347	1,267	1,682	1,832
Sex offenses (except forcible rape and prostitution)	37,653	3,296	6,723	30,930	126	934	2,236	1,165	1,163	1,099	1,370	1,339	1,262
Drug abuse violations	871,342	15,849	90,586	780,756	90	2,001	13,758	16,013	24,019	34,705	51,935	54,373	50,796
Gambling	5,668	75	707	4,961	1	2	72	125	193	314	415	376	382
Offenses against the family and children	40,846	674	2,140	38,706	44	143	487	395	519	552	894	1,065	1,186
Driving under the influence	606,953	95	5,313	601,640	7	19	69	209	1,202	3,807	10,708	15,990	19,335
Liquor laws	314,311	5,329	54,206	260,105	43	461	4,825	8,016	15,324	25,537	51,246	58,596	50,028
Drunkenness	357,796	899	7,658	350,138	12	79	808	1,253	1,826	3,680	8,685	10,452	10,757
Disorderly conduct	381,490	35,015	91,862	289,628	485	8,351	26,179	18,844	19,467	18,536	16,200	15,299	14,789
Vagrancy	20,074	378	1,312	18,762	6	57	315	334	372	228	958	861	778
All other offenses (except traffic)	1,923,852	38,837	165,317	1,758,535	889	6,894	31,054	33,130	42,862	50,488	63,318	75,629	81,400
Suspicion	884	15	57	827	1	2	12	3	21	18	65	56	61
Curfew and loitering law violations	55,325	14,075	55,325	NA	160	2,216	11,699	12,228	15,406	13,616	NA	NA	NA

NA = Not available.

[1] Because of rounding, the percentages may not add to 100.0.

[2] Violent crimes are offenses of murder and nonnegligent manslaughter, forcible rape, robbery, and aggravated assault. Property crimes are offenses of burglary, larceny-theft, motor vehicle theft, and arson.

Table IV-18.   Arrests, Cities, Distribution by Age, 2011—*Continued*

(Number, percent; 8,791 agencies; 2011 estimated population 163,760,401)

Offense charged	21	22	23	24	25–29	30–34	35–39	40–44	45–49	50–54	55–59	60–64	65 and over
Total	313,421	287,085	263,214	245,965	1,042,817	784,707	569,484	530,049	480,942	352,452	181,982	81,385	52,871
Total percent distribution[1]	4.4	4.0	3.7	3.4	14.6	11.0	8.0	7.4	6.7	4.9	2.5	1.1	0.7
Murder and nonnegligent manslaughter	381	297	333	258	1,072	658	397	332	293	197	100	51	45
Forcible rape	479	388	340	336	1,567	1,200	997	878	722	506	245	122	118
Robbery	3,887	3,196	2,687	2,474	8,994	5,807	3,607	3,203	2,343	1,427	563	187	94
Aggravated assault	9,573	9,253	8,877	8,423	37,308	29,505	21,206	18,868	16,428	11,636	5,838	2,655	2,058
Burglary	7,603	6,550	5,671	5,093	20,815	15,180	10,500	10,033	8,411	5,024	2,240	714	359
Larceny-theft	32,817	29,127	25,657	23,702	100,512	76,515	56,047	53,983	47,898	33,924	17,495	7,932	5,860
Motor vehicle theft	1,588	1,403	1,366	1,224	5,262	4,105	2,799	2,377	1,683	936	363	145	55
Arson	160	130	129	127	544	401	312	277	281	211	127	51	45
Violent crime[2]	14,320	13,134	12,237	11,491	48,941	37,170	26,207	23,281	19,786	13,766	6,746	3,015	2,315
Violent crime percent distribution[1]	4.5	4.1	3.8	3.6	15.3	11.7	8.2	7.3	6.2	4.3	2.1	0.9	0.7
Property crime[2]	42,168	37,210	32,823	30,146	127,133	96,201	69,658	66,670	58,273	40,095	20,225	8,842	6,319
Property crime percent distribution[1]	4.1	3.6	3.2	2.9	12.4	9.4	6.8	6.5	5.7	3.9	2.0	0.9	0.6
Other assaults	28,376	27,425	25,877	24,878	110,149	86,529	63,865	57,301	48,777	32,880	15,848	7,023	5,292
Forgery and counterfeiting	1,640	1,668	1,656	1,657	7,756	6,311	4,416	3,749	2,710	1,789	839	347	191
Fraud	3,069	3,104	2,865	2,884	13,611	11,669	9,264	8,319	6,514	4,326	2,215	946	684
Embezzlement	576	487	449	377	1,514	1,095	905	740	563	384	197	100	39
Stolen property; buying, receiving, possessing	2,482	2,236	2,033	1,767	7,837	5,882	3,989	3,435	2,510	1,529	699	251	134
Vandalism	6,719	5,762	4,984	4,402	17,879	11,700	7,703	6,718	5,644	3,738	1,726	823	586
Weapons; carrying, possessing, etc.	4,788	4,305	3,860	3,568	14,021	9,184	5,618	4,287	3,539	2,689	1,411	770	608
Prostitution and commercialized vice	1,837	1,847	1,686	1,579	6,783	5,601	4,589	4,653	3,686	2,204	937	399	356
Sex offenses (except forcible rape and prostitution)	1,236	1,047	983	920	4,148	3,606	3,095	3,002	3,076	2,438	1,584	879	945
Drug abuse violations	45,589	40,655	36,844	34,350	139,362	100,144	64,961	57,086	48,665	32,850	15,112	5,793	2,241
Gambling	301	244	235	196	710	476	354	329	254	253	177	124	135
Offenses against the family and children	1,382	1,451	1,452	1,418	7,745	6,859	4,993	4,074	2,943	1,718	873	365	288
Driving under the influence	29,854	29,490	28,143	26,914	112,078	81,014	59,563	54,767	50,966	39,398	22,754	12,353	8,313
Liquor laws	8,467	5,549	4,351	3,561	13,913	10,707	9,006	10,676	12,497	11,019	6,199	2,737	1,553
Drunkenness	17,189	15,208	13,454	12,604	52,661	40,538	32,714	35,840	39,435	32,861	17,338	7,031	3,371
Disorderly conduct	18,152	15,700	13,677	12,144	47,789	33,253	24,384	22,902	22,459	17,224	8,943	3,915	2,798
Vagrancy	599	510	492	412	1,921	1,680	1,528	1,994	2,390	2,445	1,354	559	281
All other offenses (except traffic)	84,622	80,008	75,064	70,667	306,740	234,997	172,597	160,173	146,197	108,820	56,786	25,102	16,415
Suspicion	55	45	49	30	126	91	75	53	58	26	19	11	7
Curfew and loitering law violations	NA	NA	NA	NA	NA	NA	NA	NA	NA	NA	NA	NA	NA

NA = Not available.

[1] Because of rounding, the percentages may not add to 100.0.

[2] Violent crimes are offenses of murder and nonnegligent manslaughter, forcible rape, robbery, and aggravated assault. Property crimes are offenses of burglary, larceny-theft, motor vehicle theft, and arson.

Table IV-19. Arrests, Cities, Persons Under 15, 18, 21, and 25 Years of Age, 2011

(Number, percent; 8,791 agencies; 2011 estimated population 163,760,401)

Offense charged	Total all ages	Number of persons arrested				Percent of total all ages			
		Under 15	Under 18	Under 21	Under 25	Under 15	Under 18	Under 21	Under 25
Total	7,139,104	256,392	928,321	1,952,730	3,062,415	3.6	13.0	27.4	42.9
Murder and nonnegligent manslaughter	6,085	52	506	1,671	2,940	0.9	8.3	27.5	48.3
Forcible rape	10,837	545	1,553	2,939	4,482	5.0	14.3	27.1	41.4
Robbery	70,832	3,107	16,329	32,363	44,607	4.4	23.1	45.7	63.0
Aggravated assault	231,162	7,922	24,608	49,534	85,660	3.4	10.6	21.4	37.1
Burglary	166,221	10,307	37,188	68,028	92,945	6.2	22.4	40.9	55.9
Larceny-theft	815,356	48,915	171,212	303,887	415,190	6.0	21.0	37.3	50.9
Motor vehicle theft	38,262	1,750	8,605	14,956	20,537	4.6	22.5	39.1	53.7
Arson	6,457	1,742	2,980	3,662	4,208	27.0	46.2	56.7	65.2
Violent crime[1]	318,916	11,626	42,996	86,507	137,689	3.6	13.5	27.1	43.2
Property crime[1]	1,026,296	62,714	219,985	390,533	532,880	6.1	21.4	38.1	51.9
Other assaults	716,626	42,785	111,019	182,406	288,962	6.0	15.5	25.5	40.3
Forgery and counterfeiting	40,470	124	963	5,741	12,362	0.3	2.4	14.2	30.5
Fraud	81,037	455	3,064	11,567	23,489	0.6	3.8	14.3	29.0
Embezzlement	9,380	20	265	1,954	3,843	0.2	2.8	20.8	41.0
Stolen property; buying, receiving, possessing	52,962	1,882	8,503	18,178	26,696	3.6	16.1	34.3	50.4
Vandalism	142,860	16,579	41,921	64,476	86,343	11.6	29.3	45.1	60.4
Weapons; carrying, possessing, etc.	92,728	5,606	17,702	34,080	50,601	6.0	19.1	36.8	54.6
Prostitution and commercialized vice	41,635	64	697	5,478	12,427	0.2	1.7	13.2	29.8
Sex offenses (except forcible rape and prostitution)	37,653	3,296	6,723	10,694	14,880	8.8	17.9	28.4	39.5
Drug abuse violations	871,342	15,849	90,586	247,690	405,128	1.8	10.4	28.4	46.5
Gambling	5,668	75	707	1,880	2,856	1.3	12.5	33.2	50.4
Offenses against the family and children	40,846	674	2,140	5,285	10,988	1.7	5.2	12.9	26.9
Driving under the influence	606,953	95	5,313	51,346	165,747	*	0.9	8.5	27.3
Liquor laws	314,311	5,329	54,206	214,076	236,004	1.7	17.2	68.1	75.1
Drunkenness	357,796	899	7,658	37,552	96,007	0.3	2.1	10.5	26.8
Disorderly conduct	381,490	35,015	91,862	138,150	197,823	9.2	24.1	36.2	51.9
Vagrancy	20,074	378	1,312	3,909	5,922	1.9	6.5	19.5	29.5
All other offenses (except traffic)	1,923,852	38,837	165,317	385,664	696,025	2.0	8.6	20.0	36.2
Suspicion	884	15	57	239	418	1.7	6.4	27.0	47.3
Curfew and loitering law violations	55,325	14,075	55,325	55,325	55,325	25.4	100.0	100.0	100.0

* = Less than one-tenth of one percent.

[1] Violent crimes are offenses of murder and nonnegligent manslaughter, forcible rape, robbery, and aggravated assault. Property crimes are offenses of burglary, larceny-theft, motor vehicle theft, and arson.

Table IV-20. Arrests, Cities, Distribution by Sex, 2011

(Number, percent; 8,791 agencies; 2011 estimated population 163,760,401)

Offense charged	Number of persons arrested			Percent male	Percent female	Percent distribution[1]		
	Total	Male	Female			Total	Male	Female
Total	7,139,104	5,264,306	1,874,798	73.7	26.3	100.0	100.0	100.0
Murder and nonnegligent manslaughter	6,085	5,411	674	88.9	11.1	0.1	0.1	*
Forcible rape	10,837	10,710	127	98.8	1.2	0.2	0.2	*
Robbery	70,832	62,143	8,689	87.7	12.3	1.0	1.2	0.5
Aggravated assault	231,162	177,472	53,690	76.8	23.2	3.2	3.4	2.9
Burglary	166,221	139,732	26,489	84.1	15.9	2.3	2.7	1.4
Larceny-theft	815,356	452,166	363,190	55.5	44.5	11.4	8.6	19.4
Motor vehicle theft	38,262	31,414	6,848	82.1	17.9	0.5	0.6	0.4
Arson	6,457	5,285	1,172	81.8	18.2	0.1	0.1	0.1
Violent crime[2]	318,916	255,736	63,180	80.2	19.8	4.5	4.9	3.4
Property crime[2]	1,026,296	628,597	397,699	61.2	38.8	14.4	11.9	21.2
Other assaults	716,626	520,364	196,262	72.6	27.4	10.0	9.9	10.5
Forgery and counterfeiting	40,470	25,353	15,117	62.6	37.4	0.6	0.5	0.8
Fraud	81,037	49,307	31,730	60.8	39.2	1.1	0.9	1.7
Embezzlement	9,380	4,658	4,722	49.7	50.3	0.1	0.1	0.3
Stolen property; buying, receiving, possessing	52,962	42,096	10,866	79.5	20.5	0.7	0.8	0.6
Vandalism	142,860	115,371	27,489	80.8	19.2	2.0	2.2	1.5
Weapons; carrying, possessing, etc.	92,728	85,329	7,399	92.0	8.0	1.3	1.6	0.4
Prostitution and commercialized vice	41,635	12,653	28,982	30.4	69.6	0.6	0.2	1.5
Sex offenses (except forcible rape and prostitution)	37,653	34,635	3,018	92.0	8.0	0.5	0.7	0.2
Drug abuse violations	871,342	704,847	166,495	80.9	19.1	12.2	13.4	8.9
Gambling	5,668	5,096	572	89.9	10.1	0.1	0.1	*
Offenses against the family and children	40,846	26,859	13,987	65.8	34.2	0.6	0.5	0.7
Driving under the influence	606,953	455,176	151,777	75.0	25.0	8.5	8.6	8.1
Liquor laws	314,311	221,807	92,504	70.6	29.4	4.4	4.2	4.9
Drunkenness	357,796	293,550	64,246	82.0	18.0	5.0	5.6	3.4
Disorderly conduct	381,490	274,900	106,590	72.1	27.9	5.3	5.2	5.7
Vagrancy	20,074	16,323	3,751	81.3	18.7	0.3	0.3	0.2
All other offenses (except traffic)	1,923,852	1,451,829	472,023	75.5	24.5	26.9	27.6	25.2
Suspicion	884	682	202	77.1	22.9	*	*	*
Curfew and loitering law violations	55,325	39,138	16,187	70.7	29.3	0.8	0.7	0.9

* = Less than one tenth of one percent.

[1] Because of rounding, the percentages may not add to 100.0.

[2] Violent crimes are offenses of murder and nonnegligent manslaughter, forcible rape, robbery, and aggravated assault. Property crimes are offenses of burglary, larceny-theft, motor vehicle theft, and arson.

Table IV-21.　Arrests, Cities, Distribution by Race, 2011

(Number, percent; 8,791 agencies; 2011 estimated population 163,760,401)

Offense charged	Total arrests					Percent distribution[1]					Arrests under 18				
	Total	White	Black	American Indian or Alaskan Native	Asian or Pacific Islander	Total	White	Black	American Indian or Alaskan Native	Asian or Pacific Islander	Total	White	Black	American Indian or Alaskan Native	Asian or Pacific Islander
Total	7,112,156	4,763,093	2,174,403	107,332	67,328	100.0	67.0	30.6	1.5	0.9	923,785	599,508	302,583	12,262	9,432
Murder and nonnegligent manslaughter....................	6,072	2,601	3,329	69	73	100.0	42.8	54.8	1.1	1.2	505	209	293	3	0
Forcible rape	10,787	6,490	4,063	123	111	100.0	60.2	37.7	1.1	1.0	1,546	903	625	8	10
Robbery..............................	70,720	29,694	40,031	504	491	100.0	42.0	56.6	0.7	0.7	16,308	4,984	11,138	70	116
Aggravated assault..........................	230,587	140,821	83,879	3,192	2,695	100.0	61.1	36.4	1.4	1.2	24,536	13,468	10,582	277	209
Burglary..............................	165,849	104,236	58,890	1,312	1,411	100.0	62.8	35.5	0.8	0.9	37,085	21,317	15,189	241	338
Larceny-theft........................	812,403	551,616	237,763	13,626	9,398	100.0	67.9	29.3	1.7	1.2	170,362	108,509	56,779	2,638	2,436
Motor vehicle theft..................	38,171	22,896	14,432	471	372	100.0	60.0	37.8	1.2	1.0	8,580	4,440	3,971	92	77
Arson..................................	6,435	4,460	1,835	71	69	100.0	69.3	28.5	1.1	1.1	2,971	2,109	807	23	32
Violent crime[2]....................	318,166	179,606	131,302	3,888	3,370	100.0	56.5	41.3	1.2	1.1	42,895	19,564	22,638	358	335
Property crime[2]...................	1,022,858	683,208	312,920	15,480	11,250	100.0	66.8	30.6	1.5	1.1	218,998	136,375	76,746	2,994	2,883
Other assaults	714,191	446,161	250,022	11,116	6,892	100.0	62.5	35.0	1.6	1.0	110,596	64,710	43,847	1,258	781
Forgery and counterfeiting.............	40,340	25,768	13,896	223	453	100.0	63.9	34.4	0.6	1.1	961	622	324	4	11
Fraud..................................	80,686	50,281	28,914	741	750	100.0	62.3	35.8	0.9	0.9	3,046	1,745	1,235	35	31
Embezzlement	9,351	6,045	3,086	48	172	100.0	64.6	33.0	0.5	1.8	262	176	79	1	6
Stolen property; buying, receiving, possessing.....................	52,858	33,399	18,584	384	491	100.0	63.2	35.2	0.7	0.9	8,490	4,708	3,625	66	91
Vandalism.............................	142,263	100,941	37,541	2,422	1,359	100.0	71.0	26.4	1.7	1.0	41,708	31,468	9,276	578	386
Weapons; carrying, possessing, etc..	92,537	50,938	40,175	563	861	100.0	55.0	43.4	0.6	0.9	17,646	10,629	6,694	113	210
Prostitution and commercialized vice	41,558	22,054	18,345	242	917	100.0	53.1	44.1	0.6	2.2	695	232	454	1	8
Sex offenses (except forcible rape and prostitution)	37,546	25,966	10,587	546	447	100.0	69.2	28.2	1.5	1.2	6,694	4,515	2,071	53	55
Drug abuse violations	869,266	553,669	302,757	5,846	6,994	100.0	63.7	34.8	0.7	0.8	90,217	65,951	22,350	1,023	893
Gambling.............................	5,665	1,475	4,037	19	134	100.0	26.0	71.3	0.3	2.4	707	53	651	2	1
Offenses against the family and children	40,612	27,100	11,927	1,208	377	100.0	66.7	29.4	3.0	0.9	2,104	1,428	600	61	15
Driving under the influence	604,487	512,750	75,298	8,546	7,893	100.0	84.8	12.5	1.4	1.3	5,287	4,837	306	83	61
Liquor laws..........................	311,855	251,371	45,644	11,124	3,716	100.0	80.6	14.6	3.6	1.2	53,851	47,169	4,120	1,875	687
Drunkenness.........................	356,768	288,997	58,665	6,629	2,477	100.0	81.0	16.4	1.9	0.7	7,626	6,634	753	173	66
Disorderly conduct..........................	379,301	234,170	134,951	7,399	2,781	100.0	61.7	35.6	2.0	0.7	91,374	51,862	37,930	983	599
Vagrancy.............................	19,876	11,148	8,157	433	138	100.0	56.1	41.0	2.2	0.7	1,308	958	340	5	5
All other offenses (except traffic).............................	1,915,981	1,224,330	646,815	29,659	15,177	100.0	63.9	33.8	1.5	0.8	164,156	112,610	48,131	1,783	1,632
Suspicion	884	475	402	3	4	100.0	53.7	45.5	0.3	0.5	57	21	35	0	1
Curfew and loitering law violations.................	55,107	33,241	20,378	813	675	100.0	60.3	37.0	1.5	1.2	55,107	33,241	20,378	813	675

NA = Not available.

[1] Because of rounding, the percentages may not add to 100.0.

[2] Violent crimes are offenses of murder and nonnegligent manslaughter, forcible rape, robbery, and aggravated assault. Property crimes are offenses of burglary, larceny-theft, motor vehicle theft, and arson.

Table IV-21. Arrests, Cities, Distribution by Race, 2011—*Continued*

(Number, percent; 8,791 agencies; 2011 estimated population 163,760,401)

Offense charged	Percent distribution[1]					Arrests 18 years and over					Percent distribution[1]				
	Total	White	Black	American Indian or Alaskan Native	Asian or Pacific Islander	Total	White	Black	American Indian or Alaskan Native	Asian or Pacific Islander	Total	White	Black	American Indian or Alaskan Native	Asian or Pacific Islander
Total.................................	100.0	64.9	32.8	1.3	1.0	6,188,371	4,163,585	1,871,820	95,070	57,896	100.0	67.3	30.2	1.5	0.9
Murder and nonnegligent manslaughter........................	100.0	41.4	58.0	0.6	0.0	5,567	2,392	3,036	66	73	100.0	43.0	54.5	1.2	1.3
Forcible rape	100.0	58.4	40.4	0.5	0.6	9,241	5,587	3,438	115	101	100.0	60.5	37.2	1.2	1.1
Robbery...	100.0	30.6	68.3	0.4	0.7	54,412	24,710	28,893	434	375	100.0	45.4	53.1	0.8	0.7
Aggravated assault..........................	100.0	54.9	43.1	1.1	0.9	206,051	127,353	73,297	2,915	2,486	100.0	61.8	35.6	1.4	1.2
Burglary...	100.0	57.5	41.0	0.6	0.9	128,764	82,919	43,701	1,071	1,073	100.0	64.4	33.9	0.8	0.8
Larceny-theft	100.0	63.7	33.3	1.5	1.4	642,041	443,107	180,984	10,988	6,962	100.0	69.0	28.2	1.7	1.1
Motor vehicle theft.........................	100.0	51.7	46.3	1.1	0.9	29,591	18,456	10,461	379	295	100.0	62.4	35.4	1.3	1.0
Arson...	100.0	71.0	27.2	0.8	1.1	3,464	2,351	1,028	48	37	100.0	67.9	29.7	1.4	1.1
Violent crime[2]...............................	100.0	45.6	52.8	0.8	0.8	275,271	160,042	108,664	3,530	3,035	100.0	58.1	39.5	1.3	1.1
Property crime[2].............................	100.0	62.3	35.0	1.4	1.3	803,860	546,833	236,174	12,486	8,367	100.0	68.0	29.4	1.6	1.0
Other assaults	100.0	58.5	39.6	1.1	0.7	603,595	381,451	206,175	9,858	6,111	100.0	63.2	34.2	1.6	1.0
Forgery and counterfeiting..............	100.0	64.7	33.7	0.4	1.1	39,379	25,146	13,572	219	442	100.0	63.9	34.5	0.6	1.1
Fraud...	100.0	57.3	40.5	1.1	1.0	77,640	48,536	27,679	706	719	100.0	62.5	35.7	0.9	0.9
Embezzlement.................................	100.0	67.2	30.2	0.4	2.3	9,089	5,869	3,007	47	166	100.0	64.6	33.1	0.5	1.8
Stolen property; buying, receiving, possessing........................	100.0	55.5	42.7	0.8	1.1	44,368	28,691	14,959	318	400	100.0	64.7	33.7	0.7	0.9
Vandalism..	100.0	75.4	22.2	1.4	0.9	100,555	69,473	28,265	1,844	973	100.0	69.1	28.1	1.8	1.0
Weapons; carrying, possessing, etc..	100.0	60.2	37.9	0.6	1.2	74,891	40,309	33,481	450	651	100.0	53.8	44.7	0.6	0.9
Prostitution and commercialized vice	100.0	33.4	65.3	0.1	1.2	40,863	21,822	17,891	241	909	100.0	53.4	43.8	0.6	2.2
Sex offenses (except forcible rape and prostitution).....................	100.0	67.4	30.9	0.8	0.8	30,852	21,451	8,516	493	392	100.0	69.5	27.6	1.6	1.3
Drug abuse violations	100.0	73.1	24.8	1.1	1.0	779,049	487,718	280,407	4,823	6,101	100.0	62.6	36.0	0.6	0.8
Gambling..	100.0	7.5	92.1	0.3	0.1	4,958	1,422	3,386	17	133	100.0	28.7	68.3	0.3	2.7
Offenses against the family and children	100.0	67.9	28.5	2.9	0.7	38,508	25,672	11,327	1,147	362	100.0	66.7	29.4	3.0	0.9
Driving under the influence	100.0	91.5	5.8	1.6	1.2	599,200	507,913	74,992	8,463	7,832	100.0	84.8	12.5	1.4	1.3
Liquor laws......................................	100.0	87.6	7.7	3.5	1.3	258,004	204,202	41,524	9,249	3,029	100.0	79.1	16.1	3.6	1.2
Drunkenness....................................	100.0	87.0	9.9	2.3	0.9	349,142	282,363	57,912	6,456	2,411	100.0	80.9	16.6	1.8	0.7
Disorderly conduct.........................	100.0	56.8	41.5	1.1	0.7	287,927	182,308	97,021	6,416	2,182	100.0	63.3	33.7	2.2	0.8
Vagrancy..	100.0	73.2	26.0	0.4	0.4	18,568	10,190	7,817	428	133	100.0	54.9	42.1	2.3	0.7
All other offenses (except traffic)..	100.0	68.6	29.3	1.1	1.0	1,751,825	1,111,720	598,684	27,876	13,545	100.0	63.5	34.2	1.6	0.8
Suspicion	100.0	36.8	61.4	0.0	1.8	827	454	367	3	3	100.0	54.9	44.4	0.4	0.4
Curfew and loitering law violations	100.0	60.3	37.0	1.5	1.2	NA	NA	NA	NA	NA	NA	NA	NA	NA	NA

NA = Not available.

[1] Because of rounding, the percentages may not add to 100.0.

[2] Violent crimes are offenses of murder and nonnegligent manslaughter, forcible rape, robbery, and aggravated assault. Property crimes are offenses of burglary, larceny-theft, motor vehicle theft, and arson.

Table IV-22.   Arrest Trends, Metropolitan Counties, 2010–2011

(Number, percent change; 1,200 agencies; 2011 estimated population 46,615,313; 2010 estimated population 46,217,361)

Offense charged	Number of persons arrested								
	Total all ages			Under 18 years of age			18 years of age and over		
	2010	2011	Percent change	2010	2011	Percent change	2010	2011	Percent change
Total[1]	1,508,639	1,449,698	-3.9	148,236	135,033	-8.9	1,360,403	1,314,665	-3.4
Murder and nonnegligent manslaughter.............................	1,365	1,349	-1.2	113	88	-22.1	1,252	1,261	+0.7
Forcible rape..	2,335	2,199	-5.8	368	320	-13.0	1,967	1,879	-4.5
Robbery	8,250	7,555	-8.4	1,555	1,375	-11.6	6,695	6,180	-7.7
Aggravated assault...	51,365	48,030	-6.5	5,129	4,658	-9.2	46,236	43,372	-6.2
Burglary	35,619	35,837	+0.6	6,673	6,344	-4.9	28,946	29,493	+1.9
Larceny-theft..	105,130	109,030	+3.7	19,387	18,375	-5.2	85,743	90,655	+5.7
Motor vehicle theft	7,751	7,485	-3.4	1,474	1,320	-10.4	6,277	6,165	-1.8
Arson..	1,339	1,458	+8.9	422	525	+24.4	917	933	+1.7
Violent crime[2]..	63,315	59,133	-6.6	7,165	6,441	-10.1	56,150	52,692	-6.2
Property crime[2]	149,839	153,810	+2.7	27,956	26,564	-5.0	121,883	127,246	+4.4
Other assaults	153,363	148,775	-3.0	25,815	23,230	-10.0	127,548	125,545	-1.6
Forgery and counterfeiting	9,901	8,722	-11.9	170	177	+4.1	9,731	8,545	-12.2
Fraud..	31,077	26,632	-14.3	611	596	-2.5	30,466	26,036	-14.5
Embezzlement...	2,196	2,100	-4.4	59	40	-32.2	2,137	2,060	-3.6
Stolen property; buying, receiving, possessing.....................	11,800	11,718	-0.7	1,320	1,113	-15.7	10,480	10,605	+1.2
Vandalism...	25,396	24,805	-2.3	7,107	6,550	-7.8	18,289	18,255	-0.2
Weapons; carrying, possessing, etc.	15,464	15,132	-2.1	3,005	2,676	-10.9	12,459	12,456	*
Prostitution and commercialized vice...........................	2,379	1,942	-18.4	63	49	-22.2	2,316	1,893	-18.3
Sex offenses (except forcible rape and prostitution)...........	9,954	9,445	-5.1	1,879	1,705	-9.3	8,075	7,740	-4.1
Drug abuse violations...	190,469	182,779	-4.0	17,407	15,438	-11.3	173,062	167,341	-3.3
Gambling..	1,062	519	-51.1	29	39	+34.5	1,033	480	-53.5
Offenses against the family and children	29,521	31,610	+7.1	445	334	-24.9	29,076	31,276	+7.6
Driving under the influence......................................	165,330	159,326	-3.6	1,361	1,273	-6.5	163,969	158,053	-3.6
Liquor laws...	45,855	42,873	-6.5	10,731	10,043	-6.4	35,124	32,830	-6.5
Drunkenness..	42,210	38,417	-9.0	882	761	-13.7	41,328	37,656	-8.9
Disorderly conduct	43,599	40,957	-6.1	11,348	9,633	-15.1	32,251	31,324	-2.9
Vagrancy..	1,692	1,643	-2.9	140	44	-68.6	1,552	1,599	+3.0
All other offenses (except traffic)................................	511,120	486,464	-4.8	27,646	25,431	-8.0	483,474	461,033	-4.6
Suspicion	24	49	+104.2	5	9	+80.0	19	40	+110.5
Curfew and loitering law violations.............................	3,097	2,896	-6.5	3,097	2,896	-6.5	NA	NA	NA

* = Less than one tenth of one percent.

NA = Not available.

[1] Does not include suspicion.

[2] Violent crimes are offenses of murder and nonnegligent manslaughter, forcible rape, robbery, and aggravated assault. Property crimes are offenses of burglary, larceny-theft, motor vehicle theft, and arson.

Table IV-23.   Arrest Trends, Metropolitan Counties, by Age and Sex, 2010–2011

(Number, percent change; 1,200 agencies; 2011 estimated population 46,615,313; 2010 estimated population 46,217,361)

Offense charged	Male						Female					
	Total			Under 18			Total			Under 18		
	2010	2011	Percent change	2010	2011	Percent change	2010	2011	Percent change	2010	2011	Percent change
Total[1]	1,131,941	1,083,951	-4.2	107,333	97,411	-9.2	376,698	365,747	-2.9	40,903	37,622	-8.0
Murder and nonnegligent manslaughter	1,203	1,177	-2.2	95	74	-22.1	162	172	+6.2	18	14	-22.2
Forcible rape	2,308	2,180	-5.5	359	317	-11.7	27	19	-29.6	9	3	-66.7
Robbery	7,223	6,622	-8.3	1,415	1,251	-11.6	1,027	933	-9.2	140	124	-11.4
Aggravated assault	40,454	37,586	-7.1	3,864	3,483	-9.9	10,911	10,444	-4.3	1,265	1,175	-7.1
Burglary	30,199	30,390	+0.6	6,004	5,696	-5.1	5,420	5,447	+0.5	669	648	-3.1
Larceny-theft	64,300	66,987	+4.2	12,072	11,621	-3.7	40,830	42,043	+3.0	7,315	6,754	-7.7
Motor vehicle theft	6,369	6,142	-3.6	1,208	1,102	-8.8	1,382	1,343	-2.8	266	218	-18.0
Arson	1,114	1,196	+7.4	356	456	+28.1	225	262	+16.4	66	69	+4.5
Violent crime[2]	51,188	47,565	-7.1	5,733	5,125	-10.6	12,127	11,568	-4.6	1,432	1,316	-8.1
Property crime[2]	101,982	104,715	+2.7	19,640	18,875	-3.9	47,857	49,095	+2.6	8,316	7,689	-7.5
Other assaults	112,009	107,862	-3.7	17,158	15,238	-11.2	41,354	40,913	-1.1	8,657	7,992	-7.7
Forgery and counterfeiting	6,284	5,509	-12.3	133	128	-3.8	3,617	3,213	-11.2	37	49	+32.4
Fraud	17,080	15,182	-11.1	404	402	-0.5	13,997	11,450	-18.2	207	194	-6.3
Embezzlement	1,151	1,118	-2.9	40	21	-47.5	1,045	982	-6.0	19	19	0.0
Stolen property; buying, receiving, possessing	9,480	9,414	-0.7	1,102	934	-15.2	2,320	2,304	-0.7	218	179	-17.9
Vandalism	20,496	20,144	-1.7	5,955	5,515	-7.4	4,900	4,661	-4.9	1,152	1,035	-10.2
Weapons; carrying, possessing, etc.	13,950	13,730	-1.6	2,610	2,336	-10.5	1,514	1,402	-7.4	395	340	-13.9
Prostitution and commercialized vice	948	781	-17.6	11	10	-9.1	1,431	1,161	-18.9	52	39	-25.0
Sex offenses (except forcible rape and prostitution)	9,278	8,856	-4.5	1,679	1,556	-7.3	676	589	-12.9	200	149	-25.5
Drug abuse violations	149,542	142,682	-4.6	14,216	12,577	-11.5	40,927	40,097	-2.0	3,191	2,861	-10.3
Gambling	891	364	-59.1	16	18	+12.5	171	155	-9.4	13	21	+61.5
Offenses against the family and children	24,831	26,777	+7.8	311	223	-28.3	4,690	4,833	+3.0	134	111	-17.2
Driving under the influence	125,421	119,282	-4.9	986	918	-6.9	39,909	40,044	+0.3	375	355	-5.3
Liquor laws	32,086	29,546	-7.9	6,478	5,912	-8.7	13,769	13,327	-3.2	4,253	4,131	-2.9
Drunkenness	34,559	31,302	-9.4	660	577	-12.6	7,651	7,115	-7.0	222	184	-17.1
Disorderly conduct	31,377	29,597	-5.7	7,602	6,495	-14.6	12,222	11,360	-7.1	3,746	3,138	-16.2
Vagrancy	1,226	1,186	-3.3	100	40	-60.0	466	457	-1.9	40	4	-90.0
All other offenses (except traffic)	386,134	366,406	-5.1	20,471	18,578	-9.2	124,986	120,058	-3.9	7,175	6,853	-4.5
Suspicion	17	43	+152.9	5	8	+60.0	7	6	-14.3	0	1	NA
Curfew and loitering law violations	2,028	1,933	-4.7	2,028	1,933	-4.7	1,069	963	-9.9	1,069	963	-9.9

NA = Not available.

[1] Does not include suspicion.

[2] Violent crimes are offenses of murder and nonnegligent manslaughter, forcible rape, robbery, and aggravated assault. Property crimes are offenses of burglary, larceny-theft, motor vehicle theft, and arson.

Table IV-24. Arrests, Metropolitan Counties, Distribution by Age, 2011

(Number, percent; 1,280 agencies; 2011 estimated population 51,699,773)

Offense charged	Total all ages	Ages under 15	Ages under 18	Ages 18 and over	Under 10	10–12	13–14	15	16	17	18	19	20
Total	1,617,135	40,376	153,173	1,463,962	1,226	9,111	30,039	27,287	37,385	48,125	62,498	68,581	69,542
Total percent distribution[1]	100.0	2.5	9.5	90.5	0.1	0.6	1.9	1.7	2.3	3.0	3.9	4.2	4.3
Murder and nonnegligent manslaughter	1,566	15	111	1,455	0	1	14	19	35	42	85	87	83
Forcible rape	2,427	128	339	2,088	0	38	90	64	64	83	113	107	104
Robbery	9,744	298	1,879	7,865	6	45	247	375	519	687	792	793	629
Aggravated assault	54,787	1,744	5,350	49,437	47	459	1,238	976	1,180	1,450	1,639	1,788	1,922
Burglary	41,103	2,000	7,599	33,504	91	418	1,491	1,462	1,854	2,283	3,008	2,774	2,418
Larceny-theft	124,496	5,546	21,407	103,089	106	1,185	4,255	3,996	5,453	6,412	7,247	6,683	5,802
Motor vehicle theft	8,811	290	1,586	7,225	2	33	255	322	467	507	523	427	405
Arson	1,764	309	589	1,175	21	95	193	88	111	81	73	66	46
Violent crime[2]	68,524	2,185	7,679	60,845	53	543	1,589	1,434	1,798	2,262	2,629	2,775	2,738
Violent crime percent distribution[1]	100.0	3.2	11.2	88.8	0.1	0.8	2.3	2.1	2.6	3.3	3.8	4.0	4.0
Property crime[2]	176,174	8,145	31,181	144,993	220	1,731	6,194	5,868	7,885	9,283	10,851	9,950	8,671
Property crime percent distribution[1]	100.0	4.6	17.7	82.3	0.1	1.0	3.5	3.3	4.5	5.3	6.2	5.6	4.9
Other assaults	163,111	10,220	26,254	136,857	383	2,758	7,079	4,952	5,500	5,582	4,702	4,755	4,860
Forgery and counterfeiting	9,844	27	188	9,656	2	5	20	26	36	99	247	355	417
Fraud	29,665	98	626	29,039	3	17	78	84	185	259	509	671	779
Embezzlement	2,343	9	47	2,296	0	1	8	3	7	28	106	137	113
Stolen property; buying, receiving, possessing	13,759	244	1,326	12,433	5	34	205	248	351	483	762	770	624
Vandalism	28,225	2,608	7,555	20,670	139	721	1,748	1,361	1,700	1,886	1,816	1,541	1,297
Weapons; carrying, possessing, etc.	18,406	1,350	3,367	15,039	151	423	776	546	639	832	921	854	748
Prostitution and commercialized vice	2,387	5	61	2,326	0	1	4	10	16	30	49	107	101
Sex offenses (except forcible rape and prostitution)	10,705	915	1,976	8,729	27	257	631	341	338	382	399	400	401
Drug abuse violations	213,452	2,718	17,229	196,223	19	354	2,345	2,613	4,487	7,411	11,715	12,420	12,355
Gambling	600	7	41	559	0	2	5	6	14	14	12	7	20
Offenses against the family and children	33,272	111	384	32,888	7	22	82	70	73	130	243	313	412
Driving under the influence	171,732	26	1,325	170,407	0	5	21	55	253	991	2,731	4,048	4,873
Liquor laws	43,985	835	10,122	33,863	12	68	755	1,336	2,879	5,072	7,572	7,834	6,753
Drunkenness	38,633	114	768	37,865	0	10	104	117	173	364	1,141	1,227	1,298
Disorderly conduct	46,743	3,777	10,839	35,904	61	890	2,826	2,193	2,478	2,391	1,890	1,571	1,553
Vagrancy	2,248	18	70	2,178	0	2	16	6	12	34	72	79	93
All other offenses (except traffic)	539,545	6,097	28,406	511,139	136	1,160	4,801	5,202	7,371	9,736	14,128	18,763	21,434
Suspicion	77	5	24	53	0	1	4	4	7	8	3	4	2
Curfew and loitering law violations	3,705	862	3,705	-	8	106	748	812	1,183	848	NA	NA	NA

NA = Not available.

[1] Because of rounding, the percentages may not add to 100.0.

[2] Violent crimes are offenses of murder and nonnegligent manslaughter, forcible rape, robbery, and aggravated assault. Property crimes are offenses of burglary, larceny-theft, motor vehicle theft, and arson.

Table IV-24. Arrests, Metropolitan Counties, Distribution by Age, 2011—*Continued*

(Number, percent; 1,280 agencies; 2011 estimated population 51,699,773)

Offense charged	21	22	23	24	25–29	30–34	35–39	40–44	45–49	50–54	55–59	60–64	65 and over
Total	67,103	63,142	59,768	57,780	252,936	201,800	151,699	137,758	119,158	80,267	40,516	18,443	12,971
Total percent distribution[1]	4.1	3.9	3.7	3.6	15.6	12.5	9.4	8.5	7.4	5.0	2.5	1.1	0.8
Murder and nonnegligent manslaughter	89	66	64	77	242	208	108	107	79	63	48	29	20
Forcible rape	89	90	69	64	312	285	260	185	157	117	70	23	43
Robbery	571	441	427	410	1,375	874	498	390	335	184	104	30	12
Aggravated assault	2,087	1,944	1,842	1,874	8,404	7,131	5,308	4,937	4,379	3,146	1,608	776	652
Burglary	2,051	1,824	1,660	1,376	5,648	4,188	2,695	2,307	1,827	1,033	468	141	86
Larceny-theft	5,326	4,445	4,267	4,071	16,808	12,654	9,545	8,917	7,751	5,177	2,438	1,137	821
Motor vehicle theft	339	307	302	316	1,291	1,047	747	647	489	242	97	30	16
Arson	58	49	34	30	204	136	109	107	107	72	44	21	19
Violent crime[2]	2,836	2,541	2,402	2,425	10,333	8,498	6,174	5,619	4,950	3,510	1,830	858	727
Violent crime percent distribution[1]	4.1	3.7	3.5	3.5	15.1	12.4	9.0	8.2	7.2	5.1	2.7	1.3	1.1
Property crime[2]	7,774	6,625	6,263	5,793	23,951	18,025	13,096	11,978	10,174	6,524	3,047	1,329	942
Property crime percent distribution[1]	4.4	3.8	3.6	3.3	13.6	10.2	7.4	6.8	5.8	3.7	1.7	0.8	0.5
Other assaults	5,362	5,198	5,090	4,921	22,618	19,603	15,818	14,912	12,814	8,321	4,201	1,984	1,698
Forgery and counterfeiting	400	398	394	378	1,862	1,510	1,113	945	795	481	202	101	58
Fraud	798	863	827	879	4,676	4,673	4,231	3,591	2,938	1,798	977	464	365
Embezzlement	121	118	92	94	375	277	277	210	169	103	67	27	10
Stolen property; buying, receiving, possessing	634	581	518	496	2,159	1,792	1,261	1,136	845	512	209	72	62
Vandalism	1,239	1,043	909	841	3,453	2,463	1,662	1,497	1,300	796	438	212	163
Weapons; carrying, possessing, etc.	785	764	685	657	2,682	2,011	1,321	1,085	995	766	405	201	159
Prostitution and commercialized vice	120	114	119	88	396	307	229	236	195	129	76	33	27
Sex offenses (except forcible rape and prostitution)	345	298	256	229	1,114	990	905	895	809	585	430	315	358
Drug abuse violations	11,433	10,480	9,360	8,773	36,171	25,827	16,937	14,585	12,333	8,173	3,670	1,423	568
Gambling	10	6	10	9	61	54	72	63	57	57	42	41	38
Offenses against the family and children	557	654	790	772	5,229	6,161	5,630	4,927	3,716	2,172	848	335	129
Driving under the influence	7,232	7,415	7,336	7,175	30,765	22,938	17,560	17,048	16,246	12,250	7,003	3,523	2,264
Liquor laws	1,051	694	584	469	1,931	1,482	1,157	1,204	1,247	882	576	260	167
Drunkenness	1,567	1,531	1,432	1,355	5,762	4,673	3,676	3,931	4,212	3,266	1,685	686	423
Disorderly conduct	1,766	1,529	1,379	1,347	5,585	4,462	3,375	3,550	3,202	2,395	1,263	599	438
Vagrancy	74	101	84	77	316	271	214	236	224	163	113	40	21
All other offenses (except traffic)	22,997	22,187	21,237	20,999	93,485	75,774	56,986	50,107	41,937	27,382	13,430	5,939	4,354
Suspicion	2	2	1	3	12	9	5	3	0	2	4	1	0
Curfew and loitering law violations	NA	NA	NA	NA	NA	NA	NA	NA	NA	NA	NA	NA	NA

NA = Not available.

[1] Because of rounding, the percentages may not add to 100.0.

[2] Violent crimes are offenses of murder and nonnegligent manslaughter, forcible rape, robbery, and aggravated assault. Property crimes are offenses of burglary, larceny-theft, motor vehicle theft, and arson.

Table IV-25. Arrests, Metropolitan Counties, Persons Under 15, 18, 21, and 25 Years of Age, 2011

(Number, percent; 1,280 agencies; 2011 estimated population 51,699,773)

Offense charged	Total all ages	Number of persons arrested				Percent of total all ages			
		Under 15	Under 18	Under 21	Under 25	Under 15	Under 18	Under 21	Under 25
Total	1,617,135	40,376	153,173	353,794	601,587	2.5	9.5	21.9	37.2
Murder and nonnegligent manslaughter	1,566	15	111	366	662	1.0	7.1	23.4	42.3
Forcible rape	2,427	128	339	663	975	5.3	14.0	27.3	40.2
Robbery	9,744	298	1,879	4,093	5,942	3.1	19.3	42.0	61.0
Aggravated assault	54,787	1,744	5,350	10,699	18,446	3.2	9.8	19.5	33.7
Burglary	41,103	2,000	7,599	15,799	22,710	4.9	18.5	38.4	55.3
Larceny-theft	124,496	5,546	21,407	41,139	59,248	4.5	17.2	33.0	47.6
Motor vehicle theft	8,811	290	1,586	2,941	4,205	3.3	18.0	33.4	47.7
Arson	1,764	309	589	774	945	17.5	33.4	43.9	53.6
Violent crime[1]	68,524	2,185	7,679	15,821	26,025	3.2	11.2	23.1	38.0
Property crime[1]	176,174	8,145	31,181	60,653	87,108	4.6	17.7	34.4	49.4
Other assaults	163,111	10,220	26,254	40,571	61,142	6.3	16.1	24.9	37.5
Forgery and counterfeiting	9,844	27	188	1,207	2,777	0.3	1.9	12.3	28.2
Fraud	29,665	98	626	2,585	5,952	0.3	2.1	8.7	20.1
Embezzlement	2,343	9	47	403	828	0.4	2.0	17.2	35.3
Stolen property; buying, receiving, possessing	13,759	244	1,326	3,482	5,711	1.8	9.6	25.3	41.5
Vandalism	28,225	2,608	7,555	12,209	16,241	9.2	26.8	43.3	57.5
Weapons; carrying, possessing, etc.	18,406	1,350	3,367	5,890	8,781	7.3	18.3	32.0	47.7
Prostitution and commercialized vice	2,387	5	61	318	759	0.2	2.6	13.3	31.8
Sex offenses (except forcible rape and prostitution)	10,705	915	1,976	3,176	4,304	8.5	18.5	29.7	40.2
Drug abuse violations	213,452	2,718	17,229	53,719	93,765	1.3	8.1	25.2	43.9
Gambling	600	7	41	80	115	1.2	6.8	13.3	19.2
Offenses against the family and children	33,272	111	384	1,352	4,125	0.3	1.2	4.1	12.4
Driving under the influence	171,732	26	1,325	12,977	42,135	*	0.8	7.6	24.5
Liquor laws	43,985	835	10,122	32,281	35,079	1.9	23.0	73.4	79.8
Drunkenness	38,633	114	768	4,434	10,319	0.3	2.0	11.5	26.7
Disorderly conduct	46,743	3,777	10,839	15,853	21,874	8.1	23.2	33.9	46.8
Vagrancy	2,248	18	70	314	650	0.8	3.1	14.0	28.9
All other offenses (except traffic)	539,545	6,097	28,406	82,731	170,151	1.1	5.3	15.3	31.5
Suspicion	77	5	24	33	41	6.5	31.2	42.9	53.2
Curfew and loitering law violations	3,705	862	3,705	3,705	3,705	23.3	100.0	100.0	100.0

* = Less than one tenth of one percent.

[1] Violent crimes are offenses of murder and nonnegligent manslaughter, forcible rape, robbery, and aggravated assault. Property crimes are offenses of burglary, larceny-theft, motor vehicle theft, and arson.

Table IV-26. Arrests, Metropolitan Counties, Distribution by Sex, 2011

(Number, percent; 1,280 agencies; 2011 estimated population 51,699,773)

Offense charged	Number of persons arrested			Percent male	Percent female	Percent distribution[1]		
	Total	Male	Female			Total	Male	Female
Total	1,617,135	1,212,444	404,691	75.0	25.0	100.0	100.0	100.0
Murder and nonnegligent manslaughter	1,566	1,366	200	87.2	12.8	0.1	0.1	*
Forcible rape	2,427	2,409	18	99.3	0.7	0.2	0.2	*
Robbery	9,744	8,598	1,146	88.2	11.8	0.6	0.7	0.3
Aggravated assault	54,787	42,881	11,906	78.3	21.7	3.4	3.5	2.9
Burglary	41,103	34,916	6,187	84.9	15.1	2.5	2.9	1.5
Larceny-theft	124,496	76,102	48,394	61.1	38.9	7.7	6.3	12.0
Motor vehicle theft	8,811	7,236	1,575	82.1	17.9	0.5	0.6	0.4
Arson	1,764	1,427	337	80.9	19.1	0.1	0.1	0.1
Violent crime[2]	68,524	55,254	13,270	80.6	19.4	4.2	4.6	3.3
Property crime[2]	176,174	119,681	56,493	67.9	32.1	10.9	9.9	14.0
Other assaults	163,111	118,143	44,968	72.4	27.6	10.1	9.7	11.1
Forgery and counterfeiting	9,844	6,287	3,557	63.9	36.1	0.6	0.5	0.9
Fraud	29,665	17,100	12,565	57.6	42.4	1.8	1.4	3.1
Embezzlement	2,343	1,257	1,086	53.6	46.4	0.1	0.1	0.3
Stolen property; buying, receiving, possessing	13,759	11,089	2,670	80.6	19.4	0.9	0.9	0.7
Vandalism	28,225	22,966	5,259	81.4	18.6	1.7	1.9	1.3
Weapons; carrying, possessing, etc.	18,406	16,737	1,669	90.9	9.1	1.1	1.4	0.4
Prostitution and commercialized vice	2,387	1,021	1,366	42.8	57.2	0.1	0.1	0.3
Sex offenses (except forcible rape and prostitution)	10,705	10,047	658	93.9	6.1	0.7	0.8	0.2
Drug abuse violations	213,452	167,809	45,643	78.6	21.4	13.2	13.8	11.3
Gambling	600	437	163	72.8	27.2	*	*	*
Offenses against the family and children	33,272	28,127	5,145	84.5	15.5	2.1	2.3	1.3
Driving under the influence	171,732	128,842	42,890	75.0	25.0	10.6	10.6	10.6
Liquor laws	43,985	30,349	13,636	69.0	31.0	2.7	2.5	3.4
Drunkenness	38,633	31,533	7,100	81.6	18.4	2.4	2.6	1.8
Disorderly conduct	46,743	33,674	13,069	72.0	28.0	2.9	2.8	3.2
Vagrancy	2,248	1,658	590	73.8	26.2	0.1	0.1	0.1
All other offenses (except traffic)	539,545	407,846	131,699	75.6	24.4	33.4	33.6	32.5
Suspicion	77	64	13	83.1	16.9	*	*	*
Curfew and loitering law violations	3,705	2,523	1,182	68.1	31.9	0.2	0.2	0.3

* = Less than one tenth of one percent.

[1] Because of rounding, the percentages may not add to 100.0.

[2] Violent crimes are offenses of murder and nonnegligent manslaughter, forcible rape, robbery, and aggravated assault. Property crimes are offenses of burglary, larceny-theft, motor vehicle theft, and arson.

Table IV-27. Arrests, Metropolitan Counties, Distribution by Race, 2011

(Number, percent; 1,280 agencies; 2011 estimated population 51,699,773)

Offense charged	Total arrests					Percent distribution[1]					Arrests under 18				
	Total	White	Black	American Indian or Alaskan Native	Asian or Pacific Islander	Total	White	Black	American Indian or Alaskan Native	Asian or Pacific Islander	Total	White	Black	American Indian or Alaskan Native	Asian or Pacific Islander
Total	1,612,734	1,175,314	415,210	11,047	11,163	100.0	72.9	25.7	0.7	0.7	152,668	100,293	50,333	840	1,202
Murder and nonnegligent manslaughter......................	1,565	908	639	6	12	100.0	58.0	40.8	0.4	0.8	111	66	45	0	0
Forcible rape	2,420	1,838	558	12	12	100.0	76.0	23.1	0.5	0.5	339	240	96	1	2
Robbery.............................	9,738	4,592	5,059	42	45	100.0	47.2	52.0	0.4	0.5	1,877	524	1,345	6	2
Aggravated assault	54,720	38,860	15,077	415	368	100.0	71.0	27.6	0.8	0.7	5,339	2,993	2,273	37	36
Burglary............................	41,053	30,235	10,467	161	190	100.0	73.6	25.5	0.4	0.5	7,589	4,742	2,761	36	50
Larceny-theft	124,249	85,021	37,539	580	1,109	100.0	68.4	30.2	0.5	0.9	21,358	11,999	9,013	80	266
Motor vehicle theft......................	8,795	6,458	2,253	50	34	100.0	73.4	25.6	0.6	0.4	1,581	1,010	558	8	5
Arson	1,762	1,344	401	9	8	100.0	76.3	22.8	0.5	0.5	589	459	126	0	4
Violent crime[2]...................	68,443	46,198	21,333	475	437	100.0	67.5	31.2	0.7	0.6	7,666	3,823	3,759	44	40
Property crime[2]...................	175,859	123,058	50,660	800	1,341	100.0	70.0	28.8	0.5	0.8	31,117	18,210	12,458	124	325
Other assaults	162,747	117,612	43,042	1,028	1,065	100.0	72.3	26.4	0.6	0.7	26,182	14,963	10,938	137	144
Forgery and counterfeiting.............	9,826	6,531	3,177	21	97	100.0	66.5	32.3	0.2	1.0	188	123	60	1	4
Fraud.................................	29,586	20,632	8,633	127	194	100.0	69.7	29.2	0.4	0.7	624	420	198	2	4
Embezzlement	2,337	1,462	834	12	29	100.0	62.6	35.7	0.5	1.2	47	26	21	0	0
Stolen property; buying, receiving, possessing......................	13,738	9,997	3,623	61	57	100.0	72.8	26.4	0.4	0.4	1,325	772	540	1	12
Vandalism.........................	28,159	21,754	6,057	180	168	100.0	77.3	21.5	0.6	0.6	7,520	5,672	1,762	40	46
Weapons; carrying, possessing, etc..	18,376	12,189	6,004	72	111	100.0	66.3	32.7	0.4	0.6	3,361	2,034	1,271	19	37
Prostitution and commercialized vice	2,381	1,379	863	8	131	100.0	57.9	36.2	0.3	5.5	61	32	29	0	0
Sex offenses (except forcible rape and prostitution)......................	10,688	8,361	2,161	72	94	100.0	78.2	20.2	0.7	0.9	1,970	1,386	562	9	13
Drug abuse violations	212,965	155,615	55,032	956	1,362	100.0	73.1	25.8	0.4	0.6	17,178	13,184	3,675	128	191
Gambling...........................	597	285	263	13	36	100.0	47.7	44.1	2.2	6.0	41	24	11	0	6
Offenses against the family and children	33,172	19,603	13,247	139	183	100.0	59.1	39.9	0.4	0.6	381	264	115	1	1
Driving under the influence	170,950	146,126	21,757	1,282	1,785	100.0	85.5	12.7	0.7	1.0	1,307	1,206	79	16	6
Liquor laws.......................	43,630	37,994	4,698	536	402	100.0	87.1	10.8	1.2	0.9	10,038	9,314	505	114	105
Drunkenness	38,601	33,614	4,365	340	282	100.0	87.1	11.3	0.9	0.7	764	666	81	13	4
Disorderly conduct........................	46,609	30,614	15,466	299	230	100.0	65.7	33.2	0.6	0.5	10,812	5,877	4,845	52	38
Vagrancy...........................	2,247	1,649	586	5	7	100.0	73.4	26.1	0.2	0.3	70	41	29	0	0
All other offenses (except traffic)	538,052	377,913	152,414	4,616	3,109	100.0	70.2	28.3	0.9	0.6	28,298	19,556	8,424	135	183
Suspicion	77	34	42	1	0	100.0	44.2	54.5	1.3	0.0	24	6	18	0	0
Curfew and loitering law violations...........................	3,694	2,694	953	4	43	100.0	72.9	25.8	0.1	1.2	3,694	2,694	953	4	43

NA = Not available.

[1] Because of rounding, the percentages may not add to 100.0.

[2] Violent crimes are offenses of murder and nonnegligent manslaughter, forcible rape, robbery, and aggravated assault. Property crimes are offenses of burglary, larceny-theft, motor vehicle theft, and arson.

Table IV-27. Arrests, Metropolitan Counties, Distribution by Race, 2011—*Continued*

(Number, percent; 1,280 agencies; 2011 estimated population 51,699,773)

Offense charged	Percent distribution[1]					Arrests under 18					Percent distribution[1]				
	Total	White	Black	American Indian or Alaskan Native	Asian or Pacific Islander	Total	White	Black	American Indian or Alaskan Native	Asian or Pacific Islander	Total	White	Black	American Indian or Alaskan Native	Asian or Pacific Islander
Total	100.0	65.7	33.0	0.6	0.8	1,460,066	1,075,021	364,877	10,207	9,961	100.0	73.6	25.0	0.7	0.7
Murder and nonnegligent manslaughter	100.0	59.5	40.5	0.0	0.0	1,454	842	594	6	12	100.0	57.9	40.9	0.4	0.8
Forcible rape	100.0	70.8	28.3	0.3	0.6	2,081	1,598	462	11	10	100.0	76.8	22.2	0.5	0.5
Robbery	100.0	27.9	71.7	0.3	0.1	7,861	4,068	3,714	36	43	100.0	51.7	47.2	0.5	0.5
Aggravated assault	100.0	56.1	42.6	0.7	0.7	49,381	35,867	12,804	378	332	100.0	72.6	25.9	0.8	0.7
Burglary	100.0	62.5	36.4	0.5	0.7	33,464	25,493	7,706	125	140	100.0	76.2	23.0	0.4	0.4
Larceny-theft	100.0	56.2	42.2	0.4	1.2	102,891	73,022	28,526	500	843	100.0	71.0	27.7	0.5	0.8
Motor vehicle theft	100.0	63.9	35.3	0.5	0.3	7,214	5,448	1,695	42	29	100.0	75.5	23.5	0.6	0.4
Arson	100.0	77.9	21.4	0.0	0.7	1,173	885	275	9	4	100.0	75.4	23.4	0.8	0.3
Violent crime[2]	100.0	49.9	49.0	0.6	0.5	60,777	42,375	17,574	431	397	100.0	69.7	28.9	0.7	0.7
Property crime[2]	100.0	58.5	40.0	0.4	1.0	144,742	104,848	38,202	676	1,016	100.0	72.4	26.4	0.5	0.7
Other assaults	100.0	57.1	41.8	0.5	0.5	136,565	102,649	32,104	891	921	100.0	75.2	23.5	0.7	0.7
Forgery and counterfeiting	100.0	65.4	31.9	0.5	2.1	9,638	6,408	3,117	20	93	100.0	66.5	32.3	0.2	1.0
Fraud	100.0	67.3	31.7	0.3	0.6	28,962	20,212	8,435	125	190	100.0	69.8	29.1	0.4	0.7
Embezzlement	100.0	55.3	44.7	0.0	0.0	2,290	1,436	813	12	29	100.0	62.7	35.5	0.5	1.3
Stolen property; buying, receiving, possessing	100.0	58.3	40.8	0.1	0.9	12,413	9,225	3,083	60	45	100.0	74.3	24.8	0.5	0.4
Vandalism	100.0	75.4	23.4	0.5	0.6	20,639	16,082	4,295	140	122	100.0	77.9	20.8	0.7	0.6
Weapons; carrying, possessing, etc.	100.0	60.5	37.8	0.6	1.1	15,015	10,155	4,733	53	74	100.0	67.6	31.5	0.4	0.5
Prostitution and commercialized vice	100.0	52.5	47.5	0.0	0.0	2,320	1,347	834	8	131	100.0	58.1	35.9	0.3	5.6
Sex offenses (except forcible rape and prostitution)	100.0	70.4	28.5	0.5	0.7	8,718	6,975	1,599	63	81	100.0	80.0	18.3	0.7	0.9
Drug abuse violations	100.0	76.7	21.4	0.7	1.1	195,787	142,431	51,357	828	1,171	100.0	72.7	26.2	0.4	0.6
Gambling	100.0	58.5	26.8	0.0	14.6	556	261	252	13	30	100.0	46.9	45.3	2.3	5.4
Offenses against the family and children	100.0	69.3	30.2	0.3	0.3	32,791	19,339	13,132	138	182	100.0	59.0	40.0	0.4	0.6
Driving under the influence	100.0	92.3	6.0	1.2	0.5	169,643	144,920	21,678	1,266	1,779	100.0	85.4	12.8	0.7	1.0
Liquor laws	100.0	92.8	5.0	1.1	1.0	33,592	28,680	4,193	422	297	100.0	85.4	12.5	1.3	0.9
Drunkenness	100.0	87.2	10.6	1.7	0.5	37,837	32,948	4,284	327	278	100.0	87.1	11.3	0.9	0.7
Disorderly conduct	100.0	54.4	44.8	0.5	0.4	35,797	24,737	10,621	247	192	100.0	69.1	29.7	0.7	0.5
Vagrancy	100.0	58.6	41.4	0.0	0.0	2,177	1,608	557	5	7	100.0	73.9	25.6	0.2	0.3
All other offenses (except traffic)	100.0	69.1	29.8	0.5	0.6	509,754	358,357	143,990	4,481	2,926	100.0	70.3	28.2	0.9	0.6
Suspicion	100.0	25.0	75.0	0.0	0.0	53	28	24	1	0	100.0	52.8	45.3	1.9	0.0
Curfew and loitering law violations	100.0	72.9	25.8	0.1	1.2	NA	NA	NA	NA	NA	NA	NA	NA	NA	NA

NA = Not available.

[1] Because of rounding, the percentages may not add to 100.0.

[2] Violent crimes are offenses of murder and nonnegligent manslaughter, forcible rape, robbery, and aggravated assault. Property crimes are offenses of burglary, larceny-theft, motor vehicle theft, and arson.

Table IV-28.   Arrest Trends, Nonmetropolitan Counties, 2010–2011

(Number, percent change; 1,829 agencies; 2011 estimated population 22,667,880; 2010 estimated population 22,480,585)

Offense charged	Number of persons arrested								
	Total all ages			Under 18 years of age			18 years of age and over		
	2010	2011	Percent change	2010	2011	Percent change	2010	2011	Percent change
Total[1]	783,271	759,531	-3.0	50,454	45,759	-9.3	732,817	713,772	-2.6
Murder and nonnegligent manslaughter	619	649	+4.8	24	33	+37.5	595	616	+3.5
Forcible rape	1,444	1,368	-5.3	190	173	-8.9	1,254	1,195	-4.7
Robbery	2,027	1,872	-7.6	168	147	-12.5	1,859	1,725	-7.2
Aggravated assault	19,841	19,101	-3.7	1,354	1,220	-9.9	18,487	17,881	-3.3
Burglary	19,789	20,247	+2.3	2,932	2,722	-7.2	16,857	17,525	+4.0
Larceny-theft	36,177	39,528	+9.3	4,665	4,322	-7.4	31,512	35,206	+11.7
Motor vehicle theft	3,633	3,799	+4.6	667	562	-15.7	2,966	3,237	+9.1
Arson	791	736	-7.0	181	134	-26.0	610	602	-1.3
Violent crime[2]	23,931	22,990	-3.9	1,736	1,573	-9.4	22,195	21,417	-3.5
Property crime[2]	60,390	64,310	+6.5	8,445	7,740	-8.3	51,945	56,570	+8.9
Other assaults	75,636	73,091	-3.4	8,336	7,810	-6.3	67,300	65,281	-3.0
Forgery and counterfeiting	4,102	3,547	-13.5	53	44	-17.0	4,049	3,503	-13.5
Fraud	19,002	16,872	-11.2	290	210	-27.6	18,712	16,662	-11.0
Embezzlement	983	737	-25.0	7	13	+85.7	976	724	-25.8
Stolen property; buying, receiving, possessing	4,595	5,003	+8.9	388	417	+7.5	4,207	4,586	+9.0
Vandalism	12,168	11,745	-3.5	2,714	2,672	-1.5	9,454	9,073	-4.0
Weapons; carrying, possessing, etc.	6,481	6,644	+2.5	643	607	-5.6	5,838	6,037	+3.4
Prostitution and commercialized vice	178	141	-20.8	4	5	+25.0	174	136	-21.8
Sex offenses (except forcible rape and prostitution)	4,919	4,580	-6.9	931	863	-7.3	3,988	3,717	-6.8
Drug abuse violations	93,321	87,706	-6.0	5,253	4,898	-6.8	88,068	82,808	-6.0
Gambling	198	245	+23.7	3	18	+500.0	195	227	+16.4
Offenses against the family and children	12,801	13,405	+4.7	230	205	-10.9	12,571	13,200	+5.0
Driving under the influence	153,048	147,526	-3.6	1,240	1,071	-13.6	151,808	146,455	-3.5
Liquor laws	28,347	25,380	-10.5	6,098	5,377	-11.8	22,249	20,003	-10.1
Drunkenness	19,664	18,355	-6.7	322	299	-7.1	19,342	18,056	-6.6
Disorderly conduct	21,430	19,991	-6.7	3,864	3,323	-14.0	17,566	16,668	-5.1
Vagrancy	301	229	-23.9	12	15	+25.0	289	214	-26.0
All other offenses (except traffic)	241,361	236,693	-1.9	9,470	8,258	-12.8	231,891	228,435	-1.5
Suspicion	93	157	+68.8	2	36	+1,700.0	91	121	+33.0
Curfew and loitering law violations	415	341	-17.8	415	341	-17.8	NA	NA	NA

NA = Not available.

[1] Does not include suspicion.

[2] Violent crimes are offenses of murder and nonnegligent manslaughter, forcible rape, robbery, and aggravated assault. Property crimes are offenses of burglary, larceny-theft, motor vehicle theft, and arson.

Table IV-29. Arrest Trends, Nonmetropolitan Counties, by Age and Sex, 2010–2011

(Number, percent; 1,829 agencies; 2011 estimated population 22,667,880; 2010 estimated population 22,480,585)

Offense charged	Male						Female					
	Total			Under 18			Total			Under 18		
	2010	2011	Percent change	2010	2011	Percent change	2010	2011	Percent change	2010	2011	Percent change
Total[1]	594,096	572,344	-3.7	36,767	33,266	-9.5	189,175	187,187	-1.1	13,687	12,493	-8.7
Murder and nonnegligent manslaughter	529	546	+3.2	21	27	+28.6	90	103	+14.4	3	6	+100.0
Forcible rape	1,416	1,343	-5.2	185	169	-8.6	28	25	-10.7	5	4	-20.0
Robbery	1,769	1,655	-6.4	155	136	-12.3	258	217	-15.9	13	11	-15.4
Aggravated assault	16,024	15,463	-3.5	1,067	960	-10.0	3,817	3,638	-4.7	287	260	-9.4
Burglary	17,078	17,289	+1.2	2,662	2,481	-6.8	2,711	2,958	+9.1	270	241	-10.7
Larceny-theft	24,784	27,035	+9.1	3,263	3,078	-5.7	11,393	12,493	+9.7	1,402	1,244	-11.3
Motor vehicle theft	2,996	3,150	+5.1	524	456	-13.0	637	649	+1.9	143	106	-25.9
Arson	654	641	-2.0	159	117	-26.4	137	95	-30.7	22	17	-22.7
Violent crime[2]	19,738	19,007	-3.7	1,428	1,292	-9.5	4,193	3,983	-5.0	308	281	-8.8
Property crime[2]	45,512	48,115	+5.7	6,608	6,132	-7.2	14,878	16,195	+8.9	1,837	1,608	-12.5
Other assaults	55,851	53,368	-4.4	5,532	5,029	-9.1	19,785	19,723	-0.3	2,804	2,781	-0.8
Forgery and counterfeiting	2,473	2,013	-18.6	40	31	-22.5	1,629	1,534	-5.8	13	13	0.0
Fraud	10,113	8,952	-11.5	192	120	-37.5	8,889	7,920	-10.9	98	90	-8.2
Embezzlement	396	369	-6.8	7	10	+42.9	587	368	-37.3	0	3	
Stolen property; buying, receiving, possessing	3,829	4,075	+6.4	335	335	0.0	766	928	+21.1	53	82	+54.7
Vandalism	9,921	9,598	-3.3	2,274	2,249	-1.1	2,247	2,147	-4.5	440	423	-3.9
Weapons; carrying, possessing, etc.	5,983	6,128	+2.4	580	535	-7.8	498	516	+3.6	63	72	+14.3
Prostitution and commercialized vice	102	87	-14.7	4	4	0.0	76	54	-28.9	0	1	
Sex offenses (except forcible rape and prostitution)	4,604	4,282	-7.0	843	764	-9.4	315	298	-5.4	88	99	+12.5
Drug abuse violations	72,217	67,600	-6.4	4,213	3,917	-7.0	21,104	20,106	-4.7	1,040	981	-5.7
Gambling	167	192	+15.0	2	13	+550.0	31	53	+71.0	1	5	+400.0
Offenses against the family and children	10,128	10,651	+5.2	158	137	-13.3	2,673	2,754	+3.0	72	68	-5.6
Driving under the influence	119,463	114,092	-4.5	977	789	-19.2	33,585	33,434	-0.4	263	282	+7.2
Liquor laws	19,850	17,680	-10.9	3,656	3,231	-11.6	8,497	7,700	-9.4	2,442	2,146	-12.1
Drunkenness	15,402	14,350	-6.8	225	228	+1.3	4,262	4,005	-6.0	97	71	-26.8
Disorderly conduct	15,485	14,297	-7.7	2,566	2,257	-12.0	5,945	5,694	-4.2	1,298	1,066	-17.9
Vagrancy	238	193	-18.9	8	14	+75.0	63	36	-42.9	4	1	-75.0
All other offenses (except traffic)	182,357	177,079	-2.9	6,852	5,963	-13.0	59,004	59,614	+1.0	2,618	2,295	-12.3
Suspicion	77	121	+57.1	1	19	+1,800.0	16	36	+125.0	1	17	+1,600.0
Curfew and loitering law violations	267	216	-19.1	267	216	-19.1	148	125	-15.5	148	125	-15.5

[1] Does not include suspicion.

[2] Violent crimes are offenses of murder and nonnegligent manslaughter, forcible rape, robbery, and aggravated assault. Property crimes are offenses of burglary, larceny-theft, motor vehicle theft, and arson.

Table IV-30. Arrests, Nonmetropolitan Counties, Distribution by Age, 2011

(Number, percent; 1,952 agencies; 2011 estimated population 23,492,803)

Offense charged	Total all ages	Ages under 15	Ages under 18	Ages 18 and over	Under 10	10–12	13–14	15	16	17	18	19	20
Total	781,434	11,096	47,962	733,472	455	2,712	7,929	7,688	11,888	17,290	27,391	31,794	32,974
Total percent distribution[1]	100.0	1.4	6.1	93.9	0.1	0.3	1.0	1.0	1.5	2.2	3.5	4.1	4.2
Murder and nonnegligent manslaughter	708	5	34	674	0	1	4	8	9	12	34	31	35
Forcible rape	1,415	63	179	1,236	0	16	47	39	33	44	76	72	76
Robbery	1,981	12	169	1,812	0	1	11	16	43	98	145	166	136
Aggravated assault	19,990	370	1,307	18,683	16	102	252	202	289	446	554	614	684
Burglary	21,077	655	2,867	18,210	34	179	442	430	749	1,033	1,520	1,503	1,240
Larceny-theft	41,264	1,138	4,540	36,724	30	298	810	747	1,101	1,554	2,235	2,136	1,935
Motor vehicle theft	3,954	110	595	3,359	0	15	95	150	171	164	220	200	176
Arson	773	66	145	628	3	29	34	24	23	32	46	60	76
Violent crime[2]	24,094	450	1,689	22,405	16	120	314	265	374	600	809	883	931
Violent crime percent distribution[1]	100	2	7	93	0	1	1	1	2	3	3	4	4
Property crime[2]	67,068	1,969	8,147	58,921	67	521	1,381	1,351	2,044	2,783	4,021	3,899	3,427
Property crime percent distribution[1]	100	3	12	88	0	1	2	2	3	4	6	6	5
Other assaults	75,883	2,679	8,151	67,732	117	739	1,823	1,417	1,950	2,105	2,080	2,117	2,272
Forgery and counterfeiting	3,669	6	50	3,619	0	2	4	6	11	27	73	128	136
Fraud	17,498	37	222	17,276	1	11	25	31	59	95	226	344	424
Embezzlement	773	3	13	760	0	2	1	2	2	6	18	35	24
Stolen property; buying, receiving, possessing	5,169	91	440	4,729	2	14	75	74	115	160	239	258	257
Vandalism	12,118	937	2,753	9,365	63	292	582	462	611	743	745	722	573
Weapons; carrying, possessing, etc.	6,938	246	661	6,277	10	73	163	106	147	162	239	206	256
Prostitution and commercialized vice	152	1	5	147	0	1	0	0	3	1	7	7	4
Sex offenses (except forcible rape and prostitution)	4,690	431	885	3,805	29	134	268	152	145	157	234	211	210
Drug abuse violations	90,289	634	5,077	85,212	8	73	553	712	1,355	2,376	4,290	5,064	4,973
Gambling	249	1	18	231	0	0	1	0	12	5	11	27	31
Offenses against the family and children	13,845	74	224	13,621	5	15	54	39	48	63	146	184	241
Driving under the influence	151,218	9	1,082	150,136	0	0	9	34	251	788	2,453	3,823	4,613
Liquor laws	25,607	456	5,490	20,117	4	30	422	765	1,538	2,731	4,319	4,555	4,125
Drunkenness	18,432	25	319	18,113	3	1	21	46	77	171	526	524	576
Disorderly conduct	21,461	1,156	3,602	17,859	49	268	839	693	871	882	870	745	723
Vagrancy	254	4	28	226	0	0	4	4	5	15	5	14	12
All other offenses (except traffic)	241,469	1,776	8,701	232,768	80	394	1,302	1,448	2,168	3,309	6,069	8,039	9,158
Suspicion	189	15	36	153	1	6	8	5	13	3	11	9	8
Curfew and loitering law violations	369	96	369	NA	0	16	80	76	89	108	NA	NA	NA

NA = Not available.

[1] Because of rounding, the percentages may not add to 100.0.

[2] Violent crimes are offenses of murder and nonnegligent manslaughter, forcible rape, robbery, and aggravated assault. Property crimes are offenses of burglary, larceny-theft, motor vehicle theft, and arson.

Table IV-30. Arrests, Nonmetropolitan Counties, Distribution by Age, 2011—*Continued*

(Number, percent; 1,952 agencies; 2011 estimated population 23,492,803)

Offense charged	21	22	23	24	25–29	30–34	35–39	40–44	45–49	50–54	55–59	60–64	65 and over
Total	31,099	29,777	28,571	27,481	126,453	104,379	78,949	70,052	60,246	41,888	22,356	11,291	8,771
Total percent distribution[1]	4.0	3.8	3.7	3.5	16.2	13.4	10.1	9.0	7.7	5.4	2.9	1.4	1.1
Murder and nonnegligent manslaughter	24	25	24	27	108	93	62	51	51	47	29	16	17
Forcible rape	72	51	33	37	174	135	142	118	96	55	40	24	35
Robbery	119	118	104	72	345	225	154	95	65	34	20	10	4
Aggravated assault	707	705	628	657	3,071	2,718	2,132	1,879	1,673	1,219	687	390	365
Burglary	1,089	1,002	898	818	3,398	2,451	1,528	1,137	826	467	198	75	60
Larceny-theft	1,819	1,683	1,570	1,538	6,499	5,099	3,596	3,044	2,487	1,599	778	376	330
Motor vehicle theft	189	168	132	119	610	492	363	314	198	103	40	20	15
Arson	20	36	23	11	70	53	58	55	45	36	18	9	12
Violent crime[2]	922	899	789	793	3,698	3,171	2,490	2,143	1,885	1,355	776	440	421
Violent crime percent distribution[1]	4	4	3	3	15	13	10	9	8	6	3	2	2
Property crime[2]	3,117	2,889	2,623	2,486	10,577	8,095	5,545	4,550	3,556	2,205	1,034	480	417
Property crime percent distribution[1]	5	4	4	4	16	12	8	7	5	3	2	1	1
Other assaults	2,430	2,348	2,328	2,352	11,051	9,966	8,122	7,570	6,443	4,284	2,117	1,214	1,038
Forgery and counterfeiting	144	157	136	139	750	638	435	370	245	141	76	29	22
Fraud	414	473	518	487	2,818	3,023	2,491	2,091	1,636	1,076	620	370	265
Embezzlement	27	24	26	23	115	110	108	96	60	49	16	18	11
Stolen property; buying, receiving, possessing	224	208	224	184	928	654	502	367	313	193	92	58	28
Vandalism	523	462	442	385	1,517	1,126	808	721	568	378	204	89	102
Weapons; carrying, possessing, etc.	250	227	222	213	1,053	878	630	583	542	417	259	163	139
Prostitution and commercialized vice	5	6	5	4	22	28	13	12	8	10	7	3	6
Sex offenses (except forcible rape and prostitution)	164	139	144	88	444	418	388	375	287	239	159	145	160
Drug abuse violations	4,548	4,203	3,796	3,682	15,775	11,672	8,008	6,408	5,613	3,903	1,966	889	422
Gambling	1	5	2	5	17	25	20	25	17	20	13	9	3
Offenses against the family and children	313	350	375	366	2,496	2,665	2,279	1,788	1,271	668	279	123	77
Driving under the influence	6,099	6,016	5,874	5,477	24,747	19,605	15,738	15,449	14,936	11,787	7,074	3,706	2,739
Liquor laws	683	510	395	313	1,180	827	669	679	712	530	330	152	138
Drunkenness	739	638	625	627	2,727	2,379	1,959	1,945	2,085	1,544	744	285	190
Disorderly conduct	799	706	704	665	2,794	2,379	1,758	1,738	1,657	1,162	626	304	229
Vagrancy	6	7	10	9	34	28	16	19	22	21	16	6	1
All other offenses (except traffic)	9,683	9,503	9,328	9,180	43,685	36,672	26,954	23,107	18,382	11,891	5,948	2,807	2,362
Suspicion	8	7	5	3	25	20	16	16	8	15	0	1	1
Curfew and loitering law violations	NA	NA	NA	NA	NA	NA	NA	NA	NA	NA	NA	NA	NA

NA = Not available.

[1] Because of rounding, the percentages may not add to 100.0.

[2] Violent crimes are offenses of murder and nonnegligent manslaughter, forcible rape, robbery, and aggravated assault. Property crimes are offenses of burglary, larceny-theft, motor vehicle theft, and arson.

Table IV-31. Arrests, Nonmetropolitan Counties, Persons Under 15, 18, 21, and 25 Years of Age, 2011

(Number, percent; 1,952 agencies; 2011 estimated population 23,492,803)

Offense charged	Total all ages	Number of persons arrested				Percent of total all ages			
		Under 15	Under 18	Under 21	Under 25	Under 15	Under 18	Under 21	Under 25
Total	781,434	11,096	47,962	140,121	257,049	1.4	6.1	17.9	32.9
Murder and nonnegligent manslaughter	708	5	34	134	234	0.7	4.8	18.9	33.1
Forcible rape	1,415	63	179	403	596	4.5	12.7	28.5	42.1
Robbery	1,981	12	169	616	1,029	0.6	8.5	31.1	51.9
Aggravated assault	19,990	370	1,307	3,159	5,856	1.9	6.5	15.8	29.3
Burglary	21,077	655	2,867	7,130	10,937	3.1	13.6	33.8	51.9
Larceny-theft..	41,264	1,138	4,540	10,846	17,456	2.8	11.0	26.3	42.3
Motor vehicle theft..	3,954	110	595	1,191	1,799	2.8	15.0	30.1	45.5
Arson..	773	66	145	327	417	8.5	18.8	42.3	53.9
Violent crime[1]	24,094	450	1,689	4,312	7,715	1.9	7.0	17.9	32.0
Property crime[1]	67,068	1,969	8,147	19,494	30,609	2.9	12.1	29.1	45.6
Other assaults..	75,883	2,679	8,151	14,620	24,078	3.5	10.7	19.3	31.7
Forgery and counterfeiting....................................	3,669	6	50	387	963	0.2	1.4	10.5	26.2
Fraud..	17,498	37	222	1,216	3,108	0.2	1.3	6.9	17.8
Embezzlement..	773	3	13	90	190	0.4	1.7	11.6	24.6
Stolen property; buying, receiving, possessing.......................	5,169	91	440	1,194	2,034	1.8	8.5	23.1	39.3
Vandalism	12,118	937	2,753	4,793	6,605	7.7	22.7	39.6	54.5
Weapons; carrying, possessing, etc.	6,938	246	661	1,362	2,274	3.5	9.5	19.6	32.8
Prostitution and commercialized vice	152	1	5	23	43	0.7	3.3	15.1	28.3
Sex offenses (except forcible rape and prostitution)............	4,690	431	885	1,540	2,075	9.2	18.9	32.8	44.2
Drug abuse violations	90,289	634	5,077	19,404	35,633	0.7	5.6	21.5	39.5
Gambling	249	1	18	87	100	0.4	7.2	34.9	40.2
Offenses against the family and children............................	13,845	74	224	795	2,199	0.5	1.6	5.7	15.9
Driving under the influence	151,218	9	1,082	11,971	35,437	*	0.7	7.9	23.4
Liquor laws...	25,607	456	5,490	18,489	20,390	1.8	21.4	72.2	79.6
Drunkenness..	18,432	25	319	1,945	4,574	0.1	1.7	10.6	24.8
Disorderly conduct..	21,461	1,156	3,602	5,940	8,814	5.4	16.8	27.7	41.1
Vagrancy	254	4	28	59	91	1.6	11.0	23.2	35.8
All other offenses (except traffic)	241,469	1,776	8,701	31,967	69,661	0.7	3.6	13.2	28.8
Suspicion...	189	15	36	64	87	7.9	19.0	33.9	46.0
Curfew and loitering law violations.........................	369	96	369	369	369	26.0	100.0	100.0	100.0

* = Less than one tenth of one percent.

[1] Violent crimes are offenses of murder and nonnegligent manslaughter, forcible rape, robbery, and aggravated assault. Property crimes are offenses of burglary, larceny-theft, motor vehicle theft, and arson.

Table IV-32.   Arrests, Nonmetropolitan Counties, Distribution by Sex, 2011

(Number, percent; 1,952 agencies; 2011 estimated population 23,492,803)

Offense charged	Number of persons arrested			Percent male	Percent female	Percent distribution[1]		
	Total	Male	Female			Total	Male	Female
Total	781,434	589,553	191,881	75.4	24.6	100.0	100.0	100.0
Murder and nonnegligent manslaughter	708	597	111	84.3	15.7	0.1	0.1	0.1
Forcible rape	1,415	1,390	25	98.2	1.8	0.2	0.2	0.1
Robbery	1,981	1,757	224	88.7	11.3	0.3	0.3	0.1
Aggravated assault	19,990	16,129	3,861	80.7	19.3	2.6	2.7	2.0
Burglary	21,077	18,011	3,066	85.5	14.5	2.7	3.1	1.6
Larceny-theft	41,264	28,254	13,010	68.5	31.5	5.3	4.8	6.8
Motor vehicle theft	3,954	3,285	669	83.1	16.9	0.5	0.6	0.3
Arson	773	668	105	86.4	13.6	0.1	0.1	0.1
Violent crime[2]	24,094	19,873	4,221	82.5	17.5	3.1	3.4	2.2
Property crime[2]	67,068	50,218	16,850	74.9	25.1	8.6	8.5	8.8
Other assaults	75,883	55,380	20,503	73.0	27.0	9.7	9.4	10.7
Forgery and counterfeiting	3,669	2,100	1,569	57.2	42.8	0.5	0.4	0.8
Fraud	17,498	9,325	8,173	53.3	46.7	2.2	1.6	4.3
Embezzlement	773	389	384	50.3	49.7	0.1	0.1	0.2
Stolen property; buying, receiving, possessing	5,169	4,208	961	81.4	18.6	0.7	0.7	0.5
Vandalism	12,118	9,878	2,240	81.5	18.5	1.6	1.7	1.2
Weapons; carrying, possessing, etc.	6,938	6,402	536	92.3	7.7	0.9	1.1	0.3
Prostitution and commercialized vice	152	93	59	61.2	38.8	*	*	*
Sex offenses (except forcible rape and prostitution)	4,690	4,383	307	93.5	6.5	0.6	0.7	0.2
Drug abuse violations	90,289	69,669	20,620	77.2	22.8	11.6	11.8	10.7
Gambling	249	193	56	77.5	22.5	*	*	*
Offenses against the family and children	13,845	10,992	2,853	79.4	20.6	1.8	1.9	1.5
Driving under the influence	151,218	117,011	34,207	77.4	22.6	19.4	19.8	17.8
Liquor laws	25,607	17,866	7,741	69.8	30.2	3.3	3.0	4.0
Drunkenness	18,432	14,433	3,999	78.3	21.7	2.4	2.4	2.1
Disorderly conduct	21,461	15,354	6,107	71.5	28.5	2.7	2.6	3.2
Vagrancy	254	217	37	85.4	14.6	*	0.1	*
All other offenses (except traffic)	241,469	181,195	60,274	75.0	25.0	30.9	30.7	31.4
Suspicion	189	148	41	78.3	21.7	*	*	*
Curfew and loitering law violations	369	226	143	61.2	38.8	*	*	0.1

* = Less than one tenth of one percent.

[1] Because of rounding, the percentages may not add to 100.0.

[2] Violent crimes are offenses of murder and nonnegligent manslaughter, forcible rape, robbery, and aggravated assault. Property crimes are offenses of burglary, larceny-theft, motor vehicle theft, and arson.

Table IV-33. Arrests, Nonmetropolitan Counties, Distribution by Race, 2011

(Number, percent; 1,952 agencies; 2011 estimated population 23,492,803)

Offense charged	Total arrests					Percent distribution[1]					Arrests under 18				
	Total	White	Black	American Indian or Alaskan Native	Asian or Pacific Islander	Total	White	Black	American Indian or Alaskan Native	Asian or Pacific Islander	Total	White	Black	American Indian or Alaskan Native	Asian or Pacific Islander
Total	774,835	639,726	107,926	24,043	3,140	100.0	82.6	13.9	3.1	0.4	47,539	38,626	6,849	1,921	143
Murder and nonnegligent manslaughter....................	704	491	181	30	2	100.0	69.7	25.7	4.3	0.3	34	18	13	2	1
Forcible rape	1,404	1,176	190	35	3	100.0	83.8	13.5	2.5	0.2	176	141	32	3	0
Robbery...	1,978	1,157	737	73	11	100.0	58.5	37.3	3.7	0.6	168	72	91	5	0
Aggravated assault.........................	19,913	15,300	3,641	933	39	100.0	76.8	18.3	4.7	0.2	1,298	911	321	62	4
Burglary...	20,997	17,463	2,887	622	25	100.0	83.2	13.7	3.0	0.1	2,850	2,329	397	115	9
Larceny-theft	41,091	34,131	5,895	916	149	100.0	83.1	14.3	2.2	0.4	4,508	3,677	712	104	15
Motor vehicle theft........................	3,936	3,221	565	137	13	100.0	81.8	14.4	3.5	0.3	593	509	57	23	4
Arson	768	675	66	27	0	100.0	87.9	8.6	3.5	0.0	145	132	11	2	0
Violent crime[2]..............................	23,999	18,124	4,749	1,071	55	100.0	75.5	19.8	4.5	0.2	1,676	1,142	457	72	5
Property crime[2]............................	66,792	55,490	9,413	1,702	187	100.0	83.1	14.1	2.5	0.3	8,096	6,647	1,177	244	28
Other assaults	75,483	61,557	11,019	2,731	176	100.0	81.6	14.6	3.6	0.2	8,087	6,140	1,682	243	22
Forgery and counterfeiting.............	3,625	2,940	622	51	12	100.0	81.1	17.2	1.4	0.3	49	45	4	0	0
Fraud...	17,392	14,006	3,074	272	40	100.0	80.5	17.7	1.6	0.2	214	167	45	2	0
Embezzlement	766	648	112	5	1	100.0	84.6	14.6	0.7	0.1	13	11	2	0	0
Stolen property; buying, receiving, possessing......................	5,131	4,038	984	97	12	100.0	78.7	19.2	1.9	0.2	438	318	105	14	1
Vandalism......................................	12,060	10,155	1,457	427	21	100.0	84.2	12.1	3.5	0.2	2,735	2,358	300	73	4
Weapons; carrying, possessing, etc..	6,907	5,326	1,336	224	21	100.0	77.1	19.3	3.2	0.3	656	490	135	28	3
Prostitution and commercialized vice	151	122	19	5	5	100.0	80.8	12.6	3.3	3.3	4	4	0	0	0
Sex offenses (except forcible rape and prostitution).....................	4,657	4,095	441	111	10	100.0	87.9	9.5	2.4	0.2	872	750	106	15	1
Drug abuse violations	89,635	74,280	13,459	1,473	423	100.0	82.9	15.0	1.6	0.5	5,032	4,373	506	126	27
Gambling..	245	177	51	8	9	100.0	72.2	20.8	3.3	3.7	18	16	2	0	0
Offenses against the family and children..	13,802	10,270	3,009	501	22	100.0	74.4	21.8	3.6	0.2					
Driving under the influence	148,773	129,299	14,425	3,790	1,259	100.0	86.9	9.7	2.5	0.8	1,073	983	32	51	7
Liquor laws....................................	25,178	22,741	1,104	1,236	97	100.0	90.3	4.4	4.9	0.4	5,410	4,920	129	348	13
Drunkenness..................................	18,354	16,408	1,238	650	58	100.0	89.4	6.7	3.5	0.3	316	278	18	20	0
Disorderly conduct........................	21,291	16,747	3,423	1,073	48	100.0	78.7	16.1	5.0	0.2	3,578	2,409	974	186	9
Vagrancy.......................................	252	192	51	9	0	100.0	76.2	20.2	3.6	0.0	28	27	0	1	0
All other offenses (except traffic)..	239,790	192,650	37,866	8,594	680	100.0	80.3	15.8	3.6	0.3	8,628	6,990	1,136	482	20
Suspicion	189	125	62	1	1	100.0	66.1	32.8	0.5	0.5	36	32	4	0	0
Curfew and loitering law violations	363	336	12	12	3	100.0	92.6	3.3	3.3	0.8	363	336	12	12	3

NA = Not available.

[1] Because of rounding, the percentages may not add to 100.0.

[2] Violent crimes are offenses of murder and nonnegligent manslaughter, forcible rape, robbery, and aggravated assault. Property crimes are offenses of burglary, larceny-theft, motor vehicle theft, and arson.

Table IV-33. Arrests, Nonmetropolitan Counties, Distribution by Race, 2011—*Continued*

(Number, percent; 1,952 agencies; 2011 estimated population 23,492,803)

Offense charged	Percent distribution[1]					Arrests under 18					Percent distribution[1]				
	Total	White	Black	American Indian or Alaskan Native	Asian or Pacific Islander	Total	White	Black	American Indian or Alaskan Native	Asian or Pacific Islander	Total	White	Black	American Indian or Alaskan Native	Asian or Pacific Islander
Total	100.0	81.3	14.4	4.0	0.3	727,296	601,100	101,077	22,122	2,997	100.0	82.6	13.9	3.0	0.4
Murder and nonnegligent manslaughter	100.0	52.9	38.2	5.9	2.9	670	473	168	28	1	100.0	70.6	25.1	4.2	0.1
Forcible rape	100.0	80.1	18.2	1.7	0.0	1,228	1,035	158	32	3	100.0	84.3	12.9	2.6	0.2
Robbery	100.0	42.9	54.2	3.0	0.0	1,810	1,085	646	68	11	100.0	59.9	35.7	3.8	0.6
Aggravated assault	100.0	70.2	24.7	4.8	0.3	18,615	14,389	3,320	871	35	100.0	77.3	17.8	4.7	0.2
Burglary	100.0	81.7	13.9	4.0	0.3	18,147	15,134	2,490	507	16	100.0	83.4	13.7	2.8	0.1
Larceny-theft	100.0	81.6	15.8	2.3	0.3	36,583	30,454	5,183	812	134	100.0	83.2	14.2	2.2	0.4
Motor vehicle theft	100.0	85.8	9.6	3.9	0.7	3,343	2,712	508	114	9	100.0	81.1	15.2	3.4	0.3
Arson	100.0	91.0	7.6	1.4	0.0	623	543	55	25	0	100.0	87.2	8.8	4.0	0.0
Violent crime[2]	100.0	68.1	27.3	4.3	0.3	22,323	16,982	4,292	999	50	100.0	76.1	19.2	4.5	0.2
Property crime[2]	100.0	82.1	14.5	3.0	0.3	58,696	48,843	8,236	1,458	159	100.0	83.2	14.0	2.5	0.3
Other assaults	100.0	75.9	20.8	3.0	0.3	67,396	55,417	9,337	2,488	154	100.0	82.2	13.9	3.7	0.2
Forgery and counterfeiting	100.0	91.8	8.2	0.0	0.0	3,576	2,895	618	51	12	100.0	81.0	17.3	1.4	0.3
Fraud	100.0	78.0	21.0	0.9	0.0	17,178	13,839	3,029	270	40	100.0	80.6	17.6	1.6	0.2
Embezzlement	100.0	84.6	15.4	0.0	0.0	753	637	110	5	1	100.0	84.6	14.6	0.7	0.1
Stolen property; buying, receiving, possessing	100.0	72.6	24.0	3.2	0.2	4,693	3,720	879	83	11	100.0	79.3	18.7	1.8	0.2
Vandalism	100.0	86.2	11.0	2.7	0.1	9,325	7,797	1,157	354	17	100.0	83.6	12.4	3.8	0.2
Weapons; carrying, possessing, etc.	100.0	74.7	20.6	4.3	0.5	6,251	4,836	1,201	196	18	100.0	77.4	19.2	3.1	0.3
Prostitution and commercialized vice	100.0	100.0	0.0	0.0	0.0	147	118	19	5	5	100.0	80.3	12.9	3.4	3.4
Sex offenses (except forcible rape and prostitution)	100.0	86.0	12.2	1.7	0.1	3,785	3,345	335	96	9	100.0	88.4	8.9	2.5	0.2
Drug abuse violations	100.0	86.9	10.1	2.5	0.5	84,603	69,907	12,953	1,347	396	100.0	82.6	15.3	1.6	0.5
Gambling	100.0	88.9	11.1	0.0	0.0	227	161	49	8	9	100.0	70.9	21.6	3.5	4.0
Offenses against the family and children	100.0	87.6	10.6	1.8	0.0	13,585	10,080	2,986	497	22	100.0	74.2	22.0	3.7	0.2
Driving under the influence	100.0	91.6	3.0	4.8	0.7	147,700	128,316	14,393	3,739	1,252	100.0	86.9	9.7	2.5	0.8
Liquor laws	100.0	90.9	2.4	6.4	0.2	19,768	17,821	975	888	84	100.0	90.2	4.9	4.5	0.4
Drunkenness	100.0	88.0	5.7	6.3	0.0	18,038	16,130	1,220	630	58	100.0	89.4	6.8	3.5	0.3
Disorderly conduct	100.0	67.3	27.2	5.2	0.3	17,713	14,338	2,449	887	39	100.0	80.9	13.8	5.0	0.2
Vagrancy	100.0	96.4	0.0	3.6	0.0	224	165	51	8	0	100.0	73.7	22.8	3.6	0.0
All other offenses (except traffic)	100.0	81.0	13.2	5.6	0.2	231,162	185,660	36,730	8,112	660	100.0	80.3	15.9	3.5	0.3
Suspicion	100.0	88.9	11.1	0.0	0.0	153	93	58	1	1	100.0	60.8	37.9	0.7	0.7
Curfew and loitering law violations	100.0	92.6	3.3	3.3	0.8	NA	NA	NA	NA	NA	NA	NA	NA	NA	NA

NA = Not available.

[1] Because of rounding, the percentages may not add to 100.0.

[2] Violent crimes are offenses of murder and nonnegligent manslaughter, forcible rape, robbery, and aggravated assault. Property crimes are offenses of burglary, larceny-theft, motor vehicle theft, and arson.

Table IV-34. Arrest Trends, Suburban Areas,[1] 2010–2011

(Number, percent change; 5,946 agencies; 2011 estimated population 94,078,789; 2010 estimated population 93,327,128)

Offense charged	Number of persons arrested								
	Total all ages			Under 18 years of age			18 years of age and over		
	2010	2011	Percent change	2010	2011	Percent change	2010	2011	Percent change
Total[2]	3,408,242	3,293,344	-3.4	432,956	393,329	-9.2	2,975,286	2,900,015	-2.5
Murder and nonnegligent manslaughter	2,115	2,108	-0.3	186	149	-19.9	1,929	1,959	+1.6
Forcible rape	4,518	4,303	-4.8	720	660	-8.3	3,798	3,643	-4.1
Robbery	19,903	18,747	-5.8	4,263	3,712	-12.9	15,640	15,035	-3.9
Aggravated assault	96,844	93,287	-3.7	11,195	10,387	-7.2	85,649	82,900	-3.2
Burglary	73,208	73,455	+0.3	15,766	14,541	-7.8	57,442	58,914	+2.6
Larceny-theft	320,847	327,294	+2.0	67,907	62,601	-7.8	252,940	264,693	+4.6
Motor vehicle theft	15,027	14,547	-3.2	3,141	2,907	-7.4	11,886	11,640	-2.1
Arson	3,193	3,402	+6.5	1,427	1,582	+10.9	1,766	1,820	+3.1
Violent crime[3]	123,380	118,445	-4.0	16,364	14,908	-8.9	107,016	103,537	-3.3
Property crime[3]	412,275	418,698	+1.6	88,241	81,631	-7.5	324,034	337,067	+4.0
Other assaults	324,222	314,586	-3.0	59,322	52,919	-10.8	264,900	261,667	-1.2
Forgery and counterfeiting	21,686	19,867	-8.4	518	495	-4.4	21,168	19,372	-8.5
Fraud	58,698	50,946	-13.2	1,705	1,556	-8.7	56,993	49,390	-13.3
Embezzlement	4,334	4,268	-1.5	117	113	-3.4	4,217	4,155	-1.5
Stolen property; buying, receiving, possessing	27,005	26,981	-0.1	4,158	3,710	-10.8	22,847	23,271	+1.9
Vandalism	63,592	61,618	-3.1	20,924	18,960	-9.4	42,668	42,658	*
Weapons; carrying, possessing, etc.	33,877	32,885	-2.9	7,417	6,607	-10.9	26,460	26,278	-0.7
Prostitution and commercialized vice	4,385	3,936	-10.2	111	95	-14.4	4,274	3,841	-10.1
Sex offenses (except forcible rape and prostitution)	18,727	17,757	-5.2	3,795	3,383	-10.9	14,932	14,374	-3.7
Drug abuse violations	409,466	393,651	-3.9	48,112	43,884	-8.8	361,354	349,767	-3.2
Gambling	1,403	853	-39.2	65	84	+29.2	1,338	769	-42.5
Offenses against the family and children	41,028	42,492	+3.6	1,188	919	-22.6	39,840	41,573	+4.3
Driving under the influence	366,764	350,506	-4.4	3,594	3,259	-9.3	363,170	347,247	-4.4
Liquor laws	148,965	140,204	-5.9	32,209	30,375	-5.7	116,756	109,829	-5.9
Drunkenness	131,656	124,944	-5.1	3,766	3,326	-11.7	127,890	121,618	-4.9
Disorderly conduct	162,345	151,514	-6.7	45,285	40,486	-10.6	117,060	111,028	-5.2
Vagrancy	4,121	3,910	-5.1	390	321	-17.7	3,731	3,589	-3.8
All other offenses (except traffic)	1,035,338	1,002,782	-3.1	80,700	73,797	-8.6	954,638	928,985	-2.7
Suspicion	286	235	-17.8	42	29	-31.0	244	206	-15.6
Curfew and loitering law violations	14,975	12,501	-16.5	14,975	12,501	-16.5	NA	NA	NA

NA = Not available.

* = Less than one tenth of 1 percent.

[1] Suburban areas include law enforcement agencies in cities with less than 50,000 inhabitants and county law enforcement agencies that are within a Metropolitan Statistical Area. Suburban areas exclude all metropolitan agencies associated with a principal city.

[2] Does not include suspicion.

[3] Violent crimes are offenses of murder and nonnegligent manslaughter, forcible rape, robbery, and aggravated assault. Property crimes are offenses of burglary, larceny-theft, motor vehicle theft, and arson.

Table IV-35. Arrest Trends, Suburban Areas,[1] by Age and Sex, 2010–2011

(Number, percent change; 5,946 agencies; 2011 estimated population 94,078,789; 2010 estimated population 93,327,128)

Offense charged	Male						Female					
	Total			Under 18			Total			Under 18		
	2010	2011	Percent change	2010	2011	Percent change	2010	2011	Percent change	2010	2011	Percent change
Total[2]	2,524,699	2,427,426	-3.9	307,717	279,973	-9.0	883,543	865,918	-2.0	125,239	113,356	-9.5
Murder and nonnegligent manslaughter	1,855	1,846	-0.5	160	130	-18.8	260	262	+0.8	26	19	-26.9
Forcible rape	4,469	4,260	-4.7	704	651	-7.5	49	43	-12.2	16	9	-43.8
Robbery	17,426	16,425	-5.7	3,875	3,391	-12.5	2,477	2,322	-6.3	388	321	-17.3
Aggravated assault	75,815	72,565	-4.3	8,407	7,813	-7.1	21,029	20,722	-1.5	2,788	2,574	-7.7
Burglary	62,064	62,216	+0.2	14,045	12,849	-8.5	11,144	11,239	+0.9	1,721	1,692	-1.7
Larceny-theft	183,942	189,386	+3.0	39,229	37,461	-4.5	136,905	137,908	+0.7	28,678	25,140	-12.3
Motor vehicle theft	12,297	11,826	-3.8	2,590	2,417	-6.7	2,730	2,721	-0.3	551	490	-11.1
Arson	2,703	2,846	+5.3	1,252	1,354	+8.1	490	556	+13.5	175	228	+30.3
Violent crime[3]	99,565	95,096	-4.5	13,146	11,985	-8.8	23,815	23,349	-2.0	3,218	2,923	-9.2
Property crime[3]	261,006	266,274	+2.0	57,116	54,081	-5.3	151,269	152,424	+0.8	31,125	27,550	-11.5
Other assaults	235,463	227,238	-3.5	39,022	34,632	-11.3	88,759	87,348	-1.6	20,300	18,287	-9.9
Forgery and counterfeiting	13,597	12,378	-9.0	378	362	-4.2	8,089	7,489	-7.4	140	133	-5.0
Fraud	33,672	29,888	-11.2	1,153	1,039	-9.9	25,026	21,058	-15.9	552	517	-6.3
Embezzlement	2,221	2,213	-0.4	74	67	-9.5	2,113	2,055	-2.7	43	46	+7.0
Stolen property; buying, receiving, possessing	21,303	21,205	-0.5	3,364	3,044	-9.5	5,702	5,776	+1.3	794	666	-16.1
Vandalism	51,979	50,482	-2.9	17,728	16,136	-9.0	11,613	11,136	-4.1	3,196	2,824	-11.6
Weapons; carrying, possessing, etc.	30,741	29,905	-2.7	6,542	5,895	-9.9	3,136	2,980	-5.0	875	712	-18.6
Prostitution and commercialized vice	1,809	1,604	-11.3	35	30	-14.3	2,576	2,332	-9.5	76	65	-14.5
Sex offenses (except forcible rape and prostitution)	17,364	16,553	-4.7	3,392	3,063	-9.7	1,363	1,204	-11.7	403	320	-20.6
Drug abuse violations	324,538	310,007	-4.5	39,480	36,101	-8.6	84,928	83,644	-1.5	8,632	7,783	-9.8
Gambling	1,150	642	-44.2	44	57	+29.5	253	211	-16.6	21	27	+28.6
Offenses against the family and children	32,773	34,133	+4.1	801	548	-31.6	8,255	8,359	+1.3	387	371	-4.1
Driving under the influence	275,836	260,399	-5.6	2,651	2,391	-9.8	90,928	90,107	-0.9	943	868	-8.0
Liquor laws	104,181	96,556	-7.3	19,568	18,146	-7.3	44,784	43,648	-2.5	12,641	12,229	-3.3
Drunkenness	106,991	100,347	-6.2	2,693	2,405	-10.7	24,665	24,597	-0.3	1,073	921	-14.2
Disorderly conduct	116,311	108,205	-7.0	30,386	26,966	-11.3	46,034	43,309	-5.9	14,899	13,520	-9.3
Vagrancy	3,227	3,051	-5.5	312	258	-17.3	894	859	-3.9	78	63	-19.2
All other offenses (except traffic)	780,826	752,691	-3.6	59,686	54,208	-9.2	254,512	250,091	-1.7	21,014	19,589	-6.8
Suspicion	227	185	-18.5	35	26	-25.7	59	50	-15.3	7	3	-57.1
Curfew and loitering law violations	10,146	8,559	-15.6	10,146	8,559	-15.6	4,829	3,942	-18.4	4,829	3,942	-18.4

[1] Suburban areas include law enforcement agencies in cities with less than 50,000 inhabitants and county law enforcement agencies that are within a Metropolitan Statistical Area. Suburban areas exclude all metropolitan agencies associated with a principal city.

[2] Does not include suspicion.

[3] Violent crimes are offenses of murder and nonnegligent manslaughter, forcible rape, robbery, and aggravated assault. Property crimes are offenses of burglary, larceny-theft, motor vehicle theft, and arson.

Table IV-36.   Arrests, Suburban Area Distribution by Age, 2011[1]

(Number, percent; 6,522 agencies; 2011 estimated population 104,263,328)

Offense charged	Total all ages	Ages under 15	Ages under 18	Ages 18 and over	Under 10	10–12	13–14	15	16	17	18	19	20
Total	3,796,974	120,817	447,551	3,349,423	2,894	26,748	91,175	81,901	108,514	136,319	181,049	192,225	183,513
Total percent distribution[2]	100.0	3.2	11.8	88.2	0.1	0.7	2.4	2.2	2.9	3.6	4.8	5.1	4.8
Murder and nonnegligent manslaughter	2,604	23	194	2,410	0	1	22	35	55	81	146	151	149
Forcible rape	5,007	271	765	4,242	1	75	195	131	164	199	238	260	216
Robbery	23,424	795	4,687	18,737	16	99	680	932	1,314	1,646	2,027	1,838	1,547
Aggravated assault	107,868	3,897	11,868	96,000	114	1,014	2,769	2,122	2,602	3,247	3,540	3,812	3,923
Burglary	85,052	4,667	17,063	67,989	175	1,038	3,454	3,255	4,042	5,099	6,213	5,623	4,808
Larceny-theft	382,524	19,755	73,737	308,787	352	4,275	15,128	13,987	18,371	21,624	23,745	21,357	18,025
Motor vehicle theft	16,896	676	3,384	13,512	7	85	584	730	942	1,036	971	829	766
Arson	3,951	956	1,736	2,215	56	302	598	295	268	217	172	147	150
Violent crime[3]	138,903	4,986	17,514	121,389	131	1,189	3,666	3,220	4,135	5,173	5,951	6,061	5,835
Violent crime percent distribution[2]	100.0	3.6	12.6	87.4	0.1	0.9	2.6	2.3	3.0	3.7	4.3	4.4	4.2
Property crime[3]	488,423	26,054	95,920	392,503	590	5,700	19,764	18,267	23,623	27,976	31,101	27,956	23,749
Property crime percent distribution[2]	100.0	5.3	19.6	80.4	0.1	1.2	4.0	3.7	4.8	5.7	6.4	5.7	4.9
Other assaults	362,555	23,492	60,487	302,068	707	6,256	16,529	11,470	12,747	12,778	11,317	11,301	11,816
Forgery and counterfeiting	22,970	73	558	22,412	4	14	55	82	103	300	691	956	1,040
Fraud	58,503	229	1,678	56,825	4	40	185	266	420	763	1,363	1,845	2,024
Embezzlement	5,104	19	127	4,977	0	3	16	6	32	70	222	325	290
Stolen property; buying, receiving, possessing	31,234	934	4,322	26,912	15	154	765	827	1,117	1,444	1,977	1,918	1,576
Vandalism	70,969	8,094	21,303	49,666	338	2,349	5,407	3,889	4,484	4,836	4,678	3,937	3,393
Weapons; carrying, possessing, etc.	39,242	3,029	7,824	31,418	220	927	1,882	1,303	1,523	1,969	2,226	2,069	1,808
Prostitution and commercialized vice	5,246	14	117	5,129	0	2	12	18	34	51	123	212	227
Sex offenses (except forcible rape and prostitution)	20,424	1,820	3,896	16,528	66	504	1,250	650	679	747	846	815	803
Drug abuse violations	460,338	8,137	48,815	411,523	42	1,034	7,061	7,992	12,938	19,748	31,111	31,644	28,699
Gambling	1,432	22	89	1,343	0	3	19	15	28	24	43	49	59
Offenses against the family and children	46,626	375	1,168	45,458	17	76	282	210	260	323	533	654	788
Driving under the influence	389,342	59	3,514	385,828	4	9	46	136	716	2,603	6,848	9,961	11,870
Liquor laws	174,027	2,823	33,914	140,113	26	234	2,563	4,564	9,595	16,932	33,485	36,214	29,654
Drunkenness	144,459	406	3,485	140,974	6	27	373	585	836	1,658	4,443	5,133	4,782
Disorderly conduct	177,018	16,833	45,374	131,644	205	3,913	12,715	9,223	9,826	9,492	8,108	6,958	6,628
Vagrancy	5,044	94	371	4,673	2	13	79	71	85	121	240	224	205
All other offenses (except traffic)	1,140,091	19,498	82,569	1,057,522	476	3,753	15,269	15,778	21,094	26,199	35,709	43,964	48,238
Suspicion	571	14	53	518	1	2	11	6	17	16	34	29	29
Curfew and loitering law violations	14,453	3,812	14,453	NA	40	546	3,226	3,323	4,222	3,096	NA	NA	NA

NA = Not available.

[1] Suburban areas include law enforcement agencies in cities with less than 50,000 inhabitants and county law enforcement agencies that are within a Metropolitan Statistical Area. Suburban areas exclude all metropolitan agencies associated with a principal city.

[2] Because of rounding, the percentages may not add to 100.0.

[3] Violent crimes are offenses of murder and nonnegligent manslaughter, forcible rape, robbery, and aggravated assault. Property crimes are offenses of burglary, larceny-theft, motor vehicle theft, and arson.

Table IV-36. Arrests, Suburban Area Distribution by Age, 2011[1]—*Continued*

(Number, percent; 6,522 agencies; 2011 estimated population 104,263,328)

Offense charged	21	22	23	24	25–29	30–34	35–39	40–44	45–49	50–54	55–59	60–64	65 and over
Total	165,328	151,524	139,419	131,971	562,260	432,310	318,983	292,076	256,734	178,868	90,989	42,014	30,160
Total percent distribution[2]	4.4	4.0	3.7	3.5	14.8	11.4	8.4	7.7	6.8	4.7	2.4	1.1	0.8
Murder and nonnegligent manslaughter	138	97	129	124	441	309	184	155	149	102	62	44	30
Forcible rape	213	178	160	135	666	541	465	373	326	234	111	49	77
Robbery	1,388	1,073	943	910	3,254	2,034	1,166	1,005	788	452	218	57	37
Aggravated assault	4,312	3,994	3,767	3,740	16,521	13,579	10,145	9,218	8,142	5,771	2,936	1,419	1,181
Burglary	4,210	3,682	3,284	2,844	11,486	8,310	5,381	4,848	3,764	2,128	958	267	183
Larceny-theft	16,135	13,925	12,601	11,730	49,619	37,536	27,266	25,696	22,114	15,199	7,543	3,549	2,747
Motor vehicle theft	690	613	580	557	2,424	1,922	1,410	1,155	872	454	177	62	30
Arson	106	81	81	74	334	247	199	176	184	127	74	32	31
Violent crime[3]	6,051	5,342	4,999	4,909	20,882	16,463	11,960	10,751	9,405	6,559	3,327	1,569	1,325
Violent crime percent distribution[2]	4.4	3.8	3.6	3.5	15.0	11.9	8.6	7.7	6.8	4.7	2.4	1.1	1.0
Property crime[3]	21,141	18,301	16,546	15,205	63,863	48,015	34,256	31,875	26,934	17,908	8,752	3,910	2,991
Property crime percent distribution[2]	4.3	3.7	3.4	3.1	13.1	9.8	7.0	6.5	5.5	3.7	1.8	0.8	0.6
Other assaults	12,803	12,252	11,696	11,291	50,994	42,712	33,806	31,447	26,891	17,593	8,742	3,983	3,424
Forgery and counterfeiting	902	936	898	921	4,457	3,577	2,479	2,064	1,636	1,063	473	197	122
Fraud	1,947	1,935	1,853	1,949	9,369	8,609	7,532	6,574	5,326	3,322	1,741	816	620
Embezzlement	285	251	214	197	807	596	566	447	345	226	124	57	25
Stolen property; buying, receiving, possessing	1,447	1,367	1,200	1,051	4,664	3,629	2,480	2,263	1,653	1,010	432	142	103
Vandalism	3,166	2,722	2,284	2,043	8,234	5,565	3,803	3,407	2,864	1,852	908	438	372
Weapons; carrying, possessing, etc.	1,839	1,613	1,497	1,357	5,556	3,947	2,542	2,094	1,843	1,421	794	427	385
Prostitution and commercialized vice	225	229	208	205	856	652	531	557	457	313	172	75	87
Sex offenses (except forcible rape and prostitution)	708	595	510	441	2,152	1,834	1,646	1,600	1,522	1,116	779	509	652
Drug abuse violations	25,363	22,582	19,826	18,401	73,282	50,957	32,740	27,897	23,138	15,381	6,810	2,630	1,062
Gambling	35	24	33	28	155	122	165	135	108	129	94	81	83
Offenses against the family and children	983	1,091	1,243	1,195	7,597	8,295	7,275	6,369	4,749	2,799	1,177	465	245
Driving under the influence	17,701	17,673	16,961	16,490	68,554	50,472	38,391	37,174	36,071	27,857	15,941	8,343	5,521
Liquor laws	4,586	2,872	2,184	1,755	6,590	4,767	3,575	3,748	4,075	3,282	1,913	821	592
Drunkenness	7,203	6,249	5,408	5,040	20,884	16,269	13,054	14,278	15,367	12,351	6,410	2,659	1,444
Disorderly conduct	7,816	6,680	5,862	5,329	20,849	15,101	11,374	11,153	10,498	7,846	4,018	1,911	1,513
Vagrancy	184	195	159	140	612	506	406	500	491	392	266	99	54
All other offenses (except traffic)	50,916	48,583	45,812	44,007	191,821	150,157	110,347	97,703	83,326	56,429	28,102	12,873	9,535
Suspicion	27	32	26	17	82	65	55	40	35	19	14	9	5
Curfew and loitering law violations	NA	NA	NA	NA	NA	NA	NA	NA	NA	NA	NA	NA	NA

NA = Not available.

[1] Suburban areas include law enforcement agencies in cities with less than 50,000 inhabitants and county law enforcement agencies that are within a Metropolitan Statistical Area. Suburban areas exclude all metropolitan agencies associated with a principal city.

[2] Because of rounding, the percentages may not add to 100.0.

[3] Violent crimes are offenses of murder and nonnegligent manslaughter, forcible rape, robbery, and aggravated assault. Property crimes are offenses of burglary, larceny-theft, motor vehicle theft, and arson.

Table IV-37. Arrests, Suburban Areas,[1] Persons Under 15, 18, 21, and 25 Years of Age, 2011

(Number, percent; 6,522 agencies; 2011 estimated population 104,263,328)

Offense charged	Total all ages	Number of persons arrested				Percent of total all ages			
		Under 15	Under 18	Under 21	Under 25	Under 15	Under 18	Under 21	Under 25
Total	3,796,974	120,817	447,551	1,004,338	1,592,580	3.2	11.8	26.5	41.9
Murder and nonnegligent manslaughter	2,604	23	194	640	1,128	0.9	7.5	24.6	43.3
Forcible rape	5,007	271	765	1,479	2,165	5.4	15.3	29.5	43.2
Robbery	23,424	795	4,687	10,099	14,413	3.4	20.0	43.1	61.5
Aggravated assault	107,868	3,897	11,868	23,143	38,956	3.6	11.0	21.5	36.1
Burglary	85,052	4,667	17,063	33,707	47,727	5.5	20.1	39.6	56.1
Larceny-theft	382,524	19,755	73,737	136,864	191,255	5.2	19.3	35.8	50.0
Motor vehicle theft	16,896	676	3,384	5,950	8,390	4.0	20.0	35.2	49.7
Arson	3,951	956	1,736	2,205	2,547	24.2	43.9	55.8	64.5
Violent crime[2]	138,903	4,986	17,514	35,361	56,662	3.6	12.6	25.5	40.8
Property crime[2]	488,423	26,054	95,920	178,726	249,919	5.3	19.6	36.6	51.2
Other assaults	362,555	23,492	60,487	94,921	142,963	6.5	16.7	26.2	39.4
Forgery and counterfeiting	22,970	73	558	3,245	6,902	0.3	2.4	14.1	30.0
Fraud	58,503	229	1,678	6,910	14,594	0.4	2.9	11.8	24.9
Embezzlement	5,104	19	127	964	1,911	0.4	2.5	18.9	37.4
Stolen property; buying, receiving, possessing	31,234	934	4,322	9,793	14,858	3.0	13.8	31.4	47.6
Vandalism	70,969	8,094	21,303	33,311	43,526	11.4	30.0	46.9	61.3
Weapons; carrying, possessing, etc.	39,242	3,029	7,824	13,927	20,233	7.7	19.9	35.5	51.6
Prostitution and commercialized vice	5,246	14	117	679	1,546	0.3	2.2	12.9	29.5
Sex offenses (except forcible rape and prostitution)	20,424	1,820	3,896	6,360	8,614	8.9	19.1	31.1	42.2
Drug abuse violations	460,338	8,137	48,815	140,269	226,441	1.8	10.6	30.5	49.2
Gambling	1,432	22	89	240	360	1.5	6.2	16.8	25.1
Offenses against the family and children	46,626	375	1,168	3,143	7,655	0.8	2.5	6.7	16.4
Driving under the influence	389,342	59	3,514	32,193	101,018	*	0.9	8.3	25.9
Liquor laws	174,027	2,823	33,914	133,267	144,664	1.6	19.5	76.6	83.1
Drunkenness	144,459	406	3,485	17,843	41,743	0.3	2.4	12.4	28.9
Disorderly conduct	177,018	16,833	45,374	67,068	92,755	9.5	25.6	37.9	52.4
Vagrancy	5,044	94	371	1,040	1,718	1.9	7.4	20.6	34.1
All other offenses (except traffic)	1,140,091	19,498	82,569	210,480	399,798	1.7	7.2	18.5	35.1
Suspicion	571	14	53	145	247	2.5	9.3	25.4	43.3
Curfew and loitering law violations	14,453	3,812	14,453	14,453	14,453	26.4	100.0	100.0	100.0

* = Less than one tenth of one percent.

[1] Suburban areas include law enforcement agencies in cities with less than 50,000 inhabitants and county law enforcement agencies that are within a Metropolitan Statistical Area. Suburban areas exclude all metropolitan agencies associated with a principal city.

[2] Violent crimes are offenses of murder and nonnegligent manslaughter, forcible rape, robbery, and aggravated assault. Property crimes are offenses of burglary, larceny-theft, motor vehicle theft, and arson.

Table IV-38. Arrests, Suburban Areas,[1] Distribution by Sex, 2011

(Number, percent; 6,522 agencies; 2011 estimated population 104,263,328)

Offense charged	Number of persons arrested			Percent male	Percent female	Percent distribution[2]		
	Total	Male	Female			Total	Male	Female
Total	3,796,974	2,795,803	1,001,171	73.6	26.4	100.0	100.0	100.0
Murder and nonnegligent manslaughter	2,604	2,281	323	87.6	12.4	0.1	0.1	*
Forcible rape	5,007	4,951	56	98.9	1.1	0.1	0.2	*
Robbery	23,424	20,599	2,825	87.9	12.1	0.6	0.7	0.3
Aggravated assault	107,868	83,948	23,920	77.8	22.2	2.8	3.0	2.4
Burglary	85,052	72,282	12,770	85.0	15.0	2.2	2.6	1.3
Larceny-theft	382,524	219,103	163,421	57.3	42.7	10.1	7.8	16.3
Motor vehicle theft	16,896	13,770	3,126	81.5	18.5	0.4	0.5	0.3
Arson	3,951	3,278	673	83.0	17.0	0.1	0.1	0.1
Violent crime[3]	138,903	111,779	27,124	80.5	19.5	3.7	4.0	2.7
Property crime[3]	488,423	308,433	179,990	63.1	36.9	12.9	11.0	18.0
Other assaults	362,555	261,512	101,043	72.1	27.9	9.5	9.4	10.1
Forgery and counterfeiting	22,970	14,368	8,602	62.6	37.4	0.6	0.5	0.9
Fraud	58,503	34,334	24,169	58.7	41.3	1.5	1.2	2.4
Embezzlement	5,104	2,620	2,484	51.3	48.7	0.1	0.1	0.2
Stolen property; buying, receiving, possessing	31,234	24,589	6,645	78.7	21.3	0.8	0.9	0.7
Vandalism	70,969	57,984	12,985	81.7	18.3	1.9	2.1	1.3
Weapons; carrying, possessing, etc.	39,242	35,739	3,503	91.1	8.9	1.0	1.3	0.3
Prostitution and commercialized vice	5,246	2,110	3,136	40.2	59.8	0.1	0.1	0.3
Sex offenses (except forcible rape and prostitution)	20,424	19,048	1,376	93.3	6.7	0.5	0.7	0.1
Drug abuse violations	460,338	363,828	96,510	79.0	21.0	12.1	13.0	9.6
Gambling	1,432	1,044	388	72.9	27.1	*	*	*
Offenses against the family and children	46,626	37,144	9,482	79.7	20.3	1.2	1.3	0.9
Driving under the influence	389,342	289,642	99,700	74.4	25.6	10.3	10.4	10.0
Liquor laws	174,027	119,318	54,709	68.6	31.4	4.6	4.3	5.5
Drunkenness	144,459	116,554	27,905	80.7	19.3	3.8	4.2	2.8
Disorderly conduct	177,018	126,270	50,748	71.3	28.7	4.7	4.5	5.1
Vagrancy	5,044	3,925	1,119	77.8	22.2	0.1	0.1	0.1
All other offenses (except traffic)	1,140,091	855,192	284,899	75.0	25.0	30.0	30.6	28.5
Suspicion	571	432	139	75.7	24.3	*	*	*
Curfew and loitering law violations	14,453	9,938	4,515	68.8	31.2	0.4	0.4	0.5

* = Less than one tenth of one percent.

[1] Suburban areas include law enforcement agencies in cities with less than 50,000 inhabitants and county law enforcement agencies that are within a Metropolitan Statistical Area. Suburban areas exclude all metropolitan agencies associated with a principal city.

[2] Because of rounding, the percentages may not add to 100.0.

[3] Violent crimes are offenses of murder and nonnegligent manslaughter, forcible rape, robbery, and aggravated assault. Property crimes are offenses of burglary, larceny-theft, motor vehicle theft, and arson.

Table IV-39. Arrests, Suburban Areas,[1] Distribution by Race, 2011

(Number, percent; 6,522 agencies; 2011 estimated population 104,263,328)

Offense charged	Total arrests					Percent distribution[2]					Arrests under 18				
	Total	White	Black	American Indian or Alaskan Native	Asian or Pacific Islander	Total	White	Black	American Indian or Alaskan Native	Asian or Pacific Islander	Total	White	Black	American Indian or Alaskan Native	Asian or Pacific Islander
Total	3,783,506	2,787,465	932,130	32,490	31,421	100.0	73.7	24.6	0.9	0.8	445,669	312,083	126,314	3,105	4,167
Murder and nonnegligent															
manslaughter..........................	2,599	1,442	1,113	17	27	100.0	55.5	42.8	0.7	1.0	193	101	91	1	0
Forcible rape	4,980	3,633	1,283	26	38	100.0	73.0	25.8	0.5	0.8	761	523	231	2	5
Robbery..............................	23,391	11,393	11,741	121	136	100.0	48.7	50.2	0.5	0.6	4,682	1,526	3,112	23	21
Aggravated assault..........................	107,626	75,875	29,959	920	872	100.0	70.5	27.8	0.9	0.8	11,833	7,054	4,592	99	88
Burglary......................................	84,863	62,196	21,785	375	507	100.0	73.3	25.7	0.4	0.6	17,019	11,171	5,632	82	134
Larceny-theft.........................	380,938	267,187	106,806	3,097	3,848	100.0	70.1	28.0	0.8	1.0	73,274	45,752	26,031	537	954
Motor vehicle theft........................	16,854	12,308	4,316	128	102	100.0	73.0	25.6	0.8	0.6	3,373	2,208	1,109	32	24
Arson	3,942	2,997	902	14	29	100.0	76.0	22.9	0.4	0.7	1,733	1,305	406	3	19
Violent crime[3]................................	138,596	92,343	44,096	1,084	1,073	100.0	66.6	31.8	0.8	0.8	17,469	9,204	8,026	125	114
Property crime[3].............................	486,597	344,688	133,809	3,614	4,486	100.0	70.8	27.5	0.7	0.9	95,399	60,436	33,178	654	1,131
Other assaults	361,430	260,805	95,095	2,721	2,809	100.0	72.2	26.3	0.8	0.8	60,290	37,853	21,719	323	395
Forgery and counterfeiting..............	22,897	15,377	7,232	58	230	100.0	67.2	31.6	0.3	1.0	557	394	153	1	9
Fraud	58,261	39,446	18,118	211	486	100.0	67.7	31.1	0.4	0.8	1,668	1,010	643	5	10
Embezzlement	5,086	3,347	1,654	19	66	100.0	65.8	32.5	0.4	1.3	127	83	43	0	1
Stolen property; buying,															
receiving, possessing......................	31,161	21,765	9,036	148	212	100.0	69.8	29.0	0.5	0.7	4,319	2,633	1,621	24	41
Vandalism................................	70,691	55,089	14,528	528	546	100.0	77.9	20.6	0.7	0.8	21,197	16,601	4,273	149	174
Weapons; carrying, possessing, etc..	39,164	26,238	12,443	175	308	100.0	67.0	31.8	0.4	0.8	7,800	5,168	2,494	45	93
Prostitution and commercialized															
vice	5,235	3,328	1,588	24	295	100.0	63.6	30.3	0.5	5.6	116	68	48	0	0
Sex offenses (except forcible															
rape and prostitution).....................	20,367	15,646	4,337	175	209	100.0	76.8	21.3	0.9	1.0	3,883	2,789	1,050	22	22
Drug abuse violations.....................	459,120	339,968	113,472	2,266	3,414	100.0	74.0	24.7	0.5	0.7	48,634	39,085	8,624	381	544
Gambling....................................	1,429	792	525	20	92	100.0	55.4	36.7	1.4	6.4	89	45	37	1	6
Offenses against the family															
and children	46,430	29,866	15,817	445	302	100.0	64.3	34.1	1.0	0.7	1,158	877	269	8	4
Driving under the influence	387,646	334,580	45,370	3,075	4,621	100.0	86.3	11.7	0.8	1.2	3,486	3,224	201	29	32
Liquor laws.....................................	172,599	148,832	18,729	2,935	2,103	100.0	86.2	10.9	1.7	1.2	33,704	30,630	2,162	475	437
Drunkenness................................	143,968	123,632	18,064	1,276	996	100.0	85.9	12.5	0.9	0.7	3,468	3,120	279	43	26
Disorderly conduct........................	176,303	121,290	52,162	1,675	1,176	100.0	68.8	29.6	1.0	0.7	45,260	27,542	17,169	261	288
Vagrancy......................................	5,031	3,351	1,637	23	20	100.0	66.6	32.5	0.5	0.4	367	243	123	0	1
All other offenses (except															
traffic)...	1,136,524	795,854	320,883	11,961	7,826	100.0	70.0	28.2	1.1	0.7	82,225	60,147	20,883	505	690
Suspicion	571	312	253	3	3	100.0	54.6	44.3	0.5	0.5	53	15	37	0	1
Curfew and loitering law															
violations....................................	14,400	10,916	3,282	54	148	100.0	75.8	22.8	0.4	1.0	14,400	10,916	3,282	54	148

NA = Not available.

[1] Suburban areas include law enforcement agencies in cities with less than 50,000 inhabitants and county law enforcement agencies that are within a Metropolitan Statistical Area. Suburban areas exclude all metropolitan agencies associated with a principal city.

[2] Because of rounding, the percentages may not add to 100.0.

[3] Violent crimes are offenses of murder and nonnegligent manslaughter, forcible rape, robbery, and aggravated assault. Property crimes are offenses of burglary, larceny-theft, motor vehicle theft, and arson.

Table IV-39.   Arrests, Suburban Areas,[1] Distribution by Race, 2011—*Continued*

(Number, percent; 6,522 agencies; 2011 estimated population 104,263,328)

Offense charged	Percent distribution[2]					Arrests under 18					Percent distribution[2]				
	Total	White	Black	American Indian or Alaskan Native	Asian or Pacific Islander	Total	White	Black	American Indian or Alaskan Native	Asian or Pacific Islander	Total	White	Black	American Indian or Alaskan Native	Asian or Pacific Islander
Total	100.0	70.0	28.3	0.7	0.9	3,337,837	2,475,382	805,816	29,385	27,254	100.0	74.2	24.1	0.9	0.8
Murder and nonnegligent															
manslaughter................................	100.0	52.3	47.2	0.5	0.0	2,406	1,341	1,022	16	27	100.0	55.7	42.5	0.7	1.1
Forcible rape	100.0	68.7	30.4	0.3	0.7	4,219	3,110	1,052	24	33	100.0	73.7	24.9	0.6	0.8
Robbery...	100.0	32.6	66.5	0.5	0.4	18,709	9,867	8,629	98	115	100.0	52.7	46.1	0.5	0.6
Aggravated assault	100.0	59.6	38.8	0.8	0.7	95,793	68,821	25,367	821	784	100.0	71.8	26.5	0.9	0.8
Burglary..	100.0	65.6	33.1	0.5	0.8	67,844	51,025	16,153	293	373	100.0	75.2	23.8	0.4	0.5
Larceny-theft.................................	100.0	62.4	35.5	0.7	1.3	307,664	221,435	80,775	2,560	2,894	100.0	72.0	26.3	0.8	0.9
Motor vehicle theft.........................	100.0	65.5	32.9	0.9	0.7	13,481	10,100	3,207	96	78	100.0	74.9	23.8	0.7	0.6
Arson	100.0	75.3	23.4	0.2	1.1	2,209	1,692	496	11	10	100.0	76.6	22.5	0.5	0.5
Violent crime[3]	100.0	52.7	45.9	0.7	0.7	121,127	83,139	36,070	959	959	100.0	68.6	29.8	0.8	0.8
Property crime[3].............................	100.0	63.4	34.8	0.7	1.2	391,198	284,252	100,631	2,960	3,355	100.0	72.7	25.7	0.8	0.9
Other assaults	100.0	62.8	36.0	0.5	0.7	301,140	222,952	73,376	2,398	2,414	100.0	74.0	24.4	0.8	0.8
Forgery and counterfeiting..............	100.0	70.7	27.5	0.2	1.6	22,340	14,983	7,079	57	221	100.0	67.1	31.7	0.3	1.0
Fraud..	100.0	60.6	38.5	0.3	0.6	56,593	38,436	17,475	206	476	100.0	67.9	30.9	0.4	0.8
Embezzlement	100.0	65.4	33.9	0.0	0.8	4,959	3,264	1,611	19	65	100.0	65.8	32.5	0.4	1.3
Stolen property; buying,															
receiving, possessing.......................	100.0	61.0	37.5	0.6	0.9	26,842	19,132	7,415	124	171	100.0	71.3	27.6	0.5	0.6
Vandalism......................................	100.0	78.3	20.2	0.7	0.8	49,494	38,488	10,255	379	372	100.0	77.8	20.7	0.8	0.8
Weapons; carrying, possessing, etc..	100.0	66.3	32.0	0.6	1.2	31,364	21,070	9,949	130	215	100.0	67.2	31.7	0.4	0.7
Prostitution and commercialized															
vice	100.0	58.6	41.4	0.0	0.0	5,119	3,260	1,540	24	295	100.0	63.7	30.1	0.5	5.8
Sex offenses (except forcible															
rape and prostitution)	100.0	71.8	27.0	0.6	0.6	16,484	12,857	3,287	153	187	100.0	78.0	19.9	0.9	1.1
Drug abuse violations	100.0	80.4	17.7	0.8	1.1	410,486	300,883	104,848	1,885	2,870	100.0	73.3	25.5	0.5	0.7
Gambling.......................................	100.0	50.6	41.6	1.1	6.7	1,340	747	488	19	86	100.0	55.7	36.4	1.4	6.4
Offenses against the family															
and children	100.0	75.7	23.2	0.7	0.3	45,272	28,989	15,548	437	298	100.0	64.0	34.3	1.0	0.7
Driving under the influence	100.0	92.5	5.8	0.8	0.9	384,160	331,356	45,169	3,046	4,589	100.0	86.3	11.8	0.8	1.2
Liquor laws....................................	100.0	90.9	6.4	1.4	1.3	138,895	118,202	16,567	2,460	1,666	100.0	85.1	11.9	1.8	1.2
Drunkenness..................................	100.0	90.0	8.0	1.2	0.7	140,500	120,512	17,785	1,233	970	100.0	85.8	12.7	0.9	0.7
Disorderly conduct.........................	100.0	60.9	37.9	0.6	0.6	131,043	93,748	34,993	1,414	888	100.0	71.5	26.7	1.1	0.7
Vagrancy..	100.0	66.2	33.5	0.0	0.3	4,664	3,108	1,514	23	19	100.0	66.6	32.5	0.5	0.4
All other offenses (except															
traffic)...	100.0	73.1	25.4	0.6	0.8	1,054,299	735,707	300,000	11,456	7,136	100.0	69.8	28.5	1.1	0.7
Suspicion	100.0	28.3	69.8	0.0	1.9	518	297	216	3	2	100.0	57.3	41.7	0.6	0.4
Curfew and loitering law															
violations	100.0	75.8	22.8	0.4	1.0	NA	NA	NA	NA	NA	NA	NA	NA	NA	NA

NA = Not available.

[1] Suburban areas include law enforcement agencies in cities with less than 50,000 inhabitants and county law enforcement agencies that are within a Metropolitan Statistical Area. Suburban areas exclude all metropolitan agencies associated with a principal city.

[2] Because of rounding, the percentages may not add to 100.0.

[3] Violent crimes are offenses of murder and nonnegligent manslaughter, forcible rape, robbery, and aggravated assault. Property crimes are offenses of burglary, larceny-theft, motor vehicle theft, and arson.

Table IV-40. Police Disposition of Juvenile Offenders Taken into Custody, 2011

(Number, percent.)

Population group	Total[1]	Handled within department and released	Referred to juvenile court jurisdiction	Referred to welfare agency	Referred to other police agency	Referred to criminal or adult court	Number of agencies	2011 estimated population
Total Agencies								
Number	440,787	96,808	301,471	1,939	8,299	32,270	5,079	121,067,837
Percent[2]	100.0	22.0	68.4	0.4	1.9	7.3		
Total Cities								
Number	356,223	80,667	244,417	1,523	5,723	23,893	3,889	85,576,220
Percent[2]	100.0	22.6	68.6	0.4	1.6	6.7		
Group I (250,000 and over)								
Number	93,247	27,961	63,297	75	893	1,021	34	22,898,541
Percent[2]	100.0	30.0	67.9	0.1	1.0	1.1		
Group II (100,000 to 249,999)								
Number	51,059	11,051	38,366	392	372	878	89	13,383,057
Percent[2]	100.0	21.6	75.1	0.8	0.7	1.7		
Group III (50,000 to 99,999)								
Number	67,536	13,058	47,999	294	2,360	3,825	228	15,800,505
Percent[2]	100.0	19.3	71.1	0.4	3.5	5.7		
Group IV (25,000 to 49,999)								
Number	51,166	10,185	34,844	262	1,058	4,817	363	12,630,419
Percent[2]	100.0	19.9	68.1	0.5	2.1	9.4		
Group V (10,000 to 24,999)								
Number	50,631	9,188	33,575	251	639	6,978	763	12,153,955
Percent[2]	100.0	18.1	66.3	0.5	1.3	13.8		
Group VI (under 10,000)								
Number	42,584	9,224	26,336	249	401	6,374	2,412	8,709,743
Percent[2]	100.0	21.7	61.8	0.6	0.9	15.0		
Metropolitan Counties								
Number	71,091	14,384	47,758	329	2,466	6,154	621	26,714,862
Percent[2]	100.0	20.2	67.2	0.5	3.5	8.7		
Nonmetropolitan Counties								
Number	13,473	1,757	9,296	87	110	2,223	569	8,776,755
Percent[2]	100.0	13.0	69.0	0.6	0.8	16.5		
Suburban Areas[3]								
Number	200,557	42,914	129,133	997	5,753	21,760	3,260	61,183,744
Percent[2]	100.0	21.4	64.4	0.5	2.9	10.8		

[1] Includes all offenses except traffic and neglect cases.

[2] Because of rounding, the percentages may not add to 100.0.

[3] Suburban areas include law enforcement agencies in cities with less than 50,000 inhabitants and county law enforcement agencies that are within a Metropolitan Statistical Area. Suburban areas exclude all metropolitan agencies associated with a principal city. The agencies associated with suburban areas also appear in other groups within this table.

Table IV-41. Arrests, by State, 2011

(Number.)

State	Total all classes[1]	Violent crime[2]	Property crime[2]	Murder and non-negligent man-slaughter	Forcible rape	Robbery	Aggra-vated assault	Burglary	Larceny-theft	Motor vehicle theft	Arson	Other assaults
Alabama[3]												
Under 18	156	0	95	0	0	0	0	5	90	0	0	20
Total, all ages	2,101	15	531	0	0	11	4	17	509	5	0	234
Alaska												
Under 18	3,453	194	1,028	1	14	43	136	109	834	62	23	365
Total, all ages	39,607	2,006	3,824	32	81	225	1,668	417	3,097	266	44	5,309
Arizona												
Under 18	37,596	1,059	8,886	17	13	262	767	1,285	7,194	298	109	4,093
Total, all ages	285,528	8,589	40,144	244	196	1,736	6,413	4,615	33,888	1,402	239	24,442
Arkansas												
Under 18	8,320	318	2,374	4	25	65	224	459	1,853	54	8	1,177
Total, all ages	108,281	3,229	12,948	59	139	435	2,596	2,391	10,213	285	59	8,698
California												
Under 18	144,768	10,972	33,873	135	173	4,170	6,494	11,176	20,374	1,828	495	15,506
Total, all ages	1,183,470	107,165	147,842	1,512	1,757	17,431	86,465	52,355	84,090	10,350	1,047	82,460
Colorado												
Under 18	28,675	571	6,126	5	59	101	406	589	5,137	261	139	1,685
Total, all ages	208,352	5,701	23,445	107	400	936	4,258	2,407	19,719	1,084	235	13,764
Connecticut												
Under 18	12,505	599	2,684	4	39	276	280	404	2,061	138	81	3,409
Total, all ages	119,285	4,817	17,366	128	267	1,397	3,025	2,771	13,813	612	170	23,258
Delaware												
Under 18	4,785	360	1,191	2	8	126	224	153	990	30	18	1,203
Total, all ages	37,832	2,328	7,325	29	93	583	1,623	981	6,187	116	41	7,362
District of Columbia[4]												
Under 18	645	88	81	0	0	77	11	0	74	7	0	53
Total, all ages	8,725	157	175	0	0	118	39	0	165	10	0	225
Florida[3, 5]												
Under 18	87,025	5,729	25,887	52	205	2,071	3,401	7,631	16,850	1,293	113	12,949
Total, all ages	952,845	43,364	128,489	709	1,527	9,148	31,980	28,778	94,047	5,345	319	88,685
Georgia												
Under 18	38,046	1,805	10,603	40	44	534	1,187	2,319	7,713	483	88	5,344
Total, all ages	349,708	14,419	53,874	460	350	2,787	10,822	9,596	41,729	2,148	401	33,830
Idaho												
Under 18	10,370	142	2,393	0	9	10	123	262	2,023	73	35	1,031
Total, all ages	63,005	1,303	7,037	17	68	82	1,136	948	5,859	183	47	5,198
Illinois[6]												
Under 18	24,136	2,380	5,030	38	68	1,164	1,110	893	3,207	913	17	3,716
Total, all ages	132,863	6,939	18,924	290	409	2,524	3,716	2,570	13,683	2,610	61	19,717
Indiana												
Under 18	25,633	1,187	6,828	34	15	318	820	891	5,477	404	56	4,522
Total, all ages	194,774	8,398	30,383	243	187	1,687	6,281	4,223	24,499	1,527	134	19,091
Iowa												
Under 18	15,779	545	4,381	1	22	46	476	658	3,508	135	80	2,075
Total, all ages	105,015	3,939	14,424	33	110	202	3,594	1,924	11,985	381	134	9,459
Kansas												
Under 18	7,729	254	2,022	5	43	32	174	234	1,687	75	26	1,103
Total, all ages	78,391	2,236	7,624	44	187	189	1,816	982	6,193	382	67	11,429
Kentucky												
Under 18	8,042	399	2,763	7	31	211	150	589	2,029	97	48	1,098
Total, all ages	176,087	3,563	19,953	114	244	1,146	2,059	3,818	15,397	596	142	10,545
Louisiana												
Under 18	13,711	1,378	3,492	17	36	253	1,072	769	2,562	119	42	2,352
Total, all ages	119,085	8,420	19,892	158	208	959	7,095	3,774	15,419	577	122	15,227
Maine												
Under 18	5,342	73	1,424	0	22	19	32	256	1,055	81	32	831
Total, all ages	51,592	751	8,142	17	75	204	455	1,396	6,368	301	77	6,562
Maryland												
Under 18	30,018	2,026	7,696	9	37	910	1,070	1,379	5,589	569	159	5,776
Total, all ages	229,010	9,551	28,345	202	305	2,819	6,225	5,982	20,403	1,585	375	25,424

[1] Does not include traffic arrests.

[2] Violent crimes are offenses of murder and nonnegligent manslaughter, forcible rape, robbery, and aggravated assault. Property crimes are offenses of burglary, larceny-theft, motor vehicle theft, and arson.

[3] See 2011 Arrest Data for details. http://www.fbi.gov/about-us/cjis/ucr/crime-in-the-u.s/2011/crime-in-the-u.s.-2011/persons-arrested/persons-arrested

[4] Includes arrests reported by the Metro Transit Police. This agency has no population associated with it.

[5] The arrest category "All other offenses" for Florida also includes the arrest counts for offenses against the family and children, drunkenness, disorderly conduct, vagrancy, suspicion, curfew and loitering law violations, and runaways.

[6] Forcible rape figures for Illinois include only those data provided by Rockford. The forcible rape figures for Minnesota include only those provided by the cities of St. Paul and Minneapolis. See 2011 Arrest Data for details. http://www.fbi.gov/about-us/cjis/ucr/crime-in-the-u.s/2011/crime-in-the-u.s.-2011/persons-arrested/persons-arrested

Table IV-41. Arrests, by State, 2011—*Continued*

(Number.)

State	Forgery and counter-feiting	Fraud	Embezzle-ment	Stolen property; buying, receiving, possessing	Vandal-ism	Weapons; carrying, possessing, etc.	Prostitu-tion and commer-cialized vice	Sex offenses (except forcible rape and prosti-tution)	Drug abuse violations	Gamb-ling	Offenses against the family and children	Driving under the influence
Alabama[3]												
Under 18	0	0	0	2	0	1	0	0	27	0	0	1
Total, all ages	4	9	16	20	10	20	0	0	300	0	1	287
Alaska												
Under 18	1	19	7	1	153	29	0	41	352	0	2	57
Total, all ages	64	245	102	28	887	401	69	356	2,341	1	329	4,420
Arizona												
Under 18	18	87	5	124	2,653	265	6	294	5,008	3	157	395
Total, all ages	1,822	2,101	200	1,240	11,164	2,400	777	1,702	30,886	55	2,536	35,496
Arkansas												
Under 18	8	21	6	77	231	107	0	27	661	5	4	82
Total, all ages	557	1,952	35	693	1,125	943	166	133	8,783	18	119	7,758
California												
Under 18	109	334	13	2,246	8,717	5,978	324	1,648	12,408	20	8	658
Total, all ages	6,224	6,998	1,100	17,147	21,921	27,690	10,659	11,143	188,188	590	244	104,345
Colorado												
Under 18	27	81	2	89	1,223	406	11	199	3,240	0	63	367
Total, all ages	707	1,700	121	655	4,971	1,701	319	818	15,109	2	3,134	27,314
Connecticut												
Under 18	17	39	0	46	537	180	2	95	1,105	7	35	42
Total, all ages	899	1,297	161	445	2,310	1,244	386	560	13,667	61	1,436	8,487
Delaware												
Under 18	10	61	3	69	177	89	0	47	491	1	2	0
Total, all ages	559	1,803	186	336	880	327	29	181	5,110	6	169	242
District of Columbia[4]												
Under 18	0	0	0	4	13	18	0	0	22	0	0	0
Total, all ages	2	17	0	10	29	59	0	0	204	1	0	43
Florida[3, 5]												
Under 18	66	442	11	272	1,744	1,032	35	232	10,055	31	0	221
Total, all ages	2,983	13,992	939	3,440	7,364	5,785	4,484	2,734	130,296	315	0	43,784
Georgia												
Under 18	64	267	21	430	915	813	32	652	3,106	9	246	219
Total, all ages	4,461	6,294	406	3,679	4,147	3,971	1,524	4,032	42,812	331	4,354	31,176
Idaho												
Under 18	5	23	2	49	497	92	0	59	1,001	0	9	110
Total, all ages	158	437	54	244	1,162	427	18	275	6,558	0	658	9,161
Illinois[6]												
Under 18	4	20	0	15	1,177	915	9	51	4,595	440	14	18
Total, all ages	221	232	0	80	3,904	3,941	2,432	609	38,701	2,429	353	3,619
Indiana												
Under 18	35	44	0	212	789	323	10	214	2,319	1	37	93
Total, all ages	1,145	1,699	21	1,033	2,011	1,880	977	1,277	23,345	61	1,473	20,043
Iowa												
Under 18	27	45	8	37	989	122	1	68	1,124	0	3	129
Total, all ages	515	784	68	185	2,520	566	128	213	9,139	6	1,151	11,889
Kansas												
Under 18	23	19	14	24	344	80	1	101	922	0	16	133
Total, all ages	401	931	163	283	1,875	600	213	301	7,364	1	239	11,470
Kentucky												
Under 18	12	12	3	180	331	112	1	83	896	2	17	94
Total, all ages	1,218	1,164	333	1,812	1,236	1,082	196	394	21,383	7	4,834	22,973
Louisiana												
Under 18	10	25	1	219	623	255	3	103	1,179	5	34	34
Total, all ages	362	1,411	24	1,370	2,537	1,515	351	613	14,925	103	733	6,032
Maine												
Under 18	2	15	4	27	400	39	0	43	512	0	1	46
Total, all ages	368	755	56	198	1,487	403	26	253	5,627	3	129	5,802
Maryland												
Under 18	38	62	10	20	1,304	802	15	232	4,330	20	13	108
Total, all ages	814	1,554	289	192	3,267	3,235	1,121	1,175	41,022	225	2,054	17,402

[3] See 2011 Arrest Data for details. http://www.fbi.gov/about-us/cjis/ucr/crime-in-the-u.s/2011/crime-in-the-u.s.-2011/persons-arrested/persons-arrested

[4] Includes arrests reported by the Metro Transit Police. This agency has no population associated with it.

[5] The arrest category "All other offenses" for Florida also includes the arrest counts for offenses against the family and children, drunkenness, disorderly conduct, vagrancy, suspicion, curfew and loi-tering law violations, and runaways.

[6] Forcible rape figures for Illinois include only those data provided by Rockford. The forcible rape figures for Minnesota include only those provided by the cities of St. Paul and Minneapolis. See 2011 Arrest Data for details. http://www.fbi.gov/about-us/cjis/ucr/crime-in-the-u.s/2011/crime-in-the-u.s.-2011/persons-arrested/persons-arrested

Table IV-41. Arrests, by State, 2011—*Continued*

(Number.)

State	Liquor laws	Drunken-ness[7]	Disorderly conduct	Vagrancy	All other offenses (except traffic)	Suspi-cion	Curfew and loitering law violations	Number of agencies	2011 estimated population
Alabama[3]									
Under 18	1	1	2	0	6	0	0	1	82,012
Total, all ages	6	193	30	0	425	0	0		
Alaska									
Under 18	603	11	53	5	500	0	32	32	714,559
Total, all ages	2,603	102	1,115	7	15,362	4	32		
Arizona									
Under 18	4,606	0	2,714	60	4,372	0	2,791	85	6,128,057
Total, all ages	21,739	0	17,374	1,181	78,889	0	2,791		
Arkansas									
Under 18	194	136	666	0	1,909	0	317	189	2,163,737
Total, all ages	1,828	7,316	2,681	458	48,524	0	317		
California									
Under 18	3,707	2,944	6,950	270	29,643	0	8,440	619	37,483,185
Total, all ages	15,904	99,017	11,246	5,122	310,025	0	8,440		
Colorado									
Under 18	2,734	14	2,560	0	8,067	1	1,209	180	4,644,849
Total, all ages	11,424	1,734	9,672	160	84,671	21	1,209		
Connecticut									
Under 18	149	1	1,945	0	1,592	0	21	99	3,509,272
Total, all ages	919	4	12,458	41	29,448	0	21		
Delaware									
Under 18	239	11	311	0	414	0	106	55	907,135
Total, all ages	1,615	669	2,141	1,129	5,329	0	106		
District of Columbia[4]									
Under 18	8	1	38	0	319	0	0	1	NA
Total, all ages	1,455	70	159	103	6,016	0	0		
Florida[3, 5]									
Under 18	1,170	0	0	0	27,149	0	0	678	19,052,717
Total, all ages	27,256	0	0	0	448,935	0	0		
Georgia									
Under 18	1,067	80	3,550	96	7,988	21	718	422	9,214,519
Total, all ages	9,783	3,384	26,769	1,139	98,506	99	718		
Idaho									
Under 18	1,087	49	557	0	2,864	0	400	102	1,493,662
Total, all ages	4,076	435	2,220	15	23,169	0	400		
Illinois[6]									
Under 18	152	0	2,630	0	2,746	0	224	2	2,857,044
Total, all ages	1,060	0	11,031	110	18,337	0	224		
Indiana									
Under 18	1,956	269	2,029	10	4,092	43	620	169	4,962,299
Total, all ages	10,395	16,303	6,873	83	47,533	130	620		
Iowa									
Under 18	1,329	329	1,927	0	2,115	0	525	185	2,685,953
Total, all ages	7,261	12,158	6,155	18	23,912	0	525		
Kansas									
Under 18	1,125	2	435	0	1,111	0	0	244	2,017,057
Total, all ages	6,204	347	2,746	0	23,964	0	0		
Kentucky									
Under 18	72	196	437	22	1,244	0	68	359	4,103,435
Total, all ages	500	19,360	4,998	407	60,061	0	68		
Louisiana									
Under 18	196	43	1,935	7	1,647	9	161	110	2,433,299
Total, all ages	6,723	2,794	9,772	424	25,439	257	161		
Maine									
Under 18	894	5	148	0	845	0	33	163	1,324,187
Total, all ages	3,937	24	1,709	15	15,312	0	33		
Maryland									
Under 18	572	0	1,526	10	5,229	18	211	134	4,810,360
Total, all ages	6,129	10	6,306	136	80,150	398	211		

[3] See 2011 Arrest Data for details. http://www.fbi.gov/about-us/cjis/ucr/crime-in-the-u.s/2011/crime-in-the-u.s.-2011/persons-arrested/persons-arrested

[4] Includes arrests reported by the Metro Transit Police. This agency has no population associated with it.

[5] The arrest category All other offenses for Florida also includes the arrest counts for offenses against the family and children, drunkenness, disorderly conduct, vagrancy, suspicion, curfew and loitering law violations, and runaways.

[6] Forcible rape figures for Illinois include only those data provided by Rockford. The forcible rape figures for Minnesota include only those provided by the cities of St. Paul and Minneapolis. See 2011 Arrest Data for details. http://www.fbi.gov/about-us/cjis/ucr/crime-in-the-u.s/2011/crime-in-the-u.s.-2011/persons-arrested/persons-arrested

[7] Drunkenness is not considered a crime in some states; therefore, the figures vary widely from state to state.

Table IV-41. Arrests, by State, 2011—*Continued*

(Number.)

State	Total all classes[1]	Violent crime[2]	Property crime[2]	Murder and non-negligent man-slaughter	Forcible rape	Robbery	Aggra-vated assault	Burglary	Larceny-theft	Motor vehicle theft	Arson	Other assaults
Massachusetts												
Under 18	12,149	1,340	2,239	6	30	319	985	512	1,596	98	33	2,253
Total, all ages	137,379	11,512	18,428	90	288	1,808	9,326	3,693	13,955	697	83	21,483
Michigan												
Under 18	26,155	1,530	7,721	10	86	501	933	1,371	5,809	459	82	3,393
Total, all ages	251,200	11,856	34,176	158	589	2,141	8,968	6,045	25,970	1,895	266	27,645
Minnesota[6]												
Under 18	34,171	861	8,018	6	23	336	496	678	7,041	207	92	3,058
Total, all ages	176,051	5,140	28,405	69	152	1,196	3,723	2,993	24,268	977	167	16,327
Mississippi												
Under 18	7,915	211	2,127	13	20	115	63	491	1,531	85	20	1,118
Total, all ages	102,765	2,223	11,509	173	161	625	1,264	2,373	8,639	402	95	10,911
Missouri												
Under 18	31,503	1,171	8,236	20	52	399	700	1,260	6,608	255	113	4,860
Total, all ages	295,080	10,401	41,476	252	382	2,117	7,650	6,475	33,181	1,571	249	30,529
Montana												
Under 18	6,117	91	1,422	0	7	4	80	57	1,276	72	17	503
Total, all ages	29,678	829	4,118	10	40	45	734	225	3,698	163	32	3,557
Nebraska												
Under 18	12,640	195	3,424	7	30	61	97	264	3,005	94	61	1,609
Total, all ages	81,890	2,111	11,062	53	213	355	1,490	902	9,707	364	89	8,348
Nevada												
Under 18	16,588	655	3,317	2	23	263	367	498	2,461	74	284	1,902
Total, all ages	141,908	5,690	14,355	107	168	1,491	3,924	2,579	10,895	505	376	15,863
New Hampshire												
Under 18	5,299	85	810	0	4	12	69	70	697	19	24	915
Total, all ages	40,699	860	4,152	4	42	159	655	516	3,522	75	39	5,492
New Jersey												
Under 18	30,690	2,011	5,819	13	46	947	1,005	1,131	4,416	138	134	2,640
Total, all ages	333,136	11,947	33,726	207	279	3,561	7,900	6,584	26,191	688	263	24,331
New Mexico												
Under 18	11,525	442	3,307	5	17	42	378	437	2,660	118	92	1,489
Total, all ages	108,731	4,386	13,257	83	121	380	3,802	1,835	10,800	408	214	9,808
New York[3]												
Under 18	31,515	1,667	9,339	13	68	733	853	1,606	7,311	347	75	4,041
Total, all ages	303,435	11,306	53,185	176	402	2,851	7,877	7,376	43,965	1,607	237	33,664
North Carolina												
Under 18	40,803	1,795	10,600	37	48	628	1,082	2,904	7,388	167	141	7,144
Total, all ages	494,561	19,735	71,541	573	560	3,900	14,702	17,331	52,358	1,430	422	60,169
North Dakota												
Under 18	4,754	44	965	0	5	4	35	67	863	29	6	366
Total, all ages	26,012	495	2,936	8	30	22	435	213	2,602	109	12	1,971
Ohio												
Under 18	29,697	1,027	6,127	20	64	528	415	1,158	4,684	194	91	5,512
Total, all ages	256,625	7,642	37,720	235	474	2,795	4,138	6,542	30,043	901	234	35,107
Oklahoma												
Under 18	13,878	532	4,138	17	25	137	353	734	3,214	124	66	1,056
Total, all ages	134,295	5,155	17,945	144	231	669	4,111	2,743	14,507	513	182	8,420
Oregon												
Under 18	20,457	445	5,076	2	22	114	307	486	4,310	161	119	1,742
Total, all ages	133,414	4,289	24,655	68	229	933	3,059	2,541	20,634	1,219	261	13,538
Pennsylvania												
Under 18	67,659	4,143	10,187	28	171	1,563	2,381	1,510	7,977	536	164	6,595
Total, all ages	418,838	23,179	58,946	445	953	6,470	15,311	9,730	46,076	2,593	547	45,157
Rhode Island												
Under 18	3,844	115	741	0	13	38	64	172	532	25	12	532
Total, all ages	29,852	702	3,368	6	56	141	499	773	2,439	111	45	3,829
South Carolina												
Under 18	15,796	736	4,265	24	44	218	450	856	3,270	91	48	2,783
Total, all ages	169,884	7,870	26,954	273	322	1,309	5,966	4,479	21,521	800	154	20,486

[1] Does not include traffic arrests.

[2] Violent crimes are offenses of murder and nonnegligent manslaughter, forcible rape, robbery, and aggravated assault. Property crimes are offenses of burglary, larceny-theft, motor vehicle theft, and arson.

[3] Drunkenness is not considered a crime in some states; therefore, the figures vary widely from state to state.

[6] The arrest category "All other offenses" for Florida also includes the arrest counts for offenses against the family and children, drunkenness, disorderly conduct, vagrancy, suspicion, curfew and loitering law violations, and runaways.

Table IV-41. Arrests, by State, 2011—*Continued*

(Number.)

State	Forgery and counter-feiting	Fraud	Embezzle-ment	Stolen property; buying, receiving, possessing	Vandal-ism	Weapons; carrying, possessing, etc.	Prostitu-tion and commer-cialized vice	Sex offenses (except forcible rape and prosti-tution)	Drug abuse violations	Gamb-ling	Offenses against the family and children	Driving under the influence
Massachusetts												
Under 18	12	27	4	188	598	198	3	55	504	2	151	66
Total, all ages	578	1,181	90	1,283	3,138	1,479	860	566	10,849	15	1,962	9,887
Michigan												
Under 18	24	259	11	255	771	537	7	201	2,837	10	8	360
Total, all ages	678	4,648	917	1,588	3,125	3,926	320	862	31,486	93	3,858	29,443
Minnesota[6]												
Under 18	53	150	2	414	1,334	505	21	251	3,146	0	23	286
Total, all ages	1,081	2,382	30	1,674	3,886	1,688	885	1,331	17,727	22	644	24,543
Mississippi												
Under 18	5	49	2	94	159	104	1	25	581	6	286	72
Total, all ages	639	1,551	517	746	937	828	146	314	10,862	200	4,016	11,251
Missouri												
Under 18	26	62	7	391	1,301	369	5	452	3,245	4	55	304
Total, all ages	1,737	2,643	255	2,699	5,300	3,353	306	2,018	35,383	109	3,593	29,447
Montana												
Under 18	1	11	1	0	360	14	0	19	402	0	26	39
Total, all ages	42	171	34	6	965	71	5	61	1,790	0	321	4,251
Nebraska												
Under 18	13	56	3	115	875	117	2	127	1,319	0	17	163
Total, all ages	304	1,230	75	694	2,587	835	143	560	10,423	4	1,355	12,005
Nevada												
Under 18	14	26	6	154	982	231	70	101	1,810	6	17	75
Total, all ages	700	1,354	403	1,377	2,230	1,499	3,941	1,243	15,562	31	1,159	11,834
New Hampshire												
Under 18	2	25	5	94	318	7	1	33	580	2	4	44
Total, all ages	177	689	35	637	1,122	77	49	142	3,631	2	170	3,616
New Jersey												
Under 18	61	91	7	563	1,524	951	12	204	4,739	40	54	301
Total, all ages	1,839	3,323	211	3,327	5,227	4,081	1,086	1,298	46,377	103	14,603	26,206
New Mexico												
Under 18	3	29	14	83	371	168	1	45	1,437	4	35	139
Total, all ages	222	573	230	618	1,277	692	264	220	8,859	20	1,654	11,460
New York[3]												
Under 18	68	249	3	854	2,768	361	14	612	4,180	9	30	216
Total, all ages	2,446	5,745	116	4,773	14,771	3,065	777	3,144	56,508	160	532	35,541
North Carolina												
Under 18	47	363	22	529	1,747	1,494	17	153	3,430	1	86	498
Total, all ages	2,359	18,242	1,472	4,785	8,696	7,372	989	1,686	42,225	422	7,703	53,700
North Dakota												
Under 18	6	9	5	33	213	20	0	12	342	0	57	27
Total, all ages	65	413	41	141	466	131	10	66	2,243	0	121	4,836
Ohio												
Under 18	27	111	0	510	1,317	441	11	180	2,221	2	441	115
Total, all ages	1,109	2,550	19	3,513	4,534	3,217	1,374	734	28,943	59	3,698	36,528
Oklahoma												
Under 18	9	48	26	264	324	206	2	36	1,320	0	19	166
Total, all ages	725	1,897	437	2,083	1,240	1,764	189	538	15,931	10	831	14,563
Oregon												
Under 18	15	78	1	59	1,404	210	6	145	3,059	0	5	87
Total, all ages	761	1,625	33	409	4,655	1,744	376	1,145	19,262	1	587	14,966
Pennsylvania												
Under 18	65	174	29	453	2,749	1,210	15	528	4,655	7	42	407
Total, all ages	2,669	6,685	442	2,852	9,509	4,222	1,939	2,452	52,483	124	1,141	48,519
Rhode Island												
Under 18	4	17	2	58	301	94	0	21	388	0	84	13
Total, all ages	94	542	102	312	1,108	281	42	87	3,111	11	124	2,508
South Carolina												
Under 18	17	70	4	193	734	425	1	79	2,079	1	15	108
Total, all ages	1,552	5,124	399	2,049	3,409	1,931	524	491	26,287	240	1,040	15,674

[3] Drunkenness is not considered a crime in some states; therefore, the figures vary widely from state to state.

[6] The arrest category "All other offenses" for Florida also includes the arrest counts for offenses against the family and children, drunkenness, disorderly conduct, vagrancy, suspicion, curfew and loitering law violations, and runaways.

Table IV-41. Arrests, by State, 2011—*Continued*

(Number.)

State	Liquor laws	Drunken-ness[7]	Disorderly conduct	Vagrancy	All other offenses (except traffic)	Suspi-cion	Curfew and loitering law violations	Number of agencies	2011 estimated population
Massachusetts									
Under 18	748	175	956	0	2,620	2	8	313	5,972,351
Total, all ages	4,311	7,249	7,384	9	35,084	23	8		
Michigan									
Under 18	2,443	11	1,043	0	4,033	0	701	504	8,768,968
Total, all ages	14,923	391	8,563	261	71,740	0	701		
Minnesota[6]									
Under 18	4,390	0	4,309	44	4,709	0	2,597	325	5,344,861
Total, all ages	20,644	1	13,184	571	33,289	0	2,597		
Mississippi									
Under 18	132	54	1,178	2	1,327	14	368	93	1,675,272
Total, all ages	1,560	4,409	6,783	57	32,803	135	368		
Missouri									
Under 18	1,924	24	2,007	19	5,261	0	1,780	401	5,667,706
Total, all ages	10,269	609	13,006	276	99,891	0	1,780		
Montana									
Under 18	1,060	0	582	0	1,001	0	585	92	898,221
Total, all ages	3,915	0	3,458	4	5,495	0	585		
Nebraska									
Under 18	1,733	0	761	1	1,887	0	223	205	1,658,043
Total, all ages	10,191	0	3,761	17	15,961	1	223		
Nevada									
Under 18	1,447	29	940	40	2,808	3	1,955	23	2,432,857
Total, all ages	7,709	200	2,765	2,096	49,936	6	1,955		
New Hampshire									
Under 18	655	190	235	0	1,277	0	17	133	1,029,821
Total, all ages	3,329	2,993	1,116	50	12,343	0	17		
New Jersey									
Under 18	2,232	0	2,805	35	4,806	0	1,795	577	8,760,229
Total, all ages	7,259	0	17,791	289	128,317	0	1,795		
New Mexico									
Under 18	869	5	690	3	2,372	4	15	87	1,988,459
Total, all ages	5,084	658	3,502	5	45,917	10	15		
New York[3]									
Under 18	733	0	1,455	13	4,903	0	0	506	9,114,359
Total, all ages	3,746	0	11,322	716	61,918	0	0		
North Carolina									
Under 18	3,042	0	3,720	0	6,115	0	0	375	9,281,220
Total, all ages	29,426	0	16,003	414	147,622	0	0		
North Dakota									
Under 18	809	2	759	0	879	0	206	77	645,706
Total, all ages	4,269	332	1,698	1	5,571	0	206		
Ohio									
Under 18	1,548	22	2,126	8	7,029	2	920	439	8,496,426
Total, all ages	9,777	3,117	17,659	39	58,311	55	920		
Oklahoma									
Under 18	330	600	894	0	2,201	0	1,707	291	3,489,895
Total, all ages	1,969	19,661	2,712	166	36,352	0	1,707		
Oregon									
Under 18	2,596	0	1,348	0	3,336	0	845	137	3,694,895
Total, all ages	13,663	0	10,202	0	20,658	0	845		
Pennsylvania									
Under 18	4,835	286	11,870	97	5,610	0	13,702	1,122	11,798,317
Total, all ages	20,017	23,971	48,699	1,061	51,069	0	13,702		
Rhode Island									
Under 18	92	0	746	0	615	0	21	47	873,472
Total, all ages	625	4	2,880	1	10,100	0	21		
South Carolina									
Under 18	566	81	1,936	0	1,639	0	64	251	4,209,115
Total, all ages	7,466	8,736	13,384	858	25,346	0	64		

[3] Drunkenness is not considered a crime in some states; therefore, the figures vary widely from state to state.

[6] The arrest category "All other offenses" for Florida also includes the arrest counts for offenses against the family and children, drunkenness, disorderly conduct, vagrancy, suspicion, curfew and loitering law violations, and runaways.

[7] Forcible rape figures for Illinois include only those data provided by Rockford. The forcible rape figures for Minnesota include only those provided by the cities of St. Paul and Minneapolis. See 2011 Arrest Data for details. http://www.fbi.gov/about-us/cjis/ucr/crime-in-the-u.s/2011/crime-in-the-u.s.-2011/persons-arrested/persons-arrested

Table IV-41. Arrests, by State, 2011—*Continued*

(Number.)

State	Total all classes[1]	Violent crime[2]	Property crime[2]	Murder and non-negligent man-slaughter	Forcible rape	Robbery	Aggra-vated assault	Burglary	Larceny-theft	Motor vehicle theft	Arson	Other assaults
South Dakota												
Under 18	4,962	58	1,127	1	3	2	52	88	981	39	19	403
Total, all ages	29,023	577	3,544	14	46	35	482	361	3,025	128	30	3,697
Tennessee												
Under 18	33,318	1,958	6,587	23	75	436	1,424	1,484	4,769	276	58	5,616
Total, all ages	386,758	16,546	45,236	316	429	2,331	13,470	8,113	34,706	2,131	286	34,415
Texas												
Under 18	121,237	3,609	25,409	48	234	1,067	2,260	4,048	20,469	694	198	18,280
Total, all ages	1,026,398	30,462	128,461	640	1,708	6,495	21,619	17,960	106,018	3,883	600	105,950
Utah												
Under 18	9,426	156	2,273	1	35	18	102	143	2,089	26	15	792
Total, all ages	47,321	703	8,138	13	117	88	485	722	7,237	156	23	4,262
Vermont												
Under 18	953	35	202	0	3	0	32	38	130	32	2	212
Total, all ages	10,907	421	1,487	4	36	9	372	258	1,124	95	10	1,378
Virginia												
Under 18	28,059	876	6,110	11	45	382	438	904	4,889	182	135	4,712
Total, all ages	347,903	6,721	38,670	269	336	1,982	4,134	4,733	32,650	1,008	279	41,527
Washington												
Under 18	17,052	686	5,252	13	74	205	394	902	4,099	166	85	2,748
Total, all ages	129,201	5,295	24,813	99	454	1,139	3,603	3,765	20,072	799	177	19,230
West Virginia												
Under 18	1,882	80	470	0	7	17	56	74	359	26	11	289
Total, all ages	50,204	1,947	6,537	46	61	236	1,604	1,007	5,239	250	41	6,186
Wisconsin												
Under 18	64,921	1,411	10,267	12	135	669	595	1,235	8,575	403	54	2,972
Total, all ages	317,773	7,448	35,805	127	693	1,775	4,853	4,126	30,489	1,035	155	17,195
Wyoming												
Under 18	4,782	49	768	0	4	2	43	46	693	22	7	530
Total, all ages	34,041	560	2,735	8	31	28	493	241	2,369	94	31	2,911

[1] Does not include traffic arrests.

[2] Violent crimes are offenses of murder and nonnegligent manslaughter, forcible rape, robbery, and aggravated assault. Property crimes are offenses of burglary, larceny-theft, motor vehicle theft, and arson.

Table IV-41. Arrests, by State, 2011—*Continued*

(Number.)

State	Forgery and counter-feiting	Fraud	Embezzle-ment	Stolen property; buying, receiving, possessing	Vandal-ism	Weapons; carrying, possessing, etc.	Prostitu-tion and commer-cialized vice	Sex offenses (except forcible rape and prosti-tution)	Drug abuse violations	Gamb-ling	Offenses against the family and children	Driving under the influence
South Dakota												
Under 18	4	34	4	20	240	27	0	29	654	0	167	73
Total, all ages	111	562	29	76	600	128	19	73	3,694	6	335	5,269
Tennessee												
Under 18	56	143	19	43	1,319	599	12	197	2,768	63	63	137
Total, all ages	2,387	9,055	745	730	4,706	3,532	2,390	913	40,911	365	3,006	25,559
Texas												
Under 18	130	289	15	99	3,592	977	108	600	13,561	19	74	660
Total, all ages	6,025	11,801	490	729	11,431	9,637	6,493	4,061	126,695	368	5,191	85,715
Utah												
Under 18	9	18	0	54	583	104	7	177	968	0	5	53
Total, all ages	336	473	9	249	1,486	493	64	471	5,207	1	699	3,184
Vermont												
Under 18	1	6	1	9	85	8	0	8	92	0	2	13
Total, all ages	42	231	47	116	346	15	2	25	1,041	0	309	2,264
Virginia												
Under 18	49	153	26	152	1,000	387	3	204	2,685	1	45	173
Total, all ages	2,194	6,731	1,621	1,010	4,852	3,749	783	1,083	35,416	73	2,205	28,950
Washington												
Under 18	16	27	1	197	1,096	343	16	129	2,204	3	3	107
Total, all ages	935	731	53	1,888	4,270	1,549	239	616	12,570	5	574	11,101
West Virginia												
Under 18	2	3	3	10	81	28	0	15	184	0	0	24
Total, all ages	435	785	138	340	923	391	98	152	6,798	23	86	5,356
Wisconsin												
Under 18	48	153	2	501	2,803	932	13	975	3,634	73	266	349
Total, all ages	1,156	3,684	168	1,480	8,302	3,799	457	2,510	24,140	148	2,287	28,798
Wyoming												
Under 18	4	8	1	9	207	37	0	14	570	0	7	59
Total, all ages	84	196	3	56	662	118	13	151	3,205	2	213	4,970

Table IV-41.   Arrests, by State, 2011—*Continued*

(Number.)

State	Liquor laws	Drunken-ness[7]	Disorderly conduct	Vagrancy	All other offenses (except traffic)	Suspi-cion	Curfew and loitering law violations	Number of agencies	2011 estimated population
South Dakota									
Under 18	1,040	14	333	0	529	0	206	106	686,820
Total, all ages	4,658	113	1,984	262	3,080	0	206		
Tennessee									
Under 18	940	308	3,499	0	7,013	0	1,978	446	6,086,443
Total, all ages	7,548	20,339	11,877	19	154,501	0	1,978		
Texas									
Under 18	4,296	2,594	16,704	643	23,056	0	6,522	1,020	23,937,315
Total, all ages	23,842	117,766	32,867	1,814	310,078	0	6,522		
Utah									
Under 18	1,064	31	578	3	2,026	0	525	79	1,230,046
Total, all ages	4,415	1,172	1,669	21	13,744	0	525		
Vermont									
Under 18	102	1	81	0	95	0	0	61	456,140
Total, all ages	358	3	592	1	2,229	0	0		
Virginia									
Under 18	1,840	203	983	0	6,460	0	1,997	323	8,003,311
Total, all ages	12,312	33,460	5,345	240	118,964	0	1,997		
Washington									
Under 18	1,569	5	387	2	2,209	0	52	189	3,886,312
Total, all ages	4,994	29	3,548	30	36,677	2	52		
West Virginia									
Under 18	106	13	37	0	467	0	70	247	1,498,772
Total, all ages	1,710	3,037	1,033	11	14,148	0	70		
Wisconsin									
Under 18	5,269	0	12,710	17	18,203	0	4,323	342	5,284,971
Total, all ages	27,068	12	48,195	2,712	98,086	0	4,323		
Wyoming									
Under 18	717	5	218	3	1,235	0	341	61	548,033
Total, all ages	3,285	2,679	1,257	27	10,564	9	341		

[7] Drunkenness is not considered a crime in some states; therefore, the figures vary widely from state to state.

SECTION V:
LAW ENFORCEMENT PERSONNEL

LAW ENFORCEMENT PERSONNEL

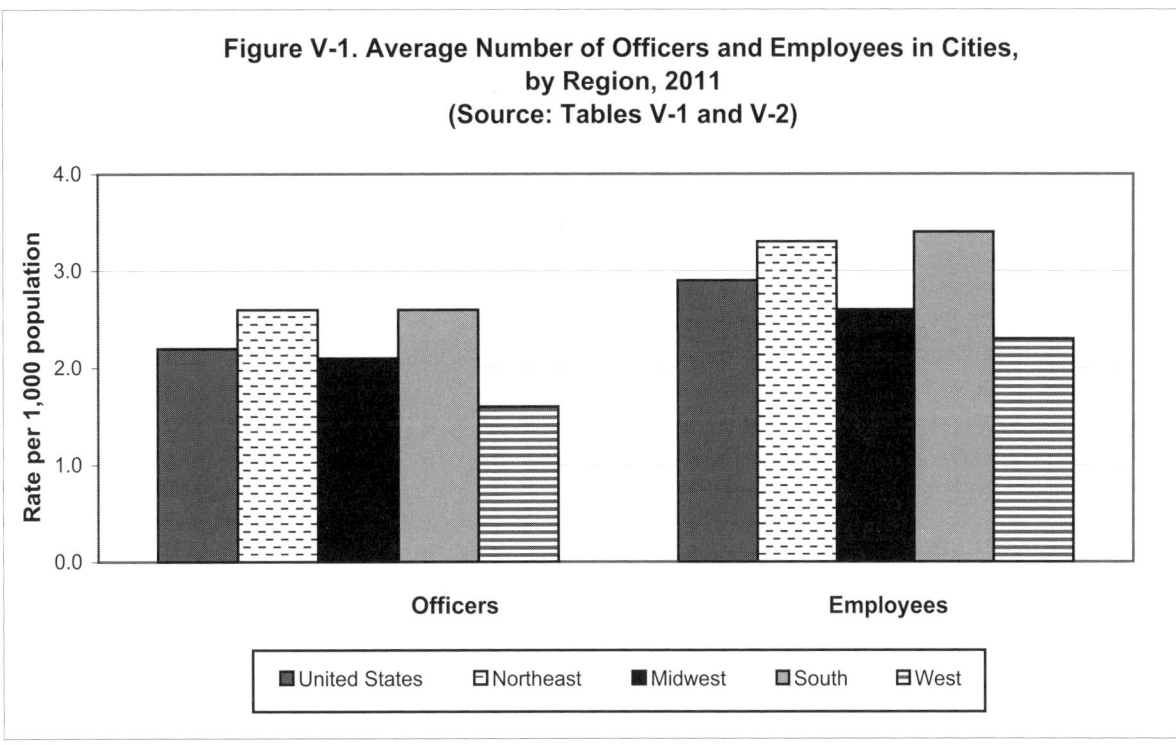

Figure V-1. Average Number of Officers and Employees in Cities, by Region, 2011 (Source: Tables V-1 and V-2)

The Uniform Crime Reporting (UCR) program defines law enforcement officers as individuals who ordinarily carry a firearm and a badge, have full arrest powers, and are paid from governmental funds set aside specifically for sworn law enforcement representatives. Because of law enforcement's varied service requirements and functions, as well as the distinct demographic traits and characteristics of jurisdictions, readers should use caution when comparing staffing levels between agencies based on police employment data from the UCR program. In addition, the data presented here reflect existing staff levels and should not be interpreted as preferred officer strengths recommended by the FBI. Also note that the totals given for sworn officers for any particular agency reflect not only the patrol officers on the street but also officers assigned to various other duties such as those in administrative and investigative positions and those assigned to special teams.

Each year, law enforcement agencies across the United States report the total number of sworn law enforcement officers and civilians in their agencies as of October 31 to the UCR program. Civilian employees include personnel such as clerks, radio dispatchers, meter attendants, stenographers, jailers, correctional officers, and mechanics provided that they are full-time employees of the agency.

This section of *Crime in the United States* presents those data as the number and rate of law enforcement officers and civilian employees throughout the United States. In 2011, 698,460 sworn officers and 303,524 civilians provided law enforcement services to more than 293 million people nationwide. These law enforcement personnel were employed by 14,633

state, city, university and college, metropolitan and nonmetropolitan county, and other law enforcement agencies. Of the slightly more than 1 million law enforcement employees, 73.4 percent were male. (Table V-5)

The data in this section are broken down by geographic region and division, population group, state, city, university and college, metropolitan and nonmetropolitan county, and other law enforcement agencies. (Information about geographic regions and divisions and population groups can be found in Appendix III.) UCR program staff compute the rate of sworn officers and law enforcement employees by taking the number of employees (sworn officers only or in combination with civilians), dividing by the population for which the agency provides law enforcement service, and multiplying by 1,000.

- Tables V-1 and V-2 present the number and rate of law enforcement personnel per 1,000 inhabitants collectively employed by agencies, broken down by geographic region and division by population group

- Tables V-3 and V-4 provide a count of law enforcement agencies by population group, based on the employment rate ranges for sworn officer and civilian employees per 1,000 inhabitants

- Table V-5 provides the number of total officers, the percentage of male and female sworn officers, and the civilian employees by population group

- Table V-6 lists the percentage of full-time civilian law enforcement employees by population group

- Table V-7 breaks down by state the number of sworn law enforcement officers and civilians employed by state law enforcement agencies

- Table V-8 provides the number of total officers, the percentage of male and female sworn officers, and the civilian employees by state

- Tables V-9 to V-11 list the number of law enforcement employees for cities, universities and colleges, and metropolitan and nonmetropolitan counties

- Table V-12 supplies employee data for those law enforcement agencies that serve the nation's transit systems, parks and forests, schools and school districts, hospitals, and so on

The demographic traits and characteristics of a jurisdiction affect its requirements for law enforcement service. For instance, a village between two large cities may require more law enforcement than a community of the same size with no urban center nearby. A town with legal gambling may have different law enforcement needs than a town near a military base. A city largely made up of college students may have different law enforcement needs than a city whose residents are mainly retirees.

Similarly, the functions of law enforcement agencies are diverse. Employees of these agencies patrol local streets and major highways, protect citizens in the nation's smallest towns and largest cities, and conduct investigations on offenses at the local and state level. State police in one area may enforce traffic laws on state highways and interstates; in another area, they may be responsible for investigating violent crimes. Sheriff's departments may collect tax monies, serve as the enforcement authority for local and state courts, administer jail facilities, or carry out some combination of these duties. This has an impact on an agency's staffing levels.

Because of the differing service requirements and functions, care should be taken when drawing comparisons between and among the staffing levels of law enforcement agencies. The data in this section are not intended as recommended or preferred officer strength; they should be used merely as guides. Adequate staffing levels can be determined only after careful study of the conditions that affect the service requirements in a particular jurisdiction.

Rate

The UCR program computes these rates by taking the number of employees, dividing by the population of the agency's jurisdiction, and multiplying by 1,000.

An examination of the 2011 law enforcement employee data by population group showed that the nation's cities had a collective rate of 2.9 law enforcement employees per 1,000 inhabitants. Cities with fewer than 10,000 inhabitants had the highest rate of law enforcement employees, with a rate of 4.5 per 1,000 inhabitants. Cities with 50,000 to 99,999 inhabitants had the lowest rate of law enforcement employees (2.1 per 1,000 in population). The nation's largest cities, those with 250,000 or more inhabitants, averaged 3.5 law enforcement employees for every 1,000 inhabitants. (Table V-1) These rates are either consistent or within a tenth of their 2010 levels.

Sworn Personnel

An analysis of the 2011 data showed that law enforcement agencies in the cities in the Northeast and the South had the highest rate of sworn officers—each at a rate of 2.6 per 1,000 inhabitants, followed by the Midwest (2.1), and the West (1.6). (Table V-2) Each of these rates has dropped one-tenth since 2010.

By population group in 2011, there were 2.2 sworn officers for each 1,000 resident population in the nation's cities collectively. This rate has dropped by a tenth after remaining constant from 2007 through 2010. Cities with fewer than 10,000 inhabitants had the highest rate at 3.5 sworn officers per 1,000 inhabitants. The nation's largest cities, those with 250,000 or more inhabitants, averaged 2.7 officers per 1,000 inhabitants, slightly lower than in 2009 and the same as in 2010. (Table V-2)

Males accounted for 88.2 percent of all full-time sworn law enforcement officers in 2011, the same percentage as 2010. Cities with populations of 1 million and over employed the highest percentage (18.0) of full-time female officers. Of the city population groups, cities with populations of 10,000 to 24,999 inhabitants employed the highest percentage (92.3) of male officers. In metropolitan counties, 86.4 percent of officers were male, and in nonmetropolitan counties, 92.7 percent of officers were male. (Table V-5)

Civilian Employees

Civilian employees provide a myriad of services to the nation's law enforcement and criminal justice agencies. Among other duties, they dispatch officers, provide administrative and record-keeping support, and query local, state, and national databases.

In 2011, 30.3 percent of all law enforcement employees in the nation were civilians. Female employees accounted for 60.8 percent of all full-time civilian law enforcement employees in 2011. In cities, civilians made up 22.1 percent of law enforcement agencies employees. Civilians made up 41.0 percent of law enforcement employees in metropolitan counties, 41.1 percent of law enforcement employees in nonmetropolitan counties, and 34.1 percent of law enforcement employees in suburban areas. (Table V-5)

Table V-1.   Full-Time Law Enforcement Employees,[1] by Geographic Region and Division and Population Group, 2011

(Number, rate per 1,000 inhabitants)

Geographic region/division	Total (11,234 cities; population 197,246,457)	Group I (75 cities, 250,000 and over; population 56,398,148)	Group II (196 cities, 100,000 to 249,999; population 29,447,050)	Group III (428 cities, 50,000 to 99,999; population 29,634,590)	Group IV (828 cities, 25,000 to 49,999; population 28,652,012)	Group V (1,834 cities, 10,000 to 24,999; population 29,005,261)
Total						
Number of employees...........	568,786	199,012	67,506	63,556	62,758	67,544
Average number of employees per 1,000 inhabitants............	2.9	3.5	2.3	2.1	2.2	2.3
Northeast						
Number of employees...........	146,598	62,580	9,452	15,549	17,898	19,254
Average number of employees per 1,000 inhabitants............	3.3	5.6	3.2	2.3	2.2	2.1
New England						
Number of employees...........	34,206	2,719	4,613	6,001	6,593	7,421
Average number of employees per 1,000 inhabitants............	2.6	4.4	3.1	2.3	2.2	2.2
Middle Atlantic						
Number of employees...........	112,392	59,861	4,839	9,548	11,305	11,833
Average number of employees per 1,000 inhabitants............	3.5	5.7	3.2	2.4	2.2	2.0
Midwest						
Number of employees...........	114,645	34,168	8,840	12,692	16,191	18,467
Average number of employees per 1,000 inhabitants............	2.6	3.6	2.1	1.9	2.0	2.1
East North Central						
Number of employees...........	81,917	26,325	5,623	8,908	12,629	13,047
Average number of employees per 1,000 inhabitants............	2.6	3.8	2.1	1.9	2.0	2.1
West North Central						
Number of employees...........	32,728	7,843	3,217	3,784	3,562	5,420
Average number of employees per 1,000 inhabitants............	2.5	3.1	2.0	1.7	1.9	2.1
South						
Number of employees...........	194,364	53,497	29,481	20,201	19,093	22,979
Average number of employees per 1,000 inhabitants............	3.4	3.2	2.7	2.7	2.7	3.0
South Atlantic						
Number of employees...........	91,706	21,601	15,317	11,226	9,025	10,624
Average number of employees per 1,000 inhabitants............	3.8	4.2	2.8	2.9	2.9	3.2
East South Central						
Number of employees...........	32,439	7,208	4,606	2,028	4,057	5,110
Average number of employees per 1,000 inhabitants............	3.4	2.9	3.4	2.9	2.8	3.2
West South Central						
Number of employees...........	70,219	24,688	9,558	6,947	6,011	7,245
Average number of employees per 1,000 inhabitants............	2.9	2.7	2.3	2.3	2.4	2.7
West						
Number of employees...........	113,179	48,767	19,733	15,114	9,576	6,844
Average number of employees per 1,000 inhabitants............	2.3	2.6	1.8	1.7	1.8	2.1
Mountain						
Number of employees...........	41,022	16,774	6,642	4,577	3,909	2,530
Average number of employees per 1,000 inhabitants............	2.6	2.8	2.0	2.1	1.9	2.4
Pacific						
Number of employees...........	72,157	31,993	13,091	10,537	5,667	4,314
Average number of employees per 1,000 inhabitants............	2.1	2.5	1.6	1.6	1.7	1.9

[1] Full-time law enforcement employees include civilians.

Table V-1.　Full-Time Law Enforcement Employees,[1] by Geographic Region and Division and Population Group, 2011—*Continued*

(Number, rate per 1,000 inhabitants)

Geographic region/division	Group VI (7,873 cities, under 10,000; population 24,109,396)	Total city agencies	2011 estimated city population	County[2] (3,399 agencies; population 95,812,483)	Total city and county agencies	2011 estimated total agency population	Suburban Area[3] (7,630 agencies; population 125,240,573)
Total							
Number of employees	108,410	11,234	197,246,457	433,198	14,633	293,058,940	465,194
Average number of employees per 1,000 inhabitants	4.5			4.5			3.7
Northeast							
Number of employees	21,865	2,592	44,795,747				
Average number of employees per 1,000 inhabitants	3.3						
New England							
Number of employees	6,859	803	12,963,908				
Average number of employees per 1,000 inhabitants	3.7						
Middle Atlantic							
Number of employees	15,006	1,789	31,831,839				
Average number of employees per 1,000 inhabitants	3.2						
Midwest							
Number of employees	24,287	3,272	44,800,021				
Average number of employees per 1,000 inhabitants	3.3						
East North Central							
Number of employees	15,385	2,060	31,447,185				
Average number of employees per 1,000 inhabitants	3.3						
West North Central							
Number of employees	8,902	1,212	13,352,836				
Average number of employees per 1,000 inhabitants	3.4						
South							
Number of employees	49,113	3,960	57,830,484				
Average number of employees per 1,000 inhabitants	6.4						
South Atlantic							
Number of employees	23,913	1,700	23,920,448				
Average number of employees per 1,000 inhabitants	7.7						
East South Central							
Number of employees	9,430	902	9,433,738				
Average number of employees per 1,000 inhabitants	5.2						
West South Central							
Number of employees	15,770	1,358	24,476,298				
Average number of employees per 1,000 inhabitants	5.6						
West							
Number of employees	13,145	1,410	49,820,205				
Average number of employees per 1,000 inhabitants	5.3						
Mountain							
Number of employees	6,590	631	15,834,272				
Average number of employees per 1,000 inhabitants	5.3						
Pacific							
Number of employees	6,555	779	33,985,933				
Average number of employees per 1,000 inhabitants	5.4						

[1] Full-time law enforcement employees include civilians.

[2] The designation county is a combination of both metropolitan and nonmetropolitan counties.

[3] Suburban areas include law enforcement agencies in cities with less than 50,000 inhabitants and county law enforcement agencies that are within a Metropolitan Statistical Area. Suburban areas exclude all metropolitan agencies associated with a principal city. The agencies associated with suburban areas also appear in other groups within this table.

Table V-2.   Full-Time Law Enforcement Officers, by Geographic Region and Division and Population Group, 2011

(Number, rate per 1,000 population.)

Geographic region/division	Total (11,234 cities; population 197,246,457)	Group I (75 cities, 250,000 and over; population 56,398,148)	Group II (196 cities, 100,000 to 249,999; population 29,447,050)	Group III (428 cities, 50,000 to 99,999; population 29,634,590)	Group IV (828 cities, 25,000 to 49,999; population 28,652,012)	Group V (1,834 cities, 10,000 to 24,999; population 29,005,261)
Total						
Number of officers	442,931	153,550	51,553	49,229	49,876	54,462
Average number of officers per 1,000 inhabitants	2.2	2.7	1.8	1.7	1.7	1.9
Northeast						
Number of officers	116,256	46,034	7,858	12,872	15,008	16,328
Average number of officers per 1,000 inhabitants	2.6	4.1	2.6	1.9	1.8	1.8
New England						
Number of officers	28,101	2,156	3,833	5,107	5,485	6,056
Average number of officers per 1,000 inhabitants	2.2	3.5	2.6	1.9	1.8	1.8
Middle Atlantic						
Number of officers	88,155	43,878	4,025	7,765	9,523	10,272
Average number of officers per 1,000 inhabitants	2.8	4.1	2.7	2.0	1.9	1.7
Midwest						
Number of officers	94,837	29,440	7,194	10,280	12,914	15,013
Average number of officers per 1,000 inhabitants	2.1	3.1	1.7	1.5	1.6	1.7
East North Central						
Number of officers	68,777	23,491	4,599	7,230	10,097	10,635
Average number of officers per 1,000 inhabitants	2.2	3.4	1.7	1.6	1.6	1.7
West North Central						
Number of officers	26,060	5,949	2,595	3,050	2,817	4,378
Average number of officers per 1,000 inhabitants	2.0	2.4	1.6	1.4	1.5	1.7
South						
Number of officers	150,062	42,222	22,616	15,510	14,943	17,949
Average number of officers per 1,000 inhabitants	2.6	2.5	2.1	2.0	2.1	2.3
South Atlantic						
Number of officers	70,637	16,280	11,797	8,679	7,143	8,510
Average number of officers per 1,000 inhabitants	3.0	3.2	2.2	2.3	2.3	2.6
East South Central						
Number of officers	25,743	6,085	3,485	1,602	3,252	4,000
Average number of officers per 1,000 inhabitants	2.7	2.5	2.5	2.3	2.2	2.5
West South Central						
Number of officers	53,682	19,857	7,334	5,229	4,548	5,439
Average number of officers per 1,000 inhabitants	2.2	2.2	1.8	1.7	1.8	2.0
West						
Number of officers	81,776	35,854	13,885	10,567	7,011	5,172
Average number of officers per 1,000 inhabitants	1.6	1.9	1.2	1.2	1.3	1.6
Mountain						
Number of officers	28,963	11,465	4,779	3,192	2,925	1,930
Average number of officers per 1,000 inhabitants	1.8	1.9	1.5	1.5	1.5	1.8
Pacific						
Number of officers	52,813	24,389	9,106	7,375	4,086	3,242
Average number of officers per 1,000 inhabitants	1.6	1.9	1.1	1.1	1.3	1.4

Table V-2. Full-Time Law Enforcement Officers, by Geographic Region and Division and Population Group, 2011—*Continued*

(Number, rate per 1,000 population.)

Geographic region/division	Group VI (7,873 cities, under 10,000; population 24,109,396)	Total city agencies	2011 estimated city population	County[1] (3,399 agencies; population 95,812,483)	Total city and county agencies	2011 estimated total agency population	Suburban area[2] (7,630 agencies; population 125,240,573)
Total							
Number of officers	84,261	11,234	197,246,457	255,529	14,633	293,058,940	306,562
Average number of officers per 1,000 inhabitants	3.5			2.7			2.4
Northeast							
Number of officers	18,156	2,592	44,795,747				
Average number of officers per 1,000 inhabitants	2.8						
New England							
Number of officers	5,464	803	12,963,908				
Average number of officers per 1,000 inhabitants	3.0						
Middle Atlantic							
Number of officers	12,692	1,789	31,831,839				
Average number of officers per 1,000 inhabitants	2.7						
Midwest							
Number of officers	19,996	3,272	44,800,021				
Average number of officers per 1,000 inhabitants	2.7						
East North Central							
Number of officers	12,725	2,060	31,447,185				
Average number of officers per 1,000 inhabitants	2.7						
West North Central							
Number of officers	7,271	1,212	13,352,836				
Average number of officers per 1,000 inhabitants	2.8						
South							
Number of officers	36,822	3,960	57,830,484				
Average number of officers per 1,000 inhabitants	4.8						
South Atlantic							
Number of officers	18,228	1,700	23,920,448				
Average number of officers per 1,000 inhabitants	5.9						
East South Central							
Number of officers	7,319	902	9,433,738				
Average number of officers per 1,000 inhabitants	4.1						
West South Central							
Number of officers	11,275	1,358	24,476,298				
Average number of officers per 1,000 inhabitants	4.0						
West							
Number of officers	9,287	1,410	49,820,205				
Average number of officers per 1,000 inhabitants	3.8						
Mountain							
Number of officers	4,672	631	15,834,272				
Average number of officers per 1,000 inhabitants	3.7						
Pacific							
Number of officers	4,615	779	33,985,933				
Average number of officers per 1,000 inhabitants	3.8						

[1] The designation county is a combination of both metropolitan and nonmetropolitan counties.

[2] Suburban areas include law enforcement agencies in cities with less than 50,000 inhabitants and county law enforcement agencies that are within a Metropolitan Statistical Area. Suburban areas exclude all metropolitan agencies associated with a principal city. The agencies associated with suburban areas also appear in other groups within this table.

Table V-3.   Full-Time Law Enforcement Employees,[1] by Rate Range, 2011

(Number, rate per 1,000 population.)

Rate range	Total cities[2] (10,052 cities; population 197,246,457)	Group I (75 cities, 250,000 and over; population 56,398,148)	Group II (196 cities, 100,000 to 249,999; population 29,447,050)	Group III (428 cities, 50,000 to 99,999; population 29,634,590)	Group IV (828 cities, 25,000 to 49,999; population 28,652,012)	Group V (1,834 cities, 10,000 to 24,999; population 29,005,261)	Group VI (6,691 cities, under 10,000; population 24,109,396)
Total Cities							
Number..	10,052	75	196	428	828	1,834	6,691
Percent[3]	100.0	100.0	100.0	100.0	100.0	100.0	100.0
0.1–0.5							
Number..	122	0	0	0	2	6	114
Percent..	1.2	0.0	0.0	0.0	0.2	0.3	1.7
0.6–1.0							
Number..	505	0	1	7	23	53	421
Percent..	5.0	0.0	0.5	1.6	2.8	2.9	6.3
1.1–1.5							
Number..	1,314	3	39	82	124	238	828
Percent..	13.1	4.0	19.9	19.2	15.0	13.0	12.4
1.6–2.0							
Number..	2,051	15	55	132	243	437	1,169
Percent..	20.4	20.0	28.1	30.8	29.3	23.8	17.5
2.1–2.5							
Number..	1,932	16	46	111	223	477	1,059
Percent..	19.2	21.3	23.5	25.9	26.9	26.0	15.8
2.6–3.0							
Number..	1,317	15	27	48	119	310	798
Percent..	13.1	20.0	13.8	11.2	14.4	16.9	11.9
3.1–3.5							
Number..	871	7	13	26	54	150	621
Percent..	8.7	9.3	6.6	6.1	6.5	8.2	9.3
3.6–4.0							
Number..	560	3	7	14	29	83	424
Percent..	5.6	4.0	3.6	3.3	3.5	4.5	6.3
4.1–4.5							
Number..	345	8	7	5	2	29	294
Percent..	3.4	10.7	3.6	1.2	0.2	1.6	4.4
4.6–5.0							
Number..	275	4	0	1	7	26	237
Percent..	2.7	5.3	0.0	0.2	0.8	1.4	3.5
5.1 and over							
Number..	760	4	1	2	2	25	726
Percent..	7.6	5.3	0.5	0.5	0.2	1.4	10.9

[1] Full-time law enforcement employees include civilians.

[2] The number of agencies used to compile these figures differs from other tables that include data about law enforcement employees because agencies with no resident population are excluded from this table. These agencies include those associated with universities and colleges and other agencies, as well as some state agencies that have concurrent jurisdiction with other local law enforcement.

[3] Because of rounding, the percentages may not add to 100.0.

Table V-4.　Full-Time Law Enforcement Officers, by Rate Range, 2011

(Number, rate per 1,000 population.)

Rate range	Total cities[1] (10,052 cities; population 197,246,457)	Group I (75 cities, 250,000 and over; population 56,398,148)	Group II (196 cities, 100,000 to 249,999; population 29,447,050)	Group III (428 cities, 50,000 to 99,999; population 29,634,590)	Group IV (828 cities, 25,000 to 49,999; population 28,652,012)	Group V (1,834 cities, 10,000 to 24,999; population 29,005,261)	Group VI (6,691 cities, under 10,000; population 24,109,396)
Total Cities							
Number..	10,052	75	196	428	828	1,834	6,691
Percent[2]	100.0	100.0	100.0	100.0	100.0	100.0	100.0
0.1–0.5							
Number..	137	0	0	0	4	8	125
Percent..	1.4	0.0	0.0	0.0	0.5	0.4	1.9
0.6–1.0							
Number..	737	2	27	55	72	102	479
Percent..	7.3	2.7	13.8	12.9	8.7	5.6	7.2
1.1–1.5							
Number..	2,064	14	69	147	247	478	1,109
Percent..	20.5	18.7	35.2	34.3	29.8	26.1	16.6
1.6–2.0							
Number..	2,625	24	48	137	312	639	1,465
Percent..	26.1	32.0	24.5	32.0	37.7	34.8	21.9
2.1–2.5							
Number..	1,690	11	30	55	112	354	1,128
Percent..	16.8	14.7	15.3	12.9	13.5	19.3	16.9
2.6–3.0							
Number..	1,000	9	13	19	64	144	751
Percent..	9.9	12.0	6.6	4.4	7.7	7.9	11.2
3.1–3.5							
Number..	586	3	8	11	10	62	492
Percent..	5.8	4.0	4.1	2.6	1.2	3.4	7.4
3.6–4.0							
Number..	368	6	0	2	5	28	327
Percent..	3.7	8.0	0.0	0.5	0.6	1.5	4.9
4.1–4.5							
Number..	241	4	1	2	0	11	223
Percent..	2.4	5.3	0.5	0.5	0.0	0.6	3.3
4.6–5.0							
Number..	138	1	0	0	0	3	134
Percent..	1.4	1.3	0.0	0.0	0.0	0.2	2.0
5.1 and over							
Number..	466	1	0	0	2	5	458
Percent..	4.6	1.3	0.0	0.0	0.2	0.3	6.8

[1] The number of agencies used to compile these figures differs from other tables that include data about law enforcement employees because agencies with no resident population are excluded from this table. These agencies include those associated with universities and colleges (see Table V-10) and other agencies (see Table V-12), as well as some state agencies that have concurrent jurisdiction with other local law enforcement.

[2] Because of rounding, the percentages may not add to 100.0.

Table V-5.   Full-Time Law Enforcement Employees, by Population Group, Percent Male and Female, 2011

(Number, percent.)

Population group	Total law enforcement employees	Percent law enforcement employees		Total officers	Percent officers		Total civilians	Percent civilians		Number of agencies	2011 estimated population
		Male	Female		Male	Female		Male	Female		
Total Agencies...............................	1,001,984	73.4	26.6	698,460	88.2	11.8	303,524	39.2	60.8	14,633	293,058,940
Total Cities	568,786	75.7	24.3	442,931	88.1	11.9	125,855	31.8	68.2	11,234	197,246,457
Group I (250,000 and over).......................	199,012	72.0	28.0	153,550	83.4	16.6	45,462	33.8	66.2	75	56,398,148
1,000,000 and over (Group I subset)	107,522	70.6	29.4	81,805	82.0	18.0	25,717	34.1	65.9	10	25,247,146
500,000 to 999,999 (Group I subset)..........	54,212	74.8	25.2	42,633	84.9	15.1	11,579	37.3	62.7	25	17,298,847
250,000 to 499,999 (Group I subset)..........	37,278	72.4	27.6	29,112	84.9	15.1	8,166	27.8	72.2	40	13,852,155
Group II (100,000 to 249,999)	67,506	73.4	26.6	51,553	88.0	12.0	15,953	26.2	73.8	196	29,447,050
Group III (50,000 to 99,999)........................	63,556	76.5	23.5	49,229	90.4	9.6	14,327	28.6	71.4	428	29,634,590
Group IV (25,000 to 49,999)........................	62,758	78.1	21.9	49,876	91.2	8.8	12,882	27.2	72.8	828	28,652,012
Group V (10,000 to 24,999)	67,544	79.6	20.4	54,462	92.3	7.7	13,082	26.8	73.2	1,834	29,005,261
Group VI (under 10,000)	108,410	79.4	20.6	84,261	91.1	8.9	24,149	38.7	61.3	7,873	24,109,396
Metropolitan Counties...................	300,568	69.5	30.5	177,406	86.4	13.6	123,162	45.2	54.8	1,285	68,238,191
Nonmetropolitan Counties..................	132,630	72.1	27.9	78,123	92.7	7.3	54,507	42.6	57.4	2,114	27,574,292
Suburban Areas[1].........................	465,194	72.9	27.1	306,562	88.4	11.6	158,632	43.0	57.0	7,630	125,240,573

[1] Suburban areas include law enforcement agencies in cities with less than 50,000 inhabitants and county law enforcement agencies that are within a Metropolitan Statistical Area. Suburban areas exclude all metropolitan agencies associated with a principal city. The agencies associated with suburban areas also appear in other groups within this table.

Table V-6.   Full-Time Civilian Law Enforcement Employees, by Population Group, 2011

(Number, percent.)

Population group	Percent civilian employees	Number of agencies	2011 estimated population
Total Agencies	30.3	14,633	293,058,940
Total Cities	22.1	11,234	197,246,457
Group I (250,000 and over)..	22.8	75	56,398,148
1,000,000 and over (Group I subset)..............................	23.9	10	25,247,146
500,000 to 999,999 (Group I subset)	21.4	25	17,298,847
250,000 to 499,999 (Group I subset)	21.9	40	13,852,155
Group II (100,000 to 249,999)..	23.6	196	29,447,050
Group III (50,000 to 99,999)	22.5	428	29,634,590
Group IV (25,000 to 49,999)	20.5	828	28,652,012
Group V (10,000 to 24,999)	19.4	1,834	29,005,261
Group VI (under 10,000)..	22.3	7,873	24,109,396
Metropolitan Counties	41.0	1,285	68,238,191
Nonmetropolitan Counties	41.1	2,114	27,574,292
Suburban Areas[1]...	34.1	7,630	125,240,573

[1] Suburban areas include law enforcement agencies in cities with less than 50,000 inhabitants and county law enforcement agencies that are within a Metropolitan Statistical Area. Suburban areas exclude all metropolitan agencies associated with a principal city. The agencies associated with suburban areas also appear in other groups within this table.

Table V-7.   Full-Time State Law Enforcement Employees, by Selected State, 2011

(Number.)

State/Agency	Total law	Total officers		Total civilians	
		Male	Female	Male	Female
Alabama					
Highway Patrol	1,275	656	14	163	442
Other state agencies	274	213	9	11	41
Alaska					
State Troopers	623	359	14	108	142
Arizona					
Department of Public Safety	1,837	1,040	56	294	447
Arkansas					
Other state agencies	34	29	1	0	4
California					
Highway Patrol	10,455	6,854	563	1,237	1,801
Other state agencies[1]	1,226	893	209	36	88
Colorado					
State Patrol	1,008	703	43	79	183
Other state agencies	280	48	5	84	143
Connecticut					
State Police	1,524	965	76	206	277
Other state agencies	37	27	1	7	2
Delaware					
State Police	890	581	71	105	133
Other state agencies	669	277	108	61	223
Florida					
Highway Patrol	2,282	1,580	204	148	350
Other state agencies	2,866	1,246	169	484	967
Georgia					
Department of Public Safety	1,458	944	45	216	253
Other state agencies	1,097	346	82	214	455
Idaho					
State Police	455	252	12	45	146
Illinois					
State Police	3,119	1,699	193	455	772
Other state agencies	431	266	23	80	62
Indiana					
State Police	1,764	1,160	61	220	323
Other state agencies	8	7	0	0	1
Iowa					
Department of Public Safety	927	595	41	142	149
Other state agencies	769	489	16	105	159
Kansas					
Highway Patrol	769	489	16	105	159
Other state agencies	511	302	16	67	126
Kentucky					
State Police	1,809	1,021	25	381	382
Other state agencies	85	48	6	9	22
Louisiana					
State Police	1,627	1,075	52	145	355
Other state agencies	36	29	5	0	2
Maine					
State Police	428	277	20	61	70
Other state agencies[1]	48	21	1	16	10
Maryland					
State Police	2,114	1,322	95	361	336
Other state agencies	1,743	858	136	448	301

Note: Caution should be used when comparing data from one state to that of another. The responsibilities of the various state police, highway patrol, and department of public safety agencies range from full law enforcement duties to only traffic patrol, which can impact both the level of employment for agencies as well as the ratio of sworn officers to civilians employed. Any valid comparison must take these factors and the other identified variables affecting crime into consideration.

[1] The total employee count includes employees from agencies that are not represented in other law enforcement employee tables.

Table V-7.   Full-Time State Law Enforcement Employees, by Selected State, 2011—*Continued*

(Number.)

State/Agency	Total law	Total officers		Total civilians	
		Male	Female	Male	Female
Massachusetts					
State Police	2,495	1,892	157	173	273
Other state agencies[1]	382	294	47	18	23
Michigan					
State Police	2,309	1,405	177	329	398
Minnesota					
State Patrol	762	499	58	107	98
Other state agencies	51	11	0	33	7
Mississippi					
Other state agencies	76	57	5	2	12
Missouri					
State Highway Patrol	2,243	1,077	56	488	622
Other state agencies	324	281	22	0	21
Montana					
Highway Patrol	300	231	9	17	43
Other state agencies	24	21	0	0	3
Nebraska					
State Patrol	703	445	25	78	155
Nevada					
Highway Patrol	909	430	54	143	282
New Hampshire					
State Police	534	332	36	49	117
Other state agencies	32	16	4	4	8
New Jersey					
State Police	4,004	2,637	104	591	672
Other state agencies	314	237	21	36	20
Port Authority of New York and New Jersey[2]	930	791	79	14	46
New Mexico					
State Police	626	461	21	38	106
Other state agencies	216	109	7	64	36
New York					
State Police	5,417	4,155	375	370	517
Other state agencies	240	198	22	6	14
North Carolina					
Highway Patrol	2,203	1,649	48	269	237
Other state agencies	694	507	61	52	74
North Dakota					
Highway Patrol	189	136	5	18	30
Ohio					
Highway Patrol	2,495	1,346	131	500	518
Other state agencies	487	382	51	17	37
Oklahoma					
Department of Public Safety	1,358	748	17	259	334
Other state agencies	72	30	5	25	12
Oregon					
State Police	774	560	48	82	84
Other state agencies	56	34	12	0	10

[1] The total employee count includes employees from agencies that are not represented in other law enforcement employee tables.

[2] Data reported are the number of law enforcement employees for the state of New Jersey.

Table V-7.　Full-Time State Law Enforcement Employees, by Selected State, 2011—_Continued_

(Number.)

State/Agency	Total law	Total officers		Total civilians	
		Male	Female	Male	Female
Pennsylvania					
State Police	7,643	4,764	245	1,164	1,470
Other state agencies	288	239	11	21	17
Rhode Island					
State Police	278	211	19	28	20
Other state agencies	82	62	4	11	5
South Carolina					
Highway Patrol	986	776	24	61	125
Other state agencies[1]	1,181	744	140	107	190
South Dakota					
Highway Patrol	252	151	5	60	36
Other state agencies	161	44	4	42	71
Tennessee					
Department of Safety	1,573	751	33	223	566
Other state agencies	1,041	582	74	114	271
Texas					
Department of Public Safety	8,127	3,269	194	1,598	3,066
Utah					
Highway Patrol	546	408	17	29	92
Other state agencies	142	122	9	7	4
Vermont					
State Police	588	289	36	134	129
Other state agencies	92	77	3	3	9
Virginia					
State Police	2,526	1,750	99	218	459
Other state agencies	761	489	59	83	130
Washington					
State Patrol	2,179	979	79	551	570
Other state agencies	6	4	0	0	2
West Virginia					
State Police	1,009	629	18	130	232
Other state agencies	191	150	3	12	26
Wisconsin					
State Patrol	644	429	48	70	97
Other state agencies	503	404	60	12	27
Wyoming					
Highway Patrol	360	188	8	60	104

Note: Caution should be used when comparing data from one state to that of another. The responsibilities of the various state police, highway patrol, and department of public safety agencies range from full law enforcement duties to only traffic patrol, which can impact both the level of employment for agencies as well as the ratio of sworn officers to civilians employed. Any valid comparison must take these factors and the other identified variables affecting crime into consideration.

[1] The total employee count includes employees from agencies that are not represented in other law enforcement employee tables.

Table V-8.   Full-Time Law Enforcement Employees, by State, 2011

(Number.)

State	Total law enforcement employees	Total officers		Total civilians		Number of agencies	2011 estimated population
		Male	Female	Male	Female		
Alabama	16,185	10,019	756	2,015	3,395	342	4,463,637
Alaska	1,990	1,179	106	238	467	40	722,151
Arizona	20,759	10,810	1,259	3,880	4,810	108	6,123,315
Arkansas	9,074	5,265	498	1,321	1,990	276	2,925,872
California	116,797	67,432	10,152	13,729	25,484	463	32,336,199
Colorado	16,700	9,864	1,391	1,834	3,611	235	5,061,016
Connecticut	10,254	7,570	785	820	1,079	103	3,580,709
Delaware	3,139	1,954	320	317	548	54	906,750
District of Columbia	4,919	3,303	1,012	277	327	2	617,996
Florida	71,906	38,145	6,468	9,772	17,521	357	18,108,630
Georgia	34,432	21,368	3,964	3,156	5,944	458	9,110,316
Hawaii	3,733	2,666	294	232	541	4	1,374,810
Idaho	4,251	2,588	171	289	1,203	108	1,580,103
Illinois	46,335	27,917	5,163	6,459	6,796	690	11,898,578
Indiana	15,851	9,878	761	2,511	2,701	244	6,119,628
Iowa	7,573	4,676	400	910	1,587	235	2,990,283
Kansas	10,058	6,004	590	1,433	2,031	320	2,541,382
Kentucky	9,063	6,572	473	825	1,193	287	3,695,575
Louisiana	20,593	12,702	2,870	1,583	3,438	181	4,006,987
Maine	2,819	2,121	136	214	348	135	1,327,672
Maryland	20,453	13,402	2,050	1,981	3,020	131	5,655,068
Massachusetts	19,771	14,962	1,363	1,425	2,021	341	6,489,247
Michigan	23,744	15,366	2,322	2,766	3,290	603	9,850,684
Minnesota	13,409	7,749	1,040	1,895	2,725	321	5,263,708
Mississippi	6,216	3,669	367	861	1,319	134	2,014,546
Missouri	20,158	13,062	1,424	2,171	3,501	560	5,911,375
Montana	3,022	1,793	114	465	650	112	996,168
Nebraska	4,893	3,147	389	367	990	156	1,797,644
Nevada	8,325	4,357	472	1,291	2,205	26	2,247,950
New Hampshire	3,473	2,413	221	243	596	155	1,196,658
New Jersey	36,854	26,133	2,424	3,242	5,055	538	8,520,270
New Mexico	6,181	4,063	441	578	1,099	112	2,010,149
New York	81,795	52,646	8,292	7,412	13,445	449	19,218,297
North Carolina	33,061	20,504	2,573	4,608	5,376	513	9,653,354
North Dakota	1,864	1,215	145	173	331	103	678,227
Ohio	30,000	19,423	2,197	3,433	4,947	617	10,255,737
Oklahoma	11,978	7,178	561	1,816	2,423	337	3,791,508
Oregon	10,057	5,502	610	1,721	2,224	213	3,837,283
Pennsylvania	31,245	23,120	2,684	2,062	3,379	966	9,530,934
Rhode Island	3,091	2,308	182	264	337	48	1,051,302
South Carolina	15,689	10,207	1,383	1,530	2,569	384	4,678,921
South Dakota	2,833	1,441	102	559	731	138	821,001
Tennessee	25,784	14,594	1,501	4,448	5,241	453	6,399,226
Texas	89,839	49,119	6,267	14,895	19,558	1,023	25,494,380
Utah	6,965	4,475	338	907	1,245	135	2,808,993
Vermont	1,503	1,040	107	115	241	68	372,484
Virginia	23,443	16,163	2,189	1,384	3,707	280	8,093,016
Washington	14,315	9,277	990	1,446	2,602	259	6,813,350
West Virginia	4,417	3,324	116	369	608	353	1,843,538
Wisconsin	18,968	11,077	1,729	2,449	3,713	393	5,704,599
Wyoming	2,207	1,402	134	155	516	70	567,714

Table V-9. Full-Time Law Enforcement Employees, by Selected State and City, 2011

(Number.)

State/City	Population	Total law enforcement employees	Total officers	Total civilians	State/City	Population	Total law enforcement employees	Total officers	Total civilians
Alabama					East Brewton	2,490	7	5	2
Abbeville	2,701	17	11	6	Eclectic	1,006	9	5	4
Adamsville	4,544	32	19	13	Elberta	1,505	6	5	1
Addison	762	3	3	0	Enterprise	26,690	69	50	19
Alabaster	30,498	74	61	13	Eufaula	13,200	50	35	15
Albertville	21,262	64	38	26	Eutaw	2,948	9	8	1
Alexander City	14,947	66	48	18	Evergreen	3,963	19	17	2
Aliceville	2,498	9	8	1	Fairfield	11,171	44	30	14
Andalusia	9,058	40	30	10	Fairhope	15,400	58	34	24
Anderson	283	1	1	0	Falkville	1,285	5	5	0
Anniston	23,217	128	91	37	Fayette	4,641	11	11	0
Arab	8,089	37	26	11	Flomaton	1,447	11	6	5
Ardmore	1,200	11	7	4	Florala	1,990	8	8	0
Argo	4,091	5	5	0	Florence	39,508	134	107	27
Ariton	768	1	1	0	Foley	14,688	86	60	26
Arley	359	3	2	1	Fort Deposit	1,350	5	5	0
Ashford	2,158	9	5	4	Fort Payne	14,079	33	28	5
Ashland	2,047	14	9	5	Fultondale	8,420	34	26	8
Ashville	2,223	5	5	0	Gardendale	13,960	38	29	9
Athens	22,002	57	46	11	Geneva	4,473	12	11	1
Atmore	10,243	32	27	5	Georgiana	1,746	14	8	6
Attalla	6,077	25	21	4	Geraldine	900	3	3	0
Auburn	53,637	112	106	6	Glencoe	5,185	8	6	2
Baker Hill	280	3	3	0	Goodwater	1,482	5	2	3
Bay Minette	8,083	29	21	8	Gordo	1,758	4	4	0
Bayou La Batre	2,570	20	15	5	Greenville	8,174	36	29	7
Bear Creek	1,075	1	1	0	Grove Hill	1,578	5	5	0
Beatrice	302	1	1	0	Guin	2,387	5	5	0
Berry	1,154	3	3	0	Gulf Shores	9,788	53	40	13
Bessemer	27,588	133	103	30	Guntersville	8,236	46	33	13
Birmingham	213,258	1,163	877	286	Gurley	805	6	6	0
Blountsville	1,692	5	5	0	Haleyville	4,193	17	13	4
Boaz	9,597	32	22	10	Hamilton	6,918	14	13	1
Brantley	813	4	4	0	Hammondville	490	1	1	0
Brent	4,971	5	5	0	Hanceville	2,996	15	11	4
Brewton	5,434	32	24	8	Harpersville	1,645	12	9	3
Bridgeport	2,430	10	6	4	Hartford	2,637	13	8	5
Brookside	1,370	4	4	0	Hartselle	14,324	37	29	8
Brundidge	2,086	13	9	4	Hayneville	936	2	2	0
Butler	1,903	6	6	0	Headland	4,532	15	11	4
Calera	11,676	33	27	6	Heflin	3,497	13	12	1
Camden	2,030	8	7	1	Helena	16,874	24	21	3
Carrollton	1,024	4	4	0	Henagar	2,355	8	4	4
Centre	3,506	11	10	1	Hokes Bluff	4,307	7	7	0
Centreville	2,791	6	6	0	Hollywood	1,005	2	2	0
Chatom	1,294	6	6	0	Hoover	82,012	223	158	65
Cherokee	1,053	2	2	0	Hueytown	16,183	43	35	8
Chickasaw	6,135	25	21	4	Huntsville	180,972	492	395	97
Childersburg	5,200	15	13	2	Ider	726	5	4	1
Citronelle	3,924	10	7	3	Irondale	12,408	38	31	7
Clanton	8,660	28	26	2	Jackson	5,253	27	21	6
Clayhatchee	592	1	1	0	Jacksons Gap	832	1	1	0
Cleveland	1,309	1	1	0	Jacksonville	12,608	33	26	7
Clio	1,406	3	3	0	Jemison	2,597	10	10	0
Collinsville	1,993	9	4	5	Killen	1,113	5	5	0
Columbiana	4,217	12	8	4	Kimberly	2,724	7	6	1
Coosada	1,230	3	3	0	Kinston	543	1	1	0
Cordova	2,105	7	5	2	Lafayette	3,017	15	14	1
Cottonwood	1,295	3	3	0	Lake View	1,952	4	3	1
Courtland	612	6	6	0	Lanett	6,499	30	27	3
Creola	1,935	11	7	4	Leeds	11,830	33	27	6
Crossville	1,871	4	4	0	Leighton	733	3	3	0
Cuba	348	1	1	0	Level Plains	2,095	5	5	0
Cullman	14,846	67	48	19	Lincoln	6,296	18	17	1
Dadeville	3,246	15	14	1	Linden	2,133	7	7	0
Daleville	5,320	22	16	6	Lineville	2,407	12	8	4
Daphne	21,674	76	46	30	Lipscomb	2,221	8	5	3
Dauphin Island	1,244	17	10	7	Littleville	1,016	9	5	4
Decatur	55,951	147	126	21	Livingston	3,502	10	7	3
Demopolis	7,519	32	29	3	Louisville	521	4	4	0
Dothan	65,811	224	150	74	Loxley	1,640	19	14	5
Double Springs	1,088	6	6	0	Luverne	2,813	14	10	4
Douglas	748	4	4	0	Madison	43,145	108	78	30
Dozier	331	1	1	0	Maplesville	711	4	4	0

Table V-9.   Full-Time Law Enforcement Employees, by Selected State and City, 2011—*Continued*

(Number.)

State/City	Population	Total law enforcement employees	Total officers	Total civilians	State/City	Population	Total law enforcement employees	Total officers	Total civilians
Margaret	4,449	4	4	0	Southside	8,452	16	10	6
Marion	3,704	6	5	1	Spanish Fort	6,831	24	20	4
Midfield	5,391	16	12	4	Springville	4,100	10	10	0
Midland City	2,355	7	4	3	Steele	1,048	3	3	0
Millbrook	14,710	42	32	10	St. Florian	415	3	2	1
Millport	1,054	1	1	0	Sulligent	1,936	6	6	0
Millry	549	4	3	1	Sumiton	2,532	14	8	6
Mobile	251,869	723	561	162	Summerdale	866	7	6	1
Montevallo	6,353	16	12	4	Sylacauga	12,810	40	38	2
Montgomery	206,754	676	530	146	Sylvania	1,846	4	4	0
Moody	11,782	20	19	1	Talladega	15,751	41	38	3
Morris	1,868	8	6	2	Tallassee	4,842	26	20	6
Moulton	3,488	11	11	0	Tarrant	6,428	26	22	4
Moundville	2,439	8	7	1	Taylor	2,386	2	2	0
Mountain Brook	20,511	62	49	13	Thomasville	4,229	18	13	5
Muscle Shoals	13,209	43	34	9	Thorsby	1,990	5	5	0
Napier Field	356	2	2	0	Town Creek	1,105	3	3	0
New Brockton	1,152	4	2	2	Triana	498	2	2	0
New Hope	2,824	6	6	0	Trinity	2,105	6	6	0
New Site	777	1	1	0	Troy	18,120	68	49	19
Newton	1,518	4	3	1	Trussville	20,029	59	45	14
Newville	542	1	1	0	Tuscaloosa	90,903	358	284	74
Northport	23,442	80	61	19	Tuscumbia	8,464	24	17	7
Notasulga	970	7	4	3	Tuskegee	9,912	32	20	12
Odenville	3,602	9	8	1	Union Springs	3,999	21	13	8
Ohatchee	1,176	5	5	0	Valley	9,570	34	24	10
Oneonta	6,599	21	20	1	Valley Head	561	3	2	1
Opelika	26,604	103	82	21	Vance	1,536	3	3	0
Opp	6,691	27	21	6	Vernon	2,010	7	7	0
Orange Beach	5,467	48	34	14	Vestavia Hills	34,197	70	68	2
Owens Crossroads	1,528	6	6	0	Weaver	3,053	11	8	3
Oxford	21,451	56	48	8	Webb	1,437	2	2	0
Ozark	14,979	36	30	6	Wedowee	827	7	7	0
Parrish	987	8	4	4	West Blocton	1,246	2	2	0
Pelham	21,455	83	67	16	Wetumpka	6,559	37	28	9
Pell City	12,756	34	31	3	Winfield	4,740	11	10	1
Phenix City	32,980	105	80	25	Woodstock	1,435	3	3	0
Phil Campbell	1,154	2	2	0					
Pickensville	611	2	1	1	**Alaska**				
Piedmont	4,901	14	10	4	Anchorage	296,955	535	390	145
Pinckard	650	1	1	0	Bethel	6,187	21	13	8
Pine Hill	980	5	5	0	Bristol Bay Borough	1,015	9	4	5
Pleasant Grove	10,159	24	19	5	Cordova	2,278	11	5	6
Powell	960	2	2	0	Craig	1,222	10	5	5
Prattville	34,123	85	76	9	Dillingham	2,370	21	8	13
Priceville	2,671	5	5	0	Fairbanks	32,089	47	44	3
Ragland	1,647	3	3	0	Haines	1,743	10	5	5
Rainbow City	9,648	32	21	11	Homer	5,091	20	12	8
Rainsville	4,972	16	11	5	Hoonah	773	6	3	3
Ranburne	411	2	2	0	Juneau	31,825	84	47	37
Red Bay	3,173	12	8	4	Kenai	7,225	27	18	9
Reform	1,710	5	5	0	Ketchikan	8,192	33	23	10
River Falls	529	2	1	1	Klawock	768	3	3	0
Riverside	2,219	3	3	0	Kodiak	6,238	39	18	21
Roanoke	6,103	28	23	5	Kotzebue	3,257	16	7	9
Robertsdale	5,301	26	13	13	Nome	3,661	17	11	6
Rockford	479	2	1	1	North Pole	2,154	15	14	1
Rogersville	1,263	5	5	0	North Slope Borough	9,596	63	36	27
Russellville	9,877	23	19	4	Palmer	6,041	29	16	13
Samson	1,949	6	5	1	Petersburg	3,000	15	9	6
Saraland	13,470	45	34	11	Sand Point	993	5	4	1
Sardis City	1,712	4	4	0	Seldovia	259	1	1	0
Satsuma	6,198	19	15	4	Seward	2,740	24	10	14
Scottsboro	14,841	69	46	23	Sitka	9,037	31	17	14
Section	774	2	2	0	Skagway	936	8	4	4
Selma	20,856	67	50	17	Soldotna	4,236	15	13	2
Sheffield	9,083	35	29	6	St. Paul	487	6	3	3
Shorter	476	6	3	3	Togiak	831	2	2	0
Silverhill	709	4	4	0	Unalaska	4,453	23	13	10
Sipsey	439	1	1	0	Valdez	4,046	17	9	8
Skyline	855	4	2	2	Wasilla	7,969	45	22	23
Slocomb	1,990	6	6	0	Whittier	224	3	3	0
Snead	839	4	4	0	Wrangell	2,411	14	6	8
Somerville	727	3	3	0					

Table V-9.   Full-Time Law Enforcement Employees, by Selected State and City, 2011—*Continued*

(Number.)

State/City	Population	Total law enforcement employees	Total officers	Total civilians
Arizona				
Apache Junction	36,347	85	54	31
Avondale	77,317	157	107	50
Benson	5,177	25	15	10
Bisbee	5,654	19	14	5
Buckeye	51,596	92	68	24
Bullhead City	40,100	115	75	40
Camp Verde	11,027	29	18	11
Casa Grande	49,259	106	78	28
Chandler	239,466	473	319	154
Chino Valley	10,970	28	23	5
Clarkdale	4,155	5	5	0
Clifton	3,358	11	6	5
Colorado City	4,889	12	7	5
Coolidge	11,992	38	29	9
Cottonwood	11,424	46	31	15
Douglas	17,624	44	30	14
Eagar	4,954	10	8	2
El Mirage	32,247	49	41	8
Eloy	16,866	39	27	12
Flagstaff	66,802	158	112	46
Florence	25,897	42	27	15
Fredonia	1,333	4	4	0
Gilbert	211,404	326	220	106
Glendale	229,931	542	401	141
Globe	7,639	31	25	6
Goodyear	66,199	129	95	34
Hayden	1,029	6	5	1
Holbrook	5,125	16	13	3
Huachuca City	1,879	10	5	5
Jerome	450	5	5	0
Kearny	1,978	8	6	2
Kingman	28,465	78	53	25
Lake Havasu City	53,271	115	84	31
Mammoth	1,446	8	5	3
Marana	35,456	104	78	26
Maricopa	44,098	56	49	7
Mesa	445,256	1,136	750	386
Miami	1,863	8	5	3
Nogales	21,132	76	59	17
Oro Valley	41,592	126	97	29
Page	7,350	31	20	11
Paradise Valley	13,001	33	25	8
Parker	3,127	13	11	2
Payson	15,518	40	26	14
Peoria	156,246	273	183	90
Phoenix	1,466,097	4,169	3,079	1,090
Pima	2,421	5	5	0
Pinetop-Lakeside	4,343	25	16	9
Prescott	40,407	85	67	18
Prescott Valley	39,372	73	60	13
Quartzsite	3,729	10	9	1
Safford	9,701	24	20	4
Sahuarita	25,617	47	40	7
San Luis	25,866	47	31	16
Scottsdale	220,462	658	406	252
Sedona	10,173	35	25	10
Show Low	10,811	43	31	12
Sierra Vista	44,509	91	62	29
Snowflake-Taylor	9,839	22	14	8
Somerton	14,489	30	22	8
South Tucson	5,732	18	17	1
Springerville	1,989	9	7	2
St. Johns	3,529	12	9	3
Superior	2,877	12	9	3
Surprise	119,181	177	123	54
Tempe	164,008	475	336	139
Thatcher	4,934	12	11	1
Tolleson	6,638	40	30	10
Tombstone	1,400	10	5	5
Tucson	527,479	1,240	949	291
Wellton	2,923	5	5	0
Wickenburg	6,453	22	15	7
Willcox	3,810	18	10	8
Williams	3,066	16	9	7
Winslow	9,792	35	26	9
Yuma	94,381	236	160	76
Arkansas				
Alma	5,460	19	11	8
Altheimer	991	2	2	0
Arkadelphia	10,795	27	22	5
Arkansas City	369	1	1	0
Ashdown	4,759	13	11	2
Ash Flat	1,090	3	3	0
Atkins	3,039	6	5	1
Augusta	2,216	6	6	0
Austin	2,053	3	3	0
Bald Knob	2,919	11	7	4
Barling	4,684	10	10	0
Bay	1,815	4	3	1
Bearden	973	2	2	0
Beebe	7,370	18	12	6
Bella Vista	26,661	34	25	9
Benton	30,913	75	55	20
Bentonville	35,568	83	58	25
Berryville	5,397	13	11	2
Blytheville	15,738	59	38	21
Bono	2,147	4	4	0
Booneville	4,020	12	8	4
Bradford	765	3	3	0
Brinkley	3,212	17	13	4
Bryant	16,814	48	38	10
Bull Shoals	1,965	5	4	1
Cabot	23,956	50	37	13
Caddo Valley	640	4	4	0
Camden	12,275	38	22	16
Cammack Village	774	5	4	1
Caraway	1,289	3	3	0
Carlisle	2,231	9	5	4
Cave City	1,918	3	3	0
Cave Springs	1,742	4	4	0
Centerton	9,587	12	11	1
Charleston	2,513	4	4	0
Cherokee Village	4,706	9	8	1
Clarendon	1,677	4	4	0
Clarksville	9,247	22	18	4
Clinton	2,622	9	8	1
Conway	59,354	142	109	33
Corning	3,403	12	8	4
Cotter	977	3	2	1
Crossett	5,549	23	15	8
Danville	2,427	6	5	1
Dardanelle	4,781	14	10	4
Decatur	1,712	6	6	0
De Queen	6,644	16	13	3
Dermott	2,911	13	7	6
Des Arc	1,730	4	4	0
De Valls Bluff	624	1	1	0
De Witt	3,317	14	8	6
Diamond City	788	1	1	0
Diaz	1,328	2	2	0
Dierks	1,142	3	3	0
Dover	1,388	4	4	0
Dumas	4,742	22	12	10
Earle	2,432	7	5	2
El Dorado	19,027	64	48	16
Elkins	2,668	6	6	0
England	2,846	12	7	5
Etowah	354	1	1	0
Eudora	2,286	8	4	4
Eureka Springs	2,089	16	10	6
Fairfield Bay	2,356	16	7	9
Farmington	6,019	11	10	1
Fayetteville	74,137	162	112	50
Flippin	1,365	6	6	0
Fordyce	4,333	12	8	4
Forrest City	15,487	45	33	12

Table V-9.   Full-Time Law Enforcement Employees, by Selected State and City, 2011—*Continued*

(Number.)

State/City	Popula-tion	Total law enforce-ment employees	Total officers	Total civilians	State/City	Popula-tion	Total law enforce-ment employees	Total officers	Total civilians
Fort Smith	86,861	216	166	50	Paris	3,559	14	9	5
Gassville	2,094	4	4	0	Parkin	1,113	2	2	0
Gentry	3,182	10	8	2	Pea Ridge	4,830	11	11	0
Glenwood	2,245	3	3	0	Perryville	1,471	4	4	0
Gosnell	3,575	8	8	0	Piggott	3,878	9	8	1
Gould	843	1	1	0	Pine Bluff	49,454	173	149	24
Gravette	2,343	9	8	1	Plainview	613	1	1	0
Greenbrier	4,742	14	9	5	Plummerville	832	3	3	0
Green Forest	2,782	10	7	3	Pocahontas	6,658	14	13	1
Greenland	1,269	4	4	0	Pottsville	2,859	5	5	0
Greenwood	9,020	22	20	2	Prescott	3,321	11	10	1
Greers Ferry	898	4	3	1	Quitman	768	4	4	0
Gurdon	2,229	4	3	1	Ravenden	474	3	2	1
Guy	713	3	2	1	Redfield	1,307	5	4	1
Hamburg	2,879	6	5	1	Rison	1,354	3	3	0
Hampton	1,334	3	3	0	Rockport	761	6	4	2
Hardy	778	3	3	0	Rogers	56,387	131	93	38
Harrisburg	2,305	4	4	0	Rose Bud	486	2	2	0
Harrison	13,041	41	29	12	Russellville	28,131	62	56	6
Hazen	1,479	7	5	2	Salem	1,647	2	2	0
Heber Springs	7,219	24	14	10	Searcy	23,031	64	46	18
Helena-West Helena	12,375	45	32	13	Sheridan	4,638	28	14	14
Hermitage	836	2	2	0	Sherwood	29,746	88	63	25
Highfill	587	2	2	0	Siloam Springs	15,153	44	30	14
Highland	1,053	3	3	0	Smackover	1,879	5	4	1
Hope	10,171	34	24	10	Springdale	70,325	162	119	43
Horseshoe Bend	2,201	5	5	0	Stamps	1,706	3	3	0
Hot Springs	35,459	133	103	30	Star City	2,291	6	5	1
Hoxie	2,801	5	4	1	Stuttgart	9,397	26	19	7
Huntsville	2,364	8	7	1	Swifton	804	2	2	0
Jacksonville	28,579	91	76	15	Texarkana	30,145	111	86	25
Jonesboro	67,772	155	144	11	Trumann	7,298	24	16	8
Judsonia	2,034	4	3	1	Tuckerman	1,876	4	3	1
Kensett	1,660	4	4	0	Van Buren	22,963	52	41	11
Lake City	2,098	4	4	0	Vilonia	3,844	8	8	0
Lakeview	747	2	2	0	Waldron	3,645	9	8	1
Lake Village	2,594	18	9	9	Walnut Ridge	4,927	9	8	1
Leachville	2,008	4	4	0	Ward	4,098	9	8	1
Lepanto	1,907	8	4	4	Warren	6,048	19	13	6
Lewisville	1,290	2	2	0	West Fork	2,335	6	5	1
Little Flock	2,605	6	5	1	West Memphis	26,444	94	74	20
Little Rock	194,988	620	505	115	White Hall	5,568	16	14	2
Lonoke	4,277	16	11	5	Wynne	8,430	19	17	2
Lowell	7,382	23	15	8					
Luxora	1,187	2	2	0	**California**				
Magnolia	11,665	26	18	8	Alameda	74,680	130	84	46
Malvern	10,396	21	18	3	Albany	18,757	34	25	9
Mansfield	1,148	3	3	0	Alhambra	84,066	128	84	44
Marianna	4,146	18	10	8	Alturas	2,860	6	5	1
Marion	12,438	27	24	3	Anaheim	340,218	527	374	153
Marked Tree	2,585	12	8	4	Anderson	10,049	26	16	10
Marmaduke	1,119	4	4	0	Antioch	103,575	124	96	28
Marvell	1,195	8	4	4	Arcadia	57,027	93	63	30
Maumelle	17,293	38	29	9	Arcata	17,434	37	27	10
Mayflower	2,251	8	6	2	Arroyo Grande	17,455	32	24	8
McCrory	1,742	5	5	0	Arvin	19,531	27	18	9
McGehee	4,251	25	7	18	Atascadero	28,643	37	27	10
McRae	687	2	2	0	Atherton	6,995	24	18	6
Mena	5,780	14	13	1	Atwater	28,499	41	31	10
Mineral Springs	1,217	3	3	0	Auburn	13,487	28	21	7
Monette	1,512	3	3	0	Avenal	15,687	17	15	2
Monticello	9,539	27	21	6	Azusa	46,906	87	62	25
Morrilton	6,818	33	22	11	Bakersfield	351,568	486	347	139
Mountain Home	12,542	34	26	8	Baldwin Park	76,276	98	70	28
Mountain View	2,769	9	8	1	Banning	29,951	42	31	11
Murfreesboro	1,653	3	3	0	Barstow	22,905	50	37	13
Nashville	4,662	17	16	1	Bear Valley	5,233	21	8	13
Newport	7,939	20	14	6	Beaumont	37,311	75	56	19
North Little Rock	62,775	221	186	35	Bell	35,894	40	28	12
Ola	1,291	3	3	0	Bell Gardens	42,567	73	51	22
Osceola	7,816	38	23	15	Belmont	26,139	42	31	11
Ozark	3,712	11	9	2	Belvedere	2,092	9	8	1
Pangburn	606	2	2	0	Benicia	27,314	51	34	17
Paragould	26,311	51	41	10	Berkeley	113,903	261	165	96

Table V-9.   Full-Time Law Enforcement Employees, by Selected State and City, 2011—*Continued*

(Number.)

State/City	Population	Total law enforcement employees	Total officers	Total civilians	State/City	Population	Total law enforcement employees	Total officers	Total civilians
Beverly Hills	34,510	162	112	50	Folsom	73,052	104	77	27
Bishop	3,925	17	12	5	Fontana	198,374	268	181	87
Blythe	21,062	31	22	9	Fort Bragg	7,359	19	15	4
Brawley	25,246	49	36	13	Fortuna	12,066	26	17	9
Brea	39,744	131	94	37	Foster City	30,926	49	36	13
Brentwood	52,086	77	60	17	Fountain Valley	55,963	76	56	20
Brisbane	4,332	14	11	3	Fowler	5,635	12	10	2
Broadmoor	4,225	9	9	0	Fremont	216,606	265	166	99
Buena Park	81,477	128	83	45	Fresno	500,480	952	751	201
Burbank	104,555	239	156	83	Fullerton	136,750	211	142	69
Burlingame	29,145	49	33	16	Galt	23,925	45	34	11
Calexico	39,025	57	38	19	Gardena	59,521	118	93	25
California City	14,286	21	14	7	Garden Grove	172,892	221	156	65
Calipatria	7,796	4	4	0	Gilroy	49,395	85	58	27
Calistoga	5,216	14	10	4	Glendale	193,973	353	237	116
Campbell	39,812	62	40	22	Glendora	50,662	93	51	42
Capitola	10,035	28	20	8	Gonzales	8,283	14	11	3
Carlsbad	106,566	153	107	46	Grass Valley	13,011	29	22	7
Carmel	3,766	19	12	7	Greenfield	16,522	20	16	4
Cathedral City	51,802	90	53	37	Gridley	6,661	22	16	6
Ceres	45,951	67	51	16	Grover Beach	13,311	27	17	10
Chico	87,200	149	95	54	Guadalupe	7,163	14	12	2
Chino	78,900	153	102	51	Gustine	5,585	10	8	2
Chowchilla	18,940	19	14	5	Hanford	54,601	76	52	24
Chula Vista	246,783	309	219	90	Hawthorne	85,284	131	94	37
Citrus Heights	84,280	130	85	45	Hayward	145,881	294	186	108
City of Angels	3,881	7	6	1	Healdsburg	11,386	25	16	9
Claremont	35,337	58	35	23	Hemet	79,582	82	60	22
Clayton	11,025	13	11	2	Hercules	24,343	26	23	3
Clearlake	15,429	28	20	8	Hermosa Beach	19,735	58	34	24
Cloverdale	8,719	22	14	8	Hillsborough	10,952	29	22	7
Clovis	96,755	146	99	47	Hollister	35,339	32	24	8
Coalinga	13,537	30	19	11	Huntington Beach	192,226	322	204	118
Colma	1,813	23	17	6	Huntington Park	58,797	110	66	44
Colton	52,767	69	47	22	Huron	6,833	12	8	4
Colusa	6,041	9	8	1	Imperial	14,931	18	16	2
Concord	123,502	196	149	47	Indio	76,930	103	65	38
Corcoran	25,105	31	19	12	Inglewood	110,962	264	183	81
Corning	7,753	22	13	9	Ione	8,011	7	6	1
Corona	154,165	227	159	68	Irvine	214,872	278	198	80
Coronado	24,987	62	43	19	Irwindale	1,439	35	26	9
Costa Mesa	111,253	209	134	75	Isleton	813	3	2	1
Cotati	7,350	15	10	5	Jackson	4,706	10	9	1
Covina	48,358	83	55	28	Kensington	5,137	10	10	0
Crescent City	7,733	13	12	1	Kerman	13,703	21	18	3
Culver City	39,340	148	105	43	King City	13,025	20	17	3
Cypress	48,364	66	53	13	Kingsburg	11,516	20	14	6
Daly City	102,312	149	109	40	Laguna Beach	22,990	85	47	38
Davis	66,393	90	59	31	La Habra	60,947	105	68	37
Delano	53,665	73	45	28	Lakeport	4,809	11	9	2
Del Rey Oaks	1,643	6	6	0	Lake Shastina	2,437	5	4	1
Desert Hot Springs	26,243	36	31	5	La Mesa	57,736	95	66	29
Dinuba	21,705	45	35	10	La Palma	15,751	32	24	8
Dixon	18,567	28	23	5	La Verne	31,428	59	40	19
Dos Palos	5,008	7	7	0	Lemoore	24,819	36	29	7
Downey	113,086	164	114	50	Lincoln	43,322	31	22	9
East Palo Alto	28,486	43	35	8	Lindsay	11,906	21	17	4
El Cajon	100,647	183	118	65	Livermore	81,920	130	83	47
El Centro	43,099	68	45	23	Livingston	13,212	27	17	10
El Cerrito	23,826	52	43	9	Lodi	62,864	104	69	35
Elk Grove	154,814	202	128	74	Lompoc	42,933	70	48	22
El Monte	114,809	168	121	47	Long Beach	467,691	1,193	847	346
El Segundo	16,850	86	61	25	Los Alamitos	11,584	26	22	4
Emeryville	10,199	51	35	16	Los Altos	29,317	47	30	17
Escalon	7,216	12	11	1	Los Angeles	3,837,207	12,724	9,860	2,864
Escondido	145,603	208	157	51	Los Banos	36,395	57	38	19
Etna	746	1	1	0	Los Gatos	29,759	59	40	19
Eureka	27,511	77	47	30	Madera	62,138	84	59	25
Exeter	10,455	16	15	1	Mammoth Lakes	8,331	21	18	3
Fairfax	7,528	16	11	5	Manhattan Beach	35,548	94	60	34
Fairfield	106,559	176	114	62	Manteca	67,885	83	59	24
Farmersville	10,712	16	14	2	Marina	19,950	38	29	9
Ferndale	1,387	4	4	0	Martinez	36,245	49	36	13
Firebaugh	7,638	15	11	4	Marysville	12,214	31	20	11

Table V-9.   Full-Time Law Enforcement Employees, by Selected State and City, 2011—*Continued*

(Number.)

State/City	Population	Total law enforcement employees	Total officers	Total civilians	State/City	Population	Total law enforcement employees	Total officers	Total civilians
McFarland	12,856	19	11	8	San Anselmo	12,481	26	19	7
Mendota	11,143	12	10	2	San Bernardino	212,392	465	296	169
Menlo Park	32,402	70	47	23	San Bruno	41,597	57	42	15
Merced	79,886	117	85	32	Sand City	338	10	9	1
Millbrae	21,785	22	18	4	San Diego	1,316,919	2,455	1,834	621
Mill Valley	14,066	24	20	4	San Fernando	23,923	50	32	18
Milpitas	67,575	105	82	23	San Francisco	814,701	2,650	2,210	440
Modesto	203,530	297	217	80	San Gabriel	40,185	68	54	14
Monrovia	37,020	73	46	27	Sanger	24,555	36	33	3
Montclair	37,095	71	49	22	San Jose	957,062	1,456	1,103	353
Montebello	63,235	105	69	36	San Leandro	85,949	126	91	35
Monterey	28,137	59	44	15	San Luis Obispo	45,649	83	57	26
Monterey Park	60,978	95	68	27	San Marino	13,302	33	27	6
Moraga	16,204	11	10	1	San Mateo	98,350	136	102	34
Morgan Hill	38,327	50	34	16	San Pablo	29,482	71	52	19
Morro Bay	10,354	23	18	5	San Rafael	58,391	81	61	20
Mountain View	74,937	137	93	44	San Ramon	72,996	71	54	17
Mount Shasta	3,434	11	8	3	Santa Ana	328,343	601	336	265
Murrieta	104,682	127	86	41	Santa Barbara	89,449	204	134	70
Napa	77,819	109	70	39	Santa Clara	117,837	197	131	66
National City	59,271	108	80	28	Santa Cruz	60,651	108	87	21
Nevada City	3,104	13	12	1	Santa Maria	100,723	147	102	45
Newark	43,073	74	54	20	Santa Monica	90,791	388	204	184
Newman	10,344	14	11	3	Santa Paula	29,666	38	28	10
Newport Beach	86,187	202	131	71	Santa Rosa	169,788	235	164	71
Novato	52,514	69	54	15	Sausalito	7,144	23	18	5
Oakdale	20,918	31	21	10	Scotts Valley	11,716	27	19	8
Oakland	395,317	913	647	266	Seal Beach	24,452	49	31	18
Oceanside	169,050	284	203	81	Seaside	33,413	48	39	9
Ontario	165,851	320	224	96	Sebastopol	7,466	20	14	6
Orange	138,020	226	158	68	Selma	23,492	39	31	8
Orland	7,377	12	10	2	Shafter	17,188	30	21	9
Oroville	15,729	37	22	15	Sierra Madre	11,045	21	16	5
Oxnard	200,225	382	235	147	Signal Hill	11,146	49	36	13
Pacifica	37,672	39	35	4	Simi Valley	125,698	161	109	52
Pacific Grove	15,218	29	20	9	Soledad	26,041	19	16	3
Palm Springs	45,076	123	85	38	Sonora	4,961	15	10	5
Palo Alto	65,160	141	83	58	South Gate	95,506	117	80	37
Palos Verdes Estates	13,596	36	25	11	South Lake Tahoe	21,655	56	39	17
Paradise	26,526	36	24	12	South Pasadena	25,920	45	33	12
Parlier	14,664	20	16	4	South San Francisco	64,380	108	79	29
Pasadena	138,734	339	231	108	Stallion Springs	2,517	3	3	0
Paso Robles	30,143	39	27	12	St. Helena	5,882	15	11	4
Petaluma	58,622	83	62	21	Stockton	295,136	494	321	173
Piedmont	10,792	27	19	8	Suisun City	28,441	35	24	11
Pinole	18,606	39	27	12	Sunnyvale	141,728	274	203	71
Pismo Beach	7,745	33	22	11	Susanville	18,158	17	16	1
Pittsburg	64,008	93	71	22	Sutter Creek	2,530	5	5	0
Placentia	51,127	62	44	18	Taft	9,437	27	16	11
Placerville	10,511	26	17	9	Tehachapi	14,583	16	14	2
Pleasant Hill	33,542	61	44	17	Tiburon	9,067	16	13	3
Pleasanton	71,111	111	80	31	Torrance	147,148	336	215	121
Pomona	150,810	249	148	101	Tracy	83,897	124	83	41
Porterville	54,802	86	59	27	Truckee	16,370	30	26	4
Port Hueneme	21,978	32	24	8	Tulare	59,975	97	70	27
Red Bluff	14,241	31	22	9	Tulelake	1,022	3	3	0
Redding	90,917	130	98	32	Turlock	69,355	118	77	41
Redlands	69,555	111	76	35	Tustin	76,428	140	92	48
Redondo Beach	67,533	147	89	58	Twin Cities	21,428	37	31	6
Redwood City	77,718	114	87	27	Ukiah	16,264	40	26	14
Reedley	24,478	46	31	15	Union City	70,333	102	76	26
Rialto	100,337	134	98	36	Upland	74,599	103	75	28
Richmond	104,920	285	191	94	Vacaville	93,515	146	90	56
Ridgecrest	27,941	47	32	15	Vallejo	117,305	117	91	26
Rio Dell	3,408	5	5	0	Ventura	107,684	161	122	39
Rio Vista	7,447	10	9	1	Vernon	113	60	49	11
Ripon	14,465	31	22	9	Visalia	125,905	197	135	62
Riverside	307,443	511	367	144	Walnut Creek	64,927	107	76	31
Rocklin	57,644	74	49	25	Watsonville	51,801	82	65	17
Rohnert Park	41,453	73	55	18	Weed	3,002	15	10	5
Roseville	120,184	180	118	62	West Covina	107,345	138	97	41
Ross	2,443	9	9	0	Westminster	90,756	133	92	41
Sacramento	471,972	947	678	269	Westmorland	2,251	5	5	0
Salinas	152,210	195	146	49	West Sacramento	49,317	89	62	27

Table V-9.   Full-Time Law Enforcement Employees, by Selected State and City, 2011—*Continued*

(Number.)

State/City	Population	Total law enforcement employees	Total officers	Total civilians	State/City	Population	Total law enforcement employees	Total officers	Total civilians
Wheatland	3,497	7	7	0	Frisco	2,730	16	13	3
Whittier	86,334	166	116	50	Fruita	12,866	18	16	2
Williams	5,183	14	11	3	Georgetown	1,052	3	3	0
Willits	4,945	18	12	6	Glendale	4,257	39	27	12
Willows	6,238	10	9	1	Glenwood Springs	9,781	28	21	7
Winters	6,702	12	10	2	Golden	19,196	61	43	18
Woodlake	7,365	13	12	1	Granby	1,896	7	6	1
Woodland	56,120	78	62	16	Grand Junction	59,586	192	101	91
Yreka	7,856	20	14	6	Greeley	94,507	242	140	102
Yuba City	65,688	87	62	25	Green Mountain Falls	651	2	2	0
					Greenwood Village	14,168	89	64	25
Colorado					Gunnison	5,956	26	14	12
Alamosa	8,933	28	24	4	Haxtun	962	3	3	0
Arvada	108,287	216	155	61	Hayden	1,842	5	4	1
Aspen	6,774	36	26	10	Holyoke	2,353	2	2	0
Ault	1,545	6	6	0	Hotchkiss	960	3	3	0
Aurora	330,740	755	638	117	Hugo	743	2	2	0
Avon	6,559	20	18	2	Idaho Springs	1,747	9	7	2
Basalt	3,924	10	8	2	Ignacio	709	6	6	0
Bayfield	2,374	7	6	1	Johnstown	10,059	15	13	2
Berthoud	5,194	9	8	1	Kersey	1,479	3	3	0
Black Hawk	120	33	24	9	Kiowa	736	2	2	0
Boulder	99,081	257	169	88	Kremmling	1,469	4	4	0
Breckenridge	4,619	27	20	7	Lafayette	24,879	44	37	7
Brighton	33,933	73	53	20	La Junta	7,200	20	14	6
Broomfield	56,862	189	108	81	Lakeside	8	4	4	0
Brush	5,558	14	11	3	Lakewood	145,470	410	270	140
Buena Vista	2,663	9	7	2	Lamar	7,940	35	22	13
Burlington	4,328	10	9	1	La Salle	1,989	6	6	0
Calhan	794	3	3	0	Las Animas	2,452	6	5	1
Campo	111	2	2	0	La Veta	814	2	2	0
Canon City	16,686	48	35	13	Leadville	2,647	10	8	2
Carbondale	6,539	17	14	3	Limon	1,913	6	5	1
Castle Rock	49,071	73	53	20	Littleton	42,464	96	70	26
Cedaredge	2,292	7	6	1	Lochbuie	4,808	6	6	0
Centennial	102,125	155	119	36	Lone Tree	10,396	51	46	5
Center	2,269	11	5	6	Longmont	87,773	198	137	61
Central City	675	5	5	0	Louisville	18,696	36	31	5
Cherry Hills Village	6,091	23	18	5	Loveland	68,024	131	90	41
Collbran	720	1	1	0	Mancos	1,359	3	2	1
Colorado Springs	423,680	900	622	278	Manitou Springs	5,079	21	15	6
Columbine Valley	1,278	6	6	0	Manzanola	442	5	4	1
Commerce City	46,713	120	93	27	Meeker	2,518	6	6	0
Cortez	8,630	51	27	24	Milliken	5,708	10	9	1
Craig	9,629	31	24	7	Minturn	1,045	3	2	1
Crested Butte	1,513	8	7	1	Monte Vista	4,521	14	12	2
Cripple Creek	1,210	11	9	2	Montrose	19,465	55	37	18
Dacono	4,224	11	9	2	Monument	5,626	16	13	3
De Beque	513	2	2	0	Morrison	435	5	4	1
Del Norte	1,715	6	5	1	Mountain View	516	5	5	0
Delta	9,070	20	17	3	Mount Crested Butte	815	7	6	1
Denver	610,612	1,646	1,420	226	Nederland	1,470	7	6	1
Dillon	920	10	8	2	New Castle	4,597	9	8	1
Durango	17,181	63	52	11	Northglenn	36,412	71	60	11
Eagle	6,621	11	9	2	Oak Creek	899	2	2	0
Eaton	4,441	9	8	1	Olathe	1,881	6	6	0
Edgewater	5,260	17	15	2	Ouray	1,017	4	4	0
Elizabeth	1,382	6	5	1	Pagosa Springs	1,757	9	8	1
Empire	287	1	1	0	Palisade	2,739	9	8	1
Englewood	30,782	100	71	29	Palmer Lake	2,462	5	5	0
Erie	18,451	23	21	2	Paonia	1,476	4	4	0
Estes Park	5,960	29	19	10	Parachute	1,104	6	5	1
Evans	18,860	32	30	2	Parker	46,086	82	58	24
Fairplay	691	3	3	0	Platteville	2,528	6	6	0
Federal Heights	11,667	36	24	12	Pueblo	108,452	258	209	49
Firestone	10,324	23	19	4	Rangely	2,406	10	5	5
Florence	3,949	18	9	9	Ridgway	940	2	2	0
Fort Collins	146,494	263	179	84	Rifle	9,332	23	20	3
Fort Lupton	7,505	14	12	2	Rocky Ford	4,026	10	8	2
Fort Morgan	11,512	29	24	5	Salida	5,327	16	13	3
Fountain	26,296	44	40	4	Sheridan	5,763	33	28	5
Fowler	1,203	3	2	1	Silt	2,981	7	6	1
Fraser/Winter Park	2,261	9	8	1	Silverthorne	3,955	18	15	3
Frederick	8,830	17	16	1	Snowmass Village	2,875	12	9	3

Table V-9. Full-Time Law Enforcement Employees, by Selected State and City, 2011—*Continued*

(Number.)

State/City	Population	Total law enforcement employees	Total officers	Total civilians	State/City	Population	Total law enforcement employees	Total officers	Total civilians
South Fork	393	3	2	1	Norwich	40,568	90	74	16
Springfield	1,476	3	3	0	Old Saybrook	10,261	31	25	6
Steamboat Springs	12,299	34	20	14	Orange	13,982	51	40	11
Sterling	15,034	24	21	3	Plainfield	15,433	19	16	3
Stratton	669	1	1	0	Plainville	17,749	41	34	7
Telluride	2,365	12	9	3	Plymouth	12,266	23	23	0
Thornton	120,841	219	158	61	Portland	9,526	12	11	1
Timnath	636	2	2	0	Putnam	9,602	18	15	3
Trinidad	9,254	34	23	11	Redding	9,175	21	15	6
Vail	5,397	56	28	28	Ridgefield	24,684	43	37	6
Victor	404	3	3	0	Rocky Hill	19,745	40	31	9
Walsenburg	3,121	12	10	2	Seymour	16,571	41	39	2
Walsh	556	1	1	0	Shelton	39,632	61	52	9
Westminster	107,962	263	185	78	Simsbury	23,554	45	35	10
Wheat Ridge	30,691	103	72	31	Southington	43,149	87	66	21
Wiggins	909	2	2	0	South Windsor	25,757	55	42	13
Windsor	18,969	23	20	3	Stamford	122,870	291	274	17
Woodland Park	7,325	28	20	8	Stonington	18,579	47	35	12
Wray	2,383	8	7	1	Stratford	51,479	101	94	7
Yuma	3,585	8	7	1	Suffield	15,764	23	18	5
					Thomaston	7,902	14	11	3
Connecticut					Torrington	36,450	90	83	7
Ansonia	19,285	51	44	7	Trumbull	36,085	82	72	10
Avon	18,131	35	29	6	Vernon	29,233	65	52	13
Berlin	19,903	53	41	12	Wallingford	45,218	94	70	24
Bethel	18,618	47	35	12	Waterbury	110,570	353	290	63
Bloomfield	20,524	57	46	11	Waterford	19,553	54	47	7
Branford	28,078	61	49	12	Watertown	22,556	47	38	9
Bridgeport	144,496	476	421	55	West Hartford	63,385	131	124	7
Bristol	60,589	138	112	26	West Haven	55,667	133	120	13
Brookfield	16,482	41	31	10	Weston	10,198	15	14	1
Canton	10,311	20	15	5	Westport	26,440	84	65	19
Cheshire	29,315	60	48	12	Wethersfield	26,717	58	47	11
Clinton	13,285	34	24	10	Willimantic	17,770	44	40	4
Coventry	12,458	19	14	5	Wilton	18,095	47	43	4
Cromwell	14,031	35	26	9	Winchester	11,263	23	19	4
Danbury	81,043	152	145	7	Windsor	29,098	59	47	12
Darien	20,770	58	51	7	Windsor Locks	12,521	29	22	7
Derby	12,926	33	31	2	Wolcott	16,711	33	24	9
East Hampton	12,983	17	15	2	Woodbridge	9,007	34	26	8
East Hartford	51,347	158	120	38					
East Haven	29,311	52	49	3	**Delaware**				
Easton	7,504	16	15	1	Bethany Beach	1,071	10	8	2
East Windsor	11,183	30	23	7	Blades	1,254	3	3	0
Enfield	44,737	112	89	23	Bridgeville	2,069	8	8	0
Fairfield	59,514	111	105	6	Camden	3,499	9	8	1
Farmington	25,387	62	45	17	Cheswold	1,394	2	2	0
Glastonbury	34,491	73	57	16	Clayton	2,948	8	7	1
Granby	11,303	18	13	5	Dagsboro	813	3	3	0
Greenwich	61,284	176	148	28	Delaware City	1,712	3	3	0
Groton	10,408	34	27	7	Delmar	1,613	13	12	1
Groton Long Point	519	7	7	0	Dewey Beach	344	9	8	1
Groton Town	29,262	69	65	4	Dover	36,416	118	90	28
Guilford	22,416	45	37	8	Elsmere	6,194	12	11	1
Hamden	61,073	124	106	18	Felton	1,311	4	3	1
Hartford	125,006	511	440	71	Fenwick Island	383	8	7	1
Madison	18,303	38	27	11	Frankford	856	2	2	0
Manchester	58,349	151	117	34	Georgetown	6,488	13	12	1
Meriden	60,981	133	119	14	Greenwood	983	3	2	1
Middlebury	7,589	17	11	6	Harrington	3,598	11	10	1
Middletown	47,736	112	97	15	Laurel	3,746	14	13	1
Milford	52,857	123	108	15	Lewes	2,775	14	13	1
Monroe	19,515	48	38	10	Middletown	19,064	33	28	5
Naugatuck	31,921	70	58	12	Milford	9,657	37	27	10
New Britain	73,341	152	140	12	Millsboro	3,917	12	11	1
New Canaan	19,775	49	44	5	Milton	2,602	12	11	1
New Haven	130,019	527	359	168	Newark	31,776	84	68	16
Newington	30,619	64	52	12	New Castle	5,339	19	17	2
New London	27,671	112	95	17	Newport	1,066	8	7	1
New Milford	28,194	63	49	14	Ocean View	1,901	9	8	1
Newtown	27,611	50	46	4	Rehoboth Beach	1,341	26	15	11
North Branford	14,434	27	22	5	Seaford	6,999	37	26	11
North Haven	24,138	58	48	10	Selbyville	2,189	8	7	1
Norwalk	85,761	201	164	37	Smyrna	10,126	29	22	7

Table V-9. Full-Time Law Enforcement Employees, by Selected State and City, 2011—*Continued*

(Number.)

State/City	Population	Total law enforcement employees	Total officers	Total civilians	State/City	Population	Total law enforcement employees	Total officers	Total civilians
South Bethany	454	6	6	0	Florida City	11,398	45	34	11
Wilmington	71,577	384	321	63	Fort Lauderdale	167,777	657	505	152
Wyoming	1,326	3	3	0	Fort Myers	63,147	237	174	63
					Fort Pierce	42,157	145	109	36
District of Columbia					Fort Walton Beach	19,773	63	49	14
Washington	617,996	4,299	3,818	481	Fruitland Park	4,134	13	13	0
					Gainesville	126,049	354	292	62
Florida					Golden Beach	932	19	18	1
Alachua	9,182	28	20	8	Graceville	2,309	10	7	3
Altamonte Springs	42,062	116	97	19	Greenacres City	38,085	64	47	17
Altha	543	1	1	0	Green Cove Springs	7,002	24	19	5
Apalachicola	2,261	8	7	1	Gretna	1,480	5	5	0
Apopka	42,108	122	87	35	Groveland	8,848	32	23	9
Arcadia	7,741	21	16	5	Gulf Breeze	5,842	31	17	14
Astatula	1,835	5	5	0	Gulfport	12,193	37	29	8
Atlantic Beach	12,827	37	27	10	Gulf Stream	797	11	11	0
Atlantis	2,032	17	12	5	Haines City	20,815	72	49	23
Auburndale	13,691	43	35	8	Hallandale	37,619	129	93	36
Aventura	36,249	119	83	36	Havana	1,778	14	10	4
Avon Park	8,956	26	23	3	Hialeah	227,731	390	329	61
Bal Harbour Village	2,547	35	27	8	Hialeah Gardens	22,040	52	37	15
Bartow	17,534	58	38	20	Highland Beach	3,587	14	13	1
Bay Harbor Islands	5,705	29	22	7	High Springs	5,423	12	10	2
Belleair	3,922	15	14	1	Hillsboro Beach	1,901	18	14	4
Belle Isle	6,070	14	13	1	Holly Hill	11,818	33	28	5
Belleview	4,553	13	11	2	Hollywood	142,686	465	305	160
Biscayne Park	3,097	12	11	1	Holmes Beach	3,888	21	14	7
Blountstown	2,548	12	8	4	Homestead	61,337	142	103	39
Boca Raton	85,542	289	191	98	Howey-in-the-Hills	1,113	6	6	0
Bonifay	2,831	7	6	1	Indialantic	2,757	17	11	6
Bowling Green	2,970	7	7	0	Indian Creek Village	87	19	13	6
Boynton Beach	69,147	214	163	51	Indian Harbour Beach	8,337	26	19	7
Bradenton	50,221	143	118	25	Indian River Shores	3,954	22	19	3
Bradenton Beach	1,187	10	10	0	Indian Shores	3,589	13	11	2
Brooksville	7,824	27	24	3	Inglis	1,343	6	5	1
Bushnell	2,451	10	9	1	Interlachen	1,422	3	3	0
Cape Coral	156,408	298	214	84	Jacksonville	834,429	3,161	1,645	1,516
Carrabelle	2,816	5	5	0	Jacksonville Beach	21,653	76	57	19
Casselberry	26,599	61	51	10	Jasper	4,608	9	8	1
Cedar Key	712	4	4	0	Jennings	890	2	2	0
Center Hill	1,001	3	3	0	Juno Beach	3,219	17	15	2
Chattahoochee	3,702	11	10	1	Jupiter	55,908	123	107	16
Chiefland	2,276	13	11	2	Jupiter Inlet Colony	405	4	4	0
Chipley	3,654	11	10	1	Jupiter Island	828	19	15	4
Clearwater	109,153	319	229	90	Kenneth City	5,048	15	14	1
Clermont	29,134	58	54	4	Key Biscayne	12,512	42	30	12
Clewiston	7,253	29	19	10	Key Colony Beach	808	5	5	0
Cocoa	17,374	88	66	22	Key West	24,985	113	87	26
Cocoa Beach	11,384	48	32	16	Kissimmee	60,495	194	126	68
Coconut Creek	53,630	135	91	44	Lady Lake	14,116	37	27	10
Coral Gables	47,418	239	170	69	Lake Alfred	5,083	15	10	5
Coral Springs	122,746	299	199	100	Lake City	12,210	52	39	13
Cottondale	946	3	3	0	Lake Clarke Shores	3,422	11	11	0
Crescent City	1,598	6	5	1	Lake Hamilton	1,248	7	6	1
Crestview	21,264	67	52	15	Lake Helen	2,660	6	5	1
Cross City	1,752	5	5	0	Lakeland	98,750	324	214	110
Dade City	6,525	34	24	10	Lake Mary	14,010	53	37	16
Davenport	2,927	10	9	1	Lake Placid	2,253	9	7	2
Davie	93,246	231	168	63	Lake Wales	14,419	50	44	6
Daytona Beach	61,836	267	228	39	Lantana	10,565	35	28	7
Daytona Beach Shores	4,305	35	27	8	Largo	78,706	182	136	46
De Funiak Springs	5,248	28	20	8	Lauderhill	67,799	127	112	15
Deland	27,399	79	61	18	Leesburg	20,391	97	72	25
Delray Beach	61,347	210	145	65	Lighthouse Point	10,485	43	34	9
Doral	46,327	118	86	32	Live Oak	6,943	20	16	4
Dunnellon	1,757	12	9	3	Longboat Key	6,982	24	17	7
Eatonville	2,188	14	12	2	Longwood	13,843	45	40	5
Edgewater	21,033	32	28	4	Lynn Haven	18,745	36	26	10
Edgewood	2,537	13	11	2	Madison	2,882	16	15	1
El Portal	2,357	7	7	0	Maitland	15,966	50	44	6
Eustis	18,811	56	43	13	Manalapan	412	13	9	4
Fellsmere	5,268	10	9	1	Marco Island	16,637	38	33	5
Fernandina Beach	11,644	43	32	11	Margate	54,010	159	103	56
Flagler Beach	4,545	187	130	57	Marianna	6,185	25	18	7

Table V-9. Full-Time Law Enforcement Employees, by Selected State and City, 2011—*Continued*

(Number.)

State/City	Popula-tion	Total law enforce-ment employees	Total officers	Total civilians	State/City	Popula-tion	Total law enforce-ment employees	Total officers	Total civilians
Mascotte	5,171	13	12	1	St. Augustine	13,152	61	50	11
Medley	849	46	37	9	St. Augustine Beach	6,260	18	16	2
Melbourne	77,105	226	163	63	St. Cloud	35,662	107	72	35
Melbourne Beach	3,143	10	9	1	St. Pete Beach	9,473	28	22	6
Melbourne Village	671	5	5	0	St. Petersburg	248,105	743	533	210
Mexico Beach	1,087	7	7	0	Stuart	15,806	60	42	18
Miami	404,901	1,404	1,061	343	Sunny Isles Beach	21,116	59	47	12
Miami Beach	88,975	501	361	140	Sunrise	85,590	260	170	90
Miami Gardens	108,628	257	200	57	Surfside	5,822	33	27	6
Miami Shores	10,636	44	35	9	Sweetwater	13,683	46	35	11
Miami Springs	13,997	53	42	11	Tallahassee	183,848	468	346	122
Milton	8,946	26	19	7	Tampa	340,284	1,219	948	271
Miramar	123,704	263	199	64	Tarpon Springs	23,804	61	47	14
Monticello	2,540	12	8	4	Tavares	14,141	38	27	11
Mount Dora	12,539	45	30	15	Temple Terrace	24,875	71	51	20
Naples	19,803	97	68	29	Tequesta	5,706	25	19	6
Neptune Beach	7,133	27	19	8	Titusville	44,357	122	86	36
New Port Richey	15,114	44	35	9	Treasure Island	6,796	26	19	7
New Smyrna Beach	22,770	51	43	8	Trenton	2,026	4	3	1
Niceville	12,923	29	23	6	Umatilla	3,503	9	8	1
North Bay Village	7,234	32	26	6	Valparaiso	5,105	14	10	4
North Miami	59,587	142	107	35	Venice	21,031	62	45	17
North Miami Beach	42,089	136	96	40	Vero Beach	15,427	74	52	22
North Palm Beach	12,179	43	31	12	Village of Pinecrest	18,471	65	48	17
North Port	58,139	125	100	25	Virginia Gardens	2,407	8	6	2
Oakland	2,573	10	9	1	Waldo	1,029	7	6	1
Ocala	57,082	230	154	76	Wauchula	5,069	20	16	4
Ocean Ridge	1,810	18	13	5	Webster	796	3	3	0
Ocoee	36,064	88	77	11	Welaka	711	1	1	0
Okeechobee	5,698	26	20	6	West Melbourne	18,605	44	34	10
Orange City	10,743	23	21	2	West Miami	6,046	22	18	4
Orange Park	8,527	28	21	7	West Palm Beach	101,281	359	271	88
Orlando	241,548	913	702	211	White Springs	788	3	3	0
Ormond Beach	38,657	92	67	25	Wildwood	6,800	26	18	8
Oviedo	33,796	79	61	18	Williston	2,806	19	11	8
Palatka	10,702	41	34	7	Wilton Manors	11,791	38	28	10
Palm Bay	104,596	241	161	80	Windermere	2,496	13	12	1
Palm Beach	8,462	108	69	39	Winter Garden	35,039	83	68	15
Palm Beach Gardens	49,112	153	111	42	Winter Haven	34,336	104	80	24
Palm Beach Shores	1,158	16	11	5	Winter Park	28,232	105	80	25
Palmetto	12,778	48	35	13	Winter Springs	33,736	78	64	14
Palm Springs	19,186	52	40	12	Zephyrhills	13,469	40	27	13
Panama City	36,981	130	94	36					
Panama City Beach	12,182	67	51	16	**Georgia**				
Parker	4,376	10	9	1	Abbeville	2,946	8	3	5
Pembroke Pines	156,859	284	227	57	Acworth	20,694	51	38	13
Pensacola	52,631	200	152	48	Adairsville	4,709	15	13	2
Perry	7,113	24	22	2	Adel	5,404	23	19	4
Pinellas Park	49,748	119	99	20	Alamo	2,834	3	2	1
Plantation	86,113	268	173	95	Albany	78,454	202	169	33
Plant City	35,194	84	66	18	Alma	3,512	13	11	2
Ponce Inlet	3,073	10	10	0	Alpharetta	58,309	132	104	28
Port Orange	56,812	90	76	14	Alto	1,187	4	3	1
Port Richey	2,707	18	12	6	Americus	17,265	45	37	8
Port St. Joe	3,492	7	7	0	Aragon	1,265	5	4	1
Port St. Lucie	166,846	261	205	56	Arcade	1,810	4	4	0
Punta Gorda	16,868	49	34	15	Arlington	1,498	4	4	0
Riviera Beach	32,931	146	108	38	Ashburn	4,207	16	16	0
Rockledge	25,266	68	49	19	Athens-Clarke County	117,114	295	231	64
Sanford	54,300	137	120	17	Atlanta	425,533	2,069	1,693	376
Sanibel	6,557	32	22	10	Auburn	6,978	22	16	6
Sarasota	52,625	222	172	50	Austell	6,668	29	23	6
Satellite Beach	10,247	30	22	8	Avondale Estates	2,999	12	12	0
Sea Ranch Lakes	679	9	5	4	Baldwin	3,322	17	12	5
Sebastian	22,228	52	34	18	Ball Ground	1,452	2	2	0
Sebring	10,634	38	32	6	Barnesville	6,844	19	17	2
Sewall's Point	2,023	8	8	0	Barwick	391	1	1	0
Shalimar	727	3	3	0	Baxley	4,458	12	10	2
Sneads	1,874	9	5	4	Berlin	558	1	1	0
South Daytona	12,419	34	27	7	Blairsville	661	8	7	1
South Miami	11,816	57	50	7	Blythe	730	1	1	0
South Palm Beach	1,187	8	8	0	Boston	1,332	4	4	0
Springfield	9,024	21	15	6	Bowdon	2,067	10	7	3
Starke	5,523	17	16	1	Braselton	7,610	14	13	1

Table V-9. Full-Time Law Enforcement Employees, by Selected State and City, 2011—*Continued*

(Number.)

State/City	Popula-tion	Total law enforce-ment employees	Total officers	Total civilians	State/City	Popula-tion	Total law enforce-ment employees	Total officers	Total civilians
Bremen	6,309	22	20	2	Guyton	1,706	4	3	1
Brooklet	1,413	4	4	0	Hagan	1,009	4	2	2
Brunswick	15,586	71	63	8	Hahira	2,773	6	5	1
Buchanan	1,119	8	7	1	Hampton	7,079	21	19	2
Byron	4,571	22	19	3	Hapeville	6,457	38	24	14
Cairo	9,733	26	23	3	Harlem	2,701	10	7	3
Calhoun	15,856	50	42	8	Harrison	495	1	1	0
Camilla	5,431	22	19	3	Hartwell	4,528	23	18	5
Canon	815	2	2	0	Hazlehurst	4,282	13	11	2
Carrollton	24,709	76	64	12	Helen	517	12	10	2
Cartersville	19,991	64	53	11	Hinesville	33,877	99	86	13
Cave Spring	1,216	3	3	0	Hiram	3,593	24	17	7
Cedartown	9,878	35	32	3	Hoboken	535	3	2	1
Centerville	7,242	18	15	3	Hogansville	3,100	20	15	5
Chamblee	10,022	63	44	19	Holly Springs	9,310	18	18	0
Chatsworth	4,356	16	14	2	Homerville	2,488	8	7	1
Chattahoochee Hills	2,409	10	10	0	Jackson	5,111	17	12	5
Chickamauga	3,142	6	6	0	Jasper	3,733	17	15	2
Clarkesville	1,756	7	6	1	Jefferson	9,556	24	21	3
Clarkston	7,653	20	17	3	Jesup	10,348	28	26	2
Claxton	2,782	9	8	1	Johns Creek	77,738	70	61	9
Cleveland	3,455	14	13	1	Jonesboro	4,786	23	19	4
Cochran	5,218	15	14	1	Kennesaw	30,175	66	54	12
College Park	14,126	127	98	29	Kingsland	16,156	47	44	3
Collins	592	1	1	0	Kingston	645	1	1	0
Colquitt	2,018	10	9	1	LaGrange	29,978	97	79	18
Columbus	192,385	569	464	105	Lakeland	3,410	11	8	3
Commerce	6,630	26	20	6	Lavonia	2,184	14	14	0
Conyers	15,395	79	58	21	Lawrenceville	28,922	91	70	21
Cordele	11,294	32	26	6	Lilburn	11,749	35	27	8
Covington	13,291	60	50	10	Lincolnton	1,587	4	4	0
Crawfordville	541	1	1	0	Locust Grove	5,473	21	19	2
Dallas	11,696	25	18	7	Loganville	10,596	30	25	5
Dalton	33,564	96	83	13	Lookout Mountain	1,623	6	6	0
Danielsville	567	1	1	0	Louisville	2,526	6	6	0
Donalsonville	2,685	9	8	1	Ludowici	1,725	11	7	4
Doraville	8,440	57	39	18	Lumber City	1,345	1	1	0
Douglasville	31,369	113	86	27	Lumpkin	1,160	5	4	1
Dublin	16,414	63	55	8	Macon	92,554	368	289	79
Duluth	26,950	73	56	17	Madison	4,031	14	12	2
Dunwoody	46,876	55	47	8	Manchester	4,286	17	12	5
East Dublin	2,473	8	8	0	Marietta	57,324	166	132	34
East Point	34,156	163	118	45	Maysville	1,822	4	4	0
Eatonton	6,565	24	23	1	McCaysville	1,070	4	4	0
Edison	1,551	5	4	1	McDonough	22,375	45	41	4
Elberton	4,714	25	19	6	McIntyre	659	5	5	0
Ellaville	1,836	4	4	0	Meigs	1,049	5	4	1
Emerson	1,489	6	6	0	Midville	273	1	1	0
Enigma	1,295	8	6	2	Midway	2,149	7	6	1
Ephesus	433	1	1	0	Milledgeville	17,948	61	39	22
Eton	922	3	3	0	Millen	3,161	9	9	0
Euharlee	4,190	9	8	1	Milton	33,091	29	26	3
Fairburn	13,121	35	30	5	Monroe	13,408	44	40	4
Fairmount	729	5	4	1	Montezuma	3,506	12	10	2
Fayetteville	16,155	44	40	4	Monticello	2,692	6	5	1
Fitzgerald	9,172	33	26	7	Morrow	6,530	44	32	12
Flowery Branch	5,754	15	13	2	Moultrie	14,456	47	42	5
Folkston	2,535	6	5	1	Mountain City	1,102	3	3	0
Forest Park	18,711	102	80	22	Mount Zion	1,718	3	3	0
Forsyth	3,838	23	18	5	Nahunta	1,067	4	3	1
Fort Oglethorpe	9,385	32	30	2	Nashville	5,004	17	14	3
Fort Valley	9,944	27	24	3	Newnan	33,474	82	68	14
Franklin	1,006	8	7	1	Newton	663	2	2	0
Franklin Springs	965	10	10	0	Nicholls	2,835	3	2	1
Gainesville	34,249	108	95	13	Norcross	9,236	50	38	12
Garden City	8,894	45	41	4	Oakwood	4,022	16	15	1
Glennville	3,616	17	12	5	Ocilla	3,459	13	12	1
Gordon	2,044	11	11	0	Omega	1,237	5	5	0
Grantville	3,081	14	13	1	Oxford	2,162	4	4	0
Gray	3,319	11	10	1	Palmetto	4,547	16	15	1
Greensboro	3,403	22	18	4	Patterson	740	1	1	0
Greenville	888	6	5	1	Peachtree City	34,816	68	65	3
Griffin	23,954	105	92	13	Pelham	3,949	14	12	2
Grovetown	11,364	29	21	8	Pembroke	2,225	7	5	2

Table V-9.   Full-Time Law Enforcement Employees, by Selected State and City, 2011—*Continued*

(Number.)

State/City	Population	Total law enforcement employees	Total officers	Total civilians	State/City	Population	Total law enforcement employees	Total officers	Total civilians
Perry	14,021	40	35	5	**Hawaii**				
Pine Mountain	1,321	8	7	1	Honolulu	963,465	2,544	2,063	481
Pooler	19,392	34	28	6	**Idaho**				
Porterdale	1,448	5	5	0	Aberdeen	2,016	7	4	3
Port Wentworth	5,430	25	21	4	American Falls	4,506	8	7	1
Powder Springs	14,124	31	26	5	Blackfoot	12,031	29	26	3
Quitman	3,901	18	15	3	Boise	207,945	353	292	61
Ray City	1,104	2	2	0	Bonners Ferry	2,571	7	7	0
Register	177	1	1	0	Buhl	4,168	9	7	2
Remerton	1,138	9	8	1	Caldwell	46,748	79	64	15
Reynolds	1,100	6	6	0	Cascade	949	4	3	1
Richmond Hill	9,403	38	31	7	Chubbuck	14,076	33	20	13
Rincon	8,952	17	16	1	Coeur d'Alene	44,625	88	70	18
Ringgold	3,627	9	9	0	Cottonwood	910	1	1	0
Riverdale	15,333	64	49	15	Emmett	6,629	14	13	1
Roberta	1,020	2	2	0	Filer	2,536	5	5	0
Rockmart	4,254	18	16	2	Fruitland	4,736	11	10	1
Rome	36,781	98	83	15	Garden City	11,093	35	26	9
Rossville	4,159	11	10	1	Gooding	3,606	8	7	1
Royston	2,616	17	14	3	Grangeville	3,176	6	6	0
Sandersville	5,990	21	19	2	Hagerman	882	1	1	0
Sandy Springs	95,089	138	123	15	Hailey	8,048	20	19	1
Savannah-Chatham Metropolitan	226,422	767	563	204	Heyburn	3,123	6	5	1
Screven	776	2	2	0	Homedale	2,662	5	5	0
Senoia	3,351	15	13	2	Idaho City	490	1	1	0
Shiloh	451	2	1	1	Idaho Falls	57,512	128	88	40
Smyrna	51,946	101	90	11	Jerome	11,010	21	18	3
Snellville	18,482	53	43	10	Kamiah	1,309	3	3	0
Social Circle	4,318	22	19	3	Kellogg	2,143	8	7	1
Sparks	2,079	2	2	0	Ketchum	2,719	14	10	4
Sparta	1,418	13	8	5	Kimberly	3,300	6	6	0
Springfield	2,890	8	7	1	Lewiston	32,247	66	45	21
Statesboro	28,796	74	62	12	McCall	3,024	19	15	4
Statham	2,440	8	8	0	Meridian	75,922	106	84	22
St. Marys	17,346	36	34	2	Montpelier	2,626	6	5	1
Stone Mountain	5,878	19	18	1	Moscow	24,063	39	31	8
Summerville	4,594	16	15	1	Mountain Home	14,363	37	28	9
Suwanee	15,557	43	35	8	Nampa	82,459	167	116	51
Sylvester	6,269	26	23	3	Orofino	3,177	6	5	1
Tallapoosa	3,212	13	12	1	Osburn	1,572	2	2	0
Tallulah Falls	170	2	2	0	Parma	2,005	4	4	0
Temple	4,284	13	11	2	Payette	7,515	14	12	2
Tennille	1,559	10	9	1	Pinehurst	1,637	1	1	0
Thomaston	9,291	22	18	4	Pocatello	54,855	126	89	37
Thomasville	18,655	66	59	7	Ponderay	1,150	7	6	1
Thunderbolt	2,703	10	8	2	Post Falls	27,879	63	37	26
Tifton	16,565	55	46	9	Preston	5,262	7	6	1
Tignall	553	2	1	1	Priest River	1,770	6	4	2
Toccoa	8,603	32	30	2	Rathdrum	6,901	13	10	3
Toomsboro	478	1	1	0	Rexburg	25,766	37	29	8
Trion	1,851	10	9	1	Rigby	3,989	9	8	1
Tunnel Hill	867	3	3	0	Rupert	5,615	12	11	1
Tybee Island	3,029	28	19	9	Salmon	3,146	7	6	1
Tyrone	6,970	15	14	1	Sandpoint	7,446	26	21	5
Union City	19,712	73	55	18	Shelley	4,458	5	5	0
Valdosta	55,236	164	143	21	Soda Springs	3,092	8	7	1
Vidalia	10,611	37	31	6	Spirit Lake	1,967	6	5	1
Villa Rica	14,140	42	34	8	St. Anthony	3,581	4	4	0
Warm Springs	431	2	2	0	St. Maries	2,429	5	5	0
Warner Robins	67,465	140	103	37	Sun Valley	1,422	11	10	1
Washington	4,188	14	14	0	Twin Falls	44,613	98	70	28
Watkinsville	2,869	7	7	0	Weiser	5,568	16	13	3
Waverly Hall	745	3	3	0	Wendell	2,813	4	3	1
Waycross	14,842	67	58	9	Wilder	1,550	3	3	0
Waynesboro	5,842	29	22	7	**Illinois**				
West Point	3,520	21	16	5	Abingdon	3,329	5	5	0
Whigham	477	5	4	1	Addison	37,053	94	65	29
Willacoochee	1,409	5	4	1	Albany	894	1	1	0
Winder	14,285	48	41	7	Albion	1,994	3	3	0
Winterville	1,137	3	3	0	Aledo	3,651	7	6	1
Woodstock	24,211	61	52	9	Algonquin	30,136	59	49	10
Wrens	2,216	8	8	0	Alsip	19,335	52	38	14
Wrightsville	2,224	5	4	1					
Zebulon	1,189	9	6	3					

Table V-9.　Full-Time Law Enforcement Employees, by Selected State and City, 2011—*Continued*

(Number.)

State/City	Population	Total law enforcement employees	Total officers	Total civilians	State/City	Population	Total law enforcement employees	Total officers	Total civilians
Altamont	2,326	6	6	0	Centralia	13,071	34	25	9
Alton	27,949	85	60	25	Centreville	5,325	16	13	3
Amboy	2,508	4	4	0	Cerro Gordo	1,407	1	1	0
Anna	4,455	7	7	0	Chadwick	553	1	1	0
Antioch	14,473	37	27	10	Champaign	81,299	143	119	24
Arcola	2,925	6	5	1	Channahon	12,598	27	25	2
Arlington Heights	75,327	138	108	30	Charleston	21,901	34	32	2
Arthur	2,295	4	4	0	Chatham	11,535	21	15	6
Ashland	1,337	1	1	0	Chebanse	1,065	1	1	0
Ashton	975	1	1	0	Chenoa	3,226	3	3	0
Athens	1,994	3	3	0	Cherry Valley	3,172	16	15	1
Atkinson	975	1	1	0	Chester	8,612	11	8	3
Atlanta	1,697	1	1	0	Chicago	2,703,713	12,799	12,092	707
Atwood	1,228	2	2	0	Chicago Heights	30,367	108	80	28
Auburn	4,785	10	6	4	Chicago Ridge	14,348	32	28	4
Augusta	589	1	1	0	Chillicothe	6,115	13	9	4
Aurora	198,495	347	285	62	Christopher	2,389	5	5	0
Aviston	1,951	1	1	0	Clinton	7,247	14	13	1
Bannockburn	1,588	7	7	0	Coal City	5,604	12	11	1
Barrington	10,358	27	23	4	Coal Valley	3,754	7	6	1
Barrington Hills	4,222	29	19	10	Cobden	1,160	3	3	0
Bartlett	41,332	70	53	17	Colfax	1,064	1	1	0
Bartonville	6,490	16	11	5	Collinsville	25,656	63	44	19
Batavia	26,123	45	39	6	Colona	5,114	10	9	1
Beckemeyer	1,043	1	1	0	Columbia	9,736	22	15	7
Bedford Park	582	43	36	7	Cortland	4,283	3	3	0
Beecher	4,372	8	7	1	Country Club Hills	16,591	52	38	14
Belleville	44,612	99	79	20	Countryside	5,913	31	24	7
Bellwood	19,128	43	40	3	Crest Hill	20,900	26	24	2
Belvidere	25,662	42	39	3	Crestwood	10,983	4	3	1
Benld	1,561	4	4	0	Crete	8,284	20	18	2
Bensenville	18,407	39	32	7	Creve Coeur	5,467	9	7	2
Benton	7,108	11	10	1	Crystal Lake	40,866	79	66	13
Berkeley	5,225	18	14	4	Danvers	1,157	2	2	0
Berwyn	56,828	139	102	37	Darien	22,152	43	36	7
Bethalto	9,550	18	14	4	Decatur	76,351	186	158	28
Bethany	1,356	1	1	0	Deer Creek-Goodfield	1,569	1	1	0
Bloomingdale	22,084	60	45	15	Deerfield	18,280	54	39	15
Bloomington	76,841	159	125	34	Deer Park	3,210	16	15	1
Blue Island	23,777	48	39	9	De Kalb	43,994	75	60	15
Bolingbrook	73,587	146	112	34	De Pue	1,844	3	3	0
Bradley	15,943	46	33	13	De Soto	1,595	3	2	1
Braidwood	6,210	13	12	1	Des Plaines	58,540	111	91	20
Breese	4,455	7	6	1	Divernon	1,176	3	3	0
Bridgeview	16,496	39	37	2	Dixmoor	3,655	14	10	4
Brighton	2,261	4	4	0	Dixon	15,780	32	28	4
Broadview	7,956	32	25	7	Downers Grove	47,977	102	72	30
Brookfield	19,035	36	31	5	Du Quoin	6,127	15	11	4
Buffalo Grove	41,621	77	67	10	Durand	1,447	1	1	0
Buffalo-Mechanicsburg	1,097	2	2	0	Dwight	4,273	9	8	1
Burbank	29,012	62	46	16	Earlville	1,706	2	2	0
Burnham	4,219	13	9	4	East Alton	6,320	17	11	6
Burr Ridge	10,591	29	26	3	East Dubuque	1,709	6	6	0
Byron	3,764	8	7	1	East Dundee	2,869	12	11	1
Cahokia	15,287	40	30	10	East Hazel Crest	1,548	11	10	1
Cairo	2,840	9	4	5	East Moline	21,366	51	40	11
Calumet City	37,154	107	81	26	East Peoria	23,472	55	43	12
Calumet Park	7,859	23	21	2	East St. Louis	27,087	66	47	19
Camp Point	1,135	2	2	0	Edinburg	1,081	1	1	0
Campton Hills	11,165	6	6	0	Edwardsville	24,366	56	42	14
Canton	14,748	35	24	11	Effingham	12,365	35	22	13
Carbondale	25,980	84	65	19	Elburn	5,619	9	8	1
Carlinville	5,935	16	11	5	Eldorado	4,134	11	7	4
Carlyle	3,291	8	7	1	Elgin	108,514	233	179	54
Carmi	5,256	10	9	1	Elizabeth	763	1	1	0
Carol Stream	39,831	79	61	18	Elk Grove Village	33,227	99	84	15
Carpentersville	37,804	70	60	10	Elmhurst	44,254	85	66	19
Carrier Mills	1,658	2	2	0	Elmwood	2,103	1	1	0
Carrollton	2,491	6	6	0	Elmwood Park	24,958	38	32	6
Carthage	2,613	4	4	0	El Paso	2,818	5	5	0
Cary	18,326	32	28	4	Elwood	2,286	11	10	1
Casey	2,777	8	7	1	Energy	1,149	4	4	0
Caseyville	4,258	12	10	2	Erie	1,607	3	3	0
Central City	1,176	4	4	0	Essex	804	1	1	0

Table V-9. Full-Time Law Enforcement Employees, by Selected State and City, 2011—*Continued*

(Number.)

State/City	Popula-tion	Total law enforce-ment employees	Total officers	Total civilians	State/City	Popula-tion	Total law enforce-ment employees	Total officers	Total civilians
Eureka	5,311	6	6	0	Hodgkins	1,903	21	19	2
Evanston	74,710	224	164	60	Hoffman Estates	52,051	113	94	19
Evergreen Park	19,912	77	62	15	Homer	1,197	1	1	0
Fairbury	3,768	8	8	0	Hometown	4,362	5	1	4
Fairfield	5,170	16	12	4	Homewood	19,381	41	36	5
Fairmont City	2,643	8	6	2	Hoopeston	5,367	14	10	4
Fairview	524	1	1	0	Hopedale	868	1	1	0
Fairview Heights	17,129	51	42	9	Indian Head Park	3,820	9	8	1
Farmington	2,455	4	4	0	Inverness	7,421	13	12	1
Findlay	685	1	1	0	Irvington	661	1	1	0
Fisher	1,887	2	2	0	Island Lake	8,104	20	14	6
Flora	5,085	16	11	5	Itasca	8,675	29	23	6
Forest Park	14,210	55	39	16	Jacksonville	19,505	50	40	10
Forest View	700	12	9	3	Jerseyville	8,490	20	14	6
Fox Lake	10,611	26	22	4	Johnsburg	6,356	10	9	1
Fox River Grove	4,869	10	10	0	Joliet	147,877	325	251	74
Frankfort	17,836	34	30	4	Jonesboro	1,826	2	2	0
Franklin Park	18,388	44	43	1	Justice	12,965	31	24	7
Freeport	25,715	68	50	18	Kankakee	27,620	80	69	11
Fulton	3,491	9	8	1	Kenilworth	2,521	13	10	3
Galena	3,439	12	10	2	Kewanee	12,955	30	23	7
Galesburg	32,292	76	52	24	Kildeer	3,980	16	15	1
Galva	2,597	3	3	0	Kincaid	1,510	1	1	0
Geneseo	6,606	17	12	5	Kingston	1,168	2	2	0
Geneva	21,560	50	36	14	Knoxville	2,920	5	5	0
Genoa	5,209	7	6	1	Lacon	1,943	3	3	0
Georgetown	3,484	4	4	0	La Grange	15,597	42	27	15
Germantown	1,273	1	1	0	La Grange Park	13,620	26	20	6
Gibson City	3,417	9	7	2	Lake Forest	19,433	55	39	16
Gifford	978	1	1	0	Lakemoor	6,035	8	7	1
Gilberts	6,900	9	8	1	Lake Villa	8,767	18	17	1
Gillespie	3,329	9	6	3	Lakewood	3,822	9	8	1
Glasford	1,025	1	1	0	Lake Zurich	19,690	51	34	17
Glen Carbon	12,973	26	19	7	La Moille	728	1	1	0
Glencoe	8,749	42	33	9	Lansing	28,416	74	55	19
Glendale Heights	34,311	75	52	23	La Salle	9,638	29	23	6
Glen Ellyn	27,533	47	39	8	Lawrenceville	4,361	7	7	0
Glenview	44,827	78	73	5	Lebanon	4,431	11	11	0
Glenwood	8,996	22	21	1	Leland	980	1	1	0
Golf	502	4	4	0	Leland Grove	1,508	5	5	0
Grafton	676	3	3	0	Lemont	16,048	32	27	5
Grandview	1,445	2	2	0	Lenzburg	523	1	1	0
Granite City	29,939	71	60	11	Le Roy	3,571	6	6	0
Grant Park	1,335	4	4	0	Lexington	2,066	1	1	0
Granville	1,431	2	2	0	Libertyville	20,376	50	39	11
Grayslake	21,020	37	32	5	Lincoln	14,548	26	25	1
Grayville	1,671	2	2	0	Lincolnshire	7,297	31	23	8
Greenfield	1,074	2	2	0	Lincolnwood	12,628	43	32	11
Greenup	1,518	4	4	0	Lisle	22,457	49	38	11
Greenville	7,021	13	9	4	Litchfield	6,960	17	15	2
Gurnee	31,389	87	58	29	Lockport	24,914	44	37	7
Hamilton	2,960	4	4	0	Lombard	43,526	83	68	15
Hampshire	5,580	11	11	0	Loves Park	24,068	36	33	3
Hampton	1,869	4	4	0	Lynwood	9,034	28	19	9
Hanover	847	1	1	0	Lyons	10,761	40	30	10
Hanover Park	38,087	84	61	23	Machesney Park	23,570	26	25	1
Harrisburg	9,044	15	14	1	Mackinaw	1,956	1	1	0
Hartford	1,433	5	4	1	Macomb	19,346	30	27	3
Harvard	9,475	23	17	6	Madison	3,903	15	11	4
Harwood Heights	8,638	33	24	9	Mahomet	7,280	9	8	1
Havana	3,311	12	8	4	Manhattan	7,072	11	10	1
Hawthorn Woods	7,686	10	9	1	Manteno	9,232	18	17	1
Hazel Crest	14,142	33	29	4	Maple Park	1,314	1	1	0
Hebron	1,220	3	3	0	Marengo	7,671	14	14	0
Henry	2,471	4	4	0	Marion	17,245	40	30	10
Herrin	12,539	24	17	7	Marissa	1,985	4	4	0
Herscher	1,596	3	3	0	Maroa	1,806	3	3	0
Hickory Hills	14,091	36	28	8	Marquette Heights	2,833	5	5	0
Highland	9,949	25	19	6	Marseilles	5,109	14	9	5
Highland Park	29,853	73	54	19	Marshall	3,945	10	9	1
Hillsboro	6,226	8	8	0	Martinsville	1,171	2	2	0
Hillside	8,182	31	25	6	Maryville	7,510	12	12	0
Hinckley	2,076	3	3	0	Mascoutah	7,506	14	13	1
Hinsdale	16,867	27	25	2	Matteson	19,066	47	39	8

Table V-9.   Full-Time Law Enforcement Employees, by Selected State and City, 2011—*Continued*

(Number.)

State/City	Popula-tion	Total law enforce-ment employees	Total officers	Total civilians	State/City	Popula-tion	Total law enforce-ment employees	Total officers	Total civilians
Mattoon	18,611	40	36	4	Palos Hills	17,537	34	31	3
Maywood	24,163	73	60	13	Palos Park	4,862	11	10	1
McCook	229	23	18	5	Pana	5,865	13	9	4
McHenry	27,073	60	45	15	Paris	8,864	21	15	6
McLean	832	1	1	0	Park City	7,593	12	10	2
McLeansboro	2,892	5	5	0	Park Forest	22,041	53	41	12
Medora	420	1	1	0	Park Ridge	37,593	67	54	13
Melrose Park	25,487	79	70	9	Pawnee	2,747	5	5	0
Mendota	7,394	20	15	5	Paxton	4,486	6	6	0
Meredosia	1,047	1	1	0	Pecatonica	2,202	5	3	2
Metropolis	6,557	21	16	5	Pekin	34,197	62	53	9
Midlothian	14,864	29	26	3	Peoria	115,353	248	213	35
Milan	5,114	20	14	6	Peoria Heights	6,175	16	12	4
Milledgeville	1,035	2	2	0	Peotone	4,154	10	9	1
Minier	1,256	2	2	0	Peru	10,326	32	25	7
Minonk	2,084	3	3	0	Petersburg	2,267	4	4	0
Minooka	10,957	22	18	4	Phoenix	1,970	2	1	1
Mokena	18,796	33	30	3	Pinckneyville	5,665	8	7	1
Moline	43,614	102	81	21	Pittsfield	4,590	6	6	0
Momence	3,320	8	8	0	Plainfield	39,700	67	51	16
Monee	5,163	13	12	1	Plano	10,889	21	19	2
Monmouth	9,472	30	20	10	Pleasant Hill	969	1	1	0
Montgomery	18,494	30	22	8	Polo	2,362	4	4	0
Monticello	5,565	7	6	1	Pontiac	11,967	20	19	1
Morris	13,677	32	23	9	Pontoon Beach	5,854	21	15	6
Morrison	4,201	6	6	0	Posen	6,005	16	14	2
Morton	16,316	26	20	6	Potomac	752	1	1	0
Morton Grove	23,340	58	45	13	Princeton	7,683	18	17	1
Mount Carmel	7,306	16	12	4	Prophetstown	2,086	3	3	0
Mount Carroll	1,722	3	3	0	Quincy	40,755	91	76	15
Mount Morris	3,007	5	4	1	Rantoul	12,980	41	32	9
Mount Prospect	54,330	100	82	18	Richmond	1,880	3	3	0
Mount Pulaski	1,571	2	2	0	Richton Park	13,687	32	28	4
Mount Sterling	2,031	8	5	3	Ridge Farm	885	1	1	0
Mount Vernon	15,323	56	44	12	River Forest	11,206	31	28	3
Mount Zion	5,851	12	10	2	River Grove	10,258	29	23	6
Moweaqua	1,837	2	2	0	Riverside	8,902	24	19	5
Mundelein	31,158	69	52	17	Riverwoods	3,671	7	7	0
Murphysboro	7,994	22	15	7	Robinson	7,736	14	13	1
Naperville	142,280	263	164	99	Rochester	3,700	8	8	0
Nashville	3,268	7	6	1	Rockdale	1,982	3	3	0
New Athens	2,060	4	4	0	Rock Falls	9,294	26	19	7
New Baden	3,359	5	5	0	Rockford	153,331	294	264	30
New Lenox	24,467	40	36	4	Rock Island	39,135	109	82	27
Niles	29,893	67	55	12	Rolling Meadows	24,172	55	47	8
Normal	52,655	88	75	13	Romeoville	39,799	85	62	23
Norridge	14,616	52	36	16	Roodhouse	1,819	7	3	4
North Aurora	16,810	30	28	2	Roselle	22,832	42	32	10
Northbrook	33,270	89	63	26	Round Lake	18,344	25	19	6
Northfield	5,436	24	18	6	Round Lake Beach	28,260	49	42	7
Northlake	12,360	57	40	17	Round Lake Heights	2,684	6	6	0
North Pekin	1,578	4	4	0	Roxana	1,547	7	6	1
North Riverside	6,692	33	25	8	Rushville	3,202	5	5	0
Oakbrook Terrace	2,140	22	19	3	Salem	7,508	21	13	8
Oak Forest	28,046	52	40	12	Sandoval	1,278	3	3	0
Oak Lawn	56,861	129	107	22	Sandwich	7,443	20	14	6
Oakwood	1,600	1	1	0	Sauget	159	13	12	1
Oblong	1,470	1	1	0	Sauk Village	10,538	30	22	8
O'Fallon	28,366	60	45	15	Savanna	3,071	8	8	0
Oglesby	3,802	12	9	3	Schaumburg	74,450	152	113	39
Okawville	1,438	3	3	0	Schiller Park	11,829	40	33	7
Old Shawneetown	194	3	3	0	Seneca	2,378	8	4	4
Olney	9,142	14	13	1	Sesser	1,937	6	5	1
Olympia Fields	5,003	23	20	3	Shannon	759	1	1	0
Oregon	3,732	9	8	1	Shawneetown	1,243	3	3	0
Orion	1,867	3	3	0	Shelbyville	4,714	8	7	1
Orland Hills	7,171	12	12	0	Sheridan	2,143	2	2	0
Orland Park	56,938	123	95	28	Sherman	4,160	6	6	0
Oswego	30,446	56	47	9	Shiloh	12,689	17	16	1
Ottawa	18,824	46	35	11	Shorewood	15,662	28	24	4
Palatine	68,763	135	110	25	Silvis	7,502	20	14	6
Palestine	1,373	2	2	0	Skokie	64,979	139	107	32
Palmyra	700	2	2	0	Sleepy Hollow	3,314	8	7	1
Palos Heights	12,553	30	27	3	Somonauk	1,899	5	5	0

Table V-9.   Full-Time Law Enforcement Employees, by Selected State and City, 2011—*Continued*

(Number.)

State/City	Popula-tion	Total law enforce-ment employees	Total officers	Total civilians	State/City	Popula-tion	Total law enforce-ment employees	Total officers	Total civilians
South Beloit	7,916	16	15	1	Winfield	9,107	19	17	2
South Chicago Heights	4,151	11	7	4	Winnebago	3,110	5	5	0
South Elgin	22,051	40	31	9	Winnetka	12,224	34	26	8
Southern View	1,647	4	4	0	Winthrop Harbor	6,762	15	9	6
South Holland	22,096	46	44	2	Wood Dale	13,811	49	32	17
South Jacksonville	3,341	6	5	1	Woodhull	813	1	1	0
South Pekin	1,149	2	2	0	Woodridge	33,070	64	49	15
South Roxana	2,059	5	5	0	Wood River	10,689	24	18	6
Sparta	4,315	14	9	5	Woodstock	24,845	46	35	11
Springfield	116,600	279	240	39	Worden	1,047	1	1	0
Spring Grove	5,795	10	8	2	Worth	10,821	25	23	2
Spring Valley	5,575	14	11	3	Wyoming	1,433	2	2	0
St. Anne	1,261	2	2	0	Yates City	695	1	1	0
Staunton	5,151	8	5	3	Yorkville	16,972	27	24	3
St. Charles	33,073	63	52	11	Zeigler	1,806	4	4	0
St. Elmo	1,430	1	1	0	Zion	24,486	60	47	13
Sterling	15,416	40	28	12					
Stickney	6,806	21	15	6	**Indiana**				
Stockton	1,868	5	4	1	Anderson	56,416	130	117	13
Stone Park	4,961	15	15	0	Angola	8,656	19	15	4
Stonington	935	2	2	0	Auburn	12,796	27	22	5
Streamwood	39,978	67	57	10	Aurora	3,769	13	10	3
Streator	13,751	30	24	6	Austin	4,317	7	7	0
Sugar Grove	9,024	14	13	1	Avon	12,510	25	23	2
Summit	11,087	32	26	6	Bargersville	4,033	9	8	1
Sumner	3,184	2	2	0	Batesville	6,553	17	12	5
Swansea	13,470	26	21	5	Bedford	13,482	38	30	8
Sycamore	17,572	32	30	2	Berne	4,019	7	6	1
Taylorville	11,280	23	18	5	Bicknell	2,930	6	6	0
Thornton	2,345	12	11	1	Bloomington	80,816	131	97	34
Tinley Park	56,874	94	71	23	Bluffton	9,948	30	20	10
Tolono	3,457	3	3	0	Boonville	6,278	15	14	1
Tremont	2,243	3	3	0	Brazil	7,952	16	13	3
Trenton	2,723	5	5	0	Bremen	4,611	16	12	4
Troy	9,918	24	18	6	Brownsburg	21,394	49	41	8
Tuscola	4,493	8	7	1	Burns Harbor	1,162	5	4	1
University Park	7,150	25	21	4	Cannelton	1,571	3	3	0
Urbana	41,374	69	55	14	Carmel	79,596	131	110	21
Valmeyer	1,267	2	2	0	Cedar Lake	11,619	22	17	5
Vandalia	7,063	15	11	4	Charlestown	7,624	20	15	5
Venice	1,896	13	9	4	Chesterton	13,135	26	22	4
Vernon Hills	25,189	63	43	20	Clarks Hill	614	1	1	0
Vienna	1,438	4	4	0	Clarksville	21,835	48	40	8
Villa Grove	2,545	5	4	1	Clinton	4,918	8	8	0
Villa Park	21,970	49	37	12	Columbia City	8,795	20	18	2
Virginia	1,616	1	1	0	Columbus	44,286	83	75	8
Warren	1,432	4	3	1	Connersville	13,550	28	27	1
Warrensburg	1,214	2	2	0	Corydon	3,138	7	7	0
Warrenville	13,180	38	31	7	Covington	2,659	6	6	0
Washington	15,180	29	21	8	Crawfordsville	15,996	45	30	15
Washington Park	4,209	8	7	1	Crown Point	27,457	54	41	13
Waterloo	9,841	16	15	1	Culver	1,360	4	4	0
Waterman	1,511	3	3	0	Cumberland	5,195	15	13	2
Watseka	5,271	9	9	0	Danville	9,047	17	15	2
Wauconda	13,644	37	26	11	Decatur	9,453	21	17	4
Waukegan	89,346	174	133	41	Delphi	2,908	7	7	0
Wayne	2,438	5	5	0	Dunkirk	2,374	7	5	2
Wayne City	1,035	1	1	0	Dyer	16,474	32	25	7
Westchester	16,768	43	32	11	East Chicago	29,850	115	105	10
West Chicago	27,168	53	47	6	Edinburgh	4,503	16	11	5
West City	663	11	6	5	Elkhart	51,209	134	120	14
West Dundee	7,353	22	19	3	Ellettsville	6,411	9	9	0
Western Springs	13,014	27	21	6	Elwood	8,658	21	16	5
West Frankfort	8,207	18	13	5	Evansville	118,029	311	282	29
Westmont	24,759	43	37	6	Fairmount	2,969	6	5	1
West Salem	900	1	1	0	Fishers	77,186	99	91	8
Westville	3,212	4	4	0	Fort Wayne	254,987	517	456	61
Wheaton	53,053	79	63	16	Fowler	2,329	4	4	0
Wheeling	37,761	83	61	22	Frankfort	16,506	31	28	3
Williamsfield	580	1	1	0	Franklin	23,833	55	40	15
Willowbrook	8,566	24	21	3	Garrett	6,318	17	13	4
Willow Springs	5,541	20	14	6	Gas City	5,995	14	10	4
Wilmette	27,169	56	44	12	Georgetown	2,891	4	4	0
Wilmington	5,741	14	13	1	Goshen	31,881	65	59	6

Table V-9.   Full-Time Law Enforcement Employees, by Selected State and City, 2011—*Continued*

(Number.)

State/City	Popula-tion	Total law enforce-ment employees	Total officers	Total civilians	State/City	Popula-tion	Total law enforce-ment employees	Total officers	Total civilians
Greencastle	10,379	17	15	2	St. John	14,926	24	18	6
Greendale	4,543	12	10	2	Tell City	7,309	20	12	8
Greenfield	20,707	42	39	3	Terre Haute	61,095	144	134	10
Greenwood	50,045	76	56	20	Tipton	5,132	14	12	2
Griffith	16,979	38	30	8	Union City	3,602	9	8	1
Hagerstown	1,796	5	5	0	Valparaiso	31,892	55	49	6
Hammond	81,243	252	210	42	Wabash	10,720	28	27	1
Hartford City	6,252	13	12	1	Walkerton	2,155	10	6	4
Hebron	3,743	7	7	0	Warsaw	13,628	42	36	6
Highland	23,848	44	37	7	Washington	11,568	24	18	6
Hobart	29,207	70	55	15	Waterloo	2,253	5	5	0
Huntingburg	6,088	11	10	1	Westfield	30,222	44	40	4
Huntington	17,480	34	32	2	West Lafayette	29,747	65	47	18
Indianapolis	833,024	1,857	1,614	243	Westville	5,883	3	3	0
Jasonville	2,233	5	5	0	Whitestown	2,882	12	12	0
Jasper	15,115	28	21	7	Whiting	5,023	24	19	5
Jeffersonville	45,183	88	74	14	Winchester	4,960	11	11	0
Kendallville	9,912	24	17	7	Zionsville	14,232	27	26	1
Kingsford Heights	1,442	2	2	0					
Knox	3,723	7	7	0	**Iowa**				
Kokomo	45,700	124	103	21	Adel	3,701	10	9	1
Lafayette	67,483	168	131	37	Albia	3,786	7	6	1
Lake Station	12,636	30	25	5	Algona	5,589	14	10	4
La Porte	22,166	48	43	5	Altoona	14,617	25	23	2
Lawrenceburg	5,068	25	21	4	Ames	59,274	76	51	25
Lebanon	15,873	30	29	1	Anamosa	5,562	7	6	1
Ligonier	4,428	11	10	1	Ankeny	45,821	58	50	8
Linton	5,441	15	11	4	Atlantic	7,149	13	12	1
Logansport	18,490	41	40	1	Audubon	2,187	3	3	0
Long Beach	1,185	6	5	1	Belle Plaine	2,547	4	4	0
Loogootee	2,765	4	4	0	Belmond	2,388	5	5	0
Lowell	9,323	19	14	5	Bettendorf	33,391	49	45	4
Madison	12,028	33	27	6	Bloomfield	2,654	5	5	0
Marion	30,101	86	72	14	Boone	12,727	17	16	1
Martinsville	11,888	32	23	9	Burlington	25,797	56	41	15
Merrillville	35,426	62	48	14	Camanche	4,471	8	8	0
Michigan City	31,460	100	92	8	Carlisle	3,896	7	6	1
Mishawaka	48,498	131	105	26	Carroll	10,156	15	14	1
Mitchell	4,372	11	7	4	Carter Lake	3,805	10	9	1
Monticello	5,405	17	12	5	Cedar Falls	39,466	42	41	1
Mooresville	9,374	27	21	6	Cedar Rapids	126,988	265	204	61
Mount Vernon	6,721	15	14	1	Centerville	5,557	18	13	5
Muncie	70,443	104	99	5	Chariton	4,344	6	5	1
Munster	23,724	42	35	7	Charles City	7,692	19	12	7
Nappanee	6,682	21	15	6	Cherokee	5,281	9	8	1
New Albany	36,558	70	65	5	Clarinda	5,601	14	9	5
New Castle	18,207	34	32	2	Clarion	2,865	8	7	1
New Chicago	2,045	4	1	3	Clear Lake	7,818	22	16	6
New Haven	14,870	27	19	8	Clinton	27,026	49	41	8
New Whiteland	5,500	12	7	5	Clive	15,528	26	24	2
Noblesville	52,234	82	72	10	Coralville	19,006	37	33	4
North Judson	1,781	4	4	0	Council Bluffs	62,556	132	112	20
North Liberty	1,906	3	3	0	Cresco	3,888	7	7	0
North Manchester	6,143	15	11	4	Creston	7,875	15	11	4
North Vernon	6,762	20	18	2	Davenport	100,207	195	167	28
Peru	11,475	30	28	2	Decorah	8,170	20	12	8
Petersburg	2,395	4	4	0	Denison	8,341	18	13	5
Plainfield	27,772	49	44	5	Des Moines	204,498	465	360	105
Plymouth	10,084	29	24	5	De Witt	5,350	11	10	1
Portage	37,016	67	59	8	Dubuque	57,939	103	97	6
Porter	4,883	13	10	3	Dyersville	4,079	5	5	0
Portland	6,255	17	13	4	Eagle Grove	3,602	7	7	0
Princeton	8,688	17	16	1	Eldora	2,746	4	4	0
Rensselaer	5,889	15	10	5	Eldridge	5,681	10	9	1
Richmond	37,000	80	69	11	Emmetsburg	3,924	7	6	1
Rochester	6,250	16	11	5	Estherville	6,393	12	12	0
Rushville	6,373	17	12	5	Evansdale	4,776	7	6	1
Schererville	29,392	61	49	12	Fairfield	9,514	20	14	6
Scottsburg	6,781	13	13	0	Forest City	4,173	8	8	0
Seymour	17,592	56	39	17	Fort Dodge	25,338	43	40	3
Shelbyville	19,289	62	50	12	Fort Madison	11,109	20	18	2
South Bend	101,685	328	258	70	Garner	3,145	5	5	0
South Whitley	1,760	4	4	0	Glenwood	5,297	10	9	1
Speedway	11,872	47	34	13	Grinnell	9,266	17	15	2

Table V-9.   Full-Time Law Enforcement Employees, by Selected State and City, 2011—*Continued*

(Number.)

State/City	Population	Total law enforcement employees	Total officers	Total civilians	State/City	Population	Total law enforcement employees	Total officers	Total civilians
Grundy Center	2,720	4	4	0	West Des Moines	56,905	77	63	14
Hampton	4,484	11	6	5	West Liberty	3,756	8	7	1
Harlan	5,133	9	8	1	West Union	2,499	4	4	0
Hawarden	2,559	4	4	0	Williamsburg	3,084	6	6	0
Hiawatha	7,061	12	12	0	Wilton	2,817	4	4	0
Humboldt	4,715	6	6	0	Windsor Heights	4,885	15	13	2
Indianola	14,859	21	19	2	Winterset	5,217	8	8	0
Iowa City	68,217	102	79	23					
Iowa Falls	5,265	14	10	4	**Kansas**				
Jefferson	4,368	6	6	0	Abilene	6,887	18	15	3
Johnston	17,368	23	22	1	Altamont	1,087	3	3	0
Keokuk	10,836	27	24	3	Andale	934	2	2	0
Knoxville	7,351	14	12	2	Andover	11,866	29	22	7
Le Claire	3,785	8	7	1	Anthony	2,283	6	5	1
Le Mars	9,877	14	13	1	Argonia	504	1	1	0
Leon	1,987	3	3	0	Arkansas City	12,494	33	26	7
Lisbon	2,163	2	2	0	Arma	1,490	5	5	0
Manchester	5,206	13	9	4	Atchison	11,091	23	22	1
Maquoketa	6,173	17	11	6	Attica	630	1	1	0
Marengo	2,541	4	4	0	Atwood	1,202	2	2	0
Marion	34,950	50	41	9	Augusta	9,333	31	23	8
Marshalltown	27,696	59	42	17	Baldwin City	4,544	9	8	1
Mason City	28,226	51	46	5	Basehor	4,642	12	9	3
Missouri Valley	2,853	6	6	0	Baxter Springs	4,265	15	10	5
Monticello	3,816	7	6	1	Bel Aire	6,812	7	7	0
Mount Pleasant	8,713	16	14	2	Belle Plaine	1,692	5	5	0
Mount Vernon	4,530	6	6	0	Belleville	2,004	5	5	0
Muscatine	23,006	43	40	3	Beloit	3,859	8	7	1
Nevada	6,834	8	7	1	Benton	886	2	2	0
New Hampton	3,590	7	7	0	Blue Rapids	1,025	1	1	0
New London	1,907	3	3	0	Bonner Springs	7,360	25	23	2
Newton	15,334	27	22	5	Buhler	1,335	3	3	0
North Liberty	13,444	15	14	1	Burden	538	1	1	0
Norwalk	8,992	16	13	3	Burlingame	940	2	2	0
Oelwein	6,449	16	11	5	Burlington	2,691	9	7	2
Ogden	2,055	3	3	0	Burrton	907	3	2	1
Onawa	3,014	6	6	0	Caldwell	1,075	3	3	0
Orange City	6,035	7	7	0	Caney	2,217	10	6	4
Osage	3,638	6	5	1	Canton	753	1	1	0
Osceola	4,955	11	10	1	Cedar Vale	583	1	1	0
Oskaloosa	11,523	18	16	2	Chanute	9,177	20	18	2
Ottumwa	25,154	46	39	7	Chapman	1,402	3	3	0
Pella	10,406	21	14	7	Chase	480	1	1	0
Perry	7,742	20	13	7	Cheney	2,107	5	5	0
Pleasant Hill	8,831	19	17	2	Cherokee	719	1	1	0
Pleasantville	1,703	1	1	0	Cherryvale	2,382	5	5	0
Polk City	3,436	6	6	0	Chetopa	1,132	4	4	0
Prairie City	1,689	3	3	0	Claflin	649	1	1	0
Red Oak	5,772	12	10	2	Clay Center	4,362	8	6	2
Rock Rapids	2,562	1	1	0	Clearwater	2,497	7	6	1
Rock Valley	3,372	5	5	0	Coffeyville	10,360	33	26	7
Sac City	2,232	4	4	0	Colby	5,421	18	12	6
Sergeant Bluff	4,249	8	7	1	Columbus	3,333	11	9	2
Sheldon	5,215	7	7	0	Colwich	1,335	2	2	0
Shenandoah	5,177	11	8	3	Concordia	5,429	17	10	7
Sioux Center	7,085	7	7	0	Conway Springs	1,280	2	2	0
Sioux City	83,117	150	123	27	Council Grove	2,196	8	7	1
Spencer	11,292	27	19	8	Derby	22,299	52	42	10
Spirit Lake	4,865	10	9	1	Dodge City	27,514	63	47	16
St. Ansgar	1,113	1	1	0	Eastborough	778	7	7	0
State Center	1,476	1	1	0	Edwardsville	4,368	17	16	1
Storm Lake	10,656	23	19	4	El Dorado	13,104	27	24	3
Story City	3,449	5	5	0	Elkhart	2,219	3	3	0
Tama	2,892	5	5	0	Ellinwood	2,145	5	5	0
Tipton	3,238	6	6	0	Ellis	2,075	5	5	0
Urbandale	39,670	53	49	4	Ellsworth	3,140	7	6	1
Vinton	5,285	8	8	0	Elwood	1,232	5	5	0
Washington	7,304	11	10	1	Emporia	25,074	63	41	22
Waterloo	68,764	137	125	12	Enterprise	860	2	2	0
Waukee	13,862	16	14	2	Erie	1,157	4	3	1
Waukon	3,917	7	7	0	Eudora	6,175	9	8	1
Waverly	9,926	17	16	1	Fairway	3,907	10	8	2
Webster City	8,112	16	12	4	Florence	468	2	2	0
West Burlington	2,984	10	10	0	Fort Scott	8,138	28	19	9

Table V-9. **Full-Time Law Enforcement Employees, by Selected State and City, 2011**—*Continued*

(Number.)

State/City	Popula- tion	Total law enforce- ment employees	Total officers	Total civilians	State/City	Popula- tion	Total law enforce- ment employees	Total officers	Total civilians
Frankfort	731	1	1	0	Oakley	2,058	10	6	4
Fredonia	2,498	7	6	1	Oberlin	1,799	4	4	0
Frontenac	3,459	10	7	3	Olathe	126,671	189	163	26
Galena	3,105	11	7	4	Osage City	2,962	6	6	0
Garden City	26,827	87	58	29	Osawatomie	4,475	17	11	6
Garden Plain	854	2	2	0	Osborne	1,440	4	4	0
Gardner	19,244	29	26	3	Oswego	1,841	4	4	0
Garnett	3,437	8	8	0	Ottawa	12,729	31	27	4
Girard	2,807	7	6	1	Overbrook	1,065	2	2	0
Goddard	4,372	8	7	1	Overland Park	174,473	287	240	47
Goodland	4,518	10	9	1	Oxford	1,056	2	2	0
Grandview Plaza	1,570	6	6	0	Paola	5,638	21	15	6
Great Bend	16,097	33	28	5	Park City	7,343	20	18	2
Halstead	2,098	6	6	0	Parsons	10,567	29	23	6
Haven	1,245	3	3	0	Peabody	1,218	2	2	0
Hays	20,640	51	33	18	Pittsburg	20,361	54	38	16
Haysville	10,895	31	26	5	Plainville	1,915	5	5	0
Herington	2,542	8	7	1	Pleasanton	1,224	2	2	0
Hesston	3,733	7	6	1	Prairie Village	21,583	56	43	13
Hiawatha	3,192	7	6	1	Pratt	6,878	20	13	7
Highland	1,018	2	2	0	Protection	517	1	1	0
Hill City	1,483	4	4	0	Roeland Park	6,774	14	12	2
Hillsboro	3,012	5	5	0	Rolla	445	1	1	0
Hoisington	2,723	7	7	0	Rose Hill	3,956	11	9	2
Holcomb	2,107	4	3	1	Rossville	1,158	2	2	0
Holton	3,350	7	7	0	Russell	4,535	19	8	11
Holyrood	450	1	1	0	Sabetha	2,587	9	5	4
Horton	1,787	9	5	4	Salina	48,010	109	78	31
Howard	691	1	1	0	Scott City	3,840	12	7	5
Hoxie	1,209	2	2	0	Scranton	715	2	2	0
Hugoton	3,929	8	6	2	Sedan	1,131	2	2	0
Humboldt	1,965	5	5	0	Sedgwick	1,706	2	2	0
Hutchinson	42,347	105	67	38	Seneca	2,004	5	5	0
Independence	9,543	27	19	8	Shawnee	62,604	109	87	22
Inman	1,386	3	3	0	Silver Lake	1,448	2	2	0
Iola	5,740	16	15	1	South Hutchinson	2,473	10	8	2
Junction City	23,501	63	44	19	Spearville	778	1	1	0
Kechi	1,921	4	3	1	Spring Hill	5,472	12	10	2
La Crosse	1,351	3	3	0	Stafford	1,049	3	3	0
La Cygne	1,156	2	2	0	Sterling	2,343	5	5	0
Lansing	11,337	18	17	1	St. Francis	1,337	3	2	1
Larned	4,080	11	7	4	St. John	1,303	4	4	0
Leavenworth	35,475	86	64	22	St. Marys	2,644	5	5	0
Leawood	32,069	80	59	21	Stockton	1,337	5	5	0
Lebo	946	1	1	0	Tonganoxie	5,028	11	10	1
Lenexa	48,496	123	84	39	Topeka	128,283	353	290	63
Liberal	20,655	55	40	15	Troy	1,016	1	1	0
Lindsborg	3,480	7	6	1	Udall	751	1	1	0
Little River	561	1	1	0	Ulysses	6,200	12	11	1
Louisburg	4,342	7	7	0	Valley Center	6,865	18	13	5
Lyndon	1,059	2	2	0	Victoria	1,222	2	2	0
Lyons	3,763	8	7	1	Wa Keeney	1,874	5	5	0
Macksville	552	1	1	0	Wamego	4,400	12	7	5
Marion	1,939	5	4	1	Waterville	684	1	1	0
Marysville	3,315	7	6	1	Wathena	1,373	2	2	0
McLouth	886	2	2	0	Wellington	8,224	20	17	3
McPherson	13,239	33	27	6	Wellsville	1,869	4	4	0
Meade	1,732	3	3	0	Westwood	2,056	8	7	1
Medicine Lodge	2,022	7	6	1	Wichita	384,796	841	646	195
Merriam	11,073	33	28	5	Winfield	12,379	31	22	9
Minneapolis	2,045	4	4	0	Yates Center	1,426	3	3	0
Mission	9,382	28	26	2					
Moran	562	1	1	0	**Kentucky**				
Mound City	698	2	2	0	Adairville	858	3	1	2
Moundridge	1,748	3	3	0	Albany	2,047	7	7	0
Mount Hope	818	1	1	0	Alexandria	8,536	15	13	2
Mulberry	523	1	1	0	Anchorage	2,364	14	10	4
Mulvane	6,150	17	11	6	Ashland	21,834	50	46	4
Neodesha	2,502	8	7	1	Auburn	1,349	2	2	0
Newton	19,254	37	32	5	Audubon Park	1,483	8	7	1
Nickerson	1,077	1	1	0	Augusta	1,198	3	3	0
North Newton	1,770	2	2	0	Barbourville	3,187	15	14	1
Norton	2,947	3	3	0	Bardstown	11,781	26	25	1
Norwich	494	1	1	0	Beattyville	1,316	5	5	0

Table V-9.   Full-Time Law Enforcement Employees, by Selected State and City, 2011—*Continued*

(Number.)

State/City	Population	Total law enforcement employees	Total officers	Total civilians	State/City	Population	Total law enforcement employees	Total officers	Total civilians
Beaver Dam	3,433	5	5	0	Jeffersontown	26,779	60	50	10
Bellevue	5,996	11	10	1	Junction City	2,256	3	3	0
Benham	503	2	2	0	La Center	1,016	1	1	0
Benton	4,379	7	7	0	La Grange	8,138	13	13	0
Berea	13,655	32	30	2	Lakeside Park-Crestview Hills	5,856	11	10	1
Bloomfield	844	1	1	0	Lancaster	3,466	8	8	0
Brandenburg	2,661	4	4	0	Lawrenceburg	10,578	23	15	8
Brooksville	646	1	1	0	Lebanon	5,577	21	15	6
Burkesville	1,532	9	5	4	Leitchfield	6,745	15	14	1
Burnside	615	4	4	0	Lewisburg	816	1	1	0
Butler	616	1	1	0	Lexington	297,847	595	522	73
Cadiz	2,576	9	8	1	London	8,048	37	34	3
Calvert City	2,584	7	6	1	Louisville Metro	665,152	1,417	1,233	184
Campbellsville	9,171	24	22	2	Loyall	1,471	1	1	0
Caneyville	612	1	1	0	Ludlow	4,437	11	10	1
Carlisle	2,024	9	5	4	Madisonville	19,726	56	44	12
Carrollton	3,965	11	10	1	Manchester	1,264	11	11	0
Catlettsburg	1,869	8	8	0	Marion	3,060	9	6	3
Cave City	2,255	6	6	0	Mayfield	10,093	24	24	0
Central City	6,019	12	12	0	Maysville	9,073	29	21	8
Clarkson	881	1	1	0	Meadow Vale	741	1	1	0
Clay City	1,084	2	2	0	Middlesboro	10,405	26	22	4
Clinton	1,398	5	5	0	Millersburg	797	1	1	0
Cloverport	1,160	2	2	0	Monticello	6,231	11	10	1
Cold Spring	5,953	12	11	1	Morehead	6,892	28	20	8
Corbin	7,354	25	18	7	Morgantown	2,411	6	6	0
Covington	40,921	132	108	24	Mortons Gap	869	1	1	0
Cynthiana	6,446	17	16	1	Mount Sterling	6,943	24	22	2
Danville	16,330	34	32	2	Mount Vernon	2,494	9	9	0
Dawson Springs	2,783	8	5	3	Mount Washington	9,180	14	13	1
Dayton	5,375	10	9	1	Muldraugh	954	4	4	0
Earlington	1,423	1	1	0	Murray	17,864	38	32	6
Eddyville	2,572	6	6	0	New Haven	861	1	1	0
Edgewood	8,634	14	14	0	Newport	15,379	44	40	4
Edmonton	1,606	6	6	0	Nicholasville	28,209	65	58	7
Elizabethtown	28,728	55	39	16	Oak Grove	7,541	22	17	5
Elkhorn City	989	4	4	0	Olive Hill	1,610	6	6	0
Elkton	2,076	7	7	0	Owensboro	57,661	130	98	32
Elsmere	8,509	13	12	1	Owingsville	1,541	5	5	0
Eminence	2,515	6	6	0	Paducah	25,197	81	71	10
Erlanger	22,034	52	40	12	Paintsville	3,483	12	11	1
Eubank	321	2	2	0	Paris	8,612	27	25	2
Evarts	969	4	4	0	Park Hills	2,991	5	5	0
Ferguson	930	1	1	0	Pikeville	6,951	29	21	8
Flatwoods	7,474	11	10	1	Pineville	1,744	9	9	0
Florence	30,158	63	59	4	Pioneer Village	2,044	5	5	0
Fort Mitchell	8,264	10	10	0	Pippa Passes	537	2	2	0
Fort Thomas	16,438	23	22	1	Powderly	750	2	2	0
Fort Wright	5,763	12	12	0	Prestonsburg	3,277	16	16	0
Frankfort	25,703	64	59	5	Princeton	6,373	15	14	1
Franklin	8,466	25	24	1	Prospect	4,730	10	9	1
Fulton	2,462	13	9	4	Richmond	31,581	67	57	10
Georgetown	29,299	46	43	3	Russell	3,403	12	12	0
Glasgow	14,125	49	37	12	Russell Springs	2,458	9	8	1
Greensburg	2,178	6	6	0	Salyersville	1,896	2	2	0
Greenville	4,342	9	9	0	Scottsville	4,255	21	13	8
Hardinsburg	2,359	5	5	0	Sebree	1,614	1	1	0
Harlan	1,757	13	12	1	Shively	15,369	31	26	5
Harrodsburg	8,398	21	13	8	Smiths Grove	719	1	1	0
Hawesville	952	1	1	0	Somerset	11,273	43	39	4
Hazard	4,487	25	18	7	South Shore	1,130	1	1	0
Henderson	28,956	77	57	20	Springfield	2,536	12	7	5
Heritage Creek	1,083	9	9	0	Stanton	2,752	7	7	0
Hillview	8,228	12	12	0	St. Matthews	17,593	38	33	5
Hindman	782	1	1	0	Sturgis	1,911	3	3	0
Hollow Creek	788	1	1	0	Taylor Mill	6,650	12	11	1
Hopkinsville	31,795	98	71	27	Uniontown	1,009	2	2	0
Horse Cave	2,327	5	5	0	Vanceburg	1,528	6	6	0
Hyden	368	4	4	0	Versailles	8,627	37	36	1
Indian Hills	2,888	8	8	0	Villa Hills	7,541	8	7	1
Inez	722	2	2	0	Vine Grove	4,551	7	7	0
Irvine	2,734	6	6	0	Warsaw	1,626	5	5	0
Irvington	1,189	3	3	0	West Liberty	3,459	7	7	0
Jamestown	1,806	5	5	0	West Point	803	4	4	0

Table V-9. Full-Time Law Enforcement Employees, by Selected State and City, 2011—*Continued*

(Number.)

State/City	Population	Total law enforcement employees	Total officers	Total civilians	State/City	Population	Total law enforcement employees	Total officers	Total civilians
Wheelwright	785	1	1	0	Marksville	5,754	27	22	5
Wilder	3,056	7	7	0	Minden	13,202	35	35	0
Williamsburg	5,281	13	12	1	Napoleonville	666	1	1	0
Williamstown	3,952	8	7	1	New Orleans	346,974	1,609	1,349	260
Wilmore	3,711	12	11	1	New Roads	4,875	20	19	1
Winchester	18,495	44	32	12	Oak Grove	1,743	6	6	0
Wingo	636	1	1	0	Oil City	1,017	4	4	0
Worthington	1,620	4	4	0	Olla	1,398	4	4	0
					Opelousas	16,786	81	64	17
Louisiana					Patterson	6,168	29	29	0
Addis	3,626	12	11	1	Pearl River	2,529	14	10	4
Alexandria	48,159	183	149	34	Pineville	14,688	68	59	9
Amite	4,179	26	26	0	Pollock	473	4	3	1
Baker	14,022	39	37	2	Ponchatoula	6,619	28	24	4
Baldwin	2,458	8	8	0	Port Allen	5,227	18	17	1
Basile	1,838	14	9	5	Port Vincent	748	2	2	0
Bastrop	11,469	29	21	8	Rayne	8,026	20	20	0
Baton Rouge	231,592	823	647	176	Richwood	3,423	11	9	2
Berwick	4,991	12	11	1	Ruston	22,059	56	42	14
Blanchard	2,926	6	5	1	Scott	8,693	25	24	1
Bogalusa	12,344	54	33	21	Shreveport	201,134	720	616	104
Bossier City	61,876	203	162	41	Simmesport	2,181	5	5	0
Brusly	2,613	9	8	1	Slidell	27,316	109	73	36
Bunkie	4,209	13	11	2	Sorrento	1,414	8	7	1
Carencro	7,595	26	24	2	Springhill	5,317	19	19	0
Cheneyville	631	4	3	1	Sterlington	1,609	6	6	0
Church Point	4,602	15	15	0	St. Francisville	1,781	9	8	1
Clarence	504	1	1	0	St. Gabriel	6,738	20	12	8
Clinton	1,668	8	7	1	Stonewall	1,831	4	4	0
Covington	8,845	47	36	11	Sulphur	20,597	68	44	24
Crowley	13,386	42	38	4	Sunset	2,923	13	8	5
Denham Springs	10,308	40	35	5	Tallulah	7,402	17	12	5
De Quincy	3,265	14	14	0	Thibodaux	14,699	85	58	27
Dixie Inn	275	3	3	0	Tickfaw	700	4	4	0
Elton	1,138	11	11	0	Vidalia	4,338	34	26	8
Erath	2,133	9	6	3	Vinton	3,241	12	10	2
Ferriday	3,543	15	10	5	Walker	6,194	20	16	4
Florien	639	3	2	1	Washington	973	7	5	2
Folsom	723	5	4	1	Westlake	4,610	21	21	0
Franklin	7,730	23	21	2	West Monroe	13,184	76	63	13
Franklinton	3,892	23	17	6	Westwego	8,612	39	38	1
French Settlement	1,126	1	1	0	Wisner	973	2	2	0
Georgetown	330	4	3	1	Youngsville	8,179	13	13	0
Golden Meadow	2,120	6	5	1	Zachary	15,097	34	32	2
Gonzales	9,870	45	45	0					
Grambling	4,994	17	12	5	**Maine**				
Gramercy	3,646	7	7	0	Ashland	1,302	2	2	0
Greenwood	3,248	11	10	1	Auburn	23,052	57	50	7
Gretna	17,898	129	97	32	Augusta	19,134	51	39	12
Hammond	20,202	104	78	26	Baileyville	1,521	3	3	0
Harahan	9,362	26	20	6	Bangor	33,035	99	81	18
Haughton	3,486	8	8	0	Bar Harbor	5,234	17	13	4
Hodge	474	4	4	0	Bath	8,513	20	17	3
Homer	3,267	10	9	1	Belfast	6,667	13	12	1
Houma	34,035	93	76	17	Berwick	7,245	12	11	1
Independence	1,680	10	10	0	Biddeford	21,274	66	45	21
Iowa	3,023	14	10	4	Boothbay Harbor	2,165	8	7	1
Jeanerette	5,581	18	13	5	Brewer	9,481	22	21	1
Jena	3,429	6	5	1	Bridgton	5,209	8	8	0
Jennings	10,478	37	25	12	Brownville	1,250	2	2	0
Jonesboro	4,747	8	8	0	Brunswick	20,275	51	36	15
Kaplan	4,642	23	17	6	Bucksport	4,923	11	7	4
Kenner	67,312	232	172	60	Buxton	8,033	14	9	5
Kentwood	2,218	8	7	1	Calais	3,123	9	8	1
Kinder	2,500	17	17	0	Camden	4,849	12	10	2
Lafayette	121,726	313	257	56	Cape Elizabeth	9,014	14	13	1
Lake Charles	72,651	185	183	2	Caribou	8,188	17	16	1
Lake Providence	4,028	14	9	5	Carrabassett Valley	781	1	1	0
Lecompte	1,238	4	4	0	Clinton	3,486	2	2	0
Leesville	6,672	26	23	3	Cumberland	7,210	10	9	1
Lutcher	3,592	3	2	1	Damariscotta	2,218	6	5	1
Mandeville	11,666	49	36	13	Dexter	3,894	5	5	0
Mansfield	5,047	22	18	4	Dixfield	2,550	4	4	0
Marion	772	2	2	0	Dover-Foxcroft	4,212	6	6	0

Table V-9. **Full-Time Law Enforcement Employees, by Selected State and City, 2011**—*Continued*

(Number.)

State/City	Population	Total law enforcement employees	Total officers	Total civilians
East Millinocket	3,072	4	4	0
Eastport	1,331	5	5	0
Eliot	6,203	11	10	1
Ellsworth	7,740	20	16	4
Fairfield	6,734	11	10	1
Falmouth	11,184	25	18	7
Farmington	7,759	14	13	1
Fort Fairfield	3,496	4	4	0
Fort Kent	4,096	8	4	4
Freeport	7,878	14	12	2
Fryeburg	3,449	6	6	0
Gardiner	5,799	14	12	2
Gorham	16,379	25	23	2
Gouldsboro	1,737	2	2	0
Greenville	1,646	3	2	1
Hallowell	2,381	5	5	0
Hampden	7,256	12	11	1
Holden	3,076	3	3	0
Houlton	6,122	20	15	5
Islesboro	566	1	1	0
Jay	4,850	8	7	1
Kennebunk	10,797	21	19	2
Kennebunkport	3,474	17	12	5
Kittery	9,489	25	19	6
Lewiston	36,587	90	79	11
Limestone	2,314	3	3	0
Lincoln	5,084	7	6	1
Lincolnville	2,164	1	1	0
Lisbon	9,008	19	14	5
Livermore Falls	3,187	6	6	0
Machias	2,221	4	4	0
Madawaska	4,034	6	5	1
Madison	4,854	7	6	1
Mechanic Falls	3,031	5	5	0
Mexico	2,681	5	5	0
Milbridge	1,353	2	2	0
Millinocket	4,505	8	8	0
Milo	2,340	2	2	0
Monmouth	4,103	4	4	0
Mount Desert	2,053	11	7	4
Newport	3,275	7	7	0
North Berwick	4,575	9	8	1
Norway	5,013	7	6	1
Oakland	6,239	11	10	1
Ogunquit	892	11	9	2
Old Orchard Beach	8,623	21	18	3
Old Town	7,839	18	16	2
Orono	10,361	15	14	1
Oxford	4,109	6	5	1
Paris	5,182	7	7	0
Phippsburg	2,216	1	1	0
Pittsfield	4,214	6	6	0
Portland	66,185	223	162	61
Presque Isle	9,691	21	17	4
Rangeley	1,168	3	3	0
Richmond	3,411	5	5	0
Rockland	7,296	21	19	2
Rockport	3,330	6	6	0
Rumford	5,840	12	11	1
Sabattus	4,875	6	5	1
Saco	18,480	46	33	13
Sanford	20,795	45	41	4
Scarborough	18,917	53	37	16
Searsport	2,615	4	4	0
Skowhegan	8,588	14	14	0
South Berwick	7,219	12	8	4
South Portland	24,999	56	52	4
Southwest Harbor	1,764	9	5	4
Swan's Island	332	1	1	0
Thomaston	2,781	5	5	0
Topsham	8,783	13	12	1
Van Buren	2,171	3	3	0
Veazie	1,919	4	4	0
Waldoboro	5,074	9	8	1
Washburn	1,687	2	2	0
Waterville	15,720	41	31	10
Wells	9,588	31	23	8
Westbrook	17,492	42	39	3
Wilton	4,115	6	6	0
Windham	16,999	29	26	3
Winslow	7,793	10	9	1
Winthrop	6,091	12	8	4
Wiscasset	3,732	3	3	0
Yarmouth	8,348	13	12	1
York	12,527	38	27	11
Maryland				
Aberdeen	15,101	49	39	10
Annapolis	38,758	148	111	37
Baltimore	626,848	3,470	2,931	539
Baltimore City Sheriff	NA	174	133	41
Bel Air	10,216	42	30	12
Berlin	4,528	18	13	5
Berwyn Heights	3,153	9	8	1
Bladensburg	9,235	23	16	7
Boonsboro	3,368	4	4	0
Bowie	55,246	58	47	11
Brentwood	3,075	3	3	0
Brunswick	5,926	12	10	2
Cambridge	12,443	58	46	12
Capitol Heights	4,378	10	9	1
Centreville	4,326	11	10	1
Chestertown	5,302	14	13	1
Cheverly	6,232	18	16	2
Chevy Chase Village	1,972	15	9	6
Colmar Manor	1,417	5	4	1
Cottage City	1,317	5	4	1
Crisfield	2,752	14	10	4
Cumberland	21,057	54	51	3
Delmar	3,031	13	12	1
Denton	4,460	13	12	1
District Heights	5,892	13	11	2
Easton	16,096	63	46	17
Edmonston	1,459	8	6	2
Elkton	15,589	46	40	6
Fairmount Heights	1,508	2	2	0
Federalsburg	2,765	10	10	0
Forest Heights	2,470	7	5	2
Frederick	65,858	171	131	40
Frostburg	9,087	18	14	4
Fruitland	4,912	21	20	1
Glenarden	6,057	11	10	1
Greenbelt	23,287	65	51	14
Greensboro	1,949	3	3	0
Hagerstown	40,038	108	95	13
Hampstead	6,383	10	9	1
Hancock	1,560	4	3	1
Havre de Grace	13,075	44	35	9
Hurlock	2,112	12	9	3
Hyattsville	17,723	51	39	12
La Plata	8,836	17	16	1
Landover Hills	1,703	5	4	1
Laurel	25,353	83	65	18
Luke	66	1	1	0
Manchester	4,854	7	6	1
Morningside	2,034	7	6	1
Mount Rainier	8,157	21	17	4
New Carrollton	12,250	21	16	5
North East	3,606	10	9	1
Oakland	1,943	2	2	0
Ocean City	7,169	124	101	23
Ocean Pines	11,821	19	15	4
Oxford	657	3	3	0
Perryville	4,402	11	10	1
Pocomoke City	4,224	20	14	6
Port Deposit	659	3	3	0
Preston	726	1	1	0
Princess Anne	3,321	15	13	2

Table V-9.　Full-Time Law Enforcement Employees, by Selected State and City, 2011—*Continued*

(Number.)

State/City	Population	Total law enforcement employees	Total officers	Total civilians	State/City	Population	Total law enforcement employees	Total officers	Total civilians
Ridgely	1,655	5	5	0	Clinton	13,689	27	24	3
Rising Sun	2,807	7	6	1	Cohasset	7,588	20	14	6
Riverdale Park	7,022	29	20	9	Concord	17,776	41	33	8
Rock Hall	1,322	5	5	0	Dalton	6,797	10	9	1
Salisbury	30,631	115	90	25	Danvers	26,654	58	46	12
Seat Pleasant	4,585	16	14	2	Dartmouth	34,239	75	61	14
Smithsburg	3,003	5	4	1	Dedham	24,880	57	54	3
Snow Hill	2,123	9	8	1	Deerfield	5,156	8	8	0
St. Michaels	1,039	9	8	1	Dennis	14,294	49	40	9
Sykesville	4,478	7	6	1	Dighton	7,129	10	10	0
Takoma Park	16,873	54	41	13	Douglas	8,523	20	15	5
Taneytown	6,792	15	14	1	Dover	5,623	17	16	1
Thurmont	6,228	11	9	2	Dracut	29,637	43	38	5
Trappe	1,087	1	1	0	Dudley	11,459	16	13	3
University Park	2,572	8	8	0	Dunstable	3,198	8	7	1
Upper Marlboro	637	3	3	0	Duxbury	15,151	35	28	7
Westminster	18,766	52	39	13	East Bridgewater	13,878	23	20	3
					East Brookfield	2,196	4	4	0
Massachusetts					Eastham	4,986	20	14	6
Abington	16,082	26	22	4	Easthampton	16,151	32	26	6
Acton	22,058	45	35	10	East Longmeadow	15,816	26	25	1
Acushnet	10,366	17	15	2	Easton	23,253	39	31	8
Adams	8,537	19	15	4	Edgartown	4,092	18	17	1
Agawam	28,611	61	52	9	Egremont	1,232	7	7	0
Amesbury	16,382	37	30	7	Erving	1,811	6	6	0
Amherst	38,050	47	45	2	Essex	3,525	12	8	4
Andover	33,403	67	50	17	Everett	41,921	100	91	9
Aquinnah	313	4	4	0	Fairhaven	15,970	36	30	6
Arlington	43,105	80	62	18	Fall River	89,399	250	196	54
Ashburnham	6,118	14	9	5	Falmouth	31,723	60	54	6
Ashfield	1,748	1	1	0	Fitchburg	40,564	80	68	12
Ashland	16,694	33	27	6	Foxborough	16,968	37	30	7
Athol	11,655	21	16	5	Framingham	68,734	126	115	11
Attleboro	43,859	86	73	13	Franklin	31,828	52	44	8
Auburn	16,287	45	34	11	Freetown	8,924	18	18	0
Avon	4,383	19	15	4	Gardner	20,351	40	30	10
Ayer	7,472	22	17	5	Georgetown	8,233	15	11	4
Barnstable	45,468	127	112	15	Gill	1,509	2	2	0
Barre	5,431	11	7	4	Gloucester	28,964	62	57	5
Becket	1,790	2	2	0	Goshen	1,060	2	2	0
Bedford	13,401	39	28	11	Grafton	17,873	23	18	5
Belchertown	14,738	23	18	5	Granby	6,278	12	10	2
Bellingham	16,432	34	26	8	Granville	1,576	1	1	0
Belmont	24,880	56	42	14	Great Barrington	7,147	18	17	1
Berkley	6,450	6	6	0	Greenfield	17,562	34	31	3
Berlin	2,883	11	7	4	Groton	10,711	22	17	5
Bernardston	2,142	3	3	0	Groveland	6,498	11	9	2
Beverly	39,743	69	65	4	Hadley	5,282	15	11	4
Billerica	40,488	75	63	12	Halifax	7,564	12	11	1
Blackstone	9,081	19	16	3	Hamilton	7,811	14	13	1
Bolton	4,927	15	10	5	Hampden	5,170	15	10	5
Boston	621,359	2,719	2,156	563	Hanover	13,964	29	27	2
Bourne	19,874	44	38	6	Hanson	10,271	24	19	5
Boxborough	5,026	16	11	5	Hardwick	3,008	3	3	0
Boxford	8,014	13	13	0	Harvard	6,560	13	9	4
Boylston	4,382	13	10	3	Harwich	12,318	33	31	2
Braintree	35,962	84	69	15	Hatfield	3,299	2	2	0
Brewster	9,880	25	20	5	Haverhill	61,250	98	84	14
Bridgewater	26,725	49	21	28	Hingham	22,292	56	47	9
Brockton	94,380	196	177	19	Hinsdale	2,044	1	1	0
Brookfield	3,411	4	4	0	Holbrook	10,857	21	20	1
Brookline	59,090	148	126	22	Holden	17,452	27	24	3
Buckland	1,914	2	2	0	Holland	2,496	2	2	0
Burlington	24,647	71	64	7	Holliston	13,630	24	23	1
Cambridge	105,803	310	269	41	Holyoke	40,123	132	120	12
Canton	21,692	43	42	1	Hopedale	5,947	13	12	1
Carlisle	4,882	10	10	0	Hopkinton	15,016	24	19	5
Carver	11,579	19	14	5	Hubbardston	4,409	7	6	1
Charlton	13,060	22	18	4	Hudson	19,179	37	31	6
Chatham	6,162	27	21	6	Hull	10,356	30	22	8
Chelmsford	34,008	60	46	14	Ipswich	13,255	30	25	5
Chelsea	35,391	100	94	6	Kingston	12,706	29	22	7
Chicopee	55,635	129	125	4	Lakeville	10,667	17	13	4
Chilmark	871	4	4	0	Lancaster	8,104	12	11	1

Table V-9. Full-Time Law Enforcement Employees, by Selected State and City, 2011—*Continued*

(Number.)

State/City	Popula-tion	Total law enforce-ment employees	Total officers	Total civilians	State/City	Popula-tion	Total law enforce-ment employees	Total officers	Total civilians
Lanesboro	3,110	7	7	0	Plainville	8,314	19	14	5
Lawrence	76,843	139	118	21	Plymouth	56,812	118	100	18
Lee	5,979	12	11	1	Plympton	2,837	8	8	0
Lenox	5,056	11	11	0	Princeton	3,434	9	6	3
Leominster	41,007	83	66	17	Provincetown	2,960	26	17	9
Leverett	1,862	2	2	0	Quincy	92,834	214	184	30
Lexington	31,585	61	46	15	Randolph	32,308	59	56	3
Lincoln	6,401	19	13	6	Raynham	13,465	34	25	9
Littleton	8,978	22	16	6	Reading	24,898	53	40	13
Longmeadow	15,880	29	24	5	Rehoboth	11,679	26	21	5
Lowell	107,167	298	226	72	Revere	52,070	96	82	14
Ludlow	21,232	38	33	5	Rochester	5,264	10	10	0
Lunenburg	10,147	14	14	0	Rockland	17,596	41	33	8
Lynn	90,880	194	175	19	Rockport	6,994	15	15	0
Lynnfield	11,667	22	17	5	Rowley	5,892	13	11	2
Malden	59,812	111	102	9	Royalston	1,266	1	1	0
Manchester-by-the-Sea	5,167	17	14	3	Rutland	8,022	9	8	1
Mansfield	23,325	37	34	3	Salem	41,592	91	81	10
Marblehead	19,929	36	27	9	Salisbury	8,333	18	14	4
Marion	4,937	14	14	0	Sandwich	20,801	35	34	1
Marlborough	38,734	77	65	12	Saugus	26,790	70	54	16
Marshfield	25,285	45	42	3	Scituate	18,244	31	27	4
Mashpee	14,091	44	34	10	Seekonk	13,806	36	34	2
Mattapoisett	6,082	18	17	1	Sharon	17,719	35	30	5
Maynard	10,168	22	21	1	Sheffield	3,277	6	6	0
Medfield	12,097	21	17	4	Shelburne	1,905	2	2	0
Medford	56,515	98	96	2	Sherborn	4,144	16	16	0
Medway	12,830	24	19	5	Shirley	7,255	14	9	5
Melrose	27,147	44	44	0	Shrewsbury	35,825	53	42	11
Mendon	5,875	15	10	5	Somerset	18,276	39	32	7
Merrimac	6,377	10	6	4	Somerville	76,216	152	126	26
Methuen	47,543	96	83	13	Southborough	9,827	18	13	5
Middleboro	23,257	42	38	4	Southbridge	16,821	36	34	2
Middleton	9,042	14	13	1	South Hadley	17,621	31	26	5
Milford	28,170	54	44	10	Southwick	9,560	21	16	5
Millbury	13,342	21	17	4	Spencer	11,759	21	17	4
Millis	7,939	19	14	5	Springfield	153,993	550	456	94
Millville	3,209	6	5	1	Sterling	7,856	18	13	5
Milton	27,168	65	49	16	Stockbridge	1,959	6	6	0
Monson	8,612	15	11	4	Stoneham	21,568	38	36	2
Montague	8,488	20	15	5	Stoughton	27,126	54	49	5
Monterey	967	2	2	0	Stow	6,630	16	11	5
Nahant	3,431	13	12	1	Sturbridge	9,324	23	18	5
Nantucket	10,234	47	33	14	Sudbury	17,767	32	27	5
Natick	33,207	63	51	12	Sunderland	3,706	5	5	0
Needham	29,060	52	46	6	Sutton	9,018	20	15	5
New Bedford	95,649	294	249	45	Swampscott	13,871	33	32	1
New Braintree	1,005	1	1	0	Swansea	15,962	36	30	6
Newburyport	17,522	35	31	4	Taunton	56,215	110	105	5
Newton	85,665	179	138	41	Templeton	8,062	15	10	5
Norfolk	11,295	22	16	6	Tewksbury	29,138	69	56	13
North Adams	13,792	33	25	8	Tisbury	3,973	14	11	3
Northampton	28,723	68	63	5	Topsfield	6,122	13	9	4
North Andover	28,525	48	36	12	Townsend	8,980	15	13	2
North Attleboro	28,887	52	40	12	Truro	2,015	14	9	5
Northborough	14,241	27	20	7	Tyngsboro	11,361	29	23	6
Northbridge	15,803	22	17	5	Uxbridge	13,539	23	18	5
Northfield	3,050	3	3	0	Wakefield	25,084	44	43	1
North Reading	14,983	29	28	1	Walpole	24,217	39	34	5
Norton	19,147	29	28	1	Waltham	61,002	174	147	27
Norwell	10,570	29	23	6	Ware	9,932	13	13	0
Norwood	28,776	67	56	11	Wareham	21,955	59	49	10
Orange	7,887	12	11	1	Warren	5,166	10	7	3
Orleans	5,926	29	23	6	Watertown	32,110	77	64	13
Oxford	13,793	24	19	5	Wayland	13,073	29	21	8
Palmer	12,214	22	18	4	Webster	16,869	34	30	4
Paxton	4,835	19	12	7	Wellesley	28,153	56	40	16
Peabody	51,563	99	88	11	Wellfleet	2,767	17	12	5
Pelham	1,329	1	1	0	Wenham	4,905	10	9	1
Pembroke	17,946	29	27	2	Westborough	18,383	34	28	6
Pepperell	11,567	17	16	1	West Boylston	7,716	18	13	5
Petersham	1,242	2	2	0	West Bridgewater	6,958	21	20	1
Phillipston	1,692	2	2	0	West Brookfield	3,724	7	6	1
Pittsfield	45,010	105	87	18	Westfield	41,344	85	78	7

Table V-9.   Full-Time Law Enforcement Employees, by Selected State and City, 2011—*Continued*

(Number.)

State/City	Population	Total law enforcement employees	Total officers	Total civilians	State/City	Population	Total law enforcement employees	Total officers	Total civilians
Westford	22,085	50	38	12	Burr Oak	827	1	1	0
Westminster	7,321	18	13	5	Burton	29,976	34	31	3
West Newbury	4,261	7	7	0	Byron	581	1	1	0
Weston	11,330	28	23	5	Cadillac	10,347	16	15	1
Westport	15,627	31	27	4	Calumet	725	1	1	0
West Springfield	28,564	85	74	11	Cambridge Township	5,729	4	3	1
Westwood	14,707	36	26	10	Canton Township	90,105	115	83	32
Weymouth	54,071	103	86	17	Capac	1,889	1	1	0
Whitman	14,577	26	25	1	Carleton	2,343	4	3	1
Wilbraham	14,306	27	26	1	Caro	4,226	7	7	0
Williamsburg	2,497	2	2	0	Carrollton Township	6,098	8	7	1
Williamstown	7,801	16	12	4	Caseville	776	2	2	0
Wilmington	22,461	48	46	2	Caspian-Gaastra	2,391	1	1	0
Winchendon	10,363	19	14	5	Cass City	2,426	4	4	0
Winchester	21,504	46	38	8	Cassopolis	1,773	5	5	0
Winthrop	17,604	32	30	2	Cedar Springs	3,506	7	7	0
Woburn	38,352	79	74	5	Center Line	8,251	21	17	4
Worcester	182,145	465	420	45	Central Lake	951	1	1	0
Wrentham	11,022	20	18	2	Charlevoix	2,511	7	6	1
Yarmouth	23,939	71	59	12	Charlotte	9,067	18	17	1
					Cheboygan	4,863	7	7	0
Michigan					Chelsea	4,940	12	8	4
Adrian	21,117	30	27	3	Chesterfield Township	43,348	60	46	14
Adrian Township	6,030	2	2	0	Chikaming Township	3,098	6	5	1
Akron	402	1	1	0	Chocolay Township	5,899	5	4	1
Albion	8,610	19	19	0	Clare	3,116	8	7	1
Algonac	4,107	8	7	1	Clawson	11,816	18	17	1
Allegan	4,994	10	9	1	Clayton Township	7,493	6	6	0
Allen Park	28,189	42	40	2	Clay Township	9,059	16	11	5
Alma	9,376	14	14	0	Clinton	2,334	4	4	0
Almont	2,672	6	6	0	Clinton Township	96,723	118	89	29
Alpena	10,475	17	15	2	Clio	2,644	4	4	0
Ann Arbor	113,848	162	118	44	Coldwater	10,937	19	17	2
Argentine Township	6,908	5	4	1	Coleman	1,242	2	2	0
Armada	1,729	2	2	0	Coloma Township	6,498	11	8	3
Auburn	2,085	2	2	0	Colon	1,172	3	3	0
Auburn Hills	21,396	61	48	13	Columbia Township	7,414	6	6	0
Au Gres-Sims	1,982	2	2	0	Concord	1,049	2	2	0
Augusta	884	3	2	1	Constantine	2,074	8	7	1
Bad Axe	3,127	7	7	0	Corunna	3,494	4	3	1
Bancroft	545	1	1	0	Covert Township	2,886	6	6	0
Bangor	1,884	5	5	0	Croswell	2,445	5	5	0
Baraga	2,051	2	2	0	Crystal Falls	1,468	2	2	0
Baroda-Lake Township	3,842	4	3	1	Davison	5,169	8	7	1
Barry Township	3,375	4	4	0	Davison Township	19,560	20	18	2
Bath Township	11,589	12	11	1	Dearborn	98,079	213	186	27
Battle Creek	61,658	127	110	17	Dearborn Heights	57,730	93	76	17
Bay City	34,906	57	53	4	Decatur	1,818	5	5	0
Belding	5,753	8	8	0	Deckerville	829	1	1	0
Bellaire	1,085	2	2	0	Denmark Township	1,619	1	1	0
Belleville	3,988	9	7	2	Denton Township	5,553	5	5	0
Bellevue	1,281	2	2	0	Detroit	713,239	3,087	2,760	327
Benton Harbor	10,030	22	20	2	Dewitt	4,504	7	6	1
Benton Township	14,738	30	25	5	Dewitt Township	14,310	16	15	1
Berkley	14,959	34	27	7	Dowagiac	5,875	15	14	1
Berrien Springs-Oronoko Township	9,186	10	9	1	Dryden Township	4,764	4	4	0
Beverly Hills	10,259	27	23	4	Dundee	3,954	1	1	0
Big Rapids	10,593	15	14	1	Durand	3,443	4	4	0
Birch Run	1,554	6	5	1	East Grand Rapids	10,686	31	29	2
Birmingham	20,088	37	29	8	East Jordan	2,349	4	4	0
Blackman Township	37,830	34	33	1	East Lansing	48,542	83	57	26
Blissfield	3,337	5	5	0	Eastpointe	32,418	48	45	3
Bloomfield Hills	3,866	26	23	3	Eaton Rapids	5,210	11	10	1
Bloomfield Township	41,039	93	72	21	Ecorse	9,505	21	20	1
Boyne City	3,732	8	7	1	Elk Rapids	1,641	5	5	0
Breckenridge	1,327	1	1	0	Elkton	807	2	2	0
Bridgeport Township	10,506	6	5	1	Elsie	965	2	2	0
Bridgman	2,289	4	4	0	Emmett Township	11,761	22	18	4
Brighton	7,438	19	17	2	Erie Township	4,514	2	2	0
Bronson	2,347	4	4	0	Escanaba	12,606	41	30	11
Brown City	1,324	2	2	0	Essexville	3,475	6	6	0
Brownstown Township	30,604	45	35	10	Evart	1,902	4	4	0
Buchanan	4,453	9	8	1	Fair Haven Township	1,106	1	1	0
Buena Vista Township	8,669	17	16	1	Farmington	10,364	29	22	7

Table V-9.   Full-Time Law Enforcement Employees, by Selected State and City, 2011—*Continued*

(Number.)

State/City	Popula-tion	Total law enforce-ment employees	Total officers	Total civilians	State/City	Popula-tion	Total law enforce-ment employees	Total officers	Total civilians
Farmington Hills	79,680	132	100	32	Ithaca	2,908	3	3	0
Fenton	11,747	16	14	2	Jackson	33,509	60	47	13
Ferndale	19,885	49	40	9	Jonesville	2,256	5	5	0
Flat Rock	9,871	19	19	0	Kalamazoo	74,206	277	234	43
Flint	102,357	139	120	19	Kalamazoo Township	21,901	37	30	7
Flint Township	31,905	41	33	8	Kalkaska	2,018	3	2	1
Flushing	8,383	9	9	0	Keego Harbor	2,968	4	4	0
Flushing Township	10,632	6	6	0	Kentwood	48,670	76	63	13
Forsyth Township	6,159	8	7	1	Kingsford	5,129	17	17	0
Fowlerville	2,884	7	6	1	Kingston	440	1	1	0
Frankenmuth	4,940	7	7	0	Kinross Township	7,555	3	3	0
Frankfort	1,285	3	3	0	Laingsburg	1,282	1	1	0
Franklin	3,148	10	10	0	Lake Angelus	290	1	1	0
Fraser	14,469	46	37	9	Lake Linden	1,006	1	1	0
Fremont	4,078	9	8	1	Lake Odessa	2,016	4	4	0
Frost Township	1,046	1	1	0	Lake Orion	2,971	8	4	4
Fruitport	1,092	9	8	1	Lakeview	1,006	2	2	0
Galesburg	2,007	2	2	0	L'Anse	2,009	4	4	0
Garden City	27,671	30	28	2	Lansing	114,211	267	188	79
Gaylord	3,642	13	11	2	Lansing Township	8,120	15	14	1
Genesee Township	21,565	16	14	2	Lapeer	8,834	22	20	2
Gerrish Township	2,991	7	7	0	Lapeer Township	5,052	1	1	0
Gibraltar	4,652	9	8	1	Lathrup Village	4,072	8	8	0
Gladstone	4,969	9	9	0	Laurium	1,976	4	4	0
Gladwin	2,931	5	5	0	Lawton	1,899	6	6	0
Grand Beach	272	4	4	0	Leslie	1,850	3	3	0
Grand Blanc	8,270	18	16	2	Lexington	1,177	3	3	0
Grand Blanc Township	37,480	43	40	3	Lincoln Park	38,115	56	49	7
Grand Haven	10,404	36	31	5	Lincoln Township	14,680	12	11	1
Grand Ledge	7,780	15	14	1	Linden	3,988	5	5	0
Grand Rapids	187,898	382	305	77	Litchfield	1,368	3	3	0
Grandville	15,366	26	24	2	Livonia	96,869	153	124	29
Grant	893	1	1	0	Lowell	3,780	8	6	2
Grayling	1,883	5	5	0	Ludington	8,070	15	14	1
Green Oak Township	17,463	16	14	2	Luna Pier	1,435	3	3	0
Greenville	8,475	21	17	4	Mackinac Island	492	7	6	1
Grosse Ile Township	10,363	23	17	6	Mackinaw City	805	6	6	0
Grosse Pointe	5,417	25	23	2	Madison Heights	29,672	60	48	12
Grosse Pointe Farms	9,472	46	33	13	Madison Township	8,614	3	3	0
Grosse Pointe Park	11,546	44	38	6	Mancelona	1,389	2	2	0
Grosse Pointe Shores	3,006	17	17	0	Manistee	6,221	12	12	0
Grosse Pointe Woods	16,123	38	33	5	Manistique	3,095	8	8	0
Hamburg Township	21,149	15	14	1	Manton	1,286	1	1	0
Hampton Township	9,645	11	10	1	Marenisco Township	1,726	1	1	0
Hamtramck	22,406	45	45	0	Marine City	4,245	3	3	0
Hancock	4,631	7	7	0	Marlette	1,874	3	3	0
Harbor Beach	1,702	4	4	0	Marquette	21,339	38	33	5
Harbor Springs	1,193	6	5	1	Marshall	7,083	14	14	0
Harper Woods	14,225	36	34	2	Marysville	9,951	16	13	3
Hart	2,124	4	4	0	Mason	8,246	14	13	1
Hartford	2,686	5	5	0	Mattawan	1,995	5	5	0
Hastings	7,344	13	11	2	Mayville	949	2	2	0
Hazel Park	16,410	39	34	5	Melvindale	10,707	24	22	2
Hesperia	953	1	1	0	Memphis	1,182	1	1	0
Hillsdale	8,299	16	14	2	Menominee	8,593	14	13	1
Holland	33,026	66	57	9	Meridian Township	39,658	43	38	5
Holly	6,081	16	12	4	Metamora Township	4,246	5	5	0
Homer	1,667	3	3	0	Michiana	182	3	3	0
Home Township	1,340	1	1	0	Midland	41,831	47	45	2
Hopkins	610	2	2	0	Milan	5,832	13	9	4
Houghton	7,702	8	7	1	Milford	15,724	24	18	6
Howard City	1,807	2	2	0	Millington	1,071	1	1	0
Howell	9,482	20	18	2	Monroe	20,717	41	36	5
Hudson	2,305	3	3	0	Montague	2,359	5	5	0
Huntington Woods	6,233	18	17	1	Montrose Township	7,875	9	8	1
Huron Township	15,867	23	18	5	Morenci	2,218	3	3	0
Imlay City	3,594	10	9	1	Morrice	926	2	2	0
Inkster	25,350	68	59	9	Mount Morris	3,084	6	6	0
Ionia	11,385	15	13	2	Mount Morris Township	21,485	30	27	3
Iron Mountain	7,618	14	14	0	Mount Pleasant	25,996	36	30	6
Iron River	3,027	7	6	1	Mundy Township	15,071	17	14	3
Ironwood	5,383	10	10	0	Munising	2,353	4	4	0
Ishpeming	6,465	10	9	1	Muskegon	38,372	84	75	9
Ishpeming Township	3,510	1	1	0	Muskegon Heights	10,848	16	15	1

Table V-9.   Full-Time Law Enforcement Employees, by Selected State and City, 2011—*Continued*

(Number.)

State/City	Population	Total law enforcement employees	Total officers	Total civilians	State/City	Population	Total law enforcement employees	Total officers	Total civilians
Muskegon Township	17,827	15	14	1	Scottville	1,213	2	2	0
Napoleon Township	6,771	2	2	0	Sebewaing	1,758	3	3	0
Nashville	1,627	2	2	0	Shelby	2,063	3	3	0
Negaunee	4,565	8	7	1	Shelby Township	73,748	89	69	20
Newaygo	1,975	5	4	1	Shepherd	1,514	2	2	0
New Baltimore	12,075	21	16	5	Somerset Township	4,620	5	4	1
New Buffalo	1,882	8	7	1	Southfield	71,685	165	134	31
New Haven	4,638	10	9	1	Southgate	30,024	46	40	6
Niles	11,591	25	17	8	South Haven	4,400	21	19	2
North Branch	1,032	2	2	0	South Lyon	11,318	18	17	1
Northfield Township	8,239	9	9	0	South Rockwood	1,674	2	2	0
North Muskegon	3,783	7	7	0	Sparta	4,137	5	5	0
Northville	5,965	13	13	0	Spaulding Township	2,151	1	1	0
Northville Township	28,476	46	34	12	Spring Arbor Township	8,261	2	2	0
Norton Shores	23,976	31	29	2	Springfield	5,256	14	13	1
Norway	2,843	4	4	0	Spring Lake-Ferrysburg	5,211	10	9	1
Novi	55,182	83	62	21	Springport Township	2,157	1	1	0
Oak Park	29,297	66	58	8	Standish	1,508	1	1	0
Olivet	1,604	2	2	0	St. Charles	2,052	2	2	0
Onaway	879	1	1	0	St. Clair	5,481	9	9	0
Ontwa Township-Edwardsburg	6,544	6	6	0	St. Clair Shores	59,670	88	83	5
Orchard Lake	2,373	8	7	1	Sterling Heights	129,601	201	157	44
Oscoda Township	6,992	12	11	1	St. Ignace	2,450	7	6	1
Otisville	863	7	6	1	St. Johns	7,859	11	10	1
Otsego	3,953	7	6	1	St. Joseph	8,359	23	17	6
Ovid	1,602	3	3	0	St. Joseph Township	10,020	12	11	1
Owosso	15,183	22	19	3	St. Louis	7,476	7	6	1
Oxford	3,433	17	10	7	Stockbridge	1,217	1	1	0
Paw Paw	3,531	9	8	1	Sturgis	10,986	22	17	5
Pentwater	856	3	3	0	Sumpter Township	9,542	19	13	6
Perry	2,186	4	4	0	Suttons Bay	618	1	1	0
Petoskey	5,666	20	18	2	Swartz Creek	5,754	7	6	1
Pigeon	1,207	1	1	0	Sylvan Lake	1,719	3	3	0
Pinckney	2,425	4	4	0	Tawas	4,632	6	5	1
Pinconning	1,306	2	2	0	Taylor	63,083	77	60	17
Pittsfield Township	34,637	52	40	12	Tecumseh	8,515	14	12	2
Plainwell	3,801	8	7	1	Thetford Township	7,044	2	2	0
Pleasant Ridge	2,524	6	6	0	Thomas Township	11,976	8	7	1
Plymouth	9,125	17	16	1	Three Oaks	1,621	1	1	0
Plymouth Township	27,503	43	29	14	Three Rivers	7,805	19	17	2
Portage	46,257	69	53	16	Tittabawassee Township	9,719	5	4	1
Port Austin	663	1	1	0	Traverse City	14,663	30	29	1
Port Huron	30,161	57	48	9	Trenton	18,839	31	30	1
Portland	3,880	5	5	0	Troy	80,919	147	102	45
Potterville	2,615	2	2	0	Tuscarora Township	3,036	8	7	1
Prairieville Township	3,401	2	2	0	Ubly	857	2	2	0
Raisin Township	7,553	6	5	1	Unadilla Township	3,363	2	2	0
Redford Township	48,326	65	55	10	Union City	1,598	4	4	0
Reed City	2,423	4	4	0	Utica	4,753	17	13	4
Reese	1,453	2	2	0	Van Buren Township	28,799	55	41	14
Richfield Township, Genesee County	8,723	10	8	2	Vassar	2,695	4	4	0
Richfield Township, Roscommon County	3,728	7	6	1	Vernon	782	1	1	0
Richland	750	1	1	0	Vicksburg	2,904	10	9	1
Richland Township, Saginaw County	4,141	4	4	0	Walker	23,519	36	33	3
Richmond	5,731	12	9	3	Walled Lake	6,994	11	10	1
River Rouge	7,897	20	19	1	Warren	133,955	227	190	37
Riverview	12,477	34	26	8	Waterford Township	71,653	64	49	15
Rochester	12,701	27	21	6	Waterloo Township	2,854	3	3	0
Rockford	5,715	10	9	1	Wayland	4,076	6	5	1
Rockwood	3,287	7	7	0	Wayne	17,580	39	31	8
Rogers City	2,825	6	6	0	West Bloomfield Township	64,641	91	71	20
Romeo	3,593	11	7	4	West Branch	2,137	5	4	1
Romulus	23,971	51	40	11	Westland	84,031	98	77	21
Roosevelt Park	3,828	5	5	0	White Cloud	1,407	2	2	0
Rose City	653	1	1	0	Whitehall	2,704	8	8	0
Roseville	47,263	81	76	5	White Lake Township	29,996	34	24	10
Royal Oak	57,193	78	66	12	White Pigeon	1,521	4	4	0
Saginaw	51,469	109	96	13	Williamston	3,851	6	5	1
Saginaw Township	40,809	48	43	5	Wixom	13,488	23	20	3
Saline	8,803	17	13	4	Wolverine Lake	4,309	5	5	0
Sandusky	2,677	4	4	0	Woodhaven	12,865	28	27	1
Saugatuck-Douglas	2,155	9	8	1	Wyandotte	25,863	46	37	9
Sault Ste. Marie	14,133	26	24	2	Wyoming	72,071	94	82	12
Schoolcraft	1,524	3	3	0	Yale	1,954	3	3	0

Table V-9.   Full-Time Law Enforcement Employees, by Selected State and City, 2011—*Continued*

(Number.)

State/City	Popula-tion	Total law enforce-ment employees	Total officers	Total civilians	State/City	Popula-tion	Total law enforce-ment employees	Total officers	Total civilians
Ypsilanti	19,420	35	30	5	Gilbert	1,813	6	6	0
Zeeland	5,500	10	9	1	Glencoe	5,674	10	9	1
Zilwaukee	1,657	2	2	0	Glenwood	2,584	3	3	0
					Golden Valley	20,528	38	30	8
Minnesota					Goodview	4,067	4	4	0
Albany	2,581	3	2	1	Grand Rapids	10,953	21	18	3
Albert Lea	18,155	39	28	11	Granite Falls	2,919	4	4	0
Alexandria	11,155	25	20	5	Hallock	989	1	1	0
Annandale	3,253	4	4	0	Hastings	22,343	32	28	4
Anoka	17,274	33	27	6	Hermantown	9,487	16	13	3
Appleton	1,423	3	3	0	Hibbing	16,487	33	29	4
Apple Valley	49,463	58	48	10	Hokah	584	1	1	0
Aurora	1,695	4	4	0	Hopkins	17,727	36	24	12
Austin	24,909	34	31	3	Houston	987	2	2	0
Avon	1,407	3	3	0	Hoyt Lakes	2,033	5	5	0
Babbitt	1,486	4	4	0	Hutchinson	14,287	31	22	9
Baxter	7,669	15	14	1	International Falls	6,474	12	11	1
Bayport	3,498	5	5	0	Inver Grove Heights	34,141	37	31	6
Becker	4,573	6	5	1	Janesville	2,273	2	2	0
Belgrade	746	2	2	0	Jordan	5,512	9	7	2
Belle Plaine	6,712	10	8	2	Kasson	5,977	8	8	0
Bemidji	13,535	30	27	3	Kimball	768	2	2	0
Benson	3,265	7	6	1	La Crescent	4,867	8	7	1
Big Lake	10,138	14	12	2	Lake City	5,102	12	10	2
Blackduck	791	2	2	0	Lake Crystal	2,569	11	4	7
Blaine	57,627	69	58	11	Lakefield	1,707	2	2	0
Blooming Prairie	2,011	3	3	0	Lakes Area	9,481	14	12	2
Bloomington	83,533	141	112	29	Lakeville	56,386	60	52	8
Blue Earth	3,379	3	3	0	Lester Prairie	1,743	3	3	0
Brainerd	13,695	28	22	6	Le Sueur	4,089	8	7	1
Breckenridge	3,412	7	7	0	Lewiston	1,633	2	2	0
Brooklyn Center	30,336	60	48	12	Lino Lakes	20,372	30	25	5
Brooklyn Park	76,366	133	105	28	Litchfield	6,778	10	9	1
Brownton	768	2	2	0	Little Falls	8,407	15	13	2
Buffalo	15,572	21	17	4	Long Prairie	3,485	5	5	0
Burnsville	60,771	85	74	11	Madison	1,563	2	2	0
Caledonia	2,890	4	4	0	Mankato	39,612	60	49	11
Cambridge	8,174	14	13	1	Maple Grove	62,042	76	62	14
Cannon Falls	4,115	8	7	1	Mapleton	1,770	3	3	0
Centennial Lakes	10,842	17	15	2	Maplewood	38,311	56	51	5
Champlin	23,267	30	25	5	Marshall	13,786	22	19	3
Chaska	23,953	27	24	3	Medina	4,930	11	10	1
Chisholm	5,014	11	10	1	Melrose	3,626	6	5	1
Cloquet	12,218	21	19	2	Mendota Heights	11,156	18	17	1
Cold Spring	5,489	8	7	1	Milaca	2,969	5	4	1
Columbia Heights	19,646	33	27	6	Minneapolis	385,531	983	852	131
Coon Rapids	61,950	67	60	7	Minnetonka	50,118	72	55	17
Corcoran	5,421	8	7	1	Minnetrista	8,734	14	11	3
Cottage Grove	34,856	45	39	6	Montevideo	5,425	11	10	1
Crookston	7,952	17	15	2	Montgomery	2,979	5	4	1
Crosby	2,404	8	7	1	Moorhead	38,359	65	52	13
Crystal	22,322	36	30	6	Moose Lake	2,772	4	4	0
Dawson	1,552	3	3	0	Morris	5,327	10	8	2
Dayton	4,707	6	5	1	Mound	9,122	14	12	2
Deephaven-Woodland	4,110	8	7	1	Mounds View	12,249	21	19	2
Detroit Lakes	8,635	16	14	2	Mountain Iron	2,891	5	5	0
Dilworth	4,055	7	6	1	Mountain Lake	2,120	3	3	0
Duluth	86,931	174	143	31	New Brighton	21,622	33	28	5
Eagan	64,702	80	69	11	New Hope	20,496	37	30	7
Eagle Lake	2,441	2	2	0	Newport	3,462	7	7	0
East Grand Forks	8,667	23	20	3	New Prague	7,378	11	9	2
Eden Prairie	61,266	90	65	25	New Richland	1,212	2	2	0
Edina	48,311	68	50	18	New Ulm	13,626	24	21	3
Elk River	23,151	38	30	8	North Branch	10,203	12	10	2
Elmore	668	1	1	0	Northfield	20,161	26	21	5
Ely	3,487	8	7	1	North Mankato	13,497	13	12	1
Eveleth	3,747	10	9	1	North St. Paul	11,548	21	19	2
Fairmont	10,748	19	16	3	Oakdale	27,589	41	31	10
Faribault	23,532	35	30	5	Oak Park Heights	4,372	10	9	1
Farmington	21,249	28	25	3	Olivia	2,503	5	5	0
Fergus Falls	13,239	27	22	5	Orono	11,501	19	16	3
Floodwood	532	3	2	1	Ortonville	1,931	3	3	0
Forest Lake	18,517	28	25	3	Osakis	1,753	4	3	1
Fridley	27,418	43	37	6	Osseo	2,449	6	5	1

Table V-9.   Full-Time Law Enforcement Employees, by Selected State and City, 2011—*Continued*

(Number.)

State/City	Popula-tion	Total law enforce-ment employees	Total officers	Total civilians	State/City	Popula-tion	Total law enforce-ment employees	Total officers	Total civilians
Owatonna	25,797	36	33	3	Belzoni	2,243	12	10	2
Park Rapids	3,738	11	10	1	Biloxi	44,221	175	125	50
Paynesville	2,451	4	4	0	Booneville	8,776	24	22	2
Plainview	3,366	5	5	0	Brandon	21,787	55	39	16
Plymouth	71,121	77	66	11	Brookhaven	12,560	42	34	8
Princeton	4,734	13	11	2	Byhalia	1,307	14	9	5
Prior Lake	22,972	26	23	3	Byram	11,532	36	22	14
Proctor	3,081	7	6	1	Carthage	5,094	20	15	5
Ramsey	23,851	27	23	4	Charleston	2,201	11	10	1
Red Wing	16,586	31	26	5	Cleveland	12,381	52	46	6
Redwood Falls	5,295	13	11	2	Collins	2,596	13	9	4
Richfield	35,500	55	44	11	Columbia	6,607	33	22	11
Robbinsdale	14,061	26	22	4	Columbus	23,729	74	67	7
Rochester	107,593	186	130	56	Como	1,284	3	3	0
Rogers	8,663	15	13	2	Corinth	14,628	42	37	5
Roseau	2,653	6	5	1	Crenshaw	888	5	5	0
Rosemount	22,043	24	22	2	D'Iberville	9,522	27	26	1
Roseville	33,920	54	48	6	Durant	2,683	13	9	4
Sartell	15,999	17	16	1	Edwards	1,038	1	1	0
Sauk Centre	4,350	7	6	1	Eupora	2,205	6	5	1
Sauk Rapids	12,872	14	13	1	Florence	4,157	18	12	6
Savage	27,119	36	32	4	Flowood	7,853	62	56	6
Shakopee	37,362	53	45	8	Fulton	3,976	10	10	0
Silver Bay	1,902	4	4	0	Gautier	18,642	55	43	12
Silver Lake	843	2	2	0	Gloster	964	6	4	2
Slayton	2,170	4	4	0	Greenville	34,530	128	99	29
Sleepy Eye	3,627	6	6	0	Greenwood	15,262	70	55	15
South Lake Minnetonka	11,747	16	14	2	Grenada	13,141	48	44	4
South St. Paul	20,316	29	27	2	Heidelberg	721	6	5	1
Springfield	2,169	5	5	0	Hollandale	2,712	12	6	6
Spring Grove	1,340	2	2	0	Horn Lake	26,165	69	53	16
Spring Lake Park	6,461	13	11	2	Indianola	10,723	27	19	8
St. Anthony	8,289	26	23	3	Itta Bena	2,057	12	7	5
Staples	3,004	5	4	1	Iuka	3,039	12	9	3
St. Charles	3,764	4	4	0	Jackson	174,170	728	439	289
St. Cloud	66,350	122	101	21	Kosciusko	7,430	19	19	0
St. Francis	7,274	12	10	2	Laurel	18,610	77	56	21
Stillwater	18,366	24	21	3	Leland	4,498	23	16	7
St. James	4,641	8	7	1	Long Beach	14,848	51	36	15
St. Joseph	6,584	8	7	1	Louisville	6,656	27	21	6
St. Louis Park	45,599	66	51	15	Lucedale	2,934	21	15	6
St. Paul	287,665	793	596	197	Macon	2,778	9	8	1
St. Paul Park	5,320	9	9	0	Madison	24,240	96	75	21
St. Peter	11,282	19	14	5	Magee	4,425	16	12	4
Thief River Falls	8,639	17	15	2	Magnolia	2,429	7	7	0
Tracy	2,180	3	3	0	McComb	12,838	63	32	31
Two Harbors	3,774	9	8	1	McLain	443	2	1	1
Virginia	8,779	19	18	1	Meridian	41,304	109	98	11
Wabasha	2,540	6	5	1	Moss Point	13,756	36	21	15
Wadena	4,120	9	8	1	Natchez	15,852	70	45	25
Waite Park	6,767	16	13	3	New Albany	8,064	24	23	1
Warroad	1,795	6	5	1	Newton	3,386	18	12	6
Waseca	9,483	15	14	1	Ocean Springs	17,508	58	41	17
Wayzata	3,716	13	12	1	Olive Branch	33,611	90	71	19
Wells	2,361	4	4	0	Oxford	18,987	68	58	10
West Hennepin	5,313	11	9	2	Pascagoula	22,477	97	65	32
West St. Paul	19,691	30	25	5	Pass Christian	4,630	21	19	2
Wheaton	1,435	3	3	0	Pearl	25,187	85	66	19
White Bear Lake	23,981	34	27	7	Petal	10,494	30	24	6
Willmar	19,761	35	31	4	Picayune	10,919	44	31	13
Windom	4,682	9	8	1	Port Gibson	1,573	8	5	3
Winnebago	1,448	3	3	0	Purvis	2,183	11	8	3
Winona	27,805	41	37	4	Ridgeland	24,138	91	70	21
Winsted	2,373	3	3	0	Ripley	5,415	12	11	1
Woodbury	62,439	76	64	12	Saltillo	4,770	9	9	0
Worthington	12,863	32	22	10	Senatobia	8,196	24	20	4
Wyoming	7,851	10	9	1	Shelby	2,237	4	4	0
Zumbrota	3,277	4	4	0	Southaven	49,167	129	105	24
					Summit	1,711	7	6	1
Mississippi					Tupelo	34,677	113	99	14
Ackerman	1,516	5	5	0	Vaiden	737	3	1	2
Amory	7,344	23	18	5	Vicksburg	23,946	101	78	23
Batesville	7,491	47	37	10	Water Valley	3,405	10	10	0
Bay St. Louis	9,295	32	25	7	West Point	11,350	30	26	4

Table V-9. Full-Time Law Enforcement Employees, by Selected State and City, 2011—*Continued*

(Number.)

State/City	Population	Total law enforcement employees	Total officers	Total civilians	State/City	Population	Total law enforcement employees	Total officers	Total civilians
Winona	5,062	11	9	2	Chillicothe	9,550	22	16	6
Yazoo City	11,446	37	27	10	Clarkton	1,293	4	4	0
					Claycomo	1,435	15	11	4
Missouri					Clayton	15,997	59	51	8
Adrian	1,683	3	3	0	Clever	2,147	5	5	0
Advance	1,352	2	2	0	Clinton	9,041	22	21	1
Anderson	1,968	5	5	0	Cole Camp	1,125	3	3	0
Appleton City	1,131	2	2	0	Columbia	108,894	186	159	27
Arbyrd	511	1	1	0	Concordia	2,459	6	6	0
Archie	1,174	3	3	0	Conway	791	1	1	0
Arnold	20,884	56	45	11	Cool Valley	1,200	9	9	0
Ash Grove	1,477	3	3	0	Cottleville	3,086	10	10	0
Ashland	3,720	7	6	1	Country Club Hills	1,279	9	9	0
Aurora	7,535	24	18	6	Country Club Village	2,458	2	2	0
Ava	3,004	13	7	6	Crane	1,467	3	3	0
Ballwin	30,514	63	51	12	Crestwood	11,955	32	26	6
Bates City	220	1	1	0	Creve Coeur	17,898	53	49	4
Battlefield	5,610	5	5	0	Crocker	1,114	3	3	0
Bella Villa	732	2	2	0	Crystal City	4,873	21	15	6
Belle	1,551	4	4	0	Cuba	3,368	13	11	2
Bellefontaine Neighbors	10,899	32	31	1	Dellwood	5,043	17	15	2
Bellerive	189	19	18	1	Delta	440	1	1	0
Bellflower	394	1	1	0	Desloge	5,072	10	10	0
Bel-Nor	1,504	7	7	0	De Soto	6,423	20	15	5
Bel-Ridge	2,747	18	15	3	Des Peres	8,403	47	39	8
Belton	23,200	61	41	20	Dexter	7,893	22	16	6
Berkeley	9,011	60	47	13	Diamond	905	2	2	0
Bernie	1,965	9	5	4	Dixon	1,555	10	5	5
Bethany	3,304	5	5	0	Doniphan	2,004	12	8	4
Beverly Hills	576	8	5	3	Doolittle	632	1	1	0
Billings	1,039	4	4	0	Drexel	969	2	2	0
Birch Tree	681	1	1	0	Duenweg	1,125	2	2	0
Birmingham	184	4	4	0	Duquesne	1,769	6	6	0
Bloomfield	1,940	4	4	0	East Prairie	3,188	10	7	3
Blue Springs	52,766	117	85	32	Edmundson	837	11	10	1
Bolivar	10,363	25	20	5	Eldon	4,584	12	11	1
Bonne Terre	6,889	10	10	0	El Dorado Springs	3,606	11	7	4
Boonville	8,349	28	21	7	Ellington	991	3	3	0
Bourbon	1,638	6	6	0	Ellisville	9,166	20	19	1
Bowling Green	5,353	15	11	4	Ellsinore	448	1	1	0
Branson	10,558	60	44	16	Elsberry	1,941	4	4	0
Branson West	480	6	6	0	Eureka	10,226	26	22	4
Braymer	881	1	1	0	Everton	320	1	1	0
Breckenridge Hills	4,763	15	14	1	Excelsior Springs	11,124	34	23	11
Brentwood	8,084	34	26	8	Exeter	775	2	2	0
Bridgeton	11,592	64	49	15	Fair Grove	1,398	4	4	0
Brookfield	4,559	18	11	7	Fair Play	477	1	1	0
Bucklin	469	1	1	0	Fairview	384	1	1	0
Buckner	3,087	9	9	0	Farber	323	1	1	0
Buffalo	3,095	8	7	1	Farmington	16,299	34	26	8
Butler	4,234	14	9	5	Fayette	2,698	7	7	0
Butterfield Village	472	2	1	1	Ferguson	21,280	63	54	9
Byrnes Mill	2,791	5	5	0	Ferrelview	453	1	1	0
Cabool	2,154	10	6	4	Festus	11,644	39	28	11
California	4,294	7	6	1	Flordell Hills	825	9	9	0
Calverton Park	1,298	7	7	0	Florissant	52,348	110	88	22
Camdenton	3,732	17	13	4	Foley	162	2	2	0
Cameron	9,969	23	17	6	Fordland	803	2	2	0
Campbell	1,999	5	5	0	Foristell	507	8	7	1
Canton	2,386	3	2	1	Forsyth	2,263	6	5	1
Cape Girardeau	38,079	94	75	19	Fredericktown	3,999	8	8	0
Cardwell	716	2	2	0	Freeman	484	1	1	0
Carl Junction	7,472	17	12	5	Frontenac	3,774	22	21	1
Carrollton	3,798	8	7	1	Fulton	12,836	34	27	7
Carterville	1,898	7	7	0	Garden City	1,648	3	3	0
Carthage	14,430	35	28	7	Gerald	1,350	5	5	0
Caruthersville	6,190	15	14	1	Gideon	1,097	3	3	0
Cassville	3,278	11	11	0	Gladstone	25,502	66	49	17
Center	510	1	1	0	Glasgow	1,107	4	4	0
Centralia	4,042	12	7	5	Glendale	5,947	14	11	3
Chaffee	2,966	11	6	5	Glen Echo Park	161	8	5	3
Charlack	1,368	10	8	2	Gower	1,532	3	3	0
Charleston	5,969	17	12	5	Grain Valley	12,901	25	19	6
Chesterfield	47,657	93	83	10	Grandview	24,564	65	51	14

Table V-9. Full-Time Law Enforcement Employees, by Selected State and City, 2011—*Continued*

(Number.)

State/City	Population	Total law enforcement employees	Total officers	Total civilians	State/City	Population	Total law enforcement employees	Total officers	Total civilians
Greendale	653	7	7	0	Lowry City	642	2	2	0
Greenfield	1,376	3	3	0	Macon	5,491	15	13	2
Greenwood	5,240	7	6	1	Malden	4,291	14	13	1
Hallsville	1,496	2	2	0	Manchester	18,160	42	37	5
Hamilton	1,816	5	4	1	Mansfield	1,301	4	4	0
Hannibal	17,981	45	35	10	Maplewood	8,075	33	31	2
Hardin	571	1	1	0	Marble Hill	1,482	4	4	0
Harrisonville	10,055	33	25	8	Marceline	2,241	8	5	3
Hartville	615	2	2	0	Marionville	2,233	2	2	0
Hayti	2,950	10	9	1	Marshall	13,112	35	25	10
Hazelwood	25,796	84	70	14	Marshfield	6,657	10	9	1
Herculaneum	3,481	12	11	1	Marthasville	1,140	1	1	0
Hermann	2,440	13	7	6	Maryland Heights	27,572	97	79	18
Higginsville	4,814	15	9	6	Maryville	12,016	26	20	6
Highlandville	914	1	1	0	Matthews	630	2	2	0
Hillsboro	2,831	6	6	0	Maysville	1,118	1	1	0
Hillsdale	1,483	14	13	1	Mayview	213	1	1	0
Holcomb	637	2	2	0	Memphis	1,829	3	3	0
Holden	2,260	7	6	1	Merriam Woods	1,767	2	2	0
Hollister	4,442	18	12	6	Mexico	11,585	35	33	2
Holt	449	1	1	0	Milan	1,967	5	5	0
Holts Summit	3,259	11	10	1	Miller	702	1	1	0
Hornersville	665	2	2	0	Mill Spring	190	1	1	0
Houston	2,089	6	6	0	Miner	988	11	8	3
Howardville	384	4	2	2	Moberly	14,025	44	32	12
Humansville	1,052	2	2	0	Moline Acres	2,451	13	12	1
Huntsville	1,570	3	3	0	Monett	8,905	30	21	9
Iberia	739	2	2	0	Montgomery City	2,844	6	6	0
Independence	117,255	280	196	84	Morehouse	977	2	2	0
Indian Point	530	1	1	0	Mosby	191	4	3	1
Ironton	1,465	3	3	0	Moscow Mills	2,518	6	6	0
Jackson	13,808	31	22	9	Mound City	1,163	2	2	0
Jasper	934	1	1	0	Mountain View	2,729	8	7	1
Jefferson City	43,236	126	86	40	Mount Vernon	4,592	12	11	1
Jennings	14,765	33	33	0	Naylor	634	1	1	0
Jonesburg	771	1	1	0	Neosho	11,878	19	18	1
Joplin	50,332	133	122	11	Newburg	472	2	2	0
Kahoka	2,086	3	3	0	New Florence	772	2	2	0
Kansas City	461,458	1,961	1,387	574	New Haven	2,097	6	6	0
Kearney	8,411	14	13	1	New London	978	1	1	0
Kennett	10,972	28	23	5	New Madrid	3,127	6	6	0
Kimberling City	2,409	8	7	1	New Melle	477	3	3	0
King City	1,017	1	1	0	Nixa	19,091	30	25	5
Kinloch	299	4	4	0	Noel	1,839	4	4	0
Kirksville	17,569	29	26	3	Norborne	711	1	1	0
Kirkwood	27,640	69	58	11	Normandy	5,026	19	18	1
Knob Noster	2,719	13	7	6	North Kansas City	4,223	47	36	11
Ladue	8,552	32	26	6	Northwoods	4,242	28	18	10
Lake Lotawana	1,946	7	6	1	Oak Grove	7,823	15	14	1
Lake Ozark	1,592	17	11	6	Oakland	1,386	69	58	11
Lakeshire	1,437	4	4	0	Oakview Village	376	6	4	2
Lake St. Louis	14,598	40	30	10	Odessa	5,319	11	10	1
Lake Tapawingo	733	3	3	0	O'Fallon	79,617	139	107	32
Lake Winnebago	1,135	5	5	0	Old Monroe	266	1	1	0
Lamar	4,548	12	10	2	Olivette	7,765	24	23	1
La Monte	1,144	2	2	0	Oregon	860	1	1	0
Lanagan	421	2	2	0	Oronogo	2,947	4	4	0
La Plata	1,371	3	3	0	Orrick	840	2	2	0
Lathrop	2,094	4	4	0	Osage Beach	4,367	40	26	14
Laurie	948	5	5	0	Osceola	950	5	4	1
Lawson	2,482	6	5	1	Overland	16,120	60	47	13
Leadington	424	6	5	1	Owensville	2,686	5	5	0
Leadwood	1,287	6	5	1	Ozark	17,885	34	30	4
Leasburg	339	1	1	0	Pacific	7,027	25	18	7
Lebanon	14,527	41	28	13	Pagedale	3,316	14	13	1
Lee's Summit	91,696	182	127	55	Palmyra	3,608	7	6	1
Lexington	4,743	10	9	1	Park Hills	8,791	14	13	1
Liberal	762	1	1	0	Parkville	5,574	16	15	1
Liberty	29,255	54	40	14	Parma	716	4	3	1
Licking	3,135	5	5	0	Pasadena Park	472	19	18	1
Lincoln	1,194	3	3	0	Peculiar	4,625	9	8	1
Linn	1,464	3	3	0	Perry	696	1	1	0
Linn Creek	245	2	2	0	Perryville	8,255	29	25	4
Lone Jack	1,054	5	5	0	Pevely	5,504	20	14	6

Table V-9.   Full-Time Law Enforcement Employees, by Selected State and City, 2011—*Continued*

(Number.)

State/City	Population	Total law enforcement employees	Total officers	Total civilians	State/City	Population	Total law enforcement employees	Total officers	Total civilians
Piedmont	1,984	7	7	0	Terre du Lac	2,328	6	6	0
Pierce City	1,297	3	3	0	Thayer	2,251	10	6	4
Pilot Knob	749	1	1	0	Tipton	3,274	3	3	0
Pine Lawn	3,287	24	21	3	Town and Country	10,854	31	30	1
Pineville	794	5	5	0	Tracy	209	1	1	0
Platte City	4,708	12	11	1	Trenton	6,023	18	12	6
Platte Woods	386	2	2	0	Troy	10,578	25	23	2
Plattsburg	2,327	5	5	0	Union	10,241	23	21	2
Pleasant Hill	8,142	18	12	6	Unionville	1,872	4	4	0
Pleasant Valley	2,972	14	9	5	University City	35,500	91	74	17
Polo	577	2	1	1	Uplands Park	447	9	7	2
Poplar Bluff	17,085	55	44	11	Van Buren	822	3	3	0
Portageville	3,240	14	10	4	Vandalia	3,913	7	5	2
Potosi	2,670	13	11	2	Velda City	1,425	13	11	2
Purcell	409	2	2	0	Velda Village Hills	1,059	8	5	3
Purdy	1,102	2	2	0	Verona	621	2	1	1
Qulin	460	1	1	0	Versailles	2,491	10	10	0
Randolph	52	2	2	0	Viburnum	696	2	2	0
Raymore	19,276	39	27	12	Vienna	612	6	6	0
Raytown	29,633	74	53	21	Vinita Park	1,887	14	13	1
Reeds Spring	916	1	1	0	Walnut Grove	667	2	2	0
Republic	14,805	34	22	12	Wardell	429	2	1	1
Rich Hill	1,401	1	1	0	Warrensburg	18,906	37	33	4
Richland	1,870	6	5	1	Warrenton	7,909	24	21	3
Richmond	5,818	12	10	2	Warsaw	2,135	7	7	0
Richmond Heights	8,634	42	41	1	Warson Woods	1,969	8	7	1
Risco	347	1	1	0	Washington	14,033	31	28	3
Riverside	2,948	34	23	11	Waverly	852	1	1	0
Riverview	2,866	10	10	0	Waynesville	4,848	11	10	1
Rockaway Beach	844	2	2	0	Weatherby Lake	1,729	5	5	0
Rock Hill	4,652	10	9	1	Webb City	11,036	27	22	5
Rock Port	1,323	3	3	0	Webster Groves	23,079	50	47	3
Rogersville	3,084	7	7	0	Wellston	2,321	8	7	1
Rolla	19,630	59	40	19	Wellsville	1,221	4	4	0
Salem	4,968	16	11	5	Wentzville	29,176	74	56	18
Salisbury	1,624	4	3	1	Weston	1,647	5	5	0
Sarcoxie	1,335	3	3	0	West Plains	12,030	30	26	4
Savannah	5,075	5	5	0	Wheaton	699	2	2	0
Scott City	4,582	17	12	5	Willard	5,307	11	10	1
Sedalia	21,465	55	43	12	Willow Springs	2,192	7	6	1
Senath	1,773	3	3	0	Winfield	1,409	6	6	0
Seneca	2,344	6	6	0	Winona	1,340	4	4	0
Seymour	1,928	6	6	0	Woodson Terrace	4,078	20	17	3
Shelbina	1,710	4	4	0	Wright City	3,130	9	8	1
Shrewsbury	6,277	19	17	2					
Sikeston	16,377	77	64	13	**Montana**				
Silex	188	2	2	0	Baker	1,756	3	3	0
Slater	1,863	5	4	1	Belgrade	7,455	18	15	3
Smithville	8,456	15	15	0	Billings	105,095	165	140	25
Southwest City	974	3	3	0	Boulder	1,194	2	2	0
Sparta	1,762	3	3	0	Bozeman	37,611	67	60	7
Springfield	160,078	384	312	72	Bridger	714	2	2	0
St. Ann	13,067	48	36	12	Chinook	1,214	4	4	0
St. Charles	66,033	152	111	41	Colstrip	2,234	12	6	6
St. Clair	4,741	17	15	2	Columbia Falls	4,730	10	9	1
Steele	2,180	5	5	0	Columbus	1,910	5	4	1
Steelville	1,648	6	6	0	Conrad	2,593	5	5	0
Ste. Genevieve	4,426	11	10	1	Cut Bank	2,894	6	6	0
St. James	4,231	9	8	1	Dillon	4,171	8	7	1
St. John	6,541	25	23	2	East Helena	2,002	5	5	0
St. Joseph	77,059	157	115	42	Ennis	845	1	1	0
St. Louis	320,454	1,920	1,363	557	Eureka	1,046	3	3	0
St. Marys	361	1	1	0	Fort Benton	1,477	5	4	1
Stover	1,098	3	3	0	Glasgow	3,279	14	11	3
St. Peters	52,766	111	86	25	Glendive	4,979	14	9	5
Strafford	2,367	8	7	1	Great Falls	59,024	125	85	40
St. Robert	4,356	25	19	6	Hamilton	4,387	16	15	1
Sturgeon	875	2	2	0	Havre	9,393	23	17	6
Sugar Creek	3,357	22	17	5	Helena	28,440	67	48	19
Sullivan	7,107	23	16	7	Hot Springs	549	3	3	0
Summersville	504	2	2	0	Joliet	600	1	1	0
Sunset Hills	8,527	32	25	7	Kalispell	20,104	44	35	9
Sweet Springs	1,489	4	4	0	Laurel	6,778	17	13	4
Tarkio	1,589	3	3	0	Lewistown	5,953	18	13	5

Table V-9.   Full-Time Law Enforcement Employees, by Selected State and City, 2011—*Continued*

(Number.)

State/City	Population	Total law enforcement employees	Total officers	Total civilians	State/City	Population	Total law enforcement employees	Total officers	Total civilians
Libby	2,651	6	6	0	South Sioux City	13,472	28	27	1
Livingston	7,107	15	14	1	St. Paul	2,310	4	4	0
Manhattan	1,533	3	3	0	Superior	1,974	4	4	0
Miles City	8,485	25	16	9	Tekamah	1,751	3	3	0
Missoula	67,381	120	100	20	Valentine	2,761	6	5	1
Plains	1,057	3	3	0	Valley	1,892	5	4	1
Polson	4,528	14	13	1	Wahoo	4,548	6	6	0
Poplar	817	3	3	0	Wayne	5,711	10	6	4
Red Lodge	2,144	7	7	0	West Point	3,394	7	6	1
Ronan City	1,888	4	4	0	Wilber	1,872	4	4	0
Sidney	5,237	11	10	1	Wymore	1,470	3	3	0
Stevensville	1,825	2	2	0	York	7,835	19	13	6
Thompson Falls	1,325	3	3	0					
Three Forks	1,886	1	1	0	**Nevada**				
Troy	946	3	3	0	Fallon	8,679	29	19	10
West Yellowstone	1,282	12	6	6	Henderson	259,902	550	336	214
Whitefish	6,413	16	15	1	Las Vegas Metropolitan Police Department	1,458,474	4,962	2,644	2,318
Wolf Point	2,644	9	8	1	Lovelock	1,910	6	5	1
					Reno	227,120	346	288	58
Nebraska					West Wendover	4,447	20	13	7
Albion	1,665	3	3	0					
Alliance	8,567	25	18	7	**New Hampshire**				
Ashland	2,475	6	5	1	Alexandria	1,615	2	2	0
Auburn	3,491	4	4	0	Alstead	1,940	1	1	0
Aurora	4,519	9	8	1	Alton	5,257	14	12	2
Bayard	1,220	4	4	0	Amherst	11,216	18	17	1
Beatrice	12,570	31	21	10	Antrim	2,640	7	5	2
Bellevue	50,584	113	98	15	Ashland	2,079	5	5	0
Blair	8,061	20	17	3	Auburn	4,959	9	7	2
Bridgeport	1,559	4	4	0	Barnstead	4,599	3	3	0
Broken Bow	3,591	7	6	1	Barrington	8,587	11	10	1
Central City	2,960	6	5	1	Bartlett	2,792	4	3	1
Chadron	5,903	20	14	6	Bedford	21,231	47	33	14
Columbus	22,308	51	36	15	Belmont	7,366	18	15	3
Cozad	4,012	6	6	0	Bennington	1,478	2	2	0
Crete	7,022	18	11	7	Berlin	10,064	30	22	8
David City	2,932	4	4	0	Bethlehem	2,529	6	6	0
Emerson	847	2	2	0	Boscawen	3,970	7	6	1
Fairbury	3,977	7	6	1	Bow	7,529	20	14	6
Falls City	4,364	12	8	4	Bradford	1,652	3	3	0
Fremont	26,633	47	37	10	Brentwood	4,492	5	5	0
Gering	8,576	18	15	3	Bristol	3,058	10	9	1
Gordon	1,626	5	4	1	Campton	3,337	7	6	1
Gothenburg	3,606	7	6	1	Candia	3,914	8	7	1
Grand Island	48,953	88	77	11	Canterbury	2,355	2	2	0
Hastings	25,129	46	35	11	Carroll	764	4	4	0
Holdrege	5,544	16	10	6	Center Harbor	1,097	3	3	0
Imperial	2,089	4	4	0	Charlestown	5,121	8	5	3
Kearney	31,062	69	55	14	Chester	4,774	7	6	1
La Vista	15,899	39	34	5	Claremont	13,372	28	23	5
Lexington	10,321	18	16	2	Colebrook	2,304	5	5	0
Lincoln	260,685	421	327	94	Concord	42,751	91	80	11
Madison	2,460	4	4	0	Conway	10,128	30	20	10
McCook	7,767	21	16	5	Danville	4,393	5	4	1
Milford	2,109	4	4	0	Deerfield	4,286	8	7	1
Minden	2,949	4	4	0	Deering	1,915	2	2	0
Mitchell	1,717	4	4	0	Derry	33,152	70	55	15
Nebraska City	7,354	15	14	1	Dover	30,026	62	44	18
Norfolk	24,426	58	38	20	Dublin	1,599	4	3	1
North Platte	24,954	62	39	23	Dunbarton	2,762	4	3	1
Ogallala	4,779	11	10	1	Durham	14,657	20	18	2
Omaha	412,608	924	778	146	Effingham	1,467	2	2	0
O'Neill	3,738	7	6	1	Enfield	4,588	8	7	1
Ord	2,131	3	3	0	Epping	6,419	14	13	1
Papillion	19,063	42	38	4	Epsom	4,572	6	5	1
Pierce	1,783	3	3	0	Exeter	14,325	33	23	10
Plainview	1,257	2	2	0	Farmington	6,795	15	13	2
Plattsmouth	6,560	17	14	3	Fitzwilliam	2,399	3	3	0
Ralston	5,996	15	13	2	Franconia	1,105	3	3	0
Schuyler	6,266	10	8	2	Franklin	8,488	25	17	8
Scottsbluff	15,173	36	31	5	Freedom	1,491	3	3	0
Scribner	865	1	1	0	Fremont	4,289	5	4	1
Seward	7,026	13	11	2	Gilford	7,135	22	16	6
Sidney	6,817	16	14	2	Gilmanton	3,782	5	4	1

Table V-9.   Full-Time Law Enforcement Employees, by Selected State and City, 2011—*Continued*

(Number.)

State/City	Popula-tion	Total law enforce-ment employees	Total officers	Total civilians	State/City	Popula-tion	Total law enforce-ment employees	Total officers	Total civilians
Goffstown	17,674	42	28	14	Seabrook	8,704	32	25	7
Gorham	2,852	10	7	3	Somersworth	11,781	30	24	6
Grantham	2,989	5	4	1	South Hampton	815	2	2	0
Greenland	3,554	7	7	0	Strafford	3,996	4	4	0
Hampstead	8,534	8	8	0	Stratham	7,265	11	10	1
Hampton	14,996	43	34	9	Sugar Hill	564	2	2	0
Hampton Falls	2,239	4	4	0	Sunapee	3,369	5	5	0
Hancock	1,656	3	3	0	Thornton	2,493	5	4	1
Hanover	11,275	30	18	12	Tilton	3,572	17	15	2
Haverhill	4,703	8	7	1	Troy	2,148	3	3	0
Henniker	4,842	9	8	1	Wakefield	5,798	11	10	1
Hillsborough	6,019	19	13	6	Walpole	3,739	4	3	1
Hinsdale	4,051	8	7	1	Warner	2,837	5	4	1
Hooksett	13,469	33	23	10	Washington	1,124	1	1	0
Hopkinton	5,596	7	7	0	Waterville Valley	247	7	6	1
Hudson	24,499	61	45	16	Weare	8,797	12	11	1
Jaffrey	5,464	14	13	1	Webster	1,874	3	2	1
Keene	23,440	57	42	15	Wilton	3,682	9	7	2
Kingston	6,033	10	9	1	Winchester	4,347	9	8	1
Laconia	15,972	46	36	10	Windham	13,610	25	19	6
Lancaster	3,512	7	6	1	Wolfeboro	6,277	17	12	5
Lebanon	13,168	47	34	13	Woodstock	1,376	5	5	0
Lee	4,336	8	7	1					
Lincoln	1,664	15	10	5	**New Jersey**				
Lisbon	1,597	4	4	0	Aberdeen Township	18,271	41	34	7
Litchfield	8,282	12	10	2	Absecon	8,439	33	26	7
Littleton	5,936	10	9	1	Allendale	6,527	17	12	5
Londonderry	24,161	74	59	15	Allenhurst	498	13	9	4
Loudon	5,324	7	6	1	Allentown	1,834	5	5	0
Madison	2,505	5	4	1	Alpha	2,377	15	14	1
Manchester	109,708	271	207	64	Alpine	1,855	13	13	0
Marlborough	2,066	2	2	0	Andover Township	6,340	18	12	6
Meredith	6,249	18	14	4	Asbury Park	16,170	98	87	11
Merrimack	25,527	52	41	11	Atlantic City	39,690	440	331	109
Middleton	1,785	3	3	0	Atlantic Highlands	4,400	19	14	5
Milford	15,135	29	24	5	Audubon	8,848	18	17	1
Milton	4,604	8	7	1	Avalon	1,338	34	21	13
Mont Vernon	2,412	3	3	0	Avon-by-the-Sea	1,907	11	11	0
Moultonborough	4,049	12	11	1	Barnegat Township	21,006	55	44	11
Nashua	86,607	226	168	58	Barrington	7,006	15	14	1
New Boston	5,328	4	3	1	Bay Head	971	8	7	1
Newbury	2,075	4	4	0	Bayonne	63,234	219	182	37
New Durham	2,641	6	5	1	Beach Haven	1,174	12	10	2
Newfields	1,682	4	4	0	Beachwood	11,082	19	17	2
New Hampton	2,168	5	5	0	Bedminster Township	8,192	17	15	2
Newington	754	11	10	1	Belleville	36,046	105	96	9
New Ipswich	5,106	5	4	1	Bellmawr	11,622	22	20	2
New London	4,403	13	8	5	Belmar	5,813	25	19	6
Newmarket	8,948	20	13	7	Belvidere	2,690	6	5	1
Newport	6,516	18	13	5	Bergenfield	26,853	53	45	8
Newton	4,609	8	6	2	Berkeley Heights Township	13,227	30	24	6
Northfield	4,835	10	9	1	Berkeley Township	41,392	90	69	21
North Hampton	4,307	13	12	1	Berlin	7,613	17	16	1
Northumberland	2,291	4	4	0	Berlin Township	5,375	19	18	1
Northwood	4,247	9	8	1	Bernards Township	26,741	50	38	12
Nottingham	4,791	7	6	1	Bernardsville	7,733	24	18	6
Orford	1,239	2	2	0	Beverly	2,586	8	6	2
Ossipee	4,351	10	9	1	Blairstown Township	5,987	7	5	2
Pelham	12,914	27	21	6	Bloomfield	47,472	136	122	14
Pembroke	7,124	14	12	2	Bloomingdale	7,681	16	15	1
Peterborough	6,292	13	11	2	Bogota	8,214	21	16	5
Pittsfield	4,111	9	8	1	Boonton	8,375	25	20	5
Plaistow	7,619	26	18	8	Boonton Township	4,277	12	12	0
Plymouth	6,999	15	9	6	Bordentown	3,937	13	11	2
Portsmouth	21,261	83	62	21	Bordentown Township	11,405	25	23	2
Raymond	10,151	24	17	7	Bound Brook	10,437	28	23	5
Rindge	6,022	9	8	1	Bradley Beach	4,312	20	16	4
Rochester	29,791	74	58	16	Branchburg Township	14,507	25	25	0
Rollinsford	2,530	4	4	0	Brick Township	75,322	177	127	50
Rye	5,305	10	9	1	Bridgeton	25,433	77	63	14
Salem	28,814	75	58	17	Bridgewater Township	44,612	90	74	16
Sanbornton	2,970	7	6	1	Brielle	4,790	15	15	0
Sandown	5,994	7	7	0	Brigantine	9,481	46	35	11
Sandwich	1,328	2	2	0	Brooklawn	1,962	8	8	0

Table V-9. Full-Time Law Enforcement Employees, by Selected State and City, 2011—*Continued*

(Number.)

State/City	Population	Total law enforcement employees	Total officers	Total civilians	State/City	Population	Total law enforcement employees	Total officers	Total civilians
Buena	4,618	12	10	2	Fieldsboro	542	2	2	0
Burlington	9,953	35	31	4	Flemington	4,596	16	16	0
Burlington Township	22,669	52	42	10	Florence Township	12,149	25	23	2
Butler	7,564	18	17	1	Florham Park	11,735	40	33	7
Byram Township	8,378	17	16	1	Fort Lee	35,463	109	89	20
Caldwell	7,848	21	20	1	Franklin	5,062	12	12	0
Camden	77,604	314	265	49	Franklin Lakes	10,625	28	22	6
Cape May	3,619	26	21	5	Franklin Township, Gloucester County	16,876	22	19	3
Carlstadt	6,147	26	23	3	Franklin Township, Hunterdon County	3,206	5	5	0
Carney's Point Township	8,076	23	18	5	Franklin Township, Somerset County	62,507	119	103	16
Carteret	22,920	65	55	10	Freehold	12,092	34	27	7
Cedar Grove Township	12,452	29	28	1	Freehold Township	36,304	65	61	4
Chatham	8,992	22	19	3	Frenchtown	1,378	3	3	0
Chatham Township	10,487	23	21	2	Galloway Township	37,473	74	59	15
Cherry Hill Township	71,281	154	130	24	Garfield	30,588	68	61	7
Chesilhurst	1,639	8	7	1	Garwood	4,240	20	16	4
Chester	1,654	9	8	1	Gibbsboro	2,282	8	8	0
Chesterfield Township	7,725	12	11	1	Glassboro	18,641	50	46	4
Chester Township	7,864	18	17	1	Glen Ridge	7,552	28	24	4
Cinnaminson Township	15,621	25	24	1	Glen Rock	11,640	22	21	1
Clark Township	14,805	48	38	10	Gloucester City	11,494	28	26	2
Clayton	8,206	18	17	1	Gloucester Township	64,849	162	111	51
Clementon	5,017	13	12	1	Green Brook Township	7,227	25	21	4
Cliffside Park	23,673	43	43	0	Greenwich Township, Gloucester County	4,915	20	18	2
Clifton	84,416	170	141	29	Greenwich Township, Warren County	5,731	11	10	1
Clinton	2,728	10	10	0	Guttenberg	11,213	29	22	7
Clinton Township	13,523	26	24	2	Hackensack	43,157	136	111	25
Closter	8,401	20	19	1	Hackettstown	9,756	18	18	0
Collingswood	13,972	29	24	5	Haddonfield	11,632	23	21	2
Colts Neck Township	10,176	20	19	1	Haddon Heights	7,498	17	16	1
Cranbury Township	3,870	18	17	1	Haddon Township	14,756	28	26	2
Cranford Township	22,700	60	46	14	Haledon	8,346	16	14	2
Cresskill	8,602	24	20	4	Hamburg	3,288	8	8	0
Deal	752	21	17	4	Hamilton Township, Atlantic County	26,591	63	46	17
Delanco Township	4,297	10	9	1	Hamilton Township, Mercer County	88,760	205	170	35
Delaware Township	4,578	9	8	1	Hammonton	14,840	36	30	6
Delran Township	16,952	35	31	4	Hanover Township	13,758	35	28	7
Demarest	4,897	15	15	0	Harding Township	3,851	13	12	1
Denville Township	16,690	43	33	10	Hardyston Township	8,240	24	18	6
Deptford Township	30,663	67	62	5	Harrington Park	4,680	9	9	0
Dover	18,217	33	30	3	Harrison	13,665	50	39	11
Dumont	17,537	43	34	9	Harrison Township	12,458	17	16	1
Dunellen	7,251	16	16	0	Harvey Cedars	338	7	7	0
Eastampton Township	6,089	17	16	1	Hasbrouck Heights	11,881	32	29	3
East Brunswick Township	47,670	105	80	25	Haworth	3,393	11	10	1
East Greenwich Township	9,587	23	21	2	Hawthorne	18,854	34	30	4
East Hanover Township	11,194	36	32	4	Hazlet Township	20,402	44	38	6
East Newark	2,414	7	7	0	Helmetta	2,185	5	5	0
East Orange	64,484	294	237	57	High Bridge	3,660	7	7	0
East Rutherford	8,943	40	40	0	Highland Park	14,029	32	25	7
East Windsor Township	27,280	57	44	13	Highlands	5,022	16	13	3
Eatontown	12,751	46	35	11	Hillsborough Township	38,430	66	51	15
Edgewater	11,551	30	29	1	Hillsdale	10,253	20	19	1
Edgewater Park Township	8,911	10	10	0	Hillside Township	21,475	79	67	12
Edison Township	100,300	226	177	49	Hi-Nella	873	12	12	0
Egg Harbor City	4,257	15	14	1	Hoboken	50,171	160	138	22
Egg Harbor Township	43,467	105	79	26	Ho-Ho-Kus	4,092	19	15	4
Elizabeth	125,386	526	312	214	Holland Township	5,309	7	6	1
Elk Township	4,230	13	12	1	Holmdel Township	16,829	47	39	8
Elmer	1,400	2	2	0	Hopatcong	15,197	32	24	8
Elmwood Park	19,468	42	40	2	Hopewell Township	17,362	39	31	8
Emerson	7,426	20	17	3	Howell Township	51,245	100	83	17
Englewood	27,237	101	76	25	Independence Township	5,681	9	8	1
Englewood Cliffs	5,299	22	21	1	Irvington	54,105	192	153	39
Englishtown	1,853	6	6	0	Island Heights	1,679	4	4	0
Essex Fells	2,120	13	13	0	Jackson Township	55,039	91	72	19
Evesham Township	45,690	78	69	9	Jamesburg	5,935	16	12	4
Ewing Township	35,909	84	71	13	Jefferson Township	21,385	45	38	7
Fairfield Township, Essex County	7,491	36	35	1	Jersey City	248,423	945	806	139
Fair Haven	6,141	13	13	0	Keansburg	10,139	36	31	5
Fair Lawn	32,565	65	53	12	Kearny	40,819	121	114	7
Fairview	13,881	36	33	3	Kenilworth	7,940	25	24	1
Fanwood	7,342	18	17	1	Keyport	7,264	19	16	3
Far Hills	922	6	6	0	Kinnelon	10,282	17	16	1

Table V-9. Full-Time Law Enforcement Employees, by Selected State and City, 2011—*Continued*

(Number.)

State/City	Popula-tion	Total law enforce-ment employees	Total officers	Total civilians	State/City	Popula-tion	Total law enforce-ment employees	Total officers	Total civilians
Lacey Township	27,736	52	40	12	Mountainside	6,707	26	21	5
Lake Como	1,765	10	10	0	Mount Arlington	5,067	13	12	1
Lakehurst	2,663	8	7	1	Mount Ephraim	4,692	14	13	1
Lakewood Township	93,152	143	116	27	Mount Holly Township	9,568	19	18	1
Lambertville	3,919	12	10	2	Mount Laurel Township	42,003	64	57	7
Laurel Springs	1,914	7	7	0	Mount Olive Township	28,211	56	47	9
Lavallette	1,881	16	12	4	Mullica Township	6,167	13	12	1
Lawnside	2,955	9	8	1	Neptune City	4,885	19	17	2
Lawrence Township, Mercer County	33,583	77	64	13	Neptune Township	28,028	87	71	16
Lebanon Township	6,610	10	9	1	Netcong	3,243	8	8	0
Leonia	8,967	18	16	2	Newark	278,064	1,209	1,095	114
Lincoln Park	10,556	27	21	6	New Brunswick	55,365	162	134	28
Linden	40,634	153	122	31	Newfield	1,558	6	6	0
Lindenwold	17,672	43	40	3	New Hanover Township	7,410	3	3	0
Linwood	7,116	17	16	1	New Milford	16,395	37	34	3
Little Egg Harbor Township	20,132	47	39	8	New Providence	12,212	29	23	6
Little Falls Township	14,480	25	22	3	Newton	8,024	32	23	9
Little Ferry	10,661	26	22	4	North Arlington	15,443	33	26	7
Little Silver	5,970	20	16	4	North Bergen Township	60,975	123	111	12
Livingston Township	29,464	80	68	12	North Brunswick Township	40,878	93	74	19
Lodi	24,216	47	39	8	North Caldwell	6,204	19	14	5
Logan Township	6,062	20	19	1	Northfield	8,653	23	22	1
Long Beach Township	3,061	45	36	9	North Haledon	8,445	21	17	4
Long Branch	30,821	100	80	20	North Hanover Township	7,704	11	10	1
Long Hill Township	8,731	26	23	3	North Plainfield	22,009	50	45	5
Longport	898	17	14	3	Northvale	4,655	12	12	0
Lopatcong Township	8,041	15	14	1	North Wildwood	4,054	35	25	10
Lower Alloways Creek Township	1,776	13	12	1	Norwood	5,730	13	12	1
Lower Township	22,942	51	40	11	Nutley Township	28,464	86	70	16
Lumberton Township	12,601	14	12	2	Oakland	12,796	31	25	6
Lyndhurst Township	20,622	52	48	4	Oaklyn	4,051	13	12	1
Madison	15,898	35	28	7	Ocean City	11,740	72	60	12
Magnolia	4,355	14	14	0	Ocean Gate	2,018	8	7	1
Mahwah Township	25,976	61	52	9	Oceanport	5,851	15	14	1
Manalapan Township	39,001	66	53	13	Ocean Township, Monmouth County	27,382	72	60	12
Manasquan	5,917	22	16	6	Ocean Township, Ocean County	8,360	23	19	4
Manchester Township	43,213	80	62	18	Ogdensburg	2,418	6	6	0
Mansfield Township, Burlington County	8,572	13	12	1	Old Bridge Township	65,593	119	93	26
Mansfield Township, Warren County	7,751	15	14	1	Old Tappan	5,769	13	12	1
Mantoloking	297	8	7	1	Oradell	8,005	20	19	1
Mantua Township	15,268	27	25	2	Orange	30,234	127	109	18
Manville	10,378	28	22	6	Palisades Park	19,687	36	28	8
Maple Shade Township	19,195	39	34	5	Palmyra	7,423	16	15	1
Maplewood Township	23,946	71	60	11	Paramus	26,430	103	76	27
Margate City	6,375	39	29	10	Park Ridge	8,674	17	17	0
Marlboro Township	40,325	83	67	16	Parsippany-Troy Hills Township	53,415	112	93	19
Matawan	8,839	22	21	1	Passaic	70,013	190	159	31
Maywood	9,587	25	21	4	Paterson	146,685	419	357	62
Medford Lakes	4,160	9	8	1	Paulsboro	6,117	17	16	1
Medford Township	23,110	37	33	4	Peapack and Gladstone	2,591	8	7	1
Mendham	4,998	13	12	1	Pemberton	1,414	6	6	0
Mendham Township	5,889	15	13	2	Pemberton Township	28,005	57	53	4
Merchantville	3,834	15	13	2	Pennington	2,594	5	4	1
Metuchen	13,619	31	27	4	Pennsauken Township	36,004	107	89	18
Middlesex	13,680	25	25	0	Penns Grove	5,164	17	13	4
Middle Township	18,974	63	48	15	Pennsville Township	13,454	21	19	2
Middletown Township	66,743	127	100	27	Pequannock Township	15,592	37	32	5
Midland Park	7,152	15	14	1	Perth Amboy	50,983	138	109	29
Millburn Township	20,216	58	48	10	Phillipsburg	15,000	37	36	1
Milltown	6,916	18	15	3	Pine Beach	2,134	7	6	1
Millville	28,495	86	75	11	Pine Hill	10,267	22	19	3
Monmouth Beach	3,290	9	9	0	Pine Valley	12	4	4	0
Monroe Township, Gloucester County	36,249	77	59	18	Piscataway Township	56,231	100	84	16
Monroe Township, Middlesex County	39,262	69	51	18	Pitman	9,041	15	14	1
Montclair	37,794	115	101	14	Plainfield	49,974	159	137	22
Montgomery Township	22,328	35	30	5	Plainsboro Township	23,076	46	35	11
Montvale	7,870	20	19	1	Pleasantville	20,316	60	47	13
Montville Township	21,600	45	38	7	Plumsted Township	8,449	14	12	2
Moonachie	2,717	19	17	2	Pohatcong Township	3,350	15	14	1
Moorestown Township	20,795	39	34	5	Point Pleasant	18,453	36	29	7
Morris Plains	5,550	15	14	1	Point Pleasant Beach	4,681	27	22	5
Morristown	18,472	54	50	4	Pompton Lakes	11,134	26	22	4
Morris Township	22,380	44	40	4	Princeton	12,348	39	30	9
Mountain Lakes	4,174	26	13	13	Princeton Township	16,319	35	26	9

Table V-9.   Full-Time Law Enforcement Employees, by Selected State and City, 2011—*Continued*

(Number.)

State/City	Population	Total law enforcement employees	Total officers	Total civilians	State/City	Population	Total law enforcement employees	Total officers	Total civilians
Prospect Park	5,885	14	14	0	Union City	66,676	184	153	31
Rahway	27,437	83	74	9	Union Township	56,831	186	136	50
Ramsey	14,521	36	30	6	Upper Saddle River	8,235	19	15	4
Randolph Township	25,820	37	33	4	Ventnor City	10,685	49	38	11
Raritan	6,904	22	18	4	Vernon Township	24,023	38	29	9
Raritan Township	22,259	34	31	3	Verona	13,376	31	27	4
Readington Township	16,180	25	23	2	Vineland	60,926	168	142	26
Red Bank	12,247	44	37	7	Voorhees Township	29,228	52	45	7
Ridgefield	11,069	29	27	2	Waldwick	9,657	24	19	5
Ridgefield Park	12,771	36	29	7	Wallington	11,373	21	20	1
Ridgewood	25,041	46	41	5	Wall Township	26,251	75	60	15
Ringwood	12,269	24	20	4	Wanaque	11,153	25	21	4
Riverdale	3,571	18	14	4	Warren Township	15,362	35	28	7
River Edge	11,378	26	20	6	Washington Township, Bergen County	9,132	21	21	0
Riverside Township	8,106	15	15	0	Washington Township, Gloucester County	48,720	84	77	7
Riverton	2,788	5	5	0	Washington Township, Morris County	18,595	32	28	4
River Vale Township	9,691	22	20	2	Washington Township, Warren County	6,673	30	28	2
Robbinsville Township	13,687	34	25	9	Watchung	5,820	37	29	8
Rochelle Park Township	5,548	24	20	4	Waterford Township	10,684	23	21	2
Rockaway	6,459	15	14	1	Wayne Township	54,899	146	117	29
Rockaway Township	24,236	66	54	12	Weehawken Township	12,596	52	48	4
Roseland	5,838	26	25	1	Wenonah	2,286	7	7	0
Roselle	21,155	71	58	13	Westampton Township	8,842	23	22	1
Roselle Park	13,341	41	34	7	West Amwell Township	3,853	6	5	1
Roxbury Township	23,402	42	39	3	West Caldwell Township	10,795	29	23	6
Rumson	7,146	19	15	4	West Deptford Township	21,749	44	41	3
Runnemede	8,496	19	18	1	Westfield	30,417	66	54	12
Rutherford	18,121	39	37	2	West Long Branch	8,124	27	21	6
Saddle Brook Township	13,704	30	27	3	West Milford Township	25,936	51	44	7
Saddle River	3,162	22	17	5	West New York	49,873	114	104	10
Salem	5,163	26	23	3	West Orange	46,361	108	95	13
Sayreville	42,846	98	84	14	Westville	4,302	16	15	1
Scotch Plains Township	23,588	48	45	3	West Wildwood	605	2	2	0
Sea Bright	1,417	12	12	0	West Windsor Township	27,255	58	46	12
Sea Girt	1,834	13	11	2	Westwood	10,944	29	25	4
Sea Isle City	2,121	34	22	12	Wharton	6,544	21	20	1
Seaside Heights	2,897	31	22	9	Wildwood	5,343	45	37	8
Seaside Park	1,584	15	14	1	Wildwood Crest	3,281	27	21	6
Secaucus	16,318	60	53	7	Willingboro Township	31,734	73	64	9
Ship Bottom	1,160	12	11	1	Winfield Township	1,476	8	8	0
Shrewsbury	3,822	19	14	5	Winslow Township	39,630	86	71	15
Somerdale	5,168	13	13	0	Woodbridge Township	99,915	245	192	53
Somers Point	10,831	33	28	5	Woodbury	10,208	31	28	3
Somerville	12,138	35	31	4	Woodbury Heights	3,065	7	6	1
South Amboy	8,660	28	23	5	Woodcliff Lake	5,749	19	18	1
South Bound Brook	4,578	13	12	1	Woodland Park	11,858	28	25	3
South Brunswick Township	43,561	97	70	27	Woodlynne	2,988	6	5	1
South Hackensack Township	2,386	15	14	1	Wood-Ridge	7,651	24	20	4
South Harrison Township	3,173	5	5	0	Woodstown	3,517	10	8	2
South Orange	16,252	56	52	4	Woolwich Township	10,234	20	19	1
South Plainfield	23,463	63	49	14	Wyckoff Township	16,752	29	23	6
South River	16,061	39	31	8					
South Toms River	3,696	12	11	1	**New Mexico**				
Sparta Township	19,788	39	29	10	Alamogordo	30,743	107	67	40
Spotswood	8,284	23	19	4	Albuquerque	551,961	1,416	1,027	389
Springfield	15,870	48	42	6	Angel Fire	1,230	4	4	0
Springfield Township	3,425	9	8	1	Artesia	11,427	53	33	20
Spring Lake	3,003	18	13	5	Aztec	6,839	15	13	2
Spring Lake Heights	4,729	12	12	0	Bayard	2,354	7	6	1
Stafford Township	26,623	68	49	19	Belen	7,350	23	20	3
Stanhope	3,622	10	9	1	Bernalillo	8,413	23	20	3
Stone Harbor	869	22	16	6	Bloomfield	8,203	26	22	4
Stratford	7,063	17	16	1	Bosque Farms	3,948	14	13	1
Summit	21,528	54	45	9	Capitan	1,506	3	3	0
Surf City	1,209	10	10	0	Carlsbad	26,431	76	49	27
Teaneck Township	39,908	108	93	15	Carrizozo	1,007	4	3	1
Tenafly	14,536	39	33	6	Cimarron	1,032	3	3	0
Tewksbury Township	6,013	11	10	1	Clayton	3,013	15	8	7
Tinton Falls	17,952	39	37	2	Cloudcroft	682	3	3	0
Toms River Township	91,543	194	150	44	Clovis	38,198	75	56	19
Totowa	10,840	31	27	4	Corrales	8,422	16	13	3
Trenton	85,196	314	238	76	Cuba	739	5	4	1
Tuckerton	3,358	8	8	0	Deming	15,021	39	34	5
Union Beach	6,266	18	14	4	Dexter	1,280	4	4	0

Table V-9.   Full-Time Law Enforcement Employees, by Selected State and City, 2011—*Continued*

(Number.)

State/City	Population	Total law enforcement employees	Total officers	Total civilians	State/City	Population	Total law enforcement employees	Total officers	Total civilians
Edgewood	3,777	8	7	1	Brant Town	2,074	1	1	0
Espanola	10,338	36	24	12	Briarcliff Manor Village	7,902	19	19	0
Estancia	1,674	6	5	1	Brighton Town	36,774	45	39	6
Eunice	2,955	15	9	6	Brockport Village	8,404	12	11	1
Farmington	46,390	153	126	27	Bronxville Village	6,351	23	21	2
Gallup	21,921	73	59	14	Buffalo	262,484	881	736	145
Grants	9,285	15	13	2	Cairo Town	6,700	1	1	0
Hatch	1,666	10	8	2	Caledonia Village	2,211	3	3	0
Hobbs	34,504	89	66	23	Cambridge Village	1,878	4	4	0
Hurley	1,312	7	5	2	Camden Village	2,241	3	3	0
Jal	2,070	9	5	4	Camillus Town and Village	24,276	25	23	2
Las Cruces	98,710	263	183	80	Canajoharie Village	2,239	3	3	0
Las Vegas	13,907	51	34	17	Canandaigua	10,592	25	23	2
Logan	1,054	4	4	0	Canastota Village	4,826	6	5	1
Lordsburg	2,828	12	10	2	Canisteo Village	2,280	2	2	0
Los Alamos	18,151	72	34	38	Canton Village	6,342	10	8	2
Los Lunas	15,001	41	36	5	Carmel Town	34,459	41	35	6
Lovington	11,132	31	21	10	Carthage Village	3,764	3	3	0
Magdalena	948	3	3	0	Catskill Village	4,099	16	15	1
Mesilla	2,221	6	6	0	Cayuga Heights Village	3,746	7	6	1
Milan	3,281	12	7	5	Cazenovia Village	2,848	5	4	1
Moriarty	1,931	11	10	1	Centre Island Village	412	7	7	0
Portales	12,417	42	23	19	Chatham Village	1,778	3	2	1
Questa	1,790	2	1	1	Cheektowaga Town	79,194	166	125	41
Raton	6,962	22	14	8	Chester Town	8,048	14	14	0
Red River	482	3	3	0	Chittenango Village	5,104	4	3	1
Rio Rancho	88,500	202	123	79	Cicero Town	29,774	14	13	1
Roswell	48,907	112	77	35	Clarkstown Town	79,221	189	163	26
Ruidoso	8,119	39	24	15	Clayton Village	1,987	3	3	0
Ruidoso Downs	2,847	17	9	8	Clifton Springs Village	2,137	2	2	0
Santa Clara	1,705	5	4	1	Cobleskill Village	4,699	11	11	0
Santa Fe	68,707	195	152	43	Coeymans Town	7,451	9	6	3
Santa Rosa	2,880	12	7	5	Cohoes	16,241	45	34	11
Silver City	10,430	38	34	4	Colchester Town	2,086	2	2	0
Socorro	9,152	29	20	9	Colonie Town	77,950	148	107	41
Springer	1,059	1	1	0	Cooperstown Village	1,860	7	6	1
Sunland Park	14,264	27	24	3	Corning	11,233	25	21	4
Taos	5,780	24	17	7	Cornwall Town	9,671	15	12	3
Taos Ski Valley	70	3	3	0	Cortland	19,290	45	42	3
Tatum	807	10	5	5	Crawford Town	9,358	15	13	2
Texico	1,143	3	3	0	Croton-on-Hudson Village	8,106	23	21	2
Truth or Consequences	6,547	17	15	2	Cuba Town	3,258	4	4	0
Tucumcari	5,423	25	15	10	Dansville Village	4,740	6	6	0
Tularosa	2,874	11	6	5	Deerpark Town	7,937	4	4	0
					Delhi Village	3,101	4	4	0
New York					Depew Village	15,372	35	30	5
Addison Town and Village	2,607	3	3	0	Deposit Village	1,670	1	1	0
Akron Village	2,881	1	1	0	Dewitt Town	22,856	40	36	4
Albany	98,296	444	312	132	Dobbs Ferry Village	10,924	27	25	2
Albion Village	6,083	11	11	0	Dolgeville Village	2,216	2	2	0
Alexandria Bay Village	1,083	2	2	0	Dryden Village	1,898	7	6	1
Alfred Village	4,193	6	6	0	Dunkirk	12,619	36	35	1
Allegany Village	1,824	3	2	1	East Aurora-Aurora Town	13,844	21	17	4
Altamont Village	1,728	1	1	0	Eastchester Town	19,642	53	48	5
Amherst Town	117,610	181	153	28	East Fishkill Town	29,159	40	32	8
Amity Town and Belmont Village	2,318	1	1	0	East Greenbush Town	16,547	32	24	8
Amityville Village	9,566	28	26	2	East Hampton Town	19,479	90	64	26
Amsterdam	18,704	44	42	2	East Hampton Village	1,088	28	23	5
Arcade Village	2,080	6	6	0	East Rochester Village	6,617	9	8	1
Ardsley Village	4,472	19	19	0	East Syracuse Village	3,098	8	7	1
Asharoken Village	657	3	3	0	Eden Town	7,723	5	4	1
Attica Village	2,558	5	5	0	Ellenville Village	4,154	10	9	1
Auburn	27,811	74	68	6	Ellicott Town	5,205	13	12	1
Baldwinsville Village	7,411	12	11	1	Ellicottville	1,605	2	2	0
Ballston Spa Village	5,433	5	5	0	Elmira	29,331	90	78	12
Batavia	15,535	31	29	2	Elmira Heights Village	4,115	9	9	0
Bath Village	5,812	12	10	2	Elmira Town	5,986	4	4	0
Beacon	15,611	33	31	2	Elmsford Village	4,685	18	18	0
Bedford Town	17,413	43	38	5	Endicott Village	13,452	38	35	3
Bethlehem Town	33,807	59	42	17	Evans Town	16,430	30	24	6
Binghamton	47,589	138	126	12	Fairport Village	5,377	11	10	1
Blooming Grove Town	12,183	17	15	2	Fallsburg Town	12,077	17	17	0
Bolivar Village	1,052	1	1	0	Floral Park Village	15,934	47	34	13
Boonville Village	2,081	3	3	0	Florida Village	2,846	1	1	0

Table V-9.   Full-Time Law Enforcement Employees, by Selected State and City, 2011—*Continued*

(Number.)

State/City	Population	Total law enforcement employees	Total officers	Total civilians	State/City	Population	Total law enforcement employees	Total officers	Total civilians
Fort Edward Village	3,390	5	5	0	Liverpool Village	2,358	6	5	1
Fort Plain Village	2,332	4	4	0	Lloyd Harbor Village	3,676	14	13	1
Frankfort Town	5,038	3	3	0	Lloyd Town	10,912	13	10	3
Frankfort Village	2,610	5	5	0	Lockport	21,260	51	48	3
Franklinville Village	1,748	2	2	0	Long Beach	33,425	92	75	17
Fredonia Village	11,280	19	15	4	Lowville Village	3,486	6	6	0
Freeport Village	43,053	105	88	17	Lynbrook Village	19,514	54	46	8
Fulton City	11,949	36	34	2	Lyons Village	3,635	10	8	2
Garden City Village	22,472	65	52	13	Macedon Town and Village	9,189	6	5	1
Gates Town	28,528	37	30	7	Malone Village	5,938	14	14	0
Geddes Town	10,581	16	14	2	Malverne Village	8,552	23	23	0
Geneseo Village	8,067	8	8	0	Mamaroneck Town	12,031	40	39	1
Geneva	13,321	40	35	5	Mamaroneck Village	19,014	57	50	7
Glen Cove	27,085	56	52	4	Manlius Town	24,657	44	36	8
Glens Falls	14,766	36	30	6	Marlborough Town	8,848	8	6	2
Glenville Town	21,848	35	21	14	Massena Village	10,985	25	20	5
Gloversville	15,735	32	30	2	Maybrook Village	2,971	3	3	0
Goshen Town	8,266	11	10	1	Mechanicville	5,219	13	12	1
Goshen Village	5,479	20	17	3	Medina Village	6,092	12	11	1
Gouverneur Village	3,967	7	5	2	Menands Village	4,008	14	11	3
Granville Village	2,554	4	4	0	Middleport Village	1,848	3	3	0
Great Neck Estates Village	2,773	16	13	3	Middletown	28,212	83	69	14
Greece Town	96,527	104	98	6	Mohawk Village	2,743	4	4	0
Greenburgh Town	43,055	135	115	20	Monroe Village	8,402	22	18	4
Greene Village	1,587	1	1	0	Montgomery Town	8,936	14	13	1
Greenwich Village	1,785	4	4	0	Monticello Village	6,756	25	23	2
Greenwood Lake Village	3,168	9	7	2	Moriah Town	3,621	2	2	0
Groton Village	2,374	1	1	0	Mount Hope Town	7,050	4	4	0
Guilderland Town	33,734	50	34	16	Mount Kisco Village	10,926	35	33	2
Hamburg Town	45,177	78	61	17	Mount Morris Village	2,999	5	5	0
Hamburg Village	9,451	15	14	1	Mount Pleasant Town	26,294	51	42	9
Hamilton Village	4,258	4	4	0	Mount Vernon	67,594	229	198	31
Harriman Village	2,435	7	7	0	Nassau Village	1,138	1	1	0
Harrison Town	27,595	66	57	9	Newark Village	9,186	18	17	1
Hastings-on-Hudson Village	7,884	21	21	0	Newburgh	28,996	88	76	12
Haverstraw Town	36,799	77	71	6	Newburgh Town	29,935	58	48	10
Hempstead Village	54,133	148	119	29	New Castle Town	17,648	41	37	4
Herkimer Village	7,778	21	21	0	New Hartford Town and Village	20,580	22	19	3
Highland Falls Village	3,918	13	10	3	New Paltz Town and Village	14,066	27	24	3
Holley Village	1,819	2	2	0	New Rochelle	77,408	214	158	56
Homer Village	3,306	4	4	0	New Windsor Town	25,357	49	40	9
Hoosick Falls Village	3,517	2	2	0	New York	8,211,875	49,401	34,542	14,859
Hornell	8,601	22	21	1	Niagara Falls	50,419	171	153	18
Horseheads Village	6,490	13	13	0	Niagara Town	8,416	5	4	1
Hudson	6,743	31	25	6	Niskayuna Town	21,879	38	27	11
Hudson Falls Village	7,314	16	13	3	Nissequogue Village	1,757	3	3	0
Hunter Town	2,744	1	1	0	North Greenbush Town	12,129	18	16	2
Huntington Bay Village	1,431	6	6	0	Northport Village	7,434	19	15	4
Hyde Park Town	21,668	17	14	3	North Syracuse Village	6,831	11	10	1
Ilion Village	8,089	20	18	2	North Tonawanda	31,710	56	46	10
Inlet Town	334	3	2	1	Norwich	7,222	19	19	0
Irondequoit Town	51,924	57	46	11	Ogdensburg	11,178	32	27	5
Irvington Village	6,449	23	22	1	Ogden Town	19,945	15	12	3
Ithaca	30,149	79	67	12	Old Brookville Village	2,144	34	26	8
Jamestown	31,286	70	60	10	Old Westbury Village	4,692	31	26	5
Johnson City Village	15,242	33	28	5	Olean	14,517	41	34	7
Johnstown	8,782	25	24	1	Olive Town	4,439	1	1	0
Kenmore Village	15,492	25	25	0	Oneida	11,444	26	22	4
Kensington Village	1,166	6	6	0	Oneonta City	13,963	32	27	5
Kent Town	13,568	25	20	5	Orangetown Town	36,998	96	86	10
Kings Point Village	5,027	24	22	2	Ossining Village	25,173	65	56	9
Kingston	24,000	75	69	6	Oswego City	18,224	48	43	5
Kirkland Town	8,410	7	7	0	Owego Village	3,914	8	7	1
Lackawanna	18,223	53	47	6	Oxford Village	1,457	1	1	0
Lake Placid Village	2,532	13	10	3	Oyster Bay Cove Village	2,207	11	11	0
Lake Success Village	2,947	26	23	3	Painted Post Village	1,817	3	3	0
Lakewood-Busti	7,384	10	9	1	Palmyra Village	3,552	6	5	1
Lancaster Town	25,431	62	47	15	Peekskill	23,689	71	58	13
Larchmont Village	5,890	27	24	3	Pelham Manor Village	5,511	28	27	1
Le Roy Village	4,411	8	8	0	Pelham Village	6,941	28	25	3
Lewisboro Town	12,467	1	1	0	Penn Yan Village	5,182	12	11	1
Lewiston Town and Village	16,335	11	10	1	Perry Village	3,690	3	3	0
Liberty Village	4,412	20	17	3	Piermont Village	2,521	8	8	0
Little Falls	4,968	12	11	1	Plattsburgh City	20,079	55	49	6

Table V-9.   Full-Time Law Enforcement Employees, by Selected State and City, 2011—*Continued*

(Number.)

State/City	Popula-tion	Total law enforce-ment employees	Total officers	Total civilians
Pleasantville Village	7,051	22	20	2
Port Chester Village	29,097	60	58	2
Port Dickinson Village	1,648	5	4	1
Port Jervis	8,868	31	30	1
Port Washington	18,991	70	62	8
Potsdam Village	9,470	17	13	4
Poughkeepsie	32,883	130	96	34
Poughkeepsie Town	38,511	95	83	12
Pulaski Village	2,376	1	1	0
Quogue Village	971	14	13	1
Ramapo Town	84,431	130	108	22
Red Hook Village	1,970	2	2	0
Rensselaer City	9,434	29	24	5
Riverhead Town	33,657	99	85	14
Rochester	211,511	871	738	133
Rockville Centre Village	24,131	63	53	10
Rome	33,877	77	73	4
Rosendale Town	6,102	3	2	1
Rotterdam Town	29,225	58	42	16
Rouses Point Village	2,219	1	1	0
Rye	15,791	40	35	5
Rye Brook Village	9,389	28	27	1
Sag Harbor Village	2,179	15	14	1
Salamanca	5,841	15	15	0
Sands Point Village	2,687	20	20	0
Saranac Lake Village	5,430	11	11	0
Saratoga Springs	26,705	79	67	12
Saugerties Town	19,570	26	21	5
Scarsdale Village	17,243	48	42	6
Schenectady	66,432	145	105	40
Schoharie Village	926	1	1	0
Scotia Village	7,764	14	13	1
Seneca Falls Village	6,711	14	12	2
Shawangunk Town	14,396	7	7	0
Shelter Island Town	2,403	10	9	1
Sherrill	3,085	3	3	0
Sidney Village	3,918	8	8	0
Silver Creek Village	2,668	5	5	0
Skaneateles Village	2,461	4	4	0
Sleepy Hollow Village	9,914	25	25	0
Solvay Village	6,614	16	14	2
Southampton Town	50,030	137	99	38
Southampton Village	3,123	44	29	15
South Glens Falls Village	3,534	6	6	0
South Nyack Village	3,526	6	6	0
Southold Town	19,860	67	52	15
Spring Valley Village	31,488	63	55	8
St. Johnsville Village	1,740	2	2	0
Stony Point Town	15,127	28	27	1
Suffern Village	10,771	25	24	1
Syracuse	145,822	564	494	70
Tarrytown Village	11,328	38	33	5
Ticonderoga Town	5,065	7	7	0
Tonawanda	15,198	33	28	5
Tonawanda Town	58,406	152	104	48
Troy	50,354	138	124	14
Tuckahoe Village	6,515	27	24	3
Tupper Lake Village	3,683	8	8	0
Tuxedo Town	3,014	15	12	3
Ulster Town	12,382	29	25	4
Utica	62,515	198	178	20
Vernon Village	1,177	1	1	0
Vestal Town	28,169	39	35	4
Walden Village	7,009	17	14	3
Wallkill Town	27,549	40	35	5
Walton Village	3,102	6	5	1
Wappingers Falls Village	5,547	7	4	3
Warsaw Village	3,489	5	5	0
Warwick Town	19,438	37	32	5
Washingtonville Village	5,926	15	13	2
Waterford Town and Village	8,461	13	10	3
Waterloo Village	5,194	9	8	1
Watertown	27,144	68	64	4
Watervliet	10,300	29	26	3

State/City	Popula-tion	Total law enforce-ment employees	Total officers	Total civilians
Watkins Glen Village	1,867	4	4	0
Waverly Village	4,464	11	10	1
Wayland Village	1,873	1	1	0
Webb Town	1,815	5	5	0
Webster Town and Village	42,833	34	29	5
Wellsville Village	4,700	12	10	2
Westfield Village	3,238	5	5	0
Westhampton Beach Village	1,729	16	14	2
West Seneca Town	44,912	79	67	12
Whitehall Village	2,626	4	4	0
White Plains	57,109	205	194	11
Whitesboro Village	3,789	6	6	0
Whitestown Town	9,199	7	7	0
Windham Town	1,711	2	2	0
Woodbury Town	10,734	21	21	0
Woodridge Village	851	1	1	0
Woodstock Town	5,910	10	10	0
Yonkers	196,857	694	619	75
Yorktown Town	36,243	63	54	9
Yorkville Village	2,701	3	3	0
North Carolina				
Aberdeen	6,431	28	26	2
Ahoskie	5,103	22	16	6
Albemarle	16,105	52	46	6
Andrews	1,804	5	5	0
Angier	4,405	12	12	0
Apex	37,951	68	53	15
Archdale	11,560	31	25	6
Asheboro	25,329	85	78	7
Asheville	84,450	238	198	40
Atlantic Beach	1,514	19	18	1
Aurora	527	2	2	0
Ayden	4,995	22	18	4
Badin	1,999	4	4	0
Bailey	576	2	2	0
Bakersville	470	1	1	0
Bald Head Island	160	21	12	9
Banner Elk	1,041	10	9	1
Beaufort	4,090	19	18	1
Beech Mountain	324	14	10	4
Belhaven	1,709	10	6	4
Belmont	10,204	44	33	11
Benson	3,353	15	14	1
Bethel	1,597	5	5	0
Beulaville	1,312	4	4	0
Biltmore Forest	1,360	15	13	2
Biscoe	1,722	9	8	1
Black Creek	779	2	2	0
Black Mountain	7,948	21	17	4
Bladenboro	1,772	5	5	0
Blowing Rock	1,257	13	10	3
Boiling Spring Lakes	5,440	9	8	1
Boiling Springs	4,706	8	8	0
Bolton	700	3	2	1
Boone	17,339	41	34	7
Boonville	1,237	5	5	0
Brevard	7,705	28	22	6
Broadway	1,245	4	4	0
Brookford	387	1	1	0
Bryson City	1,442	8	7	1
Bunn	348	2	2	0
Burgaw	3,921	13	12	1
Burlington	50,597	162	122	40
Burnsville	1,714	8	8	0
Butner	7,687	45	40	5
Cameron	289	1	1	0
Candor	851	5	5	0
Canton	4,281	20	14	6
Cape Carteret	1,941	6	6	0
Carolina Beach	5,778	30	28	2
Carrboro	19,830	42	39	3
Carthage	2,233	11	10	1
Cary	136,949	211	173	38

Table V-9.   Full-Time Law Enforcement Employees, by Selected State and City, 2011—*Continued*

(Number.)

State/City	Population	Total law enforcement employees	Total officers	Total civilians	State/City	Population	Total law enforcement employees	Total officers	Total civilians
Caswell Beach	403	4	4	0	High Point	105,695	247	211	36
Catawba	611	1	1	0	Hillsborough	6,164	26	24	2
Chadbourn	1,880	10	9	1	Holden Beach	582	8	8	0
Chapel Hill	57,959	129	114	15	Holly Ridge	1,284	9	8	1
Charlotte-Mecklenburg[1]	789,478	2,214	1,726	488	Holly Springs	24,974	54	44	10
Cherryville	5,833	22	17	5	Hope Mills	15,368	40	34	6
China Grove	3,608	13	13	0	Hot Springs	567	1	1	0
Chocowinity	830	3	3	0	Hudson	3,824	12	11	1
Claremont	1,369	9	8	1	Huntersville	47,366	90	81	9
Clayton	16,320	46	42	4	Indian Beach	113	4	4	0
Cleveland	882	5	5	0	Jackson	520	1	1	0
Clinton	8,749	34	30	4	Jacksonville	71,034	149	120	29
Clyde	1,239	4	4	0	Jefferson	1,631	3	3	0
Coats	2,139	5	5	0	Jonesville	2,314	11	10	1
Columbus	1,012	6	6	0	Kannapolis	43,166	98	76	22
Concord	80,069	182	154	28	Kenansville	866	5	5	0
Conover	8,269	26	25	1	Kenly	1,356	8	8	0
Conway	847	1	1	0	Kernersville	23,416	80	64	16
Cooleemee	972	4	4	0	Kill Devil Hills	6,768	33	29	4
Cornelius	25,181	68	51	17	King	6,992	23	20	3
Cramerton	4,218	13	13	0	Kings Mountain	10,427	36	30	6
Creedmoor	4,176	17	13	4	Kinston	21,952	85	75	10
Dallas	4,545	16	12	4	Kitty Hawk	3,313	18	16	2
Davidson	11,083	18	17	1	Knightdale	11,546	29	28	1
Denton	1,657	6	6	0	Kure Beach	2,038	12	11	1
Dobson	1,606	6	6	0	Lake Lure	1,207	11	10	1
Drexel	1,882	5	5	0	Lake Royale	2,538	6	6	0
Duck	374	9	8	1	Lake Waccamaw	1,499	5	5	0
Dunn	9,380	51	35	16	Landis	3,148	11	10	1
Durham	231,225	618	476	142	Laurel Park	2,208	7	7	0
East Bend	620	2	2	0	Laurinburg	16,164	45	39	6
East Spencer	1,553	4	4	0	Leland	13,699	34	31	3
Eden	15,724	52	43	9	Lenoir	18,459	66	52	14
Edenton	5,067	18	15	3	Lexington	19,171	74	65	9
Elizabeth City	18,920	71	58	13	Liberty	2,690	11	10	1
Elizabethtown	3,628	17	16	1	Lilesville	543	1	1	0
Elkin	4,052	21	17	4	Lillington	3,235	12	11	1
Elon	9,538	16	15	1	Lincolnton	10,619	36	31	5
Emerald Isle	3,701	16	13	3	Littleton	683	3	3	0
Enfield	2,564	17	16	1	Locust	2,967	13	12	1
Erwin	4,461	11	10	1	Long View	4,933	15	15	0
Fair Bluff	963	3	3	0	Louisburg	3,402	14	13	1
Fairmont	2,697	15	12	3	Lowell	3,571	9	9	0
Farmville	4,713	21	16	5	Lumberton	21,815	91	81	10
Fayetteville	203,107	513	366	147	Madison	2,274	14	13	1
Fletcher	7,278	15	14	1	Maggie Valley	1,165	11	10	1
Forest City	7,571	34	32	2	Magnolia	951	2	2	0
Four Oaks	1,945	5	5	0	Maiden	3,352	15	14	1
Foxfire Village	913	2	2	0	Manteo	1,452	8	7	1
Franklin	3,894	18	17	1	Marion	7,937	26	25	1
Franklinton	2,049	9	9	0	Marshall	883	3	3	0
Fremont	1,271	4	4	0	Mars Hill	1,893	5	5	0
Fuquay-Varina	18,164	36	31	5	Marshville	2,432	7	7	0
Garner	26,071	69	64	5	Matthews	27,543	69	57	12
Garysburg	1,070	2	2	0	Maxton	2,457	16	12	4
Gaston	1,167	2	2	0	Mayodan	2,509	16	13	3
Gastonia	72,651	204	176	28	Maysville	1,032	3	3	0
Gibsonville	6,491	15	14	1	Mebane	11,537	29	22	7
Glen Alpine	1,536	3	3	0	Middlesex	832	4	4	0
Goldsboro	36,899	121	110	11	Mint Hill	23,010	30	27	3
Graham	14,332	37	34	3	Misenheimer	737	4	4	0
Granite Falls	4,782	15	13	2	Mocksville	5,115	24	22	2
Granite Quarry	2,967	7	7	0	Monroe	33,213	98	86	12
Greensboro	273,086	773	636	137	Montreat	732	5	5	0
Greenville	85,626	236	185	51	Mooresville	33,126	79	58	21
Grifton	2,650	7	7	0	Morehead City	8,771	43	37	6
Hamlet	6,577	24	20	4	Morganton	17,133	90	59	31
Havelock	20,998	36	29	7	Morrisville	18,812	34	33	1
Haw River	2,327	8	8	0	Morven	517	1	1	0
Henderson	15,563	58	50	8	Mount Airy	10,520	53	41	12
Hendersonville	13,304	49	37	12	Mount Gilead	1,196	7	7	0
Hertford	2,170	9	8	1	Mount Holly	13,829	36	30	6
Hickory	40,517	147	116	31	Mount Olive	4,647	15	14	1
Highlands	936	12	11	1	Murfreesboro	2,871	14	9	5

[1] The employee data presented in this table for Charlotte-Mecklenburg represent only Charlotte-Mecklenburg Police Department and exclude Mecklenburg County Sheriff's Office.

Table V-9.   Full-Time Law Enforcement Employees, by Selected State and City, 2011—*Continued*

(Number.)

State/City	Population	Total law enforcement employees	Total officers	Total civilians	State/City	Population	Total law enforcement employees	Total officers	Total civilians
Murphy	1,648	10	7	3	Spruce Pine	2,203	11	11	0
Nags Head	2,792	23	21	2	Stallings	14,006	24	21	3
Nashville	5,420	16	15	1	Stanfield	1,505	3	3	0
Navassa	1,524	4	4	0	Stanley	3,601	10	10	0
New Bern	29,898	111	76	35	Stantonsburg	794	3	3	0
Newland	707	5	5	0	Star	887	4	4	0
Newport	4,203	9	9	0	Statesville	24,843	96	76	20
Newton	13,132	43	35	8	Stoneville	1,069	4	4	0
Newton Grove	576	3	3	0	St. Pauls	2,061	18	13	5
Norlina	1,132	4	4	0	Sugar Mountain	201	5	5	0
North Topsail Beach	752	12	11	1	Sunset Beach	3,617	13	13	0
Northwest	744	2	2	0	Surf City	1,876	19	17	2
North Wilkesboro	4,299	25	24	1	Swansboro	2,697	9	9	0
Norwood	2,409	7	6	1	Sylva	2,621	14	13	1
Oakboro	1,883	6	6	0	Tabor City	2,543	10	9	1
Oak Island	6,869	31	25	6	Tarboro	11,560	34	28	6
Ocean Isle Beach	557	13	13	0	Taylorsville	2,125	11	11	0
Old Fort	920	3	3	0	Taylortown	731	1	1	0
Oxford	8,568	35	29	6	Thomasville	27,096	74	68	6
Parkton	442	2	2	0	Topsail Beach	373	8	7	1
Pembroke	3,011	17	13	4	Trent Woods	4,208	5	5	0
Pikeville	687	3	3	0	Troutman	2,413	14	14	0
Pilot Mountain	1,496	9	8	1	Troy	3,229	12	11	1
Pinebluff	1,354	3	3	0	Tryon	1,667	10	8	2
Pinehurst	13,290	28	23	5	Valdese	4,547	12	11	1
Pine Knoll Shores	1,356	7	7	0	Vanceboro	1,018	2	2	0
Pine Level	1,722	5	5	0	Vass	729	3	3	0
Pinetops	1,391	9	6	3	Wadesboro	5,887	30	25	5
Pineville	7,574	45	34	11	Wagram	851	2	2	0
Pink Hill	559	2	2	0	Wake Forest	30,499	66	55	11
Pittsboro	3,790	13	13	0	Wallace	3,929	18	15	3
Plymouth	3,927	13	13	0	Walnut Cove	1,443	6	6	0
Polkton	3,418	1	1	0	Walnut Creek	846	2	2	0
Princeton	1,209	4	4	0	Warrenton	873	5	4	1
Raeford	4,669	16	15	1	Warsaw	3,093	15	13	2
Raleigh	409,014	846	746	100	Washington	9,868	46	38	8
Ramseur	1,713	6	6	0	Waxhaw	9,984	21	19	2
Randleman	4,165	14	14	0	Waynesville	9,994	42	34	8
Ranlo	3,478	7	7	0	Weaverville	3,160	15	14	1
Red Springs	3,471	21	17	4	Weldon	1,676	9	9	0
Reidsville	14,704	58	50	8	Wendell	5,919	17	15	2
Richlands	1,539	5	5	0	West Jefferson	1,315	8	8	0
Rich Square	970	2	2	0	Whispering Pines	2,965	9	8	1
River Bend	3,159	5	5	0	Whitakers	753	2	2	0
Roanoke Rapids	15,954	41	37	4	White Lake	812	6	6	0
Robbins	1,111	5	5	0	Whiteville	5,462	27	24	3
Robersonville	1,507	7	7	0	Wilkesboro	3,456	23	21	2
Rockingham	9,679	37	32	5	Williamston	5,581	21	20	1
Rockwell	2,135	5	5	0	Wilmington	107,826	310	256	54
Rocky Mount	58,206	207	165	42	Wilson	49,790	133	118	15
Rolesville	3,834	12	11	1	Wilson's Mills	2,306	4	4	0
Rose Hill	1,647	4	4	0	Windsor	3,676	9	9	0
Rowland	1,050	7	6	1	Wingate	3,535	8	8	0
Roxboro	8,468	38	33	5	Winston-Salem	232,529	749	585	164
Rutherfordton	4,266	15	14	1	Winterville	9,387	19	18	1
Salisbury	34,089	94	78	16	Woodfin	6,201	14	14	0
Saluda	722	4	4	0	Woodland	819	2	2	0
Sanford	28,450	100	80	20	Wrightsville Beach	2,508	26	23	3
Scotland Neck	2,085	9	8	1	Yadkinville	2,997	13	12	1
Selma	6,150	25	23	2	Youngsville	1,172	10	9	1
Seven Devils	194	6	6	0	Zebulon	4,489	23	22	1
Shallotte	3,722	14	13	1					
Sharpsburg	2,050	8	8	0	**North Dakota**				
Shelby	20,581	82	71	11	Belfield	813	2	2	0
Siler City	7,987	26	21	5	Beulah	3,174	6	5	1
Smithfield	11,105	44	42	2	Bismarck	62,305	124	96	28
Southern Pines	12,490	40	32	8	Bowman	1,678	3	3	0
Southern Shores	2,748	11	10	1	Burlington	1,078	2	2	0
Southport	2,869	11	10	1	Cando	1,134	2	2	0
Sparta	1,792	6	6	0	Carrington	2,100	4	4	0
Spencer	3,308	13	12	1	Cavalier	1,324	4	4	0
Spindale	4,376	12	12	0	Devils Lake	7,261	18	16	2
Spring Hope	1,337	6	6	0	Dickinson	18,087	47	31	16
Spring Lake	12,116	29	26	3	Ellendale	1,418	2	2	0

Table V-9.   Full-Time Law Enforcement Employees, by Selected State and City, 2011—*Continued*

(Number.)

State/City	Population	Total law enforcement employees	Total officers	Total civilians	State/City	Population	Total law enforcement employees	Total officers	Total civilians
Fargo	107,329	162	144	18	Bethel	2,713	3	3	0
Fessenden	487	1	1	0	Bethesda	1,257	1	1	0
Grafton	4,356	11	10	1	Beverly	1,314	3	3	0
Grand Forks	53,729	97	82	15	Bexley	13,067	33	27	6
Harvey	1,813	3	3	0	Blanchester	4,246	7	7	0
Hazen	2,452	4	4	0	Bluffton	4,128	6	6	0
Hillsboro	1,630	2	2	0	Boardman	35,402	62	49	13
Jamestown	15,687	33	29	4	Bolivar	995	1	1	0
Kenmare	1,114	2	2	0	Boston Heights	1,301	5	5	0
Killdeer	764	3	3	0	Bowling Green	30,050	56	41	15
Lamoure	904	1	1	0	Brady Lake	464	1	1	0
Lincoln	2,447	1	1	0	Bratenahl	1,198	13	10	3
Linton	1,115	1	1	0	Brecksville	13,666	32	26	6
Lisbon	2,190	3	3	0	Brewster	2,114	5	5	0
Mandan	18,640	35	27	8	Bridgeport	1,832	4	4	0
Medora	114	2	2	0	Brimfield Township	10,384	16	13	3
Minot	41,577	84	61	23	Broadview Heights	19,414	40	28	12
Napoleon	805	1	1	0	Brookfield Township	8,860	8	8	0
Northwood	961	2	2	0	Brooklyn	11,177	37	29	8
Oakes	1,887	3	3	0	Brook Park	19,226	49	40	9
Rolla	1,302	4	4	0	Brookville	5,888	12	11	1
Rugby	2,924	4	4	0	Brunswick	34,280	55	41	14
Sherwood	246	1	1	0	Brunswick Hills Township	9,905	11	10	1
Stanley	1,483	3	3	0	Bryan	8,551	26	19	7
Steele	727	1	1	0	Bucyrus	12,371	21	17	4
Surrey	950	1	1	0	Burton	1,456	3	3	0
Thompson	1,003	1	1	0	Butler Township	7,874	13	12	1
Valley City	6,696	18	12	6	Cadiz	3,355	5	5	0
Wahpeton	7,897	16	14	2	Caldwell	1,749	2	2	0
Watford City	1,773	7	7	0	Cambridge	10,643	28	23	5
West Fargo	26,266	46	36	10	Camden	2,047	1	1	0
Williston	14,964	35	26	9	Campbell	8,241	14	14	0
Wishek	1,019	2	2	0	Canal Fulton	5,483	10	9	1
					Canfield	7,521	20	15	5
Ohio					Canton	73,060	186	147	39
Ada	5,956	11	8	3	Carey	3,677	10	7	3
Addyston	939	1	1	0	Carlisle	4,919	9	8	1
Akron	199,256	449	410	39	Carrollton	3,243	7	7	0
Alliance	22,338	54	41	13	Celina	10,408	22	16	6
Amberley Village	3,588	21	17	4	Centerville	24,017	52	41	11
Amelia	4,805	5	4	1	Chagrin Falls	4,116	19	11	8
American Township	12,486	1	1	0	Chardon	5,152	17	11	6
Amherst	12,030	26	20	6	Chester Township	10,263	14	13	1
Andover	1,146	3	3	0	Cheviot	8,381	10	10	0
Ansonia	1,175	2	2	0	Chillicothe	21,917	51	46	5
Arcanum	2,131	3	3	0	Cincinnati	297,160	1,151	1,038	113
Arlington Heights	746	6	4	2	Circleville	13,324	28	21	7
Ashland	20,377	33	26	7	Clayton	13,219	14	14	0
Ashtabula	19,138	32	29	3	Clay Township, Ottawa County	2,724	5	5	0
Ashville	4,100	10	10	0	Clearcreek Township	14,084	13	13	0
Athens	23,849	37	24	13	Cleveland	397,106	1,697	1,451	246
Aurora	15,559	34	26	8	Cleveland Heights	46,155	114	102	12
Austintown	29,699	46	37	9	Cleves	3,236	2	2	0
Avon	21,209	41	32	9	Clinton Township	4,112	8	8	0
Bainbridge Township	11,403	26	18	8	Clyde	6,330	16	13	3
Barberton	26,569	49	36	13	Coal Grove	2,167	14	10	4
Barnesville	4,196	7	6	1	Coitsville Township	1,393	3	3	0
Batavia	1,510	3	3	0	Coldwater	4,430	8	8	0
Bath Township, Summit County	9,709	27	20	7	Columbiana	6,389	15	11	4
Bay Village	15,662	26	24	2	Columbus	787,609	2,114	1,805	309
Bazetta Township	5,878	6	6	0	Commercial Point	1,583	2	2	0
Beachwood	11,962	56	42	14	Conneaut	12,850	21	16	5
Beavercreek	45,226	59	43	16	Copley Township	17,317	31	23	8
Beaver Township	6,716	15	11	4	Cortland	7,109	9	9	0
Bedford	13,084	41	31	10	Covington	2,586	6	5	1
Bedford Heights	10,759	53	28	25	Crestline	4,633	12	8	4
Bellaire	4,281	9	9	0	Cridersville	1,853	3	3	0
Bellbrook	6,948	17	12	5	Cuyahoga Falls	49,688	75	70	5
Bellefontaine	13,380	29	22	7	Danville	1,045	2	2	0
Bellville	1,919	4	4	0	Dayton	141,631	391	342	49
Belpre	6,446	14	9	5	Deer Park	5,740	14	10	4
Bentleyville Village	865	3	3	0	Defiance	16,506	29	26	3
Berea	19,107	37	31	6	Delaware	34,778	58	51	7
Berlin Heights	715	1	1	0	Delhi Township	29,532	31	29	2

Table V-9.   Full-Time Law Enforcement Employees, by Selected State and City, 2011—*Continued*

(Number.)

State/City	Population	Total law enforcement employees	Total officers	Total civilians	State/City	Population	Total law enforcement employees	Total officers	Total civilians
Delphos	7,106	17	13	4	Hinckley Township	7,652	11	10	1
Delta	3,105	7	6	1	Hiram	1,407	2	2	0
Dennison	2,657	4	4	0	Holland	1,765	9	9	0
Dover	12,835	22	21	1	Howland Township	17,340	21	20	1
Doylestown	3,053	8	7	1	Hubbard	7,880	16	12	4
Dublin	41,782	86	64	22	Hubbard Township	5,658	9	8	1
East Canton	1,592	2	2	0	Huber Heights	38,129	68	50	18
East Cleveland	17,856	75	56	19	Hudson	22,278	35	28	7
Eastlake	18,591	42	29	13	Huron	7,154	15	12	3
East Liverpool	11,203	24	19	5	Independence	7,138	43	32	11
East Palestine	4,724	8	6	2	Indian Hill	5,789	25	20	5
Eaton	8,413	20	15	5	Ironton	11,137	20	16	4
Edgerton	2,013	3	3	0	Jackson Center	1,463	1	1	0
Edison	437	1	1	0	Jackson Township, Mahoning County	2,116	5	5	0
Elmwood Place	2,190	2	2	0	Jackson Township, Montgomery County	3,697	5	5	0
Englewood	13,475	25	20	5	Jackson Township, Stark County	40,403	52	41	11
Enon	2,417	3	3	0	Jamestown	1,994	3	3	0
Euclid	48,956	136	93	43	Jefferson	3,122	8	7	1
Evendale	2,769	21	19	2	Johnstown	4,635	14	10	4
Fairborn	32,376	53	40	13	Junction City	820	1	1	0
Fairfax	1,700	10	9	1	Kalida	1,543	1	1	0
Fairfield	42,541	78	59	19	Kent	28,925	63	41	22
Fairfield Township	21,389	18	17	1	Kenton	8,268	13	13	0
Fairlawn	7,442	30	21	9	Kettering	56,204	109	82	27
Fairport Harbor	3,111	7	6	1	Kirtland	6,871	14	9	5
Fairview Park	16,838	25	24	1	Kirtland Hills	646	10	9	1
Fayette	1,284	3	3	0	Lagrange	2,105	6	6	0
Findlay	41,232	82	64	18	Lake Township	7,959	16	15	1
Forest	1,462	7	7	0	Lakewood	52,169	116	94	22
Forest Park	18,734	43	37	6	Lancaster	38,808	82	66	16
Fort Loramie	1,479	2	2	0	Lebanon	20,048	37	28	9
Fort Recovery	1,431	2	2	0	Leipsic	2,095	4	4	0
Fostoria	13,451	26	22	4	Lexington	4,826	13	9	4
Franklin	11,780	29	23	6	Liberty Township	12,071	23	17	6
Fredericktown	2,495	4	4	0	Lima	38,799	97	79	18
Fremont	16,746	37	32	5	Lincoln Heights	3,288	8	8	0
Gahanna	33,272	70	55	15	Linndale	179	6	4	2
Galion	10,520	20	16	4	Lithopolis	1,107	3	3	0
Gallipolis	3,644	14	13	1	Lockland	3,452	14	13	1
Garfield Heights	28,870	64	52	12	Logan	7,157	20	15	5
Gates Mills	2,272	15	11	4	London	9,911	21	17	4
Geneva	6,220	15	11	4	Lorain	64,144	117	93	24
Geneva-on-the-Lake	1,289	5	5	0	Lordstown	3,420	13	9	4
Genoa Township	23,107	28	25	3	Loudonville	2,643	9	6	3
Germantown	5,551	12	11	1	Louisville	9,183	9	8	1
German Township, Clark County	7,117	3	3	0	Loveland	12,090	18	17	1
German Township, Montgomery County	2,884	6	6	0	Lowellville	1,156	3	3	0
Gibsonburg	2,583	5	5	0	Luckey	1,013	1	1	0
Girard	9,965	17	16	1	Lynchburg	1,500	3	3	0
Glendale	2,157	7	7	0	Lyndhurst	14,011	37	28	9
Glenwillow	924	4	4	0	Macedonia	11,196	24	18	6
Gnadenhutten	1,289	2	2	0	Madeira	8,732	13	12	1
Golf Manor	3,614	10	9	1	Madison	3,186	6	5	1
Goshen Township, Clermont County	15,516	12	11	1	Madison Township, Franklin County	18,041	15	14	1
Goshen Township, Mahoning County	3,245	9	8	1	Madison Township, Lake County	15,711	19	15	4
Grandview Heights	6,541	19	15	4	Magnolia	979	2	2	0
Granville	5,650	13	10	3	Manchester	2,024	2	2	0
Greenfield	4,642	11	9	2	Mansfield	47,856	109	79	30
Greenhills	3,618	8	7	1	Maple Heights	23,155	58	42	16
Green Springs	1,369	2	2	0	Marblehead	904	2	2	0
Greenville	13,237	28	22	6	Mariemont	3,405	10	9	1
Grove City	35,601	78	61	17	Marietta	14,095	35	29	6
Groveport	5,367	21	20	1	Marion	36,864	70	56	14
Hanging Rock	221	6	3	3	Marlboro Township	4,359	4	3	1
Harrison	9,904	24	22	2	Marysville	22,110	37	31	6
Hartville	2,946	8	8	0	Mason	30,734	48	41	7
Haskins	1,189	2	2	0	Massillon	32,173	52	50	2
Heath	10,318	25	18	7	Maumee	14,296	57	43	14
Hebron	2,338	8	7	1	Mayfield Heights	19,169	43	34	9
Hicksville	3,584	8	7	1	McArthur	1,702	4	4	0
Highland Heights	8,351	28	21	7	McComb	1,649	3	3	0
Highland Hills	1,131	6	5	1	McConnelsville	1,785	4	4	0
Hilliard	28,456	63	47	16	Mechanicsburg	1,645	4	4	0
Hillsboro	6,610	17	13	4	Medina Township	8,543	7	6	1

Table V-9.   Full-Time Law Enforcement Employees, by Selected State and City, 2011—*Continued*

(Number.)

State/City	Population	Total law enforcement employees	Total officers	Total civilians	State/City	Population	Total law enforcement employees	Total officers	Total civilians
Mentor	47,194	105	76	29	Peebles	1,783	2	2	0
Mentor-on-the-Lake	7,448	13	8	5	Pemberville	1,372	1	1	0
Miami Township, Clermont County	40,878	43	40	3	Peninsula	565	3	3	0
Miami Township, Montgomery County	29,152	45	38	7	Pepper Pike	5,983	21	16	5
Middlefield	2,696	12	9	3	Perkins Township	12,211	25	20	5
Middletown	48,730	109	76	33	Perrysburg	20,638	45	33	12
Milan	1,368	3	3	0	Perrysville	736	1	1	0
Milford	6,714	16	14	2	Perry Township, Columbiana County	4,554	5	5	0
Millersport	1,045	1	1	0	Perry Township, Montgomery County	3,357	4	4	0
Milton Township	2,581	4	4	0	Perry Township, Stark County	28,324	31	24	7
Minerva	3,723	14	9	5	Pickerington	18,304	34	25	9
Minerva Park	1,273	4	4	0	Pierce Township	11,222	16	16	0
Mingo Junction	3,457	4	4	0	Pioneer	1,381	3	3	0
Minster	2,807	7	6	1	Piqua	20,537	35	31	4
Monroe	14,771	36	28	8	Plain City	4,228	8	8	0
Monroeville	1,401	4	4	0	Plymouth	1,858	3	3	0
Montgomery	10,259	24	21	3	Poland Township	12,421	12	11	1
Montpelier	4,075	9	8	1	Poland Village	2,557	4	4	0
Montville Township	11,193	12	12	0	Port Clinton	6,060	18	12	6
Moraine	6,312	35	28	7	Portsmouth	20,241	43	39	4
Moreland Hills	3,322	15	14	1	Powell	11,508	19	17	2
Mount Orab	3,667	8	7	1	Powhatan Point	1,593	3	3	0
Munroe Falls	5,016	7	6	1	Ravenna	11,733	32	24	8
Navarre	1,958	5	5	0	Reminderville	3,406	8	7	1
Nelsonville	5,396	8	8	0	Republic	549	1	1	0
New Albany	7,730	22	16	6	Reynoldsburg	35,919	67	53	14
Newark	47,608	88	73	15	Richfield	3,651	23	16	7
New Boston	2,274	13	9	4	Richland Township	9,796	4	4	0
New Bremen	2,980	6	6	0	Richmond Heights	10,554	23	17	6
Newcomerstown	3,825	10	6	4	Richwood	2,231	6	6	0
New Concord	2,493	4	4	0	Rittman	6,496	10	8	2
New Franklin	14,237	18	13	5	Riverside	25,219	29	28	1
New Lexington	4,734	12	8	4	Roaming Shores Village	1,509	2	2	0
New London	2,463	4	4	0	Rockford	1,121	2	2	0
New Miami	2,251	1	1	0	Roseville	1,853	2	2	0
New Middletown	1,622	4	4	0	Rossford	6,298	13	12	1
New Philadelphia	17,301	26	22	4	Ross Township	8,361	2	2	0
Newton Falls	4,799	10	7	3	Russells Point	1,392	3	3	0
Newtown	2,674	8	7	1	Russell Township	5,194	10	9	1
Niles	19,280	40	35	5	Russellville	561	6	5	1
North Baltimore	3,435	5	5	0	Russia	640	1	1	0
North Canton	17,501	27	20	7	Sabina	2,566	5	5	0
Northfield	3,680	9	9	0	Sagamore Hills	10,955	13	9	4
North Kingsville	2,925	4	4	0	Salem	12,312	19	19	0
North Olmsted	32,742	58	44	14	Saline Township	1,354	5	5	0
North Randall	1,028	6	6	0	Sandusky	25,812	46	45	1
North Ridgeville	29,487	45	37	8	Seaman	945	1	1	0
North Royalton	30,466	58	36	22	Sebring	4,423	10	6	4
Northwood	5,269	21	17	4	Seven Hills	11,813	18	17	1
Norton	12,094	16	15	1	Seville	2,298	6	6	0
Norwalk	17,024	28	22	6	Shadyside	3,788	5	5	0
Norwood	19,221	51	48	3	Shaker Heights	28,469	87	64	23
Oak Harbor	2,761	6	4	2	Sharon Township	2,396	10	10	0
Oak Hill	1,552	3	3	0	Sharonville	13,570	43	34	9
Oakwood, Montgomery County	9,209	35	30	5	Shawnee Township	8,713	19	12	7
Oakwood, Paulding County	608	1	1	0	Sheffield Lake	9,144	12	9	3
Oakwood Village	3,670	11	9	2	Shelby	9,324	19	15	4
Oberlin	8,292	22	16	6	Sidney	21,245	48	37	11
Olmsted Falls	9,031	16	10	6	Silverton	4,792	13	10	3
Olmsted Township	13,523	19	16	3	Smith Township	4,473	4	4	0
Ontario	6,230	24	20	4	Smithville	1,253	4	4	0
Orange Village	3,325	15	14	1	Solon	23,365	69	44	25
Oregon	20,306	58	45	13	Somerset	1,482	3	2	1
Orrville	8,386	18	14	4	South Euclid	22,311	49	39	10
Orwell	1,661	5	5	0	South Point	3,961	5	5	0
Ostrander	643	1	1	0	South Russell	3,813	9	9	0
Ottawa	4,463	8	8	0	South Zanesville	1,990	3	3	0
Owensville	795	1	1	0	Spencer	754	1	1	0
Oxford Township	2,100	12	12	0	Spencerville	2,225	4	4	0
Painesville	19,577	42	36	6	Springboro	17,422	27	24	3
Parma	81,661	156	100	56	Springdale	11,231	40	33	7
Parma Heights	20,733	37	31	6	Springfield	60,652	142	126	16
Paulding	3,608	5	4	1	Springfield Township, Hamilton County	36,346	56	50	6
Payne	1,195	1	1	0	Springfield Township, Mahoning County	6,708	8	8	0

Table V-9. Full-Time Law Enforcement Employees, by Selected State and City, 2011—*Continued*

(Number.)

State/City	Population	Total law enforcement employees	Total officers	Total civilians
Springfield Township, Summit County	17,725	24	21	3
St. Bernard	4,371	17	16	1
St. Clair Township	7,963	11	10	1
Steubenville	18,673	46	40	6
St. Henry	2,429	2	2	0
St. Marys	8,338	20	15	5
Stow	34,863	57	37	20
St. Paris	2,091	3	3	0
Strasburg	2,610	4	4	0
Streetsboro	16,040	35	27	8
Strongsville	44,783	100	73	27
Struthers	10,721	19	15	4
Sugarcreek	2,222	6	6	0
Sugarcreek Township	8,047	16	15	1
Sycamore	862	1	1	0
Sylvania	18,979	41	34	7
Sylvania Township	29,544	62	45	17
Tallmadge	17,550	26	23	3
Terrace Park	2,253	6	6	0
Thornville	992	1	1	0
Tiffin	17,976	37	27	10
Tipp City	9,696	20	17	3
Toledo	287,418	517	413	104
Toronto	5,095	10	10	0
Tremont City	375	2	2	0
Trotwood	24,449	36	34	2
Twinsburg	18,809	43	32	11
Uhrichsville	5,417	8	8	0
Union City	1,667	3	3	0
Union Township, Clermont County	46,450	66	53	13
University Heights	13,549	31	26	5
Upper Arlington	33,796	60	48	12
Upper Sandusky	6,601	17	13	4
Urbana	11,802	18	18	0
Utica	2,134	7	4	3
Valley View, Cuyahoga County	2,035	18	16	2
Valleyview, Franklin County	620	1	1	0
Vandalia	15,257	38	31	7
Van Wert	10,854	28	20	8
Vermilion	10,602	21	16	5
Vienna Township	3,983	1	1	0
Village of Leesburg	1,315	3	3	0
Wadsworth	21,583	39	30	9
Waite Hill	471	6	6	0
Walbridge	3,021	6	5	1
Walton Hills	2,283	15	12	3
Wapakoneta	9,874	19	14	5
Warren	41,587	82	66	16
Warrensville Heights	13,552	44	34	10
Warren Township	5,555	6	6	0
Washington Court House	14,202	25	20	5
Waterville	5,527	11	10	1
Wauseon	7,337	18	14	4
Waverly	4,411	10	7	3
Weathersfield	8,406	9	8	1
Wellington	4,806	9	6	3
Wellston	5,667	11	8	3
Wells Township	2,837	4	4	0
West Alexandria	1,341	3	3	0
West Carrollton	13,153	28	22	6
West Chester Township	58,638	116	89	27
Westerville	36,146	89	74	15
West Jefferson	4,225	14	11	3
West Lafayette	2,323	5	5	0
Westlake	32,753	67	49	18
West Salem	1,465	2	2	0
West Unity	1,672	8	8	0
Whitehall	18,075	58	46	12
Wickliffe	12,759	40	30	10
Willard	6,241	17	14	3
Willoughby	22,284	57	42	15
Willoughby Hills	9,492	23	17	6
Willowick	14,181	32	23	9
Wilmington	12,529	31	22	9

State/City	Population	Total law enforcement employees	Total officers	Total civilians
Winchester	1,052	3	3	0
Windham	2,211	8	8	0
Wintersville	3,927	11	9	2
Woodlawn	3,296	16	15	1
Woodmere Village	885	10	9	1
Woodville	2,137	5	5	0
Wooster	26,138	38	35	3
Worthington	13,585	45	32	13
Wyoming	8,434	21	19	2
Xenia	25,738	66	44	22
Yellow Springs	3,490	9	7	2
Youngstown	67,031	183	144	39
Zanesville	25,506	81	49	32
Oklahoma				
Achille	497	3	2	1
Ada	16,990	38	34	4
Allen	942	2	2	0
Altus	20,025	58	42	16
Alva	4,998	11	9	2
Anadarko	6,834	21	16	5
Antlers	2,479	10	5	5
Apache	1,459	7	4	3
Ardmore	24,543	66	47	19
Arkoma	2,010	6	3	3
Atoka	3,140	16	15	1
Bartlesville	36,133	74	53	21
Beaver	1,531	2	2	0
Beggs	1,335	9	3	6
Bethany	19,255	40	30	10
Bixby	21,108	32	24	8
Blackwell	7,168	22	16	6
Blanchard	7,752	18	12	6
Boise City	1,280	3	3	0
Boley	1,197	1	1	0
Bristow	4,267	18	13	5
Broken Arrow	99,908	170	126	44
Broken Bow	4,164	18	14	4
Caddo	1,008	3	3	0
Calera	2,187	8	6	2
Caney	207	4	3	1
Carnegie	1,741	9	6	3
Catoosa	7,228	12	11	1
Chandler	3,133	11	7	4
Checotah	3,371	13	10	3
Chelsea	1,985	8	3	5
Cherokee	1,514	6	2	4
Chickasha	16,208	36	28	8
Choctaw	11,265	13	12	1
Chouteau	2,119	9	8	1
Claremore	18,780	54	38	16
Clayton	830	6	2	4
Cleveland	3,286	5	5	0
Clinton	9,130	26	17	9
Coalgate	1,988	6	6	0
Colbert	1,152	5	4	1
Colcord	824	1	1	0
Collinsville	5,666	15	10	5
Comanche	1,681	4	4	0
Cordell	2,946	9	5	4
Coweta	10,049	21	14	7
Crescent	1,426	5	4	1
Cushing	7,910	22	15	7
Davenport	823	1	1	0
Davis	2,712	11	9	2
Del City	21,560	42	29	13
Dewar	898	1	1	0
Dewey	3,469	11	10	1
Dibble	887	1	1	0
Drumright	2,938	6	6	0
Duncan	23,682	53	46	7
Durant	16,026	41	38	3
Edmond	82,276	132	106	26
Elk City	11,818	35	24	11

Table V-9.   Full-Time Law Enforcement Employees, by Selected State and City, 2011—*Continued*

(Number.)

State/City	Population	Total law enforcement employees	Total officers	Total civilians	State/City	Population	Total law enforcement employees	Total officers	Total civilians
El Reno	16,928	42	30	12	Ninnekah	1,013	3	3	0
Enid	49,908	142	95	47	Noble	6,550	15	11	4
Eufaula	2,843	16	12	4	Norman	112,112	217	165	52
Fairfax	1,395	7	4	3	North Enid	869	3	3	0
Fairview	2,607	8	5	3	Nowata	3,771	12	6	6
Fletcher	1,190	1	1	0	Oilton	1,024	3	3	0
Forest Park	1,009	3	3	0	Okemah	3,258	11	7	4
Fort Gibson	4,198	10	10	0	Oklahoma City	586,208	1,281	1,020	261
Fort Supply	334	2	1	1	Okmulgee	12,453	29	22	7
Frederick	3,982	14	12	2	Oologah	1,158	3	3	0
Geary	1,294	12	6	6	Owasso	29,225	60	44	16
Glenpool	10,924	28	18	10	Pauls Valley	6,253	19	13	6
Goodwell	1,307	4	4	0	Pawhuska	3,622	12	8	4
Grove	6,694	28	20	8	Pawnee	2,220	5	5	0
Guthrie	10,300	28	21	7	Perkins	2,861	7	7	0
Guymon	11,564	27	18	9	Perry	5,181	20	13	7
Haileyville	822	3	3	0	Piedmont	5,781	13	10	3
Harrah	5,150	9	9	0	Pocola	4,099	8	5	3
Hartshorne	2,148	12	5	7	Ponca City	25,659	78	48	30
Haskell	2,028	6	6	0	Porum	735	2	2	0
Healdton	2,818	7	5	2	Poteau	8,611	28	23	5
Heavener	3,451	13	8	5	Prague	2,412	13	8	5
Hennessey	2,154	8	4	4	Pryor	9,641	29	22	7
Henryetta	5,990	17	12	5	Purcell	5,947	22	19	3
Hinton	3,230	5	5	0	Ringling	1,048	2	2	0
Hobart	3,796	14	8	6	Roland	3,203	11	6	5
Holdenville	5,833	15	10	5	Rush Springs	1,244	4	4	0
Hollis	2,082	10	6	4	Sallisaw	8,975	31	24	7
Hominy	3,603	9	5	4	Sand Springs	19,108	40	29	11
Hooker	1,939	3	3	0	Sapulpa	20,764	57	46	11
Howe	811	4	3	1	Sawyer	324	2	2	0
Hugo	5,367	17	16	1	Sayre	4,422	12	6	6
Hulbert	596	3	3	0	Seiling	869	3	3	0
Hydro	979	1	1	0	Seminole	7,568	15	12	3
Idabel	7,085	25	19	6	Shawnee	30,177	78	59	19
Jay	2,474	12	9	3	Skiatook	7,476	26	19	7
Jenks	17,105	25	19	6	Snyder	1,409	3	3	0
Jones	2,721	5	5	0	South Coffeyville	793	3	3	0
Kiefer	1,703	4	4	0	Sparks	171	1	1	0
Kingfisher	4,683	12	10	2	Spencer	3,954	9	8	1
Kingston	1,618	7	7	0	Spiro	2,187	4	4	0
Krebs	2,075	6	5	1	Stigler	2,714	12	8	4
Lahoma	618	1	1	0	Stillwater	46,177	114	73	41
Lawton	97,904	232	172	60	Stilwell	3,991	18	13	5
Lexington	2,175	10	6	4	Stonewall	475	2	2	0
Lindsay	2,870	11	7	4	Stratford	1,541	3	3	0
Locust Grove	1,438	7	3	4	Stringtown	414	5	4	1
Lone Grove	5,108	9	6	3	Stroud	2,719	12	9	3
Luther	1,234	6	6	0	Sulphur	4,982	11	9	2
Madill	3,810	12	11	1	Tahlequah	15,922	39	31	8
Mangum	3,042	10	6	4	Talihina	1,126	10	6	4
Mannford	3,109	9	7	2	Tecumseh	6,526	13	12	1
Marietta	2,654	6	5	1	Texhoma	936	2	2	0
Marlow	4,712	15	10	5	The Village	9,025	28	22	6
Maysville	1,245	6	4	2	Tishomingo	3,066	7	6	1
McAlester	18,580	56	43	13	Tonkawa	3,250	10	6	4
McCurtain	522	2	1	1	Tryon	496	1	1	0
McLoud	4,087	14	9	5	Tulsa	396,101	836	745	91
Medicine Park	386	3	2	1	Tushka	315	3	3	0
Meeker	1,156	4	4	0	Tuttle	6,083	13	10	3
Miami	13,715	42	31	11	Valliant	762	5	3	2
Midwest City	54,953	120	94	26	Verdigris	4,036	3	3	0
Minco	1,649	4	4	0	Vian	1,482	3	3	0
Moore	55,671	83	78	5	Vinita	5,804	21	15	6
Mooreland	1,203	2	2	0	Wagoner	8,412	19	13	6
Morris	1,495	2	2	0	Walters	2,578	4	4	0
Mountain View	804	2	2	0	Warner	1,659	4	4	0
Muldrow	3,503	14	8	6	Warr Acres	10,151	29	23	6
Muskogee	39,643	102	89	13	Washington	625	2	2	0
Mustang	17,581	27	20	7	Watonga	5,166	9	7	2
Newcastle	7,767	22	16	6	Waukomis	1,300	2	2	0
Newkirk	2,342	7	6	1	Waurika	2,086	3	3	0
Nichols Hills	3,750	21	16	5	Waynoka	937	3	3	0
Nicoma Park	2,419	4	4	0	Weatherford	10,949	33	22	11

Table V-9. Full-Time Law Enforcement Employees, by Selected State and City, 2011—*Continued*

(Number.)

State/City	Popula-tion	Total law enforce-ment employees	Total officers	Total civilians	State/City	Popula-tion	Total law enforce-ment employees	Total officers	Total civilians
Weleetka	1,009	11	6	5	Malin	814	1	1	0
Westville	1,657	9	5	4	Manzanita	604	3	3	0
Wetumka	1,296	6	5	1	McMinnville	32,530	41	34	7
Wewoka	3,467	10	6	4	Medford	75,704	134	100	34
Wilburton	2,873	7	6	1	Merrill	853	2	1	1
Wilson	1,742	4	4	0	Milton-Freewater	7,125	17	11	6
Woodward	12,180	43	28	15	Milwaukie	20,507	41	37	4
Wright City	770	2	2	0	Molalla	8,194	15	12	3
Wynnewood	2,236	6	5	1	Monmouth	9,635	16	13	3
Yale	1,240	6	3	3	Mount Angel	3,321	8	4	4
Yukon	22,952	60	38	22	Myrtle Creek	3,476	9	7	2
					Myrtle Point	2,541	5	5	0
Oregon					Newberg-Dundee	25,499	46	33	13
Adair Village	849	7	6	1	Newport	10,095	24	19	5
Albany	50,692	89	58	31	North Bend	9,798	23	16	7
Amity	1,631	2	2	0	North Plains	1,968	2	2	0
Ashland	20,292	33	26	7	Nyssa	3,302	8	8	0
Astoria	9,578	25	16	9	Oakridge	3,239	7	4	3
Athena	1,138	2	2	0	Ontario	11,487	31	23	8
Aumsville	3,622	7	6	1	Oregon City	32,198	47	40	7
Aurora	928	9	8	1	Pendleton	16,789	24	21	3
Baker City	9,933	16	15	1	Philomath	4,633	10	9	1
Bandon	3,099	7	6	1	Phoenix	4,586	10	8	2
Beaverton	90,759	173	137	36	Pilot Rock	1,518	3	3	0
Bend	77,455	112	88	24	Portland	589,991	1,201	956	245
Black Butte		7	6	1	Port Orford	1,145	2	2	0
Boardman	3,254	7	6	1	Prineville	9,352	25	15	10
Brookings	6,403	20	13	7	Rainier	1,915	6	5	1
Burns	2,836	5	4	1	Redmond	26,494	39	30	9
Canby	15,998	30	25	5	Reedsport	4,198	15	10	5
Cannon Beach	1,708	9	8	1	Rockaway Beach	1,326	3	3	0
Carlton	2,028	3	3	0	Rogue River	2,154	5	4	1
Central Point	17,352	32	26	6	Roseburg	21,406	41	36	5
Clatskanie	1,755	6	5	1	Salem	156,283	308	191	117
Coburg	1,046	4	3	1	Sandy	9,672	17	14	3
Columbia City	1,967	1	1	0	Scappoose	6,662	11	10	1
Condon	689	2	1	1	Seaside	6,526	27	18	9
Coos Bay	16,137	37	24	13	Sherwood	18,388	26	23	3
Coquille	3,907	8	7	1	Silverton	9,320	15	14	1
Cornelius	11,995	15	14	1	Springfield	60,035	118	65	53
Corvallis	55,042	80	53	27	Stanfield	2,065	4	4	0
Cottage Grove	9,789	26	17	9	Stayton	7,725	15	13	2
Dallas	14,738	31	20	11	St. Helens	13,020	17	16	1
Eagle Point	8,559	12	11	1	Sunriver		12	11	1
Elgin	1,729	4	3	1	Sutherlin	7,893	17	15	2
Enterprise	1,961	4	4	0	Sweet Home	9,020	22	15	7
Eugene	157,848	308	185	123	Talent	6,131	10	8	2
Fairview	9,015	17	14	3	The Dalles	13,765	25	23	2
Florence	8,556	22	14	8	Tigard	48,546	89	72	17
Forest Grove	21,307	33	29	4	Tillamook	4,988	11	8	3
Gearhart	1,478	3	3	0	Toledo	3,502	16	10	6
Gervais	2,490	8	7	1	Troutdale	16,132	27	23	4
Gladstone	11,619	18	15	3	Tualatin	26,331	47	37	10
Gold Beach	2,277	6	5	1	Turner	1,874	2	2	0
Grants Pass	34,901	79	50	29	Umatilla	6,980	12	9	3
Gresham	106,718	141	111	30	Vernonia	2,174	3	3	0
Hermiston	16,923	33	24	9	Warrenton	5,042	10	9	1
Hillsboro	92,586	164	120	44	West Linn	25,376	34	31	3
Hines	1,580	4	3	1	Weston	674	2	2	0
Hood River	7,243	14	13	1	Winston	5,436	8	7	1
Hubbard	3,207	7	6	1	Woodburn	24,336	39	31	8
Independence	8,681	14	12	2	Yamhill	1,035	3	3	0
Jacksonville	2,815	6	5	1					
John Day	1,763	4	4	0	**Pennsylvania**				
Junction City	5,449	16	10	6	Abington Township, Lackawanna County	1,749	2	2	0
Keizer	36,866	46	38	8	Abington Township, Montgomery County	55,486	113	89	24
King City	3,144	6	5	1	Adams Township, Butler County	11,689	6	6	0
Klamath Falls	21,062	43	38	5	Adams Township, Cambria County	5,991	3	3	0
La Grande	13,221	33	18	15	Akron	3,888	5	5	0
Lake Oswego	37,009	67	42	25	Albion	1,521	6	2	4
Lakeview	2,318	6	5	1	Alburtis	2,369	4	4	0
Lebanon	15,683	37	26	11	Aldan	4,165	6	6	0
Lincoln City	8,014	35	25	10	Aleppo Township	1,922	15	12	3
Madras	6,110	11	10	1	Aliquippa	9,468	18	18	0

Table V-9. Full-Time Law Enforcement Employees, by Selected State and City, 2011—*Continued*

(Number.)

State/City	Population	Total law enforcement employees	Total officers	Total civilians	State/City	Population	Total law enforcement employees	Total officers	Total civilians
Allegheny Township, Blair County	6,759	7	6	1	Buckingham Township	20,139	24	22	2
Allegheny Township, Westmoreland County	8,190	9	8	1	Buffalo Township	7,330	5	5	0
Allentown	118,408	217	197	20	Bushkill Township	8,204	17	16	1
Altoona	46,468	74	66	8	Butler	13,801	24	23	1
Ambler	6,437	15	13	2	Butler Township, Butler County	17,303	23	21	2
Ambridge	7,072	13	13	0	Butler Township, Luzerne County	9,250	9	8	1
Amity Township	12,623	13	12	1	Butler Township, Schuylkill County	6,006	4	4	0
Annville Township	4,782	8	5	3	Caernarvon Township, Berks County	4,019	9	8	1
Apollo	1,652	1	1	0	California	6,817	8	7	1
Archbald	7,006	5	5	0	Caln Township	13,861	19	18	1
Arnold	5,173	11	10	1	Cambria Township	6,118	3	3	0
Ashland	2,826	3	3	0	Cambridge Springs	2,603	3	3	0
Ashley	2,799	2	2	0	Camp Hill	7,913	11	10	1
Aspinwall	2,810	7	6	1	Canonsburg	9,021	17	17	0
Aston Township	16,645	18	16	2	Canton	1,982	3	3	0
Athens	3,378	5	4	1	Carbondale	8,919	12	12	0
Athens Township	5,268	10	9	1	Carlisle	18,742	37	32	5
Auburn	743	1	1	0	Carnegie	7,997	13	12	1
Austin	564	1	1	0	Carrolltown	856	2	2	0
Avalon	4,720	7	6	1	Carroll Township, Washinton County	5,658	2	2	0
Avonmore Boro	1,014	1	1	0	Carroll Township, York County	5,958	11	11	0
Baden	4,148	5	5	0	Carroll Valley	3,888	4	3	1
Baldwin Borough	19,830	27	25	2	Castle Shannon	8,343	13	12	1
Baldwin Township	1,998	5	5	0	Catasauqua	6,457	9	8	1
Bally	1,093	2	2	0	Catawissa	1,557	2	2	0
Bangor	5,290	10	9	1	Cecil Township	11,307	18	17	1
Barrett Township	4,238	5	5	0	Center Township	11,833	14	13	1
Beaver	4,545	10	9	1	Centerville	3,273	2	2	0
Beaver Falls	9,016	19	18	1	Central Berks Regional	9,420	15	14	1
Beaver Meadows	872	1	1	0	Chalfont	4,022	7	6	1
Bedford	2,850	5	5	0	Chambersburg	20,333	35	33	2
Bedminster Township	6,595	7	6	1	Charleroi	5,291	8	6	2
Bell Acres	1,392	3	3	0	Chartiers Township	7,843	11	11	0
Bellefonte	6,207	12	10	2	Cheltenham Township	36,910	90	79	11
Bellwood	1,834	2	2	0	Chester	34,080	112	102	10
Ben Avon	1,787	15	12	3	Chester Township	3,953	12	11	1
Ben Avon Heights	372	15	12	3	Cheswick	1,752	2	2	0
Bensalem Township	60,620	129	100	29	Chippewa Township	8,024	9	8	1
Berks-Lehigh Regional	30,614	31	30	1	Churchill	3,021	10	10	0
Berlin	2,111	2	2	0	Clairton	6,818	8	8	0
Bern Township	6,819	12	12	0	Clarion	5,293	9	8	1
Berwick	10,510	16	15	1	Clay Township	6,328	4	4	0
Bethel Park	32,416	44	38	6	Clearfield	6,235	10	6	4
Bethel Township, Berks County	4,125	2	2	0	Cleona	2,087	4	4	0
Bethlehem	75,221	184	158	26	Clifton Heights	6,673	10	9	1
Bethlehem Township	23,806	34	32	2	Coaldale	2,288	4	4	0
Biglerville	1,204	2	2	0	Coal Township	10,416	13	12	1
Birdsboro	5,179	8	7	1	Coatesville	13,142	44	35	9
Birmingham Township	4,221	4	4	0	Cochranton	1,140	2	2	0
Blairsville	3,423	3	3	0	Colebrookdale District	6,039	11	9	2
Blair Township	4,508	4	4	0	Collegeville	5,105	9	8	1
Blakely	6,585	5	5	0	Collier Township	7,103	15	14	1
Blawnox	1,437	4	4	0	Collingdale	8,814	9	8	1
Bloomsburg Town	14,902	21	15	6	Colonial Regional	19,495	26	24	2
Blythe Township	927	2	2	0	Columbia	10,433	19	16	3
Boyertown	4,068	8	7	1	Conemaugh Township, Cambria County	2,018	2	2	0
Brackenridge	3,270	4	4	0	Conemaugh Township, Somerset County	7,302	7	6	1
Bradford	8,798	22	22	0	Conewago Township, Adams County	7,108	10	9	1
Bradford Township	4,820	5	5	0	Conewango Township	3,605	4	4	0
Branch Township	1,846	1	1	0	Conneaut Lake Regional	3,597	4	3	1
Brecknock Township, Berks County	4,600	5	5	0	Conoy Township	3,204	16	14	2
Brentwood	9,674	17	15	2	Conshohocken	7,858	21	19	2
Briar Creek Township	3,026	4	4	0	Conway	2,183	2	2	0
Bridgeport	4,569	9	8	1	Conyngham	1,920	1	1	0
Bridgeville	5,164	9	8	1	Coopersburg	2,394	7	7	0
Bridgewater	706	3	3	0	Coplay	3,202	4	4	0
Brighton Township	8,253	6	6	0	Coraopolis	5,695	13	10	3
Bristol	9,757	18	16	2	Cornwall	4,125	8	7	1
Bristol Township	54,756	82	70	12	Corry	6,626	11	9	2
Brockway	2,079	2	2	0	Covington Township	2,291	3	3	0
Brookhaven	8,032	7	6	1	Cranberry Township	28,188	34	28	6
Brookville	3,937	6	5	1	Crescent Township	2,648	4	4	0
Brownsville	2,338	2	2	0	Cresson	1,716	10	10	0
Bryn Athyn	1,379	5	5	0	Cresson Township	4,350	3	2	1

Table V-9.   Full-Time Law Enforcement Employees, by Selected State and City, 2011—*Continued*

(Number.)

State/City	Population	Total law enforcement employees	Total officers	Total civilians
Croyle Township	2,346	1	1	0
Cumberland Township, Adams County	6,182	6	6	0
Cumberland Township, Greene County	6,644	4	4	0
Cumru Township	15,195	27	25	2
Curwensville	2,550	1	1	0
Dale	1,238	2	2	0
Dallas	2,813	4	4	0
Dallas Township	9,023	8	8	0
Dalton	1,238	2	2	0
Danville	4,714	9	7	2
Darby	10,721	12	11	1
Darby Township	9,294	14	14	0
Decatur Township	4,563	2	2	0
Delmont	2,695	4	4	0
Derry	2,697	3	3	0
Derry Township, Dauphin County	24,758	46	38	8
Dickson City	6,089	8	6	2
Donegal Township	2,473	2	2	0
Donora	4,796	6	6	0
Dormont	8,620	16	15	1
Douglass Township, Berks County	3,317	4	4	0
Douglass Township, Montgomery County	10,228	10	9	1
Downingtown	7,916	19	16	3
Doylestown	8,407	20	15	5
Doylestown Township	17,621	23	21	2
Dublin Borough	2,165	2	2	0
Du Bois	7,819	13	13	0
Duboistown	1,209	1	1	0
Duncannon	1,527	1	1	0
Duncansville	1,237	2	2	0
Dunmore	14,102	19	19	0
Dunnstable Township	1,011	1	1	0
Duquesne	5,583	15	14	1
Duryea	4,933	2	2	0
East Bangor	1,176	1	1	0
East Berlin	1,526	1	1	0
East Bethlehem Township	2,362	1	1	0
East Brandywine Township	6,763	10	9	1
East Buffalo Township	6,434	8	8	0
East Cocalico Township	10,343	24	22	2
East Coventry Township	6,657	8	7	1
East Deer Township	1,505	1	1	0
Eastern Adams Regional	10,735	11	10	1
Eastern Pike Regional	4,807	10	9	1
East Fallowfield Township	7,473	7	7	0
East Hempfield Township	23,597	36	33	3
East Lampeter Township	16,476	42	38	4
East Lansdowne	2,677	5	3	2
East Marlborough Township	7,048	1	1	0
East McKeesport	2,715	3	3	0
East Norriton Township	13,633	30	27	3
East Pennsboro Township	20,293	20	19	1
East Penn Township	2,890	2	2	0
East Pikeland Township	7,102	8	7	1
East Pittsburgh	1,828	1	1	0
East Taylor Township	2,735	1	1	0
Easttown Township	10,510	15	14	1
East Vincent Township	6,843	6	6	0
East Washington	2,241	1	1	0
East Whiteland Township	10,684	21	19	2
Ebensburg	3,362	3	3	0
Economy	8,999	12	11	1
Eddystone	2,418	10	9	1
Edgewood	3,128	12	10	2
Edgeworth	1,685	6	4	2
Edinboro	6,459	8	8	0
Edwardsville	4,831	5	5	0
Elizabethtown	11,582	18	16	2
Elizabeth Township	13,313	11	11	0
Elkland	1,827	2	2	0
Ellwood City	7,946	12	10	2
Emmaus	11,247	20	18	2
Emsworth	2,457	15	12	3
Ephrata	13,437	34	29	5
Erie	102,111	196	172	24
Etna	3,462	7	6	1
Everett	1,840	3	3	0
Exeter	5,670	3	3	0
Exeter Township, Berks County	25,631	33	30	3
Exeter Township, Luzerne County	2,386	7	7	0
Fairview Township, Luzerne County	4,534	5	5	0
Fairview Township, York County	16,721	18	16	2
Falls Township, Bucks County	34,409	60	53	7
Fawn Township	2,384	2	2	0
Ferguson Township	17,746	25	22	3
Ferndale	1,641	1	1	0
Findlay Township	5,076	23	16	7
Fleetwood	4,098	6	6	0
Folcroft	6,627	11	10	1
Ford City	3,001	3	3	0
Forest City	1,917	2	2	0
Forest Hills	6,539	10	10	0
Forks Township	14,768	24	23	1
Forty Fort	4,227	5	5	0
Forward Township	3,387	4	4	0
Foster Township	4,330	4	4	0
Fountain Hill	4,612	11	10	1
Fox Chapel	5,405	12	12	0
Frackville	3,817	4	4	0
Franconia Township	13,106	17	15	2
Franklin	6,566	23	17	6
Franklin Park	13,513	14	13	1
Franklin Township, Carbon County	4,276	4	4	0
Frazer Township	1,161	2	2	0
Freedom Township	3,469	2	2	0
Freeland	3,542	2	2	0
Freemansburg	2,644	2	1	1
Freeport	1,819	2	2	0
Galeton	1,153	1	1	0
Gallitzin	1,919	7	7	0
Geistown	2,475	1	1	0
Gettysburg	7,644	17	13	4
Gilpin Township	2,504	1	1	0
Glassport	4,497	6	6	0
Glenolden	7,176	11	10	1
Granville Township	5,120	9	7	2
Greencastle	4,009	6	5	1
Greenfield Township, Blair County	4,186	4	4	0
Greensburg	14,939	38	28	10
Green Tree	4,446	11	10	1
Greenville	5,938	10	9	1
Greenwood Township	1,958	1	1	0
Grove City	8,349	12	11	1
Hamburg	4,303	7	6	1
Hamiltonban Township	2,380	1	1	0
Hampden Township	28,133	24	23	1
Hanover	15,338	28	25	3
Hanover Township, Luzerne County	11,111	15	14	1
Hanover Township, Washington County	2,682	9	3	6
Harmony Township	3,207	5	5	0
Harrisburg	49,686	230	179	51
Harrison Township	10,494	21	18	3
Harveys Lake	2,800	6	6	0
Hastings	1,282	1	1	0
Hatboro	7,383	17	14	3
Hatfield Township	20,604	32	27	5
Haverford Township	48,646	82	70	12
Hazleton	25,421	44	41	3
Heidelberg	1,248	3	3	0
Heidelberg Township, Berks County	1,729	1	1	0
Hellam Township	8,744	10	8	2
Hellertown	5,917	11	10	1
Hemlock Township	2,256	6	6	0
Hempfield Township, Mercer County	3,753	6	5	1
Hermitage	16,272	32	29	3
Highspire	2,407	6	6	0
Hilltown Township	15,077	20	17	3
Hollidaysburg	5,809	11	8	3

Table V-9. Full-Time Law Enforcement Employees, by Selected State and City, 2011—*Continued*

(Number.)

State/City	Popula-tion	Total law enforce-ment employees	Total officers	Total civilians	State/City	Popula-tion	Total law enforce-ment employees	Total officers	Total civilians
Homer City	1,712	2	2	0	Lower Allen Township	18,037	20	19	1
Homestead	3,175	13	12	1	Lower Burrell	11,799	16	16	0
Honesdale	4,494	8	8	0	Lower Chichester Township	3,480	5	5	0
Honey Brook	1,718	1	1	0	Lower Frederick Township	4,855	2	2	0
Hooversville	647	1	1	0	Lower Gwynedd Township	11,441	18	17	1
Hopewell Township	12,633	16	15	1	Lower Heidelberg Township	5,531	9	8	1
Horsham Township	26,230	46	39	7	Lower Makefield Township	32,663	42	38	4
Hughestown	1,396	1	1	0	Lower Merion Township	58,009	139	124	15
Hughesville	2,135	2	2	0	Lower Milford Township	3,787	2	2	0
Hummelstown	4,552	7	7	0	Lower Moreland Township	13,023	26	21	5
Huntingdon	7,116	11	11	0	Lower Paxton Township	47,511	63	56	7
Independence Township, Beaver County	2,511	3	3	0	Lower Pottsgrove Township	12,097	19	17	2
Indiana	14,020	24	22	2	Lower Providence Township	25,517	32	32	0
Indiana Township	7,276	10	10	0	Lower Salford Township	15,007	19	17	2
Industry	1,841	12	12	0	Lower Saucon Township	10,806	17	15	2
Ingram	3,341	4	4	0	Lower Southampton Township	18,969	33	30	3
Irwin	3,986	3	3	0	Lower Swatara Township	8,294	16	15	1
Ivyland	1,044	2	2	0	Lower Windsor Township	7,406	10	9	1
Jackson Township, Butler County	3,669	10	8	2	Luzerne Township	5,984	1	1	0
Jackson Township, Cambria County	4,406	2	2	0	Lykens	1,785	1	1	0
Jackson Township, Luzerne County	4,661	4	4	0	Macungie	3,084	6	6	0
Jeannette	9,685	17	14	3	Mahanoy City	4,175	4	4	0
Jefferson Hills Borough	10,653	18	17	1	Mahanoy Township	3,162	1	1	0
Jefferson Township, Mercer County	1,886	2	2	0	Mahoning Township, Carbon County	4,319	4	4	0
Jenkins Township	4,456	2	2	0	Mahoning Township, Lawrence County	3,093	2	2	0
Jenkintown	4,436	13	11	2	Mahoning Township, Montour County	4,184	7	6	1
Jermyn	2,176	1	1	0	Malvern	3,008	6	5	1
Jim Thorpe	4,796	7	6	1	Manheim	4,873	9	8	1
Johnstown	22,572	41	37	4	Manheim Township	38,255	79	63	16
Kane	3,742	5	5	0	Manor	3,249	2	2	0
Kennedy Township	7,696	15	11	4	Manor Township, Lancaster County	19,675	19	17	2
Kennett Square	6,091	14	12	2	Mansfield	3,637	5	5	0
Kidder Township	1,941	6	6	0	Marcus Hook	2,405	7	6	1
Kilbuck Township	699	15	12	3	Marietta	2,596	16	14	2
Kingston	13,224	20	19	1	Marion Township, Beaver County	916	2	2	0
Kingston Township	7,021	11	11	0	Marion Township, Berks County	1,693	3	3	0
Kiskiminetas Township	4,815	1	1	0	Marlborough Township	3,188	3	3	0
Kittanning	4,057	9	8	1	Marple Township	23,503	32	27	5
Knox	1,150	3	3	0	Mars	1,704	1	1	0
Koppel	764	2	2	0	Martinsburg	1,964	2	2	0
Kulpmont	2,933	1	1	0	Marysville	2,542	2	2	0
Kutztown	5,028	13	11	2	Masontown	3,461	5	5	0
Laflin Borough	1,492	3	3	0	Mayfield	1,813	1	1	0
Lake City	3,041	3	3	0	McAdoo	2,307	3	3	0
Lancaster	59,511	165	142	23	McCandless	28,548	29	27	2
Lancaster Township, Butler County	2,540	1	1	0	McDonald Borough	2,156	3	3	0
Langhorne Borough	1,627	8	8	0	McKeesport	19,794	55	52	3
Lansdale	16,321	31	23	8	McKees Rocks	6,123	12	11	1
Lansdowne	10,654	19	16	3	McSherrystown	3,048	4	4	0
Lansford	3,954	10	9	1	Meadville	13,431	25	22	3
Larksville	4,494	4	4	0	Mechanicsburg	9,010	16	15	1
Latimore Township	2,588	1	1	0	Media	5,344	19	16	3
Latrobe	8,365	12	12	0	Mercer	2,008	4	4	0
Laureldale	3,923	5	5	0	Mercersburg	1,566	2	2	0
Lawrence Park Township	3,995	8	7	1	Meshoppen	565	1	1	0
Lawrence Township, Clearfield County	7,705	9	8	1	Meyersdale	2,191	2	2	0
Lebanon	25,558	48	42	6	Middleburg	1,313	3	2	1
Leechburg	2,163	3	3	0	Middlesex Township, Butler County	5,407	3	3	0
Leetsdale	1,222	5	5	0	Middlesex Township, Cumberland County	7,062	10	9	1
Leet Township	1,639	4	4	0	Middletown	8,929	21	16	5
Lehighton	5,518	10	9	1	Middletown Township	45,581	57	51	6
Lehigh Township, Northampton County	10,560	13	12	1	Midland	2,643	5	4	1
Lehman Township	3,519	2	2	0	Mifflin	644	1	1	0
Lewisburg	5,810	10	8	2	Mifflinburg	3,551	10	9	1
Lewistown	8,365	13	11	2	Mifflin County Regional	20,835	16	15	1
Liberty	2,559	1	1	0	Mifflin Township	2,329	4	4	0
Liberty Township, Adams County	1,241	1	1	0	Milford	1,024	2	2	0
Ligonier	1,578	2	2	0	Millbourne	1,163	1	1	0
Ligonier Township	6,624	4	4	0	Millcreek Township, Erie County	53,686	73	59	14
Limerick Township	18,132	17	16	1	Millersburg	2,565	5	4	1
Lincoln	1,075	2	2	0	Millersville	8,194	14	12	2
Lititz	9,399	16	13	3	Millvale	3,756	4	4	0
Littlestown	4,448	8	7	1	Millville	951	1	1	0
Logan Township	12,328	18	16	2	Minersville	4,411	5	5	0

Table V-9.   Full-Time Law Enforcement Employees, by Selected State and City, 2011—*Continued*

(Number.)

State/City	Population	Total law enforcement employees	Total officers	Total civilians	State/City	Population	Total law enforcement employees	Total officers	Total civilians
Mohnton	3,053	4	4	0	North Middleton Township	11,179	10	9	1
Monaca	5,755	9	9	0	North Strabane Township	13,451	20	19	1
Monessen	7,745	12	12	0	Northumberland	3,816	5	5	0
Monongahela	4,314	9	7	2	North Versailles Township	12,459	23	20	3
Monroeville	28,477	56	46	10	North Wales	3,239	5	4	1
Montgomery	1,584	3	3	0	Northwest Lancaster County Regional	18,190	17	15	2
Montgomery Township	24,869	43	36	7	Norwood	5,909	8	7	1
Montrose	1,622	1	1	0	Oakmont	6,323	7	7	0
Moon Township	24,262	36	30	6	O'Hara Township	8,434	16	15	1
Moore Township	9,227	9	8	1	Ohio Township	4,772	15	12	3
Moosic	5,737	10	10	0	Ohioville	3,544	2	2	0
Morris-Cooper Regional	5,660	1	1	0	Oil City	10,591	23	18	5
Morrisville	8,756	12	11	1	Old Forge	8,340	5	5	0
Morton	2,678	5	4	1	Old Lycoming Township	4,954	11	10	1
Moscow	2,032	3	3	0	Oley Township	3,632	5	5	0
Mount Carmel	5,912	9	9	0	Oliver Township	1,937	1	1	0
Mount Carmel Township	3,149	6	6	0	Olyphant	5,167	5	5	0
Mount Holly Springs	2,036	3	3	0	Orangeville Area	1,771	1	1	0
Mount Joy	7,434	14	13	1	Orwigsburg	3,109	4	4	0
Mount Lebanon	33,243	53	44	9	Overfield Township	2,833	3	3	0
Mount Oliver	3,414	10	10	0	Oxford	5,093	12	11	1
Mount Pleasant	4,468	3	3	0	Paint Township	3,159	5	4	1
Mount Pleasant Township	3,526	3	3	0	Palmerton	5,431	9	8	1
Mount Union	2,455	5	5	0	Palmer Township	20,757	33	30	3
Mountville	2,811	23	20	3	Palmyra	7,343	10	9	1
Muhlenberg Township	19,691	34	32	2	Palo Alto	1,035	1	1	0
Muncy	2,485	3	3	0	Parkesburg	3,604	10	9	1
Munhall	11,442	25	21	4	Parkside	2,335	3	3	0
Murrysville	20,143	26	21	5	Parks Township	2,753	2	2	0
Myerstown	3,072	3	3	0	Patterson Township	3,039	4	4	0
Nanticoke	10,498	14	13	1	Patton	1,775	2	2	0
Nanty Glo	2,743	2	2	0	Patton Township	15,360	19	17	2
Narberth	4,296	5	5	0	Paxtang	1,566	3	3	0
Neshannock Township	9,640	7	7	0	Pen Argyl	3,606	5	5	0
Nesquehoning	3,360	4	4	0	Penbrook	3,018	8	8	0
Nether Providence Township	13,750	17	16	1	Penndel	2,335	1	1	0
Neville Township	1,087	15	12	3	Penn Hills	42,464	55	51	4
Newberry Township	15,334	18	16	2	Pennridge Regional	10,997	15	13	2
New Bethlehem	992	4	2	2	Penn Township, Butler County	5,087	4	3	1
New Brighton	9,241	9	7	2	Penn Township, Lancaster County	8,817	8	7	1
New Britain	3,162	5	4	1	Penn Township, Perry County	3,235	6	5	1
New Britain Township	11,105	14	12	2	Penn Township, Westmoreland County	20,069	23	21	2
New Cumberland	7,300	8	7	1	Penn Township, York County	15,662	25	23	2
New Garden Township	12,022	10	9	1	Pequea Township	4,620	7	7	0
New Hanover Township	10,974	10	9	1	Perkasie	8,538	21	19	2
New Holland	5,395	13	12	1	Perryopolis	1,790	2	2	0
New Hope	2,536	11	9	2	Peters Township	21,281	23	21	2
New Kensington	13,158	22	22	0	Philadelphia	1,530,873	7,427	6,625	802
New Philadelphia	1,088	1	1	0	Phoenixville	16,492	28	27	1
Newport	1,579	2	2	0	Pine Creek Township	3,225	1	1	0
Newport Township	5,391	2	2	0	Pine Grove	2,193	1	1	0
New Sewickley Township	7,383	7	7	0	Pitcairn	3,305	5	4	1
Newton Township	2,855	1	1	0	Pittsburgh	308,609	943	880	63
Newtown	2,255	5	5	0	Pittston	7,764	7	7	0
Newtown Township, Bucks County	22,366	32	28	4	Plainfield Township	6,158	12	12	0
Newtown Township, Delaware County	12,255	19	17	2	Plains Township	9,993	20	19	1
Norristown	34,433	79	65	14	Pleasant Hills	8,294	20	18	2
Northampton	9,958	12	10	2	Plum	27,213	30	24	6
Northampton Township	39,853	49	43	6	Plumstead Township	12,482	18	16	2
North Belle Vernon	1,977	3	2	1	Plymouth Township, Montgomery County	16,578	50	43	7
North Catasauqua	2,858	4	4	0	Pocono Mountain Regional	39,202	43	38	5
North Charleroi	1,317	1	1	0	Pocono Township	11,100	18	17	1
North Cornwall Township	7,577	10	9	1	Point Marion	1,163	1	1	0
North Coventry Township	7,891	16	15	1	Point Township	3,697	5	5	0
North East, Erie County	4,308	8	7	1	Polk	819	2	2	0
Northeastern Regional	11,456	13	11	2	Portage	2,646	1	1	0
Northern Berks Regional	12,730	15	14	1	Port Allegany	2,164	3	3	0
Northern Cambria Borough	3,847	3	3	0	Port Carbon	1,895	2	2	0
Northern Regional	30,781	30	28	2	Port Vue	3,810	3	3	0
Northern York Regional	66,820	55	50	5	Pottstown	22,448	57	45	12
North Fayette Township	13,978	26	20	6	Pottsville	14,370	29	28	1
North Franklin Township	4,598	6	6	0	Pringle	982	20	19	1
North Huntingdon Township	30,707	35	29	6	Prospect Park	6,475	9	9	0
North Londonderry Township	8,094	10	9	1	Pulaski Township, Lawrence County	3,463	2	2	0

Table V-9.   Full-Time Law Enforcement Employees, by Selected State and City, 2011—*Continued*

(Number.)

State/City	Population	Total law enforcement employees	Total officers	Total civilians	State/City	Population	Total law enforcement employees	Total officers	Total civilians
Punxsutawney	5,981	10	6	4	South Centre Township	1,943	4	4	0
Pymatuning Township	3,291	5	5	0	South Coatesville	1,307	2	2	0
Quakertown	9,008	23	15	8	South Connellsville Borough	1,976	2	2	0
Quarryville	2,584	4	4	0	Southern Regional Lancaster County	3,788	7	7	0
Raccoon Township	3,074	3	3	0	Southern Regional York County	10,623	12	11	1
Radnor Township	31,632	57	47	10	South Fayette Township	14,462	18	17	1
Ralpho Township	4,335	6	6	0	South Fork	931	2	2	0
Rankin	2,129	1	1	0	South Greensburg	2,124	2	2	0
Reading	88,363	181	156	25	South Heidelberg Township	7,294	7	7	0
Redstone Township	5,584	2	2	0	South Lebanon Township	9,493	8	7	1
Reilly Township	728	1	1	0	South Londonderry Township	7,013	7	6	1
Reserve Township	3,344	6	6	0	South Park Township	13,459	18	17	1
Reynoldsville	2,768	2	2	0	Southwestern Regional	17,586	14	13	1
Rice Township	3,346	5	5	0	Southwest Greensburg	2,162	2	2	0
Richland Township, Bucks County	13,094	14	12	2	Southwest Mercer County Regional	10,569	22	21	1
Richland Township, Cambria County	12,855	21	20	1	Southwest Regional	8,174	3	2	1
Ridgway	4,091	6	5	1	South Whitehall Township	19,241	41	38	3
Ridley Park	7,024	15	10	5	South Williamsport	6,399	7	7	0
Ridley Township	30,886	37	32	5	Spring City	3,334	4	3	1
Riverside	1,938	3	3	0	Springdale	3,416	4	4	0
Roaring Brook Township	1,913	1	1	0	Springdale Township	1,641	4	4	0
Roaring Spring	2,593	3	3	0	Springettsbury Township	26,753	35	32	3
Robeson Township	7,239	7	6	1	Springfield Township, Bucks County	5,051	4	4	0
Robinson Township, Allegheny County	13,397	29	27	2	Springfield Township, Delaware County	24,288	36	31	5
Rochester	3,669	10	8	2	Springfield Township, Montgomery County	19,480	31	29	2
Rochester Township	2,811	4	4	0	Spring Garden Township	12,618	22	19	3
Rockledge	2,551	4	4	0	Spring Township, Berks County	27,205	30	29	1
Rosslyn Farms	428	2	2	0	Spring Township, Centre County	7,494	8	7	1
Ross Township	31,204	48	42	6	State College	56,608	74	61	13
Rostraver Township	11,399	15	14	1	St. Clair Boro	3,014	6	6	0
Rush Township	3,423	3	3	0	St. Clair Township	1,523	1	1	0
Sadsbury Township, Chester County	3,581	2	2	0	Steelton	6,009	9	8	1
Salem Township, Luzerne County	4,268	4	4	0	Stewartstown	2,096	6	5	1
Salisbury Township	13,548	19	17	2	Stoneboro	1,054	1	1	0
Sandy Lake	661	2	1	1	Stonycreek Township	2,853	3	3	0
Sandy Township	10,659	8	7	1	Stowe Township	6,382	8	7	1
Saxton	738	1	1	0	Strasburg	2,818	4	4	0
Sayre	5,605	14	14	0	Stroud Area Regional	34,730	62	55	7
Schuylkill Haven	5,454	8	8	0	Sugarcreek	5,311	5	4	1
Schuylkill Township, Chester County	8,543	13	11	2	Sugarloaf Township, Luzerne County	4,224	2	2	0
Scottdale	4,398	7	7	0	Sugar Notch	992	4	1	3
Scott Township, Allegheny County	17,078	21	20	1	Summerhill Township	2,475	2	2	0
Scott Township, Columbia County	5,129	11	11	0	Summit Hill	3,044	6	4	2
Scott Township, Lackawanna County	4,921	5	5	0	Summit Township	2,278	1	1	0
Scranton	76,332	170	150	20	Sunbury	9,937	14	13	1
Selinsgrove	5,672	6	5	1	Susquehanna Regional	7,780	16	14	2
Sewickley	4,388	9	7	2	Susquehanna Township, Dauphin County	24,113	41	39	2
Sewickley Heights	813	5	3	2	Swarthmore	6,214	9	9	0
Shaler Township	28,849	25	25	0	Swatara Township	23,436	52	49	3
Shamokin	7,398	13	12	1	Sweden Township	875	1	1	0
Shamokin Dam	1,691	3	3	0	Swissvale	9,012	14	14	0
Sharon Hill	5,715	10	9	1	Swoyersville	5,078	6	6	0
Sharpsburg	3,457	6	6	0	Sykesville	1,161	1	1	0
Sharpsville	4,429	6	5	1	Tamaqua	7,130	10	9	1
Shenandoah	5,087	4	4	0	Tarentum	4,544	8	7	1
Shenango Township, Lawrence County	7,503	6	6	0	Tatamy	1,207	1	1	0
Shillington	5,290	9	8	1	Taylor	6,283	6	6	0
Shippensburg	5,510	10	9	1	Telford	4,888	7	6	1
Shippingport	215	2	2	0	Throop	4,101	6	6	0
Shiremanstown	1,574	2	2	0	Tiadaghton Valley Regional	6,692	11	10	1
Shohola Township	2,483	1	1	0	Tidioute	690	1	1	0
Silver Lake Township	1,721	1	1	0	Tilden Township	3,608	2	2	0
Silver Spring Township	13,701	18	16	2	Tinicum Township, Bucks County	4,008	5	5	0
Sinking Spring	4,021	7	6	1	Tinicum Township, Delaware County	4,104	17	15	2
Slatington	4,245	7	7	0	Titusville	5,619	10	10	0
Slippery Rock	3,637	3	3	0	Towamencin Township	17,634	27	22	5
Smithton Borough	400	1	1	0	Towanda	2,928	6	6	0
Smith Township	4,490	1	1	0	Trafford	3,184	3	3	0
Solebury Township	8,720	16	14	2	Tredyffrin Township	29,426	53	47	6
Somerset	6,297	8	7	1	Troy	1,358	3	3	0
Souderton	6,639	7	6	1	Tulpehocken Township	3,284	3	3	0
South Abington Township	9,102	12	10	2	Tunkhannock	1,842	5	5	0
South Beaver Township	2,726	4	4	0	Tunkhannock Township, Wyoming County	4,287	4	4	0
South Buffalo Township	2,644	2	2	0	Turtle Creek	5,366	6	5	1

Table V-9.   Full-Time Law Enforcement Employees, by Selected State and City, 2011—Continued

(Number.)

State/City	Population	Total law enforcement employees	Total officers	Total civilians	State/City	Population	Total law enforcement employees	Total officers	Total civilians
Tyrone	5,494	14	11	3	West Penn Township	4,456	3	3	0
Union City	3,331	3	3	0	West Pikeland Township	4,037	4	4	0
Uniontown	10,405	23	23	0	West Pittston	4,884	3	3	0
Union Township, Lawrence County	5,207	4	4	0	West Pottsgrove Township	3,886	10	9	1
Upland	3,249	6	5	1	West Reading	4,225	17	15	2
Upper Allen Township	18,117	21	20	1	West Sadsbury Township	2,452	4	4	0
Upper Burrell Township	2,333	2	2	0	West Shore Regional	7,648	12	10	2
Upper Chichester Township	16,791	24	23	1	Westtown-East Goshen Regional	31,972	30	27	3
Upper Darby Township	83,059	145	126	19	West View	6,793	12	8	4
Upper Dublin Township	25,651	47	40	7	West Vincent Township	4,582	6	5	1
Upper Gwynedd Township	15,602	24	21	3	West Whiteland Township	18,332	27	25	2
Upper Makefield Township	8,216	16	15	1	West Wyoming	2,734	1	1	0
Upper Merion Township	28,486	79	61	18	West York	4,632	10	10	0
Upper Moreland Township	24,092	44	36	8	Whitehall	13,988	25	20	5
Upper Nazareth Township	6,251	4	3	1	Whitehall Township	26,823	50	44	6
Upper Perkiomen	6,815	10	9	1	White Haven Borough	1,100	2	2	0
Upper Pottsgrove Township	5,332	9	8	1	Whitemarsh Township	17,404	40	34	6
Upper Providence Township, Delaware County	10,174	14	13	1	White Oak	7,887	12	11	1
Upper Providence Township, Montgomery County	21,287	26	24	2	White Township	1,398	4	4	0
					Whitpain Township	18,935	38	30	8
Upper Saucon Township	14,855	20	19	1	Wiconisco Township	1,214	1	1	0
Upper Southampton Township	15,200	24	21	3	Wilkes-Barre	41,630	87	84	3
Upper St. Clair Township	19,290	35	28	7	Wilkes-Barre Township	2,976	15	14	1
Upper Uwchlan Township	11,263	10	10	0	Wilkinsburg	15,981	28	24	4
Upper Yoder Township	5,466	13	13	0	Wilkins Township	6,377	12	12	0
Uwchlan Township	18,146	24	22	2	Williamsburg	1,258	1	1	0
Valley Township	6,816	5	5	0	Williamsport	29,475	54	50	4
Vandergrift	5,222	8	8	0	Willistown Township	10,530	19	17	2
Vandling	753	2	2	0	Wilson	7,921	9	8	1
Vernon Township	5,648	5	4	1	Wrightsville	2,317	3	3	0
Verona	2,482	4	3	1	Wright Township	5,669	7	7	0
Versailles	1,520	3	3	0	Wyoming	3,083	4	4	0
Walker Township	1,057	1	1	0	Wyomissing	10,494	25	23	2
Walnutport	2,077	3	3	0	Yardley	2,442	3	3	0
Warminster Township	32,786	52	47	5	Yeadon	11,479	17	15	2
Warren	9,741	21	15	6	York	43,857	118	105	13
Warrington Township	23,493	32	30	2	York Area Regional	60,596	55	50	5
Warwick Township, Bucks County	14,483	19	17	2	Youngsville	1,735	2	2	0
Warwick Township, Lancaster County	17,840	14	13	1	Zelienople	3,824	10	9	1
Washington, Washington County	13,707	33	31	2					
Washington Township, Fayette County	3,914	2	2	0	**Rhode Island**				
Washington Township, Franklin County	14,054	16	14	2	Barrington	16,290	31	24	7
Washington Township, Northampton County	5,138	5	5	0	Bristol	22,927	49	38	11
Washington Township, Westmoreland County	7,446	6	6	0	Burrillville	15,936	27	21	6
Watsontown	2,358	5	5	0	Central Falls	19,353	39	33	6
Waynesboro	10,602	20	18	2	Charlestown	7,818	25	20	5
Waynesburg	4,189	9	8	1	Coventry	34,972	67	52	15
Weatherly	2,533	4	4	0	Cranston	80,290	167	138	29
Weissport	413	1	1	0	Cumberland	33,466	56	47	9
Wellsboro	3,273	6	6	0	East Greenwich	13,130	40	32	8
Wesleyville	3,352	11	10	1	East Providence	46,980	108	90	18
West Brandywine Township	7,418	4	4	0	Foster	4,600	14	8	6
West Caln Township	9,043	2	2	0	Glocester	9,734	19	14	5
West Chester	18,520	60	47	13	Hopkinton	8,178	20	15	5
West Conshohocken	1,324	11	10	1	Jamestown	5,399	16	12	4
West Deer Township	11,809	12	11	1	Johnston	28,734	88	71	17
West Earl Township	7,893	6	6	0	Lincoln	21,080	42	35	7
Western Berks Regional	4,570	5	5	0	Little Compton	3,488	13	9	4
West Fallowfield Township	2,574	2	2	0	Middletown	16,131	43	38	5
Westfield	1,067	2	2	0	Narragansett	15,849	50	38	12
West Goshen Township	21,936	32	28	4	Newport	24,641	92	77	15
West Grove Borough	2,863	2	2	0	New Shoreham	1,050	9	5	4
West Hazleton	4,609	3	2	1	North Kingstown	26,454	48	40	8
West Hempfield Township	16,205	23	20	3	North Providence	32,039	83	62	21
West Hills Regional	10,943	12	11	1	North Smithfield	11,953	26	22	4
West Homestead	1,935	14	6	8	Pawtucket	71,062	164	138	26
West Lampeter Township	15,258	16	15	1	Portsmouth	17,368	34	33	1
West Mahanoy Township	2,881	3	3	0	Providence	177,830	561	471	90
West Manchester Township	18,954	29	26	3	Richmond	7,699	15	13	2
West Manheim Township	7,769	9	8	1	Scituate	10,317	22	16	6
West Mead Township	5,266	2	2	0	Smithfield	21,404	54	40	14
West Mifflin	20,378	42	36	6	South Kingstown	30,602	68	50	18
West Newton	2,641	2	2	0	Tiverton	15,761	37	27	10
West Norriton Township	15,713	33	29	4	Warren	10,598	27	21	6

Table V-9.   Full-Time Law Enforcement Employees, by Selected State and City, 2011—*Continued*

(Number.)

State/City	Population	Total law enforcement employees	Total officers	Total civilians	State/City	Population	Total law enforcement employees	Total officers	Total civilians
Warwick	82,572	209	160	49	Georgetown	9,270	35	31	4
Westerly	22,760	60	49	11	Goose Creek	36,357	83	60	23
West Greenwich	6,128	14	9	5	Great Falls	2,002	5	5	0
West Warwick	29,156	69	57	12	Greeleyville	443	3	3	0
Woonsocket	41,137	111	97	14	Greenville	59,089	235	190	45
					Greenwood	23,492	58	51	7
South Carolina					Greer	25,812	68	52	16
Abbeville	5,298	23	19	4	Hampton	2,841	11	11	0
Aiken	29,868	110	83	27	Hanahan	18,207	45	34	11
Allendale	3,523	11	10	1	Hardeeville	2,986	19	17	2
Anderson	26,997	126	86	40	Harleyville	685	4	4	0
Andrews	2,894	9	8	1	Hartsville	7,854	35	32	3
Atlantic Beach	338	4	4	0	Hemingway	464	5	4	1
Aynor	567	7	6	1	Holly Hill	1,292	7	7	0
Bamberg	3,649	12	10	2	Honea Path	3,639	14	14	0
Barnwell	4,805	17	15	2	Inman	2,348	8	8	0
Batesburg-Leesville	5,424	26	21	5	Irmo	11,226	26	24	2
Beaufort	12,505	49	45	4	Isle of Palms	4,181	31	20	11
Belton	4,182	12	12	0	Iva	1,232	7	5	2
Bennettsville	9,175	37	33	4	Jackson	1,720	4	4	0
Bethune	338	1	1	0	Jamestown	73	5	4	1
Bishopville	3,511	15	13	2	Johnsonville	1,497	6	5	1
Blacksburg	1,870	11	10	1	Johnston	2,390	7	7	0
Blackville	2,434	11	10	1	Jonesville	922	5	3	2
Bluffton	12,676	38	35	3	Kingstree	3,367	16	14	2
Bonneau	493	3	3	0	Lake City	6,753	25	21	4
Bowman	979	5	5	0	Lake View	816	4	4	0
Branchville	1,036	4	3	1	Lamar	1,001	8	8	0
Briarcliffe Acres	462	1	1	0	Lancaster	8,625	44	35	9
Brunson	560	1	1	0	Landrum	2,404	11	10	1
Burnettown	2,704	2	2	0	Lane	514	4	2	2
Calhoun Falls	2,027	7	7	0	Latta	1,395	8	8	0
Camden	6,918	30	27	3	Laurens	9,245	33	26	7
Cameron	429	1	1	0	Lexington	18,078	51	47	4
Campobello	508	5	5	0	Liberty	3,307	16	11	5
Cayce	12,674	67	52	15	Lincolnville	1,152	1	1	0
Central	5,219	9	8	1	Loris	2,424	13	9	4
Chapin	1,462	2	2	0	Lyman	3,281	9	8	1
Charleston	121,481	526	396	130	Lynchburg	377	3	3	0
Cheraw	5,919	30	24	6	Manning	4,156	19	19	0
Chesnee	878	7	7	0	Marion	7,020	24	21	3
Chester	5,672	28	25	3	Mauldin	23,156	53	42	11
Chesterfield	1,489	6	5	1	Mayesville	740	1	1	0
Clemson	14,067	35	27	8	McBee	877	1	1	0
Clinton	8,589	37	33	4	McColl	2,199	7	6	1
Clio	734	5	3	2	McCormick	2,815	7	7	0
Clover	5,153	22	18	4	Moncks Corner	7,977	27	24	3
Columbia	130,777	444	382	62	Mount Pleasant	68,633	176	138	38
Conway	17,302	58	49	9	Mullins	4,717	23	21	2
Cottageville	771	4	3	1	Myrtle Beach	27,425	268	187	81
Coward	761	1	1	0	Newberry	10,397	33	30	3
Cowpens	2,187	5	5	0	New Ellenton	2,076	5	5	0
Darlington	6,362	29	26	3	Nichols	372	4	4	0
Denmark	3,579	11	9	2	Ninety Six	2,021	5	5	0
Dillon	6,867	27	22	5	North	763	2	2	0
Due West	1,262	6	5	1	North Augusta	21,597	76	56	20
Duncan	3,218	10	10	0	North Charleston	98,606	404	337	67
Easley	20,226	52	42	10	North Myrtle Beach	13,912	123	72	51
Edgefield	4,805	9	9	0	Orangeburg	14,127	95	71	24
Edisto Beach	419	6	6	0	Pacolet	2,261	6	5	1
Ehrhardt	551	6	3	3	Pageland	2,792	17	11	6
Elgin	1,326	7	7	0	Pamplico	1,240	4	4	0
Elloree	700	3	3	0	Pawleys Island	104	6	5	1
Estill	2,064	9	7	2	Pelion	682	3	3	0
Eutawville	319	1	1	0	Pickens	3,162	15	14	1
Fairfax	2,049	7	6	1	Pine Ridge	2,088	1	1	0
Florence	37,488	136	111	25	Port Royal	10,802	22	21	1
Folly Beach	2,647	24	19	5	Prosperity	1,194	5	5	0
Forest Acres	10,482	35	26	9	Ridgeland	4,083	17	17	0
Fort Lawn	905	3	3	0	Ridgeville	2,002	2	2	0
Fort Mill	10,937	39	34	5	Rock Hill	66,924	178	136	42
Fountain Inn	7,890	30	24	6	Salley	403	1	1	0
Gaffney	12,559	44	41	3	Saluda	3,607	11	10	1
Gaston	1,664	2	2	0	Santee	972	10	8	2

Table V-9.   Full-Time Law Enforcement Employees, by Selected State and City, 2011—*Continued*

(Number.)

State/City	Population	Total law enforcement employees	Total officers	Total civilians	State/City	Population	Total law enforcement employees	Total officers	Total civilians
Scranton	943	1	1	0	Madison	6,553	11	10	1
Seneca	8,196	46	35	11	McIntosh	175	1	1	0
Simpsonville	18,450	46	36	10	Menno	615	1	1	0
Society Hill	570	2	1	1	Milbank	3,394	6	6	0
South Congaree	2,333	7	6	1	Miller	1,507	4	4	0
Spartanburg	37,444	143	121	22	Mitchell	15,440	43	27	16
Springdale	2,667	8	8	0	Mobridge	3,507	14	7	7
Springfield	530	5	3	2	North Sioux City	2,561	8	7	1
St. George	2,108	10	10	0	Parkston	1,526	3	3	0
St. Matthews	2,045	6	6	0	Philip	788	2	2	0
St. Stephen	1,717	5	5	0	Pierre	13,812	38	24	14
Sullivans Island	1,812	9	8	1	Platte	1,245	2	2	0
Summerton	1,012	4	4	0	Rapid City	68,782	141	110	31
Summerville	43,897	109	87	22	Rosholt	428	1	1	0
Sumter	40,996	121	107	14	Scotland	851	1	1	0
Surfside Beach	3,882	27	21	6	Selby	650	1	1	0
Swansea	837	5	4	1	Sioux Falls	155,760	265	230	35
Tega Cay	7,709	22	19	3	Sisseton	2,500	7	7	0
Timmonsville	2,347	5	4	1	Spearfish	10,622	29	20	9
Travelers Rest	4,629	21	15	6	Springfield	2,013	2	2	0
Turbeville	775	3	3	0	Sturgis	6,708	19	16	3
Union	8,491	37	33	4	Summerset	1,836	3	3	0
Varnville	2,187	6	6	0	Tea	3,852	6	6	0
Wagener	806	4	4	0	Tripp	655	1	1	0
Walhalla	4,313	16	14	2	Tyndall	1,080	1	1	0
Walterboro	5,461	43	30	13	Vermillion	10,700	18	17	1
Ware Shoals	2,195	7	7	0	Viborg	792	1	1	0
Wellford	2,406	9	7	2	Wagner	1,585	5	5	0
West Columbia	15,163	68	53	15	Watertown	21,743	53	35	18
Westminster	2,446	9	9	0	Webster	1,909	5	5	0
West Pelzer	890	4	4	0	Whitewood	938	3	3	0
West Union	294	2	2	0	Winner	2,932	11	9	2
Whitmire	1,458	5	4	1	Worthing	888	1	1	0
Williamston	3,980	15	11	4	Yankton	14,630	35	24	11
Williston	3,176	9	8	1					
Winnsboro	3,591	20	20	0	**Tennessee**				
Woodruff	4,138	12	11	1	Adamsville	2,227	9	6	3
Yemassee	1,039	5	5	0	Alamo	2,483	4	4	0
York	7,826	32	25	7	Alcoa	8,525	47	40	7
					Alexandria	975	3	3	0
South Dakota					Algood	3,527	13	13	0
Aberdeen	26,408	51	43	8	Ardmore	1,224	11	7	4
Alcester	817	2	2	0	Ashland City	4,582	16	14	2
Armour	708	1	1	0	Athens	13,579	31	30	1
Avon	597	1	1	0	Atoka	8,463	18	17	1
Belle Fourche	5,662	11	10	1	Baileyton	435	2	2	0
Beresford	2,029	8	4	4	Bartlett	55,106	138	107	31
Box Elder	7,895	10	9	1	Baxter	1,377	5	5	0
Brandon	8,892	12	11	1	Bean Station	2,851	6	6	0
Brookings	22,324	38	31	7	Belle Meade	2,938	20	16	4
Burke	611	1	1	0	Bells	2,459	5	5	0
Canton	3,094	5	5	0	Benton	1,397	7	6	1
Centerville	893	1	1	0	Berry Hill	542	17	13	4
Chamberlain	2,416	6	6	0	Bethel Springs	724	3	1	2
Deadwood	1,285	14	11	3	Big Sandy	562	1	1	0
Eagle Butte	1,334	2	2	0	Blaine	1,873	1	1	0
Elk Point	1,987	4	4	0	Bluff City	1,749	8	8	0
Estelline	777	1	1	0	Bolivar	5,466	27	22	5
Faith	426	1	1	0	Bradford	1,057	5	4	1
Flandreau	2,369	9	8	1	Brentwood	37,394	72	57	15
Freeman	1,322	2	2	0	Brighton	2,760	6	6	0
Gettysburg	1,176	2	2	0	Bristol	26,943	89	67	22
Gregory	1,311	3	3	0	Brownsville	10,385	34	30	4
Groton	1,476	4	4	0	Bruceton	1,491	4	4	0
Hot Springs	3,756	7	6	1	Burns	1,481	3	3	0
Hoven	411	1	1	0	Calhoun	494	2	2	0
Huron	12,745	32	25	7	Camden	3,614	19	14	5
Jefferson	554	1	1	0	Carthage	2,327	12	7	5
Kadoka	662	1	1	0	Caryville	2,318	5	5	0
Kimball	712	1	1	0	Celina	1,508	7	5	2
Lead	3,162	6	5	1	Centerville	3,677	21	13	8
Lemmon	1,242	2	2	0	Chapel Hill	1,458	5	5	0
Lennox	2,137	4	4	0	Charleston	657	3	3	0
Leola	463	1	1	0	Chattanooga	169,187	472	370	102

Table V-9.   Full-Time Law Enforcement Employees, by Selected State and City, 2011—*Continued*

(Number.)

State/City	Population	Total law enforcement employees	Total officers	Total civilians	State/City	Population	Total law enforcement employees	Total officers	Total civilians
Church Hill	6,798	11	10	1	Jamestown	1,977	10	10	0
Clarksville	134,128	316	262	54	Jasper	3,309	8	8	0
Cleveland	41,657	97	87	10	Jefferson City	8,120	21	19	2
Clifton	2,718	5	5	0	Jellico	2,376	9	8	1
Clinton	9,930	30	28	2	Johnson City	63,722	170	143	27
Collegedale	8,357	19	19	0	Jonesborough	5,097	22	17	5
Collierville	44,362	133	98	35	Kenton	1,293	4	4	0
Collinwood	991	5	5	0	Kimball	1,408	9	9	0
Columbia	34,994	94	84	10	Kingsport	48,640	174	115	59
Cookeville	30,710	90	71	19	Kingston	5,988	13	12	1
Coopertown	4,317	3	2	1	Kingston Springs	2,781	6	5	1
Copperhill	357	1	1	0	Knoxville	180,488	485	387	98
Cornersville	1,205	4	4	0	Lafayette	4,514	20	14	6
Covington	9,120	33	32	1	La Follette	7,523	30	23	7
Cowan	1,753	5	5	0	Lake City	1,797	9	7	2
Cross Plains	1,729	3	3	0	La Vergne	32,882	65	49	16
Crossville	10,892	46	43	3	Lawrenceburg	10,522	40	36	4
Crump	1,441	4	4	0	Lebanon	26,426	88	72	16
Cumberland City	314	3	3	0	Lenoir City	8,720	26	25	1
Cumberland Gap	498	1	1	0	Lewisburg	11,200	38	27	11
Dandridge	2,837	12	11	1	Lexington	7,721	29	25	4
Dayton	7,256	20	18	2	Livingston	4,095	22	17	5
Decatur	1,612	5	5	0	Lookout Mountain	1,849	22	16	6
Decaturville	875	2	1	1	Loretto	1,729	4	4	0
Decherd	2,382	10	9	1	Loudon	5,430	15	15	0
Dickson	14,669	52	46	6	Madisonville	4,618	17	14	3
Dover	1,430	5	5	0	Manchester	10,193	40	34	6
Dresden	3,032	10	9	1	Martin	11,576	37	27	10
Dunlap	4,858	13	11	2	Maryville	27,713	54	48	6
Dyer	2,362	6	6	0	Mason	1,624	5	5	0
Dyersburg	17,300	70	61	9	Maury City	680	1	1	0
Eagleville	609	1	1	0	Maynardville	2,435	3	3	0
East Ridge	21,168	40	36	4	McEwen	1,766	7	6	1
Elizabethton	14,304	44	40	4	McKenzie	5,358	19	16	3
Elkton	583	2	2	0	McMinnville	13,728	37	33	4
Englewood	1,546	6	5	1	Medina	3,510	11	11	0
Erin	1,336	6	5	1	Memphis	652,725	2,855	2,454	401
Erwin	6,152	12	12	0	Middleton	712	4	4	0
Estill Springs	2,074	6	6	0	Milan	7,922	27	22	5
Etowah	3,521	11	10	1	Millersville	6,498	17	12	5
Fairview	7,790	19	18	1	Millington	10,268	49	36	13
Fayetteville	6,889	27	25	2	Minor Hill	542	2	2	0
Franklin	63,051	150	124	26	Monteagle	1,203	5	5	0
Friendship	674	1	1	0	Monterey	2,876	8	8	0
Gadsden	474	1	1	0	Morristown	29,400	89	83	6
Gainesboro	971	5	4	1	Moscow	561	2	2	0
Gallatin	30,551	87	64	23	Mountain City	2,554	9	9	0
Gallaway	686	3	3	0	Mount Carmel	5,478	7	7	0
Gates	653	1	1	0	Mount Juliet	23,885	57	45	12
Gatlinburg	3,980	48	40	8	Mount Pleasant	4,602	16	12	4
Germantown	39,194	108	87	21	Munford	5,980	15	14	1
Gibson	400	3	2	1	Murfreesboro	109,736	274	225	49
Gleason	1,458	6	6	0	Nashville	612,789	1,618	1,315	303
Goodlettsville	16,065	52	37	15	Newbern	3,343	18	12	6
Gordonsville	1,224	5	5	0	New Hope	1,092	1	1	0
Grand Junction	328	2	2	0	New Johnsonville	1,969	4	4	0
Graysville	1,516	6	5	1	New Market	1,346	4	4	0
Greenbrier	6,491	14	13	1	Newport	7,008	31	27	4
Greeneville	15,198	49	46	3	New Tazewell	3,064	10	10	0
Greenfield	2,202	8	7	1	Niota	725	3	3	0
Halls	2,275	7	7	0	Nolensville	5,914	7	7	0
Harriman	6,407	19	18	1	Norris	1,504	7	7	0
Henderson	6,366	14	13	1	Oakland	6,683	18	18	0
Hendersonville	51,835	121	94	27	Oak Ridge	29,595	75	59	16
Henning	954	4	4	0	Obion	1,129	3	3	0
Henry	468	2	2	0	Oliver Springs	3,260	13	9	4
Hohenwald	3,791	13	12	1	Oneida	3,786	17	12	5
Hollow Rock	724	2	2	0	Paris	10,248	34	24	10
Hornbeak	428	1	1	0	Parsons	2,394	6	6	0
Humboldt	8,528	30	25	5	Petersburg	549	2	2	0
Huntingdon	4,021	16	12	4	Pigeon Forge	5,928	63	51	12
Huntland	880	3	3	0	Pikeville	1,623	3	3	0
Jacksboro	2,038	6	6	0	Piperton	1,458	9	9	0
Jackson	65,799	255	212	43	Pittman Center	507	3	3	0

Table V-9.   Full-Time Law Enforcement Employees, by Selected State and City, 2011—*Continued*

(Number.)

State/City	Population	Total law enforcement employees	Total officers	Total civilians	State/City	Population	Total law enforcement employees	Total officers	Total civilians
Plainview	2,144	1	1	0	Alice	19,506	45	37	8
Pleasant View	4,186	5	5	0	Allen	86,019	155	108	47
Portland	11,584	33	25	8	Alpine	6,029	18	9	9
Powells Crossroads	1,334	1	1	0	Alton	12,601	20	15	5
Pulaski	7,941	28	25	3	Alvarado	3,865	23	16	7
Puryear	677	2	2	0	Alvin	24,746	78	49	29
Red Bank	11,756	25	23	2	Amarillo	194,708	371	320	51
Red Boiling Springs	1,122	6	5	1	Andrews	11,321	25	16	9
Ridgely	1,811	5	5	0	Angleton	19,259	48	36	12
Ridgetop	1,891	6	6	0	Anna	8,423	13	12	1
Ripley	8,521	31	25	6	Anson	2,481	6	6	0
Rockwood	5,612	16	15	1	Anthony	5,116	17	16	1
Rogersville	4,460	16	12	4	Aransas Pass	8,377	32	23	9
Rossville	670	6	6	0	Archer City	1,873	2	2	0
Rutherford	1,161	3	3	0	Arcola	1,677	3	3	0
Rutledge	1,132	4	4	0	Argyle	3,351	10	9	1
Saltillo	306	2	2	0	Arlington	373,128	840	640	200
Savannah	7,045	21	19	2	Arp	990	4	4	0
Scotts Hill	993	1	1	0	Athens	12,977	31	24	7
Selmer	4,436	21	19	2	Atlanta	5,794	17	13	4
Sevierville	14,941	69	55	14	Aubrey	2,650	6	6	0
Sewanee	2,332	13	9	4	Austin	807,022	2,211	1,644	567
Sharon	953	1	1	0	Azle	11,177	31	23	8
Shelbyville	20,518	45	37	8	Baird	1,527	2	2	0
Signal Mountain	7,622	16	15	1	Balch Springs	24,227	55	38	17
Smithville	4,571	13	12	1	Balcones Heights	3,003	24	19	5
Smyrna	40,335	104	76	28	Ballinger	3,846	6	6	0
Soddy-Daisy	12,829	30	25	5	Bangs	1,637	3	3	0
Somerville	3,122	11	11	0	Bastrop	7,370	24	20	4
South Carthage	1,334	4	4	0	Bay City	17,985	54	35	19
South Fulton	2,375	7	6	1	Bayou Vista	1,569	5	5	0
South Pittsburg	3,019	8	8	0	Baytown	73,313	194	142	52
Sparta	4,969	16	15	1	Beaumont	120,785	295	247	48
Spencer	1,615	3	3	0	Bedford	47,968	129	80	49
Spring City	1,999	7	7	0	Bee Cave	4,008	15	14	1
Springfield	16,588	60	38	22	Beeville	13,134	26	21	5
Spring Hill	29,298	51	42	9	Bellaire	17,210	55	41	14
Surgoinsville	1,817	2	2	0	Bellmead	10,109	20	14	6
Sweetwater	5,816	19	18	1	Bellville	4,183	12	11	1
Tazewell	2,238	6	6	0	Belton	18,599	40	30	10
Tellico Plains	888	6	5	1	Benbrook	21,681	49	40	9
Tiptonville	4,504	4	4	0	Bertram	1,381	4	4	0
Townsend	452	4	4	0	Beverly Hills	2,037	10	7	3
Tracy City	1,494	5	5	0	Big Sandy	1,371	6	6	0
Trenton	4,302	25	19	6	Big Spring	27,856	61	48	13
Trezevant	867	1	1	0	Bishop	3,200	9	5	4
Trimble	643	1	1	0	Blanco	1,776	6	5	1
Troy	1,383	4	4	0	Bloomburg	413	1	1	0
Tullahoma	18,823	42	37	5	Blue Mound	2,444	10	6	4
Tusculum	2,687	2	2	0	Boerne	10,691	45	29	16
Union City	10,993	42	34	8	Bogata	1,177	4	4	0
Vonore	1,487	9	9	0	Bonham	10,340	27	19	8
Wartburg	926	5	5	0	Borger	13,530	38	26	12
Wartrace	657	2	1	1	Bovina	1,907	4	4	0
Watauga	462	1	1	0	Bowie	5,328	20	15	5
Watertown	1,490	4	4	0	Brackettville	1,724	1	1	0
Waverly	4,142	13	12	1	Brady	5,644	16	9	7
Waynesboro	2,471	8	8	0	Brazoria	3,083	12	7	5
Westmoreland	2,226	9	6	3	Breckenridge	5,902	16	11	5
White Bluff	3,235	5	5	0	Bremond	949	2	2	0
White House	10,348	22	19	3	Brenham	16,047	38	33	5
White Pine	2,216	9	8	1	Bridge City	8,005	19	15	4
Whiteville	4,680	8	8	0	Bridgeport	6,102	22	15	7
Whitwell	1,714	6	5	1	Brookshire	4,801	20	16	4
Winchester	8,607	25	23	2	Brookside Village	1,555	4	4	0
Winfield	976	1	1	0	Brownfield	9,860	24	18	6
Woodbury	2,704	9	8	1	Brownsville	178,706	311	241	70
					Brownwood	19,694	59	38	21
Texas					Bruceville-Eddy	1,506	3	3	0
Abernathy	2,864	4	4	0	Bryan	77,804	169	132	37
Abilene	119,526	241	181	60	Buda	7,449	10	9	1
Addison	13,331	84	62	22	Bullard	2,515	8	7	1
Alamo	18,739	39	28	11	Bulverde	4,727	15	14	1
Alamo Heights	7,179	33	22	11	Burkburnett	11,038	25	19	6

Table V-9.   Full-Time Law Enforcement Employees, by Selected State and City, 2011—*Continued*

(Number.)

State/City	Population	Total law enforcement employees	Total officers	Total civilians	State/City	Population	Total law enforcement employees	Total officers	Total civilians
Burleson	37,462	71	54	17	Dilley	3,976	7	6	1
Burnet	6,113	15	14	1	Dimmitt	4,485	9	7	2
Cactus	3,246	8	6	2	Donna	16,130	37	29	8
Caddo Mills	1,366	3	3	0	Double Oak	2,927	6	6	0
Caldwell	4,190	13	12	1	Driscoll	755	7	3	4
Calvert	1,217	4	4	0	Dublin	3,731	11	7	4
Cameron	5,669	13	8	5	Dumas	15,000	31	26	5
Canton	3,656	19	14	5	Duncanville	39,335	73	60	13
Canyon	13,583	24	21	3	Eagle Lake	3,716	9	8	1
Carrollton	121,603	198	153	45	Early	2,820	8	7	1
Carthage	6,922	22	16	6	Eastland	4,043	11	9	2
Castle Hills	4,203	26	20	6	East Mountain	814	2	2	0
Castroville	2,736	11	9	2	Edcouch	3,228	13	9	4
Cedar Hill	45,975	82	64	18	Edgewood	1,471	2	2	0
Cedar Park	49,967	98	76	22	Edinburg	78,722	172	124	48
Celina	6,155	6	6	0	Edna	5,615	11	9	2
Center	5,302	27	19	8	El Campo	11,846	40	28	12
Childress	6,233	12	10	2	Electra	2,850	13	7	6
Chillicothe	722	3	2	1	Elgin	8,306	24	18	6
Cibolo	15,672	26	24	2	El Paso	662,780	1,280	1,057	223
Cisco	3,981	7	5	2	Elsa	5,779	18	13	5
Clarksville	3,354	12	8	4	Ennis	18,903	40	34	6
Cleburne	29,954	70	52	18	Euless	52,356	128	85	43
Cleveland	7,836	35	21	14	Everman	6,237	18	13	5
Clifton	3,514	9	8	1	Fairfield	3,013	15	12	3
Clint	945	1	1	0	Fair Oaks Ranch	6,112	16	15	1
Clute	11,447	40	29	11	Falfurrias	5,086	14	13	1
Clyde	3,791	10	9	1	Farmers Branch	29,218	109	74	35
Cockrell Hill	4,281	18	12	6	Farmersville	3,370	11	9	2
Coleman	4,808	18	10	8	Farwell	1,392	2	2	0
College Station	95,832	171	117	54	Ferris	2,487	13	8	5
Colleyville	23,287	39	35	4	Flatonia	1,412	5	5	0
Collinsville	1,658	3	3	0	Florence	1,160	2	2	0
Colorado City	4,233	12	6	6	Floresville	6,584	16	14	2
Columbus	3,732	11	9	2	Flower Mound	66,030	116	81	35
Comanche	4,426	10	8	2	Floydada	3,102	6	6	0
Combes	2,956	6	6	0	Forest Hill	12,615	23	17	6
Commerce	8,248	20	16	4	Forney	14,970	33	22	11
Conroe	57,390	147	111	36	Fort Stockton	8,457	30	19	11
Converse	18,581	48	33	15	Fort Worth	756,803	1,933	1,509	424
Coppell	39,472	79	62	17	Frankston	1,255	6	5	1
Copperas Cove	32,706	73	55	18	Fredericksburg	10,752	34	30	4
Corinth	20,354	31	28	3	Freeport	12,303	49	35	14
Corpus Christi	311,637	624	428	196	Freer	2,877	12	8	4
Corrigan	1,629	11	7	4	Friendswood	36,558	77	63	14
Corsicana	24,270	53	43	10	Friona	4,210	10	6	4
Cottonwood Shores	1,147	2	2	0	Frisco	119,451	196	140	56
Crandall	2,918	12	12	0	Gainesville	16,339	53	39	14
Crane	3,424	11	7	4	Galena Park	11,116	24	18	6
Crockett	7,096	17	16	1	Galveston	48,748	164	129	35
Crosbyton	1,778	3	3	0	Ganado	2,045	3	3	0
Crowell	968	1	1	0	Garden Ridge	3,328	14	14	0
Crowley	13,108	37	28	9	Garland	231,650	442	322	120
Crystal City	7,288	7	2	5	Gatesville	16,082	24	16	8
Cuero	6,985	15	14	1	Georgetown	48,397	100	72	28
Cumby	793	6	5	1	Giddings	4,984	19	14	5
Daingerfield	2,614	8	7	1	Gladewater	6,577	21	16	5
Dalhart	8,097	18	15	3	Glenn Heights	11,515	25	16	9
Dallas	1,223,021	4,052	3,511	541	Godley	1,030	7	7	0
Dalworthington Gardens	2,307	18	14	4	Gonzales	7,389	22	16	6
Danbury	1,751	4	4	0	Gorman	1,106	2	2	0
Dayton	7,394	27	18	9	Graham	9,090	23	22	1
Decatur	6,169	27	21	6	Granbury	8,146	35	29	6
Deer Park	32,684	83	59	24	Grand Prairie	179,087	327	215	112
De Kalb	1,735	6	5	1	Grand Saline	3,202	8	8	0
De Leon	2,293	5	5	0	Granger	1,449	4	3	1
Del Rio	36,340	92	68	24	Granite Shoals	5,013	8	7	1
Denison	23,159	55	45	10	Grapeland	1,520	5	5	0
Denton	115,769	204	150	54	Grapevine	47,309	128	92	36
Denver City	4,573	13	8	5	Greenville	26,095	70	51	19
DeSoto	50,079	86	59	27	Gregory	1,947	4	4	0
Devine	4,442	11	9	2	Groesbeck	4,419	9	8	1
Diboll	4,876	20	14	6	Groves	16,484	23	21	2
Dickinson	19,073	44	31	13	Gruver	1,219	2	2	0

Table V-9.   Full-Time Law Enforcement Employees, by Selected State and City, 2011—*Continued*

(Number.)

State/City	Population	Total law enforcement employees	Total officers	Total civilians	State/City	Population	Total law enforcement employees	Total officers	Total civilians
Gun Barrel City	5,791	19	14	5	Kenedy	3,365	8	7	1
Hale Center	2,299	3	3	0	Kennedale	6,905	24	17	7
Hallettsville	2,604	8	7	1	Kermit	5,828	17	10	7
Hallsville	3,652	5	4	1	Kerrville	22,817	67	51	16
Haltom City	43,301	89	72	17	Kilgore	13,248	43	33	10
Hamlin	2,169	8	4	4	Killeen	130,613	316	227	89
Harker Heights	27,262	57	45	12	Kingsville	26,765	64	49	15
Harlingen	66,214	166	128	38	Kirby	8,168	17	12	5
Haskell	3,392	2	2	0	Kountze	2,168	7	6	1
Hawk Cove	493	1	1	0	Kress	730	1	1	0
Hawkins	1,305	5	5	0	Kyle	28,606	50	36	14
Hawley	647	1	1	0	Lacoste	1,143	2	2	0
Hearne	4,553	17	12	5	Lacy-Lakeview	6,626	22	14	8
Heath	7,067	18	17	1	La Feria	7,456	17	13	4
Hedwig Village	2,611	21	16	5	Lago Vista	6,168	22	15	7
Helotes	7,495	22	20	2	La Grange	4,739	10	10	0
Hemphill	1,223	3	3	0	La Grulla	1,656	6	4	2
Hempstead	5,891	18	15	3	Laguna Vista	3,183	7	7	0
Henderson	14,001	41	33	8	La Joya	4,069	16	11	5
Hereford	15,693	31	25	6	Lake Dallas	7,255	23	15	8
Hewitt	13,834	30	22	8	Lake Jackson	27,414	60	44	16
Hickory Creek	3,315	11	11	0	Lakeside	1,335	4	4	0
Hidalgo	11,434	43	29	14	Lakeview, Harris County	6,382	17	13	4
Highland Park	8,744	69	52	17	Lakeway	11,631	40	29	11
Highland Village	15,373	35	29	6	Lake Worth	4,680	34	27	7
Hill Country Village	1,006	11	11	0	La Marque	14,814	40	28	12
Hillsboro	8,634	36	25	11	Lamesa	9,620	23	16	7
Hitchcock	7,107	22	16	6	Lampasas	6,822	28	18	10
Holliday	1,795	3	3	0	Lancaster	37,126	64	50	14
Hollywood Park	3,126	12	11	1	La Porte	34,511	105	75	30
Hondo	8,988	19	17	2	Laredo	241,059	499	425	74
Hooks	2,827	7	7	0	La Vernia	1,056	7	7	0
Horizon City	17,087	24	20	4	La Villa	1,998	7	6	1
Horseshoe Bay	3,490	18	16	2	Lavon	2,266	7	7	0
Houston	2,143,628	6,531	5,294	1,237	League City	85,318	138	102	36
Howe	2,655	4	4	0	Leander	27,079	51	35	16
Hubbard	1,453	4	4	0	Leonard	2,032	5	5	0
Hudson	4,831	5	5	0	Leon Valley	10,365	33	24	9
Hudson Oaks	1,697	12	11	1	Levelland	13,827	34	23	11
Hughes Springs	1,797	5	5	0	Lewisville	97,295	193	136	57
Humble	15,451	78	58	20	Liberty	8,574	27	17	10
Huntington	2,163	5	5	0	Lindale	4,919	20	14	6
Huntsville	39,359	58	51	7	Linden	2,030	6	5	1
Hurst	38,123	115	74	41	Little Elm	26,443	37	34	3
Hutchins	5,450	22	17	5	Littlefield	6,506	19	12	7
Hutto	15,007	28	24	4	Live Oak	13,407	45	31	14
Idalou	2,297	5	5	0	Livingston	5,447	25	18	7
Ingleside	9,585	22	15	7	Llano	3,300	10	9	1
Ingram	1,842	7	6	1	Lockhart	12,965	36	25	11
Iowa Park	6,489	17	11	6	Lockney	1,881	2	2	0
Irving	220,841	482	336	146	Lometa	874	1	1	0
Italy	1,902	4	3	1	Lone Star	1,614	5	4	1
Itasca	1,679	7	7	0	Longview	82,148	217	158	59
Jacinto City	10,775	26	20	6	Lorena	1,727	6	5	1
Jacksboro	4,606	11	9	2	Lorenzo	1,171	2	2	0
Jacksonville	14,850	38	28	10	Los Fresnos	5,659	21	15	6
Jamaica Beach	1,004	5	5	0	Lott	775	4	4	0
Jarrell	1,005	2	2	0	Lubbock	234,404	488	378	110
Jasper	7,750	28	22	6	Lufkin	35,805	95	74	21
Jefferson	2,150	4	3	1	Luling	5,525	22	15	7
Jersey Village	7,780	37	28	9	Lumberton	12,194	18	15	3
Johnson City	1,691	4	4	0	Lyford	2,666	2	2	0
Jones Creek	2,063	3	3	0	Lytle	2,544	7	7	0
Jonestown	1,873	9	8	1	Madisonville	4,489	14	12	2
Joshua	6,034	15	14	1	Magnolia	1,422	12	10	2
Jourdanton	3,952	8	8	0	Malakoff	2,373	6	6	0
Junction	2,628	5	5	0	Manor	5,143	16	14	2
Karnes City	3,106	8	7	1	Mansfield	57,554	205	85	120
Katy	14,399	60	44	16	Manvel	5,288	14	10	4
Kaufman	6,844	24	16	8	Marble Falls	6,205	38	23	15
Keene	6,234	17	11	6	Marlin	6,093	18	14	4
Keller	40,461	79	49	30	Marshall	24,018	65	51	14
Kemah	1,810	22	17	5	Mart	2,255	4	4	0
Kemp	1,178	5	5	0	Martindale	1,139	3	3	0

Table V-9.   Full-Time Law Enforcement Employees, by Selected State and City, 2011—*Continued*

(Number.)

State/City	Population	Total law enforcement employees	Total officers	Total civilians	State/City	Population	Total law enforcement employees	Total officers	Total civilians
Mathis	5,046	18	12	6	Perryton	8,987	18	11	7
McAllen	132,610	403	270	133	Pflugerville	47,924	99	76	23
McGregor	5,092	16	9	7	Pharr	71,881	175	126	49
McKinney	133,876	194	153	41	Pilot Point	3,937	6	6	0
Meadows Place	4,758	16	15	1	Pinehurst	2,141	8	6	2
Melissa	4,794	9	8	1	Pittsburg	4,592	12	10	2
Memorial Villages	11,359	39	33	6	Plainview	22,661	40	32	8
Memphis	2,338	4	4	0	Plano	265,309	489	336	153
Mercedes	15,898	44	36	8	Pleasanton	9,122	24	18	6
Meridian	1,524	2	2	0	Point Comfort	753	1	1	0
Merkel	2,644	3	3	0	Ponder	1,424	1	1	0
Mesquite	142,766	305	228	77	Port Aransas	3,553	21	14	7
Mexia	7,616	28	18	10	Port Arthur	54,950	162	125	37
Midland	113,486	221	172	49	Port Isabel	5,111	25	18	7
Midlothian	18,417	41	28	13	Portland	15,417	35	24	11
Milford	743	3	3	0	Port Lavaca	12,506	26	20	6
Mineola	4,610	18	12	6	Port Neches	13,314	21	18	3
Mineral Wells	17,141	38	28	10	Poteet	3,329	8	7	1
Mission	78,679	195	140	55	Poth	1,948	3	3	0
Missouri City	68,775	111	88	23	Pottsboro	2,205	7	7	0
Monahans	7,099	16	11	5	Premont	2,709	6	6	0
Mont Belvieu	3,916	15	10	5	Presidio	4,519	5	4	1
Montgomery	634	7	7	0	Primera	4,156	9	8	1
Morgans Point Resort	4,258	8	7	1	Princeton	6,950	11	11	0
Mount Pleasant	15,892	38	27	11	Progreso	5,623	8	8	0
Muleshoe	5,267	12	8	4	Prosper	9,621	18	11	7
Munday	1,327	3	3	0	Queen City	1,507	6	6	0
Murphy	18,081	32	22	10	Quinlan	1,423	4	4	0
Mustang Ridge	879	4	4	0	Quitman	1,847	6	6	0
Nacogdoches	33,690	78	61	17	Ralls	1,985	3	3	0
Naples	1,407	4	4	0	Rancho Viejo	2,488	7	7	0
Nash	3,022	10	9	1	Ranger	2,520	7	6	1
Nassau Bay	4,086	13	12	1	Ransom Canyon	1,119	3	3	0
Navasota	7,197	26	19	7	Raymondville	11,521	22	13	9
Nederland	17,916	36	24	12	Red Oak	10,996	25	23	2
Needville	2,882	6	6	0	Refugio	2,951	9	8	1
New Boston	4,646	12	9	3	Reno	3,233	4	3	1
New Braunfels	58,955	123	100	23	Richardson	101,311	240	152	88
New Deal	811	2	2	0	Richland Hills	7,965	24	17	7
Nixon	2,435	5	4	1	Richmond	11,925	38	28	10
Nocona	3,097	9	5	4	Richwood	3,584	8	8	0
Nolanville	4,349	5	5	0	Riesel	1,028	4	4	0
Northlake	1,760	9	9	0	Rio Grande City	14,125	35	27	8
North Richland Hills	64,676	155	107	48	Rio Hondo	2,406	6	5	1
Oak Ridge	144	2	2	0	Rising Star	853	1	1	0
Oak Ridge North	3,113	16	16	0	River Oaks	7,583	24	18	6
Odessa	102,043	198	144	54	Roanoke	6,087	38	29	9
O'Donnell	848	1	1	0	Robinson	10,730	29	21	8
Olmos Park	2,284	12	12	0	Robstown	11,729	35	26	9
Olney	3,354	7	6	1	Rockdale	5,713	17	11	6
Olton	2,262	3	3	0	Rockport	8,950	27	25	2
Onalaska	1,801	6	6	0	Rockwall	38,279	86	68	18
Orange	18,986	56	42	14	Rollingwood	1,442	6	6	0
Orange Grove	1,346	5	5	0	Roma	9,970	34	25	9
Overton	2,608	9	6	3	Roman Forest	1,570	8	8	0
Ovilla	3,565	10	9	1	Roscoe	1,350	1	1	0
Oyster Creek	1,134	9	5	4	Rosebud	1,442	4	4	0
Paducah	1,211	5	1	4	Rose City	513	1	1	0
Palacios	4,817	16	11	5	Rosenberg	31,262	80	63	17
Palestine	19,106	40	34	6	Rowlett	57,382	109	73	36
Palmer	2,042	13	9	4	Royse City	9,546	16	15	1
Palmhurst	2,662	14	10	4	Runaway Bay	1,313	4	4	0
Palm Valley	1,331	5	5	0	Rusk	5,668	13	11	2
Palmview	5,575	25	18	7	Sabinal	1,731	4	4	0
Pampa	18,373	36	26	10	Sachse	20,757	41	29	12
Panhandle	2,504	4	4	0	Saginaw	20,223	42	35	7
Pantego	2,444	17	12	5	Salado	2,171	4	4	0
Paris	25,701	86	62	24	San Angelo	95,161	216	163	53
Parker	3,891	7	7	0	San Antonio	1,355,339	3,002	2,324	678
Pasadena	152,179	334	260	74	San Augustine	2,152	7	7	0
Pearland	93,172	177	134	43	San Benito	24,760	47	39	8
Pearsall	9,338	15	13	2	San Diego	4,582	6	5	1
Pecos	8,965	41	20	21	Sanger	7,062	15	14	1
Penitas	4,496	12	8	4	San Juan	34,568	56	44	12

Table V-9.   Full-Time Law Enforcement Employees, by Selected State and City, 2011—*Continued*

(Number.)

State/City	Popula-tion	Total law enforce-ment employees	Total officers	Total civilians	State/City	Popula-tion	Total law enforce-ment employees	Total officers	Total civilians
San Marcos	45,839	126	95	31	Trenton	648	2	2	0
San Saba	3,164	4	4	0	Trinity	2,754	10	6	4
Sansom Park Village	4,785	15	11	4	Trophy Club	8,193	15	14	1
Santa Anna	1,122	2	2	0	Troup	1,908	9	8	1
Santa Fe	12,479	27	21	6	Troy	1,680	5	5	0
Santa Rosa	2,933	6	6	0	Tulia	5,072	13	8	5
Schertz	32,127	67	51	16	Tye	1,268	4	4	0
Schulenburg	2,912	8	7	1	Tyler	98,939	240	190	50
Seabrook	12,203	41	32	9	Universal City	18,920	39	29	10
Seagoville	15,147	29	22	7	University Park	23,553	52	39	13
Seagraves	2,468	4	4	0	Uvalde	16,082	48	37	11
Sealy	6,146	20	18	2	Valley Mills	1,228	2	2	0
Seguin	25,705	70	52	18	Valley View	773	3	3	0
Selma	5,657	29	26	3	Van	2,687	6	6	0
Seminole	6,565	12	11	1	Van Alstyne	3,110	14	9	5
Seven Points	1,486	11	7	4	Vernon	11,234	32	21	11
Seymour	2,798	8	6	2	Victoria	63,909	145	110	35
Shallowater	2,536	5	5	0	Vidor	10,802	30	22	8
Shamrock	1,950	7	3	4	Waco	127,431	322	241	81
Shavano Park	3,099	17	16	1	Waelder	1,087	4	4	0
Shenandoah	2,179	24	23	1	Wake Village	5,608	9	8	1
Sherman	39,332	85	61	24	Waller	2,375	10	9	1
Silsbee	6,750	21	16	5	Wallis	1,278	3	3	0
Sinton	5,784	12	11	1	Watauga	23,991	50	32	18
Slaton	6,250	16	10	6	Waxahachie	30,244	70	53	17
Smithville	3,897	13	9	4	Weatherford	25,781	74	59	15
Snyder	11,438	22	20	2	Webster	10,619	63	47	16
Socorro	32,687	39	27	12	Weimar	2,196	8	7	1
Somerset	1,665	3	3	0	Weslaco	36,421	76	55	21
Somerville	1,405	5	5	0	West	2,866	7	7	0
Sonora	3,091	6	4	2	West Columbia	3,987	15	9	6
Sour Lake	1,851	8	7	1	West Lake Hills	3,127	19	13	6
South Houston	17,340	38	29	9	West Orange	3,515	11	9	2
Southlake	27,134	62	54	8	Westover Hills	696	13	10	3
South Padre Island	2,875	38	28	10	West Tawakoni	1,609	4	4	0
Southside Place	1,751	9	5	4	West University Place	15,098	33	22	11
Spearman	3,439	4	4	0	Westworth	2,524	18	13	5
Springtown	2,714	16	11	5	Wharton	9,018	32	22	10
Spring Valley	3,793	23	18	5	Whitehouse	7,821	19	13	6
Spur	1,346	2	2	0	White Oak	6,605	19	15	4
Stafford	18,065	60	44	16	Whitesboro	3,873	13	8	5
Stagecoach	549	3	3	0	White Settlement	16,455	50	36	14
Stamford	3,190	9	8	1	Whitewright	1,638	5	5	0
Stanton	2,544	3	3	0	Whitney	2,131	7	6	1
Stephenville	17,483	53	36	17	Wichita Falls	106,753	278	189	89
Stratford	2,059	4	4	0	Willis	5,781	14	12	2
Sugar Land	80,475	173	149	24	Willow Park	4,066	17	12	5
Sullivan City	4,086	13	8	5	Wills Point	3,598	12	11	1
Sulphur Springs	15,774	40	29	11	Wilmer	3,759	16	12	4
Sunray	1,967	8	6	2	Windcrest	5,477	22	15	7
Sunrise Beach Village	728	4	4	0	Wink	960	1	1	0
Sunset Valley	765	13	13	0	Winnsboro	3,506	13	9	4
Surfside Beach	492	6	6	0	Winters	2,616	4	4	0
Sweeny	3,762	7	7	0	Wolfe City	1,442	3	3	0
Sweetwater	11,135	27	22	5	Wolfforth	3,747	10	9	1
Taft	3,112	11	10	1	Woodbranch	1,309	5	3	2
Tahoka	2,729	4	4	0	Woodville	2,640	10	9	1
Tatum	1,414	5	5	0	Woodway	8,630	35	25	10
Taylor	15,511	35	26	9	Wortham	1,096	3	3	0
Teague	3,635	8	7	1	Wylie	42,299	46	41	5
Temple	67,493	163	134	29	Yoakum	5,937	17	10	7
Terrell	16,149	46	36	10	Yorktown	2,136	4	4	0
Terrell Hills	4,981	15	14	1					
Texarkana	37,177	105	93	12	**Utah**				
Texas City	46,048	116	88	28	Alta	390	8	4	4
The Colony	37,092	79	53	26	American Fork/Cedar Hills	36,755	38	32	6
Thorndale	1,364	2	2	0	Blanding	3,440	6	5	1
Thrall	857	5	5	0	Bountiful	43,373	51	36	15
Three Rivers	1,887	8	7	1	Brian Head	85	5	5	0
Tioga	820	2	2	0	Brigham City	18,244	29	25	4
Tolar	695	1	1	0	Cedar City	29,414	42	34	8
Tomball	10,979	57	42	15	Centerfield	1,393	1	1	0
Tom Bean	1,067	5	4	1	Centerville	15,631	20	17	3
Tool	2,287	12	9	3	Clearfield	30,693	44	31	13

Table V-9. Full-Time Law Enforcement Employees, by Selected State and City, 2011—*Continued*

(Number.)

State/City	Population	Total law enforcement employees	Total officers	Total civilians
Clinton	20,820	17	16	1
Cottonwood Heights	34,078	42	37	5
Draper	43,090	43	36	7
East Carbon	1,326	4	4	0
Enoch	5,915	6	4	2
Ephraim	6,253	5	5	0
Fairview	1,271	1	1	0
Farmington	18,628	17	14	3
Garland	2,446	4	4	0
Grantsville	9,065	12	10	2
Gunnison	3,348	3	3	0
Harrisville	5,674	9	8	1
Heber	11,581	15	13	2
Helper	2,243	6	6	0
Hildale	2,779	12	7	5
Hurricane	14,013	20	19	1
Ivins	6,883	12	10	2
Kamas	1,846	2	2	0
Kanab	4,395	8	7	1
Kaysville	27,827	22	20	2
La Verkin	4,138	4	4	0
Layton	68,610	106	75	31
Lehi	48,322	44	40	4
Lindon	10,264	15	14	1
Logan	49,104	96	62	34
Lone Peak	25,562	21	19	2
Mantua	700	1	1	0
Mapleton	8,133	9	8	1
Minersville	925	1	1	0
Moab	5,143	20	15	5
Monticello	2,010	3	3	0
Moroni	1,450	1	1	0
Mount Pleasant	3,323	4	4	0
Murray	47,648	82	76	6
Naples	1,789	7	6	1
Nephi	5,493	10	8	2
North Ogden	17,692	21	18	3
North Park	12,336	11	9	2
North Salt Lake	16,637	20	18	2
Ogden	84,423	165	135	30
Orem	90,033	122	88	34
Park City	7,704	41	30	11
Parowan	2,844	3	3	0
Payson	18,647	19	17	2
Perry	4,599	5	4	1
Pleasant Grove	34,156	33	25	8
Pleasant View	8,133	9	8	1
Price	8,883	21	17	4
Provo	114,659	146	99	47
Richfield	7,697	14	13	1
Riverdale	8,589	22	19	3
Roosevelt	6,163	13	11	2
Roy	37,596	45	40	5
Salem	6,547	10	9	1
Salina	2,537	5	4	1
Salt Lake City	190,038	558	414	144
Sandy	89,149	143	107	36
Santa Clara	6,119	10	9	1
Santaquin/Genola	10,700	11	11	0
Saratoga Springs	18,124	27	23	4
Smithfield	9,678	9	8	1
South Jordan	51,391	58	50	8
South Ogden	16,851	27	22	5
South Salt Lake	24,073	69	59	10
Spanish Fork	35,360	31	28	3
Springdale	539	4	3	1
Springville	30,035	31	27	4
St. George	74,304	144	104	40
Stockton	628	1	1	0
Sunset	5,221	8	8	0
Syracuse	24,801	21	19	2
Taylorsville City	59,784	66	61	5
Tooele	32,215	39	33	6
Tremonton	7,795	12	10	2
Vernal	9,264	24	21	3
Washington	19,123	26	21	5
Wellington	1,708	3	3	0
West Bountiful	5,367	10	9	1
West Jordan	105,713	133	94	39
West Valley	131,979	233	189	44
Willard	1,806	2	2	0
Woods Cross	9,949	15	13	2
Vermont				
Barre	9,062	24	18	6
Barre Town	7,933	7	6	1
Bellows Falls	3,151	12	8	4
Bennington	15,781	32	25	7
Berlin	2,890	7	6	1
Brandon	3,970	7	7	0
Brattleboro	12,059	38	24	14
Bristol	3,898	3	3	0
Burlington	42,464	128	94	34
Castleton	4,722	4	4	0
Chester	3,157	5	4	1
Colchester	17,086	36	28	8
Dover	1,125	6	5	1
Essex	19,609	33	27	6
Fair Haven	2,737	4	4	0
Hardwick	3,013	5	4	1
Hartford	9,963	33	24	9
Hinesburg	4,401	5	5	0
Ludlow	1,965	9	5	4
Lyndonville	1,208	3	3	0
Manchester	4,396	13	9	4
Middlebury	8,505	16	14	2
Milton	10,363	16	15	1
Montpelier	7,864	24	16	8
Morristown	5,233	10	10	0
Newport	4,594	12	10	2
Northfield	6,214	6	5	1
Norwich	3,418	5	4	1
Randolph	4,783	6	6	0
Richmond	4,086	4	4	0
Rutland	16,513	45	37	8
Shelburne	7,152	19	11	8
South Burlington	17,924	41	34	7
Springfield	9,383	15	15	0
St. Albans	6,926	33	23	10
St. Johnsbury	7,611	15	9	6
Stowe	4,319	11	11	0
Swanton	6,434	4	4	0
Thetford	2,591	3	3	0
Vergennes	2,591	6	6	0
Vernon	2,208	5	4	1
Waterbury	5,070	2	2	0
Weathersfield	2,828	1	1	0
Williston	8,708	15	12	3
Wilmington	1,878	7	6	1
Windsor	3,557	8	7	1
Winhall	770	6	5	1
Winooski	7,275	23	16	7
Woodstock	3,051	3	3	0
Virginia				
Abingdon	8,289	28	26	2
Alexandria	141,638	399	300	99
Altavista	3,491	14	13	1
Amherst	2,258	5	5	0
Appalachia	1,775	6	6	0
Ashland	7,311	27	24	3
Bedford	6,296	27	24	3
Berryville	4,235	10	9	1
Big Stone Gap	5,681	16	15	1
Blacksburg	43,129	79	62	17
Blackstone	3,664	18	13	5
Bloxom	392	1	1	0
Bluefield	5,509	22	17	5

Table V-9.   Full-Time Law Enforcement Employees, by Selected State and City, 2011—*Continued*

(Number.)

State/City	Population	Total law enforcement employees	Total officers	Total civilians	State/City	Population	Total law enforcement employees	Total officers	Total civilians
Boykins	571	1	1	0	Middleburg	681	5	5	0
Bridgewater	5,711	9	9	0	Middletown	1,280	2	2	0
Bristol	18,048	70	50	20	Mount Jackson	2,018	4	4	0
Broadway	3,735	4	4	0	Narrows	2,053	4	4	0
Buena Vista	6,729	16	15	1	New Market	2,172	5	5	0
Burkeville	437	1	1	0	Newport News	182,878	536	398	138
Cape Charles	1,021	5	5	0	Norfolk	245,704	808	721	87
Cedar Bluff	1,151	3	3	0	Norton	4,005	24	15	9
Charlottesville	43,994	144	117	27	Onancock	1,278	4	4	0
Chase City	2,379	10	9	1	Onley	522	5	5	0
Chatham	1,284	3	3	0	Orange	4,777	17	15	2
Chesapeake	224,864	495	354	141	Parksley	852	2	2	0
Chilhowie	1,802	6	6	0	Pearisburg	2,819	8	7	1
Chincoteague	2,976	14	10	4	Pembroke	1,141	3	3	0
Christiansburg	21,292	73	57	16	Pennington Gap	1,802	6	6	0
Clarksville	1,153	8	7	1	Petersburg	32,807	163	117	46
Clifton Forge	3,930	12	10	2	Poquoson	12,295	22	21	1
Clintwood	1,431	4	4	0	Portsmouth	96,676	335	242	93
Coeburn	2,165	7	7	0	Pound	1,049	4	4	0
Colonial Beach	3,584	16	11	5	Pulaski	9,195	36	27	9
Colonial Heights	17,619	52	48	4	Purcellville	7,819	14	13	1
Covington	6,032	28	17	11	Quantico	486	2	2	0
Crewe	2,354	5	4	1	Radford	16,604	48	37	11
Culpeper	16,575	46	38	8	Remington	605	1	1	0
Damascus	824	5	5	0	Rich Creek	783	1	1	0
Danville	43,569	136	129	7	Richlands	5,893	21	15	6
Dayton	1,548	8	7	1	Richmond	206,654	885	727	158
Dublin	2,564	10	9	1	Roanoke	98,191	300	256	44
Dumfries	5,020	8	6	2	Rocky Mount	4,856	22	20	2
Edinburg	1,053	2	2	0	Rural Retreat	1,501	1	1	0
Elkton	2,759	7	6	1	Salem	25,098	92	64	28
Emporia	5,998	37	26	11	Saltville	2,102	3	3	0
Exmore	1,477	5	5	0	Shenandoah	2,401	5	5	0
Fairfax City	22,835	82	65	17	Smithfield	8,186	26	22	4
Falls Church	12,479	38	30	8	South Boston	8,239	30	27	3
Farmville	8,314	28	27	1	South Hill	4,706	22	20	2
Franklin	8,685	42	29	13	Stanley	1,709	4	4	0
Fredericksburg	24,576	96	71	25	Staunton	24,030	67	51	16
Front Royal	14,612	43	34	9	Stephens City	1,851	4	4	0
Galax	7,126	38	24	14	St. Paul	982	4	4	0
Gate City	2,058	6	6	0	Strasburg	6,474	21	19	2
Glade Spring	1,473	3	3	0	Suffolk	85,595	245	185	60
Glasgow	1,147	1	1	0	Tappahannock	2,403	11	10	1
Glen Lyn	116	1	1	0	Tazewell	4,682	15	13	2
Gordonsville	1,514	7	6	1	Timberville	2,552	4	4	0
Gretna	1,282	4	4	0	Victoria	1,746	6	5	1
Grottoes	2,700	6	5	1	Vienna	15,874	50	39	11
Grundy	1,033	6	6	0	Vinton	8,195	24	22	2
Halifax	1,325	4	4	0	Virginia Beach	443,226	945	776	169
Hampton	139,078	374	277	97	Warrenton	9,726	23	21	2
Harrisonburg	49,498	104	87	17	Warsaw	1,530	3	2	1
Haymarket	1,803	6	5	1	Waverly	2,175	11	6	5
Haysi	504	2	2	0	Waynesboro	21,257	55	43	12
Herndon	23,570	70	54	16	Weber City	1,343	5	5	0
Hillsville	2,713	13	12	1	West Point	3,345	10	9	1
Honaker	1,466	4	3	1	White Stone	356	1	1	0
Hopewell	22,861	73	59	14	Williamsburg	14,236	39	36	3
Hurt	1,320	2	2	0	Winchester	26,516	100	76	24
Independence	958	2	2	0	Windsor	2,657	6	6	0
Jonesville	1,046	2	2	0	Wise	3,325	14	13	1
Kenbridge	1,272	6	5	1	Woodstock	5,158	16	15	1
Kilmarnock	1,505	5	5	0	Wytheville	8,309	42	28	14
La Crosse	611	1	1	0					
Lawrenceville	1,455	6	6	0	**Washington**				
Lebanon	3,465	12	11	1	Aberdeen	17,161	48	35	13
Leesburg	43,125	101	85	16	Airway Heights	6,210	15	14	1
Lexington	7,126	18	16	2	Algona	3,061	9	8	1
Louisa	1,574	6	6	0	Anacortes	16,026	31	24	7
Luray	4,953	13	11	2	Arlington	18,207	29	24	5
Lynchburg	76,471	187	160	27	Asotin	1,271	2	2	0
Manassas	38,273	117	84	33	Auburn	71,281	112	97	15
Manassas Park	14,444	42	30	12	Bainbridge Island	23,386	28	21	7
Marion	6,039	21	19	2	Battle Ground	17,847	26	21	5
Martinsville	13,986	55	50	5	Bellevue	124,283	209	173	36

Table V-9. Full-Time Law Enforcement Employees, by Selected State and City, 2011—*Continued*

(Number.)

State/City	Population	Total law enforcement employees	Total officers	Total civilians	State/City	Population	Total law enforcement employees	Total officers	Total civilians
Bellingham	82,154	160	109	51	Mabton	2,322	2	2	0
Black Diamond	4,216	11	9	2	Maple Valley	23,040	21	17	4
Blaine	4,757	13	10	3	Marysville	60,962	83	53	30
Bonney Lake	17,647	35	27	8	Mattawa	4,507	3	3	0
Bothell	34,031	84	58	26	McCleary	1,679	3	3	0
Bremerton	38,321	70	57	13	Medina	3,016	9	8	1
Brewster	2,407	8	6	2	Mercer Island	23,055	35	31	4
Brier	6,182	9	7	2	Mill Creek	18,530	26	23	3
Buckley	4,906	14	9	5	Milton	7,077	14	13	1
Burien	33,836	68	51	17	Monroe	17,575	41	31	10
Burlington	8,520	28	23	5	Montesano	4,038	10	8	2
Camas	19,659	27	23	4	Morton	1,144	4	3	1
Castle Rock	2,013	6	5	1	Moses Lake	20,686	42	34	8
Centralia	16,592	40	33	7	Mossyrock	771	2	2	0
Chehalis	7,373	21	16	5	Mountlake Terrace	20,221	38	28	10
Cheney	10,756	19	13	6	Mount Vernon	32,241	55	43	12
Chewelah	2,648	6	5	1	Moxee	3,360	5	5	0
Clarkston	7,342	15	14	1	Mukilteo	20,572	32	28	4
Cle Elum	1,901	9	8	1	Napavine	1,794	2	2	0
Clyde Hill	3,031	8	7	1	Newcastle	10,543	9	7	2
Colfax	2,849	7	6	1	Normandy Park	6,434	12	11	1
College Place	8,903	13	10	3	North Bend	5,821	8	6	2
Colville	4,746	12	10	2	Oak Harbor	22,421	40	27	13
Connell	4,275	6	6	0	Ocean Shores	5,656	13	11	2
Cosmopolis	1,675	5	4	1	Odessa	924	2	2	0
Coulee City	571	1	1	0	Olympia	47,207	89	62	27
Coulee Dam	1,115	7	7	0	Omak	4,921	13	11	2
Coupeville	1,860	5	5	0	Oroville	1,712	6	5	1
Covington	17,851	20	17	3	Orting	6,852	10	10	0
Des Moines	30,139	49	37	12	Othello	7,480	22	16	6
Dupont	8,328	12	9	3	Pacific	6,710	12	10	2
Duvall	6,800	16	15	1	Palouse	1,014	3	3	0
East Wenatchee	13,397	24	21	3	Pasco	60,719	76	64	12
Eatonville	2,801	6	5	1	Port Angeles	19,337	59	32	27
Edgewood	9,534	6	6	0	Port Orchard	11,319	24	22	2
Edmonds	40,332	61	52	9	Port Townsend	9,256	18	15	3
Ellensburg	18,459	36	27	9	Poulsbo	9,344	19	16	3
Elma	3,156	8	7	1	Prosser	5,804	17	11	6
Enumclaw	10,836	28	15	13	Pullman	30,267	39	28	11
Ephrata	7,784	19	15	4	Puyallup	37,603	74	54	20
Everett	104,635	232	190	42	Quincy	6,856	17	15	2
Everson	2,520	6	6	0	Raymond	2,927	7	6	1
Federal Way	90,707	149	122	27	Reardan	580	1	1	0
Ferndale	11,594	18	16	2	Redmond	54,993	124	83	41
Fife	9,317	55	31	24	Renton	92,354	149	122	27
Fircrest	6,599	9	9	0	Republic	1,090	3	2	1
Forks	3,587	12	5	7	Richland	48,812	70	59	11
Gig Harbor	7,238	19	17	2	Ridgefield	4,838	8	7	1
Goldendale	3,460	10	9	1	Ritzville	1,699	4	4	0
Grand Coulee	1,004	8	8	0	Rosalia	559	1	1	0
Grandview	11,032	24	18	6	Roy	805	2	2	0
Granger	3,297	5	5	0	Royal City	2,174	3	3	0
Granite Falls	3,417	9	7	2	Ruston	761	3	3	0
Hoquiam	8,863	20	17	3	Sammamish	46,498	28	22	6
Issaquah	30,911	59	31	28	SeaTac	27,331	57	43	14
Kalama	2,381	5	5	0	Seattle	618,209	1,804	1,305	499
Kelso	12,112	28	25	3	Sedro Woolley	10,705	17	14	3
Kenmore	20,781	19	15	4	Selah	7,259	15	14	1
Kennewick	75,077	104	87	17	Sequim	6,710	21	18	3
Kent	93,861	186	131	55	Shelton	9,988	21	18	3
Kettle Falls	1,620	5	4	1	Shoreline	53,839	68	51	17
Kirkland	49,552	122	92	30	Snohomish	9,241	23	18	5
Kittitas	1,403	2	2	0	Snoqualmie	10,837	17	14	3
La Center	2,844	10	8	2	Soap Lake	1,538	3	3	0
Lacey	43,058	65	54	11	South Bend	1,663	5	4	1
Lake Forest Park	12,796	22	18	4	Spokane	212,194	377	275	102
Lake Stevens	28,509	32	27	5	Spokane Valley	91,163	98	97	1
Lakewood	59,075	117	102	15	Springdale	289	1	1	0
Langley	1,051	3	3	0	Stanwood	6,329	13	11	2
Liberty Lake	7,710	10	9	1	Steilacoom	6,079	9	8	1
Long Beach	1,414	7	6	1	Sumas	1,328	6	6	0
Longview	37,223	65	54	11	Sumner	9,599	26	19	7
Lynden	12,138	18	14	4	Sunnyside	16,107	56	31	25
Lynnwood	36,398	102	71	31	Tacoma	201,510	421	378	43

Table V-9.   Full-Time Law Enforcement Employees, by Selected State and City, 2011—_Continued_

(Number.)

State/City	Popula-tion	Total law enforce-ment employees	Total officers	Total civilians	State/City	Popula-tion	Total law enforce-ment employees	Total officers	Total civilians
Tenino	1,722	5	4	1	Gary	969	2	2	0
Tieton	1,210	2	2	0	Gassaway	909	1	1	0
Toledo	736	2	2	0	Gauley Bridge	615	3	2	1
Tonasket	1,048	4	3	1	Gilbert	451	6	4	2
Toppenish	9,089	27	16	11	Glasgow	906	2	2	0
Tukwila	19,407	83	67	16	Glen Dale	1,528	9	4	5
Tumwater	17,644	29	24	5	Glenville	1,539	3	2	1
Twisp	933	3	3	0	Grafton	5,171	7	4	3
Union Gap	6,142	19	16	3	Grantsville	562	2	2	0
University Place	31,633	17	16	1	Grant Town	614	1	1	0
Vader	631	1	1	0	Granville	782	13	12	1
Vancouver	164,329	205	184	21	Hamlin	1,143	5	4	1
Walla Walla	32,229	70	42	28	Handley	349	1	1	0
Wapato	5,075	18	11	7	Harpers Ferry/Bolivar	1,332	5	4	1
Warden	2,734	5	4	1	Harrisville	1,878	1	1	0
Washougal	14,316	20	18	2	Henderson	271	1	1	0
Wenatchee	32,426	50	40	10	Hinton	2,679	4	4	0
Westport	2,132	8	6	2	Huntington	49,201	112	103	9
West Richland	11,996	16	14	2	Hurricane	6,292	17	15	2
White Salmon	2,259	7	6	1	Iaeger	302	1	1	0
Wilbur	898	2	2	0	Kenova	3,220	10	6	4
Winlock	1,360	2	2	0	Kermit	407	1	1	0
Winthrop	400	3	3	0	Keyser	5,446	15	10	5
Woodinville	11,110	16	12	4	Keystone	282	1	1	0
Woodland	5,595	12	10	2	Kimball	194	3	1	2
Yakima	92,496	172	131	41	Kingwood	2,943	2	2	0
Yelm	6,955	15	13	2	Lewisburg	3,835	13	11	2
Zillah	3,011	9	7	2	Logan	1,781	11	8	3
					Lumberport	877	2	2	0
West Virginia					Mabscott	1,410	4	4	0
Albright	299	2	1	1	Madison	3,080	5	4	1
Alderson	1,186	2	2	0	Man	760	2	2	0
Anawalt	226	1	1	0	Mannington	2,066	4	4	0
Anmoore	771	5	1	4	Marmet	1,505	5	5	0
Ansted	1,406	2	2	0	Martinsburg	17,249	60	48	12
Athens	1,049	1	1	0	Mason	969	4	4	0
Barboursville	3,969	20	18	2	Matewan	500	1	1	0
Barrackville	1,304	2	2	0	Matoaka	227	1	1	0
Bayard	290	2	2	0	McMechen	1,928	3	3	0
Beckley	17,637	65	45	20	Monongah	1,045	1	1	0
Belington	1,923	2	2	0	Montgomery	1,640	6	5	1
Belle	1,262	4	4	0	Moorefield	2,547	9	8	1
Benwood	1,422	10	6	4	Morgantown	29,698	74	64	10
Berkeley Springs	625	3	3	0	Moundsville	9,330	22	18	4
Bethlehem	2,502	4	4	0	Mount Hope	1,416	8	5	3
Bluefield	10,460	29	22	7	Mullens	1,561	6	6	0
Bradshaw	337	1	1	0	New Cumberland	1,104	3	3	0
Bramwell	364	1	1	0	New Haven	1,562	2	2	0
Bridgeport	8,159	32	29	3	New Martinsville	5,373	14	10	4
Buckhannon	5,646	9	8	1	Nitro	7,187	19	18	1
Burnsville	511	2	2	0	Nutter Fort	1,595	6	6	0
Cameron	947	2	2	0	Oak Hill	7,740	16	14	2
Capon Bridge	355	2	2	0	Oceana	1,396	5	5	0
Cedar Grove	998	2	2	0	Paden City	2,636	4	3	1
Ceredo	1,452	9	6	3	Parkersburg	31,532	74	63	11
Chapmanville	1,258	4	4	0	Parsons	1,487	1	1	0
Charleston	51,466	187	161	26	Paw Paw	509	1	1	0
Charles Town	5,266	18	15	3	Pennsboro	1,172	1	1	0
Chesapeake	1,556	4	4	0	Petersburg	2,470	5	2	3
Chester	2,588	7	6	1	Philippi	2,970	6	6	0
Clarksburg	16,599	51	47	4	Piedmont	877	1	1	0
Clendenin	1,229	4	4	0	Pineville	669	3	3	0
Danville	692	1	1	0	Point Pleasant	4,356	10	9	1
Davy	421	1	1	0	Pratt	603	1	1	0
Delbarton	580	2	2	0	Princeton	6,440	23	19	4
Dunbar	7,917	13	11	2	Rainelle	1,507	3	1	2
East Bank	960	3	3	0	Ranson	4,446	14	13	1
Eleanor	1,520	2	2	0	Ravenswood	3,881	9	8	1
Elkins	7,103	12	9	3	Reedsville	594	1	1	0
Fairmont	18,728	40	34	6	Rhodell	173	1	1	0
Fairview	409	1	1	0	Richwood	2,054	4	4	0
Farmington	375	1	1	0	Ridgeley	676	3	3	0
Fayetteville	2,896	10	9	1	Ripley	3,256	9	8	1
Follansbee	2,990	7	7	0	Rivesville	935	2	2	0
Fort Gay	706	4	4	0	Romney	1,850	4	3	1

Table V-9. Full-Time Law Enforcement Employees, by Selected State and City, 2011—*Continued*

(Number.)

State/City	Population	Total law enforcement employees	Total officers	Total civilians	State/City	Population	Total law enforcement employees	Total officers	Total civilians
Ronceverte	1,767	7	7	0	Butler	1,849	8	7	1
Rowlesburg	585	1	1	0	Caledonia	24,813	32	29	3
Salem	1,588	2	2	0	Campbellsport	2,025	1	1	0
Shepherdstown	1,736	7	5	2	Campbell Township	4,333	4	4	0
Shinnston	2,204	8	8	0	Cashton	1,107	2	2	0
Sistersville	1,398	4	4	0	Cedarburg	11,462	26	19	7
Smithers	814	4	3	1	Chenequa	593	9	8	1
Sophia	1,346	5	5	0	Chetek	2,231	6	5	1
South Charleston	13,467	41	39	2	Chilton	3,950	6	6	0
Spencer	2,325	6	6	0	Chippewa Falls	13,721	30	24	6
St. Albans	11,058	25	23	2	Cleveland	1,491	2	2	0
Star City	1,827	6	5	1	Clinton	2,163	6	6	0
St. Marys	1,862	4	4	0	Clintonville	4,579	15	11	4
Stonewood	1,808	2	2	0	Colby-Abbotsford	4,180	7	6	1
Summersville	3,577	18	17	1	Columbus	5,013	12	11	1
Sutton	995	2	1	1	Coon Valley	768	1	1	0
Sylvester	160	1	1	0	Cornell	1,473	2	2	0
Terra Alta	1,479	1	1	0	Cottage Grove	6,219	12	11	1
Triadelphia	812	1	1	0	Crandon	1,928	3	2	1
Vienna	10,763	22	17	5	Cross Plains	3,553	6	5	1
Wardensville	271	1	1	0	Cuba City	2,095	4	3	1
Wayne	1,415	2	2	0	Cudahy	18,347	42	31	11
Webster Springs	777	2	2	0	Cumberland	2,179	4	4	0
Weirton	19,771	38	35	3	Darien	1,587	6	5	1
Welch	2,409	6	5	1	Darlington	2,462	5	5	0
Wellsburg	2,809	6	6	0	Deforest	8,975	19	16	3
West Logan	425	1	1	0	Delafield	7,116	16	14	2
Weston	4,115	8	6	2	Delavan	8,500	22	17	5
Westover	3,988	9	9	0	Delavan Town	5,308	12	11	1
West Union	826	1	1	0	Denmark	2,132	2	2	0
Wheeling	28,522	83	80	3	De Pere	23,904	39	34	5
White Sulphur Springs	2,447	7	6	1	Dodgeville	4,713	10	9	1
Williamson	3,195	10	8	2	Durand	1,939	3	3	0
Williamstown	2,912	7	6	1	Eagle River	1,404	5	5	0
Winfield	2,304	2	2	0	Eagle Village	1,958	3	3	0
					East Troy	4,300	7	7	0
Wisconsin					Eau Claire	66,170	132	95	37
Adams	1,976	4	4	0	Edgar	1,485	1	1	0
Albany	1,022	3	3	0	Edgerton	5,485	12	10	2
Algoma	3,181	6	6	0	Eleva	673	1	1	0
Altoona	6,735	13	12	1	Elkhart Lake	971	3	3	0
Amery	2,915	7	6	1	Elkhorn	10,128	19	16	3
Antigo	8,270	18	15	3	Elk Mound	882	1	1	0
Appleton	72,939	132	107	25	Ellsworth	3,298	6	5	1
Arcadia	2,938	5	5	0	Elm Grove	5,960	25	17	8
Ashland	8,252	21	19	2	Elroy	1,448	3	3	0
Ashwaubenon	17,037	54	47	7	Evansville	5,034	12	9	3
Athens	1,110	1	1	0	Everest	17,111	28	25	3
Avoca	640	1	1	0	Fall Creek	1,321	2	2	0
Bangor	1,465	2	2	0	Fall River	1,719	2	2	0
Baraboo	12,100	34	28	6	Fennimore	2,508	5	5	0
Barron	3,438	6	6	0	Fitchburg	25,370	56	44	12
Bayfield	489	3	3	0	Fond du Lac	43,208	79	73	6
Bayside	4,408	20	13	7	Fontana	1,679	7	6	1
Beaver Dam	16,285	35	30	5	Fort Atkinson	12,422	24	18	6
Belleville	2,395	5	5	0	Fountain City	863	1	1	0
Beloit	37,127	86	74	12	Fox Lake	1,526	3	3	0
Beloit Town	7,695	10	9	1	Fox Point	6,730	18	17	1
Berlin	5,548	13	12	1	Fox Valley Metro	16,991	33	30	3
Big Bend	1,296	3	3	0	Franklin	35,605	74	58	16
Black River Falls	3,638	7	6	1	Frederic	1,142	1	1	0
Blair	1,372	2	2	0	Freedom	5,867	2	2	0
Bloomer	3,554	7	6	1	Geneva Town	5,015	7	6	1
Bloomfield	6,305	7	7	0	Genoa City	3,055	5	4	1
Blue Mounds	859	5	4	1	Germantown	19,835	41	30	11
Boscobel	3,245	6	6	0	Gillett	1,392	9	4	5
Brandon-Fairwater	1,256	1	1	0	Glendale	12,928	47	43	4
Brillion	3,162	8	7	1	Grafton	11,509	27	21	6
Brodhead	3,307	12	8	4	Grand Chute	21,010	33	29	4
Brookfield	38,085	81	64	17	Grand Rapids	7,679	7	5	2
Brookfield Township	6,143	14	13	1	Grantsburg	1,347	3	3	0
Brown Deer	12,051	34	29	5	Green Bay	104,510	225	186	39
Burlington	10,510	27	21	6	Greendale	14,107	36	28	8
Burlington Town	6,530	3	2	1	Greenfield	36,880	77	58	19

Table V-9.   Full-Time Law Enforcement Employees, by Selected State and City, 2011—*Continued*

(Number.)

State/City	Population	Total law enforcement employees	Total officers	Total civilians	State/City	Population	Total law enforcement employees	Total officers	Total civilians
Green Lake	964	2	2	0	Neshkoro	436	1	1	0
Hales Corners	7,726	19	16	3	New Berlin	39,756	84	68	16
Hartford	14,285	29	25	4	New Glarus	2,181	3	3	0
Hartland	9,150	18	16	2	New Holstein	3,250	7	6	1
Hayward	2,328	10	9	1	New Lisbon	2,565	4	4	0
Hazel Green	1,261	2	2	0	New London	7,327	19	17	2
Highland	846	1	1	0	New Richmond	8,411	15	15	0
Hillsboro	1,423	2	2	0	Niagara	1,631	4	4	0
Hobart-Lawrence	10,512	6	4	2	North Fond du Lac	5,036	13	11	2
Holmen	9,044	11	10	1	North Hudson	3,784	6	5	1
Horicon	3,671	7	6	1	Oak Creek	34,601	79	58	21
Hortonville	2,723	6	5	1	Oconomowoc	15,828	28	22	6
Hudson	12,774	25	22	3	Oconomowoc Town	8,445	12	10	2
Hurley	1,554	7	6	1	Oconto	4,533	8	7	1
Independence	1,342	4	4	0	Oconto Falls	2,904	5	5	0
Iron Ridge	933	1	1	0	Omro	3,532	7	6	1
Iron River	1,128	3	3	0	Onalaska	17,813	28	25	3
Jackson	6,782	11	10	1	Oregon	9,271	17	15	2
Janesville	63,852	114	102	12	Osceola	2,579	7	6	1
Jefferson	8,008	17	14	3	Oshkosh	66,371	115	97	18
Juneau	2,826	5	4	1	Osseo	1,708	4	4	0
Kaukauna	15,529	25	24	1	Palmyra	1,789	3	3	0
Kenosha	99,650	208	199	9	Park Falls	2,473	8	7	1
Kewaskum	4,021	7	7	0	Pepin	841	1	1	0
Kewaunee	2,965	6	6	0	Peshtigo	3,517	7	6	1
Kiel	3,754	8	7	1	Pewaukee Village	8,202	19	17	2
Kohler	2,129	8	7	1	Phillips	1,484	5	5	0
Kronenwetter	7,241	7	6	1	Plainfield	866	2	2	0
La Crosse	51,544	105	87	18	Platteville	11,273	24	18	6
Ladysmith	3,429	10	9	1	Pleasant Prairie	19,805	32	30	2
Lake Delton	2,927	21	19	2	Plover	12,176	22	19	3
Lake Geneva	7,684	31	22	9	Plymouth	8,482	16	16	0
Lake Hallie	6,476	7	6	1	Portage	10,369	26	22	4
Lake Mills	5,733	10	10	0	Port Washington	11,299	24	19	5
Lancaster	3,885	6	6	0	Poynette	2,539	5	4	1
Lodi	3,063	6	5	1	Prairie du Chien	5,937	13	12	1
Lomira	2,441	3	3	0	Prescott	4,277	9	8	1
Luxemburg	2,526	2	2	0	Pulaski	3,554	10	9	1
Madison	234,225	552	447	105	Racine	79,204	239	202	37
Manawa	1,377	3	3	0	Reedsburg	9,240	28	20	8
Manitowoc	33,883	71	63	8	Rhinelander	7,832	20	17	3
Maple Bluff	1,319	6	6	0	Rice Lake	8,475	19	18	1
Marathon City	1,531	2	2	0	Richland Center	5,207	13	11	2
Marinette	11,016	27	23	4	Ripon	7,767	20	14	6
Marion	1,265	3	3	0	River Falls	15,065	24	22	2
Markesan	1,482	3	3	0	River Hills	1,604	12	12	0
Marshall Village	3,879	7	6	1	Rome Town	2,732	8	7	1
Marshfield	19,201	46	39	7	Rosendale	1,068	1	1	0
Mauston	4,442	9	8	1	Rothschild	5,292	12	10	2
Mayville	5,176	9	7	2	Sauk Prairie	4,574	16	14	2
McFarland	7,842	16	14	2	Saukville	4,470	13	11	2
Medford	4,345	10	9	1	Seymour	3,466	6	6	0
Menasha	17,429	34	28	6	Shawano	9,346	21	19	2
Menomonee Falls	35,781	78	58	20	Sheboygan	49,503	110	81	29
Menomonie	16,335	35	27	8	Sheboygan Falls	7,809	16	14	2
Mequon	23,233	43	35	8	Shiocton	925	2	1	1
Merrill	9,703	25	22	3	Shorewood	13,219	29	24	5
Middleton	17,518	46	36	10	Shorewood Hills	1,572	8	6	2
Milton	5,570	13	11	2	Silver Lake	2,422	5	4	1
Milwaukee	597,426	2,586	1,862	724	Siren	810	3	3	0
Mineral Point	2,498	5	5	0	Slinger	5,090	10	9	1
Minocqua	4,404	15	10	5	Somerset	2,646	6	5	1
Mishicot	1,448	1	1	0	South Milwaukee	21,248	39	33	6
Mondovi	2,789	4	4	0	Sparta	9,563	19	17	2
Monona	7,566	25	20	5	Spencer	1,933	3	3	0
Monroe	10,874	35	26	9	Spooner	2,694	8	7	1
Montello	1,502	3	2	1	Spring Green	1,635	4	3	1
Mosinee	4,005	8	7	1	Stanley	3,624	4	4	0
Mount Horeb	7,040	11	10	1	St. Croix Falls	2,142	5	5	0
Mount Pleasant	26,311	45	41	4	Stevens Point	26,833	57	42	15
Mukwonago	7,387	21	14	7	St. Francis	9,406	26	21	5
Muskego	24,240	47	37	10	Stoughton	12,666	26	20	6
Neenah	25,612	51	41	10	Strum	1,119	2	2	0
Neillsville	2,474	7	6	1	Sturgeon Bay	9,184	22	20	2

Table V-9.   Full-Time Law Enforcement Employees, by Selected State and City, 2011—*Continued*

(Number.)

State/City	Population	Total law enforcement employees	Total officers	Total civilians	State/City	Population	Total law enforcement employees	Total officers	Total civilians
Sturtevant	7,000	11	10	1	**Wyoming**				
Summit	4,694	8	8	0	Afton	1,926	4	4	0
Sun Prairie	29,492	71	50	21	Alpine	835	1	1	0
Superior	27,363	65	60	5	Basin	1,295	3	3	0
Theresa	1,267	2	2	0	Buffalo	4,622	20	11	9
Thiensville	3,249	8	7	1	Casper	55,761	126	84	42
Three Lakes	2,140	4	4	0	Cheyenne	59,944	119	97	22
Tomah	9,133	22	20	2	Cody	9,597	24	21	3
Tomahawk	3,412	8	7	1	Cokeville	539	3	3	0
Town of East Troy	4,039	7	6	1	Diamondville	743	4	3	1
Town of Madison	6,306	18	16	2	Douglas	6,169	22	14	8
Town of Menasha	18,579	31	25	6	Evanston	12,458	33	27	6
Trempealeau	1,536	2	2	0	Evansville	2,564	12	10	2
Twin Lakes	6,015	19	13	6	Gillette	29,321	85	54	31
Two Rivers	11,763	28	24	4	Glenrock	2,597	12	6	6
Valders	966	1	1	0	Green River	12,616	38	28	10
Verona	10,665	22	20	2	Greybull	1,862	6	5	1
Viroqua	4,381	11	9	2	Guernsey	1,156	2	2	0
Walworth	2,828	19	12	7	Hanna	848	1	1	0
Washburn	2,126	7	7	0	Hulett	386	2	2	0
Waterloo	3,348	9	8	1	Jackson	9,654	34	26	8
Watertown	23,965	50	36	14	Kemmerer	2,677	8	7	1
Waukesha	71,026	149	117	32	La Barge	555	3	3	0
Waunakee	12,150	19	17	2	Lander	7,547	19	18	1
Waupaca	6,095	14	13	1	Laramie	31,064	77	49	28
Waupun	11,389	19	17	2	Lovell	2,379	10	6	4
Wausau	39,276	76	70	6	Lusk	1,580	4	4	0
Wautoma	2,228	7	6	1	Lyman	2,132	5	4	1
Wauwatosa	46,598	115	92	23	Mills	3,489	15	12	3
West Allis	60,674	155	130	25	Moorcroft	1,017	5	4	1
West Bend	31,213	72	55	17	Newcastle	3,560	13	7	6
Westby	2,210	3	3	0	Pine Bluffs	1,138	6	3	3
Westfield	1,259	3	3	0	Powell	6,365	24	15	9
West Milwaukee	4,224	23	18	5	Rawlins	9,333	29	19	10
West Salem	4,820	7	6	1	Riverton	10,700	39	28	11
Whitefish Bay	14,171	26	24	2	Rock Springs	23,221	66	45	21
Whitehall	1,565	4	4	0	Saratoga	1,704	10	6	4
Whitewater	14,453	33	23	10	Sheridan	17,584	43	28	15
Williams Bay	2,575	8	7	1	Sundance	1,192	3	3	0
Winneconne	2,360	6	5	1	Thermopolis	3,033	13	7	6
Wisconsin Dells	2,690	19	13	6	Torrington	6,553	21	14	7
Wisconsin Rapids	18,447	41	36	5	Upton	1,109	3	3	0
Woodruff	2,064	6	5	1	Wheatland	3,656	9	8	1
					Worland	5,531	10	10	0

Table V-10.   Full-Time Law Enforcement Employees, by Selected State and University or College, 2011

(Number.)

State and university/college	Campus	Student enrollment[1]	Total law enforcement employees	Total officers	Total civilians
Alabama					
Alabama State University............................		5,705	41	30	11
Auburn University	Montgomery	5,817	15	10	5
Calhoun Community College		12,134	9	8	1
Faulkner State Community College		4,620	4	4	0
Jacksonville State University		9,504	19	14	5
Troy University		28,322	17	11	6
University of Alabama..................................	Birmingham	17,543	163	86	77
	Huntsville	7,614	20	13	7
	Tuscaloosa	30,127	80	66	14
University of Montevallo		3,045	17	8	9
University of North Alabama		7,209	15	13	2
University of South Alabama		14,776	43	27	16
University of West Alabama		5,094	9	6	3
Alaska					
University of Alaska	Anchorage	18,154	21	15	6
	Fairbanks	9,855	17	10	7
Arizona					
Arizona State University..............................	Main Campus	70,440	124	65	59
Arizona Western College		8,545	12	7	5
Central Arizona College...............................		7,117	9	6	3
Northern Arizona University.......................		25,197	27	17	10
Pima Community College		36,823	33	26	7
University of Arizona		39,086	99	57	42
Yavapai College..		8,410	10	9	1
Arkansas					
Arkansas State University............................	Beebe	4,683	5	4	1
	Jonesboro	13,415	24	19	5
Arkansas Tech University		9,815	14	12	2
Henderson State University.........................		3,708	9	8	1
Northwest Arkansas Community College...		8,365	16	11	5
Southern Arkansas University.....................		3,379	8	7	1
Southern Arkansas University Tech.............		1,851	4	4	0
University of Arkansas	Fayetteville	21,405	42	34	8
	Little Rock	13,176	38	27	11
	Medical Sciences	2,836	46	35	11
	Monticello	3,638	9	8	1
	Pine Bluff	3,428	20	14	6
University of Central Arkansas....................		11,444	34	25	9
California					
Allan Hancock College		12,108	5	4	1
California State Polytechnic University	Pomona	20,747	32	18	14
	San Luis Obispo	18,360	37	18	19
California State University...........................	Bakersfield	7,906	15	11	4
	Channel Islands	3,828	24	13	11
	Chico	15,989	28	16	12
	Dominguez Hills	13,854	23	16	7
	East Bay	12,889	23	13	10
	Fresno	20,932	29	20	9
	Fullerton	35,590	34	23	11
	Long Beach	33,416	45	23	22
	Los Angeles	20,142	31	18	13
	Monterey Bay	4,790	19	13	6
	Northridge	35,272	37	22	15
	Sacramento	27,033	37	21	16
	San Bernardino	16,400	24	16	8
	San Jose[2]		66	26	40
	San Marcos	9,722	39	17	22
	Stanislaus	8,305	20	11	9
College of the Sequoias		13,470	5	4	1
Contra Costa Community College...............		7,975	32	22	10
Cuesta College..		11,335	7	6	1
El Camino College		24,756	32	25	7
Foothill-De Anza College		41,104	17	9	8
Humboldt State University		7,903	18	11	7
Marin Community College...........................		7,353	9	8	1
Pasadena Community College......................		27,023	15	7	8
Riverside Community College......................		20,585	25	18	7
San Bernardino Community College...........		13,822	17	9	8
San Diego State University...........................		29,187	43	22	21
San Francisco State University		29,718	47	26	21
San Jose/Evergreen Community College		21,671	10	4	6

[1] The student enrollment figures provided by the United States Department of Education are for the 2010 school year, the most recent available. The enrollment figures include full-time and part-time students.

[2] Student enrollment figures were not available.

Table V-10. Full-Time Law Enforcement Employees, by Selected State and University or College, 2011—*Continued*

(Number.)

State and university/college	Campus	Student enrollment[1]	Total law enforcement employees	Total officers	Total civilians
Santa Rosa Junior College		24,879	27	14	13
Solano Community College		11,801	5	3	2
Sonoma State University		8,395	20	11	9
State Center Community College District		38,821	18	15	3
University of California	Berkeley	35,833	106	64	42
	Davis	31,392	70	47	23
	Hastings College of Law	1,304	14	14	0
	Irvine	26,994	46	32	14
	Los Angeles	38,157	95	58	37
	Merced	4,381	20	11	9
	Riverside	20,692	36	26	10
	San Diego	29,176	65	30	35
	San Francisco	3,024	112	46	66
	Santa Barbara	22,218	44	29	15
	Santa Cruz	17,187	38	17	21
Ventura County Community College District		13,711	14	13	1
West Valley-Mission College		22,783	15	9	6
Colorado					
Adams State College		3,237	7	6	1
Arapahoe Community College		9,961	10	7	3
Auraria Higher Education Center[2]			37	26	11
Colorado School of Mines		5,287	9	8	1
Colorado State University	Fort Collins	30,155	44	31	13
	Pueblo	7,379	3	2	1
Fort Lewis College		3,853	9	7	2
Pikes Peak Community College		15,299	18	16	2
Red Rocks Community College		9,826	3	3	0
University of Colorado	Boulder	32,697	62	41	21
	Colorado Springs	9,745	28	16	12
	Denver	24,108	58	27	31
University of Northern Colorado		13,030	22	15	7
Connecticut					
Central Connecticut State University		12,477	26	20	6
Eastern Connecticut State University		5,606	22	16	6
Southern Connecticut State University		11,964	33	26	7
University of Connecticut	Health Center[2]		30	14	16
	Storrs, Avery Point, and Hartford[2]		86	70	16
Western Connecticut State University		6,582	24	17	7
Yale University		11,701	96	81	15
Delaware					
Delaware State University		3,757	36	19	17
University of Delaware		21,177	78	50	28
Florida					
Edison State College		16,951	12	6	6
Florida A&M University		13,284	59	34	25
Florida Atlantic University		28,270	68	41	27
Florida Gulf Coast University		12,015	18	13	5
Florida International University		42,197	72	47	25
Florida State University	Tallahassee	40,416	72	58	14
New College of Florida		801	18	12	6
Pensacola Junior College		11,676	13	8	5
Santa Fe College		15,745	21	16	5
Tallahassee Community College		14,739	28	13	15
University of Central Florida		56,106	90	59	31
University of Florida		49,827	132	80	52
University of North Florida		16,153	37	28	9
University of South Florida	St. Petersburg	3,944	16	11	5
	Tampa	40,431	57	41	16
University of West Florida		11,599	28	18	10
Georgia					
Abraham Baldwin Agricultural College		3,284	10	10	0
Agnes Scott College		917	16	9	7
Armstrong Atlantic State University		7,682	27	19	8
Atlanta Metropolitan College		3,037	15	8	7
Augusta State University		6,919	23	17	6
Berry College		2,087	17	13	4
Clark Atlanta University		3,941	43	16	27
College of Coastal Georgia		3,438	15	15	0
Dalton State College		5,988	17	14	3

[1] The student enrollment figures provided by the United States Department of Education are for the 2010 school year, the most recent available. The enrollment figures include full-time and part-time students.

[2] Student enrollment figures were not available.

Table V-10.   Full-Time Law Enforcement Employees, by Selected State and University or College, 2011—*Continued*

(Number.)

State and university/college	Campus	Student enrollment[1]	Total law enforcement employees	Total officers	Total civilians
Darton College		5,879	7	6	1
Emory University		13,381	68	50	18
Fort Valley State University		3,728	42	16	26
Gainesville State College		8,883	9	9	0
Georgia College and State University		6,737	22	15	7
Georgia Gwinnett College		5,380	24	20	4
Georgia Institute of Technology		20,720	94	74	20
Georgia Military College		1,549	5	3	2
Georgia Perimeter College		25,113	102	52	50
Georgia Southern University		19,691	45	39	6
Georgia State University		31,533	142	67	75
Gordon College		5,009	12	11	1
Kennesaw State University		23,452	63	35	28
Macon State College		6,232	6	5	1
Medical College of Georgia[2]			46	32	14
Mercer University		8,236	31	22	9
Middle Georgia College		3,496	19	17	2
Morehouse College		2,586	49	18	31
Morehouse School of Medicine		329	5	5	0
Morris Brown College[2]			4	2	2
North Georgia College and State University		5,912	19	12	7
Savannah State University		4,080	45	18	27
Southern Crescent Technical College		6,227	4	3	1
Southern Polytechnic State University		5,514	17	14	3
South Georgia College		2,214	9	5	4
Spelman College		2,177	23	13	10
University of Georgia		34,677	98	76	22
University of West Georgia		11,283	28	20	8
Valdosta State University		12,898	31	23	8
Wesleyan College		690	5	5	0
West Georgia Technical College		8,092	6	6	0
Young Harris College		820	5	4	1
Illinois					
Benedictine University		6,892	20	13	7
Black Hawk College		6,677	11	10	1
Chicago State University		7,354	37	27	10
College of DuPage		26,722	20	15	5
Elgin Community College		12,214	15	12	3
Governors State University		5,660	9	5	4
Harper College		16,060	17	11	6
Illinois State University		21,134	31	24	7
John A. Logan College		7,431	9	7	2
Joliet Junior College		15,676	22	13	9
Lake Land College		8,234	5	5	0
Loyola University		15,951	53	30	23
Moraine Valley Community College		17,387	22	15	7
Northeastern Illinois University		11,746	28	23	5
Northern Illinois University		23,850	100	70	30
Northwestern University	Chicago[2]		17	16	1
	Evanston[2]		71	29	42
Oakton Community College		11,837	12	11	1
Parkland College		9,715	20	14	6
Rock Valley College		8,849	16	13	3
Southern Illinois University	Carbondale	20,037	52	34	18
	Edwardsville	14,133	48	35	13
	School of Medicine[2]		12	5	7
South Suburban College		7,161	14	10	4
Southwestern Illinois College		13,221	22	16	6
Triton College		15,253	15	11	4
University of Illinois	Chicago	27,850	134	81	53
	Springfield	5,174	21	15	6
	Urbana	43,862	75	61	14
Waubonsee College		10,428	4	4	0
Western Illinois University		12,585	30	25	5
Indiana					
Ball State University		22,083	35	28	7
Indiana State University		11,494	33	23	10
Indiana University	Bloomington	42,464	50	41	9
	Indianapolis	30,566	49	41	8
	New Albany	7,178	10	7	3
Marian University		2,357	11	6	5
Purdue University		41,063	53	39	14

[1] The student enrollment figures provided by the United States Department of Education are for the 2010 school year, the most recent available. The enrollment figures include full-time and part-time students.

[2] Student enrollment figures were not available.

Table V-10.   Full-Time Law Enforcement Employees, by Selected State and University or College, 2011—*Continued*

(Number.)

State and university/college	Campus	Student enrollment[1]	Total law enforcement employees	Total officers	Total civilians
Iowa					
Iowa State University		28,682	39	32	7
University of Iowa		29,518	71	42	29
University of Northern Iowa		13,201	27	18	9
Kansas					
Emporia State University		6,262	9	9	0
Fort Hays State University		11,883	10	8	2
Kansas City Community College		7,556	14	13	1
Pittsburg State University		7,130	16	13	3
University of Kansas	Main Campus	28,697	48	25	23
	Medical Center[2]		67	31	36
Washburn University		7,230	19	14	5
Wichita State University		14,577	36	23	13
Kentucky					
Eastern Kentucky University		16,567	31	25	6
Kentucky State University		2,851	21	13	8
Morehead State University		8,541	41	16	25
Murray State University		10,412	22	14	8
Northern Kentucky University		15,716	22	16	6
University of Kentucky		27,108	139	49	90
University of Louisville		21,234	79	41	38
Western Kentucky University		20,897	37	27	10
Louisiana					
Delgado Community College		18,767	34	25	9
Louisiana State University	Baton Rouge	29,451	62	59	3
	Health Sciences Center, New Orleans	2,699	28	28	0
	Health Sciences Center, Shreveport	839	53	38	15
	Shreveport	4,498	10	9	1
Louisiana Tech University		11,743	17	16	1
McNeese State University		8,935	17	12	5
Nicholls State University		7,082	16	11	5
Northwestern State University		9,244	23	18	5
Southeastern Louisiana University		15,338	35	24	11
Southern University and A&M College	Baton Rouge	6,897	39	21	18
	New Orleans	3,165	14	14	0
Tulane University		12,144	130	94	36
University of Louisiana	Lafayette	16,763	26	24	2
	Monroe	8,801	27	20	7
University of New Orleans		11,276	23	23	0
Maine					
University of Maine	Farmington	2,430	6	5	1
	Orono	11,501	25	17	8
University of Southern Maine		9,654	19	11	8
Maryland					
Bowie State University		5,578	29	15	14
Coppin State University		3,800	46	22	24
Frostburg State University		5,470	20	16	4
Hagerstown Community College		4,715	2	2	0
Morgan State University		7,805	59	41	18
Salisbury University		8,397	27	17	10
St. Mary's College		2,017	13	8	5
Towson University		21,840	59	38	21
University of Baltimore		6,501	40	14	26
University of Maryland	Baltimore City	6,349	147	56	91
	Baltimore County	12,888	33	23	10
	College Park	37,641	136	88	48
	Eastern Shore	4,540	19	15	4
Massachusetts					
Amherst College		1,794	17	12	5
Assumption College		2,764	26	17	9
Bentley University		5,684	39	24	15
Boston College		14,868	66	53	13
Boston University		32,727	68	52	16
Brandeis University		5,642	25	23	2
Bridgewater State College		11,201	39	21	18
Bristol Community College		8,893	9	6	3

[1] The student enrollment figures provided by the United States Department of Education are for the 2010 school year, the most recent available. The enrollment figures include full-time and part-time students.

[2] Student enrollment figures were not available.

Table V-10.   Full-Time Law Enforcement Employees, by Selected State and University or College, 2011—*Continued*

(Number.)

State and university/college	Campus	Student enrollment[1]	Total law enforcement employees	Total officers	Total civilians
Bunker Hill Community College		12,271	11	10	1
Clark University		3,451	16	12	4
Dean College		1,266	14	7	7
Emerson College		4,566	22	18	4
Fitchburg State College		6,771	17	13	4
Framingham State University		5,953	19	15	4
Hampshire College		1,529	15	11	4
Harvard University		27,594	101	62	39
Holyoke Community College		7,404	12	12	0
Lasell College		1,798	16	14	2
Massachusetts College of Art		2,446	30	8	22
Massachusetts College of Liberal Arts		1,974	12	9	3
Massachusetts Institute of Technology		10,566	54	51	3
Massasoit Community College		8,053	17	15	2
Merrimack College		2,168	19	13	6
Mount Holyoke College		2,344	20	15	5
Northeastern University		29,519	83	54	29
North Shore Community College		7,985	19	18	1
Quinsigamond Community College		8,922	14	13	1
Salem State University		9,993	26	22	4
Smith College		3,113	17	14	3
Springfield College		5,364	38	16	22
Tufts University	Medford	10,480	68	39	29
University of Massachusetts	Amherst	27,569	79	62	17
	Dartmouth	9,432	41	25	16
	Harbor Campus, Boston	15,454	30	24	6
	Medical Center, Worcester	1,158	25	18	7
Wellesley College		2,546	17	14	3
Wentworth Institute of Technology		3,845	19	13	6
Western New England University		3,734	29	16	13
Westfield State University		5,885	22	16	6
Worcester Polytechnic Institute		5,360	25	18	7
Michigan					
Central Michigan University		28,292	27	22	5
Delta College		11,572	11	8	3
Eastern Michigan University		23,565	40	29	11
Ferris State University		14,381	18	14	4
Grand Rapids Community College		17,870	17	13	4
Grand Valley State University		24,541	19	15	4
Kirtland Community College		1,958	1	1	0
Lansing Community College		21,969	15	12	3
Macomb Community College		24,468	37	30	7
Michigan State University		46,985	105	71	34
Michigan Technological University		6,971	16	11	5
Mott Community College		11,850	8	5	3
Northern Michigan University		9,417	23	19	4
Oakland Community College		28,925	24	23	1
Oakland University		19,053	28	22	6
Saginaw Valley State University		10,656	13	11	2
University of Michigan	Ann Arbor	41,924	89	54	35
	Dearborn	8,599	24	9	15
	Flint	8,138	26	12	14
Western Michigan University		25,045	58	24	34
Minnesota					
University of Minnesota	Duluth	11,729	11	9	2
	Morris	1,811	5	3	2
	Twin Cities	51,721	64	50	14
Mississippi					
Coahoma Community College		2,741	11	10	1
East Mississippi Junior College		5,433	4	4	0
Mississippi State University		19,644	39	31	8
Northeast Mississippi Community College		3,627	7	7	0
University of Mississippi	Oxford	17,085	52	32	20
Missouri					
Lincoln University		3,349	17	13	4
Metropolitan Community College		21,244	47	24	23
Mineral Area College		3,958	18	8	10
Missouri Southern State University		5,802	9	6	3
Missouri University of Science and Technology		7,205	21	12	9
Missouri Western State University		6,095	12	9	3

[1] The student enrollment figures provided by the United States Department of Education are for the 2010 school year, the most recent available. The enrollment figures include full-time and part-time students.

Table V-10.   Full-Time Law Enforcement Employees, by Selected State and University or College, 2011—*Continued*

(Number.)

State and university/college	Campus	Student enrollment[1]	Total law enforcement employees	Total officers	Total civilians
Northwest Missouri State University...........		7,142	13	11	2
Southeast Missouri State University............		11,033	27	18	9
St. Charles Community College...................		8,202	11	8	3
St. Louis Community College	Florissant Valley	7,436	11	9	2
	Meramec	11,430	12	9	3
Three Rivers Community College................		3,730	6	5	1
Truman State University.............................		6,035	11	10	1
University of Central Missouri		11,351	20	17	3
University of Missouri	Columbia	32,341	50	34	16
	Kansas City	15,259	44	28	16
	St. Louis	16,791	27	21	6
Washington University		13,820	46	27	19
Montana					
Montana State University		13,081	35	19	16
University of Montana.................................		15,642	24	12	12
Nebraska					
Metropolitan Community College	Douglas County	18,523	22	14	8
University of Nebraska................................	Kearney	6,753	8	7	1
	Lincoln	24,610	57	35	22
Nevada					
Truckee Meadows Community College.......		12,587	9	5	4
University of Nevada	Las Vegas	28,203	53	35	18
New Hampshire					
University of New Hampshire		15,095	32	18	14
New Jersey					
Brookdale Community College...................		15,783	22	14	8
Essex County College		13,424	49	12	37
Kean University		15,939	51	26	25
Middlesex County College		12,887	16	11	5
Monmouth University		6,506	46	21	25
Montclair State University		18,402	45	36	9
New Jersey Institute of Technology		8,934	62	31	31
Richard Stockton College of New Jersey		7,879	26	17	9
Rowan University.......................................		11,300	60	22	38
Rutgers University	Camden	6,158	36	19	17
	Newark	11,798	43	39	4
	New Brunswick	38,912	83	47	36
Stevens Institute of Technology...................		5,629	21	16	5
The College of New Jersey...........................		7,115	29	20	9
University of Medicine and Dentistry	Camden[2]		18	11	7
	Newark	6,813	123	42	81
	New Brunswick[2]		36	20	16
William Paterson University.........................		11,339	42	29	13
New Mexico					
Eastern New Mexico University..................		5,075	9	8	1
New Mexico Highlands University		3,750	14	3	11
New Mexico State University		18,600	30	16	14
University of New Mexico...........................		28,688	47	31	16
Western New Mexico University..................		3,506	5	4	1
New York					
Cornell University.......................................		20,939	65	46	19
Ithaca College..		6,949	38	20	18
Rensselaer Polytechnic Institute		6,704	39	27	12
State University of New York	Albany	17,615	68	43	25
	Binghamton	14,895	39	28	11
	Buffalo	29,117	68	61	7
	Downstate Medical Center	1,702	126	34	92
	Maritime College	1,880	11	6	5
	Stony Brook	24,363	141	64	77
	Upstate Medical Center[2]		111	13	98
State University of New York Agricultural and Technical College.............	Alfred	3,709	16	11	5
	Canton	3,655	10	9	1
	Cobleskill	2,566	11	10	1
	Farmingdale	6,858	26	17	9
State University of New York College.........	Brockport	8,589	18	16	2
	Buffalo	12,419	30	29	1

[1] The student enrollment figures provided by the United States Department of Education are for the 2010 school year, the most recent available. The enrollment figures include full-time and part-time students.

[2] Student enrollment figures were not available.

Table V-10.   Full-Time Law Enforcement Employees, by Selected State and University or College, 2011—*Continued*

(Number.)

State and university/college	Campus	Student enrollment[1]	Total law enforcement employees	Total officers	Total civilians
	Cortland	7,358	25	19	6
	Environmental Science and Forestry	2,682	11	10	1
	Fredonia	5,772	16	15	1
	Geneseo	5,665	16	12	4
	New Paltz[2]		27	24	3
	Old Westbury	4,355	21	18	3
	Oneonta	5,989	26	17	9
	Optometry	303	17	6	11
	Oswego	8,297	24	20	4
	Plattsburgh	6,441	21	15	6
	Potsdam	4,413	14	12	2
	Purchase	4,167	29	25	4
	Technology[2]		12	10	2
	Utica-Rome[2]		16	11	5
North Carolina					
Appalachian State University		17,222	40	26	14
Beaufort County Community College		1,911	3	3	0
Belmont Abbey College		1,734	10	10	0
Davidson College		1,742	10	9	1
Duke University		15,016	153	59	94
East Carolina University		27,783	67	51	16
Elizabeth City State University		3,307	20	11	9
Elon University		5,709	15	14	1
Fayetteville State University		5,781	34	17	17
Methodist University		2,416	8	7	1
North Carolina Agricultural and Technical State University		10,795	58	26	32
North Carolina Central University		8,645	54	27	27
North Carolina School of the Arts		872	19	13	6
North Carolina State University	Raleigh	34,376	53	40	13
Queens University		2,524	14	7	7
University of North Carolina	Asheville	3,967	19	12	7
	Chapel Hill	29,390	92	48	44
	Charlotte	25,063	44	35	9
	Greensboro	18,771	52	30	22
	Pembroke	6,944	21	16	5
	Wilmington	13,071	44	30	14
Wake Forest University		7,162	43	22	21
Western Carolina University		9,407	23	19	4
Winston-Salem State University		6,333	31	15	16
North Dakota					
North Dakota State College of Science		2,833	4	4	0
North Dakota State University		14,407	24	15	9
University of North Dakota		14,194	14	12	2
Ohio					
Bowling Green State University		17,706	32	24	8
Capital University		3,629	11	8	3
Cleveland State University		17,386	39	24	15
College of Mount St. Joseph		2,475	10	7	3
Columbus State Community College		30,513	49	20	29
Cuyahoga Community College		31,250	35	27	8
Hocking College		6,533	5	5	0
Kent State University		26,589	38	30	8
Lakeland Community College		9,831	11	10	1
Miami University		17,472	32	23	9
Muskingum University		2,290	5	5	0
Notre Dame College		2,091	6	5	1
Ohio State University	Columbus	56,064	55	48	7
	Marion	1,816	1	1	0
	Newark	2,562	7	1	6
	Wooster[2]		5	5	0
Ohio University		25,108	30	23	7
Otterbein University		3,080	10	9	1
Sinclair Community College		21,994	26	22	4
University of Akron		27,076	43	37	6
University of Cincinnati		32,283	92	54	38
University of Rio Grande		2,299	7	6	1
University of Toledo		23,085	42	33	9
Wright State University		18,447	26	18	8
Youngstown State University		15,084	24	19	5

[1] The student enrollment figures provided by the United States Department of Education are for the 2010 school year, the most recent available. The enrollment figures include full-time and part-time students.

[2] Student enrollment figures were not available.

Table V-10. Full-Time Law Enforcement Employees, by Selected State and University or College, 2011—*Continued*

(Number.)

State and university/college	Campus	Student enrollment[1]	Total law enforcement employees	Total officers	Total civilians
Oklahoma					
Cameron University		6,330	11	11	0
East Central University		4,906	5	5	0
Northeastern Oklahoma A&M College		2,353	9	8	1
Northeastern State University	Broken Arrow[2]		8	7	1
	Tahlequah	9,558	20	15	5
Oklahoma City University		3,750	17	12	5
Oklahoma State University	Main Campus	23,667	43	32	11
	Okmulgee	3,888	8	7	1
	Tulsa[2]		9	7	2
Rogers State University		4,486	4	4	0
Seminole State College		2,337	2	2	0
Southeastern Oklahoma State University		4,172	9	7	2
Southwestern Oklahoma State University		5,259	6	5	1
Tulsa Community College		20,577	16	10	6
University of Central Oklahoma		17,101	22	16	6
University of Oklahoma	Health Sciences Center	3,847	55	40	15
	Norman	26,476	71	40	31
Pennsylvania					
Bloomsburg University		10,091	22	18	4
California University		9,400	18	14	4
Clarion University		7,315	15	10	5
Dickinson College		2,414	19	14	5
East Stroudsburg University		7,387	17	15	2
Edinboro University		8,642	15	14	1
Elizabethtown College		2,417	17	5	12
Indiana University		15,126	25	18	7
Kutztown University		10,707	21	16	5
Lehigh University		7,051	31	22	9
Lock Haven University		5,451	12	10	2
Mansfield University		3,411	12	9	3
Millersville University		8,729	18	15	3
Moravian College		2,032	13	8	5
Pennsylvania State University	Altoona	4,147	11	9	2
	Beaver	906	6	6	0
	Behrend	4,359	11	7	4
	Berks	2,771	9	8	1
	Harrisburg	4,224	8	7	1
	Hazleton	1,303	5	5	0
	McKeesport[2]		4	3	1
	Mont Alto	1,252	6	6	0
	Schuylkill	1,034	4	4	0
	University Park	45,233	72	48	24
Shippensburg University		8,326	20	17	3
Slippery Rock University		8,852	20	16	4
University of Pittsburgh	Bradford	1,629	7	6	1
	Greensburg	1,803	7	6	1
	Johnstown	2,965	14	13	1
	Pittsburgh	28,823	133	73	60
	Titusville	514	6	6	0
West Chester University		14,490	21	21	0
Rhode Island					
Brown University		8,705	84	47	37
University of Rhode Island		16,294	30	25	5
South Carolina					
Benedict College		3,137	26	21	5
Bob Jones University		3,794	12	3	9
Clemson University		19,453	35	27	8
Coastal Carolina University		8,706	71	27	44
College of Charleston		11,532	60	28	32
Columbia College		1,367	13	11	2
Denmark Technical College		1,033	4	4	0
Erskine College		811	2	2	0
Francis Marion University		4,032	14	13	1
Greenville Technical College		14,879	2	1	1
Lander University		3,060	15	13	2
Medical University of South Carolina		2,556	76	56	20
Midlands Technical College		12,078	5	5	0
Presbyterian College		1,266	6	5	1
South Carolina State University		4,362	33	21	12
Spartanburg Methodist College		790	5	5	0

[1] The student enrollment figures provided by the United States Department of Education are for the 2010 school year, the most recent available. The enrollment figures include full-time and part-time students.

[2] Student enrollment figures were not available.

Table V-10. Full-Time Law Enforcement Employees, by Selected State and University or College, 2011—*Continued*

(Number.)

State and university/college	Campus	Student enrollment[1]	Total law enforcement employees	Total officers	Total civilians
The Citadel..		3,402	20	16	4
Trident Technical College............................		15,790	32	27	5
University of South Carolina	Aiken	3,254	11	10	1
	Columbia	29,599	86	58	28
	Upstate	5,492	15	14	1
Winthrop University		5,998	22	15	7
South Dakota					
South Dakota State University.....................		12,816	14	9	5
Tennessee					
Austin Peay State University		10,723	24	13	11
Christian Brothers University......................		1,828	15	9	6
East Tennessee State University..................		14,952	27	20	7
Middle Tennessee State University		26,430	38	31	7
Northeast State Community College		6,775	5	5	0
Southwest Tennessee Community College..		13,362	29	17	12
Tennessee State University		8,930	71	43	28
Tennessee Technological University		11,538	21	14	7
University of Memphis		22,420	36	32	4
University of Tennessee...............................	Chattanooga	10,781	24	15	9
	Health Science Center[2]		57	25	32
	Knoxville	30,300	83	50	33
	Martin	8,467	17	13	4
Vanderbilt University		12,714	145	86	59
Volunteer State Community College...........		8,989	7	6	1
Walters State Community College		6,959	9	9	0
Texas					
Abilene Christian University.........................		4,728	16	15	1
Alamo Community College District............		60,983	84	65	19
Alvin Community College		5,794	12	10	2
Amarillo College		11,878	14	12	2
Angelo State University		6,856	22	11	11
Austin College		1,314	8	7	1
Baylor Health Care System[2]			177	61	116
Baylor University	Waco	14,900	33	26	7
Blinn College		17,755	18	16	2
Brookhaven College		12,784	25	17	8
Central Texas College		26,055	8	8	0
College of the Mainland		4,352	8	7	1
Eastfield College		12,919	18	17	1
El Paso Community College		29,909	45	38	7
Grayson County College		5,284	3	2	1
Hardin-Simmons University		2,313	8	7	1
Houston Baptist University		2,597	13	10	3
Houston Community College		60,303	105	62	43
Lamar University	Beaumont	14,385	33	21	12
Laredo Community College		10,029	21	19	2
McLennan Community College		9,913	17	8	9
Midwestern State University		6,426	15	10	5
Mountain View College		8,460	11	11	0
North Lake College		12,018	21	20	1
Paris Junior College		6,197	4	4	0
Prairie View A&M University		8,781	38	23	15
Rice University...		5,879	31	25	6
Richland College		19,201	19	19	0
Southern Methodist University		10,938	34	26	8
South Plains College		9,900	6	6	0
Southwestern University		1,373	7	6	1
Stephen F. Austin State University..............		12,954	47	26	21
St. Mary's University		4,105	19	17	2
Sul Ross State University		3,129	9	7	2
Tarleton State University		11,121	14	13	1
Texas A&M International University		6,853	22	17	5
Texas A&M University.................................	College Station	49,129	118	59	59
	Commerce	10,787	25	18	7
	Corpus Christi	10,033	28	15	13
	Galveston	1,867	9	8	1
	Kingsville	9,673	14	10	4
	San Antonio[2]		13	11	2
Texas Christian University		9,142	42	28	14
Texas Southern University		9,557	61	30	31
Texas State Technical College	Harlingen	5,779	13	9	4
	Marshall	949	3	3	0
	Waco	4,975	18	16	2

[1] The student enrollment figures provided by the United States Department of Education are for the 2010 school year, the most recent available. The enrollment figures include full-time and part-time students.

[2] Student enrollment figures were not available.

Table V-10. Full-Time Law Enforcement Employees, by Selected State and University or College, 2011—*Continued*

(Number.)

State and university/college	Campus	Student enrollment[1]	Total law enforcement employees	Total officers	Total civilians
Texas State University	San Marcos	32,572	40	33	7
Texas Tech University	Lubbock	31,637	85	47	38
Texas Woman's University		14,180	39	19	20
Trinity University		2,498	27	15	12
Tyler Junior College		11,738	20	14	6
University of Houston	Central Campus	38,752	151	41	110
	Clearlake	8,099	25	13	12
	Downtown Campus	12,900	37	18	19
University of Mary Hardin-Baylor...............		2,956	10	9	1
University of North Texas	Denton	36,305	87	45	42
	Health Science Center	1,579	21	11	10
University of Texas......................................	Arlington	32,975	99	29	70
	Austin	51,195	143	55	88
	Brownsville	15,230	45	16	29
	Dallas	17,128	53	21	32
	El Paso	22,106	49	20	29
	Health Science Center, San Antonio	3,310	113	30	83
	Health Science Center, Tyler[2]		14	7	7
	Houston[2]		339	91	248
	Medical Branch	2,660	89	47	42
	Pan American	18,744	43	19	24
	Permian Basin	4,063	15	10	5
	San Antonio	30,258	105	49	56
	Southwestern Medical School	2,499	130	40	90
	Tyler	6,476	17	9	8
West Texas A&M University.........................		7,839	14	10	4
Utah					
Brigham Young University...........................		33,841	38	28	10
College of Eastern Utah.............................		2,172	1	1	0
Southern Utah University		8,024	6	5	1
University of Utah..		30,819	100	31	69
Utah State University		16,472	17	11	6
Utah Valley University		32,670	10	8	2
Weber State University................................		24,048	10	9	1
Vermont					
University of Vermont		13,554	29	22	7
Virginia					
Christopher Newport University..................		4,916	23	16	7
College of William and Mary		8,000	23	18	5
Emory and Henry College		980	4	2	2
Ferrum College...		1,484	9	8	1
George Mason University		32,562	73	54	19
Hampton University		5,254	40	24	16
James Madison University		19,434	41	31	10
J. Sargeant Reynolds Community College ..		12,629	21	12	9
Longwood University		4,831	23	15	8
Lord Fairfax Community College		7,005	3	3	0
Norfolk State University		6,964	37	24	13
Northern Virginia Community College		48,996	53	47	6
Old Dominion University.............................		24,466	69	54	15
Radford University		9,007	37	23	14
Richard Bland College		1,587	7	7	0
Thomas Nelson Community College		11,086	14	10	4
University of Mary Washington....................		5,203	21	15	6
University of Richmond		4,405	34	22	12
University of Virginia...................................		24,391	118	51	67
University of Virginia's College at Wise		1,990	10	9	1
Virginia Commonwealth University		32,027	198	79	119
Virginia Military Institute		1,569	9	8	1
Virginia Polytechnic Institute and State University		31,006	75	52	23
Virginia State University..............................		5,634	36	21	15
Virginia Western Community College		8,778	8	8	0

[1] The student enrollment figures provided by the United States Department of Education are for the 2010 school year, the most recent available. The enrollment figures include full-time and part-time students.

[2] Student enrollment figures were not available.

Table V-10.   Full-Time Law Enforcement Employees, by Selected State and University or College, 2011—*Continued*

(Number.)

State and university/college	Campus	Student enrollment[1]	Total law enforcement employees	Total officers	Total civilians
Washington					
Central Washington University		11,614	12	11	1
Eastern Washington University		11,534	13	12	1
Evergreen State College		4,833	15	9	6
University of Washington		42,451	82	46	36
Washington State University	Pullman	26,308	22	17	5
	Vancouver[2]		6	3	3
Western Washington University		14,979	20	15	5
West Virginia					
Bluefield State College		2,063	2	2	0
Concord University		2,822	11	7	4
Fairmont State University		4,709	10	7	3
Glenville State College		1,827	5	3	2
Marshall University		14,192	22	20	2
Potomac State College		1,836	6	5	1
Shepherd University		4,234	10	9	1
West Liberty State College		2,738	5	5	0
West Virginia State University		3,190	10	8	2
West Virginia Tech		1,211	6	5	1
West Virginia University		29,306	58	49	9
Wisconsin					
University of Wisconsin	Eau Claire	11,413	10	9	1
	Green Bay	6,636	13	6	7
	La Crosse	10,135	16	13	3
	Madison	42,180	111	63	48
	Milwaukee	30,470	64	44	20
	Oshkosh	13,629	11	9	2
	Parkside	5,160	11	8	3
	Platteville	7,928	9	7	2
	River Falls	6,902	10	4	6
	Stevens Point	9,500	4	2	2
	Stout	9,339	9	8	1
	Superior	2,856	7	2	5
	Whitewater	11,557	15	14	1
Wyoming					
Sheridan College		3,888	2	2	0
University of Wyoming		12,911	25	14	11

[1] The student enrollment figures provided by the United States Department of Education are for the 2010 school year, the most recent available. The enrollment figures include full-time and part-time students.

[2] Student enrollment figures were not available.

Table V-11. Full-Time Law Enforcement Employees, by Selected State Metropolitan and Nonmetropolitan Counties, 2011

(Number.)

State/County	Total law enforcement employees	Total officers	Total civilians	State/County	Total law enforcement employees	Total officers	Total civilians
Alabama—Metropolitan Counties				**Arizona—Nonmetropolitan Counties**			
Autauga	64	25	39	Apache	83	29	54
Bibb	12	11	1	Cochise	195	83	112
Blount	38	35	3	Gila	141	50	91
Calhoun	57	53	4	Graham	75	21	54
Chilton	59	30	29	Greenlee	42	16	26
Colbert	54	31	23	La Paz	82	29	53
Elmore	93	46	47	Navajo	148	53	95
Etowah	164	66	98	Santa Cruz	116	40	76
Geneva	28	11	17				
Greene	27	12	15	**Arkansas—Metropolitan Counties**			
Hale	11	9	2	Benton	217	136	81
Henry	15	10	5	Cleveland	12	9	3
Houston	89	61	28	Craighead	107	30	77
Jefferson	573	440	133	Crawford	63	31	32
Lawrence	51	30	21	Crittenden	149	40	109
Lee	158	71	87	Faulkner	153	51	102
Limestone	105	41	64	Franklin	21	10	11
Lowndes	41	13	28	Garland	135	50	85
Madison	342	111	231	Grant	17	14	3
Mobile	487	167	320	Jefferson	173	55	118
Montgomery	175	129	46	Lincoln	21	8	13
Morgan	173	55	118	Lonoke	55	26	29
Russell	97	40	57	Madison	17	9	8
Shelby	204	118	86	Miller	64	25	39
St. Clair	48	42	6	Perry	18	10	8
Tuscaloosa	199	98	101	Poinsett	41	13	28
Walker	91	32	59	Pulaski	512	133	379
				Saline	92	44	48
Alabama—Nonmetropolitan Counties				Sebastian	148	111	37
Baldwin	282	102	180	Washington	293	153	140
Barbour	33	14	19				
Bullock	12	5	7	**Arkansas—Nonmetropolitan Counties**			
Butler	11	9	2	Arkansas	10	10	0
Chambers	52	23	29	Ashley	45	21	24
Cherokee	43	22	21	Baxter	50	32	18
Choctaw	14	6	8	Boone	56	23	33
Clarke	36	13	23	Bradley	6	4	2
Clay	23	7	16	Calhoun	12	6	6
Cleburne	28	12	16	Carroll	22	19	3
Coffee	42	20	22	Chicot	8	7	1
Coosa	23	12	11	Clark	28	14	14
Covington	28	26	2	Clay	22	12	10
Crenshaw	9	7	2	Cleburne	39	23	16
Cullman	137	77	60	Columbia	36	18	18
Dale	41	22	19	Conway	36	17	19
Dallas	50	25	25	Cross	38	16	22
De Kalb	87	36	51	Dallas	24	5	19
Escambia	93	26	67	Desha	7	6	1
Fayette	17	12	5	Drew	11	10	1
Franklin	48	17	31	Fulton	14	6	8
Jackson	72	33	39	Greene	49	16	33
Lamar	19	7	12	Hempstead	52	21	31
Macon	37	18	19	Hot Spring	27	15	12
Marengo	26	10	16	Howard	24	10	14
Monroe	53	18	35	Independence	76	50	26
Perry	19	8	11	Izard	27	13	14
Pickens	32	8	24	Jackson	21	12	9
Pike	26	16	10	Johnson	34	14	20
Randolph	36	15	21	Lafayette	21	7	14
Sumter	24	7	17	Lawrence	28	15	13
Tallapoosa	55	24	31	Lee	10	5	5
Washington	18	8	10	Little River	17	12	5
Wilcox	29	9	20	Logan	25	12	13
				Marion	20	18	2
Arizona—Metropolitan Counties				Mississippi	93	34	59
Coconino	229	55	174	Monroe	13	5	8
Maricopa	3,210	688	2,522	Montgomery	16	8	8
Mohave	277	92	185	Nevada	16	5	11
Pinal	620	207	413	Newton	8	6	2
Yavapai	170	121	49	Ouachita	39	15	24
Yuma	347	89	258	Phillips	18	15	3

Table V-11.   Full-Time Law Enforcement Employees, by Selected State Metropolitan and Nonmetropolitan Counties, 2011—*Continued*

(Number.)

State/County	Total law enforcement employees	Total officers	Total civilians	State/County	Total law enforcement employees	Total officers	Total civilians
Pike	21	8	13	Sierra	16	11	5
Polk	24	11	13	Siskiyou	100	77	23
Pope	38	31	7	Tehama	106	72	34
Prairie	17	7	10	Trinity	34	19	15
Randolph	20	10	10	Tuolumne	128	64	64
Scott	28	8	20				
Searcy	12	9	3	**Colorado—Metropolitan Counties**			
Sevier	29	14	15	Adams	496	353	143
Sharp	31	13	18	Arapahoe	511	248	263
St. Francis	39	20	19	Boulder	344	214	130
Stone	18	9	9	Clear Creek	72	27	45
Union	59	27	32	Douglas	423	286	137
Van Buren	32	14	18	Elbert	33	29	4
White	96	49	47	El Paso	636	418	218
Woodruff	14	6	8	Gilpin	46	29	17
Yell	26	14	12	Jefferson	801	551	250
				Larimer	367	160	207
California—Metropolitan Counties				Mesa	217	94	123
Alameda	1,599	950	649	Park	55	28	27
Butte	282	108	174	Teller	47	33	14
Contra Costa	920	618	302	Weld	320	86	234
El Dorado	333	159	174				
Fresno	942	734	208	**Colorado—Nonmetropolitan Counties**			
Imperial	265	177	88	Alamosa	43	29	14
Kern	1,118	838	280	Archuleta	35	16	19
Kings	206	69	137	Baca	11	4	7
Los Angeles	16,768	9,197	7,571	Bent	19	8	11
Madera	99	69	30	Chaffee	45	16	29
Marin	282	183	99	Cheyenne	10	5	5
Merced	237	116	121	Conejos	21	7	14
Monterey	381	283	98	Costilla	9	6	3
Napa	130	103	27	Crowley	11	6	5
Orange	3,459	1,948	1,511	Custer	22	9	13
Placer	405	216	189	Delta	64	29	35
Riverside	3,729	2,021	1,708	Dolores	7	5	2
Sacramento	1,879	1,193	686	Eagle	73	45	28
San Benito	58	27	31	Fremont	85	36	49
San Bernardino	3,029	1,706	1,323	Garfield	138	47	91
San Diego	3,692	2,196	1,496	Grand	48	19	29
San Francisco	1,043	873	170	Gunnison	28	13	15
San Joaquin	691	284	407	Hinsdale	4	3	1
San Luis Obispo	359	150	209	Huerfano	24	11	13
San Mateo	601	322	279	Jackson	7	4	3
Santa Barbara	600	430	170	Kiowa	7	6	1
Santa Clara	1,563	1,189	374	Kit Carson	29	7	22
Santa Cruz	313	138	175	Lake	16	8	8
Shasta	205	131	74	La Plata	127	98	29
Solano	415	107	308	Las Animas	30	14	16
Sonoma	610	444	166	Lincoln	21	9	12
Stanislaus	509	385	124	Logan	50	24	26
Sutter	127	99	28	Mineral	4	3	1
Tulare	653	484	169	Moffat	33	16	17
Ventura	1,194	727	467	Montezuma	71	28	43
Yolo	242	81	161	Montrose	114	53	61
Yuba	168	133	35	Morgan	50	23	27
				Otero	11	9	2
California—Nonmetropolitan Counties				Ouray	8	8	0
Alpine	18	15	3	Phillips	4	4	0
Amador	95	49	46	Pitkin	42	24	18
Calaveras	92	51	41	Prowers	32	9	23
Colusa	65	34	31	Rio Blanco	31	16	15
Del Norte	55	27	28	Rio Grande	15	10	5
Glenn	52	18	34	Routt	47	42	5
Humboldt	212	166	46	Saguache	19	8	11
Inyo	53	34	19	San Juan	4	3	1
Lake	139	51	88	San Miguel	34	30	4
Lassen	62	45	17	Sedgwick	12	6	6
Mariposa	69	55	14	Summit	58	51	7
Mendocino	138	111	27	Washington	44	12	32
Modoc	23	16	7	Yuma	19	8	11
Mono	49	28	21				
Nevada	173	66	107	**Delaware—Metropolitan Counties**			
Plumas	61	31	30	New Castle County Police Department	442	325	117

Table V-11. Full-Time Law Enforcement Employees, by Selected State Metropolitan and Nonmetropolitan Counties, 2011—*Continued*

(Number.)

State/County	Total law enforcement employees	Total officers	Total civilians	State/County	Total law enforcement employees	Total officers	Total civilians
Florida—Metropolitan Counties				Bartow	231	199	32
Alachua	495	280	215	Bibb	345	279	66
Baker	140	45	95	Brantley	38	20	18
Bay	274	213	61	Brooks	48	19	29
Brevard	1,179	500	679	Bryan	70	43	27
Broward	2,996	1,535	1,461	Butts	72	40	32
Charlotte	374	254	120	Carroll	181	99	82
Clay	535	262	273	Catoosa	138	72	66
Collier	914	565	349	Chattahoochee	13	7	6
Escambia	1,105	717	388	Cherokee	400	332	68
Flagler	187	130	57	Clarke	171	149	22
Gadsden	75	50	25	Clayton	355	271	84
Gilchrist	52	26	26	Clayton County Police Department	393	339	54
Hernando	506	322	184	Cobb	732	466	266
Hillsborough	3,326	1,246	2,080	Cobb County Police Department	642	584	58
Indian River	481	332	149	Columbia	361	303	58
Jefferson	52	22	30	Coweta	223	147	76
Lake	449	290	159	Crawford	34	16	18
Lee	899	548	351	Dade	24	22	2
Leon	356	241	115	Dawson	106	61	45
Manatee	1,067	696	371	DeKalb	794	624	170
Marion	758	548	210	DeKalb County Police Department	1,271	972	299
Martin	510	249	261	Dougherty	62	53	9
Miami-Dade	4,266	3,024	1,242	Dougherty County Police Department	47	39	8
Nassau	209	106	103	Douglas	320	285	35
Okaloosa	342	248	94	Echols	9	8	1
Orange	1,962	1,351	611	Effingham	122	73	49
Osceola	593	383	210	Fayette	227	149	78
Palm Beach	3,236	1,459	1,777	Floyd	130	78	52
Pasco	1,135	489	646	Floyd County Police Department	74	69	5
Pinellas	1,269	743	526	Forsyth	366	285	81
Polk	1,537	594	943	Fulton	930	783	147
Santa Rosa	259	179	80	Fulton County Police Department	193	141	52
Sarasota	916	395	521	Glynn	50	37	13
Seminole	1,079	397	682	Glynn County Police Department	128	114	14
St. Johns	542	261	281	Gwinnett County Police Department	984	713	271
St. Lucie	595	243	352	Hall	463	290	173
Volusia	720	418	302	Haralson	67	61	6
Wakulla	86	57	29	Harris	52	50	2
				Heard	42	21	21
Florida—Nonmetropolitan Counties				Henry	292	252	40
Bradford	48	33	15	Henry County Police Department	251	217	34
Calhoun	22	14	8	Jasper	31	17	14
Citrus	366	213	153	Jones	72	49	23
Columbia	173	93	80	Lamar	54	27	27
DeSoto	75	54	21	Lanier	12	9	3
Dixie	74	28	46	Lee	90	47	43
Franklin	73	34	39	Liberty	129	66	63
Glades	148	98	50	Long	21	18	3
Gulf	42	27	15	Lowndes	242	159	83
Hamilton	57	18	39	Madison	60	38	22
Hardee	96	43	53	McDuffie	50	33	17
Hendry	143	73	70	McIntosh	69	53	16
Highlands	311	130	181	Meriwether	60	34	26
Holmes	32	20	12	Monroe	97	52	45
Jackson	81	61	20	Murray	67	40	27
Lafayette	10	9	1	Newton	228	141	87
Levy	145	61	84	Oconee	87	57	30
Liberty	23	17	6	Oglethorpe	48	19	29
Madison	75	33	42	Paulding	268	34	234
Monroe	478	214	264	Pickens	84	74	10
Okeechobee	108	75	33	Rockdale	204	186	18
Putnam	177	110	67	Spalding	175	94	81
Sumter	251	171	80	Twiggs	43	21	22
Suwannee	102	57	45	Walton	180	158	22
Taylor	66	57	9	Whitfield	191	166	25
Union	18	12	6	Worth	34	25	9
Walton	227	158	69				
Washington	74	52	22	**Georgia—Nonmetropolitan Counties**			
				Appling	49	16	33
Georgia—Metropolitan Counties				Atkinson	12	7	5
Augusta-Richmond	722	653	69	Baldwin	120	60	60
Baker	8	7	1	Banks	53	31	22
Barrow	188	141	47	Ben Hill	36	31	5

Table V-11.   Full-Time Law Enforcement Employees, by Selected State Metropolitan and Nonmetropolitan Counties, 2011—*Continued*

(Number.)

State/County	Total law enforce-ment employees	Total officers	Total civilians	State/County	Total law enforce-ment employees	Total officers	Total civilians
Berrien	27	23	4	Canyon	209	110	99
Bleckley	40	13	27	Franklin	15	12	3
Bulloch	119	51	68	Gem	24	13	11
Calhoun	15	6	9	Jefferson	32	17	15
Camden	123	59	64	Kootenai	163	89	74
Charlton	32	18	14	Nez Perce	43	23	20
Clinch	13	9	4	Owyhee	20	11	9
Coffee	123	54	69	Power	17	9	8
Cook	43	19	24				
Crisp	72	67	5	**Idaho—Nonmetropolitan Counties**			
Decatur	34	29	5	Adams	25	19	6
Dodge	35	19	16	Bear Lake	12	6	6
Dooly	65	25	40	Benewah	17	9	8
Early	52	45	7	Bingham	51	32	19
Elbert	58	53	5	Blaine	27	18	9
Emanuel	31	13	18	Bonner	49	35	14
Evans	20	10	10	Boundary	21	11	10
Fannin	44	42	2	Butte	12	4	8
Franklin	59	32	27	Camas	6	4	2
Gordon	86	76	10	Caribou	15	9	6
Grady	47	19	28	Cassia	53	33	20
Greene	51	33	18	Clark	7	3	4
Habersham	39	37	2	Clearwater	24	16	8
Hancock	42	16	26	Custer	12	6	6
Hart	40	27	13	Elmore	42	21	21
Irwin	21	13	8	Fremont	27	18	9
Jackson	161	108	53	Gooding	18	13	5
Jeff Davis	42	17	25	Idaho	32	22	10
Jefferson	45	42	3	Jerome	23	17	6
Johnson	17	8	9	Latah	40	25	15
Laurens	100	59	41	Lemhi	9	8	1
Lumpkin	72	63	9	Lewis	10	5	5
Morgan	54	26	28	Lincoln	9	6	3
Peach	65	31	34	Madison	33	23	10
Pierce	30	14	16	Minidoka	30	19	11
Polk County Police Department	40	37	3	Oneida	13	8	5
Pulaski	35	25	10	Payette	32	17	15
Putnam	66	35	31	Shoshone	28	17	11
Rabun	53	51	2	Teton	24	12	12
Schley	7	3	4	Twin Falls	66	44	22
Seminole	28	15	13	Valley	29	15	14
Stephens	66	33	33	Washington	20	12	8
Stewart	8	4	4				
Talbot	12	8	4	**Illinois—Metropolitan Counties**			
Taliaferro	14	8	6	Alexander	11	7	4
Tattnall	34	19	15	Bond	19	11	8
Telfair	16	14	2	Boone	91	35	56
Thomas	77	42	35	Calhoun	9	5	4
Tift	111	49	62	Champaign	154	54	100
Treutlen	19	9	10	Clinton	36	15	21
Troup	127	75	52	Cook	6,596	2,132	4,464
Turner	33	15	18	De Kalb	93	40	53
Union	39	36	3	Du Page	555	423	132
Upson	65	34	31	Ford	27	7	20
Ware	125	45	80	Grundy	65	31	34
Warren	13	6	7	Henry	64	23	41
Washington	41	24	17	Jersey	31	13	18
Wayne	54	29	25	Kane	114	86	28
Webster	6	5	1	Kankakee	198	57	141
White	65	42	23	Kendall	120	58	62
Wilcox	17	9	8	Lake	498	188	310
Wilkes	27	14	13	Macon	135	63	72
Wilkinson	27	16	11	Macoupin	49	33	16
				Madison	164	80	84
Hawaii—Nonmetropolitan Counties				Marshall	18	8	10
Hawaii Police Department	551	424	127	McHenry	391	106	285
Kauai Police Department	176	129	47	McLean	136	55	81
Maui Police Department	462	344	118	Menard	18	8	10
				Monroe	34	15	19
Idaho—Metropolitan Counties				Piatt	32	10	22
Ada	394	131	263	Rock Island	150	64	86
Bannock	66	40	26	Sangamon	200	64	136
Boise	20	11	9	Stark	13	5	8
Bonneville	95	64	31	St. Clair	181	170	11

Table V-11. Full-Time Law Enforcement Employees, by Selected State Metropolitan and Nonmetropolitan Counties, 2011—*Continued*

(Number.)

State/County	Total law enforce-ment employees	Total officers	Total civilians	State/County	Total law enforce-ment employees	Total officers	Total civilians
Tazewell	113	41	72	Delaware	107	42	65
Vermilion	87	39	48	Elkhart	179	72	107
Winnebago	344	101	243	Floyd	96	31	65
Woodford	38	37	1	Franklin	39	27	12
				Gibson	43	17	26
Illinois—Nonmetropolitan Counties				Greene	40	14	26
Adams	57	57	0	Hamilton	227	61	166
Brown	9	8	1	Hancock	70	39	31
Bureau	36	18	18	Harrison	57	22	35
Carroll	24	9	15	Hendricks	99	43	56
Cass	8	7	1	Howard	138	33	105
Christian	37	18	19	Jasper	54	23	31
Clark	18	9	9	Johnson	142	112	30
Clay	15	10	5	La Porte	159	60	99
Coles	45	24	21	Madison	98	49	49
Crawford	20	9	11	Monroe	112	36	76
Cumberland	15	6	9	Morgan	29	25	4
De Witt	45	13	32	Newton	44	18	26
Douglas	32	13	19	Ohio	9	9	0
Edgar	18	7	11	Owen	32	12	20
Edwards	7	4	3	Porter	155	65	90
Effingham	47	19	28	Posey	13	12	1
Fayette	27	11	16	Putnam	34	17	17
Franklin	48	17	31	Shelby	84	29	55
Fulton	43	21	22	St. Joseph	263	107	156
Gallatin	4	4	0	Sullivan	35	10	25
Greene	13	6	7	Tippecanoe	140	46	94
Hardin	4	2	2	Tipton	26	10	16
Henderson	8	7	1	Vanderburgh	241	102	139
Iroquois	24	13	11	Vermillion	27	9	18
Jackson	76	27	49	Vigo	89	38	51
Jasper	11	6	5	Warrick	80	38	42
Jefferson	71	21	50	Washington	35	12	23
Jo Daviess	37	19	18	Wells	39	15	24
Johnson	13	7	6	Whitley	47	15	32
Knox	59	22	37				
La Salle	112	42	70	**Indiana—Nonmetropolitan Counties**			
Lawrence	23	7	16	Adams	41	16	25
Lee	39	21	18	Blackford	30	9	21
Logan	29	19	10	Cass	51	17	34
Mason	21	9	12	Crawford	15	8	7
Massac	28	13	15	Daviess	63	19	44
McDonough	25	13	12	DeKalb	62	23	39
Montgomery	40	15	25	Dubois	36	16	20
Morgan	40	15	25	Fayette	35	11	24
Moultrie	10	9	1	Fountain	20	8	12
Ogle	68	28	40	Fulton	25	10	15
Pike	26	12	14	Grant	117	45	72
Pope	6	3	3	Henry	62	27	35
Pulaski	12	8	4	Huntington	39	14	25
Putnam	13	8	5	Jackson	53	15	38
Randolph	28	12	16	Jay	43	11	32
Richland	26	8	18	Jefferson	34	16	18
Saline	48	13	35	Knox	41	16	25
Schuyler	9	5	4	Kosciusko	77	36	41
Scott	6	2	4	LaGrange	56	18	38
Shelby	25	12	13	Lawrence	66	25	41
Stephenson	56	25	31	Marshall	58	21	37
Union	19	18	1	Martin	19	7	12
Wabash	9	4	5	Miami	49	15	34
Washington	25	10	15	Montgomery	65	19	46
Wayne	21	11	10	Noble	72	20	52
White	13	6	7	Orange	27	9	18
Whiteside	33	20	13	Parke	37	11	26
				Perry	16	7	9
Indiana—Metropolitan Counties				Pike	26	9	17
Allen	328	124	204	Pulaski	42	13	29
Bartholomew	95	40	55	Randolph	40	15	25
Benton	20	7	13	Ripley	28	10	18
Boone	60	28	32	Rush	26	11	15
Brown	38	13	25	Scott	14	12	2
Clay	43	13	30	Starke	26	12	14
Dearborn	83	30	53	Steuben	61	21	40

Table V-11. Full-Time Law Enforcement Employees, by Selected State Metropolitan and Nonmetropolitan Counties, 2011—*Continued*

(Number.)

State/County	Total law enforcement employees	Total officers	Total civilians	State/County	Total law enforcement employees	Total officers	Total civilians
Union	11	6	5	Lucas	13	5	8
Wabash	31	12	19	Mahaska	26	9	17
Warren	20	7	13	Marion	33	12	21
Wayne	113	68	45	Marshall	54	19	35
White	36	13	23	Mitchell	15	6	9
				Monona	18	8	10
Iowa—Metropolitan Counties				Monroe	11	5	6
Benton	25	12	13	Montgomery	20	8	12
Black Hawk	134	102	32	Muscatine	69	22	47
Bremer	31	11	20	O'Brien	28	9	19
Dallas	47	22	25	Osceola	12	8	4
Dubuque	86	73	13	Page	15	8	7
Grundy	16	12	4	Palo Alto	15	8	7
Guthrie	10	5	5	Plymouth	28	10	18
Harrison	27	10	17	Pocahontas	17	7	10
Johnson	84	66	18	Poweshick	25	11	14
Jones	21	8	13	Ringgold	11	5	6
Linn	177	116	61	Sac	19	8	11
Madison	15	7	8	Shelby	14	8	6
Mills	19	11	8	Sioux	37	14	23
Pottawattamie	192	49	143	Tama	22	13	9
Scott	153	44	109	Taylor	9	5	4
Story	80	31	49	Union	12	6	6
Warren	34	23	11	Van Buren	11	5	6
Washington	30	17	13	Wapello	38	10	28
Woodbury	100	35	65	Wayne	16	5	11
				Webster	27	16	11
Iowa—Nonmetropolitan Counties				Winnebago	10	6	4
Adair	14	6	8	Winneshiek	23	10	13
Adams	11	6	5	Worth	20	8	12
Allamakee	14	8	6	Wright	20	8	12
Appanoose	14	7	7				
Audubon	8	5	3	**Kansas—Metropolitan Counties**			
Boone	28	11	17	Butler	110	64	46
Buchanan	27	13	14	Doniphan	14	4	10
Buena Vista	30	13	17	Douglas	135	81	54
Butler	20	12	8	Franklin	57	27	30
Calhoun	11	6	5	Geary	86	29	57
Carroll	14	9	5	Harvey	38	17	21
Cass	11	8	3	Jackson	23	16	7
Cedar	39	11	28	Jefferson	39	23	16
Cerro Gordo	67	18	49	Johnson	576	462	114
Cherokee	17	6	11	Leavenworth	93	54	39
Chickasaw	13	8	5	Linn	21	11	10
Clarke	17	6	11	Miami	43	24	19
Clay	17	9	8	Osage	44	24	20
Clayton	27	13	14	Pottawatomie	40	23	17
Clinton	41	24	17	Riley County Police Department	193	103	90
Crawford	13	10	3	Sedgwick	513	173	340
Davis	12	5	7	Shawnee	195	112	83
Decatur	10	10	0	Sumner	43	20	23
Delaware	17	13	4	Wabaunsee	20	9	11
Des Moines	43	20	23	Wyandotte	182	65	117
Dickinson	20	9	11				
Emmet	16	8	8	**Kansas—Nonmetropolitan Counties**			
Fayette	31	9	22	Allen	37	9	28
Floyd	20	11	9	Anderson	29	9	20
Franklin	10	7	3	Barber	9	4	5
Fremont	17	7	10	Barton	40	19	21
Greene	16	7	9	Bourbon	11	9	2
Hamilton	29	10	19	Brown	23	7	16
Hancock	10	7	3	Chase	9	5	4
Hardin	27	10	17	Cherokee	49	20	29
Henry	27	12	15	Cheyenne	4	4	0
Howard	14	7	7	Clark	11	6	5
Humboldt	14	8	6	Clay	20	8	12
Ida	16	9	7	Cloud	16	9	7
Iowa	26	12	14	Coffey	31	13	18
Jackson	15	9	6	Cowley	52	22	30
Jasper	44	14	30	Crawford	69	32	37
Jefferson	30	10	20	Decatur	3	3	0
Kossuth	25	9	16	Dickinson	28	16	12
Lee	30	15	15	Edwards	10	6	4
Louisa	32	10	22	Elk	9	4	5

Table V-11.   Full-Time Law Enforcement Employees, by Selected State Metropolitan and Nonmetropolitan Counties, 2011—*Continued*

(Number.)

State/County	Total law enforcement employees	Total officers	Total civilians
Ellis	29	17	12
Ellsworth	16	8	8
Finney	92	35	57
Ford	64	27	37
Gove	4	3	1
Graham	7	3	4
Grant	16	7	9
Greenwood	21	12	9
Hamilton	12	6	6
Harper	7	6	1
Haskell	16	11	5
Hodgeman	8	4	4
Kearny	21	12	9
Kingman	17	7	10
Kiowa	19	8	11
Labette	35	17	18
Lane	10	5	5
Lincoln	12	7	5
Logan	4	3	1
Lyon	90	25	65
Marshall	20	8	12
McPherson	34	16	18
Meade	16	5	11
Mitchell	17	7	10
Montgomery	34	24	10
Morton	11	6	5
Nemaha	18	9	9
Neosho	37	14	23
Ness	12	7	5
Norton	10	5	5
Osborne	14	8	6
Ottawa	19	6	13
Pawnee	15	8	7
Pratt	14	8	6
Rawlins	8	3	5
Reno	80	43	37
Republic	13	8	5
Rush	9	4	5
Russell	19	11	8
Saline	101	47	54
Scott	7	3	4
Seward	47	16	31
Sheridan	6	3	3
Sherman	12	7	5
Smith	6	5	1
Stafford	9	4	5
Thomas	13	12	1
Trego	4	3	1
Wallace	6	2	4
Washington	15	7	8
Wichita	8	4	4
Kentucky—Metropolitan Counties			
Boone	138	130	8
Bourbon	9	8	1
Boyd	35	28	7
Bullitt	48	43	5
Campbell	12	9	3
Campbell County Police Department	32	31	1
Christian	34	30	4
Clark	17	13	4
Daviess	45	40	5
Edmonson	9	7	2
Gallatin	11	10	1
Greenup	17	15	2
Hardin	39	27	12
Henry	9	8	1
Jefferson	268	216	52
Jessamine	32	24	8
Kenton County Police Department	35	33	2
Meade	12	9	3
Nelson	30	23	7
Oldham	16	14	2
Pendleton	7	6	1
Scott	33	31	2
Shelby	25	23	2
Spencer	8	7	1
Trigg	8	5	3
Trimble	1	1	0
Warren	79	56	23
Webster	9	7	2
Woodford	13	9	4
Kentucky—Nonmetropolitan Counties			
Adair	8	6	2
Anderson	16	14	2
Barren	22	18	4
Bath	4	3	1
Bell	25	15	10
Breckinridge	10	8	2
Butler	8	6	2
Caldwell	9	7	2
Calloway	22	11	11
Carlisle	3	2	1
Carroll	5	4	1
Carter	11	9	2
Casey	8	6	2
Clinton	5	4	1
Crittenden	4	3	1
Cumberland	5	4	1
Fleming	8	8	0
Franklin	22	18	4
Fulton	4	3	1
Garrard	9	8	1
Graves	14	11	3
Grayson	11	8	3
Green	5	5	0
Harlan	24	20	4
Harrison	10	10	0
Hopkins	26	18	8
Jackson	13	6	7
Johnson	14	11	3
Knott	9	6	3
Knox	12	8	4
Laurel	33	28	5
Lawrence	9	6	3
Lee	4	2	2
Leslie	9	5	4
Letcher	13	11	2
Lewis	5	3	2
Lincoln	11	9	2
Livingston	7	6	1
Logan	19	19	0
Lyon	5	5	0
Madison	30	22	8
Magoffin	5	4	1
Marion	9	7	2
Marshall	25	22	3
McCracken	44	38	6
McCreary	8	6	2
Mercer	16	7	9
Metcalfe	6	4	2
Monroe	7	4	3
Muhlenberg	16	15	1
Nicholas	1	1	0
Owen	7	5	2
Owsley	3	2	1
Perry County Police Department	2	2	0
Pike	28	17	11
Rockcastle	4	3	1
Rowan	15	11	4
Russell	11	10	1
Taylor	14	12	2
Todd	6	4	2
Union	9	8	1
Washington	8	6	2

Table V-11.   Full-Time Law Enforcement Employees, by Selected State Metropolitan and Nonmetropolitan Counties, 2011—*Continued*

(Number.)

State/County	Total law enforcement employees	Total officers	Total civilians	State/County	Total law enforcement employees	Total officers	Total civilians
Wayne	12	10	2	Lincoln	25	23	2
Whitley	16	12	4	Oxford	22	21	1
Wolfe	4	3	1	Piscataquis	18	7	11
				Somerset	17	15	2
Louisiana—Metropolitan Counties				Waldo	20	18	2
Ascension	281	244	37	Washington	13	12	1
Bossier	375	300	75				
Caddo	658	433	225	**Maryland—Metropolitan Counties**			
Calcasieu	845	431	414	Allegany	29	27	2
Cameron	70	60	10	Anne Arundel	95	69	26
De Soto	114	95	19	Anne Arundel County Police Department	870	658	212
East Baton Rouge	876	763	113	Baltimore County	97	82	15
East Feliciana	55	55	0	Baltimore County Police Department	2,181	1,877	304
Jefferson	1,404	809	595	Calvert	125	104	21
Lafayette	634	459	175	Carroll	115	84	31
Lafourche	360	314	46	Cecil	96	84	12
Livingston	233	233	0	Charles	418	288	130
Ouachita	390	390	0	Frederick	227	166	61
Plaquemines	162	161	1	Harford	371	287	84
Pointe Coupee	95	95	0	Howard	67	49	18
Rapides	463	362	101	Howard County Police Department	626	444	182
St. Bernard	272	244	28	Montgomery	165	136	29
St. Charles	363	263	100	Montgomery County Police Department	1,551	1,143	408
St. Helena	50	25	25	Prince George's	311	223	88
St. John the Baptist	252	216	36	Prince George's County Police Department	1,853	1,558	295
St. Martin	284	134	150	Queen Anne's	50	47	3
St. Tammany	706	432	274	Somerset	22	19	3
Terrebonne	359	359	0	Washington	238	93	145
Union	54	38	16	Wicomico	104	83	21
West Baton Rouge	179	127	52				
West Feliciana	74	48	26	**Maryland—Nonmetropolitan Counties**			
				Caroline	32	29	3
Louisiana—Nonmetropolitan Counties				Dorchester	38	34	4
Acadia	105	53	52	Garrett	51	29	22
Allen	60	34	26	Kent	25	20	5
Assymption	78	46	32	St. Mary's	273	136	137
Beauregard	74	54	20	Talbot	32	29	3
Bienville	56	34	22	Worcester	57	46	11
Caldwell	31	30	1				
Claiborne	97	38	59	**Michigan—Metropolitan Counties**			
Evangeline	57	22	35	Barry	52	31	21
Jackson	185	185	0	Bay	81	36	45
Jefferson Davis	60	48	12	Berrien	161	72	89
La Salle	45	25	20	Calhoun	170	76	94
Lincoln	64	47	17	Cass	70	33	37
Morehouse	147	38	109	Clinton	59	25	34
Natchitoches	87	61	26	Eaton	135	70	65
Red River	39	20	19	Genesee	209	117	92
Sabine	77	77	0	Ingham	171	103	68
St. James	96	74	22	Ionia	53	22	31
St. Mary	198	180	18	Jackson	129	53	76
Tangipahoa	291	113	178	Kalamazoo	204	139	65
Tensas	29	29	0	Kent	499	191	308
Vermilion	130	64	66	Lapeer	77	46	31
Vernon	149	104	45	Livingston	109	63	46
Washington	90	68	22	Macomb	472	238	234
Webster	142	46	96	Monroe	158	71	87
West Carroll	20	20	0	Muskegon	111	96	15
Winn	22	22	0	Newaygo	62	25	37
				Oakland	996	806	190
Maine—Metropolitan Counties				Ottawa	223	128	95
Androscoggin	28	18	10	Saginaw	129	66	63
Cumberland	70	59	11	St. Clair	164	67	97
Penobscot	31	26	5	Van Buren	93	58	35
Sagadahoc	23	20	3	Washtenaw	297	139	158
York	30	27	3	Wayne	980	891	89
Maine—Nonmetropolitan Counties				**Michigan—Nonmetropolitan Counties**			
Aroostook	17	15	2	Alcona	25	14	11
Franklin	25	15	10	Alger	11	9	2
Hancock	18	16	2	Allegan	56	48	8
Kennebec	28	25	3	Alpena	25	12	13
Knox	20	20	0	Antrim	48	20	28

Table V-11. Full-Time Law Enforcement Employees, by Selected State Metropolitan and Nonmetropolitan Counties, 2011—*Continued*

(Number.)

State/County	Total law enforcement employees	Total officers	Total civilians	State/County	Total law enforcement employees	Total officers	Total civilians
Arenac	21	12	9	Washington	223	90	133
Baraga	13	6	7	Wright	229	137	92
Benzie	35	11	24				
Branch	49	25	24	**Minnesota—Nonmetropolitan Counties**			
Charlevoix	39	19	20	Aitkin	46	17	29
Cheboygan	35	18	17	Becker	56	21	35
Chippewa	37	15	22	Beltrami	69	30	39
Clare	29	24	5	Big Stone	8	5	3
Crawford	26	16	10	Brown	36	10	26
Delta	27	13	14	Cass	58	37	21
Dickinson	33	13	20	Chippewa	18	8	10
Emmet	46	24	22	Clearwater	24	10	14
Gladwin	40	16	24	Cook	19	11	8
Gogebic	21	14	7	Cottonwood	19	9	10
Grand Traverse	123	65	58	Crow Wing	116	36	80
Gratiot	35	19	16	Douglas	76	33	43
Hillsdale	40	25	15	Faribault	26	9	17
Houghton	28	19	9	Fillmore	31	19	12
Huron	45	21	24	Freeborn	65	24	41
Iosco	22	4	18	Goodhue	100	40	60
Iron	18	9	9	Grant	11	6	5
Isabella	48	22	26	Hubbard	42	16	26
Kalkaska	34	16	18	Itasca	68	52	16
Keweenaw	8	6	2	Jackson	25	13	12
Lake	74	17	57	Kanabec	47	19	28
Leelanau	19	18	1	Kandiyohi	102	33	69
Lenawee	97	42	55	Kittson	10	5	5
Luce	5	4	1	Koochiching	18	10	8
Mackinac	24	11	13	Lac Qui Parle	8	4	4
Manistee	32	15	17	Lake	29	17	12
Marquette	57	24	33	Lake of the Woods	8	4	4
Mason	40	20	20	Le Sueur	31	16	15
Mecosta	48	23	25	Lincoln	11	5	6
Menominee	30	13	17	Lyon	47	14	33
Midland	56	28	28	Mahnomen	18	12	6
Missaukee	28	13	15	Marshall	18	12	6
Montcalm	57	28	29	Martin	30	12	18
Montmorency	24	10	14	McLeod	57	23	34
Oceana	37	21	16	Meeker	44	20	24
Ogemaw	34	16	18	Mille Lacs	63	24	39
Ontonagon	11	8	3	Morrison	52	19	33
Osceola	37	18	19	Mower	64	21	43
Oscoda	17	11	6	Murray	13	9	4
Otsego	23	10	13	Nobles	34	12	22
Presque Isle	24	13	11	Norman	8	5	3
Roscommon	39	25	14	Otter Tail	76	31	45
Sanilac	55	24	31	Pennington	28	7	21
Schoolcraft	11	3	8	Pine	73	28	45
Shiawassee	66	31	35	Pipestone	22	12	10
St. Joseph	50	25	25	Pope	14	7	7
Tuscola	49	26	23	Red Lake	11	7	4
Wexford	49	23	26	Redwood	23	12	11
				Renville	26	10	16
Minnesota—Metropolitan Counties				Rice	48	27	21
Anoka	238	122	116	Rock	15	10	5
Benton	74	27	47	Roseau	20	9	11
Blue Earth	92	25	67	Sibley	22	11	11
Carlton	46	19	27	Steele	25	20	5
Carver	146	70	76	Stevens	13	6	7
Chisago	78	38	40	Swift	15	7	8
Clay	67	30	37	Todd	29	14	15
Dakota	157	79	78	Traverse	12	5	7
Dodge	29	22	7	Wadena	21	8	13
Hennepin	745	330	415	Waseca	27	11	16
Houston	25	12	13	Watonwan	9	8	1
Isanti	59	20	39	Wilkin	18	6	12
Nicollet	38	12	26	Winona	58	20	38
Olmsted	159	61	98	Yellow Medicine	9	8	1
Polk	27	22	5				
Ramsey	400	219	181	**Mississippi—Metropolitan Counties**			
Scott	124	40	84	DeSoto	246	101	145
Sherburne	240	81	159	George	25	16	9
Stearns	178	60	118	Lamar	76	41	35
St. Louis	231	98	133	Madison	118	50	68
Wabasha	29	17	12	Rankin	190	80	110

Table V-11. Full-Time Law Enforcement Employees, by Selected State Metropolitan and Nonmetropolitan Counties, 2011—*Continued*

(Number.)

State/County	Total law enforce-ment employees	Total officers	Total civilians	State/County	Total law enforce-ment employees	Total officers	Total civilians
Simpson	42	17	25	Platte	115	81	34
Stone	22	19	3	Polk	35	22	13
				Ray	34	13	21
Mississippi—Nonmetropolitan Counties				St. Charles	223	156	67
Adams	63	34	29	St. Louis County Police Department	1,036	788	248
Attala	13	8	5	Warren	58	32	26
Benton	15	5	10	Washington	26	18	8
Bolivar	113	18	95	Webster	26	15	11
Chickasaw	15	14	1				
Choctaw	12	6	6	**Missouri—Nonmetropolitan Counties**			
Claiborne	31	13	18	Adair	32	14	18
Clarke	13	9	4	Atchison	10	5	5
Covington	17	13	4	Audrain	41	36	5
Greene	16	8	8	Barry	35	21	14
Holmes	15	12	3	Benton	19	12	7
Humphreys	13	6	7	Butler	39	16	23
Issaquena	6	3	3	Camden	113	69	44
Itawamba	27	14	13	Carroll	9	8	1
Jones	47	41	6	Carter	10	5	5
Kemper	16	10	6	Cedar	18	11	7
Lauderdale	142	51	91	Chariton	16	12	4
Leake	17	15	2	Clark	19	7	12
Lee	127	46	81	Cooper	9	8	1
Leflore	32	24	8	Crawford	37	28	9
Lincoln	43	21	22	Dade	5	1	4
Lowndes	110	44	66	Daviess	6	5	1
Marion	20	16	4	Dent	18	13	5
Monroe	61	24	37	Douglas	12	6	6
Montgomery	8	7	1	Dunklin	12	10	2
Newton	19	10	9	Gasconade	15	14	1
Noxubee	11	9	2	Grundy	14	4	10
Oktibbeha	51	27	24	Henry	37	24	13
Panola	68	28	40	Hickory	14	9	5
Pike	56	28	28	Holt	8	5	3
Pontotoc	34	18	16	Howell	31	22	9
Prentiss	32	13	19	Iron	15	10	5
Tallahatchie	24	12	12	Johnson	55	35	20
Tippah	19	8	11	Knox	2	2	0
Tishomingo	24	13	11	Laclede	23	22	1
Union	32	17	15	Lawrence	38	29	9
Warren	59	36	23	Lewis	10	4	6
Washington	54	36	18	Linn	7	6	1
Wayne	24	12	12	Livingston	20	9	11
Webster	9	6	3	Macon	15	12	3
Winston	11	9	2	Madison	10	8	2
				Maries	11	9	2
Missouri—Metropolitan Counties				Marion	36	15	21
Andrew	15	11	4	Mercer	8	3	5
Bates	39	15	24	Miller	19	17	2
Bollinger	9	9	0	Monroe	8	7	1
Boone	76	60	16	Montgomery	18	16	2
Buchanan	108	77	31	Morgan	48	23	25
Caldwell	36	8	28	New Madrid	23	12	11
Callaway	26	24	2	Nodaway	13	11	2
Cape Girardeau	70	45	25	Oregon	10	6	4
Cass	85	68	17	Ozark	14	9	5
Christian	73	29	44	Pemiscot	38	18	20
Clay	185	112	73	Perry	30	21	9
Clinton	24	18	6	Pettis	46	28	18
Cole	79	51	28	Phelps	60	25	35
Dallas	21	18	3	Pike	25	9	16
De Kalb	11	5	6	Pulaski	29	12	17
Franklin	145	120	25	Putnam	4	3	1
Greene	265	140	125	Ralls	6	6	0
Howard	11	8	3	Randolph	36	18	18
Jackson	129	95	34	Ripley	11	9	2
Jasper	145	100	45	Saline	34	21	13
Jefferson	207	144	63	Schuyler	8	3	5
Lafayette	39	37	2	Scotland	5	2	3
Lincoln	80	39	41	Scott	37	17	20
McDonald	28	27	1	Shannon	8	4	4
Moniteau	10	5	5	Shelby	9	5	4
Newton	67	34	33	St. Clair	66	20	46
Osage	13	9	4	Ste. Genevieve	48	43	5

Table V-11. Full-Time Law Enforcement Employees, by Selected State Metropolitan and Nonmetropolitan Counties, 2011—*Continued*

(Number.)

State/County	Total law enforcement employees	Total officers	Total civilians	State/County	Total law enforcement employees	Total officers	Total civilians
St. Francois	67	55	12	Douglas	201	130	71
Stoddard	24	12	12	Lancaster	96	79	17
Stone	58	49	9	Sarpy	196	130	66
Sullivan	4	3	1	Saunders	19	11	8
Taney	51	37	14	Seward	22	12	10
Texas	13	8	5				
Vernon	21	9	12	**Nebraska—Nonmetropolitan Counties**			
Worth	4	3	1	Adams	20	18	2
Wright	11	4	7	Antelope	11	5	6
				Arthur	1	1	0
Montana—Metropolitan Counties				Banner	1	1	0
Carbon	14	9	5	Blaine	1	1	0
Cascade	45	34	11	Boone	12	5	7
Missoula	173	48	125	Box Butte	18	5	13
Yellowstone	150	52	98	Brown	9	5	4
				Buffalo	43	24	19
Montana—Nonmetropolitan Counties				Burt	5	5	0
Beaverhead	18	7	11	Butler	12	7	5
Big Horn	28	14	14	Cedar	9	4	5
Blaine	13	8	5	Chase	8	4	4
Broadwater	22	9	13	Cherry	6	5	1
Carter	5	4	1	Cheyenne	8	7	1
Chouteau	19	9	10	Colfax	14	7	7
Custer	15	6	9	Cuming	6	5	1
Daniels	3	3	0	Custer	7	6	1
Dawson	7	6	1	Dawes	13	6	7
Deer Lodge	37	28	9	Dawson	65	33	32
Fallon	10	4	6	Deuel	5	4	1
Fergus	21	9	12	Dodge	24	17	7
Flathead	107	53	54	Dundy	8	4	4
Gallatin	102	48	54	Fillmore	12	7	5
Garfield	3	2	1	Franklin	7	3	4
Glacier	28	12	16	Frontier	8	5	3
Golden Valley	2	2	0	Furnas	15	8	7
Granite	9	5	4	Gage	14	11	3
Hill	28	12	16	Garden	9	4	5
Jefferson	24	13	11	Garfield	2	2	0
Judith Basin	6	4	2	Gosper	5	4	1
Lake	58	23	35	Grant	1	1	0
Lewis and Clark	73	44	29	Greeley	3	2	1
Liberty	9	5	4	Hall	35	29	6
Lincoln	38	20	18	Hamilton	18	9	9
Madison	16	10	6	Harlan	8	4	4
McCone	6	4	2	Hayes	2	2	0
Meagher	9	4	5	Hitchcock	7	4	3
Mineral	18	7	11	Holt	6	5	1
Musselshell	9	8	1	Hooker	2	2	0
Park	16	15	1	Howard	12	5	7
Petroleum	1	1	0	Jefferson	13	7	6
Phillips	11	7	4	Johnson	13	6	7
Pondera	9	8	1	Kearney	11	6	5
Powder River	6	3	3	Keith	14	7	7
Powell	17	10	7	Keya Paha	1	1	0
Prairie	3	3	0	Kimball	9	4	5
Ravalli	61	30	31	Knox	13	4	9
Richland	41	8	33	Lincoln	53	22	31
Roosevelt	24	11	13	Logan	2	2	0
Rosebud	25	14	11	Loup	1	1	0
Sanders	20	11	9	Madison	54	27	27
Sheridan	8	7	1	McPherson	1	1	0
Silver Bow	99	50	49	Morrill	9	4	5
Stillwater	14	8	6	Nance	11	7	4
Sweet Grass	13	7	6	Nemaha	5	5	0
Teton	12	9	3	Nuckolls	7	4	3
Toole	20	12	8	Otoe	25	15	10
Treasure	2	2	0	Pawnee	5	4	1
Valley	17	8	9	Perkins	8	4	4
Wheatland	15	10	5	Phelps	26	6	20
Wibaux	2	2	0	Pierce	8	4	4
				Platte	67	21	46
Nebraska—Metropolitan Counties				Polk	11	5	6
Cass	70	51	19	Red Willow	8	6	2
Dakota	16	15	1	Rock	9	3	6
Dixon	12	7	5	Scotts Bluff	23	17	6

Table V-11. Full-Time Law Enforcement Employees, by Selected State Metropolitan and Nonmetropolitan Counties, 2011—*Continued*

(Number.)

State/County	Total law enforcement employees	Total officers	Total civilians	State/County	Total law enforcement employees	Total officers	Total civilians
Sheridan	5	4	1	Lea	50	38	12
Sherman	6	5	1	Lincoln	26	18	8
Stanton	8	7	1	Luna	36	32	4
Thayer	11	7	4	McKinley	43	31	12
Thomas	1	1	0	Mora	7	5	2
Thurston	16	8	8	Otero	61	42	19
Valley	9	4	5	Quay	8	7	1
Wayne	6	5	1	Rio Arriba	24	21	3
Webster	5	5	0	Roosevelt	17	14	3
Wheeler	1	1	0	San Miguel	9	8	1
York	23	9	14	Sierra	17	15	2
				Socorro	15	11	4
Nevada—Metropolitan Counties				Taos	26	20	6
Carson City	134	91	43	Union	6	5	1
Washoe	674	402	272				
				New York—Metropolitan Counties			
Nevada—Nonmetropolitan Counties				Albany	157	121	36
Douglas	118	105	13	Broome	66	51	15
Elko	69	53	16	Chemung	49	44	5
Humboldt	48	34	14	Dutchess	138	105	33
Nye	135	98	37	Erie	157	133	24
				Herkimer	15	6	9
New Hampshire—Metropolitan Counties				Livingston	73	49	24
Rockingham	49	25	24	Madison	39	30	9
				Monroe	314	258	56
New Hampshire — Nonmetropolitan Counties				Nassau	3,200	2,388	812
Carroll	26	13	13	Niagara	140	107	33
Cheshire	23	10	13	Oneida	118	83	35
Merrimack	35	21	14	Onondaga	267	227	40
				Ontario	98	64	34
New Jersey—Metropolitan Counties				Orange	94	83	11
Atlantic	129	105	24	Orleans	40	26	14
Bergen	516	438	78	Oswego	79	64	15
Bergen County Police Department	168	91	77	Putnam	96	82	14
Burlington	86	72	14	Rensselaer	35	33	2
Camden	176	148	28	Rockland	114	82	32
Cape May	169	135	34	Saratoga	153	112	41
Cumberland	65	59	6	Schenectady	16	10	6
Essex	459	372	87	Schoharie	28	13	15
Gloucester	100	87	13	Suffolk	406	275	131
Hudson	330	231	99	Suffolk County Police Department	3,094	2,495	599
Hunterdon	25	21	4	Tioga	50	33	17
Mercer	170	131	39	Tompkins	45	40	5
Middlesex	219	180	39	Ulster	78	57	21
Monmouth	604	445	159	Warren	112	67	45
Morris	115	85	30	Washington	47	33	14
Ocean	238	126	112	Wayne	61	53	8
Salem	213	187	26	Westchester Public Safety	337	264	73
Somerset	208	168	40				
Sussex	147	122	25	**New York—Nonmetropolitan Counties**			
Union	207	164	43	Allegany	44	25	19
Warren	22	18	4	Cattaraugus	86	64	22
				Cayuga	43	39	4
New Mexico—Metropolitan Counties				Chautauqua	107	61	46
Bernalillo	337	274	63	Chenango	39	24	15
Dona Ana	195	126	69	Clinton	23	23	0
Sandoval	60	51	9	Columbia	57	47	10
San Juan	123	96	27	Cortland	52	33	19
Torrance	19	16	3	Delaware	28	17	11
Valencia	47	37	10	Essex	29	21	8
				Franklin	14	7	7
New Mexico—Nonmetropolitan Counties				Fulton	40	24	16
Catron	10	6	4	Genesee	79	49	30
Chaves	45	35	10	Greene	33	29	4
Cibola	22	16	6	Hamilton	6	5	1
Colfax	12	10	2	Jefferson	53	44	9
Curry	28	18	10	Lewis	30	19	11
De Baca	6	6	0	Montgomery	25	19	6
Eddy	60	51	9	Otsego	18	16	2
Grant	41	38	3	Schuyler	20	17	3
Guadalupe	7	5	2	Seneca	40	30	10
Harding	2	2	0	Steuben	54	37	17
Hidalgo	11	8	3	St. Lawrence	35	34	1

Table V-11. Full-Time Law Enforcement Employees, by Selected State Metropolitan and Nonmetropolitan Counties, 2011—*Continued*

(Number.)

State/County	Total law enforcement employees	Total officers	Total civilians	State/County	Total law enforcement employees	Total officers	Total civilians
Sullivan	41	41	0	Jackson	70	48	22
Wyoming	37	29	8	Jones	24	15	9
Yates	40	26	14	Lee	86	53	33
				Lenoir	105	66	39
North Carolina—Metropolitan Counties				Lincoln	154	103	51
Alamance	264	128	136	Macon	67	48	19
Alexander	48	30	18	Martin	35	33	2
Anson	59	30	29	McDowell	65	43	22
Brunswick	197	134	63	Mitchell	19	17	2
Buncombe	350	213	137	Montgomery	54	32	22
Burke	116	87	29	Moore	114	74	40
Cabarrus	317	198	119	Northampton	51	25	26
Caldwell	120	67	53	Pamlico	38	15	23
Catawba	178	129	49	Pasquotank	43	39	4
Chatham	101	79	22	Perquimans	14	11	3
Cumberland	533	299	234	Polk	35	23	12
Currituck	101	64	37	Richmond	80	50	30
Davie	79	49	30	Robeson	250	138	112
Durham	428	168	260	Rowan	163	119	44
Edgecombe	135	53	82	Rutherford	127	73	54
Forsyth	487	210	277	Sampson	133	95	38
Franklin	95	58	37	Scotland	63	37	26
Gaston	208	119	89	Stanly	88	47	41
Gaston County Police Department	228	134	94	Surry	96	56	40
Greene	49	24	25	Swain	44	21	23
Guilford	600	252	348	Transylvania	78	61	17
Haywood	95	52	43	Tyrrell	16	10	6
Henderson	188	132	56	Vance	90	43	47
Hoke	66	58	8	Warren	64	36	28
Johnston	179	103	76	Washington	40	21	19
Madison	31	20	11	Watauga	86	47	39
Mecklenburg[1]	1,201	300	901	Wilkes	114	67	47
Nash	86	81	5	Wilson	143	86	57
New Hanover	404	307	97	Yancey	33	19	14
Onslow	260	115	145				
Orange	139	105	34	**North Dakota—Metropolitan Counties**			
Pender	104	58	46	Burleigh	82	41	41
Person	82	42	40	Cass	139	73	66
Pitt	313	121	192	Grand Forks	40	33	7
Randolph	217	155	62	Morton	37	20	17
Rockingham	138	93	45				
Stokes	60	42	18	**North Dakota—Nonmetropolitan Counties**			
Union	246	186	60	Adams	2	2	0
Wake	848	371	477	Barnes	7	6	1
Wayne	150	86	64	Benson	4	4	0
Yadkin	56	31	25	Billings	4	4	0
				Bottineau	12	8	4
North Carolina—Nonmetropolitan Counties				Bowman	3	3	0
Alleghany	27	11	16	Burke	6	5	1
Ashe	54	24	30	Cavalier	11	5	6
Avery	33	24	9	Dickey	5	4	1
Beaufort	84	49	35	Divide	6	6	0
Bertie	33	24	9	Dunn	9	8	1
Bladen	67	46	21	Eddy	5	4	1
Camden	18	17	1	Emmons	4	3	1
Carteret	82	51	31	Foster	3	3	0
Caswell	46	35	11	Golden Valley	5	4	1
Cherokee	68	26	42	Grant	4	4	0
Chowan	33	15	18	Griggs	5	4	1
Clay	42	17	25	Hettinger	4	4	0
Cleveland	144	90	54	Kidder	4	3	1
Columbus	113	63	50	Lamoure	5	4	1
Craven	118	70	48	Logan	4	2	2
Dare	142	63	79	McHenry	7	7	0
Davidson	190	126	64	McIntosh	3	3	0
Duplin	90	66	24	McKenzie	16	16	0
Gates	13	12	1	McLean	31	18	13
Graham	22	14	8	Mercer	22	14	8
Granville	94	53	41	Mountrail	19	10	9
Halifax	90	62	28	Nelson	5	4	1
Harnett	205	114	91	Oliver	3	2	1
Hertford	62	22	40	Pembina	12	7	5
Hyde	15	15	0	Pierce	8	3	5
Iredell	211	157	54	Ramsey	7	6	1

[1] The employee data presented in this table for Mecklenburg represent only Mecklenburg County Sheriff's Office employees and exclude Charlotte-Mecklenburg Police Department employees.

Table V-11.   Full-Time Law Enforcement Employees, by Selected State Metropolitan and Nonmetropolitan Counties, 2011—*Continued*

(Number.)

State/County	Total law enforcement employees	Total officers	Total civilians	State/County	Total law enforcement employees	Total officers	Total civilians
Ransom	5	4	1	Marion	33	29	4
Renville	4	4	0	Meigs	15	13	2
Richland	35	15	20	Mercer	51	25	26
Rolette	18	9	9	Monroe	20	13	7
Sargent	5	4	1	Morgan	15	9	6
Sheridan	3	3	0	Muskingum	106	69	37
Sioux	1	1	0	Noble	19	8	11
Slope	1	1	0	Paulding	22	14	8
Stark	18	15	3	Perry	15	10	5
Steele	3	3	0	Putnam	54	30	24
Stutsman	11	9	2	Ross	83	54	29
Towner	3	2	1	Sandusky	52	28	24
Traill	13	8	5	Scioto	70	38	32
Walsh	16	10	6	Seneca	80	37	43
Ward	47	22	25	Shelby	59	38	21
Wells	3	3	0	Tuscarawas	94	27	67
Williams	43	27	16	Van Wert	36	20	16
				Vinton	15	10	5
Ohio—Metropolitan Counties				Williams	20	16	4
Allen	150	71	79	Wyandot	23	12	11
Belmont	59	53	6				
Brown	44	28	16	**Oklahoma—Metropolitan Counties**			
Carroll	25	19	6	Canadian	71	46	25
Clark	152	123	29	Cleveland	87	41	46
Clermont	187	81	106	Comanche	40	29	11
Cuyahoga	1,056	159	897	Creek	66	38	28
Erie	66	35	31	Grady	14	13	1
Fairfield	133	106	27	Le Flore	17	12	5
Franklin	825	647	178	Lincoln	34	13	21
Fulton	31	20	11	Logan	52	18	34
Geauga	115	48	67	McClain	26	17	9
Greene	128	82	46	Oklahoma	749	209	540
Hamilton	826	312	514	Okmulgee	15	14	1
Lake	168	39	129	Osage	76	40	36
Licking	180	121	59	Pawnee	18	8	10
Madison	38	29	9	Rogers	83	33	50
Mahoning	215	200	15	Sequoyah	46	16	30
Miami	83	46	37	Tulsa	538	232	306
Montgomery	456	200	256	Wagoner	52	19	33
Morrow	52	21	31				
Ottawa	61	22	39	**Oklahoma—Nonmetropolitan Counties**			
Portage	128	57	71	Adair	30	9	21
Preble	38	11	27	Alfalfa	9	4	5
Richland	107	35	72	Atoka	22	7	15
Stark	178	98	80	Beaver	12	7	5
Summit	417	341	76	Beckham	33	11	22
Trumbull	137	52	85	Blaine	15	7	8
Union	54	34	20	Bryan	51	17	34
Warren	182	95	87	Caddo	28	16	12
Washington	79	40	39	Carter	21	18	3
Wood	119	73	46	Cherokee	32	23	9
				Choctaw	15	5	10
Ohio—Nonmetropolitan Counties				Cimarron	7	4	3
Adams	25	18	7	Coal	9	6	3
Ashland	68	40	28	Cotton	12	8	4
Auglaize	55	22	33	Craig	26	10	16
Champaign	19	17	2	Custer	37	14	23
Clinton	65	35	30	Delaware	41	18	23
Columbiana	29	20	9	Dewey	11	4	7
Coshocton	51	40	11	Ellis	18	6	12
Crawford	54	22	32	Garfield	61	23	38
Darke	59	35	24	Garvin	31	19	12
Defiance	33	20	13	Grant	12	5	7
Fayette	34	22	12	Greer	8	4	4
Gallia	32	22	10	Harmon	4	3	1
Guernsey	41	19	22	Harper	9	5	4
Hancock	83	33	50	Haskell	16	8	8
Henry	21	18	3	Hughes	14	7	7
Highland	45	30	15	Jackson	36	13	23
Hocking	24	19	5	Jefferson	15	6	9
Holmes	45	31	14	Johnston	27	8	19
Huron	64	20	44	Kay	20	13	7
Jackson	17	12	5	Kingfisher	14	8	6
Logan	70	37	33	Kiowa	16	7	9

Table V-11.   Full-Time Law Enforcement Employees, by Selected State Metropolitan and Nonmetropolitan Counties, 2011—*Continued*

(Number.)

State/County	Total law enforcement employees	Total officers	Total civilians
Latimer	15	11	4
Love	22	8	14
Major	13	5	8
Marshall	27	8	19
Mayes	45	20	25
McCurtain	19	16	3
McIntosh	18	11	7
Murray	10	5	5
Muskogee	37	32	5
Noble	18	5	13
Nowata	20	9	11
Okfuskee	14	6	8
Ottawa	34	14	20
Payne	82	32	50
Pittsburg	64	18	46
Pontotoc	37	15	22
Pottawatomie	27	22	5
Pushmataha	14	9	5
Roger Mills	12	7	5
Seminole	36	13	23
Stephens	60	22	38
Texas	43	12	31
Tillman	27	7	20
Washington	55	26	29
Washita	18	8	10
Woods	10	5	5
Woodward	26	9	17
Oregon—Metropolitan Counties			
Benton	75	62	13
Clackamas	426	218	208
Columbia	41	35	6
Deschutes	210	82	128
Jackson	173	117	56
Lane	345	65	280
Marion	336	85	251
Multnomah	733	105	628
Polk	60	45	15
Washington	539	240	299
Yamhill	96	45	51
Oregon—Nonmetropolitan Counties			
Baker	31	11	20
Clatsop	55	26	29
Coos	85	24	61
Crook	28	15	13
Curry	36	13	23
Douglas	144	112	32
Gilliam	7	6	1
Grant	16	5	11
Harney	17	11	6
Hood River	33	16	17
Jefferson	42	13	29
Josephine	98	35	63
Klamath	61	25	36
Lake	20	7	13
Lincoln	87	27	60
Linn	177	75	102
Malheur	60	25	35
Morrow	27	27	0
Sherman	7	6	1
Tillamook	60	56	4
Umatilla	74	49	25
Union	30	17	13
Wallowa	13	7	6
Wasco	29	16	13
Wheeler	3	3	0
Pennsylvania—Metropolitan Counties			
Allegheny	185	156	29
Allegheny County Police Department	260	202	58
Beaver	30	23	7
Berks	109	95	14
Blair	10	6	4
Butler	25	19	6
Centre	19	16	3
Cumberland	33	27	6
Erie	44	36	8
Lancaster	62	53	9
Mercer	18	15	3
Montgomery	136	115	21
Northampton	56	52	4
Pike	20	17	3
Washington	27	27	0
Westmoreland	61	52	9
York	118	108	10
Pennsylvania—Nonmetropolitan Counties			
Adams	11	9	2
Bedford	10	8	2
Clarion	11	8	3
Elk	6	5	1
Franklin	21	17	4
Greene	6	5	1
Indiana	19	16	3
Jefferson	5	4	1
Lawrence	15	11	4
Schuylkill	17	13	4
Snyder	5	5	0
Tioga	8	6	2
Warren	11	9	2
Wayne	15	12	3
South Carolina—Metropolitan Counties			
Aiken	164	130	34
Anderson	373	222	151
Berkeley	238	143	95
Calhoun	25	22	3
Charleston	750	247	503
Darlington	131	73	58
Dorchester	233	125	108
Edgefield	60	31	29
Fairfield	52	46	6
Florence	226	118	108
Greenville	493	400	93
Horry	335	265	70
Horry County Police Department	249	230	19
Kershaw	76	68	8
Laurens	120	66	54
Lexington	380	247	133
Pickens	140	101	39
Richland	545	502	43
Saluda	53	18	35
Spartanburg	332	303	29
Sumter	135	121	14
York	199	174	25
South Carolina—Nonmetropolitan Counties			
Abbeville	55	29	26
Allendale	15	13	2
Bamberg	16	13	3
Barnwell	40	25	15
Beaufort	260	234	26
Cherokee	95	49	46
Chester	107	43	64
Chesterfield	88	44	44
Clarendon	54	45	9
Colleton	121	61	60
Dillon	81	35	46
Georgetown	172	95	77
Greenwood	112	70	42
Hampton	40	35	5
Jasper	41	36	5
Lancaster	139	86	53
Lee	31	27	4
Marion	40	37	3
Marlboro	30	25	5
McCormick	37	14	23
Newberry	96	47	49
Oconee	120	83	37

Table V-11.   Full-Time Law Enforcement Employees, by Selected State Metropolitan and Nonmetropolitan Counties, 2011—*Continued*

(Number.)

State/County	Total law enforce-ment employees	Total officers	Total civilians	State/County	Total law enforce-ment employees	Total officers	Total civilians
Orangeburg	129	92	37	**Tennessee—Metropolitan Counties**			
Union	76	31	45	Anderson	163	60	103
Williamsburg	67	37	30	Blount	271	129	142
				Bradley	202	105	97
South Dakota—Metropolitan Counties				Cannon	32	13	19
Lincoln	16	14	2	Carter	94	50	44
McCook	7	6	1	Cheatham	72	36	36
Meade	52	17	35	Chester	49	14	35
Minnehaha	192	84	108	Dickson	140	58	82
Pennington	366	75	291	Fayette	92	40	52
Turner	10	8	2	Grainger	42	18	24
Union	25	9	16	Hamblen	81	31	50
				Hamilton	318	160	158
South Dakota—Nonmetropolitan Counties				Hartsville-Trousdale	36	18	18
Aurora	4	3	1	Hawkins	93	44	49
Beadle	25	6	19	Hickman	39	20	19
Bennett	5	3	2	Jefferson	94	43	51
Bon Homme	8	3	5	Knox	1,067	401	666
Brookings	22	14	8	Loudon	64	39	25
Brown	50	16	34	Macon	60	24	36
Brule	9	4	5	Madison	231	74	157
Buffalo	1	1	0	Marion	49	20	29
Butte	13	4	9	Montgomery	317	82	235
Campbell	2	2	0	Polk	49	18	31
Charles Mix	13	5	8	Robertson	137	45	92
Clark	4	4	0	Rutherford	407	200	207
Clay	11	7	4	Sequatchie	39	18	21
Codington	27	9	18	Shelby	1,845	521	1,324
Corson	4	3	1	Smith	54	25	29
Custer	11	10	1	Stewart	41	18	23
Davison	8	6	2	Sullivan	253	112	141
Day	6	3	3	Sumner	248	71	177
Deuel	8	4	4	Tipton	87	49	38
Dewey	4	3	1	Unicoi	46	23	23
Douglas	2	2	0	Union	35	21	14
Edmunds	7	4	3	Washington	207	83	124
Fall River	12	6	6	Williamson	212	109	103
Faulk	9	3	6	Wilson	225	91	134
Grant	9	3	6				
Gregory	3	2	1	**Tennessee—Nonmetropolitan Counties**			
Haakon	2	2	0	Bedford	87	36	51
Hamlin	4	4	0	Benton	39	13	26
Hand	4	3	1	Bledsoe	35	9	26
Hanson	2	2	0	Campbell	66	34	32
Harding	3	2	1	Carroll	48	24	24
Hughes	49	6	43	Claiborne	91	33	58
Hutchinson	3	3	0	Clay	19	10	9
Hyde	1	1	0	Cocke	61	33	28
Jackson	2	2	0	Coffee	85	44	41
Jerauld	4	3	1	Crockett	30	13	17
Jones	2	2	0	Cumberland	105	48	57
Kingsbury	5	4	1	Decatur	32	14	18
Lake	10	5	5	DeKalb	42	20	22
Lawrence	39	13	26	Dyer	78	35	43
Lyman	5	4	1	Fentress	33	20	13
Marshall	11	6	5	Franklin	55	35	20
McPherson	2	2	0	Gibson	73	31	42
Mellette	4	4	0	Giles	60	29	31
Miner	4	3	1	Greene	156	64	92
Moody	8	4	4	Grundy	31	17	14
Perkins	4	3	1	Hancock	33	11	22
Potter	3	2	1	Hardeman	68	27	41
Roberts	27	4	23	Hardin	49	20	29
Sanborn	3	3	0	Haywood	47	22	25
Shannon	1	1	0	Henderson	62	27	35
Spink	13	8	5	Henry	65	33	32
Stanley	6	5	1	Houston	25	12	13
Sully	3	3	0	Humphreys	38	20	18
Todd	1	1	0	Jackson	41	13	28
Tripp	5	4	1	Johnson	41	16	25
Walworth	10	3	7	Lake	21	10	11
Yankton	28	10	18	Lauderdale	63	21	42
Ziebach	2	2	0	Lawrence	90	45	45
				Lewis	29	13	16

Table V-11. Full-Time Law Enforcement Employees, by Selected State Metropolitan and Nonmetropolitan Counties, 2011—*Continued*

(Number.)

State/County	Total law enforcement employees	Total officers	Total civilians
Lincoln	61	26	35
Marshall	49	22	27
Maury	149	81	68
McMinn	84	32	52
McNairy	35	17	18
Meigs	24	14	10
Monroe	67	35	32
Moore	26	13	13
Morgan	45	18	27
Obion	62	25	37
Overton	54	23	31
Perry	35	16	19
Pickett	16	10	6
Putnam	126	62	64
Rhea	54	54	0
Roane	77	41	36
Scott	65	26	39
Sevier	116	93	23
Van Buren	15	8	7
Warren	82	42	40
Wayne	46	17	29
Weakley	44	22	22
White	60	29	31
Texas—Metropolitan Counties			
Aransas	76	22	54
Archer	17	8	9
Armstrong	7	3	4
Atascosa	79	32	47
Austin	67	31	36
Bandera	66	26	40
Bastrop	206	76	130
Bell	256	89	167
Bexar	1,675	527	1,148
Bowie	47	40	7
Brazoria	345	166	179
Brazos	226	99	127
Burleson	35	12	23
Caldwell	97	24	73
Calhoun	64	23	41
Callahan	13	5	8
Cameron	438	112	326
Carson	17	6	11
Chambers	84	39	45
Clay	19	10	9
Collin	472	146	326
Comal	247	124	123
Coryell	65	28	37
Crosby	14	5	9
Dallas	2,245	422	1,823
Delta	20	8	12
Denton	592	243	349
Ector	217	95	122
Ellis	214	80	134
El Paso	1,117	257	860
Fort Bend	733	493	240
Galveston	459	278	181
Goliad	28	13	15
Grayson	137	62	75
Gregg	246	101	145
Guadalupe	210	85	125
Hardin	61	30	31
Harris	3,705	2,212	1,493
Hays	301	116	185
Hidalgo	730	262	468
Hunt	134	128	6
Irion	8	4	4
Jefferson	408	102	306
Johnson	137	94	43
Jones	21	10	11
Kaufman	241	88	153
Kendall	74	48	26
Lampasas	33	18	15
Liberty	71	51	20
Lubbock	435	168	267

State/County	Total law enforcement employees	Total officers	Total civilians
McLennan	350	121	229
Medina	70	27	43
Midland	165	75	90
Montgomery	716	401	315
Nueces	317	69	248
Orange	138	64	74
Parker	113	82	31
Potter	205	95	110
Randall	175	80	95
Robertson	32	12	20
Rockwall	118	40	78
Rusk	75	39	36
San Jacinto	62	34	28
San Patricio	104	48	56
Smith	340	167	173
Tarrant	1,388	499	889
Taylor	215	81	134
Tom Green	166	54	112
Travis	1,533	1,136	397
Upshur	75	45	30
Victoria	184	114	70
Waller	74	47	27
Webb	283	171	112
Wichita	202	69	133
Williamson	494	215	279
Wilson	69	26	43
Wise	140	52	88
Texas—Nonmetropolitan Counties			
Anderson	80	35	45
Andrews	34	12	22
Angelina	116	45	71
Bailey	23	6	17
Baylor	7	3	4
Bee	39	20	19
Blanco	22	10	12
Borden	4	3	1
Bosque	37	17	20
Brewster	28	16	12
Briscoe	2	1	1
Brooks	36	11	25
Brown	65	25	40
Burnet	59	44	15
Camp	18	7	11
Cass	44	19	25
Castro	19	8	11
Cherokee	74	29	45
Childress	24	5	19
Cochran	14	7	7
Coke	6	5	1
Coleman	6	5	1
Collingsworth	14	4	10
Colorado	47	20	27
Comanche	29	10	19
Concho	14	7	7
Cottle	1	1	0
Crane	11	6	5
Culberson	13	8	5
Dallam	6	5	1
Dawson	19	7	12
Deaf Smith	33	11	22
Dewitt	42	12	30
Dickens	6	2	4
Dimmit	50	21	29
Donley	10	6	4
Duval	42	20	22
Eastland	27	9	18
Edwards	11	5	6
Erath	57	23	34
Falls	20	5	15
Fannin	25	18	7
Fayette	46	23	23
Fisher	9	5	4
Floyd	7	3	4
Foard	3	2	1

Table V-11. Full-Time Law Enforcement Employees, by Selected State Metropolitan and Nonmetropolitan Counties, 2011—*Continued*

(Number.)

State/County	Total law enforcement employees	Total officers	Total civilians	State/County	Total law enforcement employees	Total officers	Total civilians
Franklin	20	10	10	Ochiltree	19	8	11
Freestone	40	16	24	Oldham	11	6	5
Frio	20	12	8	Palo Pinto	53	25	28
Gaines	25	14	11	Panola	55	32	23
Garza	31	11	20	Parmer	19	6	13
Gillespie	42	28	14	Pecos	37	22	15
Glasscock	4	4	0	Polk	91	47	44
Gonzales	43	14	29	Presidio	7	7	0
Gray	43	14	29	Rains	24	10	14
Grimes	45	26	19	Reagan	19	8	11
Hale	72	23	49	Real	8	4	4
Hall	11	4	7	Red River	27	12	15
Hamilton	24	13	11	Reeves	66	17	49
Hansford	9	4	5	Refugio	41	15	26
Hardeman	12	7	5	Roberts	6	5	1
Harrison	102	48	54	Runnels	25	8	17
Hartley	5	5	0	Sabine	18	8	10
Haskell	9	3	6	San Augustine	18	8	10
Hemphill	16	10	6	San Saba	5	5	0
Henderson	151	83	68	Schleicher	12	6	6
Hill	73	33	40	Scurry	41	10	31
Hockley	26	12	14	Shackelford	15	5	10
Hood	130	47	83	Shelby	30	17	13
Hopkins	59	26	33	Sherman	10	5	5
Houston	46	20	26	Somervell	41	19	22
Howard	51	16	35	Starr	114	58	56
Hudspeth	28	10	18	Stephens	27	7	20
Hutchinson	35	12	23	Sterling	4	4	0
Jack	30	9	21	Stonewall	7	3	4
Jackson	33	14	19	Sutton	13	4	9
Jasper	48	19	29	Swisher	10	4	6
Jeff Davis	7	5	2	Terrell	12	6	6
Jim Hogg	41	23	18	Terry	32	10	22
Jim Wells	67	27	40	Throckmorton	6	2	4
Karnes	20	11	9	Titus	60	25	35
Kenedy	18	11	7	Trinity	19	11	8
Kent	6	3	3	Tyler	31	16	15
Kerr	94	45	49	Upton	23	10	13
Kimble	14	11	3	Uvalde	39	21	18
King	2	2	0	Val Verde	61	42	19
Kinney	16	7	9	Van Zandt	78	42	36
Kleberg	88	22	66	Walker	72	35	37
Knox	9	3	6	Ward	32	14	18
Lamar	76	26	50	Washington	54	35	19
Lamb	29	11	18	Wharton	73	44	29
La Salle	18	10	8	Wheeler	14	9	5
Lavaca	30	12	18	Wilbarger	18	7	11
Lee	40	12	28	Willacy	44	14	30
Leon	38	24	14	Winkler	28	9	19
Limestone	87	22	65	Wood	58	27	31
Lipscomb	10	6	4	Yoakum	22	11	11
Live Oak	34	9	25	Young	33	9	24
Llano	54	29	25	Zapata	105	49	56
Loving	3	2	1	Zavala	31	14	17
Lynn	22	7	15				
Madison	24	10	14	**Utah—Metropolitan Counties**			
Marion	15	14	1	Cache	147	112	35
Martin	8	4	4	Davis	331	139	192
Mason	9	5	4	Juab	23	8	15
Matagorda	74	34	40	Morgan	11	9	2
Maverick	93	46	47	Salt Lake County Unified Police Department	501	356	145
McCulloch	12	6	6	Summit	96	54	42
McMullen	6	5	1	Tooele	114	36	78
Menard	10	5	5	Utah	358	143	215
Milam	58	18	40	Washington	155	44	111
Mills	10	6	4	Weber	90	88	2
Mitchell	11	5	6				
Montague	29	10	19	**Utah—Nonmetropolitan Counties**			
Moore	45	17	28	Beaver	77	23	54
Morris	22	9	13	Box Elder	83	28	55
Motley	2	2	0	Carbon	46	19	27
Nacogdoches	100	51	49	Daggett	23	8	15
Navarro	128	65	63	Duchesne	55	19	36
Newton	23	12	11	Emery	40	32	8
Nolan	29	10	19	Garfield	29	6	23

Table V-11.   Full-Time Law Enforcement Employees, by Selected State Metropolitan and Nonmetropolitan Counties, 2011—*Continued*

(Number.)

State/County	Total law enforcement employees	Total officers	Total civilians	State/County	Total law enforcement employees	Total officers	Total civilians
Grand	32	17	15	Rockingham	69	55	14
Iron	33	29	4	Scott	34	26	8
Kane	50	35	15	Spotsylvania	201	159	42
Millard	50	30	20	Stafford	214	152	62
Piute	3	3	0	Surry	22	13	9
Rich	10	4	6	Sussex	42	37	5
San Juan	34	27	7	Warren	93	46	47
Sanpete	52	36	16	Washington	72	52	20
Sevier	65	52	13	York	93	87	6
Uintah	68	21	47				
Wasatch	47	39	8	**Virginia—Nonmetropolitan Counties**			
Wayne	6	6	0	Accomack	67	55	12
				Alleghany	62	43	19
Vermont—Metropolitan Counties				Augusta	77	66	11
Chittenden	12	10	2	Bath	17	17	0
Franklin	14	12	2	Bland	17	11	6
Grand Isle	7	4	3	Brunswick	33	19	14
				Buchanan	47	33	14
Vermont—Nonmetropolitan Counties				Buckingham	28	20	8
Addison	9	5	4	Carroll	33	28	5
Bennington	9	6	3	Charlotte	32	30	2
Caledonia	4	2	2	Culpeper	91	74	17
Essex	3	2	1	Dickenson	32	20	12
Lamoille	21	11	10	Essex	19	12	7
Orange	14	7	7	Floyd	28	18	10
Orleans	9	6	3	Grayson	29	23	6
Rutland	24	19	5	Greensville	34	20	14
Washington	13	11	2	Halifax	37	34	3
Windham	12	10	2	Henry	127	114	13
Windsor	12	9	3	Highland	11	7	4
				King George	42	28	14
Virginia—Metropolitan Counties				Lancaster	35	29	6
Albemarle County Police Department	138	112	26	Lee	34	34	0
Amelia	24	16	8	Lunenburg	21	14	7
Amherst	69	63	6	Madison	30	17	13
Appomattox	33	30	3	Mecklenburg	91	51	40
Arlington County Police Department	440	363	77	Middlesex	21	16	5
Bedford	81	73	8	Northampton	81	64	17
Botetourt	114	92	22	Northumberland	26	15	11
Campbell	65	57	8	Nottoway	24	13	11
Caroline	69	48	21	Orange	44	36	8
Charles City	16	9	7	Page	64	48	16
Chesterfield County Police Department	574	473	101	Patrick	38	24	14
Clarke	29	17	12	Prince Edward	30	23	7
Craig	14	9	5	Rappahannock	27	26	1
Cumberland	20	13	7	Richmond	20	12	8
Dinwiddie	42	39	3	Rockbridge	37	30	7
Fairfax County Police Department	1,719	1,391	328	Russell	49	34	15
Fauquier	127	110	17	Shenandoah	77	68	9
Fluvanna	39	27	12	Smyth	41	41	0
Franklin	91	73	18	Southampton	74	62	12
Frederick	124	107	17	Tazewell	61	44	17
Giles	33	23	10	Westmoreland	31	21	10
Gloucester	58	48	10	Wise	61	47	14
Goochland	39	29	10	Wythe	46	39	7
Greene	36	22	14				
Hanover	223	205	18	**Washington—Metropolitan Counties**			
Henrico County Police Department	744	568	176	Asotin	14	12	2
Isle of Wight	45	38	7	Benton	71	60	11
James City County Police Department	97	92	5	Chelan	64	53	11
King and Queen	20	13	7	Clark	210	132	78
King William	33	21	12	Cowlitz	53	43	10
Loudoun	636	531	105	Douglas	34	27	7
Louisa	61	48	13	Franklin	27	25	2
Mathews	20	11	9	King	343	241	102
Montgomery	117	101	16	Kitsap	145	115	30
Nelson	21	15	6	Pierce	361	300	61
New Kent	43	32	11	Skagit	92	48	44
Pittsylvania	131	113	18	Skamania	26	22	4
Powhatan	58	41	17	Snohomish	331	263	68
Prince George County Police Department	73	52	21	Spokane	179	124	55
Prince William County Police Department	699	569	130	Thurston	102	82	20
Pulaski	52	42	10	Whatcom	104	85	19
Roanoke County Police Department	139	127	12	Yakima	88	56	32

Table V-11. **Full-Time Law Enforcement Employees, by Selected State Metropolitan and Nonmetropolitan Counties, 2011**—*Continued*

(Number.)

State/County	Total law enforcement employees	Total officers	Total civilians
Washington—Nonmetropolitan Counties			
Adams	27	17	10
Clallam	43	35	8
Columbia	9	8	1
Ferry	22	7	15
Garfield	15	7	8
Grant	61	47	14
Grays Harbor	77	39	38
Island	57	33	24
Jefferson	44	23	21
Kittitas	65	34	31
Klickitat	48	19	29
Lewis	56	39	17
Lincoln	23	12	11
Mason	62	47	15
Okanogan	34	29	5
Pacific	45	18	27
Pend Oreille	19	16	3
San Juan	35	20	15
Stevens	31	26	5
Wahkiakum	16	7	9
Walla Walla	30	25	5
Whitman	22	18	4
West Virginia—Metropolitan Counties			
Berkeley	79	56	23
Boone	28	22	6
Brooke	29	17	12
Cabell	51	44	7
Clay	11	6	5
Hampshire	19	16	3
Hancock	36	26	10
Jefferson	32	26	6
Kanawha	131	102	29
Lincoln	7	6	1
Marshall	29	26	3
Mineral	15	13	2
Monongalia	63	36	27
Morgan	12	11	1
Ohio	29	28	1
Pleasants	7	6	1
Preston	26	15	11
Putnam	51	40	11
Wayne	24	21	3
Wirt	3	3	0
Wood	68	38	30
West Virginia—Nonmetropolitan Counties			
Barbour	7	7	0
Braxton	11	9	2
Calhoun	3	3	0
Doddridge	6	6	0
Fayette	35	30	5
Gilmer	7	4	3
Grant	11	8	3
Greenbrier	33	28	5
Hardy	11	9	2
Harrison	37	35	2
Jackson	23	15	8
Lewis	18	14	4
Logan	25	18	7
Marion	44	33	11
Mason	25	17	8
McDowell	16	15	1
Mercer	30	26	4
Mingo	23	20	3
Monroe	8	8	0
Nicholas	27	23	4
Pendleton	3	3	0
Pocahontas	14	8	6
Raleigh	66	45	21
Randolph	14	11	3
Ritchie	9	7	2

State/County	Total law enforcement employees	Total officers	Total civilians
Roane	9	8	1
Summers	10	6	4
Taylor	15	7	8
Tucker	4	4	0
Tyler	8	7	1
Upshur	13	11	2
Webster	8	5	3
Wetzel	10	10	0
Wyoming	26	20	6
Wisconsin—Metropolitan Counties			
Brown	325	152	173
Calumet	50	23	27
Chippewa	66	53	13
Columbia	95	40	55
Dane	536	433	103
Douglas	80	28	52
Eau Claire	89	40	49
Fond du Lac	112	57	55
Iowa	39	36	3
Kenosha	334	114	220
Kewaunee	34	32	2
La Crosse	112	41	71
Marathon	174	66	108
Milwaukee	1,243	369	874
Oconto	62	26	36
Outagamie	201	82	119
Ozaukee	100	78	22
Pierce	50	46	4
Racine	214	136	78
Rock	206	96	110
Sheboygan	146	71	75
St. Croix	84	76	8
Washington	171	72	99
Waukesha	339	161	178
Winnebago	186	128	58
Wisconsin—Nonmetropolitan Counties			
Adams	57	28	29
Ashland	39	21	18
Barron	69	28	41
Bayfield	40	19	21
Buffalo	22	13	9
Burnett	34	17	17
Clark	50	47	3
Crawford	29	28	1
Dodge	174	76	98
Door	66	32	34
Dunn	55	25	30
Florence	24	20	4
Forest	38	18	20
Grant	46	25	21
Green	57	35	22
Green Lake	43	17	26
Iron	19	11	8
Jackson	45	21	24
Jefferson	120	97	23
Juneau	46	43	3
Lafayette	25	13	12
Langlade	37	14	23
Lincoln	64	29	35
Manitowoc	102	59	43
Marinette	75	30	45
Marquette	35	33	2
Menominee	20	11	9
Monroe	49	40	9
Oneida	84	38	46
Pepin	17	7	10
Polk	73	28	45
Portage	93	49	44
Price	29	19	10
Richland	31	16	15
Rusk	31	28	3

Table V-11. Full-Time Law Enforcement Employees, by Selected State Metropolitan and Nonmetropolitan Counties, 2011—*Continued*

(Number.)

State/County	Total law enforce-ment employees	Total officers	Total civilians	State/County	Total law enforce-ment employees	Total officers	Total civilians
Sauk	144	43	101	Campbell	60	45	15
Sawyer	46	34	12	Carbon	28	18	10
Shawano	102	37	65	Converse	22	13	9
Taylor	41	18	23	Crook	18	8	10
Trempealeau	51	24	27	Fremont	40	36	4
Vernon	46	26	20	Goshen	36	24	12
Vilas	71	34	37	Hot Springs	9	7	2
Walworth	209	80	129	Johnson	13	12	1
Washburn	31	14	17	Lincoln	32	20	12
Waupaca	98	37	61	Niobrara	15	4	11
Waushara	57	23	34	Park	27	15	12
Wood	71	42	29	Platte	18	9	9
				Sheridan	27	21	6
Wyoming—Metropolitan Counties				Sublette	41	36	5
Laramie	71	54	17	Sweetwater	46	41	5
Natrona	156	120	36	Teton	37	21	16
				Uinta	37	23	14
Wyoming—Nonmetropolitan Counties				Washakie	10	9	1
Albany	43	43	0	Weston	10	8	2
Big Horn	11	10	1				

Table V-12.   Full-Time Law Enforcement Employees, by Selected State and Agency, 2011

(Number.)

State, agency	Unit/office	Total law enforcement employees	Total officers	Total civilians
Alabama, State Agencies				
Alabama Alcoholic Beverage Control Board		160	132	28
Alabama Conservation Department Marine Police		70	57	13
Alabama Department of Mental Health...		4	3	1
Alabama Public Service Commission Enforcement Division		8	7	1
State Capitol Police..		32	23	9
Alabama, Tribal Agencies				
Poarch Creek Tribal		56	50	6
Alabama, Other Agencies				
24th Judicial Circuit Drug and Violent Crime Task Force...........		4	3	1
Madison-Morgan County Strategic Counterdrug Team		3	3	0
Norfolk Southern Railway		6	6	0
Alaska, Tribal Agencies				
Metlakatla Tribal		11	7	4
Alaska, Other Agencies				
Anchorage International Airport..		58	56	2
Fairbanks International Airport		35	26	9
Arizona, Tribal Agencies				
Cocopah Tribal..		28	22	6
Colorado River Agency..		25	19	6
Fort Apache Tribal...		48	23	25
Fort McDowell Tribal...		26	20	6
Fort Mojave Tribal..		51	34	17
Gila River Indian Community...		143	112	31
Hualapai Tribal..		18	17	1
Quechan Tribal		16	10	6
Yavapai-Prescott Tribal..		13	10	3
Arizona, Other Agencies				
Tucson Airport Authority...		47	20	27
Arkansas, State Agencies				
Camp Robinson..		12	11	1
State Capitol Police		22	19	3
California, State Agencies				
Atascadero State Hospital		122	110	12
California State Fair..		6	2	4
Coalinga State Hospital..		233	212	21
Department of Parks and Recreation...	Capital	600	557	43
Fairview Developmental Center		9	6	3
Lanterman State Hospital		7	5	2
Napa State Hospital..		110	101	9
Patton State Hospital..		51	39	12
Porterville Developmental Center		55	51	4
Sonoma Developmental Center		21	11	10
California, Tribal Agencies				
Hoopa Valley Tribal		15	10	5
California, Other Agencies				
East Bay Regional Parks..	Alameda County	82	55	27
Fontana Unified School District..		57	15	42
Monterey Peninsula Airport		6	6	0
Port of San Diego Harbor..		149	127	22
San Bernardino Unified School District		76	24	52
San Francisco Bay Area Rapid Transit	Contra Costa County	266	192	74
Shasta County Marshal..		25	21	4
Stockton Unified School District		23	17	6
Twin Rivers Unified School District		29	23	6
Colorado, State Agencies				
Colorado Bureau of Investigation...		201	36	165
Colorado Mental Health Institute...		79	17	62
Colorado, Tribal Agencies				
Southern Ute Tribal		39	19	20
Colorado, Other Agencies				
Two Rivers Drug Enforcement Team		7	6	1
Connecticut, State Agencies				
State Capitol Police..		37	28	9
Connecticut, Tribal Agencies				
Mashantucket Pequot Tribal		12	11	1
Connecticut, Other Agencies				
Metropolitan Transportation Authority..		755	684	71

Table V-12.   Full-Time Law Enforcement Employees, by Selected State and Agency, 2011—*Continued*

(Number.)

State, agency	Unit/office	Total law enforcement employees	Total officers	Total civilians
Delaware, State Agencies				
Attorney General	Kent County	69	39	30
	New Castle County	292	146	146
	Sussex County	49	25	24
Division of Alcohol and Tobacco Enforcement		18	15	3
Environmental Control		11	9	2
Fish and Wildlife		31	26	5
Park Rangers		18	18	0
River and Bay Authority		57	43	14
State Capitol Police		72	45	27
State Fire Marshal		52	19	33
Delaware, Other Agencies				
Amtrak Police		14	14	0
Drug Enforcement Administration	Wilmington Resident Office	21	17	4
Wilmington Fire Department		15	10	5
District of Columbia, Other Agencies				
Metro Transit Police		620	497	123
Florida, State Agencies				
Capitol Police		101	77	24
Department of Environmental Protection, Division of Law Enforcement	Leon County	163	122	41
Department of Law Enforcement	Leon County, Tallahassee	1,586	409	1,177
Florida Game Commission	Leon County	831	663	168
State Treasurer's Office	Division of Insurance Fraud	185	144	41
Florida, Tribal Agencies				
Miccosukee Tribal		41	28	13
Seminole Tribal		226	145	81
Florida, Other Agencies				
Duval County Schools		81	71	10
Florida School for the Deaf and Blind		17	9	8
Jacksonville Aviation Authority		52	37	15
Lee County Port Authority		64	40	24
Melbourne International Airport		11	10	1
Miami-Dade County Public Schools		184	159	25
Northwest Florida Beaches International Airport		15	13	2
Palm Beach County School District		201	141	60
Sarasota-Manatee Airport Authority		14	13	1
Tampa International Airport		125	59	66
Volusia County Beach Management		52	48	4
Georgia, State Agencies				
Atlanta State Farmers Market		14	14	0
Central State Hospital		15	11	4
Georgia Bureau of Investigation	Headquarters	715	252	463
Georgia Department of Transportation	Office of Investigations	2	2	0
Georgia Forestry Commission		4	4	0
Georgia Public Safety Training Center		153	27	126
Georgia World Congress		62	33	29
Ports Authority	Savannah	119	79	40
State Board of Workers Compensation	Fraud Investigation Division	13	6	7
Georgia, Other Agencies				
Augusta Board of Education		41	36	5
Bibb County Board of Education		28	23	5
Chatham County Board of Education		45	37	8
Cherokee County Marshal		14	6	8
Cobb County Board of Education		43	41	2
DeKalb County School System		318	72	246
Dougherty County Board of Education		20	20	0
Fayette County Marshal		11	10	1
Fulton County Marshal		71	60	11
Fulton County School System		64	62	2
Glynn County School System		16	16	0
Gwinnett County Public Schools		27	23	4
Habersham County Public Schools		3	3	0
Hartsfield-Jackson Atlanta International Airport		138	120	18
Metropolitan Atlanta Rapid Transit Authority		355	305	50
Richmond County Marshal		58	49	9
Stone Mountain Park		26	22	4
Idaho, Tribal Agencies				
Coeur d'Alene Tribal		13	12	1
Nez Perce Tribal		19	15	4

Table V-12.   Full-Time Law Enforcement Employees, by Selected State and Agency, 2011—*Continued*

(Number.)

State, agency	Unit/office	Total law enforcement employees	Total officers	Total civilians
Illinois, State Agencies				
Illinois Commerce Commission.............................		18	10	8
Illinois Department of Natural Resources...................		143	127	16
Secretary of State Police................................		251	135	116
State Fire Marshal......................................		19	17	2
Illinois, Other Agencies				
Burlington Northern Santa Fe Railway....................		24	21	3
Canadian National Railway..............................		8	8	0
Capitol Airport Authority...............................		6	6	0
Crystal Lake Park District...............................		3	3	0
CSX Transportation.....................................		21	21	0
Decatur Park District...................................		5	5	0
Du Page County Forest Preserve		30	25	5
Fon Du Lac Park District		2	1	1
Fox Valley Park District		6	5	1
Indiana Harbor Belt Railroad		11	10	1
Kane County Forest Preserve		6	6	0
Lake County Forest Preserve		19	17	2
McHenry County Conservation District		13	12	1
Naperville Park District.................................		1	1	0
Norfolk Southern Railway...............................	Cook County	45	44	1
Pekin Park District.....................................		1	1	0
Rockford Park District		17	15	2
Springfield Park District		8	8	0
Union Pacific Railroad	Cook County	24	24	0
	St. Clair County	7	7	0
Will County Forest Preserve		14	12	2
Indiana, State Agencies				
Northern Indiana Commuter Transportation District		8	7	1
Indiana, Other Agencies				
Indianapolis International Airport........................		91	45	46
St. Joseph County Airport Authority		17	17	0
Kansas, State Agencies				
Kansas Bureau of Investigation..........................		243	75	168
Kansas Department of Wildlife and Parks.................		186	184	2
Kansas Lottery Security Division.........................		7	4	3
Kansas Racing Commission	Security Division	57	38	19
Securities Office	Investigation Section	5	5	0
State Fire Marshal		13	12	1
Kansas, Tribal Agencies				
Iowa Tribal		5	5	0
Kickapoo Tribal		11	6	5
Potawatomi Tribal		23	12	11
Sac and Fox Tribal		6	5	1
Kansas, Other Agencies				
Blue Valley School District		9	8	1
Johnson County Park		18	17	1
Metropolitan Topeka Airport Authority		22	17	5
Shawnee Mission Public Schools.........................		8	8	0
Topeka Fire Department.................................	Arson Investigation	3	3	0
Unified School District.................................	Auburn-Washburn	2	2	0
	Bluestem	1	1	0
	Goddard	6	5	1
	Maize	4	4	0
	Seaman	3	3	0
	Shawnee Heights	1	1	0
Kentucky, State Agencies				
Alcohol Beverage Control		61	32	29
Kentucky Horse Park		7	7	0
Unlawful Narcotics Investigation.........................	Treatment and Education	17	15	2
Kentucky, Other Agencies				
Barren County Drug Task Force		2	1	1
Cincinnati-Northern Kentucky International Airport.................		62	49	13
Clark County School System.............................		2	2	0
Fayette County Schools.................................		31	27	4
Graves County Schools		1	1	0
Greater Hardin County Narcotics Task Force		2	1	1
Jefferson County Board of Education.....................		27	21	6
Louisville Regional Airport Authority		43	38	5
McCracken County Public Schools........................		5	5	0
Montgomery County School District......................		2	2	0
Northern Kentucky Narcotics Enforcement Unit..................		3	2	1
Ohio County School System		2	1	1
Pennyrile Narcotics Task Force		13	10	3
South Central Kentucky Drug Task Force		5	5	0

Table V-12. Full-Time Law Enforcement Employees, by Selected State and Agency, 2011—*Continued*

(Number.)

State, agency	Unit/office	Total law enforcement employees	Total officers	Total civilians
Louisiana, State Agencies				
Department of Public Safety....................................	State Capitol Detail	33	32	1
Tensas Basin Levee District		3	2	1
Louisiana, Tribal Agencies				
Chitimacha Tribal		14	14	0
Coushatta Tribal		18	17	1
Tunica-Biloxi Tribal..		15	12	3
Maine, Tribal Agencies				
Passamaquoddy Indian Township		11	6	5
Penobscot Nation		8	4	4
Maryland, State Agencies				
Comptroller of the Treasury....................................	Field Enforcement Division	50	22	28
Department of Public Safety and Correctional Services.............	Internal Investigations Unit	22	17	5
General Services..	Annapolis, Anne Arundel County	59	26	33
	Baltimore City	101	34	67
Natural Resources Police		604	238	366
Springfield Hospital		44	6	38
State Fire Marshal..		74	45	29
Transit Administration...		171	151	20
Transportation Authority..		618	455	163
Maryland, Other Agencies				
Maryland-National Capital Park Police	Montgomery County	87	72	15
	Prince George's County	132	107	25
Massachusetts, State Agencies				
Division of Law Enforcement.................................	Environmental Police	113	84	29
Massachusetts Bay Transportation Authority		269	257	12
Massachusetts, Other Agencies				
Beth Israel Deaconess Medical Center		57	14	43
Michigan, Tribal Agencies				
Bay Mills Tribal..		10	8	2
Little River Band of Ottawa Indians		20	19	1
Little Traverse Bay Bands of Odawa Indians		16	11	5
Nottawaseppi Huron Band of Potawatomi		9	8	1
Pokagon Tribal..		18	16	2
Saginaw Chippewa Tribal		36	27	9
Michigan, Other Agencies				
Bishop International Airport....................................		8	7	1
Capitol Region Airport Authority...........................		18	10	8
Gerald R. Ford International Airport.......................		19	18	1
Huron-Clinton Metropolitan Authority	Hudson Mills Metropark	3	3	0
	Kensington Metropark	9	9	0
	Lower Huron Metropark	8	8	0
	Stony Creek Metropark	8	8	0
Wayne County Airport		112	103	9
Minnesota, State Agencies				
Capitol Security	St. Paul	51	11	40
Minnesota, Tribal Agencies				
Lower Sioux Tribal...		4	4	0
Mille Lacs Tribal..		23	20	3
Nett Lake Tribal		5	4	1
Red Lake Agency..		38	26	12
White Earth Tribal..		34	23	11
Minnesota, Other Agencies				
Minneapolis-St. Paul International Airport		114	79	35
Three Rivers Park District		37	25	12
Mississippi, State Agencies				
State Capitol Police..		76	62	14
Missouri, State Agencies				
Capitol Police...		31	28	3
Department of Conservation....................................		199	189	10
Department of Social Services.................................	State Technical Assistance Team	13	9	4
Division of Alcohol and Tobacco Control..................		16	15	1
State Fire Marshal..		24	22	2
State Park Rangers..		41	40	1

Table V-12.   Full-Time Law Enforcement Employees, by Selected State and Agency, 2011—*Continued*

(Number.)

State, agency	Unit/office	Total law enforcement employees	Total officers	Total civilians
Missouri, Other Agencies				
Bootheel Drug Task Force		4	4	0
Clay County Drug Task Force		4	4	0
Clay County Park Authority		8	8	0
Jackson County Drug Task Force		19	17	2
Jackson County Park Rangers		19	17	2
Lambert-St. Louis International Airport		96	79	17
Springfield-Branson Airport		10	10	0
St. Charles County Park Rangers		11	11	0
St. Peters Ranger Division		6	6	0
Montana, State Agencies				
Gambling Investigations Bureau		24	21	3
Montana, Tribal Agencies				
Blackfeet Agency		29	22	7
Crow Agency		19	14	5
Flathead Tribal		36	22	14
Fort Belknap Tribal		10	9	1
Fort Peck Assiniboine and Sioux Tribes		35	28	7
Rocky Boys Tribal		29	15	14
Nevada, Tribal Agencies				
Duckwater Tribal		2	2	0
Ely Shoshone Tribal		3	3	0
Fallon Tribal		7	6	1
Moapa Tribal		11	8	3
Pyramid Lake Tribal		14	11	3
South Fork Band Tribal		1	1	0
Walker River Tribal		7	7	0
Western Nevada Agency		8	7	1
Western Shoshone Tribal		9	8	1
Yerington Paiute Tribal		4	4	0
Nevada, Other Agencies				
Clark County School District		197	160	37
New Hamshire, State Agencies				
Liquor Commission		32	20	12
New Jersey, State Agencies				
New Jersey Transit Police		286	230	56
Palisades Interstate Parkway		28	28	0
New Jersey, Other Agencies				
Park Police	Camden County	16	16	0
	Morris County	29	28	1
	Union County	82	72	10
Prosecutor	Atlantic County	167	76	91
	Bergen County	205	112	93
	Burlington County	43	43	0
	Camden County	210	143	67
	Cape May County	73	37	36
	Cumberland County	110	41	69
	Essex County	254	137	117
	Gloucester County	91	34	57
	Hudson County	216	91	125
	Hunterdon County	53	24	29
	Mercer County	162	49	113
	Middlesex County	189	68	121
	Monmouth County	282	84	198
	Morris County	150	64	86
	Ocean County	167	73	94
	Passaic County	182	76	106
	Salem County	49	19	30
	Somerset County	113	50	63
	Sussex County	46	18	28
	Union County	236	70	166
	Warren County	59	22	37
New Mexico, State Agencies				
Motor Transportation Police		216	116	100
New Mexico, Tribal Agencies				
Acoma Tribal		19	11	8
Jemez Pueblo		10	9	1
Jicarilla Apache Tribal		25	17	8
Laguna Tribal		33	26	7
Mescalero Tribal		19	12	7
Ohkay Owingeh Tribal		9	7	2
Ramah Navajo Tribal		14	12	2
Santa Ana Tribal		22	19	3
Santa Clara Pueblo		16	9	7

Table V-12. Full-Time Law Enforcement Employees, by Selected State and Agency, 2011—*Continued*
(Number.)

State, agency	Unit/office	Total law enforcement employees	Total officers	Total civilians
New York, State Agencies				
State Park	Allegany Region	14	11	3
	Central Region	20	16	4
	Finger Lakes Region	18	16	2
	Genesee Region	10	9	1
	Long Island Region	58	56	2
	New York City Region	22	18	4
	Niagara Region	20	19	1
	Palisades Region	36	35	1
	Saratoga/Capital Region	17	16	1
	Taconic Region	10	10	0
	Thousand Island Region	15	14	1
New York, Tribal Agencies				
Oneida Indian Nation		42	36	6
New York, Other Agencies				
Board of Water	Ulster County	219	205	14
New York City Metropolitan Transportation Authority		734	667	67
Onondaga County Parks		1	1	0
Suffolk County Parks		42	41	1
North Carolina, State Agencies				
Department of Human Resources		7	7	0
Department of Wildlife		223	204	19
Division of Alcohol Law Enforcement		119	101	18
Division of Marine Fisheries		61	53	8
North Carolina Arboretum		3	3	0
State Capitol Police		58	38	20
State Fairgrounds		6	2	4
State Park Rangers	Carolina Beach	5	3	2
	Cliffs of the Neuse	9	3	6
	Crowders Mountain	6	6	0
	Dismal Swamp	4	3	1
	Elk Knob	2	2	0
	Eno River	4	4	0
	Falls Lake Recreation Area	13	10	3
	Fort Fisher	5	4	1
	Fort Macon	3	3	0
	Goose Creek	9	4	5
	Gorges	4	4	0
	Hammocks Beach	7	5	2
	Hanging Rock	11	6	5
	Haw River	2	2	0
	Jockey's Ridge	7	5	2
	Jones Lake	5	4	1
	Jordan Lake State Recreation Area	16	16	0
	Kerr Lake	10	9	1
	Lake James	5	4	1
	Lake Norman	3	3	0
	Lake Waccamaw	5	4	1
	Lumber River	9	6	3
	Mayo River	1	1	0
	Medoc Mountain	5	3	2
	Merchants Millpond	5	4	1
	Morrow Mountain	10	4	6
	Mount Mitchell	3	2	1
	New River-Mount Jefferson	8	8	0
	Pettigrew	3	3	0
	Raven Rock	3	2	1
	Singletary Lake	5	2	3
	South Mountains	8	7	1
	Stone Mountain	11	5	6
	Weymouth Woods/ Sandhills Nature Preserve	3	3	0
	William B. Umstead	8	6	2
North Carolina, Tribal Agencies				
Cherokee Tribal		59	53	6
North Carolina, Other Agencies				
Asheville Regional Airport		19	14	5
Beaufort County Alcohol Beverage Control Enforcement		1	1	0
Durham County Alcohol Beverage Control Law Enforcement Office		3	3	0
Nash County Alcohol Beverage Control Enforcement		1	1	0
Piedmont Triad International Airport		22	18	4
Pitt County Memorial Hospital		55	35	20

Table V-12. **Full-Time Law Enforcement Employees, by Selected State and Agency, 2011**—*Continued*

(Number.)

State, agency	Unit/office	Total law enforcement employees	Total officers	Total civilians
Raleigh-Durham International Airport................................		33	31	2
Triad Alcohol Beverage Control Law Enforcement....................		4	3	1
WakeMed Campus Police..		66	39	27
Wilmington International Airport....................................		13	9	4
North Dakota, Tribal Agencies				
Standing Rock Agency		28	18	10
Turtle Mountain Agency..		29	22	7
Ohio, State Agencies				
Department of Liquor Control..	Enforcement Division	103	91	12
Ohio Department of Natural Resources		384	342	42
Ohio, Other Agencies				
Butler County Metroparks..		2	2	0
Cedar Point		11	11	0
Cleveland Metropolitan Park District		77	67	10
Columbus and Franklin County Metropolitan Park District.......		52	50	2
Erie MetroParks..		4	4	0
Greater Cleveland Regional Transit Authority		104	93	11
Hamilton County Park District		35	32	3
Holden Arboretum		2	2	0
Johnny Appleseed Metropolitan Park District......................		7	7	0
Lake Metroparks..		15	13	2
Lima Park Services...	Ranger Division	4	4	0
Lorain County Metropolitan Park District		15	15	0
Mill Creek Metropark..		14	13	1
Port Columbus International Airport................................		60	43	17
Preservation Parks of Delaware County		7	7	0
Robinson Memorial Hospital		9	8	1
Sandusky County Park District		4	4	0
Toledo-Lucas County Port Authority		9	9	0
Toledo Metropolitan Park District..................................		23	23	0
Wood County Park District..		5	5	0
Oklahoma, State Agencies				
Capitol Park Police..		55	25	30
Grand River Dam Authority..	Lake Patrol	17	10	7
Oklahoma, Tribal Agencies				
Cherokee Nation		38	30	8
Chickasaw Nation..		42	32	10
Choctaw Nation..		30	29	1
Comanche Nation..		27	19	8
Eastern Shawnee Tribal..		12	11	1
Kaw Tribal		6	6	0
Kickapoo Tribal		13	12	1
Miami Agency..		6	6	0
Miami Tribal		3	3	0
Muscogee Nation Tribal..		42	34	8
Osage Nation		16	15	1
Otoe-Missouria Tribal..		16	9	7
Sac And Fox Tribal		9	9	0
Seminole Nation Lighthorse		11	9	2
Tonkawa Tribal		10	5	5
Wyandotte Nation		8	7	1
Oklahoma, Other Agencies				
Guymon Public Schools..		1	1	0
Jenks Public Schools		8	7	1
Madill Public Schools..		1	1	0
McAlester Public Schools		2	2	0
Norman Public Schools		6	5	1
Putnam City Campus		11	6	5
Oregon, State Agencies				
Liquor Commission..	Benton County	1	1	0
	Clatsop County	2	1	1
	Columbia County	1	1	0
	Coos County	2	1	1
	Douglas County	2	1	1
	Hood River County	1	1	0
	Jackson County	5	4	1
	Josephine County	1	1	0
	Klamath County	1	1	0
	Lane County	7	6	1
	Lincoln County	2	1	1
	Linn County	1	1	0
	Malheur County	1	1	0
	Marion County	6	5	1
	Multnomah County	14	11	3

Table V-12. Full-Time Law Enforcement Employees, by Selected State and Agency, 2011—*Continued*

(Number.)

State, agency	Unit/office	Total law enforcement employees	Total officers	Total civilians
	Umatilla County	2	2	0
	Washington County	6	6	0
	Yamhill County	1	1	0
Oregon, Tribal Agencies				
Burns Paiute Tribal..		4	3	1
Coquille Tribal		4	4	0
Warm Springs Tribal......................................		47	40	7
Oregon, Other Agencies				
Blue Mountain Enforcement Narcotics Team	Morrow County	6	5	1
	Umatilla County	9	8	1
Port of Portland		66	49	17
Pennsylvania, State Agencies				
Moshannon State Forest................................		7	2	5
Pennsylvania Fish and Boat Commission............................		101	94	7
State Capitol Police..		141	132	9
State Park Police...	Ohiopyle	12	5	7
	Pine Grove Furnace	2	2	0
	Presque Isle	4	4	0
	Prince Gallitzin	18	8	10
	Pymatuning	3	3	0
Pennsylvania, Other Agencies				
Allegheny County District Attorney	Criminal Investigation Division	34	28	6
Allegheny County Housing Authority................................		9	8	1
Allegheny County Port Authority....................................		52	38	14
Altoona Hospital...		18	16	2
County Detective	Beaver County	8	8	0
	Berks County	34	31	3
	Bucks County	20	16	4
	Butler County	4	4	0
	Chester County	24	21	3
	Cumberland County	6	5	1
	Dauphin County	15	12	3
	Erie County	9	8	1
	Lackawanna County	13	13	0
	Lebanon County	8	6	2
	Lehigh County	18	17	1
	Luzerne County	10	10	0
	Pike County	3	3	0
	Schuylkill County	6	6	0
	Wayne County	2	2	0
	Westmoreland County	59	15	44
	York County	11	9	2
Delaware County District Attorney	Criminal Investigation Division	41	34	7
Delaware County Park		56	55	1
Easton Area School District		7	6	1
Erie City School District		4	4	0
Erie Municipal Airport Authority		8	7	1
Fort Indiantown Gap		18	8	10
Harrisburg International Airport		17	9	8
Uniontown Hospital		14	14	0
Washington County Alternative Education................................		1	1	0
Westmoreland County Park............................		21	20	1
Wilkes-Barre Area School District		5	5	0
Rhode Island, State Agencies				
Department of Environmental Management		37	30	7
Rhode Island State Airport............................		45	36	9
South Carolina, State Agencies				
Bureau of Protective Services........................		69	64	5
Department of Mental Health........................		151	102	49
Department of Natural Resources.................	Abbeville County	3	3	0
	Aiken County	2	2	0
	Allendale County	2	2	0
	Anderson County	4	4	0
	Bamberg County	3	3	0
	Barnwell County	4	4	0
	Beaufort County	3	3	0
	Berkeley County	6	6	0
	Calhoun County	2	2	0
	Charleston County	24	24	0
	Cherokee County	3	3	0
	Chester County	2	2	0
	Chesterfield County	3	3	0
	Clarendon County	4	4	0
	Colleton County	6	5	1

Table V-12. Full-Time Law Enforcement Employees, by Selected State and Agency, 2011—*Continued*

(Number.)

State, agency	Unit/office	Total law enforcement employees	Total officers	Total civilians
	Darlington County	2	2	0
	Dillon County	2	2	0
	Dorchester County	4	4	0
	Edgefield County	3	3	0
	Fairfield County	5	5	0
	Florence County	4	4	0
	Georgetown County	5	5	0
	Greenville County	4	4	0
	Greenwood County	5	5	0
	Hampton County	3	3	0
	Horry County	7	7	0
	Jasper County	3	3	0
	Kershaw County	4	4	0
	Lancaster County	3	3	0
	Laurens County	2	2	0
	Lee County	1	1	0
	Lexington County	5	5	0
	Marion County	3	3	0
	Marlboro County	3	3	0
	McCormick County	2	2	0
	Newberry County	4	4	0
	Oconee County	5	4	1
	Orangeburg County	3	3	0
	Pickens County	5	5	0
	Richland County	42	29	13
	Saluda County	2	2	0
	Spartanburg County	5	5	0
	Sumter County	3	3	0
	Union County	3	3	0
	Williamsburg County	5	5	0
	York County	4	4	0
Employment Security Commission..		4	4	0
Forestry Commission	Aiken County	1	1	0
	Anderson County	1	1	0
	Beaufort County	1	1	0
	Berkeley County	1	1	0
	Charleston County	1	1	0
	Chester County	1	1	0
	Chesterfield County	5	5	0
	Clarendon County	1	1	0
	Dillon County	1	1	0
	Fairfield County	1	1	0
	Florence County	1	1	0
	Hampton County	2	2	0
	Horry County	1	1	0
	Jasper County	1	1	0
	Kershaw County	3	3	0
	Lexington County	3	3	0
	Oconee County	1	1	0
	Orangeburg County	1	1	0
	Pickens County	1	1	0
	Richland County	2	2	0
	Spartanburg County	1	1	0
	Sumter County	2	2	0
	Williamsburg County	3	3	0
	York County	1	1	0
South Carolina School for the Deaf and Blind..............................		1	1	0
State Museum		1	1	0
State Ports Authority..		71	31	40
State Transport Police...	Abbeville County	13	13	0
	Aiken County	43	26	17
	Allendale County	18	16	2
	Anderson County	20	16	4
	Berkeley County	14	11	3
	Cherokee County	10	10	0
	Darlington County	16	14	2
United States Department of Energy..	Savannah River Plant	53	39	14
South Carolina, Other Agencies				
Charleston County Aviation Authority		42	30	12
Columbia Metropolitan Airport...		13	13	0
Greenville-Spartanburg International Airport...............................		16	15	1
Lexington County Medical Center...		61	16	45
Whitten Center		1	1	0
South Dakota, State Agencies				
Division of Criminal Investigation...		161	48	113
South Dakota, Tribal Agencies				
Flandreau Tribal		9	8	1
Oglala Sioux Tribal..		195	52	143

Table V-12. Full-Time Law Enforcement Employees, by Selected State and Agency, 2011—*Continued*

(Number.)

State, agency	Unit/office	Total law enforcement employees	Total officers	Total civilians
Tennessee, State Agencies				
Alcoholic Beverage Commission		46	27	19
Department of Correction	Internal Affairs	15	10	5
State Fire Marshal..		27	23	4
State Park Rangers..	Bicentennial Capitol Mall	6	6	0
	Big Hill Pond	3	3	0
	Big Ridge	4	4	0
	Bledsoe Creek	2	2	0
	Booker T. Washington	3	3	0
	Burgess Falls Natural Area	5	5	0
	Cedars of Lebanon	4	4	0
	Chickasaw	4	4	0
	Cove Lake	4	4	0
	Cumberland Mountain	4	4	0
	Cumberland Trail	6	6	0
	David Crockett	4	4	0
	Davy Crockett Birthplace	3	3	0
	Dunbar Cave Natural Area	3	3	0
	Edgar Evins	4	4	0
	Fall Creek Falls	8	8	0
	Fort Loudon State Historic Park	4	4	0
	Fort Pillow State Historic Park	2	2	0
	Frozen Head Natural Area	3	3	0
	Harpeth Scenic Rivers	3	3	0
	Harrison Bay	5	5	0
	Henry Horton	4	4	0
	Hiwassee/Ocoee State Scenic Rivers	6	6	0
	Indian Mountain	2	2	0
	Johnsonville State Historic Park	1	1	0
	Long Hunter	4	4	0
	Meeman-Shelby Forest	6	6	0
	Montgomery Bell	6	6	0
	Mousetail Landing	3	3	0
	Natchez Trace	5	5	0
	Nathan Bedford Forrest	3	3	0
	Norris Dam	4	4	0
	Old Stone Fort State Archaeological Park	3	3	0
	Panther Creek	3	3	0
	Paris Landing	5	5	0
	Pickett	4	4	0
	Pickwick Landing	5	5	0
	Pinson Mounds State Archaeological Park	2	2	0
	Radnor Lake Natural Area	5	5	0
	Red Clay State Historic Park	2	2	0
	Reelfoot Lake	4	4	0
	Roan Mountain	4	4	0
	Rock Island	4	4	0
	Sgt. Alvin C. York	1	1	0
	South Cumberland Recreation Area	6	6	0
	Standing Stone	4	4	0
	Sycamore Shoals State Historic Park	2	2	0
	Tim's Ford	5	5	0
	T.O. Fuller	3	3	0
	Warrior's Path	5	5	0
TennCare Office of Inspector General...		38	14	24
Tennessee Bureau of Investigation		470	178	292
Tennessee Department of Revenue	Special Investigations Unit	46	26	20
Wildlife Resources Agency	Region 1	45	41	4
	Region 2	61	52	9
	Region 3	49	45	4
	Region 4	49	45	4

Table V-12.   Full-Time Law Enforcement Employees, by Selected State and Agency, 2011—*Continued*

(Number.)

State, agency	Unit/office	Total law enforcement employees	Total officers	Total civilians
Tennessee, Other Agencies				
Chattanooga Housing Authority		6	5	1
Chattanooga Metropolitan Airport		10	10	0
Dickson Parks and Recreation		10	3	7
Drug Task Force	1st Judicial District	5	4	1
	3rd Judicial District	5	4	1
	4th Judicial District	3	2	1
	5th Judicial District	9	8	1
	8th Judicial District	4	3	1
	9th Judicial District	2	2	0
	10th Judicial District	12	11	1
	12th Judicial District	2	2	0
	13th Judicial District	2	2	0
	14th Judicial District	3	3	0
	15th Judicial District	5	4	1
	17th Judicial District	5	5	0
	18th Judicial District	8	8	0
	19th Judicial District	9	8	1
	21st Judicial District	14	11	3
	22nd Judicial District	2	2	0
	23rd Judicial District	8	7	1
	24th Judicial District	3	2	1
	25th Judicial District	2	2	0
Knoxville Metropolitan Airport		46	27	19
Memphis International Airport		64	49	15
Metropolitan Nashville Park Police		21	21	0
Nashville International Airport		75	60	15
Smyrna/Rutherford County Airport Authority		4	4	0
Tri-Cities Regional Airport		15	14	1
West Tennessee Violent Crime Task Force		7	6	1
Texas, Other Agencies				
Amarillo International Airport		14	14	0
Dallas-Fort Worth International Airport.............................		390	251	139
Hospital District	Dallas County	83	55	28
	Tarrant County	61	43	18
Houston Metropolitan Transit Authority		203	175	28
Independent School District	Aldine	51	42	9
	Alvin	21	17	4
	Angleton	5	4	1
	Austin	95	67	28
	Barbers Hill	4	3	1
	Bay City	6	5	1
	Cedar Hill	18	5	13
	Conroe	64	46	18
	Corpus Christi	53	31	22
	East Central	10	9	1
	Ector County	27	25	2
	Edinburg	77	44	33
	El Paso	49	41	8
	Fort Bend	51	43	8
	Hallsville	1	1	0
	Humble	36	26	10
	Judson	16	15	1
	Katy	44	35	9
	Killeen	17	17	0
	Klein	54	35	19
	Laredo	98	28	70
	Lyford	2	2	0
	Midland	17	11	6
	North East	66	60	6
	Pasadena	38	31	7
	Pflugerville	16	16	0
	Rio Grande City	70	14	56
	Socorro	33	28	5
	Spring	41	39	2
	Spring Branch	37	31	6
	Taft	1	1	0
	United	166	54	112
Port of Houston Authority		72	48	24

Table V-12.   Full-Time Law Enforcement Employees, by Selected State and Agency, 2011—*Continued*

(Number.)

State, agency	Unit/office	Total law enforcement employees	Total officers	Total civilians
Utah, State Agencies				
Parks and Recreation..		58	57	1
Wildlife Resources		84	74	10
Utah, Other Agencies				
Cache-Rich Drug Task Force		4	4	0
Granite School District...		37	15	22
Utah County Attorney	Investigations Division	7	5	2
Utah Transit Authority..		50	48	2
Vermont, State Agencies				
Department of Liquor Control..	Division of Enforcement and Licensing	17	16	1
Department of Motor Vehicles...		39	28	11
Fish and Wildlife Department..	Law Enforcement Division	36	36	0
Virginia, State Agencies				
Alcoholic Beverage Control Commission................................		135	109	26
Department of Conservation and Recreation		240	101	139
Department of Game and Inland Fisheries	Enforcement Division	191	172	19
Department of Motor Vehicles...		88	72	16
Southside Virginia Training Center		18	17	1
Virginia State Capitol		89	77	12
Virginia, Other Agencies				
Norfolk Airport Authority		44	37	7
Port Authority..	Norfolk	78	71	7
Reagan National Airport...		303	211	92
Richmond International Airport..		33	25	8
Washington, State Agencies				
State Insurance Commissioner	Special Investigations Unit	6	4	2
Washington, Tribal Agencies				
Chehalis Tribal..		11	10	1
Colville Tribal...		43	31	12
Jamestown S'Klallam Tribal..		2	2	0
Kalispel Tribal..		10	10	0
La Push Tribal..		4	4	0
Lower Elwha Tribal..		9	5	4
Lummi Tribal..		25	23	2
Makah Tribal..		16	10	6
Nisqually Tribal..		17	13	4
Nooksack Tribal..		9	7	2
Port Gamble S'Klallam Tribal..		9	8	1
Puyallup Tribal..		45	30	15
Quinault Indian Nation		18	10	8
Sauk-Suiattle Tribal...		3	2	1
Shoalwater Bay Tribal...		5	5	0
Skokomish Tribal..		7	5	2
Spokane Agency...		21	15	6
Squaxin Island Tribal		15	12	3
Stillaguamish Tribal..		8	8	0
Suquamish Tribal..		17	16	1
Swinomish Tribal..		17	15	2
Tulalip Tribal..		45	30	15
Upper Skagit Tribal...		6	5	1
Yakama Nation...		34	24	10
Washington, Other Agencies				
Port of Seattle..		129	99	30
West Virginia, State Agencies				
Capitol Protective Services		37	22	15
Division of Natural Resources	Barbour County	1	1	0
	Berkeley County	1	1	0
	Braxton County	1	1	0
	Brooke County	1	1	0
	Cabell County	2	2	0
	Calhoun County	1	1	0
	Clay County	2	2	0
	Doddridge County	1	1	0
	Fayette County	2	2	0
	Gilmer County	1	1	0
	Grant County	2	2	0
	Greenbrier County	2	2	0
	Hampshire County	6	5	1
	Hancock County	1	1	0
	Harrison County	2	2	0
	Jackson County	2	2	0
	Jefferson County	2	2	0
	Kanawha County	12	6	6

Table V-12.   Full-Time Law Enforcement Employees, by Selected State and Agency, 2011—*Continued*

(Number.)

State, agency	Unit/office	Total law enforcement employees	Total officers	Total civilians
	Lincoln County	1	1	0
	Logan County	2	2	0
	Marion County	5	4	1
	Marshall County	2	2	0
	Mason County	1	1	0
	McDowell County	1	1	0
	Mercer County	3	3	0
	Mineral County	2	2	0
	Mingo County	1	1	0
	Monongalia County	3	3	0
	Monroe County	1	1	0
	Morgan County	1	1	0
	Nicholas County	1	1	0
	Ohio County	1	1	0
	Pendleton County	2	2	0
	Pleasants County	2	2	0
	Pocahontas County	2	2	0
	Preston County	2	2	0
	Putnam County	3	3	0
	Raleigh County	6	5	1
	Randolph County	6	5	1
	Ritchie County	1	1	0
	Summers County	4	4	0
	Taylor County	1	1	0
	Tucker County	1	1	0
	Tyler County	1	1	0
	Upshur County	2	2	0
	Wayne County	1	1	0
	Webster County	3	3	0
	Wetzel County	1	1	0
	Wirt County	1	1	0
	Wood County	3	2	1
	Wyoming County	1	1	0
State Fire Marshal	Kanawha County	44	32	12
West Virginia, Other Agencies				
Central West Virginia Drug Task Force		4	4	0
Eastern Panhandle Drug and Violent Crime Task Force		7	6	1
Hancock/Brooke/Weirton Drug Task Force		5	5	0
Huntington Drug and Violent Crime Task Force		12	10	2
Kanawha County Parks and Recreation		3	3	0
Logan County Drug and Violent Crime Task Force		7	6	1
Metropolitan Drug Enforcement Network Team		14	13	1
Parkersburg Narcotics and Violent Crime Task Force.................		6	6	0
Potomac Highlands Drug and Violent Crime Task Force		3	3	0
Three Rivers Drug and Violent Crime Task Force......................		2	2	0
Wisconsin, State Agencies				
Capitol Police..		44	37	7
Department of Natural Resources...............................		459	427	32
Wisconsin, Tribal Agencies				
Menominee Tribal		31	25	6
Oneida Tribal		29	22	7
St. Croix Tribal		18	12	6
Wyoming, Tribal Agencies				
Wind River Agency		27	22	5
Puerto Rico and Other Outlying Areas				
Virgin Islands..	St. Croix	311	215	96
	St. Thomas	328	232	96
Federal Agencies				
National Institutes of Health		121	94	27

SECTION VI:
HATE CRIMES

HATE CRIMES

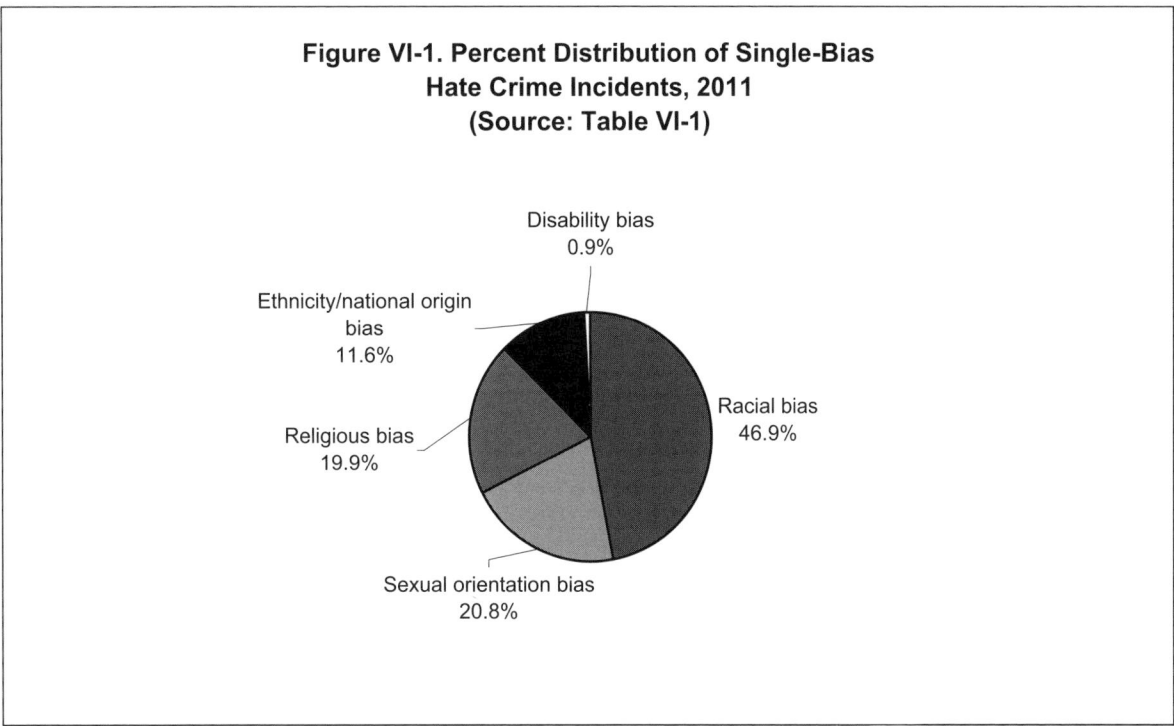

Figure VI-1. Percent Distribution of Single-Bias
Hate Crime Incidents, 2011
(Source: Table VI-1)

The Federal Bureau of Investigation (FBI) began the procedures for implementing, collecting, and managing hate crime data after Congress passed the Hate Crime Statistics Act in 1990 which required the collection of data "about crimes that manifest evidence of prejudice based on race, religion, sexual orientation, or ethnicity." In 1994, the Hate Crime Statistics Act was amended to include bias against persons with disabilities. The Church Arson Prevention Act, which was signed into law in July 1996, removed the sunset clause from the original statute and mandated that the collection of hate crime data become a permanent part of the UCR program. In 2009, Congress further amended the Hate Crime Statistics Act by passing the Matthew Shepard and James Byrd, Jr. Hate Crime Prevention Act. The amendment includes the collection of data for crimes motivated by bias against a particular gender and gender identity, as well as for crimes committed by, and crimes directed against, juveniles. The FBI is currently making plans to implement changes to collect these data. (See www.fbi.gov/about-us/cjis/ucr/hate-crime/2010/resources/hate-crime-2010-hate-crime-statistics-act for referenced legislation, as amended.)

Definitions

Hate crimes include any crime motivated by bias against race, religion, sexual orientation, ethnicity/national origin, and/or disability. Because motivation is subjective, it is sometimes difficult to know with certainty whether a crime resulted from the offender's bias. Moreover, the presence of bias alone does not necessarily mean that a crime can be considered a hate crime. Only when law enforcement investigation reveals sufficient evidence to lead a reasonable and prudent person to conclude that the offender's actions were motivated, in whole or in part, by his or her bias, should an incident be reported as a hate crime.

Data Collection

The UCR (Uniform Crime Reporting) program collects data about both single-bias and multiple-bias hate crimes. A single-bias incident is defined as an incident in which one or more offense types are motivated by the same bias. A multiple-bias incident is defined as an incident in which more than one offense type occurs and at least two offense types are motivated by different biases.

A table with selected places in the United States that did not report hate crimes in 2011 is available at http://www.fbi.gov/about-us/cjis/ucr/hate-crime/2011/tables/table-14/view.

Crimes against persons, property, or society

The UCR program's data collection guidelines stipulate that a hate crime may involve multiple offenses, victims, and offenders within one incident; therefore, the Hate Crime Statistics program is incident-based. According to UCR counting guidelines:

- One offense is counted for each victim in *crimes against persons*

- One offense is counted for each offense type in *crimes against property*

- One offense is counted for each offense type in *crimes against society*

Victims

In the UCR program, the victim of a hate crime may be an individual, a business, an institution, or society as a whole.

Offenders

According to the UCR program, the term *known offender* does not imply that the suspect's identity is known; rather, the term indicates that some aspect of the suspect was identified, thus distinguishing the suspect from an unknown offender. Law enforcement agencies specify the number of offenders, and when possible, the race of the offender or offenders as a group.

Race/ethnicity

The UCR program uses the following five racial designations in its Hate Crime Statistics program: White; Black; American Indian/Alaskan Native; Asian/Pacific Islander; and Multiple Races, Group. In addition, the UCR program uses the ethnic designations of Hispanic and Other Ethnicity/National Origin.

Agencies that participated in the Hate Crime Statistics program in 2011 represented more than 286 million inhabitants, or 91.8 percent of the nation's population, and their jurisdictions covered 49 states and the District of Columbia. The law enforcement agencies that voluntarily participate in the Hate Crime Statistics program collect details about an offender's bias motivation associated with 11 offense types already being reported to the UCR program: murder and nonnegligent manslaughter, forcible rape, aggravated assault, simple assault, and intimidation (crimes against persons); and robbery, burglary, larceny-theft, motor vehicle theft, arson, and destruction/damage/vandalism (crimes against property). The law enforcement agencies that participate in the UCR program via the National Incident-Based Reporting System (NIBRS) collect data about additional offenses for *crimes against persons* and *crimes against property*. These data appear in the category of other. These agencies also collect hate crime data for the category called *crimes against society*, which includes drug or narcotic offenses, gambling offenses, prostitution offenses, and weapon law violations.

National Volume and Percent Distribution

In 2011, 1,944 law enforcement agencies reported 6,222 hate crime incidents involving 7,254 offenses. Of these, 6,216 were single-bias offenses. An analysis of the single-bias incidents revealed 46.9 percent were racially motivated, 19.8 percent were motivated by religious bias, 20.8 percent resulted from sexual-orientation bias, 11.6 percent were based on an ethnicity/national origin bias and 0.9 percent were prompted by a disability bias. (Table VI-1)

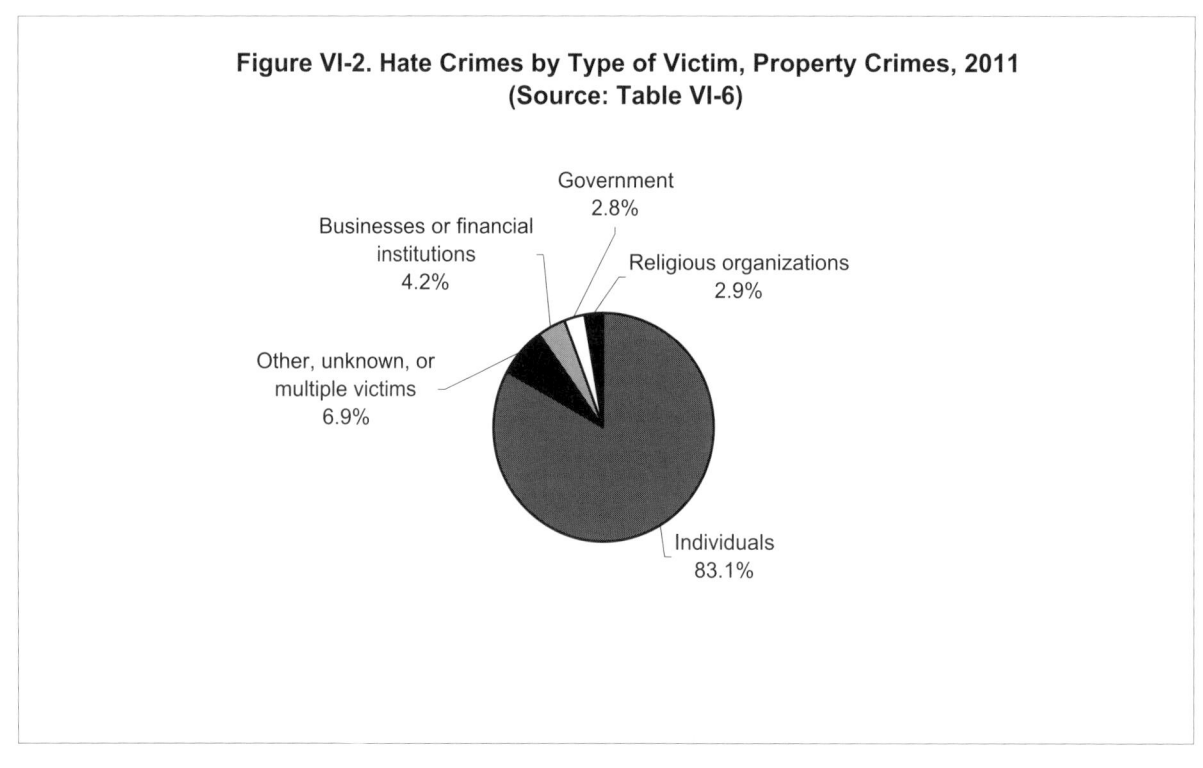

Figure VI-2. Hate Crimes by Type of Victim, Property Crimes, 2011 (Source: Table VI-6)

Government 2.8%

Businesses or financial institutions 4.2%

Religious organizations 2.9%

Other, unknown, or multiple victims 6.9%

Individuals 83.1%

The majority of the hate crime offenses that were racially motivated resulted from an anti-Black bias (72.0 percent) followed by an anti-White basis (16.7 percent). Bias against people of more than one race accounted for 4.7 percent of offenses, while anti-Asian/Pacific Islander bias accounted for 4.8 percent of racially motivated offenses, and anti-American Indian bias accounted for 1.9 percent. (Table VI-1)

Hate crimes motivated by religious bias accounted for 1,318 offenses reported by law enforcement. A breakdown of these offenses revealed 62.2 percent were motivated by anti-Jewish bias, 13.3 percent by anti-Islamic bias, 4.8 percent were anti-multiple religions or groups, 5.2 percent an anti-Catholic bias, 3.7 percent were anti-Protestant, 0.3 percent were anti-atheism/agnoticism/etc., and the remainder, 10.5 percent, of offenses were based on a bias against other religions—those not specified. (Table VI-1)

In 2011, slightly more hate crimes were committed on the basis of sexual orientation bias than on religious bias. Of the 1,508 offenses based on sexual orientation, 57.8 percent were classified as having an anti-male homosexual bias, 28.4 percent had an anti-homosexual bias, 11.1 percent had an anti-female homosexual basis, 1.5 percent had an anti-bisexual bias, and 1.1 percent had an anti-heterosexual bias. (Table VI-1)

The majority of 891 offenses that were committed on the perceived ethnicity or national origin of the victim had an anti-Hispanic basis (56.8 percent). The remaining 43.2 percent were based on bias against another ethnicity or national origin. (Table VI-1)

Other hate crime offenses were committed based on disability. The majority (60.3 percent) were classified as anti-mental disability, with the rest (39.7 percent) were classified as anti-physical disability. (Table VI-1)

Crimes Against Persons

Law enforcement agencies reported 4,623 hate crime offenses against persons in 2011. Nearly half of them (45.6 percent) involved intimidation, 34.5 percent involved simple assault, and 19.4 percent involved aggravated assault. In addition, there were four murders and seven forcible rapes. (Table VI-2)

Crimes Against Property

In 2011, hate crime offences against property totaled 2,611. Approximately 81.4 percent of offenses involved destruction/damage or vandalism. The remaining 18.6 percent of crimes against property consisted of robbery, burglary, larceny-theft, motor vehicle theft, arson, and other crimes. (Table VI-2)

Table VI-1. Incidents, Offenses, Victims, and Known Offenders, by Bias Motivation, 2011

(Number.)

Bias motivation	Incidents	Offenses	Victims[1]	Known offenders[2]
Total	6,222	7,254	7,713	5,731
Single-Bias Incidents	6,216	7,240	7,697	5,724
Race	2,917	3,465	3,645	2,787
Anti-White	504	577	593	594
Anti-Black	2,076	2,494	2,619	1,935
Anti-American Indian/Alaskan Native	61	67	70	60
Anti-Asian/Pacific Islander	138	165	175	120
Anti-multiple races, group	138	162	188	78
Religion	1,233	1,318	1,480	590
Anti-Jewish	771	820	936	287
Anti-Catholic	67	68	84	21
Anti-Protestant	44	49	51	32
Anti-Islamic	157	175	185	138
Anti-other religion	130	139	155	74
Anti-multiple religions, group	60	63	65	37
Anti-atheism/agnosticism/etc.	4	4	4	1
Sexual Orientation	1,293	1,508	1,572	1,511
Anti-male homosexual	760	871	891	978
Anti-female homosexual	137	168	174	123
Anti-homosexual	359	429	465	362
Anti-heterosexual	16	17	19	19
Anti-bisexual	21	23	23	29
Ethnicity/National Origin	720	891	939	749
Anti-Hispanic	405	506	534	452
Anti-other ethnicity/national origin	315	385	405	297
Disability	53	58	61	87
Anti-physical	19	23	26	29
Anti-mental	34	35	35	58
Multiple-Bias Incidents[3]	6	14	16	7

[1] The term victim may refer to a person, business, institution, or society as a whole.

[2] The term known offender does not imply that the identity of the suspect is known, but only that an attribute of the suspect has been identified, which distinguishes him/her from an unknown offender.

[3] In a multiple-bias incident, two conditions must be met: (a) more than one offense type must occur in the incident and (b) at least two offense types must be motivated by different biases.

Table VI-2. Incidents, Offenses, Victims, and Known Offenders, by Offense Type, 2011

(Number.)

Offense type	Incidents[1]	Offenses	Victims[2]	Known offenders[3]
Total	6,222	7,254	7,713	5,731
Crimes Against Persons	3,754	4,623	4,623	4,631
Murder and nonnegligent manslaughter	4	4	4	7
Forcible rape	7	7	7	10
Aggravated assault	677	895	895	1,095
Simple assault	1,336	1,595	1,595	1,790
Intimidation	1,720	2,106	2,106	1,711
Other[4]	10	16	16	18
Crimes Against Property	2,611	2,611	3,070	1,256
Robbery	131	131	157	288
Burglary	124	124	147	72
Larceny-theft	152	152	165	88
Motor vehicle theft	6	6	6	1
Arson	42	42	52	20
Destruction/damage/vandalism	2,125	2,125	2,510	759
Other[4]	31	31	33	28
Crimes Against Society[4]	20	20	20	34

[1] The actual number of incidents is 6,222. However, the column figures will not add to the total because incidents may include more than one offense type, and these are counted in each appropriate offense type category.

[2] The term victim may refer to a person, business, institution, or society as a whole.

[3] The term known offender does not imply that the identity of the suspect is known, but only that an attribute of the suspect has been identified, which distinguishes him/her from an unknown offender. The actual number of known offenders is 5,731. However, the column figures will not add to the total because some offenders are responsible for more than one offense type; and are, therefore, counted more than once in this table.

[4] Includes additional offenses collected in the National Incident-Based Reporting System.

Table VI-3. Offenses, Known Offender's Race, by Offense Type, 2011

(Number.)

Offense type	Total offenses	Known offender's race						Unknown offender
		White	Black	American Indian/ Alaskan Native	Asian/Pacific Islander	Multiple races, group	Unknown race	
Total	7,254	3,101	902	43	64	207	563	2,374
Crimes Against Persons	4,623	2,667	774	42	51	182	305	602
Murder and nonnegligent manslaughter	4	1	1	0	0	1	0	1
Forcible rape	7	4	1	0	0	0	1	1
Aggravated assault	895	546	193	17	10	42	43	44
Simple assault	1,595	935	338	20	20	100	78	104
Intimidation	2,106	1,173	237	5	21	39	181	450
Other[1]	16	8	4	0	0	0	2	2
Crimes Against Property	2,611	423	121	1	13	25	256	1,772
Robbery	131	49	53	1	3	12	4	9
Burglary	124	26	7	0	1	2	10	78
Larceny-theft	152	39	10	0	0	1	21	81
Motor vehicle theft	6	0	1	0	0	0	0	5
Arson	42	9	0	0	1	1	3	28
Destruction/damage/vandalism	2,125	286	46	0	8	9	215	1,561
Other[1]	31	14	4	0	0	0	3	10
Crimes Against Society[1]	20	11	7	0	0	0	2	0

[1] Includes additional offenses collected in the National Incident-Based Reporting System.

Table VI-4. Offenses, Offense Type, by Bias Motivation, 2011

(Number.)

| Bias motivation | Total offenses | Crimes against persons | | | | | Other[1] |
		Murder and nonnegligent manslaughter	Forcible rape	Aggravated assault	Simple assault	Intimidation	
Total	7,254	4	7	895	1,595	2,106	16
Single-Bias Incidents	7,240	4	7	893	1,593	2,101	16
Race	3,465	1	3	470	752	1,135	4
Anti-White	577	0	1	91	171	147	1
Anti-Black	2,494	1	1	347	500	897	3
Anti-American Indian/Alaskan Native	67	0	0	12	20	4	0
Anti-Asian/Pacific Islander	165	0	1	9	45	56	0
Anti-multiple races, group	162	0	0	11	16	31	0
Religion	1,318	0	0	36	108	291	3
Anti-Jewish	820	0	0	15	43	187	0
Anti-Catholic	68	0	0	0	3	3	0
Anti-Protestant	49	0	0	4	4	1	0
Anti-Islamic	175	0	0	14	41	70	0
Anti-other religion	139	0	0	3	8	23	3
Anti-multiple religions, group	63	0	0	0	9	7	0
Anti-atheism/agnosticism/etc.	4	0	0	0	0	0	0
Sexual Orientation	1,508	3	2	252	491	380	6
Anti-male homosexual	871	3	0	162	291	218	5
Anti-female homosexual	168	0	2	28	42	56	0
Anti-homosexual	429	0	0	60	142	99	1
Anti-heterosexual	17	0	0	2	5	3	0
Anti-bisexual	23	0	0	0	11	4	0
Ethnicity/National Origin	891	0	1	128	226	280	0
Anti-Hispanic	506	0	1	82	144	153	0
Anti-other ethnicity/national origin	385	0	0	46	82	127	0
Disability	58	0	1	7	16	15	3
Anti-physical	23	0	0	0	7	5	2
Anti-mental	35	0	1	7	9	10	1
Multiple-Bias Incidents[2]	14	0	0	2	2	5	0

[1] Includes additional offenses collected in the National Incident-Based Reporting System.

[2] In a multiple-bias incident, two conditions must be met: (a) more than one offense type must occur in the incident and (b) at least two offense types must be motivated by different biases.

Table VI-4.   Offenses, Offense Type, by Bias Motivation, 2011—*Continued*

(Number.)

Bias motivation	Crimes against property							Crimes against society[1]
	Robbery	Burglary	Larceny-theft	Motor vehicle theft	Arson	Destruction/ damage/ vandalism	Other[1]	
Total.................................	131	124	152	6	42	2,125	31	20
Single-Bias Incidents	131	124	152	6	41	2,121	31	20
Race.................................	50	52	76	5	15	868	19	15
Anti-White..	24	9	41	3	1	77	10	1
Anti-Black..	21	34	19	1	10	647	1	12
Anti-American Indian/Alaskan Native.................	1	0	11	1	0	10	6	2
Anti-Asian/Pacific Islander	1	3	5	0	1	42	2	0
Anti-multiple races, group	3	6	0	0	3	92	0	0
Religion.................................	5	29	49	0	13	780	4	0
Anti-Jewish...	3	7	13	0	3	549	0	0
Anti-Catholic..	0	4	11	0	1	46	0	0
Anti-Protestant	0	6	2	0	1	30	1	0
Anti-Islamic...	1	1	7	0	2	39	0	0
Anti-other religion.................................	1	8	3	0	5	84	1	0
Anti-multiple religions, group	0	3	11	0	1	31	1	0
Anti-atheism/agnosticism/etc.	0	0	2	0	0	1	1	0
Sexual Orientation.................................	54	17	17	0	8	275	2	1
Anti-male homosexual...............................	33	9	6	0	5	138	0	1
Anti-female homosexual.............................	3	1	1	0	0	35	0	0
Anti-homosexual.....................................	17	5	7	0	2	96	0	0
Anti-heterosexual	1	2	0	0	0	3	1	0
Anti-bisexual	0	0	3	0	1	3	1	0
Ethnicity/National Origin	22	25	8	1	5	190	2	3
Anti-Hispanic..	17	11	4	0	3	87	2	2
Anti-other ethnicity/national origin	5	14	4	1	2	103	0	1
Disability.................................	0	1	2	0	0	8	4	1
Anti-physical	0	0	1	0	0	4	4	0
Anti-mental	0	1	1	0	0	4	0	1
Multiple-Bias Incidents[2]..........................	0	0	0	0	1	4	0	0

[1] Includes additional offenses collected in the National Incident-Based Reporting System.

[2] In a multiple-bias incident, two conditions must be met: (a) more than one offense type must occur in the incident and (b) at least two offense types must be motivated by different biases.

Table VI-5. Offenses, Known Offender's Race, by Bias Motivation, 2011

(Number.)

Bias motivation	Total offenses	Known offender's race						Unknown offender
		White	Black	American Indian/ Alaskan Native	Asian/Pacific Islander	Multiple races, group	Unknown race	
Total....................................	7,254	3,101	902	43	64	207	563	2,374
Single-Bias Incidents	7,240	3,092	899	43	64	207	563	2,372
Race....................................	3,465	1,663	410	21	35	109	239	988
Anti-White..............................	577	103	287	13	5	13	47	109
Anti-Black..............................	2,494	1,416	76	4	29	89	157	723
Anti-American Indian/Alaskan Native........	67	25	15	4	0	1	6	16
Anti-Asian/Pacific Islander............	165	76	22	0	1	2	15	49
Anti-multiple races, group	162	43	10	0	0	4	14	91
Religion....................................	1,318	279	42	5	9	23	129	831
Anti-Jewish	820	139	16	1	2	7	79	576
Anti-Catholic	68	7	0	1	1	2	4	53
Anti-Protestant	49	12	0	0	0	1	9	27
Anti-Islamic	175	72	15	3	3	9	20	53
Anti-other religion	139	31	3	0	3	4	12	86
Anti-multiple religions, group	63	18	8	0	0	0	4	33
Anti-atheism/agnosticism/etc.	4	0	0	0	0	0	1	3
Sexual Orientation........................	1,508	644	343	10	12	61	128	310
Anti-male homosexual	871	358	218	7	7	43	79	159
Anti-female homosexual	168	67	47	2	2	1	9	40
Anti-homosexual	429	201	65	1	3	16	38	105
Anti-heterosexual	17	5	9	0	0	0	1	2
Anti-bisexual	23	13	4	0	0	1	1	4
Ethnicity/National Origin	891	471	96	7	8	13	61	235
Anti-Hispanic	506	290	64	5	2	7	28	110
Anti-other ethnicity/national origin	385	181	32	2	6	6	33	125
Disability....................................	58	35	8	0	0	1	6	8
Anti-physical	23	11	2	0	0	0	5	5
Anti-mental	35	24	6	0	0	1	1	3
Multiple-Bias Incidents[1]	14	9	3	0	0	0	0	2

[1] In a multiple-bias incident, two conditions must be met: (a) more than one offense type must occur in the incident and (b) at least two offense types must be motivated by different biases.

Table VI-6. Offenses, Victim Type, by Offense Type, 2011

(Number.)

Offense type	Total offenses	Victim type					Other/ unknown/ multiple
		Individual	Business/ financial institution	Government	Religious organization	Society/ public[1]	
Total..	7,254	6,016	305	206	208	20	499
Crimes Against Persons[2]	4,623	4,623	NA	NA	NA	NA	NA
Crimes Against Property	2,611	1,393	305	206	208	0	499
Robbery	131	119	3	0	0	0	9
Burglary	124	87	10	5	10	0	12
Larceny-theft	152	102	38	1	1	0	10
Motor vehicle theft	6	6	0	0	0	0	0
Arson........................	42	28	4	1	5	0	4
Destruction/damage/vandalism	2,125	1,030	243	198	192	0	462
Other[2]	31	21	7	1	0	0	2
Crimes Against Society[2]	20	NA	NA	NA	NA	20	NA

NA = Not available.
[1] The victim type society/public is collected only in the National Incident-Based Reporting System (NIBRS).
[2] Includes additional offenses collected in the NIBRS.

Table VI-7.   Victims, Offense Type, by Bias Motivation, 2011

(Number.)

Bias motivation	Total offenses	Crimes against persons					Other[1]
		Murder and nonnegligent manslaughter	Forcible rape	Aggravated assault	Simple assault	Intimidation	
Total..	7,713	4	7	895	1,595	2,106	16
Single-Bias Incidents	7,697	4	7	893	1,593	2,101	16
Race..	3,645	1	3	470	752	1,135	4
Anti-White...	593	0	1	91	171	147	1
Anti-Black..	2,619	1	1	347	500	897	3
Anti-American Indian/Alaskan Native..................	70	0	0	12	20	4	0
Anti-Asian/Pacific Islander	175	0	1	9	45	56	0
Anti-multiple races, group	188	0	0	11	16	31	0
Religion..	1,480	0	0	36	108	291	3
Anti-Jewish...	936	0	0	15	43	187	0
Anti-Catholic..	84	0	0	0	3	3	0
Anti-Protestant	51	0	0	4	4	1	0
Anti-Islamic..	185	0	0	14	41	70	0
Anti-other religion....................................	155	0	0	3	8	23	3
Anti-multiple religions, group	65	0	0	0	9	7	0
Anti-atheism/agnosticism/etc.	4	0	0	0	0	0	0
Sexual Orientation....................................	1,572	3	2	252	491	380	6
Anti-male homosexual	891	3	0	162	291	218	5
Anti-female homosexual	174	0	2	28	42	56	0
Anti-homosexual	465	0	0	60	142	99	1
Anti-heterosexual	19	0	0	2	5	3	0
Anti-bisexual	23	0	0	0	11	4	0
Ethnicity/National Origin	939	0	1	128	226	280	0
Anti-Hispanic..	534	0	1	82	144	153	0
Anti-other ethnicity/national origin	405	0	0	46	82	127	0
Disability	61	0	1	7	16	15	3
Anti-physical	26	0	0	0	7	5	2
Anti-mental	35	0	1	7	9	10	1
Multiple-Bias Incidents[2]........................	16	0	0	2	2	5	0

[1] Includes additional offenses collected in the National Incident-Based Reporting System.

[2] In a multiple-bias incident, two conditions must be met: (a) more than one offense type must occur in the incident and (b) at least two offense types must be motivated by different biases.

Table VI-7. Victims, Offense Type, by Bias Motivation, 2011—*Continued*

(Number.)

Bias motivation	Crimes against property							Crimes against society[1]
	Robbery	Burglary	Larceny-theft	Motor vehicle theft	Arson	Destruction/ damage/ vandalism	Other[1]	
Total....................	157	147	165	6	52	2,510	33	20
Single-Bias Incidents	157	147	165	6	51	2,504	33	20
Race....................	60	63	80	5	21	1,015	21	15
Anti-White....................	28	9	42	3	1	86	12	1
Anti-Black....................	24	43	21	1	16	752	1	12
Anti-American Indian/Alaskan Native................	1	0	12	1	0	12	6	2
Anti-Asian/Pacific Islander	3	5	5	0	1	48	2	0
Anti-multiple races, group	4	6	0	0	3	117	0	0
Religion....................	6	36	58	0	16	922	4	0
Anti-Jewish....................	3	8	14	0	5	661	0	0
Anti-Catholic....................	0	5	17	0	1	55	0	0
Anti-Protestant....................	0	6	2	0	1	32	1	0
Anti-Islamic....................	2	1	8	0	2	47	0	0
Anti-other religion....................	1	13	4	0	6	93	1	0
Anti-multiple religions, group	0	3	11	0	1	33	1	0
Anti-atheism/agnosticism/etc.	0	0	2	0	0	1	1	0
Sexual Orientation....................	64	21	17	0	8	325	2	1
Anti-male homosexual....................	41	9	6	0	5	150	0	1
Anti-female homosexual....................	3	1	1	0	0	41	0	0
Anti-homosexual....................	19	8	7	0	2	127	0	0
Anti-heterosexual....................	1	3	0	0	0	4	1	0
Anti-bisexual....................	0	0	3	0	1	3	1	0
Ethnicity/National Origin	27	26	8	1	6	231	2	3
Anti-Hispanic....................	22	11	4	0	4	109	2	2
Anti-other ethnicity/national origin	5	15	4	1	2	122	0	1
Disability....................	0	1	2	0	0	11	4	1
Anti-physical....................	0	0	1	0	0	7	4	0
Anti-mental....................	0	1	1	0	0	4	0	1
Multiple-Bias Incidents[2]....................	0	0	0	0	1	6	0	0

[1] Includes additional offenses collected in the National Incident-Based Reporting System.

[2] In a multiple-bias incident, two conditions must be met: (a) more than one offense type must occur in the incident and (b) at least two offense types must be motivated by different biases.

Table VI-8. Incidents, Victim Type, by Bias Motivation, 2011

(Number.)

Offense type	Total offenses	Victim type					Other/ unknown/ multiple
		Individual	Business/ financial institution	Government	Religious organization	Society/ public[1]	
Total....................	6,222	5,001	294	197	204	14	512
Single-Bias Incidents	6,216	4,996	294	196	204	14	512
Race....................	2,917	2,458	139	112	14	11	183
Religion....................	1,233	626	103	63	184	0	257
Sexual orientation....................	1,293	1,216	16	10	4	1	46
Ethnicity/national origin	720	647	35	10	2	1	25
Disability....................	53	49	1	1	0	1	1
Multiple-Bias Incidents[2]....................	6	5	0	1	0	0	0

[1] The victim type society/public is collected only in the National Incident-Based Reporting System.

[2] In a multiple-bias incident, two conditions must be met: (a) more than one offense type must occur in the incident and (b) at least two offense types must be motivated by different biases.

Table VI-9. Known Offenders,[1] by Known Offender's Race, 2011

(Number.)

Race	Number
Total	5,731
White	3,384
Black	1,195
American Indian/Alaskan Native	46
Asian/Pacific Islander	83
Multiple races, group[2]	406
Unknown race	617

[1] The term known offender does not imply that the identity of the suspect is known, but only that an attribute of the suspect has been identified, which distinguishes him/her from an unknown offender.

[2] The term multiple races, group is used to describe a group of offenders of varying races.

Table VI-10. Incidents, Bias Motivation, by Location, 2011

(Number.)

Location	Total incidents	Bias motivation					Multiple-bias incidents[1]
		Race	Religion	Sexual orientation	Ethnicity/ national origin	Disability	
Total	6,222	2,917	1,233	1,293	720	53	6
Abandoned/condemned structure	2	0	1	1	0	0	0
Air/bus/train terminal	59	32	4	14	8	1	0
Amusement park	2	0	1	0	1	0	0
Arena/stadium/fairgrounds/coliseum	2	2	0	0	0	0	0
ATM separate from bank	1	1	0	0	0	0	0
Auto dealership new/used	2	0	1	1	0	0	0
Bank/savings and loan	13	10	2	0	1	0	0
Bar/nightclub	153	66	6	64	16	1	0
Camp/campground	2	0	0	2	0	0	0
Church/synagogue/temple/mosque	276	25	237	7	7	0	0
Commercial office building	114	55	32	12	15	0	0
Construction site	8	3	2	1	2	0	0
Convenience store	79	35	10	12	22	0	0
Daycare facility	1	0	0	1	0	0	0
Department/discount store	72	39	15	12	6	0	0
Drug store/doctor's office/hospital	62	30	14	7	7	4	0
Farm facility	2	0	1	1	0	0	0
Field/woods	52	26	9	10	7	0	0
Gambling facility/casino/race track	1	0	0	0	1	0	0
Government/public building	89	51	20	10	8	0	0
Grocery/supermarket	59	36	4	6	12	1	0
Highway/road/alley/street/sidewalk	1,121	562	96	309	143	9	2
Hotel/motel/etc.	43	28	2	5	7	1	0
Industrial site	3	2	0	0	1	0	0
Jail/prison/penitentiary/corrections facility	38	24	1	7	5	1	0
Lake/waterway/beach	14	6	2	2	4	0	0
Liquor store	10	7	1	0	2	0	0
Park/playground	36	19	4	6	7	0	0
Parking/drop lot/garage	366	183	30	90	59	4	0
Rental storage facility	13	7	0	3	3	0	0
Residence/home	1,993	984	353	413	221	20	2
Rest area	5	4	0	1	0	0	0
Restaurant	115	60	11	21	23	0	0
School/college[2]	375	175	89	77	30	4	0
School—college/university	53	28	8	12	5	0	0
School—elementary/secondary	150	73	35	30	10	1	1
Service/gas station	48	25	9	3	11	0	0
Shelter—mission/homeless	1	1	0	0	0	0	0
Shopping mall	27	14	3	5	4	1	0
Specialty store (TV, fur, etc.)	48	20	11	9	7	1	0
Tribal Lands	1	0	0	1	0	0	0
Other/unknown	704	279	219	138	64	4	0
Multiple locations	7	5	0	0	1	0	1

[1] In a multiple-bias incident, two conditions must be met: (a) more than one offense type must occur in the incident and (b) at least two offense types must be motivated by different biases.

[2] The location designation school/college has been retained for agencies that have not updated their records management systems to include the new location designations of school—college/university and school—elementary/secondary, which allow for more specificity in reporting.

Table VI-11. Offenses, Offense Type, by Selected State, 2011

(Number.)

| Participating state | Total offenses | Crimes against persons | | | | | | Other[1] |
		Murder and nonnegligent manslaughter	Forcible rape	Aggravated assault	Simple assault	Intimidation	
Total	7,254	4	7	895	1,595	2,106	16
Alabama	96	0	1	9	37	20	0
Alaska	8	0	0	3	1	0	0
Arizona	231	0	0	41	43	60	0
Arkansas	18	0	0	4	5	6	0
California	1,204	1	0	185	227	286	0
Colorado	223	0	0	32	57	65	1
Connecticut	164	0	0	9	25	61	3
Delaware	21	0	0	4	1	13	0
District of Columbia	105	0	0	23	50	9	0
Florida	139	0	0	35	37	22	0
Georgia	21	0	0	4	2	6	0
Idaho	49	0	0	5	27	5	0
Illinois	89	0	0	26	17	27	0
Indiana	120	0	0	13	29	40	0
Iowa	20	0	0	6	6	4	0
Kansas	83	0	0	7	24	20	0
Kentucky	186	0	0	7	33	67	1
Louisiana	7	0	0	2	2	2	0
Maine	66	0	0	5	17	24	0
Maryland	64	0	0	23	10	1	0
Massachusetts	424	0	0	67	75	160	0
Michigan	417	0	0	49	81	173	0
Minnesota	186	0	1	17	36	91	0
Mississippi	1	0	0	0	1	0	0
Missouri	147	0	1	41	43	21	0
Montana	23	0	0	7	3	1	0
Nebraska	39	0	0	1	20	5	0
Nevada	70	0	0	24	14	13	0
New Hampshire	26	0	0	2	0	12	0
New Jersey	553	0	0	8	30	338	0
New Mexico	35	0	0	8	13	7	0
New York	566	2	0	28	199	51	0
North Carolina	129	0	0	9	22	48	0
North Dakota	32	0	0	6	9	8	0
Ohio	277	0	0	8	54	114	5
Oklahoma	38	0	1	1	18	12	0
Oregon	151	0	2	33	30	31	1
Pennsylvania	60	0	1	2	8	27	0
Rhode Island	20	0	0	1	3	2	0
South Carolina	157	0	0	24	44	25	1
South Dakota	23	0	0	1	12	0	0
Tennessee	162	0	0	14	36	51	2
Texas	189	0	0	29	54	54	2
Utah	79	1	0	9	23	6	0
Vermont	9	0	0	1	3	3	0
Virginia	166	0	0	6	42	34	0
Washington	252	0	0	29	48	74	0
West Virginia	21	0	0	7	2	2	0
Wisconsin	85	0	0	20	19	5	0
Wyoming	3	0	0	0	3	0	0

[1]Includes additional offenses collected in the NIBRS.

Table VI-11. Offenses, Offense Type, by Selected State, 2011—*Continued*

(Number.)

Participating state	Crimes against property							Crimes against society[1]
	Robbery	Burglary	Larceny-theft	Motor vehicle theft	Arson	Destruction/ damage/ vandalism	Other[1]	
Total..	131	124	152	6	42	2,125	31	20
Alabama..................................	3	3	6	0	0	17	0	0
Alaska......................................	0	0	0	0	0	4	0	0
Arizona....................................	2	9	1	0	1	73	0	1
Arkansas..................................	0	1	0	0	0	2	0	0
California.................................	39	26	4	1	8	427	0	0
Colorado..................................	6	0	12	0	2	48	0	0
Connecticut..............................	1	1	1	0	0	63	0	0
Delaware..................................	0	0	0	0	0	3	0	0
District of Columbia................	7	0	0	0	0	16	0	0
Florida.....................................	0	4	1	0	0	40	0	0
Georgia....................................	1	0	1	0	1	6	0	0
Idaho.......................................	0	1	1	0	0	9	0	1
Illinois.....................................	2	2	0	0	0	15	0	0
Indiana....................................	1	1	0	0	4	32	0	0
Iowa..	0	0	0	0	0	4	0	0
Kansas.....................................	0	1	7	1	1	20	1	1
Kentucky..................................	4	9	12	0	1	46	5	1
Louisiana.................................	0	0	0	0	0	1	0	0
Maine.......................................	0	0	0	0	0	20	0	0
Maryland..................................	1	0	0	0	1	28	0	0
Massachusetts..........................	5	2	9	0	0	101	5	0
Michigan..................................	4	7	12	0	1	78	2	10
Minnesota................................	4	1	0	0	0	36	0	0
Mississippi...............................	0	0	0	0	0	0	0	0
Missouri...................................	7	2	1	0	2	29	0	0
Montana...................................	0	0	0	0	0	12	0	0
Nebraska..................................	2	1	0	0	0	10	0	0
Nevada.....................................	1	2	1	0	1	14	0	0
New Hampshire........................	0	0	0	0	0	12	0	0
New Jersey................................	2	1	0	0	1	173	0	0
New Mexico..............................	2	0	0	0	1	4	0	0
New York..................................	8	9	9	0	3	257	0	0
North Carolina.........................	1	2	1	0	2	44	0	0
North Dakota...........................	1	0	3	0	0	5	0	0
Ohio...	10	9	15	2	1	57	2	0
Oklahoma.................................	0	0	0	0	0	6	0	0
Oregon.....................................	2	0	4	0	3	45	0	0
Pennsylvania............................	2	0	0	0	3	17	0	0
Rhode Island............................	0	4	1	0	0	8	0	1
South Carolina.........................	0	7	19	0	2	31	4	0
South Dakota...........................	1	1	1	0	0	5	1	1
Tennessee.................................	0	1	5	0	0	51	2	0
Texas..	2	2	0	0	0	46	0	0
Utah...	0	4	9	1	1	24	1	0
Vermont....................................	0	0	0	0	0	2	0	0
Virginia....................................	3	3	2	0	1	72	2	1
Washington...............................	3	5	5	1	0	82	3	2
West Virginia...........................	0	3	0	0	1	5	1	0
Wisconsin.................................	4	0	9	0	0	25	2	1
Wyoming..................................	0	0	0	0	0	0	0	0

[1] Includes additional offenses collected in the National Incident-Based Reporting System.

Table VI-12. Agency Hate Crime Reporting, by Selected State, 2011

(Number)

Participating state	Number of participating agencies	Population covered	Agencies submitting incident reports	Total number of incidents reported
Total	14,575	286,010,550	1,944	6,222
Alabama	98	2,285,487	50	83
Alaska	2	304,924	1	8
Arizona	84	6,225,041	26	192
Arkansas	259	2,804,225	10	11
California	734	37,691,912	257	1,040
Colorado	218	4,992,496	57	186
Connecticut	102	3,580,709	42	140
Delaware	56	907,135	8	15
District of Columbia	2	617,996	2	83
Florida	504	18,945,433	58	123
Georgia	521	8,600,353	8	17
Idaho	107	1,583,018	12	33
Illinois	563	9,959,109	39	69
Indiana	137	3,701,222	17	100
Iowa	212	2,904,419	12	15
Kansas	357	2,426,569	34	67
Kentucky	374	3,581,320	86	155
Louisiana	82	2,448,022	5	5
Maine	149	1,328,188	20	55
Maryland	156	5,828,289	19	49
Massachusetts	308	6,361,208	80	367
Michigan	564	9,569,653	137	346
Minnesota	180	3,992,533	44	148
Mississippi	54	748,806	1	1
Missouri	633	6,001,755	34	117
Montana	99	988,577	9	23
Nebraska	185	1,478,313	7	36
Nevada	13	2,183,002	5	59
New Hampshire	151	1,176,668	14	22
New Jersey	510	8,819,533	162	508
New Mexico	40	973,183	3	28
New York	561	19,297,804	87	544
North Carolina	516	9,655,664	49	112
North Dakota	94	666,780	8	27
Ohio	588	9,879,527	83	228
Oklahoma	319	3,790,684	17	29
Oregon	75	2,437,231	29	128
Pennsylvania	1,372	12,565,359	20	53
Rhode Island	48	1,051,302	5	20
South Carolina	341	4,668,211	65	135
South Dakota	110	731,246	7	21
Tennessee	463	6,403,353	62	144
Texas	1,027	25,629,269	57	152
Utah	125	2,775,105	29	68
Vermont	84	619,283	6	7
Virginia	408	8,087,318	54	144
Virgin Islands[1]	1		0	0
Washington	246	6,822,528	69	213
West Virginia	281	1,689,892	14	18
Wisconsin	399	5,669,896	22	76
Wyoming	63	561,000	2	2

[1] The 2011 population estimates were not available for the Virgin Islands at the time of publication.

Table VI-13. Hate Crime Incidents Per Bias Motivation and Quarter, by Selected State and Agency, 2011

(Number)

State	Agency type/name	Number of incidents per bias motivation					Number of incidents per quarter[1]				Population[2]
		Race	Religion	Sexual orient-ation	Ethnicity	Disability	1st quarter	2nd quarter	3rd quarter	4th quarter	
Alabama	**Total**	58	5	7	11	2					
	Cities										
	Abbeville	2	0	0	0	0	1	1			2,701
	Adamsville	2	0	0	0	0	1			1	4,544
	Alabaster	0	0	0	1	0	1				30,498
	Centre	1	0	0	0	0				1	3,506
	Clanton	2	0	0	0	0	1		1		8,660
	Decatur	1	0	0	2	0		1	2		55,951
	Douglas	0	0	0	1	0		1			748
	Elba	1	0	0	0	0			1		3,959
	Enterprise	2	0	0	0	0	0	0	1	1	26,690
	Foley	2	0	0	0	0	0	2	0	0	14,688
	Fort Payne	1	0	1	0	0	2				14,079
	Fultondale	1	0	0	0	0				1	8,420
	Fyffe	0	2	0	0	0	2				1,023
	Greenville	1	0	0	0	0				1	8,174
	Guntersville	0	1	0	1	0	0	1	1		8,236
	Haleyville	1	0	0	0	0	1				4,193
	Heflin	1	0	0	0	0	1				3,497
	Hoover	1	0	0	1	0	0	0	1	1	82,012
	Hueytown	1	0	0	0	0				1	16,183
	Irondale	2	0	0	0	0		2			12,408
	Jackson	1	0	0	0	0				1	5,253
	Jacksonville	1	0	0	0	0				1	12,608
	Jasper	2	0	0	0	0		0	1	1	14,421
	Lincoln	2	0	0	0	0		1	1		6,296
	Montgomery	0	0	0	1	0	1				206,754
	Mount Vernon	1	0	0	0	0				1	1,582
	Orange Beach	1	0	2	0	0		1	2		5,467
	Oxford	1	0	3	1	0	1	3		1	21,451
	Ozark	1	0	0	0	0	0			1	14,979
	Parrish	0	0	1	0	0			1		987
	Pelham	1	0	0	0	0	0	0	0	1	21,455
	Phenix City	1	0	0	0	0	1				32,980
	Piedmont	1	0	0	0	0	1				4,901
	Prattville	1	0	0	0	0	0	1			34,123
	Roanoke	3	0	0	0	1	1	1	1	1	6,103
	Saraland	2	0	0	0	0	1	1			13,470
	Sheffield	1	0	0	0	0	0	1			9,083
	Sylacauga	2	0	0	0	0	0	0	2	0	12,810
	Town Creek	0	0	0	0	1	0	1			1,105
	Tuscaloosa	1	0	0	2	0	1		2	0	90,903
	Tuscumbia	1	0	0	0	0				1	8,464
	Weaver	1	0	0	0	0			1		3,053
	Metropolitan Counties	7	1	0	1	0					
	Blount	2	0	0	0	0		1	1		
	Chilton	1	1	0	1	0	1		1	1	
	Madison	1	0	0	0	0				1	
	Tuscaloosa	3	0	0	0	0	1	1		1	
	Nonmetropolitan Counties	4	1	0	0	0					
	Coosa	0	1	0	0	0	1				
	Cullman	1	0	0	0	0			1		
	Marengo	1	0	0	0	0		1			
	Washington	2	0	0	0	0	1			1	
Alaska	**Total**	5	2	1	0	0					
	Cities	5	2	1	0	0					
	Anchorage	5	2	1	0	0	1	1	5	1	296,955
Arizona	**Total**	80	35	35	41	1					
	Cities	72	29	32	36	1					
	Apache Junction	0	0	0	2	0	0	1	0	1	36,347
	Avondale	1	0	0	1	0	0	1	1	0	77,317
	Buckeye	1	3	0	0	0	0	3	1	0	51,596
	Camp Verde	0	1	0	0	0	0	0	1	0	11,027
	Chandler	0	0	0	1	0	1	0	0	0	239,466

[1] Agencies published in this table indicated that at least one hate crime incident occurred in their respective jurisdictions during the quarter(s) for which they submitted a report to the Hate Crime Statistics Program. Blanks indicate quarters for which agencies did not submit reports.

[2] Population figures are published only for the cities. The figures listed for the universities and colleges are student enrollment and were provided by the United States Department of Education for the 2010 school year, the most recent available. The enrollment figures include full-time and part-time students.

Table VI-13. Hate Crime Incidents Per Bias Motivation and Quarter, by Selected State and Agency, 2011—*Continued*

(Number)

State	Agency type/name	Number of incidents per bias motivation					Number of incidents per quarter[1]				Popu-lation[2]
		Race	Religion	Sexual orient-ation	Ethnicity	Disability	1st quarter	2nd quarter	3rd quarter	4th quarter	
	Coolidge	1	0	0	0	0	0	1	0	0	11,992
	Gilbert	1	1	0	0	0	2	0	0	0	211,404
	Glendale	4	2	2	1	0	4	0	2	3	229,931
	Maricopa	0	0	1	1	0	0	0	0	2	44,098
	Mesa	4	3	1	0	0	2	3	1	2	445,256
	Phoenix	50	16	28	28	1	27	33	35	28	1,466,097
	Prescott Valley	0	0	0	1	0	1		0	0	39,372
	Scottsdale	3	2	0	0	0	0	1	2	2	220,462
	Somerton	1	0	0	0	0	1	0	0	0	14,489
	Surprise	1	0	0	0	0	1	0	0	0	119,181
	Tempe	2	1	0	0	0	0	2	0	1	164,008
	Wickenburg	1	0	0	0	0	0	0	1	0	6,453
	Yuma	2	0	0	1	0	1	1	0	1	94,381
	Universities and Colleges	1	2	0	2	0					
	Central Arizona College	0	1	0	0	0	1	0	0	0	7,117
	University of Arizona	1	1	0	2	0	0	1	1	2	39,086
	Metropolitan Counties	6	4	3	3	0					
	Maricopa	2	1	0	1	0	2	1	1	0	
	Mohave	0	0	1	0	0	0	1	0	0	
	Pima	3	2	0	1	0	1	2	2	1	
	Pinal	1	1	0	0	0	0	1	0	1	
	Yavapai	0	0	2	1	0	0	2	0	1	
	Other Agencies	1	0	0	0	0					
	Tucson Airport Authority	1	0	0	0	0	1	0	0	0	
Arkansas	**Total**	7	1	1	2	0					
	Cities	5	0	1	1	0					
	Benton	1	0	0	0	0	0	0	0	1	30,913
	Conway	1	0	0	0	0	0	1	0	0	59,354
	Newport	1	0	0	0	0	0	1	0	0	7,939
	Paragould	1	0	0	0	0	0	0	1	0	26,311
	Russellville	0	0	0	1	0	0	0	1	0	28,131
	Siloam Springs	0	0	1	0	0	1	0	0	0	15,153
	Texarkana	1	0	0	0	0	0	1	0	0	30,145
	Metropolitan Counties	2	0	0	1	0					
	Benton	0	0	0	1	0	0	1	0	0	
	Pulaski	2	0	0	0	0	1	1	0	0	
	Nonmetropolitan Counties	0	1	0	0	0					
	Independence	0	1	0	0	0	0	0	1	0	
California	**Total**	415	202	246	170	7					
	Cities	359	167	216	132	6					
	Alhambra	0	0	0	1	0	0	0	1	0	84,066
	Aliso Viejo	1	0	0	0	0	1	0	0	0	48,385
	Anaheim	2	1	1	1	0	2	0	2	1	340,218
	Anderson	1	0	0	0	0	0	0	1	0	10,049
	Antioch[3]	3	2	1	1	0	2	0	4	1	103,575
	Arroyo Grande	1	0	0	0	0	1	0	0	0	17,455
	Artesia	0	0	0	1	0	0	0	1	0	16,716
	Arvin	0	0	1	0	0	0	1	0	0	19,531
	Atherton	0	1	0	0	0	0	1	0	0	6,995
	Azusa	4	0	0	0	0	2	1	0	1	46,906
	Bakersfield	3	0	2	0	0	2	0	1	2	351,568
	Baldwin Park	2	0	1	1	0	2	0	2	0	76,276
	Banning	1	0	0	0	0	1	0	0	0	29,951
	Barstow	2	0	0	0	0	0	0	2	0	22,905
	Beaumont	3	0	0	2	0	3	2	0	0	37,311
	Bellflower	0	0	0	1	0	0	0	1	0	77,517
	Berkeley	0	2	2	0	0	2	1	1	0	113,903
	Beverly Hills	1	4	0	0	0	0	2	2	1	34,510
	Big Bear Lake	0	0	0	1	0	0	0	1	0	5,078
	Blythe	1	0	0	0	0	0	0	1	0	21,062
	Brentwood	0	1	2	0	0	0	1	1	1	52,086
	Burbank	1	2	1	1	0	1	3	1	0	104,555

[1] Agencies published in this table indicated that at least one hate crime incident occurred in their respective jurisdictions during the quarter(s) for which they submitted a report to the Hate Crime Statistics Program. Blanks indicate quarters for which agencies did not submit reports.

[2] Population figures are published only for the cities. The figures listed for the universities and colleges are student enrollment and were provided by the United States Department of Education for the 2010 school year, the most recent available. The enrollment figures include full-time and part-time students.

Table VI-13. Hate Crime Incidents Per Bias Motivation and Quarter, by Selected State and Agency, 2011—*Continued*

(Number)

State	Agency type/name	Number of incidents per bias motivation					Number of incidents per quarter[1]				Popu-lation[2]
		Race	Religion	Sexual orient-ation	Ethnicity	Disability	1st quarter	2nd quarter	3rd quarter	4th quarter	
	Calabasas	0	1	0	0	0	0	1	0	0	23,329
	Camarillo	1	1	0	0	0	0	1	1	0	65,968
	Campbell	1	0	0	0	0	1	0	0	0	39,812
	Carson	4	1	0	0	0	0	5	0	0	92,792
	Cathedral City	1	1	1	0	0	0	2	1	0	51,802
	Cerritos	1	0	0	0	0	0	0	0	1	49,618
	Chico	2	1	1	1	0	1	2	2	0	87,200
	Chino	0	1	0	0	0	1	0	0	0	78,900
	Chula Vista	3	1	0	2	0	1	2	1	2	246,783
	Citrus Heights	1	0	0	0	0	0	0	1	0	84,280
	Claremont	1	0	2	0	0	0	1	0	2	35,337
	Clearlake	1	0	0	0	0	0	0	1	0	15,429
	Clovis	3	0	0	0	0	0	2	1	0	96,755
	Coachella	1	1	0	0	0	0	1	1	0	41,183
	Concord	2	0	7	1	0	1	2	4	3	123,502
	Corona	1	0	0	0	0	1	0	0	0	154,165
	Costa Mesa	0	0	1	1	0	1	1	0	0	111,253
	Cotati	0	0	0	1	0	0	1	0	0	7,350
	Covina	1	0	0	0	0	1	0	0	0	48,358
	Cupertino	0	1	0	1	0	1	0	0	1	58,987
	Cypress	2	0	1	1	0	1	2	0	1	48,364
	Daly City	2	0	2	0	0	1	2	1	0	102,312
	Dana Point	1	0	0	1	0	0	0	2	0	33,743
	Davis	1	4	3	2	0	5	1	1	3	66,393
	Delano	0	0	1	0	0	0	0	0	1	53,665
	Diamond Bar	0	0	1	0	0	1	0	0	0	56,197
	Downey	0	1	0	1	0	0	0	2	0	113,086
	Dublin	1	0	0	0	0	1	0	0	0	46,577
	East Palo Alto	1	0	0	0	0	1	0	0	0	28,486
	El Cerrito	0	2	0	0	0	1	0	1	0	23,826
	Elk Grove	3	0	1	0	0	2	1	0	1	154,814
	El Monte	5	0	1	0	0	1	3	2	0	114,809
	Encinitas	0	1	1	0	0	0	1	0	1	60,218
	Escalon	1	0	1	0	0	1	0	0	1	7,216
	Escondido	4	0	0	1	0	2	2	1	0	145,603
	Eureka	2	2	0	0	0	0	0	1	3	27,511
	Fairfield	0	0	1	0	0	1	0	0	0	106,559
	Farmersville	0	0	0	1	0	0	0	0	1	10,712
	Fort Bragg	0	0	1	0	0	1	0	0	0	7,359
	Fountain Valley	2	0	1	0	0	0	0	3	0	55,963
	Fremont	0	1	0	0	0	0	1	0	0	216,606
	Fresno	1	0	0	1	0	0	2	0	0	500,480
	Fullerton	1	0	0	0	0	0	0	1	0	136,750
	Galt	0	0	0	1	0	1	0	0	0	23,925
	Garden Grove	3	1	0	0	0	1	3	0		172,892
	Glendale	2	0	1	2	0	1	0	1	3	193,973
	Grass Valley	0	0	1	0	0	0	1	0	0	13,011
	Greenfield	0	0	1	0	0	1	0	0	0	16,522
	Hawaiian Gardens	2	0	0	1	0	1	0	1	1	14,422
	Hawthorne	1	1	0	0	0	0	0	1	1	85,284
	Hayward	0	1	0	0	0	1	0	0	0	145,881
	Healdsburg	0	1	0	0	0	0	0	1	0	11,386
	Hemet	1	0	0	1	0	1	1	0	0	79,582
	Hercules	0	1	0	0	0	0	0	1	0	24,343
	Highland	1	0	0	0	0	0	0	1	0	53,728
	Huntington Beach	8	1	1	2	0	3	5	1	3	192,226
	Imperial Beach	0	0	0	1	0	1	0	0	0	26,633
	Irvine	1	1	2	3	0	5	1	1	0	214,872
	La Canada Flintridge	1	0	0	0	0	0	1	0	0	20,484
	Laguna Beach	1	0	0	0	0	0	0	1	0	22,990
	La Habra	2	0	0	0	0	0	0	1	1	60,947
	Lake Elsinore	1	0	0	0	0	0	0	0	1	52,430
	Lakewood	1	0	0	0	0	0	1	0	0	80,989
	La Mesa	0	0	2	1	0	0	2	1	0	57,736
	La Mirada	1	0	0	0	0	0	1	0	0	49,097
	Lancaster	3	0	5	0	0	1	3	1	3	158,474
	La Puente	1	0	0	0	0	0	0	0	1	40,284
	La Quinta	0	1	0	0	0	0	0	0	1	37,907
	La Verne	0	1	0	0	0	0	1	0	0	31,428
	Lemon Grove	0	0	0	1	0	0	0	1	0	25,618
	Lemoore	1	0	0	0	0	0	0	1	0	24,819
	Livermore	2	0	0	0	0	2	0	0	0	81,920

[1] Agencies published in this table indicated that at least one hate crime incident occurred in their respective jurisdictions during the quarter(s) for which they submitted a report to the Hate Crime Statistics Program. Blanks indicate quarters for which agencies did not submit reports.

[2] Population figures are published only for the cities. The figures listed for the universities and colleges are student enrollment and were provided by the United States Department of Education for the 2010 school year, the most recent available. The enrollment figures include full-time and part-time students.

Table VI-13. Hate Crime Incidents Per Bias Motivation and Quarter, by Selected State and Agency, 2011—*Continued*

(Number)

State	Agency type/name	Number of incidents per bias motivation					Number of incidents per quarter[1]				Popu-lation[2]
		Race	Religion	Sexual orient-ation	Ethnicity	Disability	1st quarter	2nd quarter	3rd quarter	4th quarter	
	Lodi	2	0	0	1	0	0	0	2	1	62,864
	Long Beach	0	3	3	0	0	3	0	2	1	467,691
	Los Angeles[3]	68	33	41	28	0	34	53	46	37	3,837,207
	Los Gatos	1	0	0	0	0	0	0	1	0	29,759
	Lynwood	1	0	0	0	0	0	0	1	0	70,592
	Malibu	0	0	0	1	0	0	1	0	0	12,794
	Manhattan Beach	1	1	0	0	0	0	0	2	0	35,548
	Marysville	2	0	0	0	0	2	0	0	0	12,214
	Menlo Park	1	0	0	0	0	1	0	0	0	32,402
	Millbrae	1	1	0	0	0	0	0	1	1	21,785
	Milpitas	0	0	1	0	0	0	1	0	0	67,575
	Mission Viejo	2	1	0	1	0	0	0	2	2	94,402
	Modesto	2	1	1	0	0	1	1	1	1	203,530
	Montclair	1	0	0	0	0	0	1	0	0	37,095
	Monterey	1	0	2	0	0	0	1	2	0	28,137
	Moreno Valley	2	0	0	0	0	0	1	0	1	195,638
	Mountain View	1	0	0	0	0	1	0	0	0	74,937
	Murrieta	3	1	0	1	0	3	1	0	1	104,682
	Napa	0	1	0	1	0	0	0	0	2	77,819
	Newark	2	0	0	2	0	2	1	1	0	43,073
	Newport Beach	0	4	0	1	0	0	3	2	0	86,187
	Norco	1	0	0	0	0	0	1	0	0	27,381
	Norwalk	3	0	1	0	0	2	0	2	0	106,790
	Novato	1	1	1	0	0	0	3	0	0	52,514
	Oakland	3	2	3	1	0	2	2	4	1	395,317
	Oceanside	4	1	0	0	0	1	3	0	1	169,050
	Ojai	0	0	1	0	0	0	1	0	0	7,549
	Ontario	1	0	0	1	0	0	1	0	1	165,851
	Orange	0	0	0	2	0	0	0	1	1	138,020
	Oxnard	1	0	1	2	0	2	1	1	0	200,225
	Pacifica	0	1	1	0	0	1	1	0	0	37,672
	Palmdale	9	0	2	1	0	2	5	5	0	154,546
	Palm Desert	0	0	1	0	0	0	0	0	1	49,015
	Palm Springs	1	3	5	1	0	4	2	0	4	45,076
	Palo Alto	2	2	0	0	0	2	2	0	0	65,160
	Paramount	1	0	0	0	0	0	0	1	0	54,734
	Parlier	1	0	0	0	0	0	1	0	0	14,664
	Patterson	1	0	0	0	0	0	0	0	1	20,653
	Perris	0	0	1	0	0	0	0	1	0	69,190
	Petaluma	1	0	0	0	0	0	1	0	0	58,622
	Pico Rivera	0	0	0	1	0	0	0	1	0	63,682
	Pinole	1	0	0	0	0	0	0	1	0	18,606
	Pittsburg	1	0	0	0	0	0	0	1	0	64,008
	Poway	1	1	1	0	0	0	1	0	2	48,373
	Rancho Cordova	0	0	0	1	0	0	1	0	0	65,538
	Rancho Palos Verdes	0	1	0	0	0	1	0	0	0	42,133
	Redding	2	0	0	0	0	1	1	0	0	90,917
	Redondo Beach	3	0	1	1	0	2	2	1	0	67,533
	Rialto	1	0	1	1	0	2	0	0	1	100,337
	Richmond	0	0	0	2	0	0	1	0	1	104,920
	Riverside	13	1	4	6	1	5	4	10	6	307,443
	Rohnert Park	2	0	0	0	0	1	1	0	0	41,453
	Rolling Hills Estates	0	0	0	1	0	1	0	0	0	8,162
	Sacramento	2	3	10	2	0	6	4	4	3	471,972
	Salinas	0	0	1	0	1	0	1	0	1	152,210
	San Bernardino	1	0	0	1	0	0	0	0	2	212,392
	San Bruno	0	1	0	0	0	0	0	1	0	41,597
	San Clemente	1	0	0	0	0	0	0	1	0	64,269
	San Diego	8	11	18	5	0	14	10	10	8	1,316,919
	San Dimas	0	1	0	0	0	0	1	0	0	33,763
	San Francisco	11	10	21	4	0	9	14	14	9	814,701
	San Gabriel	1	0	0	0	0	0	1	0	0	40,185
	Sanger	0	0	1	0	0	0	0	1	0	24,555
	San Jose	10	10	9	2	1	11	11	6	4	957,062
	San Leandro	1	0	0	0	0	0	0	1	0	85,949
	San Luis Obispo	2	0	0	1	0	2	1	0	0	45,649
	San Marcos	1	0	1	1	0	1	0	2	0	84,766
	San Mateo	0	0	2	0	0	0	0	1	1	98,350
	San Pablo	0	1	0	0	0	0	0	0	1	29,482
	San Rafael	3	0	0	0	0	2	1	0	0	58,391
	Santa Ana[3]	3	1	6	1	1	4	4	1	3	328,343
	Santa Barbara	3	0	0	0	0	1	0	2	0	89,449

[1] Agencies published in this table indicated that at least one hate crime incident occurred in their respective jurisdictions during the quarter(s) for which they submitted a report to the Hate Crime Statistics Program. Blanks indicate quarters for which agencies did not submit reports.

[2] Population figures are published only for the cities. The figures listed for the universities and colleges are student enrollment and were provided by the United States Department of Education for the 2010 school year, the most recent available. The enrollment figures include full-time and part-time students.

[3] Includes one incident reported with more than one bias motivation.

Table VI-13. Hate Crime Incidents Per Bias Motivation and Quarter, by Selected State and Agency, 2011—*Continued*

(Number)

State	Agency type/name	Number of incidents per bias motivation					Number of incidents per quarter[1]				Popu-lation[2]
		Race	Religion	Sexual orient-ation	Ethnicity	Disability	1st quarter	2nd quarter	3rd quarter	4th quarter	
	Santa Clarita	3	0	2	3	0	4	1	1	2	178,393
	Santa Cruz	10	2	3	0	0	2	3	6	4	60,651
	Santa Monica	1	3	0	1	0	0	2	1	2	90,791
	Santa Rosa	1	0	0	0	0	0	0	0	1	169,788
	Santee	5	1	0	0	0	2	0	0	4	54,041
	Saratoga	0	0	0	1	0	0	0	0	1	30,278
	Scotts Valley	1	0	1	0	0	0	0	1	1	11,716
	Selma	0	0	1	0	0	0	1	0	0	23,492
	Simi Valley	1	2	0	0	0	1	0	1	1	125,698
	Soledad	0	0	0	1	0	1	0	0	0	26,041
	Sonora	1	0	0	0	1	1	0	0	1	4,961
	South Gate	0	0	1	1	0	0	1	1	0	95,506
	South Lake Tahoe	0	0	0	0	1	1	0	0	0	21,655
	South San Francisco	1	0	0	0	0	0	0	0	1	64,380
	Stanton	1	0	0	0	0	1	0	0	0	38,635
	Stockton	2	1	0	0	0	1	0	2	0	295,136
	Sunnyvale	0	1	0	0	0	0	0	0	1	141,728
	Susanville	1	0	0	0	0	0	0	0	1	18,158
	Tehachapi	1	0	1	0	0	1	0	1	0	14,583
	Temple City	0	0	0	1	0	0	1	0	0	35,976
	Thousand Oaks	1	4	0	1	0	2	0	3	1	128,172
	Torrance	1	0	0	0	0	1	0	0	0	147,148
	Tracy	2	0	0	0	0	1	0	1	0	83,897
	Turlock	0	0	0	1	0	0	1	0	0	69,355
	Tustin	0	0	0	2	0	0	2	0	0	76,428
	Union City	0	0	2	1	0	0	0	3	0	70,333
	Upland	2	0	0	0	0	1	0	1	0	74,599
	Vallejo	1	0	1	0	0	1	1	0	0	117,305
	Ventura	1	0	0	1	0	1	0	1	0	107,684
	Victorville	2	0	0	1	0	1	1	1	0	117,266
	Visalia	0	0	0	1	0	0	1	0	0	125,905
	Vista	1	3	0	2	0	2	2	2	0	94,937
	Walnut Creek	5	8	1	1	0	3	6	2	4	64,927
	Watsonville	1	0	0	0	0	0	1	0	0	51,801
	West Covina	3	0	1	0	0	1	3	0	0	107,345
	West Hollywood	2	0	9	0	0	5	1	2	3	34,803
	Westlake Village	0	1	0	0	0	0	0	0	1	8,367
	Westminster	5	1	0	1	0	1	0	5	1	90,756
	Whittier	1	0	0	0	0	0	0	1	0	86,334
	Woodland	0	0	1	0	0	0	0	1	0	56,120
	Yorba Linda	0	1	0	0	0	0	0	0	1	64,989
	Universities and Colleges	16	5	5	5	0					
	Allan Hancock College	1	0	0	0	0	0	1	0	0	12,108
	California State University										
	Long Beach	0	0	0	1	0	1	0	0	0	33,416
	Los Angeles	1	0	0	0	0	0	1	0	0	20,142
	Northridge	1	2	1	0	0	1	2	0	1	35,272
	San Jose[4]	1	0	0	0	0	0	0	1	0	
	San Marcos	0	0	1	0	0	0	0	0	1	9,722
	Contra Costa Community College	1	0	0	0	0	1	0	0	0	7,975
	Foothill-De Anza College	0	0	0	1	0	1	0	0	0	41,104
	Humboldt State University	1	0	0	0	0	0	1	0	0	7,903
	Riverside Community College	1	0	0	0	0	0	0	0	1	20,585
	State Center Community College District	1	0	0	0	0	1	0	0	0	38,821
	University of California										
	Davis	0	0	1	0	0	1	0	0	0	31,392
	Los Angeles	0	0	1	0	0	0	1	0	0	38,157
	Medical Center, Sacramento[4]	0	0	0	1	0	1	0	0	0	
	Riverside	1	0	0	0	0	1	0	0	0	20,692
	San Diego	1	1	0	0	0	1	0	0	1	29,176
	Santa Barbara	1	0	0	0	0	0	0	0	1	22,218
	Santa Cruz	4	2	1	2	0	5	4	0	0	17,187
	West Valley-Mission College	1	0	0	0	0	0	0	0	1	22,783

[1] Agencies published in this table indicated that at least one hate crime incident occurred in their respective jurisdictions during the quarter(s) for which they submitted a report to the Hate Crime Statistics Program. Blanks indicate quarters for which agencies did not submit reports.

[2] Population figures are published only for the cities. The figures listed for the universities and colleges are student enrollment and were provided by the United States Department of Education for the 2010 school year, the most recent available. The enrollment figures include full-time and part-time students.

[4] Student enrollment figures were not available.

Table VI-13. Hate Crime Incidents Per Bias Motivation and Quarter, by Selected State and Agency, 2011—*Continued*

(Number)

State	Agency type/name	Number of incidents per bias motivation					Number of incidents per quarter[1]				Popu-lation[2]
		Race	Religion	Sexual orient-ation	Ethnicity	Disability	1st quarter	2nd quarter	3rd quarter	4th quarter	
	Metropolitan counties	30	27	23	30	1					
	Alameda	1	0	0	0	0		1	0	0	
	Butte	1	1	0	0	0	1	0	1	0	
	Contra Costa	0	2	2	0	0	2	1	1	0	
	Kern	1	0	1	2	0	0	1	2	1	
	Los Angeles	7	6	12	7	0	8	10	8	6	
	Marin	0	1	0	0	0	1	0	0	0	
	Merced	0	0	0	1	0	1	0	0	0	
	Monterey	1	0	0	1	0	0	1	0	1	
	Orange	0	1	0	0	0	0	1	0	0	
	Placer	0	1	0	0	0	1	0	0	0	
	Riverside	1	2	2	0	0	2	1	0	2	
	Sacramento	5	2	1	2	0	2	2	3	3	
	San Bernardino	0	0	0	2	0	0	1	1	0	
	San Diego	8	3	2	12	0	6	5	8	6	
	San Luis Obispo	1	0	0	0	0	0	1	0	0	
	Santa Clara	0	1	0	0	0	0	0	1	0	
	Santa Cruz	3	4	1	2	1	5	4	2	0	
	Sonoma	0	0	1	0	0	1	0	0	0	
	Sutter	0	0	1	0	0	0	0	0	1	
	Ventura	0	3	0	1	0	0	2	2	0	
	Yuba	1	0	0	0	0	0	1	0	0	
	Nonmetropolitan counties	4	3	0	0	0					
	Amador	1	0	0	0	0	0	0	0	1	
	Humboldt	0	1	0	0	0	0	1	0	0	
	Lake	1	1	0	0	0	0	1	1	0	
	Mendocino	2	0	0	0	0	1	0	1	0	
	Tuolumne	0	1	0	0	0	0	1	0	0	
Colorado	**Total**	92	32	42	20	0					
	Cities	75	26	32	18	0					
	Alamosa	0	1	1	0	0	0	0	2	0	8,933
	Aspen[3]	0	0	3	0	0	0	2	0	1	6,774
	Aurora	3	0	1	0	0	1	0	2	1	330,740
	Basalt	1	0	0	0	0	0	0	1	0	3,924
	Boulder	1	1	0	0	0	0	1	1	0	99,081
	Breckenridge	2	0	0	0	0	1	0	0	1	4,619
	Broomfield	0	1	0	0	0	1	0	0	0	56,862
	Buena Vista	0	0	1	0	0	0	0	1	0	2,663
	Canon City	0	0	1	0	0	0	0	1	0	16,686
	Centennial	4	2	1	0	0	2	1	4	0	102,125
	Colorado Springs	4	5	1	0	0	4	4	1	1	423,680
	Craig	2	0	0	0	0	0	1	1	0	9,629
	Denver	8	3	12	2	0	3	8	13	1	610,612
	Durango	3	0	3	3	0	0	4	4	1	17,181
	Englewood	1	1	0	0	0	0	1	0	1	30,782
	Estes Park	1	0	0	0	0	0	1	0	0	5,960
	Fort Collins	3	1	1	1	0	0	2	1	3	146,494
	Fort Lupton	0	0	0	1	0	0	0	1	0	7,505
	Fort Morgan	1	0	0	0	0	0	1	0	0	11,512
	Frisco	0	0	1	0	0	1	0	0	0	2,730
	Glenwood Springs	0	0	0	1	0	0	0	1	0	9,781
	Golden	0	0	0	1	0	0	1	0	0	19,196
	Grand Junction	1	2	1	0	0	2	0	1	1	59,586
	Greeley	5	1	0	4	0	2	4	4	0	94,507
	Lafayette	1	0	0	0	0			1		24,879
	La Junta	0	0	1	0	0	0	1	0	0	7,200
	Lakewood	2	0	0	1	0	0	0	3	0	145,470
	Littleton	8	0	1	0	0	0	8	0	1	42,464
	Lone Tree	7	1	0	0	0	5	2	1	0	10,396
	Longmont	3	0	0	0	0	0	2	1	0	87,773
	Loveland	1	0	0	0	0		1			68,024
	Mancos	0	0	1	0	0	1	0	0	0	1,359
	Montrose	0	0	0	1	0	0	0	1	0	19,465
	Monument	1	1	0	0	0	2	0	0	0	5,626
	Northglenn	1	0	0	0	0	0	0	1	0	36,412
	Palmer Lake	1	0	0	0	0	0	0	0	1	2,462
	Parachute	1	0	0	0	0	0	0	1	0	1,104
	Parker	1	0	0	0	0	1	0	0	0	46,086
	Pueblo	4	0	2	2	0	2	2	4	0	108,452

[1] Agencies published in this table indicated that at least one hate crime incident occurred in their respective jurisdictions during the quarter(s) for which they submitted a report to the Hate Crime Statistics Program. Blanks indicate quarters for which agencies did not submit reports.
[2] Population figures are published only for the cities. The figures listed for the universities and colleges are student enrollment and were provided by the United States Department of Education for the 2010 school year, the most recent available. The enrollment figures include full-time and part-time students.
[3] Includes one incident reported with more than one bias motivation.

Table VI-13. Hate Crime Incidents Per Bias Motivation and Quarter, by Selected State and Agency, 2011—*Continued*

(Number)

State	Agency type/name	Number of incidents per bias motivation					Number of incidents per quarter[1]				Popu-lation[2]
		Race	Religion	Sexual orient-ation	Ethnicity	Disability	1st quarter	2nd quarter	3rd quarter	4th quarter	
	Steamboat Springs	1	5	0	1	0	1	1	0	5	12,299
	Sterling	1	0	0	0	0	0	0	0	1	15,034
	Thornton	1	1	0	0	0	0	1	0	1	120,841
	Wheat Ridge	1	0	0	0	0	0	0	1	0	30,691
	Universities and Colleges	0	0	2	0	0					
	Colorado State University, Fort Collins	0	0	1	0	0	1	0	0	0	30,155
	Fort Lewis College	0	0	1	0	0	0	0	0	1	3,853
	Metropolitan Counties	14	5	4	2	0					
	Adams[3]	3	0	1	0	0	0	1	2	1	
	Arapahoe	6	2	1	0	0	3	5	1	0	
	Douglas	2	0	1	0	0	2	0	0	1	
	Larimer	2	2	1	0	0	0	1	2	2	
	Mesa	1	1	0	1	0	0	3	0	0	
	Weld	0	0	0	1	0	0	0	0	1	
	Nonmetropolitan Counties	3	1	4	0	0					
	Huerfano	0	0	1	0	0	0	0	0	1	
	Kit Carson	0	0	1	0	0	0	1	0	0	
	Logan	0	0	1	0	0	0	1	0	0	
	Moffat	1	0	0	0	0	0	1	0	0	
	Otero	0	0	1	0	0	0	0	1	0	
	Summit	2	1	0	0	0	0	2	1	0	
Connecticut..................	**Total**	63	35	24	17	1					
	Cities	58	35	20	12	1					
	Bloomfield	1	1	0	0	0	2	0	0	0	20,524
	Bridgeport	0	1	1	4	0	2	1	1	2	144,496
	Bristol	0	0	1	0	0	0	1	0	0	60,589
	Clinton	1	1	1	0	0	0	2	1	0	13,285
	Cromwell	1	1	0	0	0	1	0	0	1	14,031
	Danbury	2	0	0	1	0	3	0	0	0	81,043
	Darien	0	1	0	0	0	0	0	0	1	20,770
	East Hampton	1	0	0	0	0	0	0	0	1	12,983
	Enfield	1	0	0	0	0	0	0	1	0	44,737
	Fairfield	0	1	0	0	0	0	0	0	1	59,514
	Glastonbury	0	1	0	0	0	1	0	0	0	34,491
	Groton Town	2	3	2	0	0	1	1	1	4	29,262
	Guilford	0	1	0	0	0	0	0	0	1	22,416
	Hartford	3	0	1	1	0	2	1	2	0	125,006
	Madison	1	0	0	0	0	0	0	1	0	18,303
	Manchester	14	9	3	1	1	7	7	8	6	58,349
	Middletown	1	2	0	0	0	0	2	0	1	47,736
	Milford	3	0	0	0	0	2	0	0	1	52,857
	Naugatuck	3	0	0	1	0	0	0	2	2	31,921
	New Britain	0	1	0	0	0	0	0	0	1	73,341
	New Canaan	1	0	0	0	0	0	1	0	0	19,775
	New Haven	3	0	2	2	0	1	4	1	1	130,019
	Newington	2	4	0	1	0	0	1	4	2	30,619
	New London	6	1	1	0	0	2	2	1	3	27,671
	Norwalk	3	0	0	0	0	0	1	2	0	85,761
	Norwich	1	1	2	0	0	0	2	2	0	40,568
	Seymour	1	0	0	0	0	0	0	0	1	16,571
	Shelton	0	0	1	0	0	0	0	0	1	39,632
	Southington	1	0	1	0	0	1	1	0	0	43,149
	Stratford	1	1	0	0	0	1	0	0	1	51,479
	Torrington	1	0	0	0	0	0	0	1	0	36,450
	Wallingford	0	0	2	0	0	0	0	2	0	45,218
	Waterbury	2	1	1	0	0	2	2	0	0	110,570
	West Hartford	0	0	1	1	0	0	0	1	1	63,385
	Weston	0	1	0	0	0	0	1	0	0	10,198
	Westport	0	3	0	0	0	2	0	0	1	26,440
	Winchester	1	0	0	0	0	0	0	0	1	11,263
	Windsor Locks	1	0	0	0	0	0	0	0	1	12,521

[1] Agencies published in this table indicated that at least one hate crime incident occurred in their respective jurisdictions during the quarter(s) for which they submitted a report to the Hate Crime Statistics Program. Blanks indicate quarters for which agencies did not submit reports.

[2] Population figures are published only for the cities. The figures listed for the universities and colleges are student enrollment and were provided by the United States Department of Education for the 2010 school year, the most recent available. The enrollment figures include full-time and part-time students.

[3] Includes one incident reported with more than one bias motivation.

Table VI-13. Hate Crime Incidents Per Bias Motivation and Quarter, by Selected State and Agency, 2011—*Continued*

(Number)

State	Agency type/name	Number of incidents per bias motivation					Number of incidents per quarter[1]				Popu-lation[2]
		Race	Religion	Sexual orient-ation	Ethnicity	Disability	1st quarter	2nd quarter	3rd quarter	4th quarter	
	Universities and Colleges	3	0	4	0	0					
	Southern Connecticut State University	1	0	2	0	0	0	0	1	2	11,964
	University of Connecticut, Storrs, Avery Point, and Hartford[4]	2	0	0	0	0	1	0	0	1	
	Western Connecticut State University	0	0	2	0	0	0	0	0	2	6,582
	State Police Agencies	2	0	0	5	0					
	Connecticut State Police	2	0	0	5	0	1	5	1	0	
Delaware	**Total**	9	3	2	1	0					
	Cities	4	2	1	0	0					
	Camden	1	0	0	0	0	1	0	0	0	3,499
	Dover	2	0	0	0	0	0	1	0	1	36,416
	Newark	0	0	1	0	0	0	0	0	1	31,776
	Wilmington	1	2	0	0	0	0	2	1	0	71,577
	Metropolitan Counties	3	0	0	1	0					
	New Castle County Police Department	3	0	0	1	0	1	1	1	1	
	State Police Agencies	1	1	1	0	0					
	State Police										
	Kent County	0	0	1	0	0	0	0	1	0	
	New Castle County	1	1	0	0	0	0	2	0	0	
	Other Agencies	1	0	0	0	0					
	River and Bay Authority	1	0	0	0	0	0	0	1	0	
District of Columbia	**Total**	30	2	43	8	0					
	Cities	27	2	43	7	0					
	Washington	27	2	43	7	0	16	19	18	26	617,996
	Other Agencies	3	0	0	1	0					
	Metro Transit Police	3	0	0	1	0	2	0	1	1	
Florida	**Total**	54	29	25	16	1					
	Cities	25	18	19	8	1					
	Boca Raton	1	1	0	0	0	0	2	0	0	85,542
	Boynton Beach	0	1	1	0	0	0	0	2	0	69,147
	Dania	1	0	0	0	0	0	0	1	0	30,043
	Daytona Beach	1	0	1	0	0	0	0	2	0	61,836
	Deland	1	1	0	0	0	1	0	1	0	27,399
	Doral	1	0	0	0	0	1	0	0	0	46,327
	Fort Walton Beach	0	0	0	0	1	0	0	0	1	19,773
	Gainesville	2	8	3	0	0	3	1	4	5	126,049
	Homestead	1	0	1	1	0	3	0	0	0	61,337
	Jacksonville Beach	1	0	0	0	0	0	0	1	0	21,653
	Jupiter	1	0	0	0	0	0	1	0	0	55,908
	Key West	0	0	1	0	0	0	0	0	1	24,985
	Lake Worth	1	0	0	0	0	1	0	0	0	35,386
	Leesburg	0	0	1	0	0	0	1	0	0	20,391
	Marco Island	0	1	0	0	0	0	0	1	0	16,637
	Melbourne	1	0	2	1	0	0	3	0	1	77,105
	Miami Beach	1	1	1	0	0	3	0	0	0	88,975
	Miami Gardens	0	0	1	1	0	1	0	1	0	108,628
	Miami Shores	0	0	1	0	0	0	1	0	0	10,636
	Milton	0	0	0	1	0	0	0	1	0	8,946
	Mount Dora	0	1	0	0	0	0	0	1	0	12,539
	North Bay Village	0	0	0	1	0	0	0	0	1	7,234
	North Port	1	0	1	0	0	0	0	1	1	58,139
	Oakland Park	1	0	0	0	0	1	0	0	0	41,927
	Ocala	0	1	0	0	0	0	1	0	0	57,082
	Orlando	4	0	3	0	0	2	1	4	0	241,548
	Palm Bay	0	0	0	1	0	0	1	0	0	104,596
	Panama City	1	0	0	1	0	1	0	0	1	36,981

[1] Agencies published in this table indicated that at least one hate crime incident occurred in their respective jurisdictions during the quarter(s) for which they submitted a report to the Hate Crime Statistics Program. Blanks indicate quarters for which agencies did not submit reports.

[2] Population figures are published only for the cities. The figures listed for the universities and colleges are student enrollment and were provided by the United States Department of Education for the 2010 school year, the most recent available. The enrollment figures include full-time and part-time students.

[4] Student enrollment figures were not available.

Table VI-13. Hate Crime Incidents Per Bias Motivation and Quarter, by Selected State and Agency, 2011—*Continued*

(Number)

State	Agency type/name	Number of incidents per bias motivation					Number of incidents per quarter[1]				Popu-lation[2]
		Race	Religion	Sexual orient-ation	Ethnicity	Disability	1st quarter	2nd quarter	3rd quarter	4th quarter	
	Pensacola	1	0	1	0	0	0	0	1	1	52,631
	Port St. Lucie	0	1	0	0	0	0	0	0	1	166,846
	Royal Palm Beach	0	1	0	0	0	0	0	1	0	34,605
	Sarasota	1	0	0	0	0	0	1	0	0	52,625
	Stuart	1	0	0	0	0	0	1	0	0	15,806
	Weston	0	1	0	0	0	0	1	0	0	66,223
	Wilton Manors	1	0	1	0	0	1	0	0	1	11,791
	Winter Garden	1	0	0	1	0	1	0	1	0	35,039
	Universities and Colleges	1	1	0	0	0					
	University of Central Florida	1	0	0	0	0	0	1	0	0	56,106
	University of Florida	0	1	0	0	0	0	1	0	0	49,827
	Metropolitan Counties	27	9	6	8	0					
	Baker	0	0	1	0	0	1	0	0	0	
	Brevard	1	0	0	0	0	0	1	0	0	
	Charlotte	1	0	0	0	0	0	0	0	1	
	Clay	3	0	1	0	0	0	1	0	3	
	Collier	0	1	1	0	0	0	1	1	0	
	Escambia	0	0	0	1	0	0	0	1	0	
	Flagler	3	1	0	0	0	1	2	0	1	
	Hillsborough	2	0	0	0	0	1	0	1	0	
	Okaloosa	1	0	0	0	0	1	0	0	0	
	Orange	5	3	3	2	0	2	3	4	4	
	Osceola	1	0	0	0	0	0	0	1	0	
	Palm Beach	2	1	0	0	0	3	0	0	0	
	Pasco	3	0	0	1	0	1	2	0	1	
	Pinellas	0	0	0	1	0	1	0	0	0	
	Polk	2	1	0	1	0	2	2	0	0	
	Santa Rosa	1	0	0	1	0	0	0	0	2	
	St. Johns	1	0	0	1	0	0	1	1	0	
	Volusia	1	0	0	0	0	0	0	0	1	
	Nonmetropolitan Counties	0	1	0	0	0					
	Walton	0	1	0	0	0	1	0	0	0	
	Other Agencies	1	0	0	0	0					
	Palm Beach County School District	1	0	0	0	0	1	0	0	0	
Georgia	**Total**	11	2	4	0	0					
	Cities	4	2	3	0	0					
	Athens-Clarke County	1	1	0	0	0	2				117,114
	Atlanta	0	0	2	0	0	1	1	0	0	425,533
	Columbus	2	1	1	0	0		2	1	1	192,385
	Warner Robins	1	0	0	0	0	1	0	0	0	67,465
	Universities and Colleges	1	0	1	0	0					
	College of Coastal Georgia	1	0	0	0	0	0	0	0	1	3,438
	University of Georgia	0	0	1	0	0	0	0	0	1	34,677
	Metropolitan Counties	6	0	0	0	0					
	Catoosa	1	0	0	0	0	0	1	0	0	
	Henry County Police Department	5	0	0	0	0	1	0	1	3	
Idaho	**Total**	15	6	6	6	0					
	Cities	13	5	5	5	0					
	Boise	5	3	1	0	0	1	4	0	4	207,945
	Coeur d'Alene	3	1	0	3	0	1	2	3	1	44,625
	Hailey	1	0	0	0	0	0	1	0	0	8,048
	McCall	0	0	1	0	0	0	0	1	0	3,024
	Nampa	1	0	0	2	0	1	1	1	0	82,459
	Post Falls	3	0	0	0	0	3	0	0	0	27,879
	Rathdrum	0	0	1	0	0	0	0	1	0	6,901
	Rexburg	0	1	0	0	0	0	0	0	1	25,766
	Twin Falls	0	0	2	0	0	0	0	1	1	44,613

[1] Agencies published in this table indicated that at least one hate crime incident occurred in their respective jurisdictions during the quarter(s) for which they submitted a report to the Hate Crime Statistics Program. Blanks indicate quarters for which agencies did not submit reports.

[2] Population figures are published only for the cities. The figures listed for the universities and colleges are student enrollment and were provided by the United States Department of Education for the 2010 school year, the most recent available. The enrollment figures include full-time and part-time students.

Table VI-13. Hate Crime Incidents Per Bias Motivation and Quarter, by Selected State and Agency, 2011—*Continued*

(Number)

State	Agency type/name	Number of incidents per bias motivation					Number of incidents per quarter[1]				Popu-lation[2]
		Race	Religion	Sexual orient-ation	Ethnicity	Disability	1st quarter	2nd quarter	3rd quarter	4th quarter	
	Metropolitan Counties	2	0	0	1	0					
	Kootenai	2	0	0	1	0	0	1	1	1	
	Nonmetropolitan										
	Counties	0	1	1	0	0					
	Shoshone	0	0	1	0	0	1	0	0	0	
	Teton	0	1	0	0	0	1	0	0	0	
Illinois............................	**Total**	36	6	17	9	1					
	Cities	31	4	15	8	0					
	Alton	1	0	0	0	0	0	0	0	1	27,949
	Arlington Heights	0	0	1	0	0	1	0	0		75,327
	Aurora	2	0	0	0	0	1	0	1	0	198,495
	Beecher	1	0	0	0	0	0	0	0	1	4,372
	Bellwood	0	0	1	0	0	0	0	1		19,128
	Blue Island	1	0	0	0	0	0	1	0	0	23,777
	Cairo	0	0	1	0	0	0	0	0	1	2,840
	Carol Stream	1	0	0	0	0	0	0	0	1	39,831
	Centralia	1	0	0	0	0	0	1	0	0	13,071
	Champaign	0	0	3	1	0	1	2	1	0	81,299
	Chicago	3	2	4	1	0	4	1	3	2	2,703,713
	Danville	1	0	0	0	0	0	1	0	0	33,126
	Decatur	1	0	0	0	0	1	0	0	0	76,351
	Des Plaines	0	0	0	1	0	0	0	1	0	58,540
	East Peoria	1	0	0	0	0	0	0	0	1	23,472
	Elmhurst	1	0	0	0	0	0	0	0	1	44,254
	Joliet	0	0	0	1	0	1	0	0	0	147,877
	Leland	0	0	1	0	0	0	0	0	1	980
	Lyons	0	0	0	1	0	0	1	0	0	10,761
	Marion	2	0	0	0	0	1	1			17,245
	Mattoon	1	0	1	0	0	0	0	1	1	18,611
	Moline	1	0	0	0	0	0	1	0	0	43,614
	Normal	0	1	1	0	0	0	0	0	2	52,655
	Olney	0	0	1	1	0	0	0	2	0	9,142
	Pekin	2	0	0	0	0	0	1	1	0	34,197
	Plainfield	0	1	0	0	0	1	0	0	0	39,700
	Rockford	5	0	1	0	0	1	2	3	0	153,331
	Springfield	6	0	0	0	0	2	1	0	3	116,600
	Urbana	0	0	0	2	0	1	0	0	1	41,374
	Universities and Colleges	0	0	1	1	0					
	University of Illinois,										
	Urbana	0	0	1	0	0	0	0	0	1	43,862
	Western Illinois										
	University	0	0	0	1	0	1				12,585
	Metropolitan Counties	5	1	0	0	1					
	Kane	1	0	0	0	0	0	0	1		
	Kendall	1	0	0	0	0	0	1	0	0	
	Lake	0	1	0	0	0	0	1	0	0	
	Macon	2	0	0	0	0	0	0	2	0	
	Marshall	1	0	0	0	0	0	1	0	0	
	Peoria	0	0	0	0	1	0	1	0	0	
	Nonmetropolitan Counties	0	1	1	0	0					
	Knox	0	0	1	0	0	0	0	1	0	
	La Salle	0	1	0	0	0	1	0	0	0	
Indiana	**Total**	68	8	12	12	0					
	Cities	54	6	11	12	0					
	Bloomington	2	0	3	0	0	1	2	0	2	80,816
	Franklin	5	0	0	1	0	1	2	3	0	23,833
	Hammond	1	0	0	1	0	0	1	1	0	81,243
	Highland	1	1	0	0	0	1	0	0	1	23,848
	Indianapolis	33	3	5	10	0	11	8	21	11	833,024
	Mishawaka	1	0	2	0	0	1	0	0	2	48,498
	Muncie	3	2	1	0	0	0	0	5	1	70,443
	Portage	2	0	0	0	0			1	1	37,016
	Richmond	2	0	0	0	0	1	0		1	37,000

[1] Agencies published in this table indicated that at least one hate crime incident occurred in their respective jurisdictions during the quarter(s) for which they submitted a report to the Hate Crime Statistics Program. Blanks indicate quarters for which agencies did not submit reports.

[2] Population figures are published only for the cities. The figures listed for the universities and colleges are student enrollment and were provided by the United States Department of Education for the 2010 school year, the most recent available. The enrollment figures include full-time and part-time students.

Table VI-13. Hate Crime Incidents Per Bias Motivation and Quarter, by Selected State and Agency, 2011—*Continued*

(Number)

State	Agency type/name	Number of incidents per bias motivation					Number of incidents per quarter[1]				Popu-lation[2]
		Race	Religion	Sexual orient-ation	Ethnicity	Disability	1st quarter	2nd quarter	3rd quarter	4th quarter	
	Rushville	1	0	0	0	0	1				6,373
	Seymour	1	0	0	0	0	0	1	0	0	17,592
	Walkerton	2	0	0	0	0	0	1	0	1	2,155
	Universities and Colleges	11	2	0	0	0					
	Indiana State University	3	0	0	0	0	1	0	1	1	11,494
	Indiana University										
	Indianapolis	1	0	0	0	0	1	0	0	0	30,566
	New Albany	2	0	0	0	0	2	0	0	0	7,178
	Purdue University	5	2	0	0	0	2	2	1	2	41,063
	Metropolitan Counties	3	0	1	0	0					
	Elkhart	3	0	1	0	0	0	0	3	1	
Iowa	**Total**	7	1	6	1	0					
	Cities	4	0	3	1	0					
	Bettendorf	2	0	0	0	0	0	0	1	1	33,391
	Cedar Rapids	0	0	0	1	0	1	0	0	0	126,988
	Davenport	0	0	1	0	0	0	1	0	0	100,207
	Des Moines	1	0	0	0	0	0	0	1	0	204,498
	Grinnell	0	0	1	0	0	0	0	1	0	9,266
	Jefferson	1	0	0	0	0	1	0	0	0	4,368
	Sioux City	0	0	1	0	0	0	0	1	0	83,117
	Universities and Colleges	3	0	1	0	0					
	Iowa State University	1	0	0	0	0	0	0	0	1	28,682
	University of Iowa	2	0	1	0	0	0	2	0	1	29,518
	Metropolitan Counties	0	1	2	0	0					
	Dubuque	0	0	1	0	0	0	1	0	0	
	Johnson	0	1	0	0	0	0	0	1	0	
	Polk	0	0	1	0	0	0	0	1	0	
Kansas	**Total**	37	10	10	10	0					
	Cities	31	8	10	10	0					
	Andover	3	0	0	0	0	1	1	1	0	11,866
	Atchison	1	0	0	0	0	0	0	0	1	11,091
	Bel Aire	1	0	0	0	0	0	0	1	0	6,812
	Chanute	1	0	0	0	0	0	0	0	1	9,177
	Clay Center	0	1	0	0	0	0	0	1	0	4,362
	Derby	1	0	0	0	0	0	0	0	1	22,299
	Ellinwood	0	1	0	0	0	0	0	1	0	2,145
	Emporia	0	0	1	0	0	0	0	1	0	25,074
	Fort Scott	0	1	0	0	0	0	0	1	0	8,138
	Haysville	1	0	0	0	0	0	0	0	1	10,895
	Hutchinson	3	0	0	0	0	0	1	2	0	42,347
	Independence	2	0	0	0	0	2	0	0	0	9,543
	Iola	1	0	0	0	0	0	1	0	0	5,740
	Junction City	0	0	0	1	0	0	1	0	0	23,501
	Lansing	1	0	0	0	0	0	0	1	0	11,337
	Lawrence	1	0	1	1	0	0	1	0	2	88,200
	Leavenworth	0	1	0	0	0	0	0	0	1	35,475
	Leawood	0	0	0	1	0	0	0	1	0	32,069
	Louisburg	1	0	0	0	0	0	0	1	0	4,342
	McPherson	1	0	0	0	0	0	0	1	0	13,239
	Overland Park	3	1	1	1	0	1	3	1	1	174,473
	Pittsburg	1	0	1	0	0	0	0	1	1	20,361
	Pratt	0	0	0	1	0	0	0	1	0	6,878
	Salina	2	0	2	0	0	2	2	0	0	48,010
	Sterling	0	0	1	0	0	0	0	1	0	2,343
	Wichita	7	3	3	5	0	6	3	6	3	384,796
	Universities and Colleges	1	1	0	0	0					
	Washburn University	1	0	0	0	0	0	0	0	1	7,230
	Wichita State University	0	1	0	0	0	1	0	0	0	14,577
	Metropolitan Counties	4	0	0	0	0					
	Jefferson	1	0	0	0	0	0	0	0	1	
	Johnson	1	0	0	0	0	0	0	1	0	
	Sedgwick	1	0	0	0	0	1	0	0	0	
	Shawnee	1	0	0	0	0	1	0	0	0	

[1] Agencies published in this table indicated that at least one hate crime incident occurred in their respective jurisdictions during the quarter(s) for which they submitted a report to the Hate Crime Statistics Program. Blanks indicate quarters for which agencies did not submit reports.

[2] Population figures are published only for the cities. The figures listed for the universities and colleges are student enrollment and were provided by the United States Department of Education for the 2010 school year, the most recent available. The enrollment figures include full-time and part-time students.

Table VI-13.　Hate Crime Incidents Per Bias Motivation and Quarter, by Selected State and Agency, 2011—*Continued*

(Number)

State	Agency type/name	Number of incidents per bias motivation					Number of incidents per quarter[1]				Popu-lation[2]
		Race	Religion	Sexual orient-ation	Ethnicity	Disability	1st quarter	2nd quarter	3rd quarter	4th quarter	
	Nonmetropolitan Counties	1	1	0	0	0					
	Ford	1	0	0	0	0	0	1	0	0	
	Woodson	0	1	0	0	0	0	0	1	0	
Kentucky	**Total**	97	19	24	13	1					
	Cities	64	16	15	10	1					
	Ashland	2	1	0	0	0	1	0	1	1	21,834
	Bardstown	1	0	0	0	0	0	0	1	0	11,781
	Bellevue	0	1	0	0	0	0	1	0	0	5,996
	Berea	2	0	0	0	0	1	0	1	0	13,655
	Bowling Green	3	0	2	1	0	1	3	0	2	58,468
	Campbellsville	1	0	1	0	0	0	0	0	2	9,171
	Covington	3	1	2	1	0	1	3	2	1	40,921
	Cynthiana	3	0	0	0	0	1	0	1	1	6,446
	Dayton	1	0	0	0	0	0	1	0	0	5,375
	Elizabethtown	2	0	1	0	0	1	0	2	0	28,728
	Erlanger	0	2	0	0	0	1	1	0	0	22,034
	Florence	5	3	0	0	0	1	2	3	2	30,158
	Fort Thomas	1	0	0	0	0	0	0	1	0	16,438
	Frankfort	1	0	0	0	0	0	0	1	0	25,703
	Fulton	0	0	1	0	0	1	0	0	0	2,462
	Glasgow	0	1	0	0	0	1	0	0	0	14,125
	Graymoor-Devondale	1	0	0	0	0	0	1	0	0	2,890
	Guthrie	1	0	0	0	0	0	0	1	0	1,429
	Hopkinsville	0	0	2	0	0	0	0	2	0	31,795
	Lawrenceburg	1	0	0	0	0	0	0	0	1	10,578
	Lebanon	1	0	0	0	0	1	0	0	0	5,577
	Lexington	9	0	2	1	0	0	0	3	9	297,847
	Madisonville	2	0	0	0	0	0	1	0	1	19,726
	Morehead	2	0	0	0	0	1	0	0	1	6,892
	Mount Vernon	1	0	0	0	0	0	0	1	0	2,494
	Mount Washington	1	0	0	0	0	1	0	0	0	9,180
	Murray	1	0	2	1	0	2	0	1	1	17,864
	Newport	0	1	0	0	0	1	0	0	0	15,379
	Oak Grove	1	1	0	0	0	1	1	0	0	7,541
	Owensboro	3	1	0	1	0	3	2	0	0	57,661
	Paducah	1	0	0	1	0	0	0	1	1	25,197
	Paris	0	0	1	1	0	1	0	1	0	8,612
	Pikeville	2	0	0	0	0	1	0	1	0	6,951
	Radcliff	1	0	0	0	0	1	0	0	0	21,838
	Richmond	3	1	0	1	0	1	1	2	1	31,581
	Shelbyville	0	0	0	1	1	1	1	0	0	14,142
	Shepherdsville	1	0	0	0	0	0	0	1	0	11,300
	Shively	2	0	0	0	0	2	0	0	0	15,369
	Somerset	1	1	0	0	0	0	1	1	0	11,273
	St. Matthews	0	0	1	0	0	0	0	1	0	17,593
	Taylor Mill	1	0	0	0	0	0	0	1	0	6,650
	Versailles	0	0	0	1	0	0	0	0	1	8,627
	Vine Grove	1	0	0	0	0	1	0	0	0	4,551
	West Liberty	0	1	0	0	0	0	0	0	1	3,459
	Wilder	1	0	0	0	0	0	1	0	0	3,056
	Williamsburg	0	1	0	0	0	1	0	0	0	5,281
	Wilmore	1	0	0	0	0	0	0	1	0	3,711
	Universities and Colleges	6	0	2	0	0					
	Eastern Kentucky University	1	0	0	0	0	0	1	0	0	16,567
	Morehead State University	1	0	0	0	0	0	0	0	1	8,541
	Murray State University	0	0	1	0	0	0	0	1	0	10,412
	University of Kentucky	3	0	0	0	0	2	0	1	0	27,108
	University of Louisville	0	0	1	0	0	1	0	0	0	21,234
	Western Kentucky University	1	0	0	0	0	0	0	1	0	20,897
	Metropolitan Counties	11	1	2	1	0					
	Boone	3	0	0	0	0	2	1	0	0	
	Bourbon	1	0	0	0	0	0	0	0	1	
	Christian	0	0	1	1	0	0	0	1	1	
	Daviess	2	0	0	0	0	2	0	0	0	
	Grant	0	1	0	0	0	0	0	1	0	

[1] Agencies published in this table indicated that at least one hate crime incident occurred in their respective jurisdictions during the quarter(s) for which they submitted a report to the Hate Crime Statistics Program. Blanks indicate quarters for which agencies did not submit reports.

[2] Population figures are published only for the cities. The figures listed for the universities and colleges are student enrollment and were provided by the United States Department of Education for the 2010 school year, the most recent available. The enrollment figures include full-time and part-time students.

Table VI-13. Hate Crime Incidents Per Bias Motivation and Quarter, by Selected State and Agency, 2011—*Continued*

(Number)

State	Agency type/name	Number of incidents per bias motivation					Number of incidents per quarter[1]				Population[2]
		Race	Religion	Sexual orient-ation	Ethnicity	Disability	1st quarter	2nd quarter	3rd quarter	4th quarter	
	Hardin	1	0	0	0	0	0	0	0	1	
	Meade	1	0	0	0	0	0	1	0	0	
	Oldham County Police Department	1	0	1	0	0	1	0	0	1	
	Shelby	1	0	0	0	0	1	0	0	0	
	Woodford	1	0	0	0	0	0	0	0	1	
	Nonmetropolitan Counties	9	0	4	1	0					
	Adair	1	0	0	0	0	0	1	0	0	
	Ballard	1	0	0	0	0	0	0	0	1	
	Caldwell	0	0	1	0	0	0	0	1	0	
	Franklin	1	0	0	0	0	0	0	1	0	
	Harlan	0	0	1	0	0	0	1	0	0	
	Hart	1	0	0	0	0	0	1	0	0	
	Johnson	0	0	1	0	0	1	0	0	0	
	Laurel	1	0	0	0	0	1	0	0	0	
	McCracken	2	0	0	1	0	0	0	2	1	
	Ohio	2	0	0	0	0	0	2	0	0	
	Rowan	0	0	1	0	0	0	0	1	0	
	State Police Agencies	3	2	1	0	0					
	State Police										
	Dry Ridge	0	1	0	0	0	0	0	1	0	
	Frankfort	1	0	0	0	0	0	0	0	1	
	Madisonville	1	0	0	0	0	0	1	0	0	
	Mayfield	1	0	0	0	0	0	1	0	0	
	Morehead	0	1	0	0	0	0	0	0	1	
	Pikeville	0	0	1	0	0	0	0	1	0	
	Other Agencies	4	0	0	1	0					
	Cincinnati-Northern Kentucky International Airport	1	0	0	0	0	1	0	0	0	
	Greater Hardin County Narcotics Task Force	1	0	0	0	0	0	0	0	1	
	Jefferson County Board of Education	1	0	0	0	0	0	1	0	0	
	Laurel County Constable, District 1	1	0	0	0	0			0	1	
	Ohio County School System	0	0	0	1	0	0	1	0	0	
	Park Security	0	0	1	0	0	0	1	0	0	
Louisiana	**Total**	3	0	2	0	0					
	Cities	1	0	2	0	0					
	Gonzales	1	0	0	0	0	0	0	1	0	9,870
	Kenner	0	0	1	0	0	1	0	0	0	67,312
	Sterlington	0	0	1	0	0	1	0	0	0	1,609
	Metropolitan Counties	1	0	0	0	0					
	Lafayette	1	0	0	0	0	1	0	0	0	
	Nonmetropolitan Counties	1	0	0	0	0					
	Iberia	1	0	0	0	0	0	0	1	0	
Maine	**Total**	18	8	26	3	0					
	Cities	15	6	21	3	0					
	Augusta	0	1	1	0	0	0	1	1	0	19,134
	Biddeford	1	0	4	0	0	2	2	1	0	21,274
	Fort Kent	1	0	0	0	0	0	0	0	1	4,096
	Gorham	0	0	2	0	0	0	0	0	2	16,379
	Livermore Falls	1	0	1	0	0	0	0	1	1	3,187
	Mexico	1	0	0	1	0	2	0	0	0	2,681
	Monmouth	0	0	1	0	0	0	0	0	1	4,103
	Ogunquit	0	0	1	0	0	0	0	1	0	892
	Old Orchard Beach	1	0	0	0	0	0	0	0	1	8,623
	Portland[3]	6	3	5	2	0	2	1	8	5	66,185

[1] Agencies published in this table indicated that at least one hate crime incident occurred in their respective jurisdictions during the quarter(s) for which they submitted a report to the Hate Crime Statistics Program. Blanks indicate quarters for which agencies did not submit reports.

[2] Population figures are published only for the cities. The figures listed for the universities and colleges are student enrollment and were provided by the United States Department of Education for the 2010 school year, the most recent available. The enrollment figures include full-time and part-time students.

[3] Includes one incident reported with more than one bias motivation.

Table VI-13. Hate Crime Incidents Per Bias Motivation and Quarter, by Selected State and Agency, 2011—*Continued*

(Number)

State	Agency type/name	Number of incidents per bias motivation					Number of incidents per quarter[1]				Popu-lation[2]
		Race	Religion	Sexual orient-ation	Ethnicity	Disability	1st quarter	2nd quarter	3rd quarter	4th quarter	
	Presque Isle	0	0	1	0	0	0	0	0	1	9,691
	Rumford	0	0	1	0	0	0	0	1	0	5,840
	Saco	0	2	2	0	0	0	2	1	1	18,480
	Sanford	4	0	1	0	0	0	1	4	0	20,795
	South Portland	0	0	1	0	0	0	1	0	0	24,999
	Universities and Colleges	1	1	4	0	0					
	University of Southern Maine	1	1	4	0	0	3	1	1	1	9,654
	Metropolitan Counties	1	1	1	0	0					
	Androscoggin	0	0	1	0	0	0	1	0	0	
	Cumberland	1	0	0	0	0	0	0	0	1	
	York	0	1	0	0	0	0	0	1	0	
	State Police Agencies	1	0	0	0	0					
	State Police, Waldo County	1	0	0	0	0	0	0	1	0	
Maryland	**Total**	24	13	6	6	0					
	Cities	8	1	1	2	0					
	Baltimore	2	0	1	2	0	0	1	2	2	626,848
	Bel Air	2	0	0	0	0	1	0	0	1	10,216
	Bowie	0	1	0	0	0	0	1	0	0	55,246
	Cambridge	1	0	0	0	0	0	1	0	0	12,443
	Crisfield	1	0	0	0	0	1	0	0	0	2,752
	Cumberland	1	0	0	0	0	1	0	0	0	21,057
	Laurel	1	0	0	0	0	1	0	0	0	25,353
	Universities and Colleges	1	0	1	1	0					
	Towson University	1	0	1	1	0	2	0	0	1	21,840
	Metropolitan Counties	13	12	3	3	0					
	Anne Arundel County Police Department	0	0	1	0	0	0	0	1	0	
	Baltimore County Police Department	2	2	2	0	0	1	3	0	2	
	Carroll	0	1	0	0	0	0	1	0	0	
	Cecil	0	0	0	1	0	0	0	1	0	
	Frederick	2	0	0	1	0	2	0	0	1	
	Harford	3	0	0	0	0	1	1	0	1	
	Montgomery County Police Department	5	8	0	1	0	0	6	5	3	
	Prince George's County Police Department	0	1	0	0	0	0	1	0	0	
	Wicomico	1	0	0	0	0	0	1	0	0	
	State Police Agencies	2	0	1	0	0					
	State Police										
	Carroll County	1	0	1	0	0	1	1	0	0	
	Cecil County	1	0	0	0	0	0	1	0	0	
Massachusetts	**Total**	166	75	90	32	4					
	Cities	158	63	88	30	4					
	Acton	1	5	0	0	0	1	1	4	0	22,058
	Amesbury	1	0	0	0	0	0	0	0	1	16,382
	Amherst	0	1	0	0	0	0	0	0	1	38,050
	Andover	0	0	1	0	1	1	1	0	0	33,403
	Ashfield	0	1	0	0	0			1		1,748
	Barnstable	1	0	2	0	0	0	2	0	1	45,468
	Belchertown	0	0	1	0	0	0	0	0	1	14,738
	Belmont	1	2	0	0	1	1	2	1	0	24,880
	Beverly	0	1	1	1	0	0	3	0	0	39,743
	Boston	102	22	63	19	0	40	63	54	49	621,359
	Brewster	0	0	1	0	0	0	1	0	0	9,880
	Brockton	1	0	0	0	0	0	1	0	0	94,380
	Brookline	0	2	1	0	0	0	0	1	2	59,090
	Cambridge	11	2	2	1	1	1	4	8	4	105,803
	Chatham	0	0	1	0	0	0	0	0	1	6,162

[1] Agencies published in this table indicated that at least one hate crime incident occurred in their respective jurisdictions during the quarter(s) for which they submitted a report to the Hate Crime Statistics Program. Blanks indicate quarters for which agencies did not submit reports.
[2] Population figures are published only for the cities. The figures listed for the universities and colleges are student enrollment and were provided by the United States Department of Education for the 2010 school year, the most recent available. The enrollment figures include full-time and part-time students.

Table VI-13. Hate Crime Incidents Per Bias Motivation and Quarter, by Selected State and Agency, 2011—*Continued*

(Number)

State	Agency type/name	Number of incidents per bias motivation					Number of incidents per quarter[1]				Popu-lation[2]
		Race	Religion	Sexual orient-ation	Ethnicity	Disability	1st quarter	2nd quarter	3rd quarter	4th quarter	
	Chelmsford	1	0	0	0	0	0	0	1	0	34,008
	Chelsea	0	0	1	0	0	0	0	0	1	35,391
	Danvers	0	1	0	1	0	0	0	0	2	26,654
	Dartmouth	1	0	0	0	0	0	1	0	0	34,239
	Dennis	2	0	1	0	0	0	1	2	0	14,294
	Douglas	0	1	1	0	0	1	0	1	0	8,523
	East Longmeadow	0	1	1	0	0	0	0	1	1	15,816
	Edgartown	1	0	0	0	0	0	1	0	0	4,092
	Everett	0	1	1	0	0	0	0	1	1	41,921
	Framingham	3	1	0	0	0	0	1	0	3	68,734
	Gardner	0	1	0	0	0	0	0	1	0	20,351
	Great Barrington	0	2	0	1	0	0	1	1	1	7,147
	Greenfield	0	0	1	1	0	1	0	1	0	17,562
	Holbrook	0	0	1	0	0	0	0	0	1	10,857
	Holliston	0	1	0	0	0	1	0	0	0	13,630
	Lakeville	2	0	0	0	0	0	1	1	0	10,667
	Lawrence	1	0	0	0	0	0	1	0	0	76,843
	Leominster	1	0	0	0	0	0	0	1	0	41,007
	Lincoln	1	1	0	0	0	1	1	0	0	6,401
	Lowell	1	0	0	0	0	0	0	1	0	107,167
	Lynn	1	0	0	0	0	0	1	0	0	90,880
	Marlborough	0	0	0	1	0	0	0	1	0	38,734
	Methuen	0	1	0	0	0	0	0	0	1	47,543
	Milford	1	0	0	0	0	0	0	1	0	28,170
	Milton	1	5	0	0	0	0	0	6	0	27,168
	Natick	0	1	0	0	0	0	0	1	0	33,207
	New Bedford	0	0	1	1	0	0	1	1	0	95,649
	Newton	2	0	0	0	0	1	0	0	1	85,665
	North Adams	1	0	0	0	0	0	0	1	0	13,792
	Northampton	1	0	0	0	0	1	0	0	0	28,723
	Norton	2	0	0	0	0	1	1	0	0	19,147
	Norwell	1	0	0	0	0	1	0	0	0	10,570
	Plymouth	4	1	1	0	0	2	2	1	1	56,812
	Provincetown	0	0	1	0	0	0	0	1	0	2,960
	Randolph	1	0	0	0	0	1	0	0	0	32,308
	Revere	2	2	0	2	0	2	2	1	1	52,070
	Rutland	1	1	0	0	0	0	0	0	2	8,022
	Salem	0	2	0	0	0	0	2	0	0	41,592
	Saugus	0	0	1	0	0	0	0	1	0	26,790
	Somerset	1	0	0	0	0	0	1	0	0	18,276
	Somerville	1	0	0	0	0	0	0	0	1	76,216
	Spencer	1	1	0	0	0	1	1	0	0	11,759
	Springfield	1	0	0	0	0	0	1	0	0	153,993
	Stoneham	1	0	0	0	0	0	0	0	1	21,568
	Stoughton	0	0	0	0	1	1	0	0	0	27,126
	Taunton	0	0	0	1	0	0	0	0	1	56,215
	Upton	0	0	1	0	0	0	0	0	1	7,588
	Wayland	0	0	1	0	0	0	0	0	1	13,073
	Westfield	0	0	0	1	0	0	0	0	1	41,344
	Whitman	1	0	0	0	0	0	1	0	0	14,577
	Wilbraham	0	1	0	0	0	0	1	0	0	14,306
	Williamstown	1	0	0	0	0	0	0	0	1	7,801
	Wilmington	1	0	0	0	0	0	0	1	0	22,461
	Worcester	0	2	2	0	0	0	2	1	1	182,145
	Universities and Colleges	8	12	1	2	0					
	Boston University	1	1	0	0	0	0	2	0	0	32,727
	Clark University	0	2	0	0	0	0	1	0	1	3,451
	Hampshire College	1	0	0	0	0	0	0	1	0	1,529
	Harvard University	2	3	0	1	0	0	3	0	3	27,594
	Massachusetts Institute of Technology	1	1	0	0	0	1	0	0	1	10,566
	Northeastern University	1	2	0	1	0	1	0	1	2	29,519
	University of Massachusetts Amherst	0	3	0	0	0	1	1	1	0	27,569
	Dartmouth	0	0	1	0	0	0	1	0	0	9,432
	Harbor Campus, Boston	1	0	0	0	0	1	0	0	0	15,454
	Western New England University	1	0	0	0	0	0	1	0	0	3,734

[1] Agencies published in this table indicated that at least one hate crime incident occurred in their respective jurisdictions during the quarter(s) for which they submitted a report to the Hate Crime Statistics Program. Blanks indicate quarters for which agencies did not submit reports.

[2] Population figures are published only for the cities. The figures listed for the universities and colleges are student enrollment and were provided by the United States Department of Education for the 2010 school year, the most recent available. The enrollment figures include full-time and part-time students.

Table VI-13. Hate Crime Incidents Per Bias Motivation and Quarter, by Selected State and Agency, 2011—*Continued*

(Number)

State	Agency type/name	Number of incidents per bias motivation					Number of incidents per quarter[1]				Population[2]
		Race	Religion	Sexual orient- ation	Ethnicity	Disability	1st quarter	2nd quarter	3rd quarter	4th quarter	
	Other Agencies	0	0	1	0	0					
	Massachusetts Bay Transportation Authority, Suffolk County	0	0	1	0	0	0	0	1	0	
Michigan........................	**Total**	227	44	49	21	5					
	Cities	173	38	36	19	4					
	Adrian	0	0	1	0	0	1	0	0	0	21,117
	Albion	1	0	0	0	0	0	1	0	0	8,610
	Algonac	1	0	0	0	0	0	0	0	1	4,107
	Allen Park	1	0	0	0	0	0	0	1	0	28,189
	Ann Arbor	0	2	2	0	0	2	0	2	0	113,848
	Auburn Hills	2	0	0	0	0	0	1	1	0	21,396
	Battle Creek	4	0	0	0	0	0	0	4	0	61,658
	Bay City	0	1	0	0	0	0	0	0	1	34,906
	Birmingham	2	0	0	0	1	0	2	1	0	20,088
	Bloomfield Township	1	2	0	0	0	0	2	0	1	41,039
	Boyne City	1	1	0	0	0	0	0	1	1	3,732
	Buena Vista Township	2	0	0	0	0	1	1	0	0	8,669
	Cadillac	1	0	0	0	0	1	0	0	0	10,347
	Canton Township	2	1	1	0	0	0	0	3	1	90,105
	Caro	2	0	0	0	0	0	1	1	0	4,226
	Chelsea	0	0	1	0	0	0	0	1	0	4,940
	Chesterfield Township	2	0	0	0	0	1	0	1	0	43,348
	Clawson	1	0	0	0	0	0	0	0	1	11,816
	Clinton Township	4	0	0	0	0	1	0	1	2	96,723
	Coldwater	0	0	1	0	0	0	1	0	0	10,937
	Davison Township	1	0	0	0	0	0	0	0	1	19,560
	Dearborn	4	5	1	0	0	2	2	6	0	98,079
	Dearborn Heights	0	0	1	1	0	0	0	1	1	57,730
	Detroit	1	1	5	0	0	0	0	3	4	713,239
	East Lansing	0	0	1	0	0	0	0	1	0	48,542
	Eastpointe	2	0	1	0	0	0	0	0	3	32,418
	Emmett Township	2	0	0	0	0	1	1	0	0	11,761
	Farmington	1	1	0	0	0	1	0	1	0	10,364
	Farmington Hills	1	2	0	2	0	0	2	1	2	79,680
	Flint	1	1	0	0	0	0	1	0	1	102,357
	Flint Township	5	0	0	0	0	2	2	0	1	31,905
	Flushing Township	0	0	0	1	0	0	1	0	0	10,632
	Forsyth Township	0	0	1	0	0	1	0	0	0	6,159
	Fraser	1	0	0	0	0	0	0	0	1	14,469
	Gibraltar	1	0	0	0	0	0	1	0	0	4,652
	Grand Blanc Township	3	1	0	1	0	0	0	3	2	37,480
	Grand Haven	1	0	0	0	0	0	1	0	0	10,404
	Grand Rapids	5	0	0	1	0	2	0	3	1	187,898
	Grayling	0	0	1	0	0	1	0	0	0	1,883
	Grosse Pointe Farms	1	0	0	0	0	0	0	0	1	9,472
	Grosse Pointe Park	2	0	0	0	0	1	0	1	0	11,546
	Grosse Pointe Woods	1	0	0	0	0	0	0	0	1	16,123
	Hamburg Township	1	0	0	0	0	1	0	0	0	21,149
	Hamtramck	6	0	1	1	0	0	2	3	3	22,406
	Hancock	0	0	1	0	0	0	1	0	0	4,631
	Harper Woods	1	1	0	0	0	1	0	0	1	14,225
	Holland	3	0	0	0	0	1	0	1	1	33,026
	Holly	1	0	0	0	0	0	0	1	0	6,081
	Inkster	3	0	1	0	0	0	0	1	3	25,350
	Ironwood	0	0	1	1	0	0	1	1	0	5,383
	Jackson	3	0	0	1	0	1	2	1	0	33,509
	Kalamazoo Township	1	0	0	0	0	0	1	0	0	21,901
	Keego Harbor	1	1	0	0	0	0	0	2	0	2,968
	Kentwood	0	0	0	1	0	0	1	0	0	48,670
	Lawton	0	0	0	1	0	0	0	1	0	1,899
	Lincoln Township	0	0	0	0	1	0	0	1	0	14,680
	Livonia	7	1	1	0	0	1	1	2	5	96,869
	Mackinac Island	1	0	0	0	0	0	0	1	0	492
	Madison Heights	1	0	0	0	0	0	0	0	1	29,672
	Manton	1	0	0	0	0	0	0	1	0	1,286
	Marshall	1	0	0	0	0	1	0	0	0	7,083
	Mason	0	0	1	0	0	1	0	0	0	8,246
	Melvindale	0	1	0	0	0	0	1	0	0	10,707

[1] Agencies published in this table indicated that at least one hate crime incident occurred in their respective jurisdictions during the quarter(s) for which they submitted a report to the Hate Crime Statistics Program. Blanks indicate quarters for which agencies did not submit reports.

[2] Population figures are published only for the cities. The figures listed for the universities and colleges are student enrollment and were provided by the United States Department of Education for the 2010 school year, the most recent available. The enrollment figures include full-time and part-time students.

Table VI-13. Hate Crime Incidents Per Bias Motivation and Quarter, by Selected State and Agency, 2011—*Continued*

(Number)

State	Agency type/name	Number of incidents per bias motivation					Number of incidents per quarter[1]				Population[2]
		Race	Religion	Sexual orient-ation	Ethnicity	Disability	1st quarter	2nd quarter	3rd quarter	4th quarter	
	Meridian Township	5	1	1	0	0	0	0	3	4	39,658
	Midland	2	0	0	0	0	0	0	1	1	41,831
	Milford	1	0	0	0	0	0	0	0	1	15,724
	Monroe	1	1	0	0	0	0	0	1	1	20,717
	New Baltimore	3	1	1	1	0	2	3	1	0	12,075
	Northville Township	1	0	0	0	0	0	0	0	1	28,476
	Norton Shores	2	0	0	0	0	0	0	2	0	23,976
	Oak Park	0	3	0	0	0	0	0	0	3	29,297
	Orchard Lake	1	0	0	0	0	0	0	1	0	2,373
	Owosso	0	0	1	0	0	0	0	0	1	15,183
	Paw Paw	2	0	0	0	0	1	1	0	0	3,531
	Pinckney	1	0	2	0	0	0	2	1	0	2,425
	Pittsfield Township	2	2	1	0	1	0	2	2	2	34,637
	Plymouth Township	1	0	1	0	0	0	1	0	1	27,503
	Redford Township	1	0	0	0	0	0	0	1	0	48,326
	Reed City	1	0	0	0	0	0	1	0	0	2,423
	Rochester	1	0	0	0	0	0	0	1	0	12,701
	Romeo	0	0	0	1	0	0	1	0	0	3,593
	Roseville	9	0	2	0	0	0	0	6	5	47,263
	Saginaw	2	0	0	1	0	0	0	0	3	51,469
	Saginaw Township	2	0	0	0	0	1	1	0	0	40,809
	Saline	1	0	0	0	0	0	0	0	1	8,803
	Sault Ste. Marie	1	0	0	1	0	2	0			14,133
	Shelby Township	1	1	0	0	0	0	0	2	0	73,748
	Southfield	4	0	0	0	0	1	1	0	2	71,685
	South Lyon	0	1	1	0	0	0	1	0	1	11,318
	St. Clair Shores	1	0	0	0	0	0	0	1	0	59,670
	Sterling Heights	2	0	0	0	1	0	0	1	2	129,601
	St. Joseph	1	0	0	1	0	0	1	1	0	8,359
	Taylor	4	0	0	0	0	0	1	1	2	63,083
	Tecumseh	2	0	0	0	0	0	1	1	0	8,515
	Trenton	0	1	0	0	0	0	0	1	0	18,839
	Troy	3	0	2	0	0	0	0	2	3	80,919
	Union City	0	0	0	1	0	1	0	0	0	1,598
	Utica	1	0	0	0	0	0	0	1	0	4,753
	Van Buren Township	1	0	0	0	0	0	0	0	1	28,799
	Warren	3	1	1	1	0	2	2	0	2	133,955
	Waterford Township	2	0	0	0	0	1	0	0	1	71,653
	West Bloomfield Township	6	2	0	0	0	1	2	2	3	64,641
	Westland	1	0	0	0	0	0	0	0	1	84,031
	White Cloud	2	0	0	0	0	1	0	1	0	1,407
	Wixom	1	1	0	0	0	0	1	0	1	13,488
	Wolverine Lake	0	1	0	0	0	0	1	0	0	4,309
	Wyoming	4	0	0	1	0	2	2	1	0	72,071
	Ypsilanti	3	0	0	0	0	0	0	0	3	19,420
	Universities and Colleges	8	1	3	0	0					
	Eastern Michigan University	0	0	1	0	0	0	0	1	0	23,565
	Grand Rapids Community College	2	0	0	0	0	1	0	1	0	17,870
	Michigan State University	3	0	0	0	0	0	0	0	3	46,985
	Oakland Community College	0	0	1	0	0	0	1	0	0	28,925
	University of Michigan										
	Ann Arbor	1	1	1	0	0	0	1	1	1	41,924
	Flint	1	0	0	0	0	0	1	0	0	8,138
	Western Michigan University	1	0	0	0	0	0	1	0	0	25,045
	Metropolitan Counties	39	5	8	2	1					
	Calhoun	1	0	0	0	0	1	0	0	0	
	Eaton	0	0	1	0	0	0	0	1	0	
	Jackson	3	0	0	0	0	1	1	0	1	
	Kent	3	0	0	0	0	0	1	1	1	
	Macomb	2	0	0	0	0	0	0	1	1	
	Monroe	2	0	1	0	0	2	0	0	1	
	Muskegon	0	1	0	0	0	0	1	0	0	
	Oakland	22	3	4	2	1	2	5	6	19	
	Ottawa	1	0	0	0	0	0	1	0	0	

[1] Agencies published in this table indicated that at least one hate crime incident occurred in their respective jurisdictions during the quarter(s) for which they submitted a report to the Hate Crime Statistics Program. Blanks indicate quarters for which agencies did not submit reports.

[2] Population figures are published only for the cities. The figures listed for the universities and colleges are student enrollment and were provided by the United States Department of Education for the 2010 school year, the most recent available. The enrollment figures include full-time and part-time students.

Table VI-13. Hate Crime Incidents Per Bias Motivation and Quarter, by Selected State and Agency, 2011—*Continued*

(Number)

State	Agency type/name	Number of incidents per bias motivation					Number of incidents per quarter[1]				Popu-lation[2]
		Race	Religion	Sexual orient-ation	Ethnicity	Disability	1st quarter	2nd quarter	3rd quarter	4th quarter	
	St. Clair	0	0	1	0	0	0	0	0	1	
	Van Buren	3	0	0	0	0	0	0	0	3	
	Washtenaw	2	1	0	0	0	0	2	1	0	
	Wayne	0	0	1	0	0	0	0	1	0	
	Nonmetropolitan Counties	5	0	1	0	0					
	Grand Traverse	1	0	0	0	0	0	1	0	0	
	Montcalm	0	0	1	0	0	0	0	0	1	
	Ogemaw	1	0	0	0	0	0	0	0	1	
	Ontonagon	1	0	0	0	0	0	1	0	0	
	Presque Isle	1	0	0	0	0	0	0	0	1	
	Tuscola	1	0	0	0	0	0	0	0	1	
	State Police Agencies	1	0	1	0	0					
	State Police										
	Saginaw County	1	0	0	0	0	1	0	0	0	
	Van Buren County	0	0	1	0	0	1	0	0	0	
	Other Agencies	1	0	0	0	0					
	Huron-Clinton Metropolitan Authority,										
	Stony Creek Metropark	1	0	0	0	0	0	0	1	0	
Minnesota	**Total**	72	23	34	18	1					
	Cities	69	21	32	18	1					
	Albert Lea	0	0	0	1	0	0		1		18,155
	Bemidji	1	1	0	0	0	0	1		1	13,535
	Benson	1	0	0	0	0	0	1			3,265
	Blaine	4	0	0	1	0			2	3	57,627
	Brainerd	1	0	0	0	0	1				13,695
	Brooklyn Center	0	0	0	1	0			1		30,336
	Brooklyn Park	3	0	1	0	0	1	2	1		76,366
	Coon Rapids	2	0	1	0	0	0	1	2		61,950
	Cottage Grove	0	0	1	0	0			1		34,856
	Crystal	5	0	0	0	1	2	4			22,322
	Eden Prairie	1	0	0	1	0	1			1	61,266
	Edina	1	0	0	0	0	0		1		48,311
	Elk River	1	0	0	0	0	0			1	23,151
	Fairmont	1	0	0	0	0	1				10,748
	Fridley	1	0	0	0	0	1				27,418
	Lakeville	3	0	0	0	0	0		2	1	56,386
	Mankato	0	0	0	1	0	0			1	39,612
	Maple Grove	1	0	0	1	0	1		1		62,042
	Maplewood	1	0	0	0	0	0	1			38,311
	Mendota Heights	0	0	0	1	0	0			1	11,156
	Minneapolis	11	8	19	5	0	10	13	11	9	385,531
	Montevideo	1	0	0	0	0				1	5,425
	Moorhead	1	0	0	0	0	1				38,359
	New Brighton	3	0	0	0	0	0	2	1		21,622
	New Hope	0	0	1	0	0			1		20,496
	North St. Paul	1	0	0	0	0	1				11,548
	Plymouth	2	5	0	1	0	4	1	3		71,121
	Princeton	1	0	0	0	0				1	4,734
	Red Wing	0	0	1	0	0	0	1			16,586
	Richfield	2	0	0	1	0	0			3	35,500
	Robbinsdale	0	0	1	0	0	0	1			14,061
	Rochester	7	1	2	1	0	1	5	1	4	107,593
	Savage	1	0	0	0	0	1				27,119
	South St. Paul	0	0	2	1	0	1		2		20,316
	St. Cloud	1	0	0	0	0				1	66,350
	St. Louis Park	2	3	2	1	0	2	2	3	1	45,599
	St. Paul	7	3	1	1	0	5	5		2	287,665
	Worthington	2	0	0	0	0	1		1		12,863
	Metropolitan Counties	2	0	2	0	0					
	Carlton	0	0	1	0	0	1				
	Olmsted	0	0	1	0	0	0			1	
	Washington	1	0	0	0	0		1			
	Wright	1	0	0	0	0	0		1		

[1] Agencies published in this table indicated that at least one hate crime incident occurred in their respective jurisdictions during the quarter(s) for which they submitted a report to the Hate Crime Statistics Program. Blanks indicate quarters for which agencies did not submit reports.

[2] Population figures are published only for the cities. The figures listed for the universities and colleges are student enrollment and were provided by the United States Department of Education for the 2010 school year, the most recent available. The enrollment figures include full-time and part-time students.

Table VI-13. Hate Crime Incidents Per Bias Motivation and Quarter, by Selected State and Agency, 2011—*Continued*

(Number)

State	Agency type/name	Number of incidents per bias motivation					Number of incidents per quarter[1]				Popu-lation[2]
		Race	Religion	Sexual orient-ation	Ethnicity	Disability	1st quarter	2nd quarter	3rd quarter	4th quarter	
	Nonmetropolitan Counties	1	2	0	0	0					
	McLeod	1	0	0	0	0			1		
	Mille Lacs	0	2	0	0	0				2	
Mississippi......................	**Total**	0	0	1	0	0					
	Cities	0	0	1	0	0					
	Gulfport	0	0	1	0	0	0	0	1	0	68,049
Missouri.........................	**Total**	73	8	30	6	0					
	Cities	64	7	27	6	0					
	Branson	0	0	1	0	0	0	1	0	0	10,558
	Breckenridge Hills	0	0	1	0	0	0	0	0	1	4,763
	Columbia	2	1	2	1	0	3	2		1	108,894
	Concordia	1	0	0	0	0	0	1	0	0	2,459
	Des Peres	0	0	0	1	0	1	0	0	0	8,403
	Excelsior Springs	1	0	0	0	0	0	1	0	0	11,124
	Gladstone	2	0	0	0	0	0	0	1	1	25,502
	Gower	0	0	1	0	0	0	0	1	0	1,532
	Grandview	1	0	0	0	0	0	0	1	0	24,564
	Independence	6	0	2	0	0	0	1	6	1	117,255
	Joplin	2	0	0	0	0	0	0	2	0	50,332
	Kansas City	28	3	12	4	0	8	15	11	13	461,458
	Kirksville	0	1	0	0	0		0	1		17,569
	Lee's Summit	5	0	0	0	0	2	0	1	2	91,696
	O'Fallon	1	0	0	0	0	0	0	1	0	79,617
	Ozark	1	1	0	0	0	0	1	1	0	17,885
	Poplar Bluff	1	0	0	0	0	1	0	0	0	17,085
	Raytown	2	0	2	0	0	1	2	0	1	29,633
	Rich Hill	1	0	0	0	0	0	1	0	0	1,401
	Richmond	2	0	0	0	0	0	2	0	0	5,818
	Rolla	0	0	1	0	0	0	1	0	0	19,630
	Springfield	1	0	0	0	0	1	0	0	0	160,078
	St. Joseph	1	0	0	0	0	0	0	0	1	77,059
	St. Louis	2	0	5	0	0	1	4	1	1	320,454
	St. Peters	0	1	0	0	0	0	0	0	1	52,766
	Tracy	1	0	0	0	0	0	1	0	0	209
	Warrensburg	1	0	0	0	0	0	1	0	0	18,906
	Waynesville	1	0	0	0	0	0	1	0	0	4,848
	Woodson Terrace	1	0	0	0	0	1	0	0	0	4,078
	Universities and Colleges	1	0	3	0	0					
	Lincoln University	0	0	2	0	0	0	0	0	2	3,349
	University of Missouri										
	Columbia	1	0	0	0	0		0	0	1	32,341
	Kansas City	0	0	1	0	0	0	0	1	0	15,259
	Metropolitan Counties	8	1	0	0	0					
	St. Charles	2	0	0	0	0	0	0	2	0	
	St. Louis County										
	Police Department	6	1	0	0	0	1	1	4	1	
Montana.........................	**Total**	13	4	1	4	1					
	Cities	9	3	1	4	0					
	Billings	7	2	1	2	0	3	3	4	2	105,095
	Kalispell	0	0	0	1	0	0	1	0	0	20,104
	Missoula	2	1	0	0	0	0	0	3	0	67,381
	Polson	0	0	0	1	0	0	0	0	1	4,528
	Universities and Colleges	0	1	0	0	0					
	Montana State University	0	1	0	0	0	0	0	0	1	13,081
	Metropolitan Counties	2	0	0	0	0					
	Missoula	1	0	0	0	0	0	0	1	0	
	Yellowstone	1	0	0	0	0	0	1	0	0	
	Nonmetropolitan Counties	2	0	0	0	1					
	Gallatin	0	0	0	0	1	0	0	1	0	
	Ravalli	2	0	0	0	0	1	0	1	0	

[1] Agencies published in this table indicated that at least one hate crime incident occurred in their respective jurisdictions during the quarter(s) for which they submitted a report to the Hate Crime Statistics Program. Blanks indicate quarters for which agencies did not submit reports.

[2] Population figures are published only for the cities. The figures listed for the universities and colleges are student enrollment and were provided by the United States Department of Education for the 2010 school year, the most recent available. The enrollment figures include full-time and part-time students.

Table VI-13. Hate Crime Incidents Per Bias Motivation and Quarter, by Selected State and Agency, 2011—*Continued*

(Number)

State	Agency type/name	Number of incidents per bias motivation					Number of incidents per quarter[1]				Popu-lation[2]
		Race	Religion	Sexual orient-ation	Ethnicity	Disability	1st quarter	2nd quarter	3rd quarter	4th quarter	
Nebraska	**Total**	24	2	5	5	0					
	Cities	23	2	5	5	0					
	Crete	0	0	1	0	0	0	0	0	1	7,022
	Grand Island	1	0	0	0	0	0	0	0	1	48,953
	Kearney	1	0	0	0	0	0	0	0	1	31,062
	Lincoln	14	1	4	4	0	7	6	8	2	260,685
	Omaha	6	1	0	1	0	3	1	2	2	412,608
	Papillion	1	0	0	0	0	0	0	1	0	19,063
	Nonmetropolitan Counties	1	0	0	0	0					
	Sherman	1	0	0	0	0	0	0	1	0	
Nevada...........................	**Total Cities**	32	8	11	6	0					
	Henderson	2	0	1	0	0	0	3	0	0	259,902
	Las Vegas Metropolitan Police Department	28	8	10	6	0	8	15	15	14	1,458,474
	West Wendover	2	0	0	0	0	2	0	0	0	4,447
	Universities and Colleges	0	1	0	0	0					
	University of Nevada, Las Vegas	0	1	0	0	0	0	0	0	1	28,203
	Nonmetropolitan Counties	0	0	0	0	1					
	Nye	0	0	0	0	1	1	0	0	0	
New Hampshire.............	**Total**	12	4	4	2	0					
	Cities	12	4	4	2	0					
	Bedford	0	2	0	0	0	1	0	1		21,231
	Candia	1	0	0	0	0	0	0	1	0	3,914
	Concord	1	0	1	1	0	0	1	1	1	42,751
	Derry	1	0	0	0	0	1	0	0	0	33,152
	Hudson	1	0	0	0	0	1	0	0	0	24,499
	Londonderry	1	0	0	0	0	1	0	0	0	24,161
	Manchester	1	0	0	0	0	0	0	1	0	109,708
	Merrimack	1	1	1	0	0	0	3	0	0	25,527
	Milford	1	0	0	0	0	0	0	1	0	15,135
	Northumberland	0	0	1	0	0	0	0	0	1	2,291
	Portsmouth	3	0	0	0	0	2	1	0	0	21,261
	Raymond	0	1	0	0	0	0	1	0	0	10,151
	Rye	0	0	0	1	0	0	0	1	0	5,305
	Winchester	1	0	1	0	0	0	1	1	0	4,347
New Jersey....................	**Total**	222	166	61	52	7					
	Cities	218	163	61	52	7					
	Aberdeen Township	6	1	4	0	0	3	4	1	3	18,271
	Alpine	1	0	0	0	0	0	0	0	1	1,855
	Asbury Park	1	0	0	1	0	0	1	0	1	16,170
	Atlantic City	4	1	0	0	0	5	0	0	0	39,690
	Audubon	1	0	0	0	0	0	0	0	1	8,848
	Bayonne	1	0	0	0	0	0	1	0	0	63,234
	Belleville	0	1	1	1	0		0	1	2	36,046
	Berkeley Township	2	0	0	0	0	0	1	1	0	41,392
	Boonton Township	0	0	0	1	0	0	1	0	0	4,277
	Branchburg Township	0	0	0	1	0	1	0	0	0	14,507
	Brick Township	2	0	0	0	0	0	0	1	1	75,322
	Brielle	0	1	1	0	0	0	1	1	0	4,790
	Buena	0	0	1	1	0	0	0	0	2	4,618
	Burlington	1	0	0	0	0	0	0	1	0	9,953
	Butler	0	0	0	1	0	0	0	0	1	7,564
	Byram Township	1	0	0	0	0	0	0	1	0	8,378
	Camden	0	0	1	0	0	1	0	0	0	77,604
	Cherry Hill Township	1	1	0	0	0	0	0	1	1	71,281
	Chesterfield Township	0	0	0	1	0	0	0	1	0	7,725
	Clark Township	1	0	0	0	0	0	0	0	1	14,805
	Clementon	1	0	0	0	0	0	1	0	0	5,017

[1] Agencies published in this table indicated that at least one hate crime incident occurred in their respective jurisdictions during the quarter(s) for which they submitted a report to the Hate Crime Statistics Program. Blanks indicate quarters for which agencies did not submit reports.

[2] Population figures are published only for the cities. The figures listed for the universities and colleges are student enrollment and were provided by the United States Department of Education for the 2010 school year, the most recent available. The enrollment figures include full-time and part-time students.

Table VI-13. Hate Crime Incidents Per Bias Motivation and Quarter, by Selected State and Agency, 2011—*Continued*

(Number)

State	Agency type/name	Number of incidents per bias motivation					Number of incidents per quarter[1]				Popu-lation[2]
		Race	Religion	Sexual orient-ation	Ethnicity	Disability	1st quarter	2nd quarter	3rd quarter	4th quarter	
	Cliffside Park	1	0	0	0	0	0	1	0	0	23,673
	Clinton Township	0	1	0	0	0	0	0	0	1	13,523
	Colts Neck Township	2	0	0	0	0	0	0	2	0	10,176
	Cranbury Township	0	1	0	0	0	1	0	0	0	3,870
	Cranford Township	0	1	0	0	0	1	0	0	0	22,700
	Deal	1	0	0	0	0	0	1	0	0	752
	Delran Township	0	0	1	0	0	0	0	1	0	16,952
	Denville Township	1	0	0	0	0	0	1	0	0	16,690
	East Brunswick Township	1	5	0	1	0	1	3	1	2	47,670
	Eatontown	0	0	0	1	0	0	1	0	0	12,751
	Edison Township	2	2	2	0	0	2	0	1	3	100,300
	Egg Harbor Township	1	3	0	0	0	2	0	1	1	43,467
	Elizabeth	1	1	0	0	0	2	0	0	0	125,386
	Evesham Township	2	3	2	0	0	2	3	1	1	45,690
	Ewing Township	3	0	0	0	0	1	0	0	2	35,909
	Fair Lawn	2	2	1	0	0	0	2	1	2	32,565
	Fort Lee	1	3	1	0	0	0	1	2	2	35,463
	Franklin Lakes	0	0	0	1	0	0	1	0	0	10,625
	Freehold	2	1	0	3	0	1	2	1	2	12,092
	Freehold Township	1	4	0	1	0	0	0	0	6	36,304
	Galloway Township	2	2	1	1	0	2	2	1	1	37,473
	Glassboro	5	1	0	0	0	1	0	1	4	18,641
	Gloucester Township	1	2	1	3	0	2	2	1	2	64,849
	Green Brook Township	2	0	0	0	0	0	1	1	0	7,227
	Greenwich Township, Warren County	1	0	0	0	0	1	0	0	0	5,731
	Hackensack	0	1	0	0	0	0	0	0	1	43,157
	Haddon Township	0	0	0	1	0	0	1	0	0	14,756
	Hamilton Township, Atlantic County	0	1	0	0	0	0	0	0	1	26,591
	Hammonton	1	0	0	0	0	0	0	1	0	14,840
	Hanover Township	1	0	0	0	0	0	0	0	1	13,758
	Harding Township	0	2	0	0	0	0	2	0	0	3,851
	Highland Park	1	5	1	2	0	0	0	0	9	14,029
	Hillsborough Township	1	0	0	0	0	1	0	0	0	38,430
	Hoboken	2	0	3	1	0	3	2	0	1	50,171
	Holmdel Township	2	1	0	0	0	1	2	0	0	16,829
	Howell Township	8	6	1	1	0	2	2	5	7	51,245
	Jackson Township	0	1	1	0	0	1	0	1	0	55,039
	Jersey City	4	2	2	3	0	3	5	3		248,423
	Keansburg	12	1	3	0	0	3	8	3	2	10,139
	Kearny	0	0	1	0	0	0	1	0	0	40,819
	Lacey Township	1	0	0	0	0	0	1	0	0	27,736
	Lakehurst	3	0	0	0	0	0	3	0	0	2,663
	Lakewood Township	3	18	1	3	0	2	6	7	10	93,152
	Lambertville	0	0	0	1	0	1	0	0	0	3,919
	Little Egg Harbor Township	2	0	0	0	0	1	0	1	0	20,132
	Little Falls Township	0	0	0	0	1	0	0	0	1	14,480
	Little Ferry	2	0	1	0	0	2	1	0	0	10,661
	Lodi	3	1	3	0	0	2	2	2	1	24,216
	Long Branch	0	1	0	0	0	0	1	0	0	30,821
	Lower Township	1	0	0	1	0	1	0	0	1	22,942
	Lumberton Township	1	0	0	0	0	0	0	1	0	12,601
	Manalapan Township	0	3	0	0	0	0	1	1	1	39,001
	Manasquan	1	0	0	1	0	0	0	1	1	5,917
	Manchester Township	1	0	0	0	0	0	0	0	1	43,213
	Mansfield Township, Warren County	3	3	0	1	0	1	0	1	5	7,751
	Maplewood Township	0	1	0	0	0	0	0	1	0	23,946
	Margate City	1	1	0	0	0	0	0	2	0	6,375
	Marlboro Township	4	6	0	1	0	5	3	2	1	40,325
	Matawan	0	1	1	0	0	0	2	0	0	8,839
	Maywood	0	1	0	0	0	0	0	0	1	9,587
	Medford Township	2	1	2	1	0	3	2	0	1	23,110
	Mendham Township	0	1	0	0	0	1	0	0	0	5,889
	Merchantville	1	0	0	0	0	1	0	0	0	3,834
	Metuchen	0	1	0	0	0	0	0	0	1	13,619
	Middlesex	0	1	0	0	0	0	1	0	0	13,680
	Middle Township	1	0	0	0	0	1	0	0	0	18,974
	Middletown Township	2	1	0	0	0	0	1	0	2	66,743

[1] Agencies published in this table indicated that at least one hate crime incident occurred in their respective jurisdictions during the quarter(s) for which they submitted a report to the Hate Crime Statistics Program. Blanks indicate quarters for which agencies did not submit reports.

[2] Population figures are published only for the cities. The figures listed for the universities and colleges are student enrollment and were provided by the United States Department of Education for the 2010 school year, the most recent available. The enrollment figures include full-time and part-time students.

Table VI-13. Hate Crime Incidents Per Bias Motivation and Quarter, by Selected State and Agency, 2011—*Continued*

(Number)

State	Agency type/name	Number of incidents per bias motivation					Number of incidents per quarter[1]				Popu-lation[2]
		Race	Religion	Sexual orient-ation	Ethnicity	Disability	1st quarter	2nd quarter	3rd quarter	4th quarter	
	Monroe Township, Middlesex County	7	5	0	0	0	0	0	2	10	39,262
	Montclair	5	2	3	0	0	0	0	6	4	37,794
	Montgomery Township	3	6	0	1	0	7	0	0	3	22,328
	Montville Township	0	4	1	0	0	2	0	0	3	21,600
	Moorestown Township	3	2	0	0	0	1	1	0	3	20,795
	Mount Laurel Township	2	1	0	0	0	1	1	1	0	42,003
	Mount Olive Township	1	0	0	0	0	0	0	1	0	28,211
	Mullica Township	1	0	0	0	0	1	0	0	0	6,167
	Neptune Township	13	2	4	1	0	4	5	5	6	28,028
	Newark	0	2	0	0	0	0	1	1	278,064
	New Brunswick	2	3	0	1	0	1	2	1	2	55,365
	New Providence	0	1	0	0	1	2	0	0	0	12,212
	North Arlington	1	0	0	1	0	0	1	1	0	15,443
	North Bergen Township	0	1	0	0	0	0	0	1	0	60,975
	North Brunswick Township	2	0	0	0	0	1	0	1	0	40,878
	North Hanover Township	0	1	0	0	0	1	0	0	0	7,704
	North Plainfield	0	1	1	0	0	0	0	1	1	22,009
	North Wildwood	0	0	1	0	0	0	0	1	0	4,054
	Nutley Township	1	0	0	0	0	0	0	1	0	28,464
	Oaklyn	1	0	0	0	0	1	0	0	0	4,051
	Ocean Township, Ocean County	0	0	0	1	0	0	0	0	1	8,360
	Old Bridge Township	1	1	1	1	0	0	1	1	2	65,593
	Palmyra	2	0	1	0	0	1	1	0	1	7,423
	Passaic	1	2	0	0	1	1	2	1	0	70,013
	Paterson	0	1	0	0	0	1	0	0	0	146,685
	Paulsboro	2	0	1	0	3	0	3	3	0	6,117
	Pemberton Township	3	0	0	0	0	0	3	0	0	28,005
	Pennsauken Township	0	0	1	0	0	0	1	0	0	36,004
	Phillipsburg	1	0	0	0	0	0	1	0	0	15,000
	Piscataway Township	1	2	1	1	0	1	1	0	3	56,231
	Plainsboro Township	0	2	1	1	0	1	3	0	0	23,076
	Point Pleasant	1	0	0	0	0	0	1	0	0	18,453
	Point Pleasant Beach	2	0	0	0	0	0	0	1	1	4,681
	Pompton Lakes	0	1	0	0	0	0	1	0	0	11,134
	Princeton	0	1	0	0	0	0	0	1	0	12,348
	Ramsey	0	1	0	0	0	0	0	0	1	14,521
	Randolph Township	0	0	0	1	0	0	0	1	0	25,820
	Ridgefield Park	0	0	0	0	1	0	1	0	0	12,771
	Riverdale	1	0	0	0	0	0	0	1	0	3,571
	River Edge	0	0	0	1	0	1	0	0	0	11,378
	Riverside Township	2	1	0	0	0	2	1	0	0	8,106
	Robbinsville Township	0	0	1	0	0	0	1	0	0	13,687
	Runnemede	2	0	0	0	0	1	0	0	1	8,496
	Saddle River	0	1	0	0	0	0	0	0	1	3,162
	Sea Isle City	0	0	1	0	0	0	0	1	0	2,121
	Secaucus	1	0	0	0	0	0	1	0	0	16,318
	Somers Point	1	0	0	0	0	0	0	1	0	10,831
	Somerville	0	2	0	0	0	0	2	0	0	12,138
	South Brunswick Township	3	2	0	2	0	4	1	1	1	43,561
	South Plainfield	1	1	0	0	0	0	1	0	1	23,463
	Spotswood	3	2	2	0	0	2	1	1	3	8,284
	Stafford Township	1	1	0	0	0	0	2	0	0	26,623
	Teaneck Township	2	6	1	0	0	0	5	3	1	39,908
	Tinton Falls	3	0	0	0	0	1	0	1	1	17,952
	Union City	1	2	1	0	0	0	1	2	1	66,676
	Vineland	0	1	0	0	0	0	1	0	0	60,926
	Washington	0	0	0	1	0	0	1	0	0	6,483
	Washington Township, Gloucester County	0	0	0	1	0	0	1	0	0	48,720
	Washington Township, Warren County	1	0	0	0	0	0	1	0	0	6,673
	Waterford Township	1	0	0	0	0	0	1	0	0	10,684
	Wayne Township	1	0	0	1	0	2	0	0	0	54,899
	West Deptford Township	6	0	1	0	0	1	1	1	4	21,749
	West Long Branch	2	0	1	0	0	1	0	1	1	8,124
	West Orange	0	1	0	0	0	1	0	0	0	46,361
	West Windsor Township	1	0	0	0	0	0	0	1	0	27,255
	Wildwood	1	0	0	0	0	0	0	1	0	5,343
	Winslow Township	3	0	0	1	0	2	1	0	1	39,630

[1] Agencies published in this table indicated that at least one hate crime incident occurred in their respective jurisdictions during the quarter(s) for which they submitted a report to the Hate Crime Statistics Program. Blanks indicate quarters for which agencies did not submit reports.

[2] Population figures are published only for the cities. The figures listed for the universities and colleges are student enrollment and were provided by the United States Department of Education for the 2010 school year, the most recent available. The enrollment figures include full-time and part-time students.

Table VI-13. Hate Crime Incidents Per Bias Motivation and Quarter, by Selected State and Agency, 2011—*Continued*

(Number)

State	Agency type/name	Number of incidents per bias motivation					Number of incidents per quarter[1]				Popu-lation[2]
		Race	Religion	Sexual orient-ation	Ethnicity	Disability	1st quarter	2nd quarter	3rd quarter	4th quarter	
	Woodbridge Township	0	3	0	0	0	1	0	1	1	99,915
	Woodbury	6	0	0	1	0	2	4	0	1	10,208
	State Police Agencies	4	3	0	0	0					
	State Police										
	Atlantic County	0	2	0	0	0	1	0	0	1	
	Burlington County	1	0	0	0	0	1	0	0	0	
	Cumberland County	0	1	0	0	0	0	0	0	1	
	Hunterdon County	1	0	0	0	0	0	0	0	1	
	Sussex County	2	0	0	0	0	1	0	1	0	
New Mexico	**Total**	10	3	9	6	0					
	Cities	8	3	8	6	0					
	Albuquerque	7	3	8	6	0	5	9	7	3	551,961
	Espanola	1	0	0	0	0	1	0	0	0	10,338
	Metropolitan Counties	2	0	1	0	0					
	Bernalillo	2	0	1	0	0	0	2	1	0	
New York	**Total**	145	254	107	35	3					
	Cities	92	176	88	18	2					
	Albany	3	1	1	0	0	1	3	1		98,296
	Ballston Spa Village	0	0	0	1	0	0	1	0	0	5,433
	Binghamton	0	0	1	0	0	1	0	0	0	47,589
	Brighton Town	1	0	0	0	0	0	1		0	36,774
	Buffalo	12	2	6	6	0	4	10	7	5	262,484
	Canandaigua	1	0	1	0	0	0	0	1	1	10,592
	Cheektowaga Town	2	0	0	0	0	2	0	0	0	79,194
	Chittenango Village	1	0	0	0	0	0	1	0	0	5,104
	Clarkstown Town	0	1	0	0	0	0	1		0	79,221
	Dewitt Town	1	0	0	0	0	0	1	0	0	22,856
	Dobbs Ferry Village	0	1	0	0	0	0	1	0	0	10,924
	East Rochester Village	1	0	0	0	0	0	1	0		6,617
	Fallsburg Town	0	2	0	0	0	0	0	0	2	12,077
	Fishkill Town	1	1	0	0	0	0	0		2	20,025
	Floral Park Village	1	0	0	0	0	0	1	0	0	15,934
	Freeport Village	0	1	0	0	0	1	0		0	43,053
	Garden City Village	0	1	0	0	0	0	0	1		22,472
	Greenburgh Town	0	1	0	0	0	0	0	1	0	43,055
	Guilderland Town	0	1	0	0	0	0	1	0	0	33,734
	Haverstraw Town	0	2	0	0	0	0	2	0	0	36,799
	Horseheads Village	1	0	0	0	0	0	0	0	1	6,490
	Jamestown	1	0	0	0	0	0	0	1	0	31,286
	Kingston	0	0	1	0	0	0	0	1	0	24,000
	Larchmont Village	0	0	0	1	0	1	0	0	0	5,890
	Long Beach	2	0	0	0	0	0	0	1	1	33,425
	Mamaroneck Town	0	0	1	0	0	0	0	1	0	12,031
	Medina Village	1	0	0	0	0	0	0	1	0	6,092
	Middletown	2	1	0	0	0	2	1	0	0	28,212
	Mount Morris Village	1	0	0	0	0				1	2,999
	Mount Vernon	3	0	1	0	0	2	0	0	2	67,594
	Newburgh	0	0	1	0	0	0	0	1	0	28,996
	New Castle Town	0	0	1	0	0	0	0	0	1	17,648
	New Hartford Town and Village	1	0	0	0	0	1	0	0	0	20,580
	New Rochelle	3	3	0	0	0	3	1	0	2	77,408
	New York	33	134	66	7	0	52	77	43	68	8,211,875
	Niagara Falls	3	0	2	2	0	2	0	4	1	50,419
	North Castle Town	0	1	0	0	0	0	1		0	11,894
	Oneida	1	0	0	0	0	0	0	1	0	11,444
	Oneonta City	1	0	0	0	0	1	0	0	0	13,963
	Orangetown Town	0	1	0	0	0	0	1	0		36,998
	Plattsburgh City	0	1	0	0	0	0	1	0	0	20,079
	Poughkeepsie	4	1	0	0	0	3	0	1	1	32,883
	Poughkeepsie Town	1	1	0	0	0	1	1	0	0	38,511
	Ramapo Town	0	2	0	0	0	0	1	1	0	84,431
	Rochester	0	0	3	0	0	0	2	1	0	211,511
	Saratoga Springs	1	0	0	0	0	0	0	0	1	26,705
	Schenectady	2	0	0	0	0	1	0	1	0	66,432
	Southold Town	0	0	1	0	0	0	1	0		19,860

[1] Agencies published in this table indicated that at least one hate crime incident occurred in their respective jurisdictions during the quarter(s) for which they submitted a report to the Hate Crime Statistics Program. Blanks indicate quarters for which agencies did not submit reports.

[2] Population figures are published only for the cities. The figures listed for the universities and colleges are student enrollment and were provided by the United States Department of Education for the 2010 school year, the most recent available. The enrollment figures include full-time and part-time students.

Table VI-13. Hate Crime Incidents Per Bias Motivation and Quarter, by Selected State and Agency, 2011—*Continued*

(Number)

State	Agency type/name	Number of incidents per bias motivation					Number of incidents per quarter[1]				Popu-lation[2]
		Race	Religion	Sexual orient-ation	Ethnicity	Disability	1st quarter	2nd quarter	3rd quarter	4th quarter	
	Spring Valley Village	0	0	2	0	0	0	1	1	0	31,488
	Suffern Village	1	0	0	0	0	0	1	0	0	10,771
	Tonawanda	1	0	0	0	0	1	0	0	0	15,198
	Tonawanda Town	0	0	0	0	1	1	0			58,406
	Tuckahoe Village	1	0	0	0	0	0	0	0	1	6,515
	Vestal Town	0	1	0	0	0	0	0	0	1	28,169
	White Plains	1	1	0	0	0	1	1	0	0	57,109
	Yonkers	3	14	0	1	1	0	3	1	15	196,857
	Yorktown Town	0	1	0	0	0	0	0	0	1	36,243
	Universities and Colleges	11	2	8	2	0					
	State University of New York, Albany	2	0	0	0	0	0	2			17,615
	State University of New York Agricultural and Technical College, Morrisville	2	0	0	0	0	0	0	0	2	3,454
	State University of New York College Brockport	0	1	0	0	0				1	8,589
	Buffalo	0	0	1	1	0	0	2	0	0	12,419
	Geneseo	1	1	0	0	0	2	0	0	0	5,665
	New Paltz[4]	3	0	0	0	0	0	0		3	
	Oneonta	2	0	3	0	0	0	0	2	3	5,989
	Oswego	1	0	0	0	0	1	0			8,297
	Plattsburgh	0	0	1	1	0	2	0		0	6,441
	Potsdam	0	0	1	0	0	0	0	0	1	4,413
	Purchase	0	0	2	0	0	0	1	1	0	4,167
	Metropolitan Counties	23	56	8	12	1					
	Erie	0	0	0	1	0	0	0	0	1	
	Monroe	2	1	0	0	0	0	0	2	1	
	Nassau	13	39	2	3	0	6	17	13	21	
	Niagara	0	0	1	0	0	0	0	1	0	
	Suffolk County Police Department	7	16	5	8	1	7	10	8	12	
	Wayne	1	0	0	0	0	0	0	1		
	Nonmetropolitan Counties	2	0	0	1	0					
	Cattaraugus	1	0	0	0	0	0	1			
	Otsego	0	0	0	1	0	0	1	0	0	
	Schuyler	1	0	0	0	0		1		0	
	State Police Agencies	7	3	1	0	0					
	State Police Albany County	1	0	0	0	0	0	1	0	0	
	Clinton County	2	0	0	0	0	0	1	0	1	
	Columbia County	1	0	0	0	0		1	0	0	
	Dutchess County	1	1	0	0	0		2	0	0	
	Erie County	0	0	1	0	0	0	1	0	0	
	Orleans County	0	1	0	0	0	0	0	1	0	
	Rensselaer County	1	0	0	0	0	0	1	0	0	
	Saratoga County	1	0	0	0	0	0	1	0	0	
	Ulster County	0	1	0	0	0	0	1	0	0	
	Other Agencies	10	17	2	2	0					
	New York City Metropolitan Transportation Authority	10	17	2	2	0	12	8	3	8	
North Carolina	**Total**	65	17	17	13	0					
	Cities	51	13	11	9	0					
	Albemarle	1	0	0	0	0	1	0	0	0	16,105
	Archdale	1	0	0	0	0	1	0	0	0	11,560
	Asheville	4	2	0	1	0	3	0	3	1	84,450
	Burlington	0	0	0	1	0	0	0	0	1	50,597
	Carrboro	0	1	1	0	0	0	1	1	0	19,830
	Cary	1	0	0	0	0	0	1	0	0	136,949
	Chapel Hill	2	0	1	0	0	2	0	1	0	57,959

[1] Agencies published in this table indicated that at least one hate crime incident occurred in their respective jurisdictions during the quarter(s) for which they submitted a report to the Hate Crime Statistics Program. Blanks indicate quarters for which agencies did not submit reports.
[2] Population figures are published only for the cities. The figures listed for the universities and colleges are student enrollment and were provided by the United States Department of Education for the 2010 school year, the most recent available. The enrollment figures include full-time and part-time students.
[4] Student enrollment figures were not available.

Table VI-13. Hate Crime Incidents Per Bias Motivation and Quarter, by Selected State and Agency, 2011—*Continued*

(Number)

State	Agency type/name	Number of incidents per bias motivation					Number of incidents per quarter[1]				Popu-lation[2]
		Race	Religion	Sexual orient-ation	Ethnicity	Disability	1st quarter	2nd quarter	3rd quarter	4th quarter	
	Charlotte-Mecklenburg	3	3	1	0	0	0	1	5	1	789,478
	Creedmoor	1	0	0	1	0	1	0	0	1	4,176
	Dunn	1	0	0	0	0	0	0	0	1	9,380
	Durham	2	0	1	0	0	0	1	2	0	231,225
	Fayetteville	3	0	0	1	0	3	0	0	1	203,107
	Gastonia	0	0	0	1	0	1	0	0	0	72,651
	Greensboro	11	0	1	0	0	0	2	9	1	273,086
	Hickory	0	1	0	1	0	0	1	0	1	40,517
	High Point	3	0	0	0	0	0	1	2	0	105,695
	Hope Mills	0	1	0	1	0	2	0	0	0	15,368
	Kernersville	1	0	0	0	0	0	1	0	0	23,416
	Kill Devil Hills	0	1	0	0	0	0	0	1	0	6,768
	King	1	0	2	0	0	0	2	0	1	6,992
	Lexington	1	0	0	0	0	0	1	0	0	19,171
	Long View	3	0	1	0	0	0	4	0	0	4,933
	Morganton	1	0	0	0	0	0	0	1	0	17,133
	New Bern	1	1	0	0	0	0	1	0	1	29,898
	Reidsville	1	0	1	1	0	1	0	1	1	14,704
	Rocky Mount	1	1	1	0	0	0	0	1	2	58,206
	Salisbury	2	1	0	0	0	1	1	0	1	34,089
	Shallotte	0	0	1	0	0	0	0	1	0	3,722
	Smithfield	3	1	0	0	0	1	0	1	2	11,105
	Sylva	0	0	0	1	0	0	0	0	1	2,621
	Wadesboro	1	0	0	0	0	0	0	0	1	5,887
	Williamston	1	0	0	0	0	0	0	0	1	5,581
	Wrightsville Beach	1	0	0	0	0	0	0	1	0	2,508
	Universities and Colleges	2	0	2	0	0					
	Appalachian State University	0	0	1	0	0	0	1	0	0	17,222
	North Carolina State University, Raleigh	0	0	1	0	0	0	0	0	1	34,376
	University of North Carolina, Charlotte	2	0	0	0	0	0	2	0	0	25,063
	Metropolitan Counties	11	3	4	2	0					
	Anson	1	0	0	0	0	0	0	0	1	
	Buncombe	3	1	0	0	0	1	1	2	0	
	Catawba	0	0	1	0	0	0	0	1	0	
	Currituck	0	0	1	0	0	1	0	0	0	
	Forsyth	0	0	1	0	0	1	0	0	0	
	Gaston County Police Department	4	0	0	0	0	2	0	1	1	
	Guilford	1	0	0	0	0	1	0	0	0	
	Pitt	2	2	0	2	0	0	2	1	3	
	Union	0	0	1	0	0	0	1	0	0	
	Nonmetropolitan Counties	1	1	0	2	0					
	Clay	0	0	0	1	0	0	0	1	0	
	Lenoir	0	0	0	1	0	0	0	1	0	
	Rutherford	1	0	0	0	0	1	0	0	0	
	Transylvania	0	1	0	0	0	1	0	0	0	
North Dakota	**Total**	19	3	5	0	0					
	Cities	16	3	5	0	0					
	Bismarck	2	1	1	0	0	1	0	0	3	62,305
	Fargo	5	0	2	0	0	0	2	3	2	107,329
	Grand Forks	2	0	1	0	0	2	0	1	0	53,729
	Mandan	2	1	0	0	0	0	1	0	2	18,640
	Minot	0	1	0	0	0	0	0	0	1	41,577
	West Fargo	5	0	1	0	0	1	2	1	2	26,266
	Metropolitan Counties	2	0	0	0	0					
	Morton	2	0	0	0	0	1	1	0	0	
	Nonmetropolitan Counties	1	0	0	0	0					
	Adams	1	0	0	0	0	0	0	1	0	

[1] Agencies published in this table indicated that at least one hate crime incident occurred in their respective jurisdictions during the quarter(s) for which they submitted a report to the Hate Crime Statistics Program. Blanks indicate quarters for which agencies did not submit reports.

[2] Population figures are published only for the cities. The figures listed for the universities and colleges are student enrollment and were provided by the United States Department of Education for the 2010 school year, the most recent available. The enrollment figures include full-time and part-time students.

Table VI-13. Hate Crime Incidents Per Bias Motivation and Quarter, by Selected State and Agency, 2011—*Continued*

(Number)

State	Agency type/name	Number of incidents per bias motivation					Number of incidents per quarter[1]				Popu-lation[2]
		Race	Religion	Sexual orient-ation	Ethnicity	Disability	1st quarter	2nd quarter	3rd quarter	4th quarter	
Ohio............................	**Total**	130	23	58	15	2					
	Cities	119	18	48	12	1					
	Akron	8	2	5	1	0	3	5	2	6	199,256
	Alliance	1	0	0	0	0		1			22,338
	Athens	0	1	0	0	0	1	0	0	0	23,849
	Beavercreek	0	0	1	0	0	0	0	1	0	45,226
	Beaver Township	1	0	0	0	0	0	0	0	1	6,716
	Berea	0	0	1	0	0	1	0	0	0	19,107
	Bexley	1	0	0	0	0	0	0	1	0	13,067
	Cambridge	0	0	1	0	0	0	1	0	0	10,643
	Cardington	0	0	1	0	0	0	0	0	1	2,048
	Centerville	0	1	0	0	0	0	0	0	1	24,017
	Chillicothe	0	1	1	0	0	1	1	0	0	21,917
	Cincinnati	8	0	1	0	0	1	5	2	1	297,160
	Circleville	3	0	0	1	0	0	0	2	2	13,324
	Cleveland	1	0	2	1	0	0	1	2	1	397,106
	Columbus	16	5	16	3	0	5	9	18	8	787,609
	Dayton	4	0	2	0	0	1	4	1	0	141,631
	Defiance	2	0	0	0	0	0	1	1	0	16,506
	Eaton	1	0	0	0	0	0	1	0	0	8,413
	Englewood	2	1	0	0	0	1	1	0	1	13,475
	Fairfield Township	1	0	0	0	0	1	0	0	0	21,389
	Findlay	2	0	1	0	0	2	1	0	0	41,232
	Fremont	0	0	1	0	0	1	0	0	0	16,746
	Gahanna	1	0	0	0	0	0	0	0	1	33,272
	Grove City	0	0	1	0	0	0	0	0	1	35,601
	Heath	0	0	1	0	0	1	0	0	0	10,318
	Hilliard	0	1	0	0	0	0	0	0	1	28,456
	Holland	3	0	0	0	0	0	2	1	0	1,765
	Hubbard	1	0	0	0	0	0	0	0	1	7,880
	Huber Heights	2	0	1	0	0	0	1	1	1	38,129
	Kettering	2	0	0	0	0	1	0	1	0	56,204
	London	0	1	0	0	0	1	0	0	0	9,911
	Lorain	4	1	1	0	0	0	2	2	2	64,144
	Mansfield	11	0	0	1	0	3	1	5	3	47,856
	Marysville	1	0	0	0	0	1	0	0	0	22,110
	Mason	1	0	0	0	0	0	0	1	0	30,734
	Massillon	2	0	1	0	1	2	1	1	0	32,173
	Miamisburg	1	1	0	0	0	1	0	0	1	20,196
	Miami Township, Clermont County	1	0	0	0	0	0	0	1	0	40,878
	Miami Township, Montgomery County	4	0	1	1	0	2	1	2	1	29,152
	Montgomery	1	0	0	0	0	0	1	0	0	10,259
	Moraine	2	0	0	0	0	1	0	0	1	6,312
	Mount Healthy	1	0	1	0	0	0	1	0	1	6,102
	New Albany	0	0	1	0	0	0	0	0	1	7,730
	Newcomerstown	1	0	0	0	0	1	0			3,825
	Norton	2	0	0	0	0	0	0	2	0	12,094
	Norwood	1	0	0	0	0	0	0	0	1	19,221
	Oregon	0	0	1	0	0	0	0	0	1	20,306
	Parma	2	0	0	0	0	1	0	1	0	81,661
	Piqua	1	0	0	0	0	0	0	0	1	20,537
	Portsmouth	3	0	1	1	0	1	0	3	1	20,241
	Reynoldsburg	1	0	0	0	0	0	1	0	0	35,919
	Riverside	3	0	1	0	0	0	2	1	1	25,219
	Salem	1	0	0	0	0	0	1	0	0	12,312
	Shaker Heights	0	0	1	0	0	0	1	0	0	28,469
	Sharonville	2	0	0	0	0	1	1	0	0	13,570
	Somerset	0	0	1	0	0	0	0	1	0	1,482
	South Euclid	1	0	0	0	0	0	0	1	0	22,311
	Springfield	3	1	0	1	0	2	2	0	1	60,652
	Sugarcreek Township	0	0	1	0	0	0	0	0	1	8,047
	Upper Arlington	1	0	0	0	0	0	1	0	0	33,796
	Van Wert	2	1	1	0	0	2	0	1	1	10,854
	Wadsworth	0	0	0	2	0	0	0	1	1	21,583
	Walbridge	1	0	0	0	0	0	1	0	0	3,021
	Warren Township	1	0	0	0	0	0	0	0	1	5,555
	Washington Court House	0	1	0	0	0	0	0	1	0	14,202
	Wilmington	2	0	0	0	0	0	0	0	2	12,529
	Wooster	1	0	0	0	0	0	0	0	1	26,138
	Xenia	1	0	0	0	0	0	0	0	1	25,738

[1] Agencies published in this table indicated that at least one hate crime incident occurred in their respective jurisdictions during the quarter(s) for which they submitted a report to the Hate Crime Statistics Program. Blanks indicate quarters for which agencies did not submit reports.

[2] Population figures are published only for the cities. The figures listed for the universities and colleges are student enrollment and were provided by the United States Department of Education for the 2010 school year, the most recent available. The enrollment figures include full-time and part-time students.

Table VI-13. Hate Crime Incidents Per Bias Motivation and Quarter, by Selected State and Agency, 2011—*Continued*

(Number)

State	Agency type/name	Number of incidents per bias motivation					Number of incidents per quarter[1]				Popu-lation[2]
		Race	Religion	Sexual orient-ation	Ethnicity	Disability	1st quarter	2nd quarter	3rd quarter	4th quarter	
	Universities and Colleges	2	1	0	1	0					
	Bowling Green State University	0	1	0	0	0	0	0	1	0	17,706
	Ohio State University, Columbus	2	0	0	1	0	1	2	0	0	56,064
	Metropolitan Counties	4	2	5	1	1					
	Butler	0	0	3	0	1	0	2	1	1	
	Franklin	1	0	0	0	0	0	1	0	0	
	Greene	0	1	1	0	0	0	1	0	1	
	Lucas	1	0	0	0	0	0	0	1	0	
	Madison	0	1	0	0	0	0	0	1	0	
	Montgomery	2	0	0	0	0	1	0	1	0	
	Richland	0	0	1	1	0	2	0	0	0	
	Nonmetropolitan Counties	5	2	5	1	0					
	Ashland	0	0	1	0	0	0	0	0	1	
	Coshocton	1	0	3	0	0	3	1	0	0	
	Holmes	0	1	0	0	0	0	0	0	1	
	Logan	1	0	0	0	0	0	1	0	0	
	Marion	0	1	0	1	0	0	0	2	0	
	Ross	3	0	1	0	0	0	2	0	2	
Oklahoma	**Total**	14	2	5	8	0					
	Cities	13	1	4	5	0					
	Chickasha	1	0	0	0	0	0	0	1	0	16,208
	Coweta	1	0	0	0	0	0	0	0	1	10,049
	Dewey	1	0	0	0	0	0	0	1	0	3,469
	Enid	1	0	0	0	0	0	1	0	0	49,908
	Eufaula	1	0	0	0	0	0	1	0	0	2,843
	Guthrie	1	0	0	0	0	0	0	1	0	10,300
	Lexington	1	0	0	0	0	0	0	1	0	2,175
	Norman	3	0	0	1	0	1	1	0	2	112,112
	Oklahoma City	2	1	3	3	0	2	0	5	2	586,208
	Pauls Valley	0	0	1	0	0	0	0	1	0	6,253
	Sapulpa	1	0	0	0	0	0	1	0	0	20,764
	Stroud	0	0	0	1	0	0	1	0	0	2,719
	Metropolitan Counties	0	0	1	2	0					
	McClain	0	0	0	2	0	0	1	0	1	
	Tulsa	0	0	1	0	0	0	0	0	1	
	Nonmetropolitan Counties	1	0	0	1	0					
	Pottawatomie	1	0	0	0	0	1	0	0	0	
	Tillman	0	0	0	1	0	0	0	0	1	
	Other Agencies	0	1	0	0	0					
	Putnam City Campus	0	1	0	0	0	0	0	1	0	
Oregon..........................	**Total**	54	15	40	18	1					
	Cities	47	14	36	17	0					
	Albany	0	1	0	0	0		1			50,692
	Ashland	0	0	1	0	0	1	0	0	0	20,292
	Beaverton	9	1	2	1	0	5	4	2	2	90,759
	Coos Bay	0	0	1	0	0	1	0	0	0	16,137
	Corvallis	2	0	2	1	0	2	1	2	0	55,042
	Eugene	8	2	7	5	0	9	4	6	3	157,848
	Keizer	0	4	0	0	0	0	2	0	2	36,866
	Lebanon	1	0	2	1	0	1	1	1	1	15,683
	McMinnville	0	0	2	0	0	0	1	1	0	32,530
	Medford	5	0	0	0	0	1	1	1	2	75,704
	Newberg-Dundee	0	0	0	1	0	0	0	1	0	25,499
	Portland	8	2	16	1	0	3	9	7	8	589,991
	Redmond	2	0	0	1	0	0	1	0	2	26,494
	Reedsport	0	0	0	1	0	0	1	0	0	4,198
	Roseburg	1	0	0	0	0	0	0	0	1	21,406
	Salem	2	2	1	1	0	0	5	1	0	156,283
	Springfield	2	0	0	1	0	0	3	0	0	60,035
	Stayton	1	0	0	0	0	1	0	0	0	7,725

[1] Agencies published in this table indicated that at least one hate crime incident occurred in their respective jurisdictions during the quarter(s) for which they submitted a report to the Hate Crime Statistics Program. Blanks indicate quarters for which agencies did not submit reports.

[2] Population figures are published only for the cities. The figures listed for the universities and colleges are student enrollment and were provided by the United States Department of Education for the 2010 school year, the most recent available. The enrollment figures include full-time and part-time students.

Table VI-13. Hate Crime Incidents Per Bias Motivation and Quarter, by Selected State and Agency, 2011—*Continued*
(Number)

State	Agency type/name	Number of incidents per bias motivation					Number of incidents per quarter[1]				Population[2]
		Race	Religion	Sexual orientation	Ethnicity	Disability	1st quarter	2nd quarter	3rd quarter	4th quarter	
	Tigard	4	2	2	2	0	0	6	4	0	48,546
	Toledo	2	0	0	0	0	1	0	0	1	3,502
	Woodburn	0	0	0	1	0	0	0	1	0	24,336
	Metropolitan Counties	4	1	4	1	1					
	Clackamas	1	0	0	0	0	1				
	Deschutes	1	1	0	0	0	1	1	0	0	
	Jackson	0	0	1	0	0	0	0	0	1	
	Lane	0	0	1	1	0	1	0	1	0	
	Yamhill	2	0	2	0	1	2	1	1	1	
	Nonmetropolitan Counties	2	0	0	0	0					
	Douglas	1	0	0	0	0	1	0	0	0	
	Lincoln	1	0	0	0	0	0	1	0	0	
	State Police Agencies	1	0	0	0	0					
	State Police, Marion County	1	0	0	0	0			1		
Pennsylvania	**Total**	30	8	7	8	0					
	Cities	27	6	5	7	0					
	Abington Township, Montgomery County	1	1	0	0	0	0	1	1	0	55,486
	Carlisle	1	0	0	0	0	0	0	1	0	18,742
	Cheltenham Township	0	0	1	0	0	0	0	1	0	36,910
	Christiana	3	0	0	0	0	0	3	0	0	1,172
	Economy	1	0	0	0	0	1	0	0	0	8,999
	Harrisburg	0	0	1	0	0	0	0	0	1	49,686
	Johnstown	2	0	0	0	0	0	1	1	0	22,572
	McDonald Borough	2	0	0	0	0	0	0	0	2	2,156
	Middletown	0	0	0	1	0	0	0	1	0	8,929
	North Huntingdon Township	1	0	0	0	0	0	1	0	0	30,707
	North Sewickley Township	1	0	0	0	0	1	0			5,506
	Philadelphia	7	3	0	3	0	7	3		3	1,530,873
	Pittsburgh	7	1	3	2	0	3	3	3	4	308,609
	Reading	0	1	0	0	0		0	1	0	88,363
	York Area Regional	1	0	0	1	0	0	0	1	1	60,596
	Universities and Colleges	1	2	2	0	0					
	Pennsylvania State University, University Park	1	2	1	0	0	0	0	4	0	45,233
	West Chester University	0	0	1	0	0	0	1	0	0	14,490
	State Police Agencies	2	0	0	1	0					
	State Police										
	Chester County	0	0	0	1	0	1	0	0		
	Lancaster County	1	0	0	0	0	0	0	1	0	
	Monroe County	1	0	0	0	0	1	0	0		
Rhode Island	**Total**	3	4	8	4	1					
	Cities	3	4	8	4	1					
	Johnston	0	1	2	0	0	1	0	1	1	28,734
	Pawtucket	3	1	1	0	0	1	0	2	2	71,062
	Providence	0	1	4	4	1	0	1	9		177,830
	West Warwick	0	0	1	0	0	0	0	1	0	29,156
	Woonsocket	0	1	0	0	0	0	0	1	0	41,137
South Carolina	**Total**	64	36	20	13	2					
	Cities	38	22	16	8	1					
	Abbeville	0	0	1	0	0	0	0	1	0	5,298
	Aiken	0	0	1	0	0	0	0	1	0	29,868
	Allendale	1	0	0	0	0	0	0	1	0	3,523
	Andrews	2	0	0	0	0	1	1	0	0	2,894
	Batesburg-Leesville	1	0	0	0	0	1	0	0	0	5,424
	Beaufort	3	0	0	0	0	2	1	0	0	12,505
	Briarcliffe Acres	0	1	0	0	0	1	0	0	0	462

[1] Agencies published in this table indicated that at least one hate crime incident occurred in their respective jurisdictions during the quarter(s) for which they submitted a report to the Hate Crime Statistics Program. Blanks indicate quarters for which agencies did not submit reports.

[2] Population figures are published only for the cities. The figures listed for the universities and colleges are student enrollment and were provided by the United States Department of Education for the 2010 school year, the most recent available. The enrollment figures include full-time and part-time students.

Table VI-13. Hate Crime Incidents Per Bias Motivation and Quarter, by Selected State and Agency, 2011—*Continued*

(Number)

State	Agency type/name	Number of incidents per bias motivation					Number of incidents per quarter[1]				Population[2]
		Race	Religion	Sexual orient-ation	Ethnicity	Disability	1st quarter	2nd quarter	3rd quarter	4th quarter	
	Burnettown	1	0	0	0	0	0	0	0	1	2,704
	Camden	1	0	0	0	0	1	0	0	0	6,918
	Cayce	1	0	0	0	0	0	1	0	0	12,674
	Charleston	1	0	1	0	0	1	0	0	1	121,481
	Chester	0	0	1	0	0	1	0	0	0	5,672
	Columbia	2	0	0	0	0	0	0	0	2	130,777
	Conway	1	0	0	0	0	0	0	0	1	17,302
	Easley	0	0	0	1	0	0	1	0	0	20,226
	Elgin	1	0	0	0	0	1	0	0	0	1,326
	Florence	3	0	2	0	0	0	1	3	1	37,488
	Forest Acres	1	0	0	0	0	1	0	0	0	10,482
	Goose Creek	0	0	0	1	0	0	1	0	0	36,357
	Hampton	1	0	1	0	0	0	1	0	1	2,841
	Hanahan	0	0	1	0	0	1	0	0	0	18,207
	Hardeeville	0	1	0	0	0	0	0	0	1	2,986
	Hartsville	1	0	0	0	0	1	0	0	0	7,854
	Holly Hill	1	0	0	0	0	0	1	0	0	1,292
	Isle of Palms	0	1	0	0	0	1	0	0	0	4,181
	Landrum	1	0	0	0	0	1	0	0	0	2,404
	Latta	0	1	0	0	0	0	0	0	1	1,395
	Laurens	0	0	1	1	0	0	2	0	0	9,245
	Moncks Corner	1	1	0	0	1	1	2	0	0	7,977
	Mount Pleasant	0	0	1	0	0	0	1	0	0	68,633
	Myrtle Beach	3	0	0	0	0	0	3	0	0	27,425
	North Charleston	1	0	1	0	0	0	0	2	0	98,606
	North Myrtle Beach	1	0	0	0	0	0	1	0	0	13,912
	Pickens	1	0	0	0	0	0	0	1	0	3,162
	Port Royal	1	0	0	1	0	1	0	1	0	10,802
	Rock Hill	0	0	1	0	0	0	1	0	0	66,924
	Simpsonville	0	0	1	0	0	0	1	0	0	18,450
	Spartanburg	0	0	2	0	0	0	2	0	0	37,444
	Springdale	0	0	0	1	0	0	0	1	0	2,667
	Summerville	0	1	0	0	0	0	1	0	0	43,897
	Tega Cay	0	0	0	1	0	0	0	1	0	7,709
	Union	1	0	0	0	0	0	0	0	1	8,491
	Walhalla	0	0	0	1	0	1	0	0	0	4,313
	Walterboro	4	11	1	1	0	4	5	3	5	5,461
	Westminster	1	0	0	0	0	0	1	0	0	2,446
	Winnsboro	0	5	0	0	0	0	0	2	3	3,591
	York	1	0	0	0	0	1	0	0	0	7,826
	Universities and Colleges	6	0	0	0	0					
	College of Charleston	6	0	0	0	0	2	2	0	2	11,532
	Metropolitan Counties	13	5	1	2	1					
	Anderson	3	0	1	0	0	0	2	1	1	
	Berkeley	1	0	0	0	0	0	1	0	0	
	Fairfield	1	0	0	0	1	0	0	2	0	
	Greenville	0	0	0	1	0	0	1	0	0	
	Horry County Police Department	3	2	0	0	0	0	0	2	3	
	Pickens	0	3	0	1	0	0	1	0	3	
	Richland	5	0	0	0	0	2	1	0	2	
	Nonmetropolitan Agencies	7	9	2	3	0					
	Abbeville	0	7	0	1	0	1	1	3	3	
	Chester	2	0	0	0	0	1	0	0	1	
	Chesterfield	0	0	1	0	0	0	0	1	0	
	Clarendon	1	0	0	1	0	0	0	2	0	
	Greenwood	0	2	0	1	0	0	3	0	0	
	Hampton	1	0	0	0	0	0	0	0	1	
	Lee	0	0	1	0	0	0	0	1	0	
	Union	1	0	0	0	0	0	1	0	0	
	Williamsburg	2	0	0	0	0	0	1	1	0	
	State Police Agencies	0	0	1	0	0					
	Highway Patrol, Anderson County	0	0	1	0	0	0	0	1	0	

[1] Agencies published in this table indicated that at least one hate crime incident occurred in their respective jurisdictions during the quarter(s) for which they submitted a report to the Hate Crime Statistics Program. Blanks indicate quarters for which agencies did not submit reports.

[2] Population figures are published only for the cities. The figures listed for the universities and colleges are student enrollment and were provided by the United States Department of Education for the 2010 school year, the most recent available. The enrollment figures include full-time and part-time students.

Table VI-13. Hate Crime Incidents Per Bias Motivation and Quarter, by Selected State and Agency, 2011—*Continued*

(Number)

State	Agency type/name	Number of incidents per bias motivation					Number of incidents per quarter[1]				Popu-lation[2]
		Race	Religion	Sexual orient-ation	Ethnicity	Disability	1st quarter	2nd quarter	3rd quarter	4th quarter	
South Dakota...............	**Total**	15	2	4	0	0					
	Cities	12	2	4	0	0					
	Aberdeen	1	0	0	0	0	0	0	1	0	26,408
	Rapid City	0	0	1	0	0	0	0	0	1	68,782
	Sioux Falls	10	2	1	0	0	3	4	3	3	155,760
	Yankton	1	0	2	0	0	1	2	0	0	14,630
	Metropolitan Counties	1	0	0	0	0					
	Pennington	1	0	0	0	0	0	0	0	1	
	Nonmetropolitan Counties	2	0	0	0	0					
	Codington	1	0	0	0	0	1	0	0	0	
	Yankton	1	0	0	0	0	1	0	0	0	
Tennessee.......................	**Total**	78	15	33	13	5					
	Cities	51	10	29	13	2					
	Alamo	0	0	0	0	1	0	0	1	0	2,483
	Alcoa	1	0	0	0	0	0	0	0	1	8,525
	Bartlett	0	0	0	0	1	0	0	0	1	55,106
	Bristol	1	0	0	0	0	0	0	0	1	26,943
	Brownsville	0	0	0	1	0	0	0	0	1	10,385
	Calhoun	1	0	0	0	0	0	0	1	0	494
	Centerville	0	0	1	0	0	0	0	0	1	3,677
	Chattanooga	2	0	0	0	0	0	1	0	1	169,187
	Clarksville	2	0	3	0	0	1	1	3	0	134,128
	Cleveland	3	1	0	0	0	1	2	0	1	41,657
	Coopertown	2	0	0	0	0	0	0	2	0	4,317
	Franklin	1	1	0	0	0	0	0	0	2	63,051
	Gallatin	0	0	1	0	0	0	0	1	0	30,551
	Harriman	1	0	0	0	0	0	0	1	0	6,407
	Hendersonville	1	0	1	0	0	0	1	0	1	51,835
	Humboldt	1	0	0	0	0	0	0	1	0	8,528
	Jamestown	5	0	0	0	0	0	1	3	1	1,977
	Kingsport	4	0	0	1	0	0	4	0	1	48,640
	Kingston	1	0	0	0	0	0	0	0	1	5,988
	Knoxville	0	1	1	0	0	1	0	0	1	180,488
	Lafayette	0	0	0	1	0	1	0	0	0	4,514
	Lawrenceburg	1	0	0	0	0	0	1	0	0	10,522
	Lexington	1	0	0	0	0	1	0	0	0	7,721
	Loudon	0	0	0	1	0	1	0	0	0	5,430
	Manchester	0	0	0	1	0	1	0	0	0	10,193
	McMinnville	1	0	0	0	0	1	0	0	0	13,728
	Memphis	5	0	16	1	0	2	4	11	5	652,725
	Milan	1	0	0	0	0	0	0	1	0	7,922
	Millington	3	0	0	0	0	0	0	1	2	10,268
	Morristown	0	0	0	1	0	0	1	0	0	29,400
	Moscow	1	0	0	0	0	0	0	0	1	561
	Nashville	3	5	4	3	0	3	4	5	3	612,789
	Newport	1	0	1	0	0	2	0	0	0	7,008
	Oak Ridge	0	2	0	0	0	0	1	0	1	29,595
	Portland	0	0	0	1	0	0	0	1	0	11,584
	Sevierville	1	0	0	0	0	1	0	0	0	14,941
	Springfield	1	0	0	0	0	0	1	0	0	16,588
	Spring Hill	2	0	0	0	0	1	1	0	0	29,298
	Trimble	1	0	0	0	0	0	1	0	0	643
	Union City	0	0	1	1	0	0	0	1	1	10,993
	Vonore	0	0	0	1	0	1	0	0	0	1,487
	White House	1	0	0	0	0	0	1	0	0	10,348
	Winchester	2	0	0	0	0	0	0	0	2	8,607
	Universities and Colleges	1	0	0	0	0					
	Middle Tennessee										
	State University	1	0	0	0	0	0	0	1	0	26,430
	Metropolitan Counties	23	4	4	0	3					
	Anderson	0	0	1	0	0	1	0	0	0	
	Blount	1	0	0	0	0	0	1	0	0	
	Cheatham	1	0	0	0	0	1	0	0	0	
	Hamilton	1	0	1	0	0	1	0	0	1	
	Jefferson	1	0	0	0	0	0	1	0	0	

[1] Agencies published in this table indicated that at least one hate crime incident occurred in their respective jurisdictions during the quarter(s) for which they submitted a report to the Hate Crime Statistics Program. Blanks indicate quarters for which agencies did not submit reports.

[2] Population figures are published only for the cities. The figures listed for the universities and colleges are student enrollment and were provided by the United States Department of Education for the 2010 school year, the most recent available. The enrollment figures include full-time and part-time students.

Table VI-13. Hate Crime Incidents Per Bias Motivation and Quarter, by Selected State and Agency, 2011—*Continued*

(Number)

State	Agency type/name	Number of incidents per bias motivation					Number of incidents per quarter[1]				Popu-lation[2]
		Race	Religion	Sexual orient-ation	Ethnicity	Disability	1st quarter	2nd quarter	3rd quarter	4th quarter	
	Knox	2	0	0	0	0	0	2	0	0	
	Montgomery	2	0	0	0	0	1	0	0	1	
	Rutherford	3	0	0	0	0	1	1	0	1	
	Shelby	6	2	2	0	3	2	1	7	3	
	Stewart	1	0	0	0	0	1	0	0	0	
	Sullivan	2	0	0	0	0	0	0	1	1	
	Sumner	1	0	0	0	0	0	0	1	0	
	Washington	1	1	0	0	0	0	0	2	0	
	Wilson	1	1	0	0	0	0	0	2	0	
	Nonmetropolitan Counties	2	1	0	0	0					
	Benton	1	0	0	0	0	0	1	0	0	
	Gibson	0	1	0	0	0	0	0	0	1	
	Maury	1	0	0	0	0	0	0	0	1	
	Other Agencies	1	0	0	0	0					
	Tennessee Bureau of Investigation	1	0	0	0	0	1	0	0	0	
Texas............................	**Total**	56	19	49	27	1					
	Cities	49	19	47	27	1					
	Allen	1	0	0	0	0	0	0	1	0	86,019
	Alvin	0	0	1	0	0	1	0	0	0	24,746
	Anthony	0	0	1	0	0	0	1	0	0	5,116
	Austin	2	1	1	1	0	1	1	2	1	807,022
	Beaumont	1	0	2	0	0	0	3	0	0	120,785
	Bedford	2	0	0	0	0	2	0	0	0	47,968
	Carrollton	0	0	2	0	0	2	0	0	0	121,603
	Cedar Hill	1	0	0	0	0	0	1	0	0	45,975
	Cedar Park	1	0	0	0	1	0	0	2	0	49,967
	Copperas Cove	3	0	0	0	0	1	2	0	0	32,706
	Corpus Christi	2	0	1	0	0	0	1	2	0	311,637
	Corsicana	0	0	0	1	0	1	0	0	0	24,270
	Dallas	3	2	10	1	0	2	4	8	2	1,223,021
	Denison	2	0	0	1	0	0	2	0	1	23,159
	Denton	0	0	1	1	0	1	0	0	1	115,769
	El Paso	0	0	2	0	0	0	1	1	0	662,780
	Forney	0	0	0	1	0	0	1	0	0	14,970
	Fort Worth	5	3	4	4	0	3	4	4	5	756,803
	Galveston	0	0	1	0	0	1	0	0	0	48,748
	Garland	2	1	0	9	0	0	1	1	10	231,650
	Hallettsville	0	1	0	0	0	0	0	1	0	2,604
	Henderson	1	0	2	0	0	2	0	0	1	14,001
	Houston	4	3	6	0	0	1	2	10	0	2,143,628
	Huntsville	1	0	0	0	0	0	0	1	0	39,359
	Kilgore	1	0	0	0	0	0	0	0	1	13,248
	Lake Jackson	0	0	1	0	0	0	1	0	0	27,414
	La Porte	0	0	1	0	0	1	0	0	0	34,511
	Leonard	1	0	0	0	0	0	1	0	0	2,032
	Lewisville	0	0	1	0	0	1	0	0	0	97,295
	Longview	2	0	1	0	0	0	0	2	1	82,148
	McKinney	0	1	0	0	0	0	0	1	0	133,876
	Murphy	1	0	0	0	0	0	0	1	0	18,081
	North Richland Hills	3	3	0	0	0	0	3	2	1	64,676
	Pearland	2	0	0	1	0	0	2	0	1	93,172
	Plano	1	1	0	1	0	0	2	1	0	265,309
	Reno	0	0	1	0	0	0	0	0	1	3,233
	Round Rock	0	0	0	1	0	0	0	1	0	101,989
	Royse City	1	0	0	0	0	1	0	0	0	9,546
	Sachse	1	0	1	1	0	0	2	0	1	20,757
	San Angelo	1	0	1	2	0	1	0	2	1	95,161
	San Antonio	0	0	2	0	0	0	1	0	1	1,355,339
	Snyder	0	0	1	0	0	0	0	0	1	11,438
	Terrell	1	0	0	0	0	0	0	1	0	16,149
	Texas City	1	0	0	0	0	1	0	0	0	46,048
	Tomball	1	0	1	0	0	0	0	0	2	10,979
	Victoria	0	0	0	1	0	0	0	1	0	63,909
	West Lake Hills	0	2	0	0	0	0	0	0	2	3,127
	West Tawakoni	0	0	1	0	0	1	0	0	0	1,609
	Wichita Falls	1	0	1	1	0	0	1	2	0	106,753
	Wylie	0	1	0	0	0	1	0	0	0	42,299

[1] Agencies published in this table indicated that at least one hate crime incident occurred in their respective jurisdictions during the quarter(s) for which they submitted a report to the Hate Crime Statistics Program. Blanks indicate quarters for which agencies did not submit reports.

[2] Population figures are published only for the cities. The figures listed for the universities and colleges are student enrollment and were provided by the United States Department of Education for the 2010 school year, the most recent available. The enrollment figures include full-time and part-time students.

Table VI-13. Hate Crime Incidents Per Bias Motivation and Quarter, by Selected State and Agency, 2011—*Continued*

(Number)

State	Agency type/name	Number of incidents per bias motivation					Number of incidents per quarter[1]				Popu-lation[2]
		Race	Religion	Sexual orient-ation	Ethnicity	Disability	1st quarter	2nd quarter	3rd quarter	4th quarter	
	Universities and Colleges	3	0	1	0	0					
	Sul Ross State University	0	0	1	0	0	0	0	1	0	3,129
	Texas State Technical College, Waco	1	0	0	0	0	0	1	0	0	4,975
	University of Texas, Austin	2	0	0	0	0	1	1	0	0	51,195
	Metropolitan Counties	4	0	1	0	0					
	Comal	1	0	1	0	0	0	0	1	1	
	Potter	1	0	0	0	0	1	0	0	0	
	Wichita	1	0	0	0	0	1	0	0	0	
	Williamson	1	0	0	0	0	1	0	0	0	
Utah...............	**Total**	29	16	14	8	1					
	Cities	21	12	6	6	0					
	Bountiful	1	3	0	0	0	1	1	1	1	43,373
	Brigham City	1	0	0	0	0	0	0	1	0	18,244
	Centerville	0	1	0	0	0	0	0	1	0	15,631
	Clinton	0	1	0	0	0	0	1	0	0	20,820
	Draper	2	2	0	1	0	0	1	3	1	43,090
	Layton	1	1	0	0	0	1	1	0	0	68,610
	Murray	1	0	1	0	0	0	1	1	0	47,648
	North Salt Lake	1	1	0	0	0	0	1	1	0	16,637
	Price	2	1	0	0	0	0	0	1	2	8,883
	Provo	0	0	0	1	0	0	1	0	0	114,659
	Salt Lake City	1	0	0	1	0	0	0	2	0	190,038
	Sandy	0	0	1	0	0	0	0	0	1	89,149
	South Jordan	1	0	0	0	0	0	0	0	1	51,391
	South Salt Lake	2	0	0	0	0	0	1	1	0	24,073
	St. George	0	0	1	1	0	0	1	1	0	74,304
	Syracuse	1	0	0	0	0	0	0	1	0	24,801
	Tooele	0	0	0	1	0	0	1	0	0	32,215
	Tremonton	1	0	1	1	0	1	0	1	1	7,795
	Vernal	0	0	1	0	0	0	0	1	0	9,264
	West Bountiful	0	0	1	0	0	1	0	0	0	5,367
	West Jordan	1	1	0	0	0	0	2	0	0	105,713
	West Valley	5	1	0	0	0	0	5	1	0	131,979
	Universities and Colleges	0	0	2	1	0					
	University of Utah	0	0	2	1	0	1	1	1	0	30,819
	Metropolitan Counties	5	4	5	0	1					
	Salt Lake County Unified Police Department	4	4	3	0	1	0	0	4	8	
	Tooele	0	0	1	0	0	0	1	0	0	
	Washington	1	0	1	0	0	0	0	2	0	
	Nonmetropolitan Counties	2	0	1	0	0					
	Duchesne	1	0	1	0	0	1	1	0	0	
	Uintah	1	0	0	0	0	0	0	0	1	
	Other Agencies	1	0	0	1	0					
	Utah Transit Authority	1	0	0	1	0	0	0	1	1	
Vermont........	**Total**	4	1	2	0	0					
	Cities	3	1	2	0	0					
	Berlin	1	0	0	0	0	0	0	0	1	2,890
	Brattleboro	0	0	1	0	0	0	0	1	0	12,059
	Burlington	0	0	1	0	0	0	0	1		42,464
	Colchester	1	1	0	0	0	0	1	1	0	17,086
	Swanton	1	0	0	0	0	0	0	1	0	6,434
	State Police Agencies	1	0	0	0	0					
	State Police St. Albans	1	0	0	0	0	0	0	1	0	

[1] Agencies published in this table indicated that at least one hate crime incident occurred in their respective jurisdictions during the quarter(s) for which they submitted a report to the Hate Crime Statistics Program. Blanks indicate quarters for which agencies did not submit reports.

[2] Population figures are published only for the cities. The figures listed for the universities and colleges are student enrollment and were provided by the United States Department of Education for the 2010 school year, the most recent available. The enrollment figures include full-time and part-time students.

Table VI-13. Hate Crime Incidents Per Bias Motivation and Quarter, by Selected State and Agency, 2011—*Continued*

(Number)

State	Agency type/name	Number of incidents per bias motivation					Number of incidents per quarter[1]				Popu-lation[2]
		Race	Religion	Sexual orient-ation	Ethnicity	Disability	1st quarter	2nd quarter	3rd quarter	4th quarter	
Virginia	**Total**	76	27	21	19	1					
	Cities	26	10	13	9	0					
	Alexandria	2	0	0	1	0	0	1	1	1	141,638
	Bedford	0	0	1	0	0	0	1	0	0	6,296
	Big Stone Gap	1	0	0	0	0	0	0	0	1	5,681
	Blacksburg	0	0	1	0	0	1	0	0	0	43,129
	Charlottesville	0	0	0	1	0	0	0	1	0	43,994
	Chesapeake	3	1	0	1	0	1	1	3	0	224,864
	Christiansburg	0	0	1	0	0	0	0	0	1	21,292
	Danville	0	1	0	0	0	0	0	1	0	43,569
	Emporia	1	0	0	0	0	0	0	0	1	5,998
	Farmville	0	0	1	0	0	0	0	0	1	8,314
	Hampton	1	0	0	0	0	1	0	0	0	139,078
	Harrisonburg	0	0	2	0	0	0	0	1	1	49,498
	Lynchburg	0	0	1	0	0	1	0	0	0	76,471
	Manassas Park	1	0	0	0	0	1	0	0	0	14,444
	Newport News	4	1	2	1	0	1	2	1	4	182,878
	Norfolk	2	0	0	0	0	1	0	1	0	245,704
	Portsmouth	1	1	0	0	0	0	1	0	1	96,676
	Pulaski	1	0	0	0	0	1	0	0	0	9,195
	Richmond	0	1	0	2	0	0	1	0	2	206,654
	Roanoke	2	0	0	0	0	0	1	0	1	98,191
	Strasburg	1	0	0	0	0	1	0	0	0	6,474
	Suffolk	1	0	0	0	0	0	1	0	0	85,595
	Vinton	0	0	0	1	0	0	0	0	1	8,195
	Virginia Beach	5	5	4	2	0	4	5	4	3	443,226
	Universities and Colleges	5	5	1	2	0					
	College of William and Mary	1	0	0	1	0	0	0	2	0	8,000
	George Mason University	0	0	1	1	0	0	2	0	0	32,562
	J. Sargeant Reynolds Community College	0	1	0	0	0	1	0	0	0	12,629
	Longwood University	1	0	0	0	0	0	0	1	0	4,831
	Northern Virginia Community College	1	2	0	0	0	0	2	0	1	48,996
	Radford University	0	1	0	0	0	0	0	0	1	9,007
	University of Richmond	1	0	0	0	0	0	0	0	1	4,405
	University of Virginia	0	1	0	0	0	1	0	0	0	24,391
	Virginia State University	1	0	0	0	0	0	0	1	0	5,634
	Metropolitan Counties	42	12	7	7	1					
	Albemarle County Police Department	9	0	1	0	0	3	4	1	2	
	Appomattox	0	0	0	0	1	0	1	0	0	
	Arlington County Police Department	2	0	1	1	0	0	3	1	0	
	Chesterfield County Police Department	7	0	0	1	0	1	5	2	0	
	Fairfax County Police Department	6	6	2	1	0	3	6	3	3	
	Fauquier	0	0	0	1	0	0	0	1	0	
	Henrico County Police Department	9	1	0	1	0	0	2	4	5	
	Loudoun	0	1	0	1	0	0	2	0	0	
	Louisa	1	0	0	0	0	0	0	0	1	
	Mathews	0	0	1	0	0	0	1	0	0	
	Montgomery	4	0	1	0	0	0	1	1	3	
	Pittsylvania	1	0	0	0	0	1	0	0	0	
	Prince George County Police Department	1	0	0	0	0	0	1	0	0	
	Roanoke County Police Department	1	0	0	0	0	0	0	1	0	
	Spotsylvania	0	0	0	1	0	0	0	0	1	
	Sussex	1	0	0	0	0	1	0	0	0	
	Washington	0	0	1	0	0	0	0	0	1	
	York	0	4	0	0	0	0	0	0	4	

[1] Agencies published in this table indicated that at least one hate crime incident occurred in their respective jurisdictions during the quarter(s) for which they submitted a report to the Hate Crime Statistics Program. Blanks indicate quarters for which agencies did not submit reports.

[2] Population figures are published only for the cities. The figures listed for the universities and colleges are student enrollment and were provided by the United States Department of Education for the 2010 school year, the most recent available. The enrollment figures include full-time and part-time students.

Table VI-13.   Hate Crime Incidents Per Bias Motivation and Quarter, by Selected State and Agency, 2011—*Continued*

(Number)

State	Agency type/name	Number of incidents per bias motivation					Number of incidents per quarter[1]				Popu-lation[2]
		Race	Religion	Sexual orient-ation	Ethnicity	Disability	1st quarter	2nd quarter	3rd quarter	4th quarter	
	Nonmetropolitan Counties	2	0	0	1	0					
	King George	1	0	0	0	0	0	0	1	0	
	Southampton	1	0	0	1	0	1	0	1	0	
	Other Agencies	1	0	0	0	0					
	Virginia State Capitol	1	0	0	0	0	0	0	0	1	
Washington	**Total**	93	32	52	35	1					
	Cities	68	22	41	26	1					
	Anacortes	1	0	1	0	0	0	0	2	0	16,026
	Bainbridge Island	0	0	0	1	0	0	0	1	0	23,386
	Bellevue	7	4	0	1	0	2	4	6	0	124,283
	Bellingham	2	1	2	0	0	0	2	1	2	82,154
	Bothell	0	1	0	0	0	0	0	1	0	34,031
	Bremerton	1	0	0	0	0	0	1	0	0	38,321
	Burien	0	0	0	1	0	0	1	0	0	33,836
	Burlington	0	0	1	0	0	0	0	0	1	8,520
	Camas	2	0	0	0	0	2	0	0	0	19,659
	Centralia	2	0	1	0	0	1	0	0	2	16,592
	Chehalis	0	0	1	0	0	0	1	0	0	7,373
	Cheney	0	0	1	1	0	2	0	0	0	10,756
	Covington	0	1	0	0	0	0	0	0	1	17,851
	Des Moines	0	0	0	3	0	0	3	0	0	30,139
	East Wenatchee	0	0	1	0	0	0	1	0	0	13,397
	Edmonds	1	0	0	0	0	0	0	1	0	40,332
	Ellensburg	0	0	0	1	0	0	1	0	0	18,459
	Everett	1	0	2	0	0	0	0	1	2	104,635
	Federal Way	0	1	1	0	0	0	0	2	0	90,707
	Ferndale	1	0	2	1	0	0	2	1	1	11,594
	Garfield	0	0	1	0	0	0	1	0	0	606
	Issaquah	0	1	0	0	0	0	0	0	1	30,911
	Kennewick	0	0	2	1	0	3	0	0	0	75,077
	Kent	0	0	0	1	0	0	0	1	0	93,861
	Longview	0	0	0	1	0	0	1	0	0	37,223
	Lynden	1	0	0	0	1	1	0	1	0	12,138
	Moses Lake	0	0	0	1	0	1	0	0	0	20,686
	Mountlake Terrace	1	0	0	0	0	0	1	0	0	20,221
	Mount Vernon	2	0	0	1	0	0	0	1	2	32,241
	Newcastle	0	1	0	0	0	0	0	1	0	10,543
	Oak Harbor	1	0	0	0	0	0	1	0	0	22,421
	Omak	1	0	0	1	0	0	0	1	1	4,921
	Orting	0	0	0	1	0	0	0	1	0	6,852
	Othello	0	0	1	0	0	0	0	1	0	7,480
	Port Angeles	1	0	0	0	0	0	0	0	1	19,337
	Port Orchard	1	0	0	0	0	0	0	1	0	11,319
	Poulsbo	0	0	1	0	0	0	0	1	0	9,344
	Pullman	0	0	1	0	0	0	0	0	1	30,267
	Redmond	0	3	2	0	0	2	3	0	0	54,993
	Seattle	5	1	6	0	0	2	4	6	0	618,209
	Shelton	0	0	0	1	0	0	0	0	1	9,988
	Spokane	2	0	0	1	0	0	0	0	3	212,194
	Spokane Valley	5	1	1	0	0	4	1	0	2	91,163
	Tacoma	13	5	6	0	0	1	7	10	6	201,510
	Union Gap	0	0	0	1	0	0	0	1	0	6,142
	Vancouver	14	1	1	3	0	9	3	2	5	164,329
	Walla Walla	1	1	3	0	0	1	3	1	0	32,229
	Woodinville	0	0	1	1	0	0	1	0	1	11,110
	Yakima	2	0	2	3	0	3	2	1	1	92,496
	Universities and Colleges	3	2	2	1	0					
	Central Washington University	0	0	1	0	0	0	0	0	1	11,614
	Evergreen State College	0	1	0	0	0	0	0	0	1	4,833
	University of Washington	1	1	1	1	0	0	1	2	1	42,451
	Washington State University Pullman	1	0	0	0	0	0	0	0	1	26,308
	Vancouver[4]	1	0	0	0	0	0	0	1	0	

[1] Agencies published in this table indicated that at least one hate crime incident occurred in their respective jurisdictions during the quarter(s) for which they submitted a report to the Hate Crime Statistics Program. Blanks indicate quarters for which agencies did not submit reports.

[2] Population figures are published only for the cities. The figures listed for the universities and colleges are student enrollment and were provided by the United States Department of Education for the 2010 school year, the most recent available. The enrollment figures include full-time and part-time students.

[4] Student enrollment figures were not available.

Table VI-13. Hate Crime Incidents Per Bias Motivation and Quarter, by Selected State and Agency, 2011—*Continued*

(Number)

State	Agency type/name	Number of incidents per bias motivation					Number of incidents per quarter[1]				Population[2]
		Race	Religion	Sexual orient-ation	Ethnicity	Disability	1st quarter	2nd quarter	3rd quarter	4th quarter	
	Metropolitan Counties	20	7	8	6	0					
	Chelan	0	1	0	0	0	0	0	1	0	
	Clark	5	1	1	1	0	1	2	3	2	
	Cowlitz	1	0	0	0	0	0	0	0	1	
	King	4	1	1	2	0	2	0	3	3	
	Kitsap	2	0	1	2	0	2	2	0	1	
	Pierce	3	2	1	0	0	1	1	3	1	
	Skagit	1	0	0	1	0	0	1	1	0	
	Spokane	2	0	0	0	0	0	1	1	0	
	Thurston	2	2	4	0	0	5	0	2	1	
	Nonmetropolitan Counties	2	1	1	1	0					
	Clallam	1	0	0	0	0	1	0	0	0	
	Lewis	1	0	0	0	0	0	0	1	0	
	Mason	0	0	1	0	0	0	0	0	1	
	San Juan	0	0	0	1	0	0	1	0	0	
	Walla Walla	0	1	0	0	0	0	0	0	1	
	Other Agencies	0	0	0	1	0					
	Port of Seattle	0	0	0	1	0	0	1	0	0	
West Virginia	**Total**	12	1	3	1	1					
	Cities	4	0	3	1	1					
	Charleston	0	0	1	0	0	0	0	1	0	51,466
	Fairmont	1	0	0	0	1	0	1	1	0	18,728
	Moorefield	0	0	1	0	0	0	0	1	0	2,547
	Parkersburg	0	0	1	1	0	0	0	1	1	31,532
	Princeton	1	0	0	0	0	0	0	1	0	6,440
	Weirton	1	0	0	0	0	1	0	0	0	19,771
	Wheeling	1	0	0	0	0	1	0	0	0	28,522
	Universities and Colleges	1	1	0	0	0					
	West Virginia University	1	1	0	0	0	1	1	0	0	29,306
	Metropolitan Counties	2	0	0	0	0					
	Brooke	1	0	0	0	0	1	0	0	0	
	Wood	1	0	0	0	0	0	0	1	0	
	Nonmetropolitan Counties	4	0	0	0	0					
	Fayette	2	0	0	0	0	2	0	0	0	
	Raleigh	1	0	0	0	0	0	0	0	1	
	Tucker	1	0	0	0	0	1	0	0	0	
	State Police Agencies	1	0	0	0	0					
	State Police, Keyser	1	0	0	0	0	0	0	1	0	
Wisconsin	**Total**	49	4	16	6	1					
	Cities	44	4	14	5	1					
	Appleton	3	0	0	0	0	0	2	0	1	72,939
	Caledonia	1	0	0	0	0	0	1	0	0	24,813
	Everest	4	0	0	0	0	0	0	4	0	17,111
	Fond du Lac	2	2	0	0	0	1	1	1	1	43,208
	Fox Valley Metro	0	0	0	0	1	0	1	0	0	16,991
	Green Bay	1	0	1	0	0	0	0	0	2	104,510
	Hayward	1	0	0	0	0	0	0	1	0	2,328
	Kenosha	1	0	0	0	0	0	0	0	1	99,650
	Madison	8	1	5	2	0	3	4	5	4	234,225
	Manitowoc	3	0	1	0	0	1	1	1	1	33,883
	Milwaukee	15	1	5	3	0	4	9	9	2	597,426
	Minocqua	1	0	0	0	0	0	1	0	0	4,404
	Oak Creek	1	0	0	0	0	0	1	0	0	34,601

[1] Agencies published in this table indicated that at least one hate crime incident occurred in their respective jurisdictions during the quarter(s) for which they submitted a report to the Hate Crime Statistics Program. Blanks indicate quarters for which agencies did not submit reports.

[2] Population figures are published only for the cities. The figures listed for the universities and colleges are student enrollment and were provided by the United States Department of Education for the 2010 school year, the most recent available. The enrollment figures include full-time and part-time students.

Table VI-13. Hate Crime Incidents Per Bias Motivation and Quarter, by Selected State and Agency, 2011—*Continued*

(Number)

State	Agency type/name	Number of incidents per bias motivation					Number of incidents per quarter[1]				Popu-lation[2]
		Race	Religion	Sexual orient-ation	Ethnicity	Disability	1st quarter	2nd quarter	3rd quarter	4th quarter	
	Rhinelander	0	0	2	0	0	2				7,832
	Seymour	1	0	0	0	0	0	0	0	1	3,466
	Wausau	1	0	0	0	0	1	0	0	0	39,276
	West Allis	1	0	0	0	0	0	0	1	0	60,674
	Metropolitan Counties	2	0	2	1	0					
	Chippewa	0	0	1	1	0	0	2	0	0	
	Dane	1	0	1	0	0	0	0	1	1	
	Kenosha	1	0	0	0	0	0	0	0	1	
	Nonmetropolitan Counties	3	0	0	0	0					
	Portage	1	0	0	0	0	1	0	0	0	
	Sawyer	2	0	0	0	0	0	0	1	1	
Wyoming........................	**Total**	1	0	1	0	0					
	Cities	1	0	1	0	0					
	Green River	1	0	0	0	0	1	0	0	0	12,616
	Riverton	0	0	1	0	0	0	0	0	1	10,700

[1] Agencies published in this table indicated that at least one hate crime incident occurred in their respective jurisdictions during the quarter(s) for which they submitted a report to the Hate Crime Statistics Program. Blanks indicate quarters for which agencies did not submit reports.

[2] Population figures are published only for the cities. The figures listed for the universities and colleges are student enrollment and were provided by the United States Department of Education for the 2010 school year, the most recent available. The enrollment figures include full-time and part-time students.

APPENDIXES

APPENDIX I. CRIME TRENDS

In 2011, crime in the United States continued its trend of decline. Violent crimes declined by a rate of 3.8 percent, while property crime fell by 0.5 percent. The violent crime category includes murder, forcible rape, robbery, and aggravated assault, while property crimes include burglary, larceny-theft, and motor vehicle theft. Arson is also a property crime, but data for arson are not included in property crime totals due to variable participation from the reporting agencies.

Types of Crimes in 2011

The trend and the types of crimes committed in the United States not only continues to cover the main categories of murder, forcible rape, robbery, aggravated assault, burglary, larceny-theft, motor vehicle theft, and arson described in this publication's earlier chapters, but we are also facing an continuous increase in crimes committed through cyberspace and the Internet. These crimes are classified as scams or Internet fraud.

As Internet use has become a mainstay in our society and the world, the occurrence and development of Internet-based crimes has become widespread. As individuals, businesses, and organizations look for and implement efficient and effective ways to deter the ability of criminals to attack through cyberspace, new ways of victimizing Internet users continue to evolve.

Internet Fraud

The Internet Fraud Complaint Center—a partnership between the National White Collar Crime Center (NW3C), the Bureau of Justice Assistance (BJA), and the Federal Bureau of Investigation (FBI)—was established May 8, 2000, to address the ever-increasing incidence of online fraud. Just three years later, in response to the exponential increase in cyber crime of all types, the center changed its name to the Internet Crime Complaint Center (IC3®). With more than two million complaints received since its inception, IC3 serves as the nation's portal for reporting Internet crime and suspicious activity.

In 2011, the Internet Crime Complaint Center (IC3) actively pursued its mission to address crimes committed using the Internet, providing services to both victims of online crimes and to law enforcement. IC3 marked the third consecutive year of receiving more than 300,000 complaints, a 3.4 percent increase over 2010. The adjusted dollar loss of complaints was $485.3 million.[1]

The 2011 IC3 Internet Crime Report reveals both the scope of online crime and IC3's battle against it. The most common victim complaints included FBI-related scams, identity theft and advance fee fraud.[2] IC3 received and processed more than 26,000 complaints per month. Based on victim complaints, the top five states were California (34,169), Florida (20,034), Texas (18,477), New York (15,056) and Ohio (12,661). Victims in California reported the highest dollar losses with a total of $70.5 million. The average financial loss for reporting victims was $4,187.

IC3 serves as a powerful conduit for law enforcement to share information and pursue cases that often span jurisdictional boundaries. Collaboration within this partnership has produced a number of technological advancements to streamline the way complaints are processed and referred to investigators. Initially established as simply a convenient method for citizens to report Internet crime information, IC3 has evolved into a vital resource for both victims of online crime and for law enforcement across the country that investigate and prosecute a wide range of cases.

Below are recent scams and cyber crimes reported by the IC3 and the FBI in recent FBI press releases, and tips on ways to avoid becoming a victim of these crimes. Any type of cyber attack should be immediately reported to the local FBI office as well as to the IC3's website at www.IC3.gov. The IC3's complaint database links complaints together to refer them to the appropriate law enforcement agency for case consideration. The complaint information is also used to identify emerging trends and patterns. Information about recent Internet and cyber crime can be found at http://www.fbi.gov/scams-safety/e-scams.

Mystery/Secret Shopper Schemes

The IC3 has been alerted to an increase in employment schemes pertaining to mystery/secret shopper positions. Many retail and service corporations hire evaluators to perform secret or random checks on themselves or their competitors, and fraudsters are capitalizing on this employment opportunity. Victims have reported to the IC3 that they were contacted via email message and U.S. mail to apply to be a mystery shopper. Applicants are asked to send a résumé and are purportedly subject to an extensive background check before being accepted as a mystery shopper. The employees are sent a check with instructions to shop at a specified retailer for a specific length of time and spend a specific amount on merchandise from the store. The employees receive instructions to take note of the store's

---

[1] iC3 Internet Crime Complaint Center, 2011 Internet Crime Report, www.ic3.gov/media/annualreport/2011_IC3Report.pdf .
Methodology of evaluating loss amounts: FBI IC3 Unit staff reviewed for validity all complaints that reported a loss of more than $100,000. Analysts also converted losses reported in foreign currencies to dollars. The final amounts of all reported losses above $100,000 for which the complaint information did not support the loss amount were excluded from the statistics.

[2] Complaint category statistics that are based on the perceptions of the complaints are not typically accurate for statistical purposes. The statistics pulled from the complaints themselves, however, are considerably more accurate as they are categorized and grouped through the IC3 automated system. IC3 does not verify complaint data.

environment, color, payment procedures, gift items, and shopping/carrier bags and report back to the employer. The second evaluation is the ease and accuracy of wiring money from the retail location. The money to be wired is also included in the check sent to the employee. The remaining balance is the employee's payment for the completion of the assignment. After merchandise is purchased and money is wired, the employees are advised by the bank the check cashed was counterfeit, and they are responsible for the money lost in addition to bank fees incurred.

In other versions of the scheme, applicants are requested to provide bank account information to have money directly deposited into their accounts. The fraudster then has acquired access to these victims' accounts and can withdraw money, which makes the applicant a victim of identity theft.

Tips

The IC3 provides tips to help users avoid becoming a victim of employment schemes associated with mystery/secret shopping. They can also be found at http://www.ic3.gov/media/2010/100120.aspx:

- Do not respond to unsolicited (spam) email messages

- Do not open links contained within an unsolicited email message

- Be cautious of email messages claiming to contain pictures in attached files, as the files may contain viruses. Only open attachments from known senders. Scan all attachments for viruses, if possible

- Avoid filling out forms contained in email messages that ask for personal information

- Always compare the link in the email message to the link you are actually directed to and determine if they match and will lead you to a legitimate site

- There are legitimate mystery/secret shopper programs available. Research the legitimacy on companies hiring mystery shoppers. Legitimate companies will not charge an application fee and will accept applications online

- No legitimate mystery/secret shopper program will send payment in advance and ask the employee to send a portion of it back

Work from Home Scams

Consumers continue to lose money from work-from-home scams that assist cyber criminals to move stolen funds. Worse yet, due to their deliberate or unknowing participation in the scams, these individuals may face criminal charges. Work-from-home scam victims are often recruited by organized cyber criminals through newspaper ads, online employment services, unsolicited email messages or "spam," online and social networking sites advertising work-from-home opportunities. Once recruited, however, rather than becoming an employee of a legitimate business, the consumer is actually a "mule" for cyber criminals who use the consumer's or other victim's accounts to steal and launder money.

Fraudulent Classified Ads and Auction Sales

Internet criminals post classified ads and auctions for products they do not have and make the scam work by using stolen credit cards. Fraudsters receive an order from a victim, charge the victim's credit card for the amount of the order, then use a separate stolen credit card for the actual purchase. They pocket the purchase price obtained from the victim's credit card and have the merchant ship the item directly to the victim. Consequently, an item purchased from an online auction but received directly from the merchant is a strong indication of fraud. Victims of such a scam not only lose the money paid to the fraudster, but may be liable for receiving stolen goods.

Shoppers may help avoid these scams by using caution and not providing financial information directly to the seller, as fraudulent sellers will use this information to purchase items for their schemes. Always use a legitimate payment service to ensure a safe, legitimate purchase.

Diligently check each seller's rating and feedback along with their number of sales and the dates on which feedback was posted. Be wary of a seller with 100 percent positive feedback, with a low total number of feedback postings, or with all feedback posted around the same date and time.

Phishing and Smishing Schemes

In phishing schemes, the fraudster poses as a legitimate entity and uses email messages and scam websites to obtain victims' personal information, such as account numbers, user names, passwords, and so on. Smishing is the act of sending fraudulent text messages to bait a victim into revealing personal information.

Be leery of email messages or text messages that indicate a problem or question regarding your financial accounts. In this scam, fraudsters direct victims to follow a link or call a number to update an account or correct a purported problem. The link directs the victim to a fraudulent website or message that appears legitimate. Instead, the site allows the fraudster to steal any personal information the victim provides.

Smishing schemes involve fraudsters calling victims' cell phones and offering to lower the interest rates for credit cards the victims do not even possess. If a victim asserts that they do not own the credit card, the caller hangs up. These fraudsters call from TRAC cell phones that do not have voicemail, or the phone provides a constant busy signal when called, rendering these calls virtually untraceable.

Another scam involves fraudsters directing victims, via email, to a spoofed website. A spoofed website is a fake site that misleads the victim into providing personal information, which is routed to the scammer's computer.

Tips to avoid becoming a victim of cyber fraud. These can be found at http://www.fbi.gov/scams-safety/e-scams:

- Do not respond to unsolicited (spam) email messages

- Do not open links contained within an unsolicited email messages

- Be cautious of email messages claiming to contain pictures in attached files, as the files may contain viruses. Only open attachments from known senders. Scan the attachments for viruses, if possible

- Avoid filling out forms contained in email messages that ask for personal information

- Always compare the link in the email message with the link to which you are directed and determine whether they match and will lead you to a legitimate site

- Log directly onto the official website for the business identified in the email message, instead of "linking" to it from an unsolicited email message. If the email message appears to be from you bank, credit card issuer, or other company you deal with frequently, your statements or official correspondence from the business will provide the proper contact information

- Contact the actual business that supposedly sent the email message to verify whether the email message is genuine

- If you are asked to act quickly, or there is an emergency, it may be a scam. Fraudsters create a sense of urgency to get you to act quickly

- Verify any requests for personal information from any business or financial institution by contacting them using the main contact information

- Remember, if it looks too good to be true, it probably is

Prize Sweepstakes or Lottery Schemes

Prize sweepstakes or lottery scheme perpetrators use counterfeit checks that bear legitimate-looking logos of various financial institutions to fool victims into sending money to the fraudsters.

Fraudsters tell victims they've won a sweepstakes or lottery, but to receive a lump sum payout, they must pay the taxes and processing fees up front. Fraudsters direct individuals to call a telephone number to initiate a letter of instructions. The letter alleges that the victim may elect to take an advance on the winnings to make the required up-front payment. The letter includes a check in the amount of the alleged taxes and fees along with processing instructions. Ultimately, victims believe they are using the advance to make the required up-front payment, but in reality they are falling prey to the scheme.

The victim deposits the check into their own bank, which credits the account for the amount of the check before the check clears. The victim immediately withdraws the money and wires it to the fraudsters. Afterwards, the check proves to be counterfeit and the bank pulls the respective funds from the victim's account, leaving the victim liable for the amount of the counterfeit check plus any additional fees the bank may charge.

Persons may fall victim to this scheme due to the allure of easy money and the apparent legitimacy of the check the fraudsters included in the letter of instruction. The alleged cash prizes and locations of the financial institutions vary.

Tips to avoid being scammed (from http://www.ic3.gov/preventiontips.aspx#item-11):

- Be cautious when dealing with individuals outside of your own country

- Be leery if you do not remember entering a lottery or sweepstakes

- Beware of lotteries or sweepstakes that charge a fee prior to delivering your prize

- Be wary of demands to send additional money as a requirement to be eligible for future winnings

It is a violation of federal law to play a foreign lottery via mail or phone

Charitable Contribution Schemes

The FBI warns the public to be aware of and report any instances of alleged fraudulent activity related to relief operations and funding for victims. Criminals exploit these tragedies by sending fraudulent email messages and creating phony websites designed to solicit contributions.

The National Center for Disaster Fraud was created by the Department of Justice to investigate, prosecute, and deter fraud in the wake of Hurricane Katrina, when billions of dollars in federal disaster relief poured into the Gulf Cost region. Its mission has expanded to include suspected fraud from any natural or manmade disaster. More than 20 federal agencies, including the FBI, participate in the National Center for Disaster Fraud, which allows the center to act as a centralized clearinghouse of information related to disaster relief fraud.

Use due diligence before giving contributions to anyone soliciting donations or individuals offering to provide assistance to those affected by the tornadoes. Solicitations can originate from email messages, websites, door-to-door collections, flyers, mailings, telephone calls, and other similar methods.

Before making a donation of any kind, consumers should adhere to the following guidelines (from http://www.fbi.gov/sandiego/press-releases/2012/tips-on-avoiding-fraudulent-charitable-contribution-schemes):

- Do not respond to any unsolicited (spam) incoming email messages, including requests to open links contained within those messages, because they may contain computer viruses

- Be skeptical of individuals representing themselves as members of charitable organizations or officials asking for donations via email messages or social networking sites

- Beware of organizations with copycat names similar to but not exactly the same as those of reputable charities

- Be cautious of email messages that claim to show pictures of the disaster areas in attached files because the files may contain viruses. Only open attachments from known senders

- Ensure that contributions are received and used for intended purposes by making contributions directly to known organizations rather than relying on others to make the donation on your behalf

- Do not be pressured into making contributions; reputable charities do not use such tactics

- Be aware of whom you are dealing with when providing your personal and financial information. Providing such information may compromise your identity and make you vulnerable to identity theft

- Avoid cash donations if possible. Pay by credit card or write a check directly to the charity. Do not make checks payable to individuals.

- Verify websites. Legitimate charities do not normally solicit donations via money transfer services. Most legitimate charities' websites end in .org rather than .com.

Scareware

Scareware is malicious software that poses as legitimate computer security software and purports to detect a variety of threats on the affected computer that do not actually exist. Users are then informed they must purchase what they are told is anti-virus software to repair their computers. The users are then barraged with aggressive and disruptive notifications until they supply their credit card number and pay for the worthless "anti-virus" product. The product is, in fact, fake.

The FBI has seized more than 40 computers, servers, and bank accounts linked to scareware schemes.

The scareware scheme used a variety of ruses to trick consumers into infecting their computers with the malicious scareware products, including web pages featuring fake computer scans. Once the scareware was downloaded, victims were notified that their computers were infected with a range of malicious software, such as viruses and Trojans, and badgered into purchasing the fake anti-virus software to resolve the non-existent problem at a cost of up to $129. In one scheme, which was based in Kyiv, Ukraine, an estimated 960,000 users were victimized by this scareware scheme, leading to $72 million in actual losses.

As of June 2011, more than 1 million scareware victims had lost over $74 million.[3]

Online Vehicle Shopping Scams

Online vehicle shoppers are being victimized by fraudulent vehicle sales and false claims of vehicle protection programs (VPP). In fraudulent vehicle sales, criminals attempt to sell vehicles they do not own. They create an attractive deal by advertising vehicles for sale at prices below book value. Often sellers state that they need to sell the vehicle because they are moving for work, to include military deployments.

Because of the alleged pending move, criminals refuse to meet the victim in person or allow a vehicle inspection, and they often attempt to rush the sale. To make the deal appear legitimate, the criminal instructs the victim to send full or partial payment to a third-party agent via a wire transfer payment service and to fax the payment receipt to the seller as proof of payment.

The criminal pockets the payment but does not deliver the vehicle. Criminals also attempt to make their scams appear valid by misusing the names of reputable companies and programs.

In a new twist, criminals use a live-chat feature in email correspondence and electronic invoices. As live-chat assistants, the criminals answer victims' questions and assure them the deals are safe, claiming that safeguards are in place to reimburse buyers for any loss. The criminals falsely assert that their sales are protected by liability insurance coverage up to $50,000.

Automotive shoppers should exercise due diligence before engaging in transactions to purchase vehicles advertised online. In particular, shoppers should be cautious of the following situations (from http://www.ic3.gov/media/2011/110815.aspx):

- Sellers who want to move the transaction from one platform to another (for example, from Craigslist to eBay Motors)

- Sellers who claim that a buyer protection program offered by a major Internet company covers an auto transaction conducted outside that company's site

[3] June 22, 2011. "'Scareware' Distributors Targeted: 12 Nations Coordinate Anti-Cyber Crime Effort." http://www.fbi.gov/news/stories/2011/june/cyber_062211

- Sellers who push for speedy completion of the transaction and request payments via quick wire transfer payment systems

- Sellers who refuse to meet in person, or refuse to allow the buyer to physically inspect the vehicle before the purchase

- Transactions in which the seller and vehicle are in different locations. Criminals often claim to have been transferred for work reasons, deployed by the military, or moved because of a family circumstance, and could not take the vehicle with them

- Vehicles advertised at well below their market value. Remember, if it looks too good to be true, it probably is

Timeshare Marketing Scams

Timeshare owners across the country are being scammed out of millions of dollars by unscrupulous companies that promise to sell or rent the unsuspecting victim; timeshares. In the typical scam, timeshare owners receive unexpected or uninvited telephone calls or email messages from criminals posing as sales representatives for a timeshare resale company. The representative promises a quick sale, often within 60 to 90 days. The sales representatives often use high-pressure sales tactics to add a sense of urgency to the deal. Some victims have reported that sales representatives pressured them by claiming there was a buyer waiting in the wings, either on the other line or present in the office.

Timeshare owners who agree to sell are told that they must pay an upfront fee to cover anything from listing and advertising fees to closing costs. Many victims have provided credit cards to pay the fees ranging from a few hundred to a few thousand dollars. Once the fee is paid, timeshare owners report that the company becomes evasive—calls go unanswered, numbers are disconnected, and websites are inaccessible.

In some cases, timeshare owners who have been defrauded by a timeshare sales scheme have been subsequently contacted by an unscrupulous timeshare fraud recovery company as well. The representative from the recovery company promises assistance in recovering money lost in the sales scam. Some recovery companies require an up-front fee for services rendered, while other promise no fees will be paid unless a refund is obtained for the timeshare owner. The IC3 has identified some instances where people involved with the recovery company also have a connection to the resale company, raising the possibility that timeshare owners are being scammed twice by the same people.

If you are contacted by someone offering to sell or rent your timeshare, the IC3 recommends using caution. Listed below are tips you can use to avoid becoming a victim of a timeshare scheme (from http://www.ic3.gov/media/2012/120125.aspx):

- Be wary if a company asks you for up-front fees to sell or rent your timeshare

- Read the fine print of any sales contract or rental agreement provided

- Check with the Better Business Bureau to ensure the company is reputable

To obtain more information on Internet schemes, visit www.LooksTooGoodToBeTrue.com. Also, anyone who believes they have been a victim of this type of scam should promptly report it to the IC3's website at www.IC3.gov.

Payday Loan Telephone Collection Scams

The typical payday loan scam involves a caller who claims that the victim is delinquent on a payday loan and must make payment to avoid legal consequences. Callers pose as representatives of the FBI, "Federal Legislative Department," various law firms, or other legitimate-sounding agencies and claim to be collecting debt for companies such as United Cash Advance, U.S. Cash Advance, U.S. Cash Net, or other Internet check-cashing services. The fraudsters relentlessly call the victim's home, cell phone, and place of employment in attempts to obtain payment. The callers refuse to provide information regarding the alleged payday loan or any documentation and become verbally abusive when questioned.

One of the most insidious aspects of this scam is that the callers have accurate information about the victims, including Social Security numbers, dates of birth, addresses, employer information, bank account numbers, and names and telephone numbers of relatives and friends. The method by which the fraudsters obtained the personal information is unclear, but victims often relay that they had completed online applications for other loans or credit cards before the calls began.

The Internet Crime Complaint Center has observed variations of the scam in which the caller tells the victim that there are outstanding warrants for the victim's arrest. The caller claims that the basis of the warrants is non-payment of the underlying loan and/or hacking; if it's the latter, the caller tells the victim that he or she is wanted for hacking into a business" computer system to steal customer information. The caller will then demand payment via debit/credit card; in other cases, the caller further instructs victims to obtain a prepaid card to cover the payment.

The high-pressure collection tactics used by the fraudsters have also evolved. In one complaint, a person posed as a process server and appeared at the victim's job. In another instance, a phony process server came to a victim's home. In both cases, after claiming to be serving a court summons, the alleged process server said the victim could avoid going to court if he or she provided a debit card number for repayment of the loan.

If you are contacted by someone who is trying to collect a debt that you do not owe, you should take the following steps (from http://www.ic3.gov/media/2012/120221.aspx).

- Contact your local law enforcement agencies if you feel you are in immediate danger

- Contact your bank(s) and credit card companies

- Contact the three major credit bureaus and request an alert be put on your file

- If you have received a legitimate loan and want to verify that you do not have any outstanding obligation, contact the loan company directly

- File a complaint at www.IC3.gov

Malware Installed on Travelers' Laptops Through Software Updates on Hotel Internet Connections

Analysis from the FBI and other government agencies demonstrates that malicious actors are targeting travelers abroad through pop-up windows while they are establishing an Internet connection in their hotel rooms.

Travelers' laptops are being infected with malicious software when using hotel Internet connections abroad. In this attack, the traveler attempts to set up the hotel room Internet connection and is presented with a pop-up window notifying the traveler to update a widely used software product. If the traveler selects to accept and install the update, malicious software is installed on the laptop. The pop-up window appears to be offering a routine update to a legitimate software product for which updates are frequently available.

The FBI recommends that all government, private industry, and academic personnel who travel abroad take extra caution before updating software products through their hotel Internet connection. Checking the author or digital certificate of any prompted update to see if it corresponds to the software vendor may reveal an attempted attack. The FBI also recommends that travelers perform software updates on laptops immediately before traveling, and that they download software updates directly from the software vendor's website if updates are necessary while abroad.

Tips for Online Shopping

As more and more individuals purchase merchandise online via company web sties or auction sites, users need to take precautions to ensure safe and reliable transactions. Safeguard online purchases by following these general tips to protect you on auction sites and to avoid credit card fraud.

Tips to Avoid Internet Auction Fraud (from http://www.fbi.gov/scams-safety/fraud/internet_fraud)

- Understand as much as possible about how the auction works, what your obligations are as a buyer, and what the seller's obligations are before you bid.

- Find out what actions the website/company takes if a problem occurs and consider insuring the transaction and shipment.

- Learn as much as possible about the seller, especially if the only information you have is an e-mail address. If it is a business, check the Better Business Bureau where the seller/business is located.

- Examine the feedback on the seller.

- Determine what method of payment the seller is asking from the buyer and where he/she is asking to send payment.

- If possible, purchase items online using your credit card, because you can often dispute the charges if something goes wrong.

- Be cautious when dealing with sellers outside the United States. If a problem occurs with the auction transaction, it could be much more difficult to rectify.

- Ask the seller about when delivery can be expected and whether the merchandise is covered by a warranty or can be exchanged if there is a problem.

- Make sure there are no unexpected costs, including whether shipping and handling is included in the auction price.

- There should be no reason to give out your social security number or driver's license number to the seller.

Tips to Avoid Credit Card Fraud

- Ensure a site is secure and reputable before providing your credit card number online

- Don't trust a site just because it claims to be secure

- If purchasing merchandise, ensure it is from a reputable source

- Promptly reconcile credit card statements to avoid unauthorized charges

- Do your research to ensure legitimacy of the individual or company

- Beware of providing credit card information when requested through unsolicited emails

The FBI warns to be cautious when making transactions over the Internet—making purchases, investments, doing business with unknown Internet companies, or doing business with foreign countries (419 fraud—a letter from a foreign country or government asking for your cooperation with moving large sums of money to overseas bank accounts). Some of these sites could be fraudulent or be scams to get access to your bank accounts and money. The FBI advises us to do our homework and confirm the legitimacy of any business or site that we contemplate transacting business with over the Internet.

APPENDIX II. METHODOLOGY

Submitting Uniform Crime Reporting (UCR) program data to the Federal Bureau of Investigation (FBI) is a collective effort on the part of city, county, state, tribal, and federal law enforcement agencies to present a nationwide view of crime. Law enforcement agencies in 46 states and the District of Columbia voluntarily contribute crime data to the UCR program through their respective state UCR programs. For those states that do not have a state program, local agencies submit crime statistics directly to the FBI. The state UCR programs function as liaisons between local agencies and the FBI. Many states have mandatory reporting requirements, and many state programs collect data beyond the scope of the UCR program to address crime problems specific to their particular jurisdictions. In most cases, state programs also provide direct and frequent service to participating law enforcement agencies, make information readily available for statewide use, and help streamline the national program's operations.

Criteria for State UCR programs

The criteria established for state programs ensure consistency and comparability in the data submitted to the national program, as well as regular and timely reporting. These criteria are:

1. The state program must conform to the national UCR program standards, definitions, and information required.

2. The state criminal justice agency must have a proven, effective, statewide program and have instituted acceptable quality control procedures.

3. The state crime reporting must cover a percentage of the population at least equal to that covered by the national UCR program through direct reporting.

4. The state program must have adequate field staff assigned to conduct audits and to assist contributing agencies in record-keeping practices and crime-reporting procedures.

5. The state program must furnish the FBI with all of the detailed data regularly collected by the FBI from individual agencies that report to the state program in the form of duplicate returns, computer printouts, and/or appropriate electronic media.

6. The state program must have the proven capability (tested over a period of time) to supply all the statistical data required in time to meet publication deadlines of the national UCR program.

Data Completeness and Quality

National program staff members contact the state UCR program in connection with crime-reporting matters and, when necessary and approved by the state, they contact individual contributors within the state. To fulfill its responsibilities in connection with the UCR program, the FBI reviews and edits individual agency reports for completeness and quality. Upon request, they conduct training programs within the state on law enforcement record-keeping and crime-reporting procedures. The FBI conducts an audit of each state's UCR data collection procedures once every three years, in accordance with audit standards established by the federal government. Should circumstances develop in which the state program does not comply with the aforementioned requirements, the national program may institute a direct collection of data from law enforcement agencies within the state.

Reporting Procedures

Offenses known and value of property—Law enforcement agencies tabulate the number of Part I offenses reported based on records of all reports of crime received from victims, officers who discover infractions, or other sources, and submit these reports each month to the FBI directly or through their state UCR programs. Part I offenses include murder and nonnegligent manslaughter, forcible rape, robbery, aggravated assault, burglary, larceny-theft, motor vehicle theft, and arson. Each month, law enforcement agencies also submit to the FBI the value of property stolen and recovered in connection with the offenses and detailed information pertaining to criminal homicide.

Unfounded offenses and clearances—When, through investigation, an agency determines that complaints of crimes are unfounded or false, the agency eliminates that offense from its crime tally through an entry on the monthly report. The report also provides the total number of actual Part I offenses, the number of offenses cleared, and the number of clearances that involve only offenders under the age of 18. (Law enforcement can clear crimes in one of two ways: by the arrest of at least one person who is charged and turned over to the court for prosecution or by exceptional means—when some element beyond law enforcement's control precludes the arrest of a known offender.)

Persons arrested—In addition to reporting Part I offenses each month, law enforcement agencies also provide data on the age, sex, and race of persons arrested for Part I and Part II offenses. Part II offenses encompass all crimes, except traffic violations, that are not classified as Part I offenses.

Officers killed or assaulted—Each month, law enforcement agencies also report information to the UCR program regarding law enforcement officers killed or assaulted, and each year they report the number of full-time sworn and civilian law enforcement personnel employed as of October 31.

Hate crimes—At the end of each quarter, law enforcement agencies report summarized data on hate crimes; that is specific offenses that were motivated by an offender's bias against the perceived race, religion, ethnic or national origin, sexual orientation, or physical or mental disability of the victim. Those agencies participating in the UCR program's National Incident-Based Reporting System (NIBRS) submit hate crime data monthly.

Editing Procedures

The UCR program thoroughly examines each report it receives for arithmetical accuracy and for deviations in crime data from month to month and from present to past years that may indicate errors. UCR staff members compare an agency's monthly reports with its previous submissions and with reports from similar agencies to identify any unusual fluctuations in the agency's crime count. Considerable variations in crime levels may indicate modified records procedures, incomplete reporting, or changes in the jurisdiction's geopolitical structure.

Evaluation of trends—Data reliability is a high priority of the FBI, which brings any deviations or arithmetical adjustments to the attention of state UCR programs or the submitting agencies. Typically, FBI staff members study the monthly reports to evaluate periodic trends prepared for individual reporting units. Any significant increase or decrease becomes the subject of a special inquiry. Changes in crime reporting procedures or annexations that affect an agency's jurisdiction can influence the level of reported crime. When this occurs, the FBI excludes the figures for specific crime categories or totals, if necessary, from the trend tabulations.

Training for contributors—In addition to the evaluation of trends, the FBI provides training seminars and instructional materials on crime reporting procedures to assist contributors in complying with UCR standards. Throughout the country, representatives from the national program coordinate with representatives of state programs and law enforcement personnel and hold training sessions to explain the purpose of the program, the rules of uniform classification and scoring, and the methods of assembling the information for reporting. When an individual agency has specific problems with compiling its crime statistics and its remedial efforts are unsuccessful, personnel from the FBI's Criminal Justice Information Services Division may visit the contributor to aid in resolving the problems.

UCR Handbook—The national UCR program publishes the *Uniform Crime Reporting (UCR) Handbook* (revised 2004), which details procedures for classifying and scoring offenses and serves as the contributing agencies' basic resource for preparing reports. The national staff also produces letters to UCR contributors, state program bulletins, and UCR newsletters as needed. These publications provide policy updates and new information, as well as clarification of reporting issues.

The final responsibility for data submissions rests with the individual contributing law enforcement agency. Although

the FBI makes every effort through its editing procedures, training practices, and correspondence to ensure the validity of the data it receives, the accuracy of the statistics depends primarily on the adherence of each contributor to the established standards of reporting. Deviations from these established standards that cannot be resolved by the national UCR program may be brought to the attention of the Criminal Justice Information Systems Committees of the International Association of Chiefs of Police and the National Sheriffs' Association.

Population Estimation

The FBI calculated 2011 state growth rates using the U.S. Census Bureau's 2010 decennial state/national population figures and 2011 provisional state/national population estimates. The FBI then estimated population figures for city jurisdictions by applying the 2011 state growth rate to the 2010 U.S. Census Bureau data.

For the 2010 population estimates used in this report, the FBI computed individual rates of growth from one year to the next for every city/town and county using 2000 decennial population counts and 2001 through 2009 population estimates from the U.S. Census Bureau. Each agency's rates of growth were averaged; that average was then applied and added to its 2009 Census population estimate to derive the agency's 2010 population estimate.

NIBRS Conversion

Thirty-two state programs are certified to provide their UCR data in the expanded National Incident-Based Reporting System (NIBRS) format. For presentation in this book, the NIBRS data were converted to the historical Summary Reporting System data. The UCR program staff constructed the NIBRS database to allow for such conversion so that UCR's long-running time series could continue.

Crime Trends

By showing fluctuations from year to year, trend statistics offer the data user an added perspective from which to study crime. Percent change tabulations in this publication are computed only for reporting agencies that provided comparable data for the periods under consideration. The FBI excludes from the trend calculations all figures except those received for common months from common agencies. Also excluded are unusual fluctuations of data that the FBI determines are the result of such variables as improved records procedures, annexations, and so on.

Caution to Users

Data users should exercise care in making any direct comparison between data in this publication and those in prior issues of *Crime in the United States*. Because of differing levels of participation from year to year and reporting problems that require the FBI to estimate crime counts for certain contributors, some data may not be comparable. In addition, this publication may contain updates to data provided in prior years' publications.

For information about the FBI's caution against ranking, including warnings about variables affecting crime and characteristics of jusridictions, please see http://www .fbi.gov/about-us/cjis/ucr/crime-in-the-u.s/2011/crime-in-the -u.s.-2011/caution-against-ranking.

Offense Estimation

Some tables in this publication contain statistics for the entire United States. Because not all law enforcement agencies provide data for complete reporting periods, the FBI includes estimated crime numbers in these presentations. The FBI estimates data for three areas: Metropolitan Statistical Areas (MSAs), cities outside MSAs, and nonmetropolitan counties; and computes estimates for participating agencies that do not provide 12 months of complete data. For agencies supplying 3 to 11 months of data, the national UCR program estimates for the missing data by following a standard estimation procedure using the data provided by the agency. If an agency has supplied less than 3 months of data, the FBI computes estimates by using the known crime figures of similar areas within a state and assigning the same proportion of crime volumes to nonreporting agencies. The estimation process considers the following: population size covered by the agency; type of jurisdiction; for example, police department versus sheriff's office; and geographic location.

Estimation of State-Level Data

In response to various circumstances, the FBI calculates estimated offense totals for certain states. For example, some states do not provide forcible rape figures in accordance with UCR guidelines. In addition, problems at the state level have, at times, resulted in no useable data. Also, the conversion of the National Incident-Based Reporting System (NIBRS) data to Summary data has contributed to the need for unique estimation procedures. A summary of state-specific and offense-specific estimation procedures can be found online at http://www.fbi.gov/about-us/cjis/ucr/ crime-in-the-u.s/2010/crime-in-the-u.s.-2010/methodology.

APPENDIX III. OFFENSE DEFINITIONS

The Uniform Crime Reporting (UCR) program divides offenses into two groups. Contributing agencies submit information on the number of Part I offenses known to law enforcement; those offenses cleared by arrest or exceptional means; and the age, sex, and race of persons arrested for each of these offenses. Contributors provide only arrest data for Part II offenses. These are definitions of offenses set forth by the UCR.

The UCR program collects data on Part I offenses to measure the level and scope of crime occurring throughout the nation. The program's founders chose these offenses because (1) they are serious crimes, (2) they occur with regularity in all areas of the country, and (3) they are likely to be reported to police.

Part I offenses include criminal homicide, forcible rape, robbery, aggravated assault, burglary, larceny-theft, motor vehicle theft, and arson.

Criminal homicide—a.) Murder and nonnegligent manslaughter: the willful (nonnegligent) killing of one human being by another. Deaths caused by negligence, attempts to kill, assaults to kill, suicides, and accidental deaths are excluded. The program classifies justifiable homicides separately and limits the definition to (1) the killing of a felon by a law enforcement officer in the line of duty; or (2) the killing of a felon, during the commission of a felony, by a private citizen. b.) Manslaughter by negligence: the killing of another person through gross negligence. Deaths of persons due to their own negligence, accidental deaths not resulting from gross negligence, and traffic fatalities are excluded.

Forcible rape—The carnal knowledge of a female forcibly and against her will. Assaults and attempts to commit rape by force or threat of force are also included. Statutory rape (no force used—female victim is under the age of consent) and other sex offenses are excluded. Sexual attacks on males are counted as aggravated assaults or sex offenses, depending on the circumstances and the extent of any injuries.

Robbery—The taking or attempted taking of anything of value from the care, custody, or control of a person or persons by force or threat of force or violence and/or by putting the victim in fear.

Aggravated assault—An unlawful attack by one person upon another for the purpose of inflicting severe or aggravated bodily injury. This type of assault usually is accompanied by the use of a weapon or by means likely to produce death or great bodily harm. Simple assaults are excluded.

Burglary (breaking or entering)—The unlawful entry of a structure to commit a felony or a theft. Attempted forcible entry is included.

Larceny-theft (except motor vehicle theft)—The unlawful taking, carrying, leading, or riding away of property from the possession or constructive possession of another. Examples are thefts of bicycles or automobile parts and accessories, shoplifting, pocket-picking, or the stealing of any property or article that is not taken by force and violence or by fraud. Attempted larcenies are included. Embezzlement, confidence games, forgery, worthless checks, and the like, are excluded.

Motor vehicle theft—The theft or attempted theft of a motor vehicle. A motor vehicle is self-propelled and runs on land surface and not on rails. Motorboats, construction equipment, airplanes, and farming equipment are specifically excluded from this category.

Arson—Any willful or malicious burning or attempt to burn, with or without intent to defraud, a dwelling house, public building, motor vehicle, aircraft, personal property of another, and the like.

The **Part II** offenses for which only arrest data are collected, are:

Other assaults, also known as other assaults (simple)— Assaults and attempted assaults that are not of an aggravated nature and do not result in serious injury to the victim. Included in this category are stalking, intimidation, coercion, and hazing.

Forgery and counterfeiting—The altering, copying, or imitating of something, without authority or right, with the intent to deceive or defraud by passing the copy or thing altered or imitated as that which is original or genuine; or the selling, buying, or possession of an altered, copied, or imitated thing with the intent to deceive or defraud. Attempts are included.

Fraud—The intentional perversion of the truth for the purpose of inducing another person or other entity in reliance upon it to part with something of value or to surrender a legal right. Fraudulent conversion and obtaining of money or property by false pretenses. Confidence games and bad checks, except forgeries and counterfeiting, are included.

Embezzlement—The unlawful misappropriation or misapplication by an offender of money, property, or some other thing of value entrusted to that offender's care, custody, or control.

Stolen property; buying, receiving, possessing—Buying, receiving, possessing, selling, concealing, or transporting any property with the knowledge that it has been unlawfully taken, as by burglary, embezzlement, fraud, larceny, robbery, and the like. Attempts are included.

Vandalism—To willfully or maliciously destroy, injure, disfigure, or deface any public or private property, real or personal, without the consent of the owner or person having custody or control by cutting, tearing, breaking, marking, painting, drawing, covering with filth, or any other such means as may be specified by local law. Attempts are included.

Weapons; carrying, possessing, and the like—The violation of laws or ordinances prohibiting the manufacture, sale, purchase, transportation, possession, concealment, or use of firearms, cutting instruments, explosives, incendiary devices, or other deadly weapons. Attempts are included.

Prostitution and commercialized vice—The unlawful promotion of or participation in sexual activities for profit, including attempts. To solicit customers or transport persons for prostitution purposes; to own, manage, or operate a dwelling or other establishment for the purposes of providing a place where prostitution is performed; or to otherwise assist or promote prostitution.

Sex offenses (except forcible rape, prostitution, and commercialized vice)—Offenses against chastity, common decency, morals, and the like. Incest, indecent exposure, and statutory rape, as well as attempts are included.

Drug abuse violations—The violation of laws prohibiting the production, distribution, and/or use of certain controlled substances. The unlawful cultivation, manufacture, distribution, sale, purchase, use, possession, transportation, or importation of any controlled drug or narcotic substance. Arrests for violations of state and local laws, specifically those relating to the unlawful possession, sale, use, growing, manufacturing, and making of narcotic drugs. The following drug categories are specified: opium or cocaine and their derivatives (morphine, heroin, codeine); marijuana; synthetic narcotics—manufactured narcotics that can cause true addiction (demerol, methadone); and dangerous nonnarcotic drugs (barbiturates, benzedrine).

Gambling—To unlawfully bet or wager money or something else of value; assist, promote, or operate a game of chance for money or some other stake; possess or transmit wagering information; manufacture, sell, purchase, possess, or transport gambling equipment, devices, or goods; or tamper with the outcome of a sporting event or contest to gain a gambling advantage.

Offenses against the family and children—Unlawful nonviolent acts by a family member (or legal guardian) that threaten the physical, mental, or economic well-being or morals of another family member and that are not classifiable as other offenses, such as assault or sex offenses. Attempts are included.

Driving under the influence—Driving or operating a motor vehicle or common carrier while mentally or physically impaired as the result of consuming an alcoholic beverage or using a drug or narcotic.

Liquor laws—The violation of state or local laws or ordinances prohibiting the manufacture, sale, purchase, transportation, possession, or use of alcoholic beverages, not including driving under the influence and drunkenness. Federal violations are excluded.

Drunkenness—To drink alcoholic beverages to the extent that one's mental faculties and physical coordination are substantially impaired. Excludes driving under the influence.

Disorderly conduct—Any behavior that tends to disturb the public peace or decorum, scandalize the community, or shock the public sense of morality.

Vagrancy—The violation of a court order, regulation, ordinance, or law requiring the withdrawal of persons from the streets or other specified areas; prohibiting persons from remaining in an area or place in an idle or aimless manner; or prohibiting persons from going from place to place without visible means of support.

All other offenses—All violations of state or local laws not specifically identified as Part I or Part II offenses, except traffic violations.

Suspicion—Arrested for no specific offense and released without formal charges being placed.

Curfew and loitering laws (persons under 18 years of age)—Violations by juveniles of local curfew or loitering ordinances.

APPENDIX IV. GEOGRAPHIC AREA DEFINITIONS

The program collects crime data and supplemental information that make it possible to generate a variety of statistical compilations, including data presented by reporting areas. These statistics enable data users to analyze local crime data in conjunction with those for areas of similar geographic location or population size. The reporting areas that the program uses in its data breakdowns include community types, population groups, and regions and divisions. For community types, the program considers proximity to metropolitan areas using the designations established by the U.S. Office of Management and Budget (OMB). (Generally, sheriffs, county police, and state police report crimes within counties but outside of cities; local police report crimes within city limits.) The number of inhabitants living in a locale (based on the U.S. Census Bureau's figures) determines the population group into which the program places it. For its geographic breakdowns, the program divides the United States into regions and divisions.

Regions and Divisions

The map below illustrates the nine divisions that make up the four regions of the United States. The program uses this widely recognized geographic organization when compiling the nation's crime data. The regions and divisions are as follows:

Northeast
New England—Connecticut, Maine, Massachusetts, New Hampshire, Rhode Island, and Vermont

Middle Atlantic—New York, New Jersey, and Pennsylvania

Midwest

East North Central—Illinois, Indiana, Michigan, Ohio, and Wisconsin

West North Central—Iowa, Kansas, Minnesota, Missouri, Nebraska, North Dakota, and South Dakota

South
South Atlantic—Delaware, District of Columbia, Florida, Georgia, Maryland, North Carolina, South Carolina, Virginia, and West Virginia

East South Central—Alabama, Kentucky, Mississippi, and Tennessee

West South Central—Arkansas, Louisiana, Oklahoma, and Texas

West
Mountain—Arizona, Colorado, Idaho, Montana, Nevada, New Mexico, Utah, and Wyoming

Pacific—Alaska, California, Hawaii, Oregon, and Washington

Community Types

To assist data users who wish to analyze and present uniform statistical data about metropolitan areas, the program uses reporting units that represent major population centers. The program compiles data for the following three types of communities:

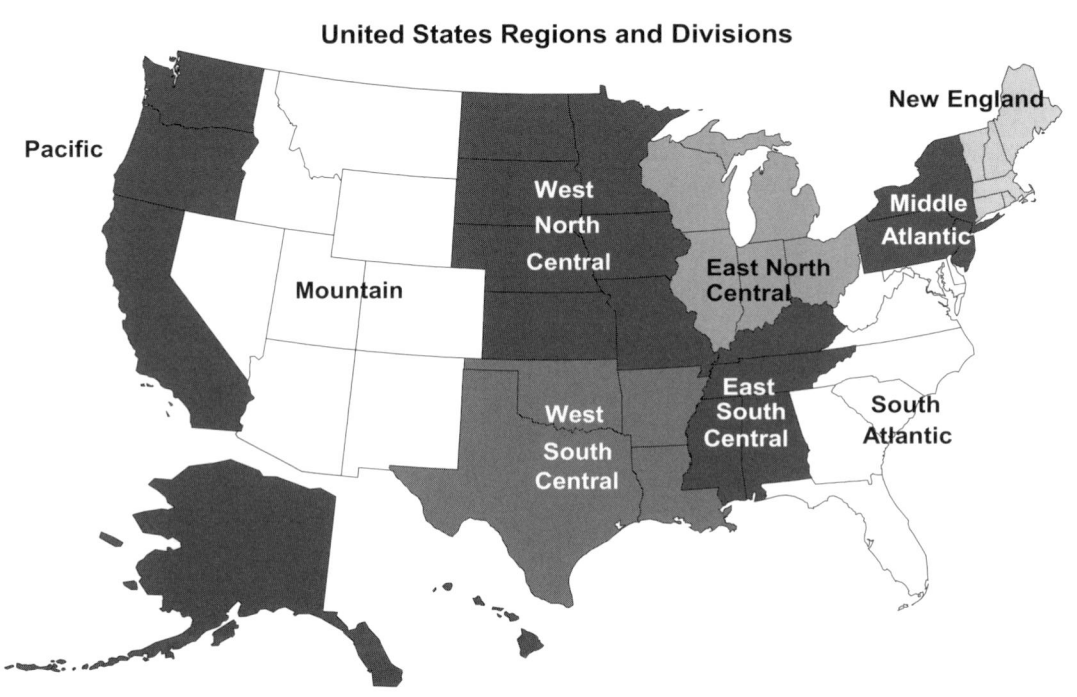

United States Regions and Divisions

Metropolitan Statistical Areas (MSAs)—Each MSA contains a principal city or urbanized area with a population of at least 50,000 inhabitants. MSAs include the principal city, the county in which the city is located, and other adjacent counties that have a high degree of economic and social integration with the principal city and county (as defined by the OMB), which is measured through commuting. In the program, counties within an MSA are considered metropolitan counties. In addition, MSAs may cross state boundaries.

Some presentations in this publication refer to Metropolitan Divisions, which are subdivisions of an MSA that consists of a core with "a population of at least 2.5 million persons. A Metropolitan Division consists of one or more main/secondary counties that represent an employment center or centers, plus adjacent counties associated with the main county or counties through commuting ties," (*Federal Register* 65 [249]). Also, some tables reference suburban areas, which are subdivisions of MSAs that exclude the principal cities but include all the remaining cities (those having fewer than 50,000 inhabitants) and the unincorporated areas of the MSAs.

Because the elements that comprise MSAs, particularly the geographic compositions, are subject to change, the program discourages data users from making year-to-year comparisons of MSA data.

Cities Outside MSAs—Ordinarily, cities outside MSAs are incorporated areas. In 2010, cities outside MSAs made up 6.5 percent of the nation's population.

Nonmetropolitan Counties Outside MSAs—Most nonmetropolitan counties are composed of unincorporated areas.

Metropolitan and nonmetropolitan community types are further illustrated in the following table:

Metropolitan	Nonmetropolitan
Principal cities (50,000+ inhabitants) Suburban cities	Cities outside metropolitan areas
Metropolitan counties	Nonmetropolitan counties

Population Groups

The program uses the following population group designations:

Individual law enforcement agencies are the source of UCR data. The number of agencies included in each population group may vary from year to year because of population growth, geopolitical consolidation, municipal incorporation, and so on. In noncensus years, the program estimates population figures for individual jurisdictions. (A more comprehensive explanation of population estimations can be found in Appendix I.)

The categories below show the number of agencies contributing to the program within each population group for 2011:

Population Group	Political Label	Population Range
I	City	250,000 or more
II	City	100,000 to 249,999
III	City	50,000 to 99,999
IV	City	25,000 to 49,999
V	City	10,000 to 24,999
VI	City[1]	Fewer than 10,000
VIII (Nonmetropolitan county)	County[2]	N/A
IX (Metropolitan county)	County[2]	N/A

Population Group	Number of Agencies	Population Covered
I	63	42,961,084
II	169	25,126,615
III	395	27,503,319
IV	707	24,481,191
V	1,525	24,108,467
VI[1,2]	5,932	19,579,725
VIII (Nonmetropolitan county)[2]	1,958	22,251,821
IX (Metropolitan county)[2]	1,280	51,699,773
Total	18,108	308,745,538

[1]Includes universities and colleges to which no population is attributed.
[2]Includes state police agencies to which no population is attributed.

APPENDIX V. THE NATION'S TWO CRIME MEASURES

The Department of Justice administers two statistical programs to measure the magnitude, nature, and impact of crime in the nation: the Uniform Crime Reporting (UCR) program and the National Crime Victimization Survey (NCVS). Each of these programs produces valuable information about aspects of the nation's crime problem. Because the UCR and NCVS programs are conducted for different purposes, use different methods, and focus on somewhat different aspects of crime, the information they produce together provides a more comprehensive panorama of the nation's crime problem than either could produce alone.

Uniform Crime Reporting (UCR) program

The UCR program, administered by the Federal Bureau of Investigation (FBI), was created in 1929 and collects information on the following crimes reported to law enforcement authorities: murder and nonnegligent manslaughter, forcible rape, robbery, aggravated assault, burglary, larceny-theft, motor vehicle theft, and arson. Law enforcement agencies also report arrest data for 20 additional crime categories.

The UCR program compiles data from monthly law enforcement reports and from individual crime incident records transmitted directly to the FBI or to centralized state agencies that report to the FBI. The program thoroughly examines each report it receives for reasonableness, accuracy, and deviations that may indicate errors. Large variations in crime levels may indicate modified records procedures, incomplete reporting, or changes in a jurisdiction's boundaries. To identify any unusual fluctuations in an agency's crime counts, the program compares monthly reports to previous submissions of the agency and to those for similar agencies.

The FBI annually publishes its findings in a preliminary release in the spring of the following calendar year, followed by a detailed annual report, *Crime in the United States*, issued in the fall. (The printed copy of *Crime in the United States* is now published by Bernan.) In addition to crime counts and trends, this report includes data on crimes cleared, persons arrested (age, sex, and race), law enforcement personnel (including the number of sworn officers killed or assaulted), and the characteristics of homicides (including age, sex, and race of victims and offenders; victim-offender relationships; weapons used; and circumstances surrounding the homicides). Other periodic reports are also available from the UCR program.

The state and local law enforcement agencies participating in the UCR program are continually converting to the more comprehensive and detailed National Incident-Based Reporting System (NIBRS). The NIBRS provides detailed information about each criminal incident in 22 broad categories of offenses.

The UCR program presents crime counts for the nation as a whole, as well as for regions, states, counties, cities, towns, tribal law enforcement areas, and colleges and universities. This allows for studies among neighboring jurisdictions and among those with similar populations and other common characteristics.

National Crime Victimization Survey

The NCVS, conducted by the Bureau of Justice Statistics (BJS), began in 1973. It provides a detailed picture of crime incidents, victims, and trends. After a substantial period of research, the BJS completed an intensive methodological redesign of the survey in 1993. It conducted this redesign to improve the questions used to uncover crime, update the survey methods, and broaden the scope of crimes measured. The redesigned survey collects detailed information on the frequency and nature of the crimes of rape, sexual assault, personal robbery, aggravated and simple assault, household burglary, theft, and motor vehicle theft. It does not measure homicide or commercial crimes (such as burglaries of stores).

Twice a year, Census Bureau personnel interview household members in a nationally representative sample of approximately 40,000 households (about 75,000 people). Approximately 150,000 interviews of individuals 12 years of age and over are conducted annually. Households stay in the sample for 3 years, and new households rotate into the sample on an ongoing basis.

The NCVS collects information on crimes suffered by individuals and households, whether or not those crimes were reported to law enforcement. It estimates the proportion of each crime type reported to law enforcement, and it summarizes the reasons that victims give for reporting or not reporting.

The survey provides information about victims (age, sex, race, ethnicity, marital status, income, and educational level); offenders (sex, race, approximate age, and victim-offender relationship); and crimes (time and place of occurrence, use of weapons, nature of injury, and economic consequences). Questions also cover victims' experiences with the criminal justice system, self-protective measures used by victims, and possible substance abuse by offenders. Supplements are added to the survey periodically to obtain detailed information on specific topics, such as school crime.

The BJS published the first data from the redesigned NCVS in a June 1995 bulletin. The publication of NCVS data includes *Criminal Victimization in the United States*, an annual report that covers the broad range of detailed information collected by the NCVS. The bureau also publishes detailed reports on topics such as crime against women, urban crime, and gun use in crime. The National Archive of Criminal Justice Data at the University of Michigan archives the NCVS data files to help researchers perform independent analyses.

Comparing the UCR program and the NCVS

Because the BJS designed the NCVS to complement the UCR program, the two programs share many similarities. As much as their different collection methods permit, the two measure the same subset of serious crimes with the same definitions. Both programs cover rape, robbery, aggravated assault, burglary, theft, and motor vehicle theft; both define rape, robbery, theft, and motor vehicle theft virtually identically. (Although rape is defined analogously, the UCR program measures the crime against women only, and the NCVS measures it against both sexes.)

There are also significant differences between the two programs. First, the two programs were created to serve different purposes. The UCR program's primary objective is to provide a reliable set of criminal justice statistics for law enforcement administration, operation, and management. The BJS established the NCVS to provide previously unavailable information about crime (including crime not reported to police), victims, and offenders.

Second, the two programs measure an overlapping but nonidentical set of crimes. The NCVS includes crimes both reported and not reported to law enforcement. The NCVS excludes—but the UCR program includes—homicide, arson, commercial crimes, and crimes committed against children under 12 years of age. The UCR program captures crimes reported to law enforcement but collects only arrest data for simple assaults and sexual assaults other than forcible rape.

Third, because of methodology, the NCVS and UCR have different definitions of some crimes. For example, the UCR defines burglary as the unlawful entry or attempted entry of a structure to commit a felony or theft. The NCVS, not wanting to ask victims to ascertain offender motives, defines burglary as the entry or attempted entry of a residence by a person who had no right to be there.

Fourth, for property crimes (burglary, theft, and motor vehicle theft), the two programs calculate crime rates using different bases. The UCR program rates for these crimes are per capita (number of crimes per 100,000 persons), whereas the NCVS rates for these crimes are per household (number of crimes per 1,000 households).

Because the number of households may not grow at the same annual rate as the total population, trend data for rates of property crimes measured by the two programs may not be comparable. In addition, some differences in the data from the two programs may result from sampling variation in the NCVS and from estimating for nonresponsiveness in the UCR program.

The BJS derives the NCVS estimates from interviewing a sample and are, therefore, subject to a margin of error. The bureau uses rigorous statistical methods to calculate confidence intervals around all survey estimates, and describes trend data in the NCVS reports as genuine only if there is at least a 90-percent certainty that the measured changes are not the result of sampling variation. The UCR program bases its data on the actual counts of offenses reported by law enforcement agencies. In some circumstances, the UCR program estimates its data for nonparticipating agencies or those reporting partial data. Apparent discrepancies between statistics from the two programs can usually be accounted for by their definitional and procedural differences, or resolved by comparing NCVS sampling variations (confidence intervals) of crimes said to have been reported to police with UCR program statistics.

For most types of crimes measured by both the UCR program and the NCVS, analysts familiar with the programs can exclude those aspects of crime not common to both from analysis. Resulting long-term trend lines can be brought into close concordance. The impact of such adjustments is most striking for robbery, burglary, and motor vehicle theft, whose definitions most closely coincide.

With robbery, the BJS bases the NCVS victimization rates on only those robberies reported to the police. It is also possible to remove UCR program robberies of commercial establishments, such as gas stations, convenience stores, and banks, from analysis. When users compare the resulting NCVS police-reported robbery rates and the UCR program noncommercial robbery rates, the results reveal closely corresponding long-term trends.

Conclusion

Each program has unique strengths. The UCR program provides a measure of the number of crimes reported to law enforcement agencies throughout the country. The program's Supplementary Homicide Reports provide the most reliable, timely data on the extent and nature of homicides in the nation. The NCVS is the primary source of information on the characteristics of criminal victimization and on the number and types of crimes not reported to law enforcement authorities.

By understanding the strengths and limitations of each program, it is possible to use the UCR program and NCVS to achieve a greater understanding of crime trends and the nature of crime in the United States. For example, changes in police procedures, shifting attitudes towards crime and police, and other societal changes can affect the extent to which people report and law enforcement agencies record crime. NCVS and UCR program data can be used in concert to explore why trends in reported and police-recorded crime may differ.

INDEX

INDEX